THE BLUE GUIDES

Albania
Austria
Belgium and Luxembourg
China
Cyprus
Czechoslovakia
Denmark
Egypt

FRANCE
France
Paris and Versailles
Burgundy
Loire Valley
Midi-Pyrénées
Normandy
South West France
Corsica

GERMANY
Berlin and Eastern Germany
Western Germany

GREECE
Greece
Athens and environs
Crete

HOLLAND
Holland
Amsterdam

Hungary
Ireland

ITALY
Northern Italy
Southern Italy
Florence
Rome and environs
Venice
Tuscany
Umbria
Sicily

Jerusalem
Malta and Gozo
Mexico
Morocco
Moscow and Leningrad
Portugal

SPAIN
Spain
Barcelona
Madrid

Sweden
Switzerland

TURKEY
Turkey
Istanbul

UK
England
Scotland
Wales
London
Museums and Galleries
   of London
Oxford and Cambridge
Country Houses of England
Gardens of England
Literary Britain and Ireland
Victorian Architecture in
   Britain
Churches and Chapels
   of Northern England
Churches and Chapels
   of Southern England
Channel Islands

USA
New York
Boston and Cambridge

The effigy of Edward, the Black Prince, in Canterbury Cathedral

The publishers and the author welcome comments, suggestions and corrections for the next edition of Blue Guide England. Writers of the most helpful letters will be awarded a free Blue Guide of their choice.

BLUE GUIDE

England

Ian Ousby

Atlas, maps and plans by John Flower

A&C Black
London

WW Norton
New York

Eleventh edition 1995

Published by A & C Black (Publishers) Ltd
35 Bedford Row, London WC1R 4JH

A CIP catalogue record of this book is available from the British Library.

ISBN 0–7136–3874–5

Published in the United States of America by
WW Norton and Company, Inc
500 Fifth Avenue, New York, NY 10110

Published simultaneously in Canada by
Penguin Books Canada Limited
10 Alcorn Avenue, Toronto, Ontario M4V 3BE

ISBN 0–393–31340–9 USA

The author and the publishers have done their best to ensure the accuracy of all the
information in Blue Guide England; however, they can accept no responsibility for any
loss, injury or inconvenience sustained by any traveller as a result of information or
advice contained in the guide.

For permission to reproduce the photographs in this guide the publishers would like
to thank the following: Susan Benn pages 59, 90, 92, 115, 119, 161, 172, 225, 257, 281,
317, 335, 395, 403, 503, 549; A.F. Kersting pages 86, 143, 168, 217, 339, 349, 447, 605,
667; Royal Pavilion, Art Gallery and Museums, Brighton page 103; The Syndics of
Cambridge University Library page 435; Roman Baths and Museum, Bath page 207;
National Trust Photographic Library pages 271, 413; Trustees of the British Museum
page 312; Dean and Chapter of Lincoln page 356; The Shakespeare Birthplace Trust
page 439; Stamford Museum page 474–5; Birmingham Museums and Art Gallery page
490; Ironbridge Gorge Museum Trust page 525; Peak District National Park page 537;
Merseyside Photo Libary page 563; City of Salford Museums and Art Gallery page
578; Peter Hollings page 585; York Civic Trust page 653; Dean and Chapter of Durham
page 682; Newcastle upon Tyne City Council page 689; Skipton Castle page 705.

Ian Ousby attended Cambridge and Harvard Universities and taught in
Britain and the USA before becoming a freelance writer. His books on
literature include *Bloodhounds of Heaven: The Detective in English Fiction
from Goodwin to Doyle* and *The Cambridge Guide to Literature in English.*
His interest in travel has produced *The Englishman's England: Taste, Travel
and the Rise of Tourism* and *James Plumptre's Britain: The Journals of a
Tourist in the 1790s* as well as Blue Guides to *Literary Britain and Ireland,*
and *Burgundy.* He is also a regular broadcaster on BBC radio.

Printed in England by Butler and Tanner

PREFACE

This new, eleventh edition of 'Blue Guide England' has the same goal as its predecessors: to guide travellers through the vast wealth of England's cultural, historic and natural resources in a way that will help them better appreciate what they see and better judge what is most worth seeing. It seeks to include as much as a single volume can reasonably contain of the best or most characteristic in landscape, architecture, archaeology, art and history—all those aspects which, combined in the present life of the nation, give England its distinctive flavour. Of course, the result can no more claim to be comprehensive than previous editions did. It does not try to catalogue every historic inn or Victorian mill or safari park, any more than it gives, at the local level, detailed advice about where to eat, sleep, golf, swim, fish, sail, hang-glide or windsurf. Yet I hope it will prove full enough to grant readers the power of choosing for themselves, particularly in stepping aside from well-beaten paths to discover that England has more to offer than any single guide could possibly capture.

In the tenth edition of this guide I paid tribute to the help I had received from: Lewis Braithwaite, Christopher Chippindale, Graham Coster, L.J.F. Keppie and Ann Stonehouse; the staff of Cambridge University Library and Cambridgeshire Central Library; the late Stuart Rossiter, who wrote many previous editions of 'Blue Guide England', and Ylva French, author of 'Blue Guide London'; and, at the Blue Guide offices, Gemma Davies, Ann Douglas, David Jones and Tom Neville. My thanks to all of them again. Work on this edition has lengthened the list of my obligations to include: Dr P.D. Baker; Frances Gapper, Patience Gapper and Sally Drury, authors of 'Blue Guide Country Houses of England'; Stephen Humphrey and the rest of the team who wrote 'Blue Guide Churches and Chapels Northern England' and 'Blue Guide Churches and Chapels Southern England'; Sue Reid; Geoffrey Tyack and Steven Brindle, authors of 'Blue Guide Country Houses of England'; John Tomes; and F.T. Dunn, R.J.M. Tolhurst and W.J.A. Wilberforce, conscientious readers who took the trouble to contact me with useful suggestions and corrections.

I have also been greatly helped by the following experts on particular sites and places: D.W. Davidge, Head Custodian, Alexander Keiller Museum, Avebury; David Apps, BAA; Yvonne C.R. Beckles, Manager, Tourist Information Centre, Bath; Julia Naismith, Publicity Officer, Holburne Museum and Crafts Study Centre, Bath; Stephen Clews, Curator, Roman Baths Museum and Pump Room, Bath; Susan Sloman, Keeper of Art, Victoria Art Gallery, Bath; Lynda Smith, Tourist Information Centre, Bedford; Ruth Bannister, Parish Administrator, Beverley Minster; Patricia Ferrins, Senior Information Assistant, Birmingham Convention and Visitor Bureau; Evelyn A. Silber, Birmingham Museums and Art Gallery; Dr J.H. Andrew, Keeper, Museum of Science and Industry, Birmingham; Paul Spencer-Longhurst, Curator, Barber Institute of Fine Arts, University of Birmingham; John Ward, Tourist Information Centre, Boston; Mary Hatcher, Tourist Information Centre, Bradford; Bob Barton, British Tourist Authority; Warwick Toone, Director of Arts and Leisure Services, Brighton; Jess Tunstall, Broads Authority; Paula Sunshine, Tourist Information Centre, Bury St Edmunds; Professor Sir Hans Kornberg, Master, Christ's College, Cambridge; M.J. Allen, Bursar, Churchill College, Cambridge; Michael McCrum, Master, Corpus Christi College, Cambridge; Dr Peter Mathias, Master, Downing College, Cambridge; Dr A.S. Bendall, Archivist,

Emmanuel College, Cambridge; W.F. Northam, Keeper (Administration), Fitzwilliam Museum, Cambridge; Juliet d'A. Campbell, Mistress, Girton College, Cambridge; Joachim Whaley, Senior Tutor, Gonville and Caius College, Cambridge; Lord Renfrew of Kaimsthorn, Master, Jesus College, Cambridge; Derek Buxton, Tourist Liaison Officer, King's College, Cambridge; Sir David Calcutt, Magdalene College, Cambridge; Dr Onora O'Neill, Principal, Newnham College, Cambridge; Sir John Meurig Thomas, Master, Peterhouse, Cambridge; The Lord Lewis, Warden, Robinson College, Cambridge; Sir Terence English, St Catharine's College, Cambridge; Malcolm Underwood, Archivist, St John's College, Cambridge; M.J. Tilby, Senior Tutor, Selwyn College, Cambridge; R.C. Andrew, Bursar, Sidney Sussex College, Cambridge; A.P. Simm, Junior Bursar, Trinity College, Cambridge; Sir John Lyons, Master, Trinity Hall, Cambridge; Dr E.S. Leedham-Green, Deputy Keeper of Manuscripts and University Archives, University Library, Cambridge; Rupert Douglas, Principal Tourism Officer, Carlisle; The Reverend Canon R.C. Johns, Carlisle Cathedral; Peter Rollins, Chief Tourism Officer, Cheltenham; Gerald Tattum, Tourism Development Officer, Chester; R.E. Waite, Principal Tourism Officer, Chichester; Karen Elmer, Community Services, Colchester; Susan Mileham, Interpretation and Visitor Services Manager, Herbert Art Gallery and Museum, Coventry; J. Weir, Dartmoor National Park Authority; Marion Nixon, Tourism Officer, Derby; Jonathan Platt, Senior Keeper of Industry and Technology, Derby; Susannah Cooper, Press Officer, Eastbourne; Alison Curtis-Smith, Tourist Office Supervisor, Ely; Kim Robbins, Public Relations Officer, English Heritage; Pamela Read, Tourist Information Centre, Exeter; Brian Pearce, Interpretation Officer, Exmoor National Park; Arthur Perceval, Honorary Director, Fleur de Lis Heritage Centre, Faversham; Philip Cooke, Chief Tourism and Marketing Officer, Gloucester; R. Faers, Tourist Information Manager, Gloucester; A. Henderson, Tourist Information Centre, Guildford; Stuart F. Mackay, Head of Marketing and Sales, Harrogate; Victoria Williams, Museum Curator, Hastings; Dr David J. Breeze, Chief Inspector of Ancient Monuments, Historic Scotland; Simon R. Green, Hull City Museums and Art Galleries; H.A. Sandall, Information Assistant, Tourist Information Centre, Ipswich; Jane Sedge, Senior Assistant Curator, Ipswich Borough Council Museums and Galleries; June Collister, Isle of Man Tourist Information; Phil Philo, Langbaurgh Museum Services, Kirkleatham; Cathy Bryon-Edmond, Tourism Officer, Kirklees Metropolitan Council; Lynne Johnson, Assistant to the Information Retrieval Officer, Lake District National Park Authority; Kairen P. Brown, Manager, Promotions and Tourism Division, Leeds; J. Howard, Tourist Information Centre, Lewes; Diane Broach, Tourist Information Centre, Lichfield; R.H. Wood, Curator, Usher Gallery, Lincoln; E.F. Greenwood, Keeper, Liverpool Museum; Linda Woodrow, Marketing and Events Officer, Lowestoft; T.A. Rattenbury, Tourist Information Centre, Lyme Regis; Henry Middleton, Maidstone Museum and Art Gallery; Maria Hannah, Marketing and Visitor Services, Manchester; Catharine Braithwaite, Gallery Services Officer, Manchester City Art Galleries; Alison Vincent, Press and Publicity Officer, Museum of Science and Industry, Manchester; Penny Hamilton, Gallery Services Officer, Whitworth Art Gallery, Manchester; Pam Wilsher, General Manager, Merseyside Tourism and Conference Bureau; Barbara Stephenson, Librarian, City and Tourist Information Services, Newcastle upon Tyne; John Millard, Senior Curator, Newcastle Museums; Rosemary O'Donoghue, Administrative Officer, Norfolk Museums Service; M.P. Bryan, Information Officer, North York Moors

National Park; Sue Kay, Tourism Development Officer, Northampton; Anne Leuchars, Information Officer, Northumberland National Park; Pam Petersen, Manager, Tourist Information Centre, Norwich; Joan Witten, Office of Population and Census Studies; Julia Maltby, Ordnance Survey; Heather Armitage, Tourist Information Centre, Oxford; N. Aubertin-Potter, Sub-Librarian, Codrington Library, All Souls College, Oxford; R.I.H. Charlton, Publications Officer, Ashmolean Museum, Oxford; John Jones, Dean and Archivist, Balliol College, Oxford; David Vaisey, Librarian, Bodleian Library, Oxford; Mark Curthoys, Archivist, Christ Church, Oxford; P.R. Baker, Bursar, Hertford College, Oxford; Dr P.M. North, Principal, Jesus College, Oxford; G.B. Richardson, Warden, Keble College, Oxford; Dr J.M. Roberts, Warden, Merton College, Oxford; Caroline Dalton, Archivist, New College, Oxford; Brigadier M.J.F. Stephens, Domestic Bursar, Oriel College, Oxford; T.A. Wyndham Lewis, Bursar, Pembroke College, Oxford; Dr W. Hayes, Principal, St John's College, Oxford; Dr G. Marshall, Provost, The Queens' College, Oxford; Bryan Ward-Perkins, Fellow Archivist, Trinity College, Oxford; Professor Peter Bayley, University College, Oxford; R.G. Smethurst, Provost, Worcester College, Oxford; J.H. Greenwood, Peak National Park; Pam Weaver, Tourist Information Centre, Penzance; Linda Willis, Tourism Officer, Peterborough; Canon Higham, Peterborough Cathedral; Jane Bailey, Tourist Information Centre, Poole; Brian Manning, Director of Leisure Services, Preston; Heather Fletcher, Tourism and Marketing Services, Royal Tunbridge Wells; Nicholas Bates, Cathedral Administrator, St Albans; Clare Bury, Tourism Development Officer, Salisbury; Mary Pocock, Salisbury District Leisure and Tourism Services; Janet Barnes, Principal Keeper, Ruskin Gallery, Sheffield; Wendy Briggs, Manager, Tourist Information Centre, Sheffield; Alison Patrick, Tourism and Publicity Officer, Shrewsbury; Betsy P. Jenkinson, Marketing Services Division, Directorate of Leisure, Tourism and Amenities, Southampton; Margot Heller, Keeper of Art and Exhibitions, Southampton; K.M. Lawford, Tourist Information Centre, Taunton; Sandra DuPont, Visitors' Officer, Tewkesbury Abbey; Nicola Wood, Publicity Officer, Thanet District Council; Helen Wilson, Sales and Publications Assistant, English Riviera Tourist Board, Torquay; S. Jackson, Assistant Tourism and Marketing Manager, Leisure Services Department, Worcester; Jane Lee, Tourism Services, York; Karen Turnpenny, Marketing Officer, National Railway Museum, York; Richard Green, Curator, York City Art Gallery; Sian Lewis, Yorkshire Museum, York; S.M. Hounsham, Publications Officer, Yorkshire Dales National Park.

To all of them, my thanks, as well as to the many other custodians, enthusiasts and passers-by who have informed my travels, and to future readers of this book who will, I hope, be as kind as past ones have been in contacting me with suggestions, comments and help for future editions.

BLUE GUIDES

The Blue Guide series began in 1915, and in 1918 Muirhead Guide-Books Limited published 'Blue Guide London and its Environs'. The first edition of 'Blue Guide England' appeared in 1920. Findlay and James Muirhead already had extensive experience of guide-book publishing: before the First World War they had been the editors of the English editions of the German Baedekers, and by 1915 they had acquired the copyright of most of the famous 'Red' Handbooks from John Murray.

An agreement made with the French publishing house Hachette et Cie in 1917 led to the translation of Muirhead's London Guide, which became the first 'Guide Bleu'—Hachette had previously published the blue-covered 'Guides Joanne'. Subsequently, Hachette's 'Guide Bleu Paris et ses Environs' was adapted and published in London by Muirhead. The collaboration between the two publishing houses continued until 1933.

In 1931 Ernest Benn Limited took over the Blue Guides, appointing Russell Muirhead, Findlay Muirhead's son, editor in 1934. The Muirheads' connection with Blue Guides ended in 1963 when Stuart Rossiter, who had been working on the Guides since 1954, became house editor, revising and compiling several of the books himself.

The Blue Guides are now published by A & C Black, who acquired Ernest Benn in 1984, so continuing the tradition of guide-book publishing which began in 1826 with 'Black's Economical Tourist of Scotland'. The Blue Guide series continues to grow: there are now more than 50 titles in print with revised editions appearing regularly and many new Blue Guides in preparation.

'Blue Guides' is a registered trademark.

CONTENTS

NORTH MIDLANDS

NORTHERN ENGLAND

Maps and Plans

Road map of England *at the back of the book*

Ground Plans

HOW TO USE THE GUIDE

The way this guide is organised will be familiar to readers of previous editions or other Blue Guides. It divides England into regions (South-Eastern, South-Western and so forth), each defined and characterised in a brief introduction and then explored in routes for drivers. These routes are not designed as suggested outings with some particular tourist attraction or famous sight in view, but as journeys between major points on the map. They avoid motorways in favour of long-established roads which have carried the traffic of history, usually not the fastest way but likely to be the most interesting. Many routes have alternative sections (A, B, etc.) which offer different ways of making the trip between the same two places or touring the same area. Detours from main routes and excursions from stopping-points along the way widen the scope of what is described.

Though it involves some overlapping of routes (indicated by crossreferences), this system has the merit of grouping places close to each other on the map close to each other on the page. It serves the habitual traveller on the look-out for ways of relieving the journey and the tourist in search of places worth particular attention or detour. The comprehensive index encourages readers to follow their own plan.

Type. The main routes are described in large type. Smaller type is used for detours and excursions, for technical or historical background, and, generally speaking, for descriptions of greater detail or less importance.

Abbreviations. Most of the forms used are generally accepted and selfexplanatory, but the following may require explanation:

b.	born
C	century
c	circa (about)
cf.	compare
d.	died
DoE	Department of the Environment
EH	English Heritage
fl.	floruit (flourished)
ft	foot (feet)
in	inch(es)
m	mile(s)
NGS	National Gardens Scheme
NT	National Trust
No.	Number
OS	Ordnance Survey
St	Saint
St.	Street
TI	Tourist Information
yd	yard(s)

Asterisks. Single asterisks indicate points of special interest or excellence. Double asterisks are used sparingly, for things worth travelling the length of the country to see.

Distances in miles are given cumulatively from the starting-point of the route or detour. Road straightening, one-way systems and bypasses ensure that they are at best approximate.

Maps and plans. The town plans and cathedral floor plans included in the text give detailed guidance. The road map of England at the back of the book is designed for general reference and planning only, not as a substitute for the motorists' maps now available in a bewildering variety of scales and formats. The paperbound Motoring Atlas (1:190,080 or 1in to 3m) published annually by Ordnance Survey is particularly useful. Those who prefer sheet maps can use the OS Routemaster series (1:250,000 or 1in to 4m) or the Michelin maps 402, 403 and 404 (1:400,000 or 1in to 6.30m).

None of these maps is adequate to the local detail in the text. The OS Landranger maps (1:50,000 or 1¼in to 1m) are by far the best for getting to know an area of some size with proper intimacy. The OS Tourist series (1:63,360 or 1in to 1m) or OS Outdoor Leisure series (1:25,000 or 2½in to 1m) cover particularly popular areas.

Population figures, rounded off to the nearest hundred, are given as a rough indication of the facilities which the traveller can expect to find. They are taken from the 1981 census, the general results of the 1991 census not being available at the time of going to press.

Tourist Information Centres (TI) are noted in the text, and street addresses given for those in major cities. The readily identifiable *i* symbol on local signposts makes them easy to find. They provide information about local attractions, opening times, special events, transport and accommodation. Those in large or popular cities frequently offer walking tours with accredited guides. Many centres can make provisional reservations at local hotels and guesthouses, and many major ones are linked by the Book-a-Bed-Ahead-Service. Those described as 'seasonal' are in general open from Easter to the end of October. (See also Useful Organisations: British Tourist Authority and English Tourist Board.)

Opening times for museums, galleries, historic buildings, country houses, etc., can vary from year to year, so that arrangements specified by anything except an annual publication quickly become dated. This guide does not attempt to offer information that might be misleading by the time the reader encounters it. It merely adds the word 'open' after sites to confirm that there is public access at certain times, if the description in the text does not otherwise make that fact clear. The phrase 'limited opening' (usually appearing in connection with privately owned country houses) warns that the building is open only one or two days a week during a short summer season, for a total of less than about 40 days a year.

Those intent on visiting a particular property are therefore urged to check in advance of any proposed trip. Tourist Information Centres can supply up-to-date information about opening times, and there are two useful annual index publications, 'Historic Houses, Castles and Gardens' and 'Museums and Galleries'. The National Trust and English Heritage issue annual handbooks to their properties.

Otherwise, a few general guidelines can be offered. The traveller will fare much better between Easter (or the beginning of April) and the end of October, dates marking the outer limits of the tourist season. In the winter, the following are likely to be closed: many National Trust buildings (though not necessarily their grounds); most privately owned country houses; and some smaller museums. Even in the tourist season smaller NT properties tend to close for one or two days a week, and only the largest privately owned country houses are open every day of the week. Public holidays add to the restrictions. Virtually all sites are closed on Christmas Day, Boxing

Day and New Year's Day. Policy for Christmas Eve and the other Bank Holidays varies—Good Friday and the May Day Bank Holiday being especially unpredictable in their effect—but in general properties administered by national or local government are more likely to close.

English Heritage has a standardised system of opening times for its properties (except some in Greater London). It is indicated in the text by the following phrases:

All year: Good Friday or 1 April (whichever is earlier) to 30 September, open daily 10.00–18.00. 1 October to Maundy Thursday or 31 March (whichever is earlier), open Tuesday to Sunday 10.00–16.00. *Summer season*: Good Friday or 1 April (whichever is earlier) to 30 September, open daily 10.00–18.00.

Many smaller open-air English Heritage properties, simply marked 'EH' in the text, are open at any reasonable time. Some English Heritage properties otherwise open standard hours may in fact close one or two days a week, particularly in winter; some close for lunch, usually 13.00–14.00. Properties are closed on Christmas Eve, Christmas Day, Boxing Day and New Year's Day.

Parish churches rarely have official opening hours, but many are kept locked as a protection against vandalism. There is usually a notice outside giving instructions for obtaining the key.

See Useful Organisations for further details of English Heritage and the National Trust.

PRACTICAL INFORMATION

The notes in this section are mainly for foreign visitors.

Roads and driving. Current driving licences issued by foreign countries are valid for up to 12 months. International Driving Permits can also be used. Car hire companies usually require that drivers have at least one year's driving experience and hold a licence free from endorsement. Some companies also insist that drivers are at least 21 and not more than 65 years old.

Road regulations are summarised in 'The Highway Code', published by Her Majesty's Stationery Office (HMSO). The rule of the road is: drive on the left and overtake on the right. Drivers from countries which keep to the right should be particularly careful when entering roundabouts, remembering to go round clockwise rather than anti-clockwise and also to give way to any traffic already on the roundabout. The wearing of seat belts is compulsory for driver and passengers.

There are four types of road in Britain: motorways, 'A' roads, 'B' roads and 'unclassified' roads. All but the last are numbered on signs and maps. Motorways, labelled 'M' and signposted in white and blue, are communication arteries engineered for speed rather than interest; they usually have three lanes in each direction. Learner drivers, riders of small motorcycles, cyclists and pedestrians cannot use them. Drivers can stop in emergencies only, on the 'hard shoulder' to the left of the left-hand lane. 'A' roads generally follow more interesting and historic routes, though dual carriageways, straightening of bends, bypasses round towns and ring roads round cities can make some of them almost as fast as motorways. 'B' roads, secondary routes used by local traffic, are narrower and more likely to wind but also more likely to bring the traveller in contact with the real character of the landscape. Unclassified roads, identified on road signs only by their destination, vary from pleasantly empty country lanes to one-lane funnels cluttered with slow-moving tractors. The majority are too small to appear on motoring atlases but OS Landranger maps usefully subdivide them into categories which give the traveller some idea of what to expect.

Unless otherwise indicated, the speed limit is 30mph in built-up areas (i.e. those with street lighting), 60mph on single carriageways and 70mph on dual carriageways and motorways.

The Automobile Association (AA) and the Royal Automobile Club (RAC) offer a wide range of useful services to members, particularly in the event of breakdown, as well as issuing many publications available to non-members. Temporary membership of one or the other is often included in car-hire terms. Members of the American Automobile Association (AAA) and of other clubs affiliated to the Alliance Internationale de Tourisme (AIT) receive membership benefits from the AA. Members of clubs affiliated to the AIT and the Fédération Internationale de l'Automobile (FIA) can use the RAC rescue services without charge. The AA headquarters is at Fanum House, Basingstoke, Hampshire RG21 2EA; phone 01256 20123. The RAC headquarters is at RAC House, M1 Cross, Brent Terrace, London NW2 1LT; phone 0181 208 4311.

Railways. The Inter-City network of British Rail (BR) has many trains leaving London at hourly intervals and reaching speeds of up to 125mph. Typical journey times from London are: less than 1 hour to Brighton;

1–1½ hours to Bath, Cambridge, Canterbury, Dover, Oxford and Salisbury; 1½–2 hours to Birmingham, Bournemouth, Bristol, Cardiff and Portsmouth; 2–3 hours to Chester, Exeter, Leeds, Lincoln, Liverpool, Manchester, Norwich, Sheffield and York; 3–4 hours to Plymouth and Penzance; and about 5 hours to Edinburgh. Inter-City trains with sleeping cars serve longer routes from London to Scotland and the South-West. The Motorail service enables travellers to transport their car by the same train. Because the main railway network radiates from London like spokes from the hub of a wheel, journeys between provincial centres may be much slower and involve changing trains.

BritRail passes allow unlimited travel for periods of 4, 8, 15 or 22 days or one month. They are available only to foreign visitors and must be bought before arrival in Britain. RailRover tickets, which can be bought in Britain, allow unlimited travel for 7 or 14 days, either in specified regions or throughout the entire network.

Coaches. Long-distance coaches provide a cheaper but slower alternative to travel by rail. National Express, the largest operator, has the centre of its network at London's Victoria Coach Station and major interchanges at Bristol, Birmingham, Leeds and Manchester. Typical journey times are: London–Brighton 1¾ hours; London–Birmingham, the busiest route, 2½ hours; Leeds–Manchester 1½ hours; Newcastle–Penzance 12½ hours. The BritExpress card for foreign visitors brings a reduction on fares for periods of 8, 15 or 21 days.

Accommodation. England offers a wide range of accommodation: hotels, inns, guesthouses, bed and breakfast (B&B), farmhouse accommodation, self-catering holiday accommodation, Youth Hostels, and camping and caravan sites. The best hotels compare favourably with the best anywhere. Some of the 'country house' hotels and older inns in country towns occupy buildings of architectural interest. However, by international standards the average hotel in the average provincial town charges too much and provides too little. Those who do not demand the full range of hotel facilities will appreciate the excellent value, as well as the informal atmosphere, offered by bed and breakfast and farmhouse accommodation.

The English Tourist Board operates a classification scheme for accommodation to indicate the range and sophistication of the facilities provided, awarding Crowns for hotels, Moons for lodges by major roads and motorways, keys for self-catering accommodation, and Qs for caravan and camping parks. The services offered by Tourist Information Centres are described in Notes On Using This Guide.

A wide range of annual publications is issued by the English Tourist Board, the British Tourist Authority, the Automobile Association and the Royal Automobile Club. Egon Ronay's guide to 'Hotels and Restaurants' and the Consumers' Association's 'Good Hotel Guide' are reliable and demanding in their standards. The Youth Hostels Association and the annual accommodation guide issued by the Ramblers' Association are listed under Useful Organisations.

Food. Breakfast and tea are still the best meals to be had in England, and they are not hard to come by. Otherwise, travellers will find greater choice and higher standards than the poor international reputation of English food might lead them to expect. Many public houses (pubs) serve cheap lunches and dinners. Italian, Chinese and Indian restaurants have brought welcome variety to even the smaller towns.

Egon Ronay's 'Just a Bite' and 'Good Food in Pubs and Bars' are useful guides to simpler fare. (Connoisseurs of pubs for their own sake will appreciate the Consumers' Association's 'Good Pub Guide' and the 'Good Beer Guide' published by CAMRA, the Campaign for Real Ale.) Egon Ronay's 'Hotels and Restaurants' and the Consumers' Association 'Good Food Guide' serve the needs of the gourmet.

Money. The pound sterling (£), the standard unit of currency, is divided into 100 pence (p). There are notes for £50, £20, £10 and £5; a small, goldcoloured coin for £1; 'silver' coins for 50p, 20p, 10p and 5p; and 'copper' coins for 2p and 1p.

Banks are usually open Monday to Friday 09.30 to 15.30 and, in some cases, Saturday 09.30 to 12.00. Outside these hours Bureaux de Change can also be found at airports, major railway stations, large hotels and department stores and travel agencies.

VAT. Value Added Tax ('vee-ay-tee' or 'vat') is a sales tax added to a wide range of goods and services, currently at a rate of 15 per cent. It should already be included in the prices quoted by hotels and restaurants. Major shops in London and other centres with a substantial tourist trade operate the Retail Export Scheme, which allows foreign visitors to get a refund for VAT on certain goods (but not hotel accommodation, car hire, etc.).

Tipping. Most hotels and many restaurants include a service charge in the bill. Add 10–15 per cent if it is not included. Taxi drivers and hairdressers expect a tip of 10–15 per cent, and porters 30–50p per suitcase. Cloakroom attendants and barmen in hotel cocktail bars expect some change to be left on the plate. Do not tip in pubs, cinemas or theatres.

Post. Post Offices are usually open Monday to Friday 09.00–17.30 and Saturday 09.00–12.30. Stamps are also available from the machines outside major Post Offices, hotel desks and many corner shops. Inland letters can be sent at a first-class rate or at a slower and cheaper second-class rate. European mail automatically goes airmail or by the quickest route, but airmail stickers and extra stamps are required for the service outside Europe.

Telephones. British Telecom is the major operator of Britain's phone system, though it now has a significant competitor in Mercury. Many public phone boxes accept only phonecards, available from Post Offices, newsagents and corner shops. The cost of BT inland calls is governed by distance and time of day: Monday to Friday 08.00 to 18.00 (expensive); and all other times including the weekend (less expensive, but still not cheap). International calls can usually be dialled directly. Rates to most countries are cheaper between 20.00 and 08.00 Monday to Friday and at the weekend.

Summer Time. British Summer Time, one hour ahead of Greenwich Mean Time, is adopted between the end of March and the end of October. The changes forward and back are always made at midnight on a Saturday, though the exact dates vary from year to year. They do not coincide with changes on the Continent.

Bank Holidays. The calendar of public holidays is: New Year's Day; Good Friday; Easter Monday; the first Monday in May (May Day Bank Holiday);

the last Monday in May (Spring or Whitsun Bank Holiday); the last Monday in August (Summer or August Bank Holiday); Christmas Day; and Boxing Day (26 December). If any of the moveable festivals or anniversaries should fall on a Sunday, the Monday afterwards is treated as a Bank Holiday instead.

Medical services. Visitors can use the accident and emergency services of the National Health Service free of charge. The NHS charges for hospital care and urgent treatment of visitors to Britain unless there is a reciprocal arrangement with their country of origin. Countries with such an arrangement include the EC and most other European countries, Australia, New Zealand and Hong Kong. Visitors should check their eligibility before starting their journey and visitors from non-reciprocal countries (e.g. USA, Canada, Switzerland, Japan) should take out medical insurance.

USEFUL ORGANISATIONS

Automobile Association (AA). See Practical Information: Roads and Driving.

British Rail (BR). See Practical Information: Railways.

The **British Tourist Authority** (BTA), the statutory agency responsible for encouraging tourism to Britain from overseas, maintains offices abroad to provide information for prospective visitors. It also runs the British Travel Centre, 12 Regent St., Piccadilly Circus, London SW1Y 4PQ (phone 0171-730 3400), which books rail, coach and air travel, sightseeing tours, theatre tickets and accommodation as well as providing information about the whole country. For other information services in England, see English Tourist Board below.

BTA overseas offices include:

Australia: 8th Floor, University Centre, 210 Clarence St., Sydney, NSW 2000; phone (02) 267 4555; fax (02) 267 4442.

Canada: 111 Avenue Rd, Suite 450, Toronto, Ontario M5R 3J8; phone (416) 925 6326; fax (416) 961 2175.

Ireland: 123 Lower Baggot St., Dublin 2; phone 010 3531 661 4188.

New Zealand: Suite 305, 3rd Floor, Dilworth Building, Corner Queen and Durham Streets, Auckland 1; phone (09) 303 1446; fax (09) 377 6965.

Singapore: 24 Raffles Place, 20-01 Clifford Centre, Singapore 0104; phone 5352966; fax 5344703.

South Africa: (visitors) Lancaster Gate, Hyde Lane, Hyde Park, Sandton 2196; (postal address) PO Box 41896, Graighall 2024; phone (011) 325 0343.

USA (Atlanta): 2580 Cumberland Parkway, Suite 470, Atlanta, Georgia 30339-3909; phone (404) 432 9635; fax (404) 432 9641.

USA (Chicago): 625 North Michigan Avenue, Suite 1510, Chicago, Illinois 60611; phone (312) 787 0490; fax (312) 787 7746.

USA (Los Angeles): 350 South Figueroa St., Suite 450, Los Angeles, California 90071; phone (213) 628 3525; fax (213) 687 6621.

USA (New York): 551 Fifth Avenue, Suite 701, New York, New York 10176; phone (212) 986 2200; fax (212) 986 1188.

The **British Waterways Board** is responsible for 2000 miles of inland waterways in England, Scotland and Wales. Inquiries to Willow Grange,

Church Road, Watford, Hertfordshire WD1 3QA; phone 01923 201239; fax 01923 226081.

The **Countryside Commission** is the official adviser to the government on protecting the countryside. It is responsible for designating Areas of Outstanding Natural Beauty, Heritage Coasts and National Parks in England and Wales. The National Parks in England are: Dartmoor, Exmoor, the Lake District, the Norfolk and Suffolk Broads, Northumberland, the Peak District, the North York Moors and the Yorkshire Dales. Largely made up of privately owned land but subject to special planning control, they are administered by separate National Park Authorities. The Commission is also responsible for creating and maintaining the Pennine Way and other long-distance paths for walkers: the Cleveland Way, Offa's Dyke Path, the Peddars' Way and Norfolk Coast Path, the Ridgeway Path, the North Downs Way, the South Downs Way, the South West Coast Path and the Wolds Way.

Further information is available from the Commission's headquarters at John Dower House, Crescent Place, Cheltenham, Gloucestershire GL50 3RA; phone 01242 521381; fax 01242 584270.

English Heritage (EH) is responsible for protecting the country's architectural heritage and administering nationally owned historic properties, except royal palaces and parks. More than 350 properties are open to the public, including prehistoric monuments (Stonehenge), Roman ruins (most of Hadrian's Wall), castles, abbeys, etc. Details of annual membership or life membership, which give free admission, are available at all staffed sites or from the membership department at PO Box 1BB, London W1A 1BB (phone 0171 973 3400). For opening times, see 'Notes On Using This Guide'.

The head office is at Keysign House, 429 Oxford Street, London W1R 2HD; phone 0171 973 3000; fax 0171 973 3430. Regional offices are:

London: The Iveagh Bequest, Kenwood, Hampstead Lane, London NW3 7JR; phone 0181 348 1286.

Midlands (Bedfordshire, Cambridgeshire, Derbyshire, Essex, Hereford & Worcester, Hertfordshire, Leicestershire, Lincolnshire, Norfolk, Northamptonshire, Nottinghamshire, the eastern part of Oxfordshire, Shropshire, Staffordshire, Suffolk, Warwickshire, West Midlands): Hazelrigg House, 33 Marefair, Northampton NN1 1SR; phone 01604 730320.

North (Cheshire, Cleveland, Cumbria, Durham, Lancashire, Northumberland, Tyne and Wear, North Yorkshire, South Yorkshire): Bessie Surtees House, 41–44 Sandhill, Newcastle upon Tyne NE1 3JF; phone 0191 261 1585.

South-East (Hampshire, Isle of Wight, Kent, Surrey, East and West Sussex): 1 High Street, Tonbridge, Kent TN9 1SG; phone 01732 778000.

South-West (Avon, Cornwall, Devon, Dorset, Gloucestershire, Isles of Scilly, the western part of Oxfordshire, Somerset, Wiltshire): 7–8 King St., Bristol, Avon BS1 4EQ; phone 0117 9750700.

English Nature is the official body responsible for nature conservation in England, Scotland and Wales. Its functions include the management of nature reserves and sites of special scientific interest. Further information is available from Northminster House, Peterborough PE1 1UA; phone 01733 340345; fax 01733 68834.

The **English Tourist Board** (ETB), which works in conjunction with the British Tourist Authority (see above) to promote tourism, provides information services for visitors in England. Much of its operation is carried out through regional Tourist Boards and local Tourist Information Centres, where the wide range of ETB publications can be obtained. The regional Tourist Boards are:

Cumbria Tourist Board: Ashleigh, Holly Rd, Windermere, Cumbria LA23 2AQ; phone 01539 44444; fax 01539 444041.

East Anglia Tourist Board (Bedfordshire, Cambridgeshire, Essex, Hertfordshire, Norfolk, Suffolk): Topplesfield Hall, Hadleigh, Suffolk IP7 5DN; phone 01473 822922; fax 01473 823063.

East Midlands Tourist Board (Derbyshire, Leicestershire, Lincolnshire, Northamptonshire, Nottinghamshire): Exchequergate, Lincoln LN2 1PZ; phone 01522 531521/3; fax 01522 532501.

Heart of England Tourist Board (Gloucestershire, Hereford and Worcester, Shropshire, Staffordshire, Warwickshire, West Midlands): Woodside, Larkhill Road, Worcester WR5 2EF; phone 01905 763436; fax 01905 763450.

London Tourist Board: 26 Grosvenor Gardens, London SW1W 0DU; phone: 0171 730 3450; fax 0171 730 9367.

Northumbria Tourist Board (Cleveland, Durham, Northumberland, Tyne and Wear): Aykley Heads, Durham DH1 5UX; phone 0191 384 6905; fax 0191 386 0899.

North West Tourist Board (Cheshire, Greater Manchester, Lancashire, Merseyside, the Derbyshire High Peak): Swan House, Swan Meadow Road, Wigan Pier, Wigan, Lancashire WN3 5BB; phone 01942 821222; fax 01942 82002.

South East England Tourist Board (Kent, Surrey, East Sussex, West Sussex): The Old Brew House, Warwick Park, Tunbridge Wells, Kent TN2 5TU; phone 01892 540766; fax 01892 511008.

Southern Tourist Board (Berkshire, Buckinghamshire, Hampshire, Isle of Wight, Oxfordshire, part of Dorset): 40 Chamberlayne, Eastleigh, Hampshire SO5 5JH; phone 01703 620006; fax 01703 620010.

West Country Tourist Board (Avon, Cornwall, Devon, Isles of Scilly, Somerset, Wiltshire, part of Dorset): 60 St David's Hill, Exeter EX4 4SY; phone 01392 76351; fax 01392 420891.

Yorkshire and Humberside Tourist Board (Humberside, North Yorkshire, South Yorkshire, West Yorkshire): 312 Tadcaster Rd, York YO2 2HF; phone 01904 707961; fax 01904 701414.

The **Forestry Commission** is the government department responsible for carrying out Britain's forestry policy, through support and control of private development and through management of its own estates, which run to almost 700,000 acres in England. They include ancient woodlands like the New Forest, the Forest of Dean and Sherwood Forest as well as forests grown since the 1940s. The Commission provides a generous range of amenities for tourists: information centres, forest drives, walks and specialist trails, picnic sites, sports facilities, and cabin and camping areas. The Commission's headquarters are at 231 Corstophine Rd, Edinburgh EH12 7AT; phone 0131 334 0303; fax 0131 334 4473.

National Express. See Practical Information: Coaches.

The **National Gardens Scheme** (NGS) arranges the opening, on selected days each summer, of gardens not usually open to the public. All proceeds go to charity. A booklet is available from booksellers and newsagents or directly from the NGS, Hatchlands Park, East Clandon, Guildford, Surrey GU4 7RT; phone 01483 211535; fax 01483 211537.

National Parks. See Countryside Commission.

The **National Trust** (NT) is an independent charity dedicated to preserving places of historic interest or natural beauty in England, Wales and Northern Ireland. (There is a separate National Trust for Scotland.) Founded in 1895, it has grown into the largest conservation society and private landowner in

Britain. About 190 historic houses, including nearly 90 large country houses, are open to the public, together with prehistoric, Roman and industrial sites, churches, chapels and barns, gardens and landscaped parks, many acres of countryside and many miles of coastline. For opening times see 'Notes On Using This Guide'. Annual membership or life membership, which give free admission to most properties, are available at all staffed sites or from PO Box 39, Bromley, Kent BR1 1NH (phone 0181 464 1111). Members of the Royal Oak Foundation, the NT's affiliate in the USA, receive membership privileges; contact 285 West Broadway, Suite 400, New York, New York 10013.

The NT head office is at 36 Queen Anne's Gate, London SW1H 9AS; phone 0171 222 9251; fax 0171 233 3037. Regional offices are:

Cornwall: Lanhydrock Park, Bodmin PL30 4DE; phone 01208 74281.

Devon: Killerton House, Broadclyst, Exeter EX5 3LE; phone 01392 881691.

East Anglia (Cambridgeshire, Essex, Norfolk, Suffolk): Blickling, Norwich NR11 6NF; phone 01263 733471.

East Midlands (Derbyshire, Leicestershire, Lincolnshire, Northamptonshire, Nottinghamshire, South Humberside, and those parts of Cheshire, Greater Manchester, Staffordshire, South Yorkshire and West Yorkshire in the Peak District National Park): Clumber Park Stableyard, Worksop, Nottinghamshire S80 3BE; phone 01909 486411.

Kent and East Sussex (includes SE Greater London): Scotney Castle, Lamberhurst, Tunbridge Wells, Kent TN3 8JN; phone 01892 890651.

Mercia (Cheshire, Merseyside, Shropshire, most of Greater Manchester and Staffordshire, part of West Midlands): Attingham Park, Shrewsbury, Shropshire SY4 4TP; phone 01743 77343.

Northumbria (Durham, Northumberland, Tyne and Wear): Scots' Gap, Morpeth, Northumberland NE61 4EG; phone 01670 74691.

North-West (Cumbria, Lancashire): The Hollens, Grasmere, Ambleside, Cumbria LA22 9QZ; phone 01539 435599.

Severn (Gloucestershire, Hereford and Worcester, Warwickshire, part of West Midlands): Mythe End House, Tewkesbury, Gloucestershire GL20 6EB; phone 01684 850051.

Southern (Hampshire, Isle of Wight, SW Greater London, Surrey, West Sussex): Polesden Lacey, Dorking, Surrey RH5 6BD; phone 01372 453401.

Thames and Chilterns (Bedfordshire, Berkshire, Buckinghamshire, Hertfordshire, London N of the Thames, Oxfordshire): Hughenden Manor, High Wycombe, Buckinghamshire HP14 4LA; phone 01494 528051.

Wessex (Avon, Dorset, Somerset, Wiltshire): Eastleigh Court, Bishopstrow, Warminster, Wiltshire BA12 9HW; phone 01985 847777.

Yorkshire (Cleveland, North Humberside, North Yorkshire, most of South Yorkshire and West Yorkshire): Goddards, 27 Tadcaster Rd, Dringhouses, York YO2 2QG; phone 01904 702021.

The **Ramblers' Association** provides information about walking in the countryside. Members also receive a yearbook containing a useful guide to bed and breakfast accommodation near long-distance footpaths. Further details from 1–5 Wandsworth Road, London SW8 2XX; phone 0171 582 6878; fax 0171 587 3799.

Royal Automobile Club (RAC). See Practical Information: Roads and Driving.

The **Youth Hostels Association** (YHA) maintains more than 260 hostels. Members of the YHA get world-wide access to hostels. Further details, including terms of membership, can be obtained from Trevelyan House, 8 St Stephen's Hill, St Albans, Hertfordshire AL1 2DY; phone 01727 55215; fax 01727 44126.

HISTORICAL INFORMATION

Prehistoric Periods

Neolithic	c 3500 BC–c 1700 BC
Bronze Age	c 1700 BC–c 650 BC
Iron Age	c 650 BC–AD 43

English History

55–54 BC	Julius Caesar makes two expeditions to Britain after subjugating Gaul.
c AD 10	Cunobelin (Cymbeline), ruler of the Trinovantes, establishes his capital at Camulodunum (Colchester).
AD 43	Roman conquest of Britain begins.
AD 50	Caractacus, British leader, captured.
AD 60–61	Unsuccessful rebellion by Boudicca (Boadicea), ruler of the Iceni.
122	Hadrian's Wall begun after the Emperor's visit to Britain.
140–141	Antonine Wall built in Scotland; abandoned c 163.
209	St Alban martyred.
409	Roman rule in Britain ends.
c 449	Angles, Saxons and Jutes invade in force, establishing in the next 150 years the separate kingdoms of Kent, Sussex, Wessex, Mercia, Bernicia and Deira (merged as Northumbria), Essex and East Anglia.
539	Date which the 10C Welsh 'Annales Cambriae' gives for the death of the British leader Arthur at the Battle of Camlan.
563	St Columba founds a monastery on Iona (Hebrides).
597–616	Kent becomes the leading English kingdom under King Ethelbert. He is converted to Christianity by Augustine at the beginning of the Saint's mission to England. Augustine founds a monastery and later an archepiscopal see at Canterbury.
617–685	Supremacy of Northumbria, notably under Kings Edwin and Oswald (rulers in 616–632 and 633–641). Paulinus baptises Edwin at York in 627. Oswald helps St Aidan establish his monastery at Lindisfarne in 635.
664	Roman and Celtic churches meet at the Synod of Whitby, their decisions generally favouring Rome.
c 730–821	Mercian supremacy, notably under Kings Ethelbald and Offa (rulers in 716–757 and 757–796). Offa's Dyke defines the Mercian boundary with Wales.
731	Bede completes his 'Historia Ecclesiastica' at Jarrow.
793	Lindisfarne sacked by Danish raiders.
829	Egbert, King of Wessex (802–839), establishes supremacy for the Wessex dynasty, which lasts during the next two centuries of Danish invasions.
878	After his great victory at Edington, Alfred the Great concedes much of Eastern England to Danish control

	(the Danelaw). It is largely reconquered by his son Edward the Elder.
991	Ethelred the Unready introduces a tax, later known as Danegeld, to buy off the invading armies.
1016	Canute (Cnut), King of Denmark, becomes King of England.
1042	Wessex dynasty restored by Edward the Confessor.
1066	Norman Conquest. Harold II, after defeating the Norwegians at Stamford Bridge, is himself defeated by William of Normandy at Hastings.
1085–1086	'Domesday Book' compiled.
1087	Death of William I (William the Conqueror); accession of William II (William Rufus).
1100	William Rufus dies, killed by an arrow while hunting in the New Forest; accession of his brother, Henry I.
1135	Death of Henry I; accession of his nephew Stephen. The challenge to his claim from Henry's daughter Matilda, leads to civil war.
1154	Death of Stephen; accession of Matilda's son, Henry II, inaugurates the Plantagenet dynasty.
1167	Expulsion of English students from Paris encourages the growth of universities at Oxford and, apparently slightly later, Cambridge.
1170	Thomas Becket murdered in Canterbury Cathedral.
1171–1172	Henry II lays claim to Ireland, awarding land to Norman knights.
1189	Death of Henry II; accession of Richard I (the Lionheart), largely absent on the Third Crusade and as a prisoner on the Continent.
1199	Death of Richard the Lionheart; accession of his brother John.
1215	King John compelled by barons to sign Magna Carta, designed to protect feudal rights and baronial privileges against royal abuse.
1216	Death of King John; accession of Henry III, with the Earl of Pembroke acting as Regent during his minority.
1249	University College, Oxford, founded; followed by Merton College (1264) and Balliol (before 1266) in Oxford and Peterhouse (1281–1284) in Cambridge.
1265	Defeat and death of Simon de Montfort at the Battle of Evesham ends the barons' rebellion.
1272	Death of Henry III; accession of Edward I.
1277–1283	Edward I conquers Wales.
1290	Edward's first queen, Eleanor of Castile, dies; Eleanor Crosses are built to mark the route of her funeral procession from Lincoln to Westminster Abbey.
1307	Edward I dies on his way to confront Scottish army led by Robert Bruce; accession of Edward II.
1312	Edward II's favourite Piers Gaveston is executed by the barons.
1327	Edward II deposed by his queen, Isabella of France, and her lover Mortimer and murdered at Berkeley Castle; accession of his son as Edward III.
1337	Hundred Years' War against France begins.
c 1343	Geoffrey Chaucer born.
1348–1349	Black Death (mainly bubonic plague) reaches England.
1351	Statute of Labourers fixes wages in response to the labour shortage caused by the Black Death.
1377	Death of Edward III; accession of Richard II, son of Edward III's eldest son, the Black Prince.

1381	Peasants' Revolt, led by Wat Tyler, defeated.
c 1382	First complete translation of the Bible into English, by the religious reformer John Wyclif, or his Lollard followers, appears; revised edition in 1388.
1399	Richard II deposed by John of Gaunt's son, Henry of Bolingbroke; he dies at Pontefract Castle in 1400. As Henry IV, Bolingbroke inaugurates the Lancastrian dynasty.
1400	Geoffrey Chaucer dies.
1401–1417	Persecution of the Lollards, followers of the religious reformer John Wyclif.
1403	Rebellion by the Earl of Northumberland and his son Henry Percy (Hotspur), joining with Owen Glendower of Wales, defeated at Shrewsbury.
1413	Death of Henry IV; accession of Henry V.
1415	Henry V resumes Hundred Years' War. English victory at Agincourt.
1422	Death of Henry V; accession of Henry VI.
1450	Jack Cade's rebellion defeated.
1455	First Battle of St Albans begins the Wars of the Roses, between the Lancastrian and Yorkist factions.
1461	Henry VI deposed; the Duke of York assumes the throne as Edward IV.
1470–1471	Henry VI briefly returns to the throne. Edward IV wins a decisive Yorkist victory over the Lancastrians at Tewkesbury. Henry VI murdered.
1476	William Caxton sets up his printing press at Westminster.
1483	Death of Edward IV. His child heir, Edward V, and his younger son Richard, Duke of York, are murdered in the Tower of London, possibly by their uncle, who assumes the throne as Richard III.
1485	Death of Richard III at Bosworth Field ends the Wars of the Roses. The victor, Henry VII, initiates the Tudor dynasty.
1509	Death of Henry VII; accession of Henry VIII.
1513	English army defeats and kills James IV of Scotland at Flodden.
1534–1540	English Reformation: Henry VIII breaks with the papacy, declaring himself head of the Church and dissolving the monasteries.
1547	Death of Henry VIII; his ten-year-old son by Jane Seymour succeeds to the throne as Edward VI, with Somerset as Lord Protector.
1549	'Book of Common Prayer' issued; revised versions appear in 1552 and 1559, and a final text in 1662.
1553	Death of Edward VI; accession of Mary I, daughter of Henry VIII and Catherine of Aragon. She reunites the English church with Rome and persecutes Protestants.
1558	Protestantism restored with the death of Mary I and the accession of Elizabeth I, daughter of Henry VIII and Anne Boleyn.
1564	Shakespeare born.
1587	Execution of Mary, Queen of Scots.
1588	Spanish Armada defeated.
1599	First Globe Theatre built in Southwark.
1603	Death of Elizabeth I without a direct heir. Accession of James I (James VI of Scotland and the son of Mary, Queen of Scots) unites the crowns of England and Scotland and initiates the Stuart dynasty.

1605	Gunpowder plot, Roman Catholic conspiracy to blow up the Houses of Parliament, discovered. Its anniversary, 5 November, enters the English calendar as Guy Fawkes Day.
1611	Authorised (King James) Version of the Bible issued.
1616	Shakespeare dies.
1620	'Mayflower' sails from Plymouth.
1625	Death of James I; accession of Charles I.
1629–1640	Charles I rules without Parliament.
1642	Civil War, between the King and Parliament, begins.
1644	Royalists defeated at Marston Moor.
1645	Royalists defeated at Naseby.
1646	Charles I surrenders to the Scots.
1649	Charles I executed and the Commonwealth declared.
1653–1658	Oliver Cromwell rules as Lord Protector.
1660	Monarchy restored with the return of Charles II from exile. Royal Society founded.
1665–1666	Great Plague.
1666	Great Fire of London.
1685	Death of Charles II; accession of his Roman Catholic brother as James II. The Duke of Monmouth's Protestant rebellion is defeated at Sedgemoor.
1688	Glorious Revolution deposes James II in favour of his nephew William III, of the House of Orange, and daughter Mary II.
1689	The Bill of Rights consolidates the power of Parliament, reduces the power of the monarchy and debars Roman Catholics from the throne.
1694	Death of Mary II. Bank of England established.
1701–1713	War of the Spanish Succession. Duke of Marlborough defeats French at Blenheim, 1704.
1702	Death of William III; accession of Queen Anne, James II's second daughter.
1707	Parliamentary union of England and Scotland.
1714	Death of Queen Anne without immediate heir. The throne passes to the House of Hanover in the person of George I.
1715	Unsuccessful Jacobite rebellion in Scotland led by James II's son, the 'Old Pretender'.
1720	South Sea Bubble ruins many investors.
1721–1742	Whig ministry of Sir Robert Walpole, often described as the first Prime Minister.
1727	Death of George I; accession of his son, George II.
1745–1746	Unsuccessful Jacobite rebellion led by Charles Edward Stuart (the 'Young Pretender' or 'Bonnie Prince Charlie'), defeated at Culloden.
1756–1763	Seven Years' War.
1759	British Museum opened. James Brindley begins the Bridgewater Canal; Manchester–Worsley section opened in 1761.
1760	Death of George II; accession of his grandson, George III.
1769	James Watt patents his steam engine.
1775–1783	American War of Independence.
1779	World's first iron bridge built at Coalbrookdale in Shropshire.
1785	'The Times' begins publication, as 'The Daily Universal Register'.

1787	The Marylebone Cricket Club (MCC) founded; it moves to Lord's in 1814.
1800–1815	Napoleonic Wars. Nelson defeats Franco-Spanish fleet at Trafalgar, 1805; Peninsula Campaign, 1808–1814; Wellington defeats Napoleon at Waterloo, 1815.
1811	Because of George III's insanity the future George IV becomes Prince Regent, with full royal powers.
1811–1816	Luddite riots by workers who attack the new machinery introduced in knitting and weaving.
1819	Peterloo massacre at mass meeting in Manchester.
1820	Regency ends with the death of George III and accession of the Prince Regent as George IV.
1824	National Gallery opened in Pall Mall; it moves to Trafalgar Square in 1838.
1825	Stockton and Darlington railway opened.
1829	Catholic emancipation. Metropolitan Police Force founded.
1830	Death of George IV; accession of his younger brother, William IV. Liverpool and Manchester railway opened.
1831	Captain Swing riots by agricultural workers.
1832	First Reform Act extends the franchise and redistributes parliamentary seats to give the new industrial towns greater representation.
1834	Tolpuddle Martyrs, six Dorset farmworkers, sentenced to transportation for trying to organise an illegal trade union.
1837	Death of William IV; accession of his niece, Queen Victoria.
1838–1842	Chartist agitation for extension of vote to all adult males.
1839	'Penny post' begins.
1840	Queen Victoria marries Prince Albert of Saxe-Coburg and Gotha.
1846	Corn Laws repealed.
1847	Factory Act limits the working day to ten hours.
1850	Roman Catholic hierarchy re-established under Archbishop of Westminster.
1851	Great Exhibition.
1854–1856	Crimean War.
1861	Prince Albert dies.
1863	The Metropolitan Line, first section of London's Underground system, opened.
1867	Second Reform Act extends the franchise.
1868	Trades Union Congress (TUC) formed in Manchester.
1877	Queen Victoria proclaimed Empress of India. Society for the Protection of Ancient Buildings formed.
1882	Ancient Monuments Protection Act, the first law of its kind, gives a measure of protection to Stonehenge and 28 other prehistoric ruins.
1895	National Trust founded.
1897	Queen Victoria's Diamond Jubilee.
1899–1902	Second South African (Boer) War.
1901	Death of Queen Victoria; accession of Edward VII.
1903	Letchworth, the first 'garden city', begun.
1908	Herbert Asquith's Liberal government introduces old age pensions.
1910	Death of Edward VII; accession of George V. In 1917 he renounces all German titles and adopts the name of Windsor for the royal family.
1914–1918	First World War.

1918	Vote given to all men over 21 and all women over 30.
1921	Most of Ireland achieves independence as Irish Free State (Eire); as Northern Ireland, six counties of Ulster remain part of the United Kingdom.
1922	British Broadcasting Corporation (BBC) founded.
1924	First Labour government takes office, under Ramsay MacDonald.
1926	General Strike.
1929	Vote given to all women over 21.
1932	Green Belt established round London to control the spread of suburbs.
1936	Death of George V. The Prince of Wales briefly succeeds as Edward VIII but abdicates before being crowned; his younger brother becomes George VI. Jarrow Hunger March to London by the unemployed. BBC begins TV broadcasting.
1939–1945	Second World War.
1945	Election of Clement Attlee's Labour government, responsible for nationalising public services and other major industries, and for creating much of the Welfare State.
1949	National Parks Commission (later the Countryside Commission) established, with the power to designate parks and outstanding areas of natural beauty in England and Wales.
1951	Festival of Britain, held a century after the Great Exhibition and designed to revive national morale after World War II.
1952	Death of George VI; accession of Elizabeth II.
1956	Calder Hall, the world's first industrial-size nuclear power station, opened at Windscale (Sellafield) in Cumbria.
1959	M1, Britain's first motorway, opened.
1962	National Theatre opened.
1969	First significant discovery of North Sea oil; first supply brought ashore in 1975.
1971	Decimal currency introduced.
1973	Britain joins the European Community ('Common Market').
1979	Margaret Thatcher elected; she is twice re-elected before resigning in 1991.
1982	Falklands War.

English Sovereigns

House of Wessex

Egbert	802–839
Ethelwulf	839–855
Ethelbald	855–860
Ethelbert	860–866
Ethelred I	866–871
Alfred the Great	871–899
Edward the Elder	899–924
Athelstan	924–939
Edmund I	939–946

Eadred	946–955
Eadwig	955–959
Edgar	959–975
Edward the Martyr	975–979
Ethelred II (the Unready)	979–1016
Edmund II (Ironside)	1016

House of Skjoldung
Canute (Cnut)	1016–1035
Harold I	1035–1040
Harthacnut	1040–1042

House of Wessex
Edward the Confessor	1042–1066
Harold II	1066

House of Normandy
William I (the Conqueror)	1066–1087
William II (Rufus)	1087–1100
Henry I	1100–1135
Stephen	1135–1154

House of Plantagenet
Henry II	1154–1189
Richard I (the Lionheart)	1189–1199
John	1199–1216
Henry III	1216–1272
Edward I	1272–1307
Edward II	1307–1327
Edward III	1327–1377
Richard II	1377–1399

House of Lancaster
Henry IV	1399–1413
Henry V	1413–1422
Henry VI	1422–1461 and 1470

House of York
Edward IV	1461–1470 and 1471–1483
Edward V	1483
Richard III	1483–1485

House of Tudor
Henry VII	1485–1509
Henry VIII	1509–1547
Edward VI	1547–1553
Mary I	1553–1558
Elizabeth I	1558–1603

House of Stuart
James I	1603–1625
Charles I	1625–1649
[Commonwealth and Protectorate	1649–1660]
Charles II	1660–1685
James II	1685–1688
William III and Mary II	1688–1694

| William III | 1694–1702 |
| Anne | 1702–1714 |

House of Hanover

George I	1714–1727
George II	1727–1760
George III	1760–1820
[Regency	1811–1820]
George IV	1820–1830
William IV	1830–1837
Victoria	1837–1901

House of Saxe-Coburg

| Edward VII | 1901–1910 |

House of Windsor

George V	1910–36
Edward VIII	1936
George VI	1936–1952
Elizabeth II	1952–

ARCHITECTURAL INFORMATION

Saxon: c 400–c 1066. Shares many characteristics with Norman, notably round arches and square towers, but is generally smaller in scale and simpler in detail. Narrow vertical strips of stone used for external decoration and 'long and short work' at the corners are distinctive features.

Examples: Barton-upon-Humber, Bradford-on-Avon, Brixworth, Cambridge (St Bene't), Deerhurst, Dover (St Mary de Castro), Earls Barton, Escomb, Greensted-juxta-Ongar, Hexham Abbey (crypt), Jarrow, Lastingham (crypt), Monkwearmouth, Repton, Ripon Cathedral (crypt), Wing. Crosses at Bewcastle, Gosforth, Sandbach.

Norman: c 1050–c 1150. The style called Romanesque on the Continent. It uses round arches, square towers and simple vaulting. Vigorous carving of detail relieves the bold, weighty masses.

Examples: Barfreston, Bristol Cathedral (chapter house), Canterbury Cathedral (crypt), Durham Cathedral, Ely Cathedral (nave), Iffley, Kilpeck, Norwich Cathedral (tower, nave, transepts), Peterborough Cathedral (except W front), Rochester Cathedral (W front, nave), Romsey Abbey, Ruardean, Southwell Minster (nave, transepts, etc.), Winchester Cathedral (transepts).

Transitional. The mid 12C style which combines elements of Norman and Early English, e.g. round and pointed arches.

Examples: Chichester Cathedral (retrochoir), Fountains Abbey (nave).

Early English: c 1150–c 1280. The first phase of Gothic, which is distinguished from earlier styles by the pointed arch, the rib vault and the flying buttress. Early English differs from later Gothic in its use of simple lancet windows and love of dogtooth moulding.

Examples: Beverley Minster (choir, transepts), Canterbury Cathedral (E end), Durham Cathedral (Chapel of the Nine Altars), Fountains Abbey (Chapel of the Nine Altars), Hexham Abbey (choir, transepts), Lincoln Cathedral (especially the Angel Choir), Rievaulx Abbey (especially the choir), Ripon Cathedral (W front), Salisbury Cathedral, Wells Cathedral (W front and nave), Winchester Cathedral (retrochoir), Worcester Cathedral (E end).

Decorated: c 1280–c 1350. The second phase of Gothic, marked by the use of window tracery (developing from geometric to flowing patterns), the ogee curve and elaborately carved ornament (particularly striking on bosses, capitals and monuments).

Examples: Beverley Minster (Percy tomb), Bristol Cathedral (choir), Ely Cathedral (octagon, Lady Chapel), Exeter Cathedral, Gloucester Cathedral (tomb of Edward II), Howden, Norwich Cathedral (cloisters), Patrington, Selby Abbey (choir), Southwell Minster (chapter house), Wells Cathedral (especially the retrochoir, Lady Chapel and chapter house), York Minster (chapter house).

Perpendicular: c 1350–c 1550. The last phase of Gothic, coinciding with the appearance of the Flamboyant style in France but markedly different in its stress on verticals and horizontals. Perpendicular enlarges windows, progressively flattening their arches and reducing wall space. Lierne vaults and fan vaults make roof patterns more complex.

Examples: Beverley Minster (W front), Bristol (St Mary Redcliffe), Cambridge (King's College Chapel), Gloucester Cathedral (exterior and choir), Manchester Cathedral,

Sherborne Abbey, Westminster Abbey (Henry VII's Chapel), Windsor (St George's Chapel), and many parish churches in Norfolk, Suffolk, the Cotswolds and Somerset.

Renaissance: late 16C–early 17C. Building energy goes mainly into country houses, which preserve the medieval central hall but celebrate their freedom from the need for defence or fortification in a display of windows. Stylistically, they mix memories of Perpendicular with classical motifs from the French, Italian and Dutch Renaissance, commonly interpreted with more enthusiasm than sophistication.

Examples: Audley End, Blickling Hall, Burghley House, Burton Constable, Hardwick Hall, Hatfield House, Kirby Hall, Knole, Longleat, Montacute House, Parham, Wollaton Hall.

Laudian Gothic: 17C Gothic, as much survival as revival, tempered by classical detail. It is chiefly seen in church and university architecture, particularly at Oxford. The name refers to Charles I's archbishop but the style continues into the age of Baroque.

Examples: Cambridge (Peterhouse Chapel), Leeds (St John's), Oxford (All Souls College, Wadham College).

Baroque: late 17C–mid 18C. Marked by the use of curved forms to create spatial complexity and illusion and by exuberant decoration. In the hands of Wren, Hawksmoor and Vanbrugh, English Baroque is notably eclectic, often demonstrating its underlying classicism and periodically betraying its lingering fondness for Gothic.

Examples: Birmingham Cathedral, Blenheim Palace, Castle Howard, London (Royal Naval College at Greenwich, St Paul's Cathedral), Oxford (The Queen's College, Radcliffe Camera), Seaton Delaval Hall.

Palladianism: 17C–18C. An ideal of classical correctness and proportion derived from the work of Andrea Palladio (1508–80), introduced to England in the 1620s by Inigo Jones and revived in the 1720s by the 3rd Earl of Burlington, partly through his protégés Colen Campbell and William Kent. Its distinctive features, often assimilated into the looser vocabulary of English classicism, include the portico, the arcaded ground floor, the giant pilaster, and the open two-armed staircase.

Examples: Bath (work of John Wood the Elder and John Wood the Younger), Buxton (The Crescent), Cambridge (Senate House), Hagley Hall, Harewood House, Holkham Hall, Houghton Hall, London (Banqueting House in Whitehall, Chiswick House, Marble Hill House in Twickenham), Stourhead, Stowe, York (Assembly Rooms).

Gothick: mid 18C–early 19C revival of Gothic, sometimes called 'Strawberry Hill Gothic' (after the example of Horace Walpole's house) or 'Rococo Gothic'. Unlike its Victorian counterpart, it treats Gothic as a source of picturesque detail rather than as a system of structural principles. Its inherent playfulness, manifest in sham ruins and follies, connects it with the taste for Chinoiserie and Oriental fantasy flourishing at the same time.

Examples: Arbury Hall, Ashridge, Audley End (chapel), Lacock Abbey, Stansted Park (chapel).

Greek Revival: mid 18C–mid 19C. A return to the Greek example of simplicity and dignity in reaction against the eclectic tendencies of 18C classicism. The textbook purity advocated by James 'Athenian' Stuart in the 1750s gave way to the freer approach of Sir John Soane and C.R.

Cockerell. Like Palladianism, the Greek Revival extends the range of classicism in England rather than remaining an entirely distinct school.

Examples: Cambridge (Downing College), Chester Castle, Great Packington (church), Liverpool (St George's Hall, Bank of England), London (British Museum), Manchester (Bank of England), Oxford (Ashmolean Museum and Taylorian Institution), Shugborough.

Gothic Revival. The Victorian Gothic Revival followed Pugin and Ruskin in admiring medieval architecture for its purity as much as for its picturesqueness and in finding it a source of moral values as well as structural principles. In practice, churches range from scholarly correctness (Scott) through eclecticism (Bodley, Pearson) to wilful, creative eccentricity (Butterfield). Public buildings sometimes cultivate the Venetian Gothic praised by Ruskin, and country houses tend towards the baronial.

Examples: Brighton (St Bartholomew's), Cambridge (St John's College Chapel), Clumber Park (church), Hoar Cross (church), Knighthayes Court, Lancing College (especially the chapel), Liverpool Cathedral, London (Houses of Parliament, Albert Memorial), Manchester Town Hall, Oxford (Keble College, University Museum), Rugby School, Scarborough (St Martin-on-the-Hill), Skelton (church), Studley Royal (church), Truro Cathedral.

Art Nouveau: late 1880s–1914. Partly inspired by Ruskin, Morris and the Arts and Crafts movement, it was determined to avoid the 19C habit of revival and find new means of expression. As its love of the flowing, undulating or swirling line suggests, Art Nouveau belonged as much to the decorative arts as to architecture.

Examples: Art Nouveau was principally a continental movement and England has no buildings to compare with the work of Gaudi in Barcelona (or, for that matter, Mackintosh in Glasgow).

Art Deco: 1920s and 1930s. A Jazz Age style, influencing interior decoration and fashion as much as architecture, it drew freely on the various ingredients of 'international modernism' (Cubism, Futurism, Expressionism) to create functional and inventive effects.

Examples: London (Michelin Building), Bexhill (De La Warr Pavilion).

Brutalism: post World War II. A style influenced by Le Corbusier (none of whose buildings are in England), particularly in its love of bold, dramatic shapes and rough texture. It is epitomised by the work of James Stirling.

Examples: Cambridge (History Faculty Building), Leicester (Department of Engineering) and Oxford (Florey Building of Queen's College).

Post-modernism: 1970s to the present. A term, popularised by Charles Jencks, for the reaction against the functionalist approach of 'international modernism'. Though partly anticipated by Brutalism, Post-modernism has favoured a witty, eclectic approach under the influence of Robert Venturi.

The most famous example is the Sainsbury wing of London's National Gallery.

FURTHER READING

In addition to the specialised guidebooks recommended in earlier sections, there are two useful annual digests: *Whitaker's Almanac* and *Britain: An Official Handbook*, the latter prepared by the Central Office of Information and published by Her Majesty's Stationery Office (HMSO).

Rather than attempting a systematic bibliography, the suggestions below record those books which the present editor has found interesting or useful. They include standard general surveys and reference books but omit many specialist or local studies and all studies of individual figures.

Geology and Landscape. Two books make an ideal introduction: A.E. Trueman's *Geology and Scenery in England and Wales* (Pelican edition revised by J.B. Whittow and J.R. Hardy, 1971) and W.G. Hoskins's *The Making of the English Landscape* (Pelican edition 1970).

History and Archaeology. The one-volume *Oxford Illustrated History of Britain*, edited by Kenneth O. Morgan (1984), and *The Cambridge Historical Encyclopedia of Great Britain and Ireland*, edited by Christopher Haigh (1985), make good general introductions. The Pelican History of England runs to nine volumes by different hands, many times reprinted and revised.

Frank Barlow, *The Feudal Kingdom of England 1042–1216* (3rd edition 1972); Peter Hunter Blair, *An Introduction to Anglo-Saxon England* (2nd edition 1977); Richard Bradley, *The Prehistoric Settlement of Britain* (1978); Asa Briggs, *The Age of Improvement 1783–1867* (1959); Barry Cunliffe, *Iron Age Communities in Britain* (2nd edition 1978); A.G. Dickens, *The English Reformation* (1964); Sheppard Frere, *Britannia: A History of Roman Britain* (2nd edition 1974); E.J. Hobsbawm, *The First Industrial Nation* (1969); J.P. Kenyon, *The Stuarts* (1958); J.H. Plumb, *The Growth of Political Stability in England 1675–1725* (1967) and *The First Four Georges* (revised edition 1974); F.M. Stenton, *Anglo-Saxon England* (3rd edition 1971); E.P. Thompson, *The Making of the English Working Class* (1963); Malcolm Todd, *Roman Britain 55 BC–AD 400: The Province Beyond Ocean* (1981); C.V. Wedgwood, *The King's Peace 1637–41* (1955) and *The King's War 1641–47* (1958); P. Williams, *The Tudor Regime* (1979); G.M. Young, *Victorian England: Portrait of an Age* (1936).

For urban, industrial and transport history: Asa Briggs, *Victorian Cities* (1963); Charles Hadfield, *English Canals* (5th edition 1974) and the ensuing series of regional canal histories; Michael Robbins, *The Railway Age* (1962); L.T.C. Rolt, *Victorian Engineering* (1970); H.J. Dyos and M. Wolff (editors), *The Victorian City* (1973).

Architecture and Landscape Gardening. The county volumes in the Buildings of England series, edited and largely written by Sir Nikolaus Pevsner, are indispensable. *A History of English Architecture*, by Peter Kidson, Peter Murray and Paul Thompson (revised Pelican edition 1979), makes a useful introduction.

Jean Bony, *The English Decorated Style: Gothic Architecture Transformed 1250–1350* (1979); R.W. Brunskill, *Traditional Buildings of Britain: An Introduction to Vernacular Architecture* (1981); Kenneth Clark, *The Gothic Revival: An Essay in the History of Taste* (3rd edition 1962); Alec Clifton-Taylor, *English Parish Churches as Works of Art* (1974) and *The Pattern of English Building* (3rd edition 1971); J. Mordaunt Crook, *The Greek Revival: Neo-Classical Attitudes in British Architecture 1760–1870* (1972); Gillian Darley, *Villages of Vision* (1975); Roger Dixon and Stefan Muthesius, *Victorian Architecture* (1978); Mark Girouard, *Life in the English Country House: A Social and Architectural History* (1978) and *The Victorian Country House* (revised edition 1979); Christopher Hussey, *The Picturesque* (1927) and *English Gardens and Landscapes 1700–1750* (1967); Edward Hyams, *The English Garden* (1964); Robert Furneaux Jordan, *Victorian Architecture* (1966); Stefan Muthesius, *The English Terraced House*

(1982); Roy Strong, *The Renaissance Garden in England* (1979); John Summerson, *Architecture in Britain: 1530–1830* (Pelican History of Art, 6th edition 1977); Geoffrey Webb, *Architecture in Britain: The Middle Ages* (Pelican History of Art, 1956).

Painting and Sculpture. *The Genius of British Painting*, ed. David Piper (1975) is a good general introduction. *The Oxford History of English Art* includes several notable volumes.

Martin Hardie, *Water-Colour Painting in Britain* (3 vols, 1966–68); Louis Hawes, *Presences of Nature: British Landscape 1780–1830* (1982); Andrew Hemingway, *The Norwich School of Painters 1803–1833* (1979); Luke Herrmann, *British Landscape Painting of the Eighteenth Century* (1973); Tim Hilton, *The Pre-Raphaelites* (1970); John Murdoch, Jim Murrell, Patrick J. Noon and Roy Strong, *The English Miniature* (1981); Ronald Paulson, *Emblem and Expression: Meaning in English Art of the Eighteenth Century* (1975); Sir Nikolaus Pevsner, *The Englishness of English Art* (1956); David Piper, *The English Face* (1957); Graham Reynolds, *A Concise History of Watercolours* (1971); Michael Rosenthal, *British Landscape Painting* (1982); Lawrence Stone, *Sculpture in Britain: The Middle Ages* (Pelican History of Art, 2nd edition 1972); Roy Strong, *The English Icon: Elizabethan and Jacobean Portraiture* (1969) and *The English Renaissance Miniature* (1983); Margaret Whinney, *Sculpture in Britain: 1530–1830* (Pelican History of Art, 1964).

Literature. The 5th edition of *The Oxford Companion to English Literature*, edited by Margaret Drabble (1985), is a standard reference book, though the present author may be forgiven for preferring *The Cambridge Guide to Literature in English*, edited by Ian Ousby (1993).

Travel books. Very few stand out from the vast list. William Cobbett's *Rural Rides* (1830) is matchless. The four-volume *Torrington Diaries*, written in the 1780s and 1790s and edited this century by C. Bruyn Andrews (reprinted 1970), and Henry James's *English Hours* (1905) deserve a wider audience. Ian Ousby's *The Englishman's England* (1990) studies the history of travel and tourism.

LONDON

The capital lies about 40 miles inland from the mouth of the Thames, cut in two from E to W by the winding course of the river. In its full extent Greater London covers 625 square miles and consists of 33 separate boroughs, including the Cities of London and Westminster. It houses about 6.8 million people. Though this number is regularly swollen by the influx of commuters and tourists, population density is still much lower than in many of the world's other major cities. Nearly one-third of London is still free of major building, and the visitor will quickly appreciate the parks and open spaces that relieve even the most crowded neighbourhoods.

The central part on which the tourist concentrates is a small fraction of Greater London: a strip less than two miles deep and about four miles wide as the crow flies, lying mainly on the N bank of the river and stretching from Kensington Gardens in the W to Tower Bridge and the Tower of London in the E. The West End, spreading from the political centre at Westminster, includes the shopping areas of Knightsbridge, Kensington High St., Oxford St., Piccadilly and Covent Garden; the restaurant and theatre land of Piccadilly Circus and Leicester Square; and a host of museums and galleries, among them the South Kensington group, the Tate Gallery on Millbank, the National Gallery and National Portrait Gallery by Trafalgar Square, and the British Museum in Bloomsbury. The square mile of the City, dominated by banking and finance, is best known to tourists for St Paul's Cathedral and the Tower of London.

'Blue Guide London' and the 'Blue Guide Museums and Galleries of London' give a fuller description than the condensed and selective account below, which is intended for the stranger whose visit to the city is one stage in the exploration of England as a whole. It is divided into three sections: the West End; the City, the East End and the South Bank; and Outer London. These dispense with the walking tours used to describe cities elsewhere in this guide and list the main sights in alphabetical order. The asterisks and double asterisks which elsewhere mark items or places of special interest are not used, since inclusion in these lists constitutes a recommendation in itself. The nearest tube (underground railway) stations are indicated. For opening times, see the general remarks in Notes On Using This Guide; special peculiarities are noted in the text below. Since arrangements are liable to change, visitors with only limited time to spend in London are urged to check in advance.

The TI Centres managed by the London Tourist Board can advise about opening hours and many other matters. They are located at: the underground station concourse of Heathrow Airport, Terminals 1, 2 and 3; Liverpool Street Station, EC2; Selfridges, Oxford St., W1; and the forecourt of Victoria Station, SW1. The City of London Information Centre is at St Paul's Churchyard, EC4. The general number of Visitorcall, a 24-hour recorded information service, is 0839 123 456; to order a free card listing the phone numbers of individual services call 0171 971 0026. (Calls cost 36p per minute cheap rate, 48p per minute at all other times.) The All-Britain Travel Centre run by the British Tourist Authority at 12 Regent St., Piccadilly Circus, SW1 books rail, coach and air travel, sightseeing tours, theatre tickets and accommodation, as well as providing information about the whole country. Of the Outer London boroughs described in Route 3, Greenwich and Richmond also have TI Centres.

1

The West End

Apsley House: see Hyde Park and Kensington Gardens.

Banqueting House, Whitehall, SW1. Tube: Westminster (Circle, District), Charing Cross (Northern, Bakerloo, Jubilee). DoE monument. Closed Mondays and at short notice for government functions. The one surviving relic of the old Palace of Whitehall, it was built for James I by Inigo Jones in 1625. Revolutionary for its date, his Palladian design exercised a lasting influence on English public buildings. The main hall has a magnificent painted ceiling (1629–34) by Rubens. Charles I was executed outside the hall in 1649—though not, perhaps, on the exact spot now marked with a plaque.

British Museum, Great Russell St., Bloomsbury, WC1. Tube: Tottenham Court Road (Central, Northern), Holborn (Central, Piccadilly). Sir Robert Smirke's Greek Revival building (1823–47), with its great colonnaded entrance, houses the national collection of antiquities. Since the first bequest from Sir Hans Sloane in the 18C, its holdings of archaeology and art have grown to such size and variety that no single visit can begin to do them justice. The summary below lists the various departments, with a brief selection of their most famous items.

Greek and Roman: the Elgin Marbles, including the sculptures from the Parthenon. Western Asiatic: Assyrian reliefs and sculptures. Egyptian: the Rosetta Stone. Oriental: a matchless display of Chinese ceramics. Prints and Drawings: cartoons by Michelangelo and Raphael. Coins and Medals. Prehistoric and Romano-British: the Mildenhall Treasure. Medieval and later: the Sutton Hoo Treasure, and the Waddesdon Bequest of 14–17C objets d'art. The **British Library**, due to move to Euston Road, is still housed in the British Museum at present. There are tours of its domed Reading Room, not otherwise open to casual visitors. The public exhibition galleries display illuminated manuscripts (the Lindisfarne Gospels), historical and literary manuscripts (two of the four extant original copies of Magna Carta; Shakespeare's signature) and specimens of early printing (a Gutenberg Bible). The British Museum's ethnographic collection is displayed at the Museum of Mankind and the natural history collection at the Natural History Museum, both separately described below.

Buckingham Palace and **St James's Park**, SW1. Tube: Victoria (Circle, District, Victoria), St James's Park (Circle, District), Hyde Park Corner (Piccadilly), Charing Cross (Northern, Bakerloo, Jubilee). Palace: open daily August to early October. Royal Mews: open Wednesday and Thursday afternoons except Ascot Week and state occasions. Queen's Gallery: closed Mondays.

The palace has been the sovereign's London residence since 1837. The dull Edwardian façade facing the Queen Victoria Memorial and the Mall has never deterred tourists. They have come in even greater numbers since the state rooms, with their sumptuous decoration and fine collection of art, were first opened to the public in 1993 to help pay for repairs to Windsor Castle after its disastrous fire. The ceremony of Changing the Guard takes place at 11.30 every day from April to early August and on alternate days from August to March. On the Saturday nearest 11 June the Queen and other members of the royal household travel in procession along the Mall to Horse Guards Parade for the ceremony of Trooping the Colour, which marks the Queen's official birthday.

St James's Park, S of the Mall, is one of the most attractive London parks, laid out in an aristocratic surrounding of palaces and government buildings and commanding a famous view towards Westminster. Ornamental wildfowl frequent the lake in the centre and Duck Island, at the E end, is their breeding ground. A band plays in the park from June to September.

In Buckingham Gate and Buckingham Palace Rd, around the corner from the Palace in the direction of Victoria Station, are: the *Royal Mews*, with the Queen's horses, state coaches, harnesses and liveries; and the *Queen's Gallery*, with changing displays drawn from the royal art collections.

Carlyle's House, 24 Cheyne Row, Chelsea, SW3. Tube: Sloane Square (Circle, District), South Kensington (Circle, District, Piccadilly). NT. Open from April to end of October; closed Mondays (except Bank Holiday Mondays) and Tuesdays. Thomas Carlyle and his wife Jane Welsh Carlyle lived in this Georgian terraced house from 1834 until their deaths. Filled with furniture, pictures and mementoes from their long residence, its rooms still radiate the atmosphere of dignified simplicity they established.

Chelsea Royal Hospital: see Royal Hospital.

Courtauld Institute Galleries, Somerset House, The Strand, WC2. Tube: Aldwych (Piccadilly), Temple (Circle, District). Part of the University of London, the galleries have notably strong collections of the French Impressionists and Post-Impressionists, early Italian painters, and Tiepolo and Rubens.

Covent Garden, WC2. Tube: Covent Garden (Piccadilly), Leicester Square (Northern, Piccadilly). Laid out in the style of an Italian piazza by Inigo Jones in 1631–39, Covent Garden was for centuries London's main fruit and vegetable market. This moved to Battersea in 1974 but the 19C *Central Market Building*, with its iron and glass roofs, has been restored as the centrepiece of a lively, fashionable area of shops, restaurants, winebars and street entertainment. At the SE corner of the Piazza the *Flower Market Building* houses the *London Transport Museum*, with horse, motor and trolley buses, trams and railway rolling stock, and London Transport posters. The *Theatre Museum* (closed Mondays) displays the Victoria and Albert Museum's theatre collection. *St Paul's*, Inigo Jones's church (rebuilt to his original design in 1795) on the W side of the Piazza, contains monuments testifying to Covent Garden's long connection with artists and actors. E of the Piazza are the *Royal Opera House*, Bow St., the home of the Royal Ballet and Royal Opera companies, and the *Theatre Royal*, Drury Lane, on the site of the theatres managed by Garrick and Sheridan.

Dickens House, 48 Doughty St., Bloomsbury, WC1. Tube: Russell Square (Piccadilly). Closed Sundays. Dickens rented this terraced house in 1837–39, the period of 'Oliver Twist' and 'Nicholas Nickleby'. The fine collection of memorabilia—portraits, furniture, personal relics, letters, manuscripts, and an extensive Dickens library—has not entirely banished the atmosphere of a family home.

Geological Museum, Exhibition Rd, South Kensington, SW7. Tube: South Kensington (Circle, District, Piccadilly). Its highlights include: a magnificent collection of gemstones, in both their natural state and various stages of cutting; an excellent audio-visual display, 'The Story of the Earth'; exhibits illustrating the regional geology of Great Britain; and the world's largest display of metalliferous ores.

Houses of Parliament, Parliament Square, Westminster, SW1. Tube: Westminster (Circle, District). The Houses of Parliament and Westminster Hall are no longer open for tours, except when organised by a Member of Parliament (MP) or peer. However, visitors are admitted to the Strangers' Galleries (public galleries) during debates. The House of Commons usually sits from 14.30 on Monday to Thursday and from 09.30 on Fridays; the House of Lords sits from 14.40 on Tuesdays, Wednesdays and some Mondays, from 15.00 on Thursdays and from 11.00 on some Fridays. Tickets can be obtained from the appropriate MP, peer or foreign embassy in London; those without tickets should queue outside St Stephen's entrance. There are short recesses at Christmas and Easter and a summer recess from the end of July to the middle of October. The official State Opening of Parliament by the Queen usually takes place in early November.

The handsome Gothic Revival buildings (1840–50; Sir Charles Barry and A.W.N. Pugin) are best seen from Westminster Bridge, the Thames or the Albert Embankment on the opposite side of the river. The stately façade is enlivened by rich decoration and three striking towers. The *Clock Tower* at the N end is recognised throughout the world as an emblem of London; strictly speaking, the name 'Big Ben' refers to the hour bell and not the clock. The *House of Lords* occupies the N half of the building and the *House of Commons* the S.

The formal term, the Palace of Westminster, is a reminder that Parliament stands on a site used by monarchs as their chief London residence from the reign of Edward the Confessor (or perhaps earlier) until Henry VIII's time. The beautiful *Westminster Hall*, interrupting the Parliament Square façade, survived the fire which destroyed most of the medieval buildings in 1834. Originally built in 1097, the Hall was remodelled in 1394–1492, when the magnificent oak roof was added. It was the scene of Richard II's deposition in 1399 and the trials of Sir Thomas More in 1535 and Charles I in 1649. Across the road from the Victoria Tower is another survival of the medieval palace, the low, moated *Jewel Tower* (EH, all year), with fine original bosses and an exhibition which includes capitals from Westminster Hall. *Victoria Tower Gardens*, with fine river views, also have memorials to the suffragettes Emmeline Pankhurst and her daughter Christabel.

Hyde Park and Kensington Gardens, mainly W2. Tube: Marble Arch (Central), Hyde Park Corner (Piccadilly), Queensway (Central) and High Street Kensington (Circle, District) among others. Apsley House/Wellington Museum: closed Mondays. Hyde Park merges with its western neighbour, Kensington Gardens, to form a large open space of more than 600 acres, still green and pleasant despite the tower blocks on the skyline round its edges. The *Serpentine*, an artificial lake with waterfowl, and its continuation as the *Long Water* cut diagonally across. **Marble Arch** (1828; John Nash) stands among the busy traffic islands at the NE corner of Hyde Park. Nearby is *Speakers' Corner*, where open-air orators gather on Sundays. **Hyde Park Corner**, at the SE end, is marked by Decimus Burton's *Wellington Arch* (1828). The Duke of Wellington lived from 1817 until his death in 1852 at *Apsley House* ('No. 1, London'), now handsomely restored as the **Wellington Museum**. Built by Robert Adam in 1771–78 and remodelled by

Benjamin Wyatt in the 1820s, it contains portraits and relics of Wellington and his contemporaries which form a vivid record of the Napoleonic period, and superb paintings presented to the Duke from the Spanish royal collection (Goya, Murillo, Rubens and Velasquez). The sandtrack for riders known as *Rotten Row* leads from Hyde Park Corner through the park, between Knightsbridge and the Serpentine. The *Serpentine Gallery* holds exhibitions of modern art. Long Water stretches to the N, with a statue of Peter Pan (1912) on its bank. Sir Gilbert Scott's massively elaborate *Albert Memorial* (1863–72) stands on the S edge of Kensington Gardens, looking across Kensington Gore to the domed **Royal Albert Hall** (1867–71). Though many types of public event take place here, the Hall is particularly famous for the Promenade concerts in July–September.

Kensington Palace (DoE monument), on the W side of the Gardens, was the sovereign's residence from 1689 until 1760. Queen Victoria, born here in 1819, lived at the palace until her accession in 1837. It is still the London home for various members of the Royal Family, though parts are open to the public. The original building of 1605 was altered by Sir Christopher Wren and Nicholas Hawksmoor in 1689–96. Externally, it is much as they left it, but the interior was sumptuously remodelled by Colen Campbell in 1718–21 and William Kent in 1722–24. The state apartments contain paintings and furniture from the royal collection. The ground floor has a display of court dress and uniforms.

Kensington Gardens: see Hyde Park and Kensington Gardens.

London Planetarium: see Madame Tussaud's Waxworks.

London Transport Museum: see Covent Garden.

Madame Tussaud's Waxworks, Marylebone Rd, NW1. Tube: Baker Street (Circle, Metropolitan, Bakerloo, Jubilee). Open all day Sunday as well as weekdays. The most famous waxworks in the world, it exhibits historical tableaux and figures of contemporary celebrities. Among the murderers and assassins in the Chamber of Horrors are death masks and historical items from the French Revolution. An inclusive ticket also admits visitors to the adjoining *London Planetarium*.

Museum of Mankind, 6 Burlington Gardens, Piccadilly, W1. Tube: Piccadilly Circus (Bakerloo, Piccadilly), Green Park (Victoria, Piccadilly, Jubilee). The British Museum's ethnographic collection, particularly strong in material illustrating the tribal societies of West Africa, Oceania and North and South America, is shown in a series of imaginatively staged exhibitions. They are changed approximately every year.

National Gallery, Trafalgar Square, WC2. Tube: Charing Cross (Northern, Bakerloo, Jubilee), Leicester Square (Northern, Piccadilly). William Wilkins's original building (1838) and Robert Venturi's Sainsbury Wing (1991) house the national collection of European art from the 15C to the early 20C. It is large and rich enough to defeat anyone attempting a single comprehensive tour. The selection below lists some of the most famous works usually on view. Since pictures are often moved and rooms rearranged, they are given alphabetically by schools and artists.

British: Constable (The Haywain; Salisbury Cathedral); Gainsborough, Thomas (Mrs Siddons); Hogarth (Marriage à la Mode); Turner (The Fighting Téméraire Tugged to her Last Berth; Rain, Steam, and Speed—The Great Western Railway). Dutch: Hobbema (The Avenue, Middleharnis);

Rembrandt (two self-portraits); Vermeer (Young Woman Seated at a Virginal; Young Woman Standing at a Virginal). Flemish: Van Dyck (portrait of Charles I); Rubens (an outstanding collection, including The Rape of the Sabine Women). French, 17C: Claude (superb group of classical landscapes). French Impressionists: Monet (The Thames below Westminster; Water Lilies); Renoir (The Umbrellas). German: Holbein (The Ambassadors). Italian, 13–15C: Giovanni Bellini (Doge Leonardo Loredan); Botticelli (Mystic Nativity; Venus and Mars); Leonardo da Vinci ('Virgin of the Rocks'); Piero della Francesca (Baptism of Christ); Uccello (Battle of San Romano; St George and the Dragon). Italian, 16C: Raphael (Pope Julius II); Titian (Bacchus and Ariadne). Netherlandish: Van Eyck (The Arnolfini Marriage). Spanish: Goya (Duke of Wellington); Velasquez (The 'Rokeby' Venus).

National Portrait Gallery, 2 St Martin's Place, WC2. Tube: Leicester Square (Northern, Piccadilly), Charing Cross (Northern, Bakerloo, Jubilee). Around the corner from the National Gallery the emphasis is on the sitters rather than the artists, though Holbein, Van Dyck, Hogarth, Reynolds and Gainsborough are all represented. Arranged chronologically (beginning on the second floor), the collection offers a pageant of the famous in all walks of life from the Middle Ages to the present.

Natural History Museum, Cromwell Rd, South Kensington, SW7. Tube: South Kensington (Circle, District, Piccadilly). Alfred Waterhouse's elaborate Romanesque building (1873–81), with its fine terracotta panels, is as impressive as the collections it houses. These consist of fossil and living plants and animals, minerals, rocks and meteorites, though the exhibitions on particular themes added in recent years show an increasing bias towards biology and man. The most popular exhibits are the dinosaurs in the vast Central Hall, dominated by the 85ft-long plaster-cast skeleton of Diplodocus carnegii.

Palace of Westminster: see Houses of Parliament.

Queen's Gallery: see Buckingham Palace and St James's Park.

Regent's Park, NW1. Tube: Regent's Park (Bakerloo), Baker Street (Circle, Metropolitan, Bakerloo, Jubilee) and, for the zoo, Mornington Crescent and Camden Town (both Northern). The London Waterbus Company runs a service along Regent's Park Canal from Camden Lock and Little Venice to the zoo (daily from April to October, weekends in winter).

Originally a royal hunting ground, Regent's Park was laid as an aristocratic 'garden suburb' by John Nash from 1812 onwards, and named after the Prince Regent, who contemplated building a country house here. A road known as the Outer Circle runs around the outside; its S half is flanked by monumental Regency terraces, largely by Nash. The S part of the park itself contains a large artificial lake, the home of many wildfowl, and the pretty *Queen Mary's Gardens*, enclosed by the Inner Circle. The open-air theatre stages performances of Shakespeare in the summer. In the N part of the park lie the *Regent's Canal* and the **Regent's Park Zoo**, officially the Gardens of the Zoological Society of London. Founded in 1825 and opened to the public in 1847, it pioneered the exhibition of exotic animals. Part of its large collection has been transferred to the more spacious Whipsnade Zoo (Route 52B). A major redevelopment programme began in 1993.

Royal Academy of Arts, Burlington House, Piccadilly, W1. Tube: Piccadilly Circus (Bakerloo, Piccadilly), Green Park (Victoria, Piccadilly, Jubilee). Although it maintains its school of art, the Royal Academy is now known above all for its exhibitions. The annual Summer Exhibition (May–August) shows contemporary British painting, sculpture, architecture and engraving which have not previously been exhibited; its tone is conservative. At other times the Academy mounts loan exhibitions. The building is in origin a mid-17C house, remodelled by Colen Campbell for the 3rd Earl of Burlington in c 1717–20 and expanded in the 19C.

Royal Albert Hall: see Hyde Park and Kensington Gardens.

Royal Hospital, Royal Hospital Rd, Chelsea, SW3. Tube: Sloane Square (Circle, District). Wren designed the handsome brick buildings of this refuge for old and disabled soldiers in 1682–92. It still houses about 420 pensioners, who wear scarlet uniforms in summer and dark blue ones in winter. Visitors can see the grounds, chapel, hall and museum. The Chelsea Flower Show takes place each May in *Ranelagh Gardens*, to the E.

Royal Mews: see Buckingham Palace and St James's Park.

Royal Opera House: see Covent Garden.

St James's Park: see Buckingham Palace and St James's Park.

Science Museum, Exhibition Rd, South Kensington, SW7. Tube: South Kensington (Circle, District, Piccadilly). It displays a remarkable collection of machinery and industrial plant, working models, and scientific apparatus and instruments of virtually every kind. These include historic steam, oil, turbine and wind engines, railway locomotives ('Puffing Billy', 1813) and rolling stock, cars and aircraft. A special exhibit is devoted to the fringes of present-day knowledge, including space flight. The top floors house the *Wellcome Museum of the History of Medicine*.

Serpentine Gallery: see Hyde Park and Kensington Gardens.

Sir John Soane's Museum, 13 Lincoln's Inn Fields, WC2. Tube: Holborn (Central, Piccadilly). Closed Sundays and Mondays. The architect Sir John Soane (1753–1837) created this small museum in his home on the N side of Lincoln's Inn Fields, leaving his unmistakable imprint on the ingeniously contrived layout of the rooms and the richly varied collections which crowd them. Two series of paintings by Hogarth and the sarcophagus of Seti I are outstanding. For the rest of Lincoln's Inn, see Route 2, Inns of Court.

South Kensington Museums: see Geological Museum, Natural History Museum, Science Museum and Victoria and Albert Museum.

Tate Gallery, Millbank, SW1. Tube: Pimlico (Victoria). Opened in 1897 thanks to the generosity of the sugar magnate Sir Henry Tate, the gallery houses the national collection of British paintings from the 16C onwards, and modern paintings and sculpture, both British and foreign, from the Impressionists to the present day. The main building contains a representative collection of the British schools of landscape and portrait painting, with outstanding groups of work by Reynolds, Gainsborough, Stubbs, Blake, Samuel Palmer, Constable, the Pre-Raphaelites and Whistler. The collection of 20C British art includes groups of work by the Bloomsbury Group and the Vorticists and, among sculptors, Moor and Hepworth. Of foreign schools and artists, the French Impressionists and Picasso and Braque are particularly well represented. James Stirling's Clore Gallery (1987) displays items from the matchless collection of Turner's work which the artist bequeathed to the nation.

Theatre Museum: see Covent Garden.

Victoria and Albert Museum, Cromwell Rd, South Kensington, SW7. Tube: South Kensington (Circle, District, Piccadilly). The 'V and A' houses an unrivalled collection of applied and decorative art, probably the largest and certainly the most bewilderingly various in the world. Several miles of exhibition space contain paintings, sculpture, ceramics, woodwork, metal-work, jewellery, armour, textiles, carpets and furniture of most periods and many cultures. The displays are divided into two categories: the popular Primary Galleries, where works of art in different media are grouped together by period, style or nationality; and, for the specialist, the Study Galleries concentrating on works of the same type or medium. Exhibits include rooms reconstructed from demolished London buildings or designed especially for the museum (notably by William Morris and Philip Webb). The paintings, prints, drawings and photographs, largely but not exclusively housed in the new Henry Cole Wing, include cartoons by Raphael, English and Continental portrait miniatures, and work by Constable.

Wallace Collection, Hertford House, Manchester Square, W1. Tube: Bond Street (Central, Jubilee). Though not as well known to tourists as the National Gallery, the Tate Gallery or the Victoria and Albert Museum, the Wallace Collection is the single most important art collection in London. Remarkable for the choiceness and variety of its contents, it is particularly notable for 18C French painting (Boucher, Fragonard, Watteau); furniture and porcelain; works by Titian, Velasquez, Rubens, Van Dyck, Rembrandt, Hals (Laughing Cavalier), Poussin (Dance to the Music of Time), Hobbema, Canaletto and Bonington; and European arms and armour. The setting is an 18C town house and the arrangement of the exhibition rooms gracefully exploits its atmosphere, juxtaposing paintings with furniture, sculpture and smaller works of art.

Wellcome Museum of the History of Medicine: see Science Museum.

Wellington Museum: see Hyde Park and Kensington Gardens.

Westminster Abbey, Broad Sanctuary, Westminster, SW1. Tube: Westminster, St James's Park (both Circle, District). The Abbey has unique importance as the church where most English monarchs have been crowned and buried. Although Saxon and Norman monasteries stood on the site, the present building is largely Early English, begun by Henry III in 1245 and continued after 1388 in harmony with the earlier work. The W towers and façade were built by Hawksmoor to Wren's design in c 1735. Inside, the grand proportions and delicate details of Henry Yevele's nave are almost overwhelmed by the monuments which make the Abbey England's chief memorial to its famous dead. The tombs of sovereigns from Henry III (d. 1272) to George II (d. 1760) lie in the richest parts of the Abbey, at the E end: the *Chapel of Henry VII* (1503–19), a supreme example of late Perpendicular architecture, and the *Chapel of St Edward the Confessor*, built by Henry III to house the mutilated shrine of the king who had rebuilt the Abbey in 1065. The S Transept is more famous as *Poets' Corner*, overflowing with graves and memorials of writers from Chaucer onwards. The monastic buildings off the cloister include: the 12C *Chapter House* (EH, all year plus Mondays in winter); the 11C *Pyx Chamber* (EH, all year plus Mondays in winter), with an exhibition of Abbey treasures; and the *Norman Undercroft*, with a museum displaying the effigies used at royal funeral processions.

Zoological Gardens: see Regent's Park.

2

The City, East End and South Bank

All Hallows by the Tower: see the Tower of London.

Barbican, London Wall, EC2. Tube: Barbican (Circle, Metropolitan, closed Sundays), St Paul's (Central), Moorgate (Circle, Metropolitan, Northern). The 60-acre modern complex of public and residential buildings stands near the site of the N gate of a 2C Roman fort and the Roman city wall, heightened in the Middle Ages. Parts of the wall have been exposed, and a signposted walk follows its course along London Wall to the Tower of London (see below). The **Museum of London** (closed Mondays), at the SW corner, uses imaginative displays to present the capital's history and its social and domestic life from earliest times to the recent past. The **Barbican Centre**, beyond the partly medieval church of *St Giles without Cripplegate* to the N, includes the *Royal Shakespeare Company Theatre*, with its large main auditorium and the smaller Pit auditorium; the *Concert Hall* of the London Symphony Orchestra; and the *Barbican Art Gallery* (closed Mondays except Bank Holidays), with changing exhibitions of modern art and selections from the City of London's outstanding collection.

Bethnal Green Museum of Childhood, Cambridge Heath Rd, E2. Tube: Bethnal Green (Central). Closed Fridays. A branch of the Victoria and Albert Museum, it displays one of the world's largest collections of toys, dolls, etc., with a particularly fine group of dolls' houses.

City churches: see St Paul's Cathedral.

Dr Johnson's House, 17 Gough Square, EC4. Tube: Blackfriars (Circle, District), Chancery Lane (Central). Closed Sundays. This early 18C building, in a little square off the N side of Fleet St., is the only one of Samuel Johnson's many London addresses to survive. His home from 1749 to 1758, it contains portraits, letters and personal relics.

Geffrye Museum, Kingsland Rd, Shoreditch, E2. Tube: Liverpool Street (Central, Circle, Metropolitan), and then bus or 1m walk. Closed Mondays except Bank Holidays. A small museum of domestic and interior design, with rooms illustrating the main changes of style from 1600 to the 1930s, it is well worth a visit despite its out-of-the-way location. It occupies a group of early 18C almshouses.

George Inn, Borough High St., Southwark, SE1. Tube: London Bridge (Northern). Both an NT property and a working pub, the George is the only galleried inn still standing in London and the only survivor of the great coaching inns on Borough High St. which appear in the pages of Chaucer, Shakespeare and Dickens. In its present form the façade dates from c 1676.

Globe Theatre: see Shakespeare Globe Museum.

Gray's Inn: see Inns of Court.

Hayward Gallery: see South Bank Centre.

Imperial War Museum, Lambeth Rd, SE1. Tube: Lambeth North (Bakerloo), Elephant and Castle (Northern, Bakerloo). It is devoted to all aspects of 20C warfare and to the part played by Britain and the Commonwealth in the two World Wars. As well as weaponry, military vehicles, uniforms, medals, documents, photographs and posters, the displays include an important collection of 20C art (Sargent, Paul Nash, Wyndham Lewis, Stanley Spencer, John Piper).

Inner Temple: see Inns of Court.

Inns of Court, off Fleet St., EC4 and High Holborn, WC1. Tube: Temple (Circle, District), Chancery Lane (Central). The four great inns of court, which originated in the 13C, hold the exclusive right of conferring the rank of barrister in England and Wales. Each has a dining hall, library and chapel, set among squares, courts and gardens like those of Oxford and Cambridge colleges. Visitors are usually admitted freely to the precincts (except the Inner Temple and Middle Temple gardens) and to the Temple Church; ask at the Porters' Lodges about admission to other buildings. The inns lie close to the boundary between the City of Westminster and the City of London, marked by Temple Bar at the junction of Fleet St. with the Strand. Immediately to the S are the **Middle Temple** and the **Inner Temple**, on land that belonged to the Knights Templar. The **Temple Church** is one of five remaining round churches in England. Its round part, which contains Templar effigies, was consecrated in 1185; the chancel was added in 1240. **Lincoln's Inn**, N of Fleet St. on Chancery Lane, has the dignified 17C New Square, restored 17C Chapel and 16C Old Hall. Beyond lie Lincoln's Inn Fields, central London's largest square; for Sir John Soane's Museum on the N side, see Route 1. **Gray's Inn**, N of High Holborn, has gardens said to have been laid out by its most famous Treasurer, Sir Francis Bacon, whose statue stands in South Square. The heavily restored half-timbered façade of **Staple Inn**, on the S side of Holborn, is the most picturesque relic of the nine subordinate Inns of Chancery, dissolved in the 19C.

Lincoln's Inn: see Inns of Court.

Middle Temple: see Inns of Court.

Monument, Monument St., EC3. Tube: Monument (Circle, District). Closed Sunday afternoons in winter. Sir Christopher Wren designed this fluted Doric column topped by a flaming urn to commemorate the Great Fire of 1666, which started in nearby Pudding Lane. A winding staircase leads to the upper gallery (202ft), worth the climb for its view.

Museum of London: see Barbican.

Museum of the Moving Image: see South Bank Centre.

National Film Theatre: see South Bank Centre.

Royal Festival Hall: see South Bank Centre.

Royal National Theatre: see South Bank Centre.

Royal Shakespeare Company Theatre: see Barbican.

St Paul's Cathedral, EC4. Tube: St Paul's (Central), Mansion House (Circle, District). Despite the modern office blocks, Sir Christopher Wren's church still just manages to dominate the top of Ludgate Hill. Built in 1675–1710 to replace the medieval cathedral destroyed in the Great Fire of 1666, it combines a Gothic ground plan with classical details and baroque elements of which the most striking is the great central dome. Nicholas Stone's statue of John Donne survives from the old building. The *Crypt* contains the tombs of Nelson and Wellington and *Painters' Corner*. Wren lies beneath a terse epitaph in the N transept. A staircase leads up the dome to the *Whispering Gallery* and fine views from the *Stone Gallery* and *Golden Gallery*.

Visitors dismayed by the crowds St Paul's often attracts can seek out the City churches Wren and Hawksmoor built after the Great Fire. Many have been restored after wartime bomb damage. They include: to the E, *St Vedast* (Foster Lane), *St Mary-le-Bow* (Cheapside), *St Stephen* (Walbrook), Hawksmoor's *St Mary Woolnoth* (Lombard St. and King William St.), *St Michael* and *St Peter* (Cornhill); near the Thames to the S, *St Andrew-by-the-Wardrobe* (Queen Victoria St.), *St James Garlickhythe* (Upper Thames St.), *St Magnus the Martyr* (Lower Thames St.), and the shell of *St Dunstan-in-the-East* (off Lower Thames St.); and along Fleet St. to the W, *St Bride* (with an interesting crypt museum) and *St Clement Danes*. See also the Monument.

Shakespeare Globe Museum, Bear Gardens, Bankside, Southwark, SE1. Tube: London Bridge (Northern). The museum is devoted to the history of Bankside in the Elizabethan and Jacobean eras, when it was the centre of London's theatre district. Displays include a full working replica of the Cockpit theatre (1616), used for workshop productions. Points of interest nearby include the site of the Rose Theatre on Rose Alley, discovered in 1989 and rescued from modern redevelopment only after the most vigorous campaign. A plaque on the wall in Park St. marks the approximate site of Shakespeare's Globe Theatre, built in 1599. It burned down in 1613, and the second Globe was demolished in 1644. On the nearby riverfront the Shakespeare Globe Trust is building a replica of the first Globe, together with a small indoor theatre designed by Inigo Jones (due to open in 1995).

South Bank Centre, SE1. Tube: Waterloo (Northern, Bakerloo), Embankment (Circle, District, Northern, Bakerloo). The post-war complex of cultural institutions around the S ends of Waterloo Bridge and Hungerford Bridge includes: the **Royal Festival Hall** and two smaller concert halls, the *Queen Elizabeth Hall* and the *Purcell Room*; the **Hayward Gallery**, with changing exhibitions of contemporary art; the **Museum of the Moving Image**, devoted to the history of film and television; the **National Film Theatre**; and the **Royal National Theatre**, with its three auditoria (the Olivier, the Lyttelton and the Cottesloe).

Southwark Cathedral, Borough High St., SE1. Tube: London Bridge (Northern). This fascinating church (raised to cathedral status in 1905) lies at the S end of London Bridge, hemmed in by Borough Market, the railway and the river. Its choir and retrochoir, begun in 1207, are perhaps the earliest Gothic work in London. The monuments, a homely contrast to the grand collection in Westminster Abbey, include the tomb of John Gower (d. 1408). The 20C memorial to Shakespeare is a reminder of the church's close tie with the 16–17C theatres on neighbouring Bankside (see Shakespeare Globe Museum). The cathedral was also connected with the Bishops of Winchester. A fragment of their 13C palace survives on nearby Clink St. (EH).

Temple Church: see Inns of Court.

Tower Bridge, EC3. Tube: Tower Hill (District, Circle). Built in 1886–94, Tower Bridge spans the Thames immediately below the Tower of London. The road connecting its towers is formed by drawbridges which can be raised to allow vessels up the river. The high-level walkway, reached by lift or stairs from the N tower, offers panoramic views. The N and S towers contain exhibitions about the design of the bridge and the history of the City's bridges, and the steam engines which operated the bridge before electrification are on view in a museum outside the S tower.

Tower of London, Tower Hill, EC3. Tube: Tower Hill (District, Circle). DoE monument. Closed Sundays from November to February; Jewel House closed in February. The Tower of London dates from about 1078, when William the Conqueror began to build the White Tower near the Roman E wall of the city. It contains *St John's Chapel*, the oldest example of Norman church architecture to survive in London. The castle was turned into a great concentric fortress in the reign of Henry III (1216–72); the outer curtain wall and the moat, now drained, were added by Edward I in 1275–85. In its time the Tower has been fortress, royal residence and state prison for people ranging from Sir Thomas More, Sir Walter Raleigh and Guy Fawkes to Rudolf Hess. Those secretly murdered here include Henry VI in 1471, the Duke of Clarence in 1478, and Edward V and his brother, 'the little Princes in the Tower', apparently in 1483. The remarkably well-preserved buildings contain the Crown Jewels and a uniquely important collection of European and Oriental arms and armour. The Tower is still maintained as an arsenal, with a garrison. The Changing of the Guard takes place on Tower Green at 11.00 daily in summer and on alternate days in winter. Quite distinct from these soldiers are the Yeoman Warders, or 'Beefeaters', with their famous costume said to date from the time of Henry VII or Edward VI. They conduct guided tours on fine days.

A section of the Roman wall, heightened in the Middle Ages, stands near Tower Hill tube station in Wakefield Gardens (EH). A signposted walk follows its course to the Barbican (see above). Beyond Tower Hill, to the W, is the church of **All Hallows by the Tower**. Its 17C brick tower, from which Pepys watched the Great Fire in 1666, survived the bombs that destroyed much of the building in World War II. The undercroft contains an interesting museum of Roman and Saxon remains.

3

Outer London

Chiswick, W4. Tube: Hammersmith (Piccadilly, District), Ravenscourt Park (District). British Rail: Chiswick Station, from Waterloo. Like Richmond and Kew further upstream, Chiswick became fashionable in the 18C as a suburb of or country retreat from London. The Queen Anne and early Georgian houses make Chiswick Mall, by the river S of the Great West Rd, one of the most attractive streets of its period. Hogarth is buried in the churchyard of *St Nicholas*, with the 3rd Earl of Burlington's protégés Colen Campbell and William Kent, and, from a later generation, Whistler. *Hogarth's House* (closed Tuesdays, also first two weeks of September and last three weeks of December), his summer residence from 1749, survives on the busy Great West Rd beyond the Hogarth roundabout. It contains a large collection of his engravings. *Chiswick House* (EH, all year plus Mondays in winter), SW on Burlington Lane, is a lovely Palladian villa built by Burlington in 1725–29; much of the ornate decoration is by Kent, who also laid out the gardens.

Greenwich, SE10. British Rail: Greenwich or Maze Hill Stations, from Charing Cross. Docklands Light Railway from Tower Hill to Island Gardens. River launches from Westminster, Charing Cross or Tower Piers. On the S bank of the river downstream from central London, Greenwich has splendid buildings to remind the visitor of its royal and naval connections. The tea-clipper 'Cutty Sark' (1869) and Sir Francis Chichester's 'Gipsy Moth IV' (1966) are berthed by Greenwich Pier; both are open, and the 'Cutty Sark' contains a fine collection of ships' figureheads. The riverfront is dominated by the graceful baroque outline of the *Royal Naval College* (grounds, Painted Hall and Chapel open afternoons, except Thursdays; hours liable to change at short notice), on the site of the palace which became a favourite residence of the Tudors. The present buildings were begun by John Webb in 1664 as a new palace for Charles II and continued by Wren from 1694 onwards as the Greenwich Hospital for disabled seamen. They include the Painted Hall, decorated by Sir James Thornhill, and the Chapel, rebuilt by 'Athenian' Stuart in 1779–89. Forming part of the same architectural group on the other side of Romney Rd are the buildings of the *National Maritime Museum* (admission fee includes Old Royal Observatory). The group now embraces Inigo Jones's *Queen's House*, completed for Henrietta Maria in 1635 and extended by John Webb in 1662. The collections illustrate virtually every aspect of Britain's naval history.

Greenwich Park climbs steeply to the top of the hill, where the *Old Royal Observatory* was the first headquarters of the Royal Observatory, founded in 1675 by Charles II. Outside the gate a 24-hour clock shows Greenwich Mean Time. The Greenwich Meridian, marking the earth's prime meridian (0° longitude), crosses the courtyard. The buildings include *Flamsteed House*, with its red time-ball, built by Wren for the first Astronomer Royal, Sir John Flamsteed. They house a collection of astronomical instruments. On the W side of the Park is *Ranger's House* (EH, all year plus Mondays in winter), once the Earl of Chesterfield's home, with musical instruments and a collection of portraits.

Hampstead, NW3. Tube: Hampstead (Northern). Though now an affluent and fashionable suburb, Hampstead has been lucky in keeping much of its village charm and in keeping the high-lying *Hampstead Heath*, one of London's largest and most rugged open spaces. Flask Walk and Well Walk, leading E from Hampstead High St. towards the Heath, are famously picturesque streets; their names recall the village's brief popularity as a spa. *Keats House*, in Keats Grove to the S, was the poet's home from 1818 until he left England in 1820; it contains a large array of memorabilia. *Fenton House* (NT), entered from Hampstead Grove N of the High St., is a late 17C house with collections of European and Oriental ceramics and musical instruments, often played by music students. Spaniards Rd and Hampstead Lane lead round the N edge of the Heath, passing the 16C *Spaniards Inn* on the way to *Kenwood* (EH, all year plus Mondays in winter), remodelled by Robert Adam in 1767–69. It houses the Iveagh Bequest, principally of English, Dutch and Flemish paintings, with outstanding works by Rembrandt, Vermeer, Gainsborough, Reynolds and Romney. The grounds make a lovely venue for summer evening concerts. **Highgate**, on the E side of Hampstead Heath, can be reached separately via Archway tube station (Northern line). *Highgate Cemetery*, though badly overgrown, is still one of the most impressive Victorian graveyards in England. It consists of a W part (guided tours only) with catacombs and an E part (more freely open) with the tombs of George Eliot and Karl Marx among others.

Hampton Court Palace, Surrey. British Rail: Hampton Court Station. River launches from Westminster Pier in summer. Also on Route 62B, along the Thames from London to Oxford. DoE monument. The Tudor and Baroque buildings, art collection, gardens and riverside setting make the Palace one of the most popular tourist attractions in the London area. A royal residence until the 18C, it was begun by Cardinal Wolsey in 1514 and surrendered after his fall in 1529 to Henry VIII. The Great Gatehouse in the mellow brick frontage, the large Base Court and the Clock Court beyond reflect the original layout of Wolsey's palace, as expanded and adapted by Henry VIII. His additions include the fan-vaulted ceiling of Anne Boleyn's Gateway and the curious astronomical clock. The E and S wings, replacing several Tudor courtyards, were built for William III by Sir Christopher Wren. Highlights of the building include: the State Apartments on the first floor, keeping much of their original furniture and decorations and displaying works from the royal collection; the Royal Chapel, built by Wolsey and embellished by Henry VIII; the Great Watching Chamber; the Great Hall (1531–36), with its magnificent hammerbeam roof; and the Tudor kitchens. The gardens, occupying a small part of Hampton Court Park, were laid out in their present formal style for William III, though the old Tennis Court (where Real Tennis is played) was originally built for Henry VIII and the Maze planted in the reign of Queen Anne. The Lower Orangery contains paintings by Mantegna.

Richmond upon Thames and **Kew**, Surrey. Tube: Richmond, Kew Gardens (both District). British Rail: Richmond, Kew Bridge, from Waterloo. River launches from Westminster Pier in summer. The site of a royal palace from the 14C to the 17C and a fashionable country retreat in the 18C, Richmond is one of Greater London's most attractive suburbs. Richmond Green is made particularly handsome by the 17–18C houses that surround it, and Richmond Hill commands a famous view of the Thames valley. *Richmond Park*, enclosed as a royal hunting ground in the 17C, has 2500 acres of natural parkland with red and fallow deer. *Ham House* (NT), by the river to the S and approached from Petersham Rd, is a 17C house which keeps its grand interior decoration, furniture and portraits.

Kew, to the N, is famous for the *Royal Botanic Gardens* which have grown from modest beginnings in 1759 to the present world-wide collection of plants. The buildings in the lovely 300-acre grounds include *Kew Palace* (DoE monument), built in 1631 and made a royal residence by George III; Sir William Chambers's *Orangery*, now housing a museum, and *Pagoda*, both built in 1761; and the famous greenhouses, notably Decimus Burton's *Palm House* (1844–48) and *Temperate House* (1860–99).

There are several points of interest on the opposite bank of the Thames from Richmond and Kew. *Marble Hill House* (EH, all year plus Mondays in winter), reached via Richmond Bridge, is a wonderfully complete example of a Palladian villa, designed in 1723–29 by Roger Morris for George II's mistress Henrietta Howard, Countess of Suffolk. *Syon House* (open Good Friday to end of September, except Fridays and Saturdays, and Sundays in October), reached via Kew Bridge, has a castellated Tudor exterior which contrasts with the state rooms grandly remodelled by Robert Adam in 1761, among the best surviving examples of his work. The collection of portraits include work by Van Dyck, Lely, Reynolds and Gainsborough. The grounds, laid out by Capability Brown, include the *Butterfly House*.

Windsor: see Route 49A.

SOUTH-EASTERN ENGLAND

South-Eastern England stretches from London and the Thames Estuary down to the English Channel, its W boundary being defined for present purposes by the Southampton road. It includes the counties of Kent, Surrey, East and West Sussex, the greater part of Hampshire, and the Isle of Wight (now a separate county in itself). The region has thus a double aspect, facing towards both the capital and the sea. Its coastline is fringed with ports, fortresses, seaside resorts and retirement communities, and its centre crossed by the great arteries which have carried foreign invasion, pilgrimage, commerce and tourism over the centuries. In the N the shadow of London falls heavily across the landscape. Kent and Surrey, both 'Home Counties' sharing a border with the capital, have lost ground to Greater London and the influence of the capital still reaches far beyond even their technical boundaries. Surrey has suffered the sadder fate. Despised until the 19C as 'a barren county of heaths, firs and unprofitable soil', it owes much of its present appearance to the railway and the commuter. A pleasantly provincial atmosphere survives in only a few towns—like Farnham and Guildford—and only the occasional beauty spot among the otherwise suburbanised landscape can attract the visitor.

The major roads, and hence the routes suggested in this book, cross the region from N to S, but the basic contours of the land go from W to E. The great chalk belt centred in Wiltshire and the Salisbury Plain continues into Hampshire and separates into two distinct ranges of downland. The North Downs run between Farnham and Guildford as the narrow ridge of the Hog's Back and then achieve their greatest heights—the lovely Box Hill (596ft) near Dorking, for example—as they head towards Rochester and the Medway river. Here they swing towards the S coast, their ridge for part of the distance making the track known as the Pilgrims' Way, and finally confront the sea as the famous white cliffs of Dover. This cliff scenery extends S to Folkestone and N to Deal, appearing again in a modified form to enliven the tip of the Isle of Thanet around Ramsgate and Margate. The South Downs begin dramatically at Butser Hill (889ft) near Petersfield in Hampshire and end at the sea at Beachy Head and the Seven Sisters, near Eastbourne, with scenery that rivals the cliffs of Dover. But for much of their way across Sussex, particularly between Arundel and Lewes, they become the 'blunt, bow-headed, whale-backed downs' which for many people typify the look of South-Eastern England. It is a gentle landscape, with clean air and short, springy turf, inevitably suggesting 'mutton and pleasantness'.

The rivers cut through both ranges of downland, sometimes in steep and narrow valleys, running N into the Thames Estuary or S into the English Channel. Towns grew up at these junctions, where travellers along the chalk ridges had to descend to ford the water and where roads following the later routes along the valleys had to cross the downland. Thus, in the N, Guildford stands on the Wey, Leatherhead and Dorking on the Mole, Maidstone and Rochester on the Medway and Canterbury on the Stour. In the S, Winchester stands on the Itchen, Arundel on the Arun and Lewes on the Ouse.

The broad oval ring of the North and South Downs gives South-Eastern England its general character. The traveller from London to the coast—say, Brighton—is aware of crossing two distinctive chalk ridges, even on the most smoothly contoured of modern roads. The N outcrop overlooks the

London Basin and the flat, often marshy countryside of the Thames Estuary, here similar in character to the N shore in Essex. On the SW edge, in Hampshire, the Downs yield to the wide reaches of Southampton Water and the great heaths and woodlands of the New Forest. Offshore, on the Isle of Wight, the chalk reappears in some of the region's most dramatic scenery.

Between the North and South Downs lies the Weald, an area still thickly wooded in places and once covered by an immense forest, whose chief relic is at Ashdown. In the W its sandstone landscape gives South-Eastern England its highest point at Leith Hill (965ft) near Dorking. In Sussex the forest provided timber for shipbuilding and charcoal for smelting iron. Before it moved to the coalfields of the Midlands and the North in the 19C, the iron industry left its mark in the wealthy ironmasters' houses (like Bateman's, later Rudyard Kipling's home, at Burwash) and the occasional iron furnishings in the churches (like the grille in the Fitzalan Chapel at Arundel). In Kent the Weald makes a charming countryside of small farms and market gardens, of orchards and hop-fields with their distinctive cowled oast-houses. This region, sometimes called the Vale of Kent, trails down to the sea at the flat, changing coastline of Romney Marsh.

The Weald has also given South-Eastern England its best building materials. Otherwise, the area is not well endowed. Kentish ragstone, a limestone quarried near Maidstone, was used for Rochester Castle and the Westgate at Canterbury, and for parish churches, whose tall towers often combine the stone with knapped local flint in chequerboarded patterns. Wealden sandstone made the churches around Tunbridge Wells, and the more attractive Horsham slates used for roofing. Yet both these stones are of limited and mainly local use, and leave South-Eastern England poor by comparison to its western neighbours. It is notable that for major buildings the materials did not come from the mainland at all: Caen stone was brought from Normandy for Canterbury Cathedral, Quarr stone from the Isle of Wight for Chichester and Winchester.

But the Weald had clay and timber. The clay made warm red bricks and tiles (often hung as cladding for outside walls) which give even the humbler buildings their sturdy and cheerful look. Oak and Spanish chestnut from the forest went into the abundance of half-timbered houses, confirming Kent in particular as a county that makes up for its comparative lack of great estates or country houses by the richness of its smaller farm buildings and the pleasing irregularity of its older townscapes. The so-called Wealden house, built from the 14C onwards, is a distinctive local feature. Here the central hall is open and two-storied, and only the upper floors at either wing are jettied outwards towards the front; the eaves of the roof are carried across the central gap by an overhanging brace.

The timber, brick and tile houses of the Weald, like the hop-fields and orchards of Kent or the soft contours of the South Downs, make for a cosily settled landscape, a peculiarly English kind of prettiness. Its small-scale charms attract the long-distance commuters, whose affluence has often helped to keep these pleasing effects well groomed. The coast, alternating between chalk cliff and low-lying, sometimes marshy ground, has a different atmosphere and a different sort of history. First impressions are likely to be dominated by the resorts that grew up in the late 18C and 19C, when sea air and sea water were first alleged to be health-giving. At points it seems that the coastline from Whitstable to Bognor has become a continuous chain of seaside amusements, man-made cliffs of boarding houses and depressingly regular blocks of retirement bungalows. These developments have long since crowded out the small packet stations and fishing villages once fringing the coast: Brighthelmston has vanished beneath the Regency and Victorian splendours of Brighton. It is only in the occasional place—like the old part of Hastings—that an older, and more authentic, whiff of the sea still lingers.

Yet the resorts never erased reminders of the coast's fragile history of invasion and defence. At Richborough, where the Romans probably first landed in AD 43, and at Reculver the invaders built fortresses to guard the navigable channel which then separated the Isle of Thanet from the mainland. The Normans, who marked the scene of their victory with the splendid Battle Abbey, consolidated the sites their predecessors had chosen. Rochester Castle, emphatically commanding the Medway, is founded partly on the Roman city walls. Dover Castle has a Roman pharos (probably the oldest building to survive in England) as well as a Norman keep. At Pevensey, where William the Conqueror first landed, and at Portchester near Portsmouth the Norman work stands inside Roman fortifications.

The earliest parts of Southampton's fine city walls also belong to the Norman period, but the later additions and reinforcements speak of the continuing need for defence along the coast. In 1278 Edward I granted the first charter to the Cinque Ports, a system of maritime defence modelled on the 'Saxon Shore' of the Romans, naming Dover, Sandwich, Hythe, Romney and Hastings. Henry VII began Portsmouth's long history of royal dock-yards and garrisons, while his successor performed the same service for Chatham. Fear of invasion by the Catholic powers of Europe also led Henry VIII to add to the coast's already impressive defences, most notably with the elegantly geometric Deal Castle. The threat of Napoleonic invasion created Martello towers—still to be seen at Dymchurch on Romney Marsh and between Hastings and Eastbourne—and, later in the 19C thoughts of the French again prompted Lord Palmerston's forts at Portsmouth.

Nor, alas, did the tradition stop in the present century. In Kent, which gained the sinister nickname of 'Bomb Alley' during World War I, Dover Castle provided shelter from cross-Channel shell fire. Portsmouth, like so many cities in the region a victim of heavy air raids, became one of the main D-Day assembly points. Hurst Castle, built by Henry VIII on a pebble spit guarding the W end of the Solent and already much altered in the 19C, again saw military service. So long a tradition makes the Channel Tunnel a welcome change in how the English regard their neighbours across the narrow waters.

4

London to Dover via Rochester and Canterbury

Directions. Total distance 71m. In its main lines the route follows A2. To (7m) Blackheath. A207 to (16m) Dartford. A2 to (28m) **Rochester**, (29m) **Chatham**, (39m) Sittingbourne, (46m) Ospringe (for **Faversham**), (56m) **Canterbury** (bypassed) and (71m) **Dover**.

A2 leaves London by the Old Kent Rd, (4m) *New Cross* and (7m) *Blackheath*. It then bypasses the centres of Bexleyheath and Dartford by the Rochester Way. A207 follows the line of Watling St., the old Dover road since Roman times, and offers a shorter route, up Shooter's Hill and down through Bexleyheath. At (14m) *Crayford* it bears right. 16m: **Dartford** (42,000 inhabitants; TI), a busy town on the Darent, has a fine galleried inn of 1703. Wat Tyler's rising probably started here, and another inn (renamed after him) in the High St. claims to be a meeting place of his supporters. The *Church*, on the river, has a strong Norman tower with 14C upper storey.

Its spacious but over-restored interior contains a late 15C mural of St George and the Dragon. The Spilman tomb, with inscriptions in German, was erected to his wife (d. 1607) by Sir John Spilman or Spielmann (d. 1626), who built one of the earliest paper mills in England; according to popular belief 'foolscap' paper was so called from a jester ('Spielmann') forming part of his arms and used by him as a watermark. A tablet in the S aisle commemorates the Cornish engineer Richard Trevithick (1771–1833), who died in poverty and was carried to his grave by his workmates.

Beyond the town A207 passes over the approach to the Dartford–Purfleet tunnel and rejoins A2, here motorway in all but name and again following the Roman alignment.

An alternative road (A226) from Dartford to Rochester diverges left from Watling St., ¾m from the church. This follows the course known to both Shakespeare and Dickens when the Roman road had decayed. 2m: *Horns Cross*, in a region of chalk pits and cement works. A little to the left, looking out across the Thames is *Stone* •church, a beautiful building of c 1245 with a chancel higher than its nave. The richly sculptured interior of the chancel, with exquisite windows and blind arcading, shares many features with Westminster Abbey. The Wylshire chantry (NE) is a 16C addition; the vault was restored by G.E. Street. 3m: *Greenhithe*, with a quaint riverfront, was the scene of Sir John Franklin's departure on his ill-fated polar voyage in 1845. *Ingress Abbey* was enlarged in the 19C with stone from old London Bridge. 5m: *Northfleet* has a large 14C church on a bluff, with a contemporary rood screen.

7m: **Gravesend** (53,000 inhabitants; TI) is the pilot station for vessels using the Port of London. It still maintains a maritime appearance, with old inns and weatherboarded houses on its narrow High St. The views of the river from near Town and Terrace Piers or (better) from Gordon Terrace, further E, are famous. The gardens here mark the site of Fort House, General Gordon's home in 1865–71. In one corner stands the *Milton Chantry* (EH, keykeeper), whose 18C exterior conceals a 14C building used as the chapel of a leper hospital and the chantry of the de Valence family. A statue (and windows in *St George's Church* W of the piers) commemorate the burial here of Pocohontas (d. 1617), the Indian princess who saved the life of Captain John Smith, coloniser of Virginia. Leonard Calvert (son of Lord Baltimore, the founder of Maryland) set sail from Gravesend in 1633; so did the Quaker George Fox in 1671 and Charles and John Wesley in 1735 on their American journeys. A tablet recalls Strindberg's residence here in 1839.

At (10m) *Chalk* Dickens spent his honeymoon. The road descends *Gad's Hill* (wide view from the Sir John Falstaff inn), where Falstaff encountered the 'rogues in buckram' ('1 Henry IV', II, iv). At *Gad's Hill Place*, an 18C red-brick house now a school, Dickens lived from 1857 until his death in 1870. The railway passes beneath the ridge in a tunnel originally built for a canal (1819–24). A2 rejoins the Roman road in Strood. 15m: *Rochester*, see below.

On the bleak peninsula lying between the Thames and the Medway to the E of Chalk are (3m) *Higham* church, with a 14C *door, screen and pulpit, and (5m) *Cooling Castle*, with a 14C gatehouse, the home of Sir John Oldcastle, the supposed original of Falstaff. In the nearby churchyard are the 18C gravestones commemorating the children of the Comport family which appear in the first chapter of Dickens's 'Great Expectations'. The marsh country where the opening scenes of the novel are laid stretches N to the Thames. It is well seen from the remote village of *Cliffe*, 1½m NW of Cooling. The large 13C church has wall paintings of the martyrdom of St Edmund and of Christ in Majesty. The peninsula ends as the *Isle of Grain*.

A2 crosses the Gravesend–Wrotham road 4m N of *Meopham* (pronounced 'Meppam'), birthplace of the naturalist John Tradescant (1608–62), where the church of 1325 has a late 14C aisle and a pulpit (1682) from St Margaret's, Westminster. The road skirts *Cobham Park*, on the right, landscaped by Repton.

Cobham Hall (now a girls' public school; limited opening) is a mainly Elizabethan mansion with a central block of 1662–72 and archaising additions by the Reptons and James Wyatt. At the SW entrance to the park is the delightful village of *Cobham*, whose church has the largest collection of *brasses in England (14–16C). Near the Leather Bottle inn, now pleasantly cluttered with Dickens relics, Mr Pickwick discovered his wonderful inscribed stone. The New College Almshouses (open) evolved in 1598 from a college founded in 1362. On Sole St. is the Tudor Yeoman's House (NT, hall open by appointment). At the W end of the village is Owletts (NT), a modest house of Charles II's reign.

At 26m the M2 diverges right and A2 continues into the centre of (28m) *Strood*, linked to Rochester by parallel bridges and now officially amalgamated with that city. In Knight Rd, S of the High St., is *Temple Manor*, a 13C hall of the Knights Templar with 16C additions (EH, keykeeper).

A228 leads NE. *Frindsbury*, right at ½m, has a flint church with Norman chancel and 13C wall paintings. 2m: *Upnor Castle* (EH, summer season) stands by the Medway on an unclassified road off A228. It was built in 1559–67 to protect Chatham dockyards on the opposite bank of the river. After the Dutch raid of 1667 proved its ineffectiveness, it became a magazine for Ordnance stores. The 13C church of (4m) *Hoo St Werburgh*, right of A228, has a shingled spire.

28m: **ROCHESTER** (52,500 inhabitants) owes its long history to its strategic position guarding Watling Street where it crosses the Medway. An important centre for Belgic civilisation, it became a fortified Roman camp, Durobrivae, and the Saxon Hroffeceaster, a bishop's see from the 7C. The Normans chose it as the site for a massive castle. The history of later centuries of travel along the London–Dover road is manifest in the handsome High St. Rochester is officially united with neighbouring Strood and Chatham as the city of Rochester upon Medway.

TI: Eastgate Cottage, High St. **Railway Stations**: Rochester and Chatham, ½m apart. **Annual Events**: Dickens Festival in June; Medway Sports Festival in July; Medway Arts Festival in July/August.

Visitors. Charles II spent a night here in 1660 on his way from Dover, Pepys stayed in 1667 in the aftermath of the Dutch raid on the Medway and James II took ship from here on his escape in 1688. Dickens knew the city well from his childhood in Chatham and his later years at Gad's Hill; it appears in 'Pickwick Papers', 'Great Expectations' and 'The Mystery of Edwin Drood'.

A tour of Rochester naturally begins at its most distinctive landmark, the *Castle (EH, all year). Perhaps the mightiest example of Norman military architecture in England, it stands on a site originally fortified by the Romans. The square five-storied keep, built c 1127 by William de Corbeuil, Archbishop of Canterbury, stands 120ft high with walls of coursed rubble averaging 12ft in thickness. Visitors can climb to the top for a panoramic view. The round SE turret was built to repair damage done when King John recaptured the castle from the rebellious barons in 1215. The keep is protected by a curtain wall following the line of the Roman wall in places; it was built c 1087 by Bishop Gundulf and partly rebuilt in the 14C.

The modest **Cathedral** stands in stocky contrast to the castle keep. It dates mainly from the 11–14C and is like Canterbury in having double transepts, a raised choir, and a presbytery with a large crypt underneath. Externally, the most striking feature is the Norman W front with its elaborate recessed *doorway, perhaps the best of its kind in England. The tympanum and figures of Solomon and the Queen of Sheba on the shafts were added c 1175.

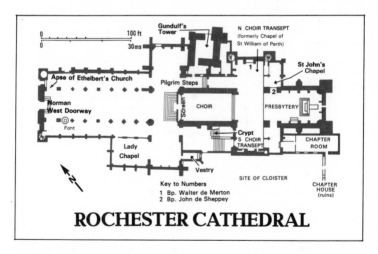

ROCHESTER CATHEDRAL

The first bishop was consecrated by Augustine of Canterbury in 604, making Rochester the second oldest see in England. The place where the apse of the original Saxon church stood is marked at the W end of the present nave; remains of a second Saxon church have been discovered beneath the N transept. Gundulf, the second Norman bishop (who built the White Tower at London), began a new church in 1082. His work can be seen in the nave, the crypt and the N tower bearing his name (originally detached and taller than it is now). The popularity of the shrine to St William of Perth, a pilgrim murdered in 1201, encouraged later rebuilding. The presbytery, E transepts and choir belong to the early 13C. The N transept dates from c 1250, the early Decorated S transept from c 1280, and the two E bays of the nave from c 1300. The central tower and spire were added c 1343, though it needed 20C rebuilding to restore their original appearance.

The six W bays of the *Nave* are Norman, creating a sombre effect unrelieved by the Perpendicular windows and clerestory. The elaborately adorned triforium passage opens on both nave and aisles. Remarkable, too, is the way that later builders reconstructed the triforium arches in the Norman style when the E bays and tower arch were altered. The *Lady Chapel* (c 1490) is off the S aisle, its great arch into the transept now closed by a modern altar screen. The *S Transept* has a brass memorial to Dickens, who wished to be buried in the cathedral, and a monument to Richard Watts (see below).

A peculiarity of the raised Early English *Choir* is the lack of aisle arcades. The figures on the choir screen are a memorial to Dean Scott (1811–97), of Liddell and Scott's Greek lexicon. The details on the corbels and the lovely shafts of Purbeck and Petworth marble should be noted. The stalls and *monks' benches (with modern book desks) are early 13C and probably the oldest in England (cf. Winchester). Opposite the 19C bishop's throne is part of a 13C wall painting showing the Wheel of Fortune. The *N Choir Transept*, formerly the Chapel of St William of Perth, contains the heavily restored tomb of Bishop Walter de Merton (d. 1277), founder of the Oxford college, with an Elizabethan effigy in alabaster. In the arch between *St John's Chapel* at the E end and the *Presbytery* is the tomb, with coloured effigy, of Bishop John de Sheppey (d. 1360). The *S Choir Transept* has a remarkable Decorated *doorway (c 1340) leading to the Chapter Room.

From the S choir aisle a flight of steps descends to the *Crypt*, one of the largest and most beautiful in England. It has fine Early English vaulting, with great variety of spans, and some medieval graffiti on the piers. The two W bays, with piers of tufa and a white stone, probably Barnack, and ribless quadripartite vaulting, are early Norman. The fragments of medieval glass in the E window came partly from Canterbury.

SE of the choir are the ruins of the *Chapter House* and remains of the Norman *Cloister* built by Bishop Ernulf (1115–24). The ruined 14C *Bishop's Gate* was the W entrance to the cloister.

The cathedral and castle confront each other across the charming little Boley Hill. The High St. lies immediately beyond Chertsey Gate at its N end, but it is worth following a less direct route and heading in the opposite direction. On Bakers Walk, skirting the castle grounds to the right, are the *Old Hall*, the home of Richard Watts (see below) visited by Elizabeth I in 1573, and *Satis House*, a 16C building with a Regency front which gave its name to Miss Havisham's home in 'Great Expectations'. From further up Boley Hill a lane leads left past the 15C *Prior's Gate* and the 18C *Minor Canon Row*, fictional home of Mr Crisparkle in 'Edwin Drood' and real home of the actress Dame Sybil Thorndike in her childhood. Beyond the 19C buildings of the *King's School*, refounded by Henry VIII after the Dissolution, the *Archdeaconry* (enlarged in 1661) and *Oriel House* (1758), the splendid avenue of *The Vines* leads left. Its name remembers the monks' vineyard once cultivated here. Crow Lane is opposite the Tudor *Restoration House*, so called because of the tradition that Charles II slept here on his way from Dover to London in 1660. Dickens apparently had it in mind for 'Satis House' in 'Great Expectations'.

Crow Lane descends to the High St. To the right is *Eastgate House*, a brick Elizabethan building that became the 'Nuns' House' of 'Edwin Drood'. It now contains the *Charles Dickens Centre*, with audio-visual displays stressing the most popular aspects of the novelist's work. In the garden is the Swiss chalet which Dickens used as his study in the grounds of Gad's Hill Place. Opposite the museum is a gabled Tudor building claimed as the home of Mr Pumblechook in 'Great Expectations' and Mr Sapsea, the mayor in 'Edwin Drood'.

Rochester town

The High St. leads NW back towards the river. The demolition of Free
School Lane (on the right) has revealed a long stretch of the old city wall
with a corner bastion. An alley on the opposite side of the High St. leads to
a garden alongside another stretch of the Roman and medieval wall.
Beyond *La Providence*, a rebuilt group of almshouses on the right, is *Watts'
Charity* (open), founded in 1579 by Richard Watts 'for Six Poor Travellers,
who, not being rogues or proctors, may receive gratis for one night lodging,
entertainment, and fourpence each' but discontinued in 1947. On the left
is *Chertsey* (or *College*) *Gate*, Jasper's home in 'Edwin Drood', leading to

Boley Hill; the half-timbered building next to it is identified with the verger's house where the mysterious Dick Datchery came to lodge in the same novel. On the right of the High St., further on, are the old *Corn Exchange* (1706) and the *George Inn*, with a 14C undercroft. The 17C *Guildhall*, containing the local museum, has a plaster ceiling and portraits of Queen Anne by Kneller and Sir Cloudesley Shovel (d. 1707), MP for Rochester. The panelled council chamber is outstanding. At the *Royal Victoria and Bull Hotel*, opposite, the Pickwickians stayed in the doubtful company of Mr Jingle, and Pip had a memorable encounter with Bentley Drummle in 'Great Expectations'.

The High St. ends at the bridge (1970), at least the sixth to have spanned the Medway at this point. On the Esplanade, in the shadow of the castle to the left, the balustrade uses stone from the 14C bridge demolished in 1857. Remains of the Roman walls are also visible. The *Bridge Chapel* (1387) was heavily restored in 1937 and is now used as the boardroom of the Bridge Wardens.

29m: Chatham (62,000 inhabitants), Rochester's neighbour on the Medway, was for long one of the chief naval stations in Great Britain.

Henry VIII was the first to use Chatham for naval purposes, and by the time of Charles II it had become pre-eminent. In 1667 the Dutch fleet commanded by Admiral de Ruyter destroyed and captured ships here but did not damage the town. The Great Lines were begun in 1715 to protect the dockyards from attack by land; their keypoint, Fort Amherst, was finished in 1782. The Royal Navy finally left Chatham in 1984. Dickens's childhood homes were in The Brook (now gone) and at 2 (now 11) Ordnance Terrace, on a height above the railway station.

Chatham High St. continues Rochester High St. *Sir John Hawkins Hospital*, founded in 1595 and rebuilt in the 19C, stands opposite a restored Norman chapel, once part of a leper hospital. Medway St. bears left to the *Town Hall*, with lawns stretching to the river and a view of Rochester. Behind rise the derelict Great Lines, where a path climbs to the *Royal Naval Memorial* (Lorimer, 1924; Maufe, 1952), giving a wide view of the Medway towns. Dock Rd continues above the Medway to *St Mary's*, a 19C church incorporating Norman details; it now houses the *Medway Heritage Centre*, whose exhibition traces the history of the river and the Medway towns. Opposite is a mounted statue of Lord Kitchener (d. 1916), removed from Khartoum in 1960. *Fort Amherst*, built in 1756 and extended by prisoners in 1802–11, contains a museum and barrack rooms recreating conditions during the Napoleonic Wars. Further on is the former **Royal Naval Dockyard** (open).

The 85-acre site, first developed by the Navy in 1547, now holds about 60 buildings of historic interest. Note particularly: the *Main Gate* (1720) with huge Royal Arms added later on both sides; the *Dockyard Church* (1808); the *Ropery* (1785); the *Sail Loft* (1734); the steam *Saw Mills* by Sir Marc Brunel (1813–24); *Medway House* (1703) and the *Officers' Terrace* in the residential centre; and *3 Slip* (1838), with a splendid timber roof. The basins give good views of Upnor Castle across the river.

In **Gillingham** (pronounced 'Jillingham'; 93,700 inhabitants; seasonal TI at Farthing Corner on M2), on the hill above Chatham dockyard, are the *Brompton Barracks*, an early 19C quadrangle. It includes a statue of General Gordon (d. 1885) on camel-back, by Onslow Ford (1890), and the *Royal Engineers' Museum*, with relics of the General.

33½m: *Rainham* has a good 14C church tower. **36m:** *Newington*, in a cherry-growing district, has a church with a handsome Perpendicular tower, a Tudor font cover and brasses. At *Lower Halstow*, 2m N, the Saxon church, remodelled in the 13C, has a leaden *font of c 1150. **37m:** *Key Street* crossroads.

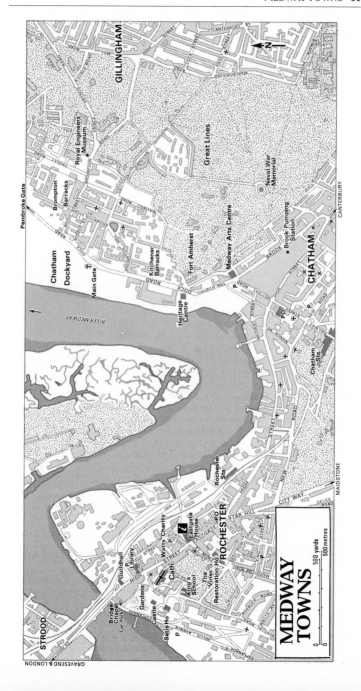

MEDWAY TOWNS

0   500 yards
0   500 metres

GRAVESEND & LONDON

STROOD

Bridge
Chapel
Car Park

Castle
Satis Ho
Guildhall
Library
Watts Charity
Eastgate
House
King's School
The Vines
Restoration Ho
Cath
Gardens
ROCHESTER
Star Hill
City Way
Delice Road
Maidstone Road
Rochester Sta.

RIVER MEDWAY

Chatham
Dockyard
Main Gate
Pembroke Gate

Royal Engineers
Museum
Brompton
Barracks
Kitchener
Barracks
Fort Amherst
Heritage
Centre
Medway Arts Centre

GILLINGHAM
Canterbury St
Marlborough Road
Page St

Great Lines

Naval War
Memorial

Brook Pumping
Station
CHATHAM
Chatham Sta.
Brook
Canterbury
Maidstone

A249 diverges left for the Isle of Sheppey, via Kingsferry Bridge over the Swale, an arm of the Thames in which St Augustine baptised 10,000 people in 597. 7m: *Queenborough*, a decayed port, was named from Queen Philippa, wife of Edward III. 10m: **Sheerness** (33,400 inhabitants; TI) a port at the mouth of the Medway, has the relics of a naval dockyard abandoned by the Admiralty in 1960. They include a dignified boatstore of 1861, one of the earliest iron-framed buildings. James II embarked here in an unsuccessful attempt to escape from England. Offshore is the *Nore*, a sandbank buoyed for safety at least since the 16C. The pressed crews were brought to man the ships of the Royal Navy here; they revolted in the Great Mutiny of 1797.

B2008 and B2231 run across the northern part of the island to (9m) *Leysdown*, on the estuary of the Thames. B2008 passes (3¼m) *Minster*, where the *abbey church of St Mary and St Sexburga, founded in 664, has a Saxon window in the N aisle. It contains the monument of Sir Robert Shurland (d. c 1300) and the fine brasses (c 1325) of Sir Roger de Northwode and his lady. The abbey gatehouse has been restored. The low clay cliffs to the E are rich in fossils. At (5½m) *Eastchurch*, on B2231, the church has a Perpendicular rood screen and a memorial window (1912) to the first aviators killed in a flying accident. The ruins of the 16C manor house of *Shurland* lie ½m NE. The desolate marshland on the S of the island is given over to sheep and hares. *Harty*, on the SE corner, has a remote and touchingly simple church.

39m: Sittingbourne (33,600 inhabitants) is a dull place but the ancient borough of *Milton Regis*, 1m N, has an old Court Hall and a good 17C building now serving as the Post Office. The large 14C church, ¾m out on the Sheppey road, has a massive tower. On Crown Quay Lane to the E is the *Dolphin Yard Sailing Barge Museum*. *Bredgar*, 4m SW beyond the motorway, has a Decorated collegiate church and chantry cottages of c 1392.

The orchard country begins beyond Sittingbourne. 42m: *Teynham* is the first place where cherries and apples were grown in Kent. 46m: *Ospringe* has a 13C church with saddleback Victorian tower, a vineyard nearby, and an early 16C building incorporating fragments of a 13C 'Maison Dieu' or pilgrims' shelter (EH, phone keykeeper, 0634 842852). Faversham is 1m to the left.

Faversham (16,500 inhabitants; TI) is an old town and port which belonged to the Cinque Ports confederation (see Dover). It has over 400 listed buildings and the longest-established 'open house' scheme in the UK, giving access to 15–25 properties on the first three Saturdays in July. The *Fleur de Lis Heritage Centre*, in a former 16C inn in Preston St., evokes the town's history. In the Market Place, where the market is held on Tuesdays, Fridays and Saturdays, is the handsome *Guildhall* (1814) on timber arcades (1574). In Court St., leading N, is Kent's only surviving major brewery, Shepherd Neame, in 18–19C buildings. *Abbey St., largely 15–18C, continues N, running parallel to the Creek. Near the end is *Arden's House*, the former abbey guesthouse (c 1520), where Thomas Arden was murdered by his wife in 1551, an event chronicled in the Elizabethan melodrama 'Arden of Feversham'. The site of the Cluniac abbey founded in 1147 by King Stephen, and the base of his tomb, were located in 1965. At the end of Abbey St., on Standard Quay, a 17C warehouse reconstituted from the abbey refectory overlooks Thames sailing barges preserved by private enthusiasts. A path from Abbey Place, by Arden's House, leads back past the *Old Grammar School* of 1587, now a masonic hall (open by appointment), to the *Parish Church*. The second biggest in Kent, it was enlarged with aisled transepts in 1315 (contemporary pillar *paintings), and given an unexpected Grecian nave in 1754 and a distinctive crown spire in 1797. The choir stalls have misericords and poppyheads. Kent's largest brass commemorates Henry Hatch (d. 1533).

Westbrook Walk, at the end of West St. opposite Stonebridge Pond, leads to *Chart Gunpowder Mills* (1760), oldest of their kind in the world and restored as a memorial to 300 years of explosives manufacture (ended in 1935). Overlooking the pond is *Davington Priory*, comprising the plain Norman church and some domestic buildings of a nunnery founded in 1153. In Tanners St., off West St., is the RC church, with paintings by Edward Ardizzone and the national shrine of St Jude. The church of *Preston*, just beyond the railway station, has a fine 13C chancel and alabaster monument (1629) to the grandparents of the second Earl of Cork (Robert Boyle, who formulated Boyle's Law).

The *Stone Chapel* (EH), just N of A2 opposite Syndale Valley Rd on the W of Faversham, incorporates part of a 3C Roman shrine. *Doddington Place*, 5m SW via Syndale Valley Rd, has gardens (open) noted for azaleas and rhododendrons. *Brogdale* (open), S of M2, is the national fruit collection, with more than 2500 varieties of apple, as well as pears, plums, apricots, peaches and cherries. *Belmont* (limited opening), 2m beyond Brogdale, is a late 18C house by Samuel Wyatt, with a superb staircase hall and orangery and the largest private collection of clocks and watches in the UK. The western entrance lodge is the first British building to draw inspiration from American architecture. The gardens of *Mount Ephraim* (open), 3m E of Faversham, were first laid out at the beginning of this century. *Perry Wood*, 3m SE, has 150 acres of woodland with walks, views and rhododendrons. *Oare Marshes* and the *South Swale Nature Reserves*, on either side of the creek mouth NW and NE of Faversham, are internationally important for their bird life.

48m: at *Brenley Corner* roundabout A2 is joined by M2.

For A299 NE to Whitstable and Herne Bay, see Route 6. An unclassified road leads right from Brenley Corner to (1m) *Boughton under Blean*, where Chaucer's pilgrims were joined by the Canon Yeoman. The Hawkins monument in the church has vigorous reliefs by Evesham (1618). 1½m beyond is *Selling*, with a church containing good Early English glass.

Beyond Brenley Corner the present course of the A2 bypasses *Boughton Street*, on the left at 49m, its handsome main street once again peaceful, and *Dunkirk*, left at 50m, where the 19C church has a plaque commemorating Courtenay's rebellion of 1838, which met its end in Bossenden wood to the N. At (51½m) *Harbledown* the hilly road gives particularly good views. The Hospital of St Nicholas, founded for lepers by Archbishop Lanfranc, has an 11C chapel and rebuilt almshouses. The hill to the S is crowned by a Belgic fort. On St Thomas's Hill to the N (named after a vanished chapel dedicated to Becket) is the *University of Kent*, founded in 1961. 56m: **Canterbury** (bypassed), see Route 5.

58m: *Patrixbourne*, left of the road, has a church with a *doorway of c 1175 and 16–17C Swiss glass.

At *Bekesbourne*, ½m beyond, are the remains of a palace of the Archbishops of Canterbury. It is worth continuing another 3m NE, beyond A257, to *Wickhambreaux*, which has a charming group of buildings around its village green. There is an Art Nouveau window (1896) by Arild Rosenkrantz in the church.

59½m: *Bishopsbourne* church has a monument to the judicious Richard Hooker (1554–1600), rector here from 1595. Oswalds was the home of Joseph Conrad (1857–1924) from 1919. For the Elham Valley, see Route 5.

At 63½m B2046 leads left and an unclassified road branches right through *Womenswold* to (3m) **Barfreston**. The *church, probably built 1170–80, has the most ornate Norman work in Kent. Note in particular the richly flowing carving of the S doorway. On sideroads about 4m N of Barfreston is *Goodnestone Park*, where Jane Austen was a visitor. Its gardens are open.

64½m: *Broome Park* (not open) is a fine house of 1635–38, once the seat of Lord Kitchener and probably the 'Tappington' of the 'Ingoldsby Legends'. 67½m: The church at *Coldred* (left) has an Early English bell gable.

From *Lydden*, right of A2, B2060 leads to (2m) *Temple Ewell*, where King John met Pandulf, the Pope's legate, preparatory to resigning his throne at Dover. B2060 then runs W along the valley past the pleasant public parks of *Kearnsey Abbey* (2½m; left) and *Russell Gardens* to (4½m) *Alkham*, where the beautiful 13C church has fine wall arcading in the N aisle. From *River*, 1½m S of Kearnsey, a similar trip leads down the next valley. At ½m are the remains of the Premonstratensian *St Radegund's Abbey* (not open).

71m: **DOVER** (32,800 inhabitants) has for centuries been England's main gateway to the Continent as well as a crucial point in its defence against invasion. It lies on low ground at the mouth of the Dour and stretches up the narrow valley which here interrupts the line of the white cliffs, fortified to the E by Dover Castle, probably England's best-known coastal garrison.

TI: Townwall St. Visitorcall provides a 24-hour recorded information service: to order a free card listing the phone numbers of individual services call 071 971 0076. (Calls cost 36p per minute cheap rate, 48p per minute at all other times.) **Buses**: from Pencester Rd to all destinations. **Railway Stations**: Dover Priory, for all services; Marine (for Western Docks). **Ferry Services**: From the Car Ferry Terminal (Eastern Docks) to Calais.

History. Dover (the Roman Dubrae or Dubris), in all ages an important landing place, was the starting-point of Watling Street, the Roman road to London via Canterbury. In the 3–4C it became a fortress guarding the 'Saxon Shore', which extended from The Wash to Spithead. In 1190 Richard I assembled his knights here before starting on the Third Crusade. The castle came to be regarded as the 'Key of England', and in 1216 successfully withstood a long siege by the Dauphin and King John's rebellious barons. The French, however, pillaged Dover in about 1295. It was captured by Parliament in 1642. Charles II landed here at the Restoration in 1660.

In World War I Dover was the headquarters of the Dover Patrol, in which British and American destroyers combined to protect navigation against German submarines and mines. In World War II it played a prominent part in the evacuation from Dunkirk, and was one of the first places to be bombed in the Battle of Britain. From 1940 to 1944 the town was under continual shell fire, the casemates of the castle providing shelter for the population.

The **Straits of Dover**, 17m wide between Dover and Cape Gris Nez, are the narrowest part of the Channel. Here, in sight of the town, the Spanish Armada of 1588 received its first shattering blow. Captain Webb swam from Dover to (21m) Calais in 1875 in 21¾hrs, and more recently the Straits have been swum many times, mostly in the reverse direction. Louis Blériot was the first man to fly an aeroplane across the Channel (1909) and the Hon. C.S. Rolls the first to cross and recross in a single flight (1910), but they were preceded by François Blanchard, who flew from Dover to Guines in his balloon in 1785.

Dover is the chief of the **Cinque Ports**, a system of maritime defence modelled on the 'Saxon Shore' ports of the Romans. The name (pronounced 'Sink') dates back to the 11C or earlier, and the first charter was granted by Edward I in 1278. It named five ports—Dover, Sandwich, Hythe, Romney and Hastings—which, in return for various privileges and immunities, were bound to supply ships for the royal fleet when required. Rye and Winchelsea were added as 'Ancient Towns', and various other places as 'Limbs' or 'Members'. The Cinque Ports are under the nominal jurisdiction of a Lord Warden, whose official residence is at Walmer Castle; the post has been held by William Pitt, the Duke of Wellington and Sir Winston Churchill, and is now held by HM the Queen Mother.

*****Dover Castle** (EH, all year plus Mondays in winter) commands the summit of the cliff E of the town. Motorists reach it from Castle Hill Rd, through

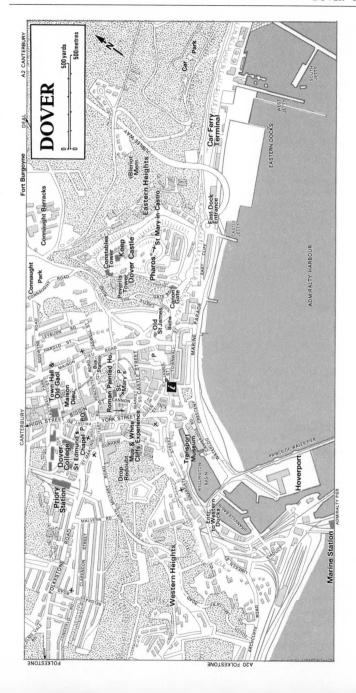

Constable's Tower (1227). The route passes 'Queen Elizabeth's Pocket Pistol', a bronze cannon 23ft long, presented by Charles V to Henry VIII; it was cast in Utrecht in 1544 and bears a Low Dutch inscription. Pedestrians approach from the bombed Norman church of *St James* at the beginning of Castle Hill Rd and enter through *Canon Gate*. The *Pharos*, perhaps the oldest standing building in England (c AD 50), is a relic of the original Roman fortress; its octagonal belfry was added by Humphrey of Gloucester. The ancient church of *St Mary-in-Castro*, built of Roman bricks, is Saxon but was badly restored in 1860. The *Keep* was built by Henry II (1181–87), with walls 17–22ft thick. It contains an armoury and a late Norman chapel. Many of the rooms have inscriptions scratched by prisoners of war during Marlborough's campaigns. From the top storey, with a fine *view, a well descends into the thickness of the wall and down into the cliff for 289ft. *Hellfire Corner* (guided tours only) was excavated in the rock below the castle in Napoleonic times and used as the base for planning the evacuation of Dunkirk.

The town is best explored from Market Square. Nearby is the *Dover Museum and White Cliffs Experience*, on the site of the Roman Classis Britannica fort, whose remains can be seen below the present building. The museum has important collections of local archaeology and history. Aimed at a less serious audience, the White Cliffs Experience uses the latest technological gimmickry (audio-visual displays, tableaux, etc.) to recreate the history of the port from Romano-British times to World War II. Cannon St. leads N from Market Square, passing New St., on the left, where the *Roman Painted House* (open) is a well-preserved town house with *wall paintings and an underfloor heating system. *St Mary's Church*, on the right-hand side of Cannon St., has a Norman tower. It contains memorials to the actor Samuel Foote (1720–77) and the poet Charles Churchill (1732–64), who died at Boulogne. Further N, in Biggin St., is the Victorian *Town Hall* incorporating the fine *Maison Dieu Hall* (open), a 14C enlargement of the pilgrims' hostel founded c 1221 by Hubert de Burgh; the restored 13C chapel at the E end was changed in the 19C into a Sessions Hall. Beneath the Town Hall are the cells of the 19C jail (guided tours). *Maison Dieu House*, now the public library, was built in 1665 for the Agent Victualler of the Navy.

In Priory Rd, the tiny restored *Chapel of St Edmund*, consecrated in 1253, was formerly attached to the Maison Dieu; dissolved in 1544, it was reconsecrated in 1968. Near Priory Station is *Dover College*, whose buildings include the refectory, dormitory and gatehouse of *St Martin's Priory*, a Benedictine foundation of 1130.

At the harbour, S of Market Square, the well laid-out Marine Parade leads to the **Eastern Docks**, with the car ferry terminal. It passes monuments to Captain Webb and C.S. Rolls, as well as remains of the fortifications added by Henry VII. A path climbs to the **Eastern Heights**, which give an excellent view of the harbour and hoverport. On *North Fall Meadow*, E of the Castle, a memorial marks the spot where Blériot landed. A cliff walk continues past a radar station to (3m) the *South Foreland*, with its lighthouse, and (4m) *St Margaret's Bay* (Route 6).

The **Western Docks**, with the Hoverport, were developed on the site of the original river mouth. They lie beyond the elegant Waterloo Crescent and Cambridge Rd, where the *Transport Museum* displays vintage vehicles. The **Western Heights** are occupied by the *Citadel* and other Napoleonic and 19C fortifications. Left of the road near the summit are the foundations of a 12C *Church of the Knights Templar* (EH). Here King John made submission to Pandulf, the Pope's legate, in 1213. A deep cleft separates the Western Heights from **Shakespeare Cliff** (350ft; footpath), so called from traditional association with a famous passage in 'King Lear' (IV, vi). At its base is the supplementary ventilation system of the *Channel Tunnel*, for which see Folkestone (Route 7). It is approached via Snargate St. (A20); the return from its W end can be made by the beach at low tide.

From Dover to *Deal*, *Sandwich* and *Ramsgate*, see Route 6; to *Folkestone*, see Route 7.

5

Canterbury

CANTERBURY (34,400 inhabitants) is not the county town of Kent nor even its largest population centre, but it is certainly its most important old city. Its situation on the banks of the Stour at a convenient staging point between London and Dover made the growth of a major settlement inevitable. The Roman town became the capital of a Saxon kingdom and, with the arrival of Augustine in 597, this in turn developed into a centre for Christianity in England. With the martyrdom of Thomas Becket in 1170 the importance of both city and cathedral increased, as they became the goal for the most famous of all English pilgrimages. In the 20C Canterbury has suffered wartime bombing and almost equally disastrous post-war city planning. Yet for all this, it still keeps a prosperous market atmosphere that dates back to Roman times. The cathedral that dominates the visitor's first impression is only the most conspicuous of many buildings, domestic as well as ecclesiastical, which bear witness to its medieval status.

TI: 34 St Margaret's St. **Bus Station**: St George's Lane. **Railway Stations**: Canterbury East, for London via Faversham and for Dover; Canterbury West, for London via Ashford, and for Maidstone and Ramsgate. **Theatres**: Marlowe Theatre, The Friars; Gulbenkian Theatre, University campus. **Annual Event**: Festival of music and drama in October.

History. The Roman Durovernum, at the junction of military roads from Lympne, Dover and Richborough, was renamed Cantwarabyrig (borough of the men of Kent) by the Saxons and became the capital of Ethelbert, King of Kent c 560. To this court, where the Frankish Queen Bertha was already a Christian, St Augustine and his fellow missionaries were welcomed in 597; the king granted to them and to Bertha the use of a church, and was himself baptised with many of his subjects. In 598 Augustine founded a Benedictine monastery, which became the burial place of the kings and early sainted archbishops, afterwards named St Augustine's Abbey. On his later return to England as 'bishop of the English' he established another church which became the first cathedral; a monastery was afterwards organised as the priory of Christ Church by Lanfranc. With the murder of Archbishop Thomas Becket in 1170 and his canonisation three years later the fame of the cathedral eclipsed that of St Augustine's Abbey and the ecclesiastical supremacy of the archbishops was definitely established. As 'the holy blissful martyr', St Thomas drew English and foreign pilgrims, including Louis VII of France, to his miracle-working shrine until its demolition by Henry VIII in 1538. The holiday aspect of the pilgrimage is immortalised in Chaucer's 'Canterbury Tales'. The latest reckoning makes the present archbishop, George Carey, the 103rd.

Canterbury was attacked by German aircraft in May and June 1942. The cathedral escaped serious damage, but a large area SE of the centre was destroyed. This quarter was replanned disastrously in the styleless manner of the 1950s with the eccentric conservation of a few church towers. Excavations in the bombed area unearthed the foundations of a Roman theatre (the second to be identified in Britain). A pre-Roman settlement of c 200 BC and a Saxon colony of the 5C have also been traced, proving a continuous occupation of 2000 years.

Natives, residents and visitors. Geoffrey Chaucer (c 1343–1400) did not live to complete the poem that would have brought his pilgrims to Canterbury, but he himself was a visitor in his capacity as the king's Clerk of Works when the cathedral nave was being rebuilt. The birthplace of Christopher Marlowe (1564–93) at 57 St George's St. was destroyed by bombs in 1942 but the tower of the nearby church where he was baptised still stands. R.H. Barham (1788–1845), author of 'The Ingoldsby Legends', was born at 61 Burgate (destroyed; plaque). Dickens, a frequent visitor, sent David Copperfield to Dr Strong's school in Canterbury and made the Wickfields and Uriah Heep natives of the city; the former Sun Inn, near Christ Church Gate, has been identified with the hotel where the Micawbers stayed. Joseph Conrad (1857–1924) is buried in the Roman Catholic cemetery.

THE CATHEDRAL AND ITS PRECINCTS. The modern approach diverges from the old Dover road, which passed through the city from NW to SE, becoming the High St. in the centre. Rheims Way now channels traffic round the S walls, giving a good view of the cathedral and passing on the left, *St Mildred's Church* and the *Castle* (both described under Stour St. below).

The best way to reach the cathedral is by following the traditional pilgrims' route from the High St. along Mercery Lane, an alley once lined with shops selling healing water from Becket's Well in the cathedral crypt, medallions of St Thomas and other souvenirs of pilgrimage. In Butter Market stands the War Memorial of 1921 and the main entrance to the cathedral precincts, *Christ Church Gate, a beautiful Perpendicular structure commemorating Arthur, Prince of Wales (1486–1502). It was built in 1517—not 1507, the date mistakenly carved when it was restored in the 1930s. The gates themselves are of c 1662.

The *Cathedral is the mother church of Anglican Christianity and the seat of the Archbishop of Canterbury, Primate of All England. Its architectural importance, however, does not quite match its ecclesiastical rank. The grandest aspect of the building, undoubtedly, is the exterior. The silhouette of its two low W towers and tall central *tower, all in lovely grey Caen stone, makes a commanding view whether it is seen at close quarters from Christ Church Gate or from the outskirts of the city (Rheims Way or the walls by the Dane John Gardens, for example). The inside of the cathedral lacks any feature as striking and its interest lies mainly in details, like the excellent stained glass and the profusion of tombs. Unfortunately, appreciation of them is made difficult by the crowds of visitors and the distinctly commercial atmosphere.

Despite its long history and continuous importance, the cathedral as it stands today is largely the creation of two distinct periods: 1070–1184 and 1391–1505. The oldest parts are fragments of the church raised by Lanfranc, the first Norman archbishop (1070–89), on the ruins of Augustine's original church. This hasty reconstruction quickly proved too small and was replaced with a grander building, supervised by Priors Ernulf and Conrad, between 1096 and 1130. The next stage in the cathedral's history came in the wake of Thomas Becket's murder in 1170 and his canonisation three years later. The French mason William of Sens and his successor, William the Englishman, added the E transepts and remodelled the E end in honour of the saint (1175–84). For some 200 years the cathedral remained in this state, until 1391, when Henry Yevele began to replace the unambitious nave and W transepts which had survived from Lanfranc's

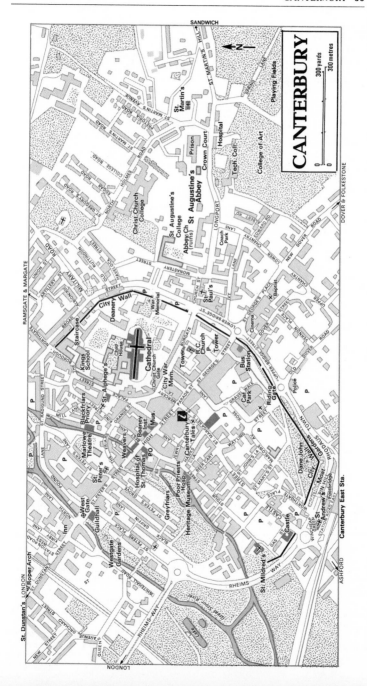

CANTERBURY

time. The work was finished with the completion of Bell Harry, the noble Perpendicular central tower, by John Wastell in 1505.

The main entrance is by the *SW Porch* (1418), probably built to commemorate the English victory at Agincourt in 1415, but a tour of the interior best starts from the W end. Yevele's *Nave* has lost its original stained glass but still impresses by its lightness, its stately simplicity and by the vista it offers towards the E, where a flight of steps ascends to the choir screen and a second flight approaching the altar can be glimpsed beyond. Under the NW tower is the 'Corinthian Throne' (1704) carved by Grinling Gibbons. In the N aisle are the ornate font (1639) and Nicholas Stone's monument to the organist and composer Orlando Gibbons, who died suddenly on his way through Canterbury in 1625. An elaborate 15C screen, with the crowned figures of six monarchs and its original iron gates, separates the nave and choir.

This spot gives a good view of Yevele's *West* (or *Nave*) *Transepts* with their great *windows. The NW window was donated by Edward IV (d. 1483), who is portrayed in the glass; the SW window has 15C tracery and glass, with some 12C glass from the clerestory of the choir. The NW transept was the scene of Becket's martyrdom. The four knights who murdered him entered by the door from the cloisters, and a slab in the pavement marks the spot where the archbishop is believed to have fallen. The adjoining *Lady Chapel* is late Perpendicular (1449–68) with rich fan vaulting. St Michael's Chapel, the corresponding chapel in the SW transept, has a fine group of monuments, notably those to Margaret Holland (d. 1437) and Archbishop Stephen Langton, who helped the barons persuade King John to sign Magna Carta in 1215.

The *Choir*, among the longest in England, was built by William of Sens in a mixture of Norman and Early English styles. It narrows at the E end to preserve the Norman side chapels, and is separated from the aisles by beautiful and unusual *screens alternating with canopied tombs. The *Choir Aisles* and the *East* (or *Choir*) *Transepts* are mainly the work of Ernulf and Conrad, altered by William of Sens. They are rich in stained glass and monuments. A 15C fresco of the life of St Eustace can be seen on the wall by the NE transept, while St Anselm's Chapel (off the S choir aisle) has a 12C wall painting of St Paul on Malta.

The part of the cathedral E of the choir was built wholly in honour of St Thomas. Until its destruction in 1538 his shrine stood behind the High Altar in the *Trinity Chapel*, with lovely columns of coloured marble. The stained-glass *windows (1220–30) depict miracles performed by the saint. Immediately behind the High Altar is the so-called *'St Augustine's Chair', probably dating from Langton's time, in which Archbishops of Canterbury have traditionally been enthroned. Between the N piers is the resplendent *tomb of Henry IV (d. 1413) and his second wife, Joan of Navarre (d. 1437); between the piers on the S side are the tomb and effigy of Edward, the Black Prince (d. 1376), with modern reproductions of his armour. At the extreme E end of the building is the delightful circular *Corona*, added by William the Englishman, with a fine 13C window.

The lofty and spacious *Crypt*, entered from the SW or NW transept, is the main survival of Ernulf and Conrad's work, with vigorous Norman carving on the capitals of the pillars and their ornamental shafts. Especially fine is the central pillar of St Gabriel's Chapel in the SE corner; the apse preserves its *paintings of c 1130. A chapel in the S aisle is walled off to form a 'Temple' for French Protestants, who have worshipped here since 1568; it includes the beautiful Black Prince's Chantry, donated in thanks for the dispensation of 1363 that allowed him to marry his kinswoman Joan, the 'Fair Maid of Kent'. Of the same period and perhaps from the same donor is the exquisite stone screen in the adjoining chapel of Our Lady of the Undercroft. The late 12C *Crypt* beneath the Trinity Chapel and the Corona includes the site of the chapel where St Thomas was first buried; on 12 July 1174 Henry II completed his penance for the murder here. It now houses *remains from the Saxon church at Reculver (see Route 6), two 7C columns and fragments of a stone cross.

On the N side of the cathedral are the extensive monastic buildings. The Benedictine monastery founded by St Augustine was enlarged and converted into a priory by Lanfranc, and much altered and rebuilt by later archbishops.

The *Great Cloister* (1397–1414) is entered from the NW transept. Though mainly Perpendicular, it incorporates some fine Norman work and beautiful Early English arcading in the N walk, cut into by the Perpendicular vaulting. The painted vault

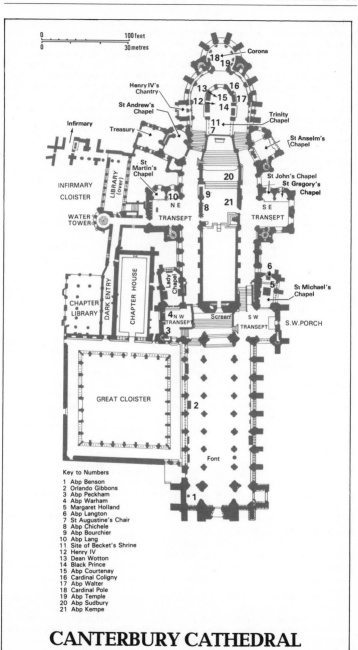

Key to Numbers
1 Abp Benson
2 Orlando Gibbons
3 Abp Peckham
4 Abp Warham
5 Margaret Holland
6 Abp Langton
7 St Augustine's Chair
8 Abp Chichele
9 Abp Bourchier
10 Abp Lang
11 Site of Becket's Shrine
12 Henry IV
13 Dean Wotton
14 Black Prince
15 Abp Courtenay
16 Cardinal Coligny
17 Abp Walter
18 Cardinal Pole
19 Abp Temple
20 Abp Sudbury
21 Abp Kempe

CANTERBURY CATHEDRAL

*bosses, which include over 800 shields, are superb; one, in the E walk, portrays Yevele, the architect. Opening off the E walk is the spacious *Chapter House*, whose lower part is the work of Prior Eastry (1304– 20), completed by Chillenden when he began the cloisters. T.S. Eliot's 'Murder in the Cathedral' was commissioned for performance here in 1935. To the NE is the rebuilt *Chapter Library* (1954), replacing a building destroyed in 1942. In the *Dark Entry*, between this and the chapter house, are two fine ranges of pillars of Lanfranc's time, some with incised decoration; these and the pillar bases in the lawn beyond the modern arcade of the library were part of the sub-vault of the *Dormitory*. The Dark Entry leads to the *Infirmary Cloister*, passing on the right a door into the crypt and a stair to the NE transept. On the left is the elaborate Norman sub-vault of the *Water Tower*, part of the ingenious water-supply system of Prior Wibert (1151–67); the upper floor is Perpendicular. The cloister is continued by the 13C sub-vault of the *Prior's Chapel*; the chapel itself was replaced after 1660 by the brick Howley Library.

The Infirmary Cloister is prolonged N by a passage below the Wolfson Library (1966) to *Prior Sellingegate* (c 1480) and the Green Court. On the E side of this square stands the *Deanery*, mixed medieval and 16C; in the SW corner is the *Archdeaconry* with a curious wooden pentice (or lean-to) of 1390 in its garden. To the E of this the *Larder Gate Building* (1951) incorporates a 15C archway and part of the monastic kitchens. This, with all the remaining buildings in the square, belongs to the **King's School**, a monastic foundation of the 7C, installed on this site by Henry VIII as a grammar school for boys. Christopher Marlowe, William Harvey, Walter Pater and Somerset Maugham were pupils here. The monastic *Brewhouse* and *Bakehouse* (1303) are incorporated in the N range. In the NW corner of the Green Court the exterior *Norman Staircase* (1151–67) leading to the hall is unique and still supremely beautiful, despite the modern roof. The adjacent *Court Gate* leads to the *Mint Yard*, the former Almonry. Its North Gate opens on Palace St., named from the Archbishop's Palace destroyed by Puritans c 1643. From then until the completion of the present modest palace on the old site in 1901, the archbishops had no official Canterbury residence.

In the E walk of the Infirmary Cloister a stately row of Norman arches marks the hall of the *Infirmary*. The more ornate arches still further E are remains of the 14C *Infirmary Chapel*. On the right of the hall is the arcaded Norman *Treasury*, while the *Choir School* on the left incorporates a refectory of 1343. Beyond the unfinished exterior of the Corona a path skirts the S side of the cathedral. It leads across the former lay cemetery, which extended from the S Porch to the exquisitely arcaded *St Anselm's Tower* and was there divided by a wall from the monks' cemetery. The grandeur and fine colouring of the SE transept are very striking from this point. Opposite the E end of the cathedral is an old walled garden, now the site of the *Kent War Memorial* (by Sir Herbert Baker). On its E side is a bastion of the old city wall, transformed into a chapel of silence, with a cenotaph, flags and inscriptions. A gate opens into Broad St., where a fine stretch of the medieval city wall still stands.

FROM THE CATHEDRAL TO ST AUGUSTINE'S ABBEY AND LONGPORT. Lady Wooton's Green leads from the opposite side of Broad St. to *St Augustine's College* (not normally open), founded for missionaries in 1848 and now occupied by the King's School. It covers part of the site of **St Augustine's Abbey**, incorporating *Fyndon's Gate* (1300–09), the great gate of the monastery, as its main entrance, as well as parts of the guest hall and, further S, the badly restored *Cemetery Gate* (1390). The remaining college buildings follow the medieval plan and are the first major work of William Butterfield. The excavated *ruins of the abbey churches and cloister (EH, all year) are reached from Longport.

The original Abbey of St Peter and St Paul, founded by St Augustine in 598 had three separate 7C churches in line. In 978 St Dunstan rededicated the abbey to the founder, and in 1049–59 Abbot Wulfric began to link the two W churches by a rotunda on the model of St-Bénigne at Dijon. All this work was demolished by the first Norman abbot, who in 1073 started a new church, completed c 1120. The abbey, which to the time of Becket ranked as the second Benedictine house in Europe, was destroyed in 1538 and a royal posting house built on the site. This was visited by Elizabeth I, Charles I (who received his bride here in June 1625) and Charles II.

The N part of the first church (*St Peter and St Paul*) lies beneath a low protective roof. King Ethelbert, Queen Bertha, St Augustine and at least eight of his early successors were buried in it, and the empty tombs of St Lawrence, St Mellitus and St Justus have been identified. The massive octagonal foundations of *Abbot Wulfric's Rotunda* are prominent to the SE. Of the *Norman church* the NW wall of the nave still stands, with Tudor additions of the 'King's House', and much of the crypt of the apsidal choir. *St Pancras*, the easternmost of the three 7C churches, built of Roman bricks, had its E end altered c 1387.

Longport continues E past, on the left, the *County Gaol* of 1808 and, on the right, the *Hospital of John Smith* (1657). *St Martin's Church* (½m), in use for Christian services before the coming of St Augustine, may stand on the site of a Romano-British church.

St Martin's Hill was occupied by Roman villas in the 4C, and possibly part of a pre-Christian building exists in the W part of the chancel S wall, especially the square-headed archway; the round-headed doorway is probably early Saxon. The nave, of Kentish rag, is plastered in the Roman fashion; the tower is 14C. Within, the 13C chancel arch and subsequent restorations obscure the antiquity of what is one of the earliest extant churches in Europe. A Norman piscina at the SE corner of the nave is beautiful in its simplicity, but most interesting is the tub-shaped *font, the lower part possibly of Saxon origin, but too late to be that in which Ethelbert was baptised. On the N wall is a 16C carving of St Martin.

FROM BURGATE TO THE WEST GATE. Burgate re-enters the walls. On the left is the tower of the ruined *St Mary Magdalene*, with a striking memorial to John Whitfield (d. 1691). To the left, further on, the Longmarket shopping precinct covers the remains of a *Roman House* (open), with a fine mosaic pavement. On St George's St. beyond stands the tower of the bombed church of *St George*, where Marlowe was baptised (tablet). St George's St. continues as High St. On the left side is *Queen Elizabeth's Guest Chamber*, a splendid Tudor house of 1573 with colourful pargetting, now a restaurant. Further, on the right, is the *Beaney Institute*, housing the *Royal Museum and Art Gallery*.

The disused church in St Margaret's St., leading to the left, houses the *Canterbury Tales*, an exhibition which seeks to bring the world of Chaucer's characters to life with the same gimmicks used by the Jorvik Viking Centre in York.

Further on, Stour St. also leads left from High St. *Greyfriars* (limited opening) was the first Franciscan friary in England, founded in 1267 and consecrated in 1325. In the 17C the Cavalier and poet Richard Lovelace lived here for a time. Further along Stour St. are the greatly altered 14C buildings of the *Poor Priests' Hospital*, now the *Museum of Canterbury's Heritage*. It displays treasures from excavations in the Roman, Saxon and medieval town, among them a Roman hoard of silver spoons, a Saxon cross and badges worn by medieval pilgrims. A more recent exhibit is Stephenson's Invicta steam engine (1830), used on the Canterbury–Whitstable railway. Stour St. continues to *St Mildred's Church*, still showing its Saxon origins despite 19C restoration. Izaak Walton was married here in 1626.

The detour can be lengthened by following Gas St., opposite the church, to the keep of the *Castle* (c 1175). Beyond, in the angle of the city walls, here offering a fine *view of the cathedral, are the gardens of the *Dane John*. The obelisk on the Dane John itself (an unexplained tumulus 80ft high) commemorates the laying out of the grounds in 1790.

Best Lane, a right turn from the High St. opposite the junction with Stour St., leads to the 13–14C refectory and undercroft of *Blackfriars* (occasionally open). The refectory was for a time used as a Baptist chapel, in which Defoe is said to have preached in 1724.

Beyond the Post Office in the High St. is the *Hospital of St Thomas*, or *Eastbridge Hospital* (open), a well-preserved hostel founded in 1180 for poor pilgrims, with a fine chapel and crypt, and a hall with an early 13C Christ in Majesty, painted in tempera. The street crosses a branch of the Stour and changes its name to St Peter's St. Overlooking the river on the right are the *Weavers' Houses*, heavily restored Tudor buildings now converted into shops, once occupied by the Huguenots who settled in Canterbury after the revocation of the Edict of Nantes (1685). At the end of St Peter's St., with the 13C *St Peter's Church* on the right, is the **West Gate**, only survivor of the seven city gates, which was built probably by Henry Yevele (1375–81). The guard chamber (open) contains a collection of arms and armour, fetters, a scold bridle, etc., and there is a good view from the top of the tower. The church of the *Holy Cross* (c 1380), beside the gate, is now the *Guildhall*; to the left are the attractive *Westgate Gardens*, with a tower of the city wall.

Outside the gate the old London road, here called St Dunstan's St., passes on the right the old *Falstaff Inn* (now a hotel and restaurant), which was a hostelry for pilgrims arriving after the city gates were closed. On the left, beyond, a 16C house (another hotel and restaurant) claims to be the home of Agnes Wickfield in Dickens's 'David Copperfield'. Further on is the 13C *St Dunstan's Church*, with the Roper vault containing the head of the sainted Sir Thomas More (1478–1535), given to his daughter Margaret Roper after 14 days' exposure on London Bridge. A brick archway opposite is the only relic of the Ropers' house.

FROM CANTERBURY TO FOLKESTONE by the Elham Valley, 20m on a winding but pretty road. To (5½m) *Bishopsbourne*, see Route 4. The route skirts Charlton Park as it branches right from A2. 7½m: *Barham*, a pleasant little village. 12½m: *Elham* (pronounced 'Eelam') has a pretty square with a fine 12–15C church. Among the interesting contents are: a 15C alabaster triptych (one panel restored), 15C and 16C stained glass, and some good 20C fittings. The Abbot's Fireside (1614; now a hotel) has an elaborate carved fireplace of 1624. At (13½m) *Lyminge* the church (c 965) adjoins the foundations of a 7C nunnery founded by Eadburg (Ethelburga), daughter of Ethelbert. 20m: *Folkestone*, see Route 7. The direct road from Canterbury to Folkestone (A260; 17m) diverges from the Dover road near Broome Park and crosses the pleasant upland common called *Swingfield Minnis*. A sideroad leads left to *St John's Commandery*, a medieval chapel of the Knights Hospitallers later converted into a farmhouse (EH, open by appointment).

FROM CANTERBURY TO MARGATE (16m; A28) and RAMSGATE (16½m; A28 and A253). To the S of (2½m) *Sturry* is *Fordwich*, the old port of Canterbury when the Stour was navigable, where the Caen stone for the cathedral was landed. The ancient town hall has a ducking stool. At (9m) *Sarre* A253 diverges right for *Ramsgate* (Route 6), passing 1m N of *Minster*, where the grand *church has a fine Norman tower and nave and an Early English chancel. Nearby is Minster Abbey (now occupied by Benedictine nuns; open). The W range dates from the late 11C or early 12C, and this incorporates the W end of the abbey church (with a spiral staircase in the tower); excavations have revealed the plan of the church, which can be seen marked out in the ground. A groin-vaulted passage and chapel are also shown. From Sarre the Margate road, A28, continues NE. (10m) *St Nicholas-at-Wade* and (16m) *Margate*, see Route 6.

From Canterbury to *Ashford*, see Route 7.

6

London to Dover via Margate, Ramsgate and the Isle of Thanet

Directions. Total distance 98m. A2, A207 and A2 again to (46m) Faversham (bypassed) and (48m) Brenley Corner, see Route 4. A299 to (56m) Whitstable and (60m) Herne Bay (both bypassed). A299, A28 to (72m) **Margate**. A255 to (75m) Broadstairs and (76½m) **Ramsgate**. A253, A256 to (83½m) Sandwich (bypassed). A258 to (89½m) Deal and (8m) **Dover** (Route 4). This alternative to Route 4 takes a longer and less direct route to Dover, avoiding Canterbury and following the 'Saxon Shore' round the Kent coast. The roads to Margate and Ramsgate are crowded in summer.

The route begins by following Route 4 to (46m) *Faversham* and the round-about at (48m) *Brenley Corner*, where A299 is taken NE towards the coast.

Some interesting villages flank the road. *Hernhill*, ¾m to the right at 48½m, has a charming little green with a typical Wealden house, the Red Lion, and a Perpendicular church. At *Graveney*, 2m left at 53m, the church is mainly 14C, with a Norman chancel, oak roof, early 16C rood screen and several brasses, one to John Martyn (d. 1436).

A299 skirts the resorts of (56m) *Whitstable* and (60m) *Herne Bay* (27,900 inhabitants; TI). Whitstable, known for its oysters, faces the Isle of Sheppey. Herne Bay (27,500 inhabitants; TI) has a more attractive seafront with an esplanade of 1830. At *Reculver*, on the coast 2m off the road at 62m, the route enters the **Isle of Thanet**.

This exposed NE corner of Kent, the vulnerable tip of the 'Saxon Shore' which the Romans defended against pirates, is called an isle because its western boundary, the river Wantsum, joins the Stour in the S and once formed a continuous navigable channel linking Reculver and Richborough. The Romans used it as part of their regular route from Boulogne (Bononia) to London and built forts at Reculver (Regulbium) and Richborough (Rutupia).

Inside the walls of the Roman fort at Reculver stand the bleak but impressive 12C towers from the church established here in 669 (EH). The rest of the Saxon church was demolished in 1809, though its ground plan is marked.

A299 joins A298 near (66m) *St Nicholas-at-Wade*, whose church has Early English carvings on Norman arches. 68m: *Birchington* is a resort now joined to Margate. The 13–14C church has brasses in the Quex chapel; also the Crispe mural monument (1651) with its six busts by J. Marshall, and a bust of Anna Crisp (d. 1708) by William Palmer. Dante Gabriel Rossetti, who died at Birchington in 1882, is commemorated by a Celtic cross in the churchyard (by Ford Madox Brown) and a window in the S aisle (by Frederic James Shields).

½m SE lies *Quex House* (open), a building of 1813 replacing the one that William III used as a stage on his journeys to and from Holland. Its grounds contain two 19C tower follies and the *Powell-Cotton Museum* of natural history and ethnography. At *Acol*, ½m further S, is the chalk pit of 'The Smuggler's Leap' ('The Ingoldsby Legends').

72m: **MARGATE** (53,300 inhabitants), a popular resort, enjoys fine sands and fresh breezes off the North Sea.

TI: 22 High St. **Buses**: bus stops in Canterbury Rd (Westbrook), The Harbour and Eastern Esplanade (Cliftonville). **Railway Station**: Station Rd, S of Marine Terrace. **Amusements**: Winter Gardens Theatre and Queens Hall (holiday shows); amusement park in Marine Terrace.

History. Once a packet station for Flushing, Margate saw the embarkation of the Elector Frederick V (King of Bohemia) and Elizabeth Stuart after their marriage in 1613. William III and the Duke of Marlborough often used its harbour. In 1588 Lord Howard of Effingham and Sir Francis Drake wrote despatches from here after the defeat of the Spanish Armada. Margate grew into a resort in the 18C. Until the coming of the railway, visitors from London came down the Thames estuary in 'Margate hoys', single-masted schooners also used to convey produce from Thanet.

The handsome quarter on the cliffs E of the old town is known as *Clifton-ville*, while to the W is *Westbrook*. A favourite spot, beside the sands and seafront, is the *Jetty* (1240ft long). The pier (1855) was damaged in the storm of 1978. In the old town is the flint church of *St John* (partly 12C) rich in brasses, of which the most striking is the skeleton commemorating Richard Notfelde (d. 1446). In King St. is a restored Tudor house (open). King St. continues inland as Dane Rd, where, at the foot of Grotto Hill, the *Grotto* (open), is fantastically decorated with shells. It is apparently a late 18C or early 19C folly.

At *Kingsgate*, 3m E via B2052, Lord Holland built an imitation Norman castle (now flats) in 1760. Across the bay is the *North Foreland* (lighthouse), the Roman Promontorium Acantium, off which Monk beat De Ruyter in 1666.
From Margate to *Canterbury*, see Route 5.

A254 leads directly to Ramsgate. A better route takes A255 SE via (75m) **Broadstairs** (TI), a quiet resort but also an expanding residential town (23,400 inhabitants). Harbour St. leads down to the charming bay through *York Gate*, a flint arch built in 1540 to protect the 'stair', or gap, in the low white cliffs.

Dickens described Broadstairs as 'one of the freest and freshest little places in the world'. Tablets mark the spots associated with him. In *Archway House*, spanning Harbour St., he wrote part of 'Barnaby Rudge'. At *Bleak House*, on top of the cliff above the pier and commanding a fine view, he planned the novel after which it was renamed and wrote much of 'David Copperfield'. Now the *Dickens and Maritime Museum*, it has a collection of Dickensiana, including the lectern he used for public readings. *Dickens House* (open), at the W end of Victoria Parade, has been identified with the home of Betsey Trotwood, though 'David Copperfield' locates it near Dover. Its exhibition traces Dickens's connection with Broadstairs. Queen Victoria stayed at *Pierremont Hall* in 1829.

76½m: **RAMSGATE** (38,200 inhabitants) is a resort spreading over two chalk cliffs and the 'gate', or valley, between them. It faces S and so is more sheltered than Margate.

TI: Argyle Centre, Queen St. **Railway Station**: off the Margate road (A254). **Ferry Services**: to Dunkerque and Ostend. **Amusements**: Granville Theatre, on the E Cliff; Argyle Centre, Queen St.; casino and amusement park on seafront.

History. Elizabeth Fry died here in 1845 and Van Gogh taught here in 1876. In 1914–18 Ramsgate came next after Dunkirk and Calais as a target for German bombardment; in 1940 it was one of the chief bases for the Dunkirk evacuation.

The *Harbour*, with an obelisk (1821) recording the departure of George IV to Hanover, is of growing commercial importance, especially for the import of cars. The yacht marina has berths for 500 craft.

At the end of W Cliff is the RC church of *St Augustine*, now part of a monastery, which A.W.N. Pugin paid for and considered his best work (1845–50). The interior, in Whitby stone, has a monument to Pugin, buried here. The church stands next to the house he designed for himself, the *Grange*, where he died in 1852. On E Cliff is the early 19C Wellington Crescent, the gigantic Granville Hotel by E.W. Pugin and, at the end of the seafront, the King George IV memorial park. *St George's Church* (1824–27), off High St., has a conspicuous tower and light interior.

From Ramsgate A253 passes the suburb of *St Lawrence*, with a 13–15C church and Norman tower. From 78½m A256 skirts *Pegwell Bay*, famous for its fossils. It is the scene of a memorable painting by William Dyce.

Beside the road is a Danish longship built and sailed in 1949 to celebrate the 1500th anniversary of Hengist and Horsa's landing at Ebbsfleet (see below). ½m further, a sideroad leads right to (1m) *St Augustine's Cross* (EH), erected in 1884 to commemorate his landing in 597. However, the exact landing place may have been at the vanished *Stonar* across the Stour from Sandwich.

Beyond (80½m) *Ebbsfleet* the skyline is dominated by the power station (1963) of *Richborough*, in a loop of the Stour, originally created in 1916 as a war-transport depot. At 82½m a toll bridge of 1797 crosses the Stour for (83½m) **Sandwich** (4200 inhabitants; seasonal TI). This charming medieval town, still largely contained within its old limits, was one of the original Cinque Ports (see Dover, Route 4), though it now lies 2m from the sea. Becket landed here in 1170 after his self-imposed exile in France, as did Richard Coeur de Lion in 1194 after his Austrian imprisonment. Thomas Paine lived in New St. for a year.

On the Quay are the *Fisher Gate* and part of the town walls, continued further W with a raised promenade. The Tudor gate-tower gave its name to the *Barbican* theatre. The attractive Upper Strand St. has the Old Customs House and, at the end, a large house (1911) by Lutyens. *St Clement's*, on higher ground to the right, has an Early English church with a low arcaded Norman tower and many interesting internal features. The fine High St. leads back towards the centre and (left) *St Peter's*, 13C with later additions. Beyond is the Cattle Market with the *Guildhall*, much extended in 1910. It contains a 17C courtroom and a museum. Further N, in Strand St., is *St Mary's* founded in the early 12C. The *King's Arms* is a timber-framed house of 1592. *Manwood Court* (c 1580), beyond, was once the grammar school.

A257 leads W out of Sandwich and in ½m a sideroad leads right to (1m) *Richborough Castle*, on the Stour (EH, all year). This is probably where the Romans landed in AD 43. A fort was built to guard Rutupia, the chief Roman port on the E coast of England until the end of the occupation. In the late 3C it became an important part of the 'Saxon Shore' defences. The ruins include the S, W and N walls of the Saxon Shore fort, 25ft high in places. Watling St., the Roman road from Canterbury, enters at the W Gate. Inside the walls are Roman and Saxon remains (1–3C AD), including the cruciform foundations of a large monument commemorating the final conquest of England in AD 81–96, a Saxon church dedicated to St Augustine, and defensive ditches. The museum has objects found during excavations. To the S is the site of a Roman amphitheatre.

Among the sandhills overlooking *Sandwich Bay*, 2½m E of the town, are the *Royal St George's* and the *Prince's Golf Links*. Further N, at the mouth of the Stour, is *Shellness* nature reserve.

89½m: **Deal** (26,000 inhabitants; TI), a 'limb' of the Cinque Ports, is a quiet coastal town with streets of 18C houses parallel to the sea. It is believed to be where Julius Caesar landed in 55 BC. William Penn sailed from here on his first voyage to America in 1682. *Old* or *Upper Deal* lies inland. St Leonard's Church has a late Norman aisled nave. The well-preserved *'Deal Castle* (EH, all year) is the most intricate of the three castles Henry VIII built to protect the safe anchorage of the Downs (see below). To the N are the scanty remains of *Sandown Castle* and, beyond, the *Royal Cinque Ports Golf Course.*

Off the coast lie the *Goodwin Sands*, dangerous sandbanks about 10m in length, marked by lightships and exposed at low water. According to legend they were once the fruitful island of Lomea, submerged by a furious storm in the 11C because the stones intended to strengthen its sea-wall had been used by the abbot of St Augustine's for the tower of Tenterden church. The *Downs*, the roadstead between the Goodwin Sands and the coast, form a natural refuge, not too safe in strong gales from the S.

90½m: *Walmer* adjoins Deal to the S. *Walmer Castle*, the third Henry VIII built in this area, became the official residence of the Lord Warden of the Cinque Ports (EH, all year but closed in January and February and when Lord Warden is in residence). The Duke of Wellington died here in 1852. His apartments have been preserved.

At 92½m B2058 diverges left for (1¾m) *St Margaret's at Cliffe*, on steep wooded cliffs in the lee of the South Foreland. The lighthouse (NT) was built in 1843 and used by Marconi for radio communications to help navigation. The old church in the landward part of the village is Norman work. On the E horn of *St Margaret's Bay* stands the granite obelisk of the Dover Patrol Monument (1921). Companion monuments stand at Cap Blanc Nez and New York Harbour. A pleasant walk along the cliffs, part of the Saxon Shore Way, leads via *Kingsdown* back to (4m) Walmer.

98m: **Dover**, see Route 4.

7

London to Dover via Maidstone and Folkestone

Directions. Total distance 78m. The route starts on A2 but soon changes to A20, followed to (4m) New Cross, (19m) Farningham, (27m) Wrotham Heath, (35m) **Maidstone**, (54m) **Ashford**, (71m) **Folkestone** and (78m) **Dover** (Route 4). M20 offers a fast alternative to A20 from (17m) Swanley, at M25, to Folkestone.

The route leaves central London by A2 (Old Kent Rd), turns right on to A20 at (4m) *New Cross* and passes through suburbs. 19m: *Farningham*, just beyond M25, is a pleasant village on the Darent. Its Early English church has a Perpendicular tower.

A225 runs S from Farningham to (9m) Sevenoaks through typical Kentish scenery. 1m: *Eynsford* has a small ruined Norman castle (c 1100) with a high curtain wall but no keep (EH). Opposite the partly Norman church a sideroad crosses the Darent by a stone bridge and leads under a railway viaduct to (½m) *'Lullingstone Roman Villa* (EH, all year). It is one of the most spectacular Roman villas in England. Excavations have found mosaic pavements in the reception room, as well as three marble busts now in the British Museum. The painted wall plaster reveals the earliest known place of Christian worship in Britain (4C). On a hillside above is a pagan funerary temple of AD 300. A private road continues to *Lullingstone Castle* (open). Its large brick gatehouse (c 1497) announces the building's Tudor origins, though they are concealed beneath elegant remodelling in Queen Anne's time. The church in the grounds has fine tombs of the Hart Dyke family. A225 continues S, passing (on the right at 4m) *Shoreham*, with a late Perpendicular church. 5½m: *Otford* has the remains of a 16C manor house of the Archbishops of Canterbury. To the left runs the so-called *Pilgrims' Way*, originally a British track, following the S slope of the Downs. 9m: *Sevenoaks*, Route 9A.

N of Farningham A225 descends the Darent valley to (4m) *Dartford* (Route 4). At (2m) *Sutton-at-Hone* the church has a monument to Sir Thomas Smyth (1558?–1625), grandly remembered as 'Governor of the East Indian and Other Companies, Treasurer of the Virginian Plantation and sometime Ambassador to the Emperor and Great Duke of Russia and Muscovy'. The house of St John's Jerusalem (12–18C) incorporates the 13C chapel of a Commandery of the Knights Hospitallers (NT, chapel and garden open). The 10–12C church of *Darenth* (¾m NE), partly built from Roman materials, has a priest's chamber above the vaulted chancel and a curious font of c 1140.

A20 passes near (21½m; left) *Brands Hatch* motor-racing circuit and at 25m descends the notorious Wrotham Hill. 26m: *Wrotham*, pronounced 'Rootam', is an attractive village with an early 14C church.

A227 leads right to (1m) *Borough Green* railway station and A25 continues to (2m) *Ightham* (pronounced 'Item'), with interesting monuments in its church. *Oldbury* (NT), ½m W on the N side of A25, is an Iron Age hill-fort. Off A227 2½m S of Ightham is *Ightham Mote* (NT). Built in the early 14C, it is everything a picturesque manor house should be: a comfortable square of timber and stone enclosing a court and surrounded by a moat. The gatehouse has a 14C lower part and upper floors built, like the S and W wings, in the mid 15C. On the opposite side of the cobbled yard stands the Great Hall, which dates from the 14C, though its large Perpendicular window was added c 1521 and the oak panelling by Norman Shaw in the 19C. To the N are more Tudor additions, notably the chapel with a painted roof. Restoration is continuing to make more rooms open to visitors. Back on A227, a sideroad leads E in ¾m to the village of *Plaxtol*. 1m E is *Old Soar Manor* (EH, summer season), the solar end of a knight's manor house of c 1290, now attached to an 18C house. A227 continues S to (5m) *Shipbourne*, a characterful village where Christopher Smart was born in 1722. For (8m) *Tonbridge*, see Route 9A.

A20 passes M20 and M26 and reaches (27m) *Wrotham Heath*, where it is joined by A25 from Sevenoaks. 2m S via B2016 is *Great Comp Garden* (open) laid out since the 1950s by the owners of the 17C house. 29m: *West Malling*, a pleasant 18C village, has the ruins of a Benedictine abbey founded in 1090 by Bishop Gundulf of Rochester (open on request, but with the restrictions of a closed order). A new abbey church was consecrated here in 1966. *St Leonard's Tower*, beyond the end of the High St., dates from c 1080 (EH). About 1m W is *Offham*, where the green has England's only surviving quintain, or post used as a mark in tilting practice.

Leybourne Castle (now the wing of a 20C house), ½m N on A228, was the home of William de Leybourne (d. 1310), England's first admiral. A tablet in the church remembers him. *Clare House* (1793), in an attractive park, is on the old road linking West Malling with (2m) *East Malling*, which has a 14–15C church, and an important Fruit Research Station (open by appointment) in Bradbourne House (rebuilt 1715).

31½m: *Ditton*. A sideroad leads left for Aylesford (see below). Just beyond, the M20 bypasses Maidstone.

35m: **MAIDSTONE** (71,800 inhabitants), the county town of Kent, lies on both banks of the Medway. Some of the streets leading off the High St. have old houses.

TI: The Gatehouse, Palace Gardens, Mill St. **Railway Stations**: Maidstone East, off Sandling Rd (A229), and Maidstone West, off Tonbridge Rd (A26). **River Cruises**: Undercliffe Boathouse (near the TI) down the Medway to Allington Lock (see below), from Easter to October. **Theatre**: Hazlitt Theatre, Earl St. **Annual Events**: Kent County Show in July at Detling Showground, 2m NE via A249; River Festival in July on the Medway in the town centre.

On the E bank of the Medway, a little S of the bridge, is the large Perpendicular church of *All Saints, chiefly built by Archbishop Courtenay (d. 1396) in connection with a secular college, suppressed in 1547, which can be seen to the S through a vaulted gate-tower. The church contains: good sedilia; stalls with misericords; a carved chancel screen (1886); the canopied tomb of Dr Wotton, first Master of the college (1417), with a wall painting of him being presented to the Virgin by saints; and a memorial (S wall) to Laurence Washington (d. 1619), George Washington's ancestor. The existing *Palace*, N of the church, is 14C with an Elizabethan E front. The small 13C gatehouse near the road is the TI Centre. Across Bishop's Way is the 14C *Palace Stable* (open), with a fine roof, housing 17–19C carriages, many of them royal. In the 18C *Town Hall* on the High St. hangs a portrait of Disraeli, who held Maidstone as his first parliamentary seat. In St Faith's St., near the East Station, the rambling 16C Chillington Manor is now the *Museum and Art Gallery*, the de facto county museum of Kent. It has costumes, ceramics (the largest collection in the county), paintings (notable Italian and Dutch works), Japanese fine and applied art, local history, natural history and relics of William Hazlitt (a native of Maidstone), as well as a gallery devoted to the Queen's Own Royal West Kent Regiment.

Otham, 3m SE of Maidstone, has timber-framed houses, notably Wardes and Stoneacre, a mainly 15C manor house (NT) with a great hall and a crownpost roof. *Sutton Valence*, on A274 5m SE, has the ruined 12C keep of its castle (EH). Off B2163 4½m S of Maidstone is *Boughton Monchelsea Place* (open), an Elizabethan mansion (1567) of Kentish ragstone, with later alterations which include Regency Gothic in the E range. The church in the handsome park was heavily restored in the 19C but has a monument by Scheemakers to Christopher Powell (d. 1742). The lychgate (1470) is one of the oldest in England. At *Loose*, by A229 3m S of Maidstone, the Wool House is a 15C half-timbered building (NT, open by appointment).

Off A20 2m NW is *Allington Castle*, a heavily restored building of the late 13C, with Tudor additions. It was the early home of Sir Thomas Wyatt (1503–42), the poet, and from here his son Sir Thomas (1521–54) set out on his rebellion against Queen Mary's Spanish marriage. It now belongs to the Carmelites and is used for religious conferences and retreats. About 2m NE of Maidstone via *Penenden Heath*, the assembly ground of the Men of Kent since Saxon times, is *Boxley*. Its partly Norman church has a memorial to Sir Francis Wyatt, who became Governor of Virginia in 1621.

FROM MAIDSTONE TO CHATHAM, 8m via A229. At *Sandling*, on the outskirts of Maidstone just before the junction with M20, a sideroad leads left to (¼m) *Allington Lock*, with a view across the Medway to Allington Castle, and the *Museum of Kent Rural Life*, with oast-house, hop garden and orchard. *Aylesford*, 1¼m beyond, has a fine river frontage, a 14C bridge, an old inn and the noble monument to Sir Thomas Colepeper (d. 1604) in its church. Sir Charles Sedley (1639–1701), poet and wit, was born in *The Friars* (½m W), which incorporated much of one of the earliest Carmelite foundations in England (1240). The Carmelites reoccupied the buildings in 1949, the first time a dispossessed order regained its old home in England. The relics of St Simon Stock (d. 1265), the first prior, were brought from Bordeaux, and in 1958–61 Adrian Gilbert Scott built a new Shrine Church for open-air services on the site of the sanctuary of the priory church (open). Left of A229 at 2m is *Kit's Coty House (EH), a dolmen with a capstone 11ft long. The long barrow survived until the 18C. A229 follows a Roman course, climbing Bluebell Hill and the North Downs, and crossing M2 to enter (8m) *Chatham* (Route 4).

FROM MAIDSTONE TO TONBRIDGE, 14m via A26 and a pleasant reach of the Medway valley. 2m: *East Barming* has a Norman church with sculptured bench-ends (c 1300). 4m: *Teston* has a medieval bridge. *West Farleigh*, on the S bank, has a well-preserved early Norman church and some large 18C houses. 5m: *Wateringbury*. At *Nettlestead*, 1m left, the tiny church has a fine series of windows. 6½m: *Mereworth Castle* (not open), modelled on Palladio's Villa Rotonda near Vicenza, was built in 1720–23 by Colen Campbell. 10m: *Hadlow* has a church with a Saxo-Norman W end, and the remains of a castle built by Walter Barton May (c 1830), including a tower 170ft high. 14m: *Tonbridge*, see Route 9A.

A20 runs E out of Maidstone and through the large village of *Bearsted*, where Edward Thomas lived in 1901–04, to (40m) the junction with B2163. Immediately to the N is *Eyhorne Manor* (not open), a typical Wealden house built in the 15C and overlaid with 17C and 18C additions. *Hollingbourne*, 1m beyond, is a charming village on the Pilgrims' Way, with the fine tomb of Lady Elizabeth Culpeper (d. 1638) in its church. B2163 S leads to *Leeds Castle (open), picturesquely sited in the middle of a lake and looking from a distance like the typical castle of romance.

The original Norman castle, begun c 1120, was greatly extended by Edward I and Eleanor of Castile after it was conveyed to the crown in 1278. To this period belong part of the Gloriette (the keep rising sheer from the lake at the N tip of the castle), the revetment wall surrounding the island and the additions to the gatehouse. The charming Fountain Court in the Gloriette was added in the reign of Edward III. Tudor contributions included the Maiden's Tower to the SE. The main part of the castle, however, was rebuilt in 1822 and most of the interiors shown are 19C or 20C reconstructions. Among the happier importations are the wood panelling from Thorpe Hall, Peterborough, in the main building and the 16C French oak staircase in the Gloriette.

42m: *Harrietsham* has a church with a Norman font and, in East St., a fine 16C Wealden House. 44m: *Lenham* is nicely grouped round the church, which has a rare armchair sedile. Sir Henry Wotton (1568–1639), poet, diplomat and wit, was born at *Boughton Malherbe*, 2½m SW, beyond *Chilston Park*, praised by Evelyn in 1666. 48m: *Charing* has a noble church and the remains of a manor house of the Archbishops of Canterbury.

Otterden Place (not open), 3½m N, is a pleasant Tudor and Georgian house beside a church rebuilt in 1753 but preserving a fine monument of 1620. B2077 leads SW from Charing through pleasant countryside and villages with timber-framed houses. *Pluckley*, at 3m, was the location of the TV series 'The Darling Buds of May', based on the work of H.E. Bates, who lived at nearby *Little Chart*. Beyond (8m) *Smarden* the road joins A274 and heads S to (12m) *Biddenden* (Route 8B).

At 52m a sideroad leads right to (⅓m) *Godinton Park* (limited opening, and by appointment). Built mainly in 1628–31, it has fine woodwork, especially the staircase and the Great Hall, which survives from the 14C building on the site.

At (54m) **Ashford** (40,000 inhabitants; TI) the church, surrounded by charming old houses, has a Perpendicular tower and monuments and brasses, including that of Elizabeth, Countess of Atholl (1375). The philosopher Simone Weil, exiled from occupied France, starved herself to death here in 1943.

FROM ASHFORD TO CANTERBURY, 14m. A28 leads NE along the Stour valley. 3m: *Kempe's Corner*. 1m to the right is *Wye*, a pretty little town which may have been the birthplace of Aphra Benn (1640–89). Among the old houses, note in particular the timber-framed Yew Trees (16–17C) on Scotton St. Wye College (1892), the agricultural school of London University, has inherited the buildings of a school and college founded by Archbishop Kempe in 1447. The crown cut in the chalk downs (right) commemorates Edward VII's coronation. *Brook*, 2¾m SE, has a Norman church with wall paintings. 4m: *Boughton Aluph*, left of the road, has a restored church with 14C nave arcades and stained glass. In the beautiful surrounding country stands *Eastwell Park* (2000 acres; lake), crossed by the Pilgrims' Way. Richard Plantagenet, Richard III's natural son, lived here after his father lost the crown at Bosworth Field, working as a bricklayer until his death in 1550. 6m: *Godmersham* has an unusual apsidal church with a Norman tower and a 12C relief of an archbishop. At Godmersham Park, backed by fine woods, Jane Austen often visited her brother Edward Knight (monument in church). 9m: *Chilham*, perched on a hill to the left of the road, is a conspicuously pretty village built in feudal fashion with a square of timber-framed houses between the flint church and the gates of the *Castle*. A keep of the original 12C building survives but the rest of the castle was built for Sir Dudley Digges in 1616. The park, landscaped by Capability Brown, is open and 'medieval banquets' are held in the keep. 11m: *Chartham* church has a fine chancel, windows with 'Kentish' tracery and good brasses, the one to Sir Robert de Septvans, d. 1306, being the oldest in Kent. The timber roof is original. 14m: *Canterbury*, see Route 5.

A20 passes between (57m) *Mersham* (pronounced 'Merzam'), where the church has monuments by Evesham and Nicholas Stone, and *Mersham le Hatch*, an Adam house of 1766 (not open). 60m: *Sellindge* church has a Norman tower. At (63m) *Newingreen* a road climbs right to *Lympne Castle* (Route 8A). The Roman Stone St. leads N to Canterbury, passing on the left *Westenhanger* racecourse and the remains of a fortified manor house. A20 bears left and passes the entrance to (65½m) *Sandling Park* (gardens open under NGS).

71m: **FOLKESTONE** (43,700 inhabitants) is an old town, once a 'limb' of the Cinque Ports and now a resort.

TI: Harbour St. **Bus Station**: Bouverie Square. **Railway Stations**: Folkestone Central, the main station; Harbour; and West, for local traffic. **Amusements**: repertory theatre at Leas Pavilion, concerts and other entertainments at Leas Cliff Hall and Rotunda Amusements.

Residents. George Grossmith, entertainer and co-author of 'The Diary of a Nobody', died here in 1912.

The *Leas*, a wide grassy promenade, extends along the top of the cliff for over 1m, with views of the sea and France, 22m away. The shrub-grown paths on the face of the beautifully planted cliff (lift) offer more sheltered walks. At the W end of the Leas the *New Metropole Arts Centre* holds temporary exhibitions of painting and sculpture. A *Road of Remembrance* descending to the harbour commemorates World War I. Near the E end of the Leas is the church of *St Mary and St Eanswyth*, largely rebuilt since its foundation in 1137 on the site of a nunnery church. The Harvey Aisle (added in 1874) and the W window, presented by over 3000 medical men, as well as a statue (1881) on the Leas, commemorate William Harvey (1578–1657), who discovered the circulation of the blood, born at Folkestone. In the chancel is a 14C canopied tomb with effigy. The site of Folkestone's ancient castle may be determined by *The Bayle* and *Bayle Pond*, near the church. In Grace Hill is the *Museum* with collections of local interest, including finds from two Roman villas excavated near the road to the Warren. Only a few narrow streets leading down to the lively harbour

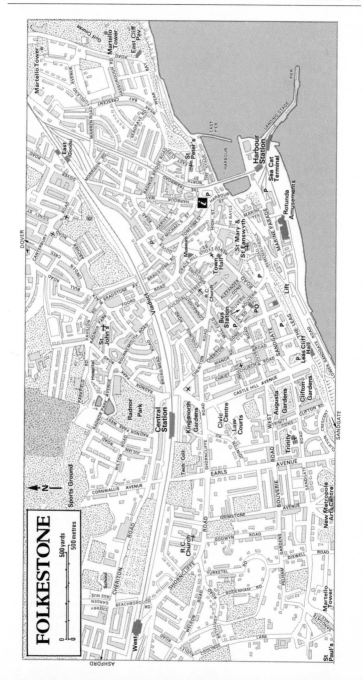

FOLKESTONE

0   500 yards
0   500 metres

survived the bombing of 1941–44 but the district has kept its nautical atmosphere.

To the E beyond the harbour is the East Cliff. Further on (1½m E) is the *Warren*, a rough expanse of tumbled chalk between the cliffs and the shore, of interest to the botanist, entomologist and fossil-gatherer. On the N rise the *Sugar Loaf, Caesar's Camp*, and other chalk hills.

From Folkestone to *Canterbury*, see Route 5; to *Hastings*, see Route 8A.

3m NW of the centre, near the M20 and the newly engineered A20, is the British terminal of the **Channel Tunnel**, linking the Kent coast with the French coast at Sangatte, near Calais. The project was agreed between Britain and France under the Treaty of Canterbury in 1986 and the contract awarded to an Anglo-French consortium, the Channel Tunnel Group and France-Manche. The tunnel was officially opened in May 1994. In fact, it consists of three tunnels: two single-track railway tunnels and a smaller service tunnel. The railway tunnels are used by passenger trains, operated by the British, French and Belgian railways, and by shuttle trains carrying cars and lorries. The exhibition centre gives further details about the project and earlier attempts to build a fixed link between Britain and France.

A20 continues across open downland, stormy in winter, to (71m) **Dover**, described in Route 4.

8

Folkestone to Hastings

The first route keeps near the coast and crosses Romney Marsh. The second heads inland through the Weald.

A. Via Rye and Winchelsea

Directions. Total distance 37m. **Folkestone**, see Route 7. A259 to (5m) **Hythe**, (14m) New Romney, (26m) **Rye**, (29m) **Winchelsea** and (37m) **Hastings** (Route 9A).

Folkestone, see Route 7. A259 passes the inconspicuous remains of Sandgate Castle, one of Henry VIII's coastal defences, on the way to (2m) *Sandgate*, Folkestone's western neighbour. Shorncliffe Camp, on the plateau above the small resort, first became an important military barracks in Napoleonic times. 5m: **Hythe** (12,700 inhabitants; seasonal TI), one of the Cinque Ports, is divided in two by the Royal Military Canal of 1804–06, beginning its 23m course to Rye. The unpretentious seafront has three Martello towers built to counter Napoleon's threat of invasion. The old village on the hillside has some interesting houses, particularly the Old Manor House at the top. The Early English church has a raised chancel above a vaulted processional path, containing over 500 skulls and other human bones, believed to have been brought from the old churchyard

(14–15C). Lionel Lukin, who invented the lifeboat in 1785, is buried in the church. A light railway runs to Dymchurch and New Romney.

1m N of Hythe is *Saltwood Castle* (open by appointment for parties only), a handsome building dating mainly from the 14C. Becket's murderers are said to have met here on their way to Canterbury, while the naming of Thorpe's Tower remembers the long imprisonment of the Lollard William Thorpe. The castle was home of Lord Clark (1903–83), art critic and historian.

10m: *Dymchurch* has a sea-wall 3m long protecting the marshes, where the Romans also built a dyke and barrier. Two Martello towers have been restored and one is now a museum (EH, keykeeper). It is the 24th of 74 which originally extended along the coast from Folkestone to Seaford. The 12C church at *Burmarsh*, 1m N in Romney Marsh, still has three of its medieval bells. 14m: **New Romney** (4600 inhabitants; seasonal TI) was one of the original Cinque Ports, though its harbour was destroyed in the 13C. The beautiful Norman and Early English church has a memorial to the children's writer E. Nesbit (1858–1924). She is buried at *St Mary in the Marsh*, 2m N, where the 13C church keeps its Norman tower.

About 3m S of A28 at 15m is *Lydd* (4700 inhabitants), whose Early English and Decorated church is sometimes known as 'the cathedral of Romney Marsh'. The chancel was destroyed by German bombs. The Perpendicular tower is particularly fine, with good vaulting. The interior incorporates remains of a Saxon church. The explosive lyddite takes its name from its development at experimental ranges here. A road goes over the shingle flats to (3m) *Dungeness*, on a bleak promontory with rough seas and good deep-sea fishing. It has a bird sanctuary, two nuclear power stations and two lighthouses; the older one (1904) is open in summer.

A259 swings inland through the marsh via (16m) *Old Romney*, with an unrestored 13C church with later additions. At 18m the road branches sharply left.

A sideroad leads right to (2m) *Ivychurch*, where the church has a handsome tower and two-storied S porch. A2070 and B2080 lead straight ahead from A259 to (1½m) the tiny village of *Snargate*. Its Early English and Perpendicular church has a curious wall painting at the W end. *Appledore*, on the bank of the Royal Military Canal 2m beyond, has a good 14C church. *Horne's Place Chapel*, 1½m N, is the 14C domestic chapel of a manor house (EH, Wednesdays only 10.00–17.00).

19m: *Brookland* •church has a detached weatherboarded steeple in the shape of a pyramid and a Norman lead font. The road zigzags through the irrigation system of the marshes, passing (on the right) the waterways feeding into the sea from Rye.

26m: **Rye** (4300 inhabitants; seasonal TI), the larger of the two 'Ancient Towns' added to the Cinque Ports, stands on a hill looking across the salt marshes towards its neighbour, Winchelsea. The cobbled streets, narrow and sometimes hilly, have many attractive buildings of the 15–18C.

Rye has lost most of its former importance through alteration of the coast. The Rye potteries are well known. The town was twice burned down by the French (1377 and 1448) and many inhabitants still bear the names of the Huguenot fugitives who took refuge here. John Fletcher, the dramatist, was born in 1579 at a house in Lion St., now a tea-shop.

The approach at the N end is through *Land Gate*, the last of three in the wall erected by Edward III. On top of the hill is *St Mary's*, a Norman and Early English church with Decorated and Perpendicular windows and flying buttresses. The altar table is wrongly alleged to be made of wood from the Armada. The pendulum of the great clock is probably the oldest in England still at work with its original mechanism

(1561–62). The W window commemorates Archbishop Benson (1829–96). 40 Church Square, a small building of c 1263, was a house of the *Friars of the Sack*, and to the SE is the turreted *Ypres Tower* (locally 'Wipers', a pronunciation made familiar by British soldiers in Flanders), built c 1250 by Peter of Savoy and sold in 1430 to John de Ypres. It houses a local history museum. *Flushing Inn*, in a square N of the church, has an interesting cellar and 16C mural painting. *Lamb House* (NT) in West St., facing the W end of St Mary's, was the home of Henry James from 1898 onwards, and afterwards of E.F. Benson, author of the 'Lucia' and 'Dodo' novels. The romantic Mermaid St., which leads off West St., has the early 16C *Mermaid Hotel*. In High St. is *Peacocke's School* (1636), where Thackeray's Denis Duval was a pupil. The *Monastery* in Conduit Hill, off High St., was originally part of a late Decorated Augustinian Friary.

Rye: West Street, with Lamb House in the background

Rye Harbour, 1½m S, is a quiet fishing port at the mouth of the Rother. Across the river towards *Camber* is the Rye Golf Course. At the beginning of the harbour road a footpath leads over the marshes to *Camber Castle*, one of Henry VIII's coastal defences, made irrelevant by the changed course of the river and dismantled in 1642.

29m: **Winchelsea**, Rye's companion 'Ancient Town', lies on a knoll rising over the marshes and the river Brede. The original town and harbour were destroyed by the sea's encroachments and the 'new' Winchelsea was founded by Edward I in 1283, rebuilt on the regular lines of a French 'bastide'. It has long since shrunk to the dimensions of a village but its buildings still 'plead haughtily for honours gone'. It is the opening scene of Thackeray's 'Denis Duval'.

St Thomas Becket, occupying one of the 'squares' laid out by Edward I, is the most important Decorated church in Sussex (begun c 1300). The nave has vanished or was never built. The church contains beautiful sedilia and fine 14C tombs of the Alards. Part of the window tracery is of the so-called 'Kentish' pattern. The modern glass is by Douglas Strachan (1928–33). The old *Court Hall*, opposite, is a museum of Winchelsea's history and the history of the Cinque Ports. Of the wall that once surrounded the town, *Strand Gate* is at the beginning of the road to Rye, and *Pipe Well* (or *Land Gate*) is to the NW. *New Gate* is now some distance S.

31m: *Icklesham* has a fine Norman *church with 14C chancel. 37m: **Hastings**, see Route 9A.

B. Via Tenterden

Directions. Total distance 48m. **Folkestone**, see Route 7. A259 to (5m) **Hythe**. A261, B2067 to (7½m) Lympne. B2067 to (27m) **Tenterden**. A28 to (48m) **Hastings** (Route 9A).

Folkestone, see Route 7. To (2m) *Sandgate* and (5m) *Hythe*, see Route 8A. A261 leaves Hythe and B2067 heads left at 6m for (7½m) *Lympne*, pronounced 'Lim'. S of the road and the village, on the edge of the escarpment overlooking Romney Marsh, stands *Lympne Castle* (open), once a residence of the Archdeacons of Canterbury. The original 13–15C buildings, two towers connected by a central block, were incorporated into a larger house in 1906. The views from the towers and the gardens include the scanty remains of *Stutfall Castle*, castrum of the Roman Portus Lemanis. The nearby church, probably built by Archbishop Lanfranc (d. 1089), has been much restored. *Port Lympne* (open), to the W of the village, is an early 20C house by Sir Herbert Baker. Its grounds are now a zoo.

B2067 continues W along the line of the escarpment, with the Royal Military Canal and Romney Marsh to the left and woodland to the right. For a brief period in 1511–12 Erasmus held the living of *Aldington*, 1m N of the road at 11½m. Beyond (17½m) *Ham Street* the marshes yield to the countryside of the Weald.

27m: **Tenterden** (6200 inhabitants; seasonal TI) is a dignified place still displaying the prosperity brought in successive centuries by shipbuilders, clothmakers and ironmasters. Its broad High St. is flanked by houses in brick, tile, timber and white-painted weatherboarding and by several old inns. The church has a Perpendicular tower and a roof of wood shingles. The Kent and East Sussex Light Railway runs steam trains to Hexden Bridge, 5m SW.

Smallhythe Place (NT), 2m S on B2082, is an early 16C timber-framed building, once the harbourmaster's house when Smallhythe was the port for Tenterden. It was Ellen Terry's home from 1899 until her death in 1928 and is preserved as a memorial to her.

FROM TENTERDEN TO CRANBROOK, 13m. A28 heads N. 1m to the right of the junction with A262 is *High Halden*, where the church has a timber belfry. A262 goes left to (6m) *Biddenden*, with a half-timbered street. *Headcorn*, 5m further N, also has some fine old houses. A229 leads W from Biddenden to (10m) *Sissinghurst Castle (NT)*, a mellow fragment of a Tudor mansion. It was the home of Vita Sackville-West and Sir Harold Nicolson. Her study and the long library are open, but the chief attraction of Sissinghurst is the lovely garden she created. A229 continues to the little town of (13m) **Cranbrook** (seasonal TI), with a steep High St. and the largest working windmill in England (1814). The grammar school, founded in 1576, was birthplace of the poet Phineas Fletcher (1582–1650). The present buildings are 18–20C. The Perpendicular church has some 16C glass and wooden bosses (c 1300) on the W wall.

The main route follows A28 W from Tenterden to (31m) *Rolvenden*, with a fine 14C church. *Great Maytham Hall* (limited opening), on the outskirts, is by Sir Edwin Lutyens (1909). The greater part has been converted into flats and only the main rooms on the ground floor are shown. Between 1898 and 1907 Frances Hodgson Burnett was tenant of the Georgian house that stood on the site; the walled garden claimed as the inspiration of 'The Secret Garden' can still be seen. 1m W along B2086 are the formal gardens of *Hole Park* (limited opening). Another 1½m W is *Benenden*, with a girls' public school built in the Elizabethan style in 1859. On A28 at (33m) *Newenden* the tiny church has a carved late Norman font. A28 crosses the Rother valley into East Sussex. 35m: *Northiam* has weatherboarded houses and a church with a Perpendicular spire and piers carrying Early English nave arcades. *Brickwall House* (limited opening) is 17C. *Great Dixter* (open), ¾m NW, is a half-timbered 15C house restored and enlarged by Lutyens in 1910. He also laid out the gardens.

Bodiam Castle (NT) is 5m W of Northiam. Built by Sir Edward Dalyngruge in 1385 and dismantled during the Civil War, the fortress keeps its strikingly unified appearance even though it is now a shell. A wide moat protects a rectangle of stone walls, with round towers at the corners and square ones in the middle surrounding a square inner courtyard. The great gateway on the N side is flanked by machiolated turrets; the outer portcullis is still visible, and there are grooves for two more beyond.

At (40m) *Brede* the church has the tomb of Sir Goddard Oxenbridge (1537). A28 descends the open valley of the Brede and climbs again to (42m) *Westfield*, with a Norman church. 48m: **Hastings**, see Route 9A.

9

London to Hastings

A. Via Sevenoaks

Directions. Total distance 63m. The route follows A21 but diverges for the towns and sights A21 bypasses. A2 to (4m) Lewisham. A21 to (10m) Bromley. A21, A224 to (24m) **Sevenoaks**. A225, B245 to (30m) **Tonbridge**. A21 to (53m) John's Cross. A2100 to (56m) Battle. A2100, A21 to (63m) **Hastings**.

The Old Kent Rd leaves London for New Cross and (4m) *Lewisham*, where A21 goes right for (10m) *Bromley*.

At 15m an unclassified road on the right leads through pleasant country to (3m) *Downe*. The Georgian *Down House* (open), ½m S, was Charles Darwin's home from 1842 until his death in 1882. It contains the study where he wrote 'The Origin of Species', many personal possessions, and a display about his grandfather, Erasmus Darwin (1731–1802); also paintings by Stubbs and Joseph Wright of Derby.

A21 joins A224, which climbs the North Downs to Badger's Mount and then descends into the valley of the Darent. At 20m, after crossing M25 and M26, the road branches right to bypass Sevenoaks. This route continues S for the town centre.

The sideroad leading SW (right) from the junction skirts *Chevening Park* (not open), a mid 17C house, perhaps by Inigo Jones, altered in the 18C. The wooded park has a lake where the inventive 3rd Earl Stanhope (d. 1816) launched 'the first craft ever propelled by steam'. His daughter, Lady Hester Stanhope (1776–1839), was born here.

22m: *Riverhead*, with some pleasant 18C houses.

A25 heads left for (2m) *Seal*, where the church has a 16C tower, a brass of 1395 and a bronze sculpture of a child (1908). 6m: *Ightham* and *Ightham Mote*, 2½m S, see Route 7.

24m: **Sevenoaks** (17,100 inhabitants; TI) is unexciting except for the High St. at the S end. This has an array of 17–18C houses and the church of *St Nicholas*, with 13C nave arcades and a Perpendicular chancel notable for its monuments. Donne was pluralist rector in 1616–31. *Sevenoaks School* was founded in 1432 and still inhabits 18C buildings designed by Lord Burlington. The triangular *Vine* is said to be the oldest cricket ground in England. William Pett (1710–86), the earliest known maker of cricket bats, lived at Sevenoaks.

At the S end of Sevenoaks, E of A225, is *•**Knole** (NT), one of the finest as well as the largest English mansions.

The core was built by Archbishop Thomas Bourchier (d. 1486) as a palace for himself and later Archbishops of Canterbury. In 1532 Cranmer resigned it to Henry VIII, who enlarged it, most strikingly by adding the Green Court through which visitors approach the building. Elizabeth I granted the lease to her cousin, Sir Thomas Sackville, later Earl of Dorset. When he acquired it permanently in 1603 he undertook a grand remodelling which still largely determines the visitor's impression of Knole.

Behind Henry VIII's Green Court is the front courtyard of Bourchier's palace, the Stone Court, remodelled in the 17C. The Great Hall, also remodelled, with a vigorously

Knole

carved screen and portraits by Van Dyck, occupies one side. The Great Staircase, another of Sackville's alterations, is among the best of its time. The upper rooms keep their original fittings and their 17C ˙furniture is outstanding. The small rooms include: the Brown Gallery (early English furniture and historical portraits); Lady Betty's Rooms (English carpets); the Spangle Bedroom (17C Brussels tapestries); the Venetian Bedroom; and the Leicester Gallery (with a surviving 15C fireplace). The state rooms, with fine 17C plasterwork ceilings and fireplaces, include: the Ballroom (portraits of the Sackvilles by Van Dyck, Kneller, Gainsborough, etc.); the Crimson Drawing Room (portraits by Reynolds); the Cartoon Gallery; and the King's Bedroom, fitted up for James I. The park of about 1000 acres (open free to pedestrians every day) commands a view of the Kentish Weald.

Vita Sackville-West (1892–1962), born here, wrote a history of the house and made it the setting for 'The Edwardians'. Virginia Woolf's 'Orlando' offers a deliberately fanciful evocation of Knole.

Emmetts Garden (NT), 4m SW of Sevenoaks, has fine trees and shrubs, particularly beautiful in spring and autumn, and views of the Weald.

A225 continues S from Sevenoaks to (26m; on the left) *Riverhill House* (limited opening), a small Queen Anne building later enlarged. The gardens have fine trees. A225 meets A21 at the roundabout shortly beyond. *Sevenoaks Weald*, ¾m W, was home of Edward Thomas and W.H. Davies in 1904–06. Caxton is said to have been born at the Long Barn. Sir Harold Nicolson and Vita Sackville-West made the 15–16C building a meeting place for the Bloomsbury Group in 1915–30. Virginia Woolf started 'Orlando' and Roy Campbell wrote 'The Georgiad' here. B245 leads south.

30m: **Tonbridge** (30,400 inhabitants; TI) is a market town on the Medway. Among its timbered buildings are the 15C *Chequers Inn* in the High St. and the 16C *Portreeve's House* in East St. The remains of the Norman *Castle* (open), built by William the Conqueror's kinsman Richard de Clare and enlarged in the 13C, stand above the river. *Tonbridge School* (off the High St.) was founded in 1553 by Sir Andrew Judd but the buildings it now occupies are 19C. Jane Austen's father was a master here and E.M. Forster an unhappy pupil. *Tudeley* church, 3m E, has a window by Marc Chagall (1967).

S of Tonbridge A21 climbs to (35m) *Pembury*. 37m: B2160 leads left for *Matfield*, 1½m, with early Georgian houses on the green. 39m: To the right are *Owl House Gardens* (open), with woodland walks extending to 12 acres.

A262 diverges left, passing (1m) *Finchcocks* (limited opening), a baroque house of 1725 with a collection of keyboard instruments. Concerts and courses are held here. *Goudhurst* (3m) is a hilltop village with fine views. Its church has monuments to the Culpeper (or Colepeper) family, including one in coloured wood to Sir Alexander Culpeper (d. 1537). 1½m NW, in an area famous for oaks, is *Horsmonden*, with an early 14C church containing a brass to Henry de Grofhurst (c 1340) and Sprivers Garden (NT). *Bedgebury National Pinetum* (open), off B2079 2½m S, belongs to the Royal Botanic Gardens. A262 continues E from Goudhurst for *Cranbrook* and *Sissinghurst Castle* (Route 8B).

40m: *Lamberhurst*, once the centre of the Wealden iron-smelting industry. 1½m W is *Bayham Abbey*, a ruined 13C Premonstratensian house (EH, summer season). A21 continues SE, passing *Scotney Castle* (NT) on the left. The grounds were laid out in the Picturesque manner in the 1830s, making cunning use of the ruined 14C castle, with 17C additions. The new house added by Salvin is not open. At (45m) *Flimwell* A21 enters East Sussex. *Pashley Manor* (only gardens open) is an old ironmaster's house near *Ticehurst*, to the W. About 3m E of Flimwell on A268 is *Hawkhurst*, where William Penn once owned the ironworks. The late Decorated church in the old village to the S has been kindly treated by successive restorations. For *Rolvenden*, 8m further NE, and *Bodiam Castle*, 4m SE of Hawkhurst, see Route 8B. 48m: *Hurst Green*.

A265 leads SW past the 17C *Haremere Hall*, pleasantly sited on the steep hillside, to (2m) *Etchingham*, with a Decorated church with window tracery and fragments of the original glass. It also contains good stalls, a screen and brasses. 6m: *Burwash* has a pleasant High St. and a church with a Norman tower. *Bateman's* (NT), a 17C ironmaster's house, was the home of Rudyard Kipling from 1902 until his death in 1936. The rooms include his study. The grounds contain a water-driven turbine he installed. The surrounding country, with low undulating hills, is the scene of 'Puck of Pook's Hill'. At *Brightling*, 2m S, is the pyramid tomb of Mad Jack Fuller (d. 1834).

At (53m) John's Cross the route takes the right fork, A2100, which leads S. 56m: **Battle** (TI), a pleasant little town, takes its name from the Battle of Hastings (1066), fought to the SE. The 12–15C *Church* has interesting pier capitals and fragments of 15C glass. There is also the tomb of Sir Anthony

Goudhurst: a traditional English village

Browne (see below) and his wife, a few brasses, and a memorial to Edmund Cartwright (1743–1823), inventor of an early power loom, who died at Hastings. The Market Square is dominated by the gatehouse of *Battle Abbey** (EH, all year).

William the Conqueror founded it to fulfil a vow made before the battle, on the spot where Harold erected his royal standard and afterwards fell. It was colonised by Benedictines from near Tours, and the church was consecrated to St Martin in 1094. At the Dissolution (1539) it was given to Sir Anthony Browne, who destroyed the church.

The *Gatehouse* (1339) is battlemented and turreted with Decorated arcading; the E wing is 16C. The inhabited parts of the abbey includes the *Abbot's House*, remodelled by Browne, and two towers (1540), all that remains of *Princess Elizabeth's Lodgings*. The *Abbey Church*, 224ft long, has practically disappeared except for part of the undercroft of the 14C E extension, which had five chapels. The high altar was erected on the spot where Harold's body was found. The most impressive remains are those of the *Dormitory*, S of the church, with its S wall and lancet windows. The undercroft is intact, with three Early English vaulted chambers. The lower floor formed the E side of the *Cloister*; the arcading of the W side with Perpendicular tracery is incorporated into the school house (Abbot's House). Remains of the *Parlour* adjoin the Dormitory to the N. Beyond them, to the right, a broad walk commands a view of the battlefield, including the heights of Senlac and of Telham (across the valley), where the Normans encamped the night before the battle.

At *Sedlescombe*, 2m NE, is a Pestalozzi Village for refugee children founded in 1960. *Ashburnham* church (1665), 3m W of Battle, has tombs and ironwork from an industry that flourished until 1825. The Place, home of the Ashburnham family for about 800 years until 1935, is a Church of England College.

63m: **HASTINGS** (74,800 inhabitants) has two aspects to its history and present character. The first is the old town to the E, which recovered from burning and looting by William the Conqueror's troops to become the leading Cinque Port in the 12C. Even after losing several harbours to the encroaching sea, it remained a lively fishing port. The second Hastings is the resort to the W, which developed with adjoining **St Leonards** in the early 19C, growing into a byword for genteel propriety.

TI: 4 Robertson Terrace; (seasonal) The Fishmarket. **Railway Stations**: Hastings Central, at the W end of Havelock Rd; St Leonards Warrior Square, at the end of King's Rd; West St Leonards, at the W end of the double town; Ore, 1m NE, the terminus of the electric line. **Bus Station**: Queen's Rd. **Amusements**: White Rock and Pier Pavilions (concerts, dancing, etc.); Stables Theatre, The Bourne. **Annual Event**: Music Festival in March.

The *Old Town* of Hastings, the fishing port between the West Hill and the East Hill, keeps narrow streets and ancient houses. Survivals include *The Fishmarket*, the tall storing-sheds for nets, and the *Fishermen's Church*, now a fishing museum, on Rock-a-Nore Rd. The Perpendicular church of *St Clement*, near the S end of the High St., has two brasses (1563 and 1601). Rossetti married Lizzie Siddal here in 1860. *Old Town Hall* nearby is a museum of local history. At the other end of the High St., with many good houses, is *St Mary Star of the Sea* (1882), an RC church built mainly by the poet Coventry Patmore, who lived at Old Hastings House. Beyond are the old *Stables* of c 1700, now a theatre. To the E is *All Saints*, a Perpendicular church where Titus Oates (baptised here in 1660) was briefly curate under his father. All Saints' St. contains more good houses: Sir Cloudesley Shovel often visited 125 and Garrick often stayed in a house at the sea end.

The scanty ruins of the Norman *Castle* (open) are on West Hill. *St Clement's Caves* (open), on the E slope, are said to have been used by smugglers and were certainly used as shelters in World War II.

From the centre, between the central station and the seafront, Queen's Rd leads past the 19C *Town Hall* to the pleasantly wooded *Alexandra Park* (100 acres). Cambridge Rd leads W past *White Rock Gardens* to the *Museum and Art Gallery*, with collections of Wealden pottery and Sussex ironwork and an Indian pavilion of 1886.

The seafront from the W end of Hastings to St Leonards gives an interesting picture of 19C development. E of Harold Place is Pelham Crescent (1824) by Joseph Kay, with the church of *St Mary* as its centrepiece. W of Queen's Hotel is the White Rock Pavilion and crowded pier. St Leonards was laid out by James and Decimus Burton (1828–34), with the Royal Victoria Hotel, altered now in more than name, forming the centre of a composition extending inland.

The most attractive short walk from Hastings leads from the East Hill to (¾m) *Ecclesbourne Glen* and (1¾m) *Fairlight Glen*, where the cliffs rise to 400ft and the trees descend almost to the sea. Beyond the head of the glen, ½m from the sea, the road returns to (2¼m) Hastings via the suburb of *Ore*, high up on St Helen's Down.

FROM HASTINGS TO EASTBOURNE, 17m via A259. The coast is lined with Martello towers. 5m: *Bexhill* (35,500 inhabitants; TI), a resort with an esplanade, a park and the De La Warr Pavilion, a splendid piece of Art Deco by Erich Mendelsohn and Serge Chermayeff (1935–36). The church of *St Peter* at Old Bexhill dates back to 1070 and contains a unique Saxon tombstone. The *Manor House* was once a residence of the

Bishops of Chichester. J.L. Baird (1888–1946), the pioneer of TV, lived at 1 Station Rd from 1941. 12½m: *Pevensey* (seasonal TI), on Pevensey Bay, the landing place of William the Conqueror in 1066. Beyond the Early English church is *Pevensey Castle (EH, all year), consisting of a Norman keep begun c 1080 and a gatehouse and inner bailey added in the 13C. It stands in the SE angle of an enclosure of about 10 acres, surrounded by a Roman wall, strengthened by round towers and still 20ft high in places. This was the Roman Anderida, one of the fortresses of the 'Saxon Shore', taken by the Saxons in 491. Opposite is the 14C Old Minthouse. 17m: Eastbourne, see Route 10A.

From Hastings to *Folkestone*, see Route 8.

B. Via Westerham

Directions. Total distance 69m. To (10m) Bromley, see Route 9A. A233 to (19m) **Westerham**. B2026 to (25m) Edenbridge. B2027, B2167 to (31m) Penshurst. B2176, A26 to (36m) **Tonbridge** (Route 9A). To (69m) **Hastings**, see Route 9A.

A2 and A21 lead to (10m) *Bromley* (see Route 9A), where A233 leads right. 14½m: *Biggin Hill* airfield was a fighter station in the Battle of Britain. The road climbs (16m) *Westerham Hill* (809ft; view), the highest point in Kent, and descends to cross the Pilgrims' Way and M25.

19m: **Westerham** is pleasantly situated near the source of the Darent. General Wolfe (1727–59) was born in the vicarage and spent his early boyhood at the 17C *Quebec House* (NT). Relics of him are preserved here and at *Squerryes Court* (open), a 17C mansion by A25 W of the town. There is a statue of him by Derwent Wood (1911). That of Churchill by Oscar Nemon (1969) stands on a marble plinth given by Marshal Tito. *Pitt's Cottage*, now a restaurant, was for a time the country retreat of the younger Pitt. Mr Collins's parsonage, in Jane Austen's 'Pride and Prejudice', was near Westerham.

B2076 leaves Westerham, passing on the left wooded sandy hills stretching to *Brasted* (NT; 600 acres, with pleasant walks and drives). 21m: *Chartwell* (NT) was the country home of Sir Winston Churchill in 1924–65. 22m: *Crockham Hill*, with a good view over the Weald. B2076 crosses the railway and the junction with B2027 into (25m) *Edenbridge*, with some old buildings near the bridge. B2027 leads E, passing at 27m an unclassified road leading right for (2m) *Hever*, where the church with a fine shingled spire has the beautiful tomb of Sir Thomas Boleyn (d. 1538), father of Anne, and a brass of Margaret Cheyne (d. 1419).

Hever Castle (open) is a fortified 14C house with a square moat, elaborately restored after it was bought by the American, William Waldorf Astor, in 1903. It is the reputed meeting place of Anne Boleyn (perhaps born here) and Henry VIII, who afterwards granted it to Anne of Cleves. The interior has rich Edwardian woodwork. Outside are an Italian garden and a neo-Tudor village built for Mr Astor by Frank L. Pearson as offices and guest rooms.

28m: an unclassified road leads right for *Chiddingstone* (1½m), a charming group of half-timbered houses (NT). The *Castle* (open), a 17C house remodelled as a Gothic castle c 1805, has 17C woodwork and a collection of Stuart and Jacobite relics.

29½m: *Penshurst Station*. B2176 leads S to (31m) *Penshurst*, a delightful village with buildings in the local vernacular tradition by George Devey (c 1850). A path leads past the church (with Sidney monuments) to *Penshurst

Place (open), which, despite various enlargements, is still a wonderfully complete specimen of a medieval manor house.

It was originally built by Sir John de Pulteney, several times Lord Mayor of London, in the 1340s. His *Great Hall is still the most striking feature of the house, 64ft long, with chestnut roof, 'Kentish' tracery and open hearth (though the louvre in the roof through which smoke escaped does not survive). The arrangement of the screens passage is original but the screen itself is Elizabethan. From that period, too, is the Long Gallery in the SW wing. Penshurst has been owned by the Sidneys since 1552 and its most interesting contents are probably the family portraits, including Sir Philip Sidney (born here in 1554) and Algernon Sidney (1663). The armoury has personal relics of Sir Philip. Ben Jonson was the first of many visiting poets who praised the charms of Penshurst and its owners' hospitality. An avenue in the beautiful park is named 'Sacharissa's Walk' from Lady Dorothy Sidney (d. 1684), the Sacharissa of Edmund Waller's poetry.

34m: *Bidborough* is a pleasant village with a well-sited church. 36m: **Tonbridge**, and on to (69m) **Hastings**, see Route 9A.

10

London to Eastbourne

A. Via Royal Tunbridge Wells

Directions. Total distance 66m. To (30m) **Tonbridge**, see Route 9A. A26 to (35m) **Royal Tunbridge Wells**. A267 to (43m) Mayfield. A267, A22 to (61m) Polegate. A22 to (66m) **Eastbourne**.

From London to (30m) **Tonbridge**, see Route 9A. A26 heads S. At (32½m) B2176 leads right for Penshurst (Route 9B). 33½m: *Southborough* (10,000 inhabitants), with a pleasant common. *Speldhurst*, 2m W, has windows by Morris and Burne-Jones in the church.

35m: **ROYAL TUNBRIDGE WELLS** (45,000 inhabitants), once an inland health resort, lies in an attractive district of hills and moorland where Kent and Sussex meet. It was named 'Royal' by Edward VII in 1909.

TI: The Old Fish Market, The Pantiles. **Buses**: from Mount Pleasant. **Railway Station**: Central Station, Mount Pleasant. **Theatres**: Assembly Hall, Crescent Rd; Trinity Arts Centre, Church Rd. **Annual Events**: Cricket Week in June; Carnival in July; Georgian Festivities in August; Sedan Chair Race in August.

History. The mild chalybeate waters were brought to notice by the hypochondriac Dudley, Lord North, in 1606 and enjoyed a great vogue after the Restoration, reaching the height of fashion in 1735–61, when Beau Nash came from Bath to preside as Master of Ceremonies. Tunbridge Wells long had the reputation of being the watering place of the serious-minded. Tunbridge ware is a kind of wood mosaic produced locally from the 17C until 1934.

The centre has an imposing group of buildings including the *Town Hall, Assembly Hall, Library* and *Museum*, with a collection of Tunbridge ware as well as domestic and agricultural bygones and dolls. But the main point of interest is the ***Pantiles**, a short promenade first laid out in 1638 and named from its original square tile paving (later replaced with Purbeck stone). On one side is a colonnade and some fine houses, added in the 18C and 19C. *A Day at the Wells*, in the Corn Exchange on the Lower Walk, recreates the town's Georgian heyday. At the Chalybeate Spring water can still be bought from the 'dipper', a traditional service dating back to the discovery of the spring. Opposite the N entrance to the Pantiles is the church of *King Charles the Martyr* with a plaster ceiling (1676–96). The Calverley estate to the NE was laid out by Decimus Burton in 1828–52. The Common (170 acres), with gorse and bracken, stretches to the W and N.

Short walks may be taken to *Rusthall Common*, 1m NW, with the fantastic Toad Rock, and to the *High Rocks*, 1½m SW, a curious sandstone formation. From the High Rocks a path leads near the Medway to the pretty village of (3½m) *Groombridge*, with a chapel of 1625. *Groombridge Place* (limited opening), a 17C house on a medieval site, has inspired artists as diverse as Sir Arthur Conan Doyle, in 'The Valley of Fear', and Peter Greenaway, in his film 'The Draughtsman's Contract'.

Groombridge can also be reached via A264 and B2188. *Withyam*, 3m further SW, has Sackville family monuments including C.G. Cibber's baroque *tomb of the 13-year-old Thomas Sackville (d. 1677).

Crowborough, on A26 7m SW of Tunbridge Wells, has an 18C church and vicarage. Sir Arthur Conan Doyle (1859–1930) died here at the house called Windlesham and Richard Jefferies lived at Downs Cottage. *Cobblers Garden* (open under NGS), off the Rotherfield road, is an exquisite 2-acre design by Martin Furniss. For Bayham Abbey, 6m SE of Tunbridge Wells, and Scotney Castle, on A21 2m beyond, see Route 9A.

A267 climbs into the Weald, crossing from Kent into East Sussex. 43m: **Mayfield** is a pleasant village on high ground. The Middle House Hotel dates from 1575. The convent school (open by appointment) includes part of the 14C *Old Palace*, a favourite residence of the Archbishops of Canterbury from the time of St Dunstan (d. 988). The medieval *Hall*, carefully restored as a chapel by E.W. Pugin in 1863–66, has three huge stone arches on carved corbels, carrying a timber roof. The chapel contains a 14C Crucifixion, a Madonna (c 1460) and the decorated back to the original Archbishop's throne. The 13–15C *St Dunstan's Church* has iron tomb slabs from local foundries in its pavement. 48½m: *Cross-in-Hand* is 1½m W of *Heathfield*, an untidy village whose church has the cenotaph of Lord Heathfield (d. 1790), defender of Gibraltar. A pillar in the neighbouring hamlet of *Cade Street* marks the spot where the rebel Jack Cade was mortally wounded in 1450. At 51½m *Horam* the manor is the home of Merrydown cider (guided tours by appointment). At 57m the route joins A22.

A271 leads E to (4m) *Herstmonceux*. About 1½m S of the village is *Herstmonceux Castle*, a moated 15C brick castle partly rebuilt this century. Opposite the W entrance to the grounds is a 12–13C church with a magnificent late 15C monument and the fine brass of William Fiennes (d. 1402).

2m SW of the junction of A267 and A22 is *Michelham Priory*, the moated remains of an Augustinian house founded in 1229 with Tudor additions.

61m: *Polegate* stands at the junction with A27, leading E to (5m) Pevensey (Route 9A) and W to Lewes (Route 10B). A sideroad leads S to (1½m) *Wannock*, on the left, with its glen and its old mill, and (3m) *Jevington*, which has a restored church with a massive tower. A22 continues S via (65m) *Willingdon*, left of the main road, where the 13C church has monuments and brasses.

66m: **EASTBOURNE** (83,000 inhabitants) is sheltered by the South Downs and the steep headland of Beachy Head. Beneath the town's present amorphous appearance is a history of development common among South coast resorts. The old village lies about 1m inland, its centre announced by the medieval church. The seafront first became fashionable with visitors at the end of the 18C and was systematically developed by the Duke of Devonshire in the 1850s, without much architectural distinction but with generous parks and gardens.

TI: Cornfield Rd. **Buses**: from Terminus Rd. **Railway Station**: Terminus Rd. **Annual Events**: Pre-Wimbledon Ladies Tennis Championships (Volkswagen Cup) at Devonshire Park in June; Cricket Week at the Saffrons in August; Air Festival in August.

Residents and visitors. Lewis Carroll spent his summer holidays at 7 Lushington Rd. Debussy finished 'La Mer' and the composer Frank Bridge (1879–1941) died here. The murderer Dr John Bodkin Adams (d. 1983) was a local practitioner.

The old village has the 18C *Manor House*, now containing the *Towner Art Gallery* with a good collection of Sussex pictures and 20C art, and *St Mary's*, Transitional with Decorated windows and Perpendicular tower. Beneath the 16C *Lamb Inn*, opposite, is an Early English vaulted chamber. Between the old and new towns stands *Compton Place* (1726–27; Colen Campbell) now a school but until 1954 a seat of the Dukes of Devonshire.

The *Parade* or *Esplanade* skirts the seafront in terraces at different levels. It extends eastwards past the *Pier* of 1872 to (¾m) the *Redoubt*, built to resist the threat of Napoleonic invasion and now accommodating three military museums. Westwards it leads to (1½m) *Holywell*, near the foot of Beachy Head, passing the *Wish Tower* (1804), a restored Martello tower—the 73rd of 74 along the coast—with a museum about the history of the Martello line of defence. Just inland from this point is *Devonshire Park* (13 acres), known for its tennis tournaments. Nearby is *Eastbourne College*, a boys' school.

3m SW of the pier by the zigzagging Duke's Drive, beginning just beyond Holywell, is *Beachy Head* ('Beauchef'; 575ft). The ruined *Belle Tout Lighthouse*, built in 1831 about 1m W, was superseded in 1902 by a new lighthouse at the foot of the cliff. The walk continues to (¾m) *Birling Gap*, where the cable from France comes ashore, beyond which are the cliffs known as the *Seven Sisters* (NT; 632 acres). The Downs to the NW are good for walking. For other places of interest W of Eastbourne, see Route 10B.

B.   Via East Grinstead and Lewes

Directions. Total distance 70m. A23 to (14m) Purley. A22 to (31m) **East Grinstead** and (36m) Wych Cross. A275 to (52m) **Lewes**. A27 to (65m) Polegate (Route 10A). A22 to (70m) **Eastbourne** (Route 10A).

The route takes A23 (Route 11A) out of London and changes to A22 at (14m) *Purley*, to bypass (19m) *Caterham* and leave the suburbs behind. 21m: *Godstone*, just beyond M25, has a 16C inn.

A25 leads W to (1½m) *Bletchingley*, a pretty village where the 12–15C church has a monument to Sir Richard Clayton, Lord Mayor of London (d. 1707). To the N, at *Brewer Street*, is a half-timbered 15C farmhouse and Pendell Court, a brick gabled mansion of 1624. For Redhill, 2m W of Bletchingley, see Route 11A.

A25 leads E to (4m) *Limpsfield*, an attractive village below a pleasant common. The church has a Norman tower and lancet windows. Frederick Delius (1863–1935) is buried in the churchyard. *Detillens* is a 15C hall house behind an 18C brick front. For Westerham, 3m further E on A25, see Route 9B.

27m: *Newchapel*, with the first Mormon temple in Europe (1958).

Lingfield, 2m E, has a large church rebuilt in the Perpendicular style. It contains a good collection of brasses, as well as the monument to Sir Reginald Cobham (d. 1446) and his wife. *Greathed Manor* (limited opening), 2½m SE of Lingfield, is Victorian. The church at *Crowhurst*, 2m N of Lingfield, has a wooden steeple, brasses and a local cast-iron tomb slab.

Beyond (29m) *Felbridge* A22 crosses from Surrey into Sussex. 31m: **East Grinstead** (22,300 inhabitants) is a pleasant town with a wide High St. flanked by good buildings, including several timber-framed houses. *Sackville College* (open) is a Jacobean almshouse of 1619.

Standen (NT), 2m S, is a house of 1891–94 by Philip Webb. Its interior has fine examples of the Arts and Crafts movement, including textiles and wallpaper by Morris and Co. *Hammerwood Park* (open), 3½m E of East Grinstead on A264, is a Greek Revival house of 1792, one of only two in England by Benjamin Latrobe, who emigrated to America and left his mark on Philadelphia, Baltimore and Washington DC. It is being rescued from years of neglect.

34m: *Forest Row* lies in *Ashdown Forest*, a beautiful region of wood and moorland. Ashdown House is the second of Latrobe's English houses. On the bank of the infant Medway are the ruins of *Brambletye*, a mansion built in 1631 but still Jacobean in spirit. *Kidbrooke Park* (limited opening), 1m SW, is 18C. Further W is the large *Weir Wood Reservoir* and 1½m SW the *Spring Hill Wildfowl Park* (open).

36m: *Wych Cross*, at the junction of A22 and A275, is in the heart of the forest.

An unclassified road leads 3m W to *West Hoathly*, with a 13C church and 15C Priest's House (open), now a folk museum. Nearby is *Gravetye Manor* (now a hotel), with a late Elizabethan S front, known for the gardens by William Robinson (1838–1935), pioneer of modern gardening.

From Wych Cross A22 bears left, offering an alternative route to Eastbourne via (45m) *Uckfield*, with the Maiden's Head, a fine Georgian inn. 1½m W is *Pilt Down*, site of the archaeological hoax.

The main route follows A275 to (40m) *Danehill*, where a road leads right to (1½m) *Horsted Keynes*, with a Norman church and miniature 13C effigy. The station on the Bluebell Railway (see below) is further W. At 41½m the road passes close to *Sheffield Park*, the mansion of Edward Gibbon's friend, the 1st Earl of Sheffield. Capability Brown landscaped the *gardens (NT).

Just beyond is *Sheffield Park Station*, from which the Bluebell railway runs through charming scenery to Horsted Keynes.

Gibbon (1737–84) is buried in the church of *Fletching*, 2m E, which also has the Dalyngridge brass (c 1380) and a unique brass of a glover (1450).

At 44m A275 crosses the A272. To the W lies *Chailey North Common*, once owned by Anne of Cleves (now a nature reserve), with a windmill and the Heritage Crafts School.

52m: **LEWES** (15,800 inhabitants) straddles the gap in the South Downs where the Ouse makes its way towards the sea at Newhaven. A 17C visitor

found it 'a place of good antiquity, large well built and well inhabited ...
beautified with divers handsome streets'. It still is.

TI: High St. **Bus Station**: Eastgate St. **Railway Station**: Station Rd (S of Southover Rd).
Theatre: Lewes Little Theatre, Lancaster St. **Annual Event**: Guy Fawkes's Day (5
November) is an occasion of great bonfires and firework displays, a tradition probably
dating from before the Gunpowder Plot of 1605.

History. The name comes from 'hlaew' ('hill') and indicates its strategic value to the
Saxons, who made it one of the capitals of the South Saxon kings. The importance of
Lewes increased when William de Warenne, a powerful friend of William the
Conqueror, and his wife founded the castle and the Cluniac priory (c 1075–88). Henry
III built the town walls, but in 1264 was defeated by Simon de Montfort at a battle
fought on the slope of the Downs to the W. The priory was dismantled at the
Reformation. During the reign of Mary Tudor 17 Protestant martyrs were burnt at the
stake near the present Town Hall. They are commemorated by an obelisk (1901) on
Cliffe Hill to the E.

Residents. The diarist John Evelyn (1620–1706) attended the Grammar School in
1630–37 (see Southover Grange below). Tom Paine (1737–1809) lived here in 1768–74
(see below).

The Norman **Castle** (open) stands on a height near the middle of the town,
almost blocking the pass through the Downs. It was built, unusually, with
a motte at each end of an oval bailey. Warenne's keep is now a ruin, though
it offers a good view from the town into the surrounding countryside. The
fine barbican (1334) is well preserved. At the corner of Castle Gate is the
Barbican House Museum of the Sussex Archaeological Society.

The *High St., reaching down towards the Ouse in the E and up the hill
to the W, has a medley of different periods and local styles: timber-framing,
tile-hanging, weatherboarding, and red and grey brickwork. On or just off
the stretch E of the castle are: *Pelham House*, 16C with an 18C façade in St
Andrew's Lane; the Georgian *White Hart Hotel* opposite the old *County
Hall* (now the Law Courts) of 1812; and the *Town Hall* (1893), unappetising
outside but with an Elizabethan staircase from Slaugham Manor inside
(Route 11B). The *Market Tower* (1792) is unusual. The road continues
beyond the Ouse as the charming, narrow Cliffe High St.

The W stretch of the High St., beyond the castle, passes the round tower
of *St Michael's* on the right. The 15C *Bull House* opposite was Tom Paine's
home. Another 15C building, now a bookshop, stands at the corner of Keere
St. (see below). *Shelley's Hotel* dates from the 16C and has a flagged hall.
Beyond more good houses further up is *St Anne's Church*, mainly 12C, with
a fine Norman font.

The suburb of *Southover* is reached by following Keere St. to the S,
passing fragments of the *Town Wall*. Beyond, on the right-hand side of
Southover High St., stands *Southover Grange* (1572), the childhood home
of John Evelyn; its pleasant gardens are open. The street bears right to *St
John*, which preserves the lead coffins of William de Warenne (d. 1088) and
his wife, and her carved tomb slab. The so-called *Anne of Cleves House*
(open), further on, is a patchwork of medieval, early 16C and Elizabethan.
Its collection of local history includes Sussex ironwork.

Behind the church, and bisected by the railway, lie the large but rather formless ruins
of the *Priory of St Pancras*, once the most important Cluniac house in Britain, founded
in 1075 and systematically demolished by Thomas Cromwell in 1539. The coffins of
the founders (see above) were discovered beneath the site of the high altar in 1845. A
monument in the form of a medieval helmet by Enzo Plazzotta was placed here in 1965

to mark the 700th anniversary of the Battle of Lewes. The remains are best seen from the recreation ground in Mountfield Rd.

On the Ouse bank, 1m N, is *South Malling* church (1627), where John Harvard, 'founder' of Harvard University, was married in 1636. Walks may be taken on the Downs: to *Mount Harry* (640ft), 2½m NW, above the racecourse; *Cliffe Hill*; and *Mount Caburn* (490ft; British fort), 2½m SE.

B2192 leads NE to (3m) *Ringmer*. The signpost records its connection with the wives of John Harvard and William Penn. **Glyndebourne** (1m S) has summer seasons of opera, started by John Christie in 1934. The new opera house designed by Michael Hopkins opened in 1994. 1½m further S is *Glynde*, with the 16C *Glynde Place* (open), which has Rubens's original sketch for the ceiling of the Banqueting House in Whitehall. B2192 continues from Ringmer to (7½m) *Halland*, where *Bentley* (open) is a modest house with formal gardens created by Mary Askew in 1942–70, a wildfowl reserve and a motor museum.

FROM LEWES TO EASTBOURNE VIA NEWHAVEN (20m). An unclassified road leads S to (3½m) *Rodmell*, where the 17C *Monk's House* (NT) was home of Leonard and Virginia Woolf from 1919. She killed herself in the nearby Ouse in 1941. The road passes the round church towers of *Southease* and *Piddinghoe*. 7m: **Newhaven**, a small port (9900 inhabitants) at the mouth of the Ouse. It dates from 1570, when the Ouse mouth shifted from the E to the W side of the valley. Louis-Philippe landed here in 1848. The apsidal 12C church, high above the town, is a relic of the medieval village of Meeching. A car ferry crosses from Newhaven to Dieppe. A259 crosses the Ouse and passes *Bishopstone*, on the left, with its little Saxon and Norman church and the remains of a Saxon village and cemetery. 11m: *Seaford* (17,800 inhabitants; TI), a resort whose partly Norman church has a remarkable capital by the S door and a relief of St Michael and the Dragon (c 1130–40). A cliff walk leads E over Seaford Head to *Cuckmere Haven* (2½m) while the road to Alfriston (3½m; see below) runs via 'High and Over' (or Hindover), with a fine *view. At (13¾m) *Exceat* the road crosses the Cuckmere valley near *Westdean*. The church here has two bronze busts, one of the painter Sir Oswald Birley (1880–1952) by Clare Sheridan, the other of Lord Waverley (d. 1958) by Epstein. 16¼m: *Friston* church has a Saxon window. 17m: *Eastdean*, ½m to the right, has a church with a Norman tower. 20m: *Eastbourne*, see Route 10A.

The main route takes A27 from Lewes, passing beneath Mount Caburn (see above). 55m: The turning on the left for Glynde and Glyndebourne, see above. To the right, beyond, is *Firle Place* (open), seat of the Gage family since the 16C. General Gage commanded the British forces at the start of the American War of Independence. The house contains good paintings, including the Cowper collection from Penshanger, and Sèvres porcelain. Behind rises *Firle Beacon* (718ft; *view), peppered with Neolithic and Bronze Age barrows. *West Firle* church has Gage monuments, including three made in 1595 by Gerard Johnson (or Janssen). 58m: A lane on the right leads to *Charleston Farmhouse* (open), where Vanessa Bell lived from 1916, decorating it in a distinctive fashion with Duncan Grant and making it a gathering place for the Bloomsbury Circle. 61½m: The Early English church at *Berwick* has wall paintings (1942–43), including a Crucifixion by Duncan Grant.

On the Cuckmere 2m S is **Alfriston**, with a Perpendicular church (the 'Cathedral of the Downs') and the shaft of a market cross. The 14C timber-built clergy house (open) was the first building acquired by the NT in 1896. The 15C forge is now a museum with an adjoining Heritage Centre. The 16C Star Inn has quaint carvings. *Drusillas Park* is a zoo, etc. *Lullington* church, beyond the river, is one of the smallest in England, only 16ft square.

63½m: *Wilmington* has the scanty ruins of a 14C Benedictine priory (open). A small museum illustrates rural life. In the face of the chalk downs on the right is the *Long Man of Wilmington*, a figure 240ft tall, with a staff in each hand. Its origin and purpose are uncertain, but its age is at least medieval. 65m: *Polegate* and A22 to (70m) **Eastbourne**, see Route 10A.

11

London to Brighton

A. Via Redhill

Directions. Total distance 51m. Slower but more attractive than Route 11B. For M23, see Route 11B. A23 to (14m) Purley, (21m) **Redhill** and (25m) Horley. B2036 to (37m) Cuckfield. A272, A273 to (44½m) Clayton. A23 to (51m) **Brighton**.

Vauxhall Bridge Rd and A23 lead S from central London, past Croydon, to (14m) *Purley*. 15¼m: *Couldson*. The road on the right climbs to the village of *Chipstead* (2m), with a 12–13C church. The isolated church of *Chaldon*, 3m SE, has a large tempera painting of the 'Ladder of Human Salvation' (c 1200). Beyond the M23 and M25 the road crosses the North Downs, separating the London basin from the Weald.

21m: the railway junction of **Redhill** is an eastern extension of Reigate (Route 11B).

The road to Godstone leads E via (3m) Bletchingley (Route 10B). *Outwood*, 3m SE of Redhill, has a 17C windmill and 2000 acres of NT property.

At (25m) *Horley* the route follows B2036 left, soon entering Sussex and the countryside of the Weald. 27m: *Burstow* church (1m E), partly 12C, has a memorial to John Flamsteed (d. 1719), the Astronomer Royal, rector here from 1684. 29½m: A sideroad leads left to *Worth*. The large Saxon *church keeps its original plan and masonry, with a chancel arch and rare two-light windows. The font is 13C. On the left beyond (33m) *Balcombe* is the viaduct carrying the railway across the Ouse valley. 37m: *Cuckfield* (28,300 inhabitants) lies on the Southern Forest Ridge. Henry Kingsley (1830–76) is buried in the churchyard. As it leaves the town, the road passes the gatehouse of *Cuckfield Place*, a fine mansion of c 1574 (altered in 1848), described in Harrison Ainsworth's 'Rookwood'. *Legh Manor*, beyond *Ansty* 2m SW, is a small 16C mansion. A272 leads E from Cuckfield to join (38½m) A273.

1m further E is *Haywards Heath*. *Lindfield*, to the N, has old houses in the village street. *Wakehurst Place Garden* (open), on B2028 3½m NW, is owned by NT and administered by Kew Gardens. The 460-acre park was laid out by Lord Wakehurst (d. 1936) as a second Kew, with exotic trees and shrubs, water gardens, etc.

A273 heads S through (41m) *Burgess Hill* (23,500 inhabitants) and (43½m) *Hassocks*. To the E is *Ditchling* (2m), where the artist Sir Frank Brangwyn (1867–1956) died. About 1½m SW of Hassocks is the Elizabethan house of *Danny* (limited opening). At (44½m) *Clayton* the route reaches the South Downs. On the right rises *Wolstanbury Hill* (677ft), on the left *Ditchling*

Beacon (812ft; NT) with a *view and two windmills. Clayton church has an 11C chancel arch and *wall paintings (c 1140). At 46m A273 rejoins A23.

51m: **BRIGHTON** (141,800 inhabitants) is the largest town and most famous resort in southern England. Its buildings reach 3½m inland towards the South Downs, while the seafront stretches 7m from Hove in the W (an independent borough with 90,000 inhabitants) to beyond Rottingdean in the E. Its nickname of 'London by the Sea' suggests its urban liveliness and its variegated seaside charms, ranging from Regency elegance to cheerful vulgarity.

TI: 10 Bartholomew Square; King Alfred Leisure Centre, Kingsway, Hove; Town Hall, Church Rd, Hove. Visitorcall provides a 24-hour recorded information service: to order a free card listing the phone numbers of individual services call 071 971 0076. (Calls cost 36p per minute cheap rate, 48p per minute at all other times.) **Coach Station**: Pool Valley. **Railway Stations**: Central, at the N end of Queen's Rd, for all trains; Hove, for Worthing, Portsmouth and London trains; Preston Park, for the N side of town; and London Rd. **Entertainments**: Theatre Royal, New Rd; Dome (variety), by the Royal Pavilion; Gardner Centre for the Arts, University of Sussex; and all the usual amusements along the seafront.

History. Brighton is mentioned in Domesday Book as Brighthelmston or Brithelmeston, after a more or less mythical Bishop of Selsey. It seems to have remained a fishing village for about seven centuries. The foundation of its modern prosperity was laid in the mid 18C by Dr Richard Russell of Lewes, who strongly recommended its air and sea-bathing (tablet on the Royal Albion Hotel). Fanny Burney, Mrs Thrale and Dr Johnson were among the early visitors (1770). A decisive cachet of fashion was added when George IV, then Prince of Wales, came to live here in 1786 and built the Pavilion. Brighton's growth was then rapid, towards Kemp Town in the E and Hove in the W. The railway confirmed its popularity, while making it less exclusive.

Natives, residents and visitors. Edward Carpenter (1844–1929), Aubrey Beardsley (1874–98; born in Buckingham Rd), Roger Quilter (1877–1953) and Frank Bridge (1879–1941) were natives. Herbert Spencer (1820–1903), who lived at 5 Percival Terrace, Kemp Town, R.S. Surtees (1803–64), Hablot K. Browne ('Phiz'; 1815–82), Thomas Hughes (1822–96) and the social reformer G.J. Holyoake (1817–1906) all died here. Residents include George Canning (1770–1827; tablet on the Royal Crescent Hotel), Harrison Ainsworth (1805–82) and Richard Jefferies (1848–87). Rowland Hill (1795–1879), the originator of penny postage and chairman of the Brighton Railway, introduced express and excursion services. Lewis Carroll spent his Christmas holidays at 11 Sussex Square, Kemp Town, for 25 years. William Friese-Greene (1855–1921), pioneer of the cinema, had his workshop in Middle St. Gladstone often spent his holidays at the former Lion Mansion Hotel. Metternich stayed at 42 Brunswick Terrace in 1848–49. Sir Hamilton Harty (1879–1941) died at Hove, and Sir Winston Churchill was a pupil at Lansworth House, Brunswick Rd, in 1883–85. Thackeray's 'Vanity Fair', Dickens's 'Dombey and Son' and Graham Greene's 'Brighton Rock' feature Brighton in their pages.

The centre is the *Old Steine* (pronounced 'Steen'), an open space with gardens, believed to take its name from the stone where fishermen used to dry their nets. On the W side, 55 was the residence of George IV's mistress and secret wife, Mrs Fitzherbert (d. 1837; buried in St John's, Kemp Town). The Steine is dominated by the *Royal Pavilion (open), the palace which George built for himself.

The Prince first rented a 'superior farmhouse' on the site in 1786. The next year Henry Holland enlarged it into a symmetrical neo-classical composition. In 1815–22 John Nash transformed it into the exotic fantasy whose distinctive outline startles and delights the visitor. Nash's minarets and balconies are Oriental only in the loosest sense, mixing Indian, Chinese and even Gothic with happy freedom. They surrender everywhere to ornate invention rather than to the requirements of scholarly accuracy.

Detail of the pelmet in the Music Room of the Royal Pavilion, Brighton

The result captures the spirit of the Regency at play more completely than any other building of the age. The rich interiors range from the deliberately dramatic Banqueting Room to the restrained sophistication of the Prince's private apartments.

William Porden's royal stables, with their dome (1804–08), have been converted into the *Dome Theatre*. Round the corner in Church St. is the *Public Library, Museum and Art Gallery*.

The museum has a room illustrating the archaeology and history of Sussex and also contains the Willett Collection of English pottery. The art gallery, with 18C furniture (made for Stanmer House) and silver (by Lamerie and Paul Storr), has British 19C and early 20C paintings, watercolours, Old Masters and one of the finest collections of Art Deco in the country.

The old town between the Old Steine, West St., and North St. (the main shopping street), contains The Lanes, narrow alleys with many antique shops. Brighton Square is a successful addition. The area to the N up to Trafalgar St., bounded W and E by Queen's Rd and the Victoria Gardens, has a Saturday flea market.

A broad esplanade stretches the whole length of the seafront. E of the Old Steine and Palace Pier runs Marine Parade, with attractive early 19C terraces, squares and crescents, to (1m) *Kemp Town*, the Regency development begun by Thomas Read Kemp in 1823 with Wilds and Busby as his architects and Thomas Cubitt among the builders. Sussex Square and

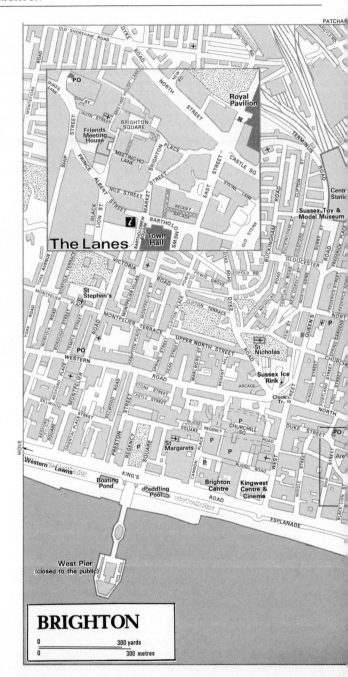

BRIGHTON

0	300 yards
0	300 metres

Lewes Crescent make a handsome centrepiece. On the level of the beach is the wide Madeira Drive, skirted by the Electric Railway, and bordered by a covered walk (½m), above which is a sheltered promenade on the cliff-side. At *Black Rock* one of Europe's largest marinas caters for pleasure boats. An undercliff walk continues to Rottingdean and Saltdean (see below).

The *Palace Pier*, immediately S of the Old Steine, replaces the Chain Pier, the first of its kind (1823), which stood a few yards further E until it was destroyed by a December storm in 1896. For many years it was the terminus of the cross-Channel service to Dieppe. The *West Pier* (1866) is closed.

W of Palace Pier, King's Rd runs to (1m) **Hove** (TI), and is prolonged to Kingsway, separated from the beach by well-kept lawns and skirting charming squares and terraces. Regency Square and Brunswick Square and Terrace have early 19C architecture. Adelaide Crescent (1830–50) and Palmeira Square are also attractive. The *Museum* is in Brooker Hall, New Church Rd.

At the start of the London Rd, N of the Old Steine, is *St Peter's*, the parish church of Brighton since 1873, by Barry (1824). In Ann St., a left turn off the London Rd, is another and better 19C church, the magnificent plain brick • *St Bartholomew* (1872–74) by Edmund Scott.

London Rd continues as Preston Rd to (1m) *Preston Park* and *Preston Manor* (open). Built in 1758 on medieval foundations, the house was given to Brighton by Sir Charles and Lady Thomas-Stanford in 1932. Most of the contents remain and the atmosphere is still that of an Edwardian family home. Collections include porcelain and silver and, in the library, the Macquoid Bequest of furniture and decorative arts.

On Dyke Rd, running NW from the centre, is the original parish church of *St Nicholas*, built in 1380 but largely rebuilt in 1853. The font (c 1170) has carvings of the Last Supper, the Baptism of Christ and the Legend of St Nicholas. The font cover is a memorial to the Duke of Wellington (1853). On the N wall, near what used to be the Thrale pew, is a tablet recording that Dr Johnson used to worship here. In the churchyard lies Nicholas Tettersell, captain of the ship that bore Charles II from Shoreham in 1651 (see below). Nearby (E) is the tomb of Martha Gunn (1727–1815), most famous of the Brighton 'bathing-women'.

Dyke Rd continues past (1m) the *Booth Natural History Museum* to (5½m) the •**Devil's Dyke**, a deep and narrow hollow in the Downs. The top of the dyke (697ft) gives a wide view. It makes a good starting-point for walks on the Downs. A pleasant descent can be made NE via the pretty hamlet of *Saddlescombe* to (1½m) Poynings (Route 11B).

The road from Brighton to Lewes (9m) via (4½m) *Falmer*, skirts *Stanmer Park*, since 1961 the **University of Sussex**, with buildings designed by Sir Basil Spence. The Gardner Centre for the Arts holds music and drama events. The public have access to the park (535 acres).

FROM BRIGHTON TO NEWHAVEN, 9m. Marine Parade leads E to Black Rock (see above), where A259 continues past *Roedean*, a girls' school founded in 1885. 3m: **Rottingdean** is at the mouth of a 'dean' (or combe) in the chalk cliffs and preserves its old village street. The church has windows by Sir Edward Burne-Jones (1833–98), who is buried in the churchyard and lived at North End House. Rudyard Kipling lived for a time at The Elms. *Ovingdean*, 1m SW, has a church with an 11C chancel, and a manor house which appears in Harrison Ainsworth's 'Ovingdean Grange'. The cliff road goes on to (4½m) *Saltdean* and (6m) the dreary *Peacehaven* (TI), a 'home fit for heroes' developed after World War I. 9m: *Newhaven*, see Route 10B.

FROM BRIGHTON TO WORTHING, 10½m by A259 (the coast road) or A57. 1m: *Hove* has Regency buildings, as well as Foredown Tower and Countryside Collection (open), with a Victorian camera obscura to view the surrounding Downs. 2m: *Portslade* and (3½m) *Southwick* are connected by wharves. At the foot of the Downs above Southwick is a Roman villa. 5m: **Shoreham-by-Sea** (20,800 inhabitants) is still important as a port. Charles II escaped from the harbour to Fécamp in 1651. *St Mary de Haura* (i.e. 'of the harbour') has a fine Transitional choir with Early English vaulting. The tower arches have unusually large capitals. In the nearby High St. is *The Marlipins*, a small medieval house now a museum. In Old Shoreham, 1m up the Adur, just below the new bridge, is the Norman church of *St Nicholas*, with a contemporary tower and a partly Saxon W end. To Horsham, see Route 12. A259 and A57 cross the Adur. 7¼m: *Lancing* has a partly Norman church. *Lancing College* has a Gothic Revival *chapel (open), begun in 1868 and completed with a huge rose window in 1977. Pupils at the school have included Evelyn Waugh. 10½m: *Worthing*, see Route 12.

B. Via Reigate

Directions. Total distance 52m. Quicker but less interesting than Route 11A. (The fastest way from London to Brighton uses the well-landscaped M23.) A217 to (21m) **Reigate**. A217, A23 to (30m) Crawley (bypassed). A23 to (34m) Handcross, (46m) Pyecombe and (52m) **Brighton** (Route 11A).

Putney Bridge crosses and A217 leads through Wandsworth. In Mitcham it swings right to bypass Sutton via (15m) *Banstead*. Beyond (16m) *Burgh Heath* it crosss the M25 (access to M23) and descends Reigate Hill (*view).

21m: **Reigate** (52,600 inhabitants with Redhill), on the southern edge of the North Downs, does not have much to detain the visitor. In the High St. is the old *Town Hall* (1728). To the N are the earthworks marking the site of the *Castle* destroyed in the Civil War. The gateway was built in 1777 out of the old stones. The parish church of *St Mary Magdalene* at the E end of the town has a nave arcade of c 1200. Lord Howard of Effingham (1536–1624), victor over the Spanish Armada in 1588, is buried beneath the chancel.

W of the town is *Reigate Priory*, on the site of an Augustinian foundation of the 13C and once Lord Howard's seat. To its S is the wooded ridge of *Reigate Park*. *Reigate Hill* (700ft) and *Colley Hill* (763ft), 1½m N and NW of the town, include about 150 acres of NT land and command views of the Weald. In easy reach are the churches of *Leigh* (3½m SW; pronounced 'Lye'), with brasses, and *Charlwood* (6½m S), with 13–15C wall paintings and a 15C screen. A25 to (6m) Dorking (Route 12) leads via (2m) *Buckland*, where the rebuilt church has a wooden belfry.

A217 heads S from Reigate, joins A23, enters Sussex and passes (26½m) *Gatwick*, with London's second airport (TI). 30m: **Crawley** (72,800 inhabitants) is bypassed to the W. Right of the road is St Leonard's Forest. 34m: *Handcross*. ½m SE are the lovely gardens of *Nymans* (NT), particularly notable for the walled garden laid out by William Robinson. *Slaugham Manor* (1m SW), now a hotel, has the ruins of a mansion probably built for the ironmaster Richard Covert (d. 1579) and dismantled in 1735. It is perhaps by Flynton, who carved Richard's tomb in the church. 45m: *Newtimber Place* (limited opening), right of the road, is a moated 17C house with a Georgian dovecote and Etruscan-style wall paintings. 46m: *Pyecombe* lies in a gap of the South Downs between Wolstanbury Hill on the left (Route 11A) and Newtimber Hill (660ft; NT). In the church the central chancel arch is Norman and the lead font dates from the late 12C. On the W side of Newtimber Hill is *Poynings* (2m) where the 14C church is on the plan of a Greek cross; and there is another lead font at *Edburton*, 2m further W. For Devil's Dyke, see Route 11A. 54m: **Brighton**, Route 11A.

12

London to Worthing

Directions. Total distance 57m. More interesting for scenery than for towns. A3 to (14m) Hook Corner. A243 to (20m) Leatherhead (bypassed). A24 to (23½m) Burford Bridge (Box Hill), (25m) **Dorking** (bypassed), (38m) **Horsham** (bypassed), (50m) Washington and (57m) **Worthing**.

The route leaves London by Putney Bridge and takes A3 as it bypasses Kingston to the S. At (14m) *Hook Corner* the route turns left on A243.

An alternative way from London (A24) runs via Morden to (15m) **Epsom** (69,200 inhabitants with Ewell). At *Epsom Downs*, 1½m NW, the Derby and the Oaks (started in 1780 and 1779) are run in May or June. The church has monuments by Flaxman and Chantrey. At (17½m) *Ashtead* the writer George MacDonald died in 1905. The church has a window of c 1500 from Herck in Belgium. A24 joins the main route at (19½m) Leatherhead.

15½m: *Chessington*, on the right, is a popular zoo and amusement park. 20m: **Leatherhead** (40,500 inhabitants) is now one of the most featureless towns in Surrey. Anthony Hope (Sir Anthony Hope Hawkins; 1863–1933) is buried in the churchyard. The Council Offices stand on the site of Kingston House, where John Wesley preached his last sermon in 1791.

FROM LEATHERHEAD TO GUILDFORD, 11½m via A246, along the N ridge of the Downs. From (2m) *Great Bookham* a sideroad leads S for 1½m to *Polesden Lacey* (NT). The house was built by Thomas Cubitt in 1824 on the site of a mansion owned by Sheridan, but owes most of its character to the handsome Edwardian alterations by Ambrose Poynter. The first-rate collection of paintings includes 17C Dutch works and British portraits (Reynolds, Raeburn). The grounds give lovely views across the North Downs, and there is a pleasant walk S to *Ranmore Common*. At (5m) *East Horsley* the church has an 11C tower and brasses. 7m: Between *West Horsley* and *East Clandon* is *Hatchlands Park* (NT), a neat brick house in the Palladian style built for Admiral Boscawen in 1756–57. The interior, by Robert Adam, contains a fine collection of keyboard instruments. The gardens were laid out by Repton, with later additions by Gertrude Jekyll. 8½m: *Clandon Park* (NT) was built by Giacomo Leoni in the 1730s. The magnificent interior, with plasterwork by Artari and chimneypieces by Rysbrack, has been restored and redecorated by John Fowler. Contents include the Gubbay collection of Chinese porcelain birds. 11½m: *Guildford*, see Route 13B.

A24 leaves Leatherhead. 22m: *Mickleham*, to the left, lies in the valley of the Mole between the chalk downs. At the church Fanny Burney was married in 1793 and George Meredith in 1864. A path leads across the Mole and through *Norbury Park*, with beeches and yews in the 'Druids' Grove', rejoining the road near Burford Bridge. *Juniper Hall*, 1m SE, now a study centre, was occupied by a group of French refugees, including General d'Arblay, who married Fanny Burney. 23½m: *Burford Bridge* spans the Mole at the foot of Box Hill. At the hotel Keats finished 'Endymion' and Stevenson stayed in 1878–86.

*Box Hill (596ft), with c 900 acres of NT property, is a spectacular expanse of down and woodland with numerous box trees from which it takes its name. A fine walk leads along the S face following the **Pilgrims' Way**, via Pebble Coombe to (6m) Reigate (Route 11B); or the ridge may be followed N across Mickleham Downs (NT) to (4m) Leatherhead. A little above Burford Bridge is *Flint Cottage*, the home from 1867 of George Meredith (1828–1909), who is buried in Dorking cemetery. At the top of the steep garden is the chalet built by Meredith as a study and bedroom in 1877. A later occupant of the cottage was Max Beerbohm, a refugee in World War II from Rapallo and from his bombed cottage at Abinger.

25m: **Dorking** (21,700 inhabitants) has little intrinsic interest but makes a good centre for walks. Vaughan Williams lived here.

A pleasant walk to the NW leads over *Ranmore Common* to (3m) *Polesden Lacey* and (5m) *Great Bookham* (see above).

*Leith Hill, 4½m SW of Dorking, is at 965ft the highest point in SE England. There is a magnificent view from the 18C tower (NT) on the summit. The surrounding woods (NT; 750 acres) are rich in bluebells and rhododendrons. Walkers can approach the hill from the Guildford road (A25) between Westcott and Wotton Hatch, or from Holmwood Station, off A24. From the summit a pleasant path leads N to Friday Street and then down the W bank of the brook to Wotton House on the A25. Motorists take the road climbing to (3½m) *Coldharbour*, a hamlet at the foot of *Anstiebury Camp* (not open), the finest prehistoric camp in Surrey, with double trenches. Beyond (4m) Coldharbour church the road crosses a beautifully wooded stretch and passes just below the conspicuous tower on the top of the hill. Further on, a right turn leads to (7½m) *Abinger Common*, with a restored 11C church, a manor house with Jacobean porch, and the old stocks on the green. *Goddards* (open by appointment) is a house by Sir Edwin Lutyens with gardens by Gertrude Jekyll. About ¾m E is *Friday Street*, a picturesque hamlet of red cottages facing a large mere. 2m SW the charming village of *Holmbury St Mary* lies beneath *Holmbury Hill* (857ft). A25 for Guildford can be joined due N of Abinger at (8½m) *Manor Farm*.

FROM DORKING TO GUILDFORD, 12m via A25. Beyond (1¼m) *Westcott* and The Rookery (left), birthplace of Malthus (1766–1834), A25 climbs to (2¾m) *Wotton*. Below the road, on the right, is the church where the diarist John Evelyn (1620–1706) is buried in the family chapel. On the left is Evelyn's home, *Wotton House* (not open); some of the surrounding woods date from his planting. 4½m: *Abinger Hammer* is a village named after an old iron furnace. E.M. Forster (1878–1969) lived at West Hackhurst (not open) and left the adjoining Piney Copse ('Forster's Wood') to the NT on his death. 5m: *Gomshall Station*. An attractive road leads S to *Peaslake* (2½m) and almost to the top of *Coneyhurst Hill* (844ft), the W summit of the Leith Hill greensand ridge. Steep and remote lanes, some of them accessible by car, cross the thickly wooded ridge to the N (*Hackhurst Downs, Netley Heath*; 270 acres NT). 6½m: A25 bypasses **Shere**, on the Tillingbourne, perhaps the prettiest village in Surrey, with a well-restored 12–15C church.

At the fork in the road beyond Shere A248 (left) offers an alternative way to Guildford. At 1m is *Albury Park* (now flats; limited opening), an originally Tudor house remodelled several times, most thoroughly by Pugin in 1846–52. The gardens John Evelyn laid out are not open to the public. The old village church, redundant since the 1840s, has traces of Saxon and Norman work. *Chilworth* (2½m) lies N of *Blackheath* (NT), a tract of open heath. *Chilworth Manor* has gardens laid out in the 17C and 18C (limited opening). 1m N of the village is *St Martha's Hill* (720ft), with the lonely *Chapel of St Martha* (*view) on the Pilgrims' Way. It was largely rebuilt in 1848.

A25 climbs to (8½m) *Newlands Corner* (500ft), on the summit of the chalk ridge, with a famous *view. Part of the Pilgrims' Way is traceable on the Downs, and to the S appears St Martha's Chapel. The road goes over *Merrow Downs* to (10m) *Merrow* and then left to (12m) *Guildford* (Route 13B).

A pleasant walk leads back from Newlands Corner to (8m) Dorking along the crest of the North Downs, via Netley Heath and Ranmore Common.

S of Dorking A24 skirts *Holmwood Common* (NT; 630 acres) and enters Sussex. About 1½m SW of (35m) *Warnham* is *Field Place* (not open), where Shelley was born in 1792.

38m: **Horsham** (bypassed) is a congested market town (25,400 inhabitants; TI). The old houses in The Causeway, at the end of West St., include the gabled 16C *Museum* with the old stocks, bullring, and whipping-post. At the end is the Early English *Church*, with Perpendicular windows, a shingle spire and interesting monuments. Horsham stone, easily split, is a traditional material for roofslabs throughout Sussex.

About 2m SW are the large but rather ineffective red-brick buildings of **Christ's Hospital**, the 'Blue Coat School' founded in London by Edward VI in 1552 and moved here in 1902. The boys still wear blue gowns, knee breeches, and yellow stockings. Pupils have included Camden, Stillingfleet, Middleton, Charles Lamb, Coleridge, Leigh Hunt and Constant Lambert. The dining hall has a painting by Verrio of the Endowment of the Royal Mathematical School in 1672. The chapel has paintings by Brangwyn.

FROM HORSHAM TO SHOREHAM, 21m. A281 leads S to (7m) *Cowfold*. The Perpendicular church, surrounded by pretty cottages, has a fine tower and the brass, 10ft long, of Prior Nelond (1433). Beyond (8¼m) *St Hugh's Charterhouse*, established by monks from the Grande-Chartreuse (1877–83), the route turns right on B2116 for (9½m) *Partridge Green*, where it takes B2135 S and crosses the Adur. Laurence Olivier (Lord Olivier; 1907–89) is buried at (12m) *Ashurst*. 16m: **Steyning**, a pleasant little town at the foot of the Downs, has an old grammar school and a *Church* founded by St Cuthman. Its most striking feature is the series of enriched late Norman arches in the nave (c 1150). The plain E arches of the nave and aisles are 100 years older. Near the Purbeck marble font is the 'Steyning Stone', probably of pre-Christian origin, rediscovered in the churchyard in 1938. Yeats wrote many of his later poems in the house on Chantry Green. About 2m W rises *Chanctonbury Ring* (783ft), a summit crowned with ancient entrenchments and a circle of beeches. Walks may be taken from Steyning along the Downs to (5m) the Devil's Dyke (Route 11A) on the E, or to (10m) Amberley (Route 13A) on the W. A283 heads S to (17m) *Bramber*, where the little Norman church has interesting capitals. It stands beside fragments of a castle (EH) including part of a tower keep built to guard the Adur estuary. St Mary's (open) is a handsome medieval house with later panelling and leather wall-hangings. *Botolphs* and *Coombes*, 1m and 2m S, have quaint little 11C churches with wall paintings of c 1100. 21m: *Shoreham*, see Route 11A.

From Horsham to *Guildford*, see Route 13B; to *Arundel*, etc., see Route 13A.

44m: *West Grinstead*, on the left, has a partly Norman church. In West Grinstead Park is 'Pope's Oak', under which the poet is said to have written 'The Rape of the Lock' at the suggestion of his host, John Caryll. On the right of A24 are the ruins of *Knepp Castle* and *Knepp Park*, with a lake 1m long. *Shipley*, on B2224 1m further W, has a restored early 19C mill (open) owned by Hilaire Belloc (1870–1953), who lived in the house nearby. 50m: *Washington*, where John Ireland died in 1962, lies below Chanctonbury Ring (see above). A fine road leads W beneath the South Downs to (2½m) *Storrington* and (6m) Amberley (Route 13A). 53m: *Findon* (bypassed) is the nearest village to Cissbury Ring (see below). A280, the 'Long Furlong' leading right for Arundel, has splendid views.

57m: **Worthing** (91,700 inhabitants; TI) is a sedate resort with many retired people. It has little of interest apart from the *Museum* in Chapel Rd, with Roman remains, English watercolours, dolls, etc.

Worthing makes a good centre for touring the South Downs and its churches. The Transitional Norman church of *Broadwater*, a suburb 1m N, has old brasses and monuments. In the nearby cemetery lie the naturalists Richard Jefferies (see below) and W.H. Hudson (1841–1922). The *church at *Sompting*, 2m NE, has been called 'the greatest architectural curiosity in the county', largely because the Saxon tower has the only English example of a 'Rhenish helm' roof. Inside are fragments of Saxon carving and a vaulted chapel built on the S side of the nave by the Templars (c 1184). Nearby is the cottage where Edward Trelawny, friend of Byron and Shelley, died in 1881. *Tarring*, 1¼m NW of Worthing's centre, has a charming High St. which includes the Parsonage Row Museum of Sussex Folklore and a famous fig garden said to have been planted by Becket. The Early English church, with a Perpendicular tower, contains a tablet to the antiquary John Selden (1584–1654), born at *Salvington*, 1m further N. *High Salvington*, another 1m N beyond A24, has a restored post mill of 1700. *Cissbury Hill* (602ft; NT), 3m N of Worthing, is crowned by *Cissbury Ring* (c 300 BC), the largest entrenchment on the South Downs.

FROM WORTHING TO CHICHESTER, 25m by the coast road (A259) past a succession of resorts. Richard Jefferies died at (2¼m) *Goring-by-Sea* in 1887. 10m: **Littlehampton** (22,200 inhabitants; seasonal TI) stands at the mouth of the Arun. 12m: *Climping* has a 13C church with a tower of 1170. To the N is *Ford*, with an open prison and a tiny Norman church. 16½m: *Felpham*, now a suburb of Bognor, has the cottage where William Blake lived in 1801–04 and the house of his patron William Hayley (1745–1820), buried in the church. 18m: **Bognor Regis** (39,500 inhabitants; TI), a resort favoured by Queen Victoria, became 'Regis' after George V convalesced in 1929 at *Aldwick*, 1½m W. A259 to (25m) *Chichester*, see Route 13A.

13

London to Portsmouth

A. Via Arundel and Chichester

Directions. Total distance 84½m. Longer and less direct than Route 13B but more interesting for architecture. To (25m) Dorking, see Route 12. A24 to (29½m) Beare Green. A29 to (42½m) Billingshurst, (47½m) Pulborough and (54½m) Whiteways Lodge. A284 to (56½m) **Arundel**. A27 to (66½m) **Chichester** (bypassed) and (84½m) **Portsmouth** (bypassed).

From London to (25m) *Dorking*, see Route 12. At (29½m) *Beare Green* A29 leads to the right. Near (33m) *Ockley* Ethelwulf of Wessex defeated the Danes in 851. Leith Hill (Route 12) rises on the right. At (38½m) *Roman Gate* a long section of the Roman Stane Street begins, leading from London to Chichester. 42½m: *Billingshurst*, with a 16C half-timbered inn. At *Coolham*, 3m SE, the 'Blue Idol' is a Quaker meeting house (now a guest house) associated with William Penn. For Shipley, 2m further, see Route 12. *Wisborough Green*, 2m W of Billingshurst on the Petworth road, is a charming village on the verge of some of the best country in Sussex. Its church has late 13C wall paintings. 47½m: **Pulborough**, on the Arun, has a large Early English and Perpendicular church with brasses.

Bignor, 7m SW (2m W of Bury, see below), in a pleasant position at the foot of the Downs, has a fine *Roman Villa (open). It was inhabited in the 2–4C and first excavated in 1811–19, when the buildings covering mosaics (mostly 4C) were erected. A museum has finds from later excavations. A footpath leads along the Arun from Pulborough to

Wiggonholt, 2m SE. *West Chiltington*, 3m E, has its stocks and whipping-post and a 12C church with wall paintings.

4m SE of Pulborough is *Parham* (open), nicely set in a deer park at the foot of the Downs. Built for the Palmer family in 1577, it is a substantial yet restrained building of grey stone, with a roof of Horsham slate. The interior includes a Great Hall and Long Gallery. The Green Room has items connected with the naturalist and explorer Sir Joseph Banks (1743–1820), among them portraits by Reynolds and Romney and a charming kangaroo by Stubbs.

FROM PULBOROUGH TO MIDHURST, 12m via A283 and A272. 1m: *Stopham*, with a narrow 14C bridge on the Arun. 5m: *Petworth* has narrow streets and good buildings of almost every period. Close to the centre stands **Petworth House** (NT), built between 1688 and 1696 in the French grand style. The Marble Hall has woodcarving by John Selden, while the small dining room (or Carved Room) has work by Grinling Gibbons. The outstanding *art collection has Greek and Roman sculpture, portraits by Van Dyck and Kneller, and works by Turner, a frequent guest. The Chapel is a pleasing mixture of 13C (from the original house on the site) and 17C (carvings by Selden). The *700-acre grounds (open all year) are among Capability Brown's finest achievements. 12m: **Midhurst**, a charming old town on the Rother, has the imposing ruins of *Cowdray House*, a Tudor mansion destroyed by fire in 1793, in Cowdray Park (open). Sir Richard Cobden (1804–65) and H.G. Wells were pupils at the 17C Grammar School (altered in 18C). The church of *Easebourne* (pronounced 'Ezburn'), 1m NE, has an effigy of Sir David Owen (d. 1535), Henry VII's uncle, and adjoins the buildings of a 13C priory of Augustinian nuns, now the church hall and vicarage. About 1m S of Midhurst an obelisk commemorates Cobden, who is buried at *West Lavington*, ¾m SE. *Trotton*, 3½m W of Midhurst, was birthplace of the dramatist Thomas Otway (1652–85). The church has a wall painting of the Last Judgement (c 1380) and brasses to the Camoy family; one of 1310 is the earliest brass in England to a woman.

A29 crosses the Arun, which meanders through rich water meadows. 48½m: *Hardham* has a church with 12C wall paintings. 52½m: *Bury*, 2m from Bignor (see above), where the novelist John Galsworthy (1867–1933) had his country home, lies opposite *Amberley*, a charming *village with a ruined castle of the Bishops of Chichester (not open) and a late Norman church. The Amberley Chalk Pits Museum displays industrial history in a former limeworks and quarry. 54½m: *Whiteways Lodge* commands a *view, with Arundel Park on the left. A284 leads S.

56½m: **Arundel** (2400 inhabitants; TI), in the gap the Arun makes in the South Downs, clusters round the base of its *Castle* (open).

Besieged by Henry I in 1102 and by Stephen in 1139, the Norman castle was finally ruined by the Parliamentarians in 1643–44. Only the Fitzalan Chapel (see below), the lower stages of the 12C Keep and the 13C Bevis Tower survive relatively unscathed. The present castle is mainly a baronial exercise of the 1790s and 1890s. The late Victorian Chapel and the Library (1801) are interesting examples of the Gothic Revival.

The parish church of *St Nicholas* (c 1380) has a rare pre-Reformation pulpit and 14C wall paintings. The *Fitzalan Chapel*, behind the altar and separated by an ancient iron grille protected with plate glass, belongs to the Duke of Norfolk, a Roman Catholic. Originally founded in 1380, it contains *monuments of the Fitzalans, previous holders of the earldom of Arundel, acquired by the Howards in 1580. The 15th Duke (1847–1917) restored the chapel and also built the conspicuous Roman Catholic cathedral church of *St Philip Neri*, with a slender flèche (1869–76; J.A. Hansom). The writer George MacDonald was pastor of the Tarrant St. chapel in 1850. *Potter's Museum of Curiosity* in the High St. is a Victorian museum of taxidermy.

Charming walks climb the banks of the Arun to (3m) *Amberley Bridge* on the W bank and to (2m) *Burpham* on the E bank, at the foot of the South Downs, with a Norman and Early English church and a promontory-fort, probably built to resist Danish sea-raiders. For *Littlehampton*, 4m S of Arundel on A284, see Route 12.

A27 runs W from Arundel, crossing the Bognor road (A29) near (60½m) *Fontwell* (TI). To the right is (½m) *Slindon*, where Archbishop Stephen Langton died in 1228 (memorial in church), with 3500 acres of NT land above it. To the left is Fontwell Park racecourse (steeplechases). 63½m: Opposite *Tangmere* is *Boxgrove*, ¼m N of the main road. The Benedictine •priory (EH) has a church with late Norman and Early English work recalling Bishop Seffrid's contributions to Chichester Cathedral. The W end of the nave is ruined. The ceiling was painted by Lambert Barnard in 1530. The De La Warr chantry was built in 1532. Of the monastic buildings to the N, the ruined guest house (c 1300) and chapter house remain.

66½m: **CHICHESTER** (24,200 inhabitants), a charming cathedral city, has many 18C houses. The Roman Noviomagus, called Cisseceaster in the 'Saxon Chronicle', it betrays its Roman origin in the four main streets meeting at right-angles in the centre.

TI: 29a South St. **Bus Station**: A286, beyond Southgate. **Railway Station**: A286, beyond Southgate. **Theatre**: Chichester Festival Theatre, Oaklands Park. **Annual Events**: Festival Theatre season May–September. Chichester Festivities (music, drama, exhibitions) in the first half of July. Racing at Goodwood Park for 18 days each year, including the Goodwood Cup in July. The Southern Cathedrals Festival of Music is held annually (in July) in rotation with Winchester and Salisbury.

The •**Cathedral** is mainly Norman and most later additions conform with its original spirit. The result may not be among the grandest English cathedrals but is certainly one of the most quietly satisfying. The exterior, a mixture of greenish limestone from the Isle of Wight and Caen stone, blends informally with the busy West St. The graceful spire, said to be the only English cathedral spire visible from the sea, dominates the town and makes a constant focus of views from the flat countryside around.

It was begun by Bishop de Luffa after the see of Selsey was moved here in c 1075. Work continued throughout the next century, interrupted by a serious fire in 1114, and the building consecrated in 1184 embodied the main structure of the present church. A second fire in 1187 prompted Bishop Seffrid II (1180–1204) to renew the inside of the clerestory, vault the roof in stone and change the Norman apse into a square retrochoir. The three porches and sacristy are Early English. The outer aisles were added and the Lady Chapel enlarged in the Decorated style (c 1300). The spire, cloister and detached belfry (unique to an English cathedral apart from the modern one at Chester) were built soon after 1400.

Visitors enter by the Early English W porch, from which the sober and harmonious proportions of the interior are immediately apparent. The arcades and gallery of Bishop de Luffa's *Nave* contrast effectively with Bishop Seffrid's light and graceful clerestory (which uses Purbeck marble) and the Decorated tracery of the aisles. The monuments include two by Flaxman, to the poet William Collins (1721–59) in the SW tower and to Agnes Cromwell (d. 1797) in St Clement's Chapel. In the N aisle are: a statue of William Huskisson, the MP killed at the opening of the Liverpool and Manchester Railway in 1830; the tomb of Richard Fitzalan, Earl of Arundel (d. 1376) and his wife; and the tomb of Joan de Vere (d.1293), daughter of Robert, Earl of Oxford.

The *S Transept* has a fine seven-light window (c 1330). Below is the tomb of Bishop Langton (1305–37); opposite, under a fine Decorated canopy, is an expressive effigy, probably of Bishop Stratford (d. 1362), on a tomb chest dating from 1846. Here also are two unusual paintings (c 1519, restored) by Lambert Barnard, a local artist employed by Bishop Sherborne (1508–36). The Early English *Sacristy* W of this transept has vaulting on exquisite corbels. The *N Transept*, long used as the parish church, has pictures of bishops by Lambert Barnard. Gustav Holst (1874–1934) is buried here. The

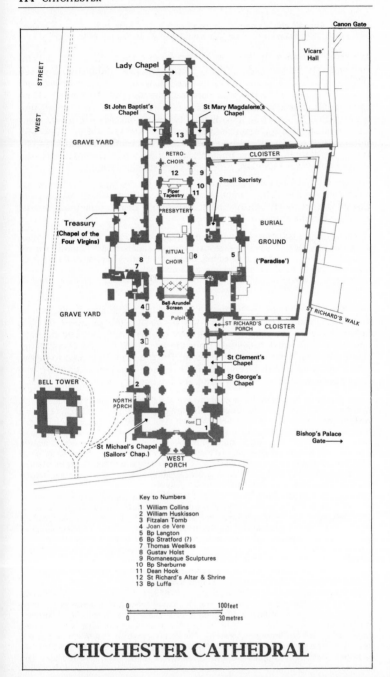

Canon Gate

Vicars' Hall

WEST STREET

Lady Chapel

St John Baptist's Chapel

St Mary Magdalene's Chapel

GRAVE YARD

13

CLOISTER

RETRO-CHOIR

12

9

Small Sacristy

10

Piper Tapestry

11

PRESBYTERY

BURIAL

GROUND

('Paradise')

Treasury (Chapel of the Four Virgins)

RITUAL CHOIR

6

5

8

7

Bell-Arundel Screen

Pulpit

ST RICHARD'S PORCH

ST RICHARD'S WALK

GRAVE YARD

4

CLOISTER

3

St Clement's Chapel

St George's Chapel

BELL TOWER

2

NORTH PORCH

Font

1

Bishop's Palace Gate→

St Michael's Chapel (Sailors' Chap.)

WEST PORCH

Key to Numbers

1 William Collins
2 William Huskisson
3 Fitzalan Tomb
4 Joan de Vere
5 Bp Langton
6 Bp Stratford (?)
7 Thomas Weelkes
8 Gustav Holst
9 Romanesque Sculptures
10 Bp Sherburne
11 Dean Hook
12 St Richard's Altar & Shrine
13 Bp Luffa

0   100 feet
0   30 metres

CHICHESTER CATHEDRAL

W wall has a memorial to Thomas Weelkes, composer of madrigals and cathedral organist in 1602–23. The *Treasury* adjoins the transept to the E. Above is the *Library* (open by appointment).

The nave is separated from the *Choir* by the Bell-Arundel Screen, a three-aisled structure attributed to Bishop Arundel (1459–78) and now restored to its original position. The choir stalls, with good misericords, date from c 1335. The most striking feature of the choir is the tapestry by John Piper (1966) covering the altar screen. The S aisle has two gracefully sculptured stone *panels (c 1140), showing Christ at the Gate of Bethany and the Raising of Lazarus. The *Chapel of St Mary Magdalene*, closing the vista, has a painting by Graham Sutherland over its altar.

The *Retrochoir* belongs to the final transition from Norman to Gothic. The interval between the Purbeck marble piers and their detached shafts is wider than in any other known example. Note the sculptural decoration in the triforium. On the N side is a window by Marc Chagall (1978). The Anglo-German tapestry (1985) was designed by Irsula Benker-Schirmer and woven in Sussex and Bavaria. On the S side is a fragment of 2C Roman mosaic, discovered under the foundations in 1969. Of the long, narrow *Lady Chapel* the two W bays belong to the original Norman church while the two E bays were added between 1288 and 1304. The first two bays show traces of the paintings by Lambert Barnard which once covered the vaults throughout the church. The simple tomb of Bishop de Luffa is in the first bay.

The *Cloisters*, entered by the beautiful Early English S porch, are 15C and irregular in both position and form. They were not built for monastic purposes and originally surrounded the cathedral's 'paradise', or burial ground. From the S walk a passage called St Richard's Walk leads to Canon Lane. In front is the *Deanery* (1725); to the right the lane ends at the 14C gateway of the *Bishop's Palace*, half of which is now a

Open-air ceremony on Palm Sunday at Chichester Cathedral

theological college. Its chapel and kitchen walls are of the 13C, the remainder 14–18C. The chapel has fine vaulting and corbels, and an exquisite painted tondo (c 1250). At the other end of the lane, beyond the 15C Vicars' Close, is the 16C *Canon Gate* into South St. By another entrance to the precincts, a few yards to the left along South St., is a 12C vaulted undercroft (now a restaurant) beneath the 14C *Vicars' Hall*.

At the centre of the town stands the rich *Market Cross* (1501), surmounted by a cupola of 1724. On the E side is a replica of a bust of Charles I; the original can be seen, with the civic plate, in the Council House. The largely Georgian North St., the finest in the city, leads past (right) *Buttermarket* (1807) by Nash and the former church of *St Olave* (now a bookshop), with early Norman features. On the outside wall of the *Council House* (1731–33; interior shown when not in use) a Roman inscription records the erection of a temple to Neptune and Minerva. Lion St. (right) leads to St Martin's Square, a delightful group of houses. *St Mary's Hospital* (open by appointment) was founded c 1158 for the care of the sick but since 1528 has been an almshouse for the aged. The *Great Hall*, formerly the infirmary but since 1680 occupied by small dwellings, has a timber roof reaching at the sides to within 6ft of the floor. To allow patients to hear mass from their beds, only a carved oak screen separates the hall from the *Chapel*, a unique arrangement in England, though it is also adopted at Beaune. Except for the partitions and chimneys, the whole dates from c 1290; the chapel has good stalls and misericords. To the N is the well-kept *Priory Park*, with the Early English choir of the *Grey Friars' Church*, later used as an assize court, and now the *Guildhall Museum* (open). William Blake was tried for sedition here in 1804 after he had ejected a soldier from his garden at Felpham. The park also contains the motte of Chichester Castle, and is surrounded by part of the *City Walls*, resting on Roman foundations and showing the extent of Roman Chichester. The N and E walls have raised footpaths.

The *Festival Theatre* (1962; Powell and Moya) in Oaklands Park is known for the drama season which Laurence Olivier first directed. The small Minerva Theatre is a recent addition to the complex.

In Little London, leading S from Priory Rd, an 18C corn store houses the *Chichester District Museum*, with displays of local geology, prehistory, Roman and Saxon finds and social history. The sculpture by John Skelton, outside, dates from 1964.

St John's Church (1812), reached by continuing S across East St. and then turning right, has an octagonal Low Church plan and monumental three-decker pulpit. Keats began 'The Eve of St Agnes' in 1819 at 11 Eastgate Square, further on.

The area SE of the Market Cross is known as *The Pallants*, with four streets intersecting the Palatinate or Archbishop's 'Peculiar', a sort of miniature city within the city. It contains some fine 18C and 19C buildings, among them *Pallant House* (1712), now open as a gallery with pictures, porcelain, glass, furniture, textiles and modern British art.

West St., opposite the cathedral, has more 18C houses. Leading from it is Chapel St., where further Roman remains came to light in 1971. West St. continues past a former church by R.C. Carpenter (1848–52), now housing shops, to the striking *John Ede's House* or Wren House (1696), now the county record office. The *County Hall* (1934) behind is inoffensive, although recent extensions in Tower St. are less harmonious. Westgate Fields, further W, gives good views of the cathedral and the walls, despite the intrusion of modern development.

Just 1¼m W of Chichester is ***Fishbourne Roman Palace** (open), a magnifcent 1C building excavated in 1961–69. It rivals the imperial palaces of Rome itself in size and grandeur. The museum houses objects found here during the excavations, as well as from a 4C town house in Chichester and a villa at nearby Chilgrove. The story of the palace is told by an audio-visual progamme.

Fishbourne could have been the base and supply depot for the Roman army: two large wooden storehouses have been discovered, with evidence of a harbour. Although a large house was built in AD 50–59, the main palace and gardens were built c AD 75. Remains of its N wing are covered by a modern building: the mosaics are the finest yet found in Britain. Parts of the W and E wings have also been uncovered, and the large garden has been replanted on the lines of the bedding trenches discovered during excavations. The S part of the garden and S wing lie under modern houses and the A29. Early in the 2C part of the palace was demolished, new mosaics were laid, and central heating installed. In c AD 285 the whole building was destroyed by fire, evidence of which can be seen in the N wing.

For several weeks in the summer Chichester becomes a starting-point for the races at *Goodwood Park* (views), 4½m N. There is also an airfield, motor circuit and golf course. **Goodwood House** itself (open), the seat of the Duke of Richmond, was built by James Wyatt (1780–1800). It contains a fine collection of portraits by Van Dyck, Lely and Kneller and pictures by Stubbs and Canaletto. The park (open daily) is noted for its cedars. Overlooking it is the *Trundle*, a prehistoric earthwork on *St Roche's Hill* (667ft). On A286 at *Singleton* is the *Weald and Downland Open Air Museum*, with 14–19C buildings rescued and reconstructed on the site. *West Dean Gardens* are open. Singleton is a secluded village. Its Norman church contains an unusual pulpit incorporated into the side of the chancel arch with two lancet openings. The chancel of the church at *Apuldram*, 1½m SW of Chichester, has triple-lancet windows with Purbeck marble shafts, a rare feature it shares with Brecon Priory in Wales.

FROM CHICHESTER TO SELSEY, 8m. B2145 crosses the fertile peninsula of Selsey ('seal's island'), mainly interesting because St Wilfrid established Christianity among the South Saxons here in 681. The saint was followed by a long line of bishops, until the Conqueror transferred the see to Chichester. 4m: *Sidlesham*. At *Pagham*, an untidy seaside village 2m E by footpath (the approach by road is from Hunston, 3m N), is a finely proportioned Early English church with lancet windows, dedicated to St Thomas Becket. 6½m: A sideroad leads left for *Church Norton* (1m). Overlooking Pagham Bay and its nature reserve (700 acres) is the romantic St Wilfrid's Chapel. The simple 13C chancel is all that remains of the church which was moved to Selsey. 8m: *Selsey* church, built in 1865, incorporates the fine nave arcades of the old church. The headland of *Selsey Bill* projects to the S. Along the shore to the W are the bungalow resorts of *Bracklesham* and *East Wittering*.

From Chichester to *Bognor* and *Worthing*, see Route 12.

69½m: *Broadbridge*. About ½m S is *Bosham* (pronounced 'Bozzam'), a pretty village and yachting centre on Chichester Harbour. The small *church appears in the Bayeux Tapestry, where Harold is shown on his way to hear mass before his ill-starred visit to Normandy. The tower, the W part of the chancel with the fine chancel arch, and possibly the nave date from the time of Edward the Confessor. The aisles are later. The chancel, with a good lancet E window, was extended in the early Norman period and again in the Early English period.

Tradition alleges that King Canute's young daughter was buried here, and a small stone coffin was found at the required spot in 1865. Some think Bosham the scene of Canute's command to the waves (cf. Southampton, Route 14A). From here a road leads to a ferry for *West Itchenor*, a picturesque yachting village.

At (73½m) *Emsworth* the route enters Hampshire. The Isle of Wight comes into view on the left. Among fine woodland 4m N is *Stansted Park* (limited opening), originally built by Talman in 1686 and rebuilt in the same style by Sir Reginald Blomfield after a fire in 1900. Most interesting is the Gothick chapel added by Lewis Way. Keats was present at its consecration in 1819, and the stained glass influenced 'The Eve of St Agnes'. 75½m: *Havant* (TI) has trebled its population to 116,650 inhabitants (with Waterloo) in 30 years.

To the S lies *Hayling Island* (seasonal TI), 4m long and 2m broad, with (2½m) *North Hayling* and the resort of (4½m) *South Hayling*. The Early English church of St Mary at South Hayling has good sculptures and lancet windows. In the churchyard is a yew 31ft in circumference. The defunct branch line from Havant to Hayling is remembered at the Hayling Billy Inn, named after the locomotive preserved outside. A ferry connects the western tip of the island with Portsmouth.

84½m: **PORTSMOUTH** (179,400 inhabitants) occupies most of Portsea Island, a narrow peninsula flanked by Langstone Harbour to the E and the magnificent Portsmouth Harbour to the W. This ideal position has made it England's chief naval base since the time of the Tudors, a history commemorated by a wealth of local museums and exhibits. In addition to the naval base and dockyard, the city includes Old Portsmouth, the resort and residential district of Southsea, and *Gosport*, technically an independent borough, on the other side of Portsmouth Harbour.

TI: The Hard; 102 Commercial Rd.; (seasonal) Clarence Esplanade, Southsea; Continental Ferry Port. **Bus Station**: The Hard. **Railway Stations**: Portsmouth and Southsea Station; Portsmouth Harbour Station (for the Isle of Wight ferry). **Ferry Services**: from Continental Ferry Port to Bilbao, Caen, Cherbourg, Le Havre and St Malo; from Portsmouth Harbour Station to Gosport and to Ryde (Isle of Wight); from Gunwharf Rd, Old Portsmouth, to Fishbourne (Isle of Wight); from Ferry Rd, Eastney, to Hayling Island. Hovercraft service from near Clarence Pier, Southsea, to Ryde. **Theatres**: Kings Theatre, Albert Rd, Southsea; Portsmouth Drama Centre, Reginald Rd, Eastney. **Annual Event**: Southsea Show on Southsea Common during the first weekend in August.

History. A small town existed at the mouth of Portsmouth Harbour soon after the Conquest, but the real history of Portsmouth began when Henry VII established the first dry dock and declared Portsmouth a Royal dockyard and garrison. Remains of the later Tudor fortifications are still an outstanding feature. Charles II was married in Government House to Catherine of Braganza in 1661. The city suffered heavily from air raids in 1941–44, and was one of the main D-Day assembly areas.

Natives, residents and visitors. Natives include: Charles Dickens (1812–7); George Meredith (1828–1909); Sir Walter Besant (1835–1901); Isambard Kingdom Brunel (1806–59); Jonas Hanway (1712–86), the philanthropist; and John Pounds (1766–1839), the crippled cobbler who founded the first 'ragged school' (1812). Fanny Price, the heroine of Jane Austen's 'Mansfield Park', had her first home here. Conan Doyle wrote his first Sherlock Holmes story, 'A Study in Scarlet', while practising as a doctor here. In 'Kipps' H.G. Wells describes his years in Portsmouth. The city's associations with Lord Nelson and other naval heroes are innumerable.

In the middle of Portsmouth, near the main railway station, is the civic centre with the Central Library, TI Centre and the restored Victorian *Guildhall*. To the N is the chief shopping area. To the SW lies Old Portsmouth; to the SE, Portsea. To the W is the naval base, dockyard and harbour. Between Old Portsmouth and the naval base is the United Services recreation ground, entered by two former town gates, the *King James Gate* (1687) in Burnaby Rd and the *Land Port* (1698) in its original position in St George's Rd (both EH).

The *Charles Dickens Birthplace Museum* is at 393 Old Commercial Rd, N of the centre. The modest house has been restored and refurnished in a style appropriate to the year

(1812) when the novelist was born here. Items on display include the couch from Gad's Hill Place (Route 4) on which he died in 1870.

HM Naval Base is entered from Portsea Hard by the Victory Gate. A town in itself, it covers over 300 acres and comprises 15 dry docks, 62 acres of fitting and repairing basins, 6000 yards of wharfage, 10 miles of railways and some fine 18C houses, including the former Navigation School ('HMS Dryad') and Admiralty House (the office of the Commander-in-Chief). In 1986 *HMS Warrior*, an iron-hulled warship launched in 1860, was permanently berthed near the Hard and Portsmouth Harbour Station. Just inside the entrance to the base is the *Exhibition* of objects retrieved from the 'Mary Rose' (see below). To the left is the *Royal Naval Museum*, occupying three Georgian storehouses and dealing with naval history from the 16C to the Falklands Campaign. In the *Old* or *King Charles's Dock* (1648) is **HMS* **Victory**, restored and fitted out almost to her appearance as at Trafalgar. Visitors can see the spot where Nelson fell and the cockpit where he died. Nearby, in a roofed-over dry dock, is the **Mary Rose* (open). This flagship, the pride of Henry VIII's navy, sank off Portsmouth in 1545; the hull was raised in 1982 and is now the object of a lengthy conservation programme. Visitors view it from an aluminium footbridge.

High St., the main street of Old Portsmouth, was devastated in 1941. The *Grammar School* founded in 1732 is largely contained in a former barracks with a fine Georgian façade. Among the few surviving old buildings is *Buckingham House* (plaque), formerly the Spotted Dog Inn, where the 1st

Old Harbour, Portsmouth

Duke of Buckingham was assassinated by John Felton in 1628. Later (1634–35) the house belonged to John Mason, founder of New Hampshire and captain of Southsea Castle. A plaque on a new building marks the site of the George Hotel, where Nelson spent the night before embarking on his last voyage. The unfinished **Cathedral**, founded in 1927, incorporates the original chancel and transepts of the church of *St Thomas of Canterbury*, dating from 1188–96, with the nave and tower rebuilt c 1693. The cupola was added in 1703. The old church now forms the sanctuary and choir. The nave and aisles, begun in 1935 by Sir Charles Nicholson, are incomplete.

The S Presbytery aisle (c 1185) contains a monument by Nicholas Stone (1631) to the Duke of Buckingham (see above), and the S choir aisle, known as the Navy Aisle (rededicated 1938), serves as a memorial to the many Royal Naval heroes. The choir, with a W gallery of 1708, contains the Corporation Pew of 1693. On the NE wall of the N transept is a mural of the Last Judgement (c 1250). In the nave is the 'Golden Barque', which served as a weather vane on the tower from 1710 to 1954. The new N tower transept contains a plaque of the Madonna by Andrea della Robbia.

Several old houses survive in St Thomas's St. N of the Cathedral, and in Lombard St. The *City Museum and Art Gallery* in Museum Rd has a collection of local paintings, including work by Clarkson Stanfield, George Smith of Chichester and the Cole family, and modern and contemporary work.

Broad St. passes on the left the *Sally Port*, the classic point of embarkation for England's naval heroes, and the 15C *Round Tower*. It continues NW to the *Point*, on the narrow entrance to the harbour, where a few alleys characteristic of the old town remain. **Portsmouth Harbour**, less than 300yd wide at its entrance, expands into a vast basin 4m long and 2m broad, giving secure anchorage to the largest vessels. A raised rampart and sea-wall walk extend E from the Round Tower towards Clarence Pier. Below the ramparts, on Governor's Green, is the *Garrison Church* (EH, keykeeper). The Early English building was originally a hospital ('Domus Dei'), with the patients in the nave and a chapel in the choir; the nave was gutted in 1941. Further on, in Pembroke Gardens, is a statue of Nelson (1951).

Beyond Clarence Pier is **Southsea**, a resort commanding views of the Isle of Wight and the shipping in Spithead. *Southsea Common*, laid out with gardens, extends the length of the esplanade. Among the memorials here are the anchor of the 'Victory' and the large *Naval War Memorial*. The *D-Day Museum* has as its centrepiece the Overlord Embroidery, 270ft long (longer than the Bayeux Tapestry), telling the story of the Normandy landings. *Southsea Castle*, built by Henry VIII and now restored, houses a museum with local archaeology, blockmaking machinery by Sir Marc Brunel and the BBC Tudor costume exhibition. Beyond are the TI Centre and the *South Parade Pier*, a centre of holiday activity. Near the Canoe Lake is *Cumberland House Museum*, mainly of natural history, with a freshwater aquarium. The former Officers' Mess (1868) of Eastney Barracks houses the *Royal Marines Museum*.

Gosport (77,300 inhabitants; TI), on the W side of the harbour, can be reached by ferry from Portsmouth (see above) or by A32 from Fareham (see below). *Holy Trinity* church has an organ brought from the demolished mansion of Canons in Middlesex, where Handel may have played it. Haslar Bridge (no vehicles) leads to *Haslar Hospital* (façade of 1746–62), with accommodation for 2000 patients. The sea-wall leads to *Fort Blockhouse* at the entrance to the harbour and opposite Portsmouth's Round Tower. The submarine base at 'HMS Dolphin' includes the *Royal Navy Submarine Museum*. Off A32 to the N is *Fort Brockhurst* (EH, all year), part of the defensive system Lord Palmerston built in the 1850s to counter the threat of French invasion.

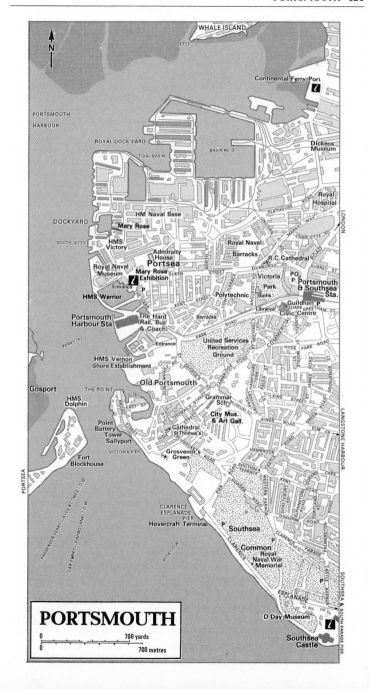

WHALE ISLAND

JETTY

Continental Ferry Port

PORTSMOUTH HARBOUR

ROYAL DOCK YARD

TIDAL BASIN

BASIN No 3

Dickens Museum

DOCKYARD

SOUTH JETTY

HM Naval Base

Mary Rose

HMS Victory

Admiralty House

Portsea

Royal Naval Museum

Mary Rose Exhibition

Entrance

HMS Warrior

Portsmouth Harbour Sta.

The Hard (Rail, Bus & Coach)

Entrance

HMS Vernon Shore Establishment

Old Portsmouth

FERRY (P)

Gosport

THE POINT

HMS Dolphin

Point Battery Tower Sallyport

Fort Blockhouse

VICTORIA PIER

QUAY

EAST ST

BROAD ST

HIGH STREET

Royal Hospital

FLATHOUSE ROAD

UNION

MARKET WAY

CHARLOTTE RD

LONDON

Royal Naval Barracks

R.C Cathedral

SURREY ST

NORTH STREET

EDINBURGH

QUEEN STREET

KENT STREET

Victoria Park

Polytechnic

Baths

Library

THE SQUARE

Guildhall Civic Centre

GREETHAM ST

PO P

Portsmouth & Southsea Sta.

PORTSMOUTH HARBOUR STATION

COMMERCIAL

HYDE PARK ROAD

Barracks

PARK ROAD

ST MICHAEL'S RD

United Services Recreation Ground

ST THOMAS'S STREET

GEORGE'S RD

CAMBRIDGE ROAD

PARK ROAD

HAMPSHIRE

PAUL'S

KING STREET

ST JAMES RD

GROSVENOR RD

Grammar Sch.

MUSEUM RD

LANDPORT

City Mus. & Art Gall.

KING STREET

KINGS ROAD

ELM GR

Cathedral (St Thomas's)

Grosvenor's Green

HAMBROOK ST

CASTLE ROAD

SOUTHSEA TERRACE

WESTERN PARADE

KENT ROAD

PIER ROAD

GORDON ROAD

OSBORNE ROAD

CLARENCE PARADE

PORTLAND ROAD

PALMERSTON

CLARENCE ESPLANADE PIER

Hovercraft Terminal

P

Southsea

Common

P

Royal Naval War Memorial

CLARENCE

LANGSTONE HARBOUR

ESPLANADE

P

SOUTHSEA & SOUTH PARADE PIER

CASTLE AVENUE

D-Day Museum

Southsea Castle

PORTSEA

PASSENGER FERRY - RYDE & COWES, O.W.

CAR FERRY - FISHBOURNE, I.O.W.

RYDE I.O.W.

Fort Widley (open), on A333 5m N of Portsmouth centre, is another part of Palmerston's fortifications. It has fine views over the Solent.

FROM PORTSMOUTH TO SOUTHAMPTON, 21m by A27. It skirts the foot of Portsdown, with Portsmouth Harbour on the left. 7¼m: **Portchester**, the Roman Portus Castra, has a magnificent *Castle* (EH, all year). The Roman *fortress, Portus Adurni, was placed here to guard the Saxon Shore. Its bastions are superb. Excavation has revealed extensive Saxon use. In the NW angle Henry II built a *castle in 1160–72, extended by Edward II and Richard II. The roof of the keep commands the entire harbour. Here Henry V mustered his Agincourt expedition. The *church in the SE angle was founded by Austin Canons in 1133. On Portsdown is a *Nelson Monument* (150ft) built by his comrades at Trafalgar. 10½m: **Fareham** (88,300 inhabitants; TI) is a market town with a fine High St. A32 leads S to (5m) Gosport (see above) and N to the Meon Valley and Alton (Route 14A). *Boarhunt*, with a late Saxon church, is 3m NE. 11m: *Titchfield* has a large church (Saxon to Perpendicular) with a splendid monument to the Southampton family by Gerard Johnson (1594). *Titchfield Abbey* (EH) was built by the 1st Earl of Southampton in 1542 on the site of the abbey church (1232–38) and incorporates its nave. Here Margaret of Anjou, just landed at Southampton, was married to Henry VI in 1445 and Charles I was arrested in 1647 before his imprisonment at Carisbrooke. 21m: *Southampton*, see Route 14A.

B. Via Guildford and Petersfield

Directions. Total distance 69m. Shorter and more scenic than Route 13A. A3 to (29m) **Guildford** (bypassed). A3100 to (33m) Godalming and (35m) Milford. A3 to (41m) **Hindhead**, (53m) **Petersfield** and (69m) **Portsmouth** (Route 13A).

Leaving London by Putney Bridge, the route joins A3 at Putney Heath. The modern course of the road bypasses Kingston, Esher and Cobham, meeting the old Portsmouth road again at (20m) *Pain's Hill*, near M25.

The old Portsmouth road, now labelled A308 and A307, passes through *Kingston upon Thames* (see 'Blue Guide London') and, beyond *Sandown Park* racecourse, becomes the High St. of (16m) *Esher* (61,400 inhabitants). Of the original Esher Place built by Bishop Waynflete in 1477–86 and occupied by Wolsey the only relic is the gatehouse (Wolsey's Tower), altered by William Kent. From Esher A244 runs W towards the Thames at Walton, Weybridge and other places described in Route 49. Off A244 ½m S of Esher lies *Claremont*, a mansion built in 1769–72 for Clive of India by Capability Brown with Henry Holland and Holland's young pupil, John Soane. The house is now a school run by Christian Scientists (limited opening). *Claremont Landscape Garden* (NT), reached by a separate entrance from A307, is one of the earliest examples of English landscaping to survive. It was begun by Sir John Vanbrugh and Charles Bridgeman before 1720 and developed by William Kent. There is a lake with an island and temple, and a curious turf amphitheatre.

From Pain's Hill A245 runs SE to (6¼m) Leatherhead (Route 12). It passes *Cobham* village, where Cedar House (NT, open by appointment) has a 15C hall. At (2½m) *Stoke d'Abernon* the church, with Saxon and Early English work and too much restoration, contains the earliest *brass in England (to Sir John d'Abernon, 1277), a brass to his son (d. 1327) and 14–16C Flemish glass.

22m: *Wisley Common*, with the pretty Bolder Mere to the left of A3 and, to the right, the *Gardens of the Royal Horticultural Society* (open). *Ockham*, 1m S, has a distinctive Victorian centre built by the 1st Lord Lovelace. The church contains a lovely seven-light E window and a monument to the 1st Lord King (d. 1734) by Rysbrack. 24m: *Ripley* is bypassed by the A3. Off the old road (B2215) lie the 13C ruins of *Newark Priory* (Augustinian, founded c 1190) on the banks of the Wey (see Route 49B).

A247 leads NW from B2215 through *Old Woking*, with an interesting church near the river, to (4m) **Woking** (81,400 inhabitants), created by the railway and still mainly a dormitory town for London commuters.

29m: **GUILDFORD** (63,000 inhabitants), the county town of Surrey, stands where the Wey cuts through the chalk ridge of the North Downs. It has pleasant hilly streets and river scenery.

TI: The Undercroft, 72 High St. **Bus Station**: near The Friary and North St. **Railway Stations**: Guildford Main Line Station, W of the river near the centre; London Rd Station off A3100. **Theatres**: Yvonne Arnaud Theatre, Millbrook; Bellerby Theatre, Leapale Lane. **Annual Event**: Surrey County Show in Stoke Park each May.

The steep *High St., descending to the river in the W, has a handsome medley of old houses. Near the top the *Royal Grammar School* keeps its 16C main building, with a library founded in 1573 by Bishop Parkhurst and containing 89 chained books (open by appointment). Beyond the junction with Chertsey St. is a fine group of buildings, beginning with the Jacobean brick *Abbot's Hospital* (guided tours available), founded in 1619 for a master, twelve brethren and ten sisters. The massive gatehouse is outstanding. Inside are some fine carved oak, stained glass of 1621 in the chapel, a portrait group by the local painter John Russell (1745–1806) and portraits of Calvin, Wyclif and Foxe. Beyond are the exuberant *Guildford House* of 1660 and the *Guildhall* (guided tours), with a Restoration frontage and clock added to a Tudor structure. *Trinity Church*, opposite, was rebuilt in the 18C. It contains the monument of Archbishop Abbot (d. 1633) from an earlier church and the cenotaph of Speaker Onslow (d. 1768), buried at Merrow. The *Angel Hotel*, a coaching inn further down the hill, has 13C cellars.

Quarry St., a left turn from the High St. as it nears the river, has more old houses and the unusual church of *St Mary*. Most of it is late Norman (1160–80) but the tower is Saxon, as the splayed openings above the tower arches inside show. A little way beyond the church is the *Castle Archway*, leading to the public gardens where the keep of the Norman *Castle* (c 1150) stands on an artificial mound. Near the archway is a small *Museum* of Surrey antiquities, ironwork, needlework and relics of Lewis Carroll (C.L. Dodgson; 1832–98). He frequently visited his sisters' home, 'The Chestnuts', on Quarry St. and is buried in Guildford cemetery.

The *Yvonne Arnaud Theatre* is in Millbrook by the Wey, overlooked by the picturesque backs of Quarry St. The church of *St Nicholas* on the other side of the river incorporates the 15C Loseley Chapel, with monuments to the More-Molyneux of Loseley.

On Stag Hill, about ¾m NW of the town centre, stands the **Cathedral** by Sir Edward Maufe.

Begun in 1936, it was consecrated in 1961 and finished in 1964. The plain exterior is of local brick, relieved only by sculptured allegorical figures. The interior, austerely effective in a modern Gothic style, is faced in stone with concrete vaults.

The N side of the hill is occupied by the *University of Surrey*, constituted in 1966 from the former Battersea Polytechnic and moved to this site.

On the Wey just S of Guildford is *St Catherine's Hill*, crowned with the ruins of an early 14C chapel and offering a good view. *Loseley House* (open), in a finely wooded park 2m SW, is a fine example of an Elizabethan manor house (1560–69). The so-called 'Nonsuch' panels of Henry VIII's reign in the great hall were probably painted for the king's tents. The Norman *church of *Compton*, 1¼m W of Loseley and 3m from

Guildford, has Saxon cells, tower and a chapel above its low vaulted sanctuary. The chapel's wooden rail may be the oldest woodwork in England. On the chancel arch is the incised figure of a Norman soldier. The painter G.F. Watts (1817–1904) lived at Limnerslease, ½m N of Compton, and his memory is kept green here by the *Watts Gallery*. The Mortuary Chapel in the new graveyard is adorned with symbolic terracotta work made by the villagers under the direction of Mrs Watts (d. 1939).

FROM GUILDFORD TO HORSHAM, 22m. A281 leads to (1½m) *Shalford*, with an 18C watermill and, near the church, the village stocks and whipping-post. The whole journey can be made on A281 but a more interesting route follows B2128 at (3m) *Bramley*, passing through (4m) *Wonersh*, with its old manor house, and (9m) *Cranleigh*, with a fine 14C church and a boys' school (1863). 22m: *Horsham*, see Route 12.

From Guildford to *Leatherhead* and to *Dorking*, see Route 12; to *Farnham*, *Alton* and *Winchester*, see Route 14A.

S of Guildford A3100 ascends the Wey. 33m: **Godalming** (18,200 inhabitants), an old town formerly a centre of the Surrey wool trade, has narrow streets, an elegant little market house and 17C half-timbered and decorated brick buildings. Aldous Huxley (1894–1963) was born here. Among its other displays, the *Museum* in the High St. commemorates Sir Edwin Lutyens and Gertrude Jekyll, who both lived and worked in the area. The large church of *St Peter and St Paul* is mainly Norman and 13C.

N of the town are the imposing buildings of *Charterhouse School* by Hardwick and others. Founded in London by Thomas Sutton in 1611, it was moved here in 1872. An old archway carved with the names of former Carthusians was brought from London. Pupils have included Crashaw, Lovelace, Isaac Barrow, Roger Williams (of Rhode Island), Steele, Addison, Wesley, Blackstone, Thomas Day (author of 'Sandford and Merton'), Grote, John Leech, Thackeray, Baden-Powell, Vaughan Williams and Max Beerbohm. The library contains many of Leech's drawings for 'Punch' and the manuscript of Thackeray's 'The Newcomes'.

Over the Wey near the A3 1½m W of Godalming are the so-called *Eashing Bridges* (NT), a medieval double bridge. On the attractive B2130 leading from Godalming to *Hascombe*, 3m SE, is (2m) the *Winkworth Arboretum* (NT), planted with rare trees and shrubs.

At (35m) *Milford* the Victorian church has stained glass by Morris and Co. Milford and Witley commons include 377 acres of NT land, with an information centre. A3100 here joins A3.

FROM MILFORD TO PETWORTH, 14m by A283. 1½m: *Witley*, where George Eliot lived from 1877 until 1880, the year of her death, at The Heights (now Rosslyn Court). 3m: *Hambledon*, left of the road, lies beneath *Hydon's Ball* (593ft; NT), a wooded hill crowned with a monument to the social reformer Octavia Hill (1838–1912). Oakhurst Cottage (NT, open by appointment) is a small timber-framed house. 4m: *Chiddingfold* is a typical Wealden village, once engaged in making glass and iron. The Crown Inn is medieval. 4½m: *Ramster* has a 20-acre garden (limited opening) laid out this century. The gardens (open under NGS) of *Vann*, 3m NE, include a water garden by Gertrude Jekyll. 14m: *Petworth*, see Route 13A.

FROM MILFORD TO MIDHURST, 16m by A286. 7m: **Haslemere** is agreeably situated between the heathery heights of Blackdown and Hindhead. A market town (13,900 inhabitants) which still boasts two 18C coaching inns, it has become the centre of a diffuse residential district. Its popularity dates from 1877, when the scientist John Tyndall (1820–93) came to live in Hindhead. Another resident, Arnold Dolmetsch (1858–1940), is commemorated by the festival of medieval music held in July. The *Educational Museum* in High St. has exhibits of British birds, geology, zoology, botany and local industries. **Blackdown** (918ft) rises 2½m S of Haslemere and commands a wide view of the Weald. The way there leaves the town by Tennyson's Lane (NT) and climbs to the right. Tennyson died in 1892 at *Aldworth*, the house he built on the E slope in 1868–69. 16m: *Midhurst*, see Route 13A.

A3 rises through heathy country. 38m: *Thursley*, to the right of the road, has a church with a timber-framed belfry, three windows of c 1030 and a font which may be Saxon. 41m: **Hindhead** rises N of Haslemere. The summit at *Gibbet Hill* (895ft) is marked by a granite cross and a pillar with an indicator showing the chief points in the magnificent *view. The spot, and the surrounding common which includes over 2000 acres of NT property, get very crowded at weekends.

The name of Gibbet Hill refers to the murder of a sailor in 1786 on the old road skirting the edge of the *Devil's Punch Bowl, a curious depression on the N side. A memorial records the crime and the fate of the assassins—an inscription listened to 'with greedy interest' by Dickens's Smike when Nicholas Nickleby read it to him. From Hindhead to *Farnham*, see Route 14A.

From Hindhead to Petersfield the road winds either side of the border between Hampshire and West Sussex. 45m: *Liphook* is a good centre for walks, for example in *Wolmer Forest* to the NW. The Fabian philosopher Sidney Webb, later Lord Passfield (1859–1947), died here at Passfield Corner. 53m: **Petersfield** (9000 inhabitants; TI) is a country town with a partly Norman church and a statue of William III on horseback (1724).

Bedales, 1m N, is a well-known co-educational school. 1½m N is *Steep*, with Edward Thomas's cottage and a memorial to him on the hill opposite. About 2½m S of Petersfield is *Buriton*, where the manor house was Gibbon's early home, and 4m SE is *Harting*, where Cardinal Pole was rector in 1526– 51 and Trollope lived in 1880–82. *Elsted* church, 2m further E, has a 13C chancel built on a Saxon nave with herringbone masonry.

On B2146 about 1½m S of Harting is *Uppark (NT), a neat box of a house designed by William Talman in 1685–90. It was badly damaged by fire in 1989 but is being restored to its original appearance. The Victorian servants' quarters in the basement are of particular interest, since H.G. Wells's mother was housekeeper here and the novelist recalled his boyhood impressions of life at Uppark in 'Tono-Bungay'.

A3 crosses the South Downs beside *Butser Hill* (887ft) and beyond (61m) *Horndean* and *Waterlooville* reaches the edge of Portsmouth. A333 leads (right) across the steep ridge of Portsdown (400ft) towards Southwick. Beyond (67m) *Hilsea* and M27 is Portsea Island, where the main part of the city stands. 69m: **Portsmouth**, see Route 13A.

14

London to Southampton

A. Via Alton and Winchester

Directions. Total distance 80m. A3 to (29m) Guildford (bypassed), see Route 13B. A31 to (39m) Farnham, (48m) **Alton** (bypassed) and (68m) **Winchester** (bypassed). A333, A33 to (80m) **Southampton**.

A3 and the course of Route 13B lead to the beginning of the Guildford bypass. After a further 3m A31 heads W along the chalk ridge known as the *Hog's Back* (350–500ft), a favourite spot with weekend tourists.

39m: **Farnham** (35,500 inhabitants; TI) is a pleasant place with Georgian houses and the *Castle of the Bishops of Winchester. Its ruined moated keep (EH, summer season) was built in 1160–75 by Bishop Henry de Blois on the site of an earlier tower whose deep well-shaft has been exposed. The Centre for International Briefing occupies the domestic buildings (limited opening). They include the Norman great hall, chapel and kitchen but owe much of their present form, particularly the fine staircase and chapel, to Bishop Morley (1662–84). Fox's Tower, in fact built by William of Waynflete (1404–75), is a lovely early brickwork.

The handsome Castle St. descends into the town. The churchyard of the large *St Andrew's* has the tomb of William Cobbett (1763–1835), probably born at the house now the *Jolly Farmers Inn*. The *Willmer House Museum* in West St., with more good Georgian buildings, is devoted to Cobbett relics and local history. Charles I spent a night at the house which has become the *Library* on the way to his trial in London.

Off B3001 2m SE, in the lovely valley of the Wey, stands *Waverley Abbey* (EH). Founded in 1128, it was the first Cistercian house in England and the 36th worldwide. The surviving ruins date from early 13C rebuilding. The name is said to have given Sir Walter Scott the title of his first novel. Beyond the river is *Moor Park* (now an Anglican education centre), where Swift worked as secretary to Sir William Temple and met Esther Johnson (Stella).

The attractive A287 runs SE from Farnham across *Frensham Common* (922 acres; NT), passing (4½m) *Frensham Pond*. The three low heather hills about 2m E are known as the *Devil's Jumps*. 6m: *Churt* was Lloyd George's home in 1925–44. *Crosswater Farm* has 6-acre woodland gardens (limited opening). 8½m: *Hindhead*, see Route 13B.

About 3m N of Farnham lies **Aldershot** (TI), an inconsiderable village before the establishment of the military camp in 1855, but now having a population of 32,700, including the troops. The camp covers about 10 square miles, with its 'Lines' barracks and military institutions of all kinds. Its history is traced by the *Military Museum* on Queen's Avenue. On the W of the town is an equestrian statue of Wellington, brought from London in 1885. Beyond A287 1m N of Farnham is the height known as *Caesar's Camp. Crondall*, off A287 4m NW of Farnham, has a fine Norman church with a brass of a priest (1381).

A31 leaves Farnham, passing on the left the turning for A325, which crosses *Alice Holt Forest* (200 acres), with the Forestry Commission's research station, and leads to the artillery camp at (10m) *Bordon*. A31 follows the course of the Wey as it enters Hampshire. At (46m) *Holybourne* Elizabeth Gaskell died in 1865.

48m: **Alton** (14,600 inhabitants; TI) has a long and attractive main street, with the *Curtis Museum*, displaying farm implements, craftsmen's tools and domestic utensils. The *Allen Gallery* in Church St., opposite, is devoted to paintings and English pottery. *St Laurence* is a large town church, mainly Perpendicular, with a Norman crossing, Saxon font and 15C pillar painting of Henry VI. The S door was riddled with bullets when the Parliamentarians shot the Royalist Colonel Boles in 1643.

The charming village of *Selborne*, on B3006 5m SE, was made famous by Gilbert White (1720–93) in 'The Natural History of Selborne'. The Wakes (open), the house where he was born and died, is preserved as a memorial to him; there are also relics of Captain Oates, the Antarctic explorer. The church has a Norman font and piers. There is a fine old yew in the churchyard, where White is buried. Selborne Hill (NT), W of the village towards Newton Valence, was the scene of many of White's observations.

49m: *Chawton* has the simple red-brick house (open) where Jane Austen lived in 1809–17, the period of her chief works.

FROM CHAWTON TO FAREHAM, 25m via A32. 3m: *East Tisted*. Rotherfield Park (limited opening) is a Gothic Revival house. The lovely Meon Valley is reached at (12½m) *West Meon*, where Thomas Lord (1755–1832) of the London cricket ground is buried. *East Meon*, a delightful village 3m E, has a *church with a black Tournai marble font like those in Winchester Cathedral and St Michael's, Southampton. The Norman tower makes a fine group with the Court House of c 1400. A ridge road running from West Meon to the Royal Naval signal school 5m SE passes the Iron Age fort known as *Old Winchester Hill* and offers good *views. 15½m: *Corhampton* has a remarkable late Saxon church with a plain Norman font and an old stone chair in the sanctuary. 17m: *Droxford* has a partly Norman church and an 18C rectory. Its railway station was headquarters of the War Cabinet immediately before D-Day in 1944. *Hambledon*, 3½m SE, claims to be the birthplace of cricket (1774). Its church is of peculiar plan and many dates. 21½m: *Wickham*, birthplace of William of Wykeham (1324–1404), has a fine square and a flour mill made from the timbers of the 'Chesapeake'. 25m: *Fareham*, see Route 13A.

59m: *New Alresford* or *Alresford* (pronounced 'Allsford') still keeps the plan laid out in 1200 by Bishop Lucy of Winchester, with *Broad St. surely the most attractive village street in Hampshire, rising towards the church tower from an artificial reservoir created by the bishop. A plaque marks the birthplace of Mary Russell Mitford (1787–1855), author of 'Our Village'. In summer, steam trains run along a reopened stretch of the 'watercress' line.

2m SW is *Tichborne*, a pleasant village with a partly Saxon church and the seat of the family embroiled in the 19C case of the 'Tichborne Claimant'. At *Hinton Ampner*, by A272 4m S, the much-altered 18C house (NT) has 17C Italian paintings, porcelain and beautiful gardens. Admiral Rodney (d. 1792) is buried at *Old Alresford*, 1m N of New Alresford on B3046. At *Northington*, 3m further N, The Grange is an ambitious Greek Revival building of c 1809 by William Wilkins (EH, exterior viewing only).

From New Alresford B3047 leads W on an alternative route (12m) into Winchester. Just S of the bridge at (4m) *Itchen Abbas* is Avington Park (limited opening). Its main frontage was created by Charles II's favourite George Brydges when he remodelled an earlier house in about 1700. The 3rd Duke of Chandos made improvements in the 1780s. Admiral Rodney spent part of his youth here. The house is now divided into flats and only the main state rooms are open.

68m: **WINCHESTER** (33,000 inhabitants) is one of the great historic cities of England. Now a county town with a cathedral and a famous boys' school, it was once capital of the Saxon kingdom and vied with London in administrative importance until the Middle Ages. Fragmentary relics of its ancient greatness survive among the handsome 18C buildings which testify to Winchester's later, more modest status as a market centre.

TI: Guildhall, The Broadway. **Bus Station**: The Broadway. **Railway Station**: off Stockbridge Rd (A272). **Theatre**: Theatre Royal, corner of Jewry St. and City Rd. **Annual Events**: Folk Festival in May; Hat Fair in July; Carnival Week in mid July; Bonfire Night Procession on 5 November. The Southern Cathedrals Festival of music is held annually (in July) in rotation with Chichester and Salisbury.

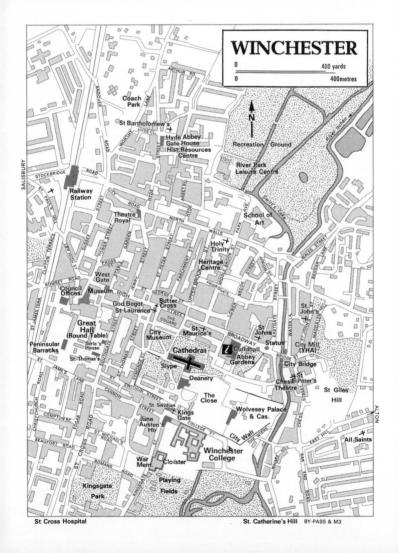

History. Winchester is successor to the British settlement of Caer Gwent, the Roman town of Venta Belgarum and the Saxon Wintanceaster, which became capital of Wessex and saw Egbert crowned as first king of all England in 829. Bishop Birinus built the first Christian church in 634, though the bishopric was not founded till 40 years later. Winchester was the capital of Alfred and of many of his successors, including Canute and the Danish kings. Edward the Confessor was crowned in the Old Minster in 1043. William the Conqueror made the city a joint capital with London and was crowned in both, an example followed by several later kings. Henry III (Henry of Winchester) was born and Henry I, Henry IV and Mary I were married here. Archbishop Stephen Langton absolved King John from excommunication at the door of the cathedral in 1213. In commerce Winchester long rivalled London, reaching its zenith by the 12C.

Since 1953 demolition and rebuilding have encouraged excavation. The course of the Iron Age defences has been traced; part of the Roman forum has been excavated on the Cathedral Green; virtually the entire site of the Old Minster, the Saxon cathedral, has been revealed; and parts of the Castle and Bishop's Palace at Wolvesey have been investigated. Work continues on the city defences and the large Roman cemeteries which extended N and E of the walls.

Residents and visitors. Izaak Walton (1593–1683), author of 'The Compleat Angler', died at 7 The Close. Jane Austen died at 8 College St. in 1817. Keats wrote his 'Ode to Autumn' and may have finished 'The Eve of St Agnes' on a visit in 1819. See also the list of famous Wykehamists under Winchester College below.

The sharp curves of Magdalen Hill descend to City Bridge across the Itchen, where part of the *City Mill* of 1744 is now a youth hostel (NT; open). The Broadway, beyond, is dominated by Hamo Thornycroft's statue of King Alfred. The *Abbey Gardens* on the left occupy the site of a convent for Benedictine nuns founded by Alfred's wife, Alswitha. *St John's Hospital* preserves a 13C chapel and an early 15C building with twin infirmaries. Further on, the High St. rises towards the West Gate. The tower of the demolished *St Maurice's Church* on the left preserves a Norman doorway. The colonnaded *Pentice* has overhanging gables, barge boards and moulded ridge tiles. The *Butter Cross* dates from the 15C but was drastically restored in the 19C. The nearby church of *St Laurence* probably occupies the site of the Conqueror's Chapel Royal. S of it stands The Square and the *City Museum*. Its display of archaeological finds from Winchester and Hampshire includes: Roman mosaic floors and painted wall plaster; Saxon objects and fragments from the Old Minster; a 12C inscription from Hyde Abbey commemorating Alfred; and a gilded reliquary of the same period. A path leads from The Square to the cathedral precincts.

The *****Cathedral** stands on low ground, its squat nave unrelieved by a tower of commanding height. It impresses on closer view, both by its size—at 556ft it is the longest medieval church in Europe—and by the richness of its interior.

Excavations N of the cathedral have located the Saxon Old Minster built by Cenwalh, King of Wessex, in 643–48. St Swithun (always spelt this way in Winchester, never 'Swithin') was buried outside its W door in 862. On 15 July 961 his remains were moved inside the church. Rain began to fall as soon as the grave was opened and continued for 40 days, thus starting the legend of the saint's control over the English summer climate. To the N was the New Minster, an abbey founded by Alfred and built by his son Edward the Elder in 903; it moved to Hyde outside the N gate of the city (see below) c 1110. To the W lay the Royal Palace. Of all this complex nothing is visible above ground, though the plan of the Old Minster has been marked out.

The present cathedral was begun by Bishop Walkelin in 1079 and consecrated in 1093. This superb Norman building was altered and extended by Bishop Godfrey de Lucy (1189–1204) in the Early English style. Bishop Edington (1346–66) rebuilt the W front and began the transformation of the nave from Norman to Perpendicular. The task was continued by the great William of Wykeham (pronounced 'Wickam'; 1367–1404)—architect, statesman and founder of Winchester College and New College, Oxford—and finished by Bishop Waynflete (1447–86). In 1905–12 Sir T.G. Jackson and Sir Francis Low used concrete to underpin the foundations, which the original builders had not carried down to sufficiently firm ground.

The core of the *Nave*, with its thick walls, bold vaulting and massive piers, is Walkelin's Norman work. Edington rebuilt the two W bays on the N side and the W bay on the S side, and Wykeham transformed the remainder, including the arcades, in the Perpendicular style. The ceiling bosses of the magnificent lierne vault include the arms of Edington and Wykeham. Against the W wall are statues of James I and Charles I by Hubert Le Sueur. In the W end of the N aisle is a stone Cantoria, or minstrels' gallery, where silverware from the treasury is displayed. On the wall of this aisle are a brass tablet and window to Jane Austen, buried beneath the pavement at this spot. In the next bay stands the 12C *font, one of only seven fonts in England of black Tournai marble, with rich carvings of Belgian workmanship. In the S arcade of the nave opposite Jane Austen's memorial is *Wykeham's Chantry, one of the cathedral's unrivalled series of chantries reflecting the development of architecture from 1366 to 1555. Edington's Chantry stands further E in the same arcade. Opposite is the Jacobean pulpit.

The *Transepts* remain much as Walkelin left them (1079–98), showing the vast scale of his design, except for later Norman rebuilding after the fall of the central tower in 1107. In the N transept the 12C Chapel of the Holy Sepulchre has *wall paintings and the W aisle, the Epiphany Chapel, has windows by Burne-Jones. In the S transept is the Venerable Chapel, with elaborate ironwork, and Prior Silkstede's Chapel (1524), with Izaak Walton's grave and a famous modern window (1914) in his memory. The S choir aisle is entered through a 12C iron *grille which may come from St Swithun's shrine (see below).

The *Choir* has magnificent *stalls (1305–10) with vigorous misericords, the oldest surviving cathedral stalls in England except for some fragments at Rochester. The desks and stools of the upper tier date from 1540. The pulpit was given by Prior Silkstede (c 1520); its carved skeins of silk make a rebus on his name. Under the tower is the marble tomb traditionally thought to be that of William Rufus. The piers, arches and clerestory of the Presbytery, prolonging the choir to the E, were rebuilt early in the 14C. Bishop Fox (1501–28) rebuilt the outer walls of its aisles, inserted the tracery of the clerestory and W window, and added the wooden lierne vault with superb bosses. He also added the screens between presbytery and aisles, which now bear six elaborate mortuary chests (four of 1525, two copied in 1661) made to contain the bones of Egbert, Canute and other pre-Conquest monarchs. The great reredos, almost certainly dating from c 1480, was mutilated at the Reformation but repaired in the 19C. The spandrels of the doors still have original work. On the E side of the reredos is the Feretory, a place for the 'feretra' or shrine for saints' relics. To its N is the Chantry of Bishop Gardiner (1555) and to its S the Chantry of Bishop Fox (1528), with a remarkable memento mori.

The large *Retrochoir* by Bishop Lucy (1189–1204) is, with the Chapel of the Holy Sepulchre, the earliest Gothic work in the building. (Except for the choir of Lincoln Cathedral, it may be the earliest pure Gothic work in England.) St Swithun's shrine stood in its centre; a new shrine was placed here in 1962. On the feretory wall at the W end are nine exquisite niches and below is the entrance to the 'Holy Hole', or vault. On either side of the retrochoir are (N) the Chantry of Bishop Waynflete (1486) and (S) the Chantry of Cardinal Beaufort (1447). The late 12C Chapel of the Guardian Angels (N) has painted *bosses of c 1240 in the roof and the effigy of Richard Weston, Earl of Portland (d. 1635), a masterpiece attributed to Francesco Fanelli. In the Lady Chapel, extended in the 15C, are late 15C woodwork and wall paintings, as well as the chair used by Mary Tudor at her wedding to Philip II of Spain in 1554. The chapel to the S, fitted up as a chantry by Bishop Langton (1501), has fine woodwork.

The impressive *Crypt* (subject to flooding and open only in the dry summer months), entered from the N transept, is in three parts. The first two are Norman, of the same date and character as the transepts. In the first and larger, under the high altar, is a well which would have been outside the original Saxon church and was probably the ancient Holy Well. The rectangular E crypt below the Lady Chapel is Early English (1189–1204).

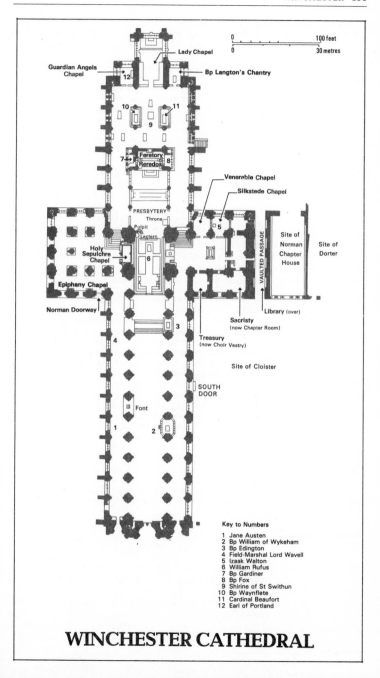

WINCHESTER CATHEDRAL

Lady Chapel

Guardian Angels Chapel

Bp Langton's Chantry

Venerable Chapel

Silkstede Chapel

Feretory
Reredos

PRESBYTERY

Throne
Pulpit
Lectern

Holy Sepulchre Chapel

Epiphany Chapel

Norman Doorway

Library (over)

Site of Norman Chapter House

Site of Dorter

VAULTED PASSAGE

Sacristy (now Chapter Room)

Treasury (now Choir Vestry)

Site of Cloister

SOUTH DOOR

Font

Key to Numbers

1 Jane Austen
2 Bp William of Wykeham
3 Bp Edington
4 Field-Marshal Lord Wavell
5 Izaak Walton
6 William Rufus
7 Bp Gardiner
8 Bp Fox
9 Shrine of St Swithun
10 Bp Waynflete
11 Cardinal Beaufort
12 Earl of Portland

0 ———— 100 feet
0 ———— 30 metres

Over the passage between the S transept and the Norman arches of the old Chapter House is the *Library* (12C, reconstructed in 1668), containing 4000 printed books and some rare manuscripts. Its chief treasure is the 12C *Winchester Bible, a magnificent illuminated Vulgate.

The Close is reached from the SW corner of the nave via the *Slype*, a passage made in 1636 to replace the right of way through the cathedral. The large and beautiful *Close* itself is partly surrounded by the ancient monastery walls. The Norman *arcade of the demolished Chapter House links the S transept to the *Deanery*, approached by a vestibule of three arches (c 1225–50). The 14C *Pilgrims' Hall* (open), with an early hammerbeam roof, stands next to the main building of the *Pilgrims' School* (1687), where the choristers' classrooms occupy the 16C Priory stables. Through the Close Gate nearby is the 13C *King's Gate*; over it is the church of *St Swithun* (rebuilt in the 16C).

Kingsgate St. is lined with old houses, mostly belonging to the College. On 9 is a tablet to the composer Samuel Sebastian Wesley, cathedral organist in 1849–64.

In College St. is the house where Jane Austen died (plaque). Further on is the great gateway (1394–97) of ***Winchester College** or *St Mary's College*, founded by William of Wykeham in 1382 and the model for the great public schools of England. The first stone of the chapel was laid in 1387 and the buildings were occupied in 1394. The school is allied with New College, Oxford, founded by Wykeham in 1379. Besides the 70 foundation scholars, who live in college, there are about 570 'commoners' in boarding houses.

The chapel, war memorial cloister and, during term, the old cloisters and chantry are open. Guided tours are available in summer.

To the left of Outer Court are the *Warden's Lodgings*, with a frontage of 1833. Within the Middle Gate is Chamber Court. The *Chapel* here still has its original fan-tracery ceiling of wood (by Hugh Herland, who designed the roof of Westminster Hall) and some original *glass portraying Richard II (now in the late 15C S chapel). The *Dining Hall* has a fine oak roof, renewed in 1819. In the passage to the *Kitchen* is a curious figure of the 'Trusty Servant', placed here in the 16C and repainted in 1809; in the *Beer Cellar* further along the passage is a *Treasury*. In the middle of Wykeham's *Cloisters* is *Fromond's Chantry* (1420–45), with an E window incorporating seven figures from the original glass of the chapel. Lord Wavell (1883–1950) is buried in the garth, while the cloister is carved with the names of Bishop Ken (1656) and other famous Wykehamists. On the wall of '*School*' (1683–87; not shown during term), sometimes ascribed to Wren, is the inscription 'aut disce, aut discede, manet sors tertia caedia' ('learn, leave, or be licked'). To the E, beyond the mill stream, is the *New Hall* (1958–60; P. Shepheard), lined with the oak panelling and screen (1680–82) from the chapel. Sir Herbert Baker's *War Memorial Cloister*, entered from Kingsgate St., commemorates over 500 Wykehamists who died in 1914–18 and 270 who died in 1939–45. Victorian buildings include the quincentenary memorial (1897; Basil Champneys), formerly a theatre, and a gymnasium and sanatorium now converted into a theatre and art school. The *College Sickhouse* dates from 1656.

Wykehamists include Sir Henry Wotton, Sir Thomas Browne, the dramatist Thomas Otway, Sydney Smith, Trollope, Dr Arnold and his son Matthew, Lord Wavell, Sir William Empson, Hugh Gaitskell, Richard Crossman and Anthony Storr.

On the left (N) side of College St. are the ruins of *Wolvesey Castle* (EH, summer season), a bishop's palace begun by William of Gifford (c 1110) and developed in its fullest form by Henry de Blois (1129–71). Of the medieval building, only the Perpendicular chapel survives, though excavation has shown that four ranges, including two great halls, enclosed a central courtyard. A wing of the neighbouring *Palace*, rebuilt by Sir Thomas Fitch for Bishop Morley in 1684, is now the bishop's residence; the rest was pulled down in 1800.

A path leading S from College Walk along the Itchen makes a pleasant route to the Hospital of St Cross (see below).

From the end of College St. another path goes between the City Wall and the river back to City Bridge (see above). Beyond the bridge, at the corner of Chesil St., is a mid 15C house claiming to be the oldest in Winchester. The 13–14C church of *St Peter* on Chesil St. has been converted into a theatre. There are good views from *St Giles Hill* to the E. *St John's Church*, ¼m N, dates from various periods between the 12C and the 16C and has aisles wider than its nave. It contains 13C wall paintings.

The main course of the walking tour is resumed at the Butter Cross, from which High St. climbs towards the West Gate. It passes, on the left, *God Begot House*, a Tudor building which has become a teashop and delicatessen. On the left is the *Old Guildhall* of 1713, now a bank, with the curfew bell-tower and a clock commemorating the Treaty of Utrecht. The *West Gate* (open) is a good specimen of medieval military architecture, the archway being 13C and the upper part c 1380. It houses a small museum with standard weights and measures, and a painted Tudor ceiling from Winchester College.

Castle Hill leads left to the *Great Hall* (open) of the castle begun by William the Conqueror and enlarged and altered by Henry III in 1222–36. Sir Walter Raleigh was tried here in 1603 beneath its clustered columns of Purbeck marble and beautiful two-light windows. At the W end, above the remains of the royal dais, hangs the romantically named 'Round Table of King Arthur', 18ft in diameter, known to have been here in 1400. It was painted in 1522 for the Emperor Charles V's visit and repainted in 1789. Next to the Great Hall rise the Law Courts; to the N are the County Council buildings (1959–60).

The *Peninsula Barracks* in Romsey Rd houses museums of the Light Infantry, the Royal Hussars, the Royal Greenjackets and the Gurkhas. Jewry St. and its prolongation as Hyde St., with some fine 17C houses, lead N for ½m to the gatehouse which is all that remains of *Hyde Abbey*. This foundation, originally known as the New Minster (see the cathedral above), moved here c 1110. The monks brought Alfred's body with them, but its final resting place is not known with certainty. Nearby *St Bartholomew's Church* has some Norman fragments.

Southgate St., opposite Jewry St., still has an 18C appearance. *Serle's House* (c 1732) is now the *Royal Hampshire Regiment Museum*. In St Cross Rd about 1m further S is the *Hospital of St Cross (open), though a more pleasant approach, suggested above, comes along the river from College Walk.

The hospital was founded by Bishop Henry de Blois for 13 poor brethren in 1136. Cardinal Beaufort added a second foundation, of 'Noble Poverty', in 1446. The brethren of the first foundation wear a black gown with a Jerusalem cross, while the others have a red gown bearing a cardinal's hat. The outer court leads to the *Beaufort Tower*, where the 'Wayfarer's Dole' of bread and ale is still supplied on request. In the inner court are the *Brethren's Houses* (c 1445), the *Refectory*, the *Kitchen*, the *Master's House*, the *Infirmary* and the *Church*, a fine example of its period (1136–c 1250). The unusual lectern dates from 1510, and in front of the altar is a brass of the Master of the Hospital (1410). The triptych in the S chapel is attributed to Mabuse (d. c 1533). Trollope's 'The Warden' undoubtedly refers to St Cross.

Across the river to the E rises *St Catherine's Hill* (255ft), commanding a fine view. At the top are a clump of trees, an Iron Age fort, the foundations of a medieval chapel and a 'mizmaze' cut in the turf. *Chilcomb*, in the valley 1m to the NE, has a small, very early Norman church. *Littleton*, off A272 2½m NW, has *Flowerdown Barrows* from a large Bronze Age burial site (EH).

FROM WINCHESTER TO NEWBURY, 25m on A34. At (3m) *Worthy Down* the route bears right. *Crawley*, 2m W, is said to be the 'Queen's Crawley' of 'Vanity Fair'. 11m: *Tufton*, on a charming reach of the Test ½m W of A34, has an 11–12C church with a 15C mural of St Christopher. At (12m) *Whitchurch* the church has an inscribed Saxon headstone and a 17C Ten Commandments board.

At Clap Gate A34 crosses the Roman Portway. Beyond (15m) *Litchfield* are the tumuli known as the *Seven Barrows* and *Beacon Hill* (858ft), both to the left. The 5th Earl of Carnarvon (1866–1923), who with Howard Carter discovered the tomb of Tutankhamen, is buried on top of Beacon Hill. 19m: *Highclere Castle* (open), the seat of the Carnarvon family, was remodelled in the Gothic style by Charles Barry in 1842. The large park was landscaped in the 18C but much altered by Victorian planting. At (20m; right) *Burghclere* the Sandham Memorial Chapel (NT), built as a World War I memorial, has murals by Stanley Spencer (1927–32). 25m: *Newbury*, see Route 20.

FROM WINCHESTER TO FAREHAM, 20m. A333 leads to (3½m) *Twyford*, where Benjamin Franklin wrote part of his autobiography. The building of the motorway over the beautiful Down caused much controversy. Beyond the village A335 branches right on an alternative route to (9m) Southampton via (3½m) *Eastleigh* (53,100 inhabitants; TI), a 19C railway town with heavy industries and Southampton's airport. A333 continues to (11½m) *Bishop's Waltham*, with the ruins of a moated palace built by Bishop Henry de Blois of Winchester in c 1135 and extended in the 15C (EH, all year). William of Wykeham died here in 1404. *Botley*, 4m SW, was Cobbett's home in 1805–17. For (16½m) *Wickham*, where the way joins A32, see the route from Chawton to Fareham above. 20m: *Fareham*, see Route 13A.

FROM WINCHESTER TO SOUTHAMPTON VIA ROMSEY, 17½m on A3090, A31 and A3057. A3090 heads SW from Winchester, with Pitt Down rising to the right. The churchyard at (5m) *Hursley* has the grave of John Keble (1792–1866), leader of the Oxford Movement and vicar of Hursley for about 30 years. He rebuilt the church from the proceeds of 'The Christian Year'; it has stained glass whose design was supervised by William Butterfield. Merdon Manor, no longer standing, was the home of Richard Cromwell (d. 1712), buried in the church with several members of his family. Beyond the village A3090 joins A31. 8m: *Ampfield* has the *Sir Harold Hillier Gardens and Arboretum* (open), begun by the nurseryman in 1953, with 160 acres of hardy plants.

10m: **Romsey** (12,900 inhabitants; TI), a small town on the Test, is famous for its *Abbey Church. A nunnery was first founded here in 907 by Edward the Elder for his daughter, St Elfleda. Remains of a later Saxon church (c 1000) have been discovered beneath the floor of the present building and can be seen through a trapdoor in the N transept. The church that survives is mainly Norman, built from 1120 onwards, with only a few later additions: the Early English bays (1230–50) at the W end of the nave, and the two 14C E windows. Indeed, Romsey keeps the character of a Norman conventual church more completely than any other building of equal size in England. The choir aisles end in apses (squared externally); the E sides of the transepts are adjoined by circular chapels. The N aisle and transept were long used as the parish church, and the reredos has paintings on wood of the Resurrection and saints (c 1500). Monuments in the S transept include a simple floor slab to Earl Mountbatten of Burma (1900–79) and an elaborate memorial of the 1650s to John St Barbe and his wife. The beautiful mouldings and original Norman triforium and clerestory of the choir are worth special attention. At the E end of the S choir aisle is a carved Saxon crucifix (c 940). Outside the S or Abbess's Door is another Saxon crucifix, the famous *Romsey Rood, ascribed to the first half of the 11C. The foundations of the Lady Chapel can be seen beyond the E end.

The so-called *King John's Hunting Box*, just E of the abbey, is a small 13C hall house. In the market place are a wrought-iron sign bracket from which two of Cromwell's soldiers were hanged and a statue of Palmerston.

His home, *Broadlands* (open), lies just S of the town and the A31. It is popular with visitors mainly for its connection with Lord Mountbatten, profusely remembered in the exhibits, and with the Prince and Princess of Wales who, like the Queen and Prince Philip, started their honeymoon here. The building itself, dating from the 16C, was converted into a pleasant Georgian mansion in 1766 by Capability Brown, who also landscaped the grounds. The collection of paintings includes several Van Dycks.

Mottisfont, off A3057 4½m NW, has a church with a Norman chancel arch and 15C stained glass. Mottisfont Abbey (NT) is a mainly 18C house built in and around the nave and cloisters of a 12C Augustinian priory. Only the monks' cellarium and a drawing room decorated by Rex Whistler in 1938 are open. The river Test runs by the pleasant gardens, notable for the walled garden with its historic roses. Florence Nightingale (1820–1910) is buried at *East Wellow*, 3m W of Romsey. Embley House (now a school), on the way from the town, was her family home in winter in 1825–96.

From Romsey A3057 heads SE to (17½m) Southampton, passing the suburb of *Maybush*, headquarters of the Ordnance Survey, established in 1741 and moved to Southampton in 1841.

The direct route from Winchester to Southampton follows A333 S to join A33. 72m: *Otterbourne*, on A31 to the left, was the lifelong home of the novelist Charlotte M. Yonge (1823–1901), who is buried outside the church her father built. There is also a memorial to John Keble, who held this parish with Hursley (see above). Beyond (74½m) *Chandler's Ford* A33 goes through the leafy suburb of *Bassett* into Southampton.

80m: **SOUTHAMPTON** (204,400 inhabitants) stands at the head of Southampton Water, the estuary of the Test, on a peninsula bounded to the E by the river Itchen. This fine natural harbour has made it a great seaport, the starting-point for famous ventures like Henry V's French expedition, the emigration of the Pilgrim Fathers and the maiden voyage of the 'Titanic'. Of the history that goes with such events, Southampton still has important reminders—particularly the fine stretches of medieval city wall— though they are dispersed among modern development.

TI: Above Bar Shopping Precinct. **Railway Stations**: Central Station, Blechynden Terrace (W of Civic Centre). Several local stations, including Southampton Airport, are served by London trains and there are special trains to the docks for some liner sailings. **Ferry services**: to Cowes, Isle of Wight, and to Cherbourg. Local ferry between Town Quay, Ocean Village and Hythe Pier. Cruises around harbour from Ocean Village. **Airport**: Southampton Airport, Eastleigh (on A335 3½m N of the city centre). Flights to Alderney, Amsterdam, Brussels, Caen, Cherbourg, Edinburgh, Glasgow, Guernsey, Liverpool and Manchester. **Theatre**: Nuffield Theatre, University of Southampton. Concerts etc. in the Turner Sims Concert Hall, The University; The Guildhall, West Marlands Rd; and the Mayflower Theatre, Commercial Rd. **Annual Events**: International Boat Show in Mayflower Park (September). The Knighthood Contest, a bowling competition dating from 1776, is held every August at the Old Green in Platform Rd, which claims to be the oldest in the world (1299).

History. The Saxon town of Hamwich superseded the Roman Clausentum (now Bitterne) on the other side of the Itchen. Both already had overseas trade, and it is said that Canute administered the famous rebuke to his courtiers at Hamwich (though Bosham has a rival claim). After the Conquest Southampton's Continental trade became of great importance. By the 15C it was the chief centre of trade wth Mediterranean ports. Part of Richard Coeur de Lion's crusading fleet and the armies that conquered at Crécy and Agincourt sailed from Southampton. In the 20C it has continued to be a chief port of embarkation for troops on foreign service, notably for D-Day in 1944. The most serious of many hostile attacks was that of 1338, when a large French, Spanish, and Genoese fleet plundered the town. The Pilgrim Fathers initially sailed for America from Southampton in 1620 in the 'Speedwell' (which had brought some of them from Holland) and the 'Mayflower'. The rise of Portsmouth and a terrible visitation of the plague (1665) conspired with other causes to diminish Southampton's prosperity, but a new era of advance was ushered in by the creation of a spa and the Napoleonic wars. This was confirmed by the coming of the railway and the building of the docks in the 1840s, when Southampton replaced Falmouth as mail-packet station for the Mediterranean and, later, North America. The 'Titanic' set sail from here in 1912. In 1940–41 the town suffered heavily from air raids. In the 1930s it was in the forefront of flying-boat design and operation; more recently the hovercraft was invented here.

Natives, residents and visitors. Natives include Isaac Watts (1674–1748), writer of hymns; Charles Dibdin (1745–1814), composer of songs; Sir John Everett Millais (1829–96), painter; George Saintsbury (1845–1933), historian and critic; and Lord Jellicoe (1859–1935), naval commander. John Alden (1599–1686), the Pilgrim Father whom Longfellow made the hero of his poem 'The Courtship of Miles Standish', was an artisan here. Jane Austen lived here after her return from Bath in 1806. The American humorist 'Artemus Ward' (C.F. Browne) died here in 1867; and R.J. Mitchell worked here on the Schneider seaplanes which led to the Spitfire.

The **Civic Centre** (1932–39; E.B. Webber) has a tall clock tower that is Southampton's most distinctive landmark. The *City Art Gallery* in the N wing has a collection which can claim to be the finest in Southern England.

Though it spans six centuries, the collection is most notable for its 20C British art. The Camden Town Group is particularly well represented. There are also works by Paul Nash, Matthew Smith, Stanley Spencer and Graham Sutherland and, as a result of the policy of acquiring contemporary British art, by Gillian Ayres, Barry Flanagan, Richard Long, Lisa Milroy and Rachel Whiteread. The permanent displays are supplemented by a lively programme of temporary exhibitions.

N of the gallery stretches *West Park*, the first of several green spaces that are a pleasant feature of the city, with a statue of Isaac Watts. Lutyens's Cenotaph looks across the road to *East Park*, with a memorial to the engineers killed in the 'Titanic' (1912). The lawns continue S and E with *Palmerston Park*, *Houndwell Park* and *Hoglands Park*.

The unimaginatively rebuilt Above Bar St. leads S from the Civic Centre. At the head of the High St. stands *Bargate, the old N gate of the city and the most elaborate city gate to survive in England. The N side still has its 13C drum towers, as well as the 15C projection with machiolated parapet. This is enlivened by 17C armorial decorations and guarded by leaden lions of 1743. The battlemented S front has three 13C arches. The taller flanking arches were pierced in 1764 and 1774. The statue above is of George III. The windows were gothicised in 1865, after the Guildhall (c 1400) on the upper floor had been made a court of justice.

Bargate now stands isolated from the old city walls (described later), warning visitors what 20C development has done to Southampton's High St. A few good buildings do survive, however, beginning (on the E side) with the *Star* and the bow-windowed *Dolphin*, rebuilt as Georgian coaching inns but both 15C in origin.

To the right of the High St. lies St Michael's Square, originally the centre of the Norman-French quarter. *St Michael* is the only medieval parish church to survive in the city, though it was altered by Francis Goodwin in 1828–29. The low central tower rests on early Norman arches but bears a disproportionately tall 18C spire. The 12C font of black Tournai marble is like the ones at Winchester Cathedral and East Meon. The screens are good modern ironwork and the Lady Chapel has a 14C Flemish brass lectern from the bombed church of Holy Rood (see below). *Tudor House* (open), a handsome timber-framed house with a banqueting hall on the W side of the square, is now a period museum. In the garden, by the ramparts of the city wall, is a rare example of a Norman merchant's house, built c 1150–75 and popularly known as *King John's House*. In the fine Bugle St., leading S, is the *Duke of Wellington Inn*, rebuilt c 1490 on 12C foundations and admirably restored. Further S is the Wool House, described later in the walking tour.

Beyond the Dolphin in High St., the ruined *Holy Rood* church has been made a memorial to men of the Merchant Navy. Philip II of Spain heard his first mass in England here in 1554 before riding to his wedding at Winchester.

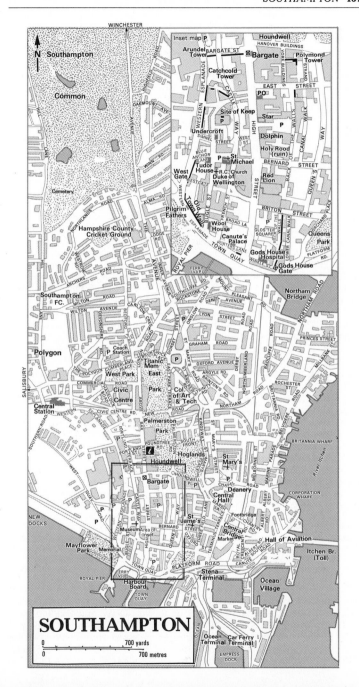

WINCHESTER

N
Southampton

Common

Cemetery

Inset map

Hampshire County
Cricket Ground

Southampton
F.C.

Polygon

West Park

Civic
Centre

Central
Station

NEW
DOCKS

Mayflower
Park

Coach
Station

Titanic
Mem
East
Park

Col.
of Art
& Tech

Palmerston
Park

Poundtree

Houndwell

Bargate

Museum
Area of
Inset

Memorial

Harbour
Board

ROYAL PIER
FERRY
(V.I.P)
TOWN QUAY

Houndwell
HANOVER BUILDINGS

Arundel
Tower
BARGATE ST
Bargate

Catchcold
Tower

Polymond
Tower

EAST
STREET

PO

Site of Keep

Star

Undercroft

Dolphin

Holy Rood
(ruin)

West
Gate

Tudor
House
R.C. Church
Duke of
Wellington

St.
Michael

Red
Lion

BERNARD
STREET

Pilgrim
Fathers

BRITON
STREET

Old
Town
Wall

Wool
House

Canute's
Palace

Queens
Park

Gods House
Hospital

TOWN QUAY

Gods House
Gate

Northam
Bridge

PRINCES STREET

GRAHAM
ROAD

OXFORD AVENUE

ROCHESTER
ROAD

BRITANNIA WHARF

St
Mary's

Deanery

Central
Hall

St
James's

BRITANNIA WHARF

CORPORATION
WHARF

River Itchen

Central
Bridge

Market

Footbridge

Hall of Aviation

Itchen Br.
(Toll)

Stena
Terminal

Ocean
Village

PLATFORM ROAD

Ocean Car Ferry
Terminal Terminal

EMPRESS
DOCK

SOUTHAMPTON

| 0 | | 700 yards |
| 0 | | 700 metres |

Further S in Lower High St. is the *Red Lion*, with a Norman cellar and 'King Henry V's courtroom'. Further on, in Porter's Lane to the right, are the remains of a long Norman house misleadingly known as *Canute's Palace*. To the left in Winkle St. stand *God's House and the Hospice of St Julian*, founded in the 12C, granted to The Queen's College, Oxford in 1343 and now housing four 'brothers' and four 'sisters' in cottages rebuilt in 1861.

The drastically restored chapel was assigned to Walloon refugees in 1567 and still has a congregation using the Anglican service in French. It contains the remains of Lord Scrope, Sir Thomas Grey and Richard, Earl of Cambridge, executed for treason outside Bargate in 1415 (see Shakespeare's 'Henry V', II, ii). Against the S wall is a strange memorial to the first Walloon minister (1569).

At the SE angle of the walls beyond are *God's House Tower* and *God's House Gateway*. The early 15C tower is now an excellent *Museum of Archaeology* with local prehistoric, Roman, Saxon and medieval finds, and pottery of later periods.

The gateway leads to Town Quay, departure point of ferries for Cowes and for Ocean Village and Hythe. Platform Rd, to the left, skirts *Queen's Park* to reach Dockgate 4, departure point of the Cherbourg ferry. Opened in 1842, the docks at the lower end of the town's peninsular are less busy now than in their first century of traffic, though ocean-going liners like the QEII still berth here. The harbour enjoys the advantage of a double tide, first via the Solent and then, two hours later, via Spithead. The old Princess Alexandra Dock has been redeveloped as *Ocean Village*, a shopping centre and 450-berth marina, with the 'S.S. Shieldhall', an old steam cargo vessel (open). There are cruises round the harbour in summer, and the local ferries connects Ocean Village with Town Quay and Hythe.

Canute Rd continues E to the Itchen Bridge, passing Albert Rd South with the *Southampton Hall of Aviation* (open). Its display includes the Sandringham Flying Boat and an exhibit tracing the work of R.J. Mitchell, designer of the Schneider seaplanes and the Spitfire.

To the W, Town Quay passes the entrance to French St., preserving a 13C merchant's house (EH, all year). The *Wool House*, further W, is a fine 14C warehouse later used as a jail for prisoners of the Napoleonic wars. It still has its original Spanish chestnut roof and has been restored as a maritime museum. Exhibits include model ships carved in bone by French prisoners. Beyond are the *Royal Pier* and *Mayflower Park*. On Western Esplanade, opposite, stands the *Pilgrim Fathers' Memorial* (1913) commemorating the sailing of the 'Mayflower' on 15 August 1620.

Western Esplanade makes a good starting-point for a tour of the surviving stretches of *Walls.

Dating from Norman times but much altered in later centuries, they formed a circuit of about 1¼m enclosing and defending the old town. About 25–30ft high, they were strengthened at intervals by towers and had seven principal gates. The N and E sides were defended by a double moat, while the S and W sides looked over the tidal estuary of the Test, since largely reclaimed at these points. The W side is the best preserved.

A flight of steps leads to a rampart walk, soon blocked by the 17C *Guard Room* (in fact, probably a merchant's storehouse). This stands next to the 14C *West Gate*, once giving directly on to West Quay, embarkation point for the Pilgrim Fathers in 1620 and probably also for Henry V's army in 1415. To the N begin the external arcades, recessed arches with holes for showering missiles on attackers, added to the defences after the French raid of 1338. The conspicuous gunports in the walls of *King John's House* (see Tudor House above) are reputedly the earliest of their kind in Britain. A medieval postern opens into Blue Anchor Lane. Simnel St has an early 14C *Undercroft*. To the N are the *Castle Watergate* and the *Castle Vault* (open for guided tours only; contact TI). A block of flats marks the site of the castle, whose bailey wall was part of the town defences. The Forty Steps mount to the rampart walk between the 15C *Catchcold Tower* and the *Arundel* (or *Windwhistle*) *Tower* at the NW corner.

Bargate St. follows the N course of the town moat, though only fragments of wall survive and the magnificent Bargate stands by itself The ruined *Polymond Tower* marks the NE corner of the walls. The line of the E wall, with a few remains, is marked by the street named Back of the Walls, leading S to God's House Tower and God's House Gate.

London Rd and The Avenue lead N to *Southampton Common*, a natural park of 350 acres, with a cemetery and the County Cricket Ground. At *Highfield*, about 1m E of the Common, is the *University of Southampton*. An institute opened here in 1862 as the result of a bequest from a local wine merchant. It was incorporated as a university college in 1902 and received its charter as a university in 1952. There are now about 5000 students, and an associated School of Navigation (at Warsash, see below). The most striking building is the copper-covered *Nuffield Theatre* (1961; Sir Basil Spence) used for both lectures and drama.

Facing Southampton Water 7m SE of the city centre is *Netley Abbey (EH, summer season), a Cistercian foundation of 1239 originally occupied by monks from Beaulieu. The picturesque ruins include the church, cloisters, chapter house and some domestic buildings. *Netley Castle*, built in the 16C to guard the Solent, was radically transformed in the 19C. *Hamble*, 1½m further SE, a yachting centre on the W side of the Hamble estuary, has a good Norman and Early English church. On the E side of the estuary is *Warsash*.

The tip of land reaching out into Southampton Water from the opposite shore is occupied by *Calshot Castle*, one of Henry VIII's coastal defences (EH, summer season). 12m from Southampton, it is reached by following A326 past (9½m) *Fawley*, with its oil refinery, and B3053.

From *Portsmouth* to Southampton, see Route 13A.

B. Via Basingstoke and Winchester

Directions. Total distance 75m. M3 provides a quick alternative way as far as Winchester. A4, A30 to (18m) Staines (bypassed). A30 to (26½m) Bagshot (bypassed), (29m) **Camberley** (bypassed) and (46m) **Basingstoke** (bypassed). A30, A33 to (63m) **Winchester** (bypassed), see Route 14A. A333, A33 to (75m) **Southampton**, see Route 14A.

A4 and then A30 lead W from London. 18m: *Staines* is bypassed. From the first roundabout on the bypass M25 leads S to M3. From the second, A308 leads NW past Runnymede to Windsor (Route 49A) and another road leads into the centre of (20m) **Egham**. The early 19C church of *St John the Baptist* preserves the remarkable monuments of Sir John Denham (d. 1638) and his two wives; the boy with the second Lady Denham grew up to be the poet Sir John Denham (1615–69). *Great Fosters*, an Elizabethan mansion further S, is now a hotel. On A30 beyond Egham stands (21m) *Royal Holloway College*, a wonderfully extravagant brick building of 1879–87 by W.H. Crossland. It was endowed by Thomas Holloway, who made his fortune from Holloway's Pills, as a college for women and later incorporated into the University of London. The picture gallery (open by appointment only) has a good collection of 19C art. 22m: *Virginia Water*, an artificial lake

1½m long, laid out in 1746 by Paul Sandby for the Duke of Cumberland, forms the S boundary of Windsor Great Park. The ruined colonnade was brought by George IV from Lepcis Magna, near Tripoli.

FROM VIRGINIA WATER TO READING, 18½m on A329. 3½m: **Ascot** is the scene of the most fashionable race meeting of the year, with the Gold Cup in June. 5m: *Bracknell* (48,800 inhabitants; TI) has the headquarters of the Meteorological Office. 10½m: *Wokingham* (24,300 inhabitants), bypassed to the N by A329(M), has the picturesque Lucas Almshouses of 1665. *Finchampstead Ridges* (60 acres; NT), 4m S, give a magnificent view to the south. 18½m: *Reading*, see Route 20.

23m: *Sunningdale*, famous for its golf course, is a residential district among fir and beech woods in the heart of the affluent 'stockbroker belt'. 26½m: *Bagshot* is bypassed.

To the S are: *Bisley* (3½m) with the camp and ranges where the National Rifle Association meets in July; *Brookwood* (5½m) and the London Necropolis, a huge cemetery with a memorial (1958) to the Commonwealth forces of World War II; and *Pirbright* (6½m), with the grave of Sir Henry Morton Stanley (1841–1904), the journalist and explorer famous for his meeting with Livingstone.

From A30 beyond Bagshot A325 leads SW to (8½m) *Aldershot* (Route 14A). It passes (3m) *Frimley*, where the American humorist Bret Harte (1839–1902) is buried in the churchyard. 7m: *Farnborough* (45,500 inhabitants) is home of the Royal Aircraft Establishment. The Farnborough International Exhibition and Flying Display is held here every two years in the first week of September. Near the station is the church built in 1887 by the Empress Eugénie (1826–1920) as a mausoleum for her husband Napoleon III, their son the Prince Imperial and herself. The adjoining abbey is occupied by Benedictines from Prinknash. On the other side of the railway is Farnborough Hill, now a convent, where the Empress died.

29m: **Camberley** (52,000 inhabitants with Frimley) lies in a heathy district largely devoted to military activities. On the right of A30 is the Royal Military Academy, Sandhurst for army officers, in beautiful grounds with a lake.

Founded in 1799 as the Royal Military College, it was merged in 1946 with the Royal Military Academy, Woolwich. The Mons Officer Cadet School was also moved here from Aldershot. The Indian Army Room in the main building contains uniforms, portraits, and medals. The *War Memorial Chapel* (1922) commemorates 4000 former cadets who fell in World War I, and a roll of honour is dedicated to 19,781 officers of the Commonwealth who fell between 1939–46. The Victory Memorial from Lüneburg Heath was brought to Sandhurst in 1958. About 2m further N is *Crowthorne*, with the public school of *Wellington College*, established in 1853, primarily for the sons of deceased officers. Nearby is *Broadmoor*, an institution for the criminally insane.

A30 crosses the Blackwater into Hampshire. 33½m: *Blackbushe Airport* is 3m N of *Fleet* (26,000 inhabitants; TI). Fleet Pond (130 acres) once provided fish for the monks of Winchester. Beyond (36m) *Hartley Wintney* B3016 leads left to *Winchfield* (1¾m), with a beautiful little church, partly robust Norman.

2m S of Winchfield is **Odiham**, with a fine High St. and the old stocks and whipping-post near the church. The town stands on the Basingstoke Canal, which runs E and N to connect with the Wey and the Thames at Weybridge. Substantial stretches of the waterway have been reclaimed, and Odiham makes a good starting-point for walks along the banks, as well as for public and charter cruises. *Odiham Castle*, 1m NW, has only the shell of its 13C keep. David II of Scotland was held here after the Battle of Neville's Cross in 1346. About 2m N of Hartley Wintney stands *Bramshill House* (now the Police Staff College, not open), a brick mansion (1612) with good gardens. It lies in the parish of *Eversley*, where Charles Kingsley was curate and then rector from 1842 until his death in 1875; he is buried in the churchyard, 1½ NE. *West Green House*, N of A30 beyond Hartley Wintney, is a small 18C building with a walled garden (NT; opening arrangements under review).

40m: *Hook* has a brick church of 1937–38 by Sir Edward Maufe. A30 next passes, on the left at 42m, the tiny Norman church of *Nately Scures* and, on the right at 43½m, the village of *Basing* (or *Old Basing*). Its large Perpendicular church has 16C monuments to the Paulet family. *Basing House* (open) was built by Sir William Paulet, 1st Marquess of Winchester (d. 1572), on the site of an earlier castle. During the Civil War it resisted the Parliamentarians for two years, finally yielding to Cromwell himself in 1645, when Inigo Jones was among the prisoners taken. Little remains intact except a gatehouse, dovecote and tithe barn. There is an exhibition showing the history of the site. A30 bypasses the centre of Basingstoke.

46m: **Basingstoke** (TI), a London 'overspill' town, has grown from a population of 25,000 in the 1960s to 67,400. *St Michael's* is a good 16C town church. The Old Town Hall in Market Place houses the *Willis Museum and Art Gallery*, with local collections and touring exhibits. In the old graveyard near the station are the ruins of the *Holy Ghost Chapel*, 13C and 16C.

*The Vyne (NT), off A340 4m N, is a splendid house with distinguished work of several periods. It was built by Lord Sandys in c 1520 and twice altered on a major scale, first by John Webb in c 1655 and then during the ownership (1754–76) of John Chute, friend to Horace Walpole. Externally, the brick entrance front belongs to the original Tudor mansion; the window surrounds, large N portico and garden pavilion are Webb's work. Inside, the most interesting features are the Palladian staircase and the Tudor chapel with original stalls and Flemish glass and tiles. There are some good chimneypieces by Webb, and the house is handsomely furnished throughout.

Upton Grey, 6m SE of Basingstoke, has a manor house with gardens (limited opening) designed by Gertrude Jekyll.

An alternative route to (23m) Winchester follows B3046 S, passing through (9m) *Chilton Candover*, with the crypt of a demolished Norman church. For (10m) *Northington*, (13m) *Old Alresford* and (14m) *New Alresford*, where A31 is followed W, see Route 14A.

The main route follows A30 and A33. Beyond (61m) *King's Worthy* the Winchester bypass leads left. *Headbourne Worthy* (right) has important Saxon work in its church, particularly a fine but damaged *rood. For (63m) **Winchester** and the continuation of the route to (75m) **Southampton**, see Route 14A.

15

Isle of Wight

Walkers need the OS Outdoor Leisure map (2½in to 1m).

The **Isle of Wight** (120,000 inhabitants) lies off the Hampshire coast opposite Southampton and Portsmouth. Separated from the mainland by the straits of the Solent on the NW and Spithead on the NE, it is shaped like an irregular lozenge about 23m wide and about 13m from N to S. Inside this small compass the scenery is both beautiful and impressively varied. The landscape of the north, for the most part low-lying and often wooded, yields to a ridge of chalk downs running across the centre of the island. This is bisected by the river Medina as it flows past Newport, the island's capital, from the wide and undulating plains in the south. The scenery grows more dramatic near the southern fringes, achieving a series of wonderful geological surprises on the coastline: the distinctive Needles and the coloured sandstone of Alum Bay in the west, the Undercliff near the southern tip and the heights of Culver Cliff in the east. Most of this fine landscape has been well preserved. The NT owns more than 3000 acres and protects another 1600. Footpaths and nature trails abound. Hardy walkers can follow the coastline almost continuously for its circuit of about 65 miles.

This natural beauty, together with the mild climate and the presence of several well-established resorts, attracts many visitors, and the island gets crowded during the summer.

History. The Isle of Wight was conquered without difficulty in AD 43 by the Romans, who called it Vectis, or Ictis, and after 449 it seems to have been settled by the Jutes. Relics of both occupations have been found. Annexed to Wessex in 661 and converted to Christianity during the next half century, the island had become the headquarters of the Danes by the end of the 10C. William the Conqueror bestowed the lordship of the island on William Fitz-Osbern, from whom it passed to the Earls of Devon. The Crown bought the lordship back in 1293 and ruled for the next several centuries by locally appointed wardens and English peers with hereditary rights. The island was still vulnerable to attack, however, and the most serious of several French raids occurred in 1377 and 1545. Henry VII put the management of the island in the hands of a Captain, a title later changed to Governor. Charles I was imprisoned here in 1647–48, for most of the time at Carisbrooke Castle.

The 19C brought happier royal connections. The island's popularity with the fashionable began during the Regency, when the Prince's patronage of the yacht club gave it the title 'Royal', and was confirmed by Queen Victoria's decision to move her summer residence from Brighton to Osborne House. Ryde had already achieved some status as a resort by the 1820s, and was followed in the 1840s and 1850s by Ventnor, Sandown and Shanklin. Such developments brought distinguished Victorians here: Tennyson, the photographer Julia Margaret Cameron and the family which produced the poet Swinburne were residents, while Dickens and the painter G.F. Watts and his wife Ellen Terry were among the visitors.

Long administratively included in Hampshire, the island is now a county in itself.

Ferry services. From Portsmouth to Ryde or Fishbourne (3m W of Ryde): passenger ferry from Portsmouth Harbour Station to Ryde; car ferry from Gunwharf Road, Old Portsmouth, to Fishbourne; hovercraft from Clarence Pier, Southsea, to Ryde. From Southampton to Cowes: car ferry and hydrofoil. From Lymington to Yarmouth: car ferry. Booking is advisable on all these routes during the summer.

The usual port of entry is **Ryde** (24,700 inhabitants with Seaview and St Helens), on a hillside overlooking Spithead.

TI: Western Esplanade. **Railway Stations**: Pier Head, Western Esplanade and St John's Rd. **Bus Station**: Western Esplanade. **Amusements**: Variety shows, concerts, etc. In Esplanade Pavilion; summer concerts in the Bandstand Enclosure. **Annual events**: Yacht racing at Fishbourne and Seaview in June, July and August.

The *Pier*, nearly ½m long, gives a fine view of Spithead and its shipping. The town still has many Regency and Victorian buildings to remind the visitor of its first development as a resort in the 19C. The most conspicuous of several churches is *All Saints'* (1868–72) by Gilbert Scott, with a tall steeple added later.

At *Binstead*, off A3054 1m W, the church was mainly rebuilt in the 19C but keeps its Early English chancel. The fine wood panelling comes from the chapel at Winchester College, and the carved altar panelling is late 16C Flemish work. The Norman doorway rebuilt as a gateway outside the church has a grotesquely carved beast. 1m further on are the scanty remains of *Quarr Abbey*, a Cistercian house founded by Baldwin de Redvers for Savigny monks in 1131. It took its name from the nearby quarries which supplied limestone for Winchester and Chichester cathedrals. The estate was sold to the Benedictines of Solesmes in 1907 and Dom Paul Bellot built a remarkable brick *church in 1911–12. *Fishbourne*, with the car ferry slip, is 3m further. It stands on the attractively wooded Wootton Creek; 1m beyond the opposite bank is *Wootton* church, with a Norman door.

2½m E of Ryde is the yachting village of *Seaview*, reached by the sea-wall and a footpath or by a toll road. 2m beyond is another sailing centre, *St Helens*, with the tower of its old church overlooking the sea and the Duver (NT), a spit of sand and shingle reaching into Bembridge Harbour. Bembridge (see below) is reached by ferry or toll road.

FROM RYDE TO NEWPORT, 8m. A3054, the main road, is dull beyond (3m) *Wootton Bridge* and a better route, with some splendid views, goes S and W from Ryde on unclassified roads via (4m) *Mersley Down* (413ft) and (5½m) *Arreton Down* (444ft). For

The Needles, at the western tip of the Isle of Wight

Arreton Manor, Haseley Manor and Newchurch, below the downs, see the route from Newport to Sandown below.

FROM RYDE TO VENTNOR, 12m by A3055. 3m: *Brading* is a quaintly decayed little town at the foot of Brading Down (407ft; view) and at the head of a once navigable inlet. The fine church (1150–1250) has a tower with an open lower stage. The many monuments include the *effigy in oak of Sir John Oglander (d. 1655) in the Oglander Chapel. On the chancel floor is an incised slab to John de Cherewin (d. 1441). The 16C rectory opposite now houses Osborn-Smith's Wax Museum, devoted to the history of the island. In the High St. is the Lilliput Museum of Antique Dolls and Toys. Under the old Town Hall are kept the stocks and whipping-post, and at the crossroads is the ring once used in bull-baiting.

About 1m SW are the remains of a *Roman Villa (open), including mosaic pavements, heating arrangements and objects unearthed during excavation. On the Down about 1m W of Brading is *Nunwell House* (open), once the seat of the Oglander family, a Jacobean and Georgian building with period furniture.

FROM BRADING TO BEMBRIDGE, 3½m. 1m: *Yaverland*, right of the road, has a Jacobean manor house next to a church with a late Norman door and chancel arch, and a well-carved modern reredos. 3½m: **Bembridge**, a yachting resort, lies at the mouth of a shallow harbour. The windmill (NT) of c 1700 is the last to survive on the island. A charming coast walk leads to (5m) *Sandown* past the *Foreland* (the E point of the island), *Whitecliff Bay* (geologically interesting) and *Culver Cliff* (254ft), the seaward end of *Bembridge Downs* (343ft; view), with its old fort and monument to Lord Yarborough (d. 1846).

7m: **Sandown** (TI), a resort with a long esplanade and a pier, lies between the white Culver Cliff and the dark red promontory of Dunnose. It is administratively combined with Shanklin (16,000 inhabitants). 9m: **Shanklin** (TI), one of the best-known resorts on the island, is built mainly on high ground away from the sea but has an esplanade and a pier. A lift operates between town level and the esplanade.

At the S end of High St. is the 'Old Village', with a few thatched cottages and rich vegetation. Above a fountain, near the Crab Inn, are some lines written by Longfellow when staying here in 1868. Keats's visit in 1819 is recorded by a plaque on Eglantine Cottage. Close by is the upper entrance of *Shanklin Chine*, a narrow wooded fissure in the sandstone, above which are the attractive *Rylstone Gardens* with views from the cliffs. The Chine is floodlit on summer evenings.

A pleasant walk leads 3m to Ventnor past (½m) the head of the small *Luccombe Chine*, (1½m) the *Landslip* and (2¼m) *Bonchurch*.

The road climbs sharply over Shanklin Down and then descends, with the Landslip on the left. 11m: *Bonchurch* is a pretty village beneath the towering downs. The tiny old church has some slight Norman remains of c 1170. In the new churchyard, higher up, is the grave of Swinburne, who used to spend his boyhood holidays at nearby East Dene, now a hostel.

12m: **Ventnor** (TI; 6500 inhabitants) was developed as a resort in the 1840s, when visitors began to seek it out for its mild winter climate. The centre of the town is laid out on a series of terraces above the sea and under *St Boniface Down* (787ft; NT), the highest point of the island. The road descends steeply to the little esplanade and pier. From the charming park, reached by the St Lawrence road, there is a cliff walk along the *Undercliff, a natural terrace consisting of a huge mass of chalk and limestone which has slipped off the blue clay beneath.

FROM VENTNOR TO FRESHWATER VIA CHALE, 17m via A3055 or 19m via A3055 and B3339. 2m: *St Lawrence*, see below. The road is bordered on the right by steep cliffs (200ft) with a fine walk along the top; the Undercliff proper is below. The road turns inland to (4m) *Niton*, a pleasant village with a 13C church, and a good centre for walking. On the S extremity of the island is *St Catherine's Lighthouse*, with one of the most powerful coast-lights in the world (open afternoons in season at the discretion of the keeper). From (5½m) *Blackgang* a footpath leads up the prominent *St Catherine's Hill* (781ft; NT), crowned by *St Catherine's Oratory*, a 14C tower used as a lighthouse or beacon (EH). *Hoy's Monument*, near the N end of the Down, celebrates the visit of Tsar Alexander in 1814. *Blackgang Chine*, left of A3055, is 400ft deep and practically bare of vegetation. From the Early English church at (6m) *Chale* A3055 continues straight along the coast to (17m) *Freshwater*, one of the few roads on the island commanding wide sea views. A more varied route follows B3399 inland through (7½m) *Chale Green*, (8½m) *Kingston* and (10½m) *Shorwell*, a pretty village with thatched, stone-built houses. The 15C church, with an early 13C door, is rich in contents: a delightful wall painting of St Christopher (c 1440); a Perpendicular stone pulpit entered through a pillar, with a canopy of 1620 and an hour-glass; a 16C brass of a priest; and many 17C Leigh monuments. Nearby are three great manor houses (not open): *Northcourt* (1615), with beautiful terraced grounds; *Westcourt* (1579), ½m W; and *Wolverton* (c 1600), ½m SW. *Yafford*, 1m SW of Shorwell, has a restored 19C watermill and farm park (open). At (12m) *Brighstone*, another stone-built village, the church has a late 13C chancel and Jacobean pulpit. 13½m: *Mottistone* has a church with coloured pillars, and a manor house of 1567 (NT; limited opening). The adjoining gardens and woods, as well as the cliffs to the S and SW, are also NT. 19m: *Freshwater*, see below.

FROM VENTNOR TO FRESHWATER AND ALUM BAY VIA NEWPORT AND YAR-MOUTH, 24½m. Beyond (2m) *St Lawrence*, with one of the smallest churches in England, an unclassified road heads inland. 3½m: *Whitwell* church has two chancels, originally separate chapels. A3020 is joined at (6m) *Godshill*, an attractive old village on a hill. The stately Perpendicular church has a rare *wall painting of Christ hanging from a lily cross and a painting of Daniel in the lions' den, a composition by Rubens probably executed by a member of his school. The monuments include a rich one to Sir John Leigh (d. 1529) and several to the Worsleys of Appuldurcombe, including Sir Richard (d. 1805), historian of the island.

The remains of *Appuldurcombe House* (EH, all year) lie 2m SE near *Wroxall*. Begun in 1701, it was clearly intended as the noblest house on the island. Today it is only a roofless shell, though there is a small museum on the site and the grounds Capability Brown landscaped in the 1780s survive.

A3020 leads to (8m) *Rookley*. To the right is *Merstone*, with a Jacobean manor house (not open). In Gatcombe Park to the left is the 13C *Gatcombe* church, with the wooden effigy of a knight. The *glass (1865–66) in the chancel is by Morris, Rossetti, Burne-Jones and Ford Madox Brown. White-croft Hospital, with its conspicuous tower, lies ½m N.

11m: **Newport** (23,600 inhabitants), the capital of the island, is a busy and attractive town built where the river Medina cuts through the central chalk ridge to flow northwards into the sea at Cowes.

TI: The Car Park, Church Litten. **Bus station**: South St. **Theatres**: Apollo Theatre, Pyle St., and Medina Theatre, Mountbatten Centre, Fairlee Rd.

Although the port is no longer the centre of trade that originally gave Newport its importance, some of its former character has been conserved. The *Quay Arts Centre* inhabits a restored warehouse in Little London. The High St. to the S has some 18C houses, notably the Red House, and the *Guildhall* (1819) by Nash. The Jacobean *Grammar School* (not open) in St

James St. was Charles I's lodging when he left Carisbrooke Castle for the conference in 1648; the Parliamentary Commissioners were housed at the Bugle Inn. The church of *St Thomas* (1854) preserves its Victorian interior, and contains a monument commissioned by Queen Victoria to Princess Elizabeth (see Carisbrooke Castle below), who is buried in the vault beneath. This, and a plaque to Prince Albert, are by Marochetti. Relics from the old church include an elaborate pulpit (1636), an alabaster effigy of 1582 and a 17C font. Behind, in St Thomas Square, is *God's Providence House* (1701), now a restaurant. Beyond, in Pyle St., is the former Victoria Methodist Church, now the Apollo Theatre, with a fine façade. In Cypress Rd, to the right of A3056 towards Sandown, is a Roman villa of 2–4C (open).

FROM NEWPORT TO SANDOWN, 8m by A3056. The road passes two country houses. 4m: *Arreton Manor* (open) is 17C with fine panelling and period furniture, as well as a museum of childhood and an adjoining 'country craft village'. The nearby church has a beautiful late 13C S chapel. 5m: *Haseley Manor* (open) is a Tudor house remodelled in the 18C. *Newchurch*, 1m left of the road at 5½m, has a church with an 18C wooden tower and a gilded 'pelican' lectern.

From Newport to *Cowes*, see below.

About 1m SW of Newport is *Carisbrooke Castle (EH, all year), on a hill about ½m S of the village.

The castle, founded on the site of a Roman fort in early Norman times, was always important as a fortress. Its chief historical interest, however, is the imprisonment here of Charles I from November 1647 to September 1648, when he was moved to Newport Grammar School and then to Hurst Castle on the mainland. His daughter Elizabeth (1635–50) died a prisoner here.

The outer entrance is an archway of 1598, leading to a stone bridge and a noble 14C *Gatehouse* with a 15C upper stage and inner doors. To the right stands the rebuilt *Chapel of St Nicholas*. The former *Governor's Lodging*, the heavily restored range of domestic buildings facing the gatehouse, consists of the *Great Hall* (with a chimneypiece of 1390), the remains of a chapel of c 1270 (with a wall painting) and the *Great Chamber*. An upper room houses the *Isle of Wight County Museum*, with an archaeological collection, local antiquities and relics of Charles I. The pottery includes some very early Neolithic examples. There is a section devoted to children (16–19C), and the oldest chamber organ in working order in Britain (1602). To the S of the Governor's Lodging is the 16C *Well House*, where a donkey treading inside a large wheel draws water from the well. Beyond is the mid 12C *Keep*, with a well 160ft deep. From the 12C *Ramparts* Roman earthworks can be seen to the S.

Carisbrooke has a priory church with the finest tower in the island (1474). The 12C arcade survives but the chancel was pulled down by Sir Francis Walsingham, Elizabeth I's Secretary of State. The 16C tomb of Lady Margaret Wadham, Jane Seymour's aunt, has interesting carvings. B3401 heads W to (15m) the *Calbourne* crossroads. In the village, to the left, the pleasant rebuilt church contains a brass of a knight (1379). The road continues over the downs (516ft) to Brighstone (2½m, see above). The main route turns right at the Calbourne crossroads for (17½m) *Shalfleet*, where the church has a huge square Norman tower, a Norman doorway with tympanum, a good roof and unusual window tracery. The remarkable S arcade is 13C. *Newtown*, 1¼m NE, is a silted former port with a little 18C town hall (NT) and a chapel of 1835 by A.F. Livesay. The estuary has a nature reserve (NT).

A3054 continues W to the tiny old port of (21m) **Yarmouth** (seasonal TI) on the Yar estuary. Near the car ferry terminal are the remains of *Yarmouth Castle*, built by Henry VIII (EH, summer season). The 17C *Church* contains a statue of Admiral Sir Robert Holmes (d. 1692), who took New York from the Dutch in 1664. The figure was begun as Louis XIV by a French sculptor and captured at sea.

A3054 continues past (2m) *Colwell Bay* to (3m) **Totland**, a pleasant little resort with a pier. B3322 continues a further 1½m to Alum Bay (see below).

An unclassified road leads left from A3054 to (23½m) *Freshwater*. The rebuilt church has a Norman doorway, and memorials to Thackeray's daughter, Lady Ritchie (d. 1919), and Tennyson (d. 1892). The poet's wife (d. 1896) is buried in the churchyard. Freshwater was also the birthplace of the physicist Robert Hooke (1653–1703). 24½m: **Freshwater Bay** is a resort where G.F. Watts and Ellen Terry spent their honeymoon in 1864.

About ¾m NW is *Farringford*, now a hotel, the mansion leased by Tennyson in 1853 and bought in 1855 out of the profits from 'Maud'. He wrote 'Crossing the Bar' on a journey across the Solent between Farringford and Aldworth, his Surrey home. There are fine walks E of Freshwater Bay, across *Afton Down* to (3m) *Brook*, with its lifeboat station and submerged forest. The coastline along this stretch is NT property.

Between Freshwater Bay and (3m) the Needles are the impressive *Freshwater Cliffs*, rising to about 400ft. They are best seen from the sea, and motor boats from Yarmouth and Totland piers make the trip to the Needles and Alum Bay, passing the cave known as *Lord Holmes's Parlour* and the recessed arch at *Scratchell's Bay*. The walk along the top of the downs above the cliffs gives a series of grand views, and *Tennyson Down* (485ft; NT) is crowned by a monument to the poet. The view near the *Needles Old Battery* (NT), a Palmerstonian fort of 1862, is striking but the remarkable contrast between the white cliff of the S side of Alum Bay and the many-coloured sands toward its centre should be seen from a boat.

Alum Bay, named after the alum formerly extracted from its clay, is famous for the brilliant colours of its vertical strata of sandstone. A granite memorial marks the site of the first permanent wireless station (1897–1900), from which Lord Kelvin sent the first paid marconigram in 1898. At the S extremity of the bay are the three isolated, pointed masses of chalk 100ft high, known as the *Needles*, with a lighthouse on the outermost.

FROM NEWPORT TO COWES, 4½m by A3020. The road keeps to high ground W of the Medina, passing *Parkhurst Prison*. At (2½m) *Northwood* is the mother church of Cowes, with a Norman doorway and Jacobean pulpit.

Cowes (19,700 inhabitants), a busy little port with the island's best harbour, is England's main yachting centre as well as a major boat-building centre.

TI: The Arcade, Fountain Quay. **Annual Events**: Yacht racing from April to September with regattas each weekend, Round-the-Island Race in June and Cowes Week in the first week of August.

The older part, *West Cowes*, on the left bank of the Medina, has a winding and hilly High St. (one way N to S) running parallel to the shore, with some quaint old shops. At its N end is the Parade, where a table commemorates the departure of the 'Ark' and the 'Dove' with the founders of Maryland in 1633. Thomas Jefferson landed here in 1784 and 1789 on his way to and from his embassy in Paris. *Cowes Castle*, further N, has been rebuilt but was originally one of Henry VIII's defences. Since 1856 it has been the headquarters of the *Royal Yacht Squadron*, the most exclusive yacht club in the world. Hard by is the Royal London Yacht Club. At the other end of High St. and in its continuation as Birmingham Rd are shipbuilding and engineering works, and Westbourne House, where Dr Arnold of Rugby was born. The newer part of West Cowes, along the Solent, has a long esplanade opened in 1926 by Edward VIII, when Prince of Wales. It extends W beyond *Egypt Point* to the resort of (1m) *Gurnard*. At *East Cowes*, on the other side of the Medina (ferry; toll), are *Norris Castle* (1799; James Wyatt), where Queen Victoria spent some youthful holidays, and the church of *St James*, with the grave of the architect John Nash (d. 1835).

Overlooking the bay about 1m SE is *Osborne House (EH, summer season, grounds 10.00–18.00, house 10.00–17.00; 1 October to 31 October, house and grounds daily 10.00–17.00). Built in an Italaniate style in 1845–51 by Prince Albert and Thomas Cubitt, it was for many years the seaside home of Queen Victoria, who died here in 1901. King Edward presented it to the nation the following year as a memorial of his mother, and one wing was made into a convalescent home for officers and civil servants. It is one of the most complete, as well as the best preserved, examples of High Victorian taste in England.

The state apartments include the Durbar Room, added in 1890 and decorated in an Indian style by J. Lockwood Kipling, the writer's father. The private suite on the first floor, kept much as it was at the Queen's death, richly evokes her domestic life with Albert. The park, much of it planted by Albert, is not open but visitors may see the *Swiss Cottage* used by the royal children, ½m E of the house. Nearby is a museum of objects collected by the Royal family on their travels and Victoria's bathing-machine.

On the bank of the river, ¾m S of Osborne, stands *Whippingham* church (1854–62), a strange medley of styles, said to have been designed by Prince Albert.

16

The New Forest

Maps: OS Outdoor Leisure map (2½in to 1m).

The *New Forest occupies the SW corner of Hampshire between Southampton Water and the Avon. It existed as such in 1016 but William the Conqueror formally established and named it c 1079. 'Forest' was a legal term implying an area subject not to common law but to the forest law, designed to safeguard wild deer for the king's hunting. ('Chase' was a similar tract not belonging to the Crown.) It was then a sparsely inhabited, infertile region of woods, thickets and open heaths. Its continued survival may have depended as much on the paucity of its soils as on the forest laws. Hunting gradually declined and from the 16C onwards tracts of land were enclosed for growing timber. Today the forest encompasses some 93,000 acres, of which 67,000 are managed by the Forestry Commission, comprising 45,000 acres of Open Forest waste where ponies and cattle graze by common right and 22,000 acres of Inclosure woodland; villages and farmland occupy the remainder.

Through a series of historical accidents the radical changes which have taken place in the English countryside over the last 200 years passed the forest by, and its Open Waste is now the largest stretch of semi-natural vegetation in lowland Britain. Its ecological importance is immense. The heaths are among the few remaining areas large enough to support a complete spectrum of heathland flora and fauna. The bogs are among the finest of their kind, with rare species of plants, birds and insects. The unenclosed woods are the best relics of relatively undisturbed deciduous forest in Britain, being mainly of oak, beech and holly. The oak and beech grown for timber in the Inclosure woodlands enjoy longer rotations than elsewhere. Both areas are rich in wildlife, providing refuges for deer, badger and foxes and habitat for breeding birds like crossbills, goldcrests and firecrests. By far the most familiar inhabitants, however, are the hardy New Forest ponies, descended from an indigenous wild breed.

The visitor will find many car parks and picnic places, crowded in summer. Waymarked trails lead into the forest's inner recesses and the many gravel tracks are open without restriction to the walker. Wild camping is not permitted. Details of camp sites can be obtained from the Forestry Commission, The Queen's House, Lyndhurst, Hampshire SO4 7NH.

Lyndhurst (TI), on A35 between Southampton and Bournemouth, is the best headquarters for visitors. Its elaborate *Church* of 1858–70 contains a painting by Lord Leighton and windows by Morris and Burne-Jones. The churchyard has the grave of Mrs Reginald Hargreaves, the original of 'Alice in Wonderland'. To the W is the *Queen's House*, former manor house of the royal manor of Lyndhurst and now the office of the Deputy Surveyor, the Forestry Commission official in charge of the forest. It adjoins the *Verderers' Hall*, where the Verderers sit every two months to hear presentments about the forest and adjudicate on matters affecting the exercise of grazing rights. The hall is open to the public only when the court is in session. Contents include an early Tudor stirrup popularly but wrongly supposed to have belonged to William Rufus, killed in the forest in 1100 (see Rufus Stone below).

A ROUNDTRIP SOUTH FROM LYNDHURST THROUGH BROCKENHURST AND BEAULIEU, 17m. A337 leads S to (4m) **Brockenhurst**, a popular starting-point for excursions.

An unclassified road, for part of its way the Rhinefield Ornamental Drive, leads W and then N to (4½m) A35 and (6½m) *Bolderwood* (see below). The forest walks leading from its car parks include (at 2m) the Ober Water Walk and (at 3½m) the Tall Trees Walk.

From Brockenhurst A337 continues S to (4¾m) **Lymington** (38,700 inhabitants; seasonal TI), a picturesque old port and yachting station at the mouth of the Lymington, which flows into the Solent. King Henry II landed here in 1154 on the way to his coronation. In 1879 Verlaine was an usher at a school next to the church, his last post in England. Car ferries cross to Yarmouth on the Isle of Wight. In the isolated church of *Boldre*, 2m NE, which has a wide nave with simple Norman arcades, Southey married his second wife in 1839. William Gilpin (1724–1804), author of 'picturesque' travel books, was vicar.

From *Keyhaven*, 4m SW of Lymington, a ferry goes to *Hurst Castle* (EH, summer season), built by Henry VIII on a pebble spit to guard the W entrance to the Solent. In 1648 Charles I was brought from the Isle of Wight and confined here for 18 days before being moved to Windsor. The castle was modernised in the 19C and 20C.

B3055 and B3054 run E from Brockenhurst through woodland and heath to (10m) *Beaulieu*, pronounced 'Bewley', a pleasant village at the head of the tidal Beaulieu river.

***Beaulieu Abbey**, a Cistercian house founded by King John in 1204, stood on the E side of the river. The chief relic of its buildings is the Early English refectory, now the *Parish Church*, with fine lancet windows, roof bosses and a beautiful reader's *pulpit. Other remains (open) are the ruined cloisters, three arches of the chapter house and the lay brothers' dormitory. The frater and cellarium house an exhibition of monastic life. A tablet in the cloisters commemorates the members of the Special Operations

Executive who trained here during World War II for their missions in Nazi-occupied territory. Only the S wall of the abbey church survives; its foundations are marked out by stones. Margaret of Anjou, Henry VI's wife, sought sanctuary here with her son Prince Edward in 1471 after the Battle of Barnet, and Perkin Warbeck found a brief refuge here in 1497.

The *Palace House* (open), originally the gatehouse, is the residence of Lord Montagu. The *National Motor Museum*, approached from the Lyndhurst road, has a superb display of motoring history from 1894 to the present. Its collection of veteran and vintage cars and motor cycles is among the finest in the world. A pleasant walk can be taken down the creek to (2¼m) *Buckler's Hard*, a pretty waterside hamlet on the Beaulieu estate, famous for its shipbuilding yard in the 18C and now much developed as a tourist attraction. There is a Maritime Museum. Several cottages contain tableaux illustrating the history of the village. *Exbury Gardens* (open), on the opposite side of the river and 4m SE of Beaulieu, have 200 acres of woodland gardens with rhododendrons, azaleas and camellias.

B3056 leads NW from Beaulieu back to (17m) Lyndhurst.

A ROUNDTRIP NORTH FROM LYNDHURST TO BOLDERWOOD, RUFUS STONE AND MINSTEAD, 17m. A35 climbs Lyndhurst Hill to the W. At the top a right turn leads through *Emery Down*, with its large village green. A left turn goes to (4m) *Bolderwood*, with the King Oak and many fir trees.

An unclassified road, for part of the way an Ornamental Drive, leads S and E to (2½m) A35, where it meets the sideroad from Brockenhurst (see above). It passes through (1m) *Mark Ash Wood*, with the finest beeches in the forest, and (2¼m) *Knightwood Inclosure*, with the Knightwood Oak, one of the oldest pollarded trees in the forest.

The unclassified road from Bolderwood passes under the A31, here dual carriageway, at 4½m. To join the NE carriageway, turn right at 5½m, cross the old aerodrome and turn right again to meet A31 at (8½m) *Stoney Cross*. Left of the way towards the Cadnam roundabout is (9½m) the *Rufus Stone*, marking the spot where it is said William Rufus was killed by an arrow glancing from a tree in 1100. According to one account he was accidentally killed by Sir Walter Tyrrel; according to another he was murdered by a dispossessed Saxon. All that is known for certain is that he died by an arrow in the forest and was hastily buried at Winchester.

A brief return on the other carriageway of the A31 from (11½m) the *Cadnam* roundabout leads to the left turn for (15m) *Minstead*, a pretty village where Conan Doyle is buried. Nearby are the gardens of *Furzey* (open), with a 16C cottage and a gallery of local crafts. E of Minstead A337 completes the return to (17m) Lyndhurst.

SOUTH-WESTERN ENGLAND

South-Western England, as defined for the purposes of this guide, stretches W from the Hampshire border and fringes of the New Forest and S from the A4, the old way from London to Bath and Bristol. It thus includes: Wiltshire; Dorset; Somerset and that part of the new county of Avon (created in 1974) which formerly belonged to Somerset; Devon; and Cornwall.

No other English country is dominated by chalk as completely as Wiltshire is. Its centre, Salisbury Plain, is also the centre from which the chalk downs of England radiate—running E to become the North and South Downs of Surrey, Kent and Sussex, SW through Dorset to the coast, and NE through the Marlborough Downs to the Berkshire Downs, the Chilterns and the Lincolnshire and Yorkshire Wolds. In Wiltshire itself the downs make a wide landscape of gently rolling hills, covered by short springy turf, ideal for grazing sheep. There are few trees, though sometimes a copse on top of a down makes a fine silhouette against the skyline. Salisbury Plain has been too thoroughly invaded by military camps and manoeuvres to show these effects at their best, and the traveller needs to go N into the Marlborough Downs around Avebury, where several of the chalk figures of horses cut into the hillsides can also be seen. The great stone circles at Avebury and Stonehenge are the most conspicuous reminders of the prehistoric culture that once flourished here.

The builders of Avebury and of the larger circle and horseshoe at Stonehenge used sarsen (grey wether), a sandstone which outcrops naturally in the region. For Salisbury Cathedral the masons could quarry their stone at nearby Chilmark. Otherwise, Wiltshire is like all chalk regions relatively poor in building stone—which may be why some of the uprights at Stonehenge are 'blue' stones brought all the way from the Presely Hills in Wales, and why the county has so little distinguished church architecture. For domestic buildings, the characteristic materials are flint and the local red bricks and tiles which make so handsome a show in, for example, the High St. of Marlborough.

Dorset, Somerset and the southern half of Avon, Wiltshire's western neighbours, are more varied in their geology, and hence their landscape and architecture, too. Of the three, Dorset presents the simplest face, its central strip made by the chalk downs continuing from Salisbury Plain. Like the Wiltshire downs, they have their prehistoric monuments (Maiden Castle, by the Dorchester–Weymouth road, must surely be the finest hill-fort in England) and their chalk hill figures, including the figure of George III near Osmington and the much older giant at Cerne Abbas, perhaps the most interesting of all these West Country carvings. To the SE of the downs is the unremarkable heathland made memorable by Thomas Hardy's Egdon Heath in 'The Return of the Native'. To the NW of the downs are fertile, clay vales which, since the spirit of Hardy pervades Dorset, inevitably remind the visitor of the Vale of the Great Dairies in 'Tess of the d'Urbervilles'. Dorset's coastline, less commercialised than the coastline of its immediate neighbours, springs several interesting surprises: the Isle of Purbeck, where the shelly limestone called Purbeck marble is quarried; the Isle of Portland, a large lump of white limestone reaching out into the Channel; the curious shingle barrier known as Chesil Bank; and the blue lias cliffs, famous for their fossils, around Lyme Regis.

The coastline of Avon and N Somerset can seem disappointing by comparison, with only the cliffs around Clevedon and Weston-super-Mare to relieve the flatness of the Severn Estuary. The variety and interest of the region lie inland: in the Mendip Hills, with their gorges and caverns, stretching from near Frome to Weston; in the Somerset Levels, with islands like Glastonbury Tor rising from the marshland; and in the Quantock Hills, eastern outlier of Exmoor, above Taunton. The fertile, orchard-growing valleys further inland, like the Vale of Taunton Deane, can seem to some eyes the quintessential Somerset landscape. From such variety comes one of the best ranges of building stone that any English region can boast. Particularly beautiful are the Bath stone which gives lightness yet dignity to the city's Georgian streets and the stone quarried at Ham Hill in the S, seen to its best effect at Montacute House. Throughout Somerset the churches are conspicuous for their tall, ornate Perpendicular towers.

Where Dorset and Somerset can still at times seem blessedly free of tourists and the worst effects of the tourist trade, Devon and Cornwall bear all too clearly the scars inflicted by the crowds of summer visitors who crawl their way down the congested A30 to the SW peninsula in search of caravan sites, clotted-cream teas, Devon cider, Cornish fudge and souvenirs of Land's End. The real attractions of the peninsula have not disappeared, but the traveller needs to pick his time and place warily. This is particularly true of the long coastline, where seaside amusements alternate with historic ports (Plymouth in the S, Barnstaple and Bideford in the N) and with a landscape rich and varied in its natural beauty: the serpentine rock of the Lizard and the wide sweep of Mount Bay in the S, for example, or the contorted granite and slate near Boscastle and Tintagel and the headland from Barnstaple (or Bideford) Bay around to Minehead.

Inland Devon has several distinct regions. Old Red Sandstone makes up the smooth plateau of Exmoor in the N, lying partly in Somerset but belonging to Devon in character. Red rock and red earth appear again in the S as part of what seems to most visitors the typically Devonian countryside, where deep lanes wind through wooded hills and combes (valleys) generously watered by a network of rivers. The houses and cottages are sometimes made of cob, or unbaked earth, whose presence beneath the whitewash or pinkwash is betrayed by the slightly rounded corners of the buildings and the use of thatch rather than a heavier roofing material. Near the centre of the county rises the bleak plateau of Dartmoor, the first and largest of the chain of granite outcrops which continues westward with Bodmin Moor and Land's End and resurfaces again as the Scilly Isles.

Together with slate, granite epitomises one side of the paradoxical nature of Cornwall, a place at once harsh and friendly. Granite and slate make the wild coastline and the dreary industrial hinterland of tin and copper mines, slate and china-clay quarries—a landscape made all the more depressing by the decline and near collapse of these industries since the 19C. Granite makes the square unadorned outlines of the parish churches, where the only decorative flourishes are carved on the woodwork inside, and the squat outlines of the low, thick-walled cottages. And yet, at the same time, Cornwall also has a mild climate and rich vegetation. The Gulf Stream brings an early spring and makes palm trees a fashionable adornment to suburban gardens. Neither granite nor palm trees are particularly English, let alone the conjunction of the two, and their presence helps underline the foreignness of Cornwall, reminding the visitor that this is a Celtic place linked by history to Brittany across the Channel as well as to its English neighbours. The ancient Cornish language, which died out in the 18C, survives in the place names. Of the most frequent Cornish prefixes, 'Tre' means 'dwelling', 'Ros' 'heath', 'Pol' 'pool', 'Lan' 'church', 'Caer' 'town' or 'fort', and 'Pen' 'summit' or 'headland'.

17

London to Salisbury and Weymouth

A. Via Dorchester

Directions. Total distance 131m. A4, A30 to (46m) Basingstoke (bypassed), or alternative way by M3, see Route 14B. A30, M3, A303, A30 to (67m) Stockbridge. A30 to (82m) **Salisbury**. A354 to (105m) Blandford Forum and (117m) Puddletown. A35 to (122m) **Dorchester**. A354 to (131m) **Weymouth**.

From London to (46m) *Basingstoke*, see Route 14B. A30 bypasses the town and joins M3, followed for 2m to A303 towards Andover (Route 19). At *Steventon*, 2½m NW of this roundabout, Jane Austen (1775–1817) was born and spent her first 25 years. 60m: At the junction with A34 the route leaves A303 for A30 again. The road crosses rich agricultural downland to (66m) *Woolbury Ring* (NT), an Iron Age hill-fort with good views, and drops into the valley of the Test at (67m) *Stockbridge*, centre of the fishing on the stream.

Danebury, another Iron Age hill-fort with good views, is 3m NW. Finds from excavation are displayed at Andover (Route 19). A3057 follows the Test S from Stockbridge, passing (3m) the turning for *Houghton*, on the opposite bank, with *Houghton Lodge Gardens* (open), which surround an 18C 'cottage ornée'. A3057 continues S via (6½m) *Mottisfont* to (10m) *Romsey* (both Route 14A).

71m: A30 crosses a tributary of the Test. At *Nether Wallop*, 1m right, the church has a 15C painting of George and the Dragon. At (74½m) *Lopcombe Corner* the road enters Wiltshire. At (76m) the Pheasant Inn, formerly The Hut, about 2m N of *Winterslow*, Hazlitt wrote the 'Winterslow Papers' and was visited by Charles and Mary Lamb. Just beyond (79m) *Figsbury Ring*, an Iron Age camp with a view of Salisbury, the road crosses the prominent line of the Roman road from Winchester to Old Sarum, a splendid walk of 21½m.

SALISBURY (36,000 inhabitants) began its prosperous but uneventful history in 1220, when the bishop's see was moved from the dry uplands of Old Sarum to this fertile spot in the valley where the Avon, the Bourne and the Nadder meet. The cathedral is famous for its close, the largest in England, and its spire, the tallest in England. Seen from the water meadows, the graceful silhouette of the spire has long been a favourite subject of painters. The area round the Market Place, to the N, preserves its medieval layout of squares known as 'chequers'. Now mainly an agricultural centre, Salisbury was once known for its cloth trade.

TI: Fish Row. **Bus Station**: Endless St. **Coach Station**: Brown St. **Railway Station**: W of the city centre, reached via Fisherton St. **Theatre**: Playhouse, Malthouse Lane. **Annual

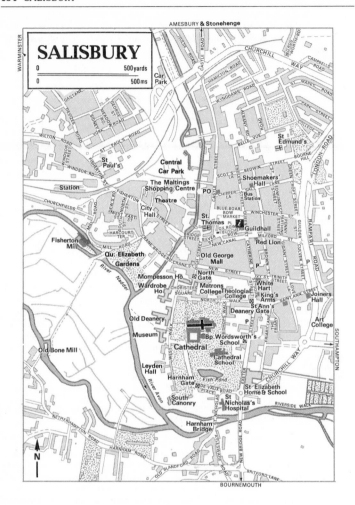

AMESBURY **& Stonehenge**

SALISBURY

0   500 yards

0   500 ms

N

BOURNEMOUTH

Events: St George's Spring Festival; the Southern Cathedrals Festival of Music is held annually (in July) in rotation with Chichester and Winchester. Salisbury Festival in September.

Residents: George Herbert (1593–1633) spent his last years at Bemerton nearby. Henry Fielding (1707–54) eloped from Salisbury with Charlotte Cradock, his first wife. Thomas Hardy portrays the city as 'Melchester' in his novels: in 'Jude the Obscure' Sue Brideshead studies at the training college in the close, while the hero works on the restoration of the cathedral.

The most striking way to reach the cathedral is by the 14C *St Ann's Gate*, leading into the North Walk of the *Close, whose spacious lawns, trees and dignified old houses make a fine setting for the great church.

The Avon marks the W boundary of the close; its other three sides have a 14C wall of stone from Old Sarum. Many houses deserve attention. The *Deanery*, in Bishop's Walk off North Walk, is mainly 13C. In Choristers' Square, beyond the end of North Walk, are the gabled, mainly 15C *Wardrobe* (housing the *Duke of Edinburgh's Royal Regimental Museum*), the 18C *Wren Hall* and *Mompesson House* (NT), with handsome plasterwork, panelling, staircase and furniture as well as a garden bounded by the close's N wall. The riverside gardens of *North Canonry*, in West Walk, are open in summer. The late 14C *King's House*, beyond, contains the *Salisbury and South Wiltshire Museum*; among the exhibits are finds from Stonehenge and other local sites, the Pitt-Rivers Collection, a display about the history of Salisbury and Old Sarum, and prints, drawings and photographs of local scenes. The old 13–18C *Bishop's Palace*, now housing the Cathedral School, is SE of the cathedral.

The *Cathedral was begun by Bishop Poore in 1220, when the cathedral at Old Sarum had become untenable, and consecrated in 1258. It was built on a virgin site and, alone among English medieval cathedrals, is of uniform design (Early English). Although the graceful *spire was the daring addition of a century later (c 1320), it fulfils the original pyramidal conception. Its apex (at 404ft the tallest in England) is 2½ft out of perpendicular. The lovely stone used in both phases of building came from the Chilmark quarry, 12m W of Salisbury.

The interior is not as satisfying as the exterior, despite its fine proportions and the harmony of the design. The chilliness of the effect was increased by the ruthless way James Wyatt (1788–89) removed screens and chapels and tidied the monuments into rows. Sir Gilbert Scott's restoration (begun in 1859) tried to minimise the damage, and some colour has been restored to the aisles by the repainting of tombs.

The *Nave*, perhaps rather narrow for its height, is divided into ten bays by clustered columns of polished Purbeck marble. The fine triforium has characteristic Early English plate tracery. In the W triple lancet window is a patchwork of 13–15C glass, some from Dijon, and the third window from the W in the S aisle has a 14C *Tree of Jesse. At the W end of the aisles is some lovely 13C grisaille glass. The *clock movement at the W end of the N aisle, probably the oldest surviving mechanism in Europe (1386), has been put in working order.

The following monuments deserve special mention (beginning at the W end of the S aisle): 1. Oldest monument in the church, brought from Old Sarum (possibly Bishop Herman, d. 1078); 2. Bishop Roger of Old Sarum (d. 1139); 3. Bishop Jocelin of Old Sarum (d. 1184); 4. Bishop Beauchamp (d. 1482); 5. Robert, Lord Hungerford (d. 1459), an elaborate effigy; 6. Base of the 13C shrine of St Osmund (the holes are the 'foramina' into which the sick were thrust to be healed); 7. Bishop de la Wyle (d. 1271); 8. *William Longespée (d. 1226), 1st Earl of Salisbury and son of Henry II (the earliest English military effigy, once brilliantly coloured). Cross to the N aisle: 9. *Sir John Cheney (d. 1509), a gigantic knight of the bodyguard of Henry VII, who fought against Richard III at Bosworth; 10. Walter, Lord Hungerford (d. 1449), a hero of Agincourt, and his wife. 11. Sir John de Montacute (d. 1390), a hero of Crécy, wearing elaborate gauntlets; 12. William Longespée, 2nd Earl of Salisbury, killed by the Saracens near Cairo (1250); 13. Diminutive effigy, probably enclosing the heart of Bishop Poore (d. 1237).

The *W Transepts* resemble the nave. The Perpendicular arches at the crossing were inserted by Bishop Beauchamp (1450–81) to strengthen the original arches against the lateral thrust of the tower and spire. In the NW arm is a bust of the naturalist and writer Richard Jefferies (d. 1887); in the SW arm is a War Memorial chapel.

In general design the *Choir* and *Presbytery* differ little from the nave. They suffered from Wyatt's determination to create a vista from end to end of the church. The paintings on the vault are repaintings (c 1870) of defaced 13C originals. The stalls have been freely restored. The throne is by Scott, though most of his furnishings were replaced in 1959 by Lord Mottistone. In front of the altar are buried the Earls of Pembroke. On the N side of the second bay from the E is the fine late Perpendicular Chantry of Bishop Audley (d. 1524), and opposite is the Hungerford Chantry (c 1429), an important example of early ironwork. In the *NE Transept* are portions of the original 13C screen and the unusual 14C *brass of Bishop Wyville (d. 1375). In the N choir aisle

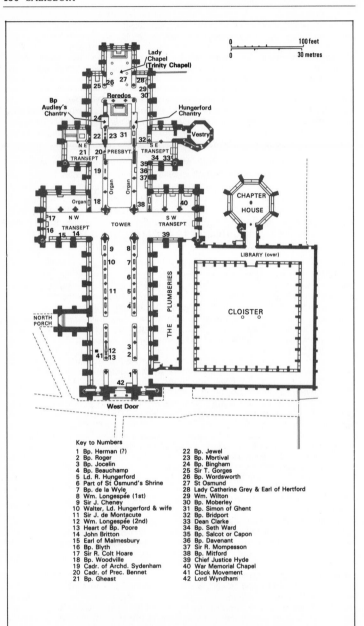

Key to Numbers

1 Bp. Herman (?)
2 Bp. Roger
3 Bp. Jocelin
4 Bp. Beauchamp
5 Ld. R. Hungerford
6 Part of St Osmund's Shrine
7 Bp. de la Wyle
8 Wm. Longespée (1st)
9 Sir J. Cheney
10 Walter, Ld. Hungerford & wife
11 Sir J. de Montacute
12 Wm. Longespée (2nd)
13 Heart of Bp. Poore
14 John Britton
15 Earl of Malmesbury
16 Bp. Blyth
17 Sir R. Colt Hoare
18 Bp. Woodville
19 Cadr. of Archd. Sydenham
20 Cadr. of Prec. Bennet
21 Bp. Gheast

22 Bp. Jewel
23 Bp. Mortival
24 Bp. Bingham
25 Sir T. Gorges
26 Bp. Wordsworth
27 St Osmund
28 Lady Catherine Grey & Earl of Hertford
29 Wm. Wilton
30 Bp. Moberley
31 Bp. Simon of Ghent
32 Bp. Bridport
33 Dean Clarke
34 Bp. Seth Ward
35 Bp. Salcot or Capon
36 Bp. Davenant
37 Sir R. Mompesson
38 Bp. Mitford
39 Chief Justice Hyde
40 War Memorial Chapel
41 Clock Movement
42 Lord Wyndham

SALISBURY CATHEDRAL

near Audley's chantry is the cenotaph of Bishop Bingham (d. 1246) and further E are the lavish monuments to Sir Thomas Gorges (d. 1610) and his wife. The *Lady Chapel*, to the E, is the earliest part of the building (1220–25). It is divided into nave and aisles by graceful clustered shafts and slender single pillars. Some of the glass is 13C and 14C. In the centre stood the shrine of St Osmund (d. 1099), Bishop of Old Sarum; his grave slab, on the S side, marks the spot where his body was first reburied after the rebuilding of the cathedral. At the E end of the S choir aisle is the imposing monument of Edward, Earl of Hertford (d. 1621) and his wife Lady Catherine (d. 1568), sister of Lady Jane Grey. Also in the S choir aisle are the finely sculptured tomb of Bishop Bridport (d. 1262) and the Mompesson tomb (1627); two windows here are Pre-Raphaelite, and in the *SE Transept* is some 13C grisaille glass. The tomb of Bishop Mitford (d. 1407), further W, has some delicate sculpture.

The SW transept leads to the well-preserved *Cloisters* (c 1270), begun by Bishop de la Wyle, unusually large for a non-monastic church. They are separated from the cathedral itself by a passage known as the Plumberies. Above the E side is the *Library* (open), built in 1446 and devoted to its present purpose in 1756. It contains almost 200 manuscripts, including an Anglo-Saxon liturgy with finely drawn capitals and a late 11C St Augustine, perhaps written by St Osmund. The octagonal *Chapter House*, entered from the E walk, was built a little after the cloisters. It contains one of the four copies of the Magna Carta. The late 13C sculptures illustrate scenes from Genesis and Exodus.

The *North* or *High St. Gate*, with the *College of Matrons* (1682) to its right, leads out of the close. The Crane Bridge goes left to *Queen Elizabeth Gardens*, by the Nadder, which give a good view of the cathedral. On the right of the High St., leading N from the close, is the *Old George*, with a remarkable roof tree and a room where Pepys slept. Old George Mall, behind, is a cleverly harmonised pedestrian precinct. Silver St., further on to the right, ends at the hexagonal 15C *Poultry Cross*. Nearby is the large civic church of *St Thomas*, also 15C, with a carved roof and a restored painting of the Last Judgement over the chancel arch. In the Market Place to the E stands a statue of Lord Herbert of Lea (1810–61) by Marochetti; another, of the blind statesman Professor Fawcett (1833–84), faces Blue Boar Row, where he was born. The *Guildhall* (1788–95), by Taylor and Pilkington, contains a portrait of the Duke of Queensberry by Raeburn.

From the NE corner Endless St. leads N to Salt Lane, on the right, with the 16C *Shoemakers' Hall* and the 15C *Pheasant Inn*.

Queen St. leads S from the Market Place. In New Canal, to the right, a cinema façade masks the *Hall of John Halle*, built by a wealthy woolstapler in 1470–83. In Milford St., to the left, is the *Red Lion Hotel*, with a pictur-esque courtyard. Queen St. is continued S as Catherine St. and St John St., passing the 18C *White Hart Hotel* (American associations) and the old *King's Arms*, where Royalists arranged the escape of Charles II after the Battle of Worcester. In St Ann's St., to the left, stands the old *Joiners' Hall* (c 1550), with a fine timbered front. Exeter St., beyond St Ann's Gate, leads to the pleasant *Riverside Walk* (left), while St Nicholas Rd (right) goes on to the Harnham Bridge, passing the remains of *St Nicholas Hospital*, founded, like the bridge, by Bishop Bingham.

Britford church, 1¼m SE of Harnham Bridge, has Saxon sculptures on the NE arch of the nave. At *Bemerton*, 1½m W of Salisbury, George Herbert spent the last three years of his life. He is buried in the old 14C church. For *Wilton House*, 3m W of Salisbury by A30, see Route 18A.

FROM SALISBURY TO STONEHENGE, 10½m. A345, the direct road, is 1m shorter but less pretty than the secondary road preferred here, which leaves Salisbury by Castle St. and follows the Avon valley. 1½m: *Stratford-sub-Castle* has a manor house once occupied by the elder Pitt, who first entered Parliament in 1735 as member for Old Sarum.

*Old Sarum (EH, all year plus Mondays in winter) stands on a low hill E of the village. It is the site successively of an Iron Age British hill-fort known to the Romans as Sorviodunum, a Saxon town, and a Norman fortress and cathedral. The bishopric of Sherborne was translated to Sarum c 1075. The cathedral begun by Bishop Herman and continued by St Osmund was consecrated in 1092 and later enlarged by Osmund's successor, Bishop Roger. A water shortage and conflict with the military authorities in the castle prompted the move to Salisbury in 1220. Sarum cathedral was razed in 1331 to provide building material for the close at Salisbury and the town gradually emptied, though a chapel survived until the 16C and the 'rotten borough' of Old Sarum returned two MPs until 1833.

Almost no traces of Roman occupation have been found, and the excavated remains are chiefly Norman. NW of the central mound where the Norman castle stood the foundations of the cathedral have been marked out. They show Bishop Roger's enlargement of the E end of the original church.

To the right of the road at (5½m) *Woodford* is *Heale House*, where Charles II hid after the Battle of Worcester. Only the gardens are open. A bridge crosses the Avon to *Durnford* (1½m), where the Norman and Early English church adjoins an early earthwork known as *Ogbury Camp*. Beyond (7m) *Lake*, reputedly the home of Sir Lancelot, is *Wilsford*, with a Norman church tower. At 9m the route turns left on A303 to (10½m) *Stonehenge* (Route 19).

A354, the Weymouth road, leads SW from Salisbury. At (85m) *Coombe Bissett* it crosses the Ebbe.

An unclassified road goes W along the valley to join A30, passing through pleasant villages: (1m) *Stratford Tony*; (5m) *Broad Chalke*, where John Aubrey (1626–97) lived at the manor house; and (11m) *Berwick St John*, beneath the heights of *White Sheet Hill* (794ft) to the N and *Winkelbury Hill* (earthwork) and *Win Green* (908ft) to the S.

92m: A354 enters Dorset, crosses Bokerley Dyke and briefly joins the line of the Roman road, leaving it again before (94m) *Handley Hill*, at the junction with B3081 from Shaftesbury to Ringwood (Route 18A). *Chettle*, to the right of the road at 98m, has Chettle House (open), a Baroque house by Thomas Archer. 105m: **Blandford Forum** (3900 inhabitants; TI), a market town on the Stour, has some fine buildings of 1735–40 by John and William Bastard, notably the town hall and the church. The pulpit is from the destroyed Wren church of St Antholin in London. The sculptor Alfred Stevens (1818–75) was a native.

Tarrant Crawford, 3m SE of Blandford, has an unspoilt 13C church with *wall paintings, mainly 14C, of St Margaret of Antioch, and the coffin slab of Bishop Poore of Salisbury, a native.

A350 leads N from Blandford to (13m) Shaftesbury (Route 18A). At 1m it gives a good view across the Stour to *Bryanston*, built by Norman Shaw as a country house in 1889–94 and now a school. *Hod Hill*, left at 3m, is a prehistoric summit fort enclosing a permanent Roman fort in its NW corner. The church at *Iwerne Courtney* or *Shroton* (4½m) has work of 1610 still in the Gothic style. *Hambledon Hill* (622ft), W of the village, is a Neolithic earthwork enjoying a fine view. *Iwerne Minster* (6m) has a church with a good spire and Norman details, and Clayesmore School, built as a country house by Alfred Waterhouse (1878).

Off A354 about 9m SW of Blandford is *Milton Abbas*, a 'model' village dating from 1780, when the 1st Earl of Dorchester cleared the old village from beside his mansion, *Milton Abbey*, ¾m NW. The house, designed in the Gothic style by Sir William Chambers, stands on the site of a monastery founded by Athelstan in 938 and incorporates the Abbot's Hall of 1498. It is now a school (open during spring and summer holidays). Beside it is the *Abbey Church*, still noble despite being reduced to its 14C choir and transepts and its 15C pinnacled tower. Inside are a rich altar screen of 1492, an elaborate 15C wooden tabernacle, two paintings from the reign of Edward

IV, interesting tombs and a brass of Sir John Tregonwell (1565). The tiny chapel of St Catherine on the hillock above was begun by Athelstan and restored under the Normans and again in the 16C. The *Park Farm Museum* deals with local history and agriculture.

A354 joins A35 at (117m) *Puddletown*. The church is rich in details: gargoyles, Norman font, three-decker pulpit, 17C W gallery and a fine group of 14–16C monuments. The village is the 'Weatherbury' of Hardy's 'Far from the Madding Crowd'. *Waterston Manor* (not open), 2m NW on B3142, was Bathsheba's home. *Ilsington* (limited opening) is a handsome house built during the reign of William and Mary.

On A35 ½m E of Puddletown stands *Athelhampton* (open), its main battlemented wing built in the 1480s and its W wing added in the next century. It stands on the legendary site of Athelstan's palace and is the 'Athelhall' of Hardy's writing. The *Great Hall keeps its original dimensions, linenfold panelling, timber roof and oriel window. The Dining Room has good 18C furniture. The beautiful formal gardens were laid out in the 1890s.

119m: In the hamlet of *Higher Bockhampton*, S of A35, stands *Hardy's Birthplace* (NT, interior open by appointment). The writer spent his childhood in this low, thatched cottage and returned in 1867, writing 'Under the Greenwood Tree' and 'Far from the Madding Crowd' here. 120m: *Stinsford*, also S of the road, is the 'Mellstock' of Hardy's work. His heart is buried in the churchyard; the rest of him lies in Westminster Abbey.

122m: **DORCHESTER** (15,000 inhabitants), the county town of Dorset, has been luckier than many county towns in keeping its character despite modern development and expansion. It preserves the market atmosphere and many of the specific features described by Hardy, who calls it 'Casterbridge'. Dorchester's appeal lies not so much in individual buildings as in the general effect of its lively but dignified streetscapes.

TI: 1 Acland Rd. **Railway Stations**: Dorchester South and Dorchester West, both S of the centre, off Weymouth Avenue.

History. The site of an Iron Age settlement became the Roman Durnovaria after about AD 70. Dorchester is rich in Roman remains (eg. Maumbury Rings) and the course of the old walls is marked by the tree-lined avenues known as 'The Walks'. In the Civil War the town was staunchly Parliamentarian, though it suffered a period of Royalist occupation. After the Battle of Sedgemoor in 1685 it was the scene of the notorious Bloody Assizes, where Judge Jeffreys sentenced 74 of Monmouth's supporters to death and 175 to transportation. The Tolpuddle Martyrs were tried here in 1834.

Residents: The Dorset poet William Barnes (1801–86) and Thomas Hardy (1840–1928).

A35 becomes B3150, leading into High East St. It climbs from the water meadows of the Frome past (all on the right) the *King's Arms*, an important location in 'The Mayor of Casterbridge', made conspicuous by its handsome portico with bow window above, and the 19C Town Hall and *Corn Exchange* to the 15C church of **St Peter**, with a statue of William Barnes outside. The church has two 14C effigies in the Hardy Chapel, a monument to the politician Denzil Holles (d. 1680) and an effective 19C reredos. From the junction outside the church Cornhill leads S, passing on the right Antelope Walk, which contains the Oak Room where Judge Jeffreys is reputed to have presided over the Bloody Assizes. Cornhill continues as South St., with (on the left) the 18C house, now Barclays Bank, which Hardy made Michael Henchard's home and *Napper's Mite*, a 17C almshouse restored as shops.

On the opposite side of the street a plaque marks the home of William Barnes, next to the architect's office where the young Hardy worked.

Weymouth Avenue leads from the junction at the bottom of South St. to *Maumbury Rings*, the largest and best preserved Roman amphitheatre in the country.

High West St. leads from St Peter's Church, beginning with the *Dorset County Museum on the right. It contains fine collections of natural history, agricultural equipment, fossils and British and Roman antiquities, including a hoard of 22,000 silver coins, a figure of a Thracian horseman and a late 4C *mosaic pavement from Hinton St Mary. There are also relics of Barnes and Hardy, among them a reconstruction of Hardy's study at Max Gate. On the opposite side of the street is the traditional lodging of Judge Jeffreys, now a café. Further up on the right is the *Old Shire Hall*, with the *Old Court* (open) where the Tolpuddle Martyrs were tried. The Top o' Town is marked by a roundabout and a statue of Hardy (1931; Eric Kennington).

From the roundabout the Bridport road leads straight ahead to the *Dorset Military Museum*, with an unusually good collection. Poundbury Rd, by the museum, leads right to (1m) *Poundbury Camp*, an Iron Age earthwork later used by the Romans. In West Walks, left from the Top o' Town roundabout, a fragment of the Roman W wall can be seen. A37 leads to (1½m) *Wolfeton House* (open), an early 16C and Elizabethan house with an irregular gatehouse, fine woodwork, fireplaces and plaster ceilings in the Parlour and Dining Room, and a stone staircase.

A352, the Wareham road, runs SE from Dorchester. After about 1m is *Max Gate* (NT; limited opening), the house Hardy designed for himself in the 1880s and lived in until his death. A right turn ½m beyond leads to *Winterbourne Came*, where Barnes was rector from 1862 until his death.

Off A354, the Weymouth road, on a conspicuous hill about 2m S of Dorchester stands *Maiden Castle (EH). It is perhaps the finest prehistoric fort in England, covering 115 acres and at one point showing eight lines of defence. Excavations have shown that the hill was occupied first as a Neolithic camp and again from c 500 BC. Most of the earthworks were built in the 1C BC, only to be stormed by the Roman general Vespasian in AD 43. The last building was a 4C Roman temple near the top of the hill.

From Dorchester to *Wimborne* and *Bournemouth*, see Route 17B; to *Sherborne*, see Route 18A; to *Exeter*, see Route 18B.

A354, the Weymouth road, climbs to the Ridgeway, with Maiden Castle on the right, and then descends through (127m) *Upwey*.

131m: **WEYMOUTH** (46,300 inhabitants), an old harbour town and resort with late Georgian buildings, stands on both sides of the Wey, the older part to the S and the newer part (once known as Melcombe Regis) to the N. The harbour divides the bay into Weymouth Bay (N) and Portland Roads (S).

TI: The King's Statue, The Esplanade. **Bus Station**: Edward St. **Railway Stations**: at junction of King St. and Queen St., and at Ferry Terminal. **Amusements**: Seaside amusements at Alexandra Gardens, Pier Bandstand, Bowleaze Cove (2m NE); summer shows, etc. in Pavilion Theatre; concerts at Harbour Pleasure Pier. **Ferry services**: to Guernsey, Jersey and (summer only) Cherbourg.

History. Weymouth's natural situation has given it a long history as a port and military base. John Endicott sailed in 1628 to found the plantation of Salem in Massachusetts, and the American assault force was launched from here on D-Day in 1944. The town's popularity as a resort began in 1789, when George III paid the first of many visits. Hardy's 'The Trumpet-Major' evokes Weymouth ('Budmouth') as a 'royal watering-place' during the Napoleonic era.

Natives: The painter Sir James Thornhill (1675–1734) and Thomas Love Peacock (1785–1866).

The old harbour town of Weymouth

The most striking landmark N of the river and the landlocked harbour is the painted and gilded *statue of George III (1810) on the Esplanade. Among the Georgian buildings to the N is the *Gloucester Hotel*, the king's summer home during his visits. Beyond the fanciful *Jubilee Clock* (1887) are, both on the left, *Greenhill Gardens* and *Lodmoor Country Park*, 70 acres of salt marshland kept as a nature reserve.

Westham Rd leads W from the king's statue to Westham Bridge and *Weymouth Museum*, with an exhibit of local history including George III's bathing-machine. *Radipole Lake*, an extension of the Wey to the N, has a bird sanctuary and swannery.

The attractive St Mary St. leads S from the king's statue to the 19C church of *St Mary*, with an altarpiece by Thornhill. The street continues to Custom House Quay, where the Town Bridge leads to the old town. In Trinity St., to the left, is *Tudor House* (limited opening), restored and fitted with appropriate furnishings. The headland to the E ends with *Nothe Gardens*, the Victorian *Nothe Fort* (open) and the old stone pier of 1824.

S of Weymouth is the **Isle of Portland** (10,900 inhabitants), a limestone peninsula 4½m long and 1¾m wide. Its rocky and almost treeless surface is pitted by the quarries that have yielded white stone for many fashionable buildings since Wren chose it to face St Paul's Cathedral. The bleak landscape is relieved by fine views out to sea and particularly across Portland Harbour. The peninsula is joined to the mainland by *Chesil Beach*, a bank of shingle about 30ft high and 200yd wide, extending 18m W to Bridport. The pebbles gradually decrease in size from E to W.

A354 passes through the suburban village of *Wyke Regis* as it leaves Weymouth and reaches Portland at (4m) *Fortuneswell*. A road branches left to *Castletown*, with a Royal Navy base and *Portland Castle*, built by Henry VIII in 1520 (EH, summer season). *Sandsfoot Castle*, his other blockhouse on the opposite shore, is in ruins. *Portland Breakwater*, built by convicts in 1849–72, is c 6000ft long and encloses the largest harbour in the kingdom (2107 acres); an inner harbour was added in 1947. A354 climbs past quarries to (5½m) *Easton*, the island's main village. *St George's church, W of the centre, was built in 1744–66 by a local mason, Thomas Gilbert. The *Tout Quarry Sculpture Park* has a remarkable display. On Wakeham Rd to the S is the *Portland Museum*, devoted to local history; the 17C building is also known as Avice's Cottage, from its connection with Hardy's 'The Well-Beloved'. *Pennsylvania Castle* (now a hotel) was built c 1800 by James Wyatt for John Penn, governor of the island and a grandson of William Penn. Its grounds include the ruins of the late 11C *Rufus Castle*. A footpath leads down to *Church Ope Cove*, where there is good swimming and a ruined watch-tower contemporary with Portland Castle. 7m: *Southwell* is the last village before the small hamlet of (8½m) *Portland Bill*, a mass of rock with a bird observatory and an old lighthouse overlooking the dangerous race offshore. Much of the area belongs to the Ministry of Defence.

FROM WEYMOUTH TO BRIDPORT, 18m by B3157, with good views of Chesil Beach. 9m: *Abbotsbury* is a charming village, popular with visitors. It has the ruins of a Benedictine abbey, with a fine 15C barn (not open) and a gable near the churchyard (EH), as well as a swannery and sub-tropical gardens (both open in summer). On a height to the S stands the 15C *St Catherine's Chapel*, with a stone vault (EH, all year plus Mondays in winter). 18m: *Bridport*, see Route 18B.

B. Via Bournemouth

Directions. Total distance 142m. A4, A30 to (46m) Basingstoke (bypassed), or alternative way by M3, see Route 14B. A30, M3, A303, A30 to (82m) **Salisbury**, see Route 17A. A338 to (98m) Ringwood. A31, A338 to (109m) **Bournemouth**. A35, A350 to (115m) Poole. A350, A35, A351 to (124m) Wareham. A352, A353 to (142m) Weymouth. OS Outdoor Leisure map (2½in to 1m) for Purbeck.

From London to (46m) *Basingstoke*, see Route 14B, and on to (82m) **Salisbury**, see Route 17A. A338 goes down the Avon valley. 88m: *Downton* has a partly Norman church and a moot, or mound, where Saxon assemblies were held (not open). *Trafalgar House* (1½m N; not open), built in 1733 and extended later in the same century, was given to Nelson's family by the nation after the Battle of Trafalgar. *Newhouse* (limited opening), at *Redlynch* 3m E, is Jacobean and Georgian. Over the Hampshire border at (90m) *Breamore* (pronounced 'Bremmer') the 10–11C *church has a stone rood and an Anglo-Saxon inscription over the archway to the S transept. The church stands in parkland near *Breamore House* (open), an Elizabethan mansion in rose-red brick, partly rebuilt after a fire in 19C.

The Great Hall overlooks the Avon valley. The Dining Room has a carved stone Renaissance fireplace and (like the bedrooms) good 16–17C furniture. Among the portraits by Thomas Hudson in the West Drawing Room is one of the earliest paintings to show cricketing equipment. The grounds contain a *Carriage Museum* and a *Countryside Museum* with agricultural machinery.

92m: *Fordingbridge* (seasonal TI), where Augustus John died in 1961, has a 13–15C church. From (98m) *Ringwood* (seasonal TI), near the W fringes of the New Forest, B3347 continues down the Avon valley to approach

Bournemouth through Christchurch; the faster route follows A31 and then A338.

109m: **BOURNEMOUTH** (158,800 inhabitants) stands at the mouth of the little Bourne valley overlooking Poole Bay. Its cliffs are interrupted by beautiful 'chines', or ravines, while its inland scenery is rich in pinewoods, well preserved in about 2000 acres of public parks and gardens. To its earlier popularity as a resort Bournemouth has added a reputation as a conference venue.

TI: Westover Rd. **Railway and Coach Station**: at Travel Interchange, off Holdenhurst Rd. Local buses from the Square, country services from the Triangle. **Amusements**: Pier Theatre; Pavilion (theatre, ballroom, etc.) on Westover Rd; Bournemouth International Centre (with two concert halls). **Airport**: at Hurn (off A338 5m N). Flights to Alderney, Guernsey and Jersey.

Natives and residents: Sir Hubert Parry (1848–1918) was born and John Keble (1792–1866) died here. Verlaine taught at St Aloysius' College in 1875–76. Robert Louis Stevenson lived in 1884–87 in a house on Alum Chine Rd whose site is now occupied by a memorial garden.

In the graveyard of *St Peter's*, E of the Square, are the tombs of William Godwin (d. 1836), his wife Mary Wollstonecraft (d. 1797), and their daughter Mary Shelley (d. 1851), author of 'Frankenstein'. Shelley's heart, retrieved from his funeral pyre at Viareggio, is buried in his wife's grave. The *Russell–Cotes Art Gallery and Museum*, on East Cliff Promenade S of the church, is housed in a late Victorian villa. Its collections include 17–20C paintings (works by Morland and Richard Wilson and Rossetti), ceramics, three rooms of Japanese art, an Irving room of theatrical relics and five period rooms.

The banks of the Bourne are attractively laid out with gardens, and behind the large *Meyrick Park*, N of the Square, stretch the remains of *Talbot Woods*, with fragrant pine trees. On the coastline to the W are *Durley Chine, Middle Chine, Alum Chine* and *•Branksome Chine. Boscombe Chine* lies to the E.

6m W on A35 is **Christchurch** (33,300 inhabitants; TI), an old town at the head of Christchurch Harbour between the Avon and the Stour. Once known as 'Twineham', it takes its present name from the magnificent *•Priory Church*, now the longest parish church in England (312ft).

The late 15C W tower (120ft high) offers a fine view from the top. There is beautiful Norman work (c 1090–1120) on the outside of the N transept. The N Porch (c 1300) is the largest in the country; under the tower is a monument to Shelley by H. Weekes (1854). The *•Nave*, built by Bishop Flambard of Durham about 1093, is a fine example of Norman work, especially in the triforium; the clerestory is Early English and the vaulting is by William Garbett (1819). The aisles are Norman, recast in the 13C. The 14C rood screen was drastically restored in 1848. The Choir is for the most part late 15C; the stalls have fanciful misericords (1200–1500), but the chief feature is the Decorated stone *•reredos representing the Tree of Jesse. Note also the Chantry of the Countess of Salisbury (beheaded 1541), the Lady Chapel (c 1405), St Michael's Loft (with a museum), the Draper Chantry (1529) at the E end of the S aisle, and Flaxman's monument to Viscountess Fitzharris (d. 1815).

Opposite the King's Arms, N of the church, are the ruins of *Christchurch Castle and Norman House* (EH). The Georgian *Red House* in Quay Rd contains a small museum of local interest. About 2m S is *Hengistbury Head*, with fine sea views, and 2m SE is *Mudeford*.

The main route leaves Bournemouth to the W through the suburbs of *Branksome* and *Parkstone*, where the Italianate church of St Osmund (1905)

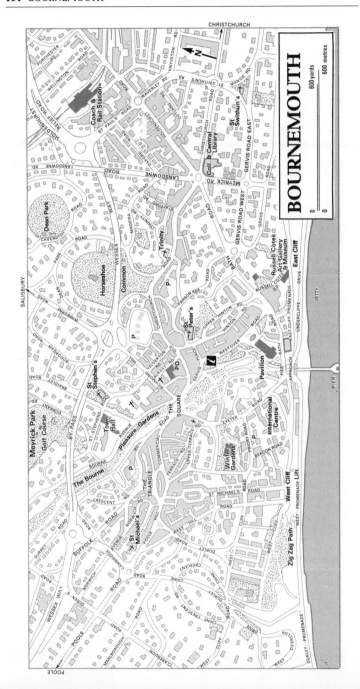

has 17C ironwork from St Mary-le-Bow in London. B3369 leads left to (2m) *Canford Cliffs* and the magnificent gardens of *Compton Acres* (open), established in the 1920s, with seven individual gardens (Japanese, Italian, Rock and Water, Heather, Roman, English and Palm Court).

115m: **Poole** (135,000 inhabitants; TI) is an old port. On the Quay, lined with warehouses, are the *Custom House* and *Poole Pottery* (open for tours). The *Waterfront Museum* is housed in a late 15C building. *Scaplen's Court* (open), in the High St., is another 15C house, arranged as a museum of domestic history. The 18C *Guildhall* (open) on Market St., off High St., has displays of local history. Ferries cross to Guernsey, Jersey, Cherbourg and St Malo.

The Quay faces **Poole Harbour**, a large and almost landlocked bay fringed with heathland. Near its narrow mouth is *Brownsea Island* (NT), reached by passenger ferry from Poole Quay and Sandbanks. It includes a nature reserve, with a heronry, waterfowl sanctuary and red squirrels, and gives fine views of the Dorset coast. The Boy Scout movement began at a trial camp here in 1907.

FROM POOLE TO DORCHESTER VIA WIMBORNE MINSTER, 27m on A349, A31 and A35.
5m: **Wimborne Minster** (5500 inhabitants; TI), an old market town on the Allen where it meets the Stour, has Georgian houses and a fine *Minster*, or collegiate church. The crossing tower, in red sandstone, is Transitional Norman and the W tower (1448–64) is Perpendicular. The most interesting features of the crowded interior, with much Norman work, are: the early 16C Flemish glass of the E window, the monument to the Duke of Somerset (d. 1444) and his wife in the choir, the chained library, and the late 16C clock in the W tower. S of the church is the *Priest's House Museum*. Near the Allen is *Deans Court Garden* (limited opening).

Canford Magna, 1½m SE, has a 12C church with the tomb of Sir Henry Layard (1817–94), excavator of Nineveh, and Canford School, built as a country house by Barry in the 1840s. In *West Moors*, 7m NE of Wimborne, is *Highbury Garden* (limited opening). On B3082 1½m NW of Wimborne stands **Kingston Lacy** (NT), a house originally built by Sir Roger Pratt in 1663–65 and transformed in 1835–40 by Charles Barry, who encased the brick exterior in Chilmark stone. Note his fine marble staircase and the library added by Robert Brettingham in the 1780s. Much of the splendid interior decoration was acquired or commissioned in Italy by William John Bankes (1786–1855), the collector and traveller. The furniture in the saloon includes items from William Beckford's Fonthill Abbey. The *art collection has Bankes family portraits by Van Dyck, Lely, Lawrence, Romney and Salvator Rosa. Many of the other pictures were collected by William Bankes; they include works by Sebastiano del Piombo (in the dining room), Giulio Romano, Jan Brueghel the Elder, Titian and Rubens (all in the saloon), and Zurbaran and Murillo (in the Spanish room). The wooded park has Red Devon cattle. B3082 continues beyond Kingston Lacy to (4m) *Badbury Rings*, an Iron Age hill-fort with good views, reputed to be the site of Arthur's last battle, Mons Badonicus; the Romans made it one of their main road junctions. B3082 ends at (9m) *Blandford Forum* (Route 17A).

A31 leads W from Wimborne along the valley of the Stour, passing (10m) the prominent Lion and Stag Gate of *Charborough Park*. At (13m) *Winterbourne Tomson* the tiny apsidal church has beautiful 18C oak fittings. A35 is joined at (16m) *Bere Regis*, the 'Kingsbere' of Hardy's 'Tess'. The interesting church has a carved timber ceiling and the burial chapel of the Turbervilles. *Woodbury Hill*, nearby, is the scene of 'Greenhill Fair' in Hardy's 'Far from the Madding Crowd'. At (19m) *Tolpuddle* the line of the Roman road from Badbury Rings crosses A35. The Tolpuddle Martyrs were five agricultural workers sentenced to transportation in 1834 for 'forming an illegal union' and now regarded as pioneers of the Trade Union movement. For (21½m) *Athelhampton*, (22m) *Puddletown* and (27m) *Dorchester*, see Route 17A.

The main route follows A350 and A35 from Poole around Hole's Bay, a branch of the harbour. At (120m) *Lytchett Minster* it bears left on A351.

124m: **Wareham** (4600 inhabitants; TI), an interesting little town on the navigable Frome, is built within an enceinte of massive Anglo-Saxon earthworks ('the Walls'), with its four main streets intersecting at right-angles. *Lady St Mary's Church* contains a stone coffin traditionally connected with King Edward the Martyr. There is also an hexagonal lead font and two remarkable little chapels. *St Martin's*, a small church on the walls, is pártly Saxon and has some badly damaged Norman wall paintings. The fine monument to T.E. Lawrence (see below) is by Eric Kennington.

The **Isle of Purbeck**, SE of Wareham, is a bold promontory of downs and heath yielding potter's clay and the shelly limestone known as Purbeck marble. A351 goes down the centre of the headland. 1m: *Stoborough*. An unclassified road leads NE to (3m) the heathland village of *Arne*, with an Early English church. The walk from Arne to *Shipstal Point*, overlooking Poole Harbour, passes through a nature reserve with deer. From Stoborough an unclassified road leads 2m SW to a ridge of the *Purbeck Hills*, with a *view from the summit. Kimmeridge and its bay (see below) lie beyond. 5m: *Corfe Castle* is a pretty village surrounding an isolated hill strategically placed in the middle of a gap in the Downs. Above it stand the striking ruins of its *Castle (NT). Lady Bankes defended it against 600 Parliamentary troops for six weeks in 1643, but it was betrayed and seized in 1646, and reduced to its present curiously shattered state by gunpowder. The mainly Norman building occupies the site of a 10C Saxon stronghold of King Edgar. Edward the Martyr was murdered at the gate by his stepmother Elfrida in 979 to clear the way to the throne for her son Ethelred. It was a favourite residence of King John, and Edward II was imprisoned here in 1326 just before his death at Berkeley Castle.

Church Knowle, 1½m SW of Corfe, has a painted triple chancel arch and a wall tomb of 1572. Sideroads continue another 3½m W via *Steeple* to the village of *Tyneham*, a good starting-point for walks to, for example, *Worbarrow Bay*. The tiny village of *Kimmeridge* lies 2½m SW of Church Knowle, near *Smedmore House* (limited opening), built mainly in the 18C, with marquetry furniture, paintings (David Cox and Copley Fielding), antique dolls and a walled garden. A private toll road runs to the secluded *Kimmeridge Bay*. The folly overlooking the beach is reputed to have suggested the 'black tower' in P.D. James' novel of that title.

Kingston, in a fine position high on the downs 2m S of Corfe Castle, has a sumptuous church by G.E. Street (1880). Chancellor Eldon, buried in the old parish church, died in 1838 at *Encombe*, 1½m SW. The area abounds in small Purbeck marble quarries. At *Sunnydown*, to the right of B3069 on the way from Kingston to Langton Matravers, some of the finest dinosaur footprints in Britain can be seen.

A351 continues to (11m) *Langton Matravers*, with a church tastefully rebuilt in 1875 and a small museum of stone crafts and local history. 11m: **Swanage** (8600 inhabitants; TI) stands on a fine bay. Its natives include John Mowlem (1788–1867), founder of the building company. He was responsible for using Wren's frontage for the Mercers' Hall in London as the façade of the *Town Hall*; he also moved the clock tower, originally erected in honour of the Duke of Wellington at the S end of London Bridge, to its present position near Swanage's pier. Other 19C survivals include the millpond in the centre of the old town and the lock-up behind the church.

A road runs on to (½m) *Peveril Point* and the coastguard station. Another road goes S to (1¼m) *Durlstone Head* and on to the *Tilly Whim Caves* (now closed), once used by smugglers. From here a spectacular walk can be taken W along the cliffs past (1½m) *Dancing Ledge* (NT), so-called from the motion of the making tide, to (4½m) *St Aldhelm's Head*, with a Norman chapel, and (5½m) the lovely little bay of *Chapman's Pool*. The Dorset Coast Path (see below) continues W to Weymouth. The return to (6m) Swanage can be made through *Worth Matravers*, where the Norman church has an impressive S door and chancel arch, and Langton Matravers.

About 3m N of Swanage is the charming village of *Studland*, with a tiny Norman church, a pretty bay and a nature reserve (NT). On the moor 1m NW of Studland is a curious perched block of ferruginous sandstone known as the *Agglestone*. A toll road continues 3m further to the floating bridge for Sandbanks and Bournemouth.

The main route follows A352 W from Wareham along the valley of the Frome. 129m: The pretty village of *Wool* has Woolbridge Manor (now a hotel), approached by a fine bridge, the home of the Turbervilles where Tess and Angel Clare spent their wedding night. The romantic but scanty ruins of *Bindon Abbey* (not open), founded by Robert de Newburgh in 1172, lie about ½m E.

About 2m N is *Bovington Camp*, the original headquarters of the Royal Tank Corps, with a Tank Museum. On the Puddletown road further N is *Clouds Hill* (NT), the cottage belonging to T.E. Lawrence (Lawrence of Arabia; 1888–1935). He is buried at *Moreton*, near B3390 to the W.
    Lulworth Cove, 5m S of Wool, is a remarkable circular bay about 500yd in diameter, almost completely landlocked by tall oolite and chalk hills. The *Dorset Coast Path leads W along the cliffs to (10m) Weymouth. To the E, on the way to the Isle of Purbeck, it passes through military firing ranges and is closed most weekdays.

At 136m the Weymouth road, A353, leaves the Dorchester road and crosses the Downs. To the right beyond (139m) *Osmington* is a figure on horseback cut into the chalk, supposed to represent George III (see 'The Trumpet Major'). Left of the road at (140m) *Overcombe* are the foundations of the small *Jordan Hill Roman Temple* (EH). 142m: **Weymouth**, see Route 17A.

18

London to Exeter

A. Via Salisbury and Yeovil

Directions. Total distance 170m. An excellent route for country houses, but A30 is congested during summer weekends and other holiday periods. At such times A303, though not free of problems, is preferable: follow the main line of Route 19 to Sparkford and then the Sparkford–Exeter detour. A4, A30 to (46m) Basingstoke (bypassed), or alternative way by M3, see Route 14B. A30, M3, A303, A30 to (82m) Salisbury, see Route 17A. A30 to (86m) Wilton, (102m) **Shaftesbury**, to (118m) **Sherborne**, (123m) **Yeovil**, (132m) Crewkerne, (141m) Chard, (154m) Honiton (bypassed) and (170m) **Exeter**.

From London to (46m) *Basingstoke*, see Route 14B, and on to (82m) *Salisbury*, see Route 17A. 86m: *Wilton* (4000 inhabitants) is a carpet-making town. The lavish Italian Romanesque church is by T.H. Wyatt (1844), with 12–16C glass from various sources. The magnificent 16–17C **Wilton House** (open) is particularly interesting for the *work of Inigo Jones and for its *art collection.

Of the house built by the 1st Earl of Pembroke in the 1540s on the site of a former abbey, only the general plan and the Holbein Porch remain (the latter moved to the grounds). The Elizabethan house that succeeded it was given an Italianate S front by Isaac de Caus (c 1633), superbly restored after a fire by Inigo Jones and his nephew-in-law John Webb (1649–52). James Wyatt's Gothic alterations (1801–14) have been modified outside but can still be seen inside. The Front Hall has a statue by Peter Scheemakers (1743) of Shakespeare, who may have acted in 'As You Like It' here in

The Palladian Bridge at Wilton House

1603. The Single Cube Room, the first of Inigo Jones's splendid state rooms, has a dado by de Critz illustrating scenes from Sir Philip Sidney's 'Arcadia', which was partly written here. The elaborately decorated Double Cube Room has a fine display of Van Dycks, among them a portrait of Charles I and one of his children. Paintings elsewhere in the house include works by Andrea del Sarto, Pieter Brueghel the Younger, Jan Brueghel the Elder, Rembrandt, Wouvermans, Rubens, Lely, Poussin, Teniers and Richard Wilson; there are also terracotta busts by Roubiliac, and furniture by Chippendale and William Kent. Apart from various amusements, the grounds contain an 18C Palladian bridge.

FROM WILTON TO WARMINSTER AND LONGLEAT, 20m by A36 and A362. A36 follows the valley of the Wylye. Though close, the river is largely hidden from view, and the prettier scenery along the S bank can be seen from a little unclassified road. At (11m) *Codford St Peter* the church has an excellently carved 9C cross shaft. At (14m) *Heytesbury* are an imposing 12–15C church restored by Butterfield and a Tudor almshouse faithfully rebuilt c 1769. Siegfried Sassoon died at Heytesbury House in 1967. *Scratchbury* and *Battlesbury*, two Iron Age forts to the right of the road further on, both give wide views. 18m: **Warminster** (15,100 inhabitants; TI) lies just below the Downs at the junction with A350, the Chippenham–Shaftesbury road (Route 20). The Georgian main street has good coaching inns, and there is an organ formerly at Salisbury Cathedral in the 14C parish *Church. Lord Weymouth School*, founded in

1707 by the Thynnes of Longleat, has a portal by Wren. Dr Arnold of Rugby was a pupil.

A362 runs W to Frome (8m, see Route 24). Below (2m) *Cley Hill*, another conspicuous Iron Age hill-fort, is the entrance to **Longleat** (open). Built for Sir John Thynne in 1559–80, with Robert Smythson among the architects, the house breaks with older traditions in the regularity of its plan and the uniform handling of all four main fronts. Inside, only the Great Hall belongs substantially to Thynne's time, with stone floor and hammerbeam ceiling. The corridors and main staircase are part of Sir Jeffrey Wyatville's alterations (1801–11) and the Italianate decoration in many of the rooms, including the former Long Gallery, was added in the 1870s. The Old Library where Bishop Ken (1637–1711) wrote his hymns is not open. Most striking of the many paintings are the portraits and, in the State Drawing Room, a Holy Family attributed to Titian. The grounds were landscaped by Capability Brown (1757–62) and Repton (c 1790). Their atmosphere is not improved by the various amusements housed in the former outbuildings or by the Safari Park, attractions which also make Longleat crowded in summer. At *Horningsham*, 1m S, the Meeting House is said to have been built in 1566 by Thynne for his Scottish Presbyterian masons and is claimed as England's oldest Dissenting place of worship.

FROM WILTON TO MERE, 25m. From *Barford St Martin*, on A30 3m W of Wilton, B3089 heads along the Nadder valley. 7m: *Dinton*. Near the church is Hyde's House (NT but not open), a building of 1725 on the probable site of the house where Edward Hyde, Earl of Clarendon (1609–74) and historian of the Civil War, was born. The neo-Grecian Philipps House (NT, open by appointment only) was built in 1813–16 by Sir Jeffrey Wyatville. Little Clarendon (NT, open by appointment only) is a late 15C house. Henry Lawes (1596–1662), composer and friend of Milton, was born at the adjoining cottage (NT, open by appointment only). 10m: *Teffont Magna* is a pretty village. The gardens of Fitz House are open on limited days in summer. S of (15m) *Fonthill Bishop* stood Fonthill Abbey, the extravagant and insecurely founded Gothick mansion built by James Wyatt in 1796–1812 for William Beckford (1759–1844), author of a fine 'Vathek'. *Tisbury*, 3m S of B3089, has a large 12–13C cruciform church with a fine 15C roof. *Wardour Castle*, 2m SW of Tisbury, is a country house by James Paine (1769–76), with a fine staircase and a chapel enlarged by Sir John Soane (1788). It is now a school (open in summer holidays). The earlier home of the Lords Arundell of Wardour is ¾m SE, near A30, at *Wardour Old Castle* (EH, summer season, daily; winter, weekends only). Built c 1393, it was badly damaged in the Civil War but preserved for its picturesque appeal. At 20m B3089 crosses A350, the Chippenham–Shaftesbury road (Route 20). At 21m B3089 joins A303 4m E of *Mere* (Route 19).

The main route follows A30 W from Wilton, through Barford St Martin and (94m) *Fovant*, where the chalk downs are carved with the emblems of the troops quartered here in 1914–18. 101m: The road enters Dorset.

102m: **Shaftesbury** (4900 inhabitants; TI), wonderfully placed on a spur 700ft high, is the picturesque relic of a town whose ancient grandeur included a castle, twelve churches and four market crosses. The house for Benedictine nuns founded by Alfred in 880 became the wealthiest nunnery in England. The scanty *Abbey Ruins* (open) are beautifully laid out and excavation has revealed the ground plan of the church. The empty tomb of Edward the Martyr (d. 978) was found in 1861 on the N side of the altar, and in 1931 a casket containing what may be his bones was unearthed nearby. Canute died here in 1035. There is an interesting little museum. *St Peter's Church* has a good 15C N parapet and 16C W porch. The formidably steep *Gold Hill commands a lovely view. At the top is the *Local History Museum*, with a collection of buttons (once the town's chief manufacture).

FROM SHAFTESBURY TO RINGWOOD, 25m on B3081, a fine scenic road across Cranborne Chase. A zigzag climbs Charlton Down to 862ft. 8m: *Tollard Royal* was King John's seat for the hunting of Cranborne Chase. Beyond (13m) *Sixpenny Handley*, where the church has 13C wall paintings, B3081 crosses A354, the Salisbury–Blandford road

(Route 17A), and then the line of the Roman Ackerley Dyke. 18m: *Cranborne*, to the left, is a small town with a Tudor and Jacobean manor house. The *gardens (limited opening) were originally laid out by John Tradescant in the 17C. *Knowlton Church and Earthworks* (EH) consist of a ruined Norman church surrounded by the remains of a henge monument. *Edmondsham House* (limited opening), about 1m S of Cranborne on a sideroad to Verwood, blends Tudor and Georgian architecture. B3081 crosses Ringwood Forest. A31 leads left to (25m) *Ringwood* (Route 17B), on the Avon and near the W fringes of the New Forest (Route 16).

From Shaftesbury to Chippenham, see Route 20.

Beyond Shaftesbury A30 crosses the fertile *Vale of Blackmore* or *Blackmoor*, watered by the Stour and the Cale, familiar to readers of Hardy's 'Tess of the d'Urbervilles'.

From (108m) *East Stour* B3092 leads S via (4m) *Marnhull*, the 'Marlott' of 'Tess', to (9m) *Sturminster Newton*, a quiet market town on the Stour, where Hardy lived in 1876–78. The poet William Barnes (1801–86) was born at *Rushay*, 1½m W. Off A357 1m E of Sturminster Newton is *Fiddleford Manor* (EH, limited opening in summer only), the hall and solar block of a 14C house altered in the early 16C; the roofs are superb. From (112m) *Henstridge*, on the A30, A357 goes 3m S to *Stalbridge*, with a tall market cross.

114m: *Purse Caundle Manor* (open), on the left, is a picturesque medieval manor house in grey stone, with Tudor additions and an attractive garden. The church of (115m) *Milborne Port* has early Norman crossing.

118m: **Sherborne** (7600 inhabitants; TI) is a handsome stone-built town with a magnificent *Abbey Church. One of the best surviving examples of Perpendicular architecture, it also incorporates remains from earlier periods.

A bishopric was established at Sherborne in 705 and moved to Old Sarum in 1075. The abbey attached to the cathedral was occupied after 998 by Benedictine monks. The 11C doorway at the W end and the four piers that support the crossing survive from the last Saxon church on the site. Of the Norman church that replaced it after 1122, there remain the S porch, the crossing arch and parts of the N and S transepts. The Lady Chapel followed in the 13C. The 15C brought an almost complete rebuilding in the Perpendicular style, starting with the choir and continuing with the nave, both of which have exceptionally rich *fan vaulting.

The monuments are striking. The Wykeham Chapel off the N transept has the tomb of Sir John Horsey (d. 1546). In the N transept a stone marks the probable grave of the poet Sir Thomas Wyatt (d. 1542). In the S transept is the Baroque memorial (1698) by John Nost to John Digby, 3rd Earl of Bristol, and his two wives. St Katherine's Chapel, on the W side, contains the tomb of John Leweston (d. 1584) and some good 15C heraldic glass. The peal of eight bells in the tower is said to be the heaviest in the world.

Sherborne School, a public school for boys refounded by Edward VI in 1550, incorporates the 15C Abbot's Hall and other monastic buildings. Pupils have included the writers John Cowper and Llewelyn Powys. The *Almshouse of St John the Baptist and St John the Evangelist*, on Trendle St. nearby, is a two-storied medieval hospital (1437). Among the pleasant row of old buildings on Half Moon St., heading E from the abbey church, is the *Museum*, with collections of local history and a Victorian dolls' house. The street ends at the early 16C *Conduit*. Cheap St. runs N, passing Newland with *Lord Digby's School* (c 1720) on the right, to The Green, with a charming 16C building known as *The Julian*.

On the S side of the Yeo ½m E are the ruins of the bishop's *Castle* built in the early 12C and briefly inhabited by Sir Walter Raleigh (EH, all year). On the opposite side of the lake stands the present *Sherborne Castle* (open), built by Raleigh in 1594. Most of the interior was remodelled in 1859–60, though there is a 17C plaster ceiling in the Red Drawing Room, a Gothick Library of c 1760 and a fine collection of Digby family portraits. The park has lovely walks and views. The Tudor manor house (open) at *Sandford Orcas*, off B3148 4m N, has good glass and furniture, and an attractive garden.

FROM SHERBORNE TO DORCHESTER, 19m by A352, through the countryside of Hardy's 'The Woodlanders'. 8½m: An unclassified road leads right, across *Batcombe Down* (*views). The remote church of *Melbury Bubb*, 4m N of the road, has a very early Norman carved *font. 9m: *Minterne Magna* with the Edwardian Minterne House (gardens open). 11m: *Cerne Abbas* is a charming village, popular with visitors, preserving the beautiful 15C gatehouse of a Benedictine abbey. The church has 14C wall paintings and a 15C screen. Above it is the *Cerne Giant* (NT), a figure 180ft long cut in the chalk. 19m: *Dorchester* (Route 17A).

121m: *Compton House* (open), N of A30, houses exotic butterflies and the Lullingstone Silk Farm. At *Bradford Abbas*, S of the road, the church has a notable W front, stone screen, font and 15C bench ends. A30 crosses the Yeo and enters Somerset. 123m: **Yeovil** (27,300 inhabitants; TI) is a busy town, badly served by modern development but keeping its old character round the Perpendicular *church.

T.S. Eliot (1888–1965) is buried and the navigator William Dampier (1652–1715) was born at *East Coker*, 3m SW.

FROM YEOVIL TO ILMINSTER, 14m by A3088 and A303. 2m: *Brympton d'Evercy* (not open), built of the local Ham Hill stone, is a satisfying mixture of styles and periods, early 16C and Elizabethan. *Odcombe*, 1m SW, was home of the eccentric traveller Sir Thomas Coryate (?1577–1617). 4m: *Montacute* has a Norman and Perpendicular church with a fine tower. *Montacute House* (NT), built for Sir Edward Phelips in the 1590s, is a masterpiece. The exterior, in Ham Hill stone weathered to a lovely gold, is enriched with balustrades, shaped gables, niches holding sculptured figures and, on the N and S sides, oriel windows marking either end of the Long Gallery. The Great Hall has a carved screen and a lively plaster frieze showing, among other scenes, a skimmington ride. Much of the panelling in the house has been renewed but the fireplaces and heraldic glass survive. Good collections of furniture and portraits (loaned by the National Portrait Gallery) have been assembled. 5½m: *Stoke-sub-Hamdon*, a charming village, has a church of outstanding interest and a 15C priory (NT, hall open). The Fleur-de-Lis inn has a fives court built in 1760. *Ham Hill*, with famous limestone quarries, has been a fort since Neolithic times. *Norton-sub-Hamdon*, 1m S, is dominated by its Perpendicular church tower. At 7m A3088 joins A303 and Route 19 for (14m) *Ilminster*.

132m: **Crewkerne** (5300 inhabitants) is a market town with a richly decorated 15C church, a grammar school founded in 1499 and almshouses of 1604 and 1707.

The pretty village of *Hinton St George*, 3m NW, has 16–19C monuments of the Poulett family in its church. The gardens (open) of *Clapton Court* are near B3165 3m SW of Crewkerne.

FROM CREWKERNE TO DORCHESTER, 21m by A356 and A37, a hilly route. A357 leaves Somerset for Dorset and climbs to (4m) *Winyard's Gap*, with NT woodland and a wide view. The road crosses *Toller Down*, where 'Far from the Madding Crowd' opens, and descends to (13m) *Maiden Newton*, where the church has a carillon of 35 bells cast in Louvain in 1882. 16m: A356 joins A37. 21m: *Dorchester* (Route 17A).

FROM CREWKERNE TO BRIDPORT, 12m by A356 and A3066. The route leaves A356 beyond (1½m) *Misterton*. 6m: **Beaminster** (pronounced 'Bemminster') is a handsome little place; its church has a stately Perpendicular tower adorned with sculptures. Thomas Fuller (1608–61) was rector of *Broadwindsor*, 3m NW. *Mapperton* (open), 2m SE , is a Tudor house enlarged in the 17C, with terraced gardens and old fish ponds. To the W of Beaminster rise *Lewesdon Hill* (894ft; NT) and *Pilsdon Pen* (909ft; *view), the highest hill in Dorset. Wordsworth lived in 1795–97 at *Racedown Lodge* (not open) below Pilsdon Pen, on B3165 (the Lyme Regis road) N of its junction with B3164 from Broadwindsor. 7m: *Parnham House* (open) is a Tudor mansion in lovely grounds. Later alterations to its exterior include the battlements and pinnacles added by Nash in 1810. The interior, including the Great Hall, is mainly the result of 20C reconstruction, though there is a carved 17C overmantel in the Strode Bedroom. Parnham also houses a furniture workshop and school for craftsmen in wood. 12m: *Bridport* (Route 18B).

A30 climbs above 750ft (view), then descends *Windwhistle Hill* between a noble avenue of beeches, skirting the grounds of *Cricket House*, built in 1804 for Admiral Hood. It now has a wildlife park. 141m: **Chard** (9400 inhabitants; TI) is a lace-making town with the former Court House of 1590 where Jeffreys sat at the 'Bloody Assizes'. Margaret Bondfield (1873–1953), the first woman cabinet minister, was born here; the painter Lucien Pissarro (1863–1944) died at *South Chard*, 2m S.

Parnham House

In the rich green valley of the Axe, off B3162 3½m SE, is *Forde Abbey (open). The house rose from the beautiful remains of a Cistercian abbey founded in 1138 and reconstructed in the Perpendicular style by the last abbot. Sir Edmund Prideaux's additions in the classical style (1649–59) blend remarkably well with the earlier work. They are seen at their best in the splendid Saloon, where Mortlake tapestries from Raphael's cartoons hang. The Chapel was formerly the abbey's chapter house. The lovely grounds extend to 25 acres. Jeremy Bentham rented Forde Abbey in 1814–17.

Axminster (seasonal TI), a pleasantly situated little town on A358 7m S of Chard, is known for making carpets. At *Musbury*, 2m SW, the church has the *Drake monument, with three pairs of polychrome stone figures (1588–1636), including the grandparents of the Duke of Marlborough. *Shute Barton*, 2m SW, is a 14–16C manor house (NT, guided tours only). The 17–18C *Loughwood Meeting House* (NT), 4m W of Axminster, was built by a local Baptist congregation.

The Exeter road grows very hilly, rising to 733ft beyond Snowdon Hill. Entering Devon, it crosses the Yarty valley and climbs past (146½m) *Yarcombe* to 874ft before being joined by A303. 154m: **Honiton** (6600 inhabitants; seasonal TI) is known for its lace, now chiefly made in the neighbouring villages, and its trout fishing. The harmonious 18C High St. has coaching inns. A375 diverges left for Sidmouth (Route 18B).

161m: A30 passes 1m N of **Ottery St Mary** (7000 inhabitants; seasonal TI), the birthplace of S.T. Coleridge (1772–1834) and the occasional childhood home of Thackeray, who made it 'Clavering St Mary' in 'Pendennis'. The town is interesting for its Early English and Decorated collegiate *church. Much of the exterior, including the transeptal towers, was copied from Exeter Cathedral by Bishop Grandisson in 1338–42. The Dorset aisle (1504–30) has fan vaulting, and the *clock keeps its original Elizabethan works. The weather vane (1335) is the oldest still working in England. The stocks still stand in the churchyard. 1m NW of Ottery is *Cadhay Manor* (limited opening), a 16C manor house behind an 18C entrance front. Its most striking feature is the courtyard in sandstone and flint chequerboarding, with statues of the Tudor monarchs over the doorways. 165m: *Clyst Honiton* and Exeter Airport (see below).

170m: **EXETER** (103,000 inhabitants), the county town of Devon, stands on rising ground on the NE bank of the Exe and is connected with the tidal estuary at Topsham by a ship canal, 5m long, begun in 1563. Despite damage from heavy wartime bombing, it remains a historic city, with a cathedral, substantial remains of its medieval walls and streets following their Roman course.

TI: Civic Centre, Paris St. and Exeter services area of M5 at Sandygate. **Bus Station**: Paris St. **Railway Stations**: St David's, off A377 NW of the centre; Central, near the Castle, ½m from St David's; St Thomas, off B3212 ½m SW of centre, for local (south Devon) trains. **Airport**: at Clyst Honiton, on A30 5m E. Flights to Belfast, Cork, Dinard, Dublin, Guernsey, Jersey, Manchester and Morlaix. **Theatres**: Barnfield, Barnfield Rd; Northcott, Exeter University. **Annual Events**: Devon County Show on Thursday–Saturday nearest to 16–18 May; Exeter Festival, first two weeks in July.

History. Exeter was the Isca Dumnoniorum of the Romans and the Escancestre of the Saxons. The city has often been attacked or besieged. The Danes stormed it in 876 and, though Athelstan built walls c 932, it was plundered again in 1003. In 1068 it submitted to William the Conqueror only after a long siege, and the castle was begun. Though occupied by Parliament at the onset of the Civil War, it was later held for the King until 1646. Bombing in 1942 destroyed 40 acres, including many old buildings.

Natives: Sir Thomas Bodley (1545–1613), Charles I's daughter Princess Henrietta (1644–70), Archbishop William Temple (1881–1944) and, probably, Nicholas Hilliard (1537–1619). Richard Hooker (1554–1600) was born at Heavitree, now a suburb to the E.

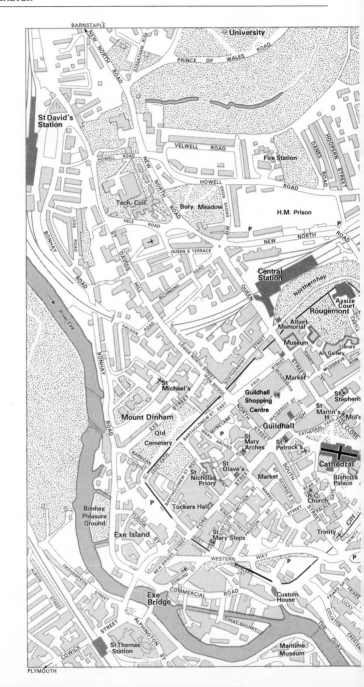

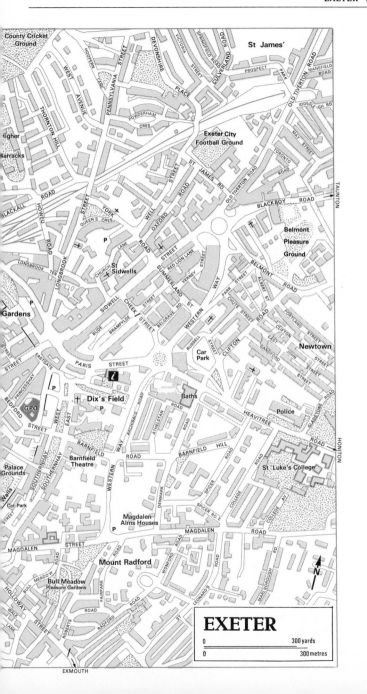

County Cricket Ground

St James'

Higher Barracks

Exeter City Football Ground

TAUNTON

BLACKBOY ROAD

Belmont Pleasure Ground

St Sidwells

Gardens

Newtown

Car Park

Paris Street

Dix's Field

Baths

Police

GPO

HEAVITREE ROAD

HONITON

Barnfield Theatre

St Luke's College

Palace Grounds

Magdalen Alms Houses

Mount Radford

Bull Meadow Pleasure Gardens

EXMOUTH

N

EXETER

| 0 | 300 yards |
| 0 | 300 metres |

The High St. keeps its Roman course but has been largely rebuilt since the German bombing. Broadgate, on the left beyond the Guildhall (see below), makes the best approach to the cathedral.

The *Cathedral, though comparatively small, is one of the most attractive in England. Except for the Norman towers, it is mainly in the Geometric Decorated style.

A Saxon monastery stood here by 680. The bishopric of Devon and Cornwall was moved from Crediton to Exeter in 1050, for its greater security. The conventual church founded by Athelstan c 932, which probably served as the earliest cathedral, was replaced by a Norman building (1112–1206). Of this the only important remains are the massive transeptal towers, unique in England except for the copies at Ottery St Mary. Bishop Bronescombe began to transform the Norman church c 1270; work continued under his successors until the time of Bishop Grandisson (d. 1369).

The many flying buttresses contrast effectively with the solid austerity of the Norman towers, to which the battlements and turrets were added in the 15C. The W façade is decorated with sculptured figures, the lower ones (with the Enthronement of the Virgin as their central subject) apparently added by Grandisson, the upper ones possibly as late as the 15C.

The most striking characteristic of the *interior is its uniform design, each detail marked by purity of style (Decorated) and answering to its counterpart with unfailing symmetry. The roof, with good bosses, forms the longest continuous stretch of Gothic vaulting in the world (over 300ft). There is a lofty clerestory but the triforium is represented by a small blank arcade. On the N side of the *Nave*, with its fine Purbeck marble pillars, is the *Minstrels' Gallery (by Bishop Grandisson). The *Transepts*, with beautiful window tracery and triforium galleries, were rebuilt by Bishops Bronescombe and Quivil (d. 1291) under the Norman towers. In the N transept are the Sylke Chantry (1508), a 15C wall painting of the Resurrection, a *clock of 1423 and a statue by Chantrey of the painter James Northcote (1746–1831). The S transept has the tomb of Hugh Courtenay, Earl of Devon (d. 1377), and his wife. From its SW corner a vestry leads to the *Chapter House*, Early English and Perpendicular with a ceiling of 1465–78. Its N and S niches contain polyester resin sculptures by Kenneth Carter (1974).

The *Choir* is separated from the nave by a triple-arched screen erected by Bishop Stapledon (d. 1326), with 17C paintings. Monuments include those of Bishops Marshall (d. 1206) and Stapledon on the N side. The stalls are 19C but with Early English misericords. The oak *Bishop's Throne and the stone sedilia are exquisite early 14C work. St James' Chapel (S), destroyed by bombing, has been beautifully rebuilt. St Andrew's Chapel (N) has a memorial window to the men of 'HMS Exeter', sunk in 1942. Bishop Oldham's Chantry (1519), in the SE corner, is decorated with owls in punning reference to the founder's name ('Owldham'). At the S side of the Lady Chapel entrance is a *wall painting (c 1500) of the Assumption and Coronation of the Virgin. The *Lady Chapel* is mainly Bronescombe's work and contains his intricately decorated tomb (1329), with its gilding and colour well restored.

On the S side of the cathedral part of the *Cloister* has been rebuilt in the original Decorated style. A wing of the rebuilt Bishop's Palace houses the *Cathedral Library* (open), entered from Palace Gate, which contains Anglo-Saxon charters, the Exeter Domesday MS and the Exeter Book, an Anglo-Saxon collection of poetry.

The **Cathedral Close** has several interesting old houses. By the 15C and 17C church of *St Martin* in the NE corner is *Mol's Coffee House* (1596), now a jeweller's. No. 5 has a 15C hall, while the *Old Law Library* at 8 occupies a 14C hall. Further on, a stone archway with a Jacobean oak door leads to a charming little quadrangle. A statue of Richard Hooker (by Alfred Drury) stands N of the cathedral.

Near the entrance to the cathedral on High St. are the much-altered *St Petrock*, with a pre-Norman tower and the *Guildhall. Dating from 1330 and thus one of the oldest civic buildings to survive in England, it has a pillared façade of 1593 projecting over the pavement. The Hall (open) has a fine roof of 1464, with corbels supposedly showing the bear and ragged

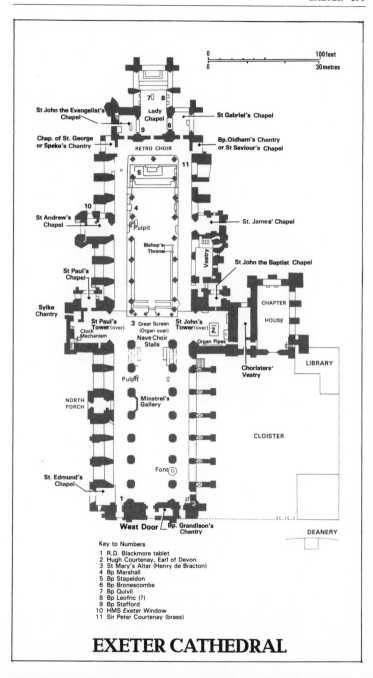

100 feet
30 metres

St John the Evangelist's Chapel

St Gabriel's Chapel

7 8

Lady Chapel

9 6

Chap. of St. George or Speke's Chantry

Bp.Oldham's Chantry or St Saviour's Chapel

RETRO CHOIR

11

5

St Andrew's Chapel

10

4

Pulpit

St. James' Chapel

Bishop's Throne

Vestry

St John the Baptist Chapel

St Paul's Chapel

Sylke Chantry

CHAPTER

HOUSE

St Paul's Tower (over)

Clock Mechanism

3 Great Screen (Organ over)

Nave Choir Stalls

St John's Tower (over)

2

Organ Pipes

LIBRARY

Choristers' Vestry

Pulpit

NORTH PORCH

Minstrel's Gallery

CLOISTER

Font

St. Edmund's Chapel

1

West Door Bp. Grandison's Chantry

DEANERY

Key to Numbers

1 R.D. Blackmore tablet
2 Hugh Courtenay, Earl of Devon
3 St Mary's Altar (Henry de Bracton)
4 Bp Marshall
5 Bp Stapeldon
6 Bp Bronescombe
7 Bp Quivil
8 Bp Leofric (?)
9 Bp Stafford
10 HMS *Exeter* Window
11 Sir Peter Courtenay (brass)

EXETER CATHEDRAL

staff of Warwick the Kingmaker, and panelled walls of 1595 ornamented with the arms of guilds, mayors, etc.

In Waterbeer St. behind the Guildhall is a tessellated pavement (covered) which may mark the site of the Roman Praetorium. Nearby is *St Pancras' Church*, with an Early English chancel and piscina, Norman font and Jacobean pulpit.

Further up High St. is *St Stephen's*, rebuilt c 1665 with an elevated chancel on an old arch called 'Stephen's Bow'. From the quiet little square behind, Bedford St. leads to Southernhay, a charming street with Georgian houses. On its W side is a fine section of the **City Wall** with bastions, revealed by bombing. In Eastgate, at the N end of Southernhay, is the entrance to the *Underground Passages* (open), probably medieval conduits for the city's water supply.

Eastgate leads back to High St. near its NE end. Castle St., almost opposite, leads N to the *Rougemont House* (open), a Georgian building with elegant bow windows and the beautiful **Rougemont Gardens**, which contain the scanty remains of William the Conqueror's *Castle*. Beyond Castle Yard (with the *County Assize Court* of 1774) stretch *Northernhay Gardens*, where another part of the old city wall can be seen. The *Prison* (1853) is prominent beyond the railway to the N.

The W part of the wall is reached via Northernhay St. and Bartholomew St. A footpath runs along the top, above the *Old Cemetery* (opened in 1637).

Queen St. leads from Northernhay's W exit back to the High St., passing the *Royal Albert Memorial Museum and Art Gallery*, with natural history and anthropology, Exeter silver, ceramics, glass, costumes from 1750 and an important collection of English paintings (works by Reynolds, Turner and Opie).

Fore St. continues from High St. down towards the Exe. A turning on the right leads to *St Mary Arches*, with Norman nave and Jacobean monuments. *St Olave's* in Fore St. has an unorthodox plan. In The Mint, a street leading to the right, is the guest wing of the Benedictine **•Priory of St Nicholas** (open), with a Norman undercroft, 13C and 15C kitchen, 15C guest hall and the prior's solar. In the garden is a 7C Celtic cross, attached for 200 years to a pier of the Exe Bridge. The Mint may take its name from the furnaces once in the undercroft. Lower down Fore St., on the right, is *Tucker's Hall* (open), the guildhouse of the 'weavers, fullers and shearmen', with a fine roof (1471) and oak panelling (1634).

The steep West St., following the line of the old wall to the left, has the interesting church of *St Mary Steps*, with a Norman font, fine rood screen and curious clock (c 1656). Next door are some 16C houses, including one moved from further W in 1961. Opposite the church stood the West Gate and a little further on was the Water Gate. On the Quay is the *Custom House* (1678–81). Beyond is the *Maritime Museum*, with a large collection of full-size boats, some of them afloat in the Canal Basin.

From the Custom House the line of the old city wall runs NE to the South Gate (removed in 1819) and along Southernhay (see above). In Magdalen St., branching right, is *Wynard's Hospital*, built c 1430, with a courtyard and a chapel sympathetically restored in the 19C. It is now a centre for voluntary organisations.

The *University of Exeter* occupies several fine mansions with beautiful grounds and new buildings by Holford in Prince of Wales Rd, about 1m N of the centre. Founded as a school of art in 1855 and incorporated as the University College of South-West England in 1922, it received its charter in 1955. The Northcott Theatre was opened in 1967.

About 1½m SW of the city, on B3212, is *Bowhill* (EH, summer season, weekdays 10.00–15.30; closed Bank Holidays and following Tuesdays). The great hall of this substantial mansion, built c 1500, has been restored.

FROM EXETER TO EXMOUTH, 11m. Leaving by South St. and passing (1m) the County Hall, the route crosses the bypass just above the Exe and the 16C *Countess of Wear Bridge* (widened 1937). 4m: *Topsham*, now a yachting centre, used to be the port of Exeter. The charming Strand has several houses in the Dutch style and a museum of local history. A ferry runs to Exminster and Turf. 5½m: A376 is joined S of *Clyst St George*. The sculptor Nicholas Stone (1586–1647) was born at *Woodbury*, 2m SE. 9m: *A La Ronde* (NT) is a 16-sided house built in 1796, with eccentric interior decorations. 11m: **Exmouth** (28,800 inhabitants; TI) has an esplanade and a view across the mouth of the Exe. A ferry runs to *Starcross* on the opposite bank, and there are excursion steamers in summer. A376 continues to Budleigh Salterton (Route 18B).

FROM EXETER TO BARNSTAPLE, 40m. A377 follows the Creed valley, passing (5m) *Newton St Cyres*, where the church has good monuments. 8m: **Crediton** (6200 inhabitants; seasonal TI), the birthplace of St Boniface or Winfrid (680–755), was the seat of the episcopal see of Devon and Cornwall from 909 until its removal to Exeter in 1050. The saint's statue is by Alan Durst (1960). The sandstone church, once collegiate, was founded in the 12C but dates mainly from the 15C. It has two good 17C tombs. At (14½m) *Morchard Road Station* B3220 for Bideford branches left. A377 enters the beautiful valley of the Taw (good fishing). 17m: *Lapford* church, on the right, has a wealth of woodwork. 21m: *Eggesford* has Chichester monuments in its church, while *Chawleigh*, 2m NE, and *Chulmleigh*, 2½m N, have rood screens. 32m: *Umberleigh* lies between two villages with interesting churches: *Atherington*, 1¼m W, has a 16C rood loft and *Chittlehampton*, 2¼m NE, dedicated to the local martyr Urith, has a *tower of 1520. *Cobbaton*, 3m N of Umberleigh, has a Combat Vehicle Museum. At 36m, where the road crosses the Taw, a lane goes straight on to (1½m) *Tawstock*, where the 14C *church has good monuments and one of the most elaborate pews in the country. 40m: *Barnstaple* (Route 26).

From Exeter to *Taunton* and *Bristol*, see Route 23; along the Exe to *Bampton*, see Route 26; to *Plymouth*, see Route 28; to *Tavistock*, see Route 29A; to Plymouth via *Princetown*, see Route 29B; to *Bodmin* and *Penzance*, see Route 32; to *Bude*, see Route 35.

B.   Via Dorchester, Lyme Regis and the Coast

Directions. Total distance 177m. A4, A30 to (46m) *Basingstoke* (bypassed) or alternative way via M3, see Route 14B. A30, M3, A303, A30 to (82m) Salisbury. A354, A35, to (122m) Dorchester, see Route 17A. A35 to (137m) **Bridport**. A35, A3052 to (146m) **Lyme Regis**. A3052 to (161m) Sidford. A3052 to (177m) **Exeter** (Route 18A).

From London to (46m) *Basingstoke*, see Route 14B, and on to (82m) *Salisbury* and (122m) *Dorchester*, see Route 17A. A35 runs W from Dorchester across downland. 126½m: The ruined prehistoric circle known as the *Nine Stones* (EH) lies S of the road as it leaves *Winterbourne Abbas*.

The countryside S of Winterbourne Abbas is rich in prehistoric remains. About 3m SW, on the Downs beyond the pretty village of *Littlebredy*, is *Kingston Russell Stone Circle* (EH). *Blackdown Hill* (776ft), 2m S of Winterbourne Abbas, is crowned by a monument of 1846 to Admiral Sir Thomas Hardy (1769–1839), flag-captain of the 'Victory' at Trafalgar. He was born at *Kingston Russell* manor house, NW of Littlebredy.

128m: *Winterbourne Poor Lot Barrows*, S of A35, are a Bronze Age group (EH). 137m: **Bridport** (6900 inhabitants; TI) is an agreeable little town 1½m

N of its harbour and beach at *West Bay*. The attractive main street has an 18C *Town Hall*. In South St., near the mainly Perpendicular *Church*, a 16C stone building houses the small *Museum and Art Gallery*; one of its displays illustrates the ancient local trade of net- and rope-making (a 'Bridport dagger' is a hangman's halter). The road grows very hilly, with some gradients of 1 in 5. 140m: *Chideock* is a charming village, with fine cliff scenery (NT) to the S. 144m: *Charmouth* is a pleasant little resort with a steep street. Both here and at Bridport Charles II was nearly taken by Parliament men on his flight from Worcester.

At *Whitchurch Canonicorum*, 2½m NE, the Norman to Perpendicular church contains the little shrine of St Candida, the only English shrine (apart from Edward the Confessor's at Westminster) to survive the Reformation unplundered.

A35 bears right for Axminster (Route 18A). The present route follows A3052 towards the coast.

146m: **LYME REGIS** (3400 inhabitants) is a charming old resort overlooking Lyme Bay and ringed by blue lias cliffs rich in fossils. The hilly streets, with many picturesque buildings, keep their Regency atmosphere.

TI: Guildhall Cottage, Church St. **Coach Stop**: Pound St. **Annual events**: Jazz Festival during the first weekend in July, Lifeboat Week at the end of July, Carnival and Regatta in the first full week of August.

History, natives and visitors. In 774 Cynewulf granted the land to the monks of Sherborne, so that they could distil salt from sea-water. The town received its royal charter from Edward I in 1284. Staunchly Parliamentarian, it withstood a two-month siege by the Royalists during the Civil War; among its defenders was the future Admiral Blake. The Duke of Monmouth landed here with three ships and 80 men on 11 June 1685 to begin his abortive rebellion against James II. Natives of Lyme include: Captain Thomas Coram (1668–1751), who established the London Foundling Hospital; Eleanor Coade (1733–1821), inventor of Coade Stone; and the geologist Mary Anning (1799–1847), who discovered the ichthyosaurus in the neighbouring cliffs in 1811. Among the visitors attracted by Lyme's popularity as a resort were Jane Austen and the artist Whistler. The town is the setting for John Fowles's novel 'The French Lieutenant's Woman' and the film derived from it.

The stone pier known as the *Cobb*, where the Duke of Monmouth disembarked, is perhaps more famous as the scene of Louisa Musgrove's accident in 'Persuasion'. Marine Parade leads NE from the Cobb to Bridge St. and the town centre, where the pleasant medley of buildings includes the *Philpot Museum*, with an important collection of fossils. The *Church*, a much altered Norman building to the N, contains a 16C tapestry commemorating the marriage of Prince Arthur and Catherine of Aragon.

About 3½m W is the *Dowlands Landslip*, where some 40 acres of ground slipped down from the cliff in 1839.

In the hilly country immediately W of Lyme A3052 crosses the border into Devon.

6m W of Lyme B3172 leads S from the main road, following the bank of the Axe and passing (1½m) *Axmouth*, with the unusual 15C tower house of *Bindon* 1m E. The breezy little resort of **Seaton** (5000 inhabitants; TI) lies 1½m further S. Delightful walks lead along the coast E to the Landslip (see above) and W via (1m) *Beer*, a fishing village with old quarries, and (3m) *Branscombe Mouth*. The good church in the romantic village of *Branscombe* lies 1½m from the sea. Over 300 acres of the Branscombe estate, including medieval farmhouses, a forge and a bakery, are NT property.

A3052 continues to (153m) *Colyford*, where the fine church has a 15C octagonal lantern, monuments and an early 10C cross. 157m: *Blackbury Camp*, on the right, is an Iron Age hill-fort (EH). At (161m) *Sidford* the route crosses the Honiton–Sidmouth road.

Sand (limited opening), in a valley off A375 2m NE, is a Tudor manor with a medieval outbuilding.

Sidmouth (12,400 inhabitants; TI), a dignified resort with many Regency villas, is delightfully situated between reddish cliffs and protected to the N by a circle of hills. Queen Victoria lived at Woolbrook Cottage (now Royal Glen Hotel) as a baby, and her father died here in 1824.

A pleasant road leads SW from Sidmouth to (4m) *Otterton*, near the popular beach at *Ladram Bay*, (4¾m) *East Budleigh* and (6¼m) the resort of **Budleigh Salterton** (4400 inhabitants; TI). Near East Budleigh are (1m W) *Hayes Barton*, the farmhouse where Sir Walter Raleigh (1552–1618) was born, and (1m N) *Bicton Park* (open), with gardens, arboretum, countryside museum and miniature railway. For Exmouth, 4m W of Budleigh Salterton, and an alternative way into Exeter, see Route 18A.

A3052 crosses the Otter at (164m) *Newton Poppleford*. 177m: **Exeter**, see Route 18A.

19

London to Taunton

Directions. Total distance 144m. Less interesting for the towns than for the landscape, historic places and Somerset churches along the way. The main route as far as Sparkford and then the detour to Exeter provide an easier alternative to Route 18A, which follows the often congested A30. A30 to (46m) Basingstoke (bypassed), or alternative way by M3, see Route 14B. A30, M3, A303 to (65m) Andover (bypassed). A303 to (79m) Amesbury (bypassed), (81m) **Stonehenge**, (105½m) Zeals (for **Stourhead** and (110m) Wincanton (bypassed). A303, A372 to (131m) Langport. A378, A358 to (144m) **Taunton**.

From London to (46m) *Basingstoke*, see Route 14B. A30 bypasses the town and joins M3, which is followed for 2m to its junction with A303. 65m: **Andover** (31,000 inhabitants; TI), bypassed to the S, is an ancient town unattractively redeveloped. The local museum incorporates a *Museum of the Iron Age*, with finds from Danebury Ring (Route 17).

A much prettier way from Basingstoke, 1m shorter, follows B3400 along the upper Test valley. 7m: *Overton* is in the rolling chalk hills praised by Cobbett. 8½m: *Laverstoke* is a model village where paper for banknotes was made for over 200 years. 11m: *Whitchurch*, on the Winchester–Newbury road, see Route 14A. 18m: *Andover*.

FROM ANDOVER TO DEVIZES, 26m by A303 to (3½m) *Weyhill* and then A342 along the NE margin of Salisbury Plain. 8m: *Ludgershall*, just across the border with Wiltshire, has a medieval cross (EH) in the main street and a fine monument to Sir Robert Brydges (d. 1558) in the church. Ludgershall Castle (EH) is the scanty ruin of an early 12C royal castle. 17m: *Upavon*, at the head of the Avon valley, has a church with a restored Norman chancel and font. The village is headquarters of RAF Air Support Command. At (21m) Chirton, on the right, the church has a Norman doorway. 22m: A342 passes

B3098 from Westbury. 24m: *Stert*, on the left, is a pleasant hamlet. 26m: *Devizes*, see Route 24.

A303 leads across the chalk ridges on the edge of **Salisbury Plain**, an undulating, almost treeless expanse about 20m long and 10m wide, lying within an area roughly defined by Andover (E), Salisbury (S), Warminster (W) and Devizes (N). It is divided from N to S by the Avon, flowing from Upavon through Amesbury to Salisbury.

The plain is the focal point from which the great chalk belts of Southern England radiate. One outcrop reaches SW through Wiltshire to the Dorset coast; another goes NE as the Marlborough Downs, the Berkshire Downs and the Chilterns. To the E lie the Hog's Back and the North Downs, the Hampshire Downs and the South Downs. This natural position at the meeting point of hills and ridgeway paths made Salisbury Plain a centre of prehistoric settlement; it is still rich in monuments and remains. The bleak and lonely appearance of the landscape, only a little altered by modern agriculture, has not been improved by the firing ranges and permanent military camps that abound. These include *Bulford* (artillery), *Netheravon* (RAF), *Upavon* (RAF), *Larkhill* (artillery) and *Tidworth*.

79m: **Amesbury** (TI) lies S of A303. The large, flint-built *Abbey Church* is Norman and Early English. Legend makes its predecessor, a Saxon nunnery founded in 980, the 'holy house at Almesbury', where the penitent Queen Guinevere sought refuge. At *Amesbury Abbey* (not open), since rebuilt, John Gay wrote 'The Beggar's Opera' in 1727 while a guest of the Duke of Queensberry.

By A303 to the NW are the prehistoric earthworks known as *Vespasian's Camp*. Near *Durrington*, off A345 1½m N, is *Woodhenge*, a Bronze Age monument with six concentric rings of wooden posts, now replaced by concrete stumps, inside a mound and ditch (EH). A345 continues N along the valley of the Avon to (7½m) *Upavon* (see above). It passes *Netheravon*, with an 18C dovecote (EH, exterior only, by written application to South-West region of EH).

81m: ****Stonehenge** ('Stanhenges', 'hanging stones'), the most famous monument of prehistoric Europe, is a circular setting of massive standing stones (EH, all year plus Mondays in winter). A surprisingly small structure, the main central ruin is only 110ft in diameter; it originally contained just 162 stones, mostly undecorated and arranged in a straightforward way. It stands isolated on the open chalk down—Emerson thought it 'like a group of brown dwarfs on the wide expanse'—but, when seen close to, the mass of its monoliths makes a striking impact.

Stonehenge is not a single-period site, but the ruins of a series of earthen monuments, now heavily eroded, and of stone structures, dating from before 3000 BC to about 1000 BC. The central portion (about 2000 BC) is unique among the relics of ancient Europe. It includes the famous trilithons, pairs of huge upright stones with a third laid crossways across their tops and held in place by mortice-and-tenon joints.

The early features at Stonehenge include a circular bank and ditch, now only 1ft deep where the visitors' path crosses it, and the Heel Stone, an unshaped upright stone by the access road on the NE. The main ruin consists of five concentric features. From the outside they are:

(1) A circle of 30 uprights, standing about 13½ft above the ground, and once supporting a continuous run of lintel stones. Sixteen uprights and five lintels remain in place.
(2) A circle of about 60 small uprights, about 5ft above the ground. Six still stand, while others are fallen and broken.

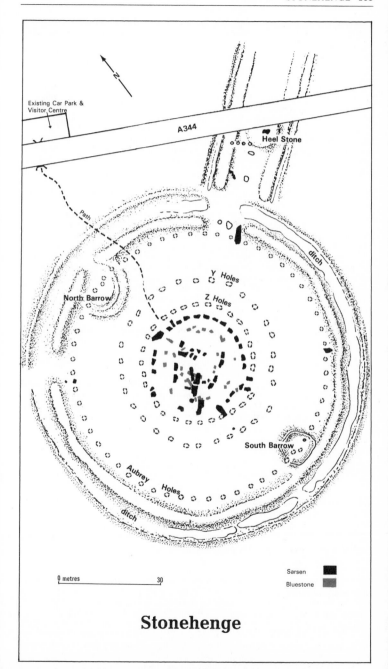

Existing Car Park &
Visitor Centre

A344

Heel Stone

Path

ditch

Y Holes

Z Holes

North Barrow

South Barrow

Aubrey Holes

ditch

0 metres   30

Sarsen

Bluestone

Stonehenge

(3) A horseshoe arrangement of five trilithons, open to the NE, the tallest standing about 24ft above the ground. Three are intact; only one upright of each of the other two stands.

(4) A horseshoe arrangement of small uprights. Six of the original 19 remain.

(5) A central stone, once erect but now lying flat, called the 'Altar Stone'.

The large circle and horseshoe are built of sarsen, a sandstone which outcrops naturally in the Avebury region to the N. It is of exceptional hardness, which both accounts for the superb state of preservation of elements and emphasises the engineering skills of its builders. The upper surface formed by the lintels of the sarsen circle was levelled to an accuracy of a very few inches, although the ground slopes; the uprights are of differing heights and the lintels of differing thicknesses. Some sarsens bear carvings of prehistoric axes and (perhaps) daggers, difficult to see unless the light is good. The small uprights are of igneous rock, brought about 200m from the Presely Hills of South-West Wales.

Stonehenge belongs, like Avebury (Route 20) and the Rollright Stones (Route 53), to the class of prehistoric monuments called 'stone rings' or 'stone circles'. It is quite exceptional in its complex plan, in the precision with which its stones have been shaped, and in its provisions of lintels. Accordingly, it has always presented grave difficulties of interpretation, and has been attributed in different centuries to giants, Romans, Danes, Phoenicians, Druids, Mycenaean Greeks and—in our own time—UFOnauts. Current archaeological opinion emphasises its comparability, in terms of the physical labour involved, with other massive sites in the region, such as Avebury, Silbury Hill (Route 20) and Durrington Walls (a huge banked enclosure 2m N, but without standing stones and now ploughed down to near-invisibility). The symmetrical layout of Stonehenge, oriented towards the NE where the sun rises on Midsummer Day, indicates that it was positioned to a solar alignment. Secure evidence for other astronomical features, or its use as a prehistoric observatory-cum-computer, is very slight.

Because of the crowds Stonehenge attracts, the centre is normally closed and visitors kept at a distance from which it is hard to see the monument properly. It is better to visit it on those winter days when the centre is open (check in advance with EH), or to follow the waymarked paths that show some of the many hundred ancient, though less spectacular, sites in the area.

In 1993 EH put forward proposals to improve the presentation of Stonehenge, now hemmed in between A303 and A344, with inadequate parking and a squalid visitor centre. The relevant stretch of A303 would be either put in a tunnel or rerouted to the S, and A344 would be closed. The eight possible sites for a new visitor centre and car park lie at or beyond the edge of the Stonehenge site.

Beyond Stonehenge A360 leads NW across the plain to (4m) *Shrewton*, where B390 goes to (14m) *Heytesbury* and (17m) *Warminster*, both on Route 18A. A360 continues to (18m) *Devizes* (Route 24) via (8m) *Tilshead*, where the church has flint and chalk banding characteristic of the local architecture. White Barrow, a Neolithic long barrow ¾m S, is NT property.

87m: *Yarnbury Castle*, on the right, is a prehistoric hill-fort. A303 descends to (89m) *Wylye*, in its river valley, where the church has a 17C pulpit. 99m: For B3089, leading SE to Wilton, see Route 18A. A303 goes on to (103m) **Mere** (TI), where Charles II rested at the Talbot Inn on his flight after the Battle of Worcester, and the poet William Barnes kept school for 12 years. The large Decorated church has 15C stalls and screens. 105½m: *Zeals*.

In the attractive village of *Stourton*, 1½m N, is **Stourhead** (NT), one of the most completely satisfying expressions of 18C culture in England. The house was built in 1721–24 for the banker Henry Hoare by Colen Campbell, pioneer of Palladianism. Thomas Atkinson added the wings in 1790–1804 and the portico was built, to Campbell's original design, in 1840; the central block was reconstructed after a fire in 1902. The interior contains furniture designed for the house by the younger Chippendale; the library has a striking 19C Wilton carpet and a plaster panel, brought from elsewhere, attributed to Grinling Gibbons. The building's severe restraint serves as foil to the magnificent Picturesque landscaping of the grounds (open all year). They were begun by Henry Hoare but owe their final appearance to the work of his son, another Henry, from 1741 onwards. A walk round the lake provides a series of artfully contrived vistas combining nature with man's work: the parish church, the 14C High Cross of Bristol (erected here in 1780), temples by Flitcroft, a Gothick cottage and a rustic grotto. The rhododendrons are a later addition. On the ridge about 2m N of the park stands *Alfred's Tower*, built in 1772 to mark the supposed site where Alfred the Great rallied his army to repel the Danes in 879.

Beyond Zeals A303 crosses the northern tip of Dorset before entering Somerset. 110m: **Wincanton** is an old coaching town famous for its race-course, at the head of the *Vale of Blackmore* or *Blackmoor*. The church porch has a curious relief of St Eligius, patron saint of smiths.

Two roads run N from Wincanton to Shepton Mallet. On B3081 lies (4½m) **Bruton**, a charming old town with a Perpendicular church (18C chancel), the King's School dating from 1519 and a packhorse bridge (Bruton Bow). Sexey's Hospital (1638) adjoins the Court House (1684), now a school. The road continues via (8m) *Evercreech*, with one of Somerset's best church towers, to (11½m) *Shepton Mallet* (Route 22). A371, 1½m longer, goes from Wincanton via (4m) the modern gardens (open) of the 18C *Hadspen House* and (5m) *Castle Cary*, where the diarist James Woodforde served as curate of his father's parish in 1771–76. There are fine churches at *Alford*, 1½m W, and *Ditcheat*, 2m NW of Castle Cary.

At 115½m A303 passes between *North Cadbury* (right), with a fine church and manor house, and *Cadbury Castle* (left), an 18-acre hill-fort and a claimant to be Arthur's Camelot. Excavations have shown that it was occupied almost continuously for nearly 4000 years, from Neolithic to Saxon times. 117½m: *Sparkford*, at the junction of the road from Frome to Yeovil. *Queen's Camel*, 1½m SW, has a fine late 14C church.

FROM SPARKFORD TO EXETER, 54m by A303 and A30. It follows the main route (see below) W from Sparkford but bear lefts on A303 after 5m. 7m: *Ilchester*, left of the road, once an important town on the Foss Way, was the Roman Lendiniae and the birthplace of Roger Bacon (1214– 94). 9m: *Tintinhull*, left of the road. Tintinhull House (NT) is early 17C with 18C additions. The small but superb garden, the only part open to the public, was laid out in the early 20C. 11m: *Martock*, 2m N on B3615, has a big church with Perpendicular tower and perhaps the best tie-beam *roof in Somerset. Among the attractive buildings nearby is the 13–14C Treasurer's House (NT, open by appointment). 12m: For A3088, leading left to Yeovil via Montacute House, see Route 18A. 13½m: *South Petherton*, N of the road, has a good church. 20m: At *Ilminster* (3700 inhabitants), a pleasant little town, the noble Perpendicular church contains the tombs of Nicholas and Dorothy Wadham (d. 1609 and 1618), founders of Wadham College, Oxford. The former school nearby is a restored 16C building. *Dillington House*, 1m NE, a 16C building with 19C alterations, was the home of Lord North while Prime Minister; it is now the Somerset College for Adult Education. *Barrington Court* (NT), off B3168 3½m NE, is an E-shaped 16C mansion built of the local Ham Hill stone, with a lively roofline. Most of the panelling inside, though appropriate, is not original to the house. The walled gardens are in the style of Gertrude Jekyll. Interesting churches in the neighbourhood include those at: *Stocklinch, Stocklinch Ottersey* (18C W gallery) and *Shepton Beauchamp* (Perpendicular tower), S and SE of Barrington Court; *Dowlish Wake*, 1½m SE of Ilminster, with the tomb of J.H. Speke (1827–64), who discovered the source of the Nile; and *Donyatt*, 2m W. A303 enters hilly country and crosses the border into Devon, joining A30 at 30m and following Route 18A to (54m) *Exeter*.

121½m: At *Yeovilton*, about 1½m S of A303, is the Royal Naval Air Station. The *Fleet Air Museum has Concorde 002 and over 50 planes illustrating the history of aviation at sea. 122½m: The route changes from A303 to A372. *Lytes Cary* (NT), about 1m N, is a small manor house built from the 14C onwards. The oldest part is the chapel, originally detached from the house; the 15C hall has a good timber roof.

Keinton Mandeville, off A37 2m N, was the birthplace of Sir Henry Irving (1838–1905). From *Barton St David*, 1m beyond, the first member of the presidential family of Adams emigrated to the USA.

162½m: *Long Sutton* has an interesting church and court house. *Somerton*, 2½m NE, is an old-fashioned little town with a fine Decorated church and a 17C market cross. It was once the capital of Somerset and residence of the West Saxon kings. At (129½m) *Huish Episcopi* the church has one of the finest towers in Somerset, a Norman doorway, and glass by Burne-Jones (1899). *Kingsbury Episcopi*, 4m S, has another lavishly decorated tower. 131m: **Langport**, overlooking the marshes of the Parrett, has a fine Perpendicular church with good stained glass and an interesting Norman carving over the S door. The Hanging Chapel, an ancient Perpendicular chapel above an archway nearby, is now a masonic temple. Walter Bagehot (1826–77) was a native of Langport.

At *Muchelney Abbey* (EH, summer season), 2m S, the foundations of the church, the early 16C abbot's house and part of the S cloister survive. To the W is a 15C Priest's House (NT, open by appointment). The church at *Low Ham*, 1¾m N of Langport, is 17C Gothic work with many strange features. The church at *High Ham*, 1¾m further N, contains splendid woodwork. The 19C Stembridge Tower Mill (NT) is the last thatched windmill in England.

A378 heads SW from Langport. 133m: At *Curry Rivel* the Perpendicular church has good parclose screens. To the N, *Red Hill* (NT) looks out over the marshes of West Sedgemoor. 136m: *Fivehead*.

The ˙church at *Ile Abbots*, 2m S, has a fine tower with original sculptures, and beautiful sedilia and piscina. See Route 24 for the villages to the N.

140m: The route changes from A378 to A358. *Hatch Court* (limited opening), 2m SE of the junction, is a Palladian house of 1755 by the amateur architect Thomas Prowse. The square central block with corner turrets is relieved by curved wings and an arcade on the S front. The interiors include a dramatic staircase hall, and there is a good collection of china.

144m: **TAUNTON** (59,100 inhabitants), the county town of Somerset, lies in the beautiful valley of Taunton Deane, known for its apples and cider.

TI: The Library, Corporation St. **Bus Station**: W of the castle. **Railway Station**: ¾m N of the town centre. **Theatre**: Brewhouse Theatre and Arts Centre, Coal Orchard. **Annual Events**: Flower Show (August); Agricultural Show (August); Carnival (October); Music and Drama Festival (November).

History. Founded c 705 by Ine, King of the West Saxons, to guard the river crossing against the Celts, Taunton remained a fortified seat of the Bishops of Winchester for more than 1000 years. The castle dates from the early 12C. Henry VII examined the pretender Perkin Warbeck here in 1497. The castle withstood three Royalist sieges in 1644–45; much of the town was destroyed by fire. On 20 June 1685, James, Duke of Monmouth, was proclaimed king in the market place. After the Battle of Sedgemoor the inhabitants suffered the cruelties of 'Kirke's Lambs' and Judge Jeffreys's Bloody Assize. The later prosperity and character of Taunton's merchant class are reflected in the town's surviving 18C buildings and Dissenting chapels. Queen's College (1843) and Taunton School (1847) are both important Dissenting foundations.

Natives: A.W. Kinglake (1809–91), author of 'Eothen', was born at Wilton House in Vivary Park.

The centre of town is the triangular, traffic-congested market place, now called Fore St., with the *Market House* of 1770–72. From the NE side Hammet St., its Georgian symmetry unpardonably spoiled, leads to *St Mary Magdalene*, one of the largest and richest Perpendicular churches in England. The richly sculptured tower, 163ft high, was reconstructed in 1858–62. The church has double aisles, figures of angels between the clerestory lights, and a glorious oak roof. To the N are Middle St., with the former *Methodist Chapel* opened by John Wesley in 1776, and the church of *St James*, with a good font and a fine tower rebuilt in 1870. On the NW side of the market, opposite Hammet St., Castle Bow leads to Castle Green and the much restored 12C *Castle*, now the *Somerset County Museum*. Exhibits include: a prehistoric collection with finds from the Iron Age lake villages at Glastonbury and Meare; Roman *mosaics from Low Ham and East Coker; and a portrait of Judge Jeffreys.

On the S side of the market place is *Tudor House* (1578), where Jeffreys lodged. High St. nearby leads S to *Vivary Park* and (left) Mary St., where the *Unitarian Chapel* has an interior of 1721. East St., leading from the market place, has *Gray's Almshouses* (1635). In East Reach, beyond, *St Margaret's Almshouses* were once a leper hospital.

Kingston St Mary, 3m N, has a fine Perpendicular church tower. The gardens of *Hestercombe House* (now owned by the Somerset County Fire Brigade), 3m NE, were laid out in 1905 by Sir Edwin Lutyens and Gertrude Jekyll. *Trull*, 2m S of Taunton, has a small church with 16C woodcarving, including a remarkably fine pulpit. *Poundisford Park* (open by appointment), near *Pitminster* 1½m further S, is a Tudor house; the Great Hall has a fine 16C plaster ceiling and a gallery above the screen.

From Taunton to *Bristol* and *Exeter*, see Route 23; to *Marlborough*, see Route 24; to *Minehead*, see Route 25B; to *Barnstaple*, see Route 26.

20

London to Bath and Bristol

Directions. Total distance 199m. M4 is the fast alternative. The detours from Newbury, Chippenham and Bristol make useful connections between SW England and the Cotswolds (particularly Route 51B). M4, A308 to (26m) Maidenhead, see Route 49A. A4 to (38½m) **Reading**, (56m) Newbury, (74m) Marlborough, (93m) Chippenham, (106m) **Bath** (Route 21) and (119m) **Bristol**.

From London to (26m) *Maidenhead*, see Route 49A. 34½m: Near *Twyford*, S of the road, is *Ruscombe*, where William Penn died in 1718.

38½m: **READING** (138,000 inhabitants; TI), the county town of Berkshire, stands on the Kennet and is cut off by the railway from the nearby Thames. A centre of the medieval cloth trade, it became known for beer, bulbs and biscuits. Nowadays it is the headquarters for many large companies. There is little to delay the tourist.

In the old centre of town is the 12C church of *St Laurence*, rebuilt but still imposing. Archbishop Laud (1553–1645), a native of Reading, was baptised in the font. The *Museum and Art Gallery* has *finds from nearby Silchester, illustrating the everyday life of a country town in Roman Britain, and finds of all ages from the Thames, including a magnificent Bronze Age *torc from Moulsford. The Forbury leads to the ruins of the Benedictine *Abbey*, founded by Henry I in 1121 and once ranking third in all England. 'Sumer is icumen in', the earliest known round for several voices, was written by a monk here c 1240. A memorial stone marks the grave of Henry I (d. 1135). The heavily restored gatehouse was once a school, where Jane Austen was a pupil in 1786. In *Reading Gaol*, adjoining the ruins, Oscar Wilde wrote 'De Profundis' (1897); the 'Ballad of Reading Gaol' is later. At Blake's Lock, on the Kennet further E, a museum deals with Reading's industrial history and waterways.

The churches of *Greyfriars* in Friar St. and *St Mary* in The Butt, both W of the old town centre, have medieval work. Watlington St. leads SE from the centre, past the 18C *Watlington House* (with a garden front of 1688), to the *Royal Berkshire Hospital*, with an Ionic façade of 1839. Mary Russell Mitford (see below) lived between 1789 and 1804 at the house in London Rd marked with a tablet.

Whiteknights Park, on Shinfield Rd 1½m S, is the site of the *University of Reading* (4400 undergraduates), which began in the centre of town in 1902, received its charter in 1926 and moved here in 1957. The campus includes the *Museum of English Rural Life*, the *Ure Museum of Greek Archaeology* and the *Cole Collection* of zoological specimens.

Three Mile Cross, 3½m S of Reading, is the scene of 'Our Village' by Mary Russell Mitford (1787–1855). She is buried at *Swallowfield*, 2½m further SE. Swallowfield Park (limited opening) is a much altered late 17C house by William Talman, architect of Chatsworth. From Three Mile Cross an unclassified road leads SW to (8m) **Silchester**, identified with Calleva Atrebatum, a flourishing Roman and pre-Roman town which seems to have contained several dyeworks. The site is enclosed by 2–3C walls 1½m in circuit and at places on the S side still 1214ft high (EH). A building, almost certainly a 4C church, has been excavated. The little Calleva Museum provides an excellent introduction to the greater collection at Reading. The interesting parish church (1m E by footpath, 2m by road) lies just inside the E gate. The earth banks of a Roman amphitheatre lie 150yd from the NE corner of the enceinte. 3½m E of Silchester church and 1½m S of Swallowfield is *Stratfield Saye House* (open), presented by the nation to the Duke of Wellington in 1815. He altered and extended the 17C house but never fulfilled his ambition of creating a Waterloo Palace to equal Blenheim. Contents include portraits, mosaic pavements from Silchester (set into the hall floor) and relics of the Duke. The Wellington Exhibition in the stables has his funeral carriage and his favourite charger, Copenhagen, is buried in the paddock nearby. The E side of the park has the Wellington Monument, with a bronze statue by Marochetti (1866).

From Reading to *Virginia Water* via *Wokingham* and *Ascot*, see Route 14B; to *London* and *Oxford* by river, see Route 49B.

A4 leaves the Thames valley and follows the tributary valley of the Kennet. 42½m: *Theale* has a large church of 1820–22 modelled on Salisbury Cathedral. About 3¼m NW, beyond *Englefield*, is *Bradfield College*, a public school founded in 1850 and noted for the Greek plays performed by the pupils. 47m: *Aldermaston* railway station.

An unclassified road on the left leads to (1¼m) *Padworth*, with a small Norman church; *Ufton Court* (not open), an Elizabethan mansion ¾m E, was home of Arabella Fermor, heroine of Pope's 'The Rape of the Lock'. *Aldermaston*, 1½m SW of its station, has a 14C wall painting and a fine monument to George Forster (d. 1526) in its church. The Atomic Weapons Research Establishment became the starting-point of an anti-nuclear protest, the Aldermaston march, in the 1950s.

From (48½m) *Woolhampton* a road climbs N to *Douai Abbey*, a Benedictine house (1903) with a boys' school transferred from Douai in France, and to

(3m) the open sandy heath of *Bucklebury Common*. The Old Vicarage gardens contain sculptures by Henry Moore and others.

56m: **Newbury** (26,400 inhabitants; TI), once a centre of the cloth trade, is known for its racecourse, about ½m SE. The Jacobean Cloth Hall, with an 18C galleried granary, is now a *Museum*; it contains collections of local history and Civil War relics. Jack of Newbury—John Smallwood, afterwards Winchcombe (d. 1520)—was a patriotic clothier who lead 150 men to Flodden in 1513; his brass can be seen in the church of *St Nicholas*, which he rebuilt. Benjamin Woodridge, the first graduate of Harvard, was rector of Newbury. The *Kennet and Avon Canal* has been restored for pleasure cruising. The N end of Newbury, called *Speenhamland*, gave its name to the allowance system of poor relief to supplement wages, first practised in 1795.

Two indecisive Civil War battles were fought nearby. A monument 1m SW marks the scene of the first (1643). The second (1644) took place 1m NW of the town, near the 14C gatehouse of *Donnington Castle* (EH, all year plus Mondays in winter).

FROM NEWBURY TO ANDOVER, 15m by A343. 4½m: *Highclere Castle*, see Route 14A. The church at (10m) *Hurstbourne Tarrant* has early 14C wall paintings. *St Mary Bourne*, 3½m SE, has a Tournai marble font. 15m: *Andover*, see Route 19.

FROM NEWBURY TO OXFORD, 25m. A34 crosses the downs, passing (9m) *East Ilsey*, once an important sheep market, and descends into the *Vale of the White Horse* (Route 51B). For (15½m) *Steventon*, (19m) *Abingdon* and on to Oxford, see Route 51A.

FROM NEWBURY TO SWINDON. The fast way is by M4, reached via A34 N of Newbury. A more interesting alternative (26m) follows B4000 up the beautiful valley of the Lambourn. 6m: *Wickham*. *Welford Hall*, 1m N, is a partly Queen Anne House in pleasant grounds. 11m: *Lambourn*, separated from the Vale of the White Horse by the Lambourn Downs, is an old town with training stables. The late Norman church has an alabaster relief of Charles I. 15m: *Ashdown House* (NT) is a tall building of unusual design, built by Lord Craven in 1660. The monumental staircase leads from ground floor to roof, where there is a view of the Downs. Above the park is *Alfred's Castle*, an Iron Age fort. Alfred fought the Danes nearby in 871. 17½m: *Ashbury* has a Norman and Early English church. At (20m) *Shrivenham* the route changes to A420. 26m: *Swindon*, see Route 51B.
   From Newbury to *Winchester*, see Route 14A.

57m: *Speen* stands on the site of the Roman Spinis. 62m: *Avington*, a quiet village on the Kennet, has a Norman church. 64m: *Hungerford*, sadly famous for the shooting massacre in 1987, is otherwise known for antique shops and angling on the Kennet.

The pretty village of *Inkpen*, 3½m SE, has a church used by the Templars, reputed to have introduced the tulips and lilies now growing wild in the area. Le Nôtre (1613–1700) stayed at the rectory and designed its gardens. *Inkpen Beacon* (954ft) and *Walbury Hill* (974ft), the highest chalk down in England, lie to the S; both give fine views. *Littlecote* (open), 3m NW of Hungerford, is a mansion of c 1500 in red brick and flint. The great hall has oak panelling and a fine collection of Cromwellian armour. Its grounds contain a Roman villa with a mosaic floor depicting Orpheus. *Ramsbury*, 3m further NW, was the seat of the Bishops of Wiltshire in the 10C. It has an unusually large 13C church. The unclassified road continues up the valley to (11½m) Marlborough via (10m) *Mildenhall* (pronounced 'Minall'), the Roman Cunetio, where the church has Saxon and Norman details and good early 19C woodwork.

Beyond (67m) *Froxfield* A4 skirts the N edge of *Savernake Forest*, a beautiful tract of oaks and beeches. *Chisbury*, S of the road at 69m, has a thatched 13C chapel (EH).

74m: **Marlborough** (5,800 inhabitants; TI) has a broad *High St., largely colonnaded and tile-hung on one side and closed at either end by church towers. Spanning the main road to the W of the town is *Marlborough College*, a public school founded in 1843. William Morris, Siegfried Sassoon, Louis MacNeice, John Betjeman and William Golding were pupils. At the graceful 18C Castle House, which sets the style for the other buildings, Thomson wrote part of his 'Spring' (1727). The grounds include Castle Mound, identified by legend as Merlin's burial place. Schoolboys cut the White Horse to the S in 1804.

An attractive walk of 6m from Marlborough to Avebury (see below) leads via *Manton*, known for its training stables, and (3m) the dolmen known as the *Devil's Den*, and then over the Downs, sprinkled with 'grey wethers' or sarsen stones, boulders left isolated by the denudation of softer strata.

A346 leads S to Andover (Route 19) via (5½m) *Burbage*, where Jane Seymour (?1509–37) was born and celebrated her marriage feast with Henry VIII at Wolf Hall.

A345 goes S across the Vale of Pewsey. The *Wansdyke*, probably a post-Roman border entrenchment, runs along the N side of the Downs. It stretches, with many gaps, from beyond Savernake Forest to Dundry Hill, S of Bristol. The *White Horse*, NW of (7m) *Pewsey*, was first cut in 1785. 9½m: *Manningford Bruce* has an early Norman church. 11m: *Upavon*, on the N edge of Salisbury Plain, see Route 19.

From Marlborough to *Glastonbury* and *Taunton*, see Route 24.

The *Wansdyke* runs parallel to A4 on the Downs to the S. 79½m: The Ridgeway path, here running N to S, crosses the road. 80m: *West Kennett*, where B4003 leads right for Avebury, has some remarkable prehistoric antiquities (EH). *Silbury Hill*, built c 2660 BC, is at 130ft high the largest artificial mound in Europe (no access to the hill itself). A footpath leads ½m S of the road to *West Kennett Long Barrow*, a chambered tomb of about 3250 BC with about 46 burials contemporary with the use of Windmill Hill. The Devizes museum has finds from excavations. At (81½m) *Beckhampton* A4 crosses the Swindon–Devizes road (Route 24). Some 400yds of Roman road survive to the SW.

Just to the N, the village of *Avebury* (seasonal TI) stands in the centre of **Avebury Stone Circles** (EH), a monument of c 2450–2200 BC 'as much surpassing Stonehenge', says Aubrey 'as a cathedral doth a parish church'.

Visitors should first turn down the village street to the *Church*, which has a reworked Saxon nave, a Saxo-Norman tub font, a rood loft of 1460 and a squint. The late 16C *Avebury Manor* (NT) has good panelling and plasterwork. At its gates is the *Avebury Museum* (EH, all year plus Mondays in winter), with finds from Avebury and Windmill Hill, providing a superb introduction to the monuments.

The remains consist mainly of a massive circular earthwork, ¾m round and about 15ft high. The fosse, originally 30ft deep, is on its inner side, suggesting a religious rather than a defensive purpose. On the inner edge stand the remains of a gigantic circle of unhewn megaliths; there were two smaller concentric circles in the enclosed area. The largest stones weigh about 60 tons. From the circle an avenue of smaller stones (NT), many re-erected, leads SE along B4003, beyond West Kennett, to a group of small stone and timber circles called *The Sanctuary* (EH), now marked out on the ground. 1½m NW via *Avebury Trusloe* is *Windmill Hill* (NT), with a Neolithic causewayed enclosure built c 3250 BC and used until c 2000.

A4 climbs the Downs. On the left are the Lansdowne Column (c 1843) and a White Horse of 1780. 87½m: *Calne* (10,300 inhabitants), known for bacon since the first factory was set up here c 1770, has a much altered 12C church.

Off A4 2½m SW is *Bowood* (open), a mansion first built in 1625 and several times altered in the 18C. The surviving part includes the S range by Robert Adam (1768–70). It contains an Orangery now serving as a picture gallery, the laboratory where Joseph Priestley discovered oxygen in 1774, and a chapel by C.R. Cockerell (1821). Among the exhibits are Lord Byron's Albanian costume and watercolours by Bonington and Turner. The grounds were laid out by Capability Brown and others. A separate garden (open in season), entered from A342, has rhododendron walks and a mausoleum by Adam. At Sloperton Cottage near *Bromham*, off A342 3m S of Bowood, Thomas Moore (1779–1852) passed most of the last 35 years of his life. A Celtic cross marks his grave in the churchyard.

93m: **Chippenham** (19,300 inhabitants; TI) is a busy country town on the Avon.

John Wood the Younger built the church of *Hardenhuish* ('Harnish'), 1m NW, in 1779. Aubrey was born at *Kington St Michael*, off A429 about 2½m NW. *Castle Combe*, 6m further W, is a pretty village with a 13C market cross and the ruins of a Saxon castle. The church has the 13C tomb of Walter de Dunstanville.

FROM CHIPPENHAM TO SHAFTESBURY, 34m by A350. 3½m: *Lacock* (NT) is a pretty village, popular with tourists. The church has a fine late Perpendicular chapel. *Lacock Abbey* (NT), on the Avon, is a pleasing amalgamation of several periods. Founded in 1232 for Augustinian canonesses, it was dissolved in 1539. Sir William Sharington demolished the church but incorporated the fine 13– 14C cloisters into his new house. Sanderson Miller added the hall and dining room to the W side in the 1750s, contributing much to the abbey's present Gothick appearance. William Henry Fox Talbot carried out his early photographic experiments here in the 1830s; the medieval barn houses a museum of photographic history. 7m: *Melksham* (9600 inhabitants; TI) is an agricultural town with a restored church, originally Norman. 11m: An unclassified road leads left to (1½m) *Steeple Ashton*, once an important wool market, which still has its lock-up and charter cross, and a restored wool merchant's house. The church has a late Perpendicular *nave of 1480 with curious corbels and fine vaulting. 16m: **Westbury** (7300 inhabitants; TI), now a railway junction, is an old town with a handsome Perpendicular church. On the Downs 2m E are *Bratton Camp*, an Iron Age hill-fort enclosing a Neolithic long barrow, and the *White Horse of Westbury*, dating in its present form from the 18C (both EH). Off A3098 2m W of Westbury is *Chalcot* (not open), a classical house of c 1680. 20m: *Warminster*, see Route 18A. 29m: *East Knoyle* was Sir Christopher Wren's birthplace. *Pyt House* (limited opening), near *Newtown* 2m SE, is an early 19C building. 34m: *Shaftesbury*, see Route 18A.

A420, running W over the Cotswolds from Chippenham, provides an alternative route to (22m) Bristol. 1½m: *Sheldon Manor* (open) was largely rebuilt in the 17C but keeps its 13C porch. The site of a deserted medieval village lies to the W. A420 enters Avon before reaching the high-lying (9m) *Marshfield*. **Dyrham Park** (NT), beyond A46 3m NW, is a mansion with a garden front of 1691 and an Italianate main extension by Talman, architect of Chatsworth. It contains a Renaissance chimneypiece, and paintings by Murillo and the Dutch masters. The deer park is open all year.

From Chippenham to *Faringdon* and also to *Cirencester*, see Route 38B.

97m: *Corsham* has 17–18C houses, a large church and *Corsham Court* (open), a mansion of 1582 altered in 1760–65 by Capability Brown for Paul Methuen. Part of the building now houses the Bath Academy of Art.

The state rooms, sumptuously furnished, contain Methuen's *collection of paintings by Italian, Flemish, Dutch and English masters. The more than 300 works include The Betrayal (Van Dyck), The Annunciation (studio of Filippo Lippi) and St John the Baptist in the Wilderness (Andrea del Sarto). The guidebook has an excellent catalogue.

A long hill leads down to (100m) *Box*, past the entrance to *Box Tunnel*, the longest railway tunnel in the world when Brunel built it in 1837. The underground quarries of Bath stone were used in 1939–45 as an aircraft factory and a refuge for treasures from the national museums. *Colerne*, 2m N, has a broken 9C cross shaft in its 13–14C church.

106m: **Bath**, see Route 21. A4 crosses the Avon. A431, an alternative road to Bristol, stays on the N bank and passes (112½m) *Bitton*, with a notable church. At *Oldland Common*, just to the NW, the church has an Ecce Homo by Murillo.

119m: **BRISTOL** (399,600 inhabitants) is an old cathedral city, port and manufacturing centre. It has imported wine from Bordeaux since the 12C and from Spain since the 15C. In the 17C and 18C it grew rich on trade with the Americas, and it still imports goods from across the Atlantic, though larger vessels now dock at Avonmouth. The City Docks, from which John and Sebastian Cabot set sail for America in 1497, have taken on new life with leisure and recreation centres. Long known for tobacco, confectionery and aircraft industries, the city produced the Bristol Boxkite in 1910 and Concorde in 1969. Despite war damage and strenuous redevelopment, Bristol preserves a few 17C houses, some gracious 18C and early 19C terraces and some splendid Victorian industrial architecture.

TI: St Nicholas Church, St Nicholas St.; Bristol Airport. **Bus and Coach Station**: Marlborough St. **Railway Stations**: Temple Meads Station (Inter-City services), SE of the centre; Parkway Station (Inter-City), near Filton, 5m NE, with access to M4 and M5. **Airport**: at Lulsgate, on A38 8m SW. Flights to Aberdeen, Amsterdam, Belfast, Brussels, Cork, Dublin, Edinburgh, Frankfurt, Glasgow, Guernsey, Jersey, Newcastle, Paris and Plymouth. **Theatres**, etc.: Theatre Royal, King St.; Hippodrome, St Augustine's Parade; Colston Hall (concerts); Arnolfini, Narrow Quay (arts complex with cinema, gallery, etc.); Watershed, Canons Rd (media centre with cinemas, galleries, etc.). **Annual Events**: North Somerset Agricultural Show (May); Bristol Harbour Regatta (August); Bristol Flower Show (August–September); International Balloon Fiesta (August–September); International Kite Festival (September).

History. Probably of late Saxon foundation, Bristol was the centre of the pre-Conquest trade in English slaves—as it became, in the 18C, the centre of the African slave trade. In the Domesday survey it already ranked next after London, York, and Winchester. The castle, where the Avon joins the Frome, was rebuilt in 1126 by Robert, Earl of Gloucester. King Stephen was held prisoner here in 1141. The summary execution of Richard II's followers before the castle gave Bristol its only scene in Shakespeare. The growing trade in cloth and wine favoured maritime daring and led to the founding of the Merchant Venturers' society. On 24 June 1497, John Cabot and his son Sebastian, who had sailed from Bristol in the 'Matthew', discovered the mainland of America, and in the next year Sebastian Cabot explored the American coast from Newfoundland to Florida. During the Civil War, Bristol was captured by Prince Rupert and became the chief Royalist stronghold in the West; but in 1645 it was stormed by the Parliamentarians under Fairfax and in 1655 its castle was slighted by Cromwell. During the Reform riots of 1831 two sides of Queen Square, with the Mansion House, custom house, bishop's palace, and gaol, were burned. The 'Great Western', Isambard Kingdom Brunel's first steam ship and pioneer of the transatlantic steam traffic, was launched at Bristol in 1838. The city was heavily attacked from the air in 1940–41.

Natives, residents and visitors: Defoe is believed to have met Alexander Selkirk, the original of Robinson Crusoe, or to have heard his story in Bristol. Thomas Chatterton (1752–70), the 'marvellous Boy', was born near St Mary Redcliffe. The actress and novelist 'Perdita' Robinson (1758–1800) was born near the cathedral and attended the school in Park St. kept by Hannah More (1745–1833) and her sisters. The painter Sir Thomas Lawrence (1769–1830) was the son of an innkeeper in Redcross St. Robert Southey (1774–1843), the son of a mercer, was born in Wine St.; he returned with Coleridge in 1794–95, when they were planning their 'Pantisocratic' society in America. Samuel Plimsoll (1824–98), 'the sailors' friend', was born at 9 Colston Parade and John Addington Symonds (1840–93) at 7 Berkeley Square. The cricketer W.G. Grace (1848–1915) was born at Downend, near Mangotsfield, 3m NE. W. Friese-Greene, pioneer of the cinema, and Cary Grant were born in Bristol.

The modern focus of movement is the Centre, an ornamental space formed in 1893 by covering over part of an arm of the Floating Harbour. The statues are of Edmund Burke, MP in 1774–80, and the benefactor Edward Colston (1636–1721). Baldwin St. leads E to Bristol Bridge, but this walking tour turns S through a Georgian quarter, partly rebuilt, bounded on three sides by the Floating Harbour. In King St. are the *Merchants' Almshouses* (1699), well restored after bombing destroyed the adjoining Hall. The Merchant Venturers' society is traceable back to the reign of Henry II. Also in this street are: the old *Free Library*, founded in 1613; the *Theatre Royal*, modelled on Wren's Drury Lane Theatre, opened in 1766, the home of the Bristol Old Vic since 1946; *Coopers Hall*, with a classical front (1744) by Halfpenny; the *St Nicholas Almshouse* (1656; rebuilt 1961); the splendid *Llandoger Trow* inn and other 17C houses. The *Old Granary* in Little King St. is an entertaining Victorian building. The new Redcliffe Way runs diagonally across Queen Square, scene of the riots of 1831, past a statue of William III by Rysbrack. At 16 David Hume was a merchant's clerk in 1734; 37 was the first American Consulate in Europe (1792).

The walk crosses the *Floating Harbour*, formed in 1803–09 by diverting a 2m stretch of the tidal Avon into a new channel. On the opposite bank stands *St Mary Redcliffe*, which Elizabeth I called 'the fairest, the goodliest, and most famous parish church in England'. Replacing a 12C church, it was built in a magnificent and harmonious Perpendicular style mainly between 1325 and 1375, the S side being older than the N; the tower is mid 13C in its lower stages, early 14C above. The church owes much to the generosity of William Canynge the elder (d. 1396) and his grandson William Canynge the younger (?1399–1474), both mayors of Bristol.

The massive tower, decorated with pinnacles and ballflower ornaments, is crowned by a spire 285ft high (the upper part is recent). The hexagonal late 13C *N Porch, unusual in ground plan and execution, has an intricately carved door and an inner porch of 1180. The S Porch dates from c 1325.

The interior is light and spacious, with elaborate vaulting and stellate tomb recesses. There is no triforium or horizontal string course. The American Chapel under the tower has some old stained glass, a fine grille (1710) by William Edney, and the so-called rib of the dun cow slain by Guy of Warwick (really a whalebone, said to have been presented to the church by Cabot in 1497). Here too is a wooden figure of Elizabeth I (c 1574). The aisled transepts are an unusual feature in parish churches, rare even in cathedrals. The S transept has monuments to Canynge the younger and his wife, and to another Canynge, as Dean of Westbury College. The tomb slab of Admiral Sir William Penn (d. 1670), father of the founder of Pennsylvania, is at the entrance to the transept; his classical monument, with his armour, is at the W end of the nave. The canopied monuments of the Medes (c 1475), and an interesting brass of their son, are in the N choir aisle. The Lady Chapel has two bays, one 25 years older than the other (1375–1400) and modern glass.

There are good brasses (kept covered) to Sir John Inyn (d. 1439), in the Lady Chapel, and, in front of the high altar, to John Brooke (d. 1512) and his wife Johanna.

Above the N porch is a muniment room where the boy poet Thomas Chatterton pretended to have discovered the Rowley MS in an old chest. Chatterton, nephew of the sexton of St Mary's, was born in Redcliffe Way nearby (house open by application to the Director, City Museum). A poor statue in the churchyard shows him in the school uniform of Colston's Hospital. In 1795 Southey and Coleridge were married to the Fricker sisters at St Mary Redcliffe.

E of the church are *Temple Meads Station* and the ruined *Temple Church*, a large Perpendicular building on the site of a church of the Knights Templar (EH, exterior viewing; key for interior available from local florist). Close by is the church of *St Thomas* by J. Allen (1792–95), with an earlier reredos (1716) and *organ loft (1730).

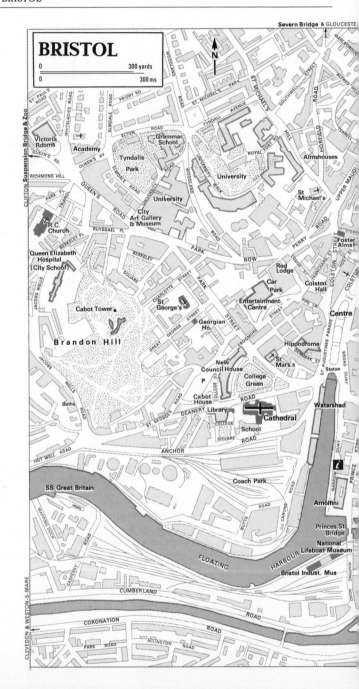

BRISTOL

0 _____ 300 yards
0 _____ 300 ms

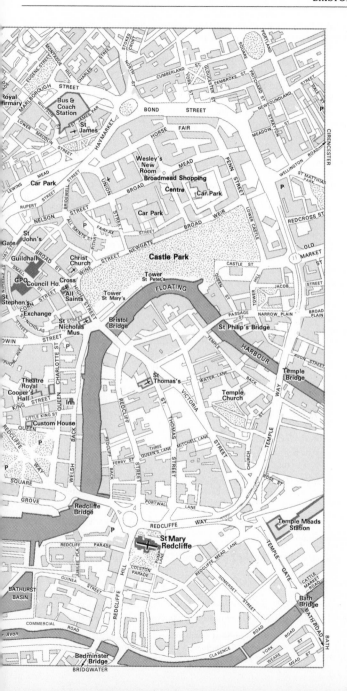

Much of the *City Docks* W of St Mary Redcliffe has been redeveloped for leisure and recreation. Prince's Wharf has the *Bristol Industrial Museum*. In Great Western Dock, further W, lies Brunel's *SS Great Britain* (open), the first ocean-going ship with screw propulsion. She made her maiden voyage to New York in 1845. In 1970 she was towed home from the Falkland Islands, where she had been wrecked in 1886, for restoration. The dock has a museum of relics from her history.

Redcliffe St. leads N from St Mary Redcliffe to (½m) *Bristol Bridge*, built in 1768 to replace the original bridge of 1247. On the left, in Baldwin St., is *St Nicholas*, a Gothick church of 1762 with a 14C crypt and an altarpiece by Hogarth, now the TI centre.

N of the bridge lies the old centre of the city. The Cross, the junction of High St., Wine St., Broad St. and Corn St., was marked until 1733 by the medieval High Cross now at Stourhead (Route 19). At the corner of Wine St. is *Christ Church*, rebuilt by Paty in 1786–90, with two Quarter Jacks of 1728 from the old church, a rood screen, and a 17C font from St Ewen's (now replaced by the Old Council House) in which Southey was baptised.

On the corner of Corn St. stood the bookshop of Joseph Cottle, friend and publisher of Coleridge, Wordsworth and Southey. On the opposite corner is the *Old Council House* by Smirke (1827). In *All Saints*, a good 15C church with two Norman bays, is the monument to Edward Colston by Gibbs and Rysbrack. The Exchange, by the elder Wood (1743), is now a market; in front are the 'Nails', four bronze tables once used by local merchants for their cash transactions (hence, perhaps, 'to pay on the nail'). Corn St. is continued by Clare St., with the elaborate tower (133ft) of *St Stephen's*, a church of 1450–90. Inside are good late medieval tomb recesses and 17C monuments of 1617. The iron gates and *sword rest, by Edney, are from St Nicholas.

Beyond the Cross, High St. continues as Broad St. On the left is the *Guildhall* (1843), now used as law courts. The *Bank of England* (1845) is by C.R. Cockerell. Further down, on the right, the façade of a 19C printing house is decorated with coloured tiles. Spanning the end of the street is *St John's Gate*, with statues of Brennus and Belinus, mythical founders of Bristol, topped by the spire of the 14C St John's.

Wine St. leads NE from the Cross. On the right a new block masks the tower of *St Mary-le-Port*; in *Castle Park* beyond is the ruined church of *St Peter*.

Union St. leads N to the church of *St James*, the nave of a late Norman priory church built in 1130 by Robert, Earl of Gloucester (d. 1157), whose tomb it contains. The W front has a rose window of unique design.

Newgate, straight on, keeps the name of the former prison where the poet Richard Savage died in 1743. The Broadmead Shopping Centre, to the left, includes *Quakers' Friars*, a square with relics of a 13C Dominican priory. The manager's office houses the Bristol Historical Tapestry. The *Register Office*, adjoining on the E, occupies the Old Friends' Meeting House (1747), on a site first occupied by the Quakers in 1670. Penn married his second wife here in 1696. Further N is the oldest Methodist chapel in England, the 'New Room' built by John Wesley in 1739. Wesley used the living quarters upstairs. His statue, by A.G. Walker (1933), stands in the courtyard.

Nelson St. leads back from Broadmead to The Centre. Christmas St., on the right, has the 13C porch of the vanished *St Bartholomew's Hospital*. The quaint Christmas Steps climb up to Colston St. from the opposite side of Rupert St. At the top are stone seats, an old inscription, and *Foster's Almshouses* (rebuilt 1861–84), with a 16C chapel dedicated to the Three Kings of Cologne. Higher up are *St Michael's*, of 1744 with a 15C tower, and the more attractive *Colston's Almshouses*, founded in 1691.

St Augustine's Parade leads S from The Centre to College Green, the former burial ground of the abbey. The *Cathedral stands on the traditional site of St Augustine's Oak, where the saint is said to have conferred with British Christians in 603. It was originally the church of an abbey founded in 1148 for Augustinian canons by Robert Fitzhardinge, Provost of Bristol. After the Dissolution it became the cathedral of the new see of Bristol, created in 1542.

The chapter house and two gateways survive from the Norman buildings. The choir was rebuilt in 1298–1363, mainly by Abbot Knowle (1306–32), connecting it with the previously detached Elder Lady Chapel built by Abbot David c 1215. The transepts were largely rebuilt after 1463, on the model of the older work. The Norman nave was allowed to fall into ruin and the church remained naveless until 1868–88, when the present nave and its two W towers were added by G.E. Street. The central tower dates from c 1450.

The cathedral is a rare example of a 'hall church': the aisles, nave and choir are all the same height, without triforium and clerestory, and the pier arches reach the full height of the building. In the aisles of the *Nave* Street copied the extraordinary vaulting of the choir. At the W end is the tomb of Sir John Young (d. 1603) and his wife Joan. The *N Transept* has rich lierne vaulting, a beautiful window and a monument to Bishop Butler (d. 1752) with an inscription by Southey. The *Elder Lady Chapel* is pure Early English, with Decorated vaulting and E window and a beautiful arcade with grotesque carvings. On the S side is the tomb of the 9th Lord Berkeley (d. 1368) and his mother.

The *Choir*, in an early Decorated style unparalleled elsewhere, has the earliest lierne vaulting in England and beautiful foliage capitals. The canopied stalls (given by Abbot Elyot, 1515–26) have been restored; the misericords and pew ends deserve attention. The organ case and front pipes date from 1685. The reredos (1899) is by Pearson. The choir aisles have skeleton vaulting, which recalls timber rather than stone construction, and stellate tomb recesses (cf. St Mary Redcliffe, above, and St David's Cathedral in Wales). The enamelled glass in the E windows was presented by Dean Glemham (1661–67). In the N choir aisle, the earlier of the two, are: a tablet to Hakluyt, prebendary in 1586–1616; a 13C coffin cover with Lombardic inscription; the tomb of Bishop Bush (d. 1558) with a 'cadaver'; and a bust of Southey by Baily. The *Eastern Lady Chapel* behind the chancel has a beautiful Decorated *E window, with original glass of c 1340, and other glass of the same date in the SW window. The reredos is partly Knowle's but with cresting added by Abbot Burton (1526–71). The chapel contains beautiful sedilia and the tombs of Abbots Newbury (1428–73), Hunt (1473–81) and Newland (1481–1515), coloured according to their original scheme. A tablet marks the grave of Bishop Butler. In the S choir aisle, with Berkeley monuments in the tomb recesses, is the beautiful Decorated entrance to the monastic *Sacristy*. It leads to the *Berkeley Chapel*, with a gilt brass *chandelier of 1450 from the Temple Church. The late Decorated *Newton Chapel*, at the W end of the S choir aisle, has 17–18C tombs of the Newton family.

The *S Transept*, with a groined roof by Abbot Hunt (1473–81), contains a sculptured coffin lid (c 1000) of the Hereford school showing the Harrowing of Hell. In the Norman S wall is the entrance to the night stair.

A door in the W wall of the S transept leads to the scanty but restored remains of the *Cloisters* (c 1480). Off the E walk is the Norman *Chapter House*, rectangular and enriched with zigzag and cable mouldings and interlaced arches. The E wall was rebuilt after the 1831 riots. The series of vestries, etc. built in 1923 as a memorial to H.O. Wills, founder of the university, occupy the site of the Dorter. The doorways of the slype and day stair are preserved. At the end is the 14C doorway of the former Bishop's Palace (not open).

W of the cathedral, leading from College Green to College Square, is the *Abbey Gateway*, late Norman and Perpendicular above. In Cloister Court, inside the gate to the left, a 13C gateway was the entrance to the Refectory, now part of the Cathedral

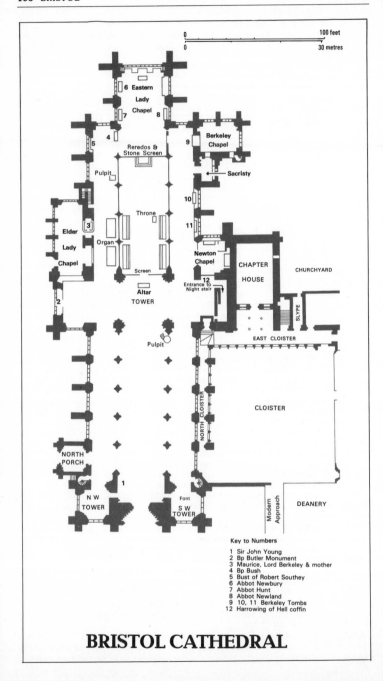

Key to Numbers

1 Sir John Young
2 Bp Butler Monument
3 Maurice, Lord Berkeley & mother
4 Bp Bush
5 Bust of Robert Southey
6 Abbot Newbury
7 Abbot Hunt
8 Abbot Newland
9 10, 11 Berkeley Tombs
12 Harrowing of Hell coffin

BRISTOL CATHEDRAL

School (refounded1542); lower down, in College Square, is another Norman gateway which led to the Abbot's Lodgings. The *Central Library* (1906; Holden) has a chimney-piece by Grinling Gibbons from the old King St. library.

On the W side of the Green is the *Council House* (1933–55; Vincent Harris). The statue of an Elizabethan seaman commemorates John Cabot. On the NE side is the lovely *St Mark's, or the Lord Mayor's Chapel.

Founded c 1230 as the chapel of a hospital for the support of a chaplain and the relief of 100 poor daily, it was taken over by the Corporation in 1541. The hospital became a school; the chapel was used by a Huguenot congregation from 1687 until 1722, when it became the Corporation's official chapel.

The nave, except for the 16C roof, and the transept arches belong to the original 13C chapel. The N transept is 19C rebuilding. The aisle, with its wagon-shaped roof, was added c 1260, the chancel, chapels and tower in the late 15C. The 16–17C French and Flemish stained glass came mostly from Fonthill Abbey (Route 18A) and Ecouen. The fine monuments include those of the founder; his nephew Robert de Gournay (d. 1269); his brother Henry, first Master of the hospital; and Sir Maurice Berkeley (d. 1464). The reredos and sedilia were restored c 1500; the sword rest (1702) was made by Edney for the Temple Church. The *Poyntz Chapel*, in the SE, is a handsome late Perpendicular chantry (c 1520), with early glass and 16C Spanish tiles.

Denmark St., behind St Mark's, leads back to St Augustine's Parade. The medieval cellars beneath the head offices of Harveys, the sherry merchants, house a museum notable for its collection of 18C glasses and Bristol Blue Glass.

Park St. climbs from College Green towards Clifton. At 43 Hannah More and her sisters kept a boarding school (1767–74) where 'Perdita' Robinson was a pupil. At 7 Great George St. (left) is the *Georgian House* (open), a merchant's house of 1789 with appropriate furnishings. Coleridge and Wordsworth probably first met here in autumn 1795. The classical *St George's*, opposite, is by Smirke (1823). *Brandon Hill* (260ft), beyond, is crowned with the *Cabot Tower* (105ft; open), built in 1897–98 to mark the quatercentenary of Cabot's expedition. On the NW slope of the hill is *Queen Elizabeth's Hospital*, a blue-coat school founded in 1590.

The *Red Lodge* (open) in Park Row, E of Park St., was built in 1578–90 and contains fine woodwork and stonecarving of the 16C and 18C, as well as a museum with contemporary furnishings.

Among the imposing group of public buildings in Queen's Rd, at the top of Park St., is the **City Museum and Art Gallery**.

It contains local and regional collections, some of national and international significance. The natural sciences, represented by major mineral and fossil specimens and by world-wide natural history material, are mostly housed in galleries which also feature aquaria and an audio-visual programme. Besides British archaeology from the South-West, there is an important display on ancient Egypt and a gallery devoted to pre-Roman and Roman glass from the Mediterranean, which complements major holdings of Bristol and British 17–20C drinking glasses and containers, and the largest collection of *Chinese glass outside China. The museum's chief treasure is the *8C BC Assyrian relief carvings from Nimrud (Iraq). High above the entrance hall hangs a modern replica of the Bristol Aircraft Company's first commercial aircraft, the 1910 Boxkite. Here too are local coins, medals and awards, and maps of the city. The art collection has European paintings, with a *portrait of Martin Luther by Cranach, Giovanni Bellini's 'Descent into Limbo' and a fine diptych by Taddeo Gaddi. The later schools include works by Vuillard, Delacroix, Redon and Renoir. The local early 19C Bristol school is strongly represented by Francis Danby, Samuel Jackson and other Bristol painters. The collection also includes: English delftware, the largest display in England; English porcelain, particularly strong in Bristol ware; and Oriental work with bronzes, porcelain, lacquer, glass and Japanese prints.

On the right rises the commanding Gothic tower (1925) of the **University of Bristol Wills Memorial Building**. The university was founded by the tobacco tycoon H.O. Wills in 1909.

In Tyndall's Park, behind, is the *Grammar School*, founded by Robert and Nicholas Thorne in 1532 and moved here in 1879. Recent university buildings have extended E beyond Woodland Rd. The *Baptist College*, originally established in 1720 in Stokes Croft owns a miniature of Cromwell and a unique copy of Tyndale's New Testament (1526). In Cotham Rd, a little to the NE, is the *Western Congregational College*, founded by the Independents in 1752 and transferred from Plymouth in 1901.

Further on in Queen's Rd the *Victoria Rooms* (1840), a well-proportioned classical building by Dyer, is the *Royal West of England Academy*.

Clifton, the high-lying residential quarter at the W end of Bristol, has a few 18C mansions and many early 19C villas and terraces. Queen's Rd and Clifton Down Rd climb to (½m) *Clifton Down* and, further N, *Durdham Down*, which together form a limestone plateau (250–300ft) above the rest of the city. They are bounded on the W by the impressive *Avon Gorge*, spanned by the graceful *Clifton Suspension Bridge* (toll), begun by Brunel in 1831 but not completed till 1864. The chains were once part of the old Hungerford Bridge in London. It is 1352ft long (702ft between the piers), 31ft wide and 245ft above high tide. The bridge commands a *view of the gorge, marred at low water by the muddy bed of the river. On the opposite side are *Nightingale Valley* and the hanging *Leigh Woods* (159 acres; NT).

On the hill above the E end of the bridge is an *Observatory* (open) with a camera obscura. From the E end a zigzag footpath descends to the *Hotwells*, a spa which attracted crowds of fashionable visitors in the 18C (see Smollett's 'Humphry Clinker' and Fanny Burney's 'Evelina'). The long Hotwell Rd leads back to (1m) College Green, passing *Holy Trinity*, by C.R. Cockerell (1828–30), gutted in 1941 and refitted by T. Burrough (1959).

In Clifton Park, ¾m NE of the bridge, is *Clifton Cathedral* (RC), a hexagonal building in reinforced concrete, completed in 1973.

Clifton Down Rd continues N from near the bridge to (¾m) *Bristol Zoo. Close by is *Clifton College*, a public school founded in 1862. Earl Haig (statue in the quadrangle), Sir Henry Newbolt, Sir A. Quiller-Couch, Robert Hichens, Roger Fry, Joyce Cary, I.A. Richards and Geoffrey Household were pupils.

At *Westbury-on-Trym*, off A4018 3m N of central Bristol, is the 15C gatehouse of a college of secular clerks where Wyclif was a prebend (NT, key available by written arrangement). The former collegiate church is mainly Perpendicular but has Early English features. The monument to Bishop Carpenter (d. 1477), responsible for the rebuilding, lies near the sanctuary. Another 15C building, in Church Rd, was probably part of the college. Indira Gandhi attended Badminton School here. Near *Henbury*, 1½m N, is *Blaise Castle House Museum* (open), a plain mansion of 1795 now containing exhibits of everyday urban and rural life. The park, landscaped by Repton, has the 18C Stratford Mill (from the 'drowned' Chew valley) and garden buildings (including a thatched dairy) by John Nash. *Blaise Castle* itself, on Henbury Hill, is a sham ruin built in 1766. *Blaise Hamlet* is a 'model' village of Picturesque cottages designed by Nash in 1810–12 (NT, cottages not open).

The Perpendicular church tower built by the Merchant Venturers in 1483 on *Dundry Hill*, 4½m S of Bristol, commands a wide *view.

FROM BRISTOL TO THE SEVERN BRIDGE. The quick route (13m) follows M32 spur to M4. A slower but slightly more interesting route (14m) leaves the city by A4, along the N bank of the Avon. 3½m: *Shirehampton* has a fine public park (NT). 6m: **Avonmouth**, where the Avon flows into the Severn, has the major docks. A402 goes up the estuary, passing on the left at 10½m the *Severn Tunnel* (railway), the longest tunnel in Britain (4m 638yd), built in 1873–86 by Brunel's pupil, Charles Richardson. 14m: *Aust* gives a good view of the *Severn Bridge* (toll), carrying M4 across to *Chepstow* and the Welsh bank of the estuary (Route 58A).

FROM BRISTOL TO CLEVEDON, 13m by A369 and B3124. A369 leaves the city by the Clifton Suspension Bridge and Leigh Woods (see above) and follows the pleasant Gordano valley. 6m: *Portbury* (left) has a large partly Norman church. M5 crosses the road. 8½m:*Portishead*, on the Severn Estuary, is the third limb of Bristol Docks. B3124 leads to 8¾m *Weston-in-Gordano*, where the church has a unique 'Palm Sunday' gallery. 13m: *Clevedon* (17,900 inhabitants) is a resort on the estuary at the foot of *Dial Hill* (296ft; view). In Old Church Rd, near the station, is a cottage doubtfully identified as the 'pretty cot' to which Coleridge brought his bride in 1795. In the old church of *St Andrew* are buried Arthur Hallam (1811–33), subject of Tennyson's 'In Memoriam', and his father Henry Hallam (1777–1859). *Clevedon Court (NT), on B3130 1½m NE, is a lovely house built in 1320 but including the tower and old hall from an earlier building. Despite Elizabethan and later additions, it keeps its medieval plan of rooms. There are good collections of Eltonware and the local Nailsea glass. Thackeray, a guest of the Elton family in 1848, used the house as model for 'Castlewood' in 'Henry Esmond'. An alternative way from Bristol to Clevedon follows B3128 and B3130 along the Yeo valley. At 9m the road passes between (left) *Tickenham* and (right) a hill crowned by *Cadbury Camp*, an entrenchment of 7 acres with a double rampart.

FROM BRISTOL TO WESTON-SUPER-MARE, 21m by A370. 12½m: *Congresbury* (pronounced 'Commsbury') has a vicarage built in 1445 and an Early English church with a fine stone spire. At *Yatton*, 1¼m N, is another good church (12–15C) and at *Claverham*, adjoining on the NE, a Friends' Meeting House of 1729. A370 crosses M5 for (21m) **Weston-super-Mare** (58,000 inhabitants; TI), a resort on the Bristol Channel with an esplanade and two piers, one leading to the rocky islet of *Birnbeck*. It is built partly on the slopes of *Worlebury Hill* (357ft; views) encircled by a toll road. On top are the remains of a British camp. Off the coast are the islets of *Steep Holme* and *Flat Holme*. On the opposite shore of the Axe is *Brean Down*, a bird sanctuary. About 4m N are the remains of *Woodspring Priory*, founded as an expiatory chapel in honour of Thomas Becket by a grandson of Reginald Fitzpurse, one of his murderers. The land to the N is NT (access from Sandy Bay). 2m S is the ruined *Uphill Old Church*.

FROM BRISTOL TO GLOUCESTER, 35m by A38. The road crosses M5 and M4. 10½m: *Thornbury* (left), the early home of the cricketer W.G. Grace (1848–1915), has a Perpendicular church. For *Berkeley*, left at 18m, and (35m) *Gloucester*, see Route 51A.

FROM BRISTOL TO CIRENCESTER, 38m. B4058 leads to (6½m) *Winterbourne*, where the heavily restored church has effigies and a brass of 1370. 9½m: *Iron Acton* has a 15C memorial cross in the churchyard. 17½m: *Wotton-under-Edge* is a pleasant little town. In *Kingswood*, off B4060 1m SW, is a late 14C gatehouse from the Cistercian abbey of 1139 (EH, key from nearby shop). B4058 climbs the wooded slopes of the Cotswolds. On the right is *Newark Park* (NT, limited opening by appointment), an Elizabethan hunting lodge. A footpath leads to *Ozleworth*, where the early Norman church has a hexagonal tower. The substantial houses of *Alderley*, 2m down the valley, were built by prosperous wool traders in the 16–18C. At the top of the ridge (21½m) the route turns right on A4135 for (28m) *Tetbury*. Thence to *Cirencester*, see Route 51B.

From Bristol to *Exeter*, see Route 23.

21

Bath

BATH (85,000 inhabitants) is one of the most beautiful cities in England, though nowadays its beauty is all too often overwhelmed by the crowds of visitors. Its long and distinguished history stems almost entirely from the natural hot springs which gush to the surface here at a constant temperature of 46.5°C. Their medicinal properties were first exploited by the Romans, whose excavated baths now make one of the chief landmarks for visitors. The city again rose to prominence as a fashionable spa in the 18C, when it was visited by almost everyone of account in literature, politics and society. The architect John Wood the Elder and his successors made Bath an enduring monument to Palladian elegance with the squares, terraces and crescents, built of the honey-coloured local stone, which rise up the steep sides of the Avon valley.

TI: The Colonnades, 1113 Bath St. **Bus Station**: Manvers St. **Railway Station**: Bath Spa Station, facing the S end of Manvers St. **Theatre**: Theatre Royal, Sawclose. **Music**: a trio plays chamber and light music in the Pump Room during morning coffee and Sunday afternoon tea. Brass and military bands give concerts in Parade Gardens on summer Sunday afternoons. **Annual Events**: Bath International Festival of Music (May and June); West of England Antiques Fair (May); Royal Bath and West Country Show (May and June); County Cricket Festival (June).

History. According to legend, the city was established by the British swineherd-prince Bladud, father of King Lear, who was expelled from court as a leper but cured himself by imitating his swine and rolling in the warm mud where the mineral waters stagnated. In about AD 44–60 the Romans built a fort here, at the junction of the Foss Way and the route from London to the Welsh frontier. Their city, with its baths and temple, dates from after AD 60. They called the settlement Aquae Sulis, from the local Celtic god Sulis, but added the name of their own healing deity, Minerva. The Saxons, who captured Bath in 577, renamed it Hat Bathum. The see of Wells was moved here between 1090 and about 1206, and its bishops are still known as Bishops of Bath and Wells. In the Middle Ages Bath was a centre of the cloth trade, as Chaucer's portrait of his 'Wife of Bath' testifies. The zenith of Bath's prosperity as a watering-place was reached during the 18C. Beau Nash (Richard Nash; 1674–1761), appointed Master of Ceremonies in 1704, introduced order and method into the social life of the place. The wealthy, self-made Ralph Allen (1693–1764) exploited the quarries of Bath stone, and a new Palladian city was designed and built by John Wood the Elder (1704–54) and his son, John Wood the Younger (1728–81). Thomas Baldwin, John Palmer, John Eveleigh and Robert Adam were among the architects who carried on the tradition until about 1800. Portraits of Bath at the height of its popularity are given by Smollett ('Humphry Clinker'), Sheridan ('The Rivals'), Fanny Burney ('Evelina'), Jane Austen ('Northanger Abbey', 'Persuasion') and Dickens ('Pickwick Papers'). Christopher Anstey's satire, 'The New Bath Guide' (1766), should not be forgotten. In the 19C, when Bath became respectable rather than fashionable, the city's character was changed but not destroyed by the arrival of Brunel's Great Western Railway and the decline of the Kennet and Avon Canal (now well restored). The Bath Festival, internationally famous for its music, was started in 1947 and the University of Bath was founded at Claverton Down in 1966.

The city has given its name to Bath chairs, Bath stone, Bath buns, Bath Oliver biscuits (invented in the 18C by a local doctor, William Oliver) and Bath chaps (cooked pigs' cheeks rolled in breadcrumbs and made into cones) but not to Bath brick, developed at Bridgwater and called after its maker.

Natives, residents and visitors. Few English cities can boast connections with so many distinguished people. They are listed here (not exhaustively) by the streets where they lived or stayed, and the streets are given in the order they are passed in the walking tours below.

WEST AND NORTH FROM THE CENTRE. *Kingsmead Square*: Bishop Butler died at Rosewell House in 1752. *Sawclose*: Beau Nash died at the house, now a restaurant, next to the Theatre Royal. *Trim St.*: General Wolfe left 5 in 1759 to take command of the assault on Quebec. *New King St.*: 9 was home of the Sheridan family, 22 of the naturalist W.H. Hudson. At 19 (now a museum) Sir William Herschel first observed the planet Uranus in 1781. *Gay St.*: 8 is associated with Mrs Piozzi (Mrs Thrale) and 30 with Josiah Wedgwood. No. 23 was the first studio of William Friese-Greene who, with John Rudge, originated cinematography in England; they are also remembered by a plaque at 10 New Bond St. *The Circus*: William Pitt, Earl of Chatham and MP for Bath, stayed at 7 and 8; the explorer David Livingstone at 13; Clive of India at 14; Gainsborough, who won his early fame in Bath, at 17; Parry, the Arctic voyager, at 27. Admiral Phillip (1738–1814), first Governor of New South Wales, spent his last years at 19. *Royal Crescent*: George Saintsbury died at 1 in 1933, Frederic Harrison at 10 in 1923. No. 5 was the home of Christopher Anstey, author of 'The New Bath Guide', and 17 of Sir Isaac Pitman, inventor of modern shorthand. From 11 Elizabeth Linley eloped with the dramatist Sheridan in 1772. *St James's Square*: at 35 Dickens, Forster and Maclise were guests of Walter Savage Landor in 1840.

NORTH AND EAST OF THE CENTRE. *Great Pulteney St*: Macaulay is associated with 1, the novelist Bulwer-Lytton with 2, the architect Thomas Baldwin with 6, Wilberforce with 36 and the evangelical writer Hannah More with 76. *Sydney Place*: Jane Austen lived with her parents at 4.

EAST OF THE CENTRE: *North Parade*: 11 was the residence of Burke, and Goldsmith stayed here in 1771; 9 was visited by Wordsworth. *Pierrepont St.*: Nelson came to 2 in 1780; at 4 Handel visited the actor James Quin. *South Parade*: at 6 the young Sir Walter Scott lived in 1777 with his uncle; at 14 Dr Johnson and Fanny Burney visited Mrs Thrale. *Old Orchard St*: Sarah Siddons achieved her first real stage success in 1775 at the Bath Theatre (now the Masonic Hall).

NORTH-EASTERN OUTSKIRTS. *Lansdown Crescent*: William Beckford moved to 20 in 1823, extending his residence to adjoining houses before his death in 1844.

The centre of Bath is formed by the Abbey, the Pump Room and the Roman Baths and Museum.

The **Abbey Church**, standing in the attractive piazza called *Abbey Churchyard*, is the last of the great English pre-Reformation churches, built in a consistent late Perpendicular style. Externally, its most striking features are the flying buttresses and the W front, with a magnificent window of seven lights flanked by turrets on which are carved ladders with angels ascending and descending.

A nunnery founded at Bath in 676 was converted into a Benedictine monastery by King Edgar, crowned there in 973. The Norman church built by Bishop John de Villula (c 1107) fell into ruin after the bishopric was restored to Wells. The smaller present church was begun in 1499 by Bishop Oliver King, but its completion was delayed by the dissolution of the monasteries and it was not consecrated until 1616. It was restored in the 19C notably by Sir Gilbert Scott in 1864–74.

The spacious interior is remarkable for the size and number of its windows; there is no triforium and the clerestory windows are unusually high. The glass is nearly all modern. Bishop King's original plan for the rich fan-tracery roof was completed when Scott extended it over the nave. At the SE angle of the choir is the small chantry of Prior Bird, notable for its carving, begun in 1515 but finished only in recent years. Apart from the altar tomb of Bishop Montagu (d. 1618) on the N side of the nave, there are no big monuments. Most of the wall tablets commemorate fashionable people who came to Bath in the 18–19C. They include: Beau Nash (d. 1761) in the S aisle; Sir Isaac

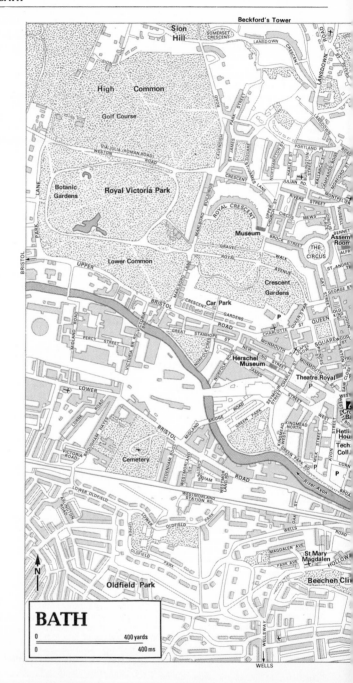

BATH

0 ———————————— 400 yards

0 ———————————— 400 ms

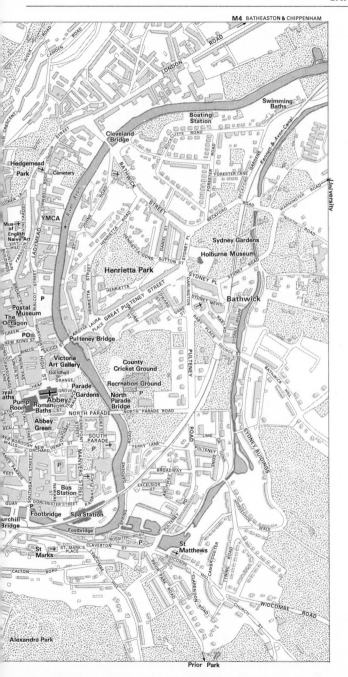

M4 BATHEASTON & CHIPPENHAM

CAMDEN ROAD

LONDON ROAD

Swimming
Baths

Boating
Station

Cleveland
Bridge

Hedgemead
Park

Cemetery

River Avon

BATHWICK STREET

CLIFFE ROAD

ROCK ROAD

FORESTER LANE

FORESTER ROAD

BECKFORD GDNS

Kennet & Avon Canal

WARMINSTER ROAD

University

YMCA

Mus
of
English
Naive Art

HAY
HILL

FOUNTAIN BUILDINGS

LADYMEAD

WALCOT STREET

BROAD ST

PARAGON

HENRIETTA STREET

HENRIETTA ROAD

HENRIETTA GDNS

DANIEL ST

SUTTON ST

Sydney Gardens

Holburne Museum

BECKFORD ROAD

SYDNEY ROAD

Henrietta Park

HENRIETTA

GREAT PULTENEY STREET

HOWARD

SYDNEY PL

DARLINGTON

Bathwick

SYDNEY MEWS

SYDNEY PL

Postal
Museum

The
Octagon

GREEN

PO

NEW BOND ST

WALLS

BRIDGE

HIGH

UNION PASS

NORTHUMBERLAND PAS

PARSONAGE

Victoria
Art Gallery

Guildhall

ORANGE GROVE

CHEAP ST

Pulteney Bridge

ARGYLE STREET

LAURA PLACE

WILLIAM ST

VANE ST

RABY PLACE

RABY

GEORGE S

BATHWICK HILL

PULTENEY

County
Cricket Ground

Recreation Ground

oyal
aths

Pump
Room

Roman
Baths

Abbey

YORK ST

ORCHARD ST

Parade
Gardens

North
Parade
Bridge

P

NORTH PARADE ROAD

LIME

GR BANK

SYDNEY BUILDINGS

BEAU ST

Abbey
Green

NEW ST

PIERREPONT ST

DUKE ST

NORTH PARADE

SOUTH
PARADE

HENRY ST

MANVERS STREET

P

FERRY LANE

PULTENEY ROAD

GR BANK

EW BOROUGH
WALLS

NEW
ORCHARD

P

GARDENS

BROADWAY

EXCELSIOR ST

ARCHWAY

AMES PARADE

REET

SOUTHGATE STREET

NEWARK ST

Bus
Station

PHILIP ST

P

SPRING

QUAY

DORCHESTER STREET

urchill
Bridge

Footbridge

Spa Station

Footbridge

ROSSITER ROAD

P

CLAVERTON

ST

St
Matthews

PULTENEY RD

WIDCOMBE HILL

CAMBRIDGE RD

TYNING ROAD

HORSESHOE WALK

St
Marks

ST. MARK'S
PLACE

VANBRUGH

CALTON ROAD

WIDCOMBE

CLARENDON ROAD

PRIOR PARK ROAD

CHURCH ROAD

WIDCOMBE ROAD

Alexandra Park

Prior Park

Pitman (d. 1897) in the N aisle; James Quin (d. 1766), with a poem by Garrick, in the N choir aisle; and the political economist Malthus (d. 1834) in the porch.

The *Vaults* house displays tracing the long history of Christian worship on the abbey site.

On the S side of Abbey Churchyard stands the **Pump Room** (open). Rebuilt in the classical style by Thomas Baldwin and John Palmer in 1792–96, it has the motto 'water is best' in Greek on its architrave. The handsome interior has a statue and a portrait of Beau Nash, and a longcase clock presented to the city in 1709 by its maker, Thomas Tompion. Windows overlook the King's Bath. A trio plays mornings and afternoons when coffee and tea are served; a fountain supplies mineral water.

The adjoining *Roman Baths and Museum embody the substantial remains of the temple and complex of baths built at the centre of Aquae Sulis, some 20ft below the present street level, between the 1C and the 4C AD. Fragments of Roman Bath were turned up during the Georgian rebuilding of the city, but excavation did not begin in earnest until 1878; it has continued to yield important discoveries up to the present.

The first major exhibit is the reconstructed pediment of the temple to Sulis Minerva, with a Romano-Celtic Gorgon's head as its centrepiece. Underground staircases and corridors lead past the *King's Bath*, named from the medieval structure placed on top of the reservoir which the Romans built to harness the hot spring. The display cases nearby contain votive offerings recovered from the spring: coins, personal jewellery and pieces of pewter scratched with prayers and curses, as well as vessels used in religious ceremonies. A walkway leads across the excavated site of the temple precinct, where part of the entrance steps to the temple can be seen. On display are: a superb head of Minerva, found beneath Stall St. in 1727; sculptured fragments later used as paving stones; two corners of the sacrificial altar, showing Hercules Bibax and Bacchus; carved reliefs of a mastiff carrying a roe deer and a hound chasing a hare; and the façade of the Four Seasons, with its Luna pediment.

Near the Roman overflow from the spring is the entrance to the baths. The *Great Bath* is now roofless, and its pillars, terrace and statues of famous Romans are 19C, but the bath itself and the surrounding pavement are well preserved. At the edge are the bases of the piers which once supported the roof. The flight of steps by which the bath was entered is visible in the murky, steaming water; and the bottom still has its floor of lead from the Mendips. Fragments displayed around the sides include part of the 3C roof vaulting, with hollow tiles.

The eastern range of baths, altered several times by the Romans, include: the tepid bath, with cooler water than the Great Bath; a little semi-circular bath probably used for curative treatment; and part of the hypocaust serving a suite of Turkish baths, a later addition to the complex. The *West Baths* have a circular bath of cold water, added in the 2C. The hypocaust, flues and stoking holes used to heat adjoining rooms also survive.

WEST AND NORTH FROM THE CENTRE AND BACK. Bath St., a perfect colonnaded thoroughfare, leads W from the Roman Baths and Stall St. to the delightful *Cross Bath*, originally medieval but rebuilt by Baldwin and Palmer (1784). The *Hot Bath* (or Old Royal Bath) to the left is by John Wood the Younger. Hetling Court continues past the back of *Hetling House* (now the Abbey Church House), one of the city's few Elizabethan houses (1570, restored 1954). A right turn on Westgate Buildings heads past Kingsmead Square, where the Baroque *Rosewell House* is by John Strahan (1736).

Gorgon's head on the pediment of the temple of Sulis Minerva, Roman Baths and Museum, Bath

Sawclose, leading N, has the *Theatre Royal*, with a façade of 1804–05 by George Dance the Younger, and the house (now a restaurant) where Beau Nash died. Queen Square, further N, was the first of John Wood the Elder's major contributions to the city (1728–34).

In New King St., off the SW corner of the square via Chapel Row and Charles St., the *Herschel Museum* was home of the astronomer and musician Sir William Herschel (1738–1822). Sheridan was living at 9 at the time of his elopement with Elizabeth Linley (1772).

From Queen's Parade, off the NW corner of the square, a flight of steps leads to a footpath curving past the back of the Circus to a superb view of the Royal Crescent (see below).

Gay St., also by the elder Wood, climbs N from Queen Square to his masterpiece, the *Circus, begun in 1754 and planned so that a true crescent faces each of its three approaches. In Bennett St., to the right, are the **Assembly Rooms** (NT), built by the younger Wood in 1769–71, gutted by fire in 1942 and since restored. They now house a *Museum of Costume* with exhibits from 1580 to the present.

On the Paragon, to the E, the 19C chapel founded by Selina, Countess of Huntingdon and its adjoining school are both open, the latter as the *Museum of English Naive Art*. Broad St., to the S, has the *Postal Museum*.

Along Brock St. to the left of the Circus is the younger Wood's masterpiece, the ***Royal Crescent** (1767–74). Its leisurely, majestic sweep is both the perfect foil to the enclosed space of the elder Wood's Circus and the final realisation of the Palladian grace to which the architects of Bath aspired. No. 1, restored and furnished by the Bath Preservation Trust, is open to the public.

The charming *Royal Victoria Park*, W of the Crescent, is the largest of many green spaces, with a botanic garden. Dickens conceived the character of Little Nell while visiting the poet Walter Savage Landor at 35 St James's Square, behind the Crescent.
  See North-Western Outskirts below for an extension of the walk N from the Crescent to Lansdown Crescent and Lansdown Hill.

NORTH AND EAST FROM THE CENTRE. High St. leads N from the abbey to Bridge St. The attractive alleyways of shops on the left include the Corridor (1825), Northumberland Place and Union Passage. On the right are munici-pal buildings whose nucleus is Baldwin's *Guildhall* of 1768–75, containing an Adam-style *Banqueting Room* (open unless otherwise booked) with Whitefriars chandeliers of 1778 and portraits of George III and Queen Charlotte. In the N wing is the **Victoria Art Gallery**.

Its permanent collection includes British and European paintings, prints, drawings and decorative arts, a proportion of which is displayed in the first floor gallery. It includes works by the local Barker family, Gainsborough, Thomas Malton and Sickert. The gallery on the ground floor houses touring and temporary exhibitions.

Bridge St. leads to the charming * *Pulteney Bridge*, flanked with shops. Built by Robert Adam in 1769–74, it is his only major contribution to the city's architecture. On the other side of the river Laura Place, with a fountain and a Victorian pillar-box, marks the start of the impressive Great Pulteney St., designed by Baldwin (1788) and unbroken on the left except for a terrace overlooking Henrietta Park. The street ends at the **Holburne Museum**, in front of Sydney Gardens.

Housed in a building of 1796–97, the collections grew from the bequest of Sir Thomas Holburne (d. 1874). Particularly strong are the English paintings, among them portraits by Gainsborough, Allan Ramsay and Raeburn and works by Stubbs, Henry and George Morland, and the Barkers of Bath. European works include 17C Italian and French as well as Flemish and Dutch paintings. Also exhibited, in an interesting juxtaposition with work by 20C British artists and craftsmen, are English and Conti-nental silver and porcelain, glass, majolica, and furniture. The Crafts Study Centre includes work by Bernard Leach (ceramics), Barron and Larcher (textiles), Irene Wellington (calligraphy) and Gimson (furniture).
  The young Jane Austen lived with her parents at 4 Sydney Place, to the right of the museum. Behind the museum lie the shady *Sydney Gardens*, laid out in 1795. Brunel's Great Western Railway and the Kennet and Avon Canal cross them.
  See Eastern Outskirts below for Sham Hill.

EAST FROM THE CENTRE. On York St., immediately S of the Pump Room and Abbey Churchyard, is the picturesque cobbled square of Abbey Green, with *Sally Lunn's House*, reputedly the oldest house in Bath (now a tea shop and restaurant), around the corner on North Parade Passage. York St. goes E to North Parade, passing *Ralph Allen's Town House*, built for the self-made magnate by the elder Wood in 1727. It originally enjoyed a clear view eastward to his folly, Sham Castle (see Eastern Outskirts below). North Parade and South Parade (reached by Pierrepont St. or Duke St.), begun in 1740, belong to one of the elder Wood's earliest grand designs for the city. To the N, at the Roman level of the city, are the pleasant *Parade Gardens*. Near *North Parade Bridge* is the so-called *Sheridan's Grotto*, a stone alcove once used as a 'post office' for lovers' letters.

NORTH-WESTERN OUTSKIRTS. About 1m NW of the centre, beyond the Royal Crescent and St James's Square, is Lansdown Crescent (1789–93; John Palmer). William Beckford lived at 20 and adjoining houses from 1823, when he left Fonthill Abbey, until his death in 1844. Somerset Place (c 1790) and Camden Crescent (c 1788), both by John Eveleigh, also command fine views of the city. On Lansdown Hill, another 1m NW, stands the neo-classical *Beckford's Tower*, built for the writer by E.H. Goodridge in 1827. It contains a small museum. The belvedere has one of the best views in the West of England. The site of the Battle of Lansdown (1643), 2½m N, is marked by an 18C monument to the Royalist victor, Sir Bevil Grenville, mortally wounded on the battlefield (EH). From *Prospect Stile*, 2m W of the tower and situated on a well defined Roman road, both Bath and Bristol are visible.

NORTH-EASTERN OUTSKIRTS. A4, the London road, heads along the N bank of the Avon. Above (2m) *Bailbrook* rises *Little Solsbury Hill* (NT) with an Iron Age hill-fort. A left turn just before *Batheaston* leads in a little over 2m to *St Catherine's*, with a 16C manor house and a church of 1490.

SOUTH-WESTERN OUTSKIRTS. The village of *Englishcombe* near the Wansdyke, off A367 4m SW of the centre, has a tithe barn and a church with grotesque Norman sculpture on its N side and a figure of a swaddled child above the chancel arch.

SOUTHERN OUTSKIRTS. *Beechen Cliff*, rising above the Avon just S of the railway station, gives the best view of the city from nearby. It is reached by crossing the Southgate footbridge and then following either Holloway or the steps climbing from Lyncombe Hill.

SOUTH-EASTERN OUTSKIRTS. Prior Park Rd climbs steeply from Claverton Rd, S of the river by the railway station. After about ½m the narrow Church St. leads left to *Widcombe*, with the lovely Widcombe Manor (not open) opposite the church. Henry Fielding wrote part of 'Tom Jones' at Widcombe Lodge. The hill continues beyond the turning for Church St. to (1m) *Prior Park* (chapel open), the Palladian mansion John Wood the Elder built for Ralph Allen in 1743. Allen's friendship with Pope, Fielding and other writers of the age makes it rich in literary associations. Altered, damaged by fire and now in use as a Catholic school, the house still has its fine chapel and a lovely Palladian bridge in the grounds (NT). *Crowe Park* (gardens open under NGS; house by appointment) is an elegant villa. From *Combe Down*, above Prior Park, a pleasant footpath leads down into Widcombe.

EASTERN OUTSKIRTS. On Bathwick Hill, c 1m beyond Sydney Gardens, is *Sham Castle*, an artificial ruin built for Ralph Allen in about 1760, with good views. The *University of Bath* lies on Claverton Down beyond. For Claverton, see the route to Bradford-on-Avon below.

FROM BATH TO BRADFORD-ON-AVON, 9m by A36 and B3108. A36, the Warminster road, follows the S bank of the canal. 2m: *Bathampton*, to the left, was Sickert's home from 1938 until his death in 1942. He is buried in the churchyard. 3½m: *Claverton*, right of A36, has Ralph Allen's grave. The manor house of 1820 by Sir Jeffrey Wyatville is an **American Museum** with 17–19C domestic interiors imported from the USA (Shaker room, Pennsylvania Dutch room, etc.) and folk art. A plaque records that Sir Winston Churchill made his first political speech here in 1897. 4½m: Just short of *Limpley Stoke* B3108 branches left across the river and the canal, climbing tortuously to the lovely stone-built town of (9m) **Bradford-on-Avon** (8800 inhabitants; TI). *St Laurence's* may be the best Saxon church in the country. The lower part probably dates from Aldhelm's foundation in c 705, the arcading above from the end of the 10C. Note in particular the flying angels over the chancel arch. The *Town Bridge* is 17C, with two 13C arches and a lock-up made from an old bridge chapel (cf. Wakefield). The *Parish Church* is Norman, Decorated and Perpendicular with some good details. *Barton Farm*, to the S, has a remarkable early 14C tithe barn (EH, phone keykeeper, 0272 750700). *South Wraxall*, 3½m N, has a fine 15C manor, and at *Great Chalfield*, 3m NE, there is another house of the same period (NT) and a church with 15C wall paintings. *Westwood*, 1½m SW of Bradford, has another good manor house (NT), built in 1400–1620, and a church with a notable tower and glass of c 1520.

The return to Bath can be made via *Farleigh Hungerford*, on A366 3½m SW, where the late 14C *Castle* (EH, all year) has the tomb of its builder and the church (1443) has his stained-glass portrait, and (2m further) *Norton St Philip*, where the 15C inn occupies the former guest house of the Abbot of Hinton Charterhouse.

For *Dyrham Park*, off A46 8m N of Bath, see Route 20.

From Bath to *London* and *Bristol*, see Route 20; to *Wells*, see Route 22.

22

Bath to Wells and the Mendip Hills

Directions. Total distance 23m. A39, the direct road from Bath to Wells via Farrington Gurney and Chewton Mendip, is shorter (20m) but less interesting. **Bath**, see Route 21. A367 to (8m) Radstock. A367, A37 to (17m) **Shepton Mallet**. A371 to (23m) **Wells**.

Bath, see Route 21. A367 follows the line of the Foss Way SW from the city. 5½m: From *Peasedown St John* unclassified roads lead left to (2m) *Wellow*, the probable birthplace of the composer John Bull (?1562–1628), which has a faithfully restored church of 1372 with a fine roof and a fresco of c 1500. About 1m S is *Stoney Littleton Long Barrow*, a Neolithic chambered burial mound (EH). 8m: *Radstock*, with the neighbouring town of *Midsomer Norton* (18,300 inhabitants together; TI), was the chief centre of the Somerset coalfield. The last pit closed in 1973. Beyond the town A367, now on a markedly Roman alignment, leaves B3139, a more direct road to Wells, on the right. At (11m) *Stratton-on-the-Fosse*, a community of Benedictine monks expelled from Douai in 1793 founded *Downside Abbey* in 1814. It includes a public school and a massive church (open) built between 1874 and 1938, with the shrine of St Oliver Plunkett. A367 climbs the Mendip Hills to (14m) *Oakhill*, beyond which it joins A37. 17m: **Shepton Mallet** (6300 inhabitants) has a market place with 15C shambles and a restored 16C cross. Old houses survive in the adjoining network of lanes. The church has a superb panelled wagon *roof. The grounds of the Bath and West Agricultural Show, held in early June, lie to the SE. A371 runs W along the pretty valley of the Sheppey. 19½m: *Croscombe* church has Jacobean woodwork.

23m: **WELLS** (9000 inhabitants; TI), with its great cathedral, is a quiet market town at the foot of the Mendip Hills. Wholly ecclesiastical in origin

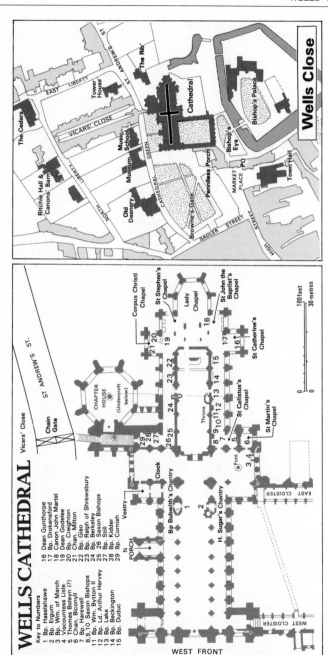

Wells Close

EAST LIBERTY — LIBERTY — ST ANDREW'S ST — EAST LIBERTY

The Cedars · Tower House · 'The Rib' · Cathedral · Bishop's Palace · Ritchie Hall & Canons' Barn · VICARS' CLOSE · Music School · GREEN · Bishop's Eye · Old Deanery · NORTH LIBERTY · Browne's Gate · CATHEDRAL GREEN · Penniless Porch · Market Place · PO · Town Hall · SADLER STREET · HIGH STREET

WELLS CATHEDRAL

ST ANDREW'S ST. · Vicars' Close · Chain Gate

Key to Numbers

1. Bp. Haselshawe
2. Bp. Ergum
3. Bp. Wm. of March
4. Viscountess Lisle
5. Thomas Boleyn (?)
6. Chan. Biconyll
7. Bp. Harewell
8, 9, 10. Saxon Bishops
11. Bp. Wm. Bytton II
12. Bp. Ld. Arthur Hervey
13. Bp. Lake
14. Bp. Beckington
15. Bp. Duduc
16. Dean Gunthorpe
17. Bp. Drokensford
18. Canon John Martel
19. Dean Godelee
20. Bp. Creighton
21. Chan. Milton
22. Bp. Giso
23. Bp. Ralph of Shrewsbury
24. Bp. Berkeley
25, 26. Saxon Bishops
27. Bp. Still
28. Bp. Kidder
29. Bp. Cornish

CHAPTER HOUSE (Undercroft below) · Corpus Christi Chapel · St Stephen's Chapel · Lady Chapel · St John the Baptist's Chapel · St Catherine's Chapel · St Calixtus's Chapel · St Martin's Chapel · Throne · Font · Clock · Bp Bubwith's Chantry · H. Sugar's Chantry · Vestry · N PORCH · WEST FRONT · WEST CLOISTER · EAST CLOISTER

100 feet · 30 metres

and development, it keeps much of its medieval character. The market place, cathedral, Bishop's Palace and the old buildings of the clergy form a harmonious group.

The irregular market place is enclosed by the 17C *Crown Hotel*, the *Town Hall* of 1779 and a N side built c 1450 by Bishop Beckington. The *Bishop's Eye* leads to the Bishop's Palace (see below) and the *Penniless Porch* to the cathedral close, known as Cathedral Green, rivalled in its calm beauty only by Salisbury close. This, however, is best entered by *Browne's Gate* (or the *Dean's Eye*) in Sadler St., where the astonishing façade of the cathedral bursts on the view. All these gates were built by Bishop Beckington.

The **Cathedral**, known for its W façade and its 'scissors arches', is wonderfully complete in all its parts. It may well be the most beautiful English cathedral.

Tradition says that a church of St Andrew was founded by King Ine c 705 near the springs which have given the city its name. In 909 Wells became the seat of the new bishopric of Somerset, but Bishop John de Villula (1088–1122) transferred the see to Bath. Under Bishop Savary (1192–1205) the title of the see was 'Bath and Glastonbury'. Bishop Jocelin (1206–42) returned to Wells and in 1219 surrendered the claim to Glastonbury, retaining the title 'Bath'. His successors ever since 1244 have been Bishops of 'Bath and Wells', and the monks of Bath and the canons of Wells had equal voices in the election of the bishops until the suppression of the abbey of Bath in 1539.

The present cathedral was begun c 1180 under Bishop Reginald. The three W bays of the choir, the transepts, and the E bays of the nave were probably finished soon after 1200. The N porch was built for Bishop Jocelin, who also completed the nave and W front, designed by Thomas Norreys (fl. 1229–49). The church was consecrated in 1239. To the Decorated style belong the chapter house (1293–1306), with its staircase and earlier undercroft (1286), and the central tower, raised to its present height in 1321. The Lady Chapel, the three E bays of the choir and the retrochoir were rebuilt by Dean Godelee c 1325. The Perpendicular W towers, designed by William de Wynford (d. 1405), were largely paid for by two bishops, the SW tower by Bishop Harewell (d. 1386) and the NW tower by Bishop Bubwith (d. 1424). The cathedral suffered at the hands of Puritans and Monmouth's rebels. It was restored in the 19C by Benjamin Ferrey and Anthony Salvin. Further restoration of the W façade was carried out in 1975–86.

The **W façade is pure Early English work challenging comparison with Reims or Amiens. Its vast screen, divided vertically by six buttresses, is made unusually wide (147ft) by placing the W towers (Perpendicular in their upper stages) not at the end of the aisles but outside them. This provides the framework for a superb display of **statues and sculptural detail by a local school of craftsmen. There were originally over 400 figures in full colour, carried in six tiers across the whole façade and round the sides of the towers. Nearly 300 remain, about half of them life-size or larger, the finest collection of medieval sculpture in England. The damage done by weather and iconoclasm prevents identification in many cases. In the tympanum of the main portal are the Virgin and Child; in the niche above, the Coronation of the Virgin. The gable has the nine orders of angels, the Apostles and the Saviour (a replacement by David Wynne, 1985).

Also on the exterior, the N side of the nave has an elegant Decorated parapet (c 1326) and Perpendicular window tracery. The *N Porch, with some exquisite carving, was built c 1213. On the N transept is a clock (15C dial repainted in the 19C) with two *figures in armour striking the quarters with their battle axes (c 1470). The Chain Gate, a Perpendicular bridge (1443–65), connects the chapter house with Vicars' Close.

On entering the cathedral from the W end, attention is immediately caught by the double straining *arch, or 'scissors arch', one of three added c 1338–48 to support the weight of the tower (completed by the addition of a spire c 1322). Like the octagon at Ely, these arches are at once a bluntly technical solution to an engineering problem and a wonderful visual coup. The rich architecture of the *Nave* makes it look taller than it is (67ft), and the unbroken row of lancets in the triforium greatly increases its apparent length. The chief decorations are the elaborate *capitals, and the medallions and carvings in the spandrels of the lancets in the triforium. The S clerestory has an early Perpendicular gallery. On the N side is the hexagonal Perpendicular chantry of Bishop Bubwith (d. 1424), with an alabaster panel of the Ascension; opposite is the chantry of Treasurer Hugh Sugar (d. 1489), with a stone pulpit of 1547 attached. The imposing lectern (1661) was a gift of Bishop Creighton; the sidelights of the W window have remains of the glass he presented.

The space beneath the tower, Early English with fan-tracery vaulting, is bounded on three sides by the scissors arches; on the fourth is a 14C screen adapted to carry the organ. The aisled transepts (c 1190) have carved *capitals. In the *N Transept* is the *clock (1386–92) with its contemporary astronomical indications and tournament of knights. In the *S Transept* are the Chapel of Calixtus, containing a tomb (c 1440) with unique representations of medieval choir vestments and alabaster *panels of the Annunciation and the Trinity, and the Chapel of St Martin, with the tomb of Chancellor William Biconyll (d. 1448). By the S wall of the transept are a 19C copy of the brass of Viscountess Lisle (d. 1464) and the tomb of Bishop William of March (d. 1302). The Saxon font comes from the earlier cathedral.

In the S choir aisle are the tombs of Bishop William Bytton II (d. 1274), with the oldest incised slab in England, and Bishop Beckington (d. 1465), with an exquisite canopy, iron screen and 'memento mori'. The effigies of Saxon bishops in the choir were probably set up c 1205 to vindicate the priority of the see of Wells over that of Bath. Both aisles keep some 14C glass; the *SE Transept* has glass (1500–25) from Rouen by pupils of Arnold of Nijmegen and also the effigy of Bishop Drokensford (d. 1329). Adjoining the SE chapel is the lofty tomb of Canon John Martel (d. c 1350).

Of the *Choir*, the first three bays (Early English, end of 12C) formed the original presbytery, the ritual choir then extending from the space under the tower to the first bays of the nave. The E portion of the choir is in a rich Geometric Decorated style. Its lierned stone vaulting recalls the wooden roofs common in Somerset. The 14C stalls, backed by a Victorian stone canopy, have 61 *misericords. The E end of the choir is formed by three arches surmounted by the E window, with *glass of c 1340 depicting a Tree of Jesse. The low screen behind the altar allows a view of the *Retrochoir* and *Lady Chapel*. Both are Decorated but the retrochoir was added later, uniting the Lady Chapel with the presbytery by four supporting pillars and ingenious vaulting. The Lady Chapel itself, finished before 1326, is an irregular octagon; its large windows are filled with fragments of superb glass (c 1320). The *NE Transept* has a sculpture of the Ascension and monuments to Bishop Creighton (d. 1672) and Chancellor Milton (d. 1337). The N choir aisle has the fine alabaster effigy of Bishop Ralph of Shrewsbury (d. 1363), the monument to Bishop Berkeley (d. 1581) and more effigies of Saxon bishops.

From the N transept an exquisite early Decorated staircase leads to the octagonal **Chapter House*, in the full Decorated style and the finest of its period in England. Probably finished c 1306, it has 32 delicate vaulting ribs springing from the central pier. The double-arched doorway, the glass in the lights of the windows, the corbels of the vaulting and the carved heads on the springers of the arcade formed by the 51 stalls are all worth attention. The staircase continues over the Chain Gate to Vicars' Close (see below).

From the S transept a doorway leads to the *Chapter Library*, built over the E walk of the cloisters in 1425. It contains 6000 books, original charters from 968 onwards and a crozier with 13C Limoges enamelling. The three-sided *Cloisters*, also entered from the S transept, were rebuilt c 1425–1508. The walls are lined with tablets moved from the cathedral, including one on the E side to the Wells composer Thomas Linley (1732–95) and his daughters, one of whom married Sheridan. The central space is known as the 'Palm Churchyard', probably because of the Palm Sunday procession which passed through it.

The ***Bishop's Palace**, S of the cathedral, is still used by the bishop; the grounds and part of the buildings are open on limited days from Easter to October and every day in August. The surrounding walls and moat were added by Bishop Ralph of Shrewsbury (1329–63). The swans in the moat find the bell-rope let down and ring the bell themselves to demand bread. Beyond the 14C gatehouse are the ruins of the magnificent *Great Hall*, built by Bishop Burnell (1274–92) and dismantled by Bishop Barlow (1549–54).

Bishop Burnell's *Chapel* is a beautiful piece of Decorated work. The *Palace* itself was built by Bishop Jocelin in 1230–40. To the SW is the long, buttressed *Bishop's Barn*, a perfect specimen of the early 15C. A path leads round the S side of the moat and back to the road, giving a good view of the finest E end in England, with the Decorated central tower, octagonal chapter house (fine gargoyles) and octagonal Lady Chapel standing clear of the choir.

On the N side of the Cathedral Green is the *Old Deanery*, partly rebuilt by Dean Gunthorpe in 1472–98. Adjoining it is the *Museum*, the rebuilt Chancellor's House, with finds from Wookey Hole and other local antiquities. Next comes the *Music School* of Wells Cathedral School, incorporating the hall of the Archdeaconry (now used as a concert hall), modernised but dating from c 1280 and with a 15C timber roof.

Further E and connected to the N side of the cathedral by the bridge over the Chain Gate is the 14C ***Vicars' Close**, built by Bishop Ralph and his successors for the College of Vicars Choral, the deputies of the canons. It consists of two rows of houses, altered but keeping their original charm. The front of 22 has been reformed as originally built. Between the Chain Gate and the close is the Vicars' Hall, or refectory (completed 1348), where the members of the college ate together. At the further end of the close is the tiny chapel, altered by Bishop Beckington. Beyond is the 14–18C *Tower House* and, opposite, the *Prebendal House*, a 15C building with a superb porch, assigned to the principal of the college.

In East Liberty and North Liberty handsome domestic buildings of many periods are now part of Wells Cathedral School.

The civic church of ***St Cuthbert** is the largest parish church in Somerset. It has a Perpendicular tower of the local type, ornate roofs, a carved pulpit of 1636 and, in the transepts, two well-carved but mutilated reredoses (one a Jesse Tree). Nearby are *Bishop Bubwith's Almshouses* (1436, with 17C additions).

The gardens of *Milton Lodge*, ½m N, have been replanted in the last 20 years.

Wells makes a good centre for touring the **Mendip Hills**. This limestone chain, about 25m long and never more than 6m wide, stretches from near Frome (Route 24) in the SE to the coast at Weston-super-Mare (Route 20). Its southern edge, marked by the course of A371, rises out of the Somerset marshes. The central plateau, most prominent between Shepton Mallet and Shipham, reaches 1066ft at Blackdown, between Cheddar and Burrington Combe. The hills are known for their gorges, caves and 'swallow-holes', though the most famous caves are now sadly commercialised. Some show traces of prehistoric settlement, while the uplands have open trenches ('scruffs') and spoil heaps from Roman lead mining.

A 35m circuit of the Mendips from Wells begins by taking a sideroad 2m NW to *Wookey Hole* (open), where the river Axe gushes to the surface. Three caves are open; twelve more have been explored. Bone remains found in the Hyaena Den show occupation from c 35,000 BC to c 12,000 BC. The caves are now owned by Madame Tussaud's, who have added a museum as well as less appropriate amusements (restored 19C paper mill, traditional fairground, penny arcade, history of waxworks exhibition). A steep unclassified road climbs the hills to (5m) *Priddy* (789ft), where the Romans mined lead. A little higher up the road joins B3135. This descends ***Cheddar Gorge**, badly cheapened by tourism, a narrow cleft winding more than 2m between limestone cliffs rising to 430ft. The cliffs are perforated by caves with delicate stalactites. *Cox's Cave* and the larger *Gough's Cave* are both open. Gough's Cave was inhabited from the Stone Age to Romano-British times; finds are displayed in the museum at the mouth. 11½m: *Cheddar* (seasonal TI) is a large village, crowded in summer, at the mouth of the gorge. The cheese for which it is famous is now widely imitated elsewhere.

Wedmore, in the marshes 4m S, gave its name to the peace concluded in 878 between Alfred and Guthrum the Dane after the Battle of Ethandune (see Edington, Route 24). The church has a fine 12C portal and a 15C St Christopher, overpainted c 1520.

A371 leads W to (13½m) *Axbridge* (TI), the centre of a strawberry-growing area. King John's Hunting Lodge is, despite its name, a Tudor merchant's house; owned by the NT, it contains a local museum. The commanding Perpendicular church has a nave roof of 1636. A371 joins A38 for about 1m (see Route 23), before branching left to (15½m) *Winscombe* and (17m) *Banwell*, where the churches both have fine Perpendicular towers and good glass. At Banwell there are also fine roofs, W gallery, pulpit and a screen of 1522. A368 runs E along the N flank of the Mendips to (23m) *Burrington*.

An alternative way back to Wells from Burrington continues along A368 through woodland to (1m) *Blagdon*, overlooking a lake-reservoir. The village gave its name to the 'Blagdon Controversy' (1800–03), provoked by charges of Methodism against Hannah More's early experiments in Sunday School education. A368 and B3114 continue along the foot of the hills, with views and good churches at (4½m) *Compton Martin* and (10m) *Chewton Mendip. Litton*, about 1m before Chewton Mendip, has *Sherborne Garden* (limited opening), made up of several gardens of different character. A39 runs directly from Chewton Mendip to (16m) Wells.

From Burrington B3134 climbs *Burrington Combe*, smaller and less plagued with tourists than Cheddar Gorge. While sheltering from a thunderstorm here, Augustus Toplady (1740–78) was inspired to write 'Rock of Ages'. The road passes just below *Blackdown* (1066ft), the highest point of the Mendips, and the centre of Roman lead mining at *Charterhouse*. At (31m) *Green Ore* the route turns S on A39 for (35m) *Wells*.

23

Bristol to Exeter

Directions. Total distance 76m. M5 follows a roughly similar line. **Bristol**, see Route 20. A38 to (32m) Bridgwater, (44m) **Taunton** (Route 19), (51m) Wellington and (58m) Waterloo Cross. B3181 to (63m) Cullompton and (67m) **Exeter** (Route 18A).

Bristol, see Route 20. A38 leaves the city by Redcliffe Hill and Bedminster. Dundry Hill and tower are on the left as the road climbs. 5½m: *Barrow Gurney*, with reservoirs.

B3130 leads left to (4½m) *Chew Magna*, a pretty place with Georgian houses and a Perpendicular church with tall tower. Near the charming village of *Chew Stoke*, 1m SW, is a reservoir formed by flooding the Chew valley. *Stanton Drew*, 1½m further E, has *three Neolithic stone circles, two avenues of standing stones, and the Cove, the remains of a burial chamber (EH, any reasonable time but closed Sundays).

8m: *Lulsgate*, with Bristol Airport, on the right.

Wrington, about 1½m NW of the road 3m further on, has one of the best Perpendicular church towers in the region. It was the birthplace of John Locke (1632–1704), remembered by a tablet in the churchyard wall, and the resting place of Hannah More (1745–1833). Barley Wood, her home in 1802–28, lies about 1m NE; she had previously lived at *Cowslip Green*, on the A38.

Between (13m) *Churchill* and (17m) *Axbridge*, A38 crosses the W outliers of the Mendip Hills, explored in Route 22. It then drops into the rich grazing flats, or 'levels', of North Somerset between the Axe and the Parrett. Part of the region is as much as 18ft below sea level. 23m: The isolated *Brent Knoll* (457ft; NT) breaks the monotony of the landscape; the Iron Age hill-fort on its summit gives a fine *view. The church in the village on its further side is Norman with Perpendicular additions; it has satirical bench ends and a monument to John Somerset (d. 1663).

At (25m) *Highbridge* a road leads right for (1¾m) **Burnham-on-Sea** (14,900 inhabitants with Highbridge; TI), a resort at the mouth of the Parrett. Its church has a white marble altarpiece carved by Grinling Gibbons as part of Wren's refurbishing of the chapel at Whitehall Palace in 1686.

32m: **Bridgwater** (30,300 inhabitants; seasonal TI) is a busy town on the Parrett, here tidal. The local red brick—called 'Bath brick' after its maker, not the city—was manufactured from the clay and sand deposited by the river. A statue of Admiral Blake (1599–1657) stands in the Cornhill outside the *Market House* (1834), with a handsome curved colonnade. The Wednesday market includes an auction still conducted in pounds, shillings and pence. Blake's birthplace, in Blake St. to the S, is now the *Museum*, with relics of the admiral, the Duke of Monmouth and the Battle of Sedgemoor, and exhibits of old Bridgwater shipping and other local industries. The church of *St Mary*, in a quiet setting behind the Market Hall, has a slender spire built in 1366 by Nicholas Waleys. Inside are wide Decorated transepts (Jacobean screen in S transept), 15C chancel roof, Perpendicular pulpit, and a painting captured from a French ship of the Armada and given to the town in the 18C. West Quay has Dutch-gabled buildings and The Lions, a fine house of c 1730. *Castle St., begun in 1723 by the Duke of Chandos, is one of the best Georgian townscapes in Somerset.

At *Enmore*, 5m SW, *Barford Park* (limited opening) is a fine 18C house. In the marshes 3m SE of Bridgwater and 1m N of *Westonzoyland* is **Sedgemoor**, where the Duke of Monmouth's rebellion against James II was crushed on 6 July 1685, less than a month after he had landed at Lyme Regis and a fortnight after he had been proclaimed king at Bridgwater. A flagstaff and memorial stones mark the field where the dead lie buried. Westonzoyland church, with a lovely *roof of c 1500, has a memorial recalling the temporary imprisonment here of 500 rebel peasants, some score of whom were hanged in chains from the belfry battlements.
    From Bridgwater to *Minehead* along the NE fringes of the Quantock Hills, see Route 25A.

36m: *North Petherton* church has a fine tower. It contains a replica of the 9C Alfred Jewel, found in nearby Parker's Field in 1693 and now in the Ashmolean Museum at Oxford (see also Burrow Mump and Athelney, Route 24). The church of (38m) *Thurloxton*, to the right, has wood furnishings of 1634.

*The Somerset marshes: looking south east over Sedgemoor from Grey-
lake, near Westonzoyland*

44m: **Taunton**, Route 19. A38 crosses the fertile valley to the smaller town
of (51m) *Wellington* (10,600 inhabitants), from which the Duke took his title.
The church has the tomb of Sir John Popham (d. 1607), the judge who tried
Raleigh.

Nynehead, 2m N, has a church with sculptures by the della Robbia and other Italian
artists, beside a manor house of 1675 (not open). *Cothay Manor* (not open), near *Thorne
St Margaret* 5m W of Wellington, is a largely unaltered 15C house. To the S of
Wellington rise the *Black Down Hills*, crowned by (2½m) the *Wellington Monument*
(NT; 900ft). *Culmstock Beacon* (819ft), at their W extremity, has a stone fire turret.

A38 soon enters Devon. At (58m) *Waterloo Cross* A373 leads past the
junction with M5 towards Tiverton (Route 26). B3181, the old A38, continues S. To its left is the Culm valley, leading to (7m) *Hemyock* at the foot of
the Black Down Hills. The road descends the river past (63m) *Cullompton*,
where the Perpendicular *church has a richly carved roof, a magnificent
tower and the beautiful 16C vaulted Lane aisle. At the hamlet of
(68½m) *Beare* the road enters a large and finely wooded stretch of NT
property. It includes *Killerton House*, reached by taking B3185 right at
Budlake, a plain Georgian building by John Johnson (1778–79) that now

contains the Paulise de Bush costume collection. The lovely hillside gardens, which have a chapel of 1841 by C.R. Cockerell, were first laid out in the late 18C. 71m: *Broadclyst* has a notable church. 73m: *Pinhoe* is on the outskirts of (76m) **Exeter** (Route 18A).

24

Marlborough to Glastonbury and Taunton

Directions. Total distance 74m. **Marlborough**, see Route 20. A4 to (7m) Beckhampton. A361 to (14m) Devizes, (24m) Trowbridge, (32m) Frome, (43m) Shepton Mallet (Route 22), (52m) **Glastonbury** and (74m) **Taunton** (Route 19). A361, running N from Beckhampton to Swindon, Lechlade, Burford, Chipping Norton and Banbury, makes an attractive link between the West Country and the Midlands.

Marlborough, see Route 20. A4 and Route 20 are followed to (7m) *Beckhampton*, just S of Avebury, where the present route turns S on A361. At 10m it crosses the line of the *Wansdyke* and at 12m passes by *Roundway Hill*, to the right. In 1643 the Parliamentarian army was defeated at Roundway Down, on the other side of the hill. 14m: **Devizes** (10,600 inhabitants; TI) stands at the mouth of the Vale of Pewsey. Once called Ad Divisas ('on the borders'), it owes its existence to the castle, since replaced, built by Bishop Roger of Sarum c 1150. It is now a busy market town with handsome 18C buildings, a *Town Hall* (1806–08) by Thomas Baldwin of Bath and a *Market Cross* (1814) by Benjamin Wyatt bearing an interesting inscription. The painter Sir Thomas Lawrence was son of the landlord at the Bear, one of several coaching inns to survive. The churches of *St John's*, with a fine tower, and *St Mary's* were founded by Bishop Roger, the former for the castle and the latter for the town; both were enlarged in the 15C. The *Museum* of the Wiltshire Archaeological and Natural History Society in Long St. has *prehistoric finds from the Wiltshire barrows, including the 'Marlborough Bucket', a Belgic wooden vat with bronze reliefs (1C BC). There are also Roman, Saxon and medieval exhibits and a natural history display. The picture gallery has a window by John Piper.

Parallel to A361 W of the town the Kennet and Avon Canal descends 237ft in 2¼m by a series of 29 locks, like a gigantic flight of stairs.

An alternative way from Devizes to Frome begins by taking A360 S. 2m: *Potterne* has a good Early English church and the late 15C timber-framed Porch House. The church at *Urchfont*, 3m SE, has a fine chancel. 5m: B3098 leads W, along the edge of Salisbury Plain. 10m: *Edington* is probably the Saxon Ethandune, where Alfred defeated the Danes in 878. The 14C *priory church is a beautiful example of the transition from Decorated to Perpendicular. Two of the monuments come from the abandoned church at *Imber*, now in the military zone of Salisbury Plain to the SE. An annual festival of church music takes place in August. B3098 passes the White Horse of Westbury and reaches (14m) *Westbury*, on the Chippenham–Shaftesbury road (Route 20). A3098 continues to (20m) *Frome*.

From Devizes to *Andover*, see Route 19.

At 21m A361 crosses A350, the Chippenham–Shaftesbury Road (Route 20). 24m: **Trowbridge** (23,000 inhabitants; TI) is the most modest of English county towns, though the handsome Georgian and Regency houses in Fore St., The Parade and Roundstone St. testify to the wealth and taste of its cloth merchants. The poet George Crabbe, a reluctant exile from Suffolk, was rector of the restored 15C church from 1813 until his death in 1832; his tomb is in the chancel. At *Holt*, on B3107 3m N, the Courts has formal 20C gardens. *Bradford-on-Avon* (Route 21) lies 3m NW of Trowbridge. 27½m: *Rode*, just over the Somerset border, was the home of Constance Kent, who confessed in 1865 to the murder of her infant half-brother here five years earlier. Rode Manor has tropical bird gardens (open).

32m: **Frome** (pronounced 'Froom'; 14,500 inhabitants) is solidly built in stone, with steep, narrow streets and a thriving market. The paved Cheap St. has a central water course. The 13C and late 14C parish church has suffered from restoration. Outside its E end is the tomb of the outspoken Bishop Ken (1637–1711).

The bishop died at *Longleat*, 4½m SE (Route 18A). Other places in easy reach of Frome include *Lullington*, 2½m N, where the church has a Norman font and N doorway, and the attractive village of *Mells*, 3½m W, where the Perpendicular *church has monuments by Burne-Jones and Sir Alfred Munnings. The restored 16C manor house (not open) belongs to the Horner family, of which 'Little Jack Horner' is said to have been a member. *Witham Friary*, 5m SW of Frome, was the site of the first Carthusian monastery in England, founded in 1178–79 by Henry II in expiation of Becket's murder. The lay brothers' chapel, now the parish church, was probably built by the 3rd prior, St Hugh of Lincoln.

33½m: A361 skirts Marston Park. The church of *Marston Bigot* has 16C German glass and a monument probably by Westmacott. 35m: *Nunney*, N of the road where it is joined by A359, has a small moated castle of 1393 (EH). *Cloford* church, off A359 1m SW, has 17C monuments to the Horner family. 41½m: *Doulting* provided the stone for Wells Cathedral. The heavily restored church has good timber roofs in the transepts. 43m: **Shepton Mallet**, see Route 22. A361 is rejoined SW of the town just before (45m) *Pilton*, built on a steep hill, with a fine partly Norman church and a Georgian manor house. 49m: *West Pinnard* has a 15C barn (NT, open by appointment).

52m: **GLASTONBURY** (6800 inhabitants), an ancient town at the base of Glastonbury Tor, is famous for the ruined abbey where history and legend combine to create a uniquely powerful atmosphere. Once the most important pilgrim shrine in England, it now attracts summer tourists in large numbers.

TI: The Tribunal, 9 High St. **Buses:** from opposite the Town Hall in Magdalene St. **Annual Events:** Anglican pilgrimage on the last Saturday in June; the Roman Catholic pilgrimage usually takes place on the previous Sunday. Carnival in mid November.

Residents. Rutland Boughton staged several of his operas at the festivals he organised here in 1914–27.

The *Abbey (open) represents the earliest Christian foundation in England. It survived Saxon, Danish and Norman conquests, and presents a continuity of religious life unparalleled elsewhere.

According to the legend, Joseph of Arimathea and 11 companions brought the chalice of the Last Supper (or the phials that held the blood of the Crucifixion) to Glastonbury in about AD 60. Here, in the Druidic Isle of Avalon or Ynyswytryn, the 'Blessed Isle', they built the Vetusta Ecclesia, or primitive church of wood and wattle. Refounded by Pope Eleutherius in 166, the settlement was visited by St Patrick (who supposedly died here in 463) and St Bridget (488). Larger churches, always carefully including the Vetusta Ecclesia, were raised by: Ine, King of the West Saxons, in 708; St Dunstan (d. 988), born and educated at Glastonbury; and Thurstin and Herlewin, the 1st Norman abbots. Under Dunstan, who became abbot c 940 and introduced the Benedictine rule, the abbey became a centre of learning and gave England many great churchmen. The Saxon kings Edmund I (d. 946), Edgar (d. 975), and Edmund Ironside (d. 1016) were buried here. Until 1154, when precedence was given to St Albans, the Abbot of Glastonbury was the premier abbot of England. The remains of Arthur and Guinevere, reputed to have been discovered here in 1191, were finally reinterred in front of the high altar in 1276, in the presence of Edward I.

In 1184 the whole abbey, including the Vetusta Ecclesia, was burned to the ground. Rebuilding began at once and, except for a few later additions, was completed in 1303. The first part to be finished was the Lady Chapel (often called St Mary's Chapel), on the exact site of the old wooden chapel and, so it is said, built in strict fidelity to the old plan. The last abbot, Richard Whiting, was executed on the Tor in 1539. After the Reformation the buildings were neglected, and were used as a stone quarry until about 1830. The ruins were bought for the Church of England in 1908.

The *Abbot's Gate*, which contains a museum, leads from the market place. Of the vast *Church* the only remains are: the two E piers of the central tower, with portions of the transeptal walls attached; one of the N transeptal chapels, with groups of floor tiles; parts of the S aisle walls of the nave and choir; and the W door. This leads into the 13C Galilee connecting the church with the late Romanesque *Lady Chapel (walls still standing), with rich carvings and interlacing arcades. Beneath is a 15C crypt connecting with an ancient well. The length of the whole range of buildings was shown to be about 590ft by the discovery of the apsidal Edgar Chapel, built by Abbot Bere, at the extreme E end. The foundations of St Dunstan's Chapel at the extreme W, and of the N porch and the Loretto Chapel on the N side of the nave, are marked on the ground, as well as the sites of the chapter house, cloisters and the sub-vaults of the refectory and dormitory. To the SW is the 14C *Abbot's Kitchen*, with a high octagonal stone roof and lantern; it contains a small display illustrating monastic life.

In High St. are the *George and Pilgrims' Inn* of 1470 (now a hotel) and the *Tribunal* (TI and EH, all year), supposedly once the abbey courthouse, with fine woodwork. It has finds from the Iron Age lake villages of Meare and Glastonbury. The church of *St John the Baptist* (1465) has a fine tower and a 15C sarcophagus from the abbey. *St Benedict's*, built on older foundations by Abbot Bere, lies W of the market place.

In Bere Lane the late 14C *Abbey Barn* (open) has emblems of the Evangelists and a fine collar-beam roof; together with the adjoining farm-house, it is now a museum of Somerset rural life. In the garden of *Chalice Well*, at the base of the Tor nearby, is the chalybeate spring once venerated for its healing powers.

The **Tor** (NT; 521ft), E of the town, commands a *view of Glastonbury, Wells and the Bristol Channel. It is crowned by the tower of the ruined chapel of *St Michael*. On *Wearyall Hill* W of the town grew the original 'Glastonbury Thorn' (*Crataegus praecox*) which, according to the legend, sprang from St Joseph's staff. The tree was cut down by the Puritans but offshoots, which blossom at Christmas, can be seen in the abbey grounds and St John's churchyard.

Meare, on B3151 3½m NW, once stood by a large lake. It has the 14C Fish House of the abbey (EH, key from Manor House farm) and the abbot's summer palace. Finds from the Iron Age lake village ½m NW are in the museums at Glastonbury and Taunton. *Butleigh*, 4m S of Glastonbury, was the birthplace of Admiral Hood (1724–1816); his monument in the church has an epitaph by Southey.

A39 runs together with A361 to (53½m) *Street* (8800 inhabitants), a little town dominated by Clark's shoe factory; there is a museum of shoemaking history. Off the road about 1½m NW lies *Sharpham Park* (not open), a manor house built by Abbot Bere and the scene of Abbot Whiting's arrest in 1539. The novelist Henry Fielding (1707–54) was born here. 57m: A361 separates from A39 and crosses King's Sedge Moor to (62m) *Othery*, where the church has a Perpendicular central tower. Westonzoyland and Sedgemoor (Route 23) lie NW. In the drained marshes to the S Alfred gathered his forces for the final struggle against the Danes in 878. The scene of his adventure with the burned cakes is laid here, and the 9C Alfred Jewel was found at nearby North Petherton (Route 23). 64m: *Burrow Mump* (NT), an isolated hill rising above the fens near *Burrow Bridge*, is the probable site of Alfred's fort. *Athelney*, 1½m SW, has a memorial pillar.

Unclassified roads run S and W from Burrow Bridge via Athelney (see above) to (4m) *Stoke St Gregory*, where the church has an early 14C octagonal crossing tower and some fine Perpendicular additions. Unclassified roads continue along the S bank of the Tone to (5½m) *North Curry*, with an imposing church framed by a handsome medley of buildings, and (9m) *Creech St Michael* church, with a wagon roof and interesting 13C details. A361 can be joined 1½m N.

At (70m) *Walford Cross*, near M5, A361 is joined by A38. When they divide 1m further on, A361 leads into Taunton from the N, A38 from the S. 74m: **Taunton**, see Route 19.

25

The Quantock Hills

The **Quantock Hills** extend from near A38 and M5 between Bridgwater and Taunton towards the sea. Formed of the Old Red Sandstone characteristic of Devon rather than Somerset geology, they are an isolated outpost of Exmoor and the Devon moorland to the W. With their clear streams, wild red deer, heather and wortleberries, and their sheltered wooded combes, they rise gently from the Vale of Taunton Deane in the S, reaching their greatest height at Will's Neck (1261ft) 2m SE of Crowcombe, and fall steeply to the narrow coastal plain and the Bristol Channel. The officially designated Area of Outstanding Natural Beauty covers about 36 square miles, of which 750 acres are NT.

The two routes suggested below are primarily for drivers and follow major roads around the fringes of the hills. A magnificent *walk of about 7m goes along the ridge from Lydeard Hill car park (½m NE of West Bagborough) to the Staple Plain car park (NT) at West Quantoxhead. It passes by Will's Neck and gives views of Dartmoor and the Black Down Hills to the S and W, Exmoor and the Brendon Hills to the W, the Mendip Hills to the E and the Somerset and Welsh coasts to the N.

Further information can be obtained from the Quantock Information Centre, Castle St., Nether Stowey and from Fyne Court, headquarters of the Somerset Trust for Nature Conservation, in Broomfield, 4½m N of Taunton.

A. Bridgwater to Minehead

Directions. Total distance 27m. **Bridgwater**, see Route 23. A39 to (8½m) **Nether Stowey**, (15m) West Quantoxhead, (18m) Williton, (25m) **Dunster** and (27m) **Minehead**.

Bridgwater, see Route 23. A39 runs along the NE fringe of the Quantocks, with flat Somerset marshland to the right. 3½m: *Cannington* is home of the Somerset College of Agriculture and Horticulture, in an Elizabethan mansion on the site of a Benedictine priory, with a collection of tropical plants in its Court Gardens (open). *Combwich*, 1½m N, is a quaint village on the banks of the Parrett. The tidal mud flats and salt marshes of *Bridgwater Bay*, another 3m NE, are a nature reserve (restricted access via the Warden). 5m: An unclassified road leads S to (1½m) *Spaxton*, where the church has carved bench ends, including one showing a fuller, or clothmaker, with his tools. 8½m: **Nether Stowey** (Quantock Information Centre) has the cottage (NT) where Coleridge lived from winter 1796 to 1798. Wordsworth came to live at Alfoxton (see below) in 1797, and the association of the two poets led to the 'Lyrical Ballads'.

A scenic road leads across the hills to Crowcombe (Route 25B). At *Ramscombe*, about 2m SW of Nether Stowey, the Forestry Commission provides a forest trail. *Stogursey*, 3m N of Nether Stowey, has a Norman priory church. *Hinkley Point*, 3m further N, has a nuclear power station.

10m: *Dodington*, right of A39, has a beautiful Elizabethan manor house (limited opening). Near (11½m) *Holford*, a good centre for walks, is *Alfoxton* (or *Alfoxden*) *House*, Wordsworth's home in 1797 and now a hotel. By the sea N of (13m) *Kilve* is a ruined 15C chantry. 14m: *East Quantoxhead* is a charming village. From (15m) *West Quantoxhead*, at the end of the walk along the hills suggested above, A39 descends to the coastal plain and (18m) *Williton*, where it is joined by A358 from Taunton (Route 25B). The Orchard Hill Museum, with agricultural tools etc., is housed in a 17C watermill. *Watchet*, 2m N, is a small port on the Bristol Channel. The Market House Museum by the harbour has exhibits of local history and geology. *Orchard Wyndham* (open by appointment) is a modest manor house. 19½m: *Washford* lies just N of *Cleeve Abbey*, founded for Cistercian monks in 1188 (EH, all year). The abbey church has largely disappeared but surviving buildings include the gatehouse of c 1530, cloisters, the excellently preserved Early English dormitory and the 15C *refectory, with a timber roof. There are also several fine doorways and tiled pavements. 22½m: *Carhampton* church has a lovely rood screen. The little resort of *Blue Anchor* lies 1m NE.

25m: **Dunster**, just inside the Exmoor National Park (with a seasonal National Park Information centre), is an attractive old place. Its many interesting buildings include the 17C *Yarn Market* in the High St., the medieval *Butter Cross* NW of the church and *Gallox Bridge*, a medieval packhorse bridge of A396 to the S (all EH). The large *Priory Church* of 1150, enlarged in the 13C and 15C, has a good roof, a *screen of 1500 and Luttrell monuments. *Dunster Castle* (NT) was built by Mohun, Earl of Somerset, c 1070 and held by the Luttrells from 1376. It owes much of its present, emphatically romantic appearance to embellishments by Anthony Salvin in 1870. The interior, with halls and library by Salvin, has late 17C plasterwork and woodcarving, and a unique series of mid 17C Dutch embossed leather hangings. Outstanding among the family portraits is Hans Eworth's painting of Sir John Luttrell (1550). On the river Avill near the grounds is the restored 18C *Castle Mill* (NT).

A396 goes up the wooded valley of the Avill to (7m) *Wheddon Cross* (see Route 27B).

27m: **MINEHEAD** (11,200 inhabitants; TI) has a picturesque quay and harbour, beneath the old village where steep lanes lead up to the 14C church (with a good screen inside). The centre of the lower town has a statue of Queen Anne (1719). There is a large holiday camp at the E end. In summer there are daily excursions from the seafront along the old West Somerset Railway to Bishop's Lydeard (Route 25B). The science-fiction writer Arthur C. Clarke was born at Minehead in 1917.

There is a nature trail on the cliffs to the NW, and a fine stretch of the Somerset and North Devon Coast Path to the W, leading past *North Hill* (*view) to (3½m) *Selworthy Beacon*. For this and other parts of Exmoor, see Route 27A.

B.   Taunton to Minehead

Directions. Total distance 24m. **Taunton**, see Route 19. A361 to (2m) Norton Fitzwarren. A358 to (5m) Bishop's Lydeard, (10½m) Crowcombe and (15m) Williton. A39 to (22m) **Dunster** and (24m) **Minehead** (Route 25A).

Taunton, see Route 19. A361 leads to (2m) *Norton Fitzwarren* (Route 26), and A358 branches right through part of the Vale of Taunton Deane and along the SW fringe of the Quantocks. 5m: *Bishop's Lydeard*, on the right, has a Perpendicular church with good woodcarving and a 14C churchyard cross. The old West Somerset Railway runs to Minehead (Route 25A).

The car park at *Lydeard Hill*, beyond *West Bagborough* 3m N, is the start of the walk along the ridge of the Quantocks suggested above.

At (6¾m) *Combe Florey*, on the left, Sydney Smith was rector from 1829 to 1845 and Evelyn Waugh (1903–66) spent his last years. *Gaulden Manor* (limited opening), near *Tolland* 3m further W, is partly 12C, with good plasterwork. It was once the home of the Turbervilles. The *Brendon Hills* appear to the left of A358. 9m: *Crowcombe*, to the right, has a Perpendicular church with good bench ends and two crosses, 12C and 14C. Opposite is the 15C Church House (open), a rare survival. A fine scenic road crosses the Quantocks to Nether Stowey (Route 25A). 11m: *Halsway Manor*, on the right, is partly medieval and partly 19C. Now a centre for folk music and dance, it is open by prior appointment. 13m: *Bicknoller* church has a carved screen and Tudor bench ends.

Stogumber, 2m SW, has attractive cottages and a Perpendicular church with a good 17C monument to Sir George Sydenham (d. 1597). The priest who prosecuted Joan of Arc came from here. *Combe Sydenham Hall* (open), in a pleasant valley 2m further W, is a mainly Elizabethan building.

At (15m) *Williton* A358 joins A39 and Route 25A to (22m) **Dunster** and (24m) **Minehead**.

26

Taunton to Barnstaple and Ilfracombe

Directions. Total distance 64m. **Taunton**, see Route 19. A361 to (20m) Bampton, (38m) South Molton, (50m) **Barnstaple** and (64m) **Ilfracombe**.

Taunton, see Route 19. A361 winds through magnificent scenery S of the Brendon Hills and Exmoor (explored in Route 27). 2m: *Norton Fitzwarren*, a centre of cider making, has a good church screen of 1509. A358 branches right, past the Quantocks to Minehead (Route 25B). 7m: *Milverton*, to the left, has a Georgian main street and a fine Perpendicular church with carved woodwork. 11m: *Wiveliscombe*. A361 enters Devon before (20m) *Bampton*, a small town with Georgian houses. It makes a good starting-point for excursions into Exmoor (Route 27B).

FROM BAMPTON TO EXETER, 21½m, following A396 down the valley of the Exe. 7m: **Tiverton** (16,500 inhabitants; TI) is an old market town on the Exe. *Tiverton Castle* (open) was begun in 1066 and keeps its 14C gatehouse, two towers and the ruins of its walls among much later addition and restoration. The fine *Church*, 15C but freely restored, contains the richly carved Greenway Chapel (1517) and an organ of 1696 by Father Smith. The *Museum* near the Town Hall has a folk collection and relics of Tiverton's lace-making industry. The old buildings of *Blundell's School* (NT, only the forecourt open), founded in 1604, stand on the bank of the Loman. R.D. Blackmore (1825–1900) was a pupil, and sent John Ridd of 'Lorna Doone' to school here. There are trips along the Grand Western Canal from Canal Hill in summer. *Knighthayes Court* (NT), 1½m N, is a spirited piece of Victorian Gothic begun in 1869 by William Burges. The richly decorated interiors are by Burges and Crace. The garden has extravagant topiary. 11¾m: *Bickleigh Bridge* dates from 1640. *Bickleigh Castle* (open), ½m S on the W bank of the Exe, has a Norman chapel and 15–17C gatehouse. Near *Cadbury*, about 3m SW of Bickleigh, is *Fursdon* (limited opening), a family house with work and contents spanning several centuries. A396 continues S to (21½m) *Exeter* (Route 18A).

A361 crosses the Exe valley. 38m: *South Molton* (seasonal TI) has a pleasant old centre with a guildhall of 1743 and a Victorian covered market. From B3226 3m N, a sideroad leads across Exmoor to (11m) *Simonsbath* (Route 27B). At *Charles*, left of B3226 another 3m N, is the rectory where R.D. Blackmore spent his boyhood. Just before (42m) *Filleigh* the road passes, on the right, the splendid mansion of *Castle Hill*, built in 1684, enlarged c 1730–40 and rebuilt after fire in 1934 (open by appointment in summer). It has 18C furniture, tapestries, porcelain and pictures. 45m: *Swimbridge* church has a notable rood screen.

50m: **BARNSTAPLE** (19,000 inhabitants), at the head of the Taw estuary, has handsome old buildings to remind the visitor of its long history as a seaport and market town. It makes a good centre for exploring North Devon.

TI: The Foyer, North Devon Library, Tuly Street. **Bus Station**: The Strand. **Railway Station**: off B3233 on the SW bank of the Taw. **Theatre:** Queen's Theatre, Boutport St. **Annual Event**: Barnstaple Fair from the Wednesday before 20 September to the following Saturday.

History. One of the four original burghs of Devon and the westernmost port in the Saxon kingdom of Wessex, Beardastaple received its first charter in 930. Athelstan

The gardens at Knighthayes Court

established a mint and garrison here and a priory at nearby Pilton. The Normans fortified the town and built the castle and keep now marked by the mound on the NE bank of the Taw. The 'staple' in Barnstaple's name shows its early importance as a market centre and this, together with its position on the estuary, assured its continuing prosperity from the 16C to the 18C. The town contributed five ships to the fleet Drake used to defeat the Spanish Armada in 1588, and thrived on the trade with North America, particularly in woollen goods and pottery. The local Barum ware is still made.

Natives and residents: John Gay (1685–1732) and the architect W.R. Lethaby (1857–1931) were Barumites. The martyr St Cuthbert Mayne (1544–77) was born at *Shirwell*, 4m NE. 'Saki' (H.H. Munro, 1870–1916) spent an unhappy childhood at *Pilton*, ½m N.

The bridge of 16 arches spanning the Taw was originally built in the 13C but widened in 1796 and 1962. There is a pleasant riverside promenade. *Queen Anne's Walk* is an 18C colonnade with a statue of Queen Anne (1708). *St Peter's Church*, restored but dating in part from the 14C, has a crooked spire and interesting monuments. The former *St Anne's Chapel* (1330), now a local museum, served as the Grammar School; its pupils included St Cuthbert Mayne, Bishop Jewel of Salisbury (1522–71) and John Gay. High St. and Boutport St., with good 17C and 18C buildings, are connected by the finely restored *Pannier Market* (1855), a vast wooden-roofed hall housing a different type of market every day of the week, except Sunday; the adjoining Butcher's Row (also 1855) originally had 33 wooden-canopied butcher's shops. *Horwood's Almshouses* and the *Maids' School* nearby, and the *Penrose Almshouses* in Litchdon St. E of the Square, are typical of 17C Barnstaple. The *Museum of North Devon*, beside the Albert Memorial Clocktower in the Square, has displays of social, mercantile and military history.

The church at *Pilton*, ½m N, has good woodwork. The gardens (open) of Marwood Hill in *Marwood*, 4m N, are notable for their camellias.

A39 leads NE from Barnstaple to (7m) *Arlington Court* (NT), a Regency house with a collection of objets d'art. The building is less interesting than the grounds (museum of horse-drawn vehicles) and the beautiful wooded setting, with nature trails and walks to the Yeo valley. A39 continues to (10m) *Blackmoor Gate* and crosses Exmoor to (21½m) *Lynton* and *Lynmouth* (Route 27A).

From Barnstaple to *Exeter*, see Route 18A. To *Okehampton*, see Route 29A. To *Penzance* via the N coast, see Route 35.

A361 follows the right bank of the Taw estuary, passing the RAF station at (53½m) *Chivenor* on the left. The church of *Heaton Punchardon*, ½m to the right, has the sumptuous tomb of Richard Coffin (d. 1523). 56½m: *Braunton* has a large church dedicated to the Celtic St Brannock, with an early tower, good bench ends and other woodwork. Nearby is a local museum. To the SW is the 'Great Field', over 300 acres still cultivated on the medieval strip system. From *Saunton*, on B3231 2m W, the Somerset and North Devon Coast Path bisects the flat peninsula to the S, with *Braunton Burrows* nature reserve occupying one of Britain's largest sand dunes. To the N, the path follows the headland round to Ilfracombe. A361 follows the valley and then climbs to 662ft at (61½m) *Mullacott Cross*. Woolacombe (see below) lies on B3343 3½m W.

64m: **ILFRACOMBE** (10,100 inhabitants) is North Devon's most popular seaside resort. Its chief merit is its natural setting among spectacular cliff scenery, with pleasant woods and glens inland.

TI: Promenade. **Bus Depot**: junction of Fore St. and Broad St. **Amusements**: Victoria Pavilion, on the Promenade. **Steamers**: to Lundy in summer, and cruises along the coast.

Holy Trinity, beyond the W end of High St., is a Norman church enlarged in 1322; it has richly carved wagon roofs. The steep turnings on the seaward side of High St. lead to *Wildersmouth Beach*, with *Capstone Hill* (181ft; view) and the *Victoria Pavilion* at its base. To the W are the *Tunnels Beaches*, reached through tunnels in the rock. To the SE of the Capstone are the *Harbour* and *Pier*, sheltered on the N side by *Lantern Hill*, with the remains of the 13C *Chapel of St Nicholas* (open) on its crest. Further SE is the sheltered *Rapparee Cove* beneath the lofty *Hillsborough* (447ft; view). At *Hele Bay*, on the other side of Hillsborough and reached from A399, is a restored 16C watermill (open). *Chambercombe Manor*, 1m SE of the centre, is a small, mainly 16–17C house.

The scenery of the headland W of Ilfracombe is superb. Much of the land is owned by the NT and crossed by the Somerset and North Devon Coast Path. Immediately W of the town is the *Torrs Walk, a zigzag 'corniche' path giving lovely views of the sea. Beyond *Flat Point* is (3m) *Lee*, a pretty village known for its fuchsias, a little inland from *Lee Bay*. From the bay a hilly footpath leads to (5m) *Bull Point Lighthouse*, and from here a road continues to (6½m) **Mortehoe**. The Early English church, with a 14C tower, contains the tomb of William de Tracey (1321), a former vicar sometimes confounded with the murderer of Thomas Becket. *Morte Point*, a rock-bound headland 1m W, commands a wild and wide view. The road goes on S past (7m) *Barricane Bay*, with its beach of minute shells, to (7½m) **Woolacombe** (seasonal TI). The Somerset and

North Devon Coast Path continues S, round (11m) *Baggy Point*, to join B3231 at (12¾m) *Croyde* for (14½m) *Saunton* (see above).

For Exmoor and the coastal route to *Minehead*, see Route 27A. For *Lundy*, see Route 35.

27

Exmoor

OS Exmoor Outdoor Leisure map (2½in to 1m).

*Exmoor is today defined by the National Park which straddles Somerset and Devon. It reaches along the N coast from near Minehead in the E to Combe Martin, just short of Ilfracombe, in the W. Its southernmost point is beyond Dulverton near the confluence of the Barle and the Exe. Inside these 267 square miles lies some of the finest countryside in England, over 17,000 acres of it owned and protected by the National Trust. There are only about 10,500 inhabitants, most of them in small villages, and only four places large enough to qualify as towns: Dunster, Porlock, and Lynton with Lynmouth in the N, and Dulverton in the S. Major roads are few, but there are more than 600 miles of public footpaths.

The region is given its distinctive character by the plateau of Old Red Sandstone and slate on which it stands, regularly reaching 1300ft and rising to its highest point at Dunkery Beacon (1704ft) S of Porlock. Its contours, at their gentlest in the Brendon Hills to the E, are everywhere less rugged than the granite tors of Dartmoor. The scenery is at its most spectacular on the coast, where the plateau abruptly meets the sea in a series of headlands interrupted only by the Vale of Porlock. England has few, if any, more beautiful stretches of coastline. The moors lie inland, including the tract known as Exmoor Forest, about 30 square miles centred on the village of Simonsbath. (Here as elsewhere in England, the term 'forest' is merely a legal one. The region was mentioned as a royal forest in a charter of King John but lost this status in 1819). The countryside is sometimes boggy, with colourless tussocky grass, grey furze, bracken and heather. This bare hill pasture supports a hardy race of horned sheep. The characteristic wildlife includes the buzzard and the wild red deer. Two herds of the native Exmoor ponies have been established in recent years by the National Park Authority to maintain the numbers of this old breed.

The rivers that drain the plateau to both N and S add much to its beauty, creating rich green pasture in the wider valleys and thickly wooded clefts in the smaller ones. The West Lyn and East Lyn, with their many tributaries, flow N to make their dramatic joint exit into the Bristol Channel between Lynton and Lynmouth. To the W is Heddon's Mouth, while to the E the lovely little valley of the Avill runs down to the sea at Dunster. The Exe, flowing S past Exeter to the English Channel at Exmouth, is joined by the Haddeo and the Barle between Dulverton and Bampton in some of the region's most delightful scenery.

The Exmoor National Park headquarters is at Exmoor House, Dulverton; there are seasonal National Park Information Centres at Dunster, County Gate, Lynmouth and Combe Martin.

A. Minehead to Ilfracombe

Directions. Total distance 37½m. This route is for motorists, but walkers can follow the magnificent scenery of the *Somerset and North Devon Coast Path all the way between Minehead and Ilfracombe. **Minehead**, see Route 25A. A39 to (6m) Porlock, (16½m) **Lynmouth** and **Lynton** and (28m) Blackmoor Gate. A399 to (33m) **Combe Martin** and (37½m) **Ilfracombe** (Route 26).

Minehead, see Route 25A. A39 undulates along the N verge of Exmoor, passing just S of (3½m) *Selworthy*, a pretty village with a green, tithe barn and fine Perpendicular church below *Selworthy Beacon* (1012ft), and (4m) *Allerford*, which has a two-arched packhorse bridge, a Museum of Rural Life and a Farm Park with rare breeds of animals. 6m: **Porlock** (the 'enclosed port') is a charming place in a fertile vale. The little 13C church of *St Dubricius* has the sumptuous tomb of Baron Harington (d. 1418) and his wife.

About 1½m W is the pretty little harbour of *Porlock Weir*. Footpaths lead another 1¾m to *Culbone* church, the smallest parish church with nave and chancel in England.
   Dunkery Beacon (1704ft; NT), a dark brown moorland hill and the highest on Exmoor, rises about 4m S of Porlock. Motorists can drive nearly all the way to the top, either by *West Luccombe* or by *Horner Woods* and *Cloutsham*. On a clear day the view from the Beacon extends from Brown Willy in Cornwall (S) to the Malvern Hills (N), and includes about 120m of the Bristol Channel. The descent can be made SE to (3½m) *Wheddon Cross* (Route 27B) or NE to (3m) *Wootton Courtenay*; the narrow, winding road S of Cloutsham goes on to (4m) *Exford* (Route 27B).

The long climb up *Porlock Hill* by A39 (1 in 4 gradient with dangerous bends) can be avoided by an easier toll road to the right, which rejoins A39 just before (9m) *Oare Post*. Here an unclassified road branches left to (1½m) Oareford (see below). Beyond the summit (1378ft) is a gentle descent through the woods of *Culbone Hill*, with fine views of the sea.

A sideroad on the left leads S to the countryside of R.D. Blackmore's 'Lorna Doone'. At (1m) *Oare* church the heroine was married to John Ridd and shot by Carver Doone. The route continues W to (2m) *Malmsmead*, with a Natural History Centre illustrating local wildlife. From here a track that quickly becomes a footpath leads S, following the course of *Badgworthy Water*. After 1m it reaches the memorial put up by Blackmore's admirers in 1969; the stream nearby has been identified with the waterslide up which John Ridd struggles in the novel. Shortly beyond is the **Doone Valley** itself, less wild and romantic than readers of 'Lorna Doone' may have been led to expect. According to tradition, the Doones were a little clan of outlaws who made their headquarters here at the end of the 17C, terrorising the local countryside until a particularly atrocious act goaded the inhabitants to crush them. The only traces of their settlement are the foundations of some huts. Blackmore, whose grandfather was rector of the adjoining parish of Oare, adapted and embellished the legend. The Doone valley lies 5m from Simonsbath (Route 27B) by a rough moorland route. Good walkers who want to see a really wild bit of Exmoor may continue NW from the Badgworthy valley for 2m, head NE after *Lank Combe* for 1½m, to the road which leads E back to (½m) Malmsmead.

A39 enters Devon at (12m) *County Gate* (1059ft; seasonal Exmoor National Park Visitor Centre). Malmsmead (see above) is about ¾m S by footpath. To the N are the beautiful grounds of *Glenthorne* and *Old Burrow* (1135ft). Beyond (15m) *Countisbury* (866ft) the road descends *Countisbury Hill* (1 in 4 gradient), with fine views. A steep path branches right to *Sillery Sands*.

16½m: **LYNTON** and **LYNMOUTH** (seasonal Exmoor National Park Visitor Centre at Lynmouth; TI at Lynton) are picturesque resorts. Lynmouth lies on the shore where the deep valleys of the East and West Lyn converge, a vulnerable position that made it the victim of devastating floods in 1952. Lynton stands on the edge of the cliff 430ft above. Steep roads and a cliff railway connect the two. The best general views of the villages are from *Hollerday Hill*, NW of Lynton, and *Summerhouse Hill* (850ft), climbed by a zigzag path beginning near the parish church in Lynmouth. Near the bridges in Lynmouth is the entrance to *Glen Lyn*, revealing the romantic cascades and fern-clad banks of the lower course of the West Lyn.

FROM LYNMOUTH TO WATERSMEET AND ROCKFORD, a walk of 4m. Tors Rd in Lynmouth quickly leads to a path on the right bank of the East Lyn, which forces its way through the narrow Watersmeet valley, thickly wooded or strewn with rocks on either side. At (1¾m) *Watersmeet* (NT) the East Lyn is joined by Hoar Oak Water; a 19C fishing lodge serves as NT shop, information centre, etc. A path follows the left bank of the valley, rising considerably above the stream. Passing through Nutcombe Wood, it emerges (3m) on the hillside, but soon re-enters the woods by a small gate. Various paths lead right to the *Long Pool*, with its fall. The main path soon reaches (4m) a bridge across the stream to *Rockford*. Hardy walkers may continue another 5m to the Doone Valley (see above) by following the S bank of the river past (1m) *Leeford* to (3m) *Malmsmead*. The return from Rockford to (3¾m) Lynmouth leads W to (½m) *Brendon* church and (1¼m) *Hillsford Bridge*, near A39.

FROM LYNTON TO COMBE MARTIN ALONG THE COAST ROAD, 12½m. The road runs inland into the *Valley of the Rocks* (walkers may take the cliff path called the *North Walk* on the seaward side of the hill). Passing Lee Abbey and Lee Bay via a toll road (superb views), the road continues steeply above (3½m) *Woody Bay*, a tiny resort enclosed by abrupt and richly wooded cliffs. A wide sweep, high above the sea (views), follows through (4½m) *Martinhoe*, then a steep descent to (6¾m) the *Hunter's Inn*, delightfully situated in the valley of the Heddon about 1m above its mouth. From here a path on either side of the Heddon leads in 1½m to *Heddon's Mouth* (NT), a small cove ringed with cliffs and connected by a beautiful cliff path with Woody Bay (2m more, see above). The road (*views*) now winds up above *Trentishoe* (1m; to the right), with a full view of the sea, to reach (9½m) a summit (989ft) between *Trentishoe Down* (1060ft; NT) to the left and *Holdstone Down* (1145ft; NT) to the right. It then descends to (10¾m) *Stony Corner* (844ft), where several roads meet. On the coast to the right are the *Great Hangman* (1043ft; NT) and the *Little Hangman* (716ft), the E pillar of Combe Martin Bay. A steep hill joins A399 at the SE end of (12½m) *Combe Martin*.

As it leaves Lynton A39 climbs the East Lyn by *Hillsford Bridge*, crosses *Beggars Roost* (947ft), and drops down to (22½m) *Barbrook* to meet the more direct road from Lynton and Lynmouth up the charming valley of the West Lyn. By *Dean Steep* A39 climbs again to 1013ft at *Martinhoe Cross*. 26m: *Parracombe*, bypassed by A39 at the foot of a steep hill, has a disused church with Georgian interior. At (28m) *Blackmoor Gate* the route turns right on A399.

A39 continues to (10m) *Barnstaple* (Route 26). B3226 heads left, with *Wistlandpound Reservoir* on the right. From it B3358 branches left across Exmoor to (8½m) *Simonsbath* (Route 27B).

33m: **Combe Martin** (seasonal TI), popular with tourists, straggles for 1½m along the road where the deep valley of the Umber makes its way to the sea. The 15C *Church*, with an Early English chancel, has a fine tower and contains a sculptured effigy of 1634. The *Pack o' Cards Inn* was reputedly built by a gambler. Further on, a road leads left to (½m) *Berrynarbor*, the birthplace of Bishop Jewel of Salisbury (1522–71), with a beautiful Perpendicular church tower. 34¾m: *Watermouth* has a 19C Gothic castle (open), much commercialised, and two caves. Beyond (36½m) *Hele Bay* the road enters (37½m) **Ilfracombe** (Route 26).

B.   Bampton to Lynton and Lynmouth

Directions. Total distance 35½m. A devious cross-country route from the S of Exmoor to the coast, with several inviting detours and alternatives. **Bampton**, see Route 26. A396, B3222 to (5¾m) Exebridge. B3222 to (8½m) **Dulverton** and (9¾m) Hele Bridge. A396 to (17m) **Wheddon Cross**. B3224, B3223 to (27m) **Simonsbath**. B3223 to (33m) Hillsford Bridge. A39 to (35½m) **Lynton** and **Lynmouth** (Route 27A).

Bampton, on A361 between Taunton and Barnstaple, see Route 26. The picturesque village of *Exebridge* can be reached directly by B3222 (2½m), but it is worth taking the longer route (5¾m) that follows A396 along the winding course of the river Exe and then branches left on B3222.

A396 continues up the valley of the Exe directly to (2¼m) Hele Bridge (see below). At 1¼m a turning on the right follows the side valley of the Haddeo E to (1m) *Bury* with its narrow hump-backed bridge.

B3222 continues NW from Exebridge up the valley of the Barle, which here marks the S boundary of Exmoor National Park, passing (6½m) *Brushford* on the left. 8½m: **Dulverton** (Exmoor National Park Visitor Centre) is a good centre for walks and fishing in the valley.

B3223 clings to the wooded banks of the Barle for ¾m and then begins to climb the hills. At 4m an unclassified road descends left into the valley where the river is crossed by (1½m) *Tarr Steps*, an old clapper bridge 180ft long, rebuilt after the floods of 1952. At 4¾m B3223 gives a fine view from the summit of *Winsford Hill* (1399ft; NT). At 6m another sideroad to the left descends into the valley at *Withypool*. At (8½m) *White Cross* B3223 joins B3224 just W of Exford (see below).

From Dulverton B3222 runs E to (9¾m) *Hele Bridge*, where A396 heads N up the Exe valley. 12m: A sideroad leads left to (2m) *Brompton Regis* and, beyond, the large *Wimbleball Lake*. At (14m) *Exton*, a typical Exmoor lowland settlement, the *Brendon Hills* begin to rise on the right. 14½m: *Coppleham Cross* marks the confluence of the Exe and the Quarme. A sideroad leads left to (1½m) *Winsford*, a hunting and fishing centre in charming surroundings on the banks of the Exe. The politician Ernest Bevin (1881–1951) was born here. A396 continues to (17m) **Wheddon Cross**.

A396 continues NW, down the wooded valley of the Avill, past (3½m) *Timberscombe* to (7m) *Dunster* (Route 25A). A sideroad leads SE from Wheddon Cross through the Brendon Hills, with particularly fine views at ¾m and 1½m. *Dunkery Beacon* (Route 27A) lies 3m NW of Wheddon Cross.

B3224 runs W to (22m) *Exford*, a fishing centre on the Exe. At (23m) *White Cross* the road is joined by B3223, which has come over Winsford Hill from Dulverton (see above). Soon afterwards it enters *Exmoor Forest* proper. 27m: **Simonsbath** takes its name from a pool in the Barle above the bridge.

B3358 runs W to (5m) *Challacombe*, where it passes between *Chapman Barrows* (1574ft) to the N and *Shoulsbury Castle* (1553ft), a prehistoric hill-fort, to the S. At 6¼m it joins B3226, which follows the edge of the National Park to (8½m) *Blackmoor Gate* (Route 27A). A minor road goes SW from Simonsbath past (3m) *Span Head* (1618ft) to (11m) *South Molton* (Route 26).

B3223 continues N from Simonsbath through the open moorland of Exmoor Forest. *Chains Barrow* (1561ft) lies to the left. 29½m: *Brendon Two Gates* (1379ft) marks the boundary with Devon and the N limit of Exmoor Forest. To the right is *Brendon Common*, with the *Doone Valley* beyond (Route 27A). The road drops down to (33m) *Hillsford Bridge*, where A39 follows the valley to (35½m) **Lynton** and **Lynmouth** (Route 27A).

28

Exeter to Plymouth

A. Via Ashburton

Directions. Total distance 43m. **Exeter**, see Route 18A. A38 to (9½m) Chudleigh, (19m) Ashburton, (21½m) Buckfastleigh, (32m) Ivybridge and (43m) **Plymouth**.

Exeter, see Route 18A. A38 is joined to the SW of the city, beyond (1½m) *Alphington*, where the church has a notable font of c 1140. 3½m: *Kennford*. 6m: A380 branches left to Newton Abbot (Route 28C). The main route follows A38 to (9½m) *Chudleigh*, with the picturesque *Chudleigh Rocks* to its S. See Route 28C for *Ugbrooke House*, near A380.

B3193, a pleasant road, goes up the Teign valley to (7½m) *Dunsford* (Route 29B). On the opposite side of the valley are *Higher Ashton* (6m from Chudleigh), where the 15C *church has fine rood and parclose screens, and *Doddiscombsleigh* (8m from Chudleigh), with 14C glass in its church.

A38 crosses the Teign and Bovey and becomes the S boundary of Dartmoor National Park (Route 29). 19m: **Ashburton**, a good starting-point for excursions across the moor, see Routes 29C and D. A38 crosses (20¾m) *Dart Bridge*. A right turn leads to (½m) **Buckfast Abbey**, founded by Canute in 1018, refounded for Cistercians by Stephen in 1147 and colonised by French Benedictines in 1882.

Nothing remains of the original building except a 12C undercroft and the 14C Abbot's Tower. The present church (open), modelled on Kirkstall and Fountains, was built by the monks themselves in 1907–38 on the old foundations. The dignified interior has: a magnificent mosaic pavement; an altar, font, and corona modelled on German

Romanesque work; and a plaque to Abbot Vonier (d. 1938) by Benno Elkan. *Hembury Castle*, an Iron Age camp surrounded by NT woodland, lies 1m NW.

From Dart Bridge the road goes on to (21½m) *Buckfastleigh* (2900 inhabitants), once famous for woollens. The late Perpendicular church has good monuments. The poet Robert Herrick is buried at (23½m) *Dean Prior*, where he was rector in 1629–47 and again in 1662–74. The road passes (25m) *Syon Abbey*, a Bridgettine nunnery since its foundation by Henry V in 1414 (formerly at Isleworth), to reach (26½m) *South Brent*, on the right, with a Norman church tower and font. *Brent Hill* (1019ft), 1m N, gives a good view and the romantic scenery of the *Dean Burn Valley*, 3m N, repays a visit. For the upper Avon valley, see Route 29C.

32m: **Ivybridge** (TI), a beautifully situated village loved by Turner, takes its name from the 13C bridge over the Erme. It makes a good starting-point for excursions on S Dartmoor.

Pleasant walks may be taken in the beautiful *Ivybridge Woods* and to (2m) *Hanger Down*, (1½m) *Western Beacon* (1088ft), or (2m) *Harford Bridge*. From the Perpendicular church at *Harford* a fine moorland walk leads along the right bank of the Erme to (3m) the *Stall Moor Circle*. There are good hut circles higher up the valley. The road from Ivybridge to (8m) *Shaugh Prior* (Route 29B) leads to (3m) *Cornwood* and thence NW, via (5m) *Tolch Moor Gate*, with the fine heights of *Pen Beacon* (1407ft) and *Shell Top* (1546ft) on the right. To *Two Bridges* over the moor, see Route 29C.

38m: *Plympton*, 4m NE of A38, is a 'Stannary' town (see introduction to Route 29) and the birthplace of Sir Joshua Reynolds (1723–92), with the old grammar school (1664) where he and his fellow artists Benjamin Haydon and James Northcote were pupils. The Guildhall where Reynolds presided as mayor, rebuilt in the 19C, is open on written application. The church of St Mary deserves a visit. Sir Christopher Wren was MP for Plympton.

Hemerdon House (limited opening), 2m NE, is an early 19C building with a collection of West Country paintings and prints. The Dartmoor Wild Life Park is at *Sparkwell*, 3m NE of Plympton.
Saltram (NT), 2m W of Plympton, is Devon's largest country house. The Tudor building was enlarged in the 1740s. Although the exterior is plain, the interior has a grand saloon and dining room by Robert Adam (1768), with ceilings by Zucchi, furniture and china, and 14 portraits by Reynolds, a frequent visitor. The kitchen remains in full working order. The landscaped park, uncomfortably close to A38, has an orangery and chapel (1776).

43m: **PLYMOUTH** (244,000 inhabitants) stands in a dramatic position at the mouths of the Plym and the Tamar and at the head of Plymouth Sound, a splendid natural haven hemmed in with islands and promontories. A major seaport and naval garrison with a long history, it is also a centre for holidaymakers.

TI: Civic Centre, Royal Parade. **Bus Station**: Bretonside for all country services; suburban services from city centre. **Railway Station**: North Rd, N of the centre. **Theatres**: Theatre Royal, Royal Parade; Athenaeum Theatre, Derry's Cross; Barbican Theatre, opposite Mayflower Steps. **Ferries**: to Roscoff and Santander. Local ferry service from Ferry Rd, Devonport, to Torpoint (for Antony House) and from Admiral's Hard, Stonehouse, to Cremyll (for Mount Edgcumbe). Pleasure cruises from the Barbican to Cawsand and from Phoenix Wharf round the warships and dockyard to the Yealm and the Tamar. **Airport**: 4m N of city centre, off A386. Flights to Aberdeen, Bristol, Cork, Glasgow, London (Heathrow), Newcastle, Paris and the Scilly Isles. **Events**: Lord Mayor's Day (May); Sutton Harbour Regatta (July); Bristol and West Drake Open Bowls Tournament (August); Naval Base Fair at HMS Drake (held every other year, usually on August Bank Holiday weekend).

History. Plymouth, known to the Domesday Book as Sutton, received its charter and its present name in 1439. It was fortified soon afterwards and ever since has played an important part in maritime history. Catherine of Aragon landed here in 1501. The town supplied seven ships to fight the Armada (1588) and the English fleet awaited the arrival of the Spaniards in Plymouth Sound. The starting-point for many expeditions by Drake, Sir Humphrey Gilbert and Sir John Hawkins (a native), Plymouth was also the last port touched by the Pilgrim Fathers on their way from Southampton to America in 1620. In the Civil War it sided with Parliament and was the only town in SW England to escape capture by the Royalists. Air raids in 1941–45 destroyed many historic buildings, though the city centre has been thoughtfully rebuilt. American troops embarked from Plymouth on D-Day in 1944, and the Falklands Task Force began and ended its expedition here in 1982.

Natives: Sir John Hawkins (1532–95); the theologian Joseph Glanvill (1636–80); the painters James Northcote (1746–1831) and Benjamin Haydon (1786–1846); the eccentric poet and parson R.S. Hawker (1830–75); the writers Henry Austin Dobson (1840–1921), Sir John Squire (1884–1958) and L.A.G. Strong (1896–1958). Captain Scott (1868–1912), born in Devonport, is commemorated by monuments on Mount Wise and St Mark's Church, Ford (Keyham).

Royal Parade, the main thoroughfare of the new city centre, runs from St Andrew's Cross in the E to Derry's Cross in the W. Halfway along, where the broad Armada Way cuts a swathe S to the Hoe, stands a flagstaff based on a bronze representation of Drake's drum. Immediately to the E is the *Guildhall* (built in 1870–74, reopened in 1959; open when not in official use), with windows by F.H. Coventry depicting the city's history and a huge Gobelins tapestry. Opposite, across the Great Square with ornamental pools, rises the *Civic Centre* of 1962 (open); a lift goes up to the belvedere on the 14th floor (*view). To the N is a modern shopping centre with the colourful *Pannier Market* (1960). Armada Way leads down to the Hoe between the Council House and the *Law Courts* (1963), with a striking entrance panel by P. Fourmaintreaux.

The *Hoe is a raised esplanade with wide lawns overlooking the Sound. A well-loved legend has Sir Francis Drake playing bowls here when the Spanish Armada was first sighted. Among the monuments are a replica (1884) of Drake's statue at Tavistock and *Smeaton's Tower* (open in summer), the upper part of the third Eddystone Lighthouse. The top of the tower gives the best view from the Hoe, which in clear weather reaches 14m S to the Breakwater and the Eddystone Lighthouse (see below). To the S is the *Plymouth Dome*, with reconstructions and high-tech displays bringing the history of Plymouth to life. To the E is the *Royal Citadel* (EH, guided tours in summer), built in 1666, with a fine gateway and a statue of George II in Roman costume; the buildings are now used by a commando regiment of the Royal Artillery. Below their walls is the *Plymouth Aquarium* (open), part of the research laboratory of the Marine Biological Association.

N of the Citadel lies the old quarter of Plymouth, with the quay known as the *Barbican*. The *Mayflower Stone and Steps* commemorate the departure of the Pilgrim Fathers in 1620. Nearby plaques remember the homecoming of the Tolpuddle Martyrs (1838) and the first seaplane flight across the Atlantic (1919). Among the historic buildings are the *Old Custom House* (1586) to the N, the *Elizabethan House* on New St., and the *Island House*, where the Pilgrim Fathers are said to have spent their last night in England, at the head of Southside St.

Southside St. and Notte St. lead to St Andrew's St., with the *Merchant's House Museum* (open), a 16–17C building now containing exhibits of

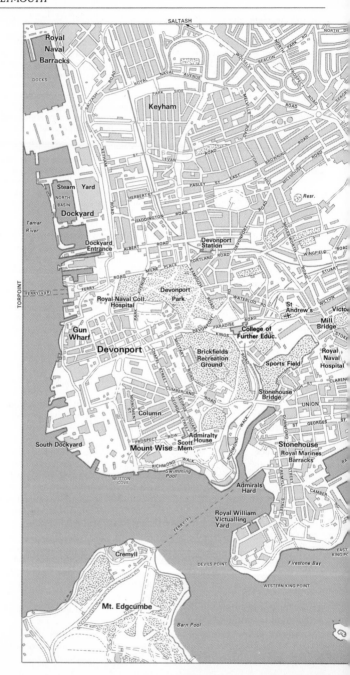

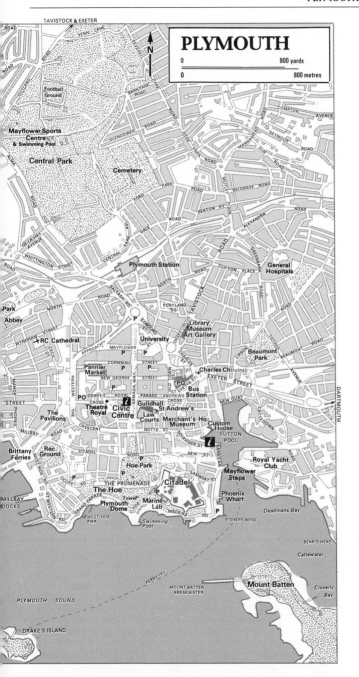

PLYMOUTH

0		800 yards
0		800 metres

TAVISTOCK & EXETER

VENN LANE

ROAD

ROAD

ROAD

OUTLAND

ALMA

Football Ground

Mayflower Sports Centre & Swimming Pool

Central Park

GLENDOWER ROAD

BARNPARK ROAD

HOLDSWORTH ROAD

PARK ROAD

FORD PARK ROAD

Cemetery

COMPTON

AVENUE

SEYMOUR

ROAD

MANNAMEAD ELM ROAD

MUTLEY PLAIN

BELGRAVE ROAD

ROAD

DE-LA-HAY AVENUE

WHITTINGTON STREET

STREET

CENTRAL PARK AVENUE

DALE ROAD

FORD

SEATON AV-NUE

ROAD

ALEXANDRA ROAD

ROAD

Park

Abbey

NORTH ROAD

SALTASH RD.

PORTLAND SQ.

TAVISTOCK

NORTH ROAD

CLIFTON PLACE

GREENBANK

General Hospitals

Plymouth Station

WYNDHAM

CECIL

TAMAR ST.

STREET

PHOENIX ST.

STREET

RC Cathedral

APPROACH

DRAKE

MAYFLOWER

CORNWALL STREET

STREET

NEW GEORGE STREET

Pannier Market

PO

DERRY'S CROSS

The Pavilions

MILLBAY ROAD

CRESCENT

THE

WESTERN

ARMADA WAY

P

University

Library Museum Art Gallery

CHARLES

Beaumont Park

BEAUMONT ROAD

CHARLES ST.

Charles Ch (ruins)

EXETER STREET

NEW QUAY

CATTEDOWN ROAD

ROYAL

PARADE

ANDREWS CROSS

ST EVANS ST.

PO

i

Bus Station

St Andrew's

Guildhall

Theatre Royal

Civic Centre

Law Courts

Merchant's Ho. Museum

NOTTE ST.

SOUTHSIDE ST.

Custom House

SUTTON POOL

i

DARTMOUTH

Brittany Ferries

Rec. Ground

CITADEL ROAD

Hoe Park

NEW ST.

LAMBHAY ST.

BARBICAN

Royal Yacht Club

Mayflower Steps

MILLBAY DOCKS

CLIFF RD.

GRAND PARADE

WEST HOE PIER

THE PROMENADE

The Hoe

Plymouth Dome

Tower

HOE

Marine Lab

MADEIRA RD.

Citadel

Phoenix Wharf

FISHERS NOSE

Deadmans Bay

BEAR'S HEAD

Cattewater

GT. WESTERN RD.

WEST HOE RD.

Swimming Pool

FERRY (P)

MOUNT BATTEN BREAKWATER

Mount Batten

Clovelly Bay

PLYMOUTH SOUND

DRAKE'S ISLAND

Plymouth's history. **St Andrew's**, the mother church of Plymouth, is 15C with a good tower.

The nave, burned by enemy action in 1941, was reconsecrated in 1957, with a W window by John Piper and Patrick Reyntiens. Chantrey's head of Zachariah Mudge (d. 1769) survived the fire. The entrails of Sir Martin Frobisher (d. 1594) and of Admiral Blake (1599–1657) are buried in or near the chancel. Captain Bligh of the 'Bounty' was baptised here.

Behind St Andrew's is *Prysten House* (open), with a galleried courtyard, built in 1498 as a merchant's house and not, as used to be believed, a monastic hostel.

From St Andrew's Cross Exeter St. leads NE, carried over the bus station by a viaduct, to the ruined 17C *Charles Church*.

In Drake Circus, N of St Andrew's Cross, are the *Public Library* and the *Museum and Art Gallery*, with work by Reynolds, Northcote and Haydon (all local men), Old Master drawings, Plymouth silver, and William Cookworthy's Plymouth and Bristol porcelain.

Union St. leads W from Derry's Cross through *Stonehouse*. On the promontory to the S are the quay at *Admiral's Hard*, the *Royal Marine Barracks* (begun 1784) and the vast *Royal William Victualling Yard* laid out by Rennie in 1826–35, with a colossal statue of William IV over the gate. Beyond (1¼m) *Stonehouse Bridge* lies **Devonport**, with its Navy dockyard. On *Mount Wise*, to the left, stand the official residences of the General in Command and the Port Admiral, and the Scott Monument of 1925 (view). Richmond Walk, below, leads to *Mutton Cove*.

The *Devonport Column*, adjoining the former *Guildhall* (1821–23), commemorates the change of name from 'Plymouth Dock' to Devonport in 1824; both are by a local architect, John Foulston. Much of the old centre has been lost to the S dockyard. The *Sailors' Rest*, founded by Agnes Weston (d. 1918) with accommodation for 1000 men, is now used by the university.

The *Dockyard* covers 300 acres and fronts on the Hamoaze, or estuary of the Tamar, which serves as a harbour for warships, including nuclear submarines. The S Dockyard and the *Gun Wharf*, built by Vanbrugh (1718–25), are connected with the *Keyham Steam Yard* in the N by railway tunnel. The largest ships can be refitted here.

The return to the city centre can be made across *Devonport Park*. St Andrew's, the mother church of Devonport, was enlarged in 1750 with ships' masts as roof piers. Immediately opposite, Devonport and Tamar High Schools occupy the former *Station Hospital* (1797). Victoria Park and North Rd are on the left. The *Royal Naval Hospital* dates from c 1762. In Wyndham St. stands the *Roman Catholic Cathedral* (1858; Joseph Hansom), a Gothic Revival building with a tall spire.

The *Eddystone Lighthouse, 14m S, was built by Sir James Douglas in 1878–82; its light, flashing twice every ½ minute, is visible for 17m. Of its predecessors, the 1st (1696–99; Winstanley) was swept away by a storm in 1703; the 2nd, of wood (1706–08; Rudyard), was destroyed by fire in 1755; and the 3rd, Smeaton's lighthouse of 1759, was removed in 1882 because the sea had eroded the rock on which it stood.

Mount Edgcumbe (open), on the Cornish peninsula, is best reached by taking the pedestrian ferry from Admiral's Hard in Stonehouse to *Cremyll*. The 16C mansion, gutted by fire in 1941 and rebuilt in 1960, is less interesting than the varied and finely wooded *grounds laid out between 1761 and 1800, with deer park, temples, amphitheatre and French, English and Italian gardens. They enjoy magnificent views over Plymouth Sound. From Cremyll the road climbs to (2½m) the twin fishing villages of

Kingsand and *Cawsand*. A fine cliff walk continues past *Penlee Point* to (2½m) *Rame Head*, with the 15C chapel of St Michael.

The ferry crossing the Hamoaze from Ferry Rd in Devonport to the Cornish coast at *Torpoint* (8400 inhabitants) gives access to *Antony House* (NT), off A374 1m inland. Standing in pleasant grounds leading down to the Lynher, the house (1711–21) has a central block of grey Pentewan stone flanked by colonnades and red-brick wings. The well-preserved interior has original panelling, furniture and portraits of the Carews. Adjoining the estate is the privately owned *Antony Woodland Garden* of 100 acres, originally established by Humphry Repton. A374 continues W to (4½m) *Sheviock*, where the 13C church has Courtenay monuments. *Portwrinkle*, 1m SW, has a long beach stretching E to Rame Head (see above). 7m: *Polbathic*. 1m NE is *St Germans*, where the striking church, with two W towers and a deep-set Norman *porch, served as Cornwall's cathedral until c 1409. Nearby is the early 19C mansion of Port Eliot, and to the W are the 17C Moyle almshouses. About 3m SW of Polbathic is the resort of *Downderry*. 12m: The road forks, A387 heading W to Looe (7m) and A374 continuing N to join A38 for Liskeard (6m), both in Route 30.

The attractive excursion up the Tamar to (19m) *Weir Head* takes c 5½hrs by boat from Phoenix Wharf. Steering through the Hamoaze between Devonport (right) and Torpoint (left), it leaves the mouth of the Lynher on the left, and enters the Tamar proper, the boundary between Devon and Cornwall. It passes under the *Royal Albert Bridge* (built for the railway by Isambard Kingdom Brunel in 1859; nearly ½m long, 100ft clearance) and then the *Tamar Suspension Bridge* (Route 30). At the W or Cornish end of these lies (4m) *Saltash*. Above the bridges the river expands into a lake ¾m wide, with the Tavy estuary to the right and Great Mis Tor visible in the distance to the N. *Landulph* (left) has the tomb of Theodore Palaeologus (d. 1636), descendant of the Byzantine emperors. On the same side, round the next bend, is *Pentillie Castle*, with its charming grounds. 14m: *Calstock* and *Cotehele House*, see Route 29A. The river makes a wide loop (3m) to the right to (17m) *Morwellham Quay*, about 1m short of the *Morwell Rocks* (300ft), on the right. 19m: *Weir Head* lies within 4m of Tavistock (Route 29A). The fine scenery higher up is accessible only by small boat.

Plymstock, about 3m SE on A379, has a 17C gun tower overlooking the Sound from Mount Batten Point (EH, contact regional office for details). The pleasant bays SE of Plymouth include *Bovisand*, *Heybrook* and *Wembury*, where the 15C church with 17C Hele and Calmady tombs overlooks the Great Mew Stone. The Hele almshouses date from 1682. The old mill (NT) on the beach at Wembury is now a café and shop. The coast W to Warren Point is NT property.

From Plymouth to *Princetown* and *Dartmoor*, see Route 29B; to *Truro* and *Penzance*, see Route 30.

B.   Via Torquay and the Coast

Directions. Total distance 70m. A380, the direct road from Exeter to (20m) Torquay, runs via Newton Abbot (Route 28C). **Exeter**, see Route 18A. A379 to (13m) Dawlish, (16m) Teignmouth, (24m) **Torquay**, (27m) Paignton, (35m) **Dartmouth**, (50m) Kingsbridge, (58m) Modbury and (70m) **Plymouth** (Route 28A).

Exeter, see Route 18A. The route leaves the city to the SW, passing (1½m) *Alphington* (Route 28A), and briefly following A38 to A379, which runs down the W bank of the Exe estuary. At (7¾m) *Kenton* the 14C church has a wonderful rood screen of c 1480. In a large deer park to the left is *Powderham Castle* (open), with the fortified mansion built by the Courtenays in 1390–1420 at its core. Much of its present appearance dates from 18C and 19C alterations. Note particularly the staircase hall (1754), with elaborate carving and plasterwork, and the music room by James Wyatt (1794–96). From (9m) *Starcross* a ferry runs to Exmouth (Route 18A). The tower of a pumping house for Brunel's experimental atmospheric railway survives here. 13m: **Dawlish** (10,800 inhabitants; TI) is a resort laid out in 1803, sheltered by the Haldon range (821ft), with the successor to Brunel's atmospheric railway skirting the beach on a viaduct. Dickens made it Nicholas Nickleby's birthplace. *Dawlish Warren*, 1½m NE, has a good sandy beach. 16m: **Teignmouth** (pronounced 'Tinmouth'; 13,300 inhabitants; TI), at the mouth of the Teign, has been a resort since the 18C. Andrew Patey of Exeter built the classical *Den Crescent* (1826) and *St Michael's* (1823), in an extravaganza of styles. Keats stayed here in 1819.

It is worth taking the walk N by the Sea Wall to (2m) the curiously formed red rocks known as the *Parson* and the *Clerk*, and also the walk to (2m) *Little Haldon* (811ft). A381 follows the Teign to (6m) Newton Abbot (Route 28C), passing on the right (2½m) *Bishopsteignton*, where the Perpendicular church has a Norman doorway and 13C tympanum.

A long bridge crosses the estuary to *Shaldon*, with Regency houses, under a bold headland called the *Ness*. The hilly Torquay road skirts the cliff above Babbacombe Bay (see below).

24m: **TORQUAY** is the largest and most popular of the three resorts which overlook Tor Bay (the others are Paignton and Brixham). Now combined as the county borough of Torbay (115,600 inhabitants), they have also been labelled the 'English Riviera' because of the mild climate and semi-tropical vegetation. Torquay itself stands on hills rising from the N shore of the bay.

TI: Vaughan Parade. **Bus Station**: Lymington Rd. **Railway Stations**: Torquay Station, off Torbay Rd (A379); Torre Station, off Newton Rd (A380). **Amusements**: Princess Theatre, Princess Gardens; Coral Island Leisure Complex, on E side of the harbour; Babbacombe Theatre, Babbacombe Downs Rd. **Ferries**: local service to Brixham. **Annual Events**: Bowls Tournament (June), Carnival (July) and Regatta (August).

Natives and residents: Elizabeth Barrett Browning made a convalescent stay here in 1838–41. Agatha Christie (1890–1976) was born here, and Sean O'Casey lived here from 1954 until his death in 1964.

Torbay Rd leads from Torquay Station at the SW end of the town, past the fine grounds of *Torre Abbey* (open), a 17–18C house built on the remains of a Premonstratensian abbey founded in 1196. Of the monastic buildings, the chapter house doorway (c 1200), 14C gatehouse, guest hall and a fine tithe barn survive. The house now contains the municipal art gallery. The road ends at (c 1m) the lively *Inner Harbour*. The *Outer Harbour*, bounded on the N by Princess Gardens, is protected from the sea by Princess Pier and Haldon Pier. Near Haldon Pier are *Aqualand*, with local and exotic marine life and the *Royal Torbay Yacht Club*. The Strand is continued NW by Fleet St. and Union St., the town's main thoroughfare. The characteristic terraces of Torquay were designed by Jacob Harvey and his sons John and William in 1811–53. *St John's* (1861–71) is a striking church by G.E. Street, decorated by Burne-Jones.

From the Strand, Torwood St. and Babbacombe Rd lead NE past the *Museum*, which contains finds from Kent's Cavern. At *Wellswood*, about 1m, a right turn on Ilsham Rd leads to *Kent's Cavern* (open), a stalactite cave inhabited between 100,000 and 8000 BC. Flint and bone implements have been discovered here.

Anstey's Cove, a pretty little bay, lies ½m N of the cavern. The return journey continues via the Bishop's Walk (cliff path; *view), Marine Drive, *Lincombe Gardens* and (2m)

Meadfoot Beach. From here the harbour can be reached via the elevated *Daddy Hole Plain* (view).

Nearly 2m N of the harbour, by the winding Babbacombe road or over *Warberry Hill* (448ft), lies the suburb of **Babbacombe**, above the coloured *Babbacombe Bay*. The splendid church of All Saints (1865–74) is by Butterfield. Babbacombe Down gives a good view of the coast. Near a miniature *Model Village* (open), a cliff railway (summer only) descends to Babbacombe beach. Beyond Babbacombe is *St Marychurch*, where the old church, with a 12C font, has been restored after bomb damage in 1943. From *Petitor* a fine walk leads along the cliffs to (1¼m) *Watcombe*, with its *Giant Rock*, and to (2m) *Maidencombe*, going on to (3m) *Labrador*, and Shaldon.

Among the points of interest W of Torquay are: (1m) *Cockington* with its Perpendicular church, 16–17C manor house, old forge and thatched cottages; *Marldon* (3m), where the Perpendicular church has monuments to the Gilberts of Compton, including Sir Humphrey Gilbert, half-brother of Sir Walter Raleigh and coloniser of Newfoundland (1583); and (4m) *Compton Castle* (NT), a fortified house of the 14–16C with courtyard, great hall, chapel and kitchen.

27m: **Paignton** (TI) is almost continuous with Torquay. The *Church* has a Norman doorway, the Kirkham Chantry (c 1526) with a fine *screen, and an old stone pulpit. The 14C *Coverdale Tower* is a fragment of a palace of the Bishops of Exeter and has no connection with the Protestant reformer Miles Coverdale. Nearby is the 15C *Kirkham House* (EH, limited opening in summer). *Oldway Mansion* (gardens and some rooms open), now the offices of Torbay Borough Council, was built by the 19C American sewing-machine millionaire Isaac Singer and further aggrandised by his son, Paris. The *Torbay and Dartmouth Steam Railway* runs to (7m) Kingswear in summer. The *Zoo and Botanical Gardens* are on the Totnes Rd. 2m further W is the *Torbay Aircraft Museum*. S of Paignton are *Goodrington Sands*. 30½m: *Churston Ferrers* church has an E window given by Agatha Christie.

Brixham (TI), 1½m E of Churston, is a resort and fishing port with an attractive harbour known for its busy fish market and trawlers (Trawler Race in June). The Old Market House on the Quay contains the *British Fisheries Museum*. A statue commemorates William of Orange's landing near here in 1688. *Brixham Museum*, next to the town hall, is devoted to local and maritime history and the history of the Coastguard Service.

34½m: *Kingswear.* Near the coast 2m S is *Coleton Fishacre Garden* (NT), with rare trees and shrubs. From Kingswear a ferry crosses the Dart to **Dartmouth** (6300 inhabitants; TI), a port on a beautiful land-locked *estuary, famous for the *Royal Naval College* (in buildings by Aston Webb) on Mount Boone to the N. Crusaders embarked from Dartmouth in 1147 and 1190, and American troops in 1944. Thomas Newcomen (1663–1729), inventor of the atmospheric steam engine, was born here; one of his engines (1725, altered in 1821) is displayed in Royal Avenue Gardens. *St Saviour* has a 15C rood screen, carved stone pulpit, and gallery of 1633 with the arms of merchant families. Note also the brass of 1408 to John Hawley (identified with Chaucer's Shipman) and the ironwork on the S door. The fine *Butterwalk* (1635–40), with carved overhangs, includes a small maritime museum. *Bayard's Cove Fort* (EH), now ruined, was built in 1509–10 to guard the inner haven. Further S, at the harbour's narrow mouth, are *St Petroc's Church*, with a Norman font, and *Dartmouth Castle* (EH, all year), built in 1481 and enlarged in the 16C. It stands opposite *Kingswear Castle* (1491–1502).

In summer there are steamers up the river Dart to (10m) Totnes (Route 28C). Opposite (3m) *Dittisham*, on the right bank, is *Greenway*, the birthplace of Sir Humphrey Gilbert (?1539–83). The *Anchor Rock*, where (according to tradition) Sir Walter Raleigh used to smoke his pipe, can be seen at low water. Beyond (6m) *Stoke Gabriel*, on the left bank, are the hanging woods of *Sharpham*, on the right bank.

Beyond Dartmouth A379 climbs steeply, passes (36¾m) *Stoke Fleming* with its conspicuous church, and reaches the shore at (38m) *Blackpool*. Beyond (39m) *Strete* the road follows a strip of shingle separating the sea from *Slapton Ley*, a narrow freshwater lagoon and nature reserve. *Slapton*, ½m N of the lagoon, has the scanty remains of a chantry (1372). At (42½m) *Torcross* the road turns abruptly inland.

From Torcross the Devon South Coast Path leads through fine cliff scenery to (4m) *Start Point*, (9m) *Prawle Point* and (14½m) *Portlemouth*, where a ferry crosses to Salcombe (see below). Portlemouth can also be reached by sideroads (about 8m) from *Chillington*, on A379 W of Torcross, via the charming village of (4m) *South Pool* or (4m) *Chivelstone*. Both have interesting churches.

50m: **Kingsbridge** (4100 inhabitants; TI), at the head of the land-locked Kingsbridge Estuary, is a busy little market town. The colonnaded *Shambles* of 1585 have an upper storey added in 1796. The church has a good monument by Flaxman.

Salcombe (2400 inhabitants; seasonal TI), on A381 6½m S, is a resort with charming scenery and rich vegetation. Once an important shipbuilding port, it has since become a sailing centre. J.A. Froude (born at Dartington near Totnes) is buried in the churchyard. At *Sharpitor*, 1½m SW, Overbecks (NT) is an Edwardian house with miscellaneous collections; the gardens, overlooking the estuary, have rare plants, shrubs and trees. The Devon South Coast Path leads along a magnificent stretch of scenery (NT), past (2m) *Bolt Head* to (8m) *Bolt Tail* and *Hope Cove*. About 4m W of Kingsbridge is the little resort of *Thurlestone*.

A379 crosses the Avon at (53½m) *Aveton Gifford*, where the fine church was almost destroyed in World War II. 58m: *Modbury* (seasonal TI) is a severe place with steep streets and slate-hung houses.

Off *Bigbury-on-Sea*, at the mouth of the Avon 5m S, is the tidal *Burgh Island*.

At 59m A379 crosses the Erme. The churches of *Ermington* (1m N) and *Holbeton* (1½m S) have twisted spires and good screens. Flete (limited opening), in Ermington, is an Elizabethan house altered by Norman Shaw. 63½m: *Yealhampton* (pronounced 'Yampton') stands at the head of the Yealm estuary. *Newton Ferrers* is attractively situated on the estuary 2m SW. The coastal scenery to the S, with the ruined church of *Revelstoke*, is magnificent.

70m: **Plymouth**, see Route 28A.

C.   Via Newton Abbot and Totnes

Directions. Total distance 47m. **Exeter**, see Route 18A. A38, A380 to (15m) **Newton Abbot** (bypassed). A381 to (24m) **Totnes**. A385 to (30m) junction with A38. A38 to (47m) **Plymouth**, see Route 28A.

Exeter, see Route 18A. A38 (Route 28A) is joined SW of the city. At 6m A380 bears left, climbing the steep *Telegraph Hill* (1 in 7). 10m: To the right of the road stands *Ugbrooke House* (open), an old place remodelled by Robert Adam in a castellated style in the 1760s, when Capability Brown landscaped the park. The handsome interior has good 18C furniture and portraits by Lely in the drawing room. Adam's chapel is claimed as the oldest Roman Catholic parish church in SW England. 15m: **Newton Abbot** (21,000 inhabitants) is a market town and railway centre. At the 14–15C *St Leonard's Tower* William of Orange is said to have been first proclaimed king after his arrival at Paignton (Route 28B) in 1688. Off A381 to the W, by the banks of the Lemon, is *Bradley Manor* (NT), a well-preserved 15C house with a Perpendicular chapel.

B3195 leads E to the coast at (4½m) Shaldon (Route 28B) via (2½m) *Combeinteignhead*, in pleasant country. At *Haccombe*, 2m SW of Combeinteignhead, the Early English church has interesting 15–17C effigies and brasses of the Carews. A382 goes up the Teign valley to (6m) Bovey Tracey and (12½m) Moretonhampstead (Route 29D), making a good approach to Dartmoor from the Torbay coast.

From Newton Abbot A380 continues to Torquay (Route 28B). The present route follows A381 S to (19m) *Ipplepen*, on the right, with a 15C church. *Torbryan*, 1m W, has the Church House Inn of 1500 and a *church with old glass and a screen of c 1430. 22½m: *Littlehempston*, on the right, has a 14C parsonage, now a farmhouse.

24m: **Totnes** (5600 inhabitants; TI) is one of the oldest and most handsome towns in England. It lies on the side of a hill with the Dart at its base, and consists mainly of one long congested *street with many Elizabethan houses. The hill leads up from the river to the *Elizabethan House Museum*, built c 1575, with a collection of furniture and domestic objects. Just beyond, the street is spanned by the arch of the *East Gate*, rebuilt c 1500. On the right stands the church of *St Mary* (1432–60), in red sandstone, with a noble tower, a splendid coloured and gilt stone *rood screen, good parclose screens and a stone pulpit. Behind it stands the charming *Guildhall* (open), a pillared 16–17C building; its interior preserves the old court room and mayor's parlour. High St. continues up the hill to *Totnes Castle* (EH, all year), with a 14C keep on the Norman motte. A walk round the circular upper storey gives a fine *view.

Off A384 about 2½m E is the picturesque ruin of *Berry Pomeroy Castle* (EH, summer season), dating largely from the 16C but with a 14C great gateway. *Bowden House*, 1m S of Totnes, is a small building of several periods, though the visitor's first impression is dominated by the Queen Anne façade (1704). Beyond the house sideroads continue 1½m SE to the attractive village of *Ashprington*, where the Avenue Cottage Gardens (open), with their woodland walks, are being recreated. The historian J.A. Froude (1818–94) was born at *Dartington*, 2m N of Totnes. *Dartington Hall* is a restored 14C manor house. The estate is now a trust with agricultural and other commercial enterprises. Here, too, are a school, a College of Arts and an Adult Education Centre. The grounds include terraces overlooking the old tiltyard; one of them has a statue by Henry Moore.

For river cruises from Totnes down the Dart to Dartmouth, see Route 28B. Sideroads follow the pretty upper valley of the Dart to (7m) Buckfastleigh (Route 28A) via (3m) *Staverton*, with a picturesque bridge. In summer the journey can be made by the *Dart Valley Railway*.

A385 leads W from Totnes to (30m) the junction with A38, where Route 28A continues to (47m) **Plymouth**.

29

Dartmoor

Walkers need the OS Outdoor Leisure map (2½in to 1m).

Dartmoor National Park lies between A30 and A38 in Devon, covering 368 square miles (24m from N to S and 23m from E to W). At its core is Dartmoor proper (300 square miles), once a royal forest and still sometimes called by that title. The tableland is the easternmost of the granite masses which punctuate the surface of SW England. Further W, they form Bodmin Moor, the Downs above St Austell, the countryside between Redruth and Helston, and the Land's End peninsula. The Scilly Isles are the remnant of the westernmost outcrop.

Dartmoor is the highest as well as the largest of these formations. Its mean elevation is about 1200ft, but some of the hills rise over 1800ft and, near Okehampton in the N, they exceed 2000ft. The characteristic grey 'tors' that crown many hills are piles of granite broken and weathered to look oddly like the ruins of human habitation. The slopes beneath these heights are covered by gorse and heather, while the low-lying country has tracts of dark peat and dangerous bog marked by the bright green of its grass. This moorland provides rough grazing for the semi-wild breed of Dartmoor ponies, and for cattle and sheep, some of which, like the ponies, are pastured all year round. The many streams that criss-cross the region flow into rivers draining the tableland to the S: the Bovey and the Teign (meeting S of Bovey Tracey to reach the sea at Teignmouth); the Dart (running past Buckfastleigh to Totnes and Dartmouth); the Avon (meandering SW after it leaves the moor at South Brent); the Erme (heading due S beyond Ivybridge); the Plym (which eventually gives its name to Plymouth); and the Tavy (running through Tavistock into the Tamar estuary at Plymouth).

In the valleys to the S the countryside grows wooded and friendly; the centres of population here, joined by the course of A38, cling to convenient river crossings. To the N, Dartmoor can be as bleak as it is isolated. The heart of the moorland is crossed by only two roads of any consequence, meeting at Two Bridges, and boasts only one town of any size, Princetown. The long-term prison here, together with the unfriendly contours of the landscape, the treacherous bogs, the frequent mists and penetrating rain, have contributed much to the moor's forbidding reputation. Its grim atmosphere is evoked by Conan Doyle's 'The Hound of the Baskervilles'.

Yet the region is also rich in historic and, especially, prehistoric remains. With its abundance of water, building stone and pasture, and its lack of the forests which then densely covered much of the surrounding lowland, Dartmoor attracted Bronze Age and Iron Age settlers. Traces of their presence survive in stone circles and rows, hut circles, cairns and trackways. Several of the chief sites are now administered by EH. Rude stone bridges ('clapper' bridges) and stone crosses marking the way to the religious houses on the borders of the moor survive from medieval times. There are also vestiges of the mining for tin, copper and manganese that once flourished here. Tavistock, Chagford, Ashburton and Plympton are the four 'Stannary' towns appointed by a charter of Edward I for the weighing and stamping of tin and the holding of monthly mining courts.

Walkers need to take special precautions: carrying a map and compass; avoiding swampy spots (bright green grass); making for a valley if overtaken by mist; and remembering that recent rain can make streams impassable. There is a large military training area in the N of Dartmoor which includes three firing ranges (marked by red and white posts, and by noticeboards at the main approaches). Maps showing these areas can be seen at local post offices, inns, etc. For information about access restrictions, write to or telephone the Range Liaison Officer, Devon Training Areas, Seaton Barracks, Tavistock Rd, Plymouth (Plymouth 772312, extension 249).

The headquarters of the Dartmoor National Park Authority, also an information centre, is at Parke, Haytor Rd, Bovey Tracey (Route 29D). The National Park's High Moorland Visitor Centre is at Princetown, and there are seasonal information centres at Okehampton and Tavistock (Route 29A), Steps Bridge, Postbridge (Route 29B), and New Bridge (Route 29C).

A. Exeter to Tavistock via Okehampton

Directions. Total distance 39m. The route follows the N and W boundaries of the National Park. **Exeter**, see Route 18A. A30 to (23m) **Okehampton** (bypassed). A30, A386 to (39m) **Tavistock**.

Exeter, see Route 18A. A30 heads W from the city. The edge of the National Park is reached at (11m) *Cheriton Bishop* on the left, where the church has a good font and woodwork.

Sideroads lead SW through (1½m) *Crockernwell* and (3m) *Drewsteignton* to (4m) *Castle Drogo* (NT), one of the last English country houses in the grand style, built in 1910–30 by Sir Edwin Lutyens for Julius Drewe, founder of the Home and Colonial Stores. Made of local granite, it dramatically exploits its site overlooking the Teign. The interior, with bare stone walls and high windows, is comfortably grand. Note particularly the main staircase and the kitchen and service rooms. The main route can be rejoined by continuing to A382, which heads NW to meet A30 near *Whiddon Down*.

18½m: *South Zeal*, a former copper-mining village with a 16C inn, lies beneath *Cosdon* or *Cawsand Beacon* (1799ft; view). *South Tawton*, 1m N, one of John Wesley's regular preaching stations, has a 15C granite church beside a 16C church house.

Sideroads lead SE from South Zeal to (1½m) *Throwleigh*, a remote parish with a fine 15–16C church and old farmhouses. Beyond the many hut circles on the moor above is a spectacular stone circle about 90ft in diameter. For *Chagford*, 5m SE of Throwleigh, see Route 29D.

At (19½m) *Sticklepath* the Finch Foundry Museum of Water Power has machinery in working order. A sideroad goes up the pretty valley of the Taw to (1¾m) *Belstone*, with tors to the S.

23m: **Okehampton** (4200 inhabitants; seasonal TI), at the confluence of the East and West Okement, is popular as a base for exploring N Dartmoor. The *Museum of Dartmoor Life* on West St. offers a good introduction to the region. The *Castle* (EH, all year), in a fine position on the river 1m SW, has late Norman work in its keep.

In the military zone to the S are (1½m) *Okehampton Camp*, (4½m) *Yes Tor* (2028ft; view) and (4¾m) *High Willhays* (2039ft), the highest point on Dartmoor. Red flags indicate when the public is excluded during artillery practice (for firing programmes, phone 0837 52939). The remote but lovely 14C church of *Bratton Clovelly* lies 7½m W of Okehampton, off B3128 (the Holsworthy road).

FROM OKEHAMPTON TO BARNSTAPLE, 29m. B3217 goes N along the West Okement valley to (12m) *Dowland*, where the little church has an early 16C oak arcade. 13½m: *Dolton* church contains a strange font made from two blocks of a 10C cross. B3217 climbs to cross B3220. At (20½m) *High Bickington* the partly Norman church has *bench ends. Beyond (22½m) *Atherington* (Route 18A) B3217 joins A377 for (29m) *Barnstaple* (Route 26). An alternative route (39m) follows A386 to (20m) *Great Torrington* and (27m) *Bideford* and A39 to Barnstaple; see Route 35.

From Okehampton to *Launceston*, *Bodmin* and *Penzance*, see Route 32.

A30 leaves Okehampton. 25½m: Beyond *Meldon*, left of the road, is *Meldon Reservoir*, formed in 1970–71 by flooding much of the steep West Okement valley. 27½m: The route follows A386 as it branches left from A30. 31m: A sideroad leads 1m W to **Lydford**, now a mere village but an important town in Saxon times. Traces of the Saxon settlement can be made out near the late 12C keep of the *Castle* (EH), used as a 'Stannary' prison. Here the Forest Courts were believed to act in accordance with the maxim 'first hang and draw, and then hear the cause, is Lydford Law'. In the 16C the town imprisoned their MP, Richard Strode, for introducing an unpopular bill; the incident led to the establishment of Parliamentary privilege. From *Lydford Gorge* (NT) a steep walk leads to the spectacular waterfall known as the *White Lady*.

For the walk from Lydford to *Merrivale* via *Mary Tavy* and *Peter Tavy*, see Route 29C.

A footpath leading E from A386 at the junction with the turning for Lydford goes to *Tavy Cleave*, a deep rocky valley with bold tors on its W side. At 2¼m it crosses the Lyd by stepping stones (beware danger signals) and heads E to (3m) *Doe Tor* and SE to (3¾m) *Hare Tor*, from which it descends to (4½m) the Cleave. Another pleasant walk starting from the same spot goes NE, crossing the Lyd by stepping stones and climbing to (1m) *Brat Tor*, in full view from the stream. 1m NE to *Great Links Tor* is another 1m NE (1924ft).

At (35m) *Mary Tavy*, the conical *Brent Tor* (1100ft; view), with a 13C chapel dedicated to St Michael de la Rupe, rises on the right.

39m: **TAVISTOCK** (seasonal TI), a stone-built 'Stannary' town, stands on the Tavy just beyond the W boundary of Dartmoor. The heavy Victorian Gothic benefactions of the 7th Duke of Bedford overshadow the chief remains of Tavistock's Benedictine *Abbey*, founded in 981: the restored main gatehouse, a fragment of the cloister (in the churchyard), the infirmary hall (now the Unitarian chapel) and the wall by the river. The W gateway stands in the vicarage garden, which also has three inscribed stones (possibly 6C), one with Oghams. The 15C church of *St Eustachius* contains the fine monument of Sir John Glanville (d. 1600).

About ½m S on the Yelverton road is a statue by Boehm of Sir Francis Drake (1542–96), born at *Crowndale*, ½m further down the Tavy.

FROM TAVISTOCK TO LISKEARD, 18½m by A390. The road crosses the Tamar by the medieval New Bridge to (14½m) *Gunnislake*. *Calstock*, by the river 2¼m S, has a graceful railway viaduct. The noble church of *Bere Ferrers* lies about 3½m further SE, near the Tavy estuary. *Cotehele House* (NT), 2m S of Gunnislake via *Albaston*, is a finely preserved medieval manor around several courtyards, built in 1485–1627. It still has original furniture, armour, 17–18C tapestries and needlework. The chapel has a clock of 1489. The watermill and cider press in the grounds have been restored. The quay by the Tamar has pleasant 18C and 19C buildings and a small shipping museum. Passing *Kit Hill* (1094ft) on the right, A390 reaches (10m) *Callington*, with a noble church. *Dupath Well* (EH, all year plus Mondays in winter), off A388 1m E, is a well house of c 1500. 18½m: *Liskeard*, see Route 30.

B.   Exeter to Plymouth via Princetown

Directions. Total distance 41m. **Exeter**, see Route 18A. B3212 to (12m) Moretonhampstead (Route 29D), (24m) Two Bridges (Route 29C), (25½m) **Princetown** and (31m) Yelverton. A386 to (41m) **Plymouth** (Route 28A).

Exeter, see Route 18A. B3212 heads SW from the city. It dips down into the valley of the Teign, here marking the E edge of Dartmoor National Park, with the pretty village of (6m) *Dunsford* on the right, and crosses the river at (6¾m) *Steps Bridge* (seasonal National Park Information). 12m: **Moretonhampstead**, see Route 29D. The Bovey is crossed before (15m) *Beetor Cross*, where roads go S to Bovey Tracey and N to Chagford, both in Route 29D. 1m further on B3212 climbs the shoulder of *Shapley Common* (1075ft), rising on the left, and gives a fine *view.

A track leads S to (1½m) *Grimspound*, a good example of a late Bronze Age settlement (EH). A wide dry-stone wall encloses about 4 acres with the remains of 24 huts. The old field pattern can be traced outside the pound. Across the valley, ½m due W, is *Challacombe Stone Row*, a triple row with what may be the remains of a stone circle. It can also be approached from Warren House Inn.

B3212 passes between tors with stone circles, stone rows and disused mines. Footpaths lead from (18m) *Warren House Inn*. 20m: *Postbridge* (seasonal National Park Information) has a fine 'clapper' bridge over the East Dart. There is another at *Bellever*, about 1m downstream.

The valley is rich in prehistoric remains. *Broadun Ring*, a group of huts inside an enclosure, is about 1½m N on the W bank of the river. The *Grey Wethers*, the two largest stone rings on the moor, are across the valley about 2m further N. For the footpaths from *Chagford*, see Route 29D.

B3212 crosses B3357 at (24m) *Two Bridges* (Route 29C). 25½m: **Princetown** (National Park High Moorland Visitor Centre) owes its existence to the *Prison* opened in 1809 by the Lord Warden of the Stannaries for prisoners of the Napoleonic wars. American prisoners were added after the war of 1812, the total number at one point being over 9000. The church was built by the men in 1814; a memorial window (1910) and a gateway (1928) commemorate the 218 Americans who died on the moor. In 1850 the building was reopened for English convicts, and part of the prison was burned down in a mutiny of 1932. Some of the surrounding moorland was cultivated by convicts before the system of hard labour was abolished. 28½m: *Yennadon Down*, to the left, commands a view with a particularly fine grouping of the tors round Burrator Reservoir, visited in the detour below. 29m: *Dousland*.

Walkhampton, ½m N, has a conspicuous church tower and 16C church house. A sideroad leads 1m S from Dousland to *Meavy*, with an old village cross. *Sheepstor*, 1¼m E, has an ancient bullring, a 15C priest's house and the tomb of Rajah Brooke of Sarawak (d. 1868). In the S side of the tor (845ft) that gives its name to the village is the *Pixies' Cave*. About 2m SE are the *Drizzlecombe* prehistoric remains (Route 29C). NW of Sheepstor is the beautiful *Burrator Reservoir* (150 acres).

31m: **Yelverton** stands on the edge of *Roborough Down* just inside the W boundary of the National Park.

*Buckland Abbey (NT) is 3m W. Built by the Cistercians in 1278, it was acquired by the Grenvilles after the dissolution of the monasteries and converted into a private house by Sir Richard Grenville in 1576. Sir Francis Drake bought the property in 1581.

The tower of the abbey church is incorporated into the house. Sir Richard Grenville's Great Hall has panelling and a fine plaster ceiling and friezes. Later additions include a handsome Georgian staircase (1772). The house is now a museum of folk art, naval history and Drake relics, of which Drake's Drum is the most famous. The grounds include the huge 14C tithe barn, now containing a display of horse-drawn vehicles. About 1m N is *Buckland Monachorum*, where the fine Perpendicular church has a monument to Lord Heathfield (d. 1790), the defender of Gibraltar.

The route takes A386 S towards Plymouth. 35m: *Bickleigh*, on the left.

About 1½m NE is *Shaugh Bridge*, at the junction of the Meavy and the Plym, with the beautiful wooded *Bickleigh Vale* (part NT). Above Shaugh Bridge is the cliff on the Plym known as the *Dewerstone Rock* (NT). For the way from *Shaugh Prior*, 1m SE, to *Ivybridge* (8m), see Route 28A.

37m: *Plymouth Airport*. 41m: **Plymouth**, see Route 28A.

C.   Ashburton to Tavistock

Directions. Total distance 20m. The route cuts across Dartmoor from SE to W with several good detours, particularly for walkers. Unclassified road to (7m) Dartmeet. B3357 to (11m) **Two Bridges** and (20m) **Tavistock** (Route 29A).

Ashburton (3600 inhabitants), on the S boundary of the National Park, lies by A38 between Exeter and Plymouth (Route 28A). It is a 'Stannary' town with many old houses, a 14–15C *Church* and a *Museum* of local antiquities and geology. The unclassified road signposted for Tavistock crosses the Dart at 1¼m by the medieval *Holne Bridge*.

About ½m beyond, where the woods of *Holne Chase* are on the right, a sideroad leads left to (1m) the picturesque village of *Holne*, birthplace of Charles Kingsley (1819–75). A good walk leads SW from Holne across the common to (2m) the Mardle and S to (2½m) *Pupers Hill* and (4m) *Hickaton Hill*, with hut circles and pounds. To the S of the hill, crossing the Abbot's Way (see below), the Avon is dammed to form a small reservoir. The river is followed to (6m) *Shipley Bridge*. A lane continues down the valley to (8½m) *South Brent* on A38 (Route 28A).

The road crosses the Dart again, by (2½m) *New Bridge* (seasonal National Park Information).

A sideroad leads N along the bank of the Dart and the Webburn to (1½m) *Buckland-in-the-Moor*, where the Early English church has a Perpendicular screen and Norman font, at the foot of *Buckland Beacon* (1282ft; view).

7m: The East and West Dart rivers unite at *Dartmeet*. Hexworthy, 1¼m S, is a fine viewpoint. B3357 leads W from Dartmeet.

11m: **Two Bridges**, at the junction of the two main roads across the moor, lies just below the confluence of the West Dart and the Cowsic. The Cowsic valley is particularly charming, and a Lich Way may be followed from Lydford Tor (2½m up the valley) to Peter Tavy (c 6m W; see below). On the Dart, 1¾m N, is *Wistman's Wood*, one of the few old groves of stunted oaks that still linger on the moor. About ¾m NE is *Crockern Tor* (1391ft), where the Tinners' Parliament was attended until 1730 by representatives of the four original 'Stannary' towns.

Another excursion can be made from *Tor Royal*, 1½m SW, to *Nun's Cross*, 3½m S, thought to have been used as a boundary mark for the Forest of Dartmoor in 1204 (mentioned in 1240), and bearing the inscriptions 'Siward' and 'Boc Lond'. Good walkers can continue by (4½m) an old mine on *Harter Tor* to (5¼m) the prehistoric remains on the Plym at *Drizzlecombe*, which include circles, rows, cairns and standing stones, and W to (7m) *Sheepstor* (Route 29B).

From Nun's Cross an old track known as Abbot's Way, running SE and then SW, leads to (1¼m) a ford on the Plym. The path on the other side is ill defined, but a SE course heads to (2½m) *Erme Head* (c 1530ft), with its mining remains. The left bank of the Erme leads to (3½m) a stream coming from some clay-works. The old railway track to the SE is followed S to (6m) the slope of *Three Barrows* (1522ft; view) and (8m) a point c ¾m E of Hartford church. From the gate about ¼m SSW a lane leads in the same direction to (10m) *Ivybridge* (Route 28A).

From Two Bridges to *Princetown* and *Plymouth*, see Route 29B.

At (13m) *Rundlestone* the road from Princetown joins B3337. 15m: *Merrivale Prehistoric Settlement* (EH), before the modern village of that name, is early Bronze Age, with hut circles, stone rows and cairns.

An easy walk to Lydford (9m) leaves the Tavistock road c 1m W at a point where a watercourse runs under the road. It strikes NNW over the common for (2m) *Cox Tor* (1452ft; view). A lane on the N side of the hill on which the tor stands leads to (2¾m) a farmhouse whence a path runs W to (3¼m) *Peter Tavy Combe, with its charming cascades. About ½m from the lower end of the combe is the village of *Peter Tavy*; from the church a lane runs N to (4¾m) *Mary Tavy*. Beyond this village A386 goes N through Blackdown. At c 1¼m a rough track on the left crosses the shoulder of *Gibbet Hill* (1159ft) to (7½m) a sideroad running NE to (9m) *Lydford* (Route 29A).

Tors rise on either side of the road before it drops down to (20m) **Tavistock** (Route 29A).

D. Ashburton to Chagford and back

Directions. Total distance 35m. A tour of E Dartmoor, partly on steep and narrow roads. **Ashburton**, see Route 29C. Unclassified roads to (6½m) Haytor Vale and (10m) **Bovey Tracey**. A382 to (17m) **Moretonhampstead**. A382 and unclassified roads to (21½m) **Chagford**. Unclassified roads and B3344 to (29m) Widecombe-in-the-Moor. Unclassified roads back to (35m) **Ashburton**.

Ashburton, see Route 29C. An unclassified road heads NE to (2m) *Ausewell Cross* and continues N past *Buckland Beacon* (1281ft; view to the W) to (4½m) *Hemsworthy Gate*, where *Rippon Tor* (1563ft), studded with cairns, stands on the right. A right turn passes the double-headed *Hay Tor* (1490ft; good views), where the tracks of a horse-operated railway opened in 1820 to serve the granite quarries can still be seen. 6½m: **Haytor Vale**.

The 14–15C parish church is at *Ilsington*, 1½m SE. John Ford (1586–?1640), the dramatist, was baptised here. N of Haytor Vale are (3m) *Becka Falls* and (4m) *Manaton*, a delightful village near Lustleigh Cleave (see below). *Hound Tor*, 1½m SE of Manaton, has the remains of a village inhabited from late Saxon times until c 1300 (EH).

The road continues E from Haytor Vale, dropping down past the nature reserve of *Yarner Wood* on the left to (10m) **Bovey Tracey** (headquarters and information centre of the Dartmoor National Park Authority), a good centre for excursions in SE Dartmoor and the lower Teign valley to the E. The Perpendicular church, dedicated to St Thomas Becket, has a remarkable coloured stone screen and pulpit. *John Cann's Rocks*, 1m NW, and *Bottor Rock*, 1½m NE, are two good view points.

A382 heads NW from Bovey Tracey. To the left are (13½m) **Lustleigh**, with an interesting church and the *Cleave*, a moorland valley about 1m W. A382 follows the valley to (17m) **Moretonhampstead**, a pleasant little town with a colonnaded almshouse of 1637. It makes a good starting-point for the moorland near the Teign. *North Bovey*, 1¾m SW, is a lovely village above the Bovey with an oak-shaded green. For B3212, the Exeter–Tavistock road, see Route 29A. At (20m) *Easton Cross* a left turn from A382 leads to (21½m) **Chagford**, a quiet and charming old 'Stannary' town which makes a good starting-point for excursions on N or E Dartmoor.

A pleasant walk of about 8m can be taken via *Teigncombe*, 2½m W, to (4m) the stone remains at *Kestor* (1433ft), then N to the *Wallabrook Clapper* and (5m) the *Scorhill Circle*. The return to Chagford passes (6m) *Gidleigh*, with a fortified mansion of c 1300. From *Batworthy*, about ½m SW of Teigncombe, another walk leads ½m to *Shovel Down*, with a stone circle and several stone rows. It can be extended SW, keeping W of *Fernworthy Forest*, via the *Grey Wethers* to *Postbridge* on B3212 (both Route 29B). Other places of interest near Chagford are: the Iron Age hill-fort at *Cranbrook Castle*, 3m NE; *Fingle Bridge* over the Teign, 4m NE; and *Castle Drogo*, 2¼m NE (Route 29A).

The return journey from Chagford goes S over Meldon Hill to (24m) *Beetor Cross*, continues S, and at 26m turns right on an unclassified road which passes some fine tors to reach (29m) **Widecombe-in-the-Moor**, a beautifully situated village made famous by the song 'Widdicombe Fair'. The fair is still held on the second Tuesday in September. The 14–16C church has a commanding tower; the church house (NT) is early 15C. The adjoining sexton's cottage is an NT and National Park Information Centre and shop. The route heads E across the Webburn, turns right for (30½m) *Hemsworthy Gate* and goes S back to (35m) *Ashburton*.

30

Plymouth to Truro and Penzance

Directions. Total distance 79m. **Plymouth**, see Route 28A. A38 to (17m) Liskeard (bypassed). A38, A390 to (28m) Lostwithiel. A390 to (36m) St Austell (bypassed). A390, A39 to (49m) **Truro**. A39, A394 to (66m) Helston. A394. A30 to (79m) **Penzance**.

Plymouth, see Route 28A, where an alternative way of starting the journey from the city (via Torpoint) is described. The main route heads NW from the centre to join A38 at the large suburb of (4m) *St Budeaux*. Its church (1563) saw the marriage of Sir Francis Drake in 1569 and contains the tomb of Sir Ferdinando Gorges (d. 1647), 1st governor of Maine. The old village lay 1¼m N on the creek leading to *Tamerton Foliot*, still with attractive waterside scenery. A38 crosses the river by the *Tamar Suspension Bridge* (toll) of 1959–61 by Mott, Hay and Anderson; the *Royal Albert Bridge* (see Route 28A) runs alongside. *Saltash* (12,700 inhabitants; TI), an old borough on the Cornish bank, is bypassed. *Trematon Castle* (open by written application), with 13C keep and gatehouse, lies 1½m SW and 2½m further on is *Ince Castle* of c 1550 (limited opening of gardens only), overlooking the beautifully wooded Lynher. A38 crosses the Lynher and then the Tiddy, and at 11m is joined by A374 from Polbathic, the end of the alternative route from Plymouth via Torpoint (Route 28A).

17m: **Liskeard** (pronounced 'Liskard'; 6300 inhabitants) has a spacious square and large Perpendicular church. It is one of Cornwall's four 'Stannary' towns, with Lostwithiel, Truro and Helston (see introduction to Route 29). Edward Gibbon became its MP in 1774.

About 2½m N lies *St Cleer*, with a holy well, giving a good view of the S part of Bodmin Moor (Route 32). The area is rich in ancient monuments (all EH): *King Doniert's Stone* (1m NW), probably a memorial to Durngarth, King of Cornwall in the 9C; the *Trevethy Quoit* (1m NE), a burial chamber of standing stones built c 3200–2500 BC; and the *Hurlers* (2m N of the Trevethy Quoit), three imperfect circles of c 2200–1400 BC. The *Cheesewring*, a pile of weathered granite slabs about 30ft high, lies ½m beyond the Hurlers. The fine church of *St Neot*, about 5m NW of Liskeard, has good glass of 1400–1532, partly restored. For *Dozmary Pool*, about 4m N of St Neot, see Route 32.

FROM LISKEARD TO LOOE AND POLPERRO, 13½m by B3254 and A387 down the Looe valley. 3m: *St Keyne* has a Mechanical Music Centre with fair organs etc. 4½m: *Duloe* has a 13C church and a stone circle. 9m: **Looe** (4500 inhabitants; TI), on both banks of its river, is a historic little port and a former haunt of smugglers, now a popular resort and centre for shark fishing. 13½m: **Polperro**, further W, a picturesque fishing village in a ravine, was also known for smuggling. A road leads W to (10½m) *Bodinnick Ferry* opposite Fowey (see below). A hilly road goes NW from Polperro via (6m) *Lanreath*, with good stalls in its church and a farm museum, to (11m) Lostwithiel (see below).
From Liskeard to *Tavistock*, see Route 29A.

19m: **Dobwalls** has a museum devoted to the wildlife painter Archibald Thorburn (1860–1935). Shortly beyond, the route changes from A38 to A390. This crosses the Fowey at (28m) **Lostwithiel** (TI), the 13C capital of Cornwall, once represented in Parliament by Joseph Addison. The *Church* has a striking 14C spire, a fine Decorated E window and *font. The medieval *Fowey Bridge* and *Stannary Court*, and the *Guildhall* of 1740, are all interesting. *Restormel Castle* (EH, summer season), high above the river 1½m N, has a circular keep of c 1200 and the ruins of a great hall added a century later.

About 2m beyond Lostwithiel B3269 branches S from A390, passing (after another 3m) the hill-fort of *Castle Dore*, which legend identifies as the palace of King Mark. *Golant*, by the river 1m E, is associated with Tristram and Iseult. The church has good woodwork. 5¼m: **Fowey** (pronounced 'Foy'; TI), a little place at the mouth of the estuary, was once a major seaport. It has a charming square and old houses. The 13–15C church of St Finnbarus has a rich tower, Norman font, good monuments and a wagon roof. Above is the 19C Place House. The ruined *St Catherine's Castle* (EH), ¾m SW, was built by Henry VIII to defend the harbour. Ferries cross the river to *Polruan* and *Bodinnick*. *Hall Walk* (NT), on the N bank of Pont Creek near Bodinnick, has a *view and memorials to the dead of World War II and to Sir Arthur Quiller-Couch ('Q'; 1863–1944), who spent much of his life at Fowey. From Hall Walk the river can be followed to Pont, before heading S to the old church of *Lanteglos*, returning to Fowey via Polruan (3½m in all). Much of the cliff scenery from Polruan E to Polperro (see above), including *Lantic Bay*, *Pencarrow Head* and *Lantivet Bay*, is NT.

At (31m) *St Blazey*, A390 reaches the rather dreary china-clay country. To the N, however, is the wooded *Luxulyan Valley*, rich in ferns and spanned by the Treffry Viaduct (c 1830). S of St Blazey are *Par*, a china-clay and granite shipping port, and *Carlyon Bay*. A390 passes the woodland garden of *Tregrehan* (open) on the way from St Blazey to (36m) **St Austell** (36,600 inhabitants with Fowey), the centre of the china-clay industry whose refuse heaps mar the surrounding district. The church has a good Perpendicular tower embellished with statues, and a Norman font.

Carthew, 2m N, has the Wheal Martyn Museum, about the china-clay industry. The handsome harbour village of *Charlestown*, 1½m SE on A3061, is familiar to TV viewers as the location of 'Poldark' and 'The Onedin Line'. B3273 runs S from St Austell to (5½m) *Mevagissey*, an attractive fishing port with cottages and a fine harbour. The church has a 17C monument with an amusing epitaph. A sideroad continues to (8m) *Gorran Haven*, pretty and unspoilt, and *Dodman Point*, a lovely gorse-covered promontory (400ft; NT). The Cornwall Coast Path leads W to (2½m) *Caerhays Castle* (limited opening of gardens only), a Gothick building of 1808 by John Nash overlooking *Veryan Bay*.

FROM ST AUSTELL TO ST MAWES, 18m. B3287 branches left from A390, the Truro road, 3m W of St Austell. A3078 then branches left from B3287. Lanes on the left lead to (11½m) *Portloe* and (12m) *Veryan*, with its early 19C 'round houses'. Between them on the coast is *Nare Head* (NT). 11½m: *Ruan High Lanes*. At (14m) *Trewithian* the road on the left leads to (18m) *St Anthony-in-Roseland*, with an attractive 12–13C church, via (15½m) the seaside village of *Portscatho*. A3078 continues via (16¼m) *St Just-in-Roseland*, with a lovely churchyard in a cove off the Fal estuary, to (18½m) **St Mawes**, with one of Henry VIII's coastal castles (EH, all year) looking across the Fal estuary to Pendennis Castle. A ferry connects St Mawes with Falmouth (see below).

The road on the right at Ruan High Lanes makes a pleasant alternative route (14¼m) to Falmouth. It crosses the Fal estuary by (4½m) *King Harry Ferry* (cars; toll). On the W bank is *Trelissick Garden* (NT), beyond which a lane leads left to the pretty village of *Feock* (1½m) and the Friends' Meeting House (1709) in the form of a thatched cottage at *Come-to-Good*. 7¼m: the road joins A39 about 4m S of Truro and the route follows the way to Falmouth suggested below.

41m: *Grampound*, on the Fal, has a wide and dignified High St. Once notorious as a 'rotten borough', it was John Hampden's first parliamentary seat (1621). 42½m: *Trewithen* (open), on the left, is a mansion of c 1715 by Thomas Edwards of Greenwich. Its gardens were laid out by George Johnstone in the 1920s, with magnolias, azaleas and rhododendrons. 44m: *Probus* church has a beautiful late Perpendicular tower. The County Demonstration Garden (open) serves an educational purpose in its examples of different garden layouts and explanations of gardening procedures.

49m: **TRURO** (16,300 inhabitants) stands on a branch of the Fal river. Historically important as a market centre and port, it became a cathedral city in the 19C.

TI: Municipal Buildings, Boscawen St. **Bus Station and Railway Station**: Station Rd, W of the centre. **River excursions**: to Falmouth via Malpas.

Natives: the actor Samuel Foote (1720–77) and the missionary Henry Martyn (1781–1812).

The Georgian terraces in Boscawen St. and Lemon St. and the houses in Prince's St. and Trafalgar Row reflect Truro's prosperity in the 18–19C. The *Museum and Art Gallery* has Cornish minerals and antiquities as well as work by the local painter John Opie (1761–1807). The **Cathedral** (1880–1910) was built by J.L. Pearson in the Early English style after the diocese of Cornwall was separated from the diocese of Devon in 1876. It stands largely on the site of Truro's 16C parish church, whose Perpendicular S aisle was incorporated in the new building as an additional S aisle to the choir.

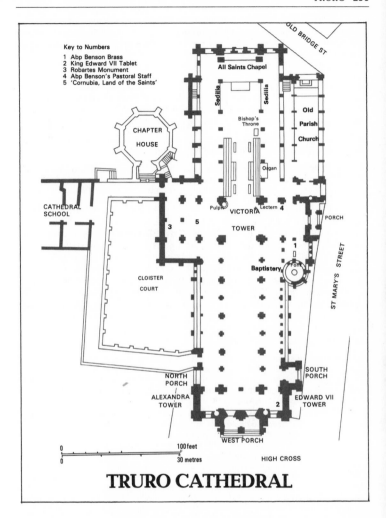

Key to Numbers
1 Abp Benson Brass
2 King Edward VII Tablet
3 Robartes Monument
4 Abp Benson's Pastoral Staff
5 'Cornubia, Land of the Saints'

TRURO CATHEDRAL

The tall circular *Baptistery* is a memorial to Henry Martyn. The N aisle has a tablet to Sir Arthur Quiller-Couch. The panoramic painting by John Miller in the N transept was unveiled in 1980.

A pleasant riverside drive leads S to (1¾m) *Malpas* (pronounced 'Mopus'; ferry), overlooking the meeting of the Truro and Tresilian rivers. A footpath leads to (2½m) *St Clement*, where there is a stone with Latin and Ogham inscriptions S of the 13C church. A lane leads back to (4m) Truro.

FROM TRURO TO FALMOUTH. BY ROAD, 11m. Beyond (4m) *Carnon Downs* A39 crosses Restronguet Creek and climbs a side valley to (5m) *Perranarworthal*. 8¼m: *Penryn* (5100 inhabitants), an old town at the head of Penryn Creek, is built of the granite for which it is famous.

BY RIVER, 11m in about 1hr. The boat descends Truro river to (1¾m) *Malpas* and enters the Fal proper. To the left are the grounds of the mainly 19C *Tregothnan House* (not open). Below is *King Harry Reach*, with a ferry and the woods of Trelissick (see above) on the left. Further down are the wide *Carrick Roads*. *Restronguet* and *Mylor Creeks* are on the right, and beyond *Trefusis Point* the boat enters Falmouth Harbour.

11m: **FALMOUTH** (18,500 inhabitants; TI) overlooks its beautiful sheltered harbour opening off Carrick Roads. It is both a well-equipped port and a popular resort, with beaches on Falmouth Bay, facing S. Its creeks are ideal for boating excursions. Several places on the estuary cultivate oysters.

Ferries (weekdays only in winter) to *St Mawes* and to *Flushing* from Prince of Wales Pier. Daily cruises in summer to *Helford* and to *Truro*.

History. Falmouth was the chief Atlantic packet station from 1689 to 1840, at first serving Corunna and, after 1702, the West Indies. The road from Exeter via Okehampton, Launceston, St Columb and Truro was devised in 1704 for the Falmouth mails.

The most interesting part of the town is by the harbour, where Market St. and Church St. have many old houses. The *Church of King Charles the Martyr*, built by Sir Peter Killigrew in 1662–65, has a fine classical interior and a tablet to Robert Burns's friend and patron, the 14th Earl of Glencairn (d. 1791). Further on, an obelisk of 1738 commemorates the powerful but extinct Killigrew family; the remains of their home, *Arwenack House*, stand opposite. At the end of the peninsula, looking across to St Mawes Castle, is **Pendennis Castle** (EH, all year), built by Henry VIII and taken by the Parliamentarians in 1645 after a five months' siege. A beautiful road leads round the promontory. The *Custom House* is one of several early 19C buildings in the Doric style; near it is the 'King's Pipe', the chimney used for burning contraband tobacco.

The lovely peninsula of *Roseland* (visited on the detour from St Austell to St Mawes above) can be reached by the ferry to St Mawes; motorists must go round by the ferry over King Harry Reach. The ferry trip from Falmouth to *Flushing* (see above) is also recommended. *Mylor* church (1½ NE of Flushing) has Norman details, a good screen and the tallest cross in Cornwall.

The *Lizard* peninsula (Route 31), to the SW, can be reached by unclassified roads passing through or near the villages of (6½m) *Constantine*, (9m) *Gweek*, at the head of the Helford river, and (10½m) *Mawgan*, with a Perpendicular church. To the E of Mawgan is *Trelowarren*, the beautifully wooded estate of the Vyvyans; it includes the Halliggye Fogou (EH, summer season), an underground tunnel of the type unique to Cornwall's Iron Age villages. The 17–19C house, with a Gothick chapel, is now mainly used as an ecumenical centre (limited opening). The Cornwall Coast Path, the walkers' route to the Lizard (c 23km), goes via (3½m) *Rosemullion Head* (NT) and (5m) the sub-tropical *Glendurgan Gardens* (NT) to (6m) *Helford Passage*, where a ferry crosses the river to Helford.

A39 heads S from Truro and A394 branches right after 7m. 66m: **Helston** (10,700 inhabitants; seasonal TI), once one of Cornwall's 'Stannary' towns, is an attractive little place above the Loe valley. The Lizard peninsula (Route 31) is reached from here. The church of 1756–62 is by Thomas Edwards. On 8 May each year crowds are attracted by the Furry Dance (or Floral Dance) in which couples, moving to a tune probably as old as the fête itself, dance along the streets and through the houses and gardens.

At *Wendron*, on B3297 3m NE, part of the Poldark Mine has been reopened as a museum to the Cornish tin-mining industry.

B3304 leads SW from Helston to (3m) the charming village of *Porthleven*, with a considerable harbour. At 1½m the road passes the beautiful grounds of *Penrose* on the bank of *Loe Pool*, which disputes the possession of King Arthur's sword Excalibur with Dozmary Pool on Bodmin Moor (Route 32). The pool is closed to the sea at its SW end by *Loe Bar*.

The strenuous coast walk to (17½m) Penzance leads via (3m) Porthleven, (5m) *Trewavas Head*, the fine bathing beach at (6½m) *Praa Sands* near the ruined *Pengersick Castle*, (10½m) *Cudden Point* and (14m) Marazion (see below). On the E side of Cudden Point is *Prussia Cove*, once a haunt of smugglers.

A394 continues to (69½m) *Breage*, where the church has late 15C mural paintings of St Christopher and a 3C Roman milestone. *Godolphin House* (limited opening), 2¼m NW, has a colonnaded front of 1635 and Tudor work inside. The road follows the curve of Mount's Bay round to (75½m) *Marazion*, deriving its name from 'marghas', the Cornish word for 'market'. Several hundred yards out to sea rises ***St Michael's Mount**, a steep crag of granite and slate resembling a smaller Mont St Michel. It is linked to the shore by a causeway uncovered for 3hrs at low tide, and reached at other times by boat from Marazion or Penzance. The island is NT; the castle that crowns it still belongs to the St Aubyn family but is open to visitors.

Identified with the Roman Ictis, from which Cornish tin was exported, St Michael's Mount became an early centre of Christianity, possibly in the 5C. There was a Celtic monastery here from the 8C, and in 1047 Edward the Confessor established a chapel and placed it under the Benedictine abbey of Mont St Michel in Normandy. The monastery was later absorbed into the castle built by the St Aubyns. Despite considerable alterations, the buildings keep their romantic appearance from the shore. The most interesting features are the 14–15C chapel, the Gothick rococo drawing room formed from the Lady Chapel, and the medieval refectory, now called the Chevy Chase Room because of the hunting scenes on its 17C plaster frieze.

The church of *St Hilary*, 2m E of Marazion, has a Decorated spire and two inscribed stones, one 4C Roman and the other 6–7C.

Beyond Marazion A394 joins A30.

79m: **PENZANCE** ('holy headland'; 19,500 inhabitants) stands on the curve of Mount's Bay. Popular as a resort and a base for excursions in the Land's End district, it still keeps some of the atmosphere of a seaport. The mild climate favours market gardening.

TI: Station Approach. **Bus Station** and **Railway Station**: by Albert Pier beyond the E end of Market Jew St. **Services**: ferries to Scilly Isles by RMV 'Scillonian III'. Helicopter service from the heliport off A30 E of the centre. Skybus from Land's End Airport. Boat trips to St Michael's Mount.

Natives and residents: Sir Humphry Davy (1778–1829), pioneer of electro-chemistry and inventor of the miners' safety lamp, was born here. The poet John Davidson (1857–1909) drowned himself here.

Market Jew St. ('Marghas Yow' or 'Thursday Market') climbs from the railway station and harbour in the E to the former *Market House* (1836), now a bank, with a statue of Sir Humphry Davy outside. Of the several interesting streets leading down towards the sea, Chapel St. has Georgian and Regency buildings, and the eccentric *Egyptian House* of 1830 (NT shop). The first announcement of the English victory at Trafalgar was made from the minstrel gallery of the *Union Hotel*. Off Morrab Rd, to the W, are: the *Library*, with rare Cornish books and prints; *Penlee Park*, with the ancient market cross and a *Museum* of natural history, Cornish antiquities and paintings by the Newlyn school; and *Morrab Gardens*, with subtropical plants.

The Esplanade goes on to (1m) **Newlyn**, a fishing village which gave its name to a school of local artists headed by Stanhope Forbes (1857–1948), responsible for the fittings (1937–41) of *St Peter's Church*. Their work can also be seen in the *Art Gallery*. The road ends at (3m) **Mousehole** (pronounced 'Mowsal'), a picturesque fishing village with the fine Elizabethan Keigwin Arms (no longer an inn). *Paul* church, ½m inland, is the burial place of Dolly Pentreath (d. 1777), usually described as the last person who spoke Cornish. From Mousehole the coast footpath leads to (5½m) *Lamorna Cove*. By B3315 near *Boleigh*, 1½m inland, are the *Tregiffian Burial Chamber* of the 3C BC (EH) and two standing stones and a stone circle, known as the *Pipers* and the *Merry Maidens*. The cliff walk can be continued to (13m) the *Logan Rock* (Route 33).

For other places of interest N and W of Penzance, see Route 33.

31

The Lizard

The Cornish peninsula S of Helston (Route 30) and the Helford river is generally known as the **Lizard**, from the headland at its tip. It stands 200–350ft above sea level, formed largely of serpentine, a greenish rock which can also be seen in the local buildings. In the centre are the breezy *Goonhilly Downs*, where the Cornish heath (Erica vagans) grows. The radio telescope and satellite communications centre make prominent landmarks. The striking cliff scenery and fine beaches of the coastline (much of it NT) are more interesting.

The peninsula is bisected from N to S by A3083, running from Helston past the naval air station at *HMS Seahawk* to (10½m) *Lizard Town*, a straggling village ¾m inland from *Lizard Point*, the southernmost point of England (49° 57′ 32″ N lat.), marked by two powerful lighthouses. B3292 runs from the main road to St Keverne and Coverack on the E coast, and B3296 runs to Mullion on the W coast; unclassified roads reach the smaller villages and coves round the coastline. Walkers will prefer to take at least part of the coastal route of about 24m suggested below, which goes down the W coast to Lizard Point and back up the E coast.

The route leaves *Helston* to the SW and skirts the W side of *Loe Pool*, by the gardens of *Penrose*, to reach the sea at (2½m) *Loe Bar* (Route 30), where the coastguard path heads left. 5½m: The 15C parish church of *Gunwalloe*, with a detached belfry, is beautifully situated in *Church Cove*. Granite boulders have been placed to protect it from further encroachment by the sea. 6½m: At *Poldhu Cove* a monument set up by the Marconi Co. marks the site of the wireless station which in 1901 transmitted the first wireless signal across the Atlantic.

A road runs inland to (1m) *Mullion*, where the Perpendicular church has elaborately carved *bench ends.

The next point on the coast is (6¾m) *Polurrian Cove*, with a good sandy beach. This is followed by (7½m) *Mullion Cove* (NT), a beautiful little fishing harbour with serpentine rocks, caves and a view of *Mullion Island* (NT). The path goes on via *Predannack Head*, *Vellan Head* and *Gew Graze* to (12½m) **Kynance Cove** (NT), with its richly coloured serpentine cliffs, fantastic rock formations and silvery sands. On the W side is *Asparagus Island*, where, when the tide is making, clouds of spray rise from the *Devil's Bellows*. The cave here is called the *Devil's Throat* or *Drawing Room*, while the two on the shore are known as the *Kitchen* and *Parlour*. The route turns inland for (14m) *Lizard Town* (see above) or continues along the coast past *Yellow Carn Cliff, Caerthilian Cove* and *Pistol Meadow*, where the bodies washed ashore from the wreck of the 'Despatch' were buried in 1809, to (14m) *Lizard Point* and its lighthouse (see above).

The coast walk goes on beyond the *Bumble Rock*, the W horn of *Housel Bay*, with the huge cavity known as the *Lion's Den*. Rounding *Bass Point*, it begins to follow the E side of the peninsula. Beyond *Hot Point* it passes *Kilcobben Cove*, with the Lizard lifeboat station. *Landewednack*, with the parish church of Lizard Town, lies inland. The *Dolor Hugo* and other caves on this part of the coast are best explored by boat. 16m: The *Devil's Frying Pan* is another circular hollow like the Lion's Den. 16¼m: *Cadgwith* is a picturesque little fishing village. Beyond the glade of *Poltesco* and (3½m) the broad *Kennack Sands* the walk rounds (21m) *Black Head*, famous for its serpentine, and reaches (22½m) *Coverack*, a charming little place. In the cove beyond *Manacle Point* is (25½m) the dreary *Porthoustock*.

Offshore are the dangerous *Manacle Rocks* and 1m inland is *St Keverne*, with the largest church in W Cornwall. The buff, green and rose-coloured stones in the pillars of its arcade are not local but may have been brought from Brittany. Many victims of shipwrecks are buried in the churchyard.

From the little fishing village of (13m) *Porthallow* or from (14½m) *Gillan*, further N, sideroads lead via (19½m) *Mawgan* (Route 30) to A3083 and (about 24m) *Helston*. The latter route passes (16½m) *Manaccan*, with an interesting church.

A road runs N from Manaccan to (1½m) *Helford*, where a ferry crosses the river to join the Falmouth road at Helford Passage (Route 30).

32

Exeter to Bodmin and Penzance

Directions. Total distance 113m. A more direct way from Exeter to Penzance than Routes 28 and 30 but less interesting, and congested in summer. **Exeter**, see Route 18A. A30 to (23m) **Okehampton** (see Route 29A), (42m) **Launceston** (bypassed), (64m) **Bodmin** (bypassed), (95m) Redruth (bypassed), (98m) Camborne (bypassed) and (113m) **Penzance** (Route 30).

Exeter, see Route 18A. A30 to (23m) **Okehampton**, see Route 29A. 32m: At *Lewtrenchard*, on the left, the writer Sabine Baring-Gould was both squire and rector from 1881 until his death in 1924. Beyond (37m) *Lifton* A30 crosses the Tamar and enters Cornwall.

42m: **Launceston** (6200 inhabitants; TI), a pleasant town once known as Dunheved ('hill-head'), rises between two hills. One is crowned by the cylindrical keep of the ruined Norman *Castle* (EH, all year). George Fox, the Quaker, was imprisoned here in 1656. On the other hill is a public park.

Both command views. The *South Gate* is the only remaining town gate. *St Mary Magdalene's Church*, with a 14C tower, has elaborate carving of 1511–24 on the outside, particularly on the S porch. *St Thomas's* preserves a Norman font. A Norman arch from the Augustinian priory now serves as entrance to the White Hart Hotel. The Georgian *Lawrence House* (NT) in Castle St. is the local history museum. The Kensey is crossed by two fine old bridges, one a footbridge 1m E.

46m: *Polyphant*, to the right of A30, is a small quarrying village which supplied stone for many Cornish churches. 49m: *Altarnun*, again to the right, has a pretty village street and the 15C *church of St Nonna, one of the best in Cornwall. The Norman font and early 16C bench ends are outstanding. There are more good bench ends at *Leaneast*, across the river Inny 2m N.

A30 crosses the wild **Bodmin Moor**, one of the granite masses which punctuate the SW peninsula, but smaller and lower than its eastern neighbour, Dartmoor. The region is dotted with ancient stones, circles and crosses; see Route 30 for those near A38 to the S. At (54m) *Bolventor* A30 passes the Jamaica Inn of Daphne du Maurier's novel. *Dozmary Pool*, about 1½m SE, is sometimes identified with the lake into which Sir Bedivere threw King Arthur's sword Excalibur (cf. Loe Pool, Route 30). About 3m NW of Bolventor rise *Brown Willy* ('Bryn Whelli'; 1377ft), the highest point in Cornwall, and its twin summit, *Rough Tor* (1311ft; NT). 59m: A road leads right to *Blisland*, with a pleasant village green and the *church of St Protus and St Hyacinth, partly Norman, with a 15C tower and an interior richly restored by F.C. Eden and Sir Ninian Comper. There is fine scenery on the moor to the N, in (2m) the valley of the De Lank river, E of the quarries, and near the *Devil's Jump* (3m further).

64m: **Bodmin** (12,100 inhabitants; TI) is the traditional county town of Cornwall, though the county council offices are now in Truro. Its 15C church is the largest medieval church in Cornwall; it has a *font of c 1200, a movable piscina of 1495, interesting woodwork and the remarkable tomb of Prior Vivian (d. 1533).

Lanhydrock (NT), overlooking the Fowey valley 2½m SE, is a 17C house largely rebuilt after a fire in 1881. The exterior is a convincing facsimile but most of the interior is Victorian in atmosphere. The gatehouse and *Long Gallery, with a richly decorated plaster ceiling, survive from the original building. At *Washaway*, 4m NW of Bodmin by A389, is *Pencarrow* (open), a Palladian house of the 1760s by Robert Allanson of York. The rich interior has good furniture and pictures, including family portraits by Reynolds. *Cardinham*, about 4m NE of Bodmin, has a good 15C church, with bench ends, and a Celtic cross.

A30 now enters the china-clay country centred on St Austell to the S (Route 30) and conical white waste dumps are seen on all sides. 67m: *Lanivet* has 6–10C carved and inscribed stones in its churchyard. 69m: *Victoria* (seasonal TI) is 1m N of *Roche*, where a chapel of 1409 is built into an outcrop of granite. *Hensbarrow* (1027ft; view) rises to the S. A30 passes the large Iron Age hill-fort of *Castle-an-Dinas* (703ft) on the right, and reaches (76½m) *Indian Queens*, where the road for Newquay (Route 35) branches to the right. At (77m) *Fraddon* A30 is joined by A39, which bears left after another mile for Truro (Route 30). 79m: *Summercourt* has a traditional fair in September.

95m: **Redruth** became the Cornish mining centre in the 19C, when the tin and copper industries flourished. It is now incorporated with (98m) **Camborne** (46,500 inhabitants together). In Redruth the house of William

Barbara Hepworth's house and studio at St Ives

Murdock (1754–1839), who first exploited gas as a source of light, has been restored as a memorial to him and to Richard Trevithick (1771–1833), the engineer who pioneered the use of high-pressure steam. Trevithick spent much of his life at *Penponds*, SW of Camborne, and was born at *Pool*, between Redruth and Camborne. The *Cornish Engines Museum* (NT) at Pool preserves beam engines used in tin mining.

SW of Redruth is *Carn Brea* (738ft), occupied from Neolithic times to the Middle Ages. At *Gwennap Pit*, a grassy hollow 1¼m SE of Redruth, John Wesley preached to large congregations of miners.

From *Portreath*, a small resort NW of Redruth, B3301 runs SW to (5½m) *Gwithian*, skirting a fine stretch of cliffs owned by NT, including *Godrevy Point*, the E horn of St Ives Bay.

105m: *Hayle* is a small port on the estuary at the head of St Ives Bay, opposite Lelant.

About 1m beyond Hayle A3074 heads round the bay to St Ives. 1m: *Lelant* is a resort, with the mother church of St Ives. 3m: *Carbis Bay*, another resort, lies to the right. The triangular monument on the hill to the left was put up in 1782 by John Knill, mayor of St Ives and a smuggler turned lawyer, who intended it as his tomb. 4½m: **St Ives** (11,000 inhabitants; TI), a resort on one of the most charming bays in England, is known for its connection with artists. The potter Bernard Leach established his workshop here, with Shoji Hamada, in 1920. Ben Nicholson and Dame Barbara Hepworth moved to St Ives in 1939, forming the centre of a group which included the local painter Peter Lanyon (1918–64). Hepworth's house and studio are now a museum of her life and work administered, like the new gallery of modern art, by the Tate Gallery. The 15C church is dedicated to St Ia, an Irish saint believed to have been martyred here in the 5C. It contains good bench ends and a Madonna by Hepworth; there is a 15C cross by the S porch. The conspicuous *Trencrom Hill* (NT; view) lies 3m S. *Towednack*, 3m SW on a lane off the Zennor road, has a plain little church with a 13C chancel arch. There are fine points on the coast SW of St Ives but the road via (4m) *Zennor*, (8m) *Morvah* and (12m) *St Just* to (18m) *Land's End*, all in Route 33, is hilly and not very interesting.

113m: **Penzance**, see Route 30.

33

The Land's End District

Maps: OS Outdoor Tourist map (2½in to 1m).

The SW peninsula of Cornwall leading to **Land's End** is a granite mass, part of the chain which starts with Dartmoor and Bodmin Moor to the E and ends with the Scilly Isles to the SW. It rises from the lowlands connecting St Ives Bay and Mount's Bay in the E to an average height of about 400ft, though some hills exceed 800ft. On the coastline the rocks have been broken and weathered by Atlantic rollers to create, particularly in the S, some of the most dramatic cliff scenery in England. The hinterland abounds in ancient stone monuments. The district is described below in a series of short routes from Penzance (Route 30). St Ives makes an alternative starting-point for excursions through the N.

FROM PENZANCE TO LAND'S END, 10m by A30. Alverton St. leads out of Penzance to A30. 2½m: *Drift*, with a reservoir to the right.

The unclassified road on the right leads to (1½m) *Sancreed*, where the churchyard has two crosses. 1¼m SW is the Iron Age village of *Carn Euny* (EH), occupied from before 400 BC until the end of the Roman period, with the relics of several huts and a *fogou, or underground chamber.

At (3¼m) *Catchall* A30 keeps to the right. Just before the top of Tregonebris Hill, on the right, is a standing stone known as the *Blind Fiddler*, while about ¼m to the left stands *Boscawen-noon*, a stone circle about 75ft in diameter. At (5½m) the village of *Crows-an-Wra* is an old cross. A sideroad leads to the right past *Carn Brea* (657ft; NT), said to enjoy the widest sea view from the mainland of the British Isles. A medieval chapel once stood on the largest of several Neolithic barrows. Further on A30 is joined by B3306 from St Just and beyond (8¾m) *Sennen* it reaches (10m) ***Land's End**.

The westernmost point of England (5° 41' 32"W long.), known to the ancients as Bolerium and in Cornish as Penwith, Land's End is a huge, turf-topped mass of granite, 60ft in height, from which a narrow ridge juts out into the sea. The *view extends 25m W to the Scilly Isles and is bounded on the N by Cape Cornwall and the Brisons rocks. Immediately in front is the *Longships Lighthouse*. To the right (N) and left (S) are the rocks known as the *Irish Lady* and the *Armed Knight*. About 9m SW is the *Wolf Rock Lighthouse*.

FROM PENZANCE TO THE LOGAN ROCK, 9m. A30 goes from Penzance to (3¼m) *Catchall*, where B3283 is followed left. 5¼m: *St Buryan* has a large collegiate church with a tall granite 15C tower and a rood screen. From (8¼m) *Treen* the coast can be reached at the rocky *Penberth Cove*, the headland fort of *Treryn Dinas* and the *Logan Rock* (NT), ¾m S, a huge mass of stone so delicately balanced that it can easily be moved. *Porthcurno*, ¾m W of the Logan Rock, has the open-air Minack Theatre, modelled on a Greek amphitheatre. *Porthcurno Cove* is the main landing station of deep-sea cables. *St Levan*, 1¼m beyond, has a small Early English and Perpendicular church with a screen and bench ends. The coastal walk continues W to (3½m) *Land's End* past some magnificent rock scenery, including *Tol Pedn Penwith* and *Pordenack*.

FROM PENZANCE TO ZENNOR, 7m. The obvious route, by B3311 to the outskirts of St Ives and then SW on B3306, is not very interesting, though at ½m B3311 passes W of the pleasant village of *Gulval*, a market-gardening centre, and at (2½m) *Castle Gate*, near the hill-fort of *Castlean-Dinas*, it gives a splendid view of Mount's Bay. A better route takes the unclassified road which branches left from B3311 at ¼m and follows the Trevaylor valley NW. On the right is (1½m) *Bleu Bridge*, a slab bridge with an inscribed stone, possibly 7C. Beyond (3m) *Newmill* a right turn leads to (4½m) the Iron Age village of *Chysauster (EH, summer season). The best excavated and most expressive site of its kind in SW England, it has four pairs of houses on either side of a main street. To the left of the main road, 1m beyond the turning for Chysauster, is the *Mulfra Quoit* dolmen. A path on the left, just short of (5½m) B3306, leads to the beehive hut at *Bosporthennis*. The bold promontory of *Gurnard's Head* lies ¾m straight ahead from the junction with B3306. The main route turns right, passing a large half-fallen dolmen on the moor to the S. 7m: *Zennor* has a 15C church with a mermaid on one of its bench ends, and the Wayside Museum of local history. D.H. Lawrence completed 'Women in Love' while living here during World War I. St Ives (Route 32) is 4m NE.

FROM PENZANCE TO MORVAH AND ST JUST, 10m. B3312 heads NW from Penzance to (2m) *Madron*, overlooking Mount's Bay, with the mother church of Penzance. There is a ruined baptistery and well 1m N. *Trengwainton Garden* (NT), ¾m SW, also has a view of the bay. An unclassified road heads NW for Morvah. Beyond (4m) *Lanyon Quoit* dolmen (NT) a path leads in ¾m to the *Ding Dong Mine*, almost certainly worked before the Christian era. On the moors to the NW are the *Mên-an-Tol* ('holed stone') and the *Mên Scryfa* ('written stone'). A little further E are the remains of the stone circle called the *Nine Maidens* (1m W of Mulfra, see above). 1m beyond the Lanyon Quoit, a track on the left goes to (1¼) the late Iron Age hill-fort known as *Chûn Castle*, with two concentric walls and a fine dolmen from an earlier date. B3306 goes left to (6m) *Morvah*. *Portheras Cove* is ¾m NW. 7m: *Trewellard* has the *Levant Steam Engine*, the oldest beam engine in Cornwall, worked from 1840 to 1930 and now restored (NT). 10m: **St Just** (4000 inhabitants), once the centre of an important mining area, has a 15C church and an amphitheatre where the old Cornish miracle plays were staged.

About 1¼m W is *Cape Cornwall* (view), with an unusual Bronze Age tomb. *Ballowall Barrow* (EH) lies to its S. Good walkers can follow the coast to (6½m) Land's End.

34

The Isles of Scilly

Maps: OS Outdoor Leisure map (1:25,000 or 2½in to 1m).

An archipelago of about 150 islands, islets and rocks 28m SW of Land's End, the **Scilly Isles** form an outlying part of the granitic mass of Cornwall. Their name (taken from Scilly Isle, one of the smallest of the group) is something of a mystery, and they are no longer exclusively identified with the Cassit-erides, or 'Tin Islands', of Herodotus. According to legend they are the only visible relic of Lyonesse, the land of Arthurian romance, which lies 40 fathoms deep between them and Cornwall. The inummerable passage graves and other *Bronze Age remains give colour to the supposition that the isles were the highlands adjoining the low alluvial plain of Lyonesse. Since 1337 they have belonged to the Duchy of Cornwall, but are admin-istered by their own all-purpose local authority, the Council of the Isles of Scilly.

The climate is very mild (mean winter temperature 8°C, summer 14°C). The permanent population is some 1900, confined to the islands of *St Mary's*, *St Martin's*, *Tresco*, *Bryher* and *St Agnes*. The chief occupations are tourism (from April to October) and the growing of early flowers (from the beginning of December onward) and early potatoes for the mainland market. Some fishing continues. Seals and seabirds abound on the unin-habited islands, and the October migration of both sea and land birds is renowned.

TI: St Mary's. **Transport to the Isles**: The RMV 'Scillonian III' of the Isles of Scilly SS Co. crosses from Penzance Dock to Hugh Town, St Mary's in about 2½hr. Daily sailings from April to mid October, except Sundays, with double sailings on Saturdays and some Wednesdays from mid May to the end of August. Winter service twice weekly. Frequent helicopter service (about 20 min.) by British Airways Helicopters Ltd from Penzance Heliport to St Mary's Airport throughout the year and to Tresco Heliport from April to September inclusive.

Air passenger services from Plymouth, Exeter and Newquay. Connecting services to Channel Islands, Cork, Gatwick and Heathrow.

Charter air passenger service from St Just (Land's End) by Isles of Scilly Skybus Ltd.

Transport between the Isles: Passenger launches connect St Mary's (Quay) with St Agnes, Bryher, Tresco and St Martin's daily from April to October inclusive, weather permitting. A freight launch provides a less frequent service from November to March.

St Mary's, the largest island (2½m by 2m), contains about three-quarters of the population. *Hugh Town*, the capital of the group, lies on the isthmus between the Garrison and the main landmass. It has a pleasant main street and a good museum. The *Garrison* has fortified walls built in 1715–46 (EH) and *Garrison Hill*, with a good view and the *Star Castle* of 1593 (now a hotel). On the W coast are the incomplete 16C fort known as *Harry's Walls* (EH), *Carn Morval* (view), and the Bronze Age burial mound and Roman village at *Bant's Carn* (EH). *McFarlands Down* in the N has a good view. On the E coast are the Bronze Age passage grave and burial mound at *Innisidgen* (EH) and *Porth Hellick Point*, near the best preserved Bronze Age burial site on the islands (EH) and the cliff fort of *Giant's Castle*. In the S are *Old Town Bay*, with the graves of 120 people lost in the wreck of the 'Schiller' in 1875, and *Peninnis Point*, with a lighthouse and a good view. Near the point is a 'logan stone' weighing over 300 tons.

Tresco lies about 1m NW of St Mary's. *Tresco Abbey* has wonderful sub-tropical •gardens (open), with the scanty remains of a Benedictine priory and the Valhalla Museum of figureheads from ships lost on the Scilly rocks. Near the N end of the island beyond *New Grimsby* is the so-called *King Charles's Castle* (EH), in fact probably built by Edward VI. The name of *Cromwell's Castle* (EH) nearby commemorates the fact that the Isles, the last Royalist stronghold, were subdued by Admiral Blake for the Cromwellians. On the N coast is *Piper's Hole*, a narrow shaft running underground for 600ft. The harbour at *Old Grimsby* on the E coast has a 16C gun battery (EH). **Bryher**, W of Tresco, is worth a visit for its rocky coast, especially at *Shipman Head* and *Hell Bay*. **Samson**, Bryher's southern neighbour, is now uninhabited. **St Helen's**, NE of Tresco and uninhabited since the 19C, has the scanty remains of a medieval church and a Celtic monastery, probably connected with St Elidius. The island's name is apparently a corruption of the saint's name. **St Martin's**, NE of Tresco, is known for its beaches. It also abounds in Bronze and Iron Age remains, and has an early navigation mark—the Day Mark of 1685—on *Chapel Down*, at the E tip. **St Agnes**, SW of St Mary's, has some good barrows, a curiously perched boulder called the *Punch Bowl*, and the old sacred well of *Sancta Warna*. On the Downs is an ancient maze, set in pebbles and known as 'Troy Town'. The disused early 18C lighthouse is the second oldest purpose-built lighthouse in the country to survive. Its fire basket is now in Tresco Abbey gardens.

The lighthouse at *Bishop Rock*, some 4m SW of St Agnes (boat trips on calm days only), guards the *Western Rocks* and particularly the *Gilstone Ledge*, where Admiral Sir Cloudesley Shovel's flagship 'Association' foundered in 1707 with the loss of 2000 men, including the admiral. The wreck was rediscovered in 1967. In 1971 treasure from the 'Hollandia', which foundered off *Gunners Rock* in 1743, yielded previously unknown Spanish-American coins and Mexican 'pieces of eight'. Many other wrecked ships have been found in the treacherous waters around the Western Rocks and the *Nor'rard Rocks* (off Bryher's W coast).

35

Penzance to Barnstaple: the North Coast of Cornwall and Devon

Directions. Total distance 117m. An excellent way for tourists who have reached Land's End by the S coast to make the return journey, this route loosely follows the course of A30 and A39. The excursions to the coast (Tintagel, Boscastle, etc.) are worth the extra miles. **Penzance**, see Route 30. A30 to (15m) Camborne and (18m) Redruth, see Route 32. A30, A3075 to (34m) **Newquay**. A392, A3059 to (41m) St Columb Major. A39 to (49m) **Wadebridge** and (60m) Camelford. B3266, B3314, B3263 to (65m) **Tintagel**. B3262 to (68m) **Boscastle**. B3262, A39 to (82½m) Stratton (**Bude**). A39 to (98m) Clovelly Cross (**Clovelly**), (108m) **Bideford** and (117m) **Barnstaple** (Route 26).

Penzance, see Route 30. A30 to (15m) *Camborne* and (18m) *Redruth*, see Route 32. The route follows A30 for a further 5m and then branches left on A3075 for Newquay.

From the same roundabout B3277 leads left to (3m) *St Agnes*. The painter John Opie (1767–1807) was born at the hamlet of *Mithian*, 1½m E. *St Agnes Beacon* (629ft; view) and much of the coastline leading to the popular little bay of *Porthtowan*, 2½m SW, are NT. B3285 continues NE from St Agnes to (7m) **Perranporth**, on Perran Bay. About 1½m N are the remains of the small *Oratory of St Piran*, restored in 1835 after having been buried in *Penhale Sands* for over 700 years. It is believed to have been built over the tomb of St Piran in the 7C. The 11C church with its cross, a little inland, was also engulfed by the sands. About 1½m E of Perranporth is the ancient amphitheatre of *St Piran's Round*.

34m: **Newquay** (20,460 inhabitants) lies on a magnificent coast. The combination of sandy beaches and Atlantic rollers has made it a centre for surfing. The landward end of the promontory ending in *Towan Head* separates Newquay Bay, with its pleasant little harbour and beaches, from Fistral Bay, overlooked by the golf course and Pentire Point.

Trerice (NT), 3m SW via A392 and A3058, is a small, well-preserved manor house of 1571. A good walk leads S and W from Newquay across the Gannel river to (2m) *Crantock*, where the church has a font recarved in 1473, and (4m) *Kelsey Head* (NT). *Holywell Bay*, 1m beyond, lies near the N edge of Penhale Sands (see above). *Cubert*, 1½m S of Crantock, has a curious church in a wild setting above the sands.

FROM NEWQUAY TO PADSTOW, 13m by B3276, a winding, hilly and often narrow road. It leaves Newquay to the N via *Porth*, the original settlement, and hugs the coast along *Watergate Bay*. From (5m) *Mawgan Porth* a sideroad leads up the *Vale of Mawgan* to *St Mawgan* (2m), a lovely village where the 13–15C church has a fine tower, a wealth of woodcarving (1450–1550) and a 14C cross in the churchyard. The nearby manor house of *Lanherne*, with a façade of 1580 and a 10C cross at its gate, is now a nunnery. The rock *scenery at (7½m) *Bedruthan Steps* is particularly impressive in rough weather. B3276 follows the coast to (9m) *Porthcothan Bay* and then turns inland to (11m) *St Merryn*. Sideroads and lanes lead NW to *Trevose Head* (2½m), with a lighthouse and a good view. *Constantine Bay* lies on its W side. *Harlyn Bay*, on the E side, has a cemetery of 400–300 BC with several graves preserved near the museum. 13m: **Padstow** ('Petrock's Stow'; seasonal TI), a decayed port on the Camel estuary, has an attractive cluster of cottages on its quay. The church has an Early English tower, a 15C font and the 17C Prideaux monument. *Prideaux Place* (open), opposite, is a partly

Elizabethan house with a fine embossed plaster ceiling in the Great Chamber. Padstow is known for its Hobby Horse festivities on May Day. A ferry crosses the estuary to Rock (see below). *Stepper Point*, 2½m N (footpath via St George's Well), has a fine view of the coast. A389 leads SE to (7m) Wadebridge (see below) via (3½m) *St Issey*, where the church has a carved reredos of c 1400 in catacleuse stone. The footpath following the derelict railway line along the Camel is shorter and more attractive.

From Newquay A392 passes S of (36m) *St Columb Minor*, with a late Decorated church tower. A3059 branches left, skirting the airport (flights to Heathrow). It joins A39 at (41m) *St Columb Major*, which has a prominent Decorated and Perpendicular church with a crudely carved font of c 1300. *Castle-an-Dinas* (Route 32) lies 2m SE. The high-lying A39, commanding wide views down to the sea, crosses the St Austell–Padstow road at (43½m) *Winnard's Perch*. At 44½m it passes, on the right, the line of standing stones called the *Nine Maidens* and at 46½m a path leads 2m across *St Breock's Downs* to a prehistoric standing stone (EH). On the downs to the N are the *Pawton* dolmen and the inscribed stone of *Nanscow*.

49m: **Wadebridge**, a market town on the Camel estuary, has a bridge dating from 1485, widened several times since. *Egloshayle*, on the opposite bank, has an Early English and Perpendicular church.

FROM WADEBRIDGE TO DELABOLE, 12m by B3314. It runs along the N bank of the estuary and, after 1½m, crosses the river Amble. 2½m: A sideroad leads left to *Rock* (3m), connected with Padstow by ferry, and *Polzeath* (6m), a sandy resort with *Pentire Point* (NT) to the N and *Trebetherick* and *Daymer Bay* to the S. On the *St Enedoc* golf course, between Trebetherick and Rock, is a 15C church recovered from the sand in 1863. Sir John Betjeman (1906–84) is buried here. B3314 continues N, then runs parallel to the coast to (6½m) *St Endellion*, where the church has a shrine carved in catacleuse by the same hand as the St Issey reredos. *Trelights*, to the NW, has *Long Cross Victorian Gardens* (open), laid out in the style of a maze. *Port Isaac*, 2m N of St Endellion, is a delightful fishing village on a little cove. A magnificent stretch of coast (NT and Cornwall North Coast Path) goes W past *Portquin* to (c 6m) Pentire Point. From (8m) *Pendoggett* B3267 leads right to St Teath and Camelford. B3314 passes below *Tregeare Rounds*, an Iron Age fort with three rings of earthworks (view). 12m: *Delabole*, where slate has been quarried for four centuries, lies 2m S of the road from Camelford to Tintagel (see below).

52m: *St Kew Highway*. The village church, over 1m N, has 15C glass and an Ogham stone. 60m: **Camelford** (seasonal TI), once regarded as the site of Camelot, is a dull place. Its mother church, with another inscribed Saxon stone, is at *Lanteglos*, 1½m SW.

A39 climbs to 1000ft, with wide but dreary views towards the highest point in Cornwall, Brown Willy (Route 32).

About 1m short of Camelford B3266 heads left, past the turning on the right for *Slaughterbridge*, the scene of a battle between Britons and Saxons in 823. B3314 and B3263 lead towards the coast. 63½m: *Trewarmett* lies inland of *Trebarwith Strand*, where Gull Rock rises out of the fine bay.

65m: **Tintagel** is deservedly one of the most famous places in Cornwall. The little village (once called Trevena) is now horribly commercialised, though the *Old Post Office* (NT), a 14C building, deserves a visit. Even the crowds of summer visitors cannot destroy the grandeur of *Tintagel Head, pronounced 'Tintadgill', a promontory connected to the mainland by a rocky neck. The scanty remains of the *Castle* (EH, all year plus Mondays in winter), perilously straddling mainland and promontory, have only slight architectural interest but complete the romantic charm of the scene. Early chroniclers and later poets have conspired to accept it as Arthur's birth-place. The castle was a stronghold of the Earls of Cornwall from c 1150 and the keep on the mainland dates from c 1236–72, but excavations have revealed traces of a Celtic monastery occupied from c 500 to c 850. A steep railed path mounts to the summit, with the remains of a small 13C chapel (perhaps incorporating some Saxon work), a freshwater spring and a natural cavern. The *view from the headland takes in the wild and rocky shore from Trevose Head in the S to Hartland Point in the N.

The *Parish Church*, dedicated to St Materiana and St Marcelliana, on the cliffs W of the village has a curious Norman font and a stone altar in the little Lady Chapel; the N wall of the nave and chancel may be Saxon. *Bossiney*, adjoining the village to the N, had Sir Francis Drake as its MP. Just to the N is *Rocky Valley*, leading left to the sea and right to *St Nectan's Kieve*, a pretty waterfall.

68m: **Boscastle** has a little *harbour (NT), now disused, flanked by steep cliffs. The name comes from the vanished Bottreaux Castle.

The magnificent walk along the coast to the N (much of it NT) goes to (5½m) *Crackington Haven* via (1m) *Pentargon Bay*, with its waterfall, and (1½m) *Beeny Cliff*, both associated with the poetry of Thomas Hardy. He met his future wife, Emma Gifford, in 1870 at *St Juliot*, 2½m E of Boscastle in the valley of the Valency river, when he was restoring the little church.

B3263 continues NE from Boscastle to rejoin A39. 78m: At *Poundstock*, W of A39, the church and 14C Guildhall make an attractive group. The Elizabethan Penfound Manor (not open) has origins in a manor of Edith, Edward the Confessor's wife. 81½m: The road divides. A39 continues straight ahead for (82½m) *Stratton*, where the fine Perpendicular church contains the tomb of Sir John Arundell (1561).

The Parliamentarians were defeated in 1643 at *Stamford Hill*, just to the NW. *Launcells*, 1m E, has a church with 15C woodwork and tiles, Norman font and Gothick pulpit.

From the road junction A3073 heads left to (82½m) **Bude** (6800 inhabitants with Stratton; TI), a resort with magnificent coastal scenery to both N and S. *Bude Haven* is protected by a breakwater ending in the *Chapel Rock*. *Compass Point*, S of the town, and *Efford Beacon*, SW, have good views.

A pleasant walk leads S along the coast to (4m) *Widemouth Bay* via (1½m) *Upton*.
  Morwenstow, where the eccentric poet R.S. Hawker was vicar from 1834 to 1875, lies on the coast about 8m N of Bude. It is reached by following the coast past *Menachurch Point* to (4½m) the *Duck Pool* at the mouth of the *Coombe Valley* (see below). The route then continues along the coast past (1m) the *Lower* and (1½m) *Higher Sharpnose Point* or turns inland for the road. Morwenstow church has an early Norman font and Norman arches with zigzag moulding. There is rhymed inscription over the door of Hawker's vicarage. *Tonacombe* (not open), a Tudor house just to the S, is Eustace Leigh's home in Kingsley's 'Westward Ho!' Good walkers can continue N to (7m) *Hartland Quay* and (9m) *Hartland Point* (see below). From Duck Pool, on the way to Morwenstow, the *Coombe Valley* leads to (3½m) Kilkhampton (see below), passing the site of Sir Richard Grenville's mansion (NT) and *Stowe Wood*.

FROM BUDE TO EXETER, 50m. A3072 runs E, crossing A39 at (2m) Stratton (see above). Further on it crosses the Tamar and the disused Bude Canal (1825), with inclined planes instead of locks, and enters Devon. 9m: *Holsworthy*, at the junction with A388 from Launceston to Bideford, has a massive Perpendicular church tower. 11m: *Stapledon*, on the left, was the birthplace of Walter de Stapledon (1261–1326), founder of Exeter College, Oxford. 14m: Sideroads lead N to *Thornbury* (3m) with the Devon Museum of Mechanical Music. 22m: *Hatherleigh* stands on the river at the junction with A386 from Okehampton to Torrington. The church of *Northlew*, 4½m SW, has

16C woodwork. B3216 rejoins A3072, which crosses the Okement 5m N of Okehampton. 28½m: *Sampford Courtenay*, a charming village, has a Perpendicular church. The Western Rising of 1549 against the Reformation began here. A3072 crosses the Taw, bypassing *North Tawton*, and joins A377 at (38m) *Copplestone*. For the rest of the way, via (42m) *Crediton* to (50m) *Exeter*, see Route 18A.

A39 leads N from Stratton. 87m: **Kilkhampton** church has a Norman S doorway and *bench ends. At 91m the road enters Devon. At (98m) *Clovelly Cross*, with the site of an Iron Age fort, B3237 goes left to **Clovelly**, a village whose picturesque charms have made it overwhelmingly popular.

It lies in a narrow rift between wooded cliffs with sweeping views of Barnstaple or Bideford Bay. The main street, far too steep for cars, descends in steps and stages past whitewashed cottages to the little cove and pier (1587). The lovely *Hobby Drive* extends SE. To the NW are the grounds of *Clovelly Court*, whose main beauty spot is *Gallantry Bower* (about 1¼m), rising sheer from the sea and giving a fine view. The rocky cove of *Mouth Mill* lies ½m beyond. The way back passes the surviving 14C wing of Clovelly Court. The *Church*, near B3237 and the visitors' car park, has Cary and Hamlyn monuments and a memorial to Charles Kingsley, who spent his boyhood at the rectory.

The road from Clovelly Cross leads W for (4m) the village of *Hartland* and (5½m) *Stoke*, where the large 14C church has a striking rood screen, font and roof, and the coast at the hamlet of (6½m) *Hartland Quay*, with contorted slate rocks. Just over ½m S is the waterfall at *Speke's Mill Mouth*. The splendid *Hartland Point*, 4½m N, is the NW tip of Devon. *Hartland Abbey* (limited opening) is a house with 18C alterations, a shrub garden and a fine woodland walk to the cliffs.

A39 continues E, past the entrance to Hobby Drive (see above), a lovely alternative approach to Clovelly. From (100m) *Buck's Cross* a lane leads down to the hamlet of *Buck's Mill* (1m). 104½m: B3236 leads left to (3m) *Westward Ho!* (see below) through *Abbotsham*, where the small 13C church has a Norman font and good bench ends.

108m: **Bideford** (pronounced 'Biddyford'; 12,200 inhabitants; TI) stands on two hills rising from the Torridge. Still a working port, it enjoyed its heyday in the 16C when the Grenvilles obtained the town charter (1573) and Bideford men made up the crew of the 'Revenge' on the Azores expedition. This era was celebrated in Kingsley's 'Westward Ho!' (1855), partly written at Bideford. The *Bridge* of 24 arches across the Torridge is medieval, but widened since then. The *Church*, rebuilt in 1864, keeps its Norman font and a monument to Sir Thomas Graynfyldd (d. 1513). The quay and Bridgeland Rd have merchants' houses of c 1690. Facing the quay is a statue of Kingsley; eight Spanish cannon stand in the nearby park. The composer Richard Mudge (1718–63) was born at Bideford.

Lundy (about 40 inhabitants) is a granite island 3m long and ¼–¾m broad in the Bristol Channel, 12m off Hartland Point. Owned by NT and administered by the Landmark Trust, it is served by steamers from (25m) Bideford all year round and from (23m) Ilfracombe (Route 26) in the summer. It has curious rock formations and is the breeding place of innumerable puffin, etc. The island remained a nest of pirates down to the reign of Queen Anne; the ruined *Marisco Castle* near the quay was the stronghold of one such ruling family. The *Shutter Rock*, off the SW end, so-called because it is believed that it would exactly fill the rifted opening of the adjacent *Devil's Lime Kiln*, was the scene of the wreck of the 'Santa Catharina' in Kingsley's 'Westward Ho!' The 19C buildings include a church, an inn and three lighthouses.

A386 leads N from the quay via (1½m) *Northam* to (3m) *Appledore*, a quaint little port still with shipyards, or to (3m) **Westward Ho!**, a resort named after Kingsley's novel. The Royal North Devon Golf Course lies to the N, separated from the sea by the curious *Pebble Ridge*. Kipling spent his unhappy schooldays here.

To the S, A386 follows the Torridge. General Monk (1608–70) was baptised at the Norman font in the church of (2m) *Landcross*. 4m: *Weare Giffard*, a former port on the opposite bank of the river, has an interesting church and 15C manor house. 7m: **Great Torrington** (4100 inhabitants), with some good Georgian houses, stands above the river. *Rosemoor Garden* (open), belonging to the Royal Horticultural Society, lies ¾m S of the centre on B3220. *Merton*, 6m SE on A386, was the birthplace of Walter de Merton, founder of the Oxford college; it is also associated with Henry Williamson's 'Tarka the Otter' (1927).

There are several churches worth visiting in the lonely country SW of Bideford, notably at *West Putford* (11½m) and *Sutcombe* (16½m).

A39 crosses Bideford bridge and follows the river N, past *Tapeley Park* (open), home of the Christie family of Glyndebourne, a much altered 18C house with Italian plaster ceilings and an Italian terraced garden. 111m: *Instow*, facing Appledore at the meeting of the Torridge and the Taw, has wide sands at low water. 117m: **Barnstaple**, see Route 26.

EASTERN ENGLAND

Eastern England is roughly defined to its W by the course of the A1 as it connects London and the South Yorkshire border, and more exactly to its S by the Thames estuary. Its long seaboard, flat for the most part and without deep-water harbours, stretches from the Thames up past the Wash to the Humber in the N. Inside these boundaries lie six counties, starting with Essex in the S and continuing up the coast with Suffolk and Norfolk, the true heart of what is traditionally called East Anglia. To their W lies Cambridgeshire, enlarged to swallow up the former Huntingdonshire and to reach as far as Peterborough. Above the Wash is Lincolnshire, still one of the largest and most varied English counties even after administrative changes gave its northern tip to an unhappy new creation, Humberside.

The region has its own distinct character. Historically, the coastline gave access to the seas of northern Europe and the ports of the Netherlands. Coastal villages became fishing centres, while the hinterland grew fat on the Flemish wool trade. Eastern England grew into a place of affluent small towns, rather than great cities or great estates, and these communities maintained a sturdy independence in religion and politics. Once the home of Queen Boudicca's Iceni, as well as the breeding ground of Kett's rebellion and the Pilgrimage of Grace, Eastern England became in the 17C a centre for radical dissent. Oliver Cromwell was a native of Huntingdonshire, while the Eastern Counties Association—formed of Essex, Suffolk and Norfolk—was a stronghold of the Parliamentary cause. Boston in Lincolnshire, connected with the Pilgrim Fathers, was only one of many towns to give its name to the map of New England.

Now that fishing has declined in the face of foreign competition and wool is no longer a staple, Eastern England is still mainly rural and agricultural. A visitor's impression of Essex in 1594 as 'fatte, fruteful, and full of profitable things' could still apply not only to that county but to most of its neighbours as well. In the S, to be sure, the London suburbs have marched into Essex. Felixstowe on the Suffolk coast flourishes as a container port, and Humberside to the N is largely industrial. In the W Peterborough continues to grow at a rate its authorities assure us is planned. But despite these developments, Eastern England still lacks major industrial or even commercial centres: even Norwich, traditionally its largest city, stands apart from the great traffic routes of England.

On the whole, Eastern England has suffered the same happy neglect from tourists as well as from industrialists and planners. Because it is not on the way to anywhere, it does not lend itself to inclusion in those brisk circuits by which foreign visitors review the pleasures of England: they proceed W from London to Oxford, Stratford-upon-Avon and Bath, or N to York and Durham. Perhaps because of its unjustified reputation for being merely a flat, wet place, Eastern England is sometimes ignored even by more leisurely travellers. It is symptomatic that Cambridge, the most obvious tourist attraction in the area, has never been able to rival Oxford in popularity.

This is not to say that Eastern England does not reward the visitor. Cambridge apart, it has much to offer in a conveniently small compass. In Norwich it has preserved a true regional capital of great antiquity; in Lincoln and Colchester it has two major Roman settlements that continued to flourish in later periods. The great Saxon monastic foundations and their

Norman successors have left major landmarks at Ely and Peterborough. These centres are connected by a network of towns and villages which together can boast perhaps the richest array of parish churches in any English region. They stand amid a landscape more varied than the popular image of the region admits—a landscape that has left its imprint on the history of English painting in the work of Constable, Gainsborough and the Norwich School.

If Eastern England seems something of a quiet corner, a place separate as well as distinct from the rest of the country, then this is no recent accident but largely the result of its natural situation. Its southern boundary, the Thames estuary, was once enforced by the dense Essex forests of which Epping Forest is the only surviving reminder. W and N lay the Lea marshes, now so thoroughly absorbed into the outskirts of London that the traveller is hardly aware of their existence. The western boundary dividing the region from the Midlands, now prosaically defined by the course of the A1, was in former times marked by the discouraging barrier of the Fens.

This flat marshland—it is only occasionally more than 20ft above sea level—stretches N from near Cambridge and Peterborough up to the Wash and continues into that part of Lincolnshire aptly named Holland. Its inland reaches are peat fen, progressively reclaimed since the Duke of Bedford called in the Dutch engineer Cornelius Vermuyden in the 17C. High-banked roads follow mathematically straight irrigation canals and rivers through a bleak landscape where the dark earth is fertile for bulbs, vegetables and grain. Near the coast the Fens become saltmarsh, made by the silting up of great river estuaries. Here the work of reclamation may date back to the Romans and had certainly been undertaken before the Norman Conquest. The tussocky grass, almost devoid of trees, makes good grazing land.

Low-lying, bounded on one side by the Fens and on the other by a sea that continually erodes its coastline, Eastern England has at its core a long outcrop of chalk running NE in modest continuation of the Chilterns in central England. Rising sharply out of the Fens in the W, it tilts down towards the coast. Nowhere flat, it is never hilly—rising above 400ft at only a few points in Suffolk and not reaching even 300ft in Norfolk. Yet it provides several distinct types of good farmland and gently rolling scenery: the Gog Magog Hills in Cambridgeshire, the open heath country of Breckland around Thetford and the fertile uplands of Norfolk. N of the Wash, it resumes in the more dramatic landscape of the Lincolnshire Wolds and continues beyond the Humber.

This varied scenery offers much to cheer the eye of both the farmer and the traveller, but it leaves the region poor in one striking respect. Eastern England has no building stone. Chalk—or clunch, as it is called when quarried for building—is too soft to withstand the weather for long. Indeed, it is too soft to wear well even indoors, as the condition of the Lady Chapel at Ely Cathedral bears heartbreaking witness. Proper stone to grace the cathedrals and churches, the Norfolk country houses and the Cambridge colleges, had to be imported. So Barnack limestone, from near Stamford, was ferried by barge down the rivers and through the Fens.

For humbler, everyday purposes the region has had to make do with local alternatives, which combine to create the characteristic appearance of its townscapes and parish churches. Flint, of course, is the oldest. It was being quarried with highly industrialised efficiency at Grime's Graves in Norfolk from about 2100 BC, and was still being knapped (or chipped into usable shape) at nearby Brandon within living memory. The round flint church towers, usually built in the 10C or 11C, are particularly distinctive: there are 114 in Norfolk, 41 in Suffolk and 8 in Essex, making 168 out of the total 180 in England as a whole. Their simple, functional air contrasts sharply with the local style of flushwork, where flint is used in combination with dressed stone to create decorative patterns. It can be seen on the Suffolk churches of Lavenham and Long Melford, as well as on the civic buildings of Norwich and King's Lynn.

Thatching makes a durable roof from reed or grass. There are about 50 thatched churches in Norfolk and about 20 in Suffolk, in addition to the thousands of houses where thatch makes a pleasant contrast with walls brightly painted in orange, yellow or pink. Timber from the Essex forests created the characteristic weatherboarding throughout the county. Further N, in Suffolk and Norfolk, it enriched the domestic architecture of towns like Lavenham and Long Melford, and was carved into the magnificent angel roofs which are the glory of so many churches. Brick, too, was being used from a very early date—at Coggleshall in Essex, for example, and Little Wenham Hall in Suffolk—and could create impressively elaborate effects at Layer Marney, Oxburgh and Tattershall. In the 19C Fletton, now a suburb of Peterborough, gave its name to one of the most famous and widely used English bricks. In Cambridgeshire and Suffolk the local brick is a yellowish white, while in Norfolk it is a warm red that contrasts cheerfully with the ubiquitous grey flint. Such modest combinations of local material, like the gentle variety of the landscape, are typical of a region that makes up in quiet charm what it may lack in the dramatic or the sublime.

36

London to Cambridge and Peterborough

Directions. Total distance 88m. The fast road to Cambridge is M11; see Route 41 for another way, via Bishop's Stortford. For A1 to Peterborough, see Route 60A. A10 to (20m) Hoddesdon (bypassed). A1170 to (24m) **Ware**. A1170, A10 to (41m) Royston. A10 to (54m) **Cambridge** (Route 37). A604 to (70m) **Huntingdon** (bypassed). A14, A1 to (83m) Norman Cross. A15 to (88m) **Peterborough**.

A10 goes N from London, crossing the North Circular Rd at (7m) *Edmonton* and M25 at (12m) *Waltham Cross*, both described in 'Blue Guide London'. 20m: *Hoddesdon* was an important stage on the coach route. Its High St. keeps some spacious houses and inns, including the Golden Lion (c 1600), with good timbering. John Loudon Macadam lived here in 1825–36. To the E, astride the river Lea, is the *Lee [sic] Valley Regional Park*, 6500 acres salvaged from the derelict land and gravel workings of 'the backyard of London'. *Rye House*, where an abortive plot to kill Charles II and his brother James was hatched in 1683, stood in the area of the park, 1m NE of Hoddesdon. Only its late 15C gatehouse survives.

B1197 leads NW to (4m) Hertford, described below, via (2m) *Hertford Heath*. *Hailey-bury College*, a public school founded in 1862, occupies the buildings (by Wilkins) of the college established by the East India Company in 1805. Clement Attlee was a pupil here.

A10 continues N, passing between Ware and Hertford on a high and windy bridge across the valley.

The main route takes A1170 to (22½m) *Great Amwell*, on the right. Its church has a Norman apse. A monument of 1800 (by Robert Mylne) to its creator, Sir Hugh Myddleton, stands in a romantic setting beside one of the springs of the New River. 24m: **Ware** (14,200 inhabitants) has reverted to its old character since the bypass opened. In the High St. is the *Priory* (Council Office), the remains of a 15C Franciscan foundation, with 17–18C additions. The Lea is lined with pleasant houses. The over-restored church has a tablet to the vicar Charles Chauncey, who became President of Harvard in 1654. Off East St. in *Bluecoat Yard* are the old Bluecoat School buildings; the original manor house is 15C with 16–17C alterations. The row of cottages (1698) was used until 1761 for the younger boys of Christ's Hospital (see below) and their 'nurses'. Among the fine 17–18C industrial buildings are Canons Maltings and Albany Corn Stores. The grammar school occupies *Amwell House* (c 1730), originally the home of the Quaker poet John Scott; his 'Grotto' (limited opening) is in Scott's Rd. Ware was the limit of John Gilpin's unwilling ride.

B1004 leads NE to (4m) *Widford*, with Blakesware Park, the 'Blakesmoor' of Lamb's 'Essays'. 3m further N is the long Georgian street of *Much Hadham*, for 900 years a manor of the Bishops of London, with a partly 15C 'palace' and 16–18C houses. At *Perry Green*, c 1m SE of Much Hadham, the former studio of the sculptor Henry Moore is open by appointment; it stands amid an *open-air exhibition of his work.

About 3m W of Ware via A119, and now almost joined to it, is **Hertford** (pronounced 'Hartford'; 21,400 inhabitants; TI), an old county town on the Lea, with a *Shire Hall* (1769) by James Adam and some fine buildings in Fore St. The scanty remains of the *Castle*, where King John of France was held in 1359, include a Norman motte and a gatehouse of 1461–65, 'gothicised' in 1787. On the Ware road are the buildings used by *Christ's Hospital School* until it moved to Horsham in 1985. Beyond the gateway of 1695 is (left) the original girls' school, a long building of 1778. Coloured figures of boys (1721) and girls adorn the street front, and another boy (from the old school at Ware) the School Hall entrance. The bust of Treasurer Lockington (c 1716) is from a demolished London church.

Bengeo, in a secluded site on the N bank of the Lea, has a small apsidal Norman church.

A414 goes SE from Hertford, rising above the Lea valley. An alternative road, B158, passes below the *County Hall* and keeps nearer the river. 2m: *Hertingfordbury* is a pretty village with a church containing Cowper monuments and one to Anne (d. 1622), wife of Lord Baltimore, founder of Maryland. 7½m: *Hatfield*, see Route 60A.

A10 continues N of Ware. Beyond (26m) *Wadesmill* a roadside obelisk commemorates Thomas Clarkson (1760–1846), who at this spot in 1785 resolved to devote his life to the abolition of slavery. 27m: *High Cross* church, by Salvin (1846), has a surprising W window of 1893. At 28½m a sideroad leads right to (¾m) *Standon* church, with an impressive W porch and detached tower. The chancel is raised above the nave under a fine arch (restored in the 19C). The *brasses include one of a merchant, John Field (d. 1474). Near (30m) *Puckeridge* A10 swings left.

An alternative route from Puckeridge (B1368; 1m shorter) runs via: (32m) *Braughing*, an important Roman road junction; (34m) *Little Hormead* (left), where the church has 12C *ironwork on its N door; (38m) *Barkway* and (40m) *Barley*, where the inn sign spans the roadway. At 49m B1368 joins A10 S of the junction with M11 and Cambridge (Route 37).

34m: *Buntingford* has a brick church of 1614–26 and a long street of 17–18C houses, notably Ward's Hospital, an almshouse founded in 1684 by Bishop Seth Ward of Salisbury, a native. At (41m) *Royston* (11,800 inhabitants), a dull town, A10 quits the line of Ermine Street.

Ermine Street continues N as A14 to (21m) *Huntingdon*. 6m: *Arrington* adjoins the park of *Wimpole Hall* (NT), Cambridgeshire's most important country house.

Wimpole is impressive for both its size and the contributions made by several generations of architects and gardeners. The park was landscaped by Bridgeman, Capability Brown and Humphry Repton; its sham ruin (1768) is by Sanderson Miller.

Sir John Soane's Yellow Drawing Room at Wimpole Hall

The S entrance avenue over 2m long, laid waste by Dutch Elm disease, has been replanted with limes. Apart from the unfortunate 19C stables, the house is restrained. The central block was begun c 1640 for Sir Thomas Chicheley, expanded later in the century and refronted by Henry Flitcroft in 1742–45. The wings were added by James Gibbs in 1719–21. Gibbs's library and chapel (with trompe l'oeil paintings by Sir James Thornhill) and Sir John Soane's *yellow drawing room and bath house (added in the 1790s) are outstanding.

The poet Matthew Prior died here in 1721 while visiting his patron, Edward Harley, Earl of Oxford. The last private owner was Mrs Elsie Bambridge, Rudyard Kipling's daughter.

The nearby parish *Church*, rebuilt by Flitcroft in 1749, has an array of monuments to the Chicheley and Hardwicke families. *Wimpole Home Farm* (NT, separate fee), built by Soane in 1794, has a Great Barn, which now houses a display of farming equipment. Rare breeds of livestock can be seen in the paddock and grounds.

Papworth Everard, 7½m further N on A14, has a famous hospital and a 'village settlement' known for its pioneering work in the training and employment of the disabled.

A10 bears NE and enters Cambridgeshire. 44m: *Melbourn* has a 13C church with an early 16C rood screen. 49m: *Harston* has an imposing flint church. 50m: *Hauxton*, a pretty village, has a church with a Norman nave and chancel, and a 13C painting of St Thomas Becket.

A10 crosses M11 and passes through (52m) *Trumpington* on the way into (54m) **Cambridge**, Route 37.

The Huntingdon road heads NW out of Cambridge, past Girton College, and becomes A604, following the line of the Roman Via Devana. 64m: *Fenstanton* has a little 17C lock-up on the green. The church has a monument to Capability Brown, who lived here from 1767 until his death in 1783.

Shortly beyond Fenstanton A1096 leads to (2m) **St Ives** (12,300 inhabitants), which claims as its founder St Ivo, a Persian missionary bishop of the 6C. On the old bridge spanning the Ouse is a 15C chapel, partly rebuilt in 1689. Cromwell, who lived here for five years, is remembered by a statue in the market place. *All Saints*, where Laurence Sterne held his first curacy, is a good 15C church. The *Norris Museum* nearby has an interesting local collection. There is charming scenery on the Great Ouse from St Ives to Huntingdon, particularly at the pretty village of *Hemingford Grey* and the 17C *Houghton Mill* (NT), with working machinery. The manor at Hemingford Grey (open by appointment), built c 1130, is supposedly the oldest continuously inhabited house in the country. The author Lucy Boston wrote about it as 'Green Knowe'.

68m: *Godmanchester* was a Roman settlement on Ermine Street. The large 13C church, built mainly of cobbles, has a 17C stone tower, a 13C mass dial and 15C misericords. The medieval Causeway has excellent houses and there is a Chinese Bridge (1827) leading to islands in the river. Island Hall (limited opening) is an 18C house. The 14C *bridge over the Great Ouse was built simultaneously from both banks, reputedly without consultation, which accounts for its misalignment in the centre. **Huntingdon** (17,500 inhabitants with Godmanchester; TI), on the N bank, is the former county town of Huntingdonshire and Cromwell's birthplace. The *Cromwell Museum*, in the former grammar school which he and Samuel Pepys attended, incorporates the W end of a 12C Hospital of St John. Almost opposite is the *George Hotel*, whose courtyard is used for open-air performances of Shakespeare in summer. To the NW the High St. passes *Cromwell House*, incorporating the house in Cromwell was born. In the other direction the street leads past the house where William Cowper lived in 1765–67 to *St Mary*, with a Perpendicular tower rebuilt in 1620.

George St. leads SW past the station to *Hinchingbrooke House* (now a school but sometimes open). Originally an Augustinian nunnery, it was turned into a dwelling after the Reformation by Cromwell's ancestors and expanded again in the late 17C. Its charm survived 19C restoration by Blore. Near the roundabout at *Brampton*, 1m beyond, is Samuel Pepys's family home (open by written appointment).

Ramsey (11800 inhabitants), 11m NE of Huntingdon, has a partly Norman church and the ruined late 14C gatehouse (NT) of an important Benedictine abbey founded in 969. The 13C Lady Chapel is now part of the grammar school.

From Huntingdon to *Thrapston*, see Route 60B; to *Ely* via *Sutton*, see Route 46B.

A14 leads NW from Huntingdon past the *Stukeley* villages, with their airfield, to join A1 at 76m. See Route 60A for the stretch of road from here to (83m) *Norman Cross*, where A15 is followed to the right. 84m: *Yaxley*, a pretty village with timbered buildings and brick and tile cottages, has a church with a tall Perpendicular steeple, medieval wall paintings and a 15C chancel screen. 87m: *Fletton*, known for the pale bricks made here since the 1880s, is an untidy suburb. Its church has Saxon *carving, perhaps from the monastery at Peterborough.

88m: **PETERBOROUGH**, an old city known to the Saxons as Medesham-stede, grew up round a great monastery founded c 650 and has been a bishop's see since the Reformation. It owed its 19C development to railway workshops and Fletton bricks. 'Planned expansion', dramatically changing its character, has raised the population to 155,000.

TI: 45 Bridge St. **Bus Station**: Queensgate. **Railway Station**: Bourges Boulevard. **Theatre**: Key Theatre, Embankment Rd. **Annual Event**: East of England Show (agricultural) in July.

Bridge St. leads from the Nene Bridge (1933) to the market place, passing the *Town Hall* (1929–33; Berry Webber). In Priestgate, opposite, are some good Georgian houses and a *Museum* with Roman remains, objects found in Whittlesey Mere and *model ships carved in bone by French prisoners at Norman Cross (see above and Route 60A). From the market place, with 17C *Guildhall*, Cowgate leads W past the Perpendicular church of *St John Baptist* (1401–07). Queensgate, N of Cowgate, has the modern shopping centre (1982).

On the other side of the square the *Western Foregate* (late 12C but much altered) leads into the *Minster Close*, in front of the W façade of the cathedral. The 13C *King's Lodging* is to the right. To the left, the chancel of the late Decorated *Becket Chapel* (c 1370) is now the song-school. On the right (S) of the close is the *Abbot's Gateway* (c 1302), leading to the *Bishop's Palace*. The figures are probably Edward I, Abbot Godfrey of Croyland and his prior. *Abbot Kirkton's Gateway* (1505), to the left, led to the Abbot's Park.

The *Cathedral* belongs to the splendid series of Fenland monasteries, originally Saxon but rebuilt after the Conquest. It is one of England's most important Norman buildings.

Founded by Peada, sub-king of Mercia (d. 656), the first monastery and its church were sacked by the Danes in 870 but rebuilt in the 10C. This second church was burned down in 1116. The present building was begun the following year and substantially completed by 1199. All this Norman work survives except for the central tower, replaced in the 14C and conserved by J.L. Pearson in 1883–86. Indeed, apart from its rough handling by Cromwell's troops, Peterborough has been unusually lucky in its later history and preserves a remarkably complete Norman church.

The visitor will first be struck by the grand exception, the W façade. Really a vast porch of three tall bays masking the original front, it was built c 1200–10; confusion

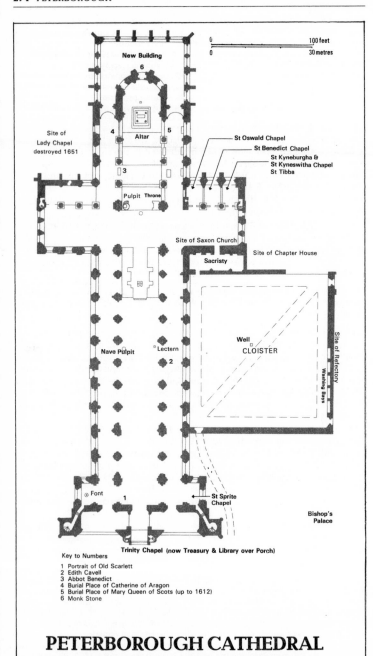

New Building

6

4   5

Site of
Lady Chapel
destroyed 1651

Altar

3

St Oswald Chapel

St Benedict Chapel

St Kyneburgha &
St Kyneswitha Chapel
St Tibba

Pulpit   Throne

Site of Saxon Church

Site of Chapter House

Sacristy

Well
CLOISTER

Site of Refectory

Nave Pulpit   Lectern

2

Washing Bays

Font

1

St Sprite
Chapel

Bishop's
Palace

Trinity Chapel (now Treasury & Library over Porch)

Key to Numbers

1 Portrait of Old Scarlett
2 Edith Cavell
3 Abbot Benedict
4 Burial Place of Catherine of Aragon
5 Burial Place of Mary Queen of Scots (up to 1612)
6 Monk Stone

0   100 feet
0   30 metres

PETERBOROUGH CATHEDRAL

was added to the richness of its effect by the Perpendicular central entrance. The *Nave keeps the forthright simplicity of the original conception, emphasised by the lack of monuments or stained glass and the uninterrupted view to the rounded apse at the E end. The painted wooden ceiling (c 1220 but repainted c 1750 and 1834) is a unique survival. To the N of the W door is an 18C copy of a naive portrait of 'Old Scarlett' (d. 1594), who 'interd two queenes within this place' (see below). On the sixth pier in the S nave a tablet remembers Nurse Edith Cavell, who went to school in Peterborough.

In the wall of the S Transept is a Saxon sculpture, probably depicting a bishop and a king (c 800), discovered in the foundations of the early Saxon church, which can be seen beneath. Though restored, the timber ceilings of both transepts are the original Norman ones.

The *Sanctuary is the oldest part of the church, though its wooden roof is Perpendicular except over the apse, where the original flat roof (painted in 1860) was kept. Beyond the apse lies the so-called 'New Building'—a square-ended retrochoir added to the E end in 1496–1508. Its intricate fan vaulting makes a striking contrast to the plain ceilings elsewhere. In the N choir aisle is the tomb of Abbot Benedict (d. 1193), who built the nave; further E is a memorial stone to Queen Catherine of Aragon (d. 1536), whose tomb was demolished by the Puritans. Behind the altar and seen from the retrochoir is the *Monk Stone. Traditionally said to be a memorial for the monks killed by the Danes in 870, it may date from a century earlier. The effigies of 12–13C abbots, brought from the ruined chapter house, are claimed as the finest Benedictine memorials in England. In the S choir aisle a slab marks the original burial place of Mary, Queen of Scots (executed at Fotheringhay in 1587), moved to Westminster Abbey in 1612.

The ruined Cloister, S of the cathedral, has 15C washing bays on its S side. From the SE corner a passage with a blind arcade, once vaulted, leads to the Early English arcade of the Infirmary, now incorporated in more recent buildings. The Almoners' Hall, S of the cloisters, illustrates the history of the site.

Excavations continue at the Bronze Age site of Flag Fen (open), E of the city. Thorpe Hall (occasionally open), a handsome mid 17C house 1m W of Peterborough, is used by the city as a cultural and leisure centre. Panelling from one of its rooms has been installed at Leeds Castle in Kent. Longthorpe Tower, 1m beyond, has early 14C domestic *murals (EH, summer season, weekends only). Castor, 2½m further W, has a beautiful Norman *church dedicated to St Kyneburga, King Peada's daughter. It has a richly decorated central tower and a wall painting of St Catherine.

Excursions from Peterborough can also be made E and N into the Fens. Whittlesey, 5m E via A605, is an old town with a fine 15C church tower and spire. The novelist L.P. Hartley was born here in 1895. Thorney, 6½m NE via A47, was the site of a Benedictine abbey founded in 972. The abbey church (1108) is now the parish church and its cloister has become a village green surrounded by houses built from monastic stone. Crowland, see Route 47A.

From Peterborough to Lincoln and the Humber, see Route 48.

37

Cambridge

CAMBRIDGE (101,200 inhabitants) is famous for its great university. It lies, nowhere more than 50ft above sea level, on the southern edge of the Fens: 'a low dirty unpleasant place', wrote the diarist John Evelyn scornfully. The disadvantages of its natural setting are offset by the buildings of the colleges. Cambridge is distinguished not just for individual triumphs like

King's College Chapel but for its array of the best in English architecture from the late medieval period through the ages of Wren and Gibbs up to the present day. The college gardens, public commons and avenues of trees all increase the beauty of the effect, particularly on the Backs, where the Cam makes its way behind several of the older colleges.

Though often crowded, and not just during the summer, Cambridge has always attracted fewer tourists than Oxford. Several days are needed to get to know the city properly. Even the most cursory inspection should include King's, Clare, St John's, Trinity, Queens' and Jesus Colleges, the Round Church and the Fitzwilliam Museum. The walks from the centre suggested below take in all the chief points of interest; the tours of the outskirts that follow are for more leisurely visitors.

TI: Wheeler St. **Bus Station**: Drummer St. **Railway Station**: 1¼m SE of the city centre (buses from St Andrew's St.). **Airport**: Marshall's Airport, Newmarket Rd. Services to Manchester and Amsterdam. **Theatres**: Arts Theatre, Peas Hill; ADC, Park St. Plays are often staged in the colleges, especially during May Week. **Annual Events**: May Week (actually about 10 days in June), with college balls, plays, concerts and the May 'Bumps' (boat races on the lower river). The Lent 'Bumps' take place in late February. The Cambridge Festival is held in late July, with music, exhibits, plays, feasts etc. Festival of Nine Lessons and Carols in King's College Chapel on Christmas Eve.

Access to colleges: In recent years the pressure of tourism has made the colleges adopt more stringent policies about opening to the public. Most of the older, river colleges now restrict access or close altogether during the Lent Term (mid April to the last week of June) and particularly during its examination period (mid May to late June). Several now charge admission fees. The TI Centre has precise details, which vary from college to college and year to year. Otherwise, the main courts, gardens and chapels are usually open, though King's College Chapel is sometimes closed for rehearsals and recording sessions. Halls are normally closed. Visitors may not enter staircases and working libraries or walk on the lawns, traditionally sacred to the feet of fellows.

History. Excavations in the Castle Hill area, N of the present centre, have revealed Belgic settlements pre-dating the Romans and a Roman camp. Soon after the Conquest the Normans built a castle, a market centre grew up S of the river and the annual trading fair on Stourbridge Common became famous. Their significance was soon eclipsed by that of the university, which probably first developed around the religious establishments of the 12C and was recognised as a seat of learning in a writ of Henry III (1231). Friction between Town and Gown culminated in the riot of 1381, when townsmen sacked several colleges. Cambridge achieved a European reputation with the arrival of Erasmus in 1510. Its wealth and well-being were increased rather than lessened by the great religious change of the 16C. It lost little during the Civil War except the plate melted down for Charles I's war chest.

Even after the coming of the railway in 1845 Cambridge never grew into an industrial centre as Oxford did, but kept its character as a Fen market town. Of late the city (as it formally became in 1951) has expanded to absorb surrounding villages and gained a reputation for computer businesses encouraged by the university's research activities.

Early names for the river were the Rhee and, more frequently, the Granta (now usually applied to the two branches above Cambridge). This gave the forms Grantebrycge (Grantabridge) and later Cantebrigge, eventually softened into Cambridge. The present name of the Cam was thus derived from the town, not the other way about.

Natives. The cricketer Sir Jack Hobbs (1882–1963). The literary critics E.M.W. Tillyard (1889–1962) and F.R. Leavis (1895–1978) were both born in Cambridge as well as pursuing their careers at the university.

The Oxbridge system. A distinguishing mark of Oxford and Cambridge, often perplexing to visitors, is the relationship between the colleges and the university. The colleges are self-governing bodies with their own endowments and statutes, responsible for admitting undergraduates, accommodating them, supervising the progress of their studies, regulating their behaviour and in general providing the focus of their social life. The university, with its widely scattered laboratories, libraries, museums, lecture rooms and administrative quarters, is strictly defined as the Chancellor and Masters—that is, the senior members as a corporate, self-governing body. It awards degrees and establishes general policy. Through the various faculties, or subject groups, into which its research and educational activities are divided, it is also responsible for providing lectures and laboratory work and for conducting examinations.

Physically, the colleges consist of rooms with communal functions (hall, chapel and library) and private rooms where the members live and work, arranged around quadrangles which are called quads at Oxford and courts at Cambridge. The college community is made up of a head, fellows and undergraduates, together with honorary fellows, graduate students and service staff of whom the most visible are the porters stationed in the lodge by the main entrance. The head is known as Master (the almost invariable term at Cambridge), Warden, Principal, Provost, Rector, Dean (at Christ Church, Oxford) or President (though at Cambridge this title occasionally denotes the Vice-Master). The fellows ('dons'), who may or may not have been graduates of the university, are some of them university teachers or administrators and some of them teachers for their college alone. All take a part in the running of the college. Undergraduates live in college, or college-owned accommodation, for most of their period of residence. Some colleges still require their students to dine in Hall a given number of times each term. The old rules governing the time by which they had to be in their rooms in the evening, when the gates were closed, have been greatly relaxed. So, too, have the regulations about wearing gowns, though some colleges still require them at formal Hall. At Cambridge the basic three-quarter length black undergraduate gown is worn unmodified at five colleges, each of the others varying it in one way or another; at Caius and Trinity the gowns are dark blue. At Oxford, scholars (undergraduates singled out for certain privileges because of academic distinction) have longer gowns than the rest (commoners), whose gowns are little more than loose sleeveless black jackets.

The ceremonial head of the university is the Chancellor, elected for life and usually an eminent public figure. At Oxford the position is held by Lord Jenkins of Hillhead, at Cambridge by His Royal Highness The Prince Philip, Duke of Edinburgh. The executive head is the Vice-Chancellor, at Oxford normally but not necessarily the head of one of the colleges, who holds office for four years at Oxford. Since 1992 Cambridge has had a full-time Vice-Chancellor, normally serving for five to seven years, who is forbidden to hold any college office. Some administrative authority rests with holders of the MA or higher degrees, known as Convocation at Oxford and the Council of the Senate at Cambridge. The wide voting rights these bodies once held have largely been confined to formal duties, such as electing the Chancellor and (at Oxford) the Professor of Poetry, a post first held by Matthew Arnold in 1858 and since then by Robert Graves, C. Day-Lewis, W.H. Auden and Seamus Heaney among others. In practice, legislative authority rests with Congregation (Oxford) and the Regent House (Cambridge), composed of all resident doctors and MAs holding teaching or administrative posts in the university or colleges. Administrative authority lies with the smaller elected bodies known at Oxford as the Hebdomadal (or weekly) Council and at Cambridge as the Council of the Senate.

The General Board of the Faculties co-ordinates educational policy and oversees the work of the various Faculty Boards, which organise courses of study, appoint teachers and conduct examinations in their separate fields. Most undergraduates read for an honours degree, usually the BA, which takes three or four years, depending on the subject. No further examination is required for an MA, which can be obtained six or more years after acceptance into the university. Full details of courses of study, first and higher degrees, etc. are given in the university handbooks, calendars and prospectuses.

The academic year, less than seven months, begins in October and is divided into three terms: Michaelmas, Lent and Easter at Cambridge; Michaelmas, Hilary and Trinity at Oxford. Examinations are held in late May and June. Degree ceremonies take place at intervals throughout the year, at Cambridge in the Senate House, at Oxford in the Sheldonian Theatre. The main ceremony at Cambridge is General Admission (two days in late June) for those graduating BA only. Commemoration, or

CAMBRIDGE

0   400 yards
0   400 metres

N

Girton College & HUNTINGDON

Fitzwilliam College

New Hall

HUNTINGDON

VICTORIA

ST. PETER'S STREET

CASTLE

ROUND HILL

St Edmund's College

Observatory & ST NEOTS

Sports Ground

Churchill College

STOREY'S WAY

Lucy Cavendish College

Westminster College

MADINGLEY

ROAD

NORTHA

WILBERFORCE

ROAD

CLARKSON

ROAD

GRANGE

ROAD

Sports Ground

Sports Ground

Fellows Garden

ADAMS

ROAD

Sports Ground

BURRELL'S WALK

GARRE

University Library

Clare College

Robinson College

HERSCHEL

ROAD

Clare Hall

King's College Choir School

King's Hostel

Fellows' Garden

QUEEN'S

CRANMER

ROAD

WEST

ROAD

Harvey Court

Selwyn College

University Arts Buildings

SIDGWICK

AVENUE

SELWYN

GDNS.

GRANGE

Newnham College

Ridley Hall

NEWNHAM

WALK

MALTIN

Wolfson College

Sports Ground

SUMMERFIELD

NEWNHAM

CLARE RD.

BARTON

ROAD

Sports Ground

Recreation Ground

GRANTCHESTER

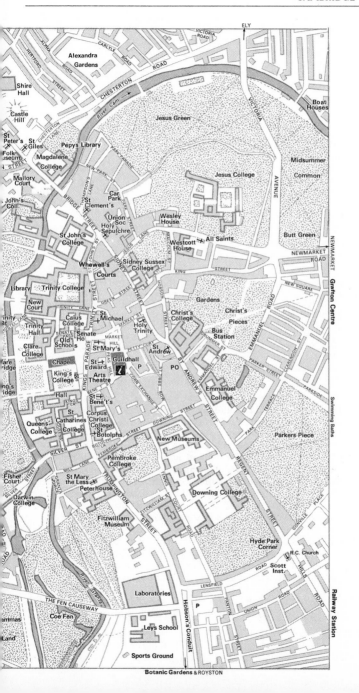

Encaenia, at Oxford is an honorary degree congregation held on the Wednesday following the end of Trinity term (early July).

From 1603 until 1950 the universities of Oxford and Cambridge each returned two members to Parliament, thus giving graduates the privilege of voting in their university as well as their home constituency. Members have included Sir Isaac Newton, William Pitt the Younger and Palmerston for Cambridge University, Peel and Gladstone for Oxford University.

The University: Cambridge has 32 colleges; the oldest is Peterhouse (1281–84) and the newest is Robinson, which received its first students in 1979. Together they educate over 9000 undergraduates. The smallest colleges are Peterhouse and Corpus Christi, with just over 200 students each, while Trinity, with over 800 undergraduates, is the largest in Cambridge or Oxford. All the colleges originally founded for men now admit women. Of the colleges founded for women only Girton is co-residential. Darwin College, St Edmund's College, Wolfson College, Lucy Cavendish College and Clare Hall are postgraduate foundations fully incorporated with the university. Hughes Hall and Homerton are 'approved foundations' (places at which students may matriculate and from which they may graduate). Westminster College, Ridley Hall, Westcott House and Wesley House are theological colleges without any formal relationship to the university.

The centre of the city is *Market Hill*, in fact a square rather than a hill, where an open market is held. The *Guildhall* of 1936–37 fills its S side.

From the SE corner lead Guildhall St., with a sculpture by Michael Ayrton, the curiously named Petty Cury (perhaps 'petite curye' or 'little cookery') and Lion Yardall—once a network of sidestreets but now a covered shopping precinct. In Peas Hill, at the SW corner of the Guildhall, is the 12C and 14C church of *St Edward King and Martyr*, where Latimer preached the Reformation. It is entered from St Edward's Passage, which has some good old houses. The nave has fine slender piers; the chancel was enlarged after 1446 to make chapels for Clare College and Trinity Hall. Peas Hill ends at the *Arts Theatre*, built and presented to Cambridge by the economist John Maynard Keynes in 1936; it should reopen after major refurbishment in late 1995 or early 1996. In Wheeler St., opposite, are the TI Centre and the 19C *Corn Exchange*, restored as a concert hall.

On the W side of Market Hill is **St Mary the Great** (Great St Mary's), the university church as well as Cambridge's main parish church. Although a church has stood here since at least the 12C, the present building dates mainly from 1478 and 1608, which saw completion of the tower (good view from the top). The nave has tall, elegant arches, a Tudor roof and fine galleries (1735). The organ, by 'Father' Smith was brought with its case from St James's, Piccadilly, in 1697. Opposite the tower end of the church is the •**Senate House**, scene of degree ceremonies and other public functions of the university. A masterly blend of Baroque ornament and Palladian restraint, it was built in 1722–30, the only part of James Gibbs's plan for a forum of university buildings to be realised. The interior (open for special exhibitions and events) has a plaster ceiling by Artari and Bagutti, woodwork by the two James Essexes, father and son, and statues of the Duke of Somerset (by Rysbrack) and Pitt (by Nollekens). The Senate House makes an admirable foil to the heavier outline of the former **Old Schools** (i.e. lecture rooms) and the old court of King's College, now housing university offices. Its main E façade, facing the green and King's Parade, was finished by Stephen Wright in 1758 but the courts behind date from c 1350–1473. The N side (1837–40; C.R. Cockerell) houses the law library.

SOUTH FROM MARKET HILL. King's Parade, the wide street that is the heart of visitors' Cambridge, begins immediately S of the Senate House and its adjoining buildings, its left-hand side a pleasant medley of shops and

Old Schools, Cambridge

domestic architecture. On the right is **King's College** (340 undergraduates), founded on the Old Schools site by Henry VI in 1441 as 'The King's College of Our Lady and St Nicholas' and re-established here four years later, in connection with Eton College.

The street frontage has a lodge and stone screen added by William Wilkins in 1828. On the S side of the *Great Court*, with its fountain, is the *Hall* (also by Wilkins, 1824–28). On the W is the stately **Fellows' Building* by Gibbs (1724), with a lovely lawn sloping down to the river; the S side is bounded by the *Library* and *Bodley's Building* (1894, completed 1928) and the N by Clare College. There is a fine view from the bridge (see also The Backs below).

MEMBERS: Christopher Tye, Francis Walsingham, Phineas and Giles Fletcher, Orlando Gibbons, Edmund Waller, Sir Robert and Horace Walpole, Sir William Temple, 'Turnip' Townshend, M.R. James, Roger Fry, E.M. Forster, John Maynard Keynes, Rupert Brooke and Salman Rushdie.

**King's College Chapel, on the N side of the Great Court, is the centrepiece of Henry VI's plan and still the crowning glory of Cambridge architecture. Work began in 1446–61 but was not resumed until 1506–15, when the stone fabric was finished under the patronage of Henry VII; the windows and woodwork were added by Henry VIII. The late Perpendicular style thus makes the transition from the last great era of medieval church building to the more secular age of the Renaissance. The rectangular plan is bold and simple, allowing for rich ornamentation of the interior, where the Tudor rose and portcullis are strongly in evidence among the carved emblems. (The rose and crown motif is probably also the Rosary and Corona of Our Lady.) Outstanding features are the delicate *fan vaulting of the roof, the 25 *windows (all 16C except for that by Clayton and Bell at the W end), the wooden organ screen (1533–36) and case (1688), and the stalls. The altarpiece is The Adoration of the Magi by Rubens, which impairs the effect of the lovely E window.

Each of the chantries, opening between the buttresses, contained an altar. The chantry at the SE corner, with Flemish glass of 1530, is a War Memorial Chapel; the one at the NE corner, with a lierne vault, was completed by 1461. The chantries N of the choir house an exhibition of the building's history.

In Bene't St., opposite the S range of King's, is *St Bene't's* (i.e. Benedict's) *Church*, with a Saxon tower and tower arch. It was the original chapel of Corpus Christi and is connected to the college by a gallery of finely toned red brick. **Corpus Christi College** (240 undergraduates) is now entered from Trumpington St., the southern continuation of King's Parade. It was founded in 1352 by the united religious guilds of Corpus Christi and the Blessed Virgin Mary.

The *Old Court*, reached from the NE corner of the New Court, is the earliest English example of a complete medieval academic quadrangle. The *New Court* is a ruthlessly symmetrical neo-Gothic creation by William Wilkins (1823–27). The *Chapel* has some 16C German glass. The portraits in the *Hall* include one of 1584 which may depict Christopher Marlowe. The *Old Library* has a manuscript collection bequeathed by Matthew Parker, master in 1554 and later Archbishop of Canterbury.

MEMBERS: Matthew Parker, Sir Nicholas Bacon, Christopher Marlowe, John Fletcher, John Cowper Powys, Llewelyn Powys, Sir George Thomson, Christopher Isherwood, E.P. Thompson.

S of Corpus Christi is *St Botolph's Church*, its dedication to the patron saint of travellers indicating that the S gate of the city, the Trumpington Gate, once stood nearby. The heavily restored 14–15C building contains a 15C painted rood screen, a handsome 17C font case and cover, and a curious monument to Dr Thomas Plaifer (d. 1609).

On the opposite side of the road a modern development by Fello Atkinson spans King's Lane and discreetly links the S end of King's with the façade of the former Bull Hotel, now part of **St Catharine's College** (380 undergraduates). The college was founded in 1473 by Robert Wodelarke, Provost of King's, but rebuilt in 1674–1757 by Robert Grumbold and James Essex, and extended in 1932–51. Its three-sided front court, of mellow brick, is separated from Trumpington St. only by iron railings (1779).

MEMBERS: Archbishop Sandys, Bishop Lightfoot, James Shirley, John Ray, Benjamin Hoadly, Malcolm Lowry, Sir Peter Hall, Ian McKellen, Howard Brenton.

Behind St Catharine's, reached by King's Lane and Queens' Lane, is *Queens' College* (460 undergraduates). The plural form in its name indicates the several stages of its foundation, first by Andrew Dokett in 1446, then again two years later under the patronage of Margaret of Anjou (whose husband, Henry VI, had just founded King's College) and finally in 1465 by Elizabeth Woodville, wife of Edward IV. Although modest in scale and ambition, Queens' is perhaps the most picturesque of all Cambridge colleges.

The magnificent *Gatehouse leads into the 15C redbrick Old Court. To the right are the *Old Chapel*, with a sundial on its wall, and the *Library*, with Jacobean bookcases; straight ahead is the *Hall*, remodelled by James Essex in 1732–34 and restored by Bodley in 1862–75. Beyond lies the charming *Cloister Court. On its N side, to the right, is the half-timbered *President's Lodge (c 1595) with a beautiful panelled gallery of c 1604. The *Mathematical Bridge*, built in the 18C and reconstructed several times since, leads across the Cam to *Fisher Court* (1936), *Cripps Court* (1972–74; Powell and Moya), *Lyon Court* (1989; Bland, Brown and Cole) and the riverside scenery of The Grove. In the small *Pump Court*, left of the Cloister Court, is the *Erasmus Tower*, above the rooms occupied by Erasmus when he taught Greek here in 1510–13. A passage from the corner of the President's Lodge leads into *Walnut Tree Court* (1617–19) and *Friars Court*, with the large *Chapel* (1890–91; Bodley) between them. Almost opposite the chapel is the *Erasmus Building* (1959–61; Basil Spence).

MEMBERS: Erasmus, St John Fisher, Sir Thomas Smith, Thomas Fuller (who moved to Sidney), Isaac Milner, Osborne Reynolds, Charles Stanford, T.H. White, Gilbert Harding, Sir David Walker, Sir John Banham, Stephen Fry.

Queens' is bounded to the S by Silver St., from which the little Laundress Lane leads left to the waterside at the end of Mill Lane. The mill pool and weir mark the division between the upper and lower river, which here changes its name to the Granta. Punts can be taken along the Backs or up to Grantchester (see below). The bulk of the *University Centre* (1964; Howell, Killick, Partridge and Amis), usually known as the Graduate Centre, does not improve the scenery on the nearside bank.

For the continuation of Silver St., see Western Outskirts below.

Silver St. leads back to Trumpington St., which continues S. On the right is the *Pitt Building* of the University Press, a conspicuous Tudor Revival building (1831–33; Blore) paid for by surplus funds collected for a statue of Pitt in London. The new buildings of the Press flank the railway line to London.

On the opposite side of the road stands **Pembroke College** (340 undergraduates), founded by the Countess of Pembroke in 1347 but largely modernised or rebuilt.

The *Chapel (1663–65) was Wren's first major work and the first major classical building of its century in Cambridge. It has a fine plaster ceiling and woodwork, and the serenity of its proportions was only a little altered by the lengthening of the E end in 1880. The *Old Library* on the left-hand side of the first court was originally the first college chapel in Cambridge (1366). *Ivy Court* (c 1614–59) was restored in 1964; to the SE is *New Court* (1882) and *Orchard Building* (1957). The fine *Gardens* have a statue of Pitt.

MEMBERS: Pembroke has produced many bishops (Ridley, Grindal, Whitgift, Andrewes, etc.) and poets: Spenser, Crashaw, Gray (see Peterhouse for the story of his migration to Pembroke), Mason and Ted Hughes. Pitt the Younger, Sumner Maine, Sir G.G. Stokes, H.F. Guggenheim, R.A. Butler (Lord Butler of Saffron Walden), Peter Cook, Ray Dolby (inventor of the Dolby sound system), Clive James, David Munrow and Christopher Hogwood were also Pembroke men.

On the right of Trumpington St. is the church of *St Mary the Less* (Little St Mary's), 14C and keeping its exquisitely flowing Decorated tracery despite later alterations. It served as the chapel of adjoining Peterhouse from its foundation until 1632, and the backs of the college's buildings are well seen from the pleasantly overgrown churchyard. **Peterhouse** (210 undergraduates) is the oldest college in Cambridge, founded by Hugh of Balsham, Bishop of Ely, in 1281. It is properly styled 'St Peter's College' and is never called 'Peterhouse College'.

In the first court is the Laudian Gothic *Chapel* (1628–32), connected with the main buildings by galleries (1709–11). The E window has its original glass and in the reredos is a 15C wooden Pietà. On the right is the dignified *Fellows' Building* by Burrough (1738–42). On the left are the *Old Library* (c 1590, extended in 1633) and the *Hall*, much altered but still substantially the original building of c 1290. It contains portraits, and glass by Morris, Burne-Jones, and Madox Brown, who also designed the windows of the *Combination Room* (1460). Beyond the Hall a path leads to the *Garden*. At the back of the second or *Gisborne Court* (1825) is *Fen Court* (1939; Hughes and Bicknell) and, to the N, the new *Library* in the former Museum of Classical Archaeology (1884). The *Master's Lodge*, a Queen Anne house of 1702, stands on the other side of Trumpington St.

MEMBERS: Cardinal Beaufort, Thomas Campion, Crashaw, Gray, Henry Cavendish, Charles Babbage, Clerk Maxwell, Lord Kelvin, James Mason. Most of the founders of molecular biology (Max Perutz, Sir Aaron Klug, Sir John Kendrew), as well as the inventors of the jet engine (Sir Frank Whittle) and the hovercraft (Sir Christopher Cockerell), are present members. Gray's rooms in the Fellows' Building, overlooking Little St Mary's, may be identified by the iron bars the poet installed to support a rope ladder in case of fire. Roused by a false alarm, he left Peterhouse in annoyance at the practical joke and became a member of Pembroke.

Just beyond Peterhouse is the *Fitzwilliam Museum, a classical building designed by George Basevi and C.R. Cockerell (1837–47) for the collections Viscount Fitzwilliam left to the university in 1816. The original building was finished in 1875 by E.M. Barry, who designed the entrance hall; since 1924 the Marlay Galleries, on the S side, and further extensions have been added. The upper galleries (open Tuesday to Friday afternoons, all day Saturday and Sunday afternoons) contain major collections of European paintings, strongly representing most periods and schools. The pictures are displayed among sculpture, furniture, ceramics, etc. of the appropriate periods. The lower galleries (open Tuesday to Friday mornings, all day Saturday and Sunday afternoons) contain West Asiatic, Egyptian, Greek and Roman antiquities; Islamic and Far Eastern art; European ceramics and other applied arts; literary and musical manuscripts; armour; and a medieval collection.

UPPER GALLERIES. From the entrance hall the staircase leads to the large *Room III*, devoted to English works. They include: portraits by Hans Eworth (*Mary Tudor), Van Dyck (Archbishop Laud), Lely, Hogarth, Allan Ramsay, Romney, Reynolds, Gainsborough (Heneage and Lucy Knight, John Kirby, Mrs John Kirby), Wright of Derby (Viscount Fitzwilliam, aged 19), Raeburn, Batoni and Carlo Dolci; genre scenes by Highmore and Hogarth; landscapes by Richard Wilson and Gainsborough; sporting paintings by Wootton and Stubbs (Gimcrack). The bust of William Pitt is by Nollekens, and the clock beside the door is by Thomas Tompion (c 1695). The gallery above contains paintings from the reserve collection.

Room II, to the right, has 19–20C English works by Madox Brown (version of Last of England), Millais, Rossetti, Holman Hunt, Edward Lear (View of the Temple of Apollo at Bassae in Arcadia), G.F. Watts, Etty, George Richmond, Augustus John (Thomas Hardy, George Bernard Shaw) and Sargent; also landscapes by Constable (Hampstead Heath, Hove Beach, Salisbury), Turner, John Martin, Inchbold, Bonington, Francis Danby, Cotman, James Stark, Joseph Stannard, John Brett and John Linnell. There are bronzes by Ricketts and Gilbert, and furniture by George Bullock and Morris and Co. *Room I* has 20C French and English paintings by Vuillard, Spencer Gore, Gilman, Bonnard, Picasso, Matisse, Paul Nash, Sir William Nicholson, Stanley Spencer (Self Portrait) and Sickert; also furniture by Hans Poelzig and bronzes by Epstein.

In *Room IV*, beyond Room III, are the French schools, with works by Delacroix (Odalisque, The Bride of Abydos), Géricault (Wounded Soldiers in a Cart), Corot (La Châtaigneraie, The Dyke), Fantin-Latour, Courbet, Fabre, Vouet, Michallon, Dujardin, Sébastien Bourdon, Marguerite Gérard, Pater, Le Brun and Oudry; also a bronze bust of Napoleon by Chaudet. French painting continues in *Room V* with examples of

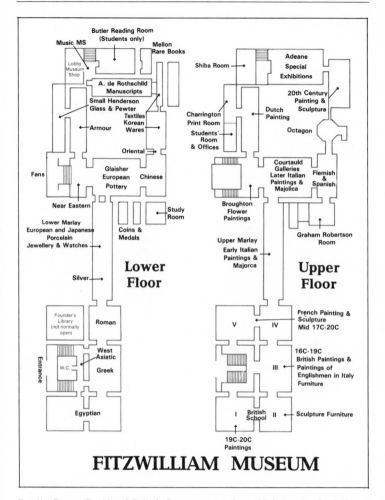

FITZWILLIAM MUSEUM

Boudin, Degas (David and Goliath, Danseuses aux Jupes Violettes, Au Café), Renoir (*Place Clichy, Le Retour des Champs, Le Coup de Vent), Monet (Les Peupliers, Le Printemps), Signac, Seurat, Cézanne, Gauguin, Pissarro and Sisley; also bronzes by Degas, Rodin and Medardo Rosso.

Room IV leads to the *Upper Marlay Gallery* (Room VI), devoted to Italian paintings, with particularly fine works by masters of the 13–15C Florentine, Sienese and North Italian schools. They include: Simone Martini (*St Geminianus, St Michael and St Augustine), Lorenzo Monaco, Filippo Lippi (Virgin and Child), the Master of the Castello Nativity, Giovanni dal Ponte, Beccafumi, Domenico Veneziano, Francesco Botticini, Ghirlandaio, Cosimo Tura, Crivelli (Virgin and Child), Cima (St Lanfranc of Pavia) and Pintoricchio. There is also an important group of cassone panels. The *Courtauld Gallery* (Room VII) continues the Italian schools, with Renaissance and Baroque works by Ludovico Carracci, Sassoferrato, Taddeo Zucarro, Annibale Carracci, Titian (*Tarquin and Lucretia, *Venus and Cupid), Tintoretto (Adoration of the Shepherds), Salvator Rosa, Francesco Guardi, Canaletto, Pittoni, Guido Reni (Ecce

Homo), Maratti, Jacopo Bassano, Veronese (*Hermes, Herse and Aglauros) and Palma Vecchio. Renaissance majolica, with bronzes and medals, are displayed in both galleries.

To the right of the Courtauld Gallery is the *Flemish and Spanish Gallery* (Room VIII), with works by Joos van Cleeve, Jan Brueghel the Elder, Pieter Brueghel the Younger (Village Fete), Murillo and Van Dyck, and *oil sketches by Rubens. The *Graham Robertson Room* and the little *Octagon*, both adjoining, are used for temporary exhibitions.

The room to the left of the Courtauld Gallery, at the head of the staircase, displays the Broughton Collection of flower paintings, as well as terracotta busts by Rysbrack, Roubiliac and Bushnell. *Room XI*, beyond, has Dutch paintings by Ruisdael, Jan Steen, Wouvermans, Franz Hals, Hobbema (*Wooded Landscape), Cuyp and Van Ostade. From it leads the *Print Room*, which usually houses temporary exhibitions, and the *Shiba Room*, with Japanese prints. The *Adeane Gallery* is used for temporary exhibitions and the *20C Gallery* beyond displays paintings (subject to change) by Léger, Picasso, Rouault, Ben Nicholson and Graham Sutherland, with sculptures by Henry Moore and Barbara Hepworth.

LOWER GALLERIES. At the foot of the stairs is the small *West Asiatic Gallery*, with superb Assyrian reliefs (9–7C BC). The *Egyptian Collection* is to the right. Room I has exhibits from the pre-Dynastic period to the Coptic period, including the shrine of the goddess Nekhbet, a granite head of Sesostris III (King of Egypt, 1878–1843 BC) and the superb portrait of Ammenemes III (King of Egypt, 1842–1797 BC). Room II contains the *Gayer-Anderson Collection, the coffin of Nekhtefmut (early 9C BC), Roman mummy-portraits, and the huge *sarcophagus lid of Ramesses III (King of Egypt, 1198–1166 BC). The *Greek Room* has representative examples of vases, seals, bronze and terracotta statuettes, sculpture including the fine Attic gravestones of Theokles and Hegemon, and a colossal caryatid head from the Inner Propylaea at Eleusis (1C BC). Among the exhibits in the *Etruscan and Roman Room* are: the Pashley sarcophagus; a head of Antinóus (AD 110–130); a child's sarcophagus (early 2C AD); a mosaic fountain niche from Baiae (c AD 50); the *cinerarium of Aelia Postumia (AD 25–50); and exquisite *seals and engraved gems. The *Lower Marlay Gallery* contains porcelain, silver and watches. At the end is the *Glaisher Gallery* with European stoneware and earthenware, and a selection of manuscripts. Off the Glaisher Gallery is the *Cripps Gallery*, with temporary exhibitions of coins and medals. Beyond are the *Chinese Collection* of ceramics and jade, and the *Gompertz Gallery* of Korean ceramics. An adjoining room displays textiles and costumes. Returning through the Glaisher Gallery we come to the *Islamic Collection*, with the adjoining *Great Britain-Sasakawa Foundation Fan Gallery*, and, beyond, the *Henderson Collection* of armour. The adjoining small room has European glass, pewter and medals. The *Rothschild Gallery* contains a miscellaneous but highly interesting medieval collection: ivories and enamels; church plate; an exquisite capital (c 1150) from Avignon; a head of Mary Magdalen in wood (late 15C Italian); and illuminated manuscripts, notably the Breton Gospel Book (9–10C), the Grey-Fitzpayn Book of Hours (c 1300) and the *Metz Pontifical, produced for a Bishop of Metz at the beginning of the 14C, the most sumptuous French liturgical manuscript of its date.

Opposite the museum is a building of 1737, formerly occupied by Fitzwilliam House (now in Huntingdon Rd; see Northern Outskirts below).

Trumpington St. ends at *Hobson's Conduit*, moved here in 1856 from its original site in Market Hill, where it had been erected in 1616, partly at the expense of Thomas Hobson (d. 1631). Hobson is the subject of two short poems by Milton. The phrase 'Hobson's choice' embalms his rule of letting out his horses for hire in strict rotation.

In Lensfield Rd, to the left, is the *Scott Polar Research Institute and Museum*, with letters, diaries and photographs from Scott's journey to the South Pole among its exhibits. The Fen Causeway leads right, to the *Engineering Laboratories* and the bleak, low-lying Coe Fen. For Trumpington Rd, to the S, see South-Western Outskirts below.

NORTH FROM MARKET HILL. Immediately N of the Senate House is **Gonville and Caius College** (460 undergraduates), shortened to 'Caius' and pronounced 'Keys'. It was founded by Edmund Gonville in 1348 and refounded by Dr Caius in 1557.

The S side of *Tree Court* (1868–70; Alfred Waterhouse) towers inappropriately over the group formed by the Senate House and Great St Mary's. It is entered from Trinity St. On its opposite side the *Gate of Virtue*, part of the symbolic 'academic path' devised by Caius, leads into *Caius Court* (1565–67). On the left is the *Gate of Honour* (1575), a charmingly eclectic little gateway leading into Senate House Passage. On the right of the court is the *Chapel* (1375, modernised in 1718), with monuments to Caius (d. 1573), Dr Legge (d. 1607) and Dr Perse (d. 1615). A passage by the chapel connects Caius Court with *Gonville Court*, built in the 15C and refaced in 1753. To the left is the *Hall*, rebuilt by Anthony Salvin in 1853.

MEMBERS: Thomas Gresham, William Harvey, Jeremy Taylor, William Wilkins, J.R. Seeley, Sir Charles Sherrington, James Elroy Flecker, David Frost, Francis Crick, Donald Davie, Sir Neville Mott, Sir Stephen Hawking, Kenneth Clarke.

The narrow, usually crowded Trinity St. continues N. Among the medley of buildings on its right-hand side, facing the frontage of Caius, is the small 14C church of *St Michael*, now converted into a meeting room.

•Trinity College (640 undergraduates) is the largest college in either Cambridge or Oxford, as well as one of the most handsome. Henry VIII established it in 1546, replacing the earlier King's Hall (1317) and Michaelhouse (1324).

The turreted brick *•Great Gatehouse* (1490–1535) belonged to King's Hall. It bears the name of Edward III and the royal coat of arms; the statue of Henry VIII on the street side and the statues of James I, Anne of Denmark and their son, the future Charles I, were added in 1615. The spacious *•Great Court* was created from the jumble of buildings belonging to the two earlier foundations by Thomas Nevile, Master from 1593 to 1615, who also placed the fountain in the centre. On the S side (left) is the *Queen's Gate* (1597), with a statue of Elizabeth I. On the N side stands the *Chapel*, completed in 1561, with 18C woodwork. In the *Ante-Chapel* are statues of *•Newton* (by Roubiliac), Bacon (by Weekes), Barrow (by Noble), Macaulay and Whewell (by Woolner) and Tennyson (by Thornycroft). W of the chapel are *King Edward III's Tower* (1428–32), a gatehouse of King's Hall rebuilt by Nevile, and the quaint little *King's Hostel*. The W side is dominated by the *•Hall*, built by Nevile in the Perpendicular style; its portraits include one by Reynolds of the Duke of Gloucester, aged six.

The screens passage leads past the Hall into *Nevile's Court*, built c 1605–12 but extended to join Wren's *•Library* of 1676–95, which fills the entire W side of the court. Wren placed the library itself on an upper floor and left an open arcade at ground level, an elegant and practical solution to the problem of storing books in the damp atmosphere by the river. On the balustrade are statues (by Cibber) representing Divinity, Law, Physics and Mathematics. The interior has few rivals among English libraries, with limewood bookcases by Grinling Gibbons and busts of Newton, Bacon (both by Roubiliac) and Tennyson (by Woolner). The statue of Byron by Thorvaldsen, at the far end, was meant for Westminster Abbey but refused a place there. The display cases contain illuminated manuscripts, autograph writings by Milton, Byron, Tennyson, Thackeray and Housman, and relics of Newton.

S of Nevile's Court is *New Court* (1825; William Wilkins), to the E of which is *Bishop's Hostel*, a separate building of 1670–71. On its W side are the beautiful *•College Grounds*, extending across to the Backs (see below). The view from the bridge (1764–68) is charming.

The college buildings extend across Trinity St. with the two *Whewell's Courts* (1860; Salvin), the *Wolfson Building* (1971) and *Blue Boar Court* (1989; Richard MacCormac).

MEMBERS: Essex, Francis Bacon, Coke, Herbert, Cowley, Marvell, Dryden, Newton, Judge Jeffreys, Porson, Melbourne, Byron, Macaulay, Kinglake, Tennyson, Arthur

Hallam (of 'In Memoriam'), Edward FitzGerald, Thackeray, Galton, Clerk Maxwell, Lord Acton, Balfour, F.W. Maitland, Charles Stanford, Sir James Frazer, A.E. Housman, Baldwin, Rutherford, Rayleigh, Eddington, Jeans, Pandit Nehru, G.E. Moore, Wittgenstein, Clive Bell, Vaughan Williams, Bertrand Russell, A.A. Milne, Vladimir Nabokov, Enoch Powell, Kim Philby, Guy Burgess, Anthony Blunt. Also members of the royal family, including Edward VII, George VI and Prince Charles. Masters of Trinity have included Archbishop Whitgift, Bishop Pearson, Dr Isaac Barrow, Richard Bentley, William Whewell, Montagu Butler, J.J. Thomson, G.M. Trevelyan, Lord Adrian and Lord Butler.

N of Trinity the street changes its name to St John's St. in deference to ***St John's College** (530 undergraduates), second in size among Oxbridge colleges only to its immediate neighbour. It replaced the 13C Hospital of St John and was founded in 1511 by Lady Margaret Beaufort, Henry VII's mother and also foundress of Christ's College. The task of carrying out her intentions was mainly performed by two of her executors, St John Fisher and Henry Hornby, Master of Peterhouse.

The *Gatehouse was built in 1510–16. Cleaning and repainting have greatly enhanced its lavish decoration: a statue of St John, the Beaufort 'yales' supporting the royal arms, Tudor rose and portcullis, forget-me-nots punning on the Beaufort motto ('Souvent me souvient'). The First Court was built by St John Fisher, but its S side (left) was rebuilt in 1772 and the large, inappropriate Chapel on the N side added by Sir Gilbert Scott in 1864–69. Between the first and second courts is the *Hall, with fine panelling, a hammerbeam roof and a portrait of Wordsworth (by Pickersgill). The *Second Court (1598–1602; Ralph Symons), built in lovely plum-coloured brick and practically unchanged, justifies Ruskin's praise of it as one of the most perfect in the university. The *Combination Room on its N side is one of the finest panelled galleries in England, with a rich plaster ceiling. The Third Court was built between 1623 and 1674. The Old Library, on its NE side, contains autograph letters, manuscripts and early printed books, including Lady Margaret's Book of Hours (early 15C French) and a vellum copy of Cranmer's Bible (1539). In 1992–94 the library was greatly extended by a new building in Chapel Court, and the lower library was modernised.

From this court two bridges cross the river: Robert Grumbold's Old Bridge (1696–1712), to the left, and the picturesque Bridge of Sighs, connecting with the Gothic New Court (1826–31; Rickman and Hutchinson) on the opposite bank. The large and beautiful College Grounds make a good approach to the Backs (see below). Beyond New Court is the Cripps Building (1966; Powell and Moya), using its position by the river and its inlet to great effect. At its N tip, near the college's back gateway into Northampton St., are the 16C Merton Hall (taking its name from the Oxford college which owned it until 1959) and the School of Pythagoras (c 1200), one of Cambridge's oldest buildings.

Behind the chapel and reached from Second Court is the partly Victorian Chapel Court, extended in 1932 by Sir Edward Maufe, who also built North Court, facing Bridge St. beyond.

MEMBERS: Sir Thomas Wyatt, Roger Ascham, Lord Burghley, Robert Greene, Thomas Nashe, Strafford, Lord Falkland, Fairfax, Herrick (who moved to Trinity Hall), Matthew Prior, Titus Oates, Sir John Herschel, Charles Churchill, Erasmus Darwin, Horne Tooke, Thomas Clarkson, Wilberforce, Wordsworth, Patrick Brontë (father of the novelists), Palmerston, William Barnes, Samuel Butler, Sir Edward Appleton, Sir John Cockcroft, Louis Leakey, Sir C. Aubrey Smith, Cecil Beaton, Glyn Daniel, Sir Nikolaus Pevsner, Sir Vivian Fuchs, Jonathan Miller, Derek Jacobi.

Still flanked by the buildings of the college, St John's St. runs N to the junction with Bridge St. and Sidney St. On the Sidney St. corner stands the ***Round Church**, as the Church of the Holy Sepulchre is usually known. Dating from c 1130, it is one of only four medieval round churches to survive in England; the others are at Northampton, Little Maplestead in Essex and the Temple in London. The Norman appearance of its circular part, like the conical roof, is almost entirely due to ruthless restoration by Salvin and the Cambridge Camden Society (the 'Ecclesiologists') in 1841. The chancel was added in the 15C, also probably the angel roof of the N aisle and choir.

Behind the Round Church are the buildings of the *Cambridge Union Society* (1866; Alfred Waterhouse), founded as a debating club in 1815.

Bridge St. leads N, passing on the right *St Clement's Church*, Early English but much altered. Beyond the bridge is **Magdalene College** (pronounced 'Maudlen'; 300 undergraduates), the only old college to have its main buildings across the river. It was refounded by Lord Audley in 1542, but its history goes back to the Benedictine hostel established c 1428 by the four great Fenland abbeys of Crowland, Ely, Ramsey and Walden, later known as Buckingham College (c 1480–1542).

The older part of the college stands on the right of Magdalene St., a narrow, crowded thoroughfare with 16C and 17C buildings. A gateway of 1585 leads to the modest, brick-built *First Court*, which keeps much of the original monastic fabric, especially on the side by the river. The *Chapel*, on the left, still has its 15C timber roof but otherwise is largely as restored in 1847–51 by John Buckler. The E window is by Pugin. The *Hall* was built c 1519, though the elegant interior with a double staircase leading up to the gallery dates from 1714. In the *Second Court* is the *Pepys Library*, its odd mixture of styles reflecting the sixty years it took to build (c 1640–1700). Since 1724 it has housed the great collection of books left to Magdalene by Samuel Pepys (d. 1702), still kept in their original shelves and original order. The chief treasure is the manuscript, in shorthand, of the 'Diary'; among the many other items are both parts of Caxton's manuscript translation of Ovid, the first collected by Pepys and the second donated to the college in 1966. The *Fellows' Garden* behind the library has sculptures of St Mary Magdalene and the Chinese God of Examinations.

On the opposite side of the road are *Benson Court* (1931–32; Sir Edwin Lutyens) and *Mallory Court*, which was converted to college use in 1925, skilfully brought together in an informal landscape with the addition of new buildings and the conversion of the medieval buildings fronting Magdalene St. (1952–58; David Roberts). *Buckingham Court* (1970), facing the Cripps Building of St John's, is also by Roberts.

MEMBERS: Henry Dunster (first President of Harvard), Pepys, Charles Kingsley, Charles Stewart Parnell, A.C. Benson, I.A. Richards, George Leigh Mallory, C.S. Lewis, Sir William Empson, Sir Michael Redgrave, Vernon Watkins.

For continuations of this route, see Northern, North-Eastern and North-Western Outskirts below.

WEST FROM MARKET HILL. Senate House Passage, between the Senate House and Caius, leads past the college's Gate of Honour to **Trinity Hall** (300 undergraduates). It was founded in 1350 by William Bateman, Bishop of Norwich, with special provisions for law students.

The main court is among the oldest in Cambridge, but its 14C buildings were given a new façade in 1730–45 by Sir James Burrough. The *Ante-Chapel* to the left (S) has three 16C brasses. Beyond the *Hall* to the W is the *Old Library* (c 1600), a lovely brick building with crow-step gables; the chained books inside are of a still earlier date. The charming *Gardens* overlook the river.

MEMBERS: Sir John Paston, Thomas Tusser, Holinshed, Bishop Gardiner, Lord Howard of Effingham, Herrick (who moved from St John's), Lord Chesterfield, Bulwer-Lytton, F.D. Maurice, Sir Leslie Stephen, Henry Fawcett, Edward Carpenter, Ronald Firbank, J.B. Priestley, Donald Maclean.

Trinity Lane leads S from the gateway of the college towards King's College Chapel. On the left it passes the back of the Old Schools and the *Gatehouse* once belonging to King's College, its lower part 15C but its upper part completed in the 19C. On the right stands **Clare College** (380 undergraduates), founded as University Hall in 1326 and refounded by Lady Elizabeth de Clare in 1338. The elegant simplicity of its architecture and the beauty of its river setting make it one of the most attractive colleges.

The *Chapel* (1763–69; Sir James Burrough and James Essex) is on the right of the lawn leading to the gateway. The skylit octagon of its ante-chapel is unique in Cambridge. The main court, rebuilt in 1638–1715 by John Westley and the Grumbold family of local craftsmen, is a wonderfully complete example of its period, its strong and simple unity varied by the small shifts of taste during the years of its building. Its W range opens on to *Clare Bridge* (1640; perhaps by Thomas Grumbold), with a splendid *view in virtually every direction. The *Fellows' Garden*, beyond, is among the best in Cambridge. See also The Backs below.

The avenue leads to Queen's Rd and, on the opposite side, Clare's *Memorial Court* (1923–34; Sir Giles Gilbert Scott), with a large War Memorial Arch. The new library in the centre (1986; Sir Philip Dowson) does its best to harmonise with the blend of monumental and domestic in Scott's original design. Nearby is a bronze Falling Warrior by Henry Moore.

MEMBERS: Bishop Latimer, Nicholas Ferrar, Lord Cornwallis, Sabine Baring-Gould, Paul Mellon, J.D. Watson.

Behind Memorial Court is the **University Library**, also by Scott (1930–34), with a tower which dominates the prospect for much of the walk from the river, and with modern extensions added to the rear. Containing over five million volumes, some 15,000 manuscripts, millions of archival items, maps, sheets of music and titles on microform, the library ranks (with the Bodleian) next in order of importance to the British Library in London. Founded in the 13C and a copyright library since 1709, it includes among its treasures: a copy of the Gutenberg Bible; a number of Caxtons, among them his 'Historyes of Troye' (1475–76), the first book printed in English, and the only known perfect copy of his 'Golden Legend' (1483); the Book of Deer (a 10C Gaelic manuscript); the 5C Codex Bezae, one of the five great uncial manuscripts of the pre-Jerome Gospels; and the Cairo Genizah fragments. It also contains many collections formed by individuals and institutions, among them the world's largest Charles Darwin archive, the Newton manuscripts, the libraries of the Bible Society and the Royal Commonwealth Society, the so-called 'Royal Library' of Bishop Moore, the library of Sir Geoffrey Keynes and the archives of the Greenwich Observatory. Exhibitions are always on public display in the entrance hall, and there are guided tours of the building each weekday at 15.00.

For Grange Rd, beyond the Library, see Western Outskirts below.

*THE BACKS. This is the familiar name for the tree-shaded grounds on the W bank of the river and, more generally, for the scenery either side of the Cam as it flows past the colleges. The most pleasant tour is by punt, from near the Silver St. bridge in the S or near Magdalene College in the N. A short excursion on foot leaves King's College by its back gateway and follows the path by the side of the Queen's Rd N to the back gateway of Clare College, whose bridge enjoys particularly charming views. The walk may be extended either by continuing up the Queen's Rd to the back gateway of Trinity College, or by entering Trinity College and St John's College through their main gateways.

SOUTH AND EAST FROM MARKET HILL. Petty Cury leads to St Andrew's St. and heads right (S). The church of *St Andrew the Great*, now disused, has a monument to Captain Cook (d. 1779) and his family. Opposite is **Christ's**

College (380 undergraduates), established in 1505 by Lady Margaret Beaufort, Henry VII's mother and later also foundress of St John's College, with the help of St John Fisher. It replaced God's House, a small college founded by William Byngham in 1436 on the site of King's College Chapel and refounded by Henry VI on the present site in 1448.

The *Gatehouse* is decorated with Beaufort insignia in even richer profusion than the gatehouse of St John's. The pleasantly irregular *First Court*, also built in 1505, was refaced in 1758–69 by James Essex, though the Master's Lodge opposite the main entrance still has its oriel window. The small *Chapel*, to the left, has stone walls from God's House. Panelled in 1701, it contains a monument by Joseph Catterns (1684) to Sir John Finch and Sir Thomas Baines. High up on the S wall is the window of Lady Margaret's oratory, now in the Master's Lodge. The *Hall* was rebuilt in 1876; its predecessor saw the earliest certain use of stage scenery in England, at a play in 1551. The *Second Court* is dominated by the *Fellows' Building* (1642), a lively piece of neo-classicism ascribed to Thomas Grumbold, one of the architects of Clare College. It opens on to the *Fellows' Garden*, which includes a mulberry tree associated (rather doubtfully) with Milton. The third court dates from 1889 to 1953, with Denys Lasdun's *New Court* (1970) reaching N to King St., where a new residential building (1993) nestles under the overhang of New Court.

MEMBERS: John Leland, Sir Walter Mildmay, Denzil Holles, Milton, Edward King ('Lycidas'), John Cleveland, Francis Quarles, Paley, H.W. Betty (the 'Infant Roscius'), Charles Darwin, Calverley, J.R. Seeley, Walter Besant, Lord Mountbatten, C.P. Snow, Anthony Storr, Lord Todd, James Meade, Lord Devlin.

Further S on St Andrew's St. is **Emmanuel College** (400 undergraduates), founded in 1584 by Sir Walter Mildmay, Elizabeth I's Chancellor of the Exchequer, primarily to train learned clergy for the Church of England. It became famous for its Puritan leanings, providing many of the philosophers and theologians called the 'Cambridge Platonists' and early emigrants to New England. Among them was John Harvard, who gave his name to the great American university.

The college occupies the site of a 13C Dominican priory. The *Front Court* no longer reveals how Ralph Symons adapted the remains in 1584–89. The entrance wing and *Hall* (left) were transformed by James Essex (1760–75), while the *Westmorland Building* (right) was refaced in 1719–22. Facing the entrance is the *Chapel*, fronted by an arcade with a gallery above, all by Wren (1677). It contains an altarpiece by Amigoni (1734), a good plaster ceiling and a memorial window to John Harvard. To the S extends the brick-built *Old Court* of 1633–34; the residential *South Block*, beyond, was completed in 1964. To the N is *New Court*; its N range was new in 1824. W of it is the kitchen, several times rebuilt; E of it is the *Old Library*, originally the chapel. The herb garden was designed by John Codrington in 1961. Beyond the large *Gardens* are the red-brick Gothic *Hostel* and *Emmanuel House* (1886–94), while the *Library*, designed as lecture rooms by Leonard Stokes in 1910, stands to the S by the Dominicans' boundary wall. The stone *North Court* (1913), also by Leonard Stokes, is on the other side of Emmanuel St.

MEMBERS: John Harvard, Archbishop Sancroft, Sir William Temple, William Law, Thomas Young, Sir F. Gowland Hopkins, Hugh Walpole, Lord Birkett, F.R. Leavis, C.N. Parkinson, Fred Hoyle. Gulliver of Swift's 'Gulliver's Travels' attends Emmanuel.

Opposite the main entrance to Emmanuel, Downing St. leads W, flanked by ponderous 19–20C buildings of the science faculties. In the *Downing Site* to the left (S) are the *Museum of Archaeology and Anthropology* and the *Sedgwick Museum*, named after Adam Sedgwick, Woodwardian Professor from 1818 to 1873. Its large fossil collection includes specimens bought from Mary Anning of Lyme Regis and Britain's oldest intact geological collection, that of Dr John Woodward (1665–1728), in its original cabinets. In the *New Museums*, the name given to the crowded and depressing medley on the right (N), is the *Museum of Zoology*. On Free School Lane, a right turn after Downing St. continues as Pembroke St., are the *Whipple Museum of the History of Science* and the original *Cavendish Physical Laboratory*, famous for the work of J.J. Thomson, Rutherford, Chadwick and Cockcroft. Just inside the nearby entrance to the New Museums is the *Mond Physical Laboratory* (1935), with a charming frieze by Eric Gill.

Further S, just after St Andrew's St. has changed its name to Regent St., is **Downing College** (360 undergraduates). It was endowed by the will of Sir George Downing (d. 1749), though legal complications delayed its foundation until 1800.

William Wilkins's design proposed severe Greek Revival buildings around a huge lawn, an effect more reminiscent of a campus than a traditional Cambridge court. In the event, only parts of the E and W ranges (1809–20) were built exactly to his plan. Their N ends were added by E.M. Barry in 1875. The N range was begun by Sir Herbert Baker (1930–31) in a badly debased version of Wilkins's style and completed, with the addition of the central *Chapel*, by A.T. Scott (1951–53). The court remains open to the S, with spacious grounds and a striking view of the *Roman Catholic Church* (1885–90) on the nearby corner of Hills Rd and Lensfield Rd. The *Combination Room* (1970) at the SW corner has a blending design in stone and pre-stressed concrete. Apart from this essay in modernism, the college has maintained its neo-classical architectural heritage with new buildings by Quinlan Terry, including the *Howard Building* (1987) and *Howard Court* (1994) at the NW corner and the *Library* (1993) at the main entrance. Downing now has the most consistent architectural tradition of any college. A detailed leaflet is available from the Porters' Lodge.

MEMBERS: J.M. Neale, C.M. Doughty, F.W. Maitland, C.S. Kenny, F.R. Leavis, Lord Goodman, Trevor Nunn, John Cleese.

Opposite Downing College is *Parker's Piece*, a large common named after Edward Parker, cook of Trinity College, who leased the land in 1587. Park Terrace, on the N side, has Regency houses. To the S lies the *University Cricket Ground*, known as 'Fenner's'. In Wollaston Rd nearby is *Hughes Hall*, a graduate college (140 students) originally founded as a women's teacher-training college in 1885.

For a continuation of this route, see South-Eastern Outskirts below.

NORTH AND EAST FROM MARKET HILL. Market St. leaves the NE corner of Market Hill. *Holy Trinity*, on the right at the junction with Sidney St., has a Regency Gothic gallery in its S transept. Jeremy Taylor was baptised here, and the Evangelical leader Charles Simeon (d. 1836) was vicar for 54 years.

Sidney St. heads N to **Sidney Sussex College** (300 undergraduates), established on the site of a Franciscan convent by the will of Frances Sidney, Countess of Sussex (d. 1589).

The original buildings by Ralph Symons were completed in 1598, but the present Gothick appearance of the college is the work of Sir Jeffrey Wyatville (1831–32), who spared only the oriel windows on the garden front. In *Hall Court*, to the left of the Porters' Lodge, the 18C *Hall* has a portrait of Cromwell which may be the one he instructed should represent him 'warts and all'. To the N is *Cloister Court*, leading to the wide and beautiful *Gardens*. Right of the Porters' Lodge is *Chapel Court*, with *Sir Francis Clerke's Building* (1628) on its S side and the *Chapel* (rebuilt by T.H. Lyon, 1912–23) on the E. A tablet in the ante-chapel records that Cromwell's head found its final resting place here in 1960. Beyond the chapel are *Garden Court* (1923; Lyon) and *South Court* (1938–39; E.R. Barrow); a covered way skirting the Master's Garden leads to *Blundell Court* (1969; Howell, Killick, Partridge and Amis). In King St., leading

E from the back gate, is *Cromwell Court* (1983; David Roberts and Whitworth, Hall and Thomas).

MEMBERS: Thomas Fuller (who moved from Queens'), Oliver Cromwell, Thomas Rymer, Sir Roger L'Estrange, Lord Owen. Duns Scotus taught at the Franciscan convent Greyfriars for a time.

Beyond Sidney Sussex are the Whewell's Courts of Trinity, on the left. Jesus Lane leads right. At the corner of Park St. to the left, beyond the classical portico of the former *Pitt Club* (now a restaurant), stand the *Amateur Dramatic Club* (ADC), founded in 1855, and the fine early 18C 'Little Trinity' guest hostel. Jesus Lane continues past *Wesley House*, a Methodist training college, on the left. Beyond is ***Jesus College**, founded in 1496 by John Alcock, Bishop of Ely, on the site of the suppressed nunnery of St Radegund. He adapted part of the conventual buildings, making its architecture among the most interesting in Cambridge.

A long passage known as 'The Chimney' approaches the college and enters by Alcock's fine, three-storied *Gatehouse*. The cock perched on a globe, above the central niche, is Alcock's rebus and appears throughout the college. From the 17–18C First Court an ogee doorway (again with Alcock's rebus) leads into **Cloister Court*, created by enlarging the nunnery's cloisters. The old entrance to the Chapter House (c 1210) survives on the E side. The cruciform **Chapel* on the S side keeps the core of the nunnery church. It is a lovely piece of Early English work, with traces of Norman in the N transept and Perpendicular windows added by Alcock. The **glass* is by Pugin and Hardman, and Madox Brown and Burne-Jones for Morris and Co. On the N side of the cloister is Alcock's *Hall*, with stairs leading from its vestibule to the *Old Library*. The buildings behind the chapel are by Waterhouse (1870) and Morley Horder (1929–35). *North Court*, in the spacious grounds, was added in 1964 to designs by David Roberts.

MEMBERS: Cranmer, Sterne, Coleridge, Malthus, Humphry Davy, Quiller-Couch, Raymond Williams, Alistair Cooke.

Opposite Jesus College is the fine church of *All Saints* (1864), by G.F. Bodley with stained gass and interior decoration by Morris and Co. It is now disused and not normally open. Next door is *Westcott House*, a Church of England training college. Jesus Lane continues to the wide space of *Midsummer Common*, stretching to the river with the college boat-houses on the opposite bank.

On Riverside, leading E from the common towards Stourbridge Common, the old sewage pumping station is now the *Cambridge Museum of Technology* (limited opening), with steam, gas and electric pumping engines. For a continuation of this route, see Eastern Outskirts below.

SOUTH-WESTERN OUTSKIRTS. The favourite short excursion is to **Grantchester**, a pretty village known for its connection with Rupert Brooke. It is best reached by the upper river (about 2m from the mill pond at the end of Mill Lane) or on foot through Grantchester Meadows (about 2m, by following Silver St., Newnham Rd and Grantchester St. from the end of the walk S from Market Hill, above). The poet is remembered in the church, which has a fine chancel and a Norman font. The *Old Vicarage* (not open), where Brooke lodged, is below the church near the river. *Byron's Pool*, ½m S, is named after Lord Byron. Walkers should continue an extra 1m from Grantchester to **Trumpington**, associated with Chaucer's 'Reeve's Tale' and still keeping its village character in the centre. The church, early 14C but heavily restored, has a *brass to Sir Roger de Trumpington (d. 1289), the second oldest in England (cf. Stoke d'Abernon, Route 13B). The drive from Cambridge goes to Trumpington first, following Trumpington Rd from the end of the walk S from Market Hill (above). It passes the *University Botanic Gardens* on the left at ¼m; they can also be entered from Hills Rd at its junction with Station Rd.

NORTHERN OUTSKIRTS. Castle St. continues N from the crossroads N of Magdalene College (at the end of the walk N from Market Hill above). On the left are the *Cambridge and County Folk Museum*, in the 16C former White Horse Inn, and the church of *St Peter*, with a Norman doorway and font surviving its rebuilding in 1781. The artificial mound of *Castle Hill*, by the *Shire Hall* to the right, was the site of pre-Roman and Roman settlements and of a castle (now demolished) built by William the Conqueror in 1068. It offers good views of the city. Castle St. continues N as Huntingdon Rd. On the left is **New Hall**, founded in 1954 as Cambridge's third college for women and still admitting women only (300 undergraduates). The stark white buildings (1962–66; Chamberlin, Powell and Bon) include a domed hall. Beyond is **Fitzwilliam College** (420 undergraduates), started in 1887 as a centre for non-collegiate students. It moved from Trumpington St. to its present buildings (by Denys Lasdun) in 1963 and became a full college in 1966.

1m further N is **Girton College**, founded by Emily Davies in 1869 as Britain's first residential college providing a university education for women. It began at Hitchin 'to avoid scandal' but moved to its present site in 1873, still safely remote from the older colleges. Since 1979 it has also admitted men (now 500 undergraduates, making it the third biggest college in Cambridge). The idiosyncratic red-brick buildings were begun by Alfred Waterhouse and completed by his son and grandson. The grounds extend to 46 acres. Virginia Woolf delivered the papers which became 'A Room of One's Own' here and at Newnham in 1928. Members include Rosamund Lehmann, Muriel Bradbrook, Q.D. Leavis, Baroness Wootton, Baroness Warnock, Kathleen Raine and Eileen Power.

Route 37 continues N to Huntingdon.

NORTH-EASTERN OUTSKIRTS. From the crossroads beyond Magdalene College, at the end of the walk N from Market Hill (above), Chesterton Lane and its continuation as Chesterton Rd head E. At (1m) the roundabout junction with Elizabeth Way stands the former *Chesterton Hall*, a much-altered Jacobean brick mansion. *Chesterton*, about ½m further E, has some pleasant river scenery and a few relics of the days before it became a suburb.

NORTH-WESTERN OUTSKIRTS. Northampton St. leads left from the crossroads N of Magdalene College (at the end of the walk N from Market Hill, above). On the right is *Kettle's Yard Art Gallery*, with a good 20C collection including work by Gaudier-Brzeska and Ben Nicholson, and on the left the back entrance to St John's College, with Merton Hall, the School of Pythagoras and the Cripps Building. At the roundabout beyond is *Westminster College*, a Presbyterian training college. The Madingley Rd heads W. On the right, Lady Margaret Rd leads to *Lucy Cavendish College*, founded in 1965, a women's college admitting graduates and mature undergraduates (80 students). In Mount Pleasant, further N, is *St Edmund's College*, mainly for graduates (70 students), founded in 1965. ¼m beyond is **Churchill College** (400 undergraduates), founded in 1960 as the national memorial to Sir Winston, with a particular emphasis on the sciences, technology and mathematics. To the traditional Cambridge plan of interlocking but spacious courts (by Richard Sheppard) the college has added the Moller Centre for Continuing Education, a sharply neo-classical building by Henning Larsen. The *Hall* has a bust of Churchill by Oscar Nemon. Sculptures on the lawns and in the courts include a fine Barbara Hepworth.

The Madingley Rd continues past the *American Military Cemetery* to (3m) *Madingley*, a pretty village with the Tudor mansion where Edward VII lived while keeping his terms at Cambridge (now a hostel and study centre).

WESTERN OUTSKIRTS. Silver St., passed on the walk S from Market Hill (above), crosses the Cam. Newnham Grange (left), once the home of the Darwin family, is now the nucleus of **Darwin College** (330 students), founded in 1964 as a graduate college by Caius, St John's and Trinity. New buildings (1968) were added to the Hermitage and the Granary, extending up to the corner of Newnham Rd. Sidgwick Avenue, straight ahead, leads to *Ridley Hall*, an Anglican training college, on the left, and **Newnham College**, founded in 1878 as the second women's college and still admitting women only (425 undergraduates). The original buildings, in red brick with handsome gables, are by Basil Champneys. Virginia Woolf delivered the papers which became 'A Room of One's Own' here and at Girton in 1928. Members include Constance Garnett, Sylvia Plath, Rosalind Franklin, Jane Grigson, Margaret Drabble and Germaine Greer. Opposite Newnham are the *University Arts Faculties*, laid out from 1952 onwards by Sir Hugh Casson and Neville Conder in a deliberately picturesque and informal manner. The *University Museum of Classical Archaeology* has a large display of plaster casts of Greek and Roman sculpture. To the N the *History Faculty Building* (1965; James Stirling) stands in aggressive contrast. The interesting *Harvey Court* of Caius College (1960; Sir Leslie Martin) is at the NE corner of the site. Sidgwick Avenue ends at **Selwyn College** (330 undergraduates), founded in 1882 for Church of England students 'willing to live economically' and recognised as a college in 1958. The original buildings are by Sir Arthur Blomfield. Members have included Malcolm Muggeridge, John Selwyn Gummer and Clive Anderson.

Grange Rd leads left past 19C Queen Anne Revival houses. Barton Rd goes right to *Wolfson College*, founded in 1965 as University College and renamed in 1973. It is principally a graduate foundation (50 undergraduates, 200 postgraduates).

The main route turns right from Selwyn and goes N along Grange Rd. In Herschel Rd to the left is *Clare Hall*, a graduate establishment (100 students) founded in 1966 by Clare College but now independent. Again to the left of Grange Rd, looking out on the tower of the University Library, is **Robinson College** (390 undergraduates). It is Cambridge's newest college, endowed in 1975 by a local businessman, David Robinson, with the largest single gift the university has ever received and opened to undergraduates in 1979. The red-brick, L-shaped buildings by Gillespie, Kidd and Coia are more in the style of a castle than a traditional Cambridge college. The chapel has windows by John Piper and an organ by Frobenius. The gardens are among the best any Cambridge college can boast.

N of Robinson College are college sports grounds and, on the left, *Wolfson Court* of Girton College (1969; David Roberts). Grange Rd ends at Madingley Rd (see North-Western Outskirts above).

SOUTH-EASTERN OUTSKIRTS. The starting-point is the large road junction beyond Downing College (at the end of the walk S and E from Market Hill above). Hills Rd goes S and crosses the railway line. Cherry Hinton Rd leads left to (2m) *Cherry Hinton*, where the church has a late Early English chancel. The main route continues on Hills Rd, passing (1m) **Homerton College** (250 undergraduates), originally a teacher-training college but now fully affiliated with the university. Beyond (2m) *Adden-brooke's Hospital* A1307 leads to the *Gog Magog Hills*, rising on the left, only 222ft high but giants indeed in the flat Cambridgeshire landscape. The Roman Via Devana crosses them and on top is (4m) *Wandlebury Camp*, an Iron Age fort (open).

It is worth continuing the drive to (10½m) *Linton*, with its zoo. At *Balsham*, 3½m N, the church is Decorated and Perpendicular, with two 15C brasses. At *Hadstock*, 2m S, the church is partly 11C with a remarkable N doorway. For Haverhill, beyond Linton at 19m, see Route 40.

EASTERN OUTSKIRTS. Jesus Lane (reached in the walk N and E from Market Hill above) continues as Maid's Causeway and the depressing Newmarket Rd. On the left just after the railway bridge is (1m) *Stourbridge Chapel*, the little Norman chapel of a hospital for lepers. *Stourbridge Common* to the N was for centuries the site of a great trading fair; it is now a dreary wasteland.

FROM CAMBRIDGE TO MILDENHALL, 22m. The route continues the drive through the Eastern Outskirts above. Newmarket Rd leads to A45 at the large roundabout, where the road for (4½m) *Stow-cum-Quy* heads N. The name is probably a corruption of 'Cow Ey' (island). B1102 continues to (6m) **Anglesey Abbey** (NT). The crypt of an Augustinian abbey is incorporated into a manor house variously owned by Thomas Hobson (see Hobson's Conduit above) and Sir George Downing, whose will endowed the college bearing his name. Today the house is badly disfigured by 20C alterations. Much more rewarding are the grounds laid out by Lord Fairhaven. At *Bottisham*, 1¼m SE, the early Decorated church has fine screens. 7½m: *Swaffham Bulbeck* has an Early English church with carved bench ends, and 16–17C houses around its green; the Commercial End built on a tributary of the Cam is a 19C development dominated by the Merchant's House. 8½m: *Swaffham Prior* has two churches in the same churchyard;

the earlier one has a Norman octagonal tower and the derelict one (restored in 1809) a Perpendicular tower. 11m: *Burwell* was a 'long street' village, and its chief glory is the late Perpendicular •church, with a clunch interior and a palimpsest brass of c 1542. *Wicken Fen* (NT), 3m N, is an untouched fenland area reserved as a sanctuary for characteristic insects and flowers. 15m: *Fordham* church has an interesting two-storied Lady Chapel on the N side. *Isleham* church, 3m NE, has a good roof, an eccentric Jacobean Communion rail and a brass to Thomas Peyton (d. 1484) and his two wives. The little Priory Church (EH) is Norman, with herringbone masonry. *Landwade* church (1445), 2m SW of Fordham, is remote and practically unrestored, with 16–18C monuments to the Cotton family. *Chippenham*, 2½m SE of Fordham, is a 'model village' built by the Thorpes of Chippenham Park. The church has old wall paintings. Chippenham Fen (NT, open by special application) is another undrained fen. 22m: *Mildenhall*, see Route 41.

From Cambridge to *Bedford*, see Route 60B; to *London* via *Stump Cross, Audley End* and *Bishop's Stortford*, see Route 41; to *London* via *Royston* and *Ware*, see Route 36; to *Huntingdon* and *Peterborough*, see Route 36; to *Ely* and *King's Lynn*, see Route 46.

38

London to Colchester, Ipswich and the East Coast

Directions. Total distance 124m. A12 is slow and congested for much of the way, particularly at summer weekends; likewise the detours to Southend, Harwich, Clacton and Felixstowe. Route 40 describes a quieter but less direct way to the coast. The route follows A12 to (15m) Gallows Corner, (31m) **Chelmsford** (bypassed), (53m) **Colchester** (bypassed), (71m) **Ipswich** (bypassed), (79m) Woodbridge (bypassed), (114m) **Lowestoft** and (124m) **Great Yarmouth**.

A12 runs NE from London through dull suburbs to (15m) *Gallows Corner*.

A127 leads E to Southend. 9m: *Laindon*, engulfed by *Basildon* (152,300 inhabitants), has a church with a unique 15C priest's house of timber against its W end. B1007 goes S over the *Langdon Hills* (387ft), with fine views of the Thames estuary (see below). 21½m: *Prittlewell* has a good 13C church and, in a delightful park, the refectory and prior's house of a 12C Cluniac priory, now a museum of local and natural history with a large collection of communications equipment. The 'south end' of the old village, standing near the mouth of the Thames, grew into the resort of **Southend-on-Sea** (156,700 inhabitants; TI). The pier, 1½m long, is the longest in the world. The more select part is *Westcliff-on-Sea*. Southchurch Hall (open) is a moated 14C manor house, with appropriate furnishings and displays of local history and medieval life. From *Southend Airport*, 2m N, passenger services fly to Guernsey, Jersey, Basle, Billund, Brussels and Ostend.

To the W of Southend is *Leigh-on-Sea*. *Hadleigh*, 2m further, has a Norman church and a ruined castle, rebuilt in 1359–70 for Edward III and made the subject of a famous painting by Constable (EH). To the S is the low-lying *Canvey Island*, protected by a sea-wall, with the methane gas terminal on its S side. A13 continues W along the estuary, passing N of *Coryton* (10m from Southend), with its oil refineries, and (15m) **Tilbury**, with its container port and passenger ferry to Gravesend on the Kent shore. *Tilbury Fort* (EH, all year) was first built by Henry VIII in 1539. Here Elizabeth I made her famous speech to the camp assembled in anticipation of the Armada in 1588 ('I know that I have the body of a weak, feeble woman, but I have the heart and stomach of a king, and of a king of England too'). Replacing the Henrician fort is a superb example of military engineering built for Charles II in 1670–83.

To the E of Southend the front extends past *Thorpe Bay* to (3½m) *Shoeburyness*. The flat deserted island of *Foulness*, overlooking *Maplin Sands* to the NE, was once chosen as the site of London's third international airport, a dubious honour later transferred to Stansted (Route 41).

Rochford, 4m N of Southend, has a Tudor mansion (not open), rebuilt by Anne Boleyn's father, and a fine brick church tower (c 1500). *Great Stambridge* church, 1½m E, partly pre-Conquest, was scene of the marriage of Governor Winthrop of Massachusetts in 1605. *Ashingdon*, 2m N of Rochford, is the probable site of the Battle of Assandun (1016), at which Canute defeated Edmund Ironside.

20m: *Brentwood* (bypassed; 55,800 inhabitants; TI) was the first staging-post on the coaching road from London, as the inn on the High St. testifies. Opposite are some typical Essex weatherboarded houses. Brentwood School, founded in 1557, keeps a block of 16C buildings. Adjoining *Shenfield*, where the church contains a remarkable oak arcade, grew round the railway junction on another road to Southend (A129; 21m). This runs via (4½m) *Billericay*, with a Chantry House where the Pilgrim Fathers assembled before leaving for America, and (15½m) *Rayleigh*, with a Norman castle mound (NT).

The brick towers and massive timberwork in the village churches are reminders of the absence of building stone and of the great forest covering Essex in the Middle Ages. At (23½m) *Mountnessing* (left) the church has huge timber struts supporting the tower. At (25m) *Ingatestone* (right) the church contains 16–17C tombs of the Petres. Their home is at the wellpreserved Tudor mansion of Ingatestone Hall (limited opening). 27m: *Margetting* church (right) has an oak steeple and 15C Jesse window.

31m: **Chelmsford** (58,200 inhabitants; TI), the county town of Essex, is a dull place. *St Mary*, now the *Cathedral*, was completed in 1424 but rebuilt after most of it collapsed in 1800. Its chief features are the beautiful S porch and the massive tower with its flèche spire (1749). The N wall of the chancel has a curious double or 'fan' arch (early 15C). The monument to Thomas Mildmay (1571) is also interesting. The *Shire Hall*, by John Johnson, is an Ionic building of 1789–92. Marconi developed his early wireless at Chelmsford and the town has a large electronics industry.

The *Museum* in Oaklands Park at Moulsham, 1m S, contains Roman and other antiquities, the Tunstill collection of English drinking glasses and a wing devoted to the Essex Regiment.

Rettendon, on A130 6m SE of Chelmsford, has the immensely varied gardens of *Hyde Hall* (open), developed since World War II and still being planted.

FROM CHELMSFORD TO MALDON AND BURNHAM-ON-CROUCH. Beyond (5m) *Danbury*, which has a sandy common and a church with three 13C wooden effigies, the road forks. A414 continues NE to (10m) **Maldon** (13,900 inhabitants; TI), a picturesque old port and yachting resort on the Blackwater. The church of *All Saints*, at the N end of the High St., has a triangular Early English tower, Decorated S aisle and 18C nave. Nearby is the 15C *Moot Hall* (open by appointment), with quaint porch and tower, used from 1556 until 1974 as the centre of local government. Attached to the tower of *St Peter* is Dr Thomas Plume's *Library* (open), a fine collection of 17C books bequeathed on his death in 1704. *St Mary*, overlooking the attractive harbour at the S end of the High St., has the remains of a 12C nave and a 17C brick tower with a white wooden steeple added a century later. The river and the sea-wall leading towards Northey Island and the Causeway reach the site of the Battle of Maldon (991), described in the Anglo-Saxon poem, where Brihtnoth was defeated by invading Vikings. From *Heybridge*, with a massive church tower, a canal and footpath lead to

(¾m) *Heybridge Basin*, frequented by yachtsmen and eel boats. *Langford*, beyond the river 1½m NW of Maldon, has the only church in England with a W apse.

From the Danbury fork B1010 leads SE. At (9½m) *Purleigh* Laurence Washington, great-great-grandfather of George Washington, was rector in 1623–43. The church tower is a Washington memorial with contributions from America. 19m: **Burnham-on-Crouch** (6300 inhabitants), on the Crouch estuary, is a centre for yachting and oyster-breeding. *Southminster*, 2½m N, has a large Perpendicular church. *Bradwell-juxta-Mare*, 5m further N, has a church with 14C details. The former rectory, Bradwell Lodge (open by appointment), is a 16C house with an 'Adam' wing. On the coast, 2m further NE, is the chapel of *St Peter-on-the-Wall*, built by St Cedd in the 7C on the ruins of the Roman fort of Othona, one of the castles of the 'Saxon Shore' (cf. Burgh Castle, below, and Brancaster, Route 45). In striking and unwelcome contrast is the nuclear power station.

From Chelmsford to *Bury St Edmunds* and *Cromer*, see Route 39.

36½m: *Hatfield Peverel* (right) has a partly Norman church. 39½m: *Witham* (left; 25,400 inhabitants) is an old town with a fine 13–15C church, 1m W, beyond the station. A plaque at 24 Newland St. marks the house where Dorothy L. Sayers lived from 1929 until her death in 1957. 43m: *Kelvedon*, on the left, has a High St. with old houses ranging from local weatherboarding to Georgian brick; more than 20 are 17C.

B1024 leads NW to *Coggleshall* (Route 41). B1023 runs SE to the Blackwater. 3m: *Tiptree* is famous for its jam. 7m: *Tolleshunt D'Arcy*, a pretty village, has a 16C moated hall with a bridge of 1585. At *Tolleshunt Major*, 2m W, by the church, is the 16C brick gatehouse and fortified wall of Beckingham Hall, rebuilt in the 18C (open by appointment). 9m: *Tollesbury* has old sail-drying sheds.

At (47m) *Marks Tey* the road is joined by A120. 48m: *Copford* has a fine Norman *church, 1m S, with an apse and a magnificent series of mural paintings showing Christ in Majesty, the raising of Jairus's daughter, signs of the Zodiac, and the Virtues (c 1150; restored). A12 swings left to bypass Colchester; the old Roman alignment of the road leads into the city.

53m: **COLCHESTER** (146,600 inhabitants) stands on a ridge above the Colne which has attracted settlement since the earliest times. It is England's oldest recorded town, and shows its historic importance in the wealth of remains from different periods: the Romano-British city walls, the Norman castle and St Botolph's priory, and many old houses, including some 200 Georgian ones.

TI: 1 Queen Street. **Bus Station**: High St. **Railway Stations**: North Station (1m N of the centre); Town Station, Magdalen St. (branch line to coast only). **Theatre**: Mercury, Balkerne Gate. **Annual Events**: Rose Show and Carnival in July; Oyster Feast in October.

History. A Bronze Age settlement (c 1100 BC) stood on the ancient ridgeway. Its strategic position led Cunobelin (Cymbeline), ruler of the Trinovantes, to make his capital here c AD 10. Claudius captured it in AD 44 and established the Colonia Camulodunum, the first Roman colony in Britain. This was stormed by Boudicca, queen of the Iceni, and after her defeat was re-established as a Roman garrison. Tradition has it that Constantine, was born here. On the departure of the Romans it became the Saxon stronghold of Colneceaster. William the Conqueror built the castle, whose keep is the largest in Europe; from the years that followed are seven surviving medieval churches within the walls and the remains of three abbeys. In the 14–17C the town was a centre of the cloth trade, its prosperity boosted by the influx of Flemish weavers in 1570. In the Civil War Colchester was staunchly Royalist, holding out against Fairfax's siege for 11 weeks.

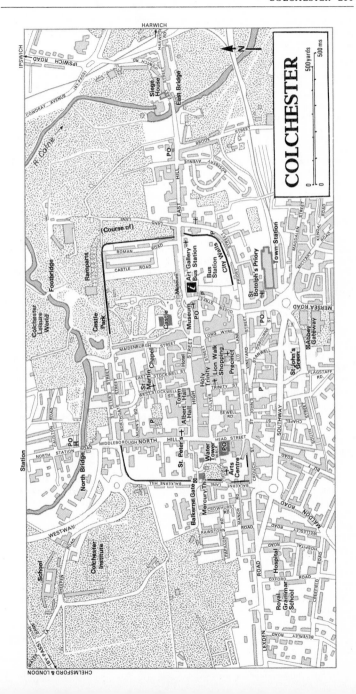

COLCHESTER

The *City Walls are the most striking witness to Colchester's Roman past. Nearly 2m in extent, and enclosing an oblong area in which the city centre still lies, they are best seen from the W side.

Probably begun in Vespasian's time but later strengthened and extended, the walls seem to have been over 20ft high, and parts are still over 10ft. The W section includes the ruined *Balkerne Gate*, most of which lies beneath the Hole-in-the-Wall Inn. *St Mary-at-the-Wall* (now the Arts Centre) keeps only the tower of the church slighted by Cromwell. Nearby is the *Water Tower* (1882), the dominant feature of the Colchester skyline, affectionately known as 'Jumbo'.

Head St. leads N, past the former King's Head inn where the Royalists surrendered in 1648, to meet North Hill with its old houses. The church of *St Peter*, partly classicised in 1758, keeps 13C ironwork on its (blocked) S door and unusual 16C brasses. The broad High St. runs W and E on the line of the ancient ridgeway and the Roman road. To the left is the *Town Hall* (1898–1902) by John Belcher; to the right the fine 15C *Red Lion Hotel*. On the left, further on, is the entrance to the park surrounding the *Castle*, a Norman building constructed in part of Roman materials (open).

The massive keep (151½ft by 110ft, with walls 12ft thick) is half as big again as the White Tower at London but lost its upper storey in 1683. Built on the platform of a Roman temple to Claudius, it contains a *Museum* with late Celtic and *Roman antiquities. The *Castle Park* includes a section of the Roman wall and gives a pleasant view of the Colne valley. An obelisk on the N side of the castle marks the spot where Lucas and Lisle, the Royalist defenders of the town, were shot by Fairfax in 1648. Adjoining the park is *Hollytrees*, a mansion of 1718, now a museum with a good collection of bygones. The *Natural History Museum* occupies an old church opposite.

High St. now passes between the pargeted *East Lodge* and the *Minories Art Gallery*, a Georgian house showing contemporary arts and crafts. Its continuation, East Hill, descends past *St James* (with a good monument of 1727) to the Colne. *Siege House*, occupied by Fairfax as his headquarters, and the *Rose and Crown* Inn are the most striking timbered buildings beyond the bridge.

Priory St. leads S from East Hill along the wall to the ruined church of *St Botolph's Priory*, an Augustinian foundation of c 1100 built mainly of Roman brick (EH). The arcaded W front has three portals, the fine one in the centre receding in five orders. Stanwell St. leads to St John's Green, with *St John's Abbey Gate*, the stately Perpendicular relic (c 1415) of a Benedictine house (EH).

A return to the centre crosses the line of the wall by Scheregate steps. On the right side of Trinity St. is *Holy Trinity Church*, with a Saxon tower built of Roman brick and a Saxon doorway. It is now a museum of rural crafts. A plaque marks the house opposite where the composer John Wilbye died in 1638; he lived for many years at Hengrave Hall (Route 41). *Tymperleys*, a half-timbered mansion next door, was the birthplace of Dr William Gilberd (1544–1603), Elizabeth I's physician. In West Stockwell St., N of the High St., are the disused Decorated church of *St Martin* and old houses, including the home of Ann and Jane Taylor, verse writers for children in the early 19C. *St Helen's Chapel* (not open), a little further to the E, dates from c 1290. It stands in the Dutch Quarter, where the Flemish weavers made their home when they arrived here in the 16C.

About 2m W of the city is *Lexden*, possibly the site of Cunobelin's, capital. The pre-Roman earthworks effectually bottle up the peninsula between the Colne and the small stream known as the Roman river. Considerable remains are still visible (EH).

The *University of Essex*, founded in 1962, is in *Wivenhoe Park*, 2m SE. About 6m SW, off B1022, and 3m from Tiptree, is *Layer Marney Tower* (open). This enormous brick gatehouse, built c 1525, is medieval in plan but Renaissance in ornament. The adjoining church has *tombs of the Lords Marney (c 1525–30), the first purely Renaissance tombs in England (cf. Oxborough, Route 39). Nearby *Layer Breton* has *Shalom Hall* (limited opening), a 19C house with collections of English portraits and French furniture and porcelain.

On the NE bank of the Colne estuary, below Colchester, are (4½m) *Wivenhoe*, with pargeting in East St., S of the church, and (10m) *Brightlingsea*, with a good church 1m inland. Opposite Brightlingsea, between the estuaries of the Colne and the Blackwater, is the island of *Mersea* with its yachting resort of *West Mersea*, 9m from Colchester via B1025. *Bourne Mill* (1591; NT), with an extravaganza of gables, lies on B1025, and a little further on is *Cannock Mill*, still in working trim.

FROM COLCHESTER TO CLACTON AND WALTON. A133 leads E to (10m) *Weeley* and then SE to (16m) **Clacton-on-Sea** (43,600 inhabitants; TI), one of the most crowded resorts in Essex. It is flanked by *Jaywick* to the W and *Holland-on-Sea* to the E. About 4½m W is the old village of *St Osyth*, where Osyth, queen of the East Saxons, was killed by the Danes c 870. A *Priory (open) on the site preserves a fine 15C gatehouse, with paintings, and other monastic buidings in a pleasant garden. On the creek below are a restored tide mill and boating lake.

From Weeley (see above) B1033 heads E via *Thorpe-le-Soken* to the quiet resort of (17m) **Frinton-on-Sea** and its homelier neighbour (17½m) **Walton-on-the-Naze** (joint population 14,700). The *Naze* is a headland to the N. Oysters are cultivated in the muddy creeks of Walton Backwaters, to the NW.

FROM COLCHESTER TO HALSTEAD. From Lexden (see above) A604 ascends the pleasant *Colne Valley. At 8m the former Chappel and Wakes Colne railway station has become the *Stour Valley Railway Centre*, with locomotives from the old Great Eastern Railway. 10m:*Earls Colne* church has a fine 16C tower, partly of brick. 13½m: *Halstead*, see Route 39.

FROM COLCHESTER TO HARWICH, 19m via A137 and B1352. At (10m) *Mistley* the 'Towers' are a fragment of Robert Adam's only English church, built in 1776 (EH, all year). 19m: **Harwich** (15,500 inhabitants; seasonal TI) is an old port and naval base on the broad estuary of the Stour and Orwell, with many 16–18C buildings. Among them is the red brick *Guildhall* (1769), with an eccentric Gothick door. On the Green is the 17C Naval Treadmill Crane. The Low Lighthouse in 'Chinese' style contrasts with the resplendent white brick High Lighthouse of 1818. Nelson stayed several times at the Three Cups Inn, while Captain Jones of the 'Mayflower' was married in Harwich and lived in King's Head St. The *Redoubt* (open) built to defend the harbour during the Napoleonic Wars is being restored. Ferry services run from Harwich to the Hook of Holland, Hamburg, Esbjerg, Kristiansand, Gothenburg, Hirtshals and Oslo; there is also a local service (passengers only) to Felixstowe (see below).

From Colchester to *Bishop's Stortford*, see Route 41.

A12 leads NE from Colchester and at (59½m) *Stratford St Mary* crosses the border into Suffolk and enters East Anglia. The Perpendicular church with flushwork is an appropriate introduction to the area. Its *N porch has an interesting window, and inside is a fine roof and 15C stained glass. There are some good 16C houses in the village. The surrounding region, with its woodlands by the banks of the Stour, is associated with John Constable (1776–1837).

Constable's birthplace in *East Bergholt*, 3m NE, does not survive but nearby are many of the scenes which, he said, 'made me a painter'. Among his favourite local subjects were: the watermills of Stratford St Mary itself; the picturesque *Flatford Mill* and *Willy Lott's Cottage*, 1m S of Bergholt (both NT but used by the Field Studies Council) and Bridge Cottage (NT), upstream, with a Constable display; and the fine 15C tower of *Stoke-by-Nayland* church, 4m W of Stratford. *Thorington Hall*, 2m SE of Stoke-by-Nayland, is a 17C house (NT, open by appointment). **Dedham**, a dignified village 1½m

E of Stratford, attracted both Constable and Sir Alfred Munnings, who lived from 1919 until his death in 1959 at *Castle House* (open). The church was built in 1492–1520 and many houses of the 16–18C survive. According to local legend the church of East Bergholt was deprived of its steeple by the devil, and so its bells are hung in a timber cage (1531) in the churchyard. *Nayland*, on the Stour 1½m S of Stoke, keeps painted panels from a 15C rood screen.

Little Wenham Hall (not open), 1½m N of (64m) *Capel St Mary*, is a very early example of Flemish brickwork (c 1250). At (67½m) *Washbrook* and *Copdock*, both with good churches, the Roman road swings N towards Venta Icenorum (Caistor St Edmund, Route 42). A12 drops into the valley of the Orwell and bypasses Ipswich.

71m: **IPSWICH** (117,000 inhabitants), the county town of E Suffolk, stands at the head of the estuary. A port and farming centre, known also for its agricultural machinery and printing works, Ipswich has too often torn down its past without putting much of worth in its place. The visitor today finds a patchwork of attractive historic buildings and unattractive town planning.

TI: St Stephen's Church, St Stephen's Lane. **Bus Station**: Dog's Head St. **Railway Station**: Burrell Rd (S of the river). **Theatre**: Wolsey Theatre, Civic Drive.

History. A prehistoric settlement grew up at the ford where the Gipping becomes navigable as the Orwell. It received its name, Gipeswic, from the Anglo-Saxons, was an important burgh by Domesday, and flourished for centuries as an agricultural centre

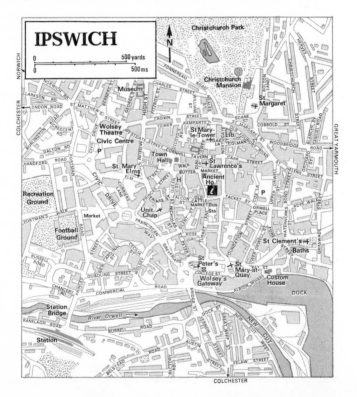

and port. Chaucer's Merchant 'wolde the see were kept for anything/Bitwixe Middleburgh and Orewelle'. It has more medieval parish churches than any English town of comparable size. From the peak of its prosperity in the 18C it remained a busy market town, its large Wet Dock handling North Sea traffic and Thames barges.

Natives and residents. Cardinal Wolsey (1475?–1530) was born here, the son of a butcher. Clara Reeve (1729–1807), Gothic novelist, was born and died here. Jeremy Collier (1650–1726), the clergyman who wrote 'A Short View of the Immorality and Profaneness of the English Stage', and H. Rider Haggard (1856–1925) attended Ipswich School.

The scale of Ipswich was greatly changed by the building of its Civic Centre. Cornhill, the traditional centre with the old *Town Hall* of 1867, lies to the E and is the natural place to start a walking tour. Tavern St. runs E. From it Dial Lane leads right, past the handsome tower of *St Lawrence*, to Butter Market. Here stands **Sparrowe's* or the *Ancient House* (1567), with a splendidly elaborate pargeted façade added in the reign of Charles II. Tavern St. continues E to the old *Great White Horse Hotel*, on the left, where Dickens stayed and Mr Pickwick had his embarrassing encounter with the lady in yellow curl papers.

Northgate St., with old houses and a 15C gateway, leads N past the *Library* (important Suffolk collections) to St Margaret's Plain. To the right is the noble flint church of *St Margaret*, with a double hammerbeam roof and a 15C clerestory. In the pleasant park adjoining stands ***Christchurch Mansion** (open), built in 1548–50, with later additions.

Rooms are furnished in styles from Tudor to Victorian, and there are good collections of furniture, ceramics and clocks. An early Tudor wing has been re-erected from elsewhere in the town. The Wingfield Room has 16C panelling from an inn in Tacket St. and Lady Drury's 'painted closet' from Hawstead Place, near Bury St Edmunds. The pictures include Tudor and Stuart portraits and works by the Suffolk painters Gainsborough and Constable. The Wolsey Art Gallery has changing exhibitions.

A return to the centre takes Oak Lane from Northgate St., past the rebuilt civic church of *St Mary-le-Tower*, with a conspicuous spire (176ft).

A second excursion from Cornhill starts by going W on Westgate St. In High St., to the right, is the *Ipswich Museum*, with collections illustrating local geology and fauna, and the prehistoric and Roman periods in East Anglia (including replicas of the Sutton Hoo and Mildenhall treasures now in the British Museum), etc. Museum St., leading left from Westgate St., has buildings fronted with Suffolk white brick. Behind the 15C church of *St Mary Elms* stands a row of medieval cottages. Off Friars St., beyond the junction with Princes St., is the handsome *Unitarian Chapel* of 1699. The courtyard leads to St Nicholas St., which goes S. At the corner with Silent St. are half-timbered houses, one identified by a plaque as Cardinal Wolsey's birthplace. St Peter's St. continues S to the church of *St Peter*, which contains a font of Tournai marble (c 1100) and the Knapp brass of 1604.

Hard by stands *Wolsey's Gateway*, the only relic of a college of secular canons founded by the Cardinal in 1527, one of 'those twins of learning, Ipswich and Oxford', that 'fell with him,/Unwilling to outlive the good that did it' (Shakespeare's 'Henry VIII', IV, ii). College St. leads E past *St Mary-at-Quay*, now the local headquarters of the Boys' Brigade, and the fine classical **Custom House* (1844) by J.M. Clarke, overlooking the Wet Dock of 1842.

Fore St. heads N, back towards the centre, passing the *Neptune Inn* and *Lord's* coal wharf, both 17C. In St Clement's Lane, to the right, the church of *St Clement* has a slender Perpendicular tower. From the N end of Fore

St. Orwell Place leads into Tacket St. Here the Salvation Army Citadel occupies the site of the theatre where Garrick made his debut as an actor proper in 1741. A kiln discovered in 1961 in nearby Cox Lane is believed to have manufactured the late Saxon pottery known as 'Thetford ware'.

At *Holbrook*, on B1080 6m S, is the Royal Hospital School, moved from Greenwich in 1933, where the sons of sailors and marines are trained for the navy. On the way there the road passes *Freston Tower* (c 1640) and *Woolverstone Hall*, now a school. Beyond, on the bank of the Orwell 7m from Ipswich, is *Pin Mill*, a favourite mooring for yachts.

FROM IPSWICH TO FELIXSTOWE, 12m via A45 across *Nacton Heath*, or 15m by the more interesting sideroad which keeps closer to the Orwell. It passes: *Nacton* church; *Orwell Park*, the home of Admiral Vernon ('Old Grog'), now a school; and *Broke Hall* (not open), the home of Admiral Sir Philip Broke (1776–1841), commander of the 'Shannon' in her encounter with the 'Chesapeake' (1813). **Felixstowe** (20,900 inhabitants; TI), 2½m long, stands on a cliff between the Orwell and the Deben. About 2m S is Felixstowe Dock, with a container port and car-ferry service to Zeebrugge. The 18C Landguard Fort stands on the site of earlier defences (EH, guided tours and limited opening of museum in summer). Across the Deben, about 2m N of Felixstowe, is *Bawdsey*, site of the first radar station (1936).

FROM IPSWICH TO SUDBURY, 21m via A1071. 5m: *Hintlesham Hall*, now a restaurant. 10m: **Hadleigh** (5900 inhabitants; TI), an old centre of the wool trade, has a large late 14C church. The Deanery Tower (1495) was the gatehouse to the palace of Archbishop Pykenham. The Guildhall (open) has a timber roof and an 18C assembly room. Thomas Woolner (1825–92), sculptor and Pre-Raphaelite, was born here. The Oxford Movement was started by the vicar of Hadleigh, Hugh Rose, in 1833. *Kersey*, 1½m NW, one of the Suffolk weaving villages, gave its name to 'Kerseymere' ('Cashmere'). The *street, with many timbered houses, dips down to a ford across the Brett. The *church has a flushwork S porch and a hammerbeam roof, and there are also remains of a 13C Augustinian priory. *Lindsey*, another weaving village 1m further W, gave its name to the cloth 'Lindsey-woolsey'. The 14C church has a tie-beam roof and wall paintings. *St James's Chapel*, ½m S, dates from the 13C and has tiny lancet windows (EH, all year). 15½m: *Boxford* has timbered houses and a wooden late Decorated porch to its church. In 1827 William Corder murdered Maria Marten in the Red Barn at *Polstead*, 2m SE. He was hanged at Bury St Edmunds (Route 39). 21m: *Sudbury*, see Route 39.

FROM IPSWICH TO NORWICH, 43m. At (4m) *Claydon* (Route 41), A140 leaves A45, following the line of the Pye Road, the Roman way from Colchester to Caistor St Edmund, to (10m) *Earl Stonham* (see Route 40). On the former airfield of *Mendlesham* (14½m; left) is a memorial to the men of the USAF. The Perpendicular church has a flushwork tower; it contains 15–17C armour, a Jacobean font cover and pulpit, and a brass to John Knyvet (1417). Hakluyt was rector of *Wetheringsett*, ¾m E of the road, from 1590 until his death. The village has timbered cottages. At (19m) *Yaxley* church is a 'sexton's wheel', used to determine voluntary fast days, one of only two in England (cf. Long Stratton below). **Eye**, 1½m E, is an attractive little town with a 16C timber-framed Guildhall. The church, with good flintwork, particularly in the tall *tower, preserves a richly painted rood screen of c 1500. To the W are the remains of the Norman castle of the Malets. Norfolk begins across the Waveney. 23m: **Scole** was an important staging post between Ipswich and Norwich at the crossing of the Great Yarmouth and Bury St Edmunds roads. The White Hart is a stately building of 1655 with Dutch gables. Remains of a Roman posting station, Villa Faustina, have been found. *Billingford*, has a restored brick cornmill (open). **Diss** (5400 inhabitants seasonal TI), 2½m W of Scole, is a little town built round a 6-acre mere. Among its buildings are the Dolphin Inn and Saracen's Head, timber-framed with overhangs, and the Victorian 'Shambles'. The church has a tall flushwork tower with processional arches at its base. John Skelton (1460–1529), poet and tutor to Henry VIII, held the living from 1498 until his death.

The *Bressingham Steam Museum*, 3m W of Diss on A1066, has traction engines and locomotives, including the Royal Scot. Bressingham Gardens (open) have hardy perennials and alpine plants. The church at *South Lopham*, 1½m further W, has a

Norman tower. *Hoxne* (pronounced 'Hoxen'), 3m SE of Diss, is a pretty village. The church has a fine tower and *wall paintings of St Christopher, the Seven Deadly Sins, and the Seven Works of Mercy. Abbey Farm, to the S, is the traditional site of the death of St Edmund, killed fighting the Danes in 869 and for many years the patron saint of England. The Roman hoard of nearly 15,000 gold and silver coins and 200 other precious objects unearthed in a field at Hoxne in 1992 is the most important Roman treasure yet found in this country.

A140 continues N from Scole to (28½m; left) *Tivetshall St Margaret*, where the church has a large Royal Arms (Elizabeth I). 32m: *Long Stratton* church has a 'sexton's wheel' (cf. Yaxley above) as well as a Jacobean font cover and pulpit. *Shelton* *church, 2m E, is a fine Perpendicular building with good brickwork (1480) by Sir Ralph Shelton. The graceful interior has a well-carved Royal Arms (William III). 34m: *Tasburgh* (on the left), a stronghold of the Iceni, has an Iron Age settlement and hill-fort. The bridge over the Tas at (35½m) *Newton Flotman* is partly medieval. The largely Elizabethan house of *Rainthorpe Hall* lies 1m SW (limited opening of gardens; house open by appointment). *Saxlingham Nethergate* church, 1½m E, has 13C glass. Venta Icenorum and *Caistor St Edumund* (Route 42) lie ½m N of (39m) *Dunston*. 43m: *Norwich*, see Route 42.

From Ipswich to *Bury St Edmunds* and *Newmarket*, see Route 41.

Beyond (76m) *Martlesham* A12 swings left to bypass Woodbridge. The old road, narrow and congested, descends to (79m) **Woodbridge** (7200 inhabitants), a charming old town on the Deben. The fine Perpendicular church has flushwork and a famous peal of bells in the tower (108ft). Inside are a 15C font and a monument to Thomas Seckford (d. 1587). The neighbouring Market Hill is dominated by the Shire Hall, originally built in 1575 though much changed. Tennyson stayed at the Bull Hotel when visiting his friend Edward FitzGerald (1809–93), who came to live at Woodbridge in 1860 and lodged over a shop on the N side of Market Hill. The surrounding streets have several more handsome inns, and New St. has a curious 18C steelyard. To the left of the main road, further on, is Little Grange, where FitzGerald spent his declining years. A pleasant walk leads along the Deben, with its yachts and tide mill.

FitzGerald lived in 1837–53 in a thatched cottage, still standing, at *Boulge*, 2½m N. He is buried in the churchyard of St Michael in the grounds of the demolished Boulge Hall nearby. On his grave blooms a descendant of the rose bush brought from Omar Khayyàm's tomb in Persia. *Grundisburgh*, 3m W of Woodbridge, is grouped round a green through which a small stream flows. In the church double hammerbeam *roofs with a multitude of angels cover the nave, S aisle and chapel. There is also a 13C wall painting of St Christopher.

FROM WOODBRIDGE TO ORFORD, 12m. From *Melton*, 1m NE of Woodbridge, A1152 crosses the Deben. To the right, on B1083 to Bawdsey, is *Sutton Hoo* (open summer weekends for guided tours), where a tumulus excavated in 1938–39 yielded the ship burial of a Saxon chieftain (c 650–70) of the Wuffingas, who ruled East Anglia at that time. The gold, silver and enamel treasures are now in the British Museum; replicas are displayed in Ipswich Museum (see above). B1084 diverges right from A1152 and crosses *Rendlesham Forest*, with oaks. 8m: *Butley* has the 14C gatehouse (now a private house) of an Augustinian priory, 1m S. Oysters are bred in the Butley river. 12m: **Orford** is a picturesque decayed seaport with a castle built by Henry II in 1165-67 (EH, all year). Its massive keep and three towers together form an irregular polygon of 18 sides. The ruined chancel of the church has a double row of Norman columns. The river Ore runs nearly parallel with the coast for 10m, separated from the sea by a narrow shingly spit. At Orfordness in 1935 Robert Watson-Watt carried out the practical experiments that gave birth to radar defence. The lonely church of *Iken*, 4½m N of Orford, commands a good view of the Alde estuary.

81m: *Ufford* church (13C) has a tabernacled *font cover, and benches with poppy heads and deep carving. 84m: *Wickham Market*, where the

Decorated church with a tall spire stands to one side of the little market square. *Charsfield*, 3m W, is the 'Akenfield' of Ronald Blythe's portrait of village life. 86m: *Little Glemham* church has a Norman doorway. Just beyond, the road skirts the park of *Glemham Hall* (not open), an 18C house on Elizabethan foundations. 91½m: *Saxmundham* is a small market town with a Decorated church containing 16C Flemish glass.

For *Leiston*, 4½m E, and *Aldeburgh*, 7½m SE, see Route 40. Beyond (95m) *Yoxford* an unclassified road on the right leads via *Westleton* to (5½m) *Dunwich*, now an attractive coastal village but an important seaport before the sea swept it away. It was the seat of the first East Anglian bishopric, established c 630, merged with that at North Elmham and transferred successively to Thetford and Norwich. Little is left of its ancient glory except the remains of a 13C Franciscan friary and the ruins of a 12C chapel near the present church, which includes materials from the last surviving old church. The local museum tells the story of Dunwich's decline. The sandy cliffs of the Heath, to the S, are NT.

101m: *Blythburgh*, on the tidal Blyth, was once a bustling port before the retreat of the sea and the silting up of the river closed it. It lies beneath one of Suffolk's finest *churches, built in 1442–73, containing original woodwork and a painted tie-beam roof with angels, used as targets by William Dowsing's crew of iconoclasts but relatively unharmed. **Southwold** (1800 inhabitants; TI), 5m E, is a charming old resort and fishing port with colourful houses. Its harbour at the mouth of the Blyth is backed by open heathland. George Orwell (1903–50) used to visit his parents' home on the High St. The Perpendicular *Church* has a notable rood screen, a panelled roof and canopied stalls.

Walberswick, 1m S across the river, has a half-ruined church as large as those at Blythburgh and Southwold.
An unclassified road running W from Blythburgh leads via (2m) *Wenhaston*, with an interesting panel of the Last Judgement dating from c 1480 in its church, to (5½m) *Halesworth*, where the Perpendicular church has good 15C brasses. About 4m SW on B1117 is *Heveningham Hall*, built in 1777–80 by Sir Robert Taylor and decorated by Wyatt, with a park by Capability Brown.

N of Blythburgh A12 skirts the fine park of *Henham* and reaches (106m) *Wrentham*. A sideroad leads 1m E to *Covehithe*, like Dunwich a port destroyed by the encroachment of the sea. Its ruined church has a smaller structure inside it, put up in 1672 to serve the needs of the reduced population. Offshore in the same year the indecisive Battle of Solebay (i.e. Southwold Bay) was fought between the Dutch fleet and the English and French under the Duke of York, later James II.

114m: **LOWESTOFT** (55,200 inhabitants), the most easterly town in England, is a resort, fishing port and ship-building centre. Thomas Nashe (1567–?1601) and Benjamin Britten (1913–76) were born here.

TI: East Point Pavilion, Royal Plain. **Bus Station**: London Rd North. **Railway Stations**: Station Square (by the harbour); also at Oulton Broad North and South. **Theatre**: Marina Theatre. **Annual Events**: Carnival Week in early August; Oulton Regatta Week in late August.

In the centre are the railway station and the harbour. Suffolk Rd, opposite the station, leads to the *Fish Market* and the trawler basin. A bascule bridge leads to the S part of town, with the *South Pier* and the newly built *East Point Pavilion*, an Edwardian-style building containing a restaurant, the TI Centre and a heritage exhibition. The long Esplanade and *South Beach* continue past *Claremont Pier*.

The old part of Lowestoft, N of the station, is reached by London Rd North. In the High St. some of the old houses preserve their bright red pantiles. Steep and narrow lanes called 'Scores' lead down towards the shore, where *Lowestoft Ness* is the most easterly point of Britain (long. 1° 45' E). At the N end of the High St. stand the *Lighthouse* and, beyond, the *Lowestoft and East Suffolk Maritime Museum* and the *Royal Naval Patrol Service Museum*. *St Margaret* at the NW edge of town, reached from the High St. by B1074 towards Somerleyton, is a spacious 15C flint building with an older tower. Thomas Nashe was baptised here.

The inner harbour, known as *Lake Lothing*, communicates by Mutford Lock with (1½m) Oulton Broad, a favourite centre for fishing and boating, with a yacht station. *Oulton* church, with a Norman chancel arch, is 1m N of the Broad. George Borrow (1803–81) wrote most of his books at his home on Oulton Broad, but the house no longer stands The *Lowestoft Museum* in the adjoining park has local archaeology and history and Lowestoft porcelain.

Blundeston, 3¼m NW, gave Dickens the name, though not the spelling, for David Copperfield's childhood home and was often visited by the poet Gray. At *Lound*, 1½m further N the church has a Perpendicular screen with a rood by Sir Ninian Comper (1914). To the W is (3m) *Somerleyton Hall* (open), built by John Thomas for the railway entrepreneur Sir Morton Peto in 1844, around a 17C manor. It has fine panelling and carving, and a maze in the gardens. The church and village were built at about the same time in an amusing eclectic style. Beyond is (4m) *Herringfleet*, with a partly Norman church and 17C hall and barn. For (5m) *St Olave's Priory* and (6m) *Fritton Decoy*, see below.

FROM LOWESTOFT TO SCOLE, 30m. A146 crosses the Waveney between Lake Lothing and Oulton Broad. 9m: **Beccles** (8900 inhabitants; seasonal TI), a town on the Waveney noted for its crayfish, has a fine Perpendicular church with a detached tower 92ft high. In 1794–97 Chateaubriand lived here as an emigré and fell in love with the parson's daughter at Bungay. At *Gillingham*, 1½m NW, is a pure early Norman church divided into five parts: Galilee, tower space, nave, chancel and apse. At *Raveningham*, 4m NW, the gardens of the Georgian Raveningham Hall are open. B1062 continues to (15m) **Bungay** (4100 inhabitants), with an octagonal market cross and two interesting churches, one of which has a pre-Norman round tower. The ruined Norman *Castle*, built by Hugh Bigod, Earl of Norfolk, in c 1165, has the remains of a keep and fore-building, and a twin-towered gatehouse added in 1294. About 2¼m SE of (19½m) *Homersfield*, at *South Elmham*, are the pre-Norman ruins called the Old Minster and wrongly claimed as the site of the East Anglian cathedral of Elmham (cf. North Elmham, Route 44A). 22m: *Harleston*. *Mendham*, 2m E, was the birthplace of Sir Alfred Munnings (1878–1959). At *Wingfield*, 5m SW of Harleston, the *church (1362) contains monuments of the Wingfield and de la Pole families. The de la Poles, Earls and Dukes of Suffolk, built the *Castle* (not open), with a handsome three-storied gatehouse of 1384 and a Tudor house behind. The Wingfields built the *College* (open), where the 18C façade conceals an older building. *Fressingfield*, 4m S of Harleston, has the 16C Fox and Goose inn, a church with fine *bench ends, roof and a Willis organ (from the Chapel Royal of the Savoy), and the grave of Archbishop Sancroft (1616–93). 30m: *Scole*, see above.

A12 runs N to (121½m) *Gorleston*, now included in the borough of Yarmouth, a seaside resort on a low cliff at the mouth of the Yare. Its sands are broad and clean and the large Decorated church, inland, has a good 15C font. From South Town, where Cotman lived as a drawing master in 1812–23, Haven Bridge crosses the Yare.

124m: **GREAT YARMOUTH** (89,100 inhabitants) is the chief town and most popular resort on the Norfolk coast. It stands on a peninsula formed by the Yare as it combines with the Waveney and the Bure to flow south from Breydon Water into the sea through a narrow mouth. Seaside Yarmouth fills the eastern edge of the peninsula, though its atmosphere imposes itself throughout the whole town. Beside the Yare is the port whose herring fleets and curing houses made 'Yarmouth bloaters' famous. The old town, originally enclosed by walls built between 1261 and 1400, keeps many handsome old buildings in brick and flint, and the distinctive 'Rows', narrow lanes running at right-angles to the river and sea to form a gridiron.

TI: Town Hall; (seasonal) Marine Parade. **Bus Station**: Wellington Rd, near Marine Parade. **Railway Station**: Vauxhall Station, reached from North Quay and Vauxhall Bridge. **Ferries**: local service across the Yare to Gorleston from just S of the Fish Wharf. **Amusements**: all the usual seaside attractions on Marine Parade.

Natives and visitors. Anna Sewell (1820–78), author of 'Black Beauty', was born on Priory Plain (see below). Dickens stayed at the Royal Hotel on Marine Parade in 1848; readers of 'David Copperfield' will remember Yarmouth's connection with the Peggottys. George Borrow often visited 169 King St., finishing 'Romany Rye' there in 1857.

On Hall Quay, by Haven Bridge, are the *Town Hall* and the *Star Hotel*, a restored Elizabethan house, once the residence of John Bradshaw, President of the court which convicted Charles I. Moored by the quayside is the 'Lydia Eva' (open), a steam drifter once used for herring fishing. South Quay has many houses of great charm, among them a refronted Tudor house claimed as scene of the conference at which Cromwell and his officers decided on Charles I's fate. It is now the *Elizabethan House Museum*. On Greyfriars Way, behind, are the scanty remains of the 13C *Greyfriars Cloisters*. The local museum nearby incorporates the walls and basement cells of the 14C *Tolhouse* (or jail). South Quay leads to the *Old Merchant's House* and the *Row 111 Houses*, good specimens of Yarmouth's 17C town houses (EH, with Greyfriars Cloisters, summer season; tours only).

The walk between Hall Quay and the large and handsome Market Place is rich in reminders of the old town, particularly on Market Row. At the NE corner of the Market Place are the almshouses called *Fishermen's Hospital* (1702). The half-timbered house (now a restaurant) in Priory Plain, just beyond, was the birthplace of Anna Sewell. The three-aisled *St Nicholas*, one of England's largest parish churches, was completely gutted in 1942. Though the outside preserves its old appearance, with 12C Norman tower and Early English W front, the interior was restored in 1957–61 by Stephen Dykes Bower. The Norman font came from the deserted church of Highway in Wiltshire, the pulpit from St George's (see below). Note also the ironwork, furnishing and glass by Brian Thomas, and the screens (1969) by Stephen Dykes Bower. The adjoining *Priory Hall*, on the S side, now a school, was originally the guesthouse of a Benedictine foundation established by Bishop Losinga. A large section of the *Town Walls*, built of brick and flint, bounds the churchyard. The *NW Tower*, now a Heritage and Information Centre for the Broads, survives on North Quay.

King St., with many good buildings, leads S from the Market Place, past *St George's* (1714), an ingeniously planned church with a cupola, now a theatre. On Blackfriars Rd, beyond the S end of King St., are two surviving towers and a stretch of the *Town Walls*.

The *Maritime Museum for East Anglia* is on Marine Parade in the centre of seaside Yarmouth. Beyond the S end of the Parade are the *South Denes*, home of Dickens's Peggotty family but now an industrial estate. The *Nelson Monument*, a Doric column of 1819, gives good views.

About 3m W of Yarmouth is **Burgh Castle** (EH). A Roman fortress on the Saxon Shore (c AD 300), it commanded the large harbour at the meeting of the Yare and Breydon Water. The three remaining landward walls are still held together by Roman mortar, though they lean at acute angles. The church to the NE has a Norman round tower, using Roman material from the castle.

FROM YARMOUTH TO BECCLES, 15m via A143 and A146. The road goes through an area whose churches have 12C round flint towers and 15C lion fonts. The one at (7m) *Fritton*, with a beautiful Norman apse, overlooks the *Fritton Decoy*, the most charming of the East Anglian lakes. 7½m: *St Olave's* has a ruined 13C Augustinian priory (EH). 9½m: *Haddiscoe* has a Norman S portal and Saxon work in the tower. 15m: *Beccles*, see above.

From Yarmouth to *Norwich*, see Route 42; to *Cromer* and *King's Lynn*, see Route 45.

39

London to Bury St Edmunds and Cromer

Directions. Total distance 142m. A12, slow and congested, to **Chelmsford**, see Route 38. A130, A131 to (42m) Braintree. A131 to (57m) Sudbury. A134 to (74m) **Bury St Edmunds**. A134, B1106 to (89m) Brandon. A1065 to (103½m) Swaffham and (119½m) Fakenham (Route 44A). A148 to (142m) **Cromer** (Route 45).

Route 38 leads to (31m) **Chelmsford**. A130 leads N and A131 turns NE. *Pleshey*, 2¾m NW of the junction, is enclosed in an earth rampart, with a huge motte and bailey on the S preserving a brick arch bridge. 38m: *Great Leighs* has the Essex showground. *Little Leighs* priory (not open), ¾m W of the road, has two gatehouses and part of a quadrangle of c 1550. 42m: **Braintree** (31,100 inhabitants; TI), at the junction of two Roman roads, was a medieval wool town. Nicholas Udall, author of 'Ralph Roister Doister', was vicar here from 1537. Bank St. leads N past old houses and inns to *Bocking*, with a good 15C church.

Black Notley, 1¾m SE, was the birthplace of the naturalist John Ray (1628–1705), buried in the churchyard. *Cressing Temple*, 3m SE, has two huge barns, one 15C and the other perhaps partly pre-Conquest. For *Bishop's Stortford* and *Colchester*, see Route 41.

49m: *Halstead* (9300 inhabitants), in the upper valley of the Colne, has an unexpectedly steep High St. The mill set up by the Courtaulds in 1826 is by the stream. *Gosfield Hall* (limited opening), 2½m W, has a brick Tudor court and panelled long gallery. It was Louis XVIII's first English home in 1807–09.

A604 leads NW towards Haverhill via (3½m) *Sible Hedingham*, where the church is the probable burial place of the condottiere Sir John Hawkwood, who was born here and died at Florence in 1394. *Castle Hedingham*, 1½m NW, has a late Norman church and a massive Norman keep of c 1100 (open).

From Halstead to *Colchester*, see Route 38.

At (51½m) *Little Maplestead*, to the left, the church, mainly early 14C, is the latest and smallest of the four medieval round churches to survive in England. (The others are at Cambridge, Northampton and the Temple in London.) 57m: **Sudbury** (9900 inhabitants; seasonal TI) has half-timbered houses from its days of silk weaving, and three striking Perpendicular churches. All have good woodwork, and *St Gregory* has a splendid font cover. The vestry of St Gregory's preserves the head of Simon of Sudbury, Archbishop of Canterbury in 1375–81, beheaded by Wat Tyler during the Peasants' Revolt. The town was the birthplace of Thomas Gainsborough (1727–88), commemorated by a statue in Market Hill. His house in Stour St. (open), with 18C furnishings, has paintings by him and his contemporaries.

Belchamp Hall (open by appointment), at *Belchamp Walter* 5m W, is a Queen Anne house with period furniture. *Edwardstone*, 6m E, was the birthplace of John Winthrop (1588–1649), first Governor of Massachusetts. His son John (1606–76), Governor of Connecticut, was born at *Groton*, 1m further, which has given its name to an American school. From Sudbury to *Ipswich*, see Route 38.

60m: *Long Melford*, see Route 40. 67m: *Bradfield Combust* was the home and burial place of Arthur Young (1741–1820), agriculturist and traveller, who went to school at Lavenham. *Rushbrooke*, 2½m NE, has a charming little church.

74m: **BURY ST EDMUNDS** (28,900 inhabitants), the historic centre of West Suffolk, has won praise over many centuries for its neat and prosperous appearance. Cobbett thought it 'the nicest town in the world'. It takes its name from the shrine of St Edmund, last king of East Anglia (d. 869). The abbey, founded in 945 and rebuilt in the 11C, became one of the noblest and wealthiest in England; it now lies ruined.

TI: 6 Angel Hill. **Buses**: from Angel Hill and St Andrew's St. **Railway Station**: Northgate St. **Theatre**: Theatre Royal, Westgate St.

History. The town owes its grid pattern to Abbot Baldwin (1065–97) who laid out the first planned town of Norman Britain, with Churchgate, the main street, in line with the high altar. In 1214 the barons, headed by Archbishop Langton, drew up the 'Petition of the Barons', the basis for Magna Carta, at the abbey church. Nowadays Bury is noted for brewing and sugar beet.

Natives and visitors. The gardener Humphry Repton (1752–1818), the diarist Henry Crabb Robinson (1775–1867) and the novelist 'Ouida' (Louise de la Ramée; 1840–1908) were natives. Edward FitzGerald attended the King Edward VI School. Visitors include Defoe, Dickens ('The Pickwick Papers') and Carlyle ('Past and Present'). William Corder, who murdered Maria Marten at Polstead (Route 38), was tried and hanged here in 1828.

The existing remains of the **Abbey** (EH, park opening hours) are reached from Angel Hill, on the E side of the town, which has the *Athenaeum*, in the Adam style, and the *Angel Hotel* (18C, with 13C cellars), where Sam Weller first met Job Trotter.

The *Abbey Gateway* (1327, rebuilt after fire in 1347) leads to a public garden with the formless ruins of the refectory, abbot's house, etc., and the 13C *Abbot's Bridge* across the Lark. Beyond the river is the former *King Edward VI School*, where FitzGerald studied. To the S are the ruined E end and transepts of the abbey church. The W front is now part of a row of houses. The *Norman Tower* is early Norman work, carved with the axe and not the chisel. Beside it is the *Cathedral of St James*, with a noble nave begun in 1438, and good 19C windows and roof; a new NW porch and cloister walk were dedicated in 1960–61 and a new chancel, by Stephen Dykes Bower, replaces that by Gilbert Scott. Across the graveyard is *St Mary*, a beautiful 15C church, with a hammerbeam *roof in the nave and a waggon roof in the choir. In the S aisle are the tomb (with skeleton effigy) and chantry ceiling of John Baret (1467) and the brass of Jankyn Smith and his wife (1487). S and N of the choir are the Drury and Carew tombs (1536 and 1501). The N or Notyngham Porch (1437) has an elaborate vault and pendant. In the NE corner of the sanctuary is a plain slab marking the grave of Mary Tudor (1496–1533), Henry VIII's sister.

The *Manor House Museum* on Honey Hill contains the Gershom-Parkington collection of clocks and watches, as well as paintings, prints, ceramics and costumes. Fornham Rd has the ruined gatehouse of *St Saviour's Hospital*, where Humphrey, Duke of Gloucester died in 1447.

Abbeygate St. (with Georgian shopfronts), or Churchgate St. (with the Independent Chapel of 1711), leads to Cornhill, the business centre of Bury. In the Traverse is *Cupola House* (1693), a dignified town mansion, the best of many 17–18C houses. Many streets have earlier houses and inns. A little below the *Market Cross*, remodelled by Adam in 1774, is the 12C *Moyses Hall*, now a museum, which may have been a Jewish merchant's house. In Guildhall St. at the other end of Cornhill is the *Guildhall*, with a porch of c 1480, and in Westgate St. is the *Theatre Royal* (NT) by Wilkins (1819).

Ickworth (NT), 3m SW, a mansion built in 1794–1830, has an unusual plan recalling the eccentricity of its owner, Frederick Hervey, Earl of Bristol and Bishop of Derry (1730–1803). The rotunda with flanking wings looks unattractive outside and creates awkward shapes inside, but the collection of furniture, silver, porcelain, paintings and sculpture (Flaxman's 'The Fury of Athamas') is distinguished. The park has pleasant walks. At *Ampton*, 5m N of Bury, Jeremy Collier was rector in 1679–84.

FROM BURY TO NORWICH, 39½m. A143 leads to (6½m) *Ixworth*, where the main street may be the start of the Peddars' Way (Route 45). The Abbey (open by prior appointment) incorporates the remains of a 12C priory and 15C prior's lodging. *Stowlangtoft* church, 2m SE, contains *bench ends and misericords, and Flemish panelling at the E end. Near (10m) *Stanton* B1111 is followed left and beyond (16m) *Garboldisham* (pronounced 'Garblesham') B1114 is followed right. At (19½m) *Kenninghall* stood a palace of the Howards, Dukes of Norfolk, demolished in 1650. It was the birthplace of the poet, Henry Howard, Earl of Surrey (1517–47), and Mary I took refuge here in 1553 before going to Framlingham. B1113 leads to (21½m) *Banham*, with a zoo and a collection of vintage cars and motorcycles. 23½m: *New Buckenham* has a Perpendicular church, the remains of a Norman chapel and a market hall with pillory, while *Old Buckenham*, to the W, has a thatched church. A140 leads into (39½m) *Norwich*, see Route 42.

From Bury to *Newmarket* and to *Ipswich*, and to *Hengrave* and *Icklingham*, see Route 41.

The main route follows A134 towards Thetford (Route 41), but soon branches left at (76½m) *Fornham St Martin* on B1106. It crosses A11 (Route 41) at (86m) *Elveden*. 89m: *Brandon* was for long a centre of flint knapping, one of the oldest trades in the world. Norfolk is beyond the Little Ouse.

Weeting, 1m N on B1106, has a 12C castle with a keep and square moat (EH). *Methwold* church, 5½m further on, has a Perpendicular crocketed steeple (120ft) and a brass to Sir Adam de Clifton (d. 1367).

A1065 crosses Thetford Chase. At 91½m B1108 branches right to (1m) *Grime's Graves, an area of Neolithic flint quarries (EH, all year). Nearly 400 shafts and pits are clustered together; one has been opened so that visitors can see the galleries radiating from the bottom. 103½m: **Swaffham** (4800 inhabitants), a market town with good Georgian buildings. The elegant Rotunda crowned with a figure of Ceres was built by the Earl of

Chalk idol found at Grime's Graves (now in the British Museum)

Oxford in 1783. The large Perpendicular church has a double hammerbeam roof and carvings of the peddlar who, tradition says, founded it.

Cockley Cley, 3m SW, has a folk museum and a reconstructed Iceni encampment. At *Oxborough*, another 4m SW, the church steeple fell in 1948 and destroyed most of the nave but spared the Bedingfield Chapel, with terracotta *monuments of c 1520 in the Italian style (cf. Layer Marney, Route 38).

Nearby is *Oxburgh Hall (NT). In the 1480s Sir Edward Bedingfield built not a castle but a square brick mansion defended by a moat and splendid castellated gatehouse. A descendant pulled down the S range in 1778 but the loss was tactfully made good in the 1830s, when the SE tower was also added and most of the windows renewed. So the outside of Oxburgh has kept its picturesque appearance. Another 19C addition, the formal French parterre by the moat, makes a pleasing contrast. Inside are the 19C library with a fireplace by A.W.N. Pugin and the turret rooms and spiral staircase of the gatehouse. Its roof offers a wide view of the flat countryside. Furnishings include: 17C embossed leather covering two staircase walls; needlework panels signed by Mary, Queen of Scots, and Bess of Hardwick; and the Sheldon tapestry, a map of neighbouring counties woven c 1647.

107½m: **Castle Acre** (left), a pleasant village with the remains of a large Cluniac *Priory founded by William de Warenne in 1090 (EH, all year). Its chief feature is the late Norman W front of the church. Note also the prior's lodging and chapel (remodelled in Tudor times and later used as a farm-house), the reredorter and the Tudor entrance gatehouse. The castle which gave its name to the village stood on huge earthworks, probably Roman (EH). The bailey gate (EH) spans the village street. The church, between castle and priory, contains painted 15C woodwork. The Peddars' Way (Route 45) can be seen to the N.

South Acre church, just to the S, contains a brass to Sir John Harsick (d. 1384) and his wife, the tomb of Lord Mayor Barkham (1621), a 14C wooden effigy and a 14C screen. At West Acre, 2¼m W, the gatehouse and barn of another priory survive near the church (with a wide 14C chancel arch). Narborough church, 2½m further SW, has a fine standing effigy of Clement Spelman, Recorder of Nottingham (d. 1679), as well as good brasses, one a palimpsest. A 14C gatehouse is the chief relic of the priory at Pentney, 1m beyond.

At 108m is the tiny Saxon church of Newton. 113m: Weasenham St Peter has a small church with flushwork. A sideroad beyond leads to (1m) Wellingham church, with a painted screen (1532).

The church of Tittleshall, 2m E, has *monuments to Sir Edward Coke (d. 1634) by Nicholas Stone; to Coke's wife, Bridget Paston (d. 1598); to Thomas Coke, Earl of Leicester (d. 1759) and his wife, with a bust by Roubiliac; and to other members of the family.

116m: The road passes the lodge gates of East Raynham Hall, sometimes ascribed to Inigo Jones, home of the agricultural pioneer 'Turnip' Townshend (Charles, 2nd Viscount Townshend; 1674–1738). 117m: The church at Toftrees has a Norman font of local type. 119½m: Fakenham, see Route 44A.

A148 heads NE via Thursford (Route 44B) to (130m) Letheringsett, with a round church tower and a watermill restored to working order (open). 132m: **Holt**, an attractive and colourful town, was the birthplace of Sir Thomas Gresham (1519–79), Lord Mayor of London and founder of the Royal Exchange, who propounded 'Gresham's Law'. Gresham's School was founded by his uncle in 1555. At 136½m A148 passes the entrance to Sheringham Hall (see Route 45). A sideroad leads right to (3m) Baconsthorpe Castle (EH, all year plus Mondays in winter), a moated and fortified manor house built by the Heydons in the 15C. The ruins include walls, towers and a gatehouse with flint facing. 142m: **Cromer**, see Route 45.

40

London to Aldeburgh

Directions. Total distance 110½m. This alternative to the A12 (Route 38) is not for the hurried. A11, A113 to (21m) Chipping Ongar. B184, A1060, B184 to (34m) Great Dunmow. B1057 to (49m) Steeple Bumpstead. B1054, A604 to (52m) Wixoe. A1092 to (55½m) **Clare** and (63m) **Long Melford**. Unclassified road to (67m) **Lavenham**. A1141 to (70m) Monks Eleigh. B1115, B1078 to (80m) **Needham Market**. B1078, A140 to (85m) Earl Stonham. A1120 to (94m) Saxtead Green. B1119 to (96m) **Framlingham**, (103m) Saxmundham (Route 38) and (107½m) Leiston. B1122 to (110½m) **Aldeburgh**

A11 goes through the E suburbs and picks up A113 at (7m) the Green Man, Leytonstone. 11m: *Chigwell* keeps its village centre with 15C church, grammar school and 17C inn, the 'Maypole' of Dickens's 'Barnaby Rudge'. 16m: The route crosses M25. 21m: *Chipping Ongar* ('Chipping' meaning 'market') has a Norman church and Saxon castle mound. *Greensted-juxta-Ongar*, 1m W, has a *church (c 845) with a remarkable nave of split oak tree trunks set upright on a sill. St Edmund's body rested here for a night in 1013 on its return from London to Bury St Edmunds, whence it had been removed in fear of the Danes. The brick choir dates from c 1500.

Stondon Massey, 2m SE of Ongar, was the home of William Byrd ('father of musick') in 1595–1623. It has an early Norman church. *Blackmore*, 2m further E, has a church with a fine timber tower, and Jericho House, built on the site of one of Henry VIII's favourite manors.

B184 from Ongar follows the ridge above the valley of the Roding, an ancient track known by its Saxon name of The Rodings (or 'clearings', hence 'road'). 23½m: *Fyfield* church has a 12C font and unusual sedilia with sculptured heads. The parishes of *Willingale Doe* and *Willingale Spain*, 2m E across the valley, have churches sharing one churchyard; St Andrew's is part Norman, and St Christopher's has good brasses. 26m (½m left) *Abbess Roding* church is 14C, with a Norman font and an 18C pulpit with fine tester. At 27½m A1060 is followed right to (28m) *Leaden Roding* church, with a weatherboarded belfry and Norman nave and chancel. To the E lie the Easters: *High Easter* church has a fine timber roof. B184 turns N and joins a Roman course (disused nearer London) on which stands (30½m) *High Roding*, where the 13C church has a 15C pulpit. *Great Canfield* church, 1m W, has a Norman chancel arch, and a 13C *wall painting of the Madonna and Child. 34m: *Great Dunmow* (4500 inhabitants), a pleasant old market town, stands above the Chelmer.

The church at *Stebbing*, 3m NE, has a stone rood screen (cf. Great Bardfield below). *Little Dunmow*, off A120 2½m SE of Great Dunmow, has the remains of *Dunmow Priory*, where, by an old custom, a flitch of bacon could be claimed by any married couple who had 'not repented them, sleeping or waking, of their marriage in a year and a day'. *Felsted*, 1m further, was a Jutish settlement. Its partly Norman church contains a 17C monument by Epiphanius Evesham to the first Lord Rich (d. 1568), founder of the school, which originally stood next to the church. Richard Cromwell was a pupil.

FROM GREAT DUNMOW TO THAXTED, 6½m by B184. 3m: *Great Easton* has the remains of a motte and bailey castle. *Little Easton* church, about 1½m SW, contains 12–15C *wall paintings, 17C German glass and 15–18C monuments. H.G. Wells lived here in

1912–30. 6½m: **Thaxted** is a picturesque town with old houses and a Jacobean Guildhall on wooden pillars (limited opening). The spacious 14–15C *church has a fine crocketed spire, pinnacled buttresses and grotesque gargoyles. The font, pulpit, N and S porches, timber roofs and organ (1703; John Harris) are all worth noting. The tower windmill, with its main machinery still intact, is now a rural museum. Thaxted was the birthplace of Samuel Purchas (1577?–1626) of the 'Pilgrimes'. Gustav Holst wrote 'The Planets' while organist at the church in 1916. *Chickney*, 3½m SW, has a primitive Norman church.

From Great Dunmow to *Bishop's Stortford* and to *Colchester*, see Route 41. B1057 winds NE from Great Dunmow through two notably attractive villages. At (41½m) *Great Bardfield* a number of local crafts have been revived. The church has a 14C stone rood screen (cf. Stebbing above). 43m: *Finchingfield* is grouped round a village green and duckpond below the squat Norman tower of the church, topped by an 18C cupola. 49m: *Steeple Bumpstead* church has a good monument to Sir Henry Bendysshe (d. 1717) and his baby son. *Haverhill* (17,100 inhabitants), a London 'overspill' town, lies 3m N. B1054 joins A1092 to cross the Stour into Suffolk at (52m) *Wixoe* and follow the valley. 53½m: *Stoke-by-Clare* is a pretty village with a large Perpendicular church containing a pulpit of 1498 and a wall painting of 1550. 55½m: **Clare** preserves many beautiful houses, some pargeted, and remains of the Augustinian priory founded in 1248, where Edward III's son Lionel, Duke of Clarence (d. 1368) was buried. Of the castle, only part of the keep still stands. The church is Perpendicular, with early Tudor work; the N chancel door has notable tracery. All the glass was destroyed by the notorious Parliamentarian, William Dowsing. A timber-framed house in the High St. contains a local museum. 58m: *Cavendish*, with a spacious green, has a church with a fine flint clerestory. It contains tombs of the Cavendishes, including Sir John (d. 1381), who built the chancel. The 15C Nether Hall is now a museum and gallery; the adjoining vineyard is also open. Across the Stour is the church of *Pentlow*, with a round tower, opposite a timbered manor house (c 1500).

63m: **Long Melford** is strikingly arranged, having church and hall around the large, attractive green at the N end and, leading S, a High St. over 2m long with many half-timbered and Georgian houses. The late Perpendicular *Church is a magnificent example of the Suffolk style, with elaborate flushwork, long nave and tall windows, and tall clerestory above. It is spacious and handsomely proportioned inside. The aisles and N chapel have 15C *glass. The Clopton Chantry, off the N aisle, contains good monuments and brasses. The Lady Chapel, attached to the E end of the church, has an ambulatory with wooden ceiling and sculptured corbels. E of the green is *Melford Hall* (NT).

It was built in the 1550s and 1560s by Sir William Cordell, Speaker of the House of Commons and Master of the Rolls, who was visited here by Elizabeth I. Its Tudor character is still shown by the exterior, a brick three-sided courtyard facing away from the green, and by the position of hall and gallery inside. Otherwise, the interior has been greatly altered, mainly by Thomas Hopper in the early 19C. His Regency library is charming.

½m N of the green is *Kentwell Hall* (open), approached by a long avenue of lime trees planted in 1678. The moated house has the same plan as Melford Hall and a similar date (shortly before 1563). Most of the interior was refurbished by Hopper after a fire in the 1820s.

From the timbered *Bull Hotel* a sideroad leads E to (67m) **Lavenham** (seasonal TI). The village is the most picturesque in Suffolk and, like Long

Melford, bears witness to the prosperity that the wool trade brought East Anglia in the late Middle Ages. Many streets have half-timbered houses, with carved angle posts and pargeting. In the Market Place is the *Guildhall* of 1529 (NT), with a corner post representing the 15th Earl of Oxford. Nearby is the *Little Hall* (open), a 15C hall house. In Water St. another hall house, the *Priory* (open), belonged to a Benedictine Order before it was enlarged into a wool merchant's home. The *Angel Hotel* has a 16C plaster ceiling and 14C wall paintings, while the *Swan* incorporates the old Wool Hall. The *Church*, magnificently sited, is of the same style as Long Melford: tall tower, long nave, generous clerestory, flushwork throughout. It was built (1480–1520) in friendly rivalry by the 14th Earl of Oxford and Thomas Spring, a wealthy clothier. It has a fine S porch, the *Spring Chantry* (1523) and the Oxford Chantry, and good misericords.

Acton church, c 3m SW, contains the *brass of Sir Robert de Bures (d. 1302), one of the oldest and best in England, and a monument to Robert Jennens (d. 1722), Marlborough's aide-de-camp. *Little Waldingfield*, c 2m E of Acton, has a fine 15C church.

A1141 leads to (68½m) *Brent Eleigh* where the church has 14C wall paintings. 70m: *Monks Eleigh* has good houses, a mill, and a large Perpendicular church. *Lindsey* and *Kersey*, 2m and 3m, SE, see Route 38.

B1115 continues E to (71m) *Chelsworth*, an attractive village on the Brett (bridge of 1754). The church contains a decorated tomb recess and a wall painting. At (72m) *Bildeston*, with good timber cottages, B1078 forks right. 75½m: *Great Bricett* church, with a Norman door, is all that remains of an Augustinian priory. 78m: *Barking* has a Decorated church with an early tie-beam roof, and parclose and *rood screens. 80m: **Needham Market** (3900 inhabitants) is a pleasant town with old houses, some dating from the 14C, lining the High St. The church contains an angel *roof.

B1078 quits the town. At the junction with A45, A140 heads N to (85m) *Earl Stonham*. The *church has a spectacular double hammerbeam roof with angels. Its Jacobean pulpit has four hour glasses, for sermons from ¼hr to 2hr. A1120 goes E to (86m) *Stonham Aspal*, whose large church has a Decorated tower. The timber-framed chancel of *Crowfield* church, 2m SE, is the only one in Suffolk.

At 89½m B1077 leads S, passing *Framsden* (windmill) on the left, to (2m) *Helmingham Hall*, with gardens and deer park (limited opening). B1079 forks left to (4m) *Otley*. The Hall (limited opening), ¼m NE, is a lovely 15–16C house, moated and timber-framed, with herringbone brick and pargeting. Bartholomew Gosnold, a descendant of the builders, settled and named Cape Cod and Martha's Vineyard in Massachusetts.

92½m: *Earl Soham* has an attractive green. 94m: *Saxtead Green* has a working windmill (EH, summer standard opening except Sunday).

Dennington, 2½m NE, has a church with *parclose screens. The bench ends include one showing a 'sciapod' (a one-legged man using his foot as a sunshade). There is a rare pyx canopy and the tomb of Lord Bardolph, who fought at Agincourt.

B1119 branches right. 96m: **Framlingham**, grouped round the triangular Market Hill, has a ruined *Castle (EH, all year). Built mainly during Edward I's reign, it is one of the earliest to use not a central keep but a surrounding curtain wall with towers at intervals. Queen Mary found refuge here with the Howards during the attempt to place Lady Jane Grey on the throne. Inside the shell stands the Poor House (1636), and the towers are adorned with Tudor chimneys. The battlements look across the Meres to the *College*, Suffolk's memorial to Prince Albert (1864), on the opposite hill. The

Aldeburgh

Church, Perpendicular and Decorated, has a covered hammerbeam roof. It contains the magnificent *monuments of the Howard family—including Henry Howard, Earl of Surrey, the poet, executed in 1547—and of Sir Robert Hitcham (d. 1636), with supporting angels. In the sanctuary is the Flodden helmet, worn at the battle by the English commander, the 2nd Duke of Norfolk. The organ has some pre-Commonwealth pipes.

103m: *Saxmundham*, see Route 38. At 107½m *Leiston* (5100 inhabitants with Sizewell) Richard Garrett built the railway engineering works and workers' cottages, and commissioned the striking church by E.B. Lamb (1853).

About 1m N are the ruins of the Premonstratensian *Leiston Abbey* (EH), which moved here from Minsmere in 1363. The church at *Theberton*, 1m further on, has a round tower, thatched roof and Norman doorway. C.M. Doughty (1843–1926) of 'Arabia Deserta' was born at Theberton Hall. To the E of Theberton, in a wild sandy area extending to low sea cliffs, is the *Minsmere* nature reserve. *Sizewell* nuclear power station, on the coast 2m E of Leiston, is being expanded by the addition of a second reactor. *Thorpeness*, on the coast 3m SE of Leiston, is a holiday village with a boating lake.

B1122 leads S to the resort of (110½m) **Aldeburgh** (2900 inhabitants; seasonal TI). It was a favourite haunt of Edward FitzGerald, while George Meredith and Wilkie Collins spent holidays here. Its atmosphere was evoked in 'The Borough' by the native poet George Crabbe (1754–1832). There is a memorial to him in the Perpendicular church. The *Moot Hall*, a half-timbered 16C building now standing amid the encroaching shingle, was the town hall of the old town washed away by the sea.

Since the 1945 production of Benjamin Britten's 'Peter Grimes', based on a poem by Crabbe, Aldeburgh has been a centre for music. Many of Britten's later operas were composed for local performance. The Aldeburgh Festival is held in June at the Maltings in *Snape*, about 5m W, converted into an opera house in 1967 and restored again after a fire in 1969.

41

London to Newmarket and Norwich

Directions. Total distance 105m. M11, the London–Cambridge motorway, provides a direct route from Wanstead/South Woodford to (38m) Stump Cross. This route follows the course the old A11, relieved of heavy traffic after Harlow but relabelled as separate roads until Stump Cross. A104, B1393 to (16½m) Epping. B1393 to (23m) Harlow. A1184 to (29½m) Bishop's Stortford. B1383 to (44m) Stump Cross. A11, A1304 to (56m) **Newmarket**. A1304, A11 to (76m) Thetford. A11 to (105m) **Norwich** (Route 42).

A104 leaves London via *Woodford* and *Epping Forest*, described in 'Blue Guide London'. B1393, followed from near the N edge of the forest, passes M25. 16½m: *Epping* (12,300 inhabitants) has a long High St. with a church of 1899 by Bodley and Garner. 23m: **Harlow** (79,800 inhabitants) was developed from 1947 onwards under the architectural supervision of Sir Frederick Gibberd. The centre incorporates sculptures by Rodin, Moore, etc. The Georgian *Passmores House* is a museum of local history, with objects unearthed during building operations. A1184 heads N to (15½m) *Sawbridgeworth* (7800 inhabitants), where the church contains good brasses. 29½m: **Bishop's Stortford** (22,800 inhabitants; TI), a market town declined into a dormitory suburb, has a fine church of c 1400 with contemporary woodwork, a few good buildings in the old centre, and a public school. The old vicarage in South Rd where Cecil Rhodes (1853–1902) was born is a museum.

FROM BISHOP'S STORTFORD TO COLCHESTER, 32m by A120, the Roman Stane Street. The road skirts the N side of *Hatfield Forest* (1049 acres; NT), once part of the old royal forests of Essex, with hornbeams and a boating lake. **Stansted Airport**, to the N, in imaginative buildings by Sir Norman Foster (1989) is London's third airport. Scheduled passenger services fly to Aberdeen, Amsterdam, Asturias, Banjul, Biarritz, Blackpool, Brussels, Bucharest, Connaught, Dijon, Dublin, Dusseldorf, Florence, Frankfurt, Glasgow, Guernsey, Helsinki, Jersey, Lille, Luxembourg, Maastricht, Manchester, Metz/Nancy, Newcastle, Nice, St Petersburg, Shannon, Stavanger, Waterford and Zaragoza. 4m: *Takeley* church has a decorative font cover and Roman material in its walls. At *Hatfield Broad Oak*, 3m S, the church contains a mailed effigy of Robert de Vere, Earl of Oxford (d. 1221). A120 continues through (9m) *Great Dunmow* (Route 40) and (17m) *Braintree* (Route 39). At *Coggleshall*, bypassed at 23m, the church has good brasses of the Paycocke family. *Paycocke's House (NT) is a richly ornamented merchant's dwelling of c 1500. The barn (NT) on Grange Hill was built by Cistercians c 1140; it is the oldest timber-framed barn to survive in Europe. At (27m) *Marks Tey* A120 joins A12 for (32m) *Colchester* (Route 38).

From Bishop's Stortford to *Ware* via *Much Hadham*, see Route 36.

B1383 continues N to (33½m) *Stansted Mountfitchet*, with a modern reconstruction (open) of its wooden motte-and-bailey castle and Norman village. 38m: **Newport** is a typical West Essex town with a long street, an old grammar school and 16–17C houses, some with pargeting. It has a fine Perpendicular church; even better is the one at *Clavering*, an attractive village on the Stort, 3½m SW.

At *Widdington*, 2m SE of Newport, is *Prior's Hall Barn (EH, summer season, weekends only), the most impressive medieval aisled barn to survive in the area.

40m: ***Audley End** (EH, summer season, Wednesday–Sunday and Bank Holidays, afternoons only) is a Jacobean mansion on the site of the Benedictine Walden Abbey.

It was built in 1603–16 for Thomas Howard, 1st Earl of Suffolk, but reduced to about a third of its original size in the 1720s by Vanbrugh, who demolished the inner and outer courtyards. With its two grand porches, the wing that survived is still imposing. Several rooms have furnishings lent by Lord Braybrooke, who sold the house to the government in 1948. Note in particular: the huge hall with splendid wood screen and plaster work; the drawing room and dining room by Robert Adam; the Gothick chapel of 1768; and the saloon with Jacobean ceiling. Among the paintings, Hans Eworth's portrait of Margaret Audley (1562) is outstanding. The park, with monuments, temples and bridges, was landscaped by Capability Brown in the 1760s. The Tea Bridge overlooks a charming waterside scene.

About 1½m E is the charming little town of **Saffron Walden** (12,500 inhabitants; TI), with a Perpendicular church and timbered buildings, including the Sun Inn (NT), a 15C house with 17C pargeting, used as headquarters by Cromwell and Fairfax. In the grounds of the interesting little museum, which contains a pillory and an Anglo-Saxon sword, are the ruins of the 12C castle. Bridge End gardens (open) at the N end of the town belonged to a house destroyed by fire. At *Hempstead*, 6m E, the highwayman Dick Turpin (1705–39) was born. In the Harvey Chapel of the church lie William Harvey (1578–1657), who discovered the circulation of the blood, and Sir Eliab Harvey (1758–1830), commander of the 'Téméraire' at Trafalgar.

At (43m) *Great Chesterford* B1383 curves sharply right across the Cam and enters Cambridgeshire, almost immediately joining the Romanised Icknield Way, on straight alignments all the way to Thetford. *Ickleton*, 1m NW, has a church with Roman monolithic columns, late Saxon details and a 'sacring' bell outside the spire.

At (44m) *Stump Cross* A1301 bears left for (14m) Cambridge (Route 37).

Duxford, W of the road at 2m, is the home of the Imperial War Museum's collection of aircraft and military vehicles (open). Near *Whittlesford* station, ¾m N, is Duxford Chapel, once part of a Hospital of St John (EH, contact regional office). 6m: *Great Shelford* church has traces of a 15C painting of Judgement Day over the chancel arch.

From *Stump Cross* the main route follows A11, crossing in succession the line of the Via Devana (Route 37), the Fleam Dyke and, on Newmarket Heath, the Devil's Ditch. The last two belong to a rampart system raised by the Angles and Mercians during the wars waged in the 6–8C for control of East Anglia. From (49½m) *Six Mile Bottom* A1304 leads to Newmarket.

56m: **Newmarket** (16,200 inhabitants; TI) is the headquarters of English horse-racing. Begun under James I, the sport has been more or less regularly practised here since the time of Charles I. On the otherwise disappointing High St., dominated by the Victorian clock tower at the top of the hill, is the *Jockey Club* (1840, restored by Richardson and Gill in 1936). The *National Horse-racing Museum*, devoted to the history of the sport, displays some good sporting art.

The most important races on the track at *Newmarket Heath*, 1½m SW, are the Two Thousand Guineas (spring), the Cesarewitch (October) and the Cambridgeshire (October). Special permission is needed to visit the training stables, but the horses are exercised on the heath in the early morning. The *National Stud* (guided tours) is near the racecourse.

At *Westley Waterless*, 5m SW, the church has the delicate *brasses of Sir John Creke and his wife (c 1325). At *Kirtling*, 4½m SE of Newmarket, the church has a fine 12C doorway and monuments to the Norths. The gatehouse (1530) of their mansion survives to the S.

FROM NEWMARKET TO IPSWICH, 41m. B1506 forks NE to (5m) *Kentford*, with a Decorated church containing 14C wall paintings. *Moulton*, 1½m SW, has a little hump-backed bridge over the Kennet marking the ancient route from Bury St Edmunds to Cambridge (EH). A45 is followed. *Risby* church, on the left at 10m, has a round Norman tower, Norman chancel arch, a good screen and wall paintings. *Little Saxham*, 2m S, has a round church tower. At 15m A45 bypasses *Bury St Edmunds* (Route 39). 19m: *Beyton* church, on the right, has a round Norman tower and (21m) *Woolpit* church has a magnificent S porch and double hammerbeam *roof. At 23m the road skirts the large *Haughley Park*, with a rebuilt Jacobean mansion and good gardens (limited opening). *Haughley*, 1½m E, has the remains of a large motte-and-bailey castle and a church with a timber roof. 27m: **Stowmarket** (10,900 inhabitants) trades in barley, and manufactures chemicals and agricultural implements. The *Museum of East Anglian Life* is an open-air display of buildings and machinery, including a 19C drainage windmill. The *Church* has a wooden spire above a square flint tower. Milton visited his tutor Thomas Young (d. 1665) at the old vicarage. The neighbourhood is rich in interesting churches: at *Combs*, 1½m S, and at *Bacton* and *Cotton*, 5m N, with notable roofs. A45 follows the Gipping valley through (31m) *Needham Market* (Route 40) to (35m) *Claydon*, with large cement works. *Little Blakenham*, 2m SW, has the 5-acre *Blakenham Woodland Garden* (open). 41m: *Ipswich*, see Route 38.

The main route rejoins A11 N of Newmarket and crosses the Lark at (65m) *Barton Mills*, where the church has 14C stained glass and a Jacobean pulpit. Beyond the village is a five-way roundabout.

A1101 goes W to (1m) *Mildenhall* (9800 inhabitants), with a Georgian High St. and 15C timber market cross. The *church, whose lovely E window dominates the street, has a Lady Chapel over the N porch and a hammerbeam *roof, carved with angels. The 'Mildenhall Treasure', a hoard of 4C Roman silver now in the British Museum, was found in 1946 at *Thistley Green*, W of the USAF base. A1101 continues into the Fens, joining (11m) A10 between Ely and Downham Market (Route 46).

From the Barton Mills roundabout A1065 leads N, passing (3m) the USAF base at *Lakenheath*. The Norman and Decorated church, W of the base, contains a memorial to Lord Kitchener (d. 1916), some of whose 17–18C ancestors lie in the churchyard. In *Hockwold Fen*, 3m N, the Roman town of Camboritum, flooded in the 2C, was discovered in 1961. Many military airfields were established in the neighbourhood in 1939–45. Memorials to the dead have been set up at *Feltwell*, 1½m N of Hockwold, and at Elveden (see below). 9m: *Brandon* and thence to *Cromer*, see Route 39.

From the Barton Mills roundabout A1101 runs SE through (2m) *Icklingham*, where the large thatched church has a Norman nave, Jacobean pulpit, 14C chest and stained glass. 7m: *Hengrave* church has a Norman tower and is crammed with monuments to the Kytsons, who built the neighbouring *Hengrave Hall* (now a conference centre), completed in 1538. The ornate bay window by John Sparke over the entrance is one of the best of its date. The arms of the Washington family, connected to the Kytsons, appear in a window. 10m: *Bury St Edmunds*, see Route 39.

A11 enters *Breckland*, the heath with gnarled Scots pines and small meres described in George Borrow's 'Lavengro'. Although much of it has been altered by forestry or enclosed for military training and airfields, an abundant bird life still inhabits the isolated ponds and rushes. 71½m: *Elveden* church is a bizarre jumble of Gothick and Art Nouveau, created by the owners of Elveden Hall (not open), an elaborate 'Moghul–Gothick' fantasy grafted on to the 18C building by the Maharaja Duleep Singh in the 1860s and extended by Lord Iveagh at the turn of the century. From Elveden to *Bury* and to *Brandon*, see Route 39. The road now skirts the edge of Thetford Chase and enters Norfolk.

76m: **Thetford** has been enlarged to 19,600 inhabitants by ugly development which makes it hard to appreciate its ancient importance as seat of the Kings of East Anglia and its bishops in 1075–94. *Castle Hill*, at the E end of the town, is the finest castle mound in the country, a Norman motte surrounded by Iron Age earthworks. Three of Thetford's five monasteries have left scanty remains: the *Priory*, founded in 1104, near the station (EH); a 12C priory of the *Canons of the Holy Sepulchre* (EH) on the Brandon road; and a *Dominican Friary* of 1340. The Friary lies behind the old *Grammar School*, which claims descent from a 7C choir school, where Tom Paine (1737–1809) was educated. He was born in a cottage behind White Hart St. (tablet), near the *Ancient House Museum*. A statue (1964) stands in front of the *Guildhall*.

Euston Hall (limited opening), 4m SE, was built c 1670 for the Earl of Arlington, a member of the Cabal, and enlarged by Matthew Brettingham in 1750–56. Its collection of paintings includes works by Van Dyck, Lely, Kneller and Stubbs. Evelyn and Kent helped to lay out the grounds. Euston gave its name to the London railway station built on the estate of the Dukes of Grafton, then owners of the Hall. The 14C church of *East Harling*, 7m E of Thetford, has medieval Norwich glass and 15–17C monuments.

A1075 leads NE from Thetford to (23m) *East Dereham* (Route 44A) via (14m) *Watton*. Near Watton are *Wayland Wood* (2m S), said to be the scene of the 'Babes in the Wood', and *Griston House* (2m SE; not open), said to be the residence of their wicked uncle.

At 90m the A11 bypasses *Attleborough* (6000 inhabitants), where the Norman and Perpendicular church has wall paintings and a magnificent *rood screen of 1475. 96m: **Wymondham** (pronounced 'Windham'), an old market town (9800 inhabitants), has one of the finest *Churches in Norfolk, originally belonging to the priory, afterwards abbey, of St Mary and St Alban (1107). In 1349 the mainly Norman nave and the Perpendicular N aisle were assigned for the use of the parishioners, who added the W tower about 1450. The E tower and the original choir, of which only fragments remain, were retained by the monks. The nave has a hammerbeam roof with angels and large bosses; part of the ceiling has been removed to show the timbering. It has a terracotta monument to Elisha Ferrers. Outstanding among the many timbered houses is the *Green Dragon*. A library occupies the 15C *Chapel of St Thomas Becket*. The *Market Cross* is a timber building of 1616. Robert Kett, leader of the brief agrarian rebellion of 1549, was a tanner at Wymondham.

About 3½m W is **Hingham**, where the fine Decorated *church has a hammerbeam roof. The Morley *monument is a triumph of deeply carved 15C work, with statues of the family. The stained glass is German (c 1500). There is a bust (1919) of Abraham Lincoln. Hingham was the home of Robert Lincoln (d. c 1540), generally accepted as the earliest known ancestor of Abraham Lincoln. Richard Lincoln of Swanton Morley (Route 44A), buried in 1620 at Hingham, disinherited his son Edward, as a result of which his grandson Samuel emigrated from Hingham in 1637, to become the first American ancestor of the President. There was an Abraham Lincoln of Norwich (b. c 1685).

105m: **Norwich**, see Route 42.

42

Norwich

NORWICH (122,300 inhabitants), the county town of Norfolk and regional capital of East Anglia, stands in a loop of the Wensum commanded by the massive castle. It preserves an irregular plan inherited from the Saxons, having neither a main street nor a central square. Surviving monuments everywhere reflect its historic importance from the Middle Ages until the Industrial Revolution, when it was the second city in England. Many old buildings use local flint in flushwork or chequerboard patterns. As well as a cathedral, Norwich boasts more than 30 pre-Reformation churches: some have already become redundant, and a total of 20 are scheduled to do so, but their preservation is guaranteed and various secular uses are being found for them (see below for details of access).

TI: Guildhall. **Buses**: from Surrey St. **Railway Station**: Thorpe Rd. **Airport**: Horsham St Faith (3½m N via A140). Direct services to Aberdeen, Amsterdam, Edinburgh and Teesside. **Theatres**: Maddermarket Theatre, St John's Alley; Theatre Royal, Theatre St.; Whiffler Open-air Theatre, Castle Gardens; Norwich Puppet Theatre, St James Cowgate; Sewell Barn Theatre, Constitution Hill.

Access to churches. The following are redundant but may be visited (details from the TI): *St Gregory*, Pottergate; *St Laurence*, St Benedict St.; *St Margaret*, St Benedict St.; *St Mary-at-Coslany*, St Mary's Plain; *St Michael-at-Coslany*, Colegate; *St Michael-at-Plea*, Redwell St.; *St Saviour*, Magdalen St. The following are usually locked but may be visited by arrangement with the vicar or other custodian: *St Augustine*, St Augustine's St.; *St George*, Colegate; *St John Maddermarket*, Pottergate; *St John de Sepulchre*, Ber St.; *St Martin-at-Palace*, Palace Plain; *St Stephen*, Rampant Horse St. Details are posted outside or may be had from the TI. A handful of churches, indicated in the walking tour below, are permanently closed. The remainder (whether still devoted to their original purpose or now in secular hands) are open, though in some cases only during limited hours.

History. A settlement near the crossing of the Wensum (Fye Bridge) above its confluence with the Yare grew by 850 into a borough trading with the Rhineland. Northwic appears on coins minted for Athelstan. In the Danish wars it was destroyed by Sweyn Forkbeard, but by the Conquest it had grown to be one of the largest boroughs in the kingdom, the fief of Gyrth Godwinsson, King Harold's brother, immediately replaced as Earl of East Anglia by a Norman. A large motte-and-bailey castle was built, driving a Norman wedge between the English areas. In 1094, when the see of Norwich was created, Bishop Losinga commandeered and razed much of the Anglo-Saxon borough to build his cathedral and moved the market site from Tombland to W of the castle. By 1140 a large community of Jews lived here freely, not confined to a ghetto. The city acquired its charters in 1194 and 1256, and its stone circuit wall (2¼m) of 1294–1320 compares in extent with that of London. In the 14C an influx of Flemish weavers helped to make Norwich the centre of the worsted trade. The city was occupied by the rebels during the Peasants' Revolt (1381) and social unrest continued (see the Paston Letters), so that again in 1549 many in Norwich sympathised with Robert Kett's insurrection. The power loom, the banking activities of the Society of Friends, and the foundation of the Norwich General Assurance brought the city into the industrial era. With the coming of the railway the vast cattle market supplied more than half the meat for London. Sporadic air attacks during World War I were followed in 1942 by the destructive 'Baedeker raids' on historic targets.

In post-war years the city has suffered changes in the cause of progress, while also fostering pioneer schemes of conservation and restoration. In 1970 the City Council designated seven Conservation Areas, including most buildings of historic and architectural interest; by 1984, there were 15 such areas, and four more are planned. Chief manufactures now are machinery and electrical equipment, boots and shoes, mustard and starch, sweets and beer, though the majority of the working population is employed in service industries. The city is known also for printing.

Natives and residents. Dame Julian of Norwich (c 1342–c 1416), mystic; members of the Paston family, authors of the 'Letters' (c 1420–1504); Robert Greene (1560–92), poet and dramatist; Sir Thomas Browne (1605–82); John 'Christmas' Beckwith (?1750–1809), organist and composer; Admiral Lord Nelson (1758–1805); Elizabeth Fry (1780–1845), prison reformer; John Crome ('Old Crome'; 1786–1821), John Sell Cotman (1784–1842) and other painters of the Norwich School; Harriet Martineau (1802–76), author and feminist; George Borrow (1803–81); Rajah Brooke of Sarawak (1803–68).

FROM THE CASTLE TO THE CATHEDRAL. A visit to Norwich may conveniently start at the *Castle, to the E of which a park and shopping mall occupy the former Cattle Market (once the castle bailey). The castle mound was raised just after the Conquest, the great stone keep perhaps being begun as early as 1094 and completed under Henry I after the model of that at Falaise. It is unique among English castles in having an exterior decoration of blank Norman arcading, accurately reproduced by Salvin in 1834–39, though in an alien stone.

It now houses a *Museum* with: *paintings by the Norwich School (Crome, Cotman, Stannard, Stark, Vincent); the largest collection of British ceramic teapots in the world; local archaeology, including the Iron Age hoard of gold torques and coins from Snettisham; Norwich silver; and Lowestoft porcelain. There are guided tours of the battlements and dungeons.

Below the castle, on the NE, the Anglia Television Centre stands at the city's busiest traffic junction. Bank Plain and its continuation Redwell St. lead N, passing (right) *St Michael-at-Plea*, with a two-storied porch entered above by a Jacobean gallery. Inside, the roof has carved angels and the font cover is Jacobean.

Across Prince's St. is the cobbled *Elm Hill, one of the finest medieval streets in England. At the top is *St Peter Hungate*, rebuilt in 1460 by John and Margaret Paston, with a cruciform hammerbeam roof and 15–16C glass. It is now a museum of church art with medieval woodwork, vestments, MSS, and bells. Beyond the bend are (left) the *Strangers' Club* (the 'strangers' being immigrant weavers), early 16C with some 17C work, (right) *Pettus House*, and beyond (left) the 17C *Flint House*. At the foot, on the corner of Wensum St., the church of *St Simon and St Jude*, aisleless with flint walls, and monuments to the Pettus family; it is now the headquarters of the Norwich Scouts and Guides movement (open).

Wensum St. leads to the right past the Maid's Head Hotel to Tombland, the old Saxon market place displaced by the Normans. *Samson and Hercules House* (1657) takes its name from the benign giants supporting the porch; the rest of the square is Georgian and pleasantly tree-shaded, with the lofty tower of *St George's Tombland* rising above the trees at the top. The 15C church has a good roof, and a relief and statuette of St George on the 17C font cover.

The *Erpingham Gate* (1420), with beautifully preserved sculpture, leads into the spacious, tree-lined cathedral Close.

To the NE of the Erpingham Gate is *Norwich School*, refounded by Edward VI, including the Chapel of St John (c 1316). Pupils include Robert Greene, Lord Nelson, George Borrow and Rajah Brooke. 'Old Crome' was drawing master here. On the N side of the cathedral is the former *Bishop's Palace*, opened in 1962 as an extension of

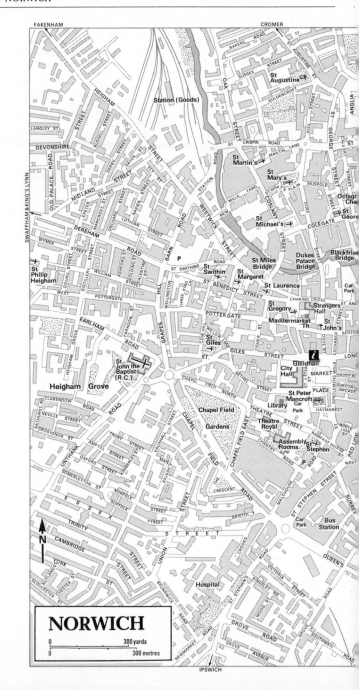

NORWICH

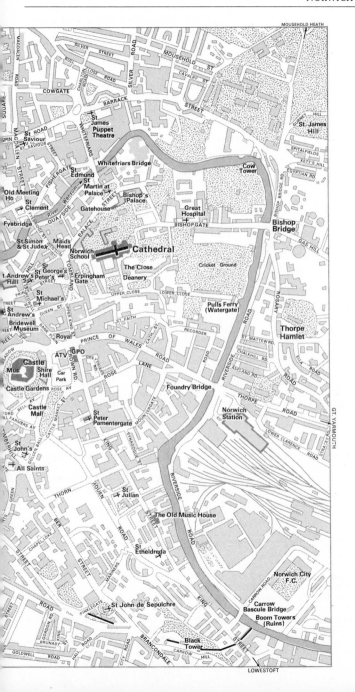

the school. The Upper Close, running E from *St Ethelbert's Gate* (c 1300; modern parapet), is continued by the Lower Close, leading to *Pull's Ferry*, the picturesque old water-gate of the cathedral precincts (restored 1948). The line of the old canal that passed beneath it, and up which the barges brought the Caen stone to build the cathedral, can still be seen.

The *Cathedral does not dominate the city as at Lincoln or Ely, but leaves that honour to the castle and occupies low ground near the river. Seen from the Close, it is nevertheless a majestic building, mainly Norman, with a soaring spire (315ft) exceeded only at Salisbury.

Building started under Bishop Losinga in 1096, two years after the see of East Anglia was moved from Thetford. Its first phase was complete by c 1145. The clerestory of the choir was rebuilt by Bishop Percy (1355–69). Bishop Alnwick (1426–36) altered the W front and completed the cloisters, begun 130 years earlier. The spire and the stone vault of nave and choir were built by Bishops Lyhart (1446–72) and Goldwell (1472–99).

The Norman style predominates, in the *tower, nave, aisles and transepts. The *Nave* has 14 bays with massive columns, clerestory and a triforium whose arches, most unusually, are almost as wide as those in the arcade below. The rhythmic unity of the effect is accentuated by the light colour of the stone and the absence of monuments. The lierne-vaulted roof is 15C, and its *bosses, telling the story of the Bible, repay close study (with the mirror trolleys provided or binoculars). The circular hole was used for letting down a censer. Two bays of the S aisle near the pulpit were made into a Perpendicular chantry by Bishop Nykke (d. 1535). The Monks' Door and the Decorated Prior's Door lead from the same aisle to the cloisters. Off the *N Transept* is St Andrew's Chapel, with 15C stained glass; the effigy in the *S Transept* may represent Bishop Losinga.

The *Choir begins W of the central tower and ends in a semi-circular apse with ambulatory and radiating chapels, a French arrangement uncommon in English churches. The presbytery, E of the tower, has been altered but preserves a plan typical of the Christian sanctuary until c 1100. The Bishop's Throne behind the high altar is 8C or earlier and may come from the Saxon cathedral at Dunwich. In the S aisle the Chapter Room has Renaissance panelling and the Bauchun Chapel remarkable roof bosses. At the E end are St Luke's Chapel (S, see below) and the Jesus Chapel (N), each formed out of two segments of a circle. Between them two fine Early English arches, from the 13C Lady Chapel, lead into the modern St Saviour's Chapel (1930–32). It contains fine 14C painted panels from St Michael-at-Plea. Even finer is the painted *retable in St Luke's Chapel, probably presented as a thank-you offering for the suppression of the Peasants' Revolt (1381). Together they form a rare survival from the East Anglian school. The so-called Bridge Chapel in the aisle was probably used for displaying relics; the vault above has paintings of 1275.

The *Cloisters, the only two-storied monastic cloister in England, were rebuilt in 1297–1430. The vault **bosses are even better than those in the nave. Nearly 400 in all, they illustrate the life of Christ and the Book of Revelation, with the Evangelists, foliage, scenes of contemporary life and Green Men. Note also the tracery of the cloister windows. At the SW corner are the Monks' Lavatories and on the E side is the Decorated entrance of the vanished Chapter House. Ruins of the Infirmary and Refectory (S side) and Guest Hall (W side) may be seen from the Close.

In May 1919 the body of Nurse Edith Cavell, shot by the Germans in 1915, was brought from Brussels and interred just E of St Luke's Chapel. A bust in Tombland commemorates her heroism.

Palace St., skirting the N wall of the precincts, gives a view through a gateway of c 1430 (good bosses) of the new *Bishop's Palace* and a surviving 14C porch of the old. Outside the gate stands the little church of *St Martin-at-Palace* with a 14C font and chandelier of 1726. *Cotman House*, opposite, was the home of J.S. Cotman. Further on, in Bishopgate, is the *Great Hospital* founded in 1249 by Bishop Walter de Suffield. The infirmary, much altered but keeping its Gothic chancel roof, houses the original wards. The attached church of *St Helen*, rebuilt c 1480, can be visited. Next to the hospital is the house Thomas Ivory built for himself. The 13C *Bishop Bridge*, at the foot of Bishopgate, is one of the oldest bridges in England still used for traffic. To the left is the brick *Cow Tower* (EH), where the cathedral collected river tolls.

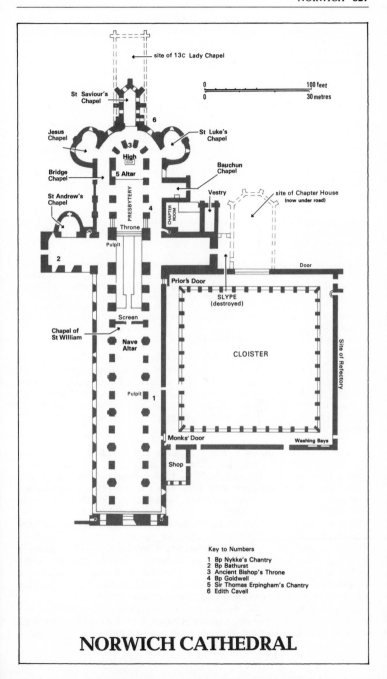

site of 13C Lady Chapel

St Saviour's Chapel

6

Jesus Chapel

St Luke's Chapel

3

High

Bauchun Chapel

Bridge Chapel

5 Altar

Vestry

site of Chapter House (now under road)

St Andrew's Chapel

PRESBYTERY

4

CHAPTER ROOM

2

Throne

Pulpit

Prior's Door

SLYPE (destroyed)

Door

Chapel of St William

Screen

Nave Altar

CLOISTER

Site of Refectory

Pulpit

1

Monks' Door

Washing Bays

Shop

0   100 feet
0   30 metres

Key to Numbers

1 Bp Nykke's Chantry
2 Bp Bathurst
3 Ancient Bishop's Throne
4 Bp Goldwell
5 Sir Thomas Erpingham's Chantry
6 Edith Cavell

NORWICH CATHEDRAL

Further N is St James's Hill, where there is a splendid view over the river valley to the cathedral, castle and city hall. *Mousehold Heath*, beyond, overlooking the city on the NE, gives the best view of Norwich (described in Chapter 14 of 'Lavengro'). Kett's followers encamped here. The heath was a favourite subject of John Crome's brush, but the famous windmill burned down in 1933.

From the cathedral Queen St. returns towards the Market Place. *St Mary-the-Less* (13C; the 'French Church'; not open), hidden in a huddle of buildings, gives a good idea of medieval conditions. A guild church, it was taken over in turn by Walloons, French Protestants, Swedenborgians, and the Scottish Apostolic Church.

FROM THE CASTLE TO THE MARKET PLACE. From Castle Meadow, to the N of the Castle Hotel, Davey Place leads into the Market Place. Expanded to its present bounds only in the last century, it is splendidly enclosed by civic grandeur of all ages, dominated by a great parish church, and filled with the colour and bustle of the stalls. The E side is Gentleman's Walk, from which *Royal Arcade* runs through to Castle St., where it has an Art Nouveau façade by Skipper.

Closing the S side is ***St Peter Mancroft**, a Perpendicular church with an elaborate tower. The turrets, crenellations, and flèche are additions by the Streets, father and son, in 1881–95. In 1715 it rang the first complete peal of 5040 changes.

The light and lofty arches of the arcade and the arrangement of the clerestory are the epitome of Norfolk Perpendicular, though the double hammerbeam roof is hidden behind ornamental coving. Note the font canopy, a 15C alabaster panel, the brasses, and the tomb chest with effigy of Francis Windham (d. 1592). The chancel has a memorial to Sir Thomas Browne (1605–82), author of 'Religio Medici', buried here. The E window is filled with 15C *glass. The sacristy contains church plate and illuminated MSS (13–14C). Outside is a statue of Browne, who lived from 1637 to his death in a house near the Lamb Inn yard.

The *City Hall* (1932–38; James and Pierce) matches the scale of the square with a tower of 202ft. The bronze lions are by A. Hardiman. To the S is the *Central Library and Record Office* (1963) with an open court and memorial to men of the US 8th Air Force lost from East Anglian bases in 1941–45. The flint *Guildhall* (1407–13) was rebuilt in 1535 with a flushwork gable. Its 16C council chamber has contemporary panelling and fittings as well as 15C glass. It is now also the TI Centre.

NORTH FROM THE MARKET PLACE ACROSS THE RIVER. London St. and Bedford St. (left) go to Bridewell Alley. The Bridewell, a flint-faced house built c 1370 on a vaulted undercroft of 1325, houses a *museum of local industries. Almost opposite is St Andrew's Church (1506), where John Robinson, pastor of the Pilgrim Fathers, was curate. It contains the tombs of Sir John Suckling's mother and other ancestors of the poet. Suckling House is a fine 16C town house. **St Andrew's Hall** and **Blackfriars' Hall** (open), built in 1440–70, together constitute the only surviving Dominican church in England. St Andrew's (the nave) has been the city's place of assembly since the Dissolution, while Blackfriars' Hall (the chancel) served as the Dutch church from the 16C to the mid 19C. The Decorated and Perpendicular windows are notable; the S walk of the cloister and the vaulted vestibule of an earlier, 13C church also survive.

Blackfriars Bridge (1783; Soane) crosses the Wensum to the N. Beyond, in the ancient 'Ward of Over-the-Water', stands *St George Colegate*, built in 1459–1513 by rich local weavers. It retains 18C fittings. John Crome is buried here.

To the W along Colegate is *St Michael-at-Coslany*, covered with flushwork tracery. Further N in St Mary's Plain, *St Mary-at-Coslany* has a Saxon round tower. The 15C roof has been restored to show the diagonal bracing. *St Martin-at-Oak* in St Martin's Lane is now a night shelter (not open to public). Further N stands *St Augustine* with a Perpendicular nave and chancel in flint and a brick tower (1687).

To the E along Colegate is the *Octagon Chapel*, originally Presbyterian, now Unitarian, by Thomas Ivory (1755), with an impressive interior. A little further on, a narrow alley leads to the *Old Meeting House* (1693), a Congregational chapel with a mellow exterior and a perfectly preserved interior. At the end of the street, *St Clement* has a slender flint tower. It contains many tablets to the Ives and Harvey families, both of whom supplied mayors for the city. To the left is Magdalen St., with *Gurney Court*, where Elizabeth Fry and Harriet Martineau were born. *St Saviour* contains a Georgian W gallery with organ, 15C font, and sword rests. Beyond, Anglia Square is a modern shopping centre. Further E is *St James Cowgate*, flint, with a brick tower perched on the W roof, a sculptured font, a screen with painted figures (1505), and 15–16C stained glass. It now houses the puppet theatre. From here Whitefriars Bridge crosses to Palace St. (above). Fishergate branches right past the Perpendicular *St Edmund*, now a store, to Fye Bridge (1822), probably the oldest crossing place of the river, and so to Tombland.

NORTH AND WEST FROM THE MARKET PLACE, AND BACK TO THE CASTLE. Dove St. leads N from the Market Place to *St John Maddermarket*, as its name suggests the centre of the dyeing trade. The fine Perpendicular tower has the four evangelists on the top battlements. Inside are a superb 18C reredos, brasses, and monuments to the Sayers and Sothertons, mayors in the 16C and 17C. The *Maddermarket Theatre* is an 18C building reconstructed as an Elizabethan theatre with apron stage. In Charing Cross is the *Strangers' Hall* (open), a merchant's house with a 15C hall over a 13C undercroft. It was the centre for immigrant weavers, then the assize judge's lodging, and is now a museum of English domestic life.

Westwards along St Benedict St. are five churches. *St Gregory* has a sculptured font, a brass eagle lectern (1496), a 14C sanctuary knocker on the vestry door and a 15C wall painting. *St Laurence* has a tall Perpendicular tower with two reliefs over the W door, and a 15C font. The Decorated *St Margaret* has an 18C painted reredos above the S door and a brass to Anne Rede (d. 1577) which is a triple palimpsest. The small *St Swithin*, with a charming Victorian bell turret, is now an arts centre. S up the narrow Three King Lane lies the round Norman tower, with an octagonal 15C upper stage, of the destroyed *St Benedict*.

Across Pottergate (left) is Cow Hill, where *St Giles* has the tallest of the Norwich towers (120ft), used as a beacon. The churchyard is planted with wisteria. Inside are an early hammerbeam roof with angels, brasses and memorials to local doctors.

In Willow Lane, close by, is the house where George Borrow spent his youth. St Giles St. continues W to the *RC Cathedral of St John the Baptist*, built in 1882–1910 by George Gilbert Scott Jr and John Oldrid Scott in a convincing Early English style, with rich marbles and fine glass.

Chapel Field Gardens leads back to Theatre St., with the *Theatre Royal* and the *Assembly Rooms* (now a restaurant and concert hall), the finest 18C building in Norwich, built by Thomas Ivory in 1754 on the foundations of the college of St Mary. Beyond, in Rampant Horse St., *St Stephen* has a flushwork tower and a Perpendicular and Tudor interior with large clerestory windows. The E window has 16C German glass. Among the memorials is one in Coade stone to Elizabeth Coppin (d. 1812), with a weeping putto. In Westlegate, across Red Lion St., is *All Saints*, in a rural setting. The font is carved with prophets and apostles. Just N is *St John Timberhill*. Prisoners from the castle jail were buried in its churchyard. The chandelier (1500) is German. Timberhill leads N to the castle.

SOUTH FROM THE CASTLE. King St. runs SE from the Prince of Wales Rd. Partly industrialised, it retains some old buildings, including the town house of the Howards. *St Peter Parmentergate* (not open) stands in a shaded churchyard. The *Dragon Hall* (open) is 14–15C, with a splendid roof. *St Julian* (rebuilt) has three Saxon windows in the N wall. A Norman doorway (from the bombed church of *St Michael-at-Thorn*, to the S) leads into the reconstructed cell of the anchoress Dame Julian. On the left is the *Old Music House* with Norman vaulting (crypt) and 15C timber roof, at one time (1633) the house of Lord Chief Justice Coke. *St Etheldreda* (now an art studio), in another lovely churchyard, has a round tower with a brick and flint octagonal upper stage. Further on, King St. passes between the *Boom Towers*, on either side of the river, and the *Black Tower* (right) where the city walls follow Carrow Hill. Their line can be traced NW to Chapel Field Gardens (see above). The direct return is along Ber St., where *St John de Sepulchre* has a Perpendicular tower, a two-storied N porch, flushwork, an East Anglian 'lion' font and a palimpsest brass. Thence to Timberhill, see above.

SOUTHERN OUTSKIRTS. **Caistor St Edmund**, or *Caister*, about 3m S, was the Roman Venta Icenorum, the chief town in the territory of the Iceni. Inside the 2C Roman enclosure of about 34 acres, which seems to have been burnt by the Saxons, is the parish church. Perpendicular, with an Early English chancel, it contains a fine carved font of c 1410 and a wall painting of St Christopher.

WESTERN OUTSKIRTS. At *Earlham*, 1½m W, is the **University of East Anglia**, opened in 1963. *Earlham Hall*, once Elizabeth Fry's home, is now an administrative building. The buildings by Denys Lasdun, with 'ziggurat' residence blocks, use the varying levels of the fine site in the Yare valley to maximum effect. The *Sainsbury Centre for Visual Arts*, built by Sir Norman Foster (1976), has an outstanding collection of modern and ethnographic art, and pre-Columbian, Asian and European antiquities.

FROM NORWICH TO YARMOUTH, 20m. A47 at first skirts the Yare. 6m: To the right, on the Yare, is the boating resort of *Brundall*. 11m: *Acle*, with a round-towered 14C church, is a convenient starting-point for the Norfolk Broads (Route 43). A47 skirts Breydon Water. 20m: *Yarmouth*, see Route 38.

From Norwich to *Ipswich*, see Route 38; to *Bury*, see Route 39; to *Newmarket* and *London*, see Route 41; to the *Norfolk Broads*, see Route 43; to *King's Lynn*, see Route 44.

43

The Norfolk Broads

Maps: OS Tourist map (1:50,000 or 1¼in to 1m), or Hamilton's 'Broads Navigation Charts and Index'.

The **Norfolk Broads** forms a triangle on the map, its apex at Norwich and its base along the coastline between Lowestoft and Sea Palling. Roads bordered by willows and dykes fringed with reeds cross the level countryside. As both its shape and its flatness would suggest, the region was once an estuary, closed at the sea by silt. There are about a dozen large broads and twice as many smaller ones, shallow lagoons formed not by the widening of rivers, from which they are mostly separated by narrow channels, but by the flooding of medieval peat diggings. The main rivers are the Yare, the Waveney and the Bure, all meeting ultimately in Breydon Water; the Ant, the Thurne and the Chet. Together they provide about 125m (200km) of navigable water. The villages are often charming, with interesting churches; there are some fine old manor houses and a few ruined abbeys and castles.

The main gateways are Norwich, Yarmouth, Lowestoft, Wroxham, Stalham and Potter Heigham. The boatyards listed in the hiring arrangements below make convenient starting-points for a tour of the waterways. Long popular with smooth-water sailors and anglers, the more popular parts of the Broads can get extremely crowded in summer.

Broads Authority (equivalent to a National Park Authority): 18 Colegate, Norwich, Norfolk NR3 1BQ. **Boats**. Yachts, cruisers and houseboats may be hired from Blake Holidays at their headquarters in Wroxham or at Acle, Beccles, Brundall, Burgh Castle, Horning, Loddon, Oulton Broad, Potter Heigham, Reedham, St Olaves, Somerleyton, South Walsham, Stalham, Sutton, Thorpe and Wayford Bridge; or from Hoseasons Holidays of Lowestoft at Acle, Beccles, Belaugh, Brundall, Burgh Castle, Hickling, Horning, Loddon, Ludham, Martham, Oulton Broad, Potter Heigham, Reedham, St Olaves, Stalham, Thorpe and Wroxham. Bed and breakfast accommodation, guest houses and small hotels are generally available for those who prefer not to sleep on board. Excursion boats ply many stretches of river. Only one trading wherry, once the characteristic vessel of the Broads, is still sailing.

Angling. The Broads and their connecting waterways are best known for bream and roach, though pike, perch and rudd are also found. Anglers must hold a National Rivers Authority rod licence but fishing on most waters is free, apart from some privately controlled Broads (Wroxham Broad and Hickling Broad, for example) where day permits are required. Information should be obtained locally, at boatyards and public houses, or directly from the National Rivers Authority, 79 Thorpe Road, Norwich NR1 1EW.

A TOUR OF THE BROADS BY ROAD FROM NORWICH, 51m. **Norwich**, see Route 42. A115 skirts Mousehold Heath and passes through the suburb of *Sprowston*, where the 14C church has a brick tower and monuments, to reach the Broads at (8m) **Wroxham**, with a bridge over the Bure. Adjoining *Hoveton* has a seasonal TI Centre. *Coltishall*, 2m NW on B1354, has a picturesque lock marking the limit of navigation. The village has 18C houses, and the church has Saxon windows and a Norman font. Right of the main road 2m N of Wroxham and Hoveton is *Beeston Hall* (open), a Gothick house of 1787. Before this, a detour leads right to (11½m) *Neatishead* and (12½m) *Barton Turf*, where the church has a good rood screen, for a glimpse of Barton Broad. Returning to the A1151, the route crosses the Ant at (16m) *Wayford Bridge* and passes (18m) *Stalham*, where the Maid's Head is a 14C inn with 18C façade, and (19m) *Sutton*. From here a left turn leads to (21m) *Hickling*, connected by a lane (¾m) with its broad. 24m: *Potter Heigham*, with 14–15C paintings in its church, leads back to Wroxham (8½m) by Ludham and Horning. A longer route follows the Yarmouth road across Heigham Bridge, on the Thurne, to (28m) *Rollesby Bridge* between Rollesby Broad and Ormesby Broad. At (30m) *Ormesby* the route turns right, then right again through (31½m) *Filby*. It then follows A1064 SW across Filby Broad and over the Bure to (37m) *Acle* (see Route 42). B1140 goes to (40m) *South Walsham*, with two churches in one churchyard. An unclassified road leads right for (41½m) *Ranworth* (seasonal TI), with glimpses of broads beyond.

Ranworth church has a painted *rood screen and lectern (both early 15C). Unclassified roads continue via (44½m) *Salhouse* back to Norwich.

A TOUR OF THE WATERWAYS FROM WROXHAM. Perhaps the most characteristic series of broads are strung along the river Bure. **Wroxham** (see road route above) is a favourite starting-point, though the river is navigable up to *Coltishall* to the NW. About 1½m below the bridge a dyke on the right leads to *Wroxham Broad (private moorings), sometimes called the 'Queen of the Broads'. On the right is *Salhouse Broad*. On the left, *Hoveton Great Broad* is a nature reserve under the auspices of English Nature. Access is by river and, on payment, a nature trail can be followed on foot. Below these is (5m) *Horning*. To the right are (6¾m) *Ranworth Broad*, a bird sanctuary which cannot be entered by boat, though the Norfolk Naturalist's Trust Centre may be visited, and (9½m) the Fleet Dyke, leading into *South Walsham Broad*. The tributary Ant, joining the Bure nearly opposite Fleet Dyke, leads via (¾m) *Ludham Bridge* and *Irstead* church, with good woodwork, to (4m) *Barton Broad*, a large, shallow lagoon with wooded banks 1½m long. About 2m N, reached via the Ant and a dyke, is *Stalham* (see road route above). The left bank of the Bure has the ruins of *St Benet's Abbey* (founded in 1020) from which the Bishop of Norwich, the only abbot in the Church of England, takes the style of 'Abbot of St Benet's at Holme'. From *Thurne Mouth*, 11¾m from Wroxham, the Thurne goes to (3½m) *Potter Heigham Bridge*, crowded in summer, and (5m) *Heigham Sound*, communicating with the shallow *Hickling Broad*, the largest of all (3m in circumference) and a noted bird sanctuary. At its N end is *Hickling Staithe*. To the NE of Heigham Sound, and connected with it by Meadow Dyke, is (1½m) *Horsey Mere* (NT), 1½m S of which is *Martham Broad*, on the opposite side of the Thurne. A dyke, 1½m above the mouth of the Thurne, leads to (¾m) *Womack Water* and (1¼m) *Ludham*, with an interesting church. Nearby, *How Hill Staithe*, on the river Ant, has the *Toad Hall Cottage Museum*, an eelcatcher's cottage with a restored Victorian interior. Tickets can be bought here for the wildlife water trail which explores the nature reserve. The lower course of the Bure, from the mouth of the Thurne to (19½m) *Acle Bridge* and (31½m) **Yarmouth** (Route 38), flows through duller country.

The Bure flows into the E end of **Breydon Water** (beware of low tides). At the SW end, near Burgh Castle, is the mouth of the Waveney, whose winding course can be followed to (18m) *Beccles* and (21m) Geldeston Lock. It passes within 1m of *Fritton Decoy* (see Route 38). The New Cut, beginning nearby, connects it with the Yare at (3½m) *Reedham* (see below). Oulton Dyke, c 5m above the New Cut, connects it with (1½m) *Oulton Broad* (see Route 38) and so with **Lowestoft**.

The Yare enters **Breydon Water** near the Waveney, and can be followed all the way to Norwich. On the N bank at 2½m is the *Berney Arms Windmill*, one of the largest Norfolk windmills to survive (EH, summer season). Beyond (6m) *Reedham*, with a fine 17C inn, is (1½m) *Hardley Dyke*, the mouth of the Chet, on the left, which can be navigated to (4m) *Loddon*, a tiny old market town with a very ancient alms box in its 15C church. Nearby are the churches of *Chedgrave* and *Heckingham*, both with Norman work, and *Hales Hall*, a late medieval manor house and barn, recently restored (limited opening of barn and garden). 9m: *Cantley Red House*, a favourite anglers' inn. About 1m beyond and to the left are the remains of *Langley Abbey* (c 1200). 13m: *Buckenham Ferry*, another gathering place for anglers. A dyke on the left leads to (¾m) *Rockland Broad*, with reed beds rich in wildfowl. 14½m: *Coldham Hall* is known for its large 'baskets' of roach and bream. About ½m off is *Brundall*, and on the left at 16¼m is the entrance to *Surlingham Broad*. The scenery from here to (21m) **Norwich** is attractive.

44

Norwich to King's Lynn

A. Via Fakenham

Directions. Total distance 47m. **Norwich**, see Route 42. A1067 to (26m) **Fakenham**. A148, A1078 to (47m) **King's Lynn** (Route 46A). A47, the direct road (43m), is fast but featureless. *North Tuddenham* (13m) was the birthplace of Matthew Vassar (1791–1868), founder of Vassar College, New York.

Norwich, see Route 42. A1067 ascends the Wensum valley, with the *Ringland* hills on the left. The church has a Perpendicular hammerbeam *roof, disguised by ribbed panelling with angels, and stained glass. *Weston Longville* church, 2m NW, has a 14C wall painting of a Tree of Jesse. James Woodforde was rector from 1774 until his death in 1803. On the right beyond (9m) *Attlebridge* is *Great Witchingham*, where the *Norfolk Wildlife Park* has European mammals in their natural habitat, as well as exotic pheasants, etc. The main road continues through the pretty hamlet of *Lenwade* and (13m; right) *Sparham*, whose 14C church has a good roof, to (15m) *Bawdeswell*, the home of Chaucer's Reeve. Its church (1955) is by Fletcher Watson. At *Elsing*, 2¾m S, is a Decorated church with the brass of its founder, Sir Hugh Hastings (d. 1347).

A detour may be taken NE on B1145 to (4m) *Reepham*. St Michael's, with a tall Perpendicular tower, dominates the little market place. A vestry connects it with a second church, St Mary's, with a Norman font and fine monument to Sir Roger de Kerdiston (d. 1337). A third church has been ruined since 1543. *Booton*, c 1½m SE, has an ambitious Gothic Revival church built in 1875–91 by the incumbent, Whitwell Elwin. At (5m) *Salle* (pronounced 'Saul') the *church is spectacular. It has a tall, decorated tower, two-storied N and S porches, an arch-braced roof with angels, bosses in the transepts, carved stalls and misericords, and a 15C 'wineglass' pulpit with Jacobean canopy. The church was built by the three local families of Brigge, Fontayne and Boleyn; Anne Boleyn is reputedly buried here. *Heydon*, 2m N of Salle, boasts a pretty village green and church with wall paintings. Heydon Hall (not open) is Tudor with 18C additions. 7m: *Cawston* church has a high tower and a superb *roof. It was built in the early 15C by Michael de la Pole, Earl of Suffolk. 11m: *Aylsham*, see Route 44B.

The main route continues via (17m) *Twyford*, with a Norman church, to (19m) *Guist*.

B1110 leads S to (3m) *North Elmham*, the seat of a bishopric founded in 673 and the only see in East Anglia from 965 to 1075, when it was moved to Thetford and thence to Norwich. N of the present church stand the ruins of the 11C Saxon cathedral and bishop's palace (EH). At *Gressenhall*, W of B1110 at 5m, the 18C workhouse contains the *Norfolk Rural Life Museum*. 9m: **East Dereham**, a market town of 11,800 people, has a parish church with painted Perpendicular ceilings in the N and S chapels, an 18C Flemish chest, and the tomb of William Cowper (1731–1800). Close to the unfinished 16C belfry a ruined chapel covers the site of the tomb of St Withburga, foundress of the church. The site of Cowper's house in the market place is occupied by the Cowper Memorial Church. Bishop Bonner's cottage (1502), with coloured pargeting, is now a museum. George Borrow (1803–81) was born at *Dumpling Green*, 1½m S. At *Shipdham*, 5m SW of Dereham, the 13C church has a two-stage lantern on its tower and contains a wooden *lectern (c 1500). In *Swanton Morley*, a pretty place 5m SW of Dereham, the Angel Inn (NT) incorporates the remains of the house where in 1615 Richard Lincoln made the will that caused his grandson Samuel, direct ancestor of Abraham Lincoln, to leave for America (cf. Hingham, Route 41). In the beautiful church of c 1370 an E window remembers the men of the adjoining RAF station.

26m: **Fakenham** (5800 inhabitants; seasonal TI), a dull little town, has a Decorated and Perpendicular church with a high tower and a notable font.

B1105 leads N via (3m) *East Barsham*, with a good early Tudor manor house, to (5m) **Walsingham**, or *Little Walsingham* (seasonal TI), noted for the ruins of an Augustinian priory (open) which once owned the shrine of Our Lady of Walsingham, commemorating the apparition of the Blessed Virgin to the lady of the manor in 1061. The pre-Reformation pilgrimage was revived in 1921 and there are now two shrines: the Anglo-Catholic shrine (1931, enlarged 1938), with a tall red-brick tower, where the image of Our Lady of Walsingham was moved from the parish church in 1931; and the Roman Catholic *Slipper Chapel*, 1½m S, a 14C building reconsecrated in 1938, with a modern *Chapel of Reconciliation* beside it. In the village are also the ruins of a late 13C *Franciscan Friary* (not open) and the parish church (restored after a fire in 1961), containing a Perpendicular font. The *Shirehall Museum* preserves an 18C court room and houses an exhibit about the history of the pilgrimage. The church at *Great Walsingham*, 1m NE, has bench ends. About 3½m NE of Walsingham are the remains of the Benedictine *Binham Priory* (EH). The nave (1091) is now the parish church. The *W front remains exquisite despite the bricking-up of the great window. It was apparently built before 1244 and is thus the earliest example of bar tracery in England. A medieval wayside cross (EH) stands on the green nearby.

From Fakenham to *Bury St Edmunds* and to *Cromer*, see Route 39.

28m: *Sculthorpe* has a Norman font of a local type. 34m: *Harpley*. 1m N is *Houghton Hall* (open), Norfolk's grandest country house and perhaps the finest example of English Palladianism.

Houghton was built in 1722–35 for Sir Robert Walpole as tangible expression of the wealth and position his career as Prime Minister to George I had won him. Colen Campbell's design followed the plan of Palladio's villas with grand simplicity: an oblong central block with rusticated ground floor and tall piano nobile above, flanked on each side by colonnades leading to servants' wings. This was elaborated in the building, most obviously by the happy addition of Thomas Ripley's domes, replacing the pedimented corners Campbell intended for the central block (cf. Holkham). William Kent was mainly responsible for the state rooms. They begin with the Stone Hall, a 40ft cube with lavish decoration including a ceiling by Artari and chimneypiece by Rysbrack. The grand proportions and rich detail set the note for the rooms that follow, culminating in the splendid saloon. Note, along the way, Kent's painted ceilings, Rysbrack's chimneypiece in the dining room and the Mortlake and Brussels tapestries. The wood carving in the common parlour is presumably from the earlier house on the site and perhaps by Gibbons. Few distinguished paintings survived the wholesale dispersal of Sir Robert's collection by his deranged grandson, the 3rd Earl of Orford, in 1779. The park was landscaped by Bridgeman. Sir Robert and his son, Horace Walpole, are buried in the little church.

Beyond Harpley A148 crosses the *Peddars' Way* (Route 45), coming from Castle Acre and Massingham Heath in the S and leading N to Ringstead

and the coast. 38½m: *Hillington* (left) has a manor house of 1627 (not open).
For *Sandringham*, 2m NW, see Route 45. At 43m a sideroad leads NW to
(1m) **Castle Rising**, perhaps the most interesting of Norfolk villages. It has
a massive Norman *Castle* of c 1150, with a keep similar to the one at
Norwich and huge earthworks covering more than 12 acres (EH, all year).
Also a beautiful late Norman church (12C) and the Jacobean *Trinity Hospital* (open), built by Henry Howard before 1614, a charity for ten elderly
women who still wear Stuart costume on Sundays. 45m: *South Wootton*
church has a fine Norman font. 47m: **King's Lynn**, see Route 46A.

Blickling Hall

B.   Via Aylsham and Fakenham

Directions. Total distance 54m. **Norwich**, see Route 42. A140 to (14m)
Aylsham. B1354 to (27m) Thursford. A148 to (33m) **Fakenham** (Route 44A).
A148, A1078 to (54m) **King's Lynn** (Route 46A).

Norwich, see Route 42. A140 heads N, passing the airport on the right, to
(14m) **Aylsham**, an old market town with 18C houses. The churchyard of
its Decorated church has a monument to Humphry Repton (1752–1818), the
landscape gardener, who lived at Sustead Hall nearby.

North Walsham, 6m NE, is a market town (7900 inhabitants) dominated by the ruined tower of its church, which has an alabaster monument to Sir William Paston (d. 1608), founder of the Paston School which Nelson attended. *Worstead*, 3m SE of Walsham, gave its name to a woollen fabric first made here by Flemish immigrants in the 12C. The 14C church has good flushwork and 15C screens. *Gunton Hall*, 5½m NW of Walsham, has a fine park (open to cars).

The main route continues NW from Aylsham on B1354, passing the lovely *Aylsham Old Hall* of 1689 (NT, not open). At 15½m it reaches ***Blickling Hall** (NT), one of England's great Jacobean houses.

It was built in 1619–27 for Sir Henry Hobart by Robert Lyminge, architect of Hatfield House in Hertfordshire, and altered by the Ivorys of Norwich in 1765–70, about the time when it passed by marriage to the Marquess of Lothian. The Ivorys' work on the exterior kept close to the spirit of the original, and so the predominating effect is still a homely Jacobean style untouched by neo-classicism. It is nowhere better displayed than by the S entrance front, a long façade of red brick with a lively skyline of gables, turrets and chimneys. Inside, the fine 17C staircase survives, though in a changed position. The dining room on the ground floor and the south drawing room above have their original fireplaces, and the latter room its original ceiling by Lyminge. The great showpiece is the *gallery, 127ft long, with a plaster ceiling whose fanciful emblems repay close study. The gardens have undergone several transformations. A formal parterre, originally 19C but redesigned in 1930, leads via an avenue of rhododendrons to a little classical temple by the Ivorys, who also built the orangery. The huge mausoleum 1m NW is by Joseph Bonomi (1793). Anne Boleyn spent her childhood in the earlier house on the site. Her family, as well as the Hobarts and Lothians, are remembered in the *Church* by the entrance; G.F. Watts's monument to the 8th Marquess of Lothian (d. 1878) is outstanding. The Perpendicular font has cheerful lions. The church at *Erpingham*, 3m NE, has 15C–17C stained glass brought from Blickling.

19½m: *Saxthorpe*. 2m N is *Mannington Hall*, a 15C moated house altered in the 19C by the eccentric 2nd Earl of Orford, with a ruined Saxon church in its lovely grounds (gardens open; house open by appointment). 27m: *Thursford*. At *Thursford Green*, c 1m NW, the *Thursford Museum* displays antique machinery (traction engines, steam engines, Wurlitzer organ, etc.). 33m: **Fakenham**, see Route 44A. 54m: **King's Lynn**, see Route 46A.

45

Great Yarmouth to Cromer and King's Lynn

Directions. Total distance 87m. The first leg of the journey avoids the main road to Cromer (34m) and takes a devious but interesting route along the coast. **Great Yarmouth**, see Route 38. A149 to (3m) Caister-on-Sea. A149, B1159 to (32m) **Cromer**. A149, A1078 to (87m) **King's Lynn** (Route 46A).

Great Yarmouth, see Route 38. A149 leads N to (3m) **Caister-on-Sea**, the site of a Roman harbour. Part of the town wall, gateway and buildings have been excavated (EH). The moated *Castle*, built c 1432, belonged to Sir John Fastolf and later to the Pastons (many of the 'Letters' were written here). It contains a motor museum. Further N B1159 goes right via *Hemsby* and (7½m) *Winterton*, with a fine 15C church tower. It turns inland to (8½m) *East Somerton*, with a ruined church in woods, and *West Somerton* church, which has a Norman round tower and 14C wall paintings. At (10m) *Horsey*, near Horsey Mere (Route 43), a barrier has been built against the sea. It has a drainage mill (NT). Through (12m) *Waxham* and (13m) *Sea Palling* the road skirts the sandy shore, regaining the coast at (18m) *Happisburgh* (pronounced 'Hazeburgh'), a pretty village with a lighthouse. The fine church has a tall tower, font and Perpendicular screen. 22m: *Bacton* has the remains of *Broomholm Priory*, now part of a farm, a Cluniac foundation of 1113 mentioned in Chaucer's 'Reeve's Tale' and Langland's 'Piers Plowman'. The attractive village is overshadowed by the terminal of the gas pipeline from the North Sea. 24m: *Paston* is a name familiar from the 15C 'Paston Letters'. A flint *barn is all that remains of their manor. The thatched church contains Paston monuments, including two by Nicholas Stone. 26m: *Mundesley* (seasonal TI) has fine sands and cliffs.

Knapton *church, 1½m inland, has a double hammerbeam roof with nearly 140 angels, and a fine font cover. *Trunch*, 1m W, has another good roof, a Perpendicular *font cover (one of only four in England) and a good screen.

The road skirts the coast via (28m) *Trimingham*, where the church has a painted choir screen, and (30m) *Overstrand*.

32m: **Cromer** (6200 inhabitants; seasonal TI), in a high but sheltered situation, is the most charming of the East Anglian seaside resorts. It became fashionable in Edwardian times, but still keeps its fishing industry, known for crabs. The 15C church has a splendid tower and tall piers and arches.

3m SW via A148 is *Felbrigg Hall*. Now NT but for 300 years previously the seat of the Windham family and its successors, it still keeps a homely atmosphere. Part of its history is written in the pleasantly inconsistent exterior, where the S range (c 1620) is vigorously Jacobean, with the motto 'Gloria Deo in Excelsis' cut in the balustrade over its three bays, and the W range (1674–87) is quiet and restrained. The story is completed inside by James Paine's alterations of 1750. Note particularly his library in the Gothick style. Of the outbuildings, the attractive brick orangery dates from 1704–05 and the stables by Donthorne were added in the 1820s. Beyond the walled garden lies wooded parkland. The church nearby has a series of *brasses (1351–1608) and monuments by Grinling Gibbons (to William Windham, d. 1686) and by Nollekens (to the politician William Windham, d. 1813). A148 continues W from Felbrigg to (1½m) the delightful wooded *Beacon Hill* (NT), which includes the highest point in Norfolk. For *Holt*, 5m beyond, see Route 39.

From Cromer to *Bury St Edmunds* and *London*, see Route 39.

The main route continues through *East Runton* and *West Runton* above cliffs which have been mostly preserved from permanent building by 'Half-Year Rights', the continuing medieval claim to common grazing; the caravans are removed in the winter. 35m: *Beeston Regis* has a fine church on the cliff edge. The 13C priory, to the W, is much ruined. 36m: *Sheringham* (5500 inhabitants; seasonal TI) is a resort known for the North Norfolk Collection of railway relics, etc., at the Victorian station. Steam locomotives run along a restored stretch of the branch line to Weybourne and beyond. *Sheringham Hall* (NT, open by appointment only) was built in 1812–17 by Humphry Repton and his son. Repton also laid out the gardens, well preserved and with magnificent rhododendrons (open all year). 39m: *Weybourne* (locally pronounced 'Webburn') has the ruins of an Augustinian priory next to the church. The high ground recedes and the salt marshes, with their abundant bird life, begin. A shingle barrier was built along the shore after the flood of 1953. 43m: Cley (pronounced 'Cly'), once a busy port, has a windmill (NT) and an 18C custom house. The large 13–15C church, ¾m inland, has an elaborate clerestory and S porch, ruined transepts and interesting brasses.

44½m: **Blakeney** is a delightful sailing village (regatta in August). The Church has a slender beacon tower at the E end, fine Early English vaulting in the chancel, and a double hammerbeam roof in the nave. A steep High St. with some charming houses leads down to the hard. The undercroft of the 14C Guildhall survives (EH). Blakeney Point (NT) and the foreshore to the N are bird sanctuaries.

At Langham, 2m S, Captain Marryat wrote several of his novels. B1156 follows the Glaven via (1m) Wiveton, with a medieval bridge and Perpendicular church, to (2m) Glandford, a pretty village with a shell museum beside the interesting church.

48½m: Stiffkey is known for its cockles ('Stewkey blues') and for a scandalous vicar in the 1930s. 52m: Wells-next-the-Sea (2400 inhabitants; seasonal TI) is an attractive little port with a rebuilt Perpendicular church. For Binham and Walsingham, see Route 44A.

About 1m S of (54m) Holkham is *Holkham Hall (open), seat of the Earls of Leicester and one of Norfolk's grandest country houses.

William Kent built Holkham in 1734–61 for Thomas Coke, the 1st Earl, whose choice of Palladianism was no doubt influenced by nearby Houghton. It consists of a central block of state rooms with corridors leading to four lower blocks of rooms for ordinary use. The material is a light-grey brick resembling stone. The most striking room is the Marble Hall, where Kent used coloured alabaster to sumptuous effect. Holkham is famous for its art collection: classical sculptures, paintings by Van Dyck, Rubens, both Poussins, Claude and Gainsborough, and a copy of Michelangelo's lost 'Bathers' cartoon. The park, with its lake, was landscaped by Capability Brown in 1762 and the formal terraces were laid out by Nesfield in 1854. To the N a monument remembers the agricultural improvements of 'Coke of Norfolk' (Thomas William Coke, 1st Earl of Leicester by the second creation, 1754–1842). The column, supported by four cows and crowned by a wheatsheaf, was put up by his tenants in 1845. The church, rebuilt in 1870, has two monuments by Nicholas Stone.

57½m: Burnham Overy Staithe is a pleasant little resort. Nelson (1758–1805) was born in the old rectory (since demolished) of Burnham Thorpe, 1m S. The church contains the font where he was christened and a lectern and rood made of wood from the 'Victory'; also the fine brass of Sir William Calthorp (d. 1420). About 1m S of Burnham Thorpe is the Augustinian Creake Abbey, founded in 1206, with remains of the 13C church and a 14C chapel (EH). The churches of North Creake and South Creake are interesting. 59m: Burnham Norton has a church with a circular tower and vestiges of a Carmelite friary (1241). The font at (60m) Burnham Deepdale has 11C carving of the labours of the months. 62m: Brancaster stands on the site of the Roman fort of Branodunum, guarding the Saxon Shore. Scolt Head (NT), a sandy and shingly island, has a ternery (strictly preserved). The church at (67m) Holme-next-the-Sea has the earliest brass with an English inscription (c 1400). The Peddars' Way, a prehistoric track improved by the Romans, reaches the sea here. It ran inland to Castle Acre and Ixworth (Route 39).

71m: **Hunstanton** (4100 inhabitants; TI), facing W across the Wash, is a resort with coloured stratified cliffs. Just S of the old lighthouse are the ruins of a chapel of St Edmund. At Old Hunstanton, 1½m N, the church has a

The Quay at Blakeney

Norman font and Le Strange monuments, including a *brass to Sir Roger (d. 1506). The church at (73½m) *Heacham* has a portrait medallion (1933) of Princess Pocohontas (1595–1617), wife of John Rolfe of Heacham Hall, whose parents are buried here. 76m: *Snettisham* and (78½m) *Dersingham* both have fine churches, the former with a tall steeple. The church at *Shernborne*, 2m E, contains a Norman font.

1½m S of Dersingham is **Sandringham House**, the country home of the Queen, more interesting for its royal connection than its architecture. It is not open when members of the royal family are in residence. Queen Victoria bought the estate for her son, the future Edward VII, and he commissioned A.J. Humbert to design the Jacobean-style building of 1870. It was expanded by the addition of a ballroom in 1883 and partly rebuilt in its upper storey after a fire in 1891. The elaborate Norwich Gates by Thomas Jekyll, at the main entrance, were a wedding present from Norfolk to Edward VII (1863). The old stables are an eclectic museum. George VI (1895–1952) was born at York Cottage and died at the house. Sandringham *Church* (late Perpendicular) contains memorials to Edward VII and other members of the royal family. At *Wolferton*, 2¾m W, the railway station built to serve Sandringham is now a museum. The church has good screens.

82½m: *Castle Rising*, see Route 44A. 87m: **King's Lynn**, see Route 46A.

46

Cambridge to Ely and King's Lynn

A.   Via Downham Market

Directions. Total distance 44m. **Cambridge**, see Route 37. A10 to (16m) **Ely** (bypassed), (33m) **Downham Market** (bypassed) and (44m) **King's Lynn**.

Cambridge, see Route 37. At (4m) *Milton*, on the right, the church has a Norman chancel arch, 17C altar rails, and monuments by Flaxman and Chantrey. 5½m: *Waterbeach* has a section of the Car Dyke, the Roman canal dug to transport fenland corn to the garrisons of Lincoln and the north. For 2m the road follows the conspicuous alignment of the Roman Akeman Street. 7m: *Denny Abbey*, on the right, was founded in 1160 by the Benedictines from Ely, taken over a century later by the Knights Templar and, after their suppression, used by the nuns of St Clare. Fragments of the church and refectory building survive (EH, summer season, daily; Sundays only in winter). 11m: *Stretham* has a 15C cross, 16–18C houses and a Decorated church. On the Old West River to the SE is a Pumping House with the original Butterfly Beam Engine of 1830 (open).

16m: **ELY** is a small city (10,300 inhabitants) built on a hill whose modest height of 70ft seems greater because of the cathedral that tops it and the flatness of the surrounding Fens.

TI: Oliver Cromwell's House, 29 St Mary's St. **Buses**: from Market St. **Railway Station**: SE of the centre.

History. According to Bede, the city acquired its name ('eel island') from the eels in the Great Ouse, E of the hill. The old 'Isle of Ely' (7m by 4m) was surrounded by marshland which only the 'Fen slodgers' who knew the tussock paths could penetrate. Hereward the Wake, 'Last of the English', held out against the invading Norman armies here until 1071, when a road was floated across the marsh on faggots.

The *Cathedral belongs to the great series of Fen monasteries established by the Saxons and rebuilt by the Normans. It differs from a foundation like Peterborough in the wealth and variety of post-Norman work, particularly the Octagon and Lady Chapel.

The first building, a 7C Benedictine abbey, was sacked by the Danes in 870. Hereward the Wake used its successor as his headquarters. The present church was begun by Abbot Simeon in 1083 and was substantially complete when the nave was finished in 1189, by which time it had been raised to cathedral rank.

The most striking part of the exterior, the W front, belongs to this period and is hence in the Norman Transitional style. Its castellated tower has two later additions: an Early English Galilee Porch at the base and a Decorated octagonal top with side turrets. Its asymmetrical appearance was caused by the fall of the NW tower in a storm in 1701.

The *Nave is a fine piece of late Norman work and, despite the massive piers of its 12 bays, seems light by comparison with the earlier naves at Durham and Gloucester. Its narrowness is emphasised by the height of the clerestory and triforium arcades. The painted ceiling is 19C but the four E bays of the S aisle keep their original 12C colouring. In this aisle are also: the Prior's Doorway (c 1140), richly ornamented outside; a Saxon cross in memory of Ovinus, vassal to Queen Etheldreda, foundress of the

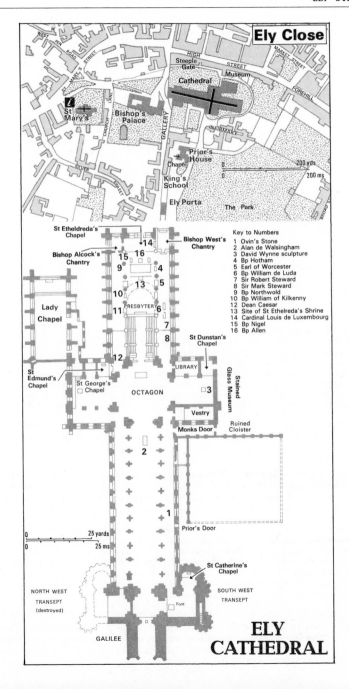

Ely Close

WEST FEN ROAD
HIGH STREET
Steeple Gate
Museum
Cathedral
MARKET STREET
FORE HILL
ST MARY'S
CHURCH LANE
St Mary's
Bishop's Palace
GALLERY
INFIRMARY
SILVER STREET
Prior's House
Chapel
King's School
Ely Porta
The Park
BROAD STREET

0 _____ 200 yds
0 _____ 200 ms

ELY CATHEDRAL

St Etheldreda's Chapel
Bishop Alcock's Chantry
14
Bishop West's Chantry
15 16
9   4
13   5
10
11   PRESBYTERY   6
Lady Chapel
7
8
St Dunstan's Chapel
12
St Edmund's Chapel
St George's Chapel
LIBRARY
Stained Glass Museum
OCTAGON
3
Vestry
Monks Door
Ruined Cloister
2
Prior's Door
1
25 yards
25 ms
St Catherine's Chapel
NORTH WEST TRANSEPT (destroyed)
Font
SOUTH WEST TRANSEPT
GALILEE

Key to Numbers
1 Ovin's Stone
2 Alan de Walsingham
3 David Wynne sculpture
4 Bp Hotham
5 Earl of Worcester
6 Bp William de Luda
7 Sir Robert Steward
8 Sir Mark Steward
9 Bp Northwold
10 Bp William of Kilkenny
11 Dean Caesar
13 Site of St Etheldreda's Shrine
14 Cardinal Louis de Luxembourg
15 Bp Nigel
16 Bp Allen

original abbey; and at the E end, another elaborate doorway, used by the monks entering from the cloisters. The lower parts of the *Transepts* are the oldest work in the cathedral (1083–1107). The E aisle of the N transept has the Chapel of St Edmund, with a 14C screen and a 12C wall painting of the saint's martyrdom. The transept leads to the *Stained Glass Museum* in the triforium and the Lady Chapel (see below).

At the junction of transepts and nave is the **Central Octagon*. The sacrist Alan de Walsingham and his carpenter, probably William Hurley, were given the chance to build it in 1322, when the original tower fell and wrecked part of the choir. The octagon takes the entire breadth of nave, transepts and choir as its base, rising on four large and four small arches. Above it, the wooden lantern is set with its angles against the faces of the stone walls. The effect, writes Nikolaus Pevsner, is 'a delight from beginning to end for anyone who feels for space as strongly as for construction'.

A 19C screen separates the Octagon from the *Choir*, which shows a clearly marked division between the three W bays by Alan de Walsingham and the delicate Early English part beyond (1234–52). The upper choir stalls are 14C with misericords but the other furnishings are the worst fruit of Gilbert Scott's 19C restoration. The aisles have monuments to medieval bishops. At the E end of the S aisle is the Chantry of Bishop West (d. 1533), combining medieval and classical motifs; the corresponding end of the N aisle is filled by the Chantry of Bishop Alcock (d. 1500), Perpendicular at its most luxuriant.

NE of the N transept is the *Lady Chapel* (1321–c 1353), another of Alan de Walsingham's happy additions. Its simple rectangle is made airy and spacious by the complex lierne-vaulted roof (at 46ft the widest medieval vault in England) and the clear glass of the broad windows. The richly carved foliage and statuettes of the wall seats are still impressive despite their badly damaged state, a result of the soft clunch (chalk) as much as the vandalism of Lord Protector Somerset's men in 1547.

The *Cloisters* are now represented mainly by the E walk, which forms the S entrance to the nave. Parts of the *Infirmary* are incorporated in Firmary Lane. The *Bishop's House*, S of the cloister, was adapted from the old guest hall and includes remains of the 12C kitchen. The other conventual buildings to survive lie further S and are part of the *King's School*, refounded at the Dissolution in 1541 but descended from the monastic school where Edward the Confessor (d. 1066) studied. The most interesting group is the *Prior's Hall* and *Prior Crauden's Chapel*, an exquisite building by Alan de Walsingham, with an original mosaic tiled floor. *Ely Porta* (the great gateway of the monastery, c 1394) leads into a street called The Gallery and so back to the cathedral. The *Bishop's Palace*, on Palace Green to the left, is mainly late 17C but preserves wings built by Bishop Alcock and a long gallery added by Bishop Goodrich (d. 1554).

The church of *St Mary*, a little W of the palace, dates from 1215. The half-timbered vicarage next to its churchyard was Oliver Cromwell's home in 1636–47, when he was farmer of the cathedral tithes and Ely's MP. It is now the TI Centre.

The *Sacrist's Gate* on the N side of the cathedral houses a museum of local history. Beyond is the High St., which leads right and continues as Forehill down to the banks of the Ouse, pleasantly cluttered with boats. A riverside walk between the two bridges passes the restored 19C *Maltings*.

FROM ELY TO NEWMARKET, 13m. A142 runs SE across the Fens. 1½m: *Stuntney* was a Bronze Age settlement. A timber track connected it with Ely. 5m: *Soham*, a large and attractive village of brick houses, was the site of a cathedral built by St Felix, the 'Apostle of East Anglia' (d. 634). The present church is 12C, with a Perpendicular tower and flushwork. The area still has many windmills. 8½m: *Fordham* (Route 37). A142 enters Suffolk near (11½m) *Exning* (right), a pleasant old village and the mother parish of Newmarket. 13½m: *Newmarket*, Route 41.

A10 runs NE from Ely. 21m: *Littleport* has a Perpendicular church with 19C additions. It enters Norfolk at (25m) *Brandon Creek*, where the Little Ouse meets the Great Ouse. 31m: *Hilgay* church has a brick tower (1794). 33m: *Denver* has a 13C church, a tower-mill (limited opening) and a sluice; the

Old Denver Sluices (1825) are by Rennie. Dorothy L. Sayers used the name for the ducal family of Lord Peter Wimsey and evoked the fenland atmosphere in 'The Nine Tailors'. 34m: **Downham Market** (4700 inhabitants) is a compact market town. The Early English church has a high tower and an excellent peal of bells.

A1122 runs E from Downham Market. 4m: *Stradsett* church, with good German stained glass of 1540, is set in the grounds of the Hall, Elizabethan with a Georgian façade. 5½m: *Fincham* has a Perpendicular church with a Norman font. The road crosses the Devil's Dyke before (10m) *Swaffham* (Route 39).

35m: *Stow Bardolph* church has 17–19C monuments of the Hare family. 38m: *Tottenhill.*

An unclassified road leads left via Magdalen Rd Station to (2½m) the Great Ouse, across which is the lonely village of *Wiggenhall St Mary Magdalen* with a Perpendicular church and 13C tower, containing good painted screens, benches, and Jacobean panelling. *Wiggenhall St Mary the Virgin* lies c 2m NW in beautiful country and has a brick church with carved early 16C benches and an eagle lectern (1518). On the E bank of the Ouse lies the church of *Wiggenhall St Germans* (also with benches), where the village has large 16–18C houses. Just to the S is *Wiggenhall St Peter* with an impressive ruined Perpendicular church standing at the 'Eau Brink'.

44m: **KING'S LYNN** (33,300 inhabitants) is an old port on the Great Ouse above its outflow into the Wash. The original parish of St Margaret grew up round the Saturday Market; a new town was laid out across the creek to the N in c 1160, with the Tuesday Market and the church of St Nicholas at its centre. Lynn has kept a townscape of 14C–19C domestic, civic and industrial buildings, particularly between its two market places and by the water. Its affinity with the Netherlands is everywhere apparent.

TI: The Old Gaol House, Saturday Market Place. **Bus Station**: Market St. **Railway Station**: Blackfriars Rd, E of the centre. **Theatre**: St George's Guildhall, King St. **Annual Event**: Festival of Music and Drama at the end of July.

Natives and residents. Fanny Burney (1752–1840) was born here while her father, Charles Burney, was organist at St Margaret's. The explorer George Vancouver (1758–98) was born behind the Friends' Meeting House in New Conduit St. The murderer Eugene Aram was arrested here in 1758.

The church of *St Margaret* in the Saturday Market was founded c 1100 by Bishop Losinga of Norwich and rebuilt in the 13C. It has 14C screens, misericords, an early Georgian pulpit, an organ by Snetzler (1754), and two of the most elaborate *brasses in England, Flemish or German in origin. The Walsoken brass (Adam de Walsoken, d. 1349) has a border of country scenes; that of Robert Braunche (d. 1364) is known as the 'Peacock Brass' from its picture of the feast Braunche gave for Edward III. Opposite, in the direction of Queen St., is a fine group consisting of the *Old Gaol House* (1784), the *Guildhall*, chequered in flint and stone (1421, with an Elizabethan addition to the left), and the *Town Hall* (1895). The Old Gaol House contains the TI Centre, through which visitors can reach a museum with displays bringing to life the town's history of crime and punishment. Adjoining is the *Town House Museum*, with recreated period rooms.

The old streets S of the Saturday Market are worth exploring. Nelson St. has *Hampton Court*, a considerably altered monastic building (c 1400). Bridge St. has the restored Jacobean *Greenland Fishery*. Further on are the 14C *Whitefriars Gateway* and the only remaining town gate, the 16C *South Gate*. E of the Saturday Market, in St James St., is the Perpendicular *Greyfriars Tower*. The Walks, beyond, has a fragment of the

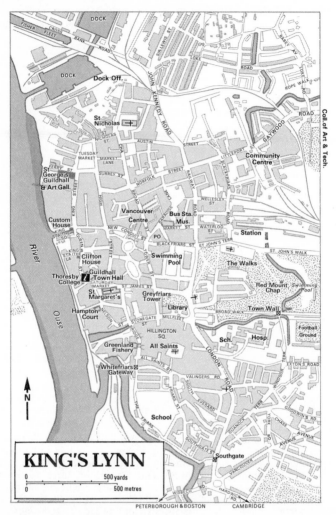

KING'S LYNN

0   500 yards

0   500 metres

PETERBOROUGH & BOSTON   CAMBRIDGE

town wall and the *Red Mount Chapel* (1482), an octagonal brick building probably used by pilgrims to Walsingham.

From the Saturday Market, Queen St. and King St. lead N to the Tuesday Market. On the left of Queen St. are *Thoresby College*, a 15C monastic house with 17C front, and *Clifton House*, a 16–17C merchant's house with a brick watch tower, a 15C undercroft and a façade remodelled by Henry Bell in c 1708. King's Staithe Lane, leading to the quay, has 16–17C warehouses and 17–18C houses. King's Staithe Square has the 17–18C *Bank House*, with a statue of Charles I. On the quay stands the *Custom House* (1683; Henry Bell), perhaps the most graceful of Lynn's buildings. The statue is of Charles II.

Purfleet St. leads right and, after crossing the High St., continues as New Conduit St. On Market St., beyond Paradise Court, are the bus station and the *Lynn Museum* of local history. It contains medieval pilgrims' badges.

King St. has a wealth of good buildings, including the 15C *St George's Guildhall*, used as a theatre in the 18C and now restored to this function. The Tuesday Market Place beyond is spacious and dignified, with the *Duke's Head* (1683–89) by Henry Bell. *St Nicholas*, off the NE corner, was built as a chapel of ease in 1146. It has a splendid S porch, benches, a 15C brass lectern and a tie-beam roof. The neighbouring streets are worth exploring.

From King's Lynn to *Norwich*, see Route 44; to *Cromer* and *Yarmouth*, see Route 45; to *Boston* and *Grimsby*, see Route 47.

B.   Via March and Wisbech

Directions. Total distance 59m. **Cambridge**, see Route 37. A10 to (16m) **Ely** (bypassed), see Route 46A. A142 to (28m) Chatteris. A141 to (36m) **March** (bypassed). A141, A47 to (46m) **Wisbech** (bypassed). A47 to (59m) **King's Lynn** (Route 46A).

Cambridge, see Route 37. A10 to (16m) **Ely**, see Route 46A. A142 runs W to (22½m) *Sutton*, on a ridge above the Fens surrounded by orchards. It has a Decorated church of c 1370.

From Sutton B1381 leads SW to (5m) *Earith*, the point from which the New Bedford River and the Old Bedford River were cut to Denver (Route 46A). On their smooth waters 17C experiments first demonstrated the curvature of the earth's surface. A1123 continues to (6½m) *Bluntisham*, where Dorothy L. Sayers was brought up at the rectory. For (9m) *St Ives* and (154m) *Huntingdon*, see Route 36.

A142 turns NW to (24m) *Mepal*, where it crosses the Bedford Rivers. At (28m) *Chatteris* (6200 inhabitants) it joins A141 from Huntingdon. Further on, A141 crosses the Forty Foot Drain, dug in the 17C by Cornelius Vermuyden. 32m: *Doddington* church, left of the road, has glass by Morris and Co., and a Dutch carving of Christ and the Woman of Samaria. 36m: **March** (14,500 inhabitants) became an important Fen town in Roman times. It declined when a new cut allowed the Nene to flow directly from Wisbech to Peterborough, but flourished again as a railway junction in the 19C. Its varied history has not given it beauty except for the church of *St Wendreda*, S of the centre. The tower is topped with a spire, the building style is a mixture of Decorated and Perpendicular, and the double hammerbeam *roof with triple ranks of angels is one of the best in the region. At (40m) *Guyhirn* A47 follows the new course of the Nene.

46m: **Wisbech** (pronounced 'Wizbeach'; 17,300 inhabitants; TI), a town of unexpected distinction, grew up when the new cut of the Nene made it the port for Peterborough. Old warehouses stand by the Nene quay and two handsome Georgian streets, *North Brink and *South Brink, line the banks of the river. The general effect recalls the tranquil landscapes of the Netherlands. The variety of the buildings makes close inspection worthwhile. North Brink has *Peckover House* (NT), built in 1722, with a rococo interior. The garden has a working orangery. E of the memorial to Thomas Clarkson (1760–1846), campaigner against slavery and a native of Wisbech, is the *Castle Estate*, begun during the 1790s in emulation of fashionable spas. It takes its name from the castle of 1072, replaced c 1658 by the mansion of John Thurloe, Secretary of State during the Protectorate. Only the entrance gates and garden walls of Thurloe's house remain and the present building is early 19C. The *Church* has, curiously, a second N aisle added in the 14C; also 15C glass, monuments, and a brass to Thomas de Braunstone (d. 1401) over 7ft long. *Walsoken* *church, in the Norfolk suburb, has one of the best Norman interiors in East Anglia and some 17C sculptures.

West Walton *church, 1½m further N, has Early English capitals and arcades like those at Lincoln. The 17C Prayer board asks for delivery from floods. The detached bell tower is 13C. *Emneth* church, 2¼m SE of Wisbech, is Norman, Early English and Perpendicular. *Leverington* church, 2m NW, is built of clunch; it has an Early English tower, a 14C porch, a 15C Jesse window and, in the NE corner, the tomb of Goldsmith's Tony Lumpkin.

A47 runs NE across the Fens passing (left at 51m) *Terrington St John*, where the 14C church is connected to a later tower by a series of rooms, a staircase and passages. The font cover dates from 1632. 55m: *Tilney All Saints* (left) has a 12C church with Norman work, a Decorated hammerbeam roof, misericords and two fonts. The Great Ouse crosses to (59m) **King's Lynn** (Route 46A).

47

King's Lynn to Boston and Grimsby

A.   Via Louth

Directions. Total distance 90m. **King's Lynn**, see Route 46A. A17 to (15m) Long Sutton. A17, A151 to (17m) Holbeach. A151 to (25m) Spalding. A16 to (41m) **Boston**, (57m) Spilsby, (73m) **Louth** and (90m) **Grimsby**.

King's Lynn, see Route 46A. A17 runs W through the flat saltmarshes below the Wash, a wide shallow bay gradually being silted up by the rivers that flow into it—the Nene, the Ouse, the Welland and the Witham. It was here that King John was overtaken by the tide, losing his baggage and treasure. The bleak landscape is relieved by splendid churches, noble in scale and often rich in woodwork. The *church at *Terrington St Clement*, N of the road at 6m, is one of the best, with many interesting details. It has a detached Perpendicular tower (characteristic of the area), a good 18C chancel screen and a font cover with paintings inside, including one of the Baptism of Christ. The church of *Walpole St Andrew* lies 2½m SW, and nearby is that of *Walpole St Peter*, with Perpendicular tracery and ornament. It has a tie-beam roof, 17C screens, misericords and a pulpit of 1620. Under the chancel is a richly groined passage, a public right of way. 10m: *Sutton Bridge* is a small river port on the Nene, over the Lincolnshire border. 13m: *Long Sutton* is a little market town whose *church has one of the oldest lead-covered spires in the country (Early English), and a 15C porch. 14½m: *Gedney* has a fine Early English *church. The tower has a Perpendicular spire, and the two-storied S porch a turret stair. Inside are 14–15C glass and coloured alabaster monuments to the Welby family. Over the S door is an ivory plaque of the Crucifixion. The desolate expanse of the Wash is well seen at *Gedney Drove End*, 5m NE. 15½m: *Fleet* church (14C) has a detached tower with spire and a Perpendicular W window. A151 heads left to (17m) **Holbeach** (4800 inhabitants), a centre of Lincolnshire's bulb-growing district. The Transitional church has a tower and spire which dominate the surrounding country. 19½m: *Whaplode* *church has a Norman chancel arch and a fine Irby monument (c 1620). The 12C tower stands at the E end of the S aisle. *Moulton*, ½m S, has an early Perpendicular rood screen, and a steeple 160ft high (c 1380). 22m: *Weston* *church is Early English with 14C transepts and a Perpendicular tower; note also the S porch. About 1½m N are the ruins of *Wykeham Chapel* (early Decorated). 24m: *Springfield Gardens* (open) has a show of bulbs in April and May.

25m: **Spalding** (18,200 inhabitants; TI), an old market-gardening town, stands on the Welland in the heart of the Fens. As at Wisbech, the flat and spacious townscape creates an atmosphere more characteristic of the Low Countries than England. From the Market Place there are walks to the river, whose banks are lined with good Georgian houses. *Ayscoughfee Hall*, a much altered 15C mansion with a beautiful garden, is a museum of agriculture and horticulture. It was the home of Maurice Johnson, founder of the 'Gentlemen's Society of Spalding', the oldest scientific and literary association in England (1710). The church of *St Mary and St Nicholas*, founded in 1284, has been much extended and its tower, with an early Perpendicular spire, looks small for the double-aisled building.

There are pumping stations and other drainage works in the surrounding Fens. The boilerhouse of the former pumping station at *Pode Hole*, 2m W, is now a drainage museum. See also Pinchbeck below.

FROM SPALDING TO CROWLAND, 9m via A1073. 3m: *Cowbit* (pronounced 'Coubitt') is a centre for Fen skating. The road crosses the fertile *Bedford Level*, named after the reclamation work of the Earl of Bedford and the Dutch engineer Vermuyden (d. 1677) in 1650–53. 9m: **Crowland** (or *Croyland*) is a pleasant town, with tree-lined streets, and the seat of an *Abbey which was, with Ely and Peterborough, one of the great Saxon foundations in Eastern England. Originally established c 716 by King Ethelbald of Mercia over the cell of the hermit St Guthlac, it was sacked by the Danes in 870, rebuilt, and burned down in 1091. What survives is a grand fragment of the Norman church raised in the early 12C by Abbot Joffrid (1109–70): the N aisle (altered in the 15C and now the parish church), the lofty arch of the central tower, the W fronts of the aisles and the attached font. Among the many details worth attention are the relief statues over the W door portraying the life of St Guthlac, the monumental slab to the master-mason William of Wermington in the W tower, and the parclose screen of 1413. The rest of the church suffered harshly after the Reformation, its E part being pulled down in 1540 and the nave and S aisle being destroyed in a bombardment by Cromwell's troops (1643).

27m: *Pinchbeck* has a large church with a 14C tower and much Perpendicular and Decorated work; the good E window is a 19C restoration by Butterfield. The alloy known as 'pinchbeck' (copper; 'false gold') is named, not from this village, but from Christopher Pinchbeck, the London watchmaker who invented it c 1720. There is a beam engine of 1833 in the *Pinchbeck Marsh* pumping station (open). 31m: *Gosberton* has another fine early Perpendicular church.

Donington, 3½m NW, was the birthplace of Matthew Flinders (1774–1814), the Australian navigator, commemorated in the fine late Decorated and early Perpendicular church.

The churches of (35m) *Sutterton*, *Algarkirk* (¾m E) and (38m) *Kirton-inHolland* are all interesting.

41m: **BOSTON** (i.e. 'St Botolph's Town'), a market town (27,000 inhabitants) near the mouth of the Witham, has both a handsome church and a lingering atmosphere to remind the visitor of the time, in the Middle Ages, when it grew rich on the wool trade with Flanders. Its great namesake in America acknowledges Boston's proud connection with the Pilgrim Fathers.

TI: Blackfriars Arts Centre. **Bus Stations**: Lincoln Lane and Tunnard St. **Railway Station**: Station St. (W of river). **Entertainments**: Theatre and Arts Centre in Blackfriars, Spain Lane; Sam Newsom Music Centre, South St. **Annual Events**: May Fair, a pleasure fair replacing the old sheep fair, in the week following 3 May; Boston Carnival on last weekend in June.

Natives and residents. John Foxe (1517–87), the martyrologist, and Jean Ingelow (1820–97), the poetess, were natives. The musician John Taverner lived here from 1537 to his death in 1545, dissolving the four local priories in his capacity as Cromwell's agent.

St Botolph, one of the largest parish churches in England, testifies to the affluence of the Boston guilds and merchants. It is made conspicuous for 20m around, both on land and sea, by its lofty Perpendicular tower and beautiful octagonal lantern (cf. Ely). The nickname of 'Boston Stump', which almost universally replaces the church's official dedication, may come from its truncated appearance when seen from a distance, or from the belief that a spire was meant to crown the lantern. A few other Perpendicular additions aside, the building is an almost pure example of flowing Decorated. The oldest part is the lower section of the tower (1309), where a tablet commemorates George Bass, surgeon of the town (born in 1771 at *Aswarby*, 4m S of Sleaford), and other Lincolnshire men who played their part in the exploration of Australia. There are fine misericords, a pulpit (1612) and several interesting tombs, including the fine slab of a Hanse merchant (1340) brought from the destroyed Franciscan church, an effigy of a knight from the church of St John, and an early 14C one of a lady with puppies playing round her feet. The SW chapel was restored in 1857 by New England Bostonians in memory of John Cotton (1584–1652), vicar here in 1612–33 before he went to America.

Boston has no other building of the first rank, but its streets and houses make an agreeable walking tour. They are redolent of the sea, with warm brick, bright paintwork and 'flood steps' in front of many doors. The Market Place, where the lively general market is held on Wednesdays and Saturdays, has the *Corporation Buildings* (1772) and the *Assembly Rooms* (1826) on the W side. In the little Mitre Lane, leading from the N end, is *Pescod Hall*, a restored 15C wool merchant's house, now a shop. South St., leading from the market to the port, has *Shodfriars Hall*, a Victorian copy of a timbered 16C building. Spain Lane, also on the left, has *Blackfriars*, part of a 13C Dominican friary, now housing a theatre. The 15C *Guildhall* on the corner (left) contains the muchaltered court where Brewster and other Pilgrim Fathers were tried in 1607 for seeking to flee the country; also shown are the cells where they were imprisoned and the old kitchens. Next door is *Fydell House* (open), a building of 1726 with a lovely carved staircase. It is owned by the Boston Preservation Trust and houses Pilgrim

Fydell House, Boston

College, an outpost of the University of Nottingham. The *Grammar School*, by Haven Bridge further on, preserves its original hall of 1567. *Hussey Tower*, behind, is a relic of a mansion of c 1500. Small lanes lead to the sea bank from which the views extend far over the Wash and inland to a superb panorama of church towers. Overlooking the Maud Foster Drain is the *Maud Foster Windmill* (limited opening) of 1815, at seven floors the tallest commercial windmill in the country.

The marsh villages near Boston have fine churches. That of *Skirbeck*, 1m SE, has an Elizabethan pulpit. Here, too, dyer's woad (Isatis tinctoria) was last grown in England; the mill for grinding it stopped work in 1932. *Fishtoft*, 1½m beyond, has village stocks and traces of Norman work in the chancel of its church. The church at *Freiston*, 3½m E, is the nave of a 12C priory church. For churches NE of Boston on A52, see Route 47B.

FROM BOSTON TO LINCOLN VIA HORNCASTLE, 39m. B1183 runs due N across the Fens to (11m) *Revesby*, the 'model' village attached to Revesby Abbey, named after the Cistercian house that was founded here from Rievaulx in 1142. The present house (not open) is Victorian and little remains of the abbey church. *East Kirkby* church, 2½m E, has fine Decorated and Perpendicular details. At (16m) *Scrivelsby* is a late Perpendicular gatehouse, the last intact remnant of *Scrivelsby Court* (open by appointment), ancient home of the Dymokes who succeeded the Marmions as lords of the manor, a position carrying the right to serve as King's Champion. The church has memorials of the Marmions and the Dymokes. 18m: **Horncastle** (4200 inhabitants; seasonal TI) stands on the site of the Roman Banovallum at the junction of the rivers Bain and Witham, by the foot of the Wolds (see below). Part of the walls of the fort have been incorporated into the *Library*. In the church of *St Mary* are the brass of Sir Lionel Dymoke, King's Champion (1519), and the monument of Sir Ingram Hopwood, 'who paid his debt to nature ... in the attempt of seizing the arch-rebel [Cromwell] in the bloody skirmish near Winceby' (1643). The scythe blades and hay knives over the door are said to have been fastened to staves for use in the battle. There was a famous August horse fair here, described by Borrow in 'Romany Rye'. The old rectory at *Somersby*, 6m NE, was the birthplace of Tennyson (1809–92). The church has a memorial to him and a remarkable churchyard cross. *Bag Enderby* church; ½m E, of which Tennyson's father was also rector, has a good font; there is another, and good monuments, at *Harrington*, 1m further. Harrington Hall is a 17C house with Tudor fragments and medieval foundations. Its walled garden is sometimes claimed as the 'High Hall Garden' of Tennyson's 'Maud'. From Horncastle to Sleaford, see Route 48.

B1190, the shortest road from Horncastle to Lincoln, runs W, crossing the Witham at (29m) *Bardney*, where excavations have laid bare the ground plan of the once wealthy Benedictine abbey and brought to light pillar bases, tomb slabs and other relics. St Oswald (d. 642) was buried here. The church of St Lawrence has an old altar slab with seven crosses. 35m: *Branston* has a late Saxon church tower. The approach to (39m) *Lincoln* (Route 48) gives fine views of the cathedral standing over the Fens.

From Boston to *Sleaford*, see Route 48.

Beyond Boston the Grimsby road runs due N across the Fens, passing through (45m) *Sibsey*, where the Norman church has an Early English tower. The *Trader Windmill*, ½m W of the village, is a brick Victorian tower mill with its machinery still intact (EH, limited opening in summer). 57m: **Spilsby** (1600 inhabitants) was the birthplace of the explorer Sir John Franklin (1787–1847), whose statue is next to the medieval *Market Cross*. The 14C *Church* has Franklin's flag and 14–16C monuments of the Willoughby and Bertie families. The one to Richard Bertie (d. 1582) and his wife is splendidly elaborate.

Spilsby stands on the edge of the Fens, with the Wolds of South Lincolnshire rising beyond. These chalk uplands, dramatic continuation of the same chalk scarp that gives Cambridgeshire its gentle Gog Magog hills and Norfolk its fertile plateau, stretch from a western escarpment by the rivers Witham and (further N) Ancholme to the flat coastal strip of marsh and sand in the east. Villages hug the valleys, while big farms spread over the high ground.

Halton Holegate, 1½m E, has a spacious Perpendicular church. *Gunby Hall* (NT), 4m further NE, is a house of 1700 in the style of Wren. It has a contemporary oak staircase, portraits by Reynolds and a walled garden. The 18C Whitegates Cottage (NT, open by appointment) on the estate is a rare surviving example of the local vernacular style. At *Old Bolingbroke*, 4m W of Spilsby via *Mavis Enderby*, only a few mounds remain of John of Gaunt's castle, where Henry IV was born in 1399 (EH). For Somersby and the other places W of Spilsby associated with Tennyson, see the detour from Boston to Lincoln above.

59m: *Partney*, with its pleasant church, was a favourite haunt of Dr Johnson when he stayed with his friend Bennet Langton at nearby Langton Hall (no longer standing). From (63m) *Ulceby Cross* A1104 leads NE to (3m) *Alford* (2600 inhabitants; seasonal TI), with a good Decorated church and a museum of Lincolnshire life in the old manor house.

Markby, 3m NE of Alford, has a thatched church and *Willoughby*, 3m S of Alford, was the birthplace of Captain John Smith of Virginia (1580–1631). For *Mablethorpe*, on the coast 6m NE of Alford, see Route 47B.

73m: **Louth** (13,300 inhabitants; TI) is dominated by its *Church, with one of the most beautiful steeples in England (1501–15). The well-proportioned interior has a magnificent high tower arch. It contains paintings and the 'Sudbury Hutch', a chest of c 1500 with portraits of Henry VII and Elizabeth of York. The town centre has 17–19C buildings, harmoniously grouped, especially in Westgate, with a lovely series of 18C doorways, and in Upgate, 16C with additions from every succeeding century. John Smith of Virginia and Sir John Franklin, as well as Tennyson and his brothers, attended the grammar school (rebuilt). The village churches in the neighbourhood are worth attention, but only scanty traces remain of *Louth Park Abbey*, a Cistercian foundation of 1139, 1½m E.

A16 follows the E edge of the Wolds and enters South Humberside. 90m: **GRIMSBY** (92,100 inhabitants; TI), or *Great Grimsby*, has been a fishing and trading port since the 11C. It remains the chief fishing port in England, though the size of the catch has greatly declined in recent years. The *Royal Docks*, built in the early 1850s, are dominated by the *Victoria Flour Mill* (1906) and the *Dock Tower* (1852), a copy of the tower on the town hall in Siena. *St James's Church* is a much altered 13C building; its most striking feature is the curious combination of clerestory and triforium.

Clee, or *Old Clee*, 1m S, has a restored church whose W tower is a fine example of Saxon work. The nave and font are Norman. For *Cleethorpes*, on the coast further S, see Route 47B. The deep-water dock at *Immingham*, 6m up the Humber from Grimsby, was first built in 1912 to handle coal from Yorkshire. It now also has an oil terminal, with oil-refining and chemical industries. A monument at *South Killingholme Haven* marks the site of the Pilgrim Fathers' embarkation for Holland in 1609.

Ashby-cum-Fenby is a pretty village 6m S of Grimsby, whose Early English church has good Decorated windows and a screen. At *East Ravendale*, 1m SW, are the remains of a Premonstratensian priory, and 2½m W of Ashby lies *Hatcliffe*, beautifully situated above a valley.

From Grimsby to *Lincoln*, see Route 48.

B. Via the Coast

Directions. Total distance 108m. **King's Lynn**, see Route 46A. To (41m) **Boston**, see Route 47A. A52 to (63m) Skegness and (81m) Mablethorpe. A1031 to (108m) **Grimsby** (Route 47A).

King's Lynn, see Route 46A. To **Boston**, see Route 47A. That route goes N into the Wolds, while the present one heads NE on A52 along the flat coastal tract. The small villages through which it passes continue the fine series of marshland churches in the earlier part of the route: (45½m) *Benington*; (47m) *Leverton*, Perpendicular with good tracery outside and a Decorated interior; (48½m) *Old Leake*, with Norman arcading; and (49½m) *Wrangle*, Perpendicular with good 14C glass. At (53m) *Friskney*, to the left, the church is Perpendicular, with some Norman work and later additions. It has a Jacobean pulpit, 14C wall paintings, and a 17C cross and graveside shelter in the graveyard. 58m: *Wainfeet All Saints*, a large, pleasant village, was the birthplace of William of Waynflete (1395–1486), Bishop of Winchester and founder of Magdalen College, Oxford. He built the Magdalen School, a fine brick building of 1484 with Victorian additions, to supply students for his college. At *Croft*, 2m NE, the Decorated *church has an early 17C pulpit, good screens and benches, a fine lectern and one of the earliest brasses in England (c 1300).

63m: **Skegness** (14,500 inhabitants; seasonal TI) is a popular resort. The *Church Farm Museum* has recreated interiors and displays of agricultural equipment. On A158 4½m inland is the Perpendicular church of *Burgh-le-*

Marsh, with a fine tower, screens and 17C pulpit. For *Gunby Hall*, 2m further, see Route 47A. Billy Butlin opened his first holiday camp in the 1930s at (66m) *Ingoldmells*. A52 here turns inland to (69m) *Hogsthorpe*, with an Early English church, and (73m) *Huttoft*, where the church has a 13C tower, good corbels, a richly carved Perpendicular font and a 14C chest. 78m: *Sutton-on-Sea* and (81m) **Mablethorpe** (joint population 7,500; TI) are less brash than Skegness. D.H. Lawrence stayed at Mablethorpe in his boyhood and remembered the holiday in 'Sons and Lovers'.

We turn inland again and take A1301. At (85m) *Theddlethorpe All Saints*, to the left, the church is built of colourful stone, with traces of every period from the early Norman. Its interesting contents include a funerary helm. The three *Saltfleetby* villages lie c 1½m N on the banks of the Great Eau, all with fine churches. At (89m) *Saltfleet* the manor house (not open) has been identified as Tennyson's 'Locksley Hall, that in the distance overlooks the sandy tracts', but a better candidate is the house so named in (92m) *North Somercotes*. Here the road veers inland to another series of fine churches: (95m) *Grainthorpe*, Perpendicular with a brick floor, 18C gallery and panelling made from old pews; (96½m) *Marshchapel*; (101m) *Tetney*, with a high Perpendicular limestone tower; and (104m) *Humberston*, 18C brick with a Perpendicular stone tower. 107m: *Cleethorpes* (35,500 inhabitants; TI), now a suburb of Grimsby, developed as a resort round the railway station (1863) built on the front. 108m: **Grimsby**, see Route 47A.

48

Peterborough to Lincoln and the Humber

Directions. Total distance 86m. **Peterborough**, see Route 36. A15 to (15m) Bourne, (33m) Sleaford and (50m) **Lincoln**. B1398, B1206 to (70m) Redbourne. A15, A18 to (75m) Brigg. A18, A15 to (86m) **Barton-upon-Humber**.

A15 leaves **Peterborough** (Route 36). 5½m: *Glinton*. Peakirk, 1½m NE, is worth visiting for the 14C wall paintings in the church of St Pega. *Helpston*, 3m W of Glinton, was the birthplace of John Clare (1793–1864). 7m: *Northborough*, the home of Clare's later years, has much of its 14C manor house. A15 crosses the Welland into Lincolnshire just S of (8m) *Market Deeping*, with some fine old houses and a 12–13C church but no longer a market. Its rectory, dating from the 13C, is the oldest inhabited parsonage in England. The composer Robert Fayrfax (1464–1521) was born here. At *Deeping St James*, to the E, the church was part of a Benedictine priory, a cell of Thorney. It has a fine 12C nave, Norman font, and a graveside shelter. The RC church near the Welland at *Deeping Gate* has two good sculptures, a 14C Crucifixion and a 15C Virgin. 15m: **Bourne** (8100 inhabitants), a typical Lincolnshire market town, is the apocryphal birthplace of Hereward the Wake. In the priory Robert Mannyng (Robert of Brunne, fl. 1300) made the translations from the Norman which laid the foundations for the English language. Lord Burghley (1520–98) was born here, in the house now the Burghley Arms, as was Monsieur Charles F. Worth of Paris (1825–95). The

Priory Church has Norman arcades. The *Town Hall* (1821) has an unusual exterior staircase. In South St. are 17C cottages and the Tudor *Red Hall*.

At *Edenham*, 3m NW on A151, the church has a fine roof and monuments of the Bertie family. 2m further on is *Grimsthorpe Castle* (open), a huge building of various dates in spacious parkland laid out by Capability Brown. Most interesting are King John's Tower, a fragment of the 13C castle, and the N front and great hall by Vanbrugh, his last work. The collection of art includes works by Holbein. The church at *Irnham*, 3½m further NW, has an Easter Sepulchre (cf. Heckington below).

20m: *Rippingale*, on the right, has a church with Geometric windows (14C) and a rare effigy of a deacon. 24m: *Folkingham*, once a town of some importance with its own quarter sessions, has a handsome square with a coaching inn. The church is Perpendicular with an excellent oak screen. Part of the early 19C House of Correction survives in the Billingborough road. At *Pickworth*, 2½m W, the church has 14C wall paintings.

To the E are (2¾m) *Billingborough* church, with a tall tower, splendid flying buttresses and florid windows, and (1m N) *Horbling*, a Georgian village with an interesting church and a votive well. *Sempringham*, 1½m S of Billingborough, was the birthplace of St Gilbert (d. 1189), founder of the only English order of monks and nuns; a Norman doorway and the nave of their church survive.

At 26m A15 crosses A52. *Threekingham*, 1m E, has a Norman church with a fine spire and Decorated windows. 31m: *Silk Willoughby* church (Decorated) has good pews and bench ends, and a Norman font. 33m: **Sleaford** (8500 inhabitants; TI) is an old market town. The *Maltings* (1892–1905), over 1000ft long, is a fine industrial building. The church of *St Denys* is noted for its flowing Decorated window tracery and ornamentation, and a 15C screen with a rood added by Sir Ninian Comper in 1918. It stands on one side of the Market Place in a harmonious group of buildings: the 15C *Vicarage*, the *Sessions House* (1831), the fine Georgian *Bristol Arms*, and the *Corn Exchange* (1857).

Ancaster, 6m SW on A153, has given its name to a famous building stone. There are a few traces of the Roman fortified station, Causennae, on Ermine Street. *Honington*, 2m further, lies on A607 from Grantham to Lincoln (Route 72). A17 leads NW from Sleaford towards Newark-on-Trent across the deserted uplands of the *Cliff* (see below and Route 72). *Rauceby*, S of the road at 4m, has a conspicuous church with fine tower and 13C broach spire. N of the road at 6m is *Cranwell RAF College*, founded in 1920. *Temple Bruer*, 2m N, with a massive Norman tower, is all that remains of a preceptory of the Knights Templar.

FROM SLEAFORD TO BOSTON, 20m. A17 leads E to (5m) *Heckington* (seasonal TI), which has a windmill with eight sails. The *church is pure late Decorated (1345–80), with flowing tracery, a magnificent Easter Sepulchre and a fine E window. *Ewerby*, 3m NW, has a 14C church with a broach spire, and *Helpringham*, 2½m S, has a Decorated steeple. A17 heads right to (12m) *Swineshead*, which has an interesting church, the old stocks and the base of a market cross. *Swineshead Abbey*, where King John stayed in 1216 after crossing the Wash, lay 1m E. 1m S of Swineshead A52 leads left to (20m) **Boston**, see Route 47A.

FROM SLEAFORD TO HORNCASTLE, 23m via A153. It crosses the Fens, through (4½m) *Anwick* and (9m) *Billinghay*, both with striking church steeples. *South Kyme*, a remote fen village S of the road, has a 13C keep, while its church is a fragment of a 12C priory. A153 crosses the Witham. 13m: **Tattershall** has the tall keep of a *Castle* (NT), built c 1440 by Baron Cromwell, Lord High Treasurer to Henry VI, perhaps 'the grandest piece of brickwork in the kingdom' (Viscount Torrington). Its walls are in places 16ft thick. There is one large main room on each floor, with some splendid fireplaces. The large collegiate *Church*, late Perpendicular, has 15–16C brasses, glass of c 1500 in the

E window and a stone choir screen. *Tattershall College* (EH) was founded by Baron Cromwell as a choir school. The village cross is 15C. 14m: *Coningsby* is supposed to have given Disraeli the title for his novel. The church has a processional path under its 15C tower. About 4m N is *Woodhall Spa* (2400 inhabitants; seasonal TI) among pines and firs. At *Kirkstead*, 1m S of Woodhall, is a fragment of a Cistercian abbey (13C) and the isolated *Chapel of St Leonard, now the parish church, a gem of Early English architecture with a choir screen of 1210. 23m: *Horncastle*, see Route 47A.

A15 continues N from Sleaford, climbing the ridge of the oolite limestone escarpment known as the Cliff (see also Route 72). At 44m it passes the turning on the left for *Aubourn*, by the Witham 4m W, where Aubourn Hall (limited opening) is Elizabethan work attributed to John Smythson Jr. A15 continues via (43¼m) *Dunston Pillar*, now ruined, built by Sir Francis Dashwood in 1751 as a land lighthouse for travellers across the heath. 47m: *Bracebridge Heath*. The church of All Saints at *Bracebridge*, by A46 to the W, has a Saxon nave and an 11C tower, perhaps pre-Norman, resembling those of St Mary-le-Wigford and St Peter-at-Gowts in Lincoln.

50m: **LINCOLN** (82,000 inhabitants), dominated by its superbly placed cathedral, stands mainly on a rocky hill rising from the river Witham on the NW edge of the Fens. Despite the growth of industry, it has kept its character and atmosphere as one of the most ancient towns in England.

TI: Castle Hill. **Bus Station**: off Melville St., by Pelham Bridge. **Railway Station**: Central Station, St Mary St. **Theatre**: Theatre Royal, Clasketgate.

History. The pre-Roman settlement guarding the gap in the oolite cliff was occupied by the Romans in AD 47, and c 80–86 it became a colony under the name of Lindum Colonia. The Saxons also left their traces, and a little later Lincoln became one of the Danelagh towns. Christianity was reintroduced by St Paulinus in 627. The bishopric dates from 1072, when Remigius transferred his bishop's stool from Dorchester-on-Thames. At the time of the Conquest, London, Winchester and York alone outranked Lincoln in importance among the cities of England, and in the 13C it was the fourth 'seaport' of the realm. The castle, built by William I was captured about 1140 by Stephen, whose conflict with Matilda surged round the city. Henry II had a second coronation here in 1158. Lincoln today is important for its heavy engineering works and for agricultural machinery. In World War I it was the birthplace of tanks.

In 1290 Queen Eleanor of Castile, wife of Edward I, died at *Harby*, 8m W of Lincoln. The successive stages of the funeral procession that bore her body to Westminster Abbey were marked by Eleanor Crosses, built between 1291 and 1294. The list varies, but began at Lincoln (see Castle and High St. below) and apparently continued with Grantham, Stamford, Geddington, Northampton, Stony Stratford, Woburn, Dunstable, St Albans, Waltham, and Cheapside and Charing Cross in London. The only ones still standing are at Geddington, Northampton and Waltham.

Natives and residents. William Byrd (1543–1623), the composer, served as organist at the cathedral from 1563 to 1572. Peter de Wint (1784–1849), the painter, lived for many years at Hilton House, Drury Lane (plaque).

A visit to Lincoln should start on Castle Hill, the high plateau marking the centre of the ancient city. On its E side the 14C *Exchequer Gate* leads to the **Cathedral**, outstanding among English churches for its wonderfully soaring position (surpassed only by Durham) and for the richly unified design that made it, in Ruskin's eyes, 'out and out the most precious piece of architecture in the British Isles'.

Its history falls into three main phases. The first began in 1072, when Bishop Remigius moved his see from Dorchester to Lincoln. Consecrated some 20 years later, this Norman cathedral was shattered by an earthquake in 1185, leaving only the central core of its W front as part of the present structure. Its fall gave Bishop Hugh (1186–1200), St Hugh of Lincoln, the chance to rebuild and extend, with Geoffrey of Noiers

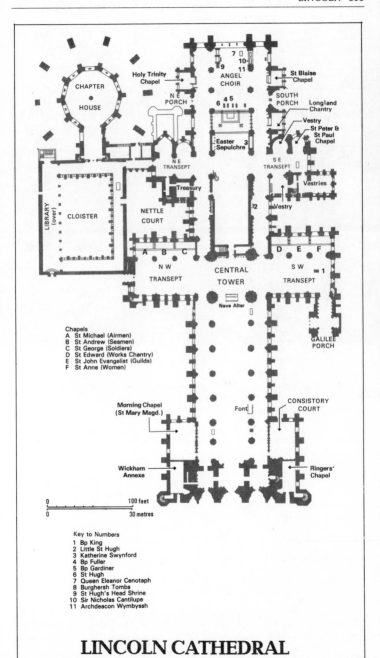

CHAPTER HOUSE

Holy Trinity Chapel

N E PORCH

ANGEL CHOIR

7
9 10
11

St Blaise Chapel

SOUTH PORCH

6 4 5

Longland Chantry

Vestry
St Peter & St Paul Chapel

Easter Sepulchre   3

N E TRANSEPT

S E TRANSEPT

Vestries

LIBRARY (over)

CLOISTER

Treasury

NETTLE COURT

Vestry

A B C

N W

TRANSEPT

CENTRAL TOWER

D E F

S W

TRANSEPT

1

Nave Altar

GALILEE PORCH

Chapels
A St Michael (Airmen)
B St Andrew (Seamen)
C St George (Soldiers)
D St Edward (Works Chantry)
E St John Evangelist (Guilds)
F St Anne (Women)

Morning Chapel
(St Mary Magd.)

Font

CONSISTORY COURT

Wickham Annexe

Ringers' Chapel

0 ——————————— 100 feet
0 ——————————— 30 metres

Key to Numbers
1 Bp King
2 Little St Hugh
3 Katherine Swynford
4 Bp Fuller
5 Bp Gardiner
6 St Hugh
7 Queen Eleanor Cenotaph
8 Burghersh Tombs
9 St Hugh's Head Shrine
10 Sir Nicholas Cantilupe
11 Archdeacon Wymbyssh

LINCOLN CATHEDRAL

The Angel Choir at Lincoln Cathedral

in charge of operations. Their work, and the work continuing under their inspiration until c 1250, was responsible for most of the present building. The third and last important stage came in 1255–80 with the addition of the Angel Choir.

The *W front consists, roughly, of a Norman block encased in a screen façade of Early English lancet work. Above the richly moulded central doorway are 11 statues of kings. The much weathered frieze of carved panels (c 1145), perhaps copied from Modena Cathedral, illustrates the Old Testament on the S side and the New Testament on the N. The SW turret is topped by a statue of St Hugh, while on the NW turret is the 'Swineherd of Stow', who contributed his savings to St Hugh's building work. The W towers belong in their lower stages to a late Norman restoration of c 1141; their upper part is late Decorated (c 1420). The magnificent *central tower, housing 'Great Tom of Lincoln', a bell weighing almost 5½ tons, rises to 271ft and commands a panoramic view. Its Geometric Decorated upper stages date from 1307–11.

On the S side, the Galilee Porch leads into the SW transept, and then to the Judgement Porch, taking its name from the striking picture of the Last Judgement in its richly decorated arch. Among the gargoyles on this part of the building is one known as the 'Devil looking over Lincoln'. The figures on the buttresses are apparently Edward I and his two wives, Eleanor and Margaret. The clear space beyond offers a good view of the E end, with its noble window, deep buttresses, lines of arcading, enriched gable and crocketed pinnacles. At the top of the gable is a sculpture of the Virgin and Child.

The doorway in the W front leads into the *Nave*, belonging to St Hugh's rebuilding, unusually wide and with delicately clustered columns. The effect would be grander if the organ over the rood screen did not block a view of the E end. The late Norman font, in the second bay of the S aisle, is one of only seven in England made from Tournai marble. The *Great* or *W Transepts*, begun by St Hugh and finished between 1220 and

1235, house six chapels. The lovely *rose windows have their original glass: the Dean's Eye, on the N, is Early English (c 1220); the flowing tracery of the Bishop's Eye, to the S, is Decorated (c 1325–50).

Elaborately carved doorways and a Decorated stone screen (c 1300) separate the nave from the fine Early English *Choir*. The S aisle passes the shrine of Little St Hugh, once said to have been ritually murdered by Jews in 1255. The magnificent canopied *choir stalls (early Perpendicular, c 1380) are among the best in England. The subjects of the misericords include the parable of the fox preaching to geese (W end of N range). The N choir aisle has a tablet to William Byrd. The *Lesser* or *E Transepts* are remarkable for their piers with detached crocketed shafts, known as the 'Trondheim Pillars' from their similarity to those at Trondheim in Norway. The Treasury by the NE transept has plate, chalices and patens.

The chief glory of the interior is the **Angel Choir*, built to replace the apsidal end of St Hugh's church when the pilgrims attracted by the saint's shrine needed more space. Queen Eleanor attended its consecration in 1280. It forms the five E bays of the present choir, and takes its name from the 30 carved angels in the spandrels of the triforium. The delicacy of these details, the richness of the bosses and the use of Purbeck marble put it among the greatest achievements of Gothic architecture in England. The 'Lincoln Imp' is a grotesque figure at the top of the last complete column on the N side. Monuments include: St Hugh, behind the altar on the N side; the battered 14C shrine of St Hugh's Head, near the Burghersh Chapel in the NE corner; and the cenotaph of Queen Eleanor (destroyed 1644, rebuilt 1891) at the E end. The great E window in the Geometric style, filled with Victorian glass, is the largest and earliest eight-light window in England.

The 13C *Cloister* is entered from the NE transept. Its E walk has the graceful polygonal *Chapter House*, with a single central shaft supporting the vaulted roof. It was the scene of the earliest meetings of the English Parliament, in the reigns of Edward I and II. The N walk, rebuilt as a Doric colonnade by Wren (c 1674), gives fine views of the cathedral. Above is the *Chapter Library* (open), with one bay of the medieval library burned in 1609 but mainly built by Wren to house Dean Honywood's collection.

The Galilee Porch leads from the cathedral into the *Close* or *Minster Yard*. At the corner nearly opposite is the 14C *Cantilupe Chantry House*; below and behind this is the arched entrance to the ruined *Old Bishop's Palace* (EH, summer season, Thursday–Monday), founded in the 12C, with 13–15C additions. Next comes the gatehouse of the *Vicars' Court*, built 1300–80 for a college of priest-vicars. E of the cathedral are the *Chancery* (14–15C) and the *Choristers' House*, and further N is the *Priory Gate*, an arch of an old gateway destroyed in 1815. The green has a statue of Tennyson by G.F. Watts. On the N side are several old houses, including the present *Bishop's House*.

On the W side of Castle Hill stands the **Castle** (open), one of the eight known to have been founded by William the Conqueror. It was started in 1068 and the walls have the herringbone masonry typical of early Norman work built near Roman remains (cf. the tower of St Albans). Unusually, the bailey wall incorporates two mottes.

The entrance is by the *Eastern Gate*, massive 14C work on top of a Norman tunnel vault. On the right is an oriel window brought from a house which stood in the High St., popularly but mistakenly known as 'John of Gaunt's Palace'. The walls enclose a garden of about six acres; on the lawn a fragment of an Eleanor Cross (see above) is preserved. To the left is the *Observatory Tower* on its motte, a Norman base with 14C upperworks and a 19C turret. Steep ladders inside lead to the roof and a dramatic *view. On the second and later motte beyond, the *Lucy Tower*, a shell keep, has the graves of prisoners from the brick *City Prison* by Carr of York and William Lumby, in use from 1787 to 1878 but now courts and a repository for archives. The prison *Chapel (open) with coffin-like pews, probably dating from the 1840s, keeps its oppressive atmosphere. The NE tower, *Cobb Hall*, is 13C and vaulted on two levels; it was the place of execution until 1868. Smirke's *Assize Courts* (1826) stand in the western part

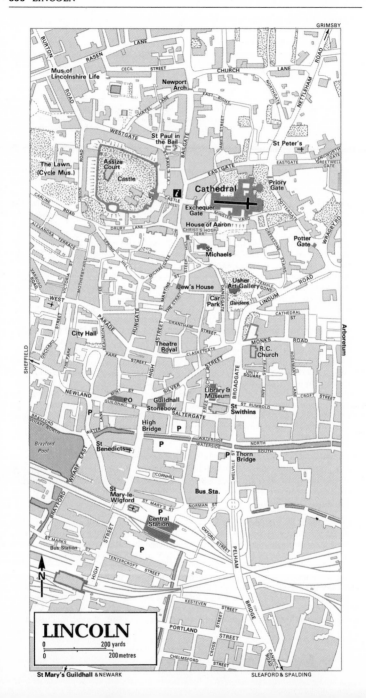

GRIMSBY

BURTON ROAD

RASEN LANE

CECIL STREET

CHURCH LANE

NORTHGATE

NETTLEHAM ROAD

Mus. of Lincolnshire Life

Newport Arch

EAST BIGHT

St Peter's

WESTGATE

St Paul in the Bail

BAILGATE

JAMES STREET

LANGWORTH GATE

GREETWELL GATE

EASTGATE

The Lawn (Cycle Mus.)

Assize Court

Castle

EASTGATE

Priory Gate

Cathedral

POTTERGATE

CASTLE HILL

Exchequer Gate

MINSTER YARD

CARLINE ROAD

UNION ROAD

DRURY LANE

House of Aaron

CHRIST'S HOSP. TERR.

Potter Gate

ALEXANDRA TERRACE

SPRING HILL

HILL

St Michaels

GREESTONE STAIRS

WRAGBY RD

YARBORO ROAD

VICTORIA STREET

MOTHERBY HILL

MICHAELGATE

Jew's House

Usher Art Gallery

WEST

FEE

ST MARTINS

THE STRAIT

DANSGATE

Car Park

Gardens

TEMPLE GDNS

LINDUM ROAD

CATHEDRAL ST

City Hall

PARADE

HUNGATE

STEEP STREET

GRANTHAM STREET

MONKS ROAD

SHEFFIELD

ORCHARD

THE PARK

BEAUMONT

PARK STREET

HIGH STREET

CLASKETGATE

R.C. Church

ROSEMARY LANE

Theatre Royal

FREE SCHOOL LANE

UNITY SQUARE

FRIARS LANE

CROFT STREET

NEWLAND

MINT LANE

SILVER STREET

BROADGATE

ST RUMBOLD ST

BRAYFORD WHARF NORTH

PO

GUILDHALL ST

Guildhall Stonebow

Library & Museum

St Swithins

Brayford Pool

WATER LANE

SALTERGATE

High Bridge

P

P

WATERSIDE

WATERSIDE NORTH

SOUTH

St Benedicts

P

P

Thorn Bridge

BRAYFORD WHARF EAST

CORNHILL

MELVILLE ST

St Mary-le-Wigford

Bus Sta.

HIGH STREET

ST. MARY'S ST.

NORMAN ST.

OXFORD STREET

PELHAM

P

Central Station

ST MARKS Bus Station

P

TENTERCROFT STREET

HIGH STREET

N

KESTEVEN STREET

BRIDGE

Arboretum

PORTLAND STREET

CROSS STREET

CANWICK ROAD

CHELMSFORD STREET

LINCOLN

0   200 yards

0   200 metres

St Mary's Guildhall & NEWARK

SLEAFORD & SPALDING

of the grounds, behind which is the *West Gate* (not open), beside the W gate of the Roman fortress.

The Lawn, across Union Rd to the W of the castle, is a new development around the 19C mental hospital. It includes the *National Cycle Museum*, an *Archaeology Centre* and a conservatory dedicated to the Lincolnshire botanist Sir Joseph Banks.

Bailgate, the centre of the Roman town, leads N from the square, with the TI Centre housed in a half-timbered building on the corner. Circles mark the bases of Roman pillars. The site of *St Paul in the Bail*, at the corner of Westgate, has been excavated to reveal the Roman forum (open). Bailgate ends at ***Newport Arch**, the N gate of the Roman city, probably dating from the early 2C. In Burton Rd, to the NW, the *Museum of Lincolnshire Life* houses a display of local history during the past 200 years.

Returning down Bailgate, the route follows East Bight to the left. This reveals a part of the Roman Wall, bends round to the right and leads into Eastgate. To the left, in front of the Eastgate Hotel, foundations of a tower of the Roman *East Gate* have been exposed. The Priory Gate (see above) and early 14C *Potter Gate* reach the busy Lindum Rd. On the right is the **Usher Art Gallery**. Its distinguished collection includes: watercolours by ***Peter de Wint** and other artists with local connections; topographical paintings of Lincolnshire which include views of the cathedral by Thomas Girtin and Turner, the latter also represented by his view of Stamford; and Benjamin West's portrait of Sir Joseph Banks. Also on display are watches, miniatures, porcelain, coins and Tennyson memorabilia. There is a continuous programme of temporary exhibitions.

Monks Rd, to the left further on, leads to the main entrance of the *Arboretum*. Beyond, on the right, is *Monks Abbey*, a small park with the remains of an Early English chapel (with Perpendicular windows), a 'cell' of St Mary's Abbey at York.

Broadgate leads S from Lindum Rd to the **City and County Museum**, in the 13C *Grey Friars Priory*. It contains local antiquities; the upper room has a 'barrel' roof. Melville St. goes on to *Pelham Bridge* (1958).

Near the junction of St Mary St. with the High St. is the church of *St Mary-le-Wigford*. It has a Saxon tower; on the outside is a Roman memorial slab with a later Saxon inscription. The nave, chancel and N aisle are Early English (c 1225). The 16C *St Mary's Conduit*, in front, was built with stones from the White Friars monastery.

In High St., just to the S, in Akrill's Passage, is a 15C timbered house. Further on is (left) *St Mary's Guildhall*, a 12C building. Beyond is the church of *St Peter-at-Gowts*, with a Saxon tower resembling St Mary-le-Wigford and a Romanesque font. About ½m further on stood the *Bar Gate*, the S entrance to the medieval city, near which rose the Eleanor Cross.

High St. leads N, passing the church of *St Benedict*, with a short late Saxon tower and a rustic 13–14C interior, to the *High Bridge*, one of the few bridges in England on which houses still stand. The original ribs can be seen from the riverside path which leads left to *Brayford Pool*, with its old quay. A short step N of the High Bridge is a fine 15C town gate, the ***Stonebow**. Its upper room, still used as the Guildhall, has a fine timber roof and contains the civic insignia (open first Saturday of each month).

High St. ends just beyond the 15C *Cardinal's Hat* at the Strait, which leads upwards to the right. At the top is **Jew's House*, one of the oldest examples of domestic architecture in England (Norman, early 12C). Steep Hill continues the ascent and a step across it forms the so-called *Reader's Rest*. Above this are *Harding House* and other timbered houses, and, on the right, the *House of Aaron the Jew*, a late Norman building with a round-headed window. Michaelgate (to the left) and Danesgate (to the right) are interesting old streets.

FROM LINCOLN TO GRIMSBY, 37m via A46. 8½m: *Snarford* church has monuments to the St Poll family. Under 1m E of (10½m) *Faldingworth* lies *Buslingthorpe*, with a church containing one of the earliest brasses in England (Sir Richard de Boselyngthorpe, c 1310). Near (16m) *Market Rasen* (2700 inhabitants) traces of Roman and pre-Roman occupation have been found. 24m: *Caistor* stands on the site of a Roman camp and has an interesting church. *Pelham's Pillar*, on top of the Wolds above Caistor, commemorates a plantation scheme by the Earl of Yarborough (1840). 37m: *Grimsby*, see Route 47A.

From Lincoln to *Grantham*, see Route 72; to *Horncastle* and *Boston*, see Route 47A.

The main route from Lincoln to the Humber heads NE for the Humber Bridge; for an alternative route NW via Gainsborough to Goole, see below.

A15 continues N from Lincoln, arrow-straight across the Fens, following the Roman Ermine Street until just before Redbourne. A more interesting road, B1398, runs parallel along the crest of the Cliff, giving wide views W across the Trent valley, especially at (54m) the junction with the Roman road from *Sturton-by-Stow*. 61m: *Glentworth* has an 11C church tower. 68m: *Kirton-in-Lindsey* is a large village with a fine Early English church tower. By the windmill to the N is the *Lincolnshire and Humberside Railway Museum*. The route turns right on B1206 to rejoin A15 at (70m) *Redbourne*. Just before (71½m) *Hibaldstow* an unclassified road leads left to the deserted medieval village of *Gainsthorpe* (EH). 75m: *Brigg* (5400 inhabitants; TI) is a small market town made prosperous by the draining of the Fens.

At *Broughton*, 3½m NW, the church has an 11C Saxon tower. 6m W of Brigg is the old iron and steel town of **Scunthorpe** (66,400 inhabitants). The Borough Museum and Art Gallery on Oswald Rd has displays of local history and a collection of prehistoric, Roman and later archaeology. 4m N via B1430 is *Normanby Hall* (open), built in the 'cubic' style in 1820 by Sir Robert Smirke, architect of the British Museum.

A18 continues NE from Brigg to (79m) the junction with M180 and A15. *Barnetby-le-Wold*, to the right, has a late Norman lead font in its 20C church. *Humberside Airport* (TI), off A18 2½m further E, has flights to Aberdeen, Amsterdam, Edinburgh, Jersey, Norwich and Teesside. A15 climbs the northern spur of the Wolds, passing (80m) *Elsham Hall Country Park* (open), before dropping down to (86m) **Barton-upon-Humber** (8500 inhabitants), a market town and decayed port with two churches. *St Peter (EH, Monday to Friday 14.00–16.00 and by appointment only at weekends) has one of the earliest church towers in England, with Saxon arcading and panels divided by strips of stone. The narthex, or W porch, is of the same date (c 1000) and its circular lights still have fragments of the original oak shutters. The rest of the building is Decorated and Perpendicular. St Mary, close by, is mainly Early English with some Transitional work. It has a brass to Simon Seman, Sheriff of London in 1433. N of the town the **Humber Bridge** (toll; TI), opened in 1981, joins the two parts of Humberside and leads to *Hull* (Route 82A).

At *Goxhill*, 4m SE of Barton-upon-Humber, the church has a fine Perpendicular tower and contains a cross-legged effigy in chain armour (c 1300). *Thornton Curtis*, 4m SE of Barton-upon-Humber, has a Norman and Early English church with a Tournai marble font. 2m E are the remains of **Thornton Abbey**, founded in 1139 for Austin Canons and rebuilt after 1264 (EH, summer season, daily; winter weekends, 10.00–16.00). They include a brick *gatehouse (1382) with five of its original statues, oak doors, an oriel window, and two sides of the chapter house (1282–1308). At *Brocklesby*,

6m SE of Thornton Curtis, the church has monuments of the Pelhams, Earls of Yarborough. In the park near the village is a circular mausoleum (1787–94) by James Wyatt.

An alternative route from (50m) Lincoln to the Humber takes A57 NW past the racecourse, with a good grandstand of 1826. The road follows the Foss Dyke cut by the Romans to connect the Trent with the Witham. 3½m S of (55m) *Saxilby* is *Doddington Hall (open).

It was built between 1593 and 1600 for Thomas Tailor, the self-made Registrar of Lincoln, and has never changed hands by sale. In all probability the architect was Robert Smythson, who built Hardwick Hall, Worksop Manor and Wollaton Hall. Modest in scale and simple in design by comparison with these great houses, Doddington is nevertheless satisfyingly confident and is lent great charm by its mellowed brickwork. The interior was remodelled in 1760–65 by Thomas Lumby, the Lincoln carpenter also responsible for the nearby village church.

At 56m A156 branches right from A57 to (59m) *Torksey*, where the Foss Dyke joins the Trent. There was a Saxon mint here. At (61m) *Marton*, it crosses Till Bridge Lane, a branch from Ermine Street. The church tower has early Norman herringbone work, and in the chancel is a 13C crucifixion. *Stow church, 2m E, is one of the largest and oldest pre-Conquest churches in England, with huge 10C crossing arches. It contains an Early English font and 13C wall paintings. *Cotes-by-Stow* church, 2m further E, has a fine rood loft. At (63m) *Knaith* Thomas Sutton, founder of Charterhouse, was born in 1532. 64m: *Lea* church has 14C glass and a 15C Crucifixion.

66m: **Gainsborough** (18,700 inhabitants) is an old market town and river port on the Trent, crossed by a bridge of 1787. Sweyn Forkbeard, King of Denmark, died here in 1014 after conquering England. Ugly red brick has largely triumphed over the picturesque charm George Eliot evoked in her portrait of the town as 'St Ogg's' in 'The Mill on the Floss'. *All Saints* church has a Perpendicular tower and a nave and chancel rebuilt in 1736–44. The *Old Hall* is a manor house rebuilt in the 1480s to entertain Richard III and rebuilt again a century later. The kitchen and great hall of the earlier building survive. The Hall is EH, open Easter Sunday to 31 October, Monday to Saturday 10.00–17.00, and 1 November to Easter Saturday, Monday to Saturday, 10.00–17.00. The 'eagre', or tidal wave on the Trent, ascends above Gainsborough. For *Bawtry*, 12m W, see Route 72.

The route follows A631 W, turning N at (69m) *Beckingham* on A161. The alluvial **Isle of Axholme** was drained by Vermuyden and his Dutch workmen (1626–28). Much of the land has been reclaimed by the flooding process known as 'warping'. Near (77½m) *Haxey*, with a 14C church, strip cultivation is much in evidence. The 'Haxey Hood', a traditional game, is played in costume on 6 January. 80½m: *Epworth* is a large village. On the road leading to Owston Ferry stands the Old Rectory (open), built in 1709 to replace an earlier building that burned down. John and Charles Wesley (1703–91 and 1707–88), founders of Methodism, spent their childhood here. 82m: *Belton* church has a 14C effigy of a knight made from a Saxon gravestone. The *Sandtoft Transport Centre*, 3m W, has trolleybuses, etc. At (87½m) *Crowle* the church has Norman traces, including a good doorway, and a Saxon cross shaft. 99m: **Goole**, see Route 81.

SOUTH MIDLANDS

Of all the regional labels with which the English make do in the absence of officially designated provinces, the term 'Midlands' is the vaguest, as well as the least appetising, stopping unpromisingly short at telling us that the area in question lacks a coastline. Yet it is still preferable to the emptily colourful coinages of the tourist industry—the Heart of England, the English Shires, and so on—even if it does require special, and to some extent arbitrary, definition. In this guide central England has been divided into the North Midlands, described in the next section, and South Midlands, described here. Its southern boundary is the valley of the Thames, and its eastern boundary the course of the A1. The third side of the triangle is formed by a line drawn roughly from the Severn and the Wye in the SW to the Wash in the NE—a rather less arbitrary boundary than it might at first sight appear. Its course begins with Gloucester, Worcester and Hereford in the W, passes through Coventry and Leicester, and ends by the A1 at Stamford. The bulk of the area thus enclosed is filled by Gloucestershire, Oxfordshire, Warwickshire, Buckinghamshire, Northamptonshire and Bedfordshire, though parts of several other counties are included at the fringes: Hereford and Worcester in the W, Berkshire in the S, Hertfordshire in the E and Leicestershire in the N.

A bird's-eye viewpoint looking N and W from London would show the land falling into an alternating rhythm of hill and plain, hill and valley, usually running crosswise to the major roads that radiate from the capital like the spokes of a wheel. The first major outcrop is of chalk, spreading N and E from the great centre of chalkland on Salisbury Plain. In the S, on the Berkshire Downs near Wantage, chalk creates the landscape of smooth, turfy contours and wide, breezy views which is familiar throughout so much of Southern England. Along its top a section of the Ridgeway Path, dotted with prehistoric monuments, overlooks the Vale of the White Horse with its ancient chalk figure cut into the soil. Further N, the gentle ridge of the Chiltern Hills runs through Buckinghamshire and into Bedfordshire before it merges into the broad swath of chalk that continues through Eastern England. The Chilterns were once densely wooded, as Burnham Beeches can still remind us, and they can still have a remote upland atmosphere in the villages N of High Wycombe or S of Stokenchurch. Yet the distinctive local character is best shown by the comfortable brick-built high streets of High Wycombe or Wendover—townscapes ready-made for the process of affluent suburbanisation which has largely overtaken them.

Beyond the Chilterns lie the vales of Oxfordshire, with the limestone ridge of the Cotswold Hills rising in the W. While the Chilterns traditionally depended on their beech forests for the local furniture industry, the Cotswolds grew rich off the lamb's back. Places like Burford, Stow-on-the-Wold, Chipping Camden, Broadway and Cirencester still testify to the prosperity the wool trade once brought. Their beauty comes from the honey-coloured local stone, a worthy rival to the Bath stone and Ham stone produced from the southern extension of the same limestone belt. Cotswold stone gives dignity to the houses and particularly to the handsome Perpendicular churches of the region; elsewhere, its warm tones can be seen in many Oxford buildings.

Approached from the E, the landscape of the Cotswolds is gentle. Its dramatic effects lie on the sharp W edge, where a series of famous viewpoints (Cleeve Hill, Birdlip and Broadway) overlook the flat country beyond. The Vale of Evesham, in the N, is a broad, fertile plain watered by the Avon and its many tributaries as its winds down from Stratford to join the Severn at Tewkesbury. By comparison to this pleasant fruit-growing country, the expanses of the Severn Vale around and, particularly, below Gloucester can seem dull and unvaried to the eye.

Where the Chilterns are chalk and the Cotswolds limestone, the Malverns, the last range of hills encountered on the journey W from London, are of hard pre-Cambrian rock. They rise with surprising suddenness from the W edge of the vale beyond Worcester, giving a foretaste of the Welsh scenery to come. Much the same can be said of the Wye valley, which marks the border with Wales as it winds down from Monmouth to Chepstow. Its tightly looping course through cliff and forest is among the most beautiful—and dramatic—inland scenery in England.

This view of the region has so far looked more W than N from London and, in doing so, it has merely followed the preference shown by generations of tourists. The Wye valley, at the W extremity, was among the first beauty spots on the itinerary of English travellers in the 18C, when lovers of the picturesque and the first Romantic poets came down the river to admire the lovely ruins of Tintern Abbey. Their spring waters made the Malvern Hills a fashionable spa resort. As for the country closer to London, the routes to Oxford and Stratford-upon-Avon via Blenheim and Woodstock or to Oxford and Cotswold villages like Bourton-on-the-Water follow a path beaten by thousands of coach tours every summer.

At first glance, it is not difficult to see why the country N of London has been less favoured. The capital has certainly left its ugly mark to the W, laying waste the scenery of the Thames valley well beyond Heathrow Airport and making the Buckinghamshire countryside of the Chilterns suburban, but even this damage can seem mild by comparison to what the traveller encounters on the routes N through Hertfordshire and Bedfordshire. Here the major roads run past an apparently endless sprawl of new towns, satellite towns and garden cities that are neither gardens nor cities. Even beyond the influence of London the region is still the graveyard of modern town planning, with Corby (in the ironstone part of Northamptonshire) a monument to yesterday's mistakes and Milton Keynes (blandly spreading over north Buckinghamshire) a reminder of how little we have learned.

Nor is the picture any more cheering in the region's historic centres. In the W, Oxford has a charm that can survive even the growth of the motor industry around it, while Warwick, as Nikolaus Pevsner says, is a 'perfect county town'. Further W, Gloucester and Worcester have been insensitively redeveloped but, like Hereford, at least have their cathedrals to commend them. In contrast, Bedfordshire, Northamptonshire and Leicestershire—lacking an ancient cathedral within their boundaries—have dull county towns. Bedford, with least to be proud of, has treated itself the best; Northampton and Leicester have all but submerged the modest historic character they possessed beneath inner ring roads and shopping centres.

The real interest of these counties will elude the traveller who sticks to major roads and heads for major destinations. Ampthill, in Bedfordshire, and Olney, in the northern tip of Buckinghamshire where it meets Bedfordshire and Northamptonshire, are just two of the many smaller places whose appeal belies their immediate surroundings and stands in pleasant contrast to their larger neighbours. Northamptonshire, and the country bordering it to the N and E, is particularly rich in this respect. The limestone belt which continues up from the Cotswolds may not create scenery to rival the Cotswolds, but it produces an equally handsome building material. Traditionally quarried at Barnack and Ketton or as roofing slabs at Collyweston, this elegant stone has helped make Northamptonshire extraordinarily rich in architecture. The county's traditional reputation for 'spires and squires' is fitting tribute to the beauty and abundance of its parish churches and country houses. The list of the handsome stone-built towns and villages begins with Oundle, Higham Ferrers, Rockingham and Duddington but has difficulty completing itself in decent compass. Stamford, just outside Northamptonshire at the junction of several counties, is a fitting climax to the region, for here the local stone and the local style have created one of the finest provincial townscapes England can boast.

49

London to Oxford: the Thames Valley

A. By road via Windsor and Henley

Directions. Total distance 60m. Windsor makes a popular day-trip from London; alternative ways by coach and rail are described in 'Blue Guide London'. M4 to (21m) Slough, for **Windsor**. A308 to (26m) Maidenhead. A4, A423 to (35m) **Henley**. A423 to (51m) Dorchester (bypassed) and (60m) **Oxford** (Route 50).

M4 leaves London, passing (junction 4) *Heathrow Airport*, the M25, and, to the N, the dreary wasteland of (21m) *Slough* (87,000 inhabitants). Junction 6 (Slough West) leads to Windsor, about 1m S.

WINDSOR (28,300 inhabitants; TI), on the S bank of the Thames, is famous for the castle where English kings and queens have lived for 900 years.

Thames St. climbs from the river and car park to the High St., which continues between the castle bastions and 18C houses, now shops. The statue of Queen Victoria at Castle Hill is by Sir Edgar Boehm (1887).

Castle Hill leads to the entrance to **Windsor Castle.

Precincts and castle open daily except Garter Day (June); State Apartments, Dolls House and Exhibition of Drawings closed when royal family is in residence (usually April and parts of March, May, June and December). All or part of the castle may be closed at short notice. The ceremony of the Changing of the Guard takes place every day except Sunday by the entrance.

The Saxon palace of Kingsbury at Old Windsor was allowed to crumble after William the Conqueror built a wooden fortress at New Windsor in 1066. Henry II rebuilt it in stone in 1165–79 and Edward III extended it, while preserving the original plan of two baileys and a mote-hill. In following centuries the castle saw royal births and marriages, and entertained several foreign monarchs during their imprisonment. Much of its present appearance dates from restoration by Sir Jeffrey Wyatville for George IV. Work is now underway to repair damage from the fire which ravaged the Private Chapel and St George's Hall in 1992.

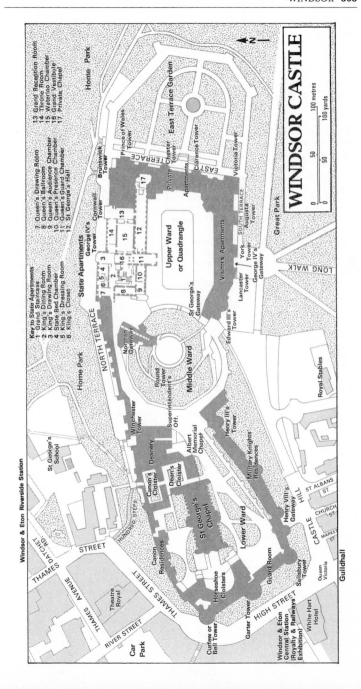

Key to State Apartments
1 Grand Staircase
2 King's Dining Room
3 King's Drawing Room
4 State Bed Chamber
5 King's Dressing Room
6 King's Closet
7 Queen's Drawing Room
8 Queen's Ballroom
9 Queen's Audience Chamber
10 Queen's Presence Chamber
11 Queen's Guard Chamber
12 St George's Hall
13 Grand Reception Room
14 Throne Room
15 Waterloo Chamber
16 Grand Vestibule
17 Private Chapel

WINDSOR CASTLE

Henry VIII's Gateway leads into the *Lower Ward*. In front is the entrance to the *Horseshoe Cloisters*, built during Edward IV's reign; at their NW corner stands the *Curfew Tower*, with a 13C interior, eight bells and an unusual clock which chimes every three hours. On the right are the houses of the Military Knights of Windsor, an order founded by Edward III as the 'Poor Knights of Windsor' at the same time as the Order of the Garter and given its present name by William IV in 1833. The central tower (1359) bears the arms of Philip and Mary.

*•**St George's Chapel** is a superb Perpendicular building, ranking with King's College Chapel in Cambridge and Henry VII's Chapel at Westminster. It was begun in 1478 by Henry Janyns for Edward IV and continued by William Vertue in 1503–11.

The *Nave* has a lierne vault with carved bosses. At the SW corner is the *Beaufort Chapel*, where the tomb of the Earl of Worcester (d. 1526) has a Flemish bronze grating, unusual in Britain. The great W window contains fine glass of 1503–09. In the NW corner is the tomb of George V (d. 1936) by Lutyens and Reid Dick, and of Queen Mary (d. 1953), with the theatrical tomb of Princess Charlotte (d. 1817) in the Urswick Chapel behind.

The *Choir* is separated from the nave by a Gothic screen (c 1785) by Henry Emlyn. The organ, originally placed centrally (as in King's College Chapel), was rebuilt in flanking sections to give a better view of the fan vaulting. In the *North Choir Aisle* is (left) the *Rutland Chapel* (1481) with effigies of George Manners (d. 1513) and his wife. To the right is the *Chantry Chapel of William, Lord Hastings* with contemporary paintings of his execution in 1483. To the left is the memorial chapel of George VI (1969). To the N of the high altar a superb pair of gates (1482) fronts the tomb of Edward IV. Above is the royal pew, a splendid wooden oriel provided by Henry VIII for Catherine of Aragon. A vault in the centre of the floor contains the remains of Henry VIII, Jane Seymour and Charles I. The stalls, in three tiers, are surmounted by the helmets, crests and banners of the 26 Knights of the Garter, whose installations have taken place at Windsor since 1348. The reverse stalls are those of the royal family, the sovereign's stall marked by the royal standard.

To the left beyond the screen, the *Bray Chapel* contains the cenotaph of the Prince Imperial, Napoleon III's son. In the *South Choir Aisle* the *Chantry of John Oxenbridge*, on the left, contains paintings of 1522, the great sword of Edward III and a simple slab marking Henry VI's tomb. On the S side of the altar is the tomb of Edward VII and Queen Alexandra (by Mackennal). The SE chapel, with the tomb of the Earl of Lincoln (d. 1585), is called the *Lincoln Chapel* or *John Schorne's Tower*, from the relics of Sir John Schorne (d. 1314), brought here in 1478.

The E wall of the ambulatory once formed the W front of Henry III's Chapel (1240–48) and retains its original doors. Beyond the floor slab of Sir Jeffry Wyatville the NE door leads through a passage to the *Dean's Cloister*, preserving arcading of Henry III's Chapel and a piece of fresco. To the N is the picturesque *Canon's Cloister* of 1353–56.

The **Albert Memorial Chapel** was rebuilt by Henry VII as a burial place for Henry VI, completed by Wolsey and converted by Queen Victoria into a memorial for Prince Albert (d. 1861), buried at Frogmore. Albert's cenotaph is by Baron Triqueti. The chapel also contains the tombs of the Duke of Clarence (d. 1892), Edward VII's elder son, by Alfred Gilbert, and of the Duke of Albany (d. 1884), Queen Victoria's youngest son. George III, Queen Charlotte and six of their sons (including George IV and William IV) are buried beneath the chapel.

To the left of the entrance to the North Terrace is the *Winchester Tower*, where Chaucer may have lived in 1390 while Master of Works at Windsor. From the North Terrace there is a view of the Home Park, Eton and Stoke Poges church.

Below is St George's School, the choir school in the building (1802) of Travers College, founded in 1795 from the bequest of Samuel Travers (d. 1725) for 'Naval Knights', an order corresponding to the Military Knights (see above) but disbanded in 1892.

The room displaying *Queen Mary's Dolls House* and the *Exhibition of Old Master Drawings* is entered from North Terrace. The dolls house was designed for Queen Mary by Lutyens; details include books and paintings by contemporary authors and artists, working plumbing and electric lighting. The exhibition of drawings displays a changing selection from the royal collection, including works by da Vinci and Holbein.

Nearby is the entrance to the ***State Apartments**, in the N wing of the Upper Ward. They contain a superb collection of paintings, furniture, sculpture and other treasures. Visitors with limited time should note that, on the whole, the finest works of art are in the rooms towards the end of the present circulation order. The position of some items is liable to change: a brochure on sale gives up-to-date details.

From the *China Gallery* climbs the *Grand Staircase*, with a statue of George IV by Chantrey, and armour made for Henry VIII and the sons of James I. The *Grand Vestibule* has relics of Napoleon and the Japanese surrender sword (early 16C) of 1945. The large *Waterloo Chamber*, built in 1830 inside a 12C court, contains portraits, mostly by Lawrence, of those instrumental in Napoleon's downfall. The *Garter Throne Room* has portraits of sovereigns in their Garter robes; the *Grand Reception Room* has Gobelins tapestries. The noble *St George's Hall*, 185ft long, where the Garter festivities are held, bears the coats of arms of the knights since 1348 on the walls and ceiling. The portraits of English sovereigns from James I to George IV are by Van Dyck, Kneller, etc., while the parallel range of busts includes work by Rysbrack, Roubiliac, Nollekens and Chantrey. The *Queen's Guard Chamber* displays a suit of armour (1585) made for Sir Christopher Hatton and busts by Leone Leoni. The *Queen's Presence Chamber* and the *Queen's Audience Chamber* both have Gobelins tapestries and ceilings by Verrio glorifying Queen Catherine of Braganza. In the former is a bust of Handel by Roubiliac, in the latter portraits of the Princes of Orange (by Honthorst) in frames carved by Grinling Gibbons. The *Queen's Ballroom* contains portraits by Van Dyck (Charles I, Henrietta Maria, their children and members of the court) with 17C furniture.

The *Queen's Drawing Room* has works by Holbein and a portrait of Elizabeth I, when princess, by an unknown artist. In the *King's Closet* are views of Venice by Canaletto and a portrait of Garrick and his wife by Hogarth. The *King's Dressing Room* contains Van Dyck's painting of Charles I from three points of view and portraits by Clouet, Memling, Dürer, Andrea del Sarto, Rembrandt, Holbein and Rubens (of himself and of Van Dyck). The *King's State Bedchamber* contains a Louis XVI bed and several Canalettos. The *King's Drawing Room* has work by Rubens (Holy Family, etc.) and a St Martin by Van Dyck. The *King's Dining Room* has a ceiling by Verrio and carvings by Gibbons.

The elliptical **Round Tower** (or Keep) gives a magnificent view. Its lower half (1170) was heightened by Wyatville. The *Queen's Private Apartments* (not open) are on the E side of the Upper Ward. The passage between the Round Tower and the Upper Ward leads through St George's Gateway to Castle Hill, near the entrance to the *Royal Stables*.

N and E of the castle is the *Home Park*, where the Royal Windsor Horse Show is held in mid May. In the S part are *Frogmore Gardens* and *Mausoleum*. The latter contains the remains of Queen Victoria and the Prince Consort; also buried here are the Duke of Windsor, Edward VIII (d. 1972), and the Duchess of Windsor, the former Mrs Simpson (d. 1986). They are usually open on the first Wednesday and Thursday in May and the Mausoleum is also open on the Wednesday nearest to 24 May, Queen Victoria's birthday. The 17C *Frogmore House* (limited opening) has been extensively restored.

The *Guildhall*, immediately S of Queen Victoria's statue on Castle Hill, was designed by Sir Thomas Fitch in 1687 and finished by Wren in 1707. It has statues of Queen Anne and Prince George of Denmark. The church of *St John the Baptist* in the High St. was rebuilt in 1822; it contains a Last Supper ascribed to Franz de Cleyn (1588–1658) and carvings by Grinling Gibbons and others. Market St. and Church St. are both cobbled, with attractive houses.

The *Royal Mews* (open) in St Alban's St. display the Queen's horses and carriages, including the Scottish State Coach used at the 1981 royal wedding, and a selection of gifts presented to the Queen for her Silver Jubilee in 1977.

Opposite Castle Hill is *Windsor and Eton Central Station*, half of which has been converted into *Madame Tussaud's Royalty and Railways Exhibition.*

The original Royal Waiting Room and large Jubilee Glass Canopy built for the present station by the Great Western Railway Co. to celebrate Queen Victoria's Diamond Jubilee have been restored. Madame Tussaud's have added life-like figures of all the personalities involved; they have restored railway carriages and built a full-size replica of the Queen-class locomotive, one of the most powerful engines of the time, which pulled the train in which foreign royal guests arrived to be received.

The *Theatre Royal, Windsor* in Thames St. was founded in 1792 with George III as its patron. The present building dates from 1815. It is the centre of the Windsor Festival, held each September, with concerts in St George's Chapel and Eton College.

The *Household Cavalry Museum* in Combermere Barracks, St Leonard's Rd, just S of central Windsor, has one of the country's largest collections of arms, saddlery, standards and uniforms.

Windsor Great Park, S of Windsor, is an area of nearly 2000 acres crossed by the road to Ascot and the Long Walk. The latter, planted with elms by Charles II and replanted after 1945 with horse chestnut and plane trees, runs straight from the castle to (2¾m) *Snow Hill*, with a huge statue of George III by Westmacott. Still inside the park, best approached via Old Windsor village along the winding Crimp Lane, is (4m) the *Savill Garden* (open), 20 acres of lovely woodland named after a former park ranger. S of the garden is Smith's Lawn, a polo ground, and beyond that the *Valley Gardens* (open). These lie on the N side of Virginia Water (Route 14B). For Runnymede to the E, see Route 49B.

Leggo have announced plans to create a theme park on the site of the former Windsor Safari Park, SW of central Windsor.

Windsor Bridge (no cars) leads to the long street forming the small town of **Eton** (3500 inhabitants) and **Eton College**, founded by Henry VI in 1440 and perhaps the most famous of all English schools. It is open to visitors during afternoons in term, and from 10.30 in the Easter and summer holidays.

The main block of fine mellow brick includes two quadrangles. The larger, School Yard, has a statue of Henry VI (1719). A frieze commemorates 1157 Etonians killed in World War I and 748 killed in World War II. Above is the *Upper School* (1689–94) with busts of eminent Etonians, damaged in 1941 but restored; the panelled walls and staircases are covered with names of boys going on to King's College, Cambridge. The *Chapel*, a Perpendicular structure begun in 1441 and completed in 1483, has a fan vault added in 1958 by Sir William Holford. A superb series of wall paintings (1479–88) has been restored; the E window is by Evie Hone (1952) and the clerestory windows are by John Piper. A museum opened in 1985.

A fine gatehouse built by Provost Lupton c 1517 leads to the second court, or *Cloisters*, with the Collegers' *Dining Hall* (1450) and the *College Library* (1725–29) above it. In the playing fields beyond is the 'wall' which gives its name to the 'wall game', a style of football peculiar to Eton.

Old Etonians include Fielding, Dr Thomas Arne, Charles James Fox, Richard Porson, the elder and younger Pitt, Sir Robert Walpole and his son Horace, Gray, Shelley, Wellington, Canning, Gladstone, A.W. Kinglake, Swinburne, Sir Leslie Stephen, Sir Hubert Parry, Robert Bridges, Captain Oates, Sir Steven Runciman, J.B.S. Haldane, M.R. James, Aldous Huxley, Cyril Connolly, Henry Green, Sir Harold Acton, George Orwell, Anthony Eden, Harold Macmillan, Ian Fleming, Lord Hailsham, Lord Carrington, Humphrey Lyttleton.

Dorney Court (open), off B3026 3m W of Eton, is a pleasant house of c 1500 in timber and brick, with a well-preserved interior.

The main route follows A308 W from Windsor to (26m) **Maidenhead** (49,000 inhabitants; TI), at the start of a beautiful stretch of the Thames extending about 7m to Marlow. Oldfield, by the river, houses the *Henry Reitlinger Bequest* (open), which includes Oriental ceramics and drawings.

FROM MAIDENHEAD TO HIGH WYCOMBE. There are two routes, by A4094 (11½m) from the bridge or by A308 and A404 (10½m) from the centre. A4094 passes Boulter's Lock (Route 49B) and (3½m) **Cookham**, a pretty riverside village where Sir Stanley Spencer (1891–1959) was born and spent most of his life, putting local scenes and people into his paintings. A gallery in the High St. is devoted to his work and life, and there is a copy of his Last Supper in the church. A4094 crosses the river to the large residential village of (4½m) *Bourne End*. The alternative way by A308 and A404 crosses the river between (4¾m) Bisham, pronounced 'Bizzum', and (5½m) Marlow. *Bisham Abbey* (not open), now the National Sports Centre, is a Tudor house incorporating the remains of an Augustinian priory. The church has a monument to Sir Philip and Sir Thomas Hoby (d. 1558 and 1566) and an armorial window of enamelled glass. **Marlow** (14,100 inhabitants; seasonal TI) is a pleasant old place with attractive houses and a suspension bridge across the Thames (1831–36; William Tierney Clark). Shelley and his wife visited Thomas Love Peacock here in 1815, and in 1817–18, when they lived at Albion House in West St., Shelley wrote 'The Revolt of Islam' and Mary Shelley 'Frankenstein'. The parish church has a curious monument to Sir Miles Hobart (d. 1632), paid for by Parliament, depicting the accident that killed him. The RC church (1845–48) is by A.W.N. Pugin.

FROM MAIDENHEAD TO BEACONSFIELD. The direct route follows the way to High Wycombe via A4094 and Bourne End described above. An interesting alternative (8m) goes via *Taplow*, off A4 2m NE of the centre of Maidenhead. Sir Stanley Spencer (see above) died here, and the church has 14–15C brasses. The road climbs steeply from the village and soon skirts, on the left, the beautiful woods of **Cliveden** (NT, open). The house, designed in 1851 by Sir Charles Barry, lies further N. It is let to Blakeney Hotels Ltd, and only three rooms are open. On the right is the estate of *Dropmore* (not open) and, beyond, *Dorneywood* (NT), presented to the nation as a residence for a Secretary of State; only the gardens are open, by written appointment. Further E is the wooded common of *Burnham Beeches* (Route 51A). Beyond (5m) *Hedsor* the road drops to join A4094, the High Wycombe road, at (6m) *Wooburn*. B4440 goes right for *Beaconsfield* (Route 51A).

A4 leads out of Maidenhead to Maidenhead Thicket, with the *Courage Shire Horse Centre* (open). A423 branches right. At *Hurley*, ½m from the river, the partly Saxon and partly Norman church was the nave of a Benedictine priory church. Remains of the cloisters and domestic buildings are incorporated in nearby houses.

35m: **Henley-on-Thames** (11,000 inhabitants; TI) is a pleasant town with timber-framed and 18C houses. The Royal Regatta takes place in June/July (see headnote to Route 49B). At its E end stands a bridge of 1786, with sculptured masks of the Thames and Isis over its central arches. The big *Church*, with a Perpendicular tower, has flint and stone chequer-boarding outside, and a monument to Dame Elizabeth Periam (d. 1621) inside. The *Chantry House* and the *Red Lion*, nearby, are 14C.

Fawley Court (open), off A4155 1m N, is a country house by Wren (1684) with alterations and additions by James Wyatt in the 1770s, when Capability Brown also landscaped the gardens. The drawing room has a plasterwork *ceiling by Grinling Gibbons. The building is now the Divine Mercy College, a school run by the Marian Fathers, who have added a museum largely devoted to their connection with Poland. In the Chilterns 5m N of Henley, off A423 and B480, is *Stonor Park* (open), a medley of most architectural periods from the 13C and for much of its history an important centre of Roman Catholicism. The 12–14C chapel, with its Gothick interior of 1757, has been used for Mass without break for eight centuries. Edmund Campion (1540–81) set up his printing press here. *Greys Court* (NT), 3m W of Henley, is a Jacobean house enclosed by the ruins of a 14C fortified mansion. It has a Tudor donkey-wheel like the one at Carisbrooke.

On A321 3¼m S of Henley, on the Berkshire bank of the Thames, is the pretty village of *Wargrave*. The church, burned down by suffragettes in 1914, was rebuilt in 1916, when Norman masonry was discovered beneath the 17C brick casing of the tower. It contains a S window by John Hayward (1962) and the monument of Thomas Day (1748–89), author of 'Sandford and Merton'. Tennyson was married in 1850 at *Shiplake*, on the opposite bank.

Beyond Henley A423 leaves the Thames valley and climbs the Chilterns to (40½m) *Nettlebed*. The countryside to the N is explored in Route 51A. Beyond the summit, the road drops past (42m) *Nuffield*, on the left, from which the Oxford car magnate William Robert Morris (1877–1963) took his title. His home at Nuffield Place (limited opening) still has an atmosphere of the 1930s.

At 43½m A423 bears left from its natural course, blocked by RAF Benson, to (46½m) *Crowmarsh Gifford*, with its little Norman church, on the Thames opposite Wallingford. It then heads right, along the E bank of the river, to (48m) *Benson*. The farming pioneer Jethro Tull (1674–1741) lived at Howbery Park, between Crowmarsh and Benson.

It is more attractive and no further to leave A423, continue on the old road for 1½m and then turn right for (46m) **Ewelme**, prettiest of the Chiltern villages, with its 15C *Church*, almshouse and school making a lovely group. In the church is the *tomb of Alice, Duchess of Suffolk (d. 1475), one of only three effigies showing a woman wearing the Order of the Garter (cf. Stanton Harcourt, Route 36B). The 15 brasses include one of her father, Thomas Chaucer (d. 1434), supposed to be the poet's son, and his wife. Note also the screens, roofs and the pyramidal *font cover; the head on the corbel above may be Edward III. Jerome K. Jerome (1859–1927), author of 'Three Men in a Boat', is buried here. The large village of (48m) *Benson* was a seat of the kings of Mercia. The airfield lies to the SE.

A423 leads to (49m) *Shillingford*. The pleasant village of *Warborough*, adjoining Shillingford to the N, has a 13C lead font in its church.

On A329 2m S of Shillingford is **Wallingford** (6300 inhabitants; TI), with narrow streets on a medieval plan, remains of the earth ramparts that encircled it, and an old bridge widened in 1809. The Town Hall dates from 1670. The site of the old castle, with the remains of St Nicholas Priory, is now given over to public gardens. The legal historian Sir William Blackstone (1723–80) is buried in the church.

A329 heads down from Wallingford to (15m) Reading, keeping to the S bank of the Thames through one of the loveliest stretches of its valley, visited by river in Route 49B. Agatha Christie (1890–1976) is buried at *Cholsey*, off A329 3m SW of Wallingford. From *Streatley*, on A329 5m S of Wallingford and at the foot of the Berkshire Downs, B4009 heads 3m W to *Aldworth*, with the remarkable 14C De la Beche *effigies in its church.

North Moreton church, 3m W of Wallingford, has 14C glass in the Stapelton chantry. From Wallingford W to Wantage, see Route 51B.

Beyond Shillingford A423 crosses the Thame, a tributary of the Thames, and bypasses (51m) **Dorchester**. Now merely a village of pleasant houses, it was a Roman military centre and an important Saxon town, the cathedral city of Wessex (634–705) and of Mercia (869–1072). A priory of Augustinian canons was founded on the site of the cathedral c 1140 and, though the other monastic buildings were destroyed at the Reformation, the *Abbey Church* survives as the parish church.

The nave and W end of the choir belong to the Norman church, probably begun before the abbey and completed c 1180. The S nave aisle and both choir aisles are in the Geometric Decorated style (1280–1320), while the E end dates from the close of the Decorated period. The low W tower and round transept arches were added in the 17C.

The three *windows at the E end are the chief glory of the building, unique in being traceried throughout and ornamented with sculptured figures. The E window, divided in two by a massive buttress, contains 14C glass. On the N side is the Jesse window, growing from a stone figure of Jesse on the windowsill. Under the S window are the canopied sedilia and piscina, with 12C glass in the little triangular windows behind. Note also the lead font (1170–80), decorated with figures of the Apostles. An 'Anglo-American' garden has been laid out on the site of the cloisters, N of the church.

Overy, ¼m SE, has some attractive cottages.

A423 runs directly from Dorchester to Oxford, but a diversion (about 4m longer) can be made on A415, following the loop of the Thames to the W. 3m: *Clifton Hampden* (Route 51B). 7m: **Abingdon** (22,700 inhabitants; TI) is a pleasant old town. It sprang up round a powerful Benedictine abbey founded in 675, and was the county town of Berkshire until 1870. The rebuilt bridge gives a striking view, with the former *Gaol* (1811), now a leisure centre, prominent in the foreground. On the N bank of the Thames are the remains of the *Abbey* (open), so closely integrated with later buildings that it is hard to distinguish them. The entrance is by the 15C gatehouse, next to the 12–15C church of *St Nicholas*. The abbey church has disappeared, and the main survivals are a range of ancillary buildings by the mill stream to the S. They include the large, square 14C hall known as the Checker (i.e. Exchequer), now fitted up as the Unicorn Theatre, and the early 16C Long Gallery. The 18C *Guildhall*, S of the abbey gatehouse, contains an art gallery with civic plate, etc. (open by appointment only). It preserves traces of the abbey hospital and includes the old grammar school of 1563. Just down Bridge St., the *Crown and Thistle* has a picturesque courtyard. In the market place stands the *County Hall* (EH) of 1677–80 by Christopher Kempster, Wren's master mason. It contains a local museum. A shopping precinct runs NW, while the attractive East St Helen St. leads to *St Helen's*, a Perpendicular church with a spire, double aisles and a Jacobean pulpit. The churchyard is surrounded by almshouses, including *Christ's Hospital*, founded in 1553 in direct succession to the ancient Guild of the Holy Cross (hall open by appointment).

At *Drayton*, on B4017 2½m S, the church has 16C alabaster carvings. *Steventon*, 1½m further on B4017, has medieval buildings, now private houses, once belonging to a Benedictine priory. The Great Hall in South Cottage (NT) is open by written application to the tenant. *Milton Manor* (open), beyond A34 1½m E of Steventon, is a modest 17–18C house in red brick, with a Gothick chapel and library. *Sutton Courtenay*, by the river 2m E of Drayton, see Route 36B. *Radley*, 2½m NE of Abingdon, has a public school founded in 1847. At *Sunningwell*, beyond A34 3m N of Abingdon, the church has a classical seven-sided porch added by Bishop Jewel of Salisbury when he was rector here in 1552. The philosopher Roger Bacon is said to have used the tower for astronomical calculations. For *Kingston Bagpuize*, 6m W of Abingdon on A415, see Route 51B.

A423, the direct road from Dorchester to Oxford, passes through (57m) *Nuneham Courtenay*. The village was moved to its present position by Earl Harcourt in 1765. *Nuneham Park* (left), with its beautiful wooded grounds, is now a conference centre. 57m: the Oxford ring road. A4144, to the W, enters the city via Folly Bridge, A4158 (E) via Magdalen Bridge. *Iffley*, on the river between the two roads, has perhaps the best-preserved small Norman parish *church in England, built c 1170. The low, square tower has fine carving on its top storey, and the W front has a beautifully ornamented doorway. The last bay of the chancel is Early English, and many of the windows were inserted in the 14–15C. The doorways to the former rood loft reveal elaborate groined archways. 60m: **Oxford**, see Route 50.

B. By River

Maps: Stanford's River Thames map (published by E. Stanford Ltd, 12–14 Long Acre, London WC2).

Rising in the Cotswolds and eventually joining the sea through its broad estuary E of London, the Thames has a total course of about 210 miles. The Thames Valley extends from Kingston-upon-Thames, near the edge of SW London, to (91½m) Oxford. The river here is ideal for boating—and hence apt to get crowded with pleasure craft in summer. Its commercial traffic is slight, its current gentle (except after floods) and its scenery unsurpassed for quiet, typically English beauty: low hills and wooded cliffs, small towns and villages, meadows and country houses with gardens and lawns sloping down to the water. The finest reaches are between Maidenhead and Marlow, Henley and Sonning, Mapledurham and Goring. Reading is the only industrial town.

Passenger boats run between most of the major points along the river. Salter Brothers Ltd of Oxford operate a twice daily service in summer between Staines and Windsor, Windsor and Marlow, Henley and Reading, Abingdon and Oxford. Kingston and Hampton Court are both connected with central London by the regular service (every day in summer, weekends in spring and autumn) from Westminster Pier. A full list of companies and their locations is given in the useful pamphlet, 'Cruising on the River Thames', obtainable from Customer Services (River Division), Thames Water, Nugent House, Vastern Rd, Reading RG1 8DB. For further information, write to: The Secretary, Upper Thames Passenger Boat Association, Turk Launches Ltd, Thames Side, Kingston-upon-Thames.

Boats for hire. Rowing boats, punts, canoes, etc. are available by the hour or day at many points, and cruisers by the day or week from the many hire firms. The best punting waters are at Staines, Maidenhead and Goring. For companies and their locations, see 'Cruising on the River Thames'. All pleasure boats must be registered with Thames Water before being used in any way on the river upstream of the Teddington boundary. Application forms are obtained from and handled by Finance Directorate (Income Section), Thames Water, address as above.

Regattas. Henley Royal Regatta is held on five days in the first week of July, over a course of about 1¼m between Temple Island and Poplar Point, just N of Henley Bridge. Founded in 1839 and now the leading amateur regatta in the world, it is a fashionable occasion. Other rowing regattas are held, mostly in July and early August, at Molesey, Marlow, Kingston, Staines, Walton, Reading, Bourne End and Goring.

Kingston-upon-Thames (see 'Blue Guide London') is 10m SW of central London, reached by British Rail from Waterloo or steamer service from Westminster Pier. 3m: *Hampton Court* (see Route 3 and 'Blue Guide London'), with the palace on the right and the mouth of the Mole on the left. Above Tagg's Island is *Hampton* (right), with Garrick's Villa. Greater London yields to Surrey and, beyond a series of reservoirs, the river reaches (6m) *Sunbury Lock*. Sunbury lies on the N bank. 7½m: *Walton Bridge*. *Walton-on-Thames* is on the S bank, with St George's Hill. At the bend in the river *Cowey Stakes* disputes with Brentford the claim to be where Julius Caesar crossed the Thames in 54 BC. The straight Desborough Channel here cuts off c 1m, but the river runs more pleasantly by *Lower Halliford*. Thomas Love Peacock (1785–1866) is buried in Halliford churchyard. *Shepperton* has a pleasant 17–18C centre. 9½m: *Shepperton Lock*.

On the left, at the mouth of the Wey, is **Weybridge** (49,200 inhabitants with Walton), which preserves the column (1794) from London's Seven Dials on its green. Between Weybridge and (19½m) Godalming the *Wey Navigation* (NT) is open to pleasure boats. It passes through a charming stretch of country at *Pyrford*, near Newark Priory and Old Woking (Route 13B), and skirts the grounds of Sutton Place.

Beyond Chertsey Bridge (1780–85) is (11½m) *Chertsey Lock*. Abbey Mead (left) recalls the famous Benedictine abbey at *Chertsey*, founded in the 7C and refounded in 1110, of which almost nothing survives. It was known especially for its floor tiles, which adorn many English churches. At (12½m) *Laleham*, on the right, Matthew Arnold (1822–88) was born and is buried beside the partly Norman church. Laleham Abbey was the home of Lord Lucan of Crimean War fame. 13½m: *Penton Hook Lock*, with a marina. 15½m: **Staines** (53,800 inhabitants), with two bridges across the Thames. Just short of (16½m) *Bell Weir Lock* the river passes under the M25; the Colne enters from the right. The right bank here belongs to Berkshire, though for most of the way to Henley it is Buckinghamshire. On the left is *Egham* (Route 14B) and, beyond, the level meadow of **Runnymede** (NT), with (18m) *Magna Carta Island*, probably the actual place where King John signed Magna Carta in 1215. The entrance pavilions were designed by Lutyens (1932). Above, on *Cooper's Hill*, rises the Commonwealth Air Forces Memorial (1953) by Sir Edward Maufe; beyond are the Magna Carta Memorial (1957) and the John F. Kennedy Memorial (1965). The S bank of the river becomes Berkshire. Just within the boundary is Beaumont College, a Roman Catholic public school founded in 1861, in a house once occupied by Warren Hastings. 19½m: *Old Windsor Lock* is at the entrance to one of three artificial cuts on the way to Oxford. 21½m: *Datchet* (left) faces the Home Park of Windsor. William Herschel moved here after receiving a pension from George III; Haydn's visit is supposed to have inspired 'The Creation'. 22½m: *Romney Lock*, with a good view of Eton College and its playing fields. 23m: *Windsor Bridge* connects **Windsor** with **Eton** (Route 49A).

Most of the riverside towns and villages between Windsor and Oxford are described more fully in the road routes: see particularly Route 49A but also the index.

Above Windsor is (24m) *Clewer*, on the left, with the headquarters of the Clewer Sisterhood and a partly Norman church. 25m: *Boveney Lock*. 27m: *Down Place*, left, was home of the publisher Jacob Tonson (d. 1736) and a meeting place of the Kit-Cat Club. At (27½m) *Monkey Island* the stream is very swift. The river passes under a bridge carrying the M4. 28m: *Bray Lock*. The large village of *Bray*, ½m further, has the picturesque Jesus Hospital (1627). In the 18C song, the time-serving Vicar of Bray boasts that he has three times changed his creed to keep his living.

Passing under Brunel's railway bridge (1837–38) and Maidenhead Bridge (1772–77) the river reaches (29½m) **Maidenhead**, opposite *Taplow*. One of the most beautiful (and popular) reaches of the river begins here. 30¼m: *Boulter's Lock*, with *Cliveden Woods* stretching along the right bank for about 2m beyond. *Hedsor* stands on high ground E of (32¼m) *Cookham Lock*. *Cookham* lies ½m beyond the lock on the left bank; on the right, 1m farther, is *Bourne End*. The fine *Quarry Wood* begins on the left just short of (36½m) *Marlow Lock*. **Marlow** is on the right bank, with the grounds of Bisham Abbey opposite. Bisham church can be reached from the riverbank. 38m: *Temple Lock*. 38½m: *Hurley Lock*. About 1m further, on the right, is *Medmenham Abbey* (not open), a ruined 13C Cistercian monastery rebuilt as a country house in the 18C.

Sir Francis Dashwood's Hell-Fire Club met here from 1745, adopting from Rabelais the motto 'Fay ce que voudras' ('Do what you please') and becoming notorious for blasphemous orgies, probably exaggerated in the telling. John Wilkes (a guest only), the poet Charles Churchill and the playwright Paul Whitehead were among the leading spirits.

42m: *Hambleden* stands 1m N of its lock. The 17C mansion of *Greenlands* (not open), further along on the right, is now an administrative staff college. Then come *Temple Island* and the Henley Regatta Course. *Fawley Court* (open), to the right, stands opposite *Remenham*, on the boundary between Buckinghamshire and Oxfordshire.

44½m: **Henley** is on the right (Oxfordshire) bank. 45½m: *Marsh Lock*. On the left is a pretty backwater. Then comes *Wargrave* on the Berkshire bank. At (48m) *Shiplake Lock* the little river Loddon joins the Thames. *Shiplake* is on the right; on the left is St Patrick's Stream, another pleasant backwater. 50½m: The charming village of *Sonning*, on the left, has an ancient bridge and a church with eight 15–17C brasses. *Sonning Lock*, just beyond the bridge, is one of the prettiest on the river. 53½m: *Caversham Lock*, near the bridges connecting **Reading** with *Caversham*, its suburb on the N bank.

About ½m before the lock the Thames is joined by the Kennet, linked with the Kennet and Avon Canal to the W, navigable to (18½m) *Newbury*.

At (57m) *Tilehurst* the church has the splendid monument of Sir Peter Vanlore (d. 1627). 58m: *Mapledurham Lock*, with a much painted mill and weir, inspired some of E.H. Shepard's drawings for Kenneth Grahame's 'The Wind in the Willows'. Close by is **Mapledurham House** (open), a manor house of 1588–1612 in patterned red brick.

Pope visited Teresa and Martha Blount here. The oak Tudor staircase and some early 17C plaster ceilings survive, with some unusual 17–18C carved wooden heads of animals in the entrance hall, and good furniture and portraits. The chapel of 1797 is in the Gothick style. The lovely grounds, which Pope may have helped to lay out, include the remains of the earlier manor house and a restored watermill.

The pretty village has almshouses of 1629 and a church restored by Butterfield in 1863, with its S aisle reserved as a Roman Catholic chapel for the owners of the manor.

The Thames enters one of its finest reaches. *Hardwick House* (not open), on the right, is delightfully situated. 60½m: *Whitchurch Lock*, with a toll bridge connecting *Whitchurch* (right) to *Pangbourne* (left), where Kenneth Grahame lived at Church Cottage from 1924 until his death in 1932. Further along, also on the left, is *Basildon*, with a low-lying church, the *Child Beale Wildlife Trust* (open) and, set on the hill, **Basildon Park** (NT), a Palladian house in Bath stone by John Carr of York (1770). It keeps its octagon room and grand staircase, as well as much of the original plasterwork. On the opposite bank is the lovely Hartslock Wood. 64½m: *Goring Lock*, with a rebuilt bridge. The ancient Icknield Way crosses the Thames at *Goring*, on the right bank. The church, with a tourelle on its Norman tower and Roman (?) tiles in the S porch, contains remnants of the chapel of an Augustinian nunnery. Beyond the pretty Berkshire village of *Streatley* both banks are in Oxfordshire. 65m: *Cleeve Lock*. Opposite (76m) *Moulsford* is *South Stoke*, with an Early English church. *North Stoke*, further on, was the home of the singer Dame Clara Butt (1873–1936).

70½m: *Wallingford Bridge*, leading from **Wallingford** to *Crowmarsh Gifford*. 71½m: *Benson Lock*. The twin *Sinodun Hills* or *Wittenham Clumps*, with an Iron Age earthwork, come into view and remain in sight for the next 8m. 72½m: *Shillingford*. 2½m further on is the mouth of the Thame. Above this point the Thames is also known, poetically but not locally, as the Isis. 75½m: *Day's Lock*. Sinodun Hills are above *Little Wittenham*, on the left bank. From the right bank a footpath leads to (1m) **Dorchester** past the Dyke Hills, an old fortification stretching from the Thame to the Thames. On the right are (76¾m) *Burcot* and (78m) *Clifton Hampden*, with a heavily restored 12–14C church on a low cliff. 78½m: *Clifton Lock*. On the backwater is the pretty village of *Long Wittenham*, where the church has a late Norman lead font and a unique piscina which doubles as the founder's monument. The river next passes *Appleford*, on the left, near the railway bridge. Didcot power station dominates the scene. 81½m: *Culham Lock*. *Culham*, on the right, is connected by a bridge with *Sutton Courtenay*, a delightful village on a pretty backwater reached from the far end of Culham Cut. The Liberal Prime Minister Herbert Asquith (1852–1928) and George Orwell (Eric Blair, 1905–50) are buried here. *Old Culham Bridge*, on another backwater, dates from 1430. **Abingdon** has a rebuilt bridge, ¼m before (84m) *Abingdon Lock*. Beyond the railway bridge are, on the right, the beautiful woods of *Nuneham Park*. 88½m: *Sandford Lock*, the deepest on the Thames, with the Radley College boathouse. 89½m: The river passes under the railway and the Oxford ring road, with Hinksey Stream branching left. 90m: *Iffley Lock*, with Iffley church on the right. The stretch from here to Folly Bridge is the scene of the 'Eights' and 'Torpid' boat races. Opposite the New Cut, an artificial mouth of the Cherwell, is the Oxford University boathouse, on the left. Christ Church Meadow appears on the right. 91½m: *Folly Bridge*, the landing place for **Oxford** (Route 50).

THE THAMES ABOVE OXFORD. Known at Oxford as the 'Upper River', it is much less crowded, despite its beauty, since the headroom at Osney Bridge is only 7½ft. 1m: *Osney Lock*. On the right is the entrance to the *Oxford Canal*, originally projected by Brindley in 1769, which runs via *Banbury* to (49m) the *Napton* junction with the Grand Union Canal (Route 52B) and continues N from (54m) the *Braunston* junction to (77m) the *Hawkesbury* junction with the Coventry Canal. 2m: On the left is *Binsey*, with St Frideswide's Well by its little 12–13C church. On the right is Port Meadow, where the burgesses of Oxford have enjoyed the right of free pasture since the time of Edward the Confessor. 3¼m: *Godstow Lock*, with the Trout Inn and the remains of the Benedictine nunnery where 'Fair' Rosamond, mistress of Henry II, was educated and buried (c 1176) after her death at Woodstock. The little village of *Wytham*, with its woods, lies ¾m W. The river goes under a bridge carrying the Oxford ring road and reaches (4½m) *King's Lock*, near another entrance to the Oxford canal. At 6m the mouth of the Evenlode is passed on the right. 7m: *Eynsham Lock*, with Swinford Bridge (1777) leading to *Eynsham*, ¾m to the right. 8½m: *Pinkhill Lock*. 11½m: *Bablock Hythe*, celebrated in Matthew Arnold's 'The Scholar Gipsy'. On the left a path leads to (1m) *Cumnor*, the scene of Amy Robsart's death. Cumnor Place is gone but the church is interesting, with one of two known contemporary statues of Elizabeth I and a memorial to Amy Robsart.

2m NW is **Stanton Harcourt**, with the remains of the 15C manor house (limited opening), abandoned when the Harcourt family seat was moved to Nuneham Courtenay in 1750. The picturesque group includes the gatehouse, kitchen and Pope's Tower, so-called because the poet stayed here in 1717–18 while translating the 'Iliad'. The church has a rare mid 13C chancel screen and the monument of Margaret Harcourt (d. 1471), one of the three known effigies of ladies wearing the Order of the Garter (cf. Ewelme, Route 49A).

12½m: From *Northmoor Lock* a footpath runs S to (1m) *Appleton*, with a manor house of c 1190 (not open). 15m: *New Bridge*, where the Windrush flows in, is medieval. R.D. Blackmore (1825–1900) was born at the pretty village of *Longworth*, 1½m SW. For *Kingston Bagpuize*, 1½m S of New Bridge, see Route 51B. 17m: *Shifford Lock* is at the entrance to a cut, which is crossed by a ford. 21m: *Tadpole Bridge*. 21½m: *Rushey Lock*. 24m: *Radcot Lock*. 26m: *Radcot Bridge* (14C) is the best surviving medieval bridge over the Thames. Stone quarried near Burford for St Paul's Cathedral was shipped from here. 27m: *Grafton Lock*. On the left, beyond, is the church of *Eaton Hastings*; for *Buscot Park*, see Route 51B. On the right is *Kelmscott* (limited opening), the 16–17C manor that William Morris made his country home from 1871 until his death in 1896. It gave its name to the Kelmscott Press in Hammersmith. It is now owned by the Society of Antiquaries. Morris is buried in the churchyard, with a tomb designed by Philip Webb. The boundary between Oxfordshire and Gloucestershire is passed before (29½m) *Buscot Lock*. 30¼m: *St John's Lock*, the last on the journey upstream. The left bank belongs briefly to the N tip of Wiltshire. 31m: **Lechlade** (Route 51B) marks the present limit of navigation. On the Thames to the W lie: (32¼m) *Inglesham*, at the entrance of the derelict Thames and Severn Canal, with a fine 14C tomb of Purbeck marble in its church; (37m) *Kempsford*, with a beautiful church tower; and (42¼m) *Cricklade* (Route 51B). See Route 51B for the river's source at *Thames Head*, near Cirencester.

50

Oxford

OXFORD (116,400 inhabitants) is famous for its university. The grouping of towers and spires makes a beautiful sight in the distance. On closer view, the colleges prove rich in examples, often excellent, of every period from the medieval to the present and of most major English architects since the Renaissance. Their combined effect—seen at its best in High St., Broad St. and the square where the Radcliffe Camera stands—is sometimes skilfully planned and sometimes happily accidental. Emphatically a city even apart from the university, Oxford is a lively but often congested place which attracts visitors for its shopping facilities and its cultural life as well as for its architecture.

Several days are needed to get to know it properly. Even the shortest tour should include Christ Church (with Oxford Cathedral), Merton, Queen's, Magdalen and New College, as well as the Sheldonian Theatre and the Ashmolean Museum. The four walks from the centre suggested below take in all the chief points of interest; the tours of the outskirts that follow are for leisurely visitors.

TI: The Old School, Gloucester Green. **Coach Station**: Gloucester Green. **Railway Station**: Botley Rd, about ½m W of Carfax. **Parking**: The Park and Ride scheme has free car parks at Pear Tree (N), Thornhill (E), Red Bridge (S) and Seacourt (W), with bus services to the city centre every 10 minutes. **Theatres**: Oxford Playhouse, Beaumont St.; Apollo Theatre, George St. **Music**: Evening services daily in the chapels of New College, Magdalen College and the Cathedral (Christ Church). **Annual Events**: Eights Week (late May), with college balls, plays, concerts and boat races on the Isis (Thames) between Iffley and Folly Bridge. Torpids, also boat races, take place in February. For the celebration of May Day, see Magdalen College.

Access to Colleges: The pressure of tourism has forced the colleges to adopt stringent policies about opening to the public. Many are closed in the morning, but most are open for at least a few hours in the afternoon. Some limit access to quads and grounds; chapels, halls, old libraries and other features of interest may or may not be open. Visitors should not enter staircases or working libraries without a prior appointment. The TI Centre can supply precise details, which vary from college to college and year to year.

History. Oxford's name (the 'ford for oxen' over the Thames at Hinksey) shows that it first owed its existence to a convenient river-crossing. Yet there was no Roman or British settlement, and the city is not mentioned in written records until the Anglo-Saxon Chronicle of 912. By then it was a trading centre with several religious foundations (the priory of St Frideswide's may date from the early 8C), where kings several times held councils of state.

Despite picturesque legends that the university was founded by the mythical British king Memphric or, at least, by Alfred the Great, nobody knows when or how it began. It is first mentioned in the 12C, when its growth was encouraged by the influx of English students expelled from Paris in 1167. The teaching body was in due time recognised as a 'studium generale', or university, with all the powers of a corporation. In 1214 the papal legate Pandulf gave it its first legal privilege, conferring immunity from lay jurisdiction—the first stage in the long and often riotous struggle between Town and Gown. The first colleges to be endowed with their own rules and privileges were University College (1249), Merton (1264) and Balliol (before 1266). They were reserved for graduates only, and until the time of Elizabeth I most students lived in the numerous halls (or hostels kept by graduate principals).

Fondly called the 'home of lost causes', the university acquired a long history of ideological turbulence. Wyclif and his Lollard followers caused controversy in the 14C. The Reformation brought first the Calvinist iconoclasm of Edward VI's reign and then the Catholic reaction under Queen Mary, when the Protestant martyrs Cranmer, Latimer and Ridley were burnt at the stake in Broad St. In the Civil War the university supported the Royalist cause while the city declared for Parliament. Oxford became the headquarters of the king and court in 1642, but in 1646 yielded to General Fairfax. After the Restoration the university settled down into the ease of the 18C, interrupted only by political disputes and the Methodist movement. Religious controversy of another kind was caused in the 1830s by the High Church tendency known as the Oxford (or Tractarian) Movement under the leadership of Pusey, Keble and Newman.

The process of democratising the university was started by the 'Extension' movement and the foundation of Ruskin College in the 19C. The academic year 1919–20 brought three important changes: the admission of women to university degrees, the dethroning of Greek as a necessary part of a university education and (after 700 years of independence) the acceptance of a government grant.

Yet perhaps the most important 20C changes have come with the rapid expansion and industrialisation of the city itself. In the 19C the university was able to resist the encroachments of the Industrial Revolution, remaining famous for the pastoral beauty of its immediate surroundings. That changed in the 1920s when William Robert Morris, later Viscount Nuffield (1877–1963), began production of the Morris car at Cowley to the SE, which became the headquarters of the Austin–Rover group. Many of the old manufacturing buildings have been pulled down, and the area is being redeveloped as a business and industrial park.

The University. The Oxbridge system is described under the entry for Cambridge (Route 37). Oxford has 35 colleges, of which 28 admit both undergraduates and graduates, with undergraduates predominating and making up a total population of about 9500. The undergraduate colleges vary both in their date of foundation, with Balliol, University College and Merton (see above) being the oldest and St Catherine's (1963) the newest, and in their size. St Catherine's is the largest (410 undergraduates) and Corpus Christi (213) the smallest. All the colleges originally founded for men now admit women as well. Of the colleges founded for women (Lady Margaret Hall, Somerville, St Hugh's, St Hilda's and St Anne's), only St Hilda's remains exclusively female. In the undergraduate population at large men outnumber women by about two to one. Six graduate colleges—Linacre, Nuffield, St Antony's, St Cross, Wolfson and the newest, Green—have been founded since 1937. All Souls, a much older foundation, admits only fellows.

In addition, five permanent private halls partake in the university's privileges and are admitted to its degrees: Campion Hall, Greyfriars, Mansfield, Regent's Park and St Benet's. Campion Hall, Greyfriars and St Benet's, primarily for members of religious orders (Jesuit, Franciscan and Benedictine respectively), admit men only. Not incorporated with the university, but enjoying a special relation to it, are Ruskin College (now primarily for students sponsored by trade unions) and five theological institutions: Ripon, St Stephen's, Wycliffe, Manchester and Blackfriars.

The centre of the old city is **Carfax** (possibly the Latin 'quadrifurcus' or the French 'quatre voies'), where four main streets join: St Aldate's, leading S to Folly Bridge over the Thames; High St., leading E to Magdalen Bridge over the Cherwell; Cornmarket, leading N and finally broadening out into St Giles; and Queen St., leading W to the Westgate shopping centre and the railway station.

The 14C tower (open) with quarter boys, at the NW angle of Carfax, is all that remains of *St Martin's*. The composer Orlando Gibbons (1583–1625) was baptised here, and Shakespeare is said to have stood sponsor to the infant William Davenant (1606–68), whose father was landlord of the Crown Tavern. At 3 opposite is the guest chamber of the inn, known as the

Painted Room (open by arrangement), where John Davenant may have entertained Shakespeare. The wall paintings date from 1450 and 1550, the panelling from 1630.

SOUTH AND EAST FROM CARFAX. St Aldate's passes (left) the Town Hall, housing the *Museum of Oxford*. Behind the largely 19C *St Aldate's Church*, on the right, is Pembroke College; opposite is the main front of Christ Church.

In Brewer St. (right) are the *Cathedral Choir School*, where Dorothy L. Sayers was born in 1893, and *Campion Hall*, for Jesuits (1936; Lutyens). In Rose Place, further on, is the *Old Palace*, built in the 16C by Robert King, last Abbot of Osney and first Bishop of Oxford, but dating in its present form from 1628 (restored 1952) and now, with its modern extension, home of the Roman Catholic chaplaincy to the university.

83 St Aldate's, opposite the entrance to Christ Church Meadow, is the original of the shop in Lewis Carroll's 'Through the Looking Glass'. St Aldate's descends to (¼m) *Folly Bridge*, rebuilt in 1825–27 by Ebenezer Perry, where the gatehouse once stood which Roger Bacon is said to have used as his observatory.

Pembroke College (350 undergraduates), founded in 1624 to supersede Broadgates Hall, is named after the Earl of Pembroke, Chancellor of the university at the time.

Dr Johnson, who studied here in 1728–29, had second-floor rooms over the gateway. The old refectory of Broadgates Hall is now the *Senior Common Room* (not open), and Johnson's desk and teapot are on display in the *Library*. The *Chapel*, originally 18C, was redecorated by C.E. Kempe in 1884 to make the most lavish neo-Renaissance interior in Oxford. The Besse Building, Beef Lane (now a paved footpath) and reconstructed 16C houses of Pembroke St. form a delightful *North Quad* (1954–62), reminiscent of a square in a small country town. The new *Library* (1974) was the gift of a family of American alumni. The *Macmillan Building* (1976) and the *Sir Geoffrey Arthur Building* (1990) were built to house more undergraduates.

MEMBERS of Broadgates Hall: Bishop Bonner, Beaumont, William Camden, John Pym and Sir Thomas Browne, who spanned the change to Pembroke. Of Pembroke: Samuel Johnson, William Shenstone, George Whitefield, Sir William Blackstone, John Lemprière (of the 'Classical Dictionary'), James Smithson (founder of the Smithsonian Institute in Washington DC), William Fulbright, Michael Heseltine.

*Christ Church (390 undergraduates), familiarly known as 'the House', is built on the largest and most aristocratic scale of any Oxford college. It was first founded by Wolsey as Cardinal College in 1525, on the site of St Frideswide's Priory. After Wolsey's fall Henry VIII refounded it as Henry VIII College, an ecclesiastical establishment only. At the Reformation this was suppressed in turn, to be refounded yet again in 1545 as Christ Church. By a unique arrangement, the remains of the old priory church became Oxford Cathedral as well as the college chapel, and the Dean (appointed by the Crown) head of both the cathedral chapter and the college.

The visitors' entrance is by the wrought-iron gates of the War Memorial Gardens and along the Broad Walk of *Christ Church Meadow* to the *Meadows Building* (1863). The buildings beyond the Meadow Gate are the remains of St Frideswide's Priory: the original frater (later the Old Library, now undergraduate rooms), the cloister and the cathedral. The Perpendicular *Cloister* (1499) was destroyed on the W side in 1525. In the E walk is the late Norman doorway of the *Chapter House*, an Early English chamber used for exhibiting church plate.

The ***Cathedral**, one of the smallest in England, owes its present Norman appearance to rebuilding in 1140–80. Of the many later alterations, the

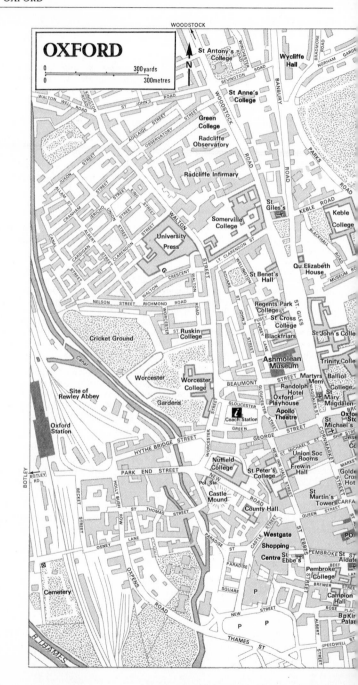

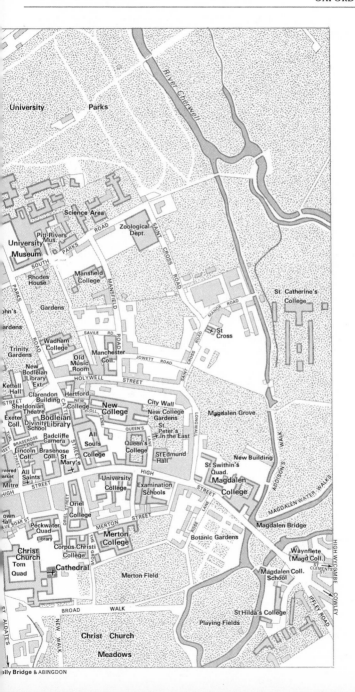

most conspicuous are the squat 13C spire and the W front and E end by Sir Gilbert Scott (1870).

In the *Nave*, the massive Norman pillars of the arcades are alternately round and octagonal; an illusion of height is given by the unusual placing of the triforium inside the main arches, with secondary arches below. The roof is 16C timberwork, the pulpit and organ screen are 17C, the stalls 19C. The N aisle has a W window with glass by Abraham van Linge (c 1630) depicting Jonah and Nineveh; the S aisle has a W window by Morris and Burne-Jones, the first of several in the cathedral. There are monuments to Bishop Berkeley (1685–1753) and the Tractarian leader Edward Pusey (1800–82).

The *Choir* has a vaulted late 15C •roof. The E end is by Scott. Like the lantern, the *Transepts* have early 16C roofs. The S end of the S transept is a conjectural restoration by Scott. St Lucy's Chapel, in the former E aisle of this transept, has a flamboyant •E window with glass (c 1330) including a representation of Becket's martyrdom from which the saint's head has been struck out. Opening from the N transept are three parallel aisles: the N choir aisle, the Lady Chapel and the Latin Chapel. Between the first two is the fragmentary base of the late 13C shrine of St Frideswide, once the goal of pilgrims, and opposite, between the Lady Chapel and the Latin Chapel, is the Perpendicular watching chamber from which the treasures of the shrine were guarded. The Latin Chapel has massive 16C oak stalls and 14C glass in the N windows; the monuments include one to Robert Burton (1577–1640) of 'The Anatomy of Melancholy'. Two of the three N aisles have E windows by Morris and Burne-Jones, while the Latin Chapel has an earlier window (1858) by Burne-Jones.

The W end of the cathedral opens into the *Great Quadrangle* (or *Tom Quad*), the largest in Oxford, begun by Wolsey as a cloister and not completed until the 1660s. The pool in the centre is known as the 'Mercury' from its statue, now a modern copy of the original 17C one by Giovanni da Bologna. On the W side is the *Great Gate* (1526), the main college entrance from St Aldate's, below the famous *Tom Tower*, added by Wren in 1681 to house 'Great Tom', the huge bell from Osney Abbey. It sounds 101 times at 21:05 every evening, once for each member of the original foundation, formerly the signal for the closing of all college gates.

The college •*Hall* (open) is entered from the bell tower (1879) near the cathedral in the SE corner of the quad. The staircase (1805; James Wyatt) has a beautiful fan-tracery •roof (1640), a very late example of the style in England. The hall itself, the largest in Oxford, was completed in Wolsey's time. It has a richly carved hammerbeam roof and portraits by Lely, Kneller, Reynolds, Gainsborough, Romney, Lawrence, Millais, Watts, Herkomer and Graham Sutherland. Henry VIII (by Sonmans) dominates, flanked by Elizabeth I (perhaps by Zucchero) and Wolsey (perhaps by Robert Greenbury). Wolsey's vast kitchen below is still in use (not open).

In the NE corner of the quad is Dr Fell's Tower, with statues of Dean John Fell (1660–86; 'I do not like thee, Dr Fell') and Dean Liddell (1855–91). Beneath it Killcanon Passage, so-called because of its cold draughts, leads to *Peckwater Quad*, built in 1706–11 on the site of the Peckwater Inn. On its S side is the splendid *Library* of 1717–72 (open by special appointment) with beautiful plasterwork ceilings, woodwork and furnishings, and some of the earliest wall bookcases to be built. It contains the manuscript of John Evelyn's diary and memorabilia of Wolsey and Lewis Carroll. On the W side of Peckwater is the entrance to the *Blue Boar Quad* (1968; Powell and Moya); on the E is *Canterbury Quad*, built in 1773–83 on the site of the old Canterbury College. The *Picture Gallery* (open) has the finest collection in Oxford of paintings and drawings, mostly 14–17C Italian.

MEMBERS include politicians and Prime Ministers (Canning, Peel, Gladstone, Salisbury, Halifax, Eden, Douglas-Home). Among other notables are: Richard Hakluyt, Sir Philip Sidney, Robert Burton, Thomas Otway, William Penn, John Locke, John and Charles Wesley, 'Monk' Lewis, Edward Pusey, John Ruskin, Lewis Carroll (C.L. Dodgson), Sir Adrian Boult, Sir William Walton, Lord David Cecil, W.H. Auden. Charles I made the Deanery his home during the Civil War.

Christ Church is left either by the gate of Canterbury Quad or by the path in Christ Church Meadow leading N from the Broad Walk across Merton Field. Both routes bring us to Merton St. and a group of three colleges: Oriel on the N side (entered from Oriel St. around the corner), Corpus Christi and Merton on the S.

Oriel College (280 undergraduates) was founded as St Mary's College in 1324 by Adam de Brome, Edward II's almoner and rector of St Mary the Virgin, used as the college chapel in the Middle Ages. In 1326 the college was refounded by Edward II and renamed the King's College. Its present name comes from La Oriole, a building on the site acquired in 1329.

The picturesque Front Quad, built between 1619 and 1642, is a good example of 17C Gothic. The *Hall* has a fine hammerbeam roof and, over the porch outside, statues of the Virgin Mary and two kings, perhaps Edward II and James I or Charles I. The *Chapel* has good woodwork. The quad to the left is 18C, with a handsome Palladian *Library* by James Wyatt (1788). St Mary's Quad incorporates the hall and chapel (c 1640) of St Mary Hall, absorbed by Oriel in 1902. The new front in the High St. was built by Basil Champneys (1909–11) from a bequest by Cecil Rhodes, whose statue it bears.

The properties on the *Island Site*, W of the college and linked to it by a tunnel forming a fourth quadrangle, have recently been renovated. Their heart is the 17C tennis court on which Charles I and Prince Rupert are said to have played. Now named the *Harris Building* and converted into student accommodation and lecture rooms, it forms the focal point of an attractive group of buildings, which includes Tackleys Inn, bought by Adam de Brome in 1324 as one of the two original college houses.

MEMBERS: Sir Walter Ralegh, William Prynne, Bishop Butler, William Collins, Gilbert White, Bishop Samuel Wilberforce, Dr Arnold, Mark Pattison, Thomas Hughes, J.A. Froude, Matthew Arnold, A.H. Clough, Cecil Rhodes, Richard Hughes, A.J.P. Taylor. The leaders of the Oxford Movement were fellows: John Keble, John Henry Newman, Edward Pusey and Richard Hurrell Froude.

Corpus Christi College (213 undergraduates) was founded in 1517 by Bishop Richard Foxe.

The gateway, with its oriel window and fan-vaulted roof, and the Front Quad date from the founder's time. The tall sundial with its perpetual calendar was put up in 1581. The attractive little *Hall* has a hammerbeam roof, the *Chapel* a striking E window and an altarpiece of the school of Rubens. The *Library* is one of the most picturesque in Oxford. Beyond, to the SE, is a small quad with cloisters on one side and the *Turner Buildings* (1706–12) on the other. The *Gardens* are small but pretty.

MEMBERS: Nicholas Udall, Reginald Pole, John Jewel, Richard Hooker, Thomas Day, John Keble, Dr Arnold, Sir Henry Newbolt, Robert Bridges, Sir Isaiah Berlin, William Waldegrave, Vikram Seth.

*Merton College (250 undergraduates) is in all essentials the oldest college in Oxford, though both University College and Balliol were endowed a few years earlier. It was founded by Walter de Merton in 1264 as a special training school for the secular as opposed to the monastic clergy. Its organisation was the model for later Oxbridge colleges.

The buildings are among the oldest and most interesting in Oxford. The gateway tower was started in 1416 but not completed until about 1465. Opposite the gate, on the S side of the Front Quad, is the *Hall*, virtually rebuilt by Scott in 1874 but with original 13C ironwork on its door. On the W side, past the old *Treasury* or *Muniment Room* (c 1288), with high-pitched stone roof, is the entrance to the picturesque **Mob Quad* (c 1288–1378). The Decorated **Chapel* (1290–94), with a Perpendicular tower added in 1450, is the oldest in Oxford. It never had a nave, and the 14C and 15C transepts now form an ante-chapel, which contains a fine Decorated piscina, old glass, and the monuments of Sir Henry Savile (d. 1622), Sir Thomas Bodley (d. 1613) by Nicholas Stone and Anthony à Wood (d. 1695). Three arches of the screen designed by Wren are in the crossing. The windows of the choir are filled with glass of c 1300. There are two brasses (c 1400 and 1471) in front of the high altar. The *Library*, in Mob Quad, is perhaps the most interesting medieval library in England. Built in 1373–78, it was the first to store books upright in shelves instead of lying them flat in presses, and it keeps many of its old fittings. In addition to manuscripts, its treasures include Chaucer's Astrolabe. Adjoining rooms display memorabilia of Sir Max Beerbohm.

The *Fellows' Quad* (1608–10) is in the elegant late Gothic style copied at Oriel, Wadham and University Colleges. To the E of the Front Quad is *St Alban's Quad* (rebuilt by Basil Champneys, 1904–10), on the site of St Alban's Hall, founded in the 13C and amalgamated with Merton in 1882.

MEMBERS: Thomas Bradwardine and other 14C philosophers and mathematicians, and John Wyclif. Other notables include Sir Thomas Bodley, Anthony à Wood, Thomas Carew, Sir Richard Steele, Lord Randolph Churchill, George Saintsbury, Sir Max Beerbohm, T.S. Eliot, Louis MacNeice, Robert Byron, Sir Angus Wilson and Sir Lennox Berkeley (born at Boar's Hill). William Harvey was Warden during the Civil War, and Henrietta Maria lodged here while the King was at Christ Church. Philip Massinger attended St Alban's Hall, and Newman was its Vice-Principal.

Oriel St., Magpie Lane, Logic Lane and the E end of Merton St. all join the High St., explored in the next walking tour.

EAST FROM CARFAX. *High St. (the High) leads in a gentle curve and changing vistas to (½m) Magdalen Bridge. The streetscape is usually obscured by traffic and shoppers, and can best be appreciated early on a Sunday morning.

The first points of interest, both on the left, are the covered market and the Mitre, a much altered 17–18C coaching inn. On the opposite corner of Turl St. stands the classical *All Saints' Church* (probably by Dean Aldrich, 1706–08), with a distinctive spire, now used as the library of Lincoln College (visited in the walk N and E from Carfax, below).

Beyond the High St. front of Brasenose, on the same side, is the church of **St Mary the Virgin**, whose Decorated *tower and spire make a familiar Oxford landmark. The tower (open) gives perhaps the best view of the city. Facing the High is an Italianate baroque porch (1637), designed by Nicholas Stone and given by Dr Morgan Owen, Archbishop Laud's chaplain. The image of the Virgin and Child inspired one of the charges against Laud at his trial in 1644. The main entrance is around the corner in Radcliffe Square.

Since at least the 14C St Mary's has been used as the university church, where the University Sermons are preached by 'select preachers' every Sunday and where the Bampton lectures are given. Cranmer, soon to become one of Oxford's Protestant martyrs, publicly repudiated his recantation here in 1556. John Wesley worshipped and preached here, as in the 19C did the leaders of the Oxford Movement. Newman was vicar from 1828 to 1843.

The tower, spire, Brome chapel and Congregation house, all on the N side, date from the early 14C. Otherwise the church was largely rebuilt in the Perpendicular style c 1463–90. The many monuments include: a slab in the choir recording the burial of Amy Robsart (d. 1560); the tomb of Adam de Brome (d. 1328), vicar and founder of Oriel College; and plaques to Dr John Radcliffe and John Aubrey.

Radcliffe Square is worth exploration before returning to the High. Its centrepiece is the *Radcliffe Camera, a Baroque rotunda with a dome rising from an octagonal base, built by James Gibbs (1737–49) to house Dr Radcliffe's science library. It has long been part of the Bodleian.

On the W side of the square is **Brasenose College** (320 undergraduates), founded in 1509 by William Smyth, Bishop of Lincoln, and Sir Richard Sutton. The name probably comes from the brazen knocker (a lion's head) of an older hall on the site, carried off to Stamford in the migration of Oxford students in 1333 and recovered only in 1890. Another derivation is from a supposed 'brasenhus', or brewery, on the site.

The gateway tower leads into the Front Quad, begun in the founder's time but given its third storey in the early 17C. The *Library* and *Chapel* were both built in 1656–66, the latter combining the classical and Gothic. Its plaster fan-tracery ceiling hides the hammerbeam roof brought from the dissolved St Mary's College. There is a pretentious monument to Walter Pater (1839–94) in the ante-chapel. The High St. front is by Sir T.G. Jackson (1886–1909); cleverly inserted W of Jackson's quad are sets of rooms by Powell and Moya (1959–61), the first of their many buildings in Oxford and Cambridge.

MEMBERS: John Foxe, Robert Burton, Elias Ashmole, John Marston, Thomas Traherne, R.H. Barham of the 'Ingoldsby Legends', Walter Pater, Earl Haig, John Buchan, Charles Morgan, John Middleton Murry, Robert Runcie (Archbishop of Canterbury), Sir William Golding, John Mortimer, Lord Scarman.

On the N side of Radcliffe Square stands the *Old Schools Quadrangle, built in 1613–19. Over the doorways are the Latin names of the disciplines formerly studied. The gate tower on the E side, designed and built by men brought from Yorkshire by Sir Henry Savile, is ornamented with columns of the five classical orders and a statue of James I. The building is now part of the **Bodleian Library**, whose exhibition room is in the doorway marked 'Scholas Naturalis Philosophiae'. The only other part open to the public is the former Divinity School, entered through the vestibule, or Proscholium, on the W side of the quadrangle near Le Sueur's statue of the Earl of Pembroke. Its vaulted *roof decorated with over 450 carved bosses is one of the marvels of Oxford, the whole building having been completed, after 60 years of construction, in 1488. Cranmer, Latimer and Ridley were examined here in 1555. The library shop is in the Proscholium. Readers are admitted to the rest of the library by ticket and must be either members of the university or suitably sponsored. Guided tours, which include visits to the university's Convocation House and the glorious Duke Humfrey's Library, are available to members of the public and take place daily in summer.

One of the oldest and most important libraries in the world, the Bodleian was first endowed by Humfrey, Duke of Gloucester (1391–1447), whose collection was dispersed in Edward VI's reign. In 1602 the library was refounded by Sir Thomas Bodley, fellow of Merton and Queen Elizabeth I's Ambassador to the Netherlands. From his collection of 2000 books, the library has grown to more than five and a half million printed books as well as over 148,000 manuscripts, more than a million maps and large collections of music and ephemera, occupying over 90 miles of shelving. It is one of the six copyright libraries entitled to receive a copy of every book published in the UK.

Hertford College, by the NE corner of Radcliffe Square, is visited on the walk N and E from Carfax (below). To reach the main entrance of All Souls College, on the E side of the square, return to the High.

All Souls College was founded in 1438 by Henry Chichele, Archbishop of Canterbury, both as a college of higher theological and legal studies and as a chantry for the souls of those killed in the French wars. It has a Warden and over 60 fellows but no undergraduates, a unique arrangement until the foundation of Nuffield College as a graduate college in 1937.

The fine front and gateway, facing the High, and the front quad are carefully restored 15C work. From the NW corner of the quad a vaulted passage leads to the Perpendicular *Chapel*, with 15C *glass in the ante-chapel, a 15C carved oak roof, an 18C screen and a stone *reredos, restored in 1872–79 after being walled up for over 200 years. The statues are 19C but the painting is original. The *North Quad* is Gothic, by Nicholas Hawksmoor (1715–40). The *Codrington Library* (not open), on its N side, contains 150,000 volumes and many drawings from Wren's office, including some for St Paul's.

MEMBERS: Thomas Linacre, Jeremy Taylor, Sir Christopher Wren, Sir William Blackstone, Max Müller, W.P. Ker, T.E. Lawrence, and other scholars and politicians too numerous to detail.

University College (375 undergraduates) lies a little further down the High, almost opposite All Souls. Though it claims Alfred the Great as founder, its first endowment was William of Durham's bequest in 1249, administered by the university until 1280. The college moved to this site about 1332.

The long curved front, with its oriels, Dutch gables and two gateway towers, is 17C Gothic. The W gateway, with statues of Queen Anne outside and James II inside, leads to the larger *Front Quad* (1634–77). The E gateway, with statues of Queen Mary outside and Dr Radcliffe inside, leads to a smaller quad built in the same style in 1716–19 from a bequest by Dr Radcliffe. In Front Quad is the *Chapel*, remodelled by Scott in 1862 but with 17C panelling, stalls and screens, and glass (1641) by Abraham van Linge. A passage from the NW corner of the quad leads to the *Shelley Memorial*, a domed chamber with a figure of the drowned poet by Onslow Ford (1893). Later additions include the *New Buildings* (1842; Barry), the *Library* (1861; Scott) and, in Logic Lane, the *Goodhart Building* (1960–61; Robert Matthew and Johnson-Marshall).

MEMBERS: Lord Herbert of Cherbury, Dr John Radcliffe, Roger Newidgate (founder of the poetry prize), Sir William Jones, Shelley (sent down after two terms for refusing to admit authorship of 'The Necessity of Atheism'), Prince Felix Youssoupoff (Rasputin's assassin), Clement Attlee, Lord Beveridge (Master), C.S. Lewis, Sir Stephen Spender, Harold Wilson (fellow), Lord Goodman (Master), Sir V.S. Naipaul, Bob Hawke, Sir Stephen Hawking, Bill Clinton.

Beyond University College are the *Examination Schools* (1876–82; Sir T.G. Jackson), now used for lectures as well. By the corner of Queen's Lane, opposite, is the graceful façade of *The Queen's College* (290 undergraduates). It was founded in 1341 by Robert de Egglesfield, chaplain to Philippa, Edward III's wife and the first of several queens to take an interest in the college. The founder provided for a Provost and 12 fellows to represent Our Lord and Apostles, and 70 'poor boys' as disciples, Oxford's first formal arrangement for the education of undergraduates.

The college was mainly rebuilt in the Baroque style between 1682 and 1765, though the identity of its architects is far from clear. The *Front Quad*, separated from the street only by a screen and gatehouse with a cupola, owes something to Nicholas Hawksmoor, though his design was greatly altered in the building. On either side of the passage leading into the *North Quad* are the *Hall* and the *Chapel*, the latter with a decorated ceiling (the painting in the apse is by Sir James Thornhill), a magnificent Baroque screen, and glass by Abraham van Linge. The North Quad, built before the Front Quad with Wren playing a part in the early designs, has the magnificent *Library* on its W side.

MEMBERS: Thomas Middleton, William Wycherley, Edmund Halley, Joseph Addison and William Collins (who both migrated to Magdalen), Jeremy Bentham, Walter Pater, Leopold Stokowski, Sidney Keyes and Lord Florey (Provost).

It is worth following Queen's Lane to **St Edmund Hall** (360 undergraduates), the last survivor of the medieval halls, dating from the 13C. It is dedicated to St Edmund of Abingdon, Archbishop of Canterbury, who taught at Oxford c 1195–1200. Controlled by Queen's College from 1557 to 1937, it achieved full collegiate status in 1957.

Three sides of the charming Front Quad were built in the 16C and 17C; the S side, on the right, was added in 1932–34. The tiny panelled *Chapel* has windows by Morris and Burne-Jones and an altarpiece by Ceri Richards (1958). The former *St Peter in the East*, further up Queen's Lane, is now the college library; the late Norman crypt is open.

MEMBERS: Thomas Hearne, Sir Robin Day, Terry Jones.

Beyond St Edmund Hall, Queen's Lane winds round to join New College Lane, explored in the walking tour N and E from Carfax (below).

The remainder of the walk along the High is dominated by the view of ***Magdalen College** (pronounced 'Maudlen'; 380 undergraduates), one of the most beautiful and spacious colleges. It was founded on the site of a former Hospital of St John in 1458 by William of Waynflete, successively headmaster of Winchester, Provost of Eton, Bishop of Winchester and Lord Chancellor.

The chief feature of the High St. front is the graceful Perpendicular *Tower, built in 1492–1505 (tradition says by Wolsey, then bursar) as the bell tower of the college chapel, though detached from it. Hymns are sung from the top at 06.00 on May morning.

The entrance is by St John's Gateway (1885). To the left are the Victorian Gothic *St Swithun's Buildings* and, beyond them, *Longwall Quad* (1932; Giles Gilbert Scott) and the *New Library*, built in 1851 as a hall for Magdalen College School. Ahead are the *President's Lodgings*, also Victorian, and the *Grammar Hall* (1614), a restored fragment of the vanished Magdalen Hall. Immediately to the right are the open-air pulpit, where a University Sermon is preached on the Sunday after St John the Baptist's Day (24 June), and the narrow entrance to the *Chaplain's Quad*, with remains of St John's Hospital and the blocked-up Pilgrim's Gate into the High.

The buildings on the E side (right) of *St John's Quad* are those planned and largely completed by William of Waynflete. The *Founder's Tower* (not open) is still part of the President's Lodgings. Under the Muniment Tower is the entrance to the *Chapel*, finished before 1483, though its interior was reorganised by Cottingham in 1820. The Lyttleton monument (1634) is by Nicholas Stone. The choir is famous for its singing; visitors are welcome to choral services (18.00 on Monday and Wednesday–Friday, 17.15 on Saturday, 11.30 and 15.15 on Sunday in term). A passage beneath the Muniment Tower leads to the *Cloisters*, with grotesque carvings on the buttresses, dating from the founder's time but heavily restored in the 19C. Stairs at the SE corner lead to the *Hall* (1474), altered but keeping its beautiful panelling, oriel and musicians' gallery above a Jacobean screen; the roof is modern. The *Old Library* (not often open) on the W side contains illuminated manuscripts and Wolsey's copy of the Gospels.

A passage on the N side leads across a wide lawn to the elegant *New Building* (1733). On the left is Magdalen's deer park, the *Grove* (not open). On the right a bridge crosses the Cherwell to a meadow with the *Water Walks*.

MEMBERS: Bishop Richard Foxe, John Colet, Cardinal Wolsey, Cardinal Pole, John Foxe, Sir Thomas Bodley, John Hampden, Joseph Addison and William Collins (both migrants from Queen's), Edward Gibbon (sent down for becoming a Catholic and later contemptuous of academic standards at Magdalen), John Wilson (Christopher North), Charles Reade, Oscar Wilde, Compton Mackenzie, C.S. Lewis, Sir John Betjeman, Henry Green, Geoffrey Household, Gilbert Ryle, Sir Rupert Cross, A.J.P. Taylor, Lord Florey, Lord Denning, Kenneth Baker, Desmond Morris, Peter Brook, Robert Hardy, Dudley Moore, Julian Barnes.

Just beyond the college *Magdalen Bridge*, built by John Gwynn in 1772–79 and widened in 1883, crosses the Cherwell.

Opposite Magdalen is the **Botanic Garden** (open), the oldest in England, founded in 1621, with a gateway by Nicholas Stone. Rose Lane, to the right of the garden, leads into Merton Field and Christ Church Meadow.

Across Magdalen Bridge, immediately to the left, are Magdalen's *Waynflete Building* (1960–61; Booth, Ledeboer and Pinckheard) and the startling *Florey Building* of Queen's College (1968–70; James Stirling). *Stone's Hospital*, an almshouse of 1697–1700, is in St Clement's St. On the right after the bridge are *Magdalen College School* and, on a pleasant riverside site, **St Hilda's College**, founded for women in 1893 and still admitting women only (340 undergraduates). Members include Barbara Castle, Dame Helen Gardner and Barbara Pym. In Iffley Rd is *Greyfriars*, a permanent private hall for Franciscan students.

NORTH AND EAST FROM CARFAX. Cornmarket St. is one of Oxford's busiest shopping streets. The Saxon tower of *St Michael's Church*, on the right, was once part of the city's defences. The four figures in the E windows are the oldest glass in Oxford (c 1290). William Morris married Jane Burden here in 1859.

In St Michael's St., to the left, are the mid Victorian buildings of the *Oxford Union Society*, founded as a social and debating club in 1823. The frescoes painted by Rossetti, Morris and other Pre-Raphaelites in 1857 have since faded.

The handsome *Broad St. leads right. On the opposite side stands **Balliol College** (350 undergraduates), founded before 1266 by John de Balliol, father of the Scottish king of the same name, as a penance for insulting the Bishop of Durham. The first statutes were given by his widow, Dervorguilla, in 1282. The college achieved its academic reputation under a series of masters of whom Benjamin Jowett (1817–93) was the most famous.

The college was virtually rebuilt in the 19C by Alfred Waterhouse (Broad St. front and E side of the Front Quad, and the Hall in Garden Quad, 1867–77), William Butterfield (Chapel, 1856–57) and Anthony Salvin (part of the W side of Garden Quad, 1852–53). In the Front Quad, the *Library* (originally the hall) is in fact 15C but was altered beyond recognition by Wyatt in the 1790s. The interior of Butterfield's *Chapel* has been toned down in the 20C. Some Anglo-Flemish glass of 1529 has been reset in the E window; other windows have glass of 1637 by Abraham van Linge. In the NW corner of the Front Quad a passage leads, past ancient wooden doors which originally stood at the Broad St. entrance, to Garden Quad. Here Waterhouse's *Hall* sits uneasily between two 1960s additions (by Oxford Architects Partnership).

MEMBERS: John Wyclif (Master in 1364), John Evelyn, Adam Smith, Robert Southey, J.G. Lockhart, Cardinal Manning, both Archbishops Temple (father and son), A.P. Stanley, Matthew Arnold, A.H. Clough, Algernon Swinburne (persuaded to leave in 1860), T.H. Green, Gerard Manley Hopkins, Andrew Lang, Arnold Toynbee, A.C. Bradley, Lord Curzon, Lord Asquith, Hilaire Belloc, Monsignor Ronald Knox, King Olav of Norway, Lord Beveridge, Harold Macmillan, Julian Huxley, Aldous Huxley, Graham Greene, L.P. Hartley, Anthony Powell, Neville Shute, Edward Heath, Denis Healey, Lord Jenkins of Hillhead, John Schlesinger.

The *Oxford Story*, on the opposite side of Broad St., is an exhibition which seeks to bring the history of the university to life with the same gimmicks of presentation used by the Jorvik Viking Centre in York.

Trinity College (280 undergraduates), E of Balliol, lies some way back from Broad St. It was founded in 1555 by Sir Thomas Pope, an Oxfordshire landowner, but incorporates part of Durham College, founded c 1286 for students from the Benedictine monasteries at Durham and elsewhere in the North. The varied yet harmonious buildings and the spacious grounds are among Oxford's most attractive.

The large and irregular Front Quad is entered through iron gates of 1737. To the right, facing Broad St., are some old cottages converted into college rooms and, beyond them, *Kettell Hall*, built as a private house by President Kettell in 1618–20. The E range and the *President's Lodgings* are by Sir T.G. Jackson (1883–87). The main gateway was built by President Bathurst in 1691–94. He was also responsible for the *Chapel, to the right, with a superb baroque interior with Victorian glass. The carved lime and juniper wood reredos may be by Grinling Gibbons. The E range of *Durham Quad*, including the *Old Library* (not open), is a 15C fragment of Durham College. The *Hall*, on the W side, is a modest building of 1618–20, redecorated with marbled paintwork in 1988. In *Garden Quad*, beyond, the N range is a much-altered building by Wren (1665–68); the E side opens out into pleasant gardens. On their S side, also reached by the gate between Jackson's buildings in the NE corner of the Front Quad, are 20C additions: the neo-classical *War Memorial Library* (1928; J. Osborne Smith) and *Cumberbatch*

Quad (1964–68; Maguire and Murray), over the underground rooms of Blackwell's bookshop.

MEMBERS: Lord Baltimore (founder of Maryland), Henry Ireton, John Aubrey, Sir John Denham, William Pitt the elder, Lord North, Walter Savage Landor (sent down in 1793), Cardinal Newman, Sir Richard Burton, Sir Arthur Quiller-Couch, James Elroy Flecker, Laurence Binyon, Monsignor Ronald Knox, Lord Goddard, Lord Clark, Terence Rattigan, Anthony Crosland, Jeremy Thorpe.

Turl St. (the Turl) leads from the S side of Broad St. opposite Trinity. On the left stands **Exeter College** (280 undergraduates), founded by Walter de Stapeldon in 1314 and refounded by Sir William Petre in 1566.

The college has been much rebuilt. The Turl St. front and main quad are essentially 17–18C but owe their present look to 19C alterations. The *Hall*, on the S of the quad, dates from 1618 and originally faced a chapel of the same date, demolished to make way for the inappropriate *Chapel* (1857) by Sir Gilbert Scott. It contains a tapestry by William Morris and Edward Burne-Jones, who first met as undergraduates here. *Palmer's Tower* (1432), facing the E end of the chapel, is the oldest part of the college. From here passages lead right to the *Library* (1856; Scott) and pleasant garden, and left into the small *Margary Quad*, with the *Thomas Wood Building* (1964; Brett and Pollen) on its W side.

MEMBERS: John Ford, the first Earl of Shaftesbury, Sir Charles Lyell, J.A. Froude, F.D. Maurice, William Morris, Edward Burne-Jones, Sir Hubert Parry, J.R.R. Tolkien, Richard Burton, Robert Robinson, Alan Bennett, Imogen Stubbs.

On the opposite side of the Turl is **Jesus College** (300 undergraduates), the first post-Reformation Oxford college, founded in 1571, nominally by Elizabeth I but really by Hugh Price, Treasurer of St David's. For many years it had a close connection with Wales.

The oldest part is the Turl St. front, rebuilt in the Perpendicular style in 1856 by Buckler, who also restored the Market St. front. The S side of the Front Quad and the N side, with the Principal's house and the chapel, were built by Sir Eubule Thelwall, Principal in 1621–30. The *Chapel*, extended in 1636, has a barrel-vaulted roof, late 17C screen and early 17C pulpit; other features date from G.E. Street's restoration in 1864. The *Hall* (c 1617), opposite the main entrance, has a carved Jacobean screen and portraits of Elizabeth I (by Nicholas Hilliard), Charles I (by Van Dyck), Charles II (attributed to Lely) and the architect John Nash (by Lawrence). The *Senior Common Room* (not open) has a portrait of Elizabeth I attributed to Zucchero and one of Canon Jenkins by Holman Hunt. The charming inner quadrangle was mainly the work of Sir Leoline Jenkins, Principal in 1661–73. The *Library* has 17C fittings. A passage on the N side leads to 20C additions, including a block by J. Fryman (1971).

MEMBERS: Lancelot Andrewes, Richard (Beau) Nash, J.R. Green, Sir John Rhys, T.E. Lawrence, Harold Wilson, Magnus Magnusson.

Further down the Turl, also on the left, is **Lincoln College** (260 undergraduates), one of the best preserved of the late medieval colleges. It was founded in 1427 by Bishop Fleming of Lincoln for training clergy to refute the Wycliffite or Lollard heresy.

The attractive N quadrangle keeps its 15C appearance. The *Hall* (1437) has its original 15C timbers and smoke louvre, and a screen and wainscoting of 1696–1700. On the right are the rooms in which John Wesley, a fellow of the college, is said to have lived and members of the Holy Club or Methodists first met (open on application to the porter). The S quadrangle (1608–31) contains the *Chapel* built by Bishop Williams of Lincoln (1629–31), with painted glass attributed to Bernard van Linge, cedar wainscoting and carved bench ends. *All Saints' Church*, at the corner of the Turl and the High, passed in the walk E from Carfax (above), was part of the college's original endowment and is now its library.

MEMBERS: Bishop Sanderson of Lincoln, Sir William Davenant, Dr John Radcliffe, John Wesley, Mark Pattison, Edward Thomas, Robert Speaight, Sir Osbert Lancaster, Lord Florey, Sir John Beazley, Egon Wellesz, Dr Seuss (Theodore Geisel), John le Carré (David Cornwell), Sir Peter Parker.

Broad St. continues E. It ends on the left with the inexpressive block of the *New Bodleian*, begun by Sir Giles Gilbert Scott in 1935, but on the right there is a handsome group of university buildings. The lovely *Old Ashmolean Museum* (open), the first public museum in the world, was built in 1678–83 for Elias Ashmole's collection of natural curiosities (see the Ashmolean, on the walk N and W from Carfax, below). It is now the *Museum of the History of Science*, with fine scientific instruments. The *Sheldonian Theatre* (open), Wren's first work, was built in 1663–69 at the expense of Archbishop Sheldon as a venue for university occasions. Degree-giving ceremonies are held here. The plan of the building, semi-circular in front and rectangular behind, imitates the Theatre of Marcellus in Rome. It is partly surrounded by railings whose stone plinths carry 13 busts, renewed in 1972. The octagonal cupola, a reconstruction of 1832 which is larger than Wren's original one, gives a famous view over the city. The ceiling inside has an allegorical painting by Robert Streeter (1669). Beyond the Sheldonian is the *Clarendon Building*, designed by Hawksmoor under Vanbrugh's influence in 1713, partly from the profits of Clarendon's 'History of the Great Rebellion'. It used to house the Clarendon Press but is now part of the Bodleian.

A short way along Parks Rd, N from the end of Broad St., is **Wadham College** (360 undergraduates), facing the gardens of Trinity. It was founded by Nicholas Wadham of Somerset and built in 1610–13 on the site of an Augustinian friary by his widow Dorothy.

The well-preserved buildings are a fine example of Jacobean Gothic. Between the hall and chapel, on the E side, is a porch with statues of Nicholas and Dorothy Wadham. The *Chapel*, altered inside in the 19C, has a Jacobean screen and an E window by Bernard van Linge (1622). The *Hall* has a hammerbeam roof, Jacobean screen and large portrait collection. The secluded *Gardens* give a lovely view of the garden front. The S quadrangle has a pleasant copper-roofed block (1954; Henry Goddard) and, E of the Foundation Building, the imposing *Library* (1977; Gillespie, Kidd and Coia). The *Bowra Building* (by Richard MacCormac) was opened in 1992.

MEMBERS: Admiral Blake, John Wilmot (Earl of Rochester), Sir Charles Sedley, Sir Christopher Wren, Francis Kilvert, Sir T.G. Jackson, Lord Birkenhead, Sir Thomas Beecham, Maurice Bowra (Warden), C. Day-Lewis, Rex Warner, Michael Foot, Melvyn Bragg, Alan Coren.

Parks Rd returns to the junction with Broad St. The handsome Holywell St., on the left, is the starting-point for a tour of the Eastern Outskirts (below). Catte St. heads S, quickly coming to **Hertford College** (350 undergraduates), with its bridge spanning New College Lane to link the old and new buildings. It began as Hart Hall, founded in 1282, afterwards Hertford College (1740–1805) but absorbed by Magdalen Hall in 1822. On the dissolution of Magdalen Hall in 1874, the college was refounded through the bequest of Thomas Charles Baring, the banker.

The oldest part of the main quad is the NE corner, where the *Old Hall* dates from the late 16C. The E range, containing the *Old Library* and *Senior Common Room*, was built early in the 17C, the present *Library* (formerly the chapel) in the 18C. Most of the rest of the college is the work of Sir T.G. Jackson, including the *Hall* and staircase (1877), the present *Chapel* (1910), the bridge (1913) and the *Octagon* (1923–26). *Holywell Quad* was completed between 1976 and 1981.

MEMBERS of Hart Hall: John Donne, John Selden, Henry Pelham. Of the original Hertford College: Charles James Fox. Of Magdalen Hall: William Tyndale, Thomas Hobbes, Lord Clarendon, Sir Matthew Hale, Sir Henry Vane and Dr John Wilkins. Of the refounded Hertford College: W.R. Inge, Evelyn Waugh.

The handsome buildings of Radcliffe Square are visited in the walk E from Carfax (above).

New College Lane goes on to ***New College** (410 undergraduates), founded in 1379 by William of Wykeham, also founder of Winchester College. Behind the modest entrance lies one of Oxford's grandest colleges; with superb Perpendicular buildings (completed c 1386).

The intimate style of the Front Quad was lost by the addition of a third storey (1674) and the modernisation of its windows (1721). The noble *Chapel*, on the N, was restored in 1877 by Sir Gilbert Scott, who introduced a hammerbeam roof. The ante-chapel has original 14C *glass, except for the insipid W window painted by Thomas Jarvis to the designs of Sir Joshua Reynolds (1778), a fine series of 23 brasses dating from 1403 to 1619, and Epstein's statue of Lazarus (1951). In the chapel itself the reconstructed stalls retain their old arm rests and misericords, including one of the founder (first stall on the S side). On the N side of the altar are the founder's *crozier and a painting of St James by El Greco. The choral services rival those at Magdalen. The *Hall*, adjoining the chapel, is the oldest and one of the finest in Oxford, with early 16C linenfold panelling and a roof by Scott (1865).

W of the chapel are the detached *Bell Tower* and the quiet *Cloisters*, with remarkable trussed rafters, memorial tablets and ten statues from the steeple of St Mary the Virgin.

A passage in the E side of the quad, under the *Founder's Library* (1778; Wyatt), leads to the handsome *Garden Quad* of 1682–1708, enclosed on its E side by a lovely wrought-iron screen (1711). The chief feature of the spacious *Gardens* is a well-preserved remnant of the old city wall, dating from Henry III's time.

The buildings facing Holywell St. to the N are by Scott (1872) and Basil Champneys (1896 and 1885). The *Sacher Building* (1961–62; David Roberts) faces E to Longwall St.

MEMBERS: Henry Chichele, William of Waynflete, William Grocyn, Sir Henry Wotton, Bishop Ken, James Woodforde, Sydney Smith, Augustus Hare, W.A. Spooner, Lionel Johnson, John Galsworthy, A.P. Herbert (last MP for the university, 1935–50), Maurice Bowra, Lord David Cecil, Hugh Gaitskell, George Woodcock, E.F. Schumacher, Len Murray, Brian Johnston, Tony Benn, John Fowles.

From the end of this walk the High (on the walk E from Carfax, above) can be joined via New College Lane and Queen's Lane, passing St Edmund Hall, or via Catte St., running S from the head of New College Lane through Radcliffe Square, or via Longwall St.

NORTH FROM CARFAX. This begins by following the previous walk up Cornmarket St. but, instead of turning right into Broad St., continues straight ahead into Magdalen St. and past the church of St Mary Magdalen, largely rebuilt by Scott. He was also responsible for the prominent *Martyrs' Memorial* (1841) outside, modelled on the Eleanor Crosses, with statues of Cranmer, Ridley and Latimer, burned at the stake in 1556 in nearby Broad St.

The memorial stands at the beginning of the broad, tree-lined thoroughfare called St Giles, with the side of Balliol College on the right. At the corner of Beaumont St., on the left, is a Greek Revival building by C.R. Cockerell (1841–45). Its E wing, facing St Giles, is occupied by the *Taylor Institution* (the 'Taylorian'), founded for the study of modern languages from the bequest of Sir Robert Taylor (d. 1788).

The central range and W wing house the ¡**Ashmolean Museum**, with the university's art and archaeological collections.

Their nucleus was 'Tradescant's Ark', collections of rarities formed by John Tradescant the Elder (d. 1638) and his son, and settled on Elias Ashmole. The Old Ashmolean on Broad St. was built to receive them. When they outgrew this building, the natural curiosities were transferred to the University Museum and the ethnographical exhibits to the Pitt-Rivers Museum (both visited later on this walk) and the remainder housed here.

Ground floor. The bookshop is on the right of the entrance and the information desk is in the Randolph Gallery (1) on the left. The Randolph Gallery contains classical sculptures, Greek, Hellenistic and Roman originals, and Roman copies, mainly from the Arundel or Pomfret marbles, including a torso of c 480–60 BC, a pedimental sculpture embodying two linear measures (Aegean of the 5C BC), and the fragment of a frieze of an Athenian temple. In the showcases are fine temporary displays of individual aspects of archaeology. To the W are: the Petrie Room (6) containing Egyptian predynastic material, mainly from Sir Flinders Petrie's excavations; the Chester Room (7), with scarabs, beads, seals, papyri, etc.; and the Egyptian Dynastic Gallery (8), which includes pottery, faience, jewellery, bronzes and glass, mostly from excavated sites. The Griffith Gallery of Egyptian sculpture (9) contains: the *shrine of Taharqa from Kawa (7C BC) decorated in bas-relief; finds from the Oxford excavations in Nubia; reliefs, stelae and sculpture; mummy cases and funerary furnishings; wall paintings and fragmentary reliefs from Tell el-Amarna; and Coptic textiles. From here a passage leads to the Marshall Room (10), with coloured Worcester porcelain (1750–83), and displays of European porcelain (12).

N of the Randolph Gallery, the Medieval Room (4) contains: the *Alfred Jewel (9C AD; cf. North Petherton, Route 23), perhaps the head of an 'aestel', or pointer, for following the lines of illuminated manuscripts; the similar Minster Lovell Jewel; Viking antiquities; local pottery; brooches; medieval tiles; the Odda Stone, the foundation stone (1056) of the Saxon chapel at Deerhurst (Route 55); and objects of historical

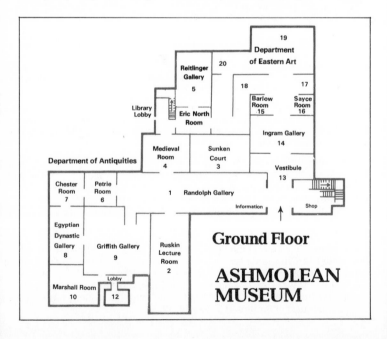

interest. To the right of the Medieval Room is the Sunken Court (3; open to students on request) containing the reserve collection of Greek vases.

Opposite the main entrance is the *Department of Eastern Art. The vestibule (13) has examples of Gandhara sculpture and other early Asian cultures to one side and early Chinese bronzes to the other. The Ingram Gallery (14) of Chinese ceramics (400 BC–14C AD) contains also pottery tomb figures (AD 618–906), a Song gilt bronze Bodhisattva and 16C cast-iron heads. The following rooms to right and left (15 and 16) show 14–20C Chinese porcelains and Chinese decorative arts. A large seated polychromed wooden Buddha dominates the end of the gallery. The room beyond (19) is devoted mainly to Japanese ceramics and other decorative arts. The Screen Gallery (20) houses Japanese fine arts and leads through a display of Indian and South Asian decorative arts to the Tibetan Room (21). On the left are stone, metal and terracotta works from India and South Asia. To the right is the Eric North Room (23), where exhibitions are usually changed monthly. The Reitlinger Gallery (24), connecting with both the Eric North Room and the Screen Gallery, displays the arts of Islam.

First floor. Beyond the small Founder's Room (35), with portraits of Elias Ashmole and his contemporaries, steps lead down to the Department of Antiquities, the many superb finds arranged for expert study rather than aesthetic appreciation. The Tradescant Room (25) has objects from the original 17C collections, and historical relics such as Guy Fawkes's lantern, Bradshaw's hat, Powhatan's mantle, etc. Displayed in the John Evans Room (27) are objects of the European Neolithic, Bronze and Iron Ages, including gold ornaments, fine collections of bronze implements, Celtic art, and a large alcove of Italian and Etruscan antiquities. The *Cretan collection in the Arthur Evans Room (28), principally from the excavations of Sir Arthur Evans at Knossos, is of special importance, and includes Minoan pottery, seals, Linear B tablets, swords, jewellery and finds from the Dictaean Cave. Fine Cycladic marble figurines, lead boat models and finds from excavations at Phylakopi on Melos are also displayed here. Beyond is the Myres Room (29) of Cypriot antiquities, with pottery, jewellery, sculpture, etc. To the right is the Drapers' Gallery (30), exhibiting material from the pre-Islamic Near East, notably finds from Jericho and Jerusalem, and 'Luristan Bronzes'. To the left the

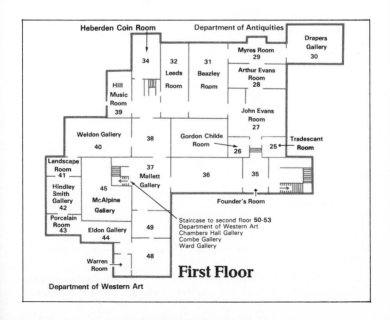

First Floor

Beazley Room (31) is devoted to Greek antiquities, including silver, bronzes, terracottas, gems, jewellery and Geometric, Orientalising and Black-and-Red figure pottery. The Leeds Room (32) houses finds from the Roman Empire and from Europe during the Dark Ages, with particular reference to Britain. A staircase descends to the Byzantine lobby (5). The Heberden Coin Room (34) contains rich collections of Greek, Roman, Oriental, medieval European coins and medals from all periods. (Students may consult the main part of the collection by appointment only.) Nearby is the Hill Music Room (39), which contains 16–18C Italian and English stringed instruments, including 'Le Messie' by Stradivarius.

This room is part of the Department of Western Art, which occupies the rest of the upper floors. Beyond the Founder's Room (see above) is the long gallery (36), containing many of the Fortnum collection of bronzes, as well as 13–16C Italian *paintings. They include two of the most famous Florentine paintings in this country, 'The Hunt in a Forest' by Uccello and 'The Forest Fire' by Piero di Cosimo, and major works by Giovanni di Paolo, Orcagna, Pintoricchio, Lorenzo di Credi, Filippo Lippi, Crivelli, Bronzino, Giovanni Bellini, Veronese, Giorgione, Tintoretto and Jacopo Bassano.

At the end is the Mallett Gallery (37) with tapestries, sculpture, Gainsborough's 'Descent from the Cross' and drawings by Michelangelo and Raphael. The Dutch Room (38) has works by 17C Dutch and Flemish painters, including Rubens, Van Dyck, Salomon van Ruysdael and Jacob van Ruisdael, Koninck, Drost and Van Goyen. The Weldon Gallery (40) is devoted mainly to 17C–early 18C Italian art, though several other schools are also represented, together with Baroque sculpture in silver, bronze and marble. Of the paintings, 'The Deposition' by Van Dyck, 'The Judgement of Hercules' by Paolo de Matteis, 'The Exposition of Moses' by Nicolas Poussin and 'The Glorification of Germanicus' by Rubens are outstanding. The adjoining room (41) brings together landscape work by Gaspard Poussin, Claude Lorrain, Corot, Richard Wilson and Constable.

The Hindley-Smith Gallery (42) displays French 19–20C painting and sculpture. Camille Pissarro is particularly well represented, and there are works by Toulouse-Lautrec, Van Gogh, Monet, Manet, Renoir, Cézanne, Bonnard, Rodin, Matisse and Picasso. The adjoining room (43) contains 20C painting. Beyond this is the Eldon Gallery (44), where a changing selection from the department's rich collection of drawings, watercolours and prints, and sometimes loan exhibitions, are displayed. Approached through the Eldon Gallery is the McAlpine Gallery (45), devoted to temporary exhibitions. A vestibule (46) at the far end of the Eldon Gallery, containing drawings by the great school of Russian stage design, gives access to the Fine Art Library (ticket holders only), the Print Room (open on application) and the small Warren Room (47) with English Delft ware.

The Farrer Gallery (48) contains one of the country's principal collections of Stuart and early Georgian silver, including pieces by Huguenot craftsmen working in London c 1705–50 (Lamerie, Platel and the Courtaulds); also examples of Italian sculpture, including works by the Della Robbia, and Gainsborough's portrait of John Drummond. The Fortnum Gallery (49) brings together Renaissance bronzes, Italian majolica and finger rings. Among the smaller works of art in these two galleries are ivories, plaquettes and Limoges enamels.

The Fortnum Gallery leads back into the Mallett Gallery (37). On the landing (50) is Dutch and English glass.

The **second floor** begins with the Chambers Hall Gallery (51) devoted to 18C paintings and sculpture, including works by Tiepolo, Guardi, Canaletto, Batoni, Panini, Reynolds, Gainsborough, Hogarth and Roubiliac. The collection of 19–20C British art in the Combe Gallery (52) includes work by Samuel Palmer and the Pre-Raphaelites, including Rossetti, Holman Hunt, Millais and Arthur Hughes. The Ward Gallery (53) has Dutch 17–18C paintings of flowers and still life, together with Dutch earthenware and glassware.

The Cast Gallery lies to the N of the museum, approached from St John's St. It contains over 250 casts of Greek and Graeco-Roman statuary, arranged in historical sequence.

The dignified Georgian Beaumont St. leads W, past the *Playhouse* (1938; Sir Edward Maufe). At the end is **Worcester College** (320 undergraduates),

St John's Garden Quad, Oxford

once known from its remoteness as 'Botany Bay'. It was founded in 1714 by Sir Thomas Cookes, but the site had been occupied first by Gloucester College (founded in 1283), the general house of studies for English Benedictines, and after the Reformation by Gloucester Hall.

The main buildings (1746–91) are neo-classical. The *Chapel*, originally by Wyatt, was redecorated—and made very dark—by Burges in 1866 with paintings and mosaics recalling his work at Cardiff Castle. On the left side of the quadrangle is a row of five small *monastic houses, relics of Gloucester College, with the arms of Benedictine abbeys over the doorways. The large and beautiful *Gardens contain a lake. On the S side are the *Nuffield Building* (1931), the *Wolfson Building* (1971; Peter Bosanquet), the *Casson Building* (1961; Sir Hugh Casson) and the *Linbury Building* (1990; Robert Maguire). The *Sainsbury Building* (1981; Richard MacCormac) is to the N.

MEMBERS of Gloucester College: Thomas Walsingham. Of Gloucester Hall: Richard Lovelace, Sir Kenelm Digby. Of Worcester College: Thomas De Quincey, Lord Sainsbury of Preston Candover, Richard Adams, Rupert Murdoch.

Along Walton St. beyond Worcester College is *Ruskin College*, founded in 1899 by Walter Vrooman and Charles Beard, American admirers of John Ruskin, for working men to study history, sociology and economics. It is not officially connected with the university. Further N are the buildings of the *Oxford University Press*.

For Nuffield College and other sites S of Worcester College, see Western Outskirts below.

Opposite the Taylorian, back on St Giles, is **St John's College** (350 undergraduates), founded in 1555 by Sir Thomas White, a Reading clothier and Lord Mayor of London, on the site of the old Cistercian college of St Bernard, which Archbishop Chichele had founded in 1437.

The Front Quad is the oldest part, being on three of its sides the remains of St Bernard's College, with a third storey added in the 17C. Over the gateway are statues of St Bernard, Chichele and White, with a statue of John the Baptist by Eric Gill (1936) on the inner side. The *Chapel* and *Hall*, on the left, are both 16C but much altered, the chapel in the 19C and the hall in the 18C. A handsome doorway and passage opposite the main entrance lead into *Canterbury Quad*, begun in 1596–97 but completed by Archbishop Laud in 1631–36. His elegant colonnades and Baroque decoration make an interesting contrast with the traditional Oxford Jacobean-Gothic style elsewhere in the quad. The bronze statues of Charles I and Henrietta Maria on the gate towers are by Le Sueur. The *Old Library* (open by written appointment only) has a portrait of Charles I, partly composed of minutely written psalms, and memorabilia of Laud.

To the S (right) of the Front Quad is *Dolphin Quad*, partly 18C and partly by Sir Edward Maufe (1948). In the N quadrangle, left of the Front Quad, the most striking building is the bold series of interlocking polygons (1958–60; Michael Powers and the Architects Co-Partnership). The NE corner of the college houses more new architecture: the *Sir Thomas White Building* (1976; Sir Philip Dowson and Arup Associates) and the *Garden Quad* (1993; Richard MacCormack and MacCormack, Jameson Prichard). The *Gardens*, laid out in the 18C, are among the best in Oxford.

MEMBERS: Edmund Campion, Archbishop Laud, Archbishop Juxon, James Shirley, A.E. Housman, Gilbert Murray, Sir Tyrone Guthrie, Robert Graves, Philip Larkin, Sir Kingsley Amis.

Opposite St John's College, N along St Giles, are *Blackfriars*, established in the 1920s for Dominican monks studying in Oxford, and *Pusey House*, a theological centre named after the Tractarian leader, with a chapel and library. Since 1981 it has also been the headquarters of **St Cross College**, a graduate college founded in 1965. In Pusey St. is *Regent's Park College*, a permanent private hall of the university and training centre for Baptist clergy. Opposite *St Benet's Hall*, another permanent private hall, stands *Queen Elizabeth House*, a 17C building used as a centre for Commonwealth studies. St Giles ends with *St Giles's Church*, mostly 12C and 13C, isolated in the fork of Woodstock Rd and Banbury Rd. These are explored in Northern Outskirts, below.

Little Clarendon St., on the left, leads to a large complex of university and faculty buildings.

The present tour heads right on Keble Rd, with science faculty buildings on the left, and around the corner into Parks Rd, where Keble College and the University Museum face each other.

Keble College (390 undergraduates) opened in 1870 as a memorial to the Tractarian leader John Keble (1792–1866) and to provide an Oxford education for 'gentlemen of slender means'. From the start, William Butterfield's *buildings* (1868–82) provoked controversy by their tense, angular shapes and bold use of polychromatic brick ('streaky bacon'); they still have the power to call forth widely differing reactions.

The vast *Chapel*, dominating the main quad, has a splendid interior. A small sidechapel houses Holman Hunt's 'The Light of the World'. The *Hall*, the longest in Oxford, has George Richmond's portrait of Keble among its paintings. The *Library* has illuminated medieval manuscripts, incunabula, and early printed books as well as Keble and Newman letters.

The **University Museum**, opposite, houses the natural science collections of the university, including some impressive prehistoric skeletons. The 'building was designed in 1855 by Benjamin Woodward with the active participation of Ruskin. Its cathedral-like interior of iron and glass is rich with decorative detail. Behind it is the *Pitt-Rivers Museum of Ethnology and Pre-History*, with exhibits from around the world, including those collected by Captain Cook.

The *University Science Area*, with a medley of 19–20C buildings, extends down South Parks Rd to the University Parks (see Eastern Outskirts, below).

Parks Rd goes N round the edge of the University Parks towards Lady Margaret Hall (see North-Eastern Outskirts, below). To the S, it passes Wadham College and joins Broad St., on the walk N and E from Carfax (above).

WESTERN OUTSKIRTS. Queen St. leads W from Carfax, away from the older colleges. Near the entrance to the large new Westgate shopping centre on the left, New Inn Hall St. leads right to **St Peter's College** (280 undergraduates), founded as a private hall in 1928 and granted full collegiate status in 1961. It incorporates a much-altered fragment of New Inn Hall, one of the oldest medieval halls. Its chapel is the church of *St Peter-le-Bailey* (1874; Basil Champneys), with an E window by John Hayward (1964). Opposite St Peter's is the old gateway of St Mary's Hall, an Augustinian house dissolved by Elizabeth I. Erasmus prepared his edition of the Greek Testament here in 1498. The site is now occupied by *Frewin Hall*, belonging to Brasenose College.

New Rd continues W from the shopping centre and the end of Queen St. On its right stands **Nuffield College**, founded in 1937 by Lord Nuffield (William Robert Morris), the car manufacturer, for graduate studies and research. It has some 38 resident fellows and about 60 students working for higher degrees. The buildings (by Austen Harrison, with Thomas Barnes and Piers Hubbard) follow the founder's preference for a traditional Cotswold style. The Chapel was planned with the help of John Piper, who also designed the altar and (with Patrick Reyntiens) the stained-glass windows. Across the road from Nuffield College, the County Hall, Assize Court and prison occupy the site of the Norman and medieval *Castle*, claimed as the birthplace of Richard I in 1157.

The area S and W of New Rd and the castle was once the site of several religious houses: Osney Abbey, Rewley Abbey, and the Franciscan house to which the medieval philosopher Roger Bacon belonged.

Worcester St. leads N from New Rd to Worcester College (see the walk N from the city centre, above).

Park End St. leads W from the end of New Rd to (¼m) the railway station.

EASTERN OUTSKIRTS. A tour starts at the E end of Broad St., on the walk N and E from Carfax (above). The old and dignified Holywell St. runs E, past (right) Bath Place and a back entrance to New College, and (left) the *Old Music Room* of 1748, the first room in Europe to be built solely for musical purposes.

On Mansfield Rd, also to the left, is *Manchester College*, a Unitarian training college which began at Manchester in 1786 and moved to Oxford in 1888. The buildings (1891–93; T. Worthington) are Gothic Revival; the chapel has windows by Morris and Burne-Jones. Beyond is *Mansfield College*, founded in Birmingham in 1838 as a Congregationalist training college but now a permanent private hall of the university. Its Gothic Revival buildings are by Basil Champneys (1887–89). Mansfield Rd ends at South Parks Rd, met again near the end of this tour.

Holywell St. continues E to meet Longwall St., running right to the High, and St Cross Rd, which is followed left. On the right is the church of *St Cross*, with a 12C chancel arch and 13C tower, and *Holywell Manor*, a much altered 15C building now used as a graduate centre by Balliol and St Anne's. The extension of Balliol opposite is named after its architect, Sir Leslie Martin, who also designed the *English Faculty*,

Bodleian Law Library and *Institute of Statistics* (1964) at the fork of St Cross Rd and Manor Rd.

Manor Rd heads right and crosses the Cherwell to reach **St Catherine's College** (410 undergraduates), founded in 1868 as a society for non-collegiate students and raised to collegiate status in 1963. Its buildings, gardens and (notably) furnishings were designed by the Danish architect Arne Jacobsen (1960–64). A.A. Milne and Edward Thomas were members of the earlier society.

St Cross Rd turns right from Manor Rd and continues between playing fields to join South Parks Rd. On the left-hand corner is the huge *Zoology and Psychology Building* in stilted concrete (1965–70; Sir Leslie Martin). Beyond are the University Science Area, the University Museum and Keble College (on the walk N from Carfax, above). On the right-hand corner is **Linacre College**, founded as a graduate society in 1926 and raised to the status of graduate college in 1965. Ahead, to the N, are the *University Parks*, with playing fields (including the university cricket ground) and a network of pleasant footpaths. To the right is an attractive walk along the Cherwell, and from the SE corner a footpath leads between two branches of the river to join (c 1m) the Marston Rd.

NORTH-EASTERN OUTSKIRTS. **Lady Margaret Hall** is beautifully situated on the N side of the University Parks. It can be reached by footpath through the Parks; alternative approaches take Parks Rd and Norham Gardens from Keble College (on walk N from Carfax, above) or Banbury Rd (Northern Outskirts, below). The first place of higher education for women in Oxford, it was founded for Anglican students in 1878 and achieved full collegiate status in 1960. It now admits men as well (340 undergraduates). Its main buildings—by Basil Champneys (1881–83), Reginald Blomfield (1896–1915) and Raymond Erith (1961)—make a harmonious neo-Georgian group. The Chapel (1931; Sir Giles Gilbert Scott) has a painting of the flagellation of Christ attributed to Taddeo Gaddi and a triptych by Burne-Jones (c 1863). The gardens stretch down to the Cherwell. Members include Barbara Hammond, Dame C.V. Wedgwood, Georgiana Battiscombe, Lady Antonia Fraser.

Also by the Cherwell, N of Lady Margaret Hall, is **Wolfson College**. It can be reached by taking Dragon School Lane from Lady Margaret Hall, or by taking Bardwell Rd from Banbury Rd (Northern Outskirts, below). Starting as a graduate society, Iffley College, in 1965, it grew into a graduate college the following year with the help of grants from the Wolfson and Ford Foundations. The first President was Sir Isaiah Berlin. The handsome white and grey concrete buildings are by Powell and Moya (1971–74).

NORTHERN OUTSKIRTS. The start is the N end of St Giles (on the walk N from Carfax, above), where Woodstock Rd and Banbury Rd fork.

On the left-hand side of Woodstock Rd is **Somerville College**, a college for women only (350 undergraduates) founded in 1879 as a non-denominational alternative to the Anglican Lady Margaret Hall. The original building, Walton House, dates from 1826; subsequent buildings are ranged around a large central quadrangle. The main entrance is through the Darbishire Quad (1932). Members include Vera Brittain, Rose Macaulay, Dorothy L. Sayers, Margaret Kennedy, Dorothy Hodgkin, Dame Janet Vaughan, Winifred Holtby, Indira Gandhi, Marghanita Laski, Margaret Thatcher, Shirley Williams, Iris Murdoch.

Immediately N of Somerville is the *Radcliffe Infirmary*, a teaching hospital founded in 1770 from the bequest of Dr John Radcliffe. Its original building is by Henry Keene. Beyond lies another of the doctor's bequests, the lovely *Radcliffe Observatory* (open by appointment), built by James Wyatt and Henry Keene in 1772–94. Since 1979 it has been the centrepiece of **Green College**, a foundation named after Dr and Mrs Cecil Green of Dallas, Texas, and devoted to advanced scientific studies.

Opposite is **St Anne's College**, founded in 1879 as a society for women studying in Oxford and granted full collegiate status in 1952. It now admits men as well (380 undergraduates). The varied buildings, dating from the 1930s onwards, include the graceful Hall (1959; Gerald Banks) and the Wolfson Building (1966; Howell, Killick, Partridge and Amis).

On the corner of Bevington Rd, beyond St Anne's, is *St Antony's College* for graduates, founded in 1948. Bevington Rd leads into Banbury Rd opposite *Wycliffe Hall*, an Anglican theological college. About ¼m N is **St Hugh's College**, founded for women in 1886 by Elizabeth Wordsworth, who also founded Lady Margaret Hall, and granted full collegiate status in 1959. It still admits women only (330 undergraduates). The main buildings (1914–36) are brick neo-Georgian; the Wolfson Building (1966) is by David Roberts. Graduates include Mary Renault.

Bardwell Rd leads E from Banbury Rd to Wolfson College (see North-Eastern Outskirts, above).

Banbury Rd leads S from Wycliffe Hall back to St Giles, passing the turning for Lady Margaret Hall (North-Eastern Outskirts, above) and the buildings of the science faculties.

OUTSKIRTS: VIEWS. The low hills around Oxford offer some good views of the city, worth hunting out among the suburbs. *Shotover Plain*, with its very steep approach road, is a large wooded country park about 3m E of Magdalen Bridge, just beyond the ring road. *Boar's Hill*, 4m SW and also beyond the ring road, has *Jarn's Mound*, a wild garden and wood made by the archaeologist Sir Arthur Evans (d. 1941). *Raleigh Park* is by the ring road and *North Hinksey*, about 1½m W. North Hinksey has an early 17C conduit house (EH).

OUTSKIRTS: RIVER SCENERY. There is a pleasant trip up the Cherwell from Magdalen Bridge to (c 4½m) *Water Eaton* and (c 6½m) *Islip*, also visited in the routes to Banbury and Bicester below. Good walks can also be taken beside the Thames upstream towards Stanton Harcourt and downstream toward Abingdon, both described in Route 49B. For the church at *Iffley*, passed on the way downstream, see Route 49A.

FROM OXFORD TO BANBURY, 23m by A423. From St Giles the Banbury Rd. leads through the N outskirts of the city and crosses the A40. Just over ½m beyond a lane goes right for (1m) *Water Eaton* on the Cherwell and, after another ½m, A43 branches right for Bicester (see below). Beyond (4½m) *Kidlington* the Oxford Canal (Route 49B) is crossed. From (12½m) *Hopcroft's Holt* B4030 leads right for (1½m) *Rousham*, a charming little village on the Cherwell. The church has interesting Norman and Decorated features. **Rousham Park** (open) is a 17C house altered in 1738 by William Kent, of less interest than the *gardens he laid out, among the best Picturesque landscaping in England. Horace Walpole found 'the sweetest little groves, glades, porticos, cascades and river imaginable' and thought Rousham 'the most engaging of Kent's works'. 13¼m: *Steeple Aston*, on the right, remains attractive despite recent development. The church includes a baroque monument of 1730. 16½m: *Deddington*, once an important market town, has mounds marking the site of its castle (EH). The church at *Somerton*, on the Cherwell 4m SE, has some remarkable 16C monuments. At (19½m) *Adderbury* the route joins Route 52A and the road from London.

FROM OXFORD TO BICESTER, 12m by A423, A43 and A421. After 4m A43 branches right from the route to Banbury (above). 5m: A road leads right for (1m) *Islip*, birthplace of Edward the Confessor (1004). The church at *Wood Eaton*, 1¾m S, has a painted 14C rood beam in its roof. The church at *Charlton-on-Otmoor*, 2½m NE of Islip, is a well-preserved example of the transition between Decorated and Perpendicular, with an early 16C rood screen and loft. 7½m: *Weston-on-the-Green* stands at the fork of A43 to Northampton and A421 for Bicester. Weston Manor, now a hotel, is a much altered 15–16C building. 12m: *Bicester*, Route 52A.

From Oxford to London via *Henley* and *Windsor*, see Routes 49A and 49B; to London via *High Wycombe*, and to *Gloucester* via *Cheltenham*, see Route 51A; to *Stratford-upon-Avon*, see Route 53; to *Worcester*, see Route 54.

51

London to Gloucester: the Cotswolds

A. Via the Chilterns, Oxford and Cheltenham

Directions. Total distance 104m. M40 covers the 40m stretch from Denham to just short of Wheatley, bypassing Beaconsfield, High Wycombe and Stokenchurch, and offering a quick way through the Chilterns. This route cuts through the centre of the Cotswolds. The hills to the S are described in Route 51B, and their N fringe in the journeys from Oxford to Stratford (Route 53) and Oxford to Worcester (Route 54). A40 to (25m) *Beaconsfield*, (29m) **High Wycombe**, (36½m) *Stokenchurch*, (55m) **Oxford** (bypassed; Route 50), (66m) *Witney* (bypassed), (73m) *Burford* (bypassed), (82m) *Northleach*, (95m) **Cheltenham**, (104m) **Gloucester**.

A40 heads NW from central London. Beyond (18m) *Uxbridge Common* it crosses the Grand Union Canal in the Colne valley and enters the **Chiltern Hills**.

This range of chalk downs runs from near Reading through the SE corner of Buckinghamshire, at 700–850ft for much of the way, reaching its highest point at Coombe Hill (852ft) near Wendover (Route 52A) and gradually petering out further N, beyond Luton. The dense beech forests encouraged the local industry of furniture-making ('Windsor' chairs), now largely centred on High Wycombe.

The only way that an MP may vacate his seat is by accepting the stewardship of the Chiltern Hundreds (Stoke, Desborough and Burnham) or that of the Manor of Northstead in Yorkshire, both offices of profit under the Crown and hence incompatible with Parliamentary duties. The nominal duty of the Steward of the Chiltern Hundreds is to protect wayfarers from bandits, who once lurked in the forests.

19m: The roundabout at *Denham* marks the start of M40. A412 heads SW to (6½m) Slough. Just beyond the roundabout, on the right, is the old village street of Denham. The church contains the brass of Dame Agnes Jordan, Abbess of Syon (c 1540), one of only two extant brasses of an abbess. M25 is passed on the way to (21m) *Gerrards Cross*, a residential suburb stretching N to Chalfont St Peter.

Off A413 4½m N is **Chalfont St Giles**, with the little cottage (open) where Milton lived in 1665–66. 'Paradise Lost' was finished and 'Paradise Regained' begun here. The church has medieval wall paintings. A413 goes on to join Route 52A at *Amersham*. Newland Park, about 2½m E of Chalfont St Giles, has the *Chiltern Open Air Museum*, with reconstructed old buildings from the Chilterns. *Jordans*, about 2m S of Chalfont St Giles, has a group of historic Quaker buildings: the meeting house built in 1688, with the graves of William Penn (1644–1718), founder of Pennsylvania, and of Milton's friend Thomas Ellwood (d. 1713) in its burial ground; Old Jordans, the 17C farmhouse (now a guesthouse of the Society of Friends) where Penn and fellow Quakers gathered before the meeting house was built; and a barn allegedly built from the timbers of the 'Mayflower'.

2m S of Gerrards Cross, just beyond M40, is the pretty village of *Fulmer*, where the church of 1610 has a rare contemporary wooden font. **Stoke Poges**, 2m further S, is known for its connection with Thomas Gray (1716–71) and for the churchyard where his 'Elegy' was probably written. There is a monument to him by James Wyatt (1799) E of the churchyard, and he is buried with his mother near the E wall of the church. The church itself dates mainly from the 14C. The 'Bicycle Window' (1643), showing a hobby horse, is a curiosity which attracts tourists. Gray's 'Ode on a Distant Prospect of Eton College' is said to have been written in his mother's garden at *Stoke Court* (not open) to the NW. A355, W of Stoke Poges, skirts the magnificent forest of ***Burnham Beeches** (444 acres) to rejoin A40 at Beaconsfield.

25m: **Beaconsfield** (pronounced 'Beckonsfield'; 11,000 inhabitants), though much developed, keeps its wide High St. of Georgian brick. The town boasts several famous residents. The poet Edmund Waller (1606–87), born at Coleshill to the N, is buried in the churchyard. Edmund Burke (1729–97), who lived here from 1768, is buried in the church. G.K. Chesterton (1874–1936), who wrote many of his Father Brown stories at Beaconsfield, is commemorated in St Theresa's RC church. For Disraeli, who derived his title from the town, see Hughenden Manor below. In Warwick Rd, N of the railway station, is the *Bekonscot Model Village* (open).

From Beaconsfield to *Maidenhead*, see Route 49A.

29m: **High Wycombe** (pronounced 'Wickam'; 60,500 inhabitants; TI), known for its furniture industry, has suffered badly from redevelopment. The 13–16C *Church* is the largest in the county. The *Guildhall* (1757) is by Henry Keene and the *Market Hall* (1761) by Robert Adam.

Penn, on B474 about 2½m NE, claims to be the ancestral home of William Penn's family. The church has a good nave roof, a 15C painted Doom and Penn brasses.

FROM HIGH WYCOMBE TO AYLESBURY. The direct route runs via West Wycombe (see below). A more attractive way (18½m), giving a much better flavour of the Chiltern countryside, begins by taking A4128 N from the centre of High Wycombe. 1½m: *Hughenden Manor* (NT) was Disraeli's country seat from 1847 until his death in 1881. He is buried in the churchyard, and the church has a monument erected by Queen Victoria. At (2m) *Hughenden Valley* the road forks. The sideroad continues straight ahead through hilly country via (5m) *Speen* and (7m) *Lacey Green* to join A4010, the West Wycombe–Aylesbury road, at (9m) *Princes Risborough*. A4128 continues from Hughenden valley to (5½m) *Prestwood* and a region closely associated with John Hampden (1594–1643), MP for Buckinghamshire and a leading supporter of the Parliamentarian cause in its conflict with Charles I. On the sideroads leading N and W of Prestwood are (6½m) the stone cross marking the parcel of land for which Hampden refused to pay the illegal 'ship money' tax and (7½m) *Hampden House* (not open), his home, rebuilt in the 18C. Close by is the church of *Great Hampden*, where he is buried; it contains the tomb of his first wife (d. 1634), with a touching epitaph, and several re-used brasses of the Hampdens. A well-preserved stretch of *Grim's Dyke*, an ancient bank and ditch of uncertain purpose, runs between Great Hampden and Lacey Green (see above). Sideroads continue N from Hampden House to join A4010 and reach Aylesbury via Stoke Mandeville. On the left is (9½m) *Chequers* (not open), the Tudor mansion used as the Prime Minister's country residence. On the right is *Coombe Hill* (852ft; NT), highest point of the Chilterns. 18½m: *Aylesbury*, see Route 52A.

From High Wycombe to *Maidenhead*, see Route 49A.

31½m: *West Wycombe* is a fascinating place, dominated by the work of Sir Francis Dashwood (1708–81), best known for his Hell-Fire Club (cf. Medmenham Abbey, Route 49B). On the hill S of A40 lies his house, *West Wycombe Park* (NT), rebuilt in a mixture of classical styles between 1740 and 1771. It has several painted ceilings, and some good 18C furniture. The *grounds are landscaped with temples around an artificial lake. The village has some charming 16–18C houses (most of them NT but not open). On the hill N of A40 is the church, originally medieval but eccentrically rebuilt by Sir Francis, with a huge gilded ball on top of its tower. At the E end is a huge hexagonal mausoleum (1765; John Bastard). Below are artificial caves (open) quarried 1750–52 and used, it is said, for the revels of the Hell-Fire Club.

FROM WEST WYCOMBE TO AYLESBURY, 16m by A4010. 1½m: *Bradenham* church has a Saxon doorway and the grave of Isaac Disraeli (1766–1848), Benjamin's father, who lived in the manor house from 1829 until his death. 7m: **Princes Risborough** is a small town below the Chiltern Hills. Opposite the church is the 17–18C *Manor House* (NT, open by appointment only). *Monks Risborough*, to the N, has an interesting Early English and Perpendicular church. Cut into the hillside opposite the village is the *Whiteleaf Cross* (NT), probably marking the junction of the Icknield Way with another important road running N to Oxford; there is a good view across the Vale of Aylesbury. *Bledlow*, a finely placed village 2m SW of Princes Risborough, has a Norman font in the church and, on the hill further SW, another chalk cross. For (12m) *Stoke Mandeville* and (16m) *Aylesbury*, see Route 52A.

Beyond (36½m) *Stokenchurch* is the crest of the Chiltern ridge (787ft), with a good view, and the long descent into Oxfordshire. 40m: *Aston Rowant*, ¾m to the right, has a church with early Norman details and a Purbeck marble font.

Some of the best Chiltern scenery is reached by the sideroads running S from A40 between Stokenchurch and Aston Rowant. The Hambleden road gives fine *views as it crosses *Ibstone Common*, with its little Norman church and windmill, before descending to (4m) *Fingest*, where the Norman church has a unique twin-gabled tower. 7m: *Hambleden*, a charming village, is 1m from the Thames and about 2m from Henley by road or footpath (Routes 49A and 49B). Another road from A40, further W, follows the crest of the Chilterns to (8m) *Nettlebed* (Route 49A) via *Christmas Common* and (6m) *Cookley Green*. Just before Cookley Green a road branches left through *Pishill* to (3m) *Stonor* (Route 49A).

From Aston Rowant B4009 heads SW to (3m) *Watlington*, with a 17C market house. *Chalgrove*, 4m NW of Watlington, was the scene of the battle where John Hampden was mortally wounded in 1643; he is commemorated by a stone obelisk.

45½m: *Milton Common*, near the end of the M40.

A329 leads NW, passing on the left (1m) *Rycote Chapel* (EH, limited opening in summer), a private chapel of 1449 with both original and 17C furnishing. 4m: **Thame** (8500 inhabitants; TI) has a pleasant High St. The large church has a fine early 14C screen and the monument of Lord Williams (d. 1559) and his wife. Nearby are the original grammar school buildings (1575) where Hampden, Dean Fell and Anthony à Wood were educated. *Long Crendon*, 2m N on B4011, keeps its 14C courthouse (NT).

49m: *Wheatley*.

Waterperry, 2½m NE, has the former gardens of Waterperry Horticultural School (open) and a charming little church with a three-decker pulpit, 18C box pews, the late 14C effigy of a knight and a palimpsest brass of c 1440 re-used c 1540 for Walter Curson and his wife. *Garsington Manor* (gardens open under NGS), 3m S of Wheatley, was in 1915–29 the home of Philip and Lady Ottoline Morrell, who made it an important literary gathering place. Yeats, Rupert Brooke, D.H. Lawrence, T.S. Eliot, Aldous Huxley and members of the Bloomsbury group were all visitors.

50½m: *Forest Hill* was the scene of Milton's unhappy first marriage. 55m: **Oxford**, see Route 50.

A40 bypasses the city to the N. 61½m: *Eynsham*, to the left, has an old village cross and a few fragments of its once famous abbey. 66m: **Witney** (14,100 inhabitants; TI), to the right of A40 on the Windrush, has a 17C butter cross, an 18C town hall and many other good Georgian buildings, including some used for the local industry of blanket-making. The large and handsome church has an Early English tower and spire, animal carvings on the porch, a large Decorated N window and 14–17C monuments.

Minster Lovell is charmingly situated on the Windrush 3m W of Witney. Near its good Perpendicular church are the picturesque ruins of the 15C *Minster Lovell Hall* (EH, summer season, Thursday to Sunday and Bank Holidays, 10.00–18.00), with great hall, solar, kitchens and a well-preserved dovecote. At *North Leigh*, on A4095 3m NE of Witney, the church contains the lovely Wilcote Chapel (c 1440). About 2m N of the village is a 4C *Roman Villa* with baths and a *mosaic floor (EH, grounds open all year; limited access to mosaic in summer).

There are many interesting churches in the lowlands S of Witney. *Brize Norton* (4m SW) has a Norman door and a fine screen. *Black Bourton* (6m SW), the birthplace of the novelist Maria Edgeworth (1767–1849), has another Norman door and wall paintings of c 1275. *Broadwell* church (8m NW) is 11–13C, and at *Langford* (¾m further) the *church has a largely Saxon tower and a Saxon carving of the Crucifixion set in the 13C porch. *Bampton*, 5½m S of Witney and 2m N of Tadpole Bridge (Route 49B), is a large stone-built village with good 17–18C houses. Its church has Norman work and an Early English *spire. At *South Leigh*, 2¾m SE of Witney, the church has 14–15C wall paintings. John Wesley preached his first sermon here in 1725.

A40 runs parallel to the Windrush as it approaches the **Cotswold Hills**, the narrow limestone ridge running NE to SW across Gloucestershire.

In the E the Cotswolds rise by easy stages from the valleys of Oxfordshire, on a line marked roughly by Chipping Norton, Burford and Cirencester. Their W edge, running

The Slaughters

past Chipping Campden, Broadway, Cheltenham and Stroud, drops abruptly away into the Vale of Evesham and the Severn Vale, with famous viewpoints at Broadway, Cleeve Hill and Birdlip. At 1031ft, Cleeve Hill is the highest point of the Cotswolds; few places are above 1000ft, and most are between 500 and 600ft. These gently wooded hills make ideal sheep pasture. The region's long connection with wool is shown by the discovery of a fulling establishment at Chedworth, one of several important Roman sites hereabouts, and by the frequency with which 'ship' (a corruption of 'sheep') turns up in the names of towns, villages and streets. The equally common prefix, 'chipping', comes from 'cheapening' and indicates a market centre. The prosperity enjoyed by the Cotswold wool trade in the 14–16C has left its permanent mark in the many handsome churches, towns and villages built of local stone weathering into rich yellows and browns. Tourists have now replaced wool as the region's staple, making much of its picturesque charm dangerously self-conscious.

73m: **Burford** (TI), on the Windrush to the N, is an attractive little place, once one of the chief Cotswold wool towns. The High St., with medieval and Renaissance merchants' houses, drops steeply to cross the river by a fine old bridge. The *Tolsey Museum* is devoted to local history. The church of **St John the Baptist*, a mixture of Norman, Early English and Perpendicular, contains many chapels and monuments, notably those of Edmund Harman (d. 1569) and his wife (N aisle), and Lord Chief Justice Tanfield (d. 1625) and his family (N chapel), perhaps by Gerard Christmas. A memorial in the S transept to Christopher Kempster (1626–1709), one of Wren's master masons, reminds us of the nearby stone quarries at Taynton, Great Barrington, etc.

Swinbrook, on the N bank of the Windrush 2½m E, has a church with grotesquely carved stalls and 17C monuments of the Fettiplaces arranged in tiers. *Asthall*, across the river, has a good church and manor house. *Shilton*, in a valley 2½m SE of Burford, has a partly Norman church with an interesting carved font. The *Cotswold Wildlife Park* (open) is off A361 2m S of Burford.

FROM BURFORD TO STOW-ON-THE-WOLD AND BACK THROUGH BOURTON-ON-THE-WATER. A424 heads NW from Burford across the border with Gloucestershire. 10m: **Stow-on-the-Wold** (TI) is the highest settlement in Gloucestershire ('Stow on the Wold/Where the wind blows cold') and probably originated as a lookout post on the Foss Way. Later a Cotswold wool town, it is now popular with visitors, as the many antique shops bear witness. Horse fairs are held in May and October. A 14C cross stands in the large market place and the old church contains a Crucifixion by Gaspard de Crayer (1610). *Oddington*, off A436 2½m E, has a restored old church with wall paintings and Norman details. The *Cotswold Farm Park* lies 6½m W of Stow off B4077. B4068, continued by A436, goes SW to rejoin A40 and the main route at (21½m) *Andoversford*. On A436 1½m E of its junction with B4068 is *Notgrove Long Barrow* (EH).

A more interesting way back from Stow-on-the-Wold takes A429, following the straight Roman course of the Foss Way over the hills. 14m: Left of the road is the pretty **Bourton-on-the-Water**, with the Windrush flowing down its main street. The *Birdland Zoo Garden*, the *Cotswolds Motor Museum*, the *Model Railway Exhibition*, the *Model Village* and the *Village Life Exhibition* cater to the large numbers of tourists. The picturesque villages of *Lower Slaughter* and *Upper Slaughter*, 1½m and 2¼m N, are also overrun with visitors in summer. Their curious name comes from the Anglo-Saxon word meaning 'slough', or muddy place. A40 is rejoined just W of (19m) *Northleach* (see below). A429 continues SW, still following the line of the Foss Way, another 10m to *Cirencester* (Route 51B). From (3m) *Fossebridge*, on the Coln, sideroads lead left (E) to the partly Saxon church of *Coln Rogers* and the Norman church of *Coln St Dennis*. **Chedworth**, 3m W of Fossebridge, has a partly Norman church and the best **Roman Villa* (NT) in England, with well-preserved baths and pavements. The local tradition is that the Romans originally planted the lilies of the valley still growing here.

For Bibury, SW of Burford, see Route 51B.

The main route follows A40 W from Burford. 78m: A sideroad on the right leads to *Sherborne*. The Dutton family monuments in the church include work by Rysbrack and the elder Westmacott and the striking effigy of Cromwell's friend John Dutton (d. 1657). He built the beautiful hunting lodge, *Lodge Park* (not open), beyond the A40 2m SW. At (82m) *Northleach* (seasonal TI) the 15C church has a splendid *porch and brasses of local wool merchants. By the junction with A429 W of the town the well-presented *Cotswold Countryside Collection* is housed in a former prison of 1789–91. See above for A429 NE to Stow-on-the-Wold via Bourton-on-the-Water and SW to Cirencester via Chedworth. At (88m) *Andoversford* A40 meets A436 from Stow (see above). There is a good view at *Kilkenny*, on A436 1½m SW. *Withington*, 3m S of Andoversford, has picturesque cottages and a church with Perpendicular tower, Perpendicular clerestory windows and Norman work. 89½m: *Whittington*, N of A40, has a church with 14C effigies and a 16C manor house (limited opening).

95m: **CHELTENHAM** (103,000 inhabitants) lies between Cleeve Hill, the highest point of the Cotswolds, and the Severn Vale. Its Regency centre recalls its days as a fashionable spa. Cheltenham is also the home of several important annual festivals, a conference venue and a tourist centre for the Cotswolds.

TI: 77 Promenade. **Bus Station**: Royal Well. **Railway Station**: Queen's Rd, about 1m W of the centre. **Airport**: at Staverton, 4m W. **Theatres**: Everyman, Regent St.; Playhouse, Bath Rd. **Annual Events**: Steeplechasing at Prestbury Park, off A435 1m N, from October to May, with the National Hunt Festival in March, including the Cheltenham Gold Cup; International Festival of Music (July); Cricket Festival (July–August); Flower Show (July–September); Festival of Literature (October).

History. Cheltenham was a small market town until the 18C, when the spa waters were 'discovered' on the site now occupied by Cheltenham Ladies' College. The seal of fashionable approval was set by George III's visit in 1788. Cheltenham's popularity was further encouraged by the Duke of Wellington and Princess (later Queen) Victoria. Byron and Jane Austen added a literary flavour. From the 1830s, Cheltenham became a favourite retirement spot for officers who had done colonial duty in the army, navy and East India Company. Their presence contributed to the town's rise as an educational centre. Today it has five public schools, of which the Gentlemen's College (1841) and the Ladies' College (1853) enjoy an international reputation.

Natives and residents. Gustav Holst (1874–1934) was born here. Edward Jenner (1749–1823), discoverer of the smallpox vaccine, lived in St George's Rd, and Tennyson wrote part of 'In Memoriam' at his house in St James's Square.

Just off the High St. in the centre of town is the old parish church of *St Mary*, with a 14C broach spire. Inside are a beautiful rose window of c 1320, a brass of 1513 on the N side of the chancel, and a tablet to Henry Skillicorne, developer of the spa, with a lengthy epitaph. The *Art Gallery and Museum* in nearby Clarence St. has 17C Dutch paintings (Brouwer, Ostade, Steen, Wouwermans, etc.), 17–20C English paintings, and work by Ernest Gimson and the Arts and Crafts Movement. Also on display are Chinese porcelain, pottery, costumes, furniture, local archaeological finds and Cotswold prints.

The tree-lined Promenade, leading SW from the High St., is the most handsome survival of Regency Cheltenham. The buildings have splendid ironwork balconies. A *terrace of c 1823 on the right now houses the *Municipal Offices* and the *TI Centre*. In front is a statue by Lady Scott of Edward Wilson, who died with Scott in the Antarctic in 1912. On Oriel Rd to the left is the *Town Hall* (1903). On St George's Rd to the right are the buildings of *Cheltenham Ladies' College*, founded in 1853; former pupils include the novelist Margaret Kennedy. Beyond the *Imperial Gardens* and the fine *Queen's Hotel* by the Jearrard brothers (1838), the Promenade continues as Montpellier Walk, with *Montpellier Gardens* and, opposite, a row of shops (1836–38) separated by caryatid figures copied from the Erechtheion at Athens. The street ends at the *Rotunda* (1817), now a bank but originally the Montpellier Spa.

Montpellier Terrace leads left to Bath Rd and *Cheltenham College*, founded in 1841. C. Day-Lewis taught here. Old Cheltonians include Lord Morley, W.E. Lecky, A.C. Bradley and Patrick White.

Clarence Rd, NE of the High St. beyond the coach station, has the *Gustav Holst Birthplace Museum*, a Regency house with memorabilia of the composer and a refurbished Victorian kitchen, nursery and servants' quarters. Evesham Rd runs N from Clarence Rd to *Pittville Park*. The *Pittville Pump Room* (open), built in 1825–30, houses the Gallery of Fashion, recreating local history from the 18C. The spa waters can still be taken here.

Leckhampton Hill (978ft), on B4070 2m S, has a view and a striking outcrop of rocks nicknamed the Devil's Chimney. *Seven Springs*, 1½m further SE, is the source of the Churn and considered by some the true head of the Thames (cf. Thames Head, Route 51B).

FROM CHELTENHAM TO BROADWAY, 15m by A46 along the edge of the Cotswolds. Beyond (2¼m) *Southam* the road climbs *Cleeve Hill* (1031ft), the highest point in the Cotswolds, with a popular view W over the Vale of Severn. *Bishop's Cleeve*, 2m NW, has a Norman *church with a well-decorated W front, a massive nave and a superb Jacobean musicians' gallery. The fine monuments include one to Richard de la Bere (d. 1636) and his wife. 7m: *Winchcombe* (seasonal TI) is a pleasant old market town with a fine late Perpendicular church, freely restored but keeping some good gargoyles. There is also a museum in the Old Town Hall, and a Railway Museum. *Sudeley Castle* (open), 1m SE, was built c 1450 but slighted in the Civil War and made habitable again in the 19C. The 19C interiors are interesting chiefly for the collection of paintings (Rubens, Van Dyck, Constable, Turner). The Dungeon Tower has a large exhibition of toys. In the pleasant Victorian gardens is the chapel, with the tomb of Catherine Parr (1512–48), Henry VIII's widow and wife of Sudley's owner, Lord Seymour. 2m S of Winchcombe, on the way to *Charlton Abbots*, is the Neolithic *Belas Knapp Long Barrow* (EH). 9m: *Hailes Abbey* (EH, all year) is a ruined Cistercian monastery, founded in 1246 and later famous with pilgrims for its relic of Christ's blood, mentioned in Chaucer's 'Pardoner's Tale'. Only a fragment of the 15C cloister survives but there is an excellent *museum with roof bosses, tiles, etc. The parish church is outstanding for its *wall paintings of c 1300. 10m: B4077 heads E towards Stow-on-the-Wold. At 1m it passes *Stanway*, with a picturesque group formed by the church, the 16–17C Stanway House (limited opening) and its striking gatehouse, once thought to be by Inigo Jones but probably the work of a local master mason. The house has a Great Hall, some 18C rooms and a 14C tithe barn. 15m: *Broadway*, see Route 54.

103m: **GLOUCESTER** (pronounced 'Gloster'; 92,100 inhabitants) lies in the Severn Vale on the E bank of the river. It attracts visitors by the relics of its medieval past, particularly the great cathedral, and its handsomely redeveloped docks. Otherwise, Gloucester is an important commercial centre which in recent years has lost some of its traditional industry but gained new businesses, notably in computer technology. The city centre has been badly redeveloped.

TI: St Michael's Tower, The Cross. **Bus Station**: off Market Parade and Bruton Way, about ½m E of the cathedral. **Railway Station**: off Bruton Way, beyond the bus station. **Airport**: Gloucester and Cheltenham Airport at Staverton, 4m NE. Passenger services to Guernsey and Jersey. **Theatre**: Olympus Theatre, King's Barton St. **Annual Events**: The Three Choirs Festival (August) rotates annually between Gloucester, Worcester

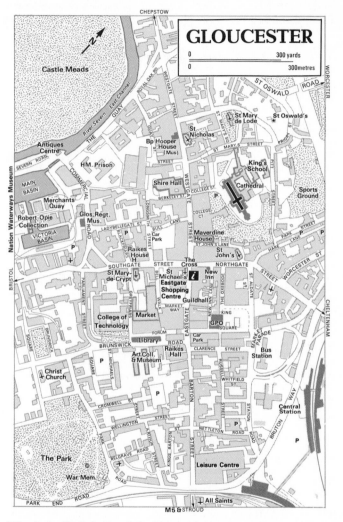

and Hereford cathedrals. Founded c 1715 and held continuously since 1724, it has given first performances of works by Elgar and Vaughan Williams.

History. In the 1C AD the Romans established a fortress here, at the lowest point where the Severn could conveniently be crossed. It quickly grew into Glevum, one of England's four coloniae, with walled fortifications and a street pattern (still apparent today) based on a central cross. After the Norman Conquest the city became a favourite with several generations of kings, receiving its first charter in 1155 and witnessing the coronation of Henry III in 1216. Gloucester sided with Parliament in the Civil War and successfully withstood a Royalist siege in 1643. At the Restoration it was punished by having its Roman walls dismantled and its boundaries greatly reduced. The Industrial Revolution transformed Gloucester into an inland port with its own dock basin (1810) and canal (1827) linked directly to the Severn estuary. Known particularly for its trade in imported timber, it also numbered railway carriage workshops and the Gloster Aircraft Company among its local industries.

Natives. John Taylor (1580–1653), the Water Poet; Robert Raikes (1735–1811), the virtual founder of Sunday Schools; George Whitefield (1714–1770), the evangelical preacher, born at the Bell Inn on Southgate St.; Sir Charles Wheatstone (1802–75), inventor of the electric telegraph; W.E. Henley (1849–1903), poet and essayist, born at 2 Eastgate St.; Ivor Gurney (1890–1937), poet and composer, born on Constitution Walk.

The centre of the city is formed, in Roman fashion, by the junction at the Cross of four streets: Northgate, Southgate, Eastgate and Westgate. The Perpendicular tower of *St Michael's* at the SE corner is now the TI Centre.

Westgate St. and College St. lead to the cathedral. The route along Westgate passes *Maverdine House*, on the right, turning a quaint façade towards a sidelane. The little College Court, beyond, has a building, now a shop and museum, claimed as the original of the Tailor of Gloucester's house in Beatrix Potter's story and the *Pilgrims' Arch* leading to College Green. Opposite College St. is the *Shire Hall* by Robert Smirke (1816), with its huge modern extension. Westgate St. continues with the interesting *Folk Museum* in a group of medieval timbered buildings on the left, including one known as Bishop Hooper's Lodging from the belief that Hooper spent his last night here in 1555 before his martyrdom in nearby St Mary's St. Opposite is the church of *St Nicholas*, with a Perpendicular spire and Norman S door.

The ***Cathedral** stands on College Green, the central tower, W façade and S entrance porch immediately proclaiming it a major achievement of Perpendicular architecture.

The plan of the present building was established by Serlo, whom William the Conqueror made abbot of a new Benedictine foundation replacing the Order which had flourished here in various forms since the 7C. Serlo's Norman church was begun in 1089 and finished soon after 1100. In 1327 the abbey accepted the body of Edward II, murdered at Berkeley Castle and refused burial at Bristol and Malmesbury. His shrine quickly began to attract pilgrims and, from the vast income which resulted, the monks rebuilt both church and abbey. Work started in 1337 and continued throughout the next hundred years. Because Gloucester's wealth enabled it to employ a court mason, the church became the first great success in the new Perpendicular style. The exterior is largely Perpendicular and in the choir a Perpendicular casing effectively disguises the Norman core. The central tower was added in 1450, and the beautiful Lady Chapel (1457–98) closed the work of the Gloucester masons. At the Dissolution Henry VIII raised the church to cathedral rank.

The *Nave* is predominantly Norman, apart from the two W bays built in 1421–37. Its great cylindrical pillars overpower the triforium and the timid Early English clerestory and vaulting (1242–45). Their exceptional height was made necessary by the original cloister outside the N wall, preventing low aisle windows and allowing light into the nave only through a lofty pier arcade. The cloister supported the N aisle when the S aisle became unsafe and had to be revaulted in 1318, the date, also, of the ballflowered tracery in the S aisle windows. The Norman vaulting and carved capitals in the N aisle should be noted, as well as the old glass in the third and fifth windows from the W end and the Perpendicular door to the cloisters at the E end. Monuments here include the elaborate family one to Mayor Machen (d. 1614) and Flaxman's graceful memorial to Mrs Morley (d. 1784).

The **Choir* projects one bay into the nave and is separated from it by a 19C screen with the organ above. It is usually entered from the S aisle, near Abbot Seabroke's Chantry (1547). Both choir and *Transepts* look pure Perpendicular, as the walls were veiled with tracery and the massive piers pared down when the Norman choir was transformed in the mid 14C. The design is a perfect unity from floor to ceiling. The tall

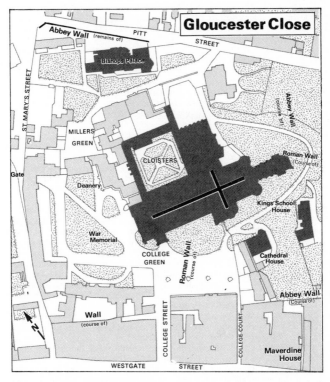

Gloucester Close

ABBEY WALL (remains of) · PITT STREET

Bishops Palace

ST MARY'S STREET

MILLERS GREEN

CLOISTERS

Abbey Wall (course of)

Roman Wall (Course of)

Gate

Deanery

Kings School House

War Memorial

COLLEGE GREEN

Roman Wall (course of)

Cathedral House

Wall (course of)

Abbey Wall (Course of)

COLLEGE STREET

COLLEGE COURT

Maverdine House

WESTGATE STREET

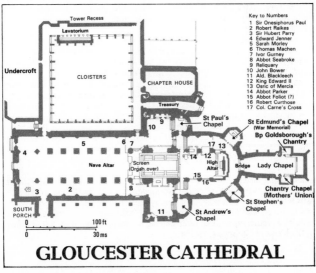

Tower Recess

Lavatorium

Undercroft

CLOISTERS

CHAPTER HOUSE

Treasury

St Paul's Chapel

Nave Altar

Screen (Organ over)

High Altar

Bridge

St Edmund's Chapel (War Memorial)

Bp Goldsborough's Chantry

Lady Chapel

Chantry Chapel (Mothers' Union)

St Stephen's Chapel

St Andrew's Chapel

SOUTH PORCH

0 _____ 100 ft
0 _____ 30 ms

Key to Numbers

1 Sir Onesiphorus Paul
2 Robert Raikes
3 Sir Hubert Parry
4 Edward Jenner
5 Sarah Morley
6 Thomas Machen
7 Ivor Gurney
8 Abbot Seabroke
9 Reliquary
10 John Bower
11 Ald. Blackleech
12 King Edward II
13 Osric of Mercia
14 Abbot Parker
15 Abbot Foliot (?)
16 Robert Curthose
17 Col. Carne's Cross

GLOUCESTER CATHEDRAL

clerestory windows; the rectilinear tracery made necessary by the size of the end windows; the one-storey design of the tracery, carried up by unbroken vaulting shafts, that covers the Norman triforium and pier arcades; the lierne *vaulting, in the complicated patterns of the choir roof, with its angel bosses, and the simpler but more subtly skilled roof of the S transept: all these are the quintessence of Perpendicular architecture. The S transept, remodelled in 1331–37, forestalls by some 20 years the evolution of Perpendicular elsewhere in England. On its E wall is the so-called Prentice Bracket, in the form of a mason's square; beside it is the Chapel of St Andrew, with a huge diagonal strut. The latest part is the N transept (restored 1368–74). On its E side is St Paul's Chapel, with a fine, restored altar screen; against its N wall is a beautiful arcaded Early English structure known as the Reliquary, now forming the door to the Treasury.

The great *E Window, the largest in the country, is said to have been donated by Lord Bradeston c 1352 to commemorate the Battle of Crécy. The light tone of the glass is as innovative as the architecture, and the walls have been made slightly wider than the chancel by tilting them outwards. The reredos is Victorian, as are the sub-stalls. The restored 14C *stalls have vigorous misericords. The W window of the choir, an unusual feature made possible by the difference in height between choir and nave, contains old glass from other windows.

Of the various tombs in the choir, the most beautiful is the *tomb of Edward II, erected by Edward III. It stands under the N arcade of the presbytery, between the monument of Osric of Mercia (founder of the first abbey in 681) and the tomb prepared for the last abbot (1539) but occupied by two bishops. The bracket tomb on the S has been assigned to Serlo, the first Norman abbot, but the figure with the church in his hand is probably Abbot Foliot (d. 1243). In front of the altar are well-preserved encaustic tiles of 1455. The NE chapel, the Chapel of St Edmund the Martyr, has fragments of a reredos of c 1450. The SE chapel is dedicated to St Stephen. The S choir aisle has the tomb of Robert Curthose (d. 1134), William the Conqueror's eldest son, with a coloured effigy in bog oak (c 1290) resting on a 15C mortuary chest.

The *Lady Chapel was the last great work at Gloucester (1457–98). It is detached from the E end of the choir to avoid obscuring the E window, and its W end diminishes in height and breadth to form a gracefully vaulted vestibule. Open tracery fills the upper part of the W arch. The exquisite lierne vaulting with leaf bosses, the crisply carved tracery of the windows and the narrow wall spaces between, the vaulting shafts, the ruined reredos, the sedilia and the remaining 15C tiles all contribute to the chapel's architectural harmony. The side chapels, with oratories or music galleries in their upper storeys, are delicately vaulted. The late 15C E window of nine lights contains old glass, some of it not designed for this window, which represented the Tree of Jesse. There are several charming monuments.

The *Choir Triforium*, reached from the N transept, contains an exhibition of the building's history. Its two halves are linked by the Whispering Gallery, running outside the E window and across the W end of the Lady Chapel. The Norman *Crypt*, entered from the S transept, consists of an apse and five chapels.

The *Cloisters (c 1370–1410), entered from the N aisle of the nave, are remarkably beautiful and well preserved. The fan-tracery vaulting, certainly the first of any extent in Britain, is claimed as an invention of the Gloucester masons. The S side has 'carrel' recesses for desks; on the N side is the lavatorium, with a towel recess in the wall opposite. The Chapter House on the E is restored Norman with a Perpendicular E window bay. On the W side of the cloisters a medieval undercroft has been turned into the cathedral shop. From here a door leads out into College Green, on the other side of which is the medieval *St Mary's Gateway*, formerly the main gateway for provisioning the abbey.

The gate leads into St Mary's St. Opposite is the memorial to Bishop Hooper, who was martyred here in 1555, watched (so the story goes) by Bishop Bonner from the little window over the gateway. The nearby church of *St Mary-de-Lode*, with its low Norman chancel, stands on the site of a Roman building. Priory Rd to the N has four 11–12C arches marking the site of *St Oswald's Priory*, founded in 909 and destroyed during the siege of Gloucester in 1643.

Berkeley St., off Westgate St. opposite College St., leads to 18C houses culminating in *Bearland House* at the end, *Bearland Lodge* on Longsmith St. to the left and *Ladybellegate House* (1705), facing the head of Lady-bellegate St. Off Ladybellegate St. is *Blackfriars* (EH, summer season, weekends only, 10.00–15.15), the church and part of the E range of a 13C Dominican friary, with a fine timber roof.

Beyond Blackfriars is Southgate St., with the partly 12C church of *St Mary-de-Crypt*. It has good brasses and the tomb of Robert Raikes, whose house on the other side of the street is now the Golden Cross Inn. George Whitefield preached his first sermon here. Behind St Mary's is *Greyfriars* (EH), the remains of the early 16C church of a Franciscan friary, with a Georgian house added to the W end. Greyfriars Walk continues past the *Eastgate Market* to Brunswick Rd.

To the left on Brunswick Rd is the **City Museum and Art Gallery**. Its archaeological collection includes a 1C bronze mirror from Birdlip, a group of Romano-British sculptures (AD 100–250) from Lower Slaughter, and Roman altars, coins, etc. from the city itself. The foundations of the Roman city wall on which the building stands have been exposed. Natural history exhibits include a beehive and aquarium. The art gallery upstairs has Georgian furniture, barometers, glass, ceramics, silver and English land-scape paintings from the 17C onwards.

Beyond the museum Brunswick Rd continues to the junction with East-gate St. Part of the Roman defences have been excavated by the corner of Constitution Walk, to the left, and on King's Walk, opposite (both open at limited times in summer). Eastgate heads back to the Cross.

The *Docks* lie SW of the Cross, reached via Southgate St. and Commercial Rd, with the *Gloucestershire Regimental Museum*. The area has been handsomely rede-veloped. The old Albert Warehouse (1851) is now the *Museum of Advertising and Packaging*, containing the large and various Robert Opie collection. The huge Llanthony Warehouse, to the S, is now the *National Waterways Museum*, with a wide range of displays, models and simulators dedicated to bringing two centuries of canal history to life. Narrowboats, barges and a steam dredger are moored at the quayside. Between the river and the canal are the remains of the 12C *Llanthony Abbey*, a daughter house of the Welsh monastery.

The **Severn Bore**, a wave caused by the incoming tide, is best seen not in Gloucester itself but below the city at places like *Epney* (see below) on the E bank or *Minsterworth* on the W bank (5m W; see also Route 55B). The larger waves usually come in spring and autumn from 07.00 to 11.00 and 19.00 to 23.00.

FROM GLOUCESTER TO BERKELEY, 17m by A38, the Bristol road, down the Vale of Severn. 5m: *Hardwicke Court* (limited opening) is a Regency house by Robert Smirke. 9m: *Frampton-on-Severn*, a charming village 1m to the right of A38, has a church with a Romanesque lead font, one of six identical ones in Gloucestershire. Beyond the canal a winding road follows the Severn back towards Gloucester, passing (2½m) *Epney*, known for its elvers, or young eels. See also the Severn Bore, above. 13m: By the Severn beyond *Slimbridge* is the *Wildfowl Trust* (open) founded by Sir Peter Scott in 1946, where many thousands of waterfowl may be seen. 16m: The little town of *Berkeley* lies 1m to the right. *Berkeley Castle* (open), entered by a bridge over the moat, still looks a feudal stronghold. Part of the circular keep and inner bailey belong to the mid 12C; the rest is mainly 14C. Edward II was murdered here in 1327. Medieval rooms include the kitchen, the Great Hall (with the original timber roof, a painted 16C screen and 17C Oudenarde tapestries) and the chapel, later made into a living room. The Early English *Church* has a 15C screen and monuments to the Berkeley family. Swift wrote the epitaph on the jester Dicky Pearce (d. 1728) in the churchyard. The house nearby where Edward Jenner (1749–1823) was born and died is now a museum devoted to his memory. There is a nuclear power station by the river (now decommissioned), and another at *Oldbury-on-Severn*, 8m S. At *Sharpness*, 1½m beyond Berkeley, the

Gloucester canal joins the Severn. For the rest of the way by A38 from Berkeley to Bristol, see Route 20.

FROM GLOUCESTER TO LEDBURY, 17m. A40 heads W towards Ross-on-Wye, crossing the Severn at 1m. *Over Bridge* (EH) was built by Telford in 1825–30. The direct way to Ledbury (another 15m) is by A417, passing W of *Ashleworth* on the Severn, with a 15C tithe barn (NT). A more interesting route keeps on A40 for another mile and then branches right on B4215, up the pretty Leadon valley. 9m: *Newent* (TI) has timbered houses and a 16C market hall. 12¾m: *Dymock*, known for its orchards and daffodils, has a large and interesting church with a S doorway of c 1130. At *Kempley*, 2m W, the little Norman church (EH, all year plus Mondays in winter) has 12–14C *frescoes. 17m: *Ledbury*, see Route 57.

From Gloucester to *Worcester*, see Route 55; to *Hereford*, see Route 56. For the *Wye Valley* and the *Forest of Dean*, W of Gloucester, see Route 58.

B.   Via the Vale of the White Horse and Cirencester

Directions. Total distance 109m. This route goes through the S Cotswolds. Route 51A, where the region is characterised more fully, cuts across the centre, and the N fringes are described in the journeys from Oxford to Stratford (Route 53) and Oxford to Worcester (Route 54). The detours from Faringdon and Cirencester described below make useful connections between the Cotswolds and SW England (Route 20). To (47½m) *Wallingford*, see Route 49A. A4130, A417 to (62½m) *Wantage*. A417, A420 to (72m) *Faringdon*. A417 to (78m) *Lechlade*, (91m) **Cirencester** and directly to (109m) **Gloucester** (Route 51A), or alternative way (8m longer) on A419 via *Stroud*.

An alternative way of starting the journey goes via (38½m) *Reading* (Route 20) and A329 along the S bank of the Thames to (47½m) *Streatley* (Route 49A). It then branches left on A417. 53½m: *Blewbury*, 3m S of *Didcot*, is a pleasant place. It has enterprisingly taken to commissioning and staging operas, with amateur performers, in its church. The painter Sir William Nicholson (1872–1949) died here. 55m: *Upton* has a small primitive Norman church. At (57m) *Harwell*, the main route described below is joined.

From London via Henley to (47½m) *Wallingford*, see Route 49A. A4130 continues to (53m) *Didcot*, with a large power station, a railway junction familiar to travellers on the Oxford and Swindon lines. The Railway Centre (open) has steam engines, rolling stock, etc., from Brunel's Great Western Railway. *East Hagbourne*, 1½m S on the way to Blewbury, is a notably pretty village. A4130 meets A34 at the roundabout S of Abingdon (Route 49A), then loops round to join A417 ½m W of *Harwell*, with a large 13–14C church. The sprawling Atomic Energy Research Establishment is on A4185 1½m S. A417 goes past (58½m) *East Hendred*, which has a curious early 14C wooden lectern in the church and a Perpendicular wayside chapel with priest's house attached. 60½m: *Ardington House* (limited opening), also in the lea of the downs S of A417, is a Baroque house built in 1719–20, with a handsome staircase hall.

62½m: **Wantage** (8800 inhabitants), in the Vale of the White Horse, was the birthplace of Alfred the Great (849–99), whose statue stands in the market place. The church has brasses and the 14C tomb of Sir William Fitzwarren, who, with his wife Dame Alice, plays a leading part in 'Dick Whittington'.

The **Vale of the White Horse** lies between Wantage and Faringdon. It is bounded on the S by the *Berkshire Downs, with the Ridgeway linking the prehistoric sites along their breezy top. This ancient British trackway follows the curve of the hills from Streatley in the E, veers S of Swindon, crosses the upper Kennet valley 1½m E of Avebury (Route 20) and joins the Wansdyke—a distance of some 40m. The Countryside Commission's 'Ridgeway Path' follows its course as much as modern roads permit, connecting with the Icknield Way in the E.

B4507 running W from Wantage, with the vale on its right and the Ridgeway on its left, gives a good introduction to the landscape and its major points of interest. ½m: A sideroad leads left to (2m) *Letcombe Bassett*. The Iron Age *Segsbury Camp* by the Ridgeway above the village gives a fine view. 2¼m: The church at *Childrey* (right) has a lead font and brasses. 3¼m: *Sparsholt* (right) has a church with a 12C doorway and 14C effigies in oak and stone. 5m: Left of the road is a perforated sarsen stone known as the *Blowing Stone*. *Kingston Lisle Park*, to the right, is partly 17C. The village church has 14C wall paintings. *Uffington*, 2m NW of Kingston Lisle, has a good Early English church. Thomas Hughes (1822–96), who describes the vale at the opening of 'Tom Brown's Schooldays', was born here. 6m: Cut into the turf of *White Horse Hill* (656ft; EH) is the horse which gives its name to the region. Popularly associated with Alfred's victory over the Danes at the Battle of Ashdown, fought somewhere along these downs in 871, it belongs in fact to the 1C BC—certainly the oldest white horse, and perhaps the oldest chalk figure, in Britain. On the W side of the hill is the hollow known as the *Manger* and the natural mound known as *Dragon Hill* (EH), from the local tradition that St George slew the dragon here. *Uffington Castle* (EH), the Iron Age earthwork on top of the hill, has a splendid *view. From here the Ridgeway leads SW to (1½m) *Wayland's Smithy* (EH), a Neolithic burial mound.

The Great Coxwell tithe barn

A417 heads across the vale. 64½m: *West Challow*, to the left, has a small 12C church. A420, the Oxford–Swindon road, is briefly followed to A417. 72m: **Faringdon** (seasonal TI) has a 17C market hall and several old inns. The *Church* has a Transitional Norman core (note the S doorway and the clustered piers at the crossing) and many good details: six-light Perpendicular windows in the N aisle, sedilia and monuments. *Faringdon House* was built by Henry Pye (1745–1813), the undistinguished Poet Laureate, who also planted the conspicuous Faringdon Clump. The folly (1935) on the hill to the E was perhaps the last folly in England.

The early 13C Cistercian *tithe barn (NT) at *Great Coxwell*, 2m SW, was called by William Morris 'the finest piece of architecture in England'.

A420 leads NE toward Oxford. 5m: *Pusey House* was the birthplace of Edward Pusey (1800–82), leader of the Oxford Movement. 8m: *Kingston Bagpuize* has a church of 1799–1800 by the entrance to *Kingston Bagpuize House* (limited opening). This handsome red-brick building with stone dressings looks early 18C, though the family date it from 1670. There are good panelling and fireplaces inside. The pleasant gardens have an early 18C gazebo. For *Longworth*, 1m NW, see Route 49B.

FROM FARINGDON TO CHIPPENHAM, 32m by A420, A3102 and A4. 12m: **Swindon** (91,000 inhabitants; TI) was created by the railway, which made it the site of a major junction and carriage works. It incorporated the market town of *Old Swindon*, on the hill 1m S. Now a business and commercial centre, it has become a road junction linking SW England with the Cotswolds and the Midlands. The *Great Western Railway Museum* on Faringdon Rd has old locomotives. The birthplace of Richard Jefferies (1848–87) at *Coate Farm*, 1½m SE, is now a museum. The church at *Lydiard Tregoze*, 6m W, has monuments to the St John family, who lived at *Lydiard Park* (open), a mansion largely rebuilt in the 1740s, with rich decorative plasterwork inside. The grounds cover more than 260 acres. 17m: *Wootton Bassett*, with modern development, has a half-timbered town hall. *Brinkworth*, 4m NW, has a 15C church with contemporary wall paintings. *Dauntsey*, 2m SW of Brinkworth, was a favourite resort of George Herbert. Beyond (22m) *Lyneham* the Chippenham road has been demoted to B4069. 32m: *Chippenham*, see Route 20.

Beyond Faringdon A417 continues NW to (75m) *Eaton Hastings* (Route 49B) and (76m) *Buscot Park* (NT). Built about 1780 and restored in the 1930s, the house has a fine collection of furniture and paintings, with work by Rembrandt and Burne-Jones, who also designed the E window in the church by the Thames. The Old Parsonage (NT, open by appointment) is early 18C. For *Kelmscott*, on the opposite bank, see Route 49B. A417 crosses the river and enters Gloucestershire. 78m: **Lechlade**, a small market town with a large Perpendicular wool church, marks the upper limit of navigation on the Thames. 82½m: **Fairford** is a small and attractive town on the Coln. The late Perpendicular church of *St Mary*, decorated on the outside with sculpture, contains 16C painted glass *windows, probably from the same Anglo-Flemish workshop that made the glass for King's College Chapel, Cambridge. The series of 28 tells the Biblical story from the Creation to the Last Judgement. There are handsome merchants' houses in the High St., and in London Rd is the birthplace of John Keble (1792–1866), a leader of the Oxford Movement.

A charming sideroad goes up the Coln valley to (2m) *Quenington*, where the church has a Norman doorway, and (5m) **Bibury**, one of the most popular Cotswold villages. Arlington Row (NT, not open) is a much-photographed group of stone-built cottages. The 17C Arlington Mill is a rural museum. The sideroad continues up the valley to join A429, the Foss Way (Route 51A). A433 leads left from Bibury to Cirencester, passing (2m) *Barnsley House* (gardens open).

91m: **Cirencester** (pronounced 'Siren-sester, 'Sisister' or 'Sisitter'; 16,000 inhabitants; TI) is the most interesting town in the Cotswolds. Once Corinium, a Roman provincial capital second in size only to London by the end of the 1C AD, it later became a market centre for the wool trade. Its medieval prosperity is shown by the parish church of *St John the Baptist*, one of the largest in England, originally Norman but largely rebuilt in the Perpendicular style. Note: the fine W tower (begun in 1400); the threestoried *S porch (c 1490); the Trinity Chapel (1430) with its brasses; the fan-vaulting of St Catherine's Chapel (1508); and the 'wineglass' pulpit of 1515, one of the few pre-Reformation pulpits to survive in England. The *Corinium Museum* has a large and well-presented collection of Roman remains: mosaics, tombstones, painted wall plaster, and fragments of stone carving which include a limestone relief of three fertility goddesses.

Excavation has revealed much of the grid system of the Roman streets, with a forum and basilica in the centre. The *Amphitheatre* (EH), one of Britain's largest, is near the bypass on the W of town. Earthworks at *Bagendon*, off A435 3m N, mark the site of Corinium's predecessor, the Belgic capital Dobunni.

Spitalgate Lane has some arches of the *Hospital of St John* founded by Henry II, but the only relic of the Augustinian abbey which he refounded is a gateway (c 1180) in Grove Lane beyond.

Immediately W of the town is *Cirencester Park* (open, with polo matches on summer weekends), laid out in a series of avenues and rides by the 1st Earl Bathurst in 1714. Pope's Seat, a rusticated pavilion, recalls frequent visits by the poet, who may have helped with the landscaping.

A419 follows the course of the Roman Ermin Way SE from Cirencester to (7½m) *Cricklade* on the upper Thames (Route 49B). Of Cricklade's two churches, St Mary's dates mainly from the early 12C while St Sampson's mixes Early English, Decorated and Perpendicular. The Perpendicular church at *Purton*, 4m S, is one of the few in England to have both a central and W tower. *Down Ampney*, 3m N of Cricklade, was the birthplace of Ralph Vaughan Williams (1872–1958).

FROM CIRENCESTER TO BRISTOL, 37m by A433, A46, A432. 2m: A429 bears left for Malmesbury (see below). A433 continues through (3m) *Thames Head*, generally regarded as the source of the Thames. 6m: *Rodmarton*, to the right, has the gardens (limited opening) of Rodmarton Manor, with topiary, etc. Nearby is the *Windmill Tump Long Barrow* (EH). 10m: **Tetbury** (seasonal TI), on a hill, has always been popular with tourists. The town hall dates from 1655, and the church (1777–81) has tall wooden pillars and contemporary pews and galleries. *Chavenage* (open), 2m NW, is a 16C house with a lovely frontage, tall windows in its great hall and 17C tapestries upstairs. The 18C chapel, separate from the house, has earlier stone carving. 13m: *Westonbirt Arboretum* (open), part of a large Forestry Commission estate on the right, has rare trees. 16m: *Didmarton* church has an 18C interior. At 18m, beyond the Worcester Lodge of Badminton Park (see below), A433 joins A46, followed S. 24m: *Old Sodbury* is at the junction with A432, followed W. *Badminton Park* (open by written appointment), 3m NE, was begun in 1682 and completed by Kent in 1740. It has Kent interiors and 18C furniture. For *Dyrham Park*, beyond M4 3m further S, see Route 20. 25m: *Chipping Sodbury* is an old market town with a broad stone-built street and a good church. At the 16C *Little Sodbury Manor* (open by written appointment), to the N, William Tyndale translated the Bible. *Horton Court* (NT), further N, has a Norman hall and late Perpendicular ambulatory. 37m: *Bristol*, see Route 20.

FROM CIRENCESTER TO CHIPPENHAM, 21m. A433, on the route to Bristol above, is followed 2m to A429, then followed left. 11m: **Malmesbury** (2600 inhabitants; TI) is a pleasant little town above the Avon. Of the abbey founded in the 7C, later one of the most powerful Benedictine foundations, only the nave of the *Abbey Church* (c 1115–40) survives. Its most striking feature is the S porch. Inside is the alleged tomb of King Athelstan (d. 940). The historian William of Malmesbury (c 1090–1143) was a monk of the abbey, as was a certain Oliver, who in the 11C made himself wings and jumped from the tower; miraculously, he was only lamed. Thomas Hobbes (1588–1679) was born here, and Joseph Addison was MP for Malmesbury in 1710–19. The market place has a cross of c 1500, and at the foot of the hill is the late 12C *St John's Hospital*. About 2m NE is *Charlton Park House* (limited opening), visited by Dryden but substantially rebuilt by the younger Matthew Brettingham in the 1770s. The church at *Garsdon*, 2m E of Malmesbury, has Washington tombs. *Luckington Court* (limited opening), on B4040 6m W, is mainly Queen Anne. 21m: *Chippenham*, see Route 20.

From Cirencester A417 follows the Roman Ermin Way across the Cotswolds to (109m) Gloucester. 99m: *Elkstone*, ½m to the right, has the best Norman *church in the region. Beyond (100m) *Birdlip* a sharp detour to the right avoids the steep descent of Birdlip Hill, with a famous *view.

Great Witcombe, on the left halfway down the hill, has a small partly Norman church. In the S part of nearby Witcombe Park is *Great Witcombe Roman Villa* (EH) with mosaic floors.

A more interesting way from Cirencester to Gloucester (8m longer) goes W on A419 past Cirencester Park and along the Stroudwater valley. 97m: *Sapperton*, about 1m N of the road, has a church largely rebuilt in the Queen Anne period, with 16–18C monuments. 103m: **Stroud** (20,900 inhabitants; TI), at the meeting of five deep valleys, was a centre of the wool trade and the West of England cloth industry, though few mills now remain. Its history is traced in the local museum.

Miserden, 7m NE by sideroads, has the delightful gardens of Miserden Park (limited opening), partly designed by Lutyens.

A46 runs S down the Nailsworth valley, past (2m) *Woodchester* where the Roman pavement is uncovered every ten years, to (4¼m) *Nailsworth*, where the poet and 'super-tramp' W.H. Davies (1871–1940) died. The *Nailsworth Ladder*, a freak hill, has a gradient of 1 in 2¼. *Avening*, 2½m SE on B4014 towards Tetbury, has a partly Norman church. Nailsworth and Avening can also be reached from Stroud by the sideroads that run across the uplands E of the valley. Much of the land is owned by NT. A46 climbs to (1m) *Rodborough Common* and (3m) *Amberley* (Glos), where Mrs Craik wrote 'John Halifax, Gentleman'. Beyond *Minchinhampton Common* to the E is (4½m) *Minchinhampton* (671ft), with a pillared market house.

The winding B4066 leads SW from Stroud. Near (4½m) *Nympsfield* are *Nympsfield Long Barrow* (EH) and *Woodchester Park* (limited opening), an unoccupied and uncompleted Gothic Revival house. 5½m: *Uley Tumulus* (EH), known as Hetty Pegler's Tump, is a Neolithic long barrow on a commanding hilltop site. 6½m: *Owlpen Manor* (limited opening) is a picturesque 16–17C house in the valley E of *Uley*. 9m: *Dursley* has 18C buildings, including the town hall. William Tyndale (1484–1536), translator of the Bible, is claimed as a native of *Nibley*, 2m S. For *Wotton-under-Edge*, 4m S of Dursley, see Route 20.

A46 goes N up the Painswick valley. On the left rises *Haresfield Beacon* (713ft; NT), with a *view over the Severn. 107m: *Painswick* (seasonal TI), a typical Cotswold town with stone-built houses, is famous for its churchyard with 18C *table-tombs and trimmed yews. The *Painswick Rococo Garden* (open) is ½m N. 110m: *Cranham Woods* lie beneath an earthwork called *Kimsbury Castle* (view).

In a hollow to the left lies *Prinknash Abbey* (pronounced 'Prinnash'; open), occupied since 1928 by Benedictine monks and known for its pottery. The site once belonged to the Abbot of Gloucester but the buildings (by F. Goodhart-Rendel and F.G. Broadbent) date mainly from the 1930s. At *Upton St Leonards*, 1½m NW of Prinknash, the church has a Norman doorway and Early English chancel.

Commanding views of the Severn Vale and the Malvern Hills, A46 drops to join A417 at (111m) *Brockworth*. Cheltenham is 6m straight ahead and Birdlip 3m E by the main road. **Gloucester** (Route 51A) is to the W at 117m.

52

London to Coventry

A.   Via Banbury and Warwick

Directions. Total distance 100m. A41 to (18½m) Watford (bypassed), (21½m) Hemel Hempstead (bypassed), (39m) Aylesbury, (56m) Bicester, (71m) **Banbury** and (90m) **Warwick** (and **Leamington Spa**). A46, A452 to (94m) Kenilworth. A429 to (99m) **Coventry**. A useful central route through the Midlands, dull in its early stages, but connecting easily with Birmingham from Warwick or Coventry. Note the alternative ways from London to Aylesbury and from Aylesbury to Banbury, and the convenient detours from Banbury or Warwick to Stratford-upon-Avon.

A404 and A413 provide an alternative route (40m) to Aylesbury, leaving London via Harrow (see the 'Blue Guide London') and the suburb of (20m) *Rickmansworth* (30,000 inhabitants). To the right of A404 before Rickmansworth is *Moor Park* (open), now a golf club-house, a mansion of the 1720s variously attributed to Giacomo Leoni and the painter Sir James Thornhill. Murals include work by Verrio belonging to the earlier house built for the Duke of Monmouth in the 1680s. 24½m: *Chenies*, on the right, is a 19C 'model' village with *monuments of the Dukes of Bedford in its church. Their former home, *Chenies Manor* (open), is a 16C brick house with magnificent chimneys and formal gardens. 26½m: The old part of **Amersham** (17,500 inhabitants), S of the railway line, has a brick market hall (1682) and almshouses (1657) and an attractive High St. The church contains 17–19C monuments of the Curwen and Drake families. The new town is 1m N at *Amersham-on-the-Hill*. At *Chesham Bois*, 1m beyond, the gardens (open under NGS) have rare plants. *Chesham*, 2m N of Amersham-on-the-Hill, is a pleasant town in the valley of the Chess.

A404 changes to A413, which crosses the Chiltern Hills (cf. Route 51A). 29m: *Little Missenden*, on the left, has a 12C church with 14C wall paintings. 31m: *Great Missenden* lies to the left in a beautiful valley. Its Decorated and Perpendicular church has a monument to Lady Boys (1638) by Nicholas Stone. Just beyond the village a road heads left towards Princes Risborough (Route 51A), passing (on the right at 2m) the turning for *Little Hampden*, where the tiny church has 14C wall paintings. 35m: **Wendover** (8,600 inhabitants; TI) is a handsome place on the Icknield Way. *Coombe Hill* (852ft; NT), the highest of the Chilterns, rises 1½m W. A413 descends into the fertile *Vale of Aylesbury* and passes (37½m) *Stoke Mandeville*, with a hospital for paraplegics, before entering (40m) *Aylesbury*.

The main route leaves London through the NW suburbs on A41, with the M1 relieving it between Hendon and M25 near King's Langley. Hertfordshire begins between (12m) *Bushey* (left) and *Elstree*. After the suburb of (18½m) *Watford* (76,000 inhabitants) and M25, the road joins the line of the Grand Union Canal (cf. Route 52B) just short of (20m) *King's Langley*. The village takes its name from the royal palace where Edmund de Langley

(1341–1402), Edward III's son, was born. The church contains the heraldic tomb used for Edward and Isabella of Castile (d. 1394), though probably designed for Richard II. Richard lay buried elsewhere in the church from 1399 to 1413. Only a fragment remains of the Dominican friary where Edward II's favourite Piers Gaveston was buried in 1315.

The hamlet of *Bedmond*, 1m E, was the birthplace of Nicholas Breakspear (d. 1159) who, as Adrian IV, became the only English pope. A tablet remembers him in the 12–13C church of *Abbot's Langley*, ½m S.

A41 bypasses (21½m) **Hemel Hempstead** (79,600 inhabitants; TI), developed after World War II. The centre, built mainly in the 1950s and 1960s, has a pleasant water-garden. The Norman church, with a lead spire, adjoins the old High St., 1½m NE. 27m: **Berkhamsted** (15,500 inhabitants; TI) has the remains of the 11C *Castle* (EH) where William the Conqueror received the submission of Edgar Atheling in 1066 and John II of France was imprisoned after the Battle of Poitiers in 1356. Natives of the town include William Cowper (1731–1800) and Graham Greene, whose father was headmaster of the school founded in 1541.

About 3m N is **Ashridge**, a Gothick mansion of 1808–1814 by James Wyatt, now a management training centre (limited opening of gardens). It stands on the site of a monastery of Bonhommes, founded in 1283, famous for possessing a drop of Christ's blood. The future Queen Elizabeth was arrested here in 1554 by Queen Mary. The park and downland (4000 acres; NT) include a monument to the 3rd Duke of Bridgewater (1736–1803), the canal-builder, and Ivinghoe Beacon (see below).

At (30m) *Cowroast Lock*, the summit lock of 44 from the Thames, A41 branches left from the Grand Union Canal. 32m: *Tring* (10,600 inhabitants) is an old town at the foot of the Chilterns. The baptismal register of the 14–16C flint church contains entries referring to the Washington family. Along Akeman St. is the *Zoological Museum*, a collection begun by the 2nd Lord Rothschild and now a department of the Natural History Museum in London. *Tring Park* was a seat of the Rothschilds.

From the station, 1¾m E of the town, the railway enters Robert Stephenson's great cutting (1834–38) through the summit of the hills. *Aldbury*, a charming village 1m further E, is the burial place of Mrs Humphry Ward (1851–1920), who lived at Stocks. About 1¼m W of Tring is *Drayton Beauchamp*, where the judicious Hooker was rector in 1584–85. The church has 14C glass in its E window.

B488 and B489 run NE to (10m) Dunstable (Route 52B), following the course of the Icknield Way and passing (3½m) *Ivinghoe*, from which Scott derived the title of 'Ivanhoe'. It has a striking 13–14C church and a post windmill of 1627 (NT), one of the oldest in Britain. *Ivinghoe Beacon* (756ft; NT) has an early Iron Age hill-fort; the view across to Whipsnade (Route 52B) is marred by a radio station.

Beyond Tring A41 enters Buckinghamshire. 39m: **Aylesbury** (48,200 inhabitants; TI), the county town, has lost much of its historic character to insensitive modern development. From the ring road Great Western St. passes beneath *Friar's Square* market, a new precinct in harsh and restless concrete incorporating at different levels the bus station, county library and municipal offices. It emerges in the old Market Square, with the original *County Hall* of 1723–40 by Thomas Harris and the *Bull's Head*, 15C behind its Victorian exterior; just off it is the *King's Head* (NT), also 15C, with a fine mullioned window. Good 17–18C houses survive, notably in Temple St. and Church St., where the former grammar school (15C but rebuilt in 1720) houses the *County Museum*, with a good collection of local antiquities. The composer Rutland Boughton (1878–1960) was born in Aylesbury.

Dinton, off A418 4¼m SW on the way to Thame, has a church with an elaborate Norman *S doorway and good brasses. *Nether Winchendon House* (limited opening), in a pretty village 2¼m W of Dinton, is a Tudor building with 18C Gothic alterations.

FROM AYLESBURY TO BANBURY VIA BUCKINGHAM, 34m by A413 and A422, an alternative to the main route, via Bicester, described below. 10m: *Winslow* is a handsome place, with *Winslow Hall* (open by appointment), a brick town house of 1700 almost certainly by Wren. 3m W is *Claydon House* (NT), partly late Tudor and partly built by Sir Thomas Robinson in 1760–80 for the 2nd Earl Verney. It contains rococo apartments designed by Lightfoot (otherwise unknown), including a 'Chinese Chippendale' room; a magnificent staircase with plasterwork by Joseph Rose; good family portraits; and memorials of Florence Nightingale, who frequently visited her sister here. The adjoining church of *Middle Claydon* has monuments of the Verneys and previous owners, the Giffards. 17m: **Buckingham** (8000 inhabitants), a quiet old town, has long been superseded as county town by Aylesbury. Built round the market place, with a Georgian town hall at the S end and the 18C jail further N, it has a 15C *Chantry Chapel* (NT), with a Norman doorway. The high-lying parish church was built in 1771–81 but completely altered in the 1860s by Sir Gilbert Scott, who was born at *Gawcott*, 1½m S. The *University of Buckingham*, opened in 1976 and granted its royal charter in 1983, is Britain's only independent university. The Hunter St. campus has restored old buildings.

The remote Perpendicular church of *Hillesden*, beyond Gawcott 4m S of Buckingham, is one of the best in the county, while the church at *Chetwode*, about 3m further W, is the chancel of an Augustinian priory, founded in 1245, with a beautiful five-light E window. Both have good stained glass. The church at *Maids' Moreton*, 1½m N of Buckingham, is a beautiful example of mid 15C work.

An avenue leads N from Buckingham to (3m) **Stowe**, formerly the home of the Dukes of Buckingham and now a public school (state rooms and grounds open at Easter and during summer holidays). The house, originally late 17C, was altered and enlarged during the ownership (1697–1749) of Sir Richard Temple, later Viscount Cobham, and again in the 1770s, when Robert Adam designed the imposing S front. The *grounds (NT), among the supreme achievements of 18C Picturesque landscaping, were designed for Temple on the grandest scale by Vanbrugh, Bridgeman, Kent and Capability Brown, with Gibbs also contributing to the many garden buildings. The scenery by the Octagon Lake, with the Palladian Bridge near its NE tip, is particularly charming.

A422 runs NW from Buckingham and enters the S tip of Northamptonshire just before (24m) **Brackley** (6600 inhabitants; TI), a pleasant old town on A43 halfway between Oxford and Northampton. The *Town Hall* (1706) stands in the middle of the broad High St. *Magdalen College School*, founded in 1548 in buildings acquired for his Oxford foundation by William of Waynflete, incorporates the much altered chapel of a Hospital of St James and St John. This, like the low-lying parish church of *St Peter*, still has medieval statues in the niches of its tower. A422 continues NW, leaving Northamptonshire for Oxfordshire beyond (31m) *Middleton Cheney*, where the church has splendid stained glass by Morris and Co., particularly the *E window of 1865. 34m: *Banbury*, see below.

The main route follows A41 from Aylesbury to (45m) *Waddesdon*. ***Waddesdon Manor** (NT) contains one of the finest private art collections in the country.

The mansion was built for Baron Ferdinand de Rothschild in 1874–80 by Hippolyte Destailleur in the style of a French château, with motifs copied from Blois and Chambord. It stands in splendid grounds landscaped by Lainé.

Many rooms have boiseries, or carved wooden panelling, brought from 18C French houses. The furniture is also mainly 18C French, with masterpieces made by Riesener for Marie Antoinette and the future Louis XVIII in 1777–90, and a bureau (1779) belonging to Beaumarchais, with inlay alluding to his works. The Savonnerie carpets, Sèvres porcelain, sculpture (by Lemoine, Clodion, Falconet and others), snuff boxes, musical instruments, etc. are of the same period. The collection of paintings includes, in the Morning Room, work by Rubens, de Hooch ('The Game of Ninepins'), Cuyp,

Dou, van der Heyden, Metsu, Terborch, Teniers and Gainsborough. Elsewhere are paintings by Watteau, Lancret, Pater and Boucher, portraits by Reynolds and Romney, and portraits of Perdita Robinson by both Gainsborough and Reynolds. The *Bachelors Wing displays 16–17C armour; 15–17C painting and sculpture; miniatures (including Anne of Denmark, by Hilliard); Renaissance jewellery; 16–17C glass; Limoges enamel; and illuminated manuscripts.

1½m N is *Quainton Railway Centre*, former depot of the Grand Central Railway, with vintage steam locomotives. *Quainton* church, 1m beyond, has many fine 17–18C monuments.

51m: A sideroad leads S from A41 to (4m) *Brill*, on an isolated hill enjoying a wide *view, with an interesting 11–14C church and an old windmill.

Wotton House, 3m NE of Brill, is early 18C with alterations by Sir John Soane in 1820. *Boarstall*, 2m W of Brill, has a 14C fortified gatehouse (NT, open by appointment) and an 18C duck decoy in natural woodland (also NT).

A41 enters Oxfordshire before (56m) **Bicester** (pronounced 'Bister'; 17,200 inhabitants), a dull town. The big church has a stained glass window (1866) by Morris and Co. 65m: *Aynho*, at the S tip of Northamptonshire, is a charming village built in creamy stone. *Aynhoe Park* (limited opening) is a 17C house altered by Sir John Soane in 1800–05. A41 crosses the Cherwell, marking the border of Oxfordshire, and joins the Oxford road at the handsome village of (67½m) *Adderbury*. The large 14C *church, with a 15C chancel, has notable carving on the outside. Adderbury House was the home of the Earl of Rochester (1647–80).

The neighbourhood has several interesting churches. *King's Sutton*, 1½m E across the Cherwell, has an elaborate Perpendicular steeple. *Bloxham*, a large, well-built village 2m W, has a magnificent *church, mainly 14C, with carving by the same masons who worked at Adderbury and stained glass by Morris and Co. *South Newington* church, 1½m beyond Bloxham, has wall paintings dating from c 1360.

71m: **Banbury** (38,200 inhabitants; TI) is a busy town with several 17C houses. It is known for its cakes and ale and for 'Banbury Cross', destroyed by Puritans in 1602 and replaced by a new one in 1859. The neo-classical church (1790–1822) is by S.P. and C.R. Cockerell, the citizens having blown up the medieval one with gunpowder.

Broughton Castle (limited opening), on B4035 3m SW, is a moated building of c 1300 remodelled as a Tudor mansion. The interior has 16C plaster ceilings, panelling and chimneypieces, including one in the French style in the room known as the Star Chamber. The chapel survives from the 14C, while the Gallery is the most striking 18C Gothick alteration. *Warkworth*, 2m E of Banbury, has the mid 14C tomb of (?) Sir John de Lyons in its church. For *Middleton Cheney*, see the alternative route from Aylesbury to Banbury, above.

FROM BANBURY TO COVENTRY VIA SOUTHAM, 27m via A423. This alternative to the main route below heads directly N from Banbury, avoiding Warwick and Leamington. 4½m: *Mollington*. Charles I defeated Waller in 1644 at *Cropredy*, on the Cherwell 2m E. A423 enters Warwickshire. 6m: *Farnborough Hall* (NT) is a 17–18C building with rococo plasterwork and attractive grounds. 9m: *Wormleighton*, 1½m to the right, has a church with a Perpendicular screen and Jacobean woodwork, and the remains of an early 17C manor house, half destroyed after Prince Rupert's stay here before Edgehill. 14m: *Southam* has an inn on the site of the 14–18C mint where trade tokens were made. The church, mainly 14–15C, has a fine clerestory and 16C timber roof. 27m: *Coventry*, see below.

FROM BANBURY TO STRATFORD-UPON-AVON. The direct route, 20m by A422, runs via the steep *Sun Rising Hill*. 3m: The 17C *Wroxton Abbey*, once the home of Lord North,

Prime Minister during the American War of Independence, is owned by Fairleigh Dickinson University. 5m: At *Alkerton*, left of A422, the gardens of Brook Cottage are open. Near the top of the hill is (8m) *Upton House* (NT), a 16–17C building with paintings by El Greco, Rembrandt, Bosch (*'Nativity'), Hogarth and Reynolds, as well as Brussels tapestries, porcelain and furniture.

A better route to Stratford (21m) follows A41, the Warwick and Birmingham road, to (5m) the pleasant village of *Warmington* and branches left on B4086. Below (7½m) *Edge Hill* (1 in 7) the first, indecisive battle of the Civil War was fought in 1642. The village has a sham castle built by Sanderson Miller in the 1740s, now a pub, overlooking the battlefield. 13m: *Compton Verney* (not open) is an 18C house, with work by Robert Adam, standing near a large lake. The road crosses the Foss Way. Beyond (16m) *Wellesbourne* B4086 leads via *Charlecote Park* into (21m) *Stratford-upon-Avon* (both Route 53).

FROM BANBURY TO NORTHAMPTON, 25m. From A422 2m E of Banbury B4525 branches NE. 7½m: *Sulgrave Manor* (open) is the English home of George Washington's ancestors, rebuilt by Lawrence Washington after he acquired it in 1539. The porch bears the family coat of arms, dubiously regarded as the origin of the 'Stars and Stripes'. The house has been restored as a Washington museum, with 16–17C furnishings and portraits of the President by Gilbert Stuart, Charles Willson Peale and Archibald Robertson. *Sulgrave* has an interesting church with brasses of Lawrence Washington (d. 1584) and his wife. 11m: At *Canons Ashby* the church is a relic of an Augustinian priory. *Canons Ashby House* (NT), the seat of the Dryden family, is mid 16C with Queen Anne alterations, and pleasant formal gardens. The Jacobean plaster ceiling in the drawing room is outstanding. At 17m B4525 crosses A5 (Route 52B) and becomes B452, joining A45 at 21m, heading E to (25m) *Northampton* (Route 59).

Beyond Banbury A41 enters Warwickshire. 76½m: *Warmington*, see the detour from Banbury to Stratford above. The *Dassett Hills* rise on the right. At 83½m is the windmill at *Chesterton*, 1½m to the right. Built in 1632, this curious structure has been attributed to the landowner Sir Edward Peyto, Inigo Jones and Nicholas Stone. Stone was certainly responsible for the monument (1639) to Sir William Peyto and his wife in the Decorated and Perpendicular parish church. A41 crosses the Foss Way.

90m: **WARWICK** (pronounced 'Warrick'; 22,000 inhabitants), an old county town known for its medieval castle, stands on a rocky hill overlooking the N bank of the Avon. It owes much of its handsome, unified appearance to rebuilding after a fire in 1694.

TI: The Court House, Jury St. **Railway Station**: Off Coventry Rd, NE of the centre. **Buses**: from Market Place.

The *East Gate*, a relic of the old town walls, is crowned with a Gothick chapel of 1788. Warwick Castle, to the S, is described at the end of this tour. Smith St. heads E, passing the birthplace of Walter Savage Landor (1775–1864) on the left. *St John's House*, on the right beyond, is a picturesque 17C building on the site of a Hospital of St John. It is now a branch of the County Museum, with costumes, domestic scenes, musical instruments and a regimental collection. From the East Gate the dignified Jury St. leads towards the centre of town. Outstanding are the Georgian *Pageant House* on the left and, at the central crossing, the *Court House* (1725–28) by Francis Smith, now the Town Council offices and TI Centre.

In Castle St., to the left, is the 16C house of Thomas Oken (d. 1573), now the *Warwick Doll Museum*.

Church St., on the right, leads to the collegiate church of **St Mary**. After the original building was largely destroyed in the fire of 1694, the tower, nave, aisles and transepts were rebuilt by Sir William Wilson in a curious mixture of Gothic and Renaissance styles.

The main points of interest are survivals from the earlier church. In the centre of the tall chancel (completed in 1392) stands the *tomb, with recumbent effigies, of Thomas Beauchamp, Earl of Warwick (d. 1369), founder of the choir, and his wife. In front of the altar is a brass to Cecilia Puckering (d. 1626) with an anagram on her name. The former chapter house, N of the choir, has the pretentious tomb of Fulke Greville, Lord Brooke (see Warwick Castle, below). The Norman crypt has massive piers.

The S transept leads to the Perpendicular *Beauchamp Chapel (1443–64). The bear and ragged staff of the Warwicks are much in evidence. Outside the entrance (a convincing pastiche of 1704) is the brass of Thomas Beauchamp, Earl of Warwick (d. 1401), who finished the choir, and his wife. In the centre of the chapel is the tomb of its founder, Richard Beauchamp, Earl of Warwick (d. 1439), and his wife, with a brass effigy surmounted by a guard of unusual design. By the N wall is the painted monument of Robert Dudley, Earl of Leicester (d. 1588), friend and Councillor to Elizabeth I, and his wife Lettice (d. 1634); his infant son, Robert Dudley (d. 1584), lies by the S wall. To the SW of the founder's tomb is the altar tomb of Ambrose Dudley, Earl of Warwick (d. 1590). The windows have contemporary glass and the stalls date from 1449. Over the W door is a painted Last Judgement of 1678, damaged in the fire. Between the chapel and the chancel is the so-called Little Chantry with fan vaulting and niches and a wooden piscina.

The High St. continues past the *Aylesford Hotel* (1696) and the *Warwick Arms Hotel* (1790), the vista being closed by the *West Gate*. The chapel above belongs to the **Lord Leycester Hospital** (open), whose half-timbered buildings are on the right.

Robert Dudley, Earl of Leicester, founded the hospital in 1571, combining the buildings of several religious guilds to provide an asylum for aged or infirm retainers and their wives. The brethren, now ex-servicemen, wear black gowns on state occasions and still retain their original silver badges of 1571. The Guildhall (c 1450) in the S range contains a small museum, while the Great Hall of King James in the W range, dating from c 1383 but named after a royal visit in 1617, has a fine oak roof. The Chapel of St James over the gateway was founded in 1383; the tower was added in 1450 and the E window in the 19C. A malthouse and the former Anchor Inn, both 17C, are now flats for the brethren.

Fragments of the town walls survive N of the West Gate, and can be seen from Friars St. and Bowling Green St. Bowling Green St. leads to the Market Place, with the 17C Market Hall housing the *County Museum*. Its collection of local geology, natural history and history includes the 17C Sheldon tapestry of Warwickshire.

Castle Hill leads to *Warwick Castle (open), above the Avon on the S side of the town. From the outside it has the satisfyingly picturesque look of a 14C fortress, while its state rooms are those of a 17–19C mansion. It is extremely popular with visitors.

Although 'The Anglo-Saxon Chronicle' records that Ethelfleda, Alfred the Great's daughter, fortified Warwick in 914, the mound to the W of the present castle is a Norman motte. This Norman fortress, an earth and timber structure built at the behest of William the Conqueror, was strengthened in stone in the 12C. The Earls of Warwick rebuilt the castle in the 14C, adding outer walls, towers and gateways. In 1604 it was granted by James I to Sir Fulke Greville, later Lord Brooke (1554–1628), who spent large sums on its repair. His 17–19C descendants, Earls of Warwick in the second creation, were largely responsible for the present appearance of the state rooms and private apartments. In 1978 the castle was bought by Madame Tussauds.

A winding approach cut through solid rock leads to the entrance via the Clock Tower and Barbican, with historical displays. To its left is the entrance to the Armoury and the massive, irregular Caesar's Tower, with dungeons in the lower storey; to its right

is the 12-sided Guy's Tower, with a good view of the castle buildings f
the other sides of the turfed Inner Court are the Bear and Clarence Tow
Norman mound (in front) and the range of domestic buildings overlooking u.
(left).

The Great Hall, originally 14C but with much 19C reconstruction, contains arms and
armour, a huge 14C cooking pot, a bust of Charles I by Rysbrack and the grotesque
'Kenilworth Buffet' of 1851. The state rooms (mostly decorated in 1770–90) contain
portraits by Van Dyck, Lely and Kneller, sculpture, furniture and china. Note the Adam
fireplace in the Cedar Drawing Room, the Italian inlaid table in the Green Drawing
Room and the Delft tapestries in the Queen Anne Bedroom. The private apartments
contain a reconstruction, with tableaux of wax figures, of a royal weekend party in
1898.

The gardens, laid out by Capability Brown in 1753, have pretty walks, peacocks and
a conservatory, now housing a 'spectacle' devised by the present management.

Mill St., with some attractive old houses, descends from the castle gate to
the river, giving a view of the castle and the broken 14C bridge. The main
Banbury road leads to the stone bridge of 1790, which gives a better •view
of the castle. On the left is the pleasant *St Nicholas's Park*. Beyond the river
is Bridgend, with some timbered buildings and, in Myton Rd to the left,
Warwick School, in 19C buildings but claiming a continuous existence since
1100.

ROYAL LEAMINGTON SPA (56,500 inhabitants), 2m E of Warwick, owes
its Regency and Victorian buildings and its handsome gardens to the former
popularity of its chalybeate and salt springs. They first attracted attention
towards the end of the 18C and the first bath was opened in 1786, but real
prosperity came in the 19C, when Dr Henry Jephson was the leading
physician. Queen Victoria bestowed the prefix 'Royal' on Leamington Spa.

TI: Jephson Lodge, The Parade. **Railway Station**: Old Warwick Rd (A425), SW of town
centre. **Buses**: from The Parade. **Theatre**: Royal Spa Centre, Newbold St.

Visitors. Ruskin was taken by his parents to consult Dr Jephson in 1841. The same
year brought Cobden to Leamington, to urge the recently bereaved John Bright to
work for the repeal of the Corn Laws. Dickens, who later gave public readings here,
made Leamington the scene of Mr Dombey's introduction to Mrs Skewton and Edith
Granger. Hawthorne stayed here while writing 'Our Old Home' in 1858.

In the middle of the town, where the Victoria Bridge crosses the river Leam,
stands the *Royal Pump Room*, with a colonnade of 1813–14 but otherwise
rebuilt in 1926. Physiotherapy treatment is still given here under the
National Health Service. Behind it are the *Royal Pump Room Gardens*; on
the other bank, York Walk leads ¾m to the large *Victoria Park*. Opposite
the Pump Room are the *Jephson Gardens*, with the *Mill Gardens* further
away, S of the river.

Bath St. leads S towards the railway station, passing *All Saints*, begun in
1843 to the design of its vicar and extended by Blomfield. The *Art Gallery
and Museum* is in Avenue Rd, to the right. It includes Dutch and Flemish
paintings (Bloemaert), 19–20C English paintings, ceramics (Delft,
Wedgwood) and 18C drinking glasses.

N of the Pump Room runs the spacious Parade, with early 19C buildings.
More of Leamington's characteristic architecture can be seen in Clarendon
Square, further N, and Lansdowne Crescent and Lansdowne Circus (NE),
reached by turning right along Warwick St.

Offchurch, 3m E, has a 13C church with Norman details.

ROM WARWICK TO STRATFORD-UPON-AVON. The direct way (8m) is by A429 and A46. A more interesting route, 1½m longer, stays on A429, crossing the Avon just before (3m) *Barford*. 5¾m: B4088, leading right, skirts the edge of *Charlecote Park* (Route 53). B4086 heads for (9½m) *Stratford-upon-Avon* (Route 53).

FROM WARWICK TO BIRMINGHAM, 20m by A41. 6m: *Baddesley Clinton*. The moated manor house (NT) dates from the 14C. For *Packwood House*, 2m W, see the detour from Stratford to Birmingham in Route 53. 10m: *Knowle* has a Perpendicular church. 11m: A41 crosses M42. 13m: *Solihull* (107,100 inhabitants; TI), now a suburb of Birmingham, has a restored 13–15C church. 20m: *Birmingham*, see Route 61.

The main route leaves Warwick by the Coventry road, heading N past a statue of Guy and the boar by Keith Godwin (1964) to (91m) *Guy's Cliffe*, where a 15C chantry with a statue of the knight is romantically situated above a pool of the Avon. Here, according to legend, Guy of Warwick lived the life of a hermit after killing the Dun Cow and the giant Colbrand and performing heroic deeds in the Holy Land. Nearby is the so-called Saxon Mill, often painted by David Cox and others. 91½m: A46 is joined near Gaveston's Cross (1832), marking the spot where Edward II's favourite, Piers Gaveston, was executed in 1312.

94m: **Kenilworth** (19,300 inhabitants; TI), left of A46, has the scanty remains of a 12C Augustinian priory and a fine Norman doorway, perhaps from the priory, inserted in the tower of the over-restored parish church. The town is usually visited for ***Kenilworth Castle** (EH, all year), a ruin in red sandstone, with Norman, 14C and Elizabethan work, made famous by Sir Walter Scott.

It was founded soon after 1120 by Geoffrey of Clinton, Treasurer of England. The keep was built in 1170–80 and the outer wall and its towers in 1203–16. John of Gaunt, Earl of Lancaster, added the Strong Tower, the Great Hall and the southern rooms in the 1390s. The castle passed to his son, Henry IV, and remained royal until Elizabeth granted it to Robert Dudley, Earl of Leicester, in 1563. He improved and enlarged the building, and entertained Elizabeth here in 1565, 1568, 1572 and 1575. The pageants of the last year are described by Scott. In 1648 the castle was awarded to the Parliamentarian Colonel Hawkesworth, who began the destruction.

Visitors can enter by Castle Green on the N side; a better approach is from the S, crossing the causeway which once dammed the artificial lake to Mortimer's Tower. The curtain wall and towers of the Outer Ward are early 13C; the stables and gatehouse at the N entrance, the only part of the castle still habitable, are the Earl of Leicester's additions. To the right of the Inner Court is the massive Norman keep. Adjoining it on the same side are the scanty remains of the kitchens, beyond which is the Strong Tower (1390), with the room of Amy Robsart, Leicester's first wife. The W side of the Inner Court is occupied by John of Gaunt's Great Hall, with two oriels at its S end. On the S side are the White Hall, or Great Chamber, and the Second Chamber, ending John of Gaunt's work. In the SE angle are Leicester's Buildings, with the rooms where Queen Elizabeth stayed in 1575. Henry VIII's Lodgings, on the E side, have practically disappeared. The garden was on the N side of the keep.

Stoneleigh Abbey (open), by the Avon 3m E of Kenilworth, is a Baroque mansion (1714–26) by Francis Smith of Warwick. The 14C gatehouse and some Norman doorways with fine mouldings survive from the Cistercian monastery founded here in 1154, while the E wing (not open) belongs to the Elizabethan house built after the Dissolution. In Smith's W range, the Card Room and Dining Room preserve their contemporary wood panelling, while the Saloon and Chapel have plasterwork decoration added later in the 18C. The Royal Agricultural Show is held in the park in early July. The parish church of *Stoneleigh* has Norman work, including the font, and monuments of the Leigh family.

From Kenilworth A429 heads directly N to Coventry. On the left shortly before it crosses (97m) A45 is the *University of Warwick*, founded in 1961 and opened in 1965. The Arts Centre (1974, enlarged in 1981 a theatre, smaller studio theatre, cinema, concert hall and the Mu with a permanent collection and temporary exhibitions.

99m: **COVENTRY** (318,000 inhabitants) looks wholly modern at first sight. It is dominated by Sir Basil Spence's cathedral, the shopping precinct, the inner ring road and all the other fruits of the rebuilding which followed the German bombing raid in 1940. In fact, the city has a long history, particularly as a centre of trade and manufacturing. The ruins of the old cathedral have been preserved next to its successor but elsewhere, with the medieval street plan all but effaced, the relics of Coventry's past—its parish churches, and the remains of its powerful religious houses and guilds—are disjointed fragments which need seeking out among the post-war development.

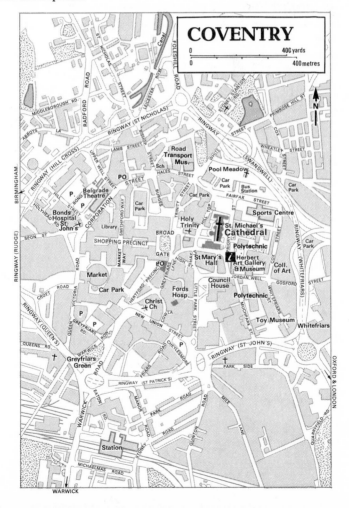

(: Bayley Lane. **Bus Station**: Pool Meadow, near the inner ring road, NE of the centre. **Railway Station**: Eaton Rd, S of the centre and the inner ring road. **Airport**: Regular flights to Dublin, Gloucester/Cheltenham, Guernsey, Jersey, Oxford and Waterford. **Theatres**: Belgrade Theatre, Corporation St.; Arts Centre, University of Warwick.

History. Coventre, the Couentrev of the Domesday Book, may derive from a Saxon convent, but its practical history begins with the foundation of a Benedictine priory in 1043 by Leofric, Earl of Mercia, and his wife Godgyfu. The legend of how Lady Godiva averted her husband's anger from the town by riding naked through its streets is first found in the 'Flores Historiarum' of 1235; the episode of Peeping Tom dates only from the 17C. After the Conquest the town prospered so greatly, as a centre of the wool trade and then of cloth-making, that by 1377 it ranked next to London, York and Bristol. After the cloth industry declined at the end of the 16C, Coventry became famous for woollen caps, silk ribbons, watches and (in the 19C) sewing-machines. Its bicycle industry was established in the 1870s and its motor industry in the 1890s. An armaments centre during both World Wars, it suffered the German air raid which devastated its old cathedral, much of the centre and many factories on the night of 14 November 1940. Rebuilding began in post-war years under the supervision of the City Architect, Sir Donald Gibson.

Natives and residents. George Eliot (1819–79) attended school at Nantglyn, 29 Warwick Row, W of Greyfriars Green, and lived with her father in 1841–49 at Bird Grove in the Foleshill Rd. Ellen Terry (1847–1928) was born in either Market St. or Smithford St. Philip Larkin was born here in 1922: 'Nothing, like something, happens anywhere'.

The centre is Broadgate, an open space laid out as a garden with a statue of Lady Godiva on horseback by Reid Dick (1949). Under the Godiva Clock is a mosaic memorial to 16C Coventry martyrs by René Antonietti (1953). The reliefs on the steel doors of the National Westminster bank are worth noting. The shopping precinct extends W of Broadgate.

To the E rise two of Tennyson's 'three tall spires' of Coventry. The nearer belongs to *Holy Trinity*, a Perpendicular church with a fine roof and tower-lantern (1667), a remarkable Perpendicular stone pulpit, and stalls with misericords from Whitefriars. The W window is by Hugh Easton (1955). Sarah Siddons was married here in 1773. Priory Row, N of the church, has pleasant old houses and fragments of the priory church demolished in 1539.

Just to the S the Perpendicular steeple dominates the remains of the old cathedral, built as the parish church of St Michael, raised to cathedral status in 1918 and largely destroyed in 1940. The shell has been rededicated as a memorial shrine and vestibule to the new **Cathedral**. Its moving desolation is heightened by the altar cross of charred roof beams (now a replica). Set against the S wall is Epstein's figure of Christ, 'Ecce Homo' (1935). In a gesture of reconciliation, the vestries were rebuilt as an international centre by German students and apprentices.

The new cathedral, designed by Sir Basil Spence and built in 1954–62, extends towards the N at right-angles to the old. (Thus its 'E end' in fact faces N, but in the description below the liturgical rather than geographical points of the compass are used.) Benjamin Britten's 'War Requiem' was written for its rededication.

The exterior, with an alternating screen of wall in pink sandstone and window set saw-toothed to the line of the building, gives marked contrasts. The roof is topped by a gilded bronze flèche, locally nicknamed 'Radio Coventry'. On the nave wall facing Priory St., by the steps leading up to the porch, is Epstein's bronze of St Michael subduing the Devil. The extended roof of the porch links old and new buildings. Their unity is further emphasised by the enormous glass screen, engraved with translucent figures by John Hutton, which takes the place of a W wall.

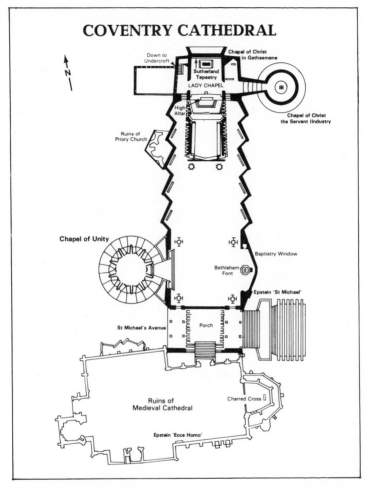

COVENTRY CATHEDRAL

N

Down to Undercroft

Chapel of Christ in Gethsemane

Sutherland Tapestry

LADY CHAPEL

High Altar

Chapel of Christ the Servant (Industry)

Ruins of Priory Church

Chapel of Unity

Baptistry Window

Bethlehem Font

Epstein 'St Michael'

St Michael's Avenue

Porch

Ruins of Medieval Cathedral

Charred Cross

Epstein 'Ecce Homo'

Since the side windows are hidden from view when the cathedral is entered from the W, attention is immediately drawn towards the altar by the immensity of Graham Sutherland's tapestry. The *Nave* has a floor of polished black and white marble, contrasting with the plain walls. The ceiling, carried on two rows of slender concrete columns, is made up of concrete ribs which form an unbroken diamond pattern, filled in with wooden louvres. The roof above is carried wholly by the outer walls. The *Baptistery*, to the right, is a shallow alcove bounded by a stained-glass •window, by John Piper and Patrick Reyntiens, extending from floor to ceiling. The font is a rough sandstone boulder from the valley of Barakat outside Bethlehem. Opposite is the entrance to the *Chapel of Unity*, shaped like a crusader's tent. Its mosaic floor was designed by the Swedish artist Einar Forseth; the windows, by Margaret Traherne, were paid for by German donors.

At the foot of each section of nave wall are the carved stone •Tablets of the Word, by Ralph Beyer. The walk down the nave reveals each pair of the ten nave windows, throwing light from their abstract colours towards the altar. They were designed by Lawrence Lee, Geoffrey Clarke and Keith New.

The *Chancel* is not formed by the traditional placing of lectern (with bronze eagle by Elizabeth Frink), pulpit and stalls. These and the bishop's throne on the left have canopies which suggest, not too happily, flocks of doves in flight. The uncased organ is on either side of the end walls of the aisles. The stone altar stands alone in front of a silver-gilt cross by Geoffrey Clarke, which cradles another cross of nails. Beyond is the *Lady Chapel*, its structural simplicity forming a foil for the *tapestry by Graham Sutherland which fills the whole E wall. Woven at Felletin, near Aubusson, in France, it depicts Christ in Glory with man at his feet. A lower panel showing Christ crucified gives the effect of a reredos to the Lady Chapel altar and, when seen from the nave, to the high altar.

To the right of the Lady Chapel is the theatrical *Chapel of Christ in Gethsemane*, separated from the aisle only by a wrought-iron crown of thorns by Sir Basil Spence. Behind the asymmetrically placed altar a kneeling angel in bronze relief is silhouetted against a rich gold mosaic, by Stephen Sykes. A short passage leads to the *Chapel of Industry* (Chapel of Christ the Servant), combining the functions of the former guild chapels. Its windows give glimpses of industrial Coventry. To the left of the Lady Chapel, steps lead down to the visitors' centre in the *Undercroft*.

John F. Kennedy House, a youth centre in the precincts, was opened in 1965 by Willy Brandt, then Chief Burgomaster of Berlin and later Chancellor of West Germany.

In Priory St., flanking the cathedral, rises *Coventry University*. S of the cathedral is *St Mary's Hall (open when not in civic use), founded in 1342 for the Merchant Guild, enlarged c 1400 for the Trinity Guild and since 1552 the property of the corporation.

Above the kitchen and vaulted crypt is the Great Hall, with the Coventry Tapestry, an early 16C Flemish work probably commemorating Henry VII and Elizabeth of York's visit in 1500. Two small chambers opening off the hall have panelling from old Coventry inns. On the S rises the 13C Caesar's Tower, perhaps a relic of the Earl of Chester's castle. The only part to be destroyed in 1940, it has been reconstructed with the old material. Mary, Queen of Scots, was imprisoned for a while in 1569 on its second floor.

Greyfriars Lane leads S from High St. past *Ford's Hospital* (1509), a half-timbered almshouse for five poor men and their wives, restored after bomb damage. Further S is the third of the three spires of Coventry, the octagonal steeple (c 1350) of *Christ Church*, the only part of the church to survive bombing in 1940.

Warwick Rd goes on to Greyfriars Green, with its gardens and a statue of Sir Thomas White (1492–1567), founder of St John's College, Oxford. Eaton Rd, on the other side of the inner ring road, continues to the station.

The **Herbert Art Gallery and Museum** is in Jordan Well.

Visitors interested in the cathedral should see Graham Sutherland's preparatory sketches for the tapestry. The Philip Allen collection of oriental ceramics illustrates the development of the potter's art over 2000 years. A history gallery tells the story of Coventry. There are also small displays of natural history and archaeology, as well as temporary exhibitions.

Whitefriars St. and a subway under the ring road lead to the **Whitefriars Museum**, comprising the E cloisters, chapter house and dormitory of a Carmelite friary founded in 1342, with a small explanatory display. The building is often used for special sculpture exhibitions and for concerts, plays, etc.

Hales St., N of the centre, begins near the inner ring road and the Pool Meadow bus station with a section of the old *City Wall* (1356, dismantled 1662), skirted by a pleasant garden, connecting the small Swanswell Gate and Cook St. Gate. Around the corner is the *Museum of British Road Transport*, with cars, motor cycles and bicycles by famous Coventry manufacturers (Daimler, Jaguar, Singer, Standard, Triumph). Corporation St. leads from the W end of Hales St., passing the *Belgrade Theatre*, whose name recalls the wartime exchange of aid between the two bombed cities. In Hill St., on the right, *Bond's Hospital* and the former buildings of *Bablake School*, both originally 16C, make a picturesque group. Close by, at the corner of Corporation St. and Fleet St., is the mid 14C *St John's Church*, with a lantern tower. The phrase 'to send to Coventry' may derive from the fate of defeated Royalist troops imprisoned in the church during the Civil War and shunned by the inhabitants. Spon St., continuing Fleet St. to the W, was a centre of the watch-making industry. It still has medieval cottages.

Wyken, in the NE suburbs, has a Norman church with a 15C wall painting of St Christopher. *Coombe Park*, about 3m E of Coventry, has formal gardens and woods. Coombe Abbey (not open) stands on the site of a Cistercian monastery and has part of its 13–15C cloisters. At *Baginton*, beyond A45 3m S of Coventry, the Lunt (open) is a reconstructed Roman fort of the 1C AD. The parish church has a good brass of Sir William Bagot (d. 1407), a minor character in Shakespeare's 'Richard II'.

FROM COVENTRY TO BIRMINGHAM, 17m by A45. A45 is joined NW of Coventry. 6m: *Meriden* has a cross said to mark the centre of England. *Berkswell*, 2m S, is a pleasant village in a rural pocket. The church has a Norman chancel and Saxon and Norman crypts. *Great Packington*, 1m NW of Meriden, has a church (1789–90) by Joseph Bonomi. The composer Richard Mudge (1717–63) died here. 8m: A45 crosses M42. 10m: *Elmdon*, with Birmingham Airport, is near the National Exhibition Centre. 17m: *Birmingham* (Route 61) is reached through the E suburbs of Yardley and Small Heath.

From Coventry to *Chester*, see Route 64.

B. Via St Albans and Rugby

Directions. Total distance 91m. M1 provides a quick alternative. A5, A5183 to (19m) **St Albans**. A5183, A5 to (32m) Dunstable. A5 to (45m) Milton Keynes, (59m) Towcester and (67m) Weedon Bec. A5, A428 to (81m) **Rugby**. A428 to (91m) **Coventry** (Route 52A).

A5 runs NW from London, following the course of the Roman Watling Street, and changes its name to A5183 beyond (11m) *Elstree*.

19m: **ST ALBANS** (72,300 inhabitants), on a hill by the Ver, is an old place with the remains of the Roman Verulamium and a largely Norman abbey church, now the cathedral. The streets round the market centre have some good old houses and inns.

TI: Town Hall. **Railway Stations**: City Station (King's Cross line), NE of the centre; Abbey Station (Warford line), S of the centre. **Theatre**: Amateur productions at Abbey Theatre, Holywell Hill. **Events**: International Organ Festival held biennially in July (1995, etc.) in the cathedral.

History. St Albans is the successor of the Roman Verulamium (see description below). It owes its name to St Alban, a Roman soldier and England's first Christian martyr, beheaded here in AD 209 for sheltering Amphibalus, the priest who had converted him. The hill where he was executed became the site of a Roman shrine, a Saxon church and a Benedictine abbey founded c 793 by Offa, King of Mercia. The abbey rose to great wealth and power, its head being the premier abbot of England between 1154 and 1396. Two important battles took place during the Wars of the Roses: Henry VI was defeated and captured at the first, near Holywell Hill in 1455, and released after Queen Margaret's victory at the second, on Bernard's Heath N of St Peter's church in 1461. The abbey church became cathedral of a new diocese in 1877.

Natives and residents. Nicholas Breakspear, who became Pope Adrian IV in 1154, was educated at St Albans. The chronicler Matthew Paris (d. 1259) was a monk here. The composer Robert Fayrfax was organist in the abbey church from 1498 until his death in 1521. Sir Francis Bacon (1561–1621) lived and died at Gorhambury (see below) and is buried in St Michael's church (see below). The dramatist James Shirley (1596–1666) taught at the grammar school. Sarah, Duchess of Marlborough (1660–1744), was born at St Albans and William Cowper was a patient here in 1764–65.

The *Clock Tower* (limited opening), dating from 1411, in the High St. is the centre of the town. In front of it stood an Eleanor Cross, destroyed in 1702. The old French Row leads N, past a 15C inn, to the *Town Hall* of 1830. The broad, tree-shaded St Peter's St., where a market is held on Wednesdays and Saturdays, goes on to *St Peter's*, a late Perpendicular church with old glass and a tablet to Edward Strong (d. 1723), Wren's master mason.

Nearly opposite the W end of St Peter's are *Pemberton's Almshouses* (1624). Hatfield Rd to the E has another group of almshouses, founded by Sarah, Duchess of Marlborough in 1736. The *Museum of St Albans*, opposite, has craft tools, workshops and period rooms, and a natural history collection. Off the E side of St Peter's St. is the *Civic Centre* with the *Alban Arena* (1968).

Passages from High St. or the attractive Holywell Hill lead to the massive, inelegant **Cathedral**, on higher ground than any other English cathedral. The central tower with its striking arcade and part of the N side of the long nave are Norman, built from Roman bricks and tiles. The ugly W front and transeptal façades are mainly 19C.

The central part, traditionally the site of Alban's martyrdom and Offa's Saxon abbey, is still substantially the church built by Paul of Caen, the first Norman abbot, in 1077–88 and dedicated in 1116. The nave was lengthened to the W in 1200–35 and the E end, which originally ended in a chevron of seven apses just E of the transepts, was rebuilt with presbytery, retrochoir and Lady Chapel between 1235 and 1326. Restoration was begun by Sir Gilbert Scott in 1856 and completed, after the church had been raised to cathedral status in 1877, by Sir Edmund Beckett (later Lord Grimthorpe) who designed and paid for the W front, the transept windows and the nave ceiling.

The plain but graceful W end of the *Nave* is Early English, abruptly joining the Norman work on the N side and continued on the S side by five Decorated bays of 1345. The W and S sides of the Norman piers have 13C and 14C *wall paintings; the westernmost, showing the Crucifixion, is probably by Walter of Colchester (c 1220), whom Matthew Paris called 'an incomparable painter'. A stone rood screen (c 1350) separates the nave from the Norman ritual *Choir* and presbytery. The choir ceiling, divided into square painted panels, dates from the late 14C; the tower ceiling was renewed in 1952, when one original panel was removed to the N presbytery aisle. There too is the *brass of Abbot Thomas de la Mare (d. 1396). A larger 18C panel from the N transept, showing Alban's martyrdom, is preserved in the S presbytery aisle. Most of the presbytery and retrochoir was rebuilt in 1257–1320; the unique wooden vault was painted c 1450. The elaborate stone reredos behind the high altar dates from 1484. The statues are 19C replacements. The altarpiece of the Resurrection is by Sir Alfred Gilbert. On the N side of the presbytery is the chantry of Abbot Ramryge (d. 1520), on the S side the chantry of Abbot Wallingford, donor of the reredos.

The tower, crossing and transepts are the best preserved part of the Norman church. The arches on their E sides led into apsidal chapels. The N transept has a 15C mural of Doubting Thomas. The large rose window on the N wall, by Lord Grimthorpe, was reglazed by Alan Younger in 1989.

Immediately E of the presbytery is *St Alban's Chapel*, with the marble pedestal of the saint's early 14C shrine, pieced together from more than 2000 fragments in 1872 and restored in 1993. On the N side is the *watching loft of c 1400, with a relic cupboard below. There are contemporary carvings on the main beams. On the S side is the *monument to Humphrey, Duke of Gloucester (d. 1447), Henry V's brother; it has a tall canopy with the only pre-Reformation statuettes of English kings and a 13C grille

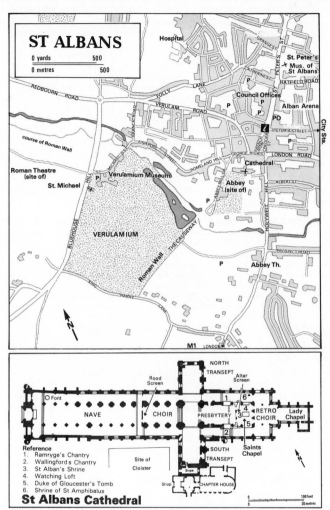

St Albans Cathedral

Reference
1. Ramryge's Chantry
2. Wallingfords Chantry
3. St Alban's Shrine
4. Watching Loft
5. Duke of Gloucester's Tomb
6. Shrine of St Amphibalus

of Sussex ironwork. On either side of the retrochoir are chapels, to St Michael (N) and Our Lady of the Tapers (S). Beyond is the *Lady Chapel* (1308–26).

A door from the S transept leads to the slype and the red-brick *Chapter House* (1982; William Whitfield).

Most of the other monastic buildings were destroyed after the Reformation but the *Abbey Gatehouse* (1361), now part of St Albans School, survives a few yards W of the cathedral. Abbey Mill Lane leads down to a bridge over the Ver, near the *Fighting Cocks Inn*, probably on the site of a boathouse of the Saxon monastery.

Beyond the river and ornamental lake are the park and playing fields on the site of the Roman **Verulamium**.

Prae Wood, on the hill to the SW, was site of a Belgic settlement of the late 1C BC. Verulamium itself was founded soon after the Roman conquest of AD 43 and became a 'municipium', the only one in Britain, two years later. Sacked by Boudicca (Boadicea) in 61, it was rebuilt on a larger scale and flourished until c 410.

To the S is part of the early 3C city wall (EH), which enclosed over 200 acres. A hypocaust with mosaic floor (AD 150 and 300) has been preserved under cover. The foundations of the basilica have been marked out beside the *Museum to the W. Finds from the site include mosaics, wall paintings on plaster, burial urns, lead coffins and a 2C bronze figurine of Venus. On the other side of A414, further W, is the *Roman Theatre*, built c 140 and enlarged several times, the last in c 300.

St Michael's Church, near the museum, has Sir Francis Bacon's tomb, with a statue showing him in a characteristic attitude ('sic sedebat'; 'thus he used to sit'). The church, founded in 948, has traces of Saxon work and a Jacobean pulpit.

St Michael's St. leads back to the town centre via Fishpool St. (with several 15–16C inns and 18C houses), Romeland Hill (the old burial ground of the abbey) and the attractive George St.

Gorhambury (limited opening), beyond the Roman theatre about 1½m W, is a late 18C house with part of Sir Francis Bacon's library, portraits and busts of the Bacon family and two fireplaces by Piranesi. In the hall are two enamelled windows from the Tudor house where Sir Francis lived and died; its ruins lie ¼m W (EH, limited opening in summer, and at other times by appointment). At *Chiswell Green*, about 2m S of St Albans on the Watford road (B4360), are the *Gardens of the Rose* (open), the showground of the Royal National Rose Society. Beyond *London Colney*, 3m SW of St Albans, there is an exhibition of de Haviland aircraft (limited opening) in the grounds of *Salisbury Hall*. The house itself (not open) is a medieval manor remodelled for Nell Gwynne by Charles II. Hawksmoor is buried at *Shenley*, 2m S of London Colney.

From St Albans to *Bedford*, *Oundle* and *Stamford*, see Route 60B.

A5183 changes its name back to A5 after it crosses M1 at 25m. *Flamstead*, ½ S of the road, is a pretty village. Bedfordshire is entered shortly before (32m) **Dunstable** (35,700 inhabitants; TI). The church of *St Peter*, incorporating the remains of an Augustinian priory founded by Henry I, is grand Norman and Early English work. Cranmer pronounced sentence of divorce against Catherine of Aragon here in 1555. Pupils of Dunstable School include Gary Cooper (1901–61).

For *Luton*, to the E, see Route 60B. At **Whipsnade**, on the Chilterns 3m SW of Dunstable, the *Zoo* run by the Zoological Society of London is a pioneer venture in keeping wild animals in uncaged freedom.

36m: *Hockliffe*, at the junction with A4012.

3m W is **Leighton Buzzard** (30,600 inhabitants), an old town united with neighbouring *Linslade* on the opposite bank of the Ouse. The Early English church has a beautiful spire, 13C ironwork on the W door and carvings on the crossing piers. The basilican *church at *Wing*, 2½m SW, has a Saxon apse, crypt and nave arches; among 16–17C Dormer monuments is the classical tomb (1552) of Sir Robert. *Ascott House* (NT), in a charming garden, has the Anthony de Rothschild collection of paintings (Cuyp, Hobbema, Gainsborough, Stubbs), furniture and Oriental porcelain. *Mentmore Towers* (limited opening), 2½m S of Wing, is a neo-Jacobean mansion built for Baron Meyer de Rothschild in 1852–54 by Sir Joseph Paxton, the architect of the Crystal Palace. It is now administrative headquarters of the Maharishi University of Natural Law. *Stewkley*, 3m NW of Wing, has a richly decorated late Norman *church (c 1150).

A4012 runs N from Hockliffe past (2m) *Milton Bryan*, the birthplace of Sir Joseph Paxton, to (4m) *Woburn*, a handsome little town. **Woburn Abbey** (open) was a pioneer among stately homes in the campaign to attract large numbers of visitors. Its atmosphere has suffered in the process. Built on the site of a Cistercian foundation, the house is largely by Henry Flitcroft (W range, 1747–61) and Henry Holland (S range, 1787–90). The sumptuous interior has an outstanding collection of paintings, with rooms devoted to Canaletto and Reynolds, work by 16–17C Dutch masters and George Gower's portrait of Elizabeth I. The grounds have various amusements, several species of deer, including the unique Père David herd, and a famous safari park.

A5 enters Buckinghamshire. 45m: **Milton Keynes** (TI), developed since 1967, has absorbed several older towns and villages, notably *Fenny Stratford, Bletchley, Wolverton* and *Stony Stratford*. Roads and roundabouts spread out from the large central shopping area just N of A5 to enclose separate developments. Walton Hall, SE, is headquarters of the *Open University*.

From Milton Keynes to *Northampton* via *Newport Pagnell*, see Route 59.

A5 crosses the Great Ouse into Northamptonshire. 51m: From the roundabout A508 leads N to (13m) Northampton via Stoke Bruerne (Route 59). A422, heading S to (7m) Buckingham (Route 52A), passes at 1m the turning for *Passenham*, where the church has misericords of 1628 and wall paintings. The remnants of Whittlewood Forest lie to the W of A5.

59m: **Towcester** (5000 inhabitants) is an old town, once important for its coaching inns, on the site of the Roman Lactodorum. *St Lawrence* has the tomb of Archdeacon Sponne (d. 1449), a local benefactor.

Easton Neston, to the E (public drive to the church), is a mansion remodelled by Wren and Hawksmoor. The church at *Slapton*, 4m SW of Towcester, has 14C wall paintings. Edith Sitwell (1887–1965) is buried at *Weedon Lois*, about 4m further W..
A43 to (11m) Brackley (Route 52A) passes (4m) *Silverstone* with its motor-racing track.

67m: *Weedon* (or Weedon Bec), properly *Weedon Bec*. At *Stowe Nine Churches*, 2m S, the church has a Saxon tower and good monuments, including one of 1617–20 to Elizabeth Lady Carey by Nicholas Stone. There are brasses and medieval monuments in the church at *Dodford*, 1¼m W of Weedon.

FROM WEEDON TO COVENTRY VIA DAVENTRY, 23m by A45. 4m: **Daventry** (17,000 inhabitants; TI) is an old town with a church of 1752–58 by David Hiorne. Charles I spent the week before Naseby at the Wheatsheaf. A BBC transmitter is prominent on the outskirts. A361, the Banbury road, leads S to the source of the Cherwell at (4½m) *Charwelton*. The church, 1m E, has 15–16C brasses and tombs of the Andrews family. 7m: *Braunston* is a waterway junction on the **Grand Union Canal**. Formed in 1929 by the union of the Grand Junction, the Regent's and six other canals (all still navigable), the Grand Union links Braunston with the Thames (S), the Nene (E) and the Trent (N) and with most centres of the Midlands. The old Grand Junction Canal, built in 1793–1805, leaves the Thames at Brentford and runs a 94m course via Watford, Berkhamsted, Tring, Leighton Buzzard, Wolverton and Weedon, closely followed by the Midland railway, to join the Oxford Canal (Route 49B) here. It has tunnels between Blisworth and Stoke Bruerne (Route 59) and E of Braunston (2042yd long). From Braunston, the N reach of the Oxford Canal connects via (23m) the Hawkesbury junction with the Coventry Canal. From the *Norton* junction, 4½m E of Braunston, the old *Grand Union* (24½m; 1814), now part of the 'Leicester Arm', runs N to the Leicestershire and Northamptonshire Union Canal at Gumley near Market Harborough, threading Crick and Husbands Bosworth tunnels and descending Foxton locks; from here the Trent may be reached. From the *Napton* junction, 5m W of Braunston, the Oxford Canal goes S to Oxford via Banbury, and the 'Birmingham Arm' of the Grand Union runs via Warwick and Kingswood (Route 53) to Birmingham. A45 enters Warwickshire and crosses M5. 12m: *Dunchurch* lies 3m S of Rugby (see below).

At (20m) *Willenhall* (nr Coventry) the suburbs of Coventry begin. *Wolston*, 3½m E, has a church with Norman work, and some remains of an old priory. 23m: *Coventry*, see Route 52A.

Beyond Weedon A5 continues along the line of the old Watling Street, closely accompanied by the Grand Union Canal (see above), the railway line and the M1. 70½m: Near *Buckby Locks* on the canal was the Roman settlement of Bannaventa. A mile further N A5 passes the junction of two arms of the Grand Union on the left, then crosses the Leicester arm and the railway line in the *Watford Gap*, by the big motorway junction. A5 leaves its Roman line near (76m) *Kilsby*.

The church at *Ashby St Ledgers*, on A361 2½m S, has 14C wall paintings. The manor house (not open) belonged to Robert Catesby and was a meeting place for conspirators in the Gunpowder Plot.

77m: A5 is left for A428. Route 64, from Coventry to Chester, picks up the A5 further N beyond Nuneaton. 78½m: *Hillmorton* church has 14C effigies. 81m: **Rugby** (60,400 inhabitants; TI) is a railway junction and industrial centre, with a public school.

Rugby School was founded in 1567, though it became eminent under the headmastership (1828–42) of Dr Thomas Arnold. The mainly 19C buildings are dominated by the work of William Butterfield. His characteristically emphatic chapel (1872) has 16C Flemish glass and windows by Morris and Co., as well as the tomb of Dr Arnold, moved from the earlier chapel. A statue by Brock commemorates Thomas Hughes (1822–96), author of 'Tom Brown's Schooldays'. A tablet on the 'Doctor's Wall' commemorates William Webb Ellis, whose 'fine disregard for the Rules of Football' originated the game of rugby. Pupils include Sir Richard Temple, Walter Savage Landor, Dean Arthur Stanley, Matthew Arnold, Thomas Hughes, Lewis Carroll, Arthur Hugh Clough, Wyndham Lewis and Rupert Brooke, a native of Rugby and son of a master.

FROM RUGBY TO LEICESTER, 21m by A426. 4m: The road crosses A5 NE of Rugby. The Roman station of Tripontium lay 1m S. At *Shawell*, 1m E, Tennyson wrote much of 'In Memoriam'. The only place of interest further along the way is (7m) **Lutterworth**, where Wyclif was rector of St Mary's from c 1374 until his death in 1384. His works were condemned in 1414 by the Council of Constance and his remains disinterred and thrown into the little river Swift. The church has two wall paintings. 21m: *Leicester*, see Route 59.

FROM RUGBY TO MARKET HARBOROUGH, 18m by B5414 and A427. B5414 crosses A5 and then M6 and M1 near their junction with each other, and follows the Avon, which here divides Northamptonshire from Leicestershire. 5m: *Swinford*. *Stanford Hall* (open), 1m to the right, is a house of 1690, with additions by Francis Smith of Warwick, in a splendid park. It has a collection of Stuart and Jacobite paintings. The early 14C church of *Stanford*, on the Northamptonshire bank of the river, contains fine 14–16C glass and good 16–17C monuments. The organ, brought from Magdalen College, Oxford, is said by tradition to have come from Whitehall Palace. At (9½m) *North Kilworth* B5414 joins A427, heading E from Lutterworth (see above). Beyond (12m) *Husbands Bosworth* the road follows the Welland. 18m: *Market Harborough*, see Route 59.

From Rugby to *Althorp* and *Northampton*, see Route 59.

A428 continues W from Rugby to (91m) **Coventry** (Route 52A).

53

Oxford to Stratford-upon-Avon

Directions. Total distance 39m. The route passes the N fringe of the Cotswolds, explored more fully in Routes 51A and 51B. **Oxford**, see Route 50. A34 to (8m) Woodstock, (18m) Chipping Norton (bypassed) and (39m) **Stratford-upon-Avon**.

Oxford, see Route 50. A34, the Woodstock road, leaves the city. 8m: **Woodstock** (2000 inhabitants; seasonal TI) is an attractive little town with Georgian houses and a *Town Hall* (1766) by Sir William Chambers in the High St. *Fletcher's House*, in Park St. opposite the church, contains the *Oxfordshire County Museum*, devoted to the archaeology, crafts and industry of the region. Further on, the Triumphal Gate leads to Woodstock's chief attraction for visitors, **Blenheim Palace** (open), the baroque mansion Sir John Vanbrugh built for the 1st Duke of Marlborough.

Blenheim Palace

It stands on the site of the royal manor of Woodstock where, in the 12C, Henry I enclosed a deer park and built a hunting lodge. Henry II enlarged it into a palace and, according to tradition, built a secluded bower for his mistress, 'Fair' Rosamond. The Black Prince (1330–76), son of Edward III, was born here. In 1554–55 the future Elizabeth I was confined in the gatehouse by her sister Mary. In 1704 Queen Anne gave the manor to John Churchill, Duke of Marlborough, as reward for his victory over the French at Blenheim that year. The decayed remains of the medieval palace were swept away and in 1705 Vanbrugh, aided by Nicholas Hawksmoor, began to build a new palace—the only building in Britain not intended for royal occupation to bear that title. It was finally completed after the duke's death in 1722 at a total cost of 300,000, of which an increasingly reluctant Parliament paid 240,000.

From the Triumphal Gate the visitors' entrance leads through the *park (2700 acres), by Capability Brown in 1764–74. The artificial lake, crossed by Vanbrugh's Grand Bridge, was formed by damming a valley of the Glyme. Near the N shore are Fair Rosamond's Well and the presumed site of the medieval Woodstock Manor. Beyond, the Victory Column (1730) stands at the head of an avenue of trees. The parterre immediately E of the palace and the water terraces on the W were added this century.

The palace itself consists of a central block linked by curved colonnades to a kitchen courtyard and a stable courtyard. Vanbrugh conceived it in his most elaborate manner, deliberately aiming to create a 'national Monument' rather than a home, even for a Duke and Duchess. To Horace Walpole it looked like 'the palace of an auctioneer who had been chosen King of Poland'. Sympathetic observers point to the romantic effect of its skyline, more reminiscent of a medieval castle than an 18C country house.

The Great Hall, with stonework by Gibbons and a painted ceiling by Thornhill, makes a restrained introduction to the otherwise lavish interior. The drawing rooms have ceilings by Hawksmoor and portraits (Kneller, Romney, Reynolds, Sargent, Van Dyck). The Saloon has a painted ceiling by Laguerre and marble doorcases by Gibbons. The State Rooms are hung with Brussels tapestries commemorating the 1st Duke's campaigns. The Long Library has a stucco ceiling, a statue of Queen Anne and a bust of the 1st Duke by Rysbrack, also responsible (with Kent) for the pompous tomb of the Duke and Duchess in the Chapel. Sir Winston Churchill (1874–1965), born in the bedroom W of the Great Hall, lies in the churchyard of *Bladon*, on the SE edge of the park.

In the Evenlode valley NW of Woodstock are the little towns of (6m) *Charlbury*, below *Wychwood Forest*, and (12m) *Shipton-under-Wychwood*.

12m: *Over Kiddington*. *Ditchley Park* (open), 1¼m left, an Anglo-American study centre, is by James Gibbs (1720–26) with decorations by Flitcroft and Kent. It stands on the site of the house where the Earl of Rochester (1647–80) was born. 18m: **Chipping Norton** (5000 inhabitants; seasonal TI), 1½m W A34, is a Cotswold market town. It has a church with Perpendicular nave and brasses, and 17C almshouses.

Great Tew, 6m E, is a charming village. Lucius Cary, Viscount Falkland (1610–43), made his house here, now vanished, the centre of a literary circle including Jonson, Suckling, Cowley and Waller. He is buried in the church, which also has a monument by Chantrey to Mary Anne Boulton (d. 1829), wife of the engineer Matthew Boulton, who bought the estate in 1816. *Hook Norton* church, 5m NE, has a carved Norman *font. Warren Hastings (1732–1818) was born at *Churchill*, 3m SW of Chipping Norton, and buried at *Daylesford*, 5m W. For *Stow-on-the-Wold*, 9m W, see Route 51A.

From Chipping Norton to *Worcester*, see Route 54.

A34 continues N to the boundary between Oxfordshire and Warwickshire. 21m: The *Rollright Stones*, ½m W of the road, are Neolithic monuments: the stone circle called the King's Men, the remains of a burial chamber called the Whispering Knights and, across the road, an outlying stone of doubtful significance, the King Stone. 26m: **Shipston-on-Stour** has 17–18C houses.

Ilmington, 4m NW, has a Norman church. *Barcheston*, 1m SE of Shipston, has a 16C alabaster monument in its church. William Sheldon began tapestry weaving in

England here in 1560. *Compton Wynyates*, the lovely Tudor mansion in a wooded hollow 5m E of Shipston, is not open.

A34 descends the valley of the Stour, keeping near the river most of the way. 27m: *Honington* is a pretty village. *Honington Hall* (limited opening) is late 17C outside and mid 18C inside. The parish church dates mainly from the 1680s.

39m: **STRATFORD-UPON-AVON** (20,900 inhabitants), thanks almost entirely to the fact that Shakespeare was born and died here, has developed from a small market town into the most popular tourist attraction in England outside London. The birthplace alone is visited by more than half a million people each year. Stratford can now claim serious attention only as the

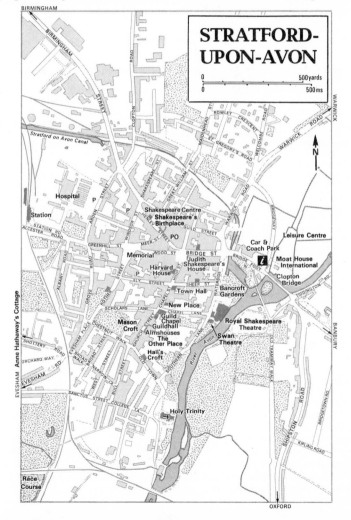

provincial home of the Royal Shakespeare Company, which operates three theatres here. The RSC, derived from the summer festival company founded by Charles Flower in 1879 with E.F. Benson as its first director, gained its international reputation with the work of Sir Peter Hall after World War II. Apart from its theatres in Stratford, it also organises productions at the Barbican in London (Route 2).

TI: Bridgefoot. **Railway Station**: off Alcester Rd, about ½m W of the centre. **Theatres**: The Royal Shakespeare Theatre and the Swan Theatre on Waterside, and the Other Place on Southern Lane, all administered by the Royal Shakespeare Company. The Stratford season lasts from mid March to January. See walking tour below for further details. **Annual Events**: Shakespeare Birthday Celebrations (April); Boat Club Annual Regatta (usually 3rd Saturday in June); Stratford-upon-Avon Festival (July), with a wide range of activities; Mop Fair (12 October).

The **Shakespeare Birthplace Trust** administers the Birthplace, Hall's Croft, the New Place estate, Anne Hathaway's Cottage (Shottery) and Mary's Arden's House (Wilmcote). An inclusive ticket for all five properties is available.

History. The poet's father John, native of Snitterfield, had moved to this 'proper little mercate town' (as Camden called it) by the early 1550s and set up business on Henley St. as a glover. Rival traditions make him a wool merchant or butcher. He achieved local eminence with his appointment as Alderman in 1565 and High Bailiff in 1567, the latter post making him a JP. In 1557 he had married Mary Arden, daughter of a yeoman from Wilmcote. William was the third of their eight children, and the eldest son. The date of his baptism, 26 April 1564, has given Englishmen a patriotic excuse for celebrating his birthday as 23 April, St George's Day. Virtually nothing can be said of his childhood or youth beyond the safe assumption that he attended the local grammar school and the fact that he married Anne Hathaway of Shottery in 1582. His first daughter, Susanna, was born in 1583 and the twins Judith and Hamnet in 1585. Neither the date nor the occasion of his leaving Stratford is known, though it evidently happened during the 'lost years' 1585–92 and is attributed by stubborn local legend to poaching adventures at Charlecote Park. He kept close ties with the town, strengthened when he bought New Place in 1597 and inherited the Henley St. house on his father's death in 1601. He retired to New Place in 1611, died at Stratford on 23 April 1616 and was buried at Holy Trinity, where he had been baptised. Hamnet had died in infancy but his wife and both daughters outlived him, continuing the family connection with Stratford. Susanna married Dr John Hall and Judith married Thomas Quiney, a vintner. Shakespeare's last direct descendant was Elizabeth Hall, who married Thomas Nash but left Stratford after his death to become Lady Bernard.

After Shakespeare's death the history of Stratford became intertwined with the growth of his reputation. The town's status as a national literary shrine was established by David Garrick's Jubilee of 1769, which celebrated Shakespeare's memory in every way except by performing any of his plays. In the 19C Stratford's rise was furthered by the public purchase of the Henley St. house and the building of the first Memorial Theatre in 1877–79. Marie Corelli made the town her home from 1901 until her death in 1924.

The old centre is formed by a gridiron of streets parallel to the river. A convenient walking tour begins at its NE corner near the *Clopton Bridge*, built by Sir Hugh Clopton in 1480–90 and widened in 1925. Bridge St. goes to its junction with High St., with *Judith Shakespeare's House*. On the right Henley St. leads to the *Shakespeare Centre* (1964), with its library. **Shakespeare's Birthplace** (open) consists of two timber-framed houses, originally part of a row but now detached. Shakespeare is presumed to have been born in the W half, now fitted up in the manner of a 16C family home. The E half is a museum illustrating his life, work and times. The garden is planted with flowers and trees mentioned in the plays.

Shakespeare's birthplace before Victorian restoration

The building dates from the late 15C or early 16C. John Shakespeare was living in the W half and apparently using it for his business by 1552. He bought the other half in 1556, and at some later point in the century the two houses were connected and a rear wing added. Shakespeare inherited it in 1601, though his mother and sister, Joan Hart, continued to live here. On her death in 1646 it passed to Susanna Hall and then to her daughter Elizabeth. When she died in 1670 it returned to the Hart family, who remained owners until the early 19C. During these vicissitudes the E half became an inn known as the Swan and later as the Swan and Maidenhead, while the W half was at one time a butcher's shop. Interest was first aroused by the 1769 Jubilee, when Garrick arbitrarily identified the first-floor bedroom in the W half as the birthroom itself. The tenants obligingly took to showing visitors an implausible collection of Shakespeare relics. The Shakespeare Birthplace Committee (predecessor of the modern Trust) bought the property in 1847 and reopened it as a museum in 1863, after substantial repairs and alterations charitably described as restoration. The annual number of visitors has grown steadily from a trickle of about 1000 in the early 19C and about 30,000 by the turn of the century to its present overwhelming flood. Entertaining accounts appear in Irving's 'Sketch Book', Hawthorne's 'Our Old Home' and James's story 'The Birthplace'.

High St. continues to *Harvard House* (open), a building of 1596 where John Harvard's mother Katherine Rogers spent her childhood. It was restored by Marie Corelli and presented to Harvard in 1909. The row of half-timbered buildings continues to Ely St. On the opposite corner, where High St.

continues as Chapel St., stands the *Town Hall* (1797). The statue of Shakespeare on the N front was presented by Garrick in 1769. Chapel St. has several old inns and, on the left at the end, the **New Place** estate (open), which consists of Nash's House and the site of New Place.

Nash's House, a half-timbered building with a reconstructed streetfront, was inherited by Shakespeare's granddaughter Elizabeth Hall from her first husband, Thomas Nash. It contains a museum of Stratford history. The garden is planted on the foundations of New Place, the late 15C house Shakespeare bought in 1597 and retired to in 1611. It was torn down in 1759 by Rev. Francis Gastrell after a dispute about rates. The gardens of New Place are entered separately from around the corner in Chapel Lane; in the central lawn is a mulberry said to be descended from the original tree planted by Shakespeare and cut down by Gastrell in 1756.

Opposite New Place, at the corner of Chapel Lane and Church St., is the *Guild Chapel*, with a late 13C chancel, a nave rebuilt by Sir Hugh Clopton in 1495 and a wall painting of the Last Judgement (c 1500). Beyond lie the *Grammar School* where Shakespeare is assumed to have been educated, in the former Guildhall, and a row of almshouses once maintained by the Guild. On the opposite side of the street is the 18C *Mason Croft*, once the home of Marie Corelli and now the Shakespeare Institute of the University of Birmingham.

From the end of Church St. Old Town leads left. *Hall's Croft* (open), a Tudor town house on the left, was the home of Shakespeare's daughter Susanna and her husband Dr John Hall. It contains Tudor and Jacobean furniture, and one room has been equipped as a 16C dispensary. Near the end of the road, among lime trees by the bank of the river, is **Holy Trinity**, usually visited because Shakespeare is buried in it.

The tower and transepts are 13C, the nave and aisles early 14C, while the chancel and nave clerestory were rebuilt in the late 15C, when the porch was added. The spire (1765) replaces the original wooden one.

The font where Shakespeare was christened is at the W end of the N aisle. In the chancel (entrance fee) a case displays copies of the registers with entries for his baptism and burial. His grave lies on the N side of the chancel, its slab bearing a doggerel inscription. On the wall above is Janssen's monument, with an epitaph celebrating Shakespeare's achievement in literature and the recoloured bust which has disappointed many visitors. Close by are the graves of Shakespeare's wife, his daughter Susanna and his sons-in-law Dr Hall and Thomas Nash. The graves of other relatives are unmarked. The chancel also contains the tombs of its builder, Dean Balsall (d. 1491), and Shakespeare's friend John Combe (d. 1614), while the Clopton Chapel at the E end of the N aisle has monuments of the Cloptons.

The centre is reached by Southern Lane and its continuation as Waterside, running alongside the river and past the Royal Shakespeare Company's three Stratford theatres. **The Other Place**, on the left, is the smallest and has the broadest repertoire, ranging from classical to contemporary plays. The **Swan Theatre** (1986; Michael Reardon), on the right, inhabits the shell of the original Memorial Theatre, built in 1877–79 but gutted by fire in 1926. Its auditorium recalls the design of Elizabethan playhouses and is used for staging the work of Shakespeare and his contemporaries. The **Royal Shakespeare Theatre** plays Shakespeare's work. The building (1932; Elizabeth Scott) has decoration by Eric Kennington and a terrace overlooking the Avon.

The *Royal Shakespeare Collection*, part of the theatre complex, has the 'Flower Portrait' of Shakespeare, either model for or copy of the Droeshout engraving in the First Folio, and a collection of theatrical relics.

Beyond the Royal Shakespeare Theatre are the pleasant *Bancroft Gardens*.

The Stratford-upon-Avon Canal, built in 1793–1816, runs N from the Bancroft Gardens to join the Worcester and Birmingham Canal at (25½m) *King's Norton*. Its S section, open to pleasure craft, rises by 36 locks with large aqueducts at *Edstone* and *Wootton Wawen* to (13½m) *Kingswood* and the Grand Union Canal (Route 52B).

Shottery, the birthplace of Shakespeare's wife, is about 1m W of Stratford, reached by a footpath. *Anne Hathaway's Cottage* (open) is a half-timbered Elizabethan farmhouse with thatched roof, with some of its 16C furniture. From Shottery a lane leads NW, crossing A422, to (2¼m more) **Wilmcote**, with *Mary Arden's House* (open), the half-timbered farmhouse where Shakespeare's mother is said to have been born. It contains 16C furniture; the barns have farm equipment.

The villages, churches and country houses in the region, several connected with Shakespeare in legend or actuality, offer relief from the atmosphere of Stratford. Shakespeare's parents were married in the church at *Aston Cantlow*, beyond Wilmcote 4½m NW of Stratford. It has a good late 13C chancel. *Tiddington*, on B4086 1½m E of Stratford, and *Alveston*, 1m further, are pretty villages. They lie on the way to (4½m) *Charlecote Park* (NT), a heavily restored Tudor mansion with an original gatehouse. Legend insists that the young Shakespeare was caught poaching deer in the park and brought before its owner, Sir Thomas Lucy. The church, rebuilt when the house was altered in the 19C, has 17C monuments to the Lucy family. At *Clifford Chambers*, by A46 1½m S of Stratford, the church has Norman details.

FROM STRATFORD TO BIDFORD-ON-AVON, 7m by A439. It leaves Stratford with Shottery (see above) to the right and, on the left, the turning for (2m) *Luddington*, where the church is the strongest claimant to be the scene of Shakespeare's marriage (cf. Temple Grafton below). 4m: *Welford*, 1m S of the road, is a pretty village with a maypole. 7m: **Bidford-on-Avon** has the former Falcon Inn, which local tradition makes the scene of a drinking bout by the youthful Shakespeare. The crab tree beneath which he slept it off has vanished. *Wixford* church, 2m N on the way to Alcester, has Norman details.

FROM STRATFORD TO ALCESTER, 8m W by A422, partly following the course of the Roman road. Shottery (see above) lies to the S . 4½m: The church at *Temple Grafton*, 1m S of the road, is sometimes claimed as the scene of Shakespeare's marriage (cf. Luddington above). 8m: **Alcester** is an old town of Roman origin, with a 17C town hall, some Tudor houses and a church made Gothick outside and classical inside in 1729–30. Off B4089 1½m NE is the 14C *Kinwarton Dovecote* (NT), with an ogee doorway. *Great Alne*, 1½m further, has an old watermill. Off A435 2m N of Alcester is *Coughton Court* (NT), the early 16C house of the RC Throckmorton family. Behind the imposing gatehouse, with wings of 1780, are the half-timbered N and S wings. The E wing was destroyed by a mob in 1688. The hall, in the gatehouse, has a fan-vaulted ceiling; other rooms have wood panelling. The staircase was brought from Harvington Hall. Family portraits include one by Largillière; there are Jacobite relics. Nearby is the Perpendicular church, with many of its original furnishings and 16C Throckmorton tombs, and a Roman Catholic church (1857) by Hansom. At *Studley*, 2m further N, the church has a Norman doorway. *Ragley Hall* (open), on A435 1¾m SW of Alcester, was begun by Robert Hooke in 1679–83, altered and decorated by Gibbs c 1750 and given a portico by James Wyatt in the 1780s. The handsome interiors, redecorated in recent years, include fine plasterwork by Gibbs, especially the baroque decoration of the *Great Hall. Among the paintings are work by George Morland, Reynolds (portrait of Horace Walpole), van Loo, Hoppner and Lely. One staircase has a mural by Graham Rust (1983), the other a large painting by Ceri Richards (1964). See above for *Wixford*, 2m S of Alcester.

FROM STRATFORD TO BIRMINGHAM, 25m by A34, following the last stage of the old coaching route from London via Oxford and Stratford, and running parallel to the Stratford-upon-Avon Canal for the first part of the journey. 6m: *Wootton Wawen*, left of the main road after the canal, has a church with a Saxon core. 8m: *Henley-in-Arden* is a quaint little town with an old market cross, a Perpendicular church, a 15C former Guildhall and the 17C White Swan. 11m: *Lapworth*, 1m to the right, has a church with Norman details. *Kingswood*, at the junction of the Stratford Canal and the Grand Union

Canal, lies 1½m further E. 13m: *Hockley Heath*. 2m E is *Packwood House* (NT), a timber-framed Tudor building with good furniture and an outstanding collection of tapestries and textiles. The topiary garden of yew trees dates from the 17C. A34 crosses M42 at 16m and passes through the suburbs of Hall Green and Sparkbrook on the way into the centre of (25m) *Birmingham* (Route 61).

From Stratford to *Banbury* and to *Warwick*, see Route 52A.

54

Oxford to Worcester: the Vale of Evesham

Directions. Total distance 58m. **Oxford**, see Route 50. A34 to (18m) Chipping Norton, see Route 53. A44 to (27m) Moreton-in-Marsh, (36m) Broadway, (42m) Evesham, (49m) Pershore and (58m) **Worcester**. Before dropping down into the Vale of Evesham, the route goes across the N fringes of the Cotswolds, explored more fully in Routes 51A and 51B.

Oxford, see Route 50, and to (18m) *Chipping Norton*, see Route 53. A44 leaves the town. 22m: A436 leads left to (5½m) *Stow-on-the-Wold* (Route 51A), passing (2½m) *Daylesford* (Route 53) and (3m) *Oddington* (Route 51A). Shortly beyond the turning for Stow a sideroad on the left leads in 1m to *Chastleton House* (NT). Built in 1603 of Cotswold stone, it has a strikingly handsome exterior, and keeps its great hall and long gallery, together with original plasterwork and furniture. 27m: **Moreton-in-Marsh** is a small market town with the Fosse Way as its High St. The Curfew Tower dates from the 16C. *Stow-on-the-Wold* lies 4m S on A429 (the Foss Way). At (29m) *Bourton-on-the-Hill* A44 reaches the crest of the Cotswolds. *Batsford Arboretum* (open), 1m N, has rare trees. At *Sezincote*, 1½m S, the house (limited opening) was built c 1805 by Cockerell and Thomas Daniell in an Indian style anticipating Brighton's Royal Pavilion; the oriental gardens (open) are by Repton.

About 4m N of A44 is **Chipping Campden** (seasonal TI), once a centre of the Cotswold wool trade and now popular with visitors for its handsome stone buildings. The broad, curving *High St.* is a picturesque medley of styles from the 14C to the 18C. Market Place, the row of buildings in the middle of the street, includes the *Town Hall*, 14C but much altered, and the *Market Hall* of 1627. The *Woolstaplers' Hall* (c 1340) is a museum of bygones. Further S are the remains of the 17C mansion built by Sir Baptist Hicks, Viscount Campden, and a group of almshouses of 1612. The church of *St James*, with its great *W tower and airy nave, typifies the Perpendicular wool churches of the region. The brasses in the chancel include one of the local wool merchant William Grevil (d. 1401). Among the elaborate monuments to the Noel and Hicks families in the S chapel is the tomb of Viscount Campden (d. 1629) and his wife, perhaps by Nicholas Stone.

Off B4081 4m NE of Chipping Campden is *Hidcote Manor Garden* (NT), created this century by Lawrence Johnston. Opposite is *Kiftsgate Court Garden* (open). *Mickleton*, on A46 just beyond the end of B4081, is a pretty village at the N fringe of the Cotswolds.

Beyond Moreton-in-Marsh A44 enters the county of Hereford and Worcester and descends Broadway Hill. 34m: *Broadway Tower* (open), in the country park ½m left of the road, was built as a folly by the Earl of Coventry in 1800. It contains exhibitions of the Cotswold wool trade and of work by William Morris, who stayed here; the top floor and roof have a wide view. 36m: **Broadway** (seasonal TI) has been made popular with tourists by its reputation as one of the most handsome villages in the country. Among the 16–18C houses on the broad, stone-built High St. are the *Lygon Arms*, now a hotel but once a manor house used by both Charles I and Cromwell as the tide of battle flowed in the neighbourhood, and the *Tudor House* (1660). The church of *St Eadburgha*, largely Perpendicular despite its ancient dedication, lies 1m S. The sideroad continues another 1¼m to *Snowshill Manor* (NT), a typical Cotswold manor house with Tudor work behind the façade of c 1700. It contains a magpie collection (Japanese Samurai armour, 18C musical instruments, early bicycles, model ships, etc.).

Buckland, off A46 2m SW, has England's oldest rectory, with a 15C great hall (open). A46 continues SW to (6m) *Hailes Abbey* and (9m) *Winchcombe* (Route 51A).

A44 crosses the **Vale of Evesham**, watered by the Avon and its many tributaries as it winds from Stratford (Route 53) in the NE to join the Severn at Tewkesbury (Route 55) in the SW. The district is known for vegetables and fruit, especially plums. *Bredon Hill* (Route 55), an outlier of the Cotswolds, rises to the left of the road. 39m: *Wickhamford* church, ½m right of A44, has the tomb of Penelope Washington (d. 1697), bearing the Washington arms. 42m: **Evesham** (15,300 inhabitants; TI) has tree-lined walks along the banks of the Avon. In the Market Place are the half-timbered 15C *Round House* and the *Town Hall*, built in 1586 but remodelled in the 19C. All that survives of the once rich Benedictine *Abbey* founded in the 8C is the Norman and Tudor gateway to the churchyard and the detached 16C *bell tower, Perpendicular at its most ornate. The abbey precinct contains two churches: the Perpendicular *St Lawrence*, now redundant, and *All Saints*, the present parish church, which is Norman beneath Perpendicular remodelling. The old *Almonry* (open), where pilgrims to St Lawrence were lodged, houses a small museum of local remains from the Romano-British period onwards.

At the Battle of Evesham (1265) the army commanded by the future Edward I defeated Simon de Montfort, who was buried in the abbey church. An obelisk (1845) marks the site of the battle about 1m N of the town. *Middle Littleton*, by B4085 3m NE, has a 13C tithe barn (NT). At *Bretforton*, off B4035 4m E of Evesham, the Fleece Inn (NT) dates partly from the 14C. At *Ashton-under-Hill*, 5½m SW of Evesham, is *Bredon Springs Garden* (open).

At (49m) **Pershore** (TI), another pleasant town on the Avon, the choir and transepts of the Benedictine *Abbey Church* are preserved as the parish church. The 14C tower, originally over the crossing, now stands at the W end of the building. Inside are the Norman crossing arches and S transept, and an early 13C apsidal E end, with vaulting built after a fire in 1288. *Strensham*, 5m SW near M5, was the birthplace of Samuel Butler (1612–80), author of 'Hudibras'.

58m: **WORCESTER** (pronounced somewhere between 'Wooster' and 'Worster'; 75,900 inhabitants) stands on the smoothly flowing Severn, looking E across the Vale of Evesham and W to the Malvern Hills. The central tower of its cathedral makes a conspicuous landmark. Many other

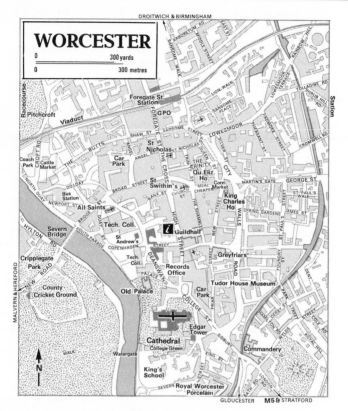

old buildings survive, but the redevelopment inflicted on much of the centre in the 1960s is notoriously insensitive.

TI: The Guildhall, High St. **Bus Station**: (town buses) Angel Place; (out-of-town services) Newport St. **Coach Station**: Croft Rd. **Railway Stations**: Foregate Street Station, ¼m N of the centre, and Shrub Hill Station, ¾m E of the centre. **Theatre**: The Swan, near Pitchcroft. **Annual Events**: The Three Choirs Festival (August) rotates annually between Worcester, Hereford and Gloucester cathedrals. Founded c 1715 and held continuously since 1724, it has given first performances to works by Elgar and Vaughan Williams. The Christmas Fayre, with crafts market, is held on the first weekend in December.

History. There are scanty traces of an Iron Age settlement (c 500 BC) and a Roman town, perhaps called Vertis, on the ridge where the cathedral stands. But the real history of Worcester began c 680, when the bishopric was founded in the Saxon Wigorna Ceaster. At the Conquest the town was important enough to be made the seat of a Norman castle. Its adherence to the Royalist cause during the Civil War won Worcester the motto 'Civitas in Bello in Pace Fidelis' ('The City Loyal in War and Peace'). It was the first city to declare for Charles I, and the last rallying point for supporters of the young Charles II, defeated at the Sidbury Gate in 1651. Known for its cloth trade in the Middle Ages, Worcester recovered from the upheavals of the Civil War to become a manufacturing centre in the 18C and early 19C. Its glove-making factories have virtually disappeared, but the city is still the home of Royal Worcester porcelain, started in 1751, and of Lea and Perrins sauce, begun at a chemist's shop in Broad St. in 1825. Berrow's 'Worcester Journal', probably established in 1690 and certainly in circulation by 1709, is the oldest English newspaper with a continuous history.

Natives and residents. The novelist Mrs Henry Wood (1814–87) was born and the madrigalist Thomas Tomkins (1572–1656) died here. Sir Edward Elgar (1857–1934), born at the nearby village of Lower Broadheath (see below), spent much of his life in Worcester and died at a house demolished in 1969. An Elgar Trail follows sites connected with his life and work in the city and surrounding region; a useful accompanying pamphlet is available from the Worcester and Malvern TI Centres.

The *Cathedral is approached from College Yard, where a few 18C houses still survive in contrast to the bleak modern development nearby. The outside of the cathedral was renewed by A.E. Perkins and Sir Gilbert Scott in 1864–74. Most of it is now Victorian, and only the rich central tower survived relatively unscathed. The real beauty of the cathedral lies within, in the great E end and the unusually interesting tombs and monuments.

The present building is the latest of several to stand on the site. It succeeds two Saxon cathedrals—the first presumably dating from the establishment of the bishopric in c 680, the second built while Oswald was bishop (961–92)—and Wulstan's cathedral of 1084–89. The chief surviving fragment of the Norman building is the crypt. Wulstan was canonised in 1203, after miracles had begun to happen at his tomb, and the resulting flow of pilgrims encouraged (and paid for) a major campaign of rebuilding. Work on the new E end began with the Lady Chapel in 1224. The remodelling of the nave, started in 1317, was finished after serious interruptions in the 1370s—the date when the central tower was also completed.

The impressive late 14C N Porch is halfway along the nine piers of the *Nave*. The two W bays (c 1160) are remarkable Transitional work, their capitals foreshadowing later foliage design and their pointed arches already Early English. The other seven bays differ entirely from them, and are not uniform. On the N side they are Decorated (1317–27) and on the S very early Perpendicular, probably built immediately before the nave vaulting was finished in 1377. The lofty triforium is also different on the N and S sides. The N aisle has a tablet and memorial window to Elgar (not buried here) in the second bay and, in the sixth, the tomb of Sir John Beauchamp and his wife (c 1400), opposite the altar tomb of Robert Wilde (d. 1607) and his wife. Beyond the Jesus Chapel, further E, is the curious tomb of Bishop Bullingham (d. 1576), not in its original place. In the S aisle the lower part of the wall belonged to the Norman nave. Five Norman recesses face the present pier arches, two of them filled with later monumental arches. The two W bays are contemporary with those of the nave. A monument to Bishop Johnson (d. 1774) by Robert Adam, with a bust by Nollekens, stands at this end of the aisle. The ashes of Stanley Baldwin (1867–1947) lie at the W entrance.

The aisleless *W Transepts* mix Norman and Perpendicular with 19C restoration. The E wall of each transept has a Norman arch. Below the one in the N transept is Roubiliac's monument to Bishop Hough (d. 1743). Here, too, are tablets to three novelists with local connections: Mrs Sherwood (1775–1851), Mrs Henry Wood (1814–87) and Francis Brett Young (1884–1954). The S transept has the Great Organ; the Little Organ (by 'Father' Smith, 1704), said to have belonged to Handel, is in the choir.

The *E end is second only to that of Beverley Minster as a work of the period 1220–60. Its quality is best seen in the Early English *Lady Chapel*, begun in 1224, with tall lancet windows and sculptured arcade below, and in the *E Transepts*. Among the sculptures in the spandrels is the Worcester Crucifix, at the E end of the S aisle, with expressive figures of the Virgin and St John (restored 1862). The piers and arches are taller at the E end than in the *Presbytery*, which is built over the Norman crypt, raising the floor level above that of transepts and Lady Chapel. Bishop Giffard (1268–1302) added the detached shafts of Purbeck marble. The late Victorian stalls incorporate 14C *misericords; the pulpit is 16C and the other furniture 19C.

The tomb of King John (d. 1216) stands in the Presbytery. It still contains his skeleton, though only the Purbeck marble *effigy is contemporary with his death. The lion at his feet bites the end of his sword, allegedly a reference to the curbing of royal power by the barons with the signature of Magna Carta. The tomb chest is probably of the

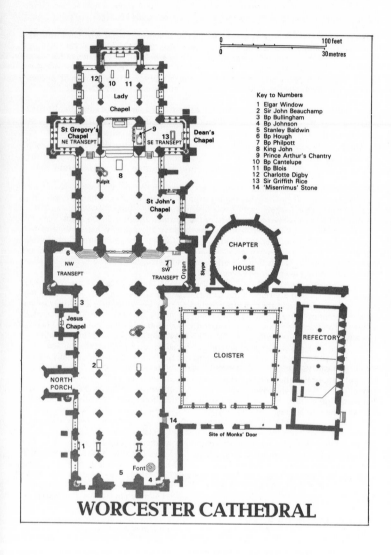

0   100 feet

0   30 metres

Key to Numbers

1 Elgar Window
2 Sir John Beauchamp
3 Bp Bullingham
4 Bp Johnson
5 Stanley Baldwin
6 Bp Hough
7 Bp Philpott
8 King John
9 Prince Arthur's Chantry
10 Bp Cantelupe
11 Bp Blois
12 Charlotte Digby
13 Sir Griffith Rice
14 'Miserrimus' Stone

12   10   11

Lady

Chapel

St Gregory's
Chapel
NE TRANSEPT

9

13   Dean's
SE TRANSEPT   Chapel

8

Pulpit

St John's
Chapel

6

NW

TRANSEPT

7

SW

TRANSEPT   Organ   Slype

CHAPTER

HOUSE

3

Jesus
Chapel

CLOISTER

REFECTORY

2

NORTH
PORCH

14

Site of Monks' Door

1

5   Font   4

WORCESTER CATHEDRAL

same date as the adjacent *Chantry of Prince Arthur, erected in 1504, two years after the prince died at Ludlow aged only 15. Within the screenwork below are two effigy tombs, probably of Bishop Giffard (see above) and a kinswoman. The Lady Chapel has the tombs of Bishop Cantelupe (d. 1266) and Bishop Blois (d. 1236). On the N wall is a tablet to Izaak Walton's second wife (d. 1662), with an epitaph by him. To the left is a sensitive monument by Chantrey to Mrs Digby (d. 1820). Opposite the NE transept,

Worcester Cathedral: the head of the effigy of King John

now St George's Chapel, is the tomb of Bishop de Cobham (d. 1327), who built the Jesus Chapel and began the new nave. The SE transept, now the Dean's Chapel, has the tombs of Sir William de Harcourt (14C) and Sir Griffith Rice (d. 1523), and a small alabaster Madonna (c 1470) by Nottingham craftsmen.

The many pillared *Crypt* is entered from the SW transept. Begun by Wulstan in 1084, it is the largest Norman crypt in England and the second oldest of the four apsidal crypts in English cathedrals (Canterbury is earlier, Winchester and Gloucester are later). Its beauty must have been even greater in its original form, extending to the E.

The *Library* (open by prior appointment), over the S aisle of the nave, has some 4000 volumes, both manuscripts and printed books of the 15–18C.

The late 14C *Cloisters* are entered from the S nave aisle or through the richly moulded late Norman door from College Green. Of the roof *bosses, those in the S walk form a Jesse Tree, representing the ancestors of Christ, while in the N walk adoring angels turn towards a central boss carved with the Virgin and Child. The tombstone inscribed 'Miserrimus' ('Most wretched man') at the W end of the N walk, which inspired Wordsworth to a sonnet, is said to be that of a Jacobite canon unable to adjust to William III's rule. The early 12C *Chapter House* on the E side, a circular building with a central shaft, set the pattern for later chapter houses (at Lincoln and Wells, for example). The walls, with Norman blind arcading, have alternate bands of green and brown stone. The windows and vaulting are Perpendicular. On the S side of the cloisters is the monks' *Refectory*, on a vaulted Norman undercroft, which became part of King's School after the Reformation. (The Refectory and Chapter House are open on application to the verger on duty.)

College Green, S of the cloisters, has 18C houses and the *Edgar Tower* (c 1350), once the great gate of the monastery.

The most interesting secular building in Worcester is the *Commandery* (open), off Sidbury SE of the cathedral. Originally founded as the Hospital of St Wulstan in 1085, it became a private house at the Reformation; what survives is mainly 15C. Its rich interior, with a great hall, contains a museum dedicated to the Civil War.

In Severn St., to the SW, are the *Royal Worcester Porcelain Works* (guided tours), founded in 1751 and occupying this site since 1840. The adjoining *Dyson Perrins Museum* (open) has a collection of antique Worcester.

Friar St. and New St., leading N from Sidbury to the Old Cornmarket, both have good timbered buildings. In Friar St. are the *Tudor House Museum*, dealing with the social and domestic life of the city, and *Greyfriars* (NT), mainly late 15C. In New St. are the early 16C *Nash House* and, at the Cornmarket end, *King Charles's House* (1577), where Charles II found momentary refuge after the Battle of Worcester.

The High St., running N from the cathedral, begins with a statue of Elgar (1981). The former church of *St Helen* on the corner of Fish St. is now the County Records Office, with the marriage contract of Shakespeare and Anne Hathaway. The *Guildhall* (open), on the left beyond, is a splendid building (1721–23) by a local pupil of Wren, Thomas White. The statues of Charles I and Charles II reflect the city's politics. The assembly room inside (1791) has portraits of George III and Queen Charlotte by Reynolds. Down Church St. to the right is *St Swithin*, with a Perpendicular tower but otherwise by E. and T. Woodward (1733–36). The remarkably complete 18C interior includes a *three-decker pulpit with mayor's chair. In Trinity St., behind, is the restored 16C *Queen Elizabeth's House*.

High St. is continued by The Cross, The Foregate and Foregate St. At the end of The Cross is the church of *St Nicholas* (1732), also by White. The Foregate has *Berkeley's Hospital*, an almshouse of 1703 in the Dutch style. The *City Museum and Art Gallery* in Foregate St. contains geology, natural history and archaeology as well as regimental collections.

Deansway, leading from the cathedral to the Worcester Bridge over the Severn, passes the 18C street frontage of the old *Bishop's Palace* and the distinctive slender spire (1791) of the demolished church of *St Andrew*, known locally as the Glover's Needle. Opposite is the former *Countess of Huntingdon's Chapel* (1804–15), with a Regency interior, restored as a concert hall for the neighbouring *Elgar School of Music*. *All Saints*, at the corner of Deansway and Bridge St., was largely rebuilt in 1739–42; it contains furnishings by Sir Aston Webb and an 18C wrought-iron sword rest from the mayor's stall. The *Worcester Bridge*, built in 1771 and since widened, gives a good general view of the city. *Pitchcroft* racecourse lies to the N. The *County Cricket Ground*, on the far bank, looks across to the cathedral.

At *Lower Broadheath*, off A44 3m W, the cottage where Elgar was born in 1857 is now a museum. *Leigh*, off A4103 5m W of Worcester, has a large 14C barn, built for Pershore Abbey (EH, summer season). *Wichenford*, near B4204 5½m NW of Worcester, has a half-timbered 17C dovecote (NT). The gardens (open) of *Spetchley Park*, 3m E of Worcester on A422 towards Stratford, include a deer park.

FROM WORCESTER TO TENBURY WELLS, 23m by A443 and A456. A443 goes up the Severn valley to (6m) *Holt Heath* and turns left. *Holt*, to the right by the river, has a Norman church and the remains of its 14–16C castle (not open). *Holt Fleet*, to the N, has a bridge by Telford (1828). 9m: S of the main road and *Great Witley* stands the ruined shell of *Witley Court* (EH, all year), a 17C house remodelled by Samuel Dawkes in the 1860s. The Italianate *chapel, now the parish church, has a painted ceiling by Antonio Bellucci brought from the vanished mansion of Canons in 1747 and a monument by Rysbrack to Lord Foley (d. 1732). Abberley Hill rises N of the village. A443 follows the Teme Valley. Near its confluence with the Rea, A456 heads to (23m) *Tenbury Wells* (Route 65).

FROM WORCESTER TO BIRMINGHAM. M5 is the fast connection between the two cities but A38 makes a more interesting journey (26m). Beyond (4m) *Martin Hussingtree* it follows a Roman course. 7m: **Droitwich** (18,000 inhabitants; TI) was known to the Romans as Salinae because of its salt springs. It was developed as a spa in the 19C by John Corbett, whose buildings give the town its characteristic brick and half-timbered style. The most interesting church is *St Peter's*, ½m S of the centre, where Edward Winslow (1595–1655), one of the Pilgrim Fathers, was baptised. *Hotel Impney* at Dodderhill, off A38 1m NE of the centre, is the château Corbett built for himself in 1869–75. *Hanbury Hall* (NT), off B4090 2½m E of Droitwich, is a Queen Anne house of 1701 with staircase and ceilings painted by Thornhill, a collection of English porcelain figures and an orangery. A38 crosses M5 and passes, on the right at 11m, the salt-working centre of *Stoke Prior*. Just beyond is the turning for the *Avoncroft Museum of Buildings* (open), with old buildings reconstructed in an open-air setting. 13m: **Bromsgrove** (43,700 inhabitants; TI) has gabled houses and a handsome Perpendicular church. A headstone in the churchyard honours two engine drivers whose locomotive blew up in 1840 while climbing the Lickey Incline (see below). A.E. Housman (1859–1936), who spent part of his childhood in Bromsgrove, was born at *Fockbury*, 1m NW. Near *Tardebigge*, 3m E of Bromsgrove, where the church has a graceful spire of 1776, the flight of locks on the Worcester and Birmingham Canal is the longest in Britain. *Redditch* (66,600 inhabitants; TI), 3m further E, is a dull place.

The road now climbs between the *Clent Hills* (1036ft; NT) on the left and the *Lickey Hills* (900ft). 17m: The large estate of *Chadwich Manor* (NT) near the top is a favourite weekend resort from Birmingham. The road passes between *Rubery*, on the left and *Rednal*, with the grave of Cardinal Newman (see Route 61). 26m: *Birmingham*, see Route 61.

From Worcester to *Gloucester*, see Route 55; to *Hereford*, see Route 57; to *Shrewsbury*, see Route 66.

55

Gloucester to Tewkesbury and Worcester

Directions. Total distance 25m. **Gloucester**, Route 51A. A38 to (10m) **Tewkesbury**, (25m) **Worcester** (Route 54).

Gloucester, see Route 51A. A38 heads N, up the Vale of Gloucester. 7½m: On the left, B4213 and the unclassified road branching from it lead to (1½m) **Deerhurst**, by the Severn, with two outstanding Saxon buildings. *St Mary belonged to a Saxon monastery with a documented history from 804. The lower half of the tower is Saxon; later herringbone work can be seen on many parts of the exterior. The nave, with Early English arcades, incorporates the original choir; its Saxon apse, not rebuilt after a 15C fire, can easily be traced outside. The E wall of the tower has a curious two-light triangularheaded window; below it are a triangular opening (like several others in the N and S walls) and a blocked door once leading to a W gallery. The *font has spiral ornamentation, probably earlier than the 9C. A unique feature of the 15C brass of Sir John and Lady Cassey in the N choir aisle is the named figure of their dog, 'Terri'. About 200 yards away, across the road and attached to a half-timbered house, is * Odda's Chapel (EH, all year plus Mondays in winter). According to a foundation stone now in Oxford's Ashmolean Museum, it dates from 1056 and was built by Earl Odda as a memorial chapel for his brother Aelfric.

10m: **Tewkesbury** (9700 inhabitants; TI), on the Warwickshire Avon close to its meeting with the Severn, is an old town with one of the most magnificent English abbey churches, half-timbered houses and pleasant riverside scenery.

The Yorkists led by Edward IV, the future Richard III and the Duke of Clarence finally defeated the Lancastrians under Margaret of Anjou at the Battle of Tewkesbury (1471), fought in the 'Bloody Meadow' ½m S of the town. Dickens's Mr Pickwick dined at the Royal Hop Pole on Church St. The town is also the setting of Mrs Craik's novel 'John Halifax, Gentleman' (1856), which uses the 18C Abbey Mill as a setting, and the birthplace of the novelist Henry Green (1905–73).

The ***Abbey Church**, almost as large as Westminster Abbey, is remarkable for its blend of Norman and Decorated and for the splendour of its medieval tombs.

The Benedictine abbey was founded in 715. The present church was begun in 1092 by Robert Fitzhamon and consecrated in 1121. Norman work was brought to a close when the upper stages of the central tower were added c 1160. The tower and nave were vaulted and the ambulatory and E end were remodelled in the first half of the 14C. The church today remains substantially as it was when it was reconsecrated after the Battle of Tewkesbury, though neglect and frequent restoration have left their mark both inside and outside. Sir Gilbert Scott's work in 1875–79 provoked William Morris to form the Society for the Protection of Ancient Buildings.

The splendid *central tower is the largest Norman tower in existence, with wide views over the surrounding vales and hills. The N Porch is impressively plain, while the W front is almost entirely taken up by a grand recessed arch rising nearly to roof height; the Perpendicular style window was added in 1686. The cluster of Decorated chapels at the E end contrasts with the austere Norman work.

The interior has even more variety. Although the great pillars of the *Nave dwarf the triforium and the Decorated clerestory and vaulting (c 1340), they justify their predominance by the grandeur of their scale. Along the centre of the nave are carved roof bosses. The tower vaulting has shields and a circle of suns representing the 'sun of York' triumphant over the Lancastrians at Tewkesbury. A brass in the pavement below marks the traditional site of the grave of Edward, the young Lancastrian Prince of Wales killed in or shortly after the battle. The Transepts are Norman with 14C windows. The beautiful S transept contains the apsidal Lady Chapel with the 'Madonna del Passeggio', after the school of Raphael; it is reputed to have belonged to Madame de Pompadour. The transept also has a memorial tablet to Mrs Craik (1826–87).

The choir is surrounded by an Ambulatory with radiating chapels added in 1330–50. On the N side is the St Margaret's Chapel, with the tomb of Sir Guy de Brienne (d. 1390), and St Edmund's Chapel, with bosses showing the saint's martyrdom. Beside it is the cenotaph of Abbot Wakeman (d. 1549), with a startling effigy. Behind the high altar is the vault where the murdered Duke of Clarence and his wife were buried in 1478. The truncated Norman pillars of the *Choir* support pointed arches and a tall superstructure with a richly groined and bossed 14C roof. The brasses, monuments and 14C *windows of the choir commemorate the Fitzhamons, De Clares, Despensers, Beauchamps and other lords of Tewkesbury in its great days. Finest of all is the Perpendicular *Beauchamp Chantry (1422), still with traces of its original colouring. Next to it is the Fitzhamon Chantry (1397), and to the E the canopied tomb and effigies of Hugh Despenser and his wife (c 1349), who largely financed the rebuilding of the choir and E end. On the S side of the high altar is the Perpendicular Despenser Chantry, also called the Trinity Chapel (c 1390, restored 1983), with some of the earliest fan vaulting in England and the kneeling figure of Edward Despenser on the roof. To the E is the tomb of Hugh Despenser's father, also Hugh (d. 1326). The old organ S of the choir stalls is known as the Milton Organ, since the poet is believed to have played it when it was at Hampton Court Palace during the Commonwealth.

The only other monastic building to survive is the 15C *Abbey House*, much altered in the 18C; the nearby gatehouse is a 19C restoration. The row of half-timbered cottages in Church St. includes two museums: the *Little Museum*, recreating the original 15C interior, and the *Countryside Museum*, in memory of the local author John Moore (1907–67).

Bredon (pronounced 'Breedon'), on B4080 3m NE, has a Norman and Decorated church and a large 14C tithe barn (NT). Above it is the rounded *Bredon Hill* (961ft), with a *view and an Iron Age hill-fort. *Elmley Castle*, on its NE flank, has an interesting church with the tomb of the 1st Earl of Coventry (d. 1699) by William Stanton.

Tredington, off A38 2½m SE of Tewkesbury, has a little Norman church. At *Stoke Orchard*, on the other side of M5 1½m further, the church has five layers of wall paintings, the earliest (early 13C) depicting the life of St James of Compostela. The sideroad continues another 2m to *Bishop's Cleeve* (Route 51A).

From Tewkesbury to *Ledbury*, see Route 57.

King John's Bridge (c 1200, rebuilt in 1963) straddles the Avon. The Severn Bridge is by Telford (1826). A38 continues up the Severn valley and passes under M50. 16m: Beyond the river about 1m left is *Upton-on-Severn* (seasonal TI), a pleasant little place with 18C houses. The White Lion is usually identified as the scene of a memorable night of errors in Fielding's 'Tom Jones'. 17½m: *Severn Stoke*. Beyond M5 about 1½m E is *Croome Court*, Capability Brown's first building (1751), now a school (not open). The nearby church has 17C monuments of the Earls of Coventry and a wooden font (1760). *Pirton* church, 1m N, has a half-timbered tower. 25m: **Worcester**, see Route 54.

56

Gloucester to Ross-on-Wye and Hereford

Directions. Total distance 30m. **Gloucester**, Route 51A. A40 to (16m) Ross-on-Wye. A49 to (30m) Hereford.

Gloucester, see Route 51A. A40 heads W, crossing the Severn at 1m. 7m: *Huntley* is on the outskirts of the *Forest of Dean*, explored in Route 58B. *May Hill* (969ft), commanding a fine view, rises on the right. Shortly beyond, A40 enters the county of Hereford and Worcester. 14m: On the left are the Decorated tower of the church at *Weston-under-Penyard* and the woods of *Penyard Park*. Just E of Weston is the site of the Roman Ariconium, where iron was smelted.

16m: **Ross-on-Wye** (7200 inhabitants; TI) is an attractive town on a hill above the E bank of the Wye. The *Prospect*, by the church, gives a good view of the horseshoe bend in the river. *St Mary's* is a large Decorated and Perpendicular building, poorly restored in 1743 and again in 1862. The E window has glass of 1430, while the E window in the N aisle has become a trellis for a climbing tree. The many good monuments include those of the Rudhalls (1530–1651). In front of the altar is the grave of John Kyrle (1637–1724), the town's most noted benefactor, praised as the Man of Ross in Pope's third 'Moral Essay'. Kyrle's house, bearing his bust, stands in the market place by the red sandstone *Market House* of 1660–74.

The 'Ross Spur', part of the unfinished M50 motorway to South Wales, provides the quickest route to Birmingham, via the junction with M5.

From Ross to the *Wye Valley* and the *Forest of Dean*, see Routes 58A and 58B.

A49, the direct road to Hereford, crosses the Wye by the *Wilton Bridge* (1597 but widened). To its N is the ruined 13–16C *Wilton Castle* (not open), destroyed by the Royalists in the Civil War. 25m: The road climbs the flank of *Aconbury Hill* (904ft), with an Iron Age hill-fort.

More attractive, and very little longer, are the sideroads which keep closer to the river between Ross and Hereford. On the E bank B4224 passes (5m) the turning for *How Caple*, where the terraced gardens (open) of How Caple Court give views across the river to the Forest of Dean and the Welsh mountains. It then goes via (9m) *Fownhope*, between the *Woolhope* hills and the Wye. On the W bank, unclassified roads lead to a charming reach at (5m) *Hoarwithy* and then join B4399 near (11m) *Holme Lacy*, where the interesting church by the river has 16–19C monuments of the Scudamore family. On its way into Hereford B4399 passes (14m) *Rotherwas Chapel* (EH, keykeeper at nearby filling station), a curious mixture of 14C, 16C and 19C work.

30m: **HEREFORD** (pronounced 'Herryford'; 47,700 inhabitants) stands on the Wye near the Welsh marches. Its strategic position gave it a long and bloody part to play in military history, culminating in its misfortunes during the Civil War. Although the castle has all but vanished, the cathedral, medieval street pattern and several old buildings survive. Hereford today is a market centre for the surrounding countryside, as well as home of a cider-making industry.

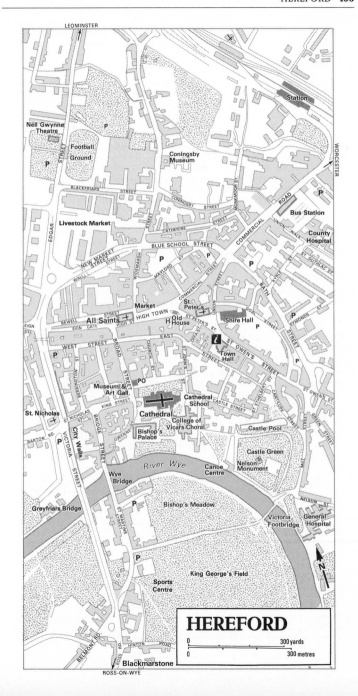

HEREFORD

| 0 | 300 yards |
| 0 | 300 metres |

TI: Town Hall, St Owen's St. **Bus Station**: Commercial Rd, NE of the centre. **Theatre**: The Nell Gwynne, Edgar St. **Annual Events**: The Three Choirs Festival (August) rotates annually between Hereford, Gloucester and Worcester cathedrals. Founded c 1715 and held continuously since 1724, it has given first performances to works by Elgar and Vaughan Williams.

History. The city's name is Saxon, meaning 'army ford', a clear indication that it was from early times a military post along the approaches to southern Wales. It was laid out near the end of the 7C, at about the same time the bishopric was founded. The first earthwork defences were built a century later to protect the area between the river and the present East and West streets. In the 10C a meeting here between Athelstan and the Welsh chieftains fixed the Wye as the border. Ralph, Edward the Confessor's nephew, built one of the first Norman castles in England on the site now known as Castle Green, but in 1055 the town was sacked and burnt by the Welsh. Under the Normans Hereford grew into an important border garrison and trading centre. It suffered badly during the troubled reign of King Stephen, and again during the struggle between Henry III and Simon de Montfort, when de Montfort held both Henry III and the future Edward I prisoner here in 1264. Stone city walls and towers, following the course of the modern inner city ring road, had been completed by the end of the 13C. In 1326 Hugh Despenser was hanged here after his capture at Neath, and Owen Tudor was executed at High Town in 1461 after the Battle of Mortimer's Cross. During the Civil War Hereford was twice taken by Parliament and unsuccessfully besieged by a Scottish army in 1645. After this the city stagnated. It was only in the 19C, with proper sewage and water supply and the arrival of the railway, that modern Hereford started to develop.

Natives and residents. Thomas Traherne (1637–74), Nell Gwynne (1650–87) and David Garrick (1717–79) were born in Hereford. David Cox was a drawing master here in 1814–26.

The commercial centre is the broad street known as High Town. The *Old House* (open), a black-and-white building of 1621, is furnished in the 17C style. In High St. to the W, *All Saints* has a distorted spire, late 14C carved oak stalls and a chained library (open by appointment only). Broad St. leads S from the church to the cathedral close. On the right at the bottom is the *City Museum and Art Gallery*, with a Roman altar and tessellated pavements, and 19C watercolours by local artists.

The *Cathedral* is a modest building of local sandstone. Its chief interest is the mixture of different styles and periods, and the unusual treasures it contains. Its chief weakness is the treatment it has suffered in the name of restoration.

The see of Hereford was detached from Lichfield towards the end of the 7C and a stone cathedral later built on the site where, according to legend, the ghost of the murdered St Ethelbert of East Anglia (d. 794) demanded burial. A later Saxon cathedral, ruined in the Welsh invasion of 1055, was rebuilt by the first Norman bishop, Robert de Losinga, beginning in 1079. His work was largely obliterated by Bishop de Reynelm (1107–15), grandly called 'founder of the church' on his tomb. Bishop Robert de Béthune (1131–48) completed the nave and restored the choir. Bishop William de Vere (1186–99) radically altered the E end, originally apsidal, and probably began the Lady Chapel, though this was not finished until c 1220. Later bishops refined details but increased the lack of unity. Peter of Aquablanca built the N transept in c 1260, Swinfield (1283–1316) the inner N porch, and Adam of Orleton (1317–27) the chapter house and central tower, rising from Norman piers and arches. Bishop Booth (1516–35) added the outer N porch. The fall of the W tower in 1786 gave James Wyatt the excuse to pull down two W bays and destroy much Norman work in the nave. In 1856–63 Sir Gilbert Scott restored the whole cathedral, reconstructing what Wyatt had destroyed at the E end. Wyatt's W front was replaced by J. Oldrid Scott's pseudo-Decorated façade in 1908.

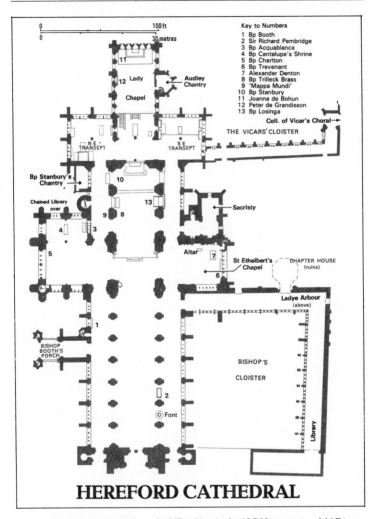

0 _____ 100 ft
0 _____ 30 metres

Key to Numbers
1 Bp Booth
2 Sir Richard Pembridge
3 Bp Acquablanca
4 Bp Cantelupe's Shrine
5 Bp Charlton
6 Bp Trevenant
7 Alexander Denton
8 Bp Trilleck Brass
9 'Mappa Mundi'
10 Bp Stanbury
11 Joanna de Bohun
12 Peter de Grandisson
13 Bp Losinga

11
12 Lady Chapel   Audley Chantry
Coll. of Vicar's Choral →
THE VICARS' CLOISTER
N E TRANSEPT   S E TRANSEPT
Bp Stanbury's Chantry →
10
Chained Library over
13
← Sacristy
9 8
4   3
Altar
5
7
St Ethelbert's Chapel   CHAPTER HOUSE (ruins)
6
Ladye Arbour (above)
1
BISHOP BOOTH'S PORCH
BISHOP'S CLOISTER
2
◉ Font
Library

HEREFORD CATHEDRAL

Externally the best view is from the NE, taking in the 13C N transept and 14C tower as well as the Lady Chapel, choir and NE transept.

The 12C *Nave* is one of the richest Norman designs in England, with massive piers and elaborate arches. Its upper part was evilly treated by Wyatt (1788), who rebuilt the triforium, clerestory and wooden vaulting. The aisles are late Decorated on Norman lower courses. The N aisle has a monument to Bishop Booth (d. 1535) and the S aisle one to Sir Richard Pembridge (d. 1375); the Norman font nearby depicts the Apostles (cf. Mitcheldean and Newnham, both Route 58B).

The *N Transept* was built c 1260 by Peter of Aquablanca, probably to house his own exquisite tomb. Here too is the shrine of St Thomas Cantilupe (d. 1282), with naturalistic foliage and figures of knights. Under the great window, one of the largest examples of Geometrical tracery in England, is the canopied tomb of Bishop Charlton (d. 1344). In striking contrast the *S Transept* keeps its Norman character. The primitive design of the E wall is probably Losinga's work (1079) and thus the oldest part of the cathedral. Three tapestries designed by John Piper hang here, and there is a triptych of the South German school (c 1530). Bishop Trevenant (d. 1404), who made the Perpendicular alterations to the transept, lies under the S window. The coloured tomb effigies nearby are of Alexander Denton (d. 1577), his wife and child. The fireplace on the W wall is Norman in origin. Until 1843 the *Tower Lantern*, with its many shafts and curious gratings, was hidden by a 15C roof.

The *Choir*, originally dedicated in 1110, has a Norman triforium below an Early English clerestory which, like the vaulting, dates from the 13C. The main arches are supported by massive piers and the capitals of the semi-detached shafts are elaborately carved. The grand Norman arch to the E, surmounted by a blind arcade, originally led to the centremost of three apses but is blocked by a pier of the processional aisle added when the E end was altered in 1186–99. The stalls and bishop's throne are 14C. A marble slab opposite the throne commemorates St Ethelbert, and there is a 14C statue of the saint on the S side of the sanctuary. The 12C wooden chair to the left of the altar is said to have been used by King Stephen in 1138. Under the carpet nearby is a brass to Bishop Trilleck (d. 1360).

In the N choir aisle hangs the *Mappa Mundi*, drawn on vellum c 1290 by Richard of Haldingham. It shows Jerusalem in the centre and Paradise at the top, with Europe (and Hereford) at the bottom left. The *Chained Library* (open), now in the former muniments room opposite the map, has nearly 1500 chained books, the largest collection in the world. Its manuscripts include two pages from a 7C Gospel of St Matthew, the Four Gospels (8C) and the Hereford Breviary (1265–70). Also opening from the N choir aisle is the Perpendicular *Chantry of Bishop Stanbury* (d. 1474), with rich fan vaulting and heraldry; his alabaster tomb is across the aisle. The S choir aisle has 14C effigies of early bishops. The *E Transepts* were built on the site of the Norman apsidal chapels between c 1190 and 1370, most of the work dating from 1290. The SE transept contains a bust by Roubiliac, probably of James Thomas (d. 1757).

The *Lady Chapel* (1220) is beautiful Early English work, especially the clustered window shafts and the (restored) lancets at the E end. On the S side is the 15C tomb of Precentor Swinfield, with his swine rebus, and behind a screen of painted stone is the *Chantry of Bishop Audley* (1492–1502). On the N side are the effigy tombs of Joanna de Bohun (d. 1327) and Sir Peter de Grandisson (d. 1358). Below the chapel is the Early English *Crypt* (open) of c 1220, the last to be built in an English cathedral. It is now the Treasury.

From the SE transept the *Vicars' Cloister*, a covered walk with a carved oak roof, leads to the quadrangular *College of Vicars Choral* (1475). The *Bishop's Cloister*, with two Perpendicular walks, leads from the S side of the nave. The remains of the ten-sided 14C *Chapter House* can be seen off the E walk, in the garden between the two cloisters. The W walk, demolished in 1760, was partly replaced by a two-storey building in 1897. The *Cathedral School*, immediately E of the cathedral, dates back to 1381. Pupils include the cathedral choristers. The *Bishop's Palace* (not open) stands between the cathedral and the river. A tablet on the wall of the bishop's garden in Gwynne St. marks the supposed site of Nell Gwynne's birthplace.

King St. and Bridge St. go on from the cathedral to the *Wye Bridge* (1490 but widened in 1826), which is relieved by the modern Greyfriars Bridge (1966) further upstream. A walk leads W along the near bank of the river to the *Herefordshire Waterworks Museum*, a 19C pumping station with its machinery in working order. *Bishop's Meadow*, with a river walk, extends E from Wye Bridge along the far bank to the Victoria Footbridge, which crosses to *Castle Green*, marking the site of Hereford's castle. The pool on its N side was part of the moat. In the middle is a column (1809) to Nelson.

St Owen's St., leading back to High Town, passes the *Town Hall* (1904) and TI Centre, the *Shire Hall* (1819; Smirke) and *St Peter's Church*, with 13C steeple and 15C stalls.

Commercial St. runs NE from High Town and becomes Commercial Rd after it crosses the ring road, marking the line of the old walls. At (c ¾m) the corner of Venns Lane beyond the railway station is the *Churchill Gardens Museum*, a Regency house exhibiting 18–19C costumes and furniture. Widemarsh St. runs N from High Town, passing a plaque marking the site of Garrick's birthplace at the corner of Maylord St. and then crossing the ring road and the line of the walls. The *St John and Coningsby Museum*, on the right at about ½m, was an almshouse for old soldiers and servants, established in 1614 on the site of a Hospital of the Order of St John. The heavily restored chapel dates from c 1200. The garden has a 14C preaching cross and other relics of a Dominican house founded in 1322. Eign Gate leads from the W end of High St. to the ring road. Victoria St., to the left, has some remains of the 13C walls. Eign St., Whitecross St. and Whitecross Rd (A438) continue W, passing (left) the *Museum of Cider* and (right) the *Bulmer Railway Centre* (limited opening), with several historic railway engines. The heavily restored *White Cross*, at 1¼m, was put up in 1361 by Bishop Charlton in gratitude for the departure of the Black Death, during which markets were held here.

Beyond *Swainshill*, 5m W on A438 to Hay-on-Wye, *The Weir* (NT) is a garden overlooking the Wye. *Kentchester*, ½m N, is the site of the Roman Castra Magna, on the road from Wroxeter near Shrewsbury to Caerleon. *Credenhill*, near A480 another ½m N, has a tablet to the poet Thomas Traherne in the church where he was rector c 1657–66. *Brinsop*, 1m further, has a small church with a Norman tympanum (c 1150) and a memorial window to Wordsworth and his sister Dorothy, several times guests at nearby Brinsop Court. At *Madley*, on B4352 6m W of Hereford, the *church has a 13C nave and 14C apse over a vaulted crypt. The 12C N porch was a transept of an earlier church. *Moccas Court* (limited opening), 5m further, is a red-brick house by Robert Adam (1775–81) in a park by Capability Brown (1778). Near *Dorstone*, on B4348 3m further W, is the prehistoric burial chamber of *Arthur's Stone* (EH). At **Kilpeck**, 7m SW of Hereford off A465 to Abergavenny, the *church has some of the richest Norman carving in the country. Note in particular the S doorway, W window, chancel arch and apse. *Kentchurch Court* (open only to parties by appointment), on sideroads 4m SW of Kilpeck, is a 14C house altered by Nash. At *Abbey Dore*, off A465 about 5m W of Kilpeck, the *church preserves the mainly Early English choir and transepts of a Cistercian abbey church (1180–c 1280). On the opposite bank of the river Dore are the gardens (open) of Abbey Dore Court. *Longtown Castle* (EH), 4m SW of Abbey Dore, has a cylindrical keep of c 1200 overlooking the Black Mountains.

From Hereford to *Worcester*, see Route 57; to *Shrewsbury*, see Route 65; to *Hay-on-Wye* and *Abergavenny*, see 'Blue Guide Wales'.

57

The Malvern Hills: Worcester to Hereford

Directions. Total distance 31m. **Worcester**, Route 54. A449 to (7m) Great Malvern and (16m) Ledbury. A438 to (31m) **Hereford**, Route 56.

An alternative, less interesting route from Worcester to (28m) Hereford on A44 and A465 swings N of the Malvern Hills via the high-lying *Bromyard Downs* and (14m) **Bromyard** (TI), with many half-timbered houses. *Lower Brockhampton House* (NT), 2m NE of Bromyard, is a late 14C manor house with a half-timbered 15C gatehouse. Only the hall and parlour are open. *Edvin Loach*, 4m N of Bromyard, has the remains of an isolated 11C church (EH).

Worcester, see Route 54. A449 heads SW and crosses the Teme at (2m) *Powick Bridge*. The ***Malvern Hills** rise sharply from the flat landscape ahead.

This narrow range of hard Pre-Cambrian rocks, mainly gneiss, runs from N to S for about 9m, separating the Severn Plain around Worcester from the rolling countryside around Hereford. There are about 20 summits, averaging only a little over 1000ft, with intervening faults eroded into hollows. The chief hills, from N to S, are West Hill, North Hill, Sugarloaf Hill, the Worcestershire Beacon (the highest point, 1395ft), the Herefordshire Beacon, Swinyard Hill, Midsummer Hill, Hollybush Hill, Ragged Stone and the Gloucester Beacon (or Chase End). Most can be climbed by easy paths. The many springs and wells have made Malvern water famous. The region is intimately connected with Elgar, whose local roots are traced by the Elgar Trail, described in a useful pamphlet available from the Worcester or Great Malvern TI Centres.

7m: **Great Malvern** (30,200 inhabitants; TI), on the slopes to the left of A449, is the chief of several places taking their name from the hills. St Ann's Well on the side of the nearby Worcestershire Beacon made the town a fashionable spa by the 1820s. It still keeps the atmosphere of an inland resort, aided by its many hotels and its public school, Malvern College, founded in 1863. The Malvern Festival, held at the Festival Theatre and Winter Gardens in late May, is largely devoted to Shaw's plays and Elgar's music.

The ***Priory Church**, with a tower recalling that of Gloucester Cathedral, looks entirely Perpendicular from the outside but its interior is largely that of the original Norman building (c 1085), with massive round piers in the nave. Much 15C glass survives, notably in the N transept window, with a portrait of Prince Arthur, Henry VII's eldest son. The choir screen is panelled with locally made 15C *tiles, and there are good monuments and misericords.

Above the church stands a restored Perpendicular gateway of the Benedictine priory where William Langland (1330?–1386?), author of 'Piers Plowman', is thought to have been educated. The opera singer Jenny Lind (1820–87) is buried in the cemetery near the railway station.

North Hill (1307ft), with a good view of the town and its church, takes about ½hr to climb from Great Malvern. On the other side of the hill, reached by B4232, *West Malvern* looks across to the Herefordshire hills. The *Royal Well* (1150ft) is nearby.

Beyond Great Malvern A449 swings round to follow the line of hills from N to S. 8m: The *Worcestershire Beacon* (1395ft), on the right, commands a *view embracing 15 counties, Hereford, Worcester and Gloucester cathedrals, the abbeys of Malvern, Tewkesbury, Deerhurst, Evesham and Pershore, the Wrekin (N) and the Brecknock Hills (W). B4232 branches right from A449 near the Beacon, making its way S via *Wyche Cutting* and the *Jubilee Drive* to rejoin the main route near (4m) the Herefordshire Beacon. 10m: *Malvern Wells* has the Holy Well (680ft). To the E is the Three Counties Showground, where the agricultural fair is held in June. At (11m) *Little Malvern* the 14C church is a relic of the Benedictine priory founded in 1171. Little Malvern Court incorporates the 14C Prior's Hall (limited opening). Elgar is buried in the Roman Catholic cemetery. The hills continue S of Little Malvern but A449 veers W to (12m) *Wynd's Point* (830ft), the pass between the main ridge and the *Herefordshire Beacon* (1114ft). On top of the Beacon is a hill-fort with medieval additions where, according to tradition, Caractacus was captured in AD 75.

A449 descends to (16m) **Ledbury** (TI), a busy little town on the slope of the hill. The 17C *Market House*, perhaps by John Abel, still stands on its original tall chestnut pillars. The *Feathers* and the *Talbot* are late 16C inns. The large *Church* is mainly 13–14C, with a massive detached tower and good monuments, notably the Skynner Tomb (1631) in the chancel and a rare 13C effigy of a priest in the N transept. In the churchyard lies Jacob

Tonson (d. 1736), publisher of Dryden and Pope. *Ledbury Park* (not open) is a gabled manor of 1590. William Langland, author of 'Piers Plowman', may have been born at Ledbury. John Masefield (1878–1967) was a native, and Elizabeth Barrett Browning (1806–61) spent much of her early life in the neighbourhood.

Bosbury, on B4220 3m N, has interesting old houses, notably the Crown inn. The church contains two Harford family tombs, one of them (1573; John Guldo) the oldest signed monument in England. *Castle Frome*, by B4214 1½m further N, has a *font of c 1150 with a vivid Baptism of Christ by the Hereford school of sculpture. At *Much Marcle*, 4½m SW of Ledbury, the monuments in the church include the beautiful effigy of Blanche Mortimer (d. 1347). *Hellen's* (opening) is a manor house dating from the 13C. Attractive lanes lead NW over Marcle Hill to Woolhope (see below) and Hereford.

FROM LEDBURY TO TEWKESBURY, 14m by A438. 2m: *Eastnor Castle* (limited opening) is a massive exercise in medievalism by Sir Robert Smirke (1812–15). As well as its collection from Italy, which includes some 17C panelling, the interior is rich in Victoriana, with decoration by Pugin (1849) and George Fox (1860s) and frescoes by G.F. Watts. The road continues across the S tip of the Malverns, passing near (7m) *Birtsmorton*, with a 12–16C moated manor (not open) where Wolsey was chaplain c 1503–7. 14m: *Tewkesbury*, see Route 55.
From Ledbury to *Gloucester*, see Route 51A.

A438 goes N and W from Ledbury through rich countryside of orchards and hop gardens. The wooded hills around *Woolhope*, to the left, command wide views; see also Route 56. 23m: *Tarrington* church has a fine 12C chancel arch. 31m: **Hereford**, see Route 56.

58

Ross-on-Wye to Chepstow

A. The Wye Valley

Directions. Distances: 26m on the direct route, 33½m including the detours to Goodrich and Symond's Yat Rock. **Ross-on-Wye**, see Route 56. A40 to (11m) **Monmouth**. A466 to (21m) Tintern and (26m) **Chepstow**.

Maps: OS Outdoor Leisure map (2½in to 1m).

The Wye (Welsh 'Gwy', water) rises in Wales on the slopes of Plynlimon, only 2m from the headwaters of the Severn, and flows SE and E via Rhayader, Builth Wells and Hay to Hereford. It then turns S, flowing past Ross-on-Wye and Monmouth to join the Severn just below Chepstow—a total course of 130m. The *valley of the lower Wye between Ross and Chepstow, where the river meanders and loops back on itself between wooded cliffs and gorges, is among the finest inland scenery in Britain. Its natural beauty is enhanced by the border castles at Goodrich and Chepstow and the incomparable Tintern Abbey.
    This reach of the river first became popular towards the end of the 18C, when tourists—Wordsworth and Coleridge among them—satisfied their eye

for the picturesque by admiring the views which William Gilpin's influential travel guide (1782) commended and their appetite for Gothic by making moonlit visits to Tintern. The tourists continue to come in large numbers, but except for the obvious beauty spots near the major roads it is not the sort of countryside that can easily be made to feel unpleasantly crowded.

Offa's Dyke, the great earthwork which the Mercian king (757–795) built along the western border of his territory between the Dee and the Severn, ran near the E bank of the Wye from Monmouth to Chepstow. The Offa's Dyke Path established by the Countryside Commission loosely follows its course and incorporates the surviving stretches of the dyke. Another long-distance walk, the Lower Wye Valley Walk, follows the river from Hereford to Chepstow (about 50m); further details are available from local TI Centres. There are also forest trails on both banks.

Ross-on-Wye, see Route 56. This route leaves the town by Wilton Bridge and joins A40, heading S. 4m: An unclassified road leads left to (¾m) *Goodrich Castle (EH, all year), standing on bedrock above the river.

It takes its name from Godric, who built the first fortress at the beginning of the 12C. Of today's ruins, the grey sandstone keep is mid 12C and the other buildings, in red sandstone, are 13C. The castle belonged to the Earls of Pembroke for most of the 13C, passing in c 1326 to the Talbots, later Earls of Shrewsbury. It was slighted after the Civil War, during which it had been held successively by the Parliamentarians and the Royalists. Wordsworth met the little girl who inspired 'We Are Seven' here in 1793.

A farm near Kerne Bridge, ½m E, preserves some domestic remains of *Flatesford Priory* (1347). Below, the river makes a long loop and the scenery becomes more varied. Its right bank belongs to Herefordshire and its left bank to Gloucestershire.

*Symond's Yat Rock (pronounced 'Sim-') lies 3m S of Goodrich. The rock (473ft) is a famous beauty spot, rising between two reaches of the Wye only 500 yards apart at their nearest point. Its peak commands a glorious view of the river as it loops through wooded scenery: to the E are the steep *Coldwell Rocks*, where the Wye makes a wide bend to the N, while to the SW the river sweeps round the Great Doward (see below). There is an orientation table, and the log cabin by the Forestry Commission car park has information about geological and forest trails. B4432 leads S into the Forest of Dean (Route 58B).

A40 continues to (6½m) *Whitchurch*, childhood home of the artist Wilson Steer (1860–1942). B4164 leads left to the popular village of (1m) **Symond's Yat** below the rocks which here wall the Wye. Beyond Whitchurch A40 skirts the hills of *Great Doward* (661ft) and *Little Doward* (700ft) to the left. On the S slope of Great Doward is *King Arthur's Cave*, reached by sideroads and paths, with signs of human use from the late Ice Age (c 12,000 BC) to Roman times, as well as fossil remains of mammoth, rhinoceros and hyena. There is an Iron Age hill-fort on Little Doward, between the cave and *Ganarew* on A40. Shortly beyond Ganarew it enters the Welsh county of Gwent, so named in 1974. It was previously Monmouthshire which, though strongly Welsh in character, had been included among English counties by Henry VIII in 1535.

11m: **Monmouth** (7400 inhabitants; seasonal TI), county town of the old Monmouthshire, is a market centre on the W bank of the Wye above its meeting with the Monnow. Probably the site of the Roman Blestium, it grew up around the 12C castle and Benedictine priory. For the most part its street plan has been unchanged since the 15C.

Natives. The chronicler Geoffrey of Monmouth (d. 1155), born here, may have been a monk at the priory. Henry V (Harry of Monmouth) is thought to have been born in the castle.

The centre is Agincourt Square, the old market. The *Shire Hall* (1724) carries a statue of Henry V; in front is one of the Hon. Charles Rolls (d. 1910), one of the founders of Rolls Royce and a native of nearby Hendre. Of the *Castle*, approached by Castle Hill roughly opposite Shire Hall, little survives apart from the early 12C keep, or Great Tower. *Great Castle House* (1673) is army property. Priory St., leading N from the square, has the *Market Hall* (rebuilt 1969) with a local history centre and relics of Nelson. *St Mary's Church*, a short way NE, stands on the site of the priory church. Largely rebuilt by G.E. Street (1881), it still has its graceful Decorated spire and, in the baptistery, 15C tiles and a cresset stone from the older church (c 1102). Monnow St. leads S from Agincourt Square to the *Monnow Bridge*, with Britain's only example of a gatehouse actually standing on a bridge. Just beyond is the small, over-restored church of *St Thomas Becket*, with a Norman chancel arch and N door (c 1180).

Across the river 1m E is *Kymin Hill* (850ft; NT), with a 'temple' built in 1800 to honour Nelson's admirals, commanding a *view over the Wye and the Monnow.
    For Usk, 13m SW, and for the route W from Monmouth to *Abergavenny* via *Raglan Castle*, see 'Blue Guide Wales'.
    From Monmouth to the *Forest of Dean* to the E, see Route 58B.

Across the Wye, A466 branches right. The valley narrows, and road and river run close together for the rest of the way. Beyond (13m) *Redbrook*, the left bank belongs to Gloucestershire and the right to Gwent. A stretch of Offa's Dyke survives on the wooded heights of the Gloucestershire side. At (16m) *Bigsweir Bridge* A40 crosses to the Gwent bank. 17½m: *Llandogo* is beautifully placed in a fold of the steep, wooded hills. There is another stretch of Offa's Dyke near (20m) *Brockweir*, a former port and shipbuilding centre on the Gloucestershire bank. For *Hewelsfield*, 2m E, see Route 58B.
    21m: *Tintern Abbey* (Cadw, Welsh Historic Monuments; open) stands on a patch of level ground by the river against a backdrop of tree-covered hills. Despite the ugliness of its immediate surroundings, it is still probably Britain's most romantic Cistercian ruin.

It was founded in 1131, but little remains of the first abbey and most of what survives today dates from the 13C and 14C. After being dissolved in 1536 the abbey mouldered quietly away until the vogue for ruins at the end of the 18C made it popular with tourists. It inspired a famous poem by Wordsworth and was painted by Turner.
    The entrance leads through an excellent exhibition centre. The *Church*, by far the most interesting of the buildings to survive, is on the far (S) side of the precinct. Its chief feature, best seen from outside the site, is the great W window of seven lights and the W doorway, with its twin trefoil-headed openings. The nave, mostly late 13C, still has its clerestory on the S side. Beyond the four large and beautiful crossing arches that once supported the tower is the superb *E window, covering almost the whole of the wall.
    The remains of the domestic buildings (1220–70) on the N side of the church are relatively unimportant. The size of the Lay Brothers' Refectory at the NW corner of the main *Cloister* is a reminder that, with the Cistercian emphasis on agriculture, lay brothers usually outnumbered monks. From the vestry on the E side of the cloister there is a door into the N transept, which incorporates remains of the original 12C church, as well as having the night stairs to the monks' dormitory and a six-light window with much of its tracery. Beyond the *Infirmary Cloister* and its attached buildings to the NE is the *Abbot's Lodging* with hall, camera and chapel.

The abbey made much use of the river as a waterway, and the neighbouring Anchor Hotel is on the site of the Watergate; a 13C arch leading to the slipway can be seen. Just W of the abbey, beside the car park, the *Guest House* and other buildings have been excavated.

Chapel Hill Walk (1½m) and *Barbadoes Walk* (2m) are waymarked walks in Tintern Forest to the W, both starting from the Forestry Commission car park ¼m up the Llanishen road.

For the surviving stretch of Offa's Dyke across the Wye SE of Tintern, see Route 58B.

Below Tintern the Wye is tidal, making so many loops and bends on its way to Chepstow as almost to double the direct distance of 4m. A40 climbs above the river. 23m: *Wyndcliff (650ft; the 'y' is pronounced long) is a popular viewpoint, reached either by steps from the car park on the main road or by the sideroad to the right ½m beyond and following the path from the car park. The view includes the Severn and the Severn Bridge, prominent to the S, the Mendips beyond and the Cotswolds in the E. 24½m: on the left is *Piercefield Park* with Chepstow racecourse.

26m: **Chepstow** (9000 inhabitants; seasonal TI) is an old town on the W bank of the Wye above its junction with the Severn. It grew up around the Norman castle, and developed into a port and shipbuilding centre in the 18C and early 19C.

The *Castle (Cadw, Welsh Historic Monuments; open), separated from the town by a ravine, stands on a steep platform of rock washed by a broad reach of the Wye.

Founded soon after the Conquest by William FitzOsbern, Earl of Hereford, it was unusual in having been built of stone from the outset. In its present form it is mainly 14C.

The gatehouse of 1225–45 is flanked by drum-towers. On the N of the inner ward are the remains of domestic buildings. This part of the castle, overhanging the cliff, gives a good view down to the river and upwards to the Great Tower. On the SE of the ward is Marten's Tower, so-called because the regicide Henry Marten was held here from 1660 until his death in 1680; Jeremy Taylor was also a prisoner, in 1655. Beyond the middle ward is the Great Tower of the original castle (1067–72); its E door and the S and W wall arcades are the oldest part of the building. The upper ward and the barbican lie beyond.

The *Museum*, across Bridge St. from the castle car park, is devoted to local history. Two bridges cross the river nearby. The road bridge dates from 1816 and the railway bridge, although modernised, was originally built by Brunel. *St Mary's Church*, ruthlessly restored in the 19C, belonged to the Benedictine priory. The Norman nave, aisle and W door survive; inside are Henry Marten's tomb and interesting monuments. The 13C *Port Wall* which enclosed the town to the S and W can be traced for much of its course, one good place being the main car park off Beaufort Square. The W gate spanning the main street, though probably more or less true to the original design, was rebuilt in 1524.

St Briavels 7m NE off B4228, has a Norman church and a 12C castle (YHA and EH; bailey open summer season, daily 13.00–16.00). The S end of Offa's Dyke is across the Wye 2m SE, between B4228 and Sedbury Cliffs.

From the *Severn Bridge*, just over 1m S of the town centre, to *Bristol*, see Route 20. From Chepstow to *Gloucester* via the *Forest of Dean*, see Route 58B.

B. The Forest of Dean

Maps: OS Outdoor Leisure map (2½in to 1m).

The **Forest of Dean** is a steeply edged plateau on the wedge of land between the lower Wye and the Severn estuary. Its average height is about 650ft, though Ruardean Hill in the N rises to 951ft. Its oak and beech woodlands were reserved as a royal forest by Edward the Confessor, and in 1938 the region became the first National Forest Park (34,000 acres). The many forest trails make excellent walking.

Its long history of mining gives the forest an added interest. The Romans first extracted iron ore from the limestone inner rim of the plateau at the Scowles, near Bream. Iron-mining flourished in the Middle Ages, with 'free miners' enjoying special rights, and lasted until the 19C. Today the old 'bell pits' are overgrown. Coal-mining was carried on near the centre of the Forest, with large-scale workings between Coleford and Cinderford. It too has been abandoned, and replanting by the Forestry Commission has helped conceal its effects, though an industrial atmosphere still lingers in some towns.

The routes suggested below head E from Monmouth and Chepstow (Route 58A) towards Gloucester (Route 51A).

FROM MONMOUTH VIA MITCHELDEAN TO A40, 16m on A4136. The road climbs round the side of *Kymin Hill* (Route 58A) and (2¾m) the *Buckstone* (951ft), with a rocking stone and a fine *view. The outskirts of the Forest of Dean begin at (3¾m) *Staunton*, where the church is partly Norman, like several on the fringes of the forest. For *Coleford*, 2m SE, see route below. 6m: B4228 and then B4432 head N through *Berry Hill* to (2½m) *Symond's Yat Rock* (Route 58A). The woodland on the left has several forest trails. A4136 continues to (11m) *Nailbridge*. At *Ruardean*, 2m NW on B4227, the church has a *carving of St George and the Dragon (c 1150) on the tympanum of the porch, by the Hereford school of sculpture. *Ruardean Hill* (951ft) makes a good viewpoint. 13½m: *Mitcheldean* keeps half-timbered houses and a 14–15C church with a distinctive slender spire rebuilt in c 1760, a carved oak roof and a Norman font showing the Apostles (cf. Newnham, below, and Hereford Cathedral). At *Abenhall*, ¾m S, the church has a 15C font with the arms of local free miners. 16m: A4136 joins A40 near *Huntley* and *May Hill*, on the way from Gloucester to Ross-on-Wye (Route 56).

FROM CHEPSTOW TO GLOUCESTER VIA COLEFORD AND CINDERFORD, 33m. A48 crosses the river and after 1m B4228 branches left. 2m: *Wintour's Leap* is a 100ft precipice with a view over the Wye. 3m: A fragment of Offa's Dyke (EH) lies between the road and the river. 4m: There is a picnic site and viewpoint in the woods to the left. At (6m) *Hewelsfield*, right of B4228, the church has a Norman tower and nave. For *Brockweir* and Offa's Dyke, left of the road, see Route 58A. 7½m: *St Briavels*, high above the Wye valley, has a partly Norman church and a 13C castle, now a youth hostel. 9½m: B4321 leads left to (¾m) *Clearwell*, where the castle is a Gothick building of 1727, now a hotel, and the *Caves* (open) are old iron mines, with a museum and geology exhibition. At *Newland*, 1½m NW, the church is known as the 'Cathedral of the Forest'. It has a Decorated spire and a 15C brass depicting a free miner. B4228 goes on to (12m) *Coleford* (TI), where

B4226 heads N and E to (15½m) *Speech House*, in the centre of the forest.
Now a hotel, it was built in 1676 as a courthouse for the Foresters of Dean.
There are forest trails in the woods to both N and S; the New Fancy Trail
leads to a good viewpoint 2m S. B4226 continues E to (18m) *Ruspidge* and
(19m) *Cinderford*, once a coal-mining centre. For the Soudley valley to the
S, see route below. The present route takes A4151 W to (19½m) *Littledean*.
Littledean Hall (open) is a 16–17C building, with oak-panelled rooms, on
older foundations. The grounds have good views. A4151 joins A48 at (22m)
Elton, on the route to (33m) Gloucester described below.

FROM CHEPSTOW TO GLOUCESTER VIA A48, 28m. A dull road following the
Severn estuary, with the forest to the N. 8m: *Lydney* has a 14C cross. The
grounds (limited opening) of *Lydney Park* have a deer park and remains of
a 12C castle and Roman temple, with a museum of objects. From *Bream*,
on B4231 3m NW, a path leads to the Roman iron workings at the Scowles.
The *Norchard Railway Centre* on B4234, 1m N of Lydney, is headquarters
of the Dean Forest Railway, with steam locomotives. 11m: *Nibley*. A big
fragment of Roman road has been exposed at *Blackpool Bridge*, on B4431
2½m NW. 11½m: *Blakeney*. B4227 leads up the Soudley Valley, with the
Dean Heritage Museum at (2m) *Lower Soudley*. 15m: *Newnham* is a
charming little town on a bend in the river. The church has a Norman font
showing the Apostles (cf. Mitcheldean, above, and Hereford Cathedral). At
(17m) *Elton* the route is joined by A4151 from Cinderford (see route above).
18½m: at *Westbury-on-Severn* the church has a separate 13C tower with
shingled 14C spire. *Westbury Court Garden* (NT) is a 17C water-garden.
23m: *Minsterworth* makes a good place to see the Severn Bore (Route 51A).
25m: A40 heads E to (28m) *Gloucester* (Route 51A).

59

London to Northampton and Leicester

Directions. Total distance 96m. Less interesting for the larger towns than
the smaller places and the detours. To (45m) Milton Keynes, see Route 52B.
A5, A508 to (64m) **Northampton**. A508 to (82m) Market Harborough. A6
to (96m) **Leicester**.

Route 52B leads along A5 to (45m) **Milton Keynes**.

An alternative to the main route to Northampton described below follows A422 N from
Milton Keynes to (5m) *Newport Pagnell* (10,800 inhabitants). *Chicheley Hall* (limited
opening), on A422 2m NE, is a lovely baroque house (1719–23) by Francis Smith of
Warwick. The outside has a richly carved frieze, capitals and doorcase. Inside, the hall
is by Henry Flitcroft, and there is handsome wood panelling in several rooms. For
Olney, further N, see the detour from Northampton to Bedford below. From Newport
Pagnell B526 leads to (7½m) *Gayhurst*. The elegant *church of c 1728, by an uniden-
tified architect, contains an expressive monument to Sir Nathan Wright and his son.
It stands beside the Elizabethan mansion (not open) where the gunpowder conspirator
Sir Everard Digby (1578–1606) lived and his son Sir Kenelm Digby (1603–65) was born.
To the left near (9m) *Stoke Goldington* the tall steeple of *Hanslope* church can be seen.
B526 joins A508 shortly before (18m) *Northampton* (see below).

The main route leaves A5 at (51m) the roundabout beyond *Stony Stratford*, heading N on A508. 57m: *Stoke Bruerne*, left of the road, is a charming place on the Grand Union Canal (Route 52B) near the S end of the Blisworth tunnel. The **Waterways Museum** is devoted to the history of the canal. In *Stoke Park* (limited opening of gardens and exterior) two pavilions and a colonnade survive from the earliest English house on a Palladian plan (1630), attributed to Inigo Jones. A508 crosses M1. The way into Northampton, after (63m) the junction with A45, passes an *Eleanor Cross, one of three which survive from the series marking the overnight stops in the funeral procession of Queen Eleanor of Castile in 1290. See Lincoln (Route 48) for further details. Just beyond is the 16–19C *Delapré Abbey*, now the County Record Office (gardens open; limited opening of public rooms), on the site of the Cluniac nunnery where the queen's body lay.

64m: **NORTHAMPTON** (186,000 inhabitants), the county town, is a dull place with nondescript modern development. It has little of interest except its churches, St Peter, All Saints and St Sepulchre.

TI: Visitor Centre, 10 St Giles Square. **Bus and Coach Station**: Greyfriars, with access from Grosvenor Centre. **Railway Station**: Castle Station, W of town centre. **Theatre**: Royal Theatre, Derngate.

History. The castle which Simon de Senlis, 1st Earl of Northampton, built in this old Saxon town soon after the Norman Conquest became a favourite resort of kings and the site of several great councils and parliaments. St Thomas Becket was tried at the castle in 1164, and Shakespeare laid the first scene of 'King John' in the great hall. A decisive battle (1460) in the Wars of the Roses was fought outside the town walls at Delapré. Northampton sided with Parliament during the Civil War, and one of Charles II's first acts was to raze its castle and walls. It suffered a disastrous fire in 1675.

Natives and residents. Robert Browne (?1550–?1633), leader of the sect which founded Congregationalism, died in Northampton jail (see St Giles's church below). Philip Doddridge (1702–51) was minister at the Congregationalist church for the last 22 years of his life. John Clare was an inmate of the county asylum from 1841 until his death in 1864. Spencer Perceval, the Prime Minister assassinated in 1812, and the rationalist reformer Charles Bradlaugh (1833–91) were MPs for Northampton. Malcolm Arnold was born here in 1921.

From Castle Station, near the site of the vanished castle, Marefair leads towards the centre. On the right is *St Peter, one of the finest late Norman churches in England, dating from c 1160. The most interesting features are the richly carved arch on the W front and, inside, the massive W tower arch and the capitals. There is also a Saxon cross shaft. The *Doddridge Church* in Doddridge St., to the left, dates from 1695. It has a monument to its former minister Philip Doddridge (d. 1751).

Further down Marefair is the Elizabethan *Hazelrigg House*, where Cromwell is supposed to have stayed before the Battle of Naseby. Gold St. continues to *All Saints, handsomely rebuilt after the fire of 1675. Its early 18C Ionic portico, with a statue of Charles II in Roman costume, was a favourite haunt of John Clare when he was allowed out of Northampton asylum. The church is nicely complemented by the *County Hall* (1682) on the opposite side of George Row. The *Guildhall* in St Giles Square is florid Victorian Gothic (1864, E.W. Godwin; enlarged in 1892 and restored in 1992). Guided tours of it are organised by the *Visitor Centre*, in restored Georgian and Victorian buildings opposite. The Centre includes an audio-visual display of the town's history. A bridge links the centre with the *Central Museum and Art Gallery* in Guildhall Rd, with work by 15–18C

Italian painters and the Norwich School, British ceramics, and displays tracing Northampton's long connection with shoemaking.

St Giles St. leads from the Guildhall to the church of *St Giles*, Perpendicular with Norman fragments. Robert Browne, founder of the Brownist sect, is buried here. The RC church of *St John* in Bridge St. uses the converted almshouse and chapel of a medieval hospital of St John. The chapel has a fine Perpendicular W window.

N of All Saints is the big Market Square, where the main market is held on Tuesdays, Wednesdays, Thursdays, Fridays and Saturdays. At the NE corner the rebuilt façade of *Welsh House* (1595) survives the destruction of much of the neighbourhood to make way for the nearby *Grosvenor Centre* and other modern development. From the NW corner Sheep St. leads past the house where Dr Doddridge had his academy to *St Sepulchre, one of only four round churches to survive in England. (The others are at the Temple in London, Cambridge and Little Maplestead in Essex.)

The tower and spire are late 14C. The round part, with its eight Norman pillars supporting late 14C arches, was built c 1100–15 by Simon de Senlis on his return from the Crusades. It resembles its prototype, the Church of the Holy Sepulchre in Jerusalem, more closely than the other English round churches. The present nave is a 13–14C enlargement of the original Norman choir, while the present choir dates from 1860–64. On the N wall is the quaint Coles brass (1640).

Further N, in Barrack Rd, is the *Roman Catholic Cathedral*, much enlarged from a church of 1844 by Pugin. Abington St., a shopping thoroughfare leading NE from the Market Square, is continued by Wellingborough Rd to the *County Cricket Ground*, on the left, and *Abington Park*, on the right. The manor house contains the *Abington Museum*, with period rooms, Chinese ceramics and natural history collections. Shakespeare's grand-daughter Lady Bernard (d. 1670) lived here and is buried in the S chapel of the old village church. In Kettering Rd, branching left from Wellingborough Rd, the 19C church of *St Matthew* has a stone Madonna and Child (1944) by Henry Moore and a painting of the Crucifixion (1946) by Graham Sutherland.

6m NW on A428 towards Rugby is **Althorp** (limited opening), the family home of the Princess of Wales and hence extremely popular with visitors. The 16C house was remodelled several times, notably in the 1730s by Roger Morris, who designed the splendid entrance hall, and in the 1780s by Henry Holland. It contains a large and distinguished *collection of pictures, furniture and china, part of it inherited from Sarah, Duchess of Marlborough. The portraits include work by Reynolds and Gainsborough in the Marlborough Room and by Van Dyck, Lely and Kneller in the Picture Gallery.

The church of *Great Brington* on the W side of the park contains the *tombs of the Spencers from 1522 onwards and is the burial place of George Washington's ancestors Laurence (d. 1616) and Robert (d. 1622), who moved from Sulgrave (Route 52A). Off A428 about 3m beyond Althorp are: *Holdenby House* (gardens opening; house open to parties by appointment), 2m E, a Tudor house where Charles I was held prisoner in 1647; *Coton Manor Gardens* (limited opening), 2m N; and *Guilsborough*, 1m beyond Coton, with glass by Morris and Co. in the church and a former school building of 1668.

FROM NORTHAMPTON TO BEDFORD VIA OLNEY, 21m by A428. 5m: *Denton*. 4m SW is *Horton*, with *The Menagerie*, a modern garden being created around an 18C folly. A428 crosses *Yardley Chase*, a wide tract of moorland with fine oaks. 7m: *Yardley Hastings*. About 1½m N is *Castle Ashby House* (open to parties of 25 or more by prior appointment), an Elizabethan mansion with additions in the 1630s, sometimes ascribed to Inigo Jones, including a lettered balustrade. It has a noted collection of furniture and paintings (Reynolds, Kneller, Raeburn). The church has interesting monuments. At *Easton Maudit*, 2m E of Castle Ashby, the antiquarian Thomas Percy of 'Percy's Reliques' was vicar from 1753 to 1782. The church has 17C monuments of the Yelvertons. Shortly beyond Yardley Hastings B5388 branches right to (10½m) **Olney** (3500 inhabitants), a charming town in the northern tip of Buckinghamshire. In the market place the house where William Cowper lived with Mrs Unwin in 1768–86 is now the *Cowper and Newton Museum*. It has relics of the poet and his friend John Newton (d. 1807), perpetual curate of Olney, as well as an exhibit of the local lace-making industry. From the river Ouse there are beautiful views of the early Decorated *Church* with its tall spire. The handsome village of *Weston Underwood*, 2m SW, was Cowper's home from 1786 until 1795. The church at *Ravenstone*, 1m further, has good 18C woodwork and the elegant tomb, perhaps by Joseph Catterns, of Lord Chancellor Finch, Earl of Nottingham (d. 1682), founder of the adjoining almshouses. B565 rejoins A428 just before (13m) *Cold Brayfield*. 14m: *Turvey* has a large, interesting church with an early 14C painted *Crucifixion and fine 16C monuments of the Mordaunts. *Clifton Reynes*, on the Ouse 3m W, has 13–14C wooden effigies in its church. From (18m) *Bromham*, with a 17C mill (open), a sideroad leads about 3m NW to *Stevington*, with an 18C post windmill. *Stagsden Bird Gardens* (open), on A422 2m SW of Bromham, is a breeding centre for pheasants, waterfowl and owls. 21m: *Bedford*, see Route 60B.

FROM NORTHAMPTON TO HIGHAM FERRERS, 15m. A45 is the faster road but A4500, the old Wellingborough road, is more convenient for the sightseer. Both run parallel to the Nene. 3½m: *Great Billing* has a pretentious monument of 1700 by John Bushnell in the church. *Little Billing*, 1m SW, has a remarkable Saxon font. 4½m: *Ecton* was the home of Benjamin Franklin's ancestors until his father left for New England in 1685. On the right at 6½m is *Earls Barton*, where the church is famous for its late Saxon *tower, the most important work to survive from this period in England. *Whiston* church, 1½m SW, is a lovely example of late Perpendicular (1534). For *Castle Ashby*, further S, see the detour from Northampton to Bedford above. 10m: **Wellingborough** (39,600 inhabitants; TI) is an old town above the Nene. The parish church of All Hallows has good misericords and modern windows by John Piper and Patrick Reyntiens. St Mary's is a florid building (1908–30) by Sir Ninian Comper. A45 is joined for the last part of the journey to (15m) *Higham Ferrers* (Route 60B).

From Northampton to *Banbury*, see Route 52A.

A508 continues due N from Northampton, past (70m) the Pitsford reservoir, to (71m) *Brixworth*, with the kennels of the Pytchley hunt. The Saxon *church, originally built c 680 with bricks from local Roman buildings, shows three distinct phases of work before the Conquest. *Spratton*, 2¼m W, has a Norman and Transitional church containing the effigy of Sir John Swinford (d. 1371), with the earliest known example of the SS collar. *Cottesbrooke Hall* (limited opening), 4m NW of Brixworth, is a well-pre-served Queen Anne building. 73m: *Lamport Hall* (limited opening), right of the road, was built by John Webb in the 1650s and extended by Francis Smith of Warwick and his son in the 1730s. 76m: The battlefield of *Naseby*, where the Parliamentarian army defeated Charles I and Prince Rupert in 1645, lies 4m W of the road beyond *Haselbech*. A column put up in 1936 marks the correct site.

The road enters Leicestershire just before (82m) **Market Harborough** (16,000 inhabitants; TI). Its market place has the grammar school of 1614 and *St Dionysius*, a Perpendicular church with a beautiful Decorated broach spire. Nearby is the house where Charles I is said to have spent the night before Naseby. The *Museum* of local history is in the council offices on Adam and Eve St.

From Market Harborough to *Rugby*, see Route 52B.

A6 continues N. 88m: *Kibworth* has 17–18C houses and a post mill of 1711. Philip Doddridge (see Northampton, above) was dissenting minister here in 1723–25.

96m: **LEICESTER** (282,300 inhabitants), the county town, is an unattrac-tive place. The pervasive effects of its industry and manufacturing—in the outer sprawl of 20C housing estates, inner ring of 19C red-brick terraces and ghastly redevelopment of the centre—make it hard to appreciate the real points of interest, chiefly its Roman remains and several museums.

TI: 26 St Martin's Walk; St Margaret's Bus Station. **Bus Station**: St Margaret's, Abbey St. **Railway Station**: London Rd, SE of the centre. **Theatres**: Haymarket Theatre and Studio Theatre, The Haymarket; The Little Theatre, Dover St.; Phoenix Art Theatre, Upper Brown St.

History. According to tradition, King Lear and his daughters lived at Leicester. The Romans made it the fortified Ratae Coritanorum. It was the seat of the East Mercian bishopric from 680 to 869, but soon afterwards became one of the five towns of the Danelagh (hence the suffix 'gate', from the Danish 'gade', which survives in street names). It was recovered by Ethelfleda, Alfred the Great's daughter, in 918. After the Norman Conquest it fell to Hugh of Grantmesnil, who built the castle, and in 1239 to Simon de Montfort, Earl of Leicester and a great local benefactor. Lancastrian kings acknowledged its importance by holding three parliaments here in the 15C and by making frequent visits to the castle, though Richard III had to sleep at an inn on his way to Bosworth Field in 1485. Prince Rupert besieged and captured Leicester during the Civil War (Bunyan was among the defending army), but Parliament recovered it after the Battle of Naseby. Later prosperity came from hosiery, encouraged by the stocking frame in the late 17C. In 1800 the population still stood at only 17,000, a reminder (if it were needed) that most of Leicester's growth belonged to the Industrial Revolution.

Natives and residents. The Chartist Thomas Cooper, C.P. Snow and Joe Orton were born here. Thomas Cook took his first step as a tour operator with a railway excursion to Loughborough and back in 1841.

The *Clock Tower* (1866), with statues of Simon de Montfort and other local benefactors, marks the hub of converging main roads which developed outside the Roman E gate. It is reached from the railway station to the SE by Granby St., the chief shopping street. From East Gates the Roman main street ran W to the Soar Bridge; the High St. follows the medieval line a little to the N. The High Cross stood where it met the old thoroughfare from N to S, now Highcross St. and its continuation, in St Nicholas Circle.

To the right Highcross St. leads past the site of the Free Grammar School of 1573 (plaque). Beyond the inner ring road are *All Saints*, an early Decorated church with a Norman W doorway, clock of c 1620 and Early English font, and, to the E, *St Margaret*, with a Perpendicular tower and chancel, and fragments of Saxon masonry at the E end of the N aisle. The fine *Great Meeting* (1708), one of England's oldest Non-conformist chapels, survives in East Bond St. behind St Margaret's Baths and the car park on Vaughan Way.

By the intrusive St Nicholas Circle stands **St Nicholas**, the oldest church in Leicester, built partly of Roman materials with an early Norman tower, a primitive Saxon nave and an Early English chancel. On the W side of the churchyard rises the **Jewry Wall** (EH), a mass of Roman masonry with bonding courses of brick and four recessed arches. It may have been the W wall of a basilica in the Roman forum, which extended E and N, or part of the later Roman baths, which can be seen in plan to the W. Beyond is the **Jewry Wall Museum**.

A museum of archaeology up to the Middle Ages, its *Roman exhibits include several mosaic pavements (notably the Peacock mosaic, and Cyparissus and his stag), large wall paintings, a wooden bucket with bronze decoration, and milestones from the Fosse Way. The columns outside come from a colonnade in the forum.

Beyond *West Bridge* over the Grand Junction Canal, St Augustine's St. leads to *Bow Bridge* over the Soar, where a plaque records the last resting place of Richard III.

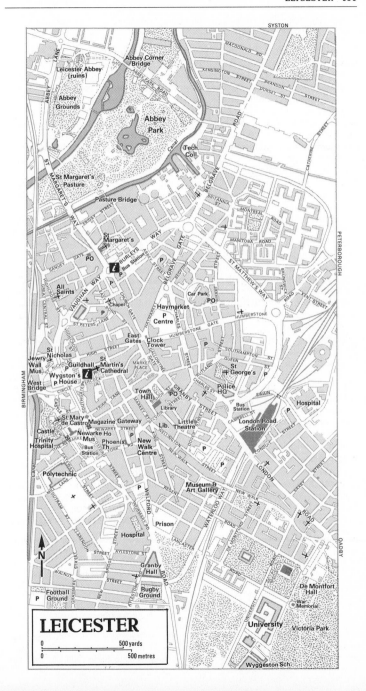

LEICESTER

| 0 | | 500 yards |
| 0 | | 500 metres |

Tradition maintains that his body, brought from Bosworth to the Greyfriars monastery, was thrown into the river at the Reformation but afterwards reburied near here.

Castle St. leads from the opposite side of St Nicholas Circle to *St Mary de Castro, a church with an unusual ground plan. The original Norman collegiate church was enlarged with a chancel in the richest late Norman style (after 1150) and, in the Early English period, with a massive tower and a wide parochial nave on the S side. Features include: the Norman N doorway, arcading in the N aisle, windows and sedilia; the Decorated roof in the original chancel; the Early English sedilia; the Perpendicular roof in the S nave; and the 13C font. The few remains of the once famous *Castle* are reached through a timber gateway (1445). *Castle House*, on the right, incorporates the domestic buildings. In Castle Yard, where Wesley used to preach, a façade of c 1698 masks the late Norman hall, divided into three in 1821, so that only the N and S ends are visible. (Now an assize court, it is open when not in use.) A doorway from the hall can be seen in the W wall of the church.

The *Turret Gateway* (1423) leads into the Newarke, the 'new work' added to the castle in 1332. The rebuilt *Trinity Hospital* was founded in 1331 by Henry of Lancaster and enlarged in 1354 by his son Henry, Duke of Lancaster, who died here in 1361. Mary Bohun (d. 1394), Henry V's mother, is buried in the partly original chapel. The *Newarke Houses Museum*, in two 16–17C buildings, illustrates the social and industrial history of Leicester since the Middle Ages, with 17C panelled rooms, a 19C street scene, and clocks and musical instruments. The splendid early 15C *Magazine Gateway*, isolated amid the traffic, houses the Museum of the Royal Leicestershire Regiment.

Southgates or the more peaceful Castle St. lead back N to St Nicholas Circle. *Wygston's House* in Applegate, E of the circle, is a museum of 18–20C costume. The old civic church of **St Martin**, raised to cathedral status in 1926, stands on a cramped site in Peacock Lane. Originally Early English, with a Perpendicular chancel, it was largely refashioned by Raphael Brandon in 1844–67. To its W is the *Guildhall* (open), a 14–16C building which originally belonged to the Guild of Corpus Christi. The great hall is imposing; the mayor's parlour has a 17C chimneypiece, woodwork and stained glass. The Town Library, whose foundation in c 1587 makes it one of the earliest free municipal libraries in England, was first installed here c 1633.

A little to the E of cathedral and Guildhall is the *Market Place*, where the main markets are held on Wednesday, Friday and Saturday. The old *Corn Exchange* has a fine outside staircase (c 1851). To the S are the *Town Hall* (1875) and the *Central Library*. King St., beyond, leads to the *New Walk*, a long tree-lined pathway laid out in 1785, with the **Museum and Art Gallery**.

It contains geology and natural history, and an ancient Egyptian gallery. The wide art collection is particularly strong in 19–20C English painters (the Bloomsbury circle, Lowry, Stanley Spencer) and the German Expressionists.

University Rd leads to the right from the end of New Walk and passes *Victoria Park*, with the *De Montfort Hall* and Lutyens's fine *War Memorial*, on the way to the **University of Leicester**, which received its charter in 1957. The main building, originally a hospital, dates from 1837; the Department of Engineering (1959–63; James Stirling and James Gowan) is conspicuous among modern additions. *Wyggeston Boys' School* can trace its origins to a charitable foundation of 1513.

Haymarket and Belgrave Gate, leading NE from the Clock Tower, are continued beyond the inner ring road by Belgrave Rd. To the left are *Abbey Park*, with a lake, and the remains of **Leicester Abbey**, where Wolsey came to die in 1530. His tomb has disappeared, and little is left of the Augustinian monastery except the conjectural foundations and the boundary wall. Further N, in Corporation Rd off Abbey Lane, a sewage pumping station with Victorian beam engines is the *Museum of Technology*. Off Belgrave Rd further N is *Belgrave Hall* (open), a Queen Anne house with charming gardens, now a period museum of coaches and agricultural equipment.

Charnwood Forest is a wooded, hilly region of granite and slate rising out of the plain NW of Leicester. A convenient tour leaves the city on A50 and branches left to (4½m) *Groby*. Elizabeth Woodville, later Edward IV's wife, lived at the manor house with her first husband, Sir John Grey. A sideroad leads N, below A50 and past the attractive Groby Pool, descending to (6½m) *Newton Linford*. *Bradgate Park* (open), with oak trees and herds of red and fallow deer, is the best place to see the natural appearance of the forest. The ruined Bradgate House was the birthplace of Lady Jane Grey, the 'nine days' queen' (1537–1554). About 2m NW of Newton are the 14C remains of *Ulverscroft Priory* (not open). The route continues to *Bardon Hill*, *Mount St Bernard* and *Grace Dieu*, described in the detour from Leicester to Burton below, or returns via *Cropton Reservoir*, *Thurcaston* (where Bishop Latimer was born in 1485) and *Rothley*.

FROM LEICESTER TO BURTON-UPON-TRENT, 25m by A50. The disused line to Swannington was Robert Stephenson's first railway (1832). 4½m: *Groby*, see above. *Kirby Muxloe*, 2½m S, has the remains of a moated, brick-built *castle begun by William, Lord Hastings in 1480 and left unfinished after Richard III executed him for treason (EH, all year). Beyond (10m) *Bardon Hill* (912ft), a famous viewpoint in Charnwood Forest on the right, A50 enters the Leicestershire coalfield. 12m: *Coalville* (30,800 inhabitants; TI) is a mining and brick-making town. *Donington-le-Heath*, 1m SW, has a restored 13C manor house (open). The Trappist monastery of *Mount St Bernard*, remotely situated in Charnwood Forest about 3m NE of Coalville, was founded in 1835, England's first new abbey since the Reformation. Its church was begun by A.W.N. Pugin in 1840 (partly open). Beyond Whitwick 3½m N of Coalville is *Grace Dieu*, with the scanty remains of a 13C Augustinian nunnery (seen in a field skirted by A512) and the manor house where Francis Beaumont (1584–1616) was born.

17m: **Ashby-de-la-Zouch** (11,500 inhabitants; TI) is a pleasant little place. Its ruined *Castle* (EH, all year), originally Norman and 14C, was refortified by William, Lord Hastings in 1474–76 and slighted by Parliamentarians during the Civil War. The late Perpendicular church of *St Helen* has a rare 15C recumbent effigy of a pilgrim, and the tombs of the 2nd Earl of Huntingdon (d. 1561) and Selina, Countess of Huntingdon (d. 1791), Wesley's friend. The 'Tournament Field' made famous by Scott's 'Ivanhoe' lies about 1m N of the town. About 2m E is *Coleorton Hall* (National Coal Board), where Wordsworth, his sister Dorothy, and Coleridge advised Sir George Beaumont (d. 1827) on the landscaping of his grounds. *Appleby Magna*, off A453 5m SW of Ashby, has an early 14C church and moated 15–16C manor house (not open). *Appleby Parva*, ¾m beyond, has a grammar school of 1693–97. From Ashby to *Derby*, see Route 68, to *Nottingham*, see Route 70. A50 passes (20m) *Swadlincote* (23,400 inhabitants). 25½m: *Burton-upon-Trent*, Route 61.

FROM LEICESTER TO GRANTHAM, 30m. A607 branches right from A46, the Foss Way, shortly before (4½m) *Syston* and follows the valley of the Wreake. The village names ending in 'by' show Danish occupation. 6m: *Quenborough*, to the right, was Prince Rupert's headquarters during the siege of Leicester. 7m: *Rearsby*. There is a fine early 14C church at *Gaddesby*, 2½m E. 8½m: *Brooksby*, where George Villiers, Duke of Buckingham, was born at the hall in 1592, has a little Perpendicular church. 15m: **Melton Mowbray**, see Route 70. A607 crosses the limestone outcrop of the Leicestershire Wolds, for which (20m) *Waltham-on-the-Wolds* is a good centre. *Sproxton*, 3m E, has a 10C cross. 26m: *Denton*, with a 13–15C church, is near *Belvoir Castle* (Route 72). 27m: *Harlaxton Manor*, one of the most extravagant 19C mansions in the country, was built to the designs of Anthony Salvin and its owner, Gregory Gregory, in the 1830s. It is now an extension college of the University of Evansville, Indiana. 30m: *Grantham*, see Route 72.

From Leicester to *Rugby*, see Route 52; to *Birmingham*, see Route 61; to *Derby* and *Sheffield*, see Route 68.

60

London to Stamford

A. Via the A1

Directions. Total distance 91m. To (21m) Hatfield, (24m) Welwyn Garden City, (32m) Stevenage, (39m) Baldock, (77m) Norman Cross and (91m) **Stamford**.

A1 bypasses the towns—including all those listed above—and becomes motorway for several stretches, though the frequent roundabouts on the non-motorway parts and the heavy lorry traffic make it unpopular with some long-distance travellers. For some of the way it follows a historic route. Ermine Street, the Roman road from London to the North, ran via Ware and Huntingdon (now A10, A14; Route 36) but coincided with A1 between Alconbury and Colsterworth, N of Stamford, before continuing (as B6403 and A15; Route 48) via Lincoln and the Humber ferry. The Great North Rd, the old coaching route, began by following the present A1000 through Barnet and Potters Bar to Hatfield and Welwyn, and then B197 between Stevenage and Baldock, but joined the present A1 between Biggleswade and Markham Moor, N of Newark. The journey up A1 is continued in Route 72 (Stamford to Doncaster) and Route 85B (Doncaster to Durham, New-castle and Berwick).

A1 becomes motorway from (15m) the junction with M25 until just short of (21m) **Hatfield** (29,000 inhabitants), developed as a 'satellite town' of London after World War II. The old town stands on the Great North Road, 1m E. Its church has the striking tomb of Lord Burghley's son Robert Cecil, 1st Earl of Salisbury (d. 1612), a small 13C effigy of a knight and a monument by Nicholas Stone (1617). In a fine park E of the town is *Hatfield House (open), one of the largest and most splendid Jacobean mansions in the country.

It was built in 1607–12 for the 1st Earl of Salisbury by Robert Lyminge, architect of Blickling Hall; like the Norfolk house, it uses red brick with stone dressings. The S front, originally the main entrance, has a stone clock tower and loggia (now closed in to form the armoury) which have been attributed to Inigo Jones. Inside, note the screen and minstrels' gallery in the Great Hall, the carved oak staircase by John Bucke, and the chimneypiece by Maximilian Colt in King James's Drawing Room. The large collection of paintings includes portraits of Elizabeth I by Isaac Oliver and Nicholas Hilliard and a delightfully informal portrait of the 1st Marchioness of Salisbury by Reynolds. In the grounds stands the surviving part of the old Palace (1497), where Elizabeth I was living in confinement when her sister Queen Mary died in 1558.

24m: **Welwyn Garden City** (pronounced 'Wellin'; 47,000 inhabitants; TI), E of the road, was begun in 1920 on the same principles as Letchworth (see below) and later expanded as a satellite town in conjunction with Hatfield. 27m: *Welwyn* (9000 inhabitants), W of A1, is the old town. Edward Young (1683–1765), author of the lugubrious 'Night Thoughts', was rector here. The railway crosses the graceful *Digswell Viaduct* (1848–50), 1m E.

A pleasant stretch of country, missed by the motorway, can be reached by taking B656 via (1½m) *Codicote*. At *Ayot St Lawrence*, 2¾m W, *Shaw's Corner* (NT) was the home of George Bernard Shaw from 1906 until his death in 1950. It remains virtually unaltered since his day. 4½m: **Knebworth House** (open) has been the ancestral home of the Lyttons since 1492. Its fantastic 19C Gothic exterior, impressive only from a distance, conceals the core of the Tudor house within. The Banqueting Hall has a fine early 17C screen and gallery, and later 17C wood panelling in the neo-classical manner. The State Drawing Room, refurbished by Edward Bulwer-Lytton, 1st Baron Lytton (1803–73), is a spirited piece of Victorian medievalism. The house also preserves the novelist's study, with mementoes of his friend Dickens. At *St Paul's Walden*, 3m NW, the church has a *choir of 1727. 9m: **Hitchin** (30,000 inhabitants; TI) is a handsome market town with narrow streets and old inns. The 12–15C parish church has good screens, a 15C font and several brasses. George Chapman (1559?–1634), playwright and translator of Homer, is said to have been born in Tilehouse St., where there are many 16–18C houses. Sir Henry Wood died at Hitchin in 1944. From Hitchin to Bedford, see Route 60B. A600 and A6001 lead via (15m) *Henlow*, with its large RAF camp, to rejoin A1 at (19m) *Biggleswade* (see below).

A1, here motorway, continues N past Stevenage and Baldock. 32m: **Stevenage** (74,000 inhabitants; TI) was developed in the 1950s as another satellite town. Edward Gordon Craig (1872–1966) was born here.

4m E is the village of *Benington*, with the *Benington Lordship Gardens* (limited opening). *Cromer*, on B1037 4m NE of Stevenage, has a 17C post windmill being restored to working order (limited opening).

39m: **Baldock** (6700 inhabitants), a pleasant old town where the Great North Road crossed the Icknield Way, has a broad High St. and a church with a fine 15C rood screen. The name is a corruption of 'Baghdad', recalling that Baldock stood on land belonging to the Knights Templar.

Ashwell, 4½m NE, has a 14C church with a striking tower which preserves a curious graffito of old St Paul's Cathedral. The Town House, now a village museum, is one of many good houses in the attractive main street.

FROM BALDOCK TO LUTON, 14m by A505. 2m: **Letchworth** (31,800 inhabitants), the first 'garden city' in England, was founded under the inspiration of Ebenezer Howard in 1903. 5m: *Hitchin*, see above. 8m: *Great Offley* has several monuments by Joseph Nollekens in the church. 14m: *Luton*, see Route 60B.
  From Baldock to *Cambridge* via *Royston*, see Route 36.

A1 enters Bedfordshire before (46m) *Biggleswade* (11,600 inhabitants), a dull town to the E.

At *Ickwell*, about 2m W of A1, the clockmaker Thomas Tompion (1638–1713) was born. The airfield at *Old Warden*, 1m further, has the *Shuttleworth Collection* (open) of historic planes and cars. Nearby is the *Swiss Garden* (open), dating from the 19C. The earlier house on the site of *Southill Park* (not open), 1½m S of Old Warden, was the birthplace of Admiral John Byng (1704–57), shot 'pour encourager les autres' after the loss of Minorca. Henry Holland designed the present house for the Whitbread family in the 1790s.

At (50m) *Sandy*, near the foot of a sandstone ridge, A1 crosses the road from Cambridge to Bedford (Route 60B). The Great Ouse is passed beyond (52½m) *Tempsford*. 57m: *Eaton Socon* lies near another route from Cambridge to Bedford. **St Neots** (21,200 inhabitants), on the far bank of the Great Ouse 1½m NE, has a fine Perpendicular church tower.

At *Colmworth*, on unclassified roads about 4½m W of A1 and Eaton Socon, the refectory of the Augustinian *Bushmead Priory* survives (EH, summer season, Saturdays 10.00–18.00, Sundays 14.00–18.00). From St Neots B1043 follows the river via (3m) *Great*

Paxton, where the church has Saxon work inside, to (8m) *Godmanchester* and (9m) *Huntingdon*, both Route 36.

From St Neots to *Higham Ferrers*, see Route 60B.

62m: *Buckden* has a Perpendicular church overshadowed by the remains of the 15C brick palace of the Bishops of Lincoln, now belonging to the RC Claretian Missionaries. Catherine of Aragon lived here between her divorce and her retirement to Kimbolton. B661 leads W to the reservoir at *Grafham Water*. 65m: A604 goes E to (1½m) *Brampton* and (3½m) *Huntingdon*, both in Route 36. Beyond (67½m) *Alconbury* A1 is joined by A14 from Huntingdon and follows the line of Ermine Street.

At *Little Gidding*, about 5½m NW of Alconbury, Nicholas Ferrar (1592–1637) founded the Anglican community remembered in T.S. Eliot's 'Four Quartets'. Ferrar's tomb stands outside the W door of the little church, largely rebuilt in the 18C.

75m: *Glatton*, W of A1, has a big, handsome church with a Perpendicular tower. 76½m: *Stilton*, also W, gave its name to the cheese, which was not made in the neighbourhood but brought by waggon from Leicestershire to be taken to London by coach. Its sale at the 17C Bell Inn ceased in 1964 after 170 years. 77m: At *Norman Cross*, now a roundabout, French prisoners were held during the Napoleonic Wars. A15 branches NE to (5m) *Peterborough*, Route 36. Beyond (81m) the intersection of A1 with A605 from Peterborough to Oundle stood the important Roman station of Durobrivae, from which Ermine Street crossed the Nene and followed a straight line to Stamford. An earlier Roman road, King Street, headed due N. At (83½m) *Wansford Station* the Nene Valley Railway preserves steam trains and

Stamford in the eighteenth century: a print by Samuel and Nathaniel Buck

operates a section of the old track running 5m E to Nene Park and Orton Mere. An extension further E towards Peterborough is planned. At (85m) *Wansford*, with a handsome old inn, Route 60B joins the route. 87m: *Wittering* church, W of the road, has a Saxon arch.

91m: **STAMFORD** (16,200 inhabitants) can fairly claim to be the most handsome town of its size in England. It stands on the Welland, between the fens of Eastern England and the limestone country of the Midlands, from which it takes its building stone. The street plan and parish churches survive from the days of its medieval importance, but Stamford's chief glory is the almost unequalled range of 17–19C houses and civic buildings.

TI: Arts Centre, 27 St Mary's St. **Bus Station**: Sheepmarket. **Railway Station**: off Station Rd in St Martin's, S of the river. **Annual Events**: Stamford Festival every July. The Stamford Shakespeare Company stages amateur productions at Tolethorpe Hall, off A6121 2m NE, from June to late August. The Three-Day Horse Trials are held in the park of Burghley House every September.

History. Standing at a convenient crossing of the river Welland, Stamford (the 'stone ford') is a natural centre for settlement. It became one of the five Danelagh towns after the Danish invasion of the 9C, and after the Conquest acquired a castle and town walls enclosing the area N of the river. The Domesday Book (1086) calls it a market, but in the Middle Ages Stamford was known for its religious foundations and parish churches. The arrival of seceding students from Oxford in 1333 briefly made it a serious competitor to the older university. After the Reformation the town developed as an important coaching stop and trading centre on the Great North Road, as its 17–19C houses still testify. It was saved from further development in the 19C by the decision to route the main railway line through Peterborough. In 1967 it became the first town in England and Wales designated a Conservation Area under the Civic Amenities Act.

Natives and residents. Daniel Lambert (1770–1809), who weighed 52 stone 11 lb (739 lb; 335 kg) at his death, is buried in the cemetery of St Martin's. John Clare (1793–1864), who worked at Burghley House in 1809, was first helped to public notice by a local bookseller. The conductor Sir Malcolm Sargent (1895–1967), a native of Stamford, is buried in the cemetery off Little Casterton Rd.

St Martin's High St., S of the river, is a fine, largely 18C streetscape giving equally handsome views towards the centre of town. The late Perpendicular church of *St Martin* contains the tombs of Lord Burghley (1520–98) and other members of the Cecil family, and late 15C *glass from Tattershall and other Lincolnshire churches. The *George*, at the foot of the hill, is a coaching inn with a sign still spanning the road.

Beyond the Welland, the hill climbs towards the Early English tower and Decorated *spire of *St Mary*. On the left is a Norman archway into St Mary's Passage and on the right the *Town Hall* (1777). The largely Perpendicular interior of St Mary's contains the elaborate monument of Sir David Phillips (d. 1506) and his wife. Beyond the church St Mary's St. goes left towards Red Lion Square (see below), but it is worth turning right instead. On the left is the former Stamford Hotel, a grand Regency building, and on the right the *Old Theatre* of 1768 where Edmund Kean and Sheridan played, now an Arts Centre. St George's Square, beyond, is a delightful backwater with the *Assembly Rooms* of 1725 (also used by the Arts Centre) and the church of *St George*. Its chancel and clerestory were rebuilt in 1449 by Sir William Bruges, first Garter King of Arms; some of the glass refers to founder members of the Garter.

Maiden Lane, with 16C buildings, leads N to the High St., where St Michael, largely 19C, has been made into shops. The *Public Library* opposite is converted from the old meat market (1804). St Paul's St., continuing High St. to the right, has *Stamford School*, founded in 1532, with a 12–13C chapel. Lord Burghley, Lord Northcliffe and Sir Malcolm Sargent were pupils. The gateway opposite is the only relic of Brazenose Hall, said to have been built for the Oxford students in 1333 and otherwise demolished in 1688. At the road fork by the hospital further E is the gateway of *Whitefriars*, founded in 1285, where Richard II held council in 1392. Opposite, a plaque commemorates the site of *Greyfriars* monastery, founded in 1220. Joan, Fair Maid of Kent, the Black Prince's wife, was buried here in 1385.

In Priory Rd, to the SE, the Benedictine *St Leonard's Priory* has remains of c 1090 and a W front of 1150.

St Paul's St. and a right turn into Star Lane return to Broad St., with many 18C houses, where the market is held on Fridays. The *Museum* on the left has local archaeology and crafts. On the right is the most impressive of Stamford's many almshouses, *Browne's Hospital*, founded c 1480.

Red Lion St. continues Broad St. down into Red Lion Square. *St John*, to the left, is Perpendicular with good woodwork. *All Saints*, immediately right, is mainly Early English with Perpendicular additions, including the tower and spire, and curious external arcading. It has fine brasses.

The little Barn Hill, leading beyond All Saints, has Queen Anne and Georgian houses. Nearby Scotgate has 17C almshouses.

The old brewery in All Saints St. is now a *Brewery Museum*. The street and its continuation, St Peter's St., lead W above the bus station and past several almshouses to the site of St Peter's Gate, dismantled in 1770 when more almshouses were built here. Petergate, running N, has the only one of Stamford's defensive towers to survive.

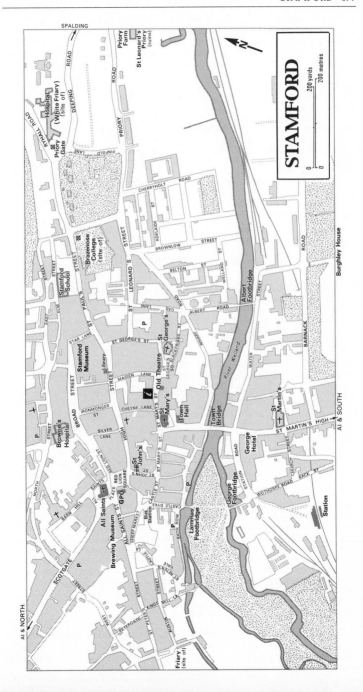

STAMFORD

Rutland Terrace has a good view of the Welland valley. Charming old lanes, such as King's Mill Lane and St Peter's Vale, lead down to the waterfront.

Burghley House (open), 1¼m SE off B1443 towards Barnack, was built for the great Lord Burghley in 1560–87. The palatial *exterior, and particularly the exuberant and fantastic skyline with its profusion of Renaissance motifs, make a wonderfully dramatic effect in the wide and graceful parkland. The interior, extensively remodelled and redecorated in the 1680s, is inevitably disappointing by comparison. The Chapel has an altarpiece by Veronese and, like other rooms, carving attributed to Grinling Gibbons. The State Rooms are dominated by massive, uninspired paintings on ceilings and walls by Antonio Laguerre. The large collection of art includes Oriental procelain, some interesting portraits and paintings by Bernard van Orley, Pieter Breughel and Jacob van Ruisdael. The grounds include Capability Brown's Deer Park and Orangery.

B1443 continues about 2m beyond Burghley to *Barnack*, famous for its building stone. The church has a Saxon *tower (c 1000) and a beautiful Early English porch and font. *Wothorpe*, by A43 1m SW of Stamford, has the remains of the 17C mansion once occupied by George Villiers, 2nd Duke of Buckingham (not open). *Little Casterton*, on the site of a Roman station 2m N of Stamford, has an Early English church.

From Stamford to *Oundle* and *Bedford*, see Route 60B; to *Rutland Water* and *Nottingham*, see Route 70; to *Doncaster*, see Route 72.

B. Via Bedford and Oundle

Directions. Total distance 93m. A devious route by comparison to Route 60A but particularly interesting beyond Bedford, with different ways of crossing Northamptonshire from Higham Ferrers to Stamford. A5, A5183 to (19m) St Albans, see Route 52B. A1081 to (30m) Luton. A6 to (49m) **Bedford** and (63m) Higham Ferrers. A605 to (77m) **Oundle**. A605, B671 to (86m) Wansford. A1 to (92m) **Stamford**, see Route 60A.

From London to (19m) *St Albans*, see Route 52B. A1081 leads N via (24m) *Harpenden* (27,900 inhabitants), with green spaces on its High St.

Bedfordshire is entered on the way to (30m) **Luton** (165,000 inhabitants; TI), traditionally a centre of straw-hat making but now known for cars and engineering. There is little of interest except the fine church of *St Mary*, NE of the station. It has a 14C tower and, inside, good Decorated work and the Wenlock Chapel (1461), with a late Perpendicular screen, remarkable double arch, monuments and brasses. Phillipa of Hainault gave the tabernacled stone font canopy (c 1330–40). The *Museum and Art Gallery* in Wardown Park has exhibits of local history, including the straw-plait and lace industries.

Luton Airport (TI), SE of the town, has passenger services to Alicante, Belfast, Dublin, the Isle of Man, Jersey, Malaga, Menorca, Paris and Tenerife.

Luton Hoo (open) stands 2m S of Luton in a fine park by Capability Brown. The house, originally built by Robert Adam in 1767–74 but altered, gutted by fire and reconstructed, is less interesting than its contents. The *Wernher collection includes medieval ivories, Renaissance bronzes and jewellery, tapestries from Beauvais and Gobelins, English porcelain and Fabergé jewellery. The many fine paintings include work by Bermejo, Lippi, Altdorfer and the 17C Dutch school (Hobbema, van Ostade, de Hooch, Metsu, Dou, Wouwermans), as well as portraits by John Hoppner and Sargent.

From Luton to *Baldock*, see Route 60A.

A6 leads N from Luton, past (40m) *Silsoe*. *Wrest Park* (EH, summer season, weekends and Bank Holidays only), ¾m E, a house of 1834–39 in the French style, has 18–19C landscaped grounds and garden buildings. Attached to the church at *Flitton*, 1½m W of Silsoe, is the mausoleum of the de Grey family with 16–19C tombs (EH, weekends only; contact keykeeper). 41m: *Clophill* lies 3m E of **Ampthill** (5800 inhabitants; TI), a handsome little town in hilly countryside. The mainly Perpendicular church has a monument to Richard Nicholls (1624–72), first English governor of New York, with the cannon ball said to have killed him at the Battle of Solebay (Route 38).

Ampthill Park, ½m W on the Woburn road, has a memorial cross with an inscription by Horace Walpole marking the site of Ampthill Castle, where Catherine of Aragon lived during the divorce proceedings in 1531–33. On a ridge N of the town, by B530, stands the elegant shell of the early 17C *Houghton House*, built for the Countess of Pembroke, Sir Philip Sidney's sister, and variously attributed to John Thorpe and Inigo Jones (EH). It is sometimes identified with the House Beautiful in Bunyan's 'Pilgrim's Progress'. About 1½m further N, on its way into Bedford, B530 passes the turning for *Houghton Conquest*, where the church has a 14C wall painting, good old glass and brasses. The church at *Marston Moretaine*, 4m NW of Ampthill, has a detached belfry and a window by Morris and Co.

A6 continues N, bypassing (46m) **Elstow**, Bunyan's birthplace (see below). The half-timbered *Moot Hall* on the handsome village green is a museum illustrating his life and times. In the church Bunyan was baptised, rang the bells and heard the sermons which stirred his conscience. The building incorporates Norman work from the church of a Benedictine nunnery founded in 1078. Over the N door is a Norman group of Christ between St Peter and St John. Inside are fine brasses of Lady Argentein (d. 1427) and Abbess Elizabeth Hervey (d. 1524).

49m: **BEDFORD** (71,600 inhabitants), the county town, has connections with Bunyan and pleasant riverside scenery.

TI: 10 St Paul's Square. **Railway Station**: Midland Rd, W of the town, for main line and Bletchley services. **Buses**: from All Hallows.

Natives and residents. John Bunyan (1628–88), born near Elstow, served in the Parliamentarian army during the Civil War and returned to follow his father's trade of tinker or brazier. In 1653 he joined a Nonconformist group in Bedford, becoming pastor in 1672 and holding the position until his death. Arrested for unlicensed preaching in 1660, he spent most of the next 12 years in the County Gaol, which stood at the corner of High St. and Silver St. Here he wrote 'Grace Abounding to the Chief of Sinners' (1666) and probably began the first part of 'Pilgrim's Progress', completed during a later spell of imprisonment in 1676–77, when he may have been held in the County Gaol again or in the Town Gaol on the old bridge. He died in London and is buried in Bunhill Fields. Bedford's Dissenting tradition continued with John Howard (1726–90), whose interest in prison reform was aroused while he was High Sheriff of Bedford, and William Hale White ('Mark Rutherford'; 1831–1913), son of a local bookseller.

The Town Bridge (1813) stands at the S end of the High St. Upstream is the *County Hall*. *The Embankment follows the tree-lined N bank of the river downstream to (½m) Russell Park. The former church of *St Mary*, S of the bridge, is now an archaeological centre. Near the bridge are the *Swan Hotel* (1794; Henry Holland) and the *Bedford Museum*, with local history, archaeology, geology and natural history. The mound in the gardens is all that survives of the Norman castle which commanded the ford over the Ouse until its destruction in 1224. The *Cecil Higgins Art Gallery*, in a finely re-created Victorian mansion, has an excellent collection including English watercolours (Turner) and drawings, porcelain and *glass.

In Mill St. behind the museum, *Howard House* belonged to the prison reformer. Nearby is the *Bunyan Meeting*, built in 1850 on the site of the barn where Bunyan used to preach. The panels on the bronze doors (1876) illustrate the 'Pilgrim's Progress'. The *Bunyan Museum* has an interesting collection of relics. A plaque in St Cuthbert's St. to the N marks the site of Bunyan's home from 1655.

High St. runs N from the Ouse Bridge through the centre of town. St Paul's Square, to the left, has a statue of John Howard and the church of *St Paul*, with the 14C stone pulpit from which Wesley preached his assize sermon in 1758 and the brass of a local benefactor, Sir William Harpur (d. 1573).

Behind are the 18–19C *Town Hall* and the *Civic Theatre* (with amateur productions), and in Harpur St. to the NW the façade (1830; Edward Blore) of the Bedford Modern School now fronts a shopping centre.

A plaque at the corner of High St. and Silver St. marks the site of the County Gaol where Bunyan served certainly his first and perhaps also his second term of imprisonment. Bunyan's statue stands at the N end of High St. The church of *St Peter* has a Norman S porch and a tower with Saxon work.

Cardington, off A603 2½m SE, was the home of John Howard after 1758. The church has a black Wedgwood font and the churchyard a memorial to victims of the R101 airship disaster in 1930; the airship hangars dominate the RAF station.

FROM BEDFORD TO HITCHIN, 17m by A600. 10m: *Shefford*. *Chicksands Priory* (limited opening), off A507 1¼m W, has the remains of a Gilbertine priory incorporated in an 18–19C house. The site is now marked by a gigantic USAF antenna, likened by Pevsner to a steel Stonehenge. For *Southill Park* and other places N of Shefford, see Route 60A. 17m: *Hitchin*, see Route 60A.

FROM BEDFORD TO CAMBRIDGE. The fast route takes A428, a brief stretch of A1 and then A45. A slightly more interesting route (29m) begins on A603. 4m: *Willington* has a 16C dovecote and stables (NT, open by appointment) and, in the church, the fine Gostwick tomb (1615). It crosses A1 (Route 60A) on the way into (8m) *Sandy*, where B1042 continues E. 12m: *Potton*. 2m E is *Cockayne Hatley*, with 17C Flemish wood carving in the church. At 19½m the route crosses A14 to join A603, passing *Wimpole Hall* (Route 36) on the way to (29m) *Cambridge* (Route 37).

From Bedford to *Northampton* via *Olney*, see Route 59.

A6 continues N. 50½m: *Clapham* has a Saxon church tower. *Felmersham*, left of the road at 54m, has a fine Early English church. *Harrold*, 4m further W, has an old Buttermarket and a lock-up on the village green. There is a large country park on the banks of the Ouse. 55m: *Bletsoe*, to the right, was the birthplace of Lady Margaret Beaufort (1443–1509), Henry VII's mother. The route enters Northamptonshire before (62m) *Rushden* (22,700 inhabitants), where the largely Decorated church has a 'strainer arch' (cf. Finedon below), a 15C screen and 17C alabaster Pemberton tombs. H.E. Bates was born here in 1905. *Hinwick House*, 3½m SW, is a Queen Anne building of local stone, with Mortlake tapestries and good portraits. At *Hinwick Hall* the first school for disabled boys opened in 1943.

63m: **Higham Ferrers** (5200 inhabitants) is a handsome little town. The Early English and Decorated *•Church* has a beautiful spire, double nave, stalls with misericords and bench ends, and, among several brasses, one of Laurence St Maur (d. 1337). The schoolhouse and bede house in the churchyard belonged to the college of secular canons founded in 1422 by Archbishop Chichele (1362–1443), a native of the town. Nearby College St. has fragments of the quadrangle, including its chapel (EH, summer season, daily; contact keykeeper in winter).

Standing at the junction of A6 with A45 and near the junction with A605, Higham Ferrers is starting-point for several interesting detours and alternative ways to Stamford.

FROM HIGHAM FERRERS TO STAMFORD VIA KETTERING, ROCKINGHAM AND UPPINGHAM, 34m. A6 starts the journey. 1½m: *Irthlingborough* (4900 inhabitants), beyond the Nene, has a church with a separate 14C bell-tower crowned by an octagon. At (4m) *Finedon* the excellent Decorated church has a 'strainer arch' across the nave (cf. Rushden above). 6m: *Burton Latimer* (5400 inhabitants) has early 14C paintings of St Catherine's martyrdom in its church. *Pytchley*, 3m W, gave its name to a famous pack of foxhounds, later moved to Brixworth (Route 59). 8m: *Barton Seagrave* has an early Norman and Early English church. 9m: **Kettering** (45,400 inhabitants; TI) is a nondescript industrial town. The late Perpendicular church has a tall spire and an early Decorated N doorway and E end. The Art Gallery in Sheep St. has travelling exhibitions and 19–20C English art, developed from the collection donated by Sir Alfred East (1849–1913), a native of Kettering. The Westfield Museum in West St. has Roman finds and displays about the local shoe-making industry. *Rushton Hall*, off A6003 4½m NW, was home of the prominent Catholic landowner Sir Thomas Tresham (1534–1605). Now a school of the Royal National Institute for the Blind, it is open by prior appointment. Nearby stands the wonderful *Triangular Lodge (EH, summer season) built in 1593–97 by Sir Thomas in symbolic expression of his faith. *Rothwell* (6400 inhabitants), on A6 4m NW of Kettering, has a market house with heraldic decorations begun by Sir Thomas in 1578 and a Transitional church with misericords.

A6003 leaves Kettering. 13m: The church at *Great Oakley*, ¾m E, has stalls with misericords from the vanished Pipewell Abbey. The route passes W of (15m) **Corby** (47,600 inhabitants; TI), which has survived the death of the steel industry that first created it in the 1930s. 17m: *Rockingham* is a stone-built village. *Rockingham Castle (open) stands on the escarpment above the Welland valley. William the Conqueror ordered the building of the castle and later kings refurbished it. It passed from royal hands in 1544, and the process of converting Rockingham into a private house has continued ever since, interrupted only by the Civil War, when Sir Lewis Watson yielded the castle to the Parliamentarians. The result is a pleasantly eclectic blend of medieval fortress and country house. Edward I's gatehouse still stands, and remains of the Norman keep survive in the gardens; the fortified walls have become a terrace with fine views. The flag tower was added by Salvin in 1838. The Great Hall has been subdivided and the present hall is mainly Tudor. The Long Gallery has portraits by Reynolds, Zoffany and Angelica Kaufmann, with mementoes of Dickens, who used Rockingham as the model for Chesney Wold in 'Bleak House'. The terrace and formal gardens, whose yew walk is noted in the novel, lead to a 19C wild garden in the ravine.

A6003 continues N into the former county of Rutland, now part of Leicestershire. 20m: To the W is *Stoke Dry*, overlooking *Eyebrook Reservoir*, with Digby monuments in its church. Sir Everard Digby (1578–1606), executed for his part in the Gunpowder Plot, was born here. *Lyddington*, 1m E of A6003, has a 15–17C bede house in the surviving part of a manor house belonging to the Bishops of Lincoln (EH, summer season). The 14C church has communion rails of 1635 which completely surround the altar, an apparently unique design adopted as a compromise during liturgical controversy. 22m: **Uppingham** (2800 inhabitants) is a pleasant little place. The church has a pulpit given by its most famous rector, Jeremy Taylor (1613–67). Uppingham School, founded in 1587, first became a leading public school under Dr Edward Thring in 1853–87. Pupils include the novelist Norman Douglas. *Preston*, 2m N, has a partly Norman church. For Oakham and Rutland Water, further N, see Route 70.

N of Uppingham A47 is followed E. At (26m) *Morcott*, where the church is mainly late Norman, A6121 leads ½m NE, to *North Luffenham*, with a handsome 13–14C church. 30½m: *Ketton*, famous for its stone, has cement works by the main road but a fine 13–14C church and pleasant houses in the older part of the village by the Chater. 34m: *Stamford*, see Route 60A.

FROM HIGHAM FERRERS TO STAMFORD VIA GEDDINGTON AND DUDDINGTON, 31m. The detour above goes to (9m) *Kettering*. A43 leads through the pleasant countryside of *Rockingham Forest*, once a royal deer forest but no longer heavily wooded. 10½m:

Weekley has 16–17C Montagu tombs in the church, and a charming almshouse (1611) and school (1624). *Warkton*, 1½m SE, has later *monuments of the Montagus, including work by Roubiliac and Robert Adam. 12m: *Geddington*, once a royal manor, has an *Eleanor Cross (EH), one of three which survive from the series marking the overnight stops in the funeral procession of Queen Eleanor of Castile in 1290. See Lincoln (Route 48) for further details. The church has a late Decorated spire, Saxon remains and fine screens. There is a heavily repaired medieval bridge. *Boughton House* (limited opening), in fine grounds 1½m SE, was grandly remodelled in the French style in 1683–1709. The State Rooms have painted ceilings by Chéron and Mortlake tapestries; the fine collection of art includes many sketches by Van Dyck. 20m: *Deene Park* (limited opening), to the left, is a mainly Tudor mansion, still with its Great Hall. The church contains the memorial of the Earl of Cardigan (d. 1868), leader of the charge of the Light Brigade at Balaclava. *Kirby Hall* (EH, all year), 2m W, is the shell of a mansion begun in 1570 but owing much of its appearance to alterations in 1638–40. These have been attributed to Inigo Jones, though Nicholas Stone is a better candidate. The route passes (26m) *Duddington* and (27m) *Collyweston*, both among the best stone-built villages in England. Collyweston is known for its roofing slabs. 29m: *Easton-on-the-Hill*, another handsome village, has an early 16C Priest's House (NT, open by appointment). The route crosses A1 to enter (31m) *Stamford*. See Route 60A.

FROM HIGHAM FERRERS TO ST NEOTS, 17m by A45. 9m: *Kimbolton* has a handsome main street. *Kimbolton Castle* (limited opening), now a school, incorporates part of the castle where Catherine of Aragon lived in 1533–36 after her divorce but owes its dignified appearance to remodelling by Vanbrugh in 1707–14. The church at *Swineshead*, 4m SW, has a Decorated choir, with misericords from a vanished priory. At 16m A45 crosses A1 on the way into (17m) *St Neots*, Route 60A.

From Higham Ferrers to *Northampton* via *Wellingborough*, see Route 59.

The main route branches right from A6 on A605 just N of Higham Ferrers. 65m: *Stanwick* church has an octagonal tower and spire. 65½m: *Raunds* (7400 inhabitants), a shoe-making town, has a 13C church with another famous *spire. 70m: *Thrapston* is a quiet place.

The Perpendicular church at *Islip*, on the Nene ¾m W, contains a tablet to Mary Washington (d. 1624). *Twywell* church, 2½m further, has early Norman features. The 15C church at *Lowick*, 1½m N of Islip, has an octagonal lantern on the *tower, fine contemporary monuments and Decorated glass.

A604, heading E from Thrapston to Huntingdon, passes (6m) *Molesworth*, with its USAF base, and (8m) *Leighton Bromswold*, 1m N of the road. The *church was rebuilt by George Herbert, incumbent in 1626–30. Nearby is the gatehouse of a vanished Jacobean mansion. 17m: *Huntingdon*, see Route 36.

73m: *Thorpe Waterville. Aldwincle*, across the Nene 1½m W, was birthplace of the historian Thomas Fuller (1608–61) and John Dryden (1631–1700). Dryden spent part of his boyhood at *Titchmarsh*, 1½m SE of Thorpe Waterville, and is remembered by a tablet in the church, with a fine Perpendicular tower. *Lilford Park* (open), 1½m N of Thorpe Waterville, has aviaries and other attractions. The Jacobean Lilford Hall is rarely open. 75m: *Barnwell*, to the right, has the ruins of a 13C castle (not open).

77m: **Oundle** (3500 inhabitants; TI) is a stone-built town with one of the tall church steeples characteristic of the region, a public school and many good 17–18C houses. The front of the Talbot Inn (1626) was built with materials from Fotheringhay Castle (see below); the oak staircase comes from the same source.

Misericords from the demolished choir of Fotheringhay can be seen in the churches at *Lower Benefield* (3m W), *Hemington* (3m SE) and *Tansor* (2m NE). The Nene between Tansor and *Cotterstock*, nearer Oundle, is particularly charming, while *Polebrook*, on the way to Hemington, has one of the best churches in the district.

Southwick Hall (limited opening), 2½m NW of Oundle, has 14C, Tudor and 18C work. A footpath from the Brigstock road, 4m SW of Oundle, leads to *Lyveden Old Bield* (not open) and *Lyveden New Bield* (NT). The old building was remodelled by Sir Thomas Tresham of Rushton (see above). His new building is an unfinished shell begun in the 1590s, shaped like a Greek cross and adorned with esoteric references to his ardent Catholicism.

80m: *Warmington* has an Early English church with its original roof, groined in wood. *Fotheringhay* lies on the other side of the Nene, 2m NW. The mound of the great keep (not open) is almost the only surviving trace of the castle where Richard III was born in 1452 and Mary, Queen of Scots, tried and executed in 1587. The early 15C collegiate church, with a lantern tower, lacks the original choir. It contains two monuments erected by Queen Elizabeth I in memory of Yorkist princes buried here. At (82m) *Elton* B671 branches left from A605. *Elton Hall* (limited opening) is a 15–19C mansion with early Bibles and work by English painters. At *Nassington*, 3m NW, the manor house (limited opening) dates from the early 13C. At (86m) *Wansford* B671 joins A1, following Route 60A to (92m) **Stamford**.

NORTH MIDLANDS

The previous section marked the upper limit of the South Midlands by a line drawn roughly from the Severn and the Wye in the SW to the Wash in the NE, passing through the centre of England. The North Midlands, explored here by routes starting from the various cities along this line, continues up to the borders of Merseyside, Greater Manchester and South Yorkshire. On the W lies the border with Wales, while in the E the course of the A1 is again used to distinguish the Midlands from Eastern England. The area thus defined includes parts of Hereford and Worcester, West Midlands, Warwickshire, Leicestershire and Lincolnshire and all of Shropshire, Cheshire, Staffordshire, Derbyshire and Nottinghamshire.

Southerners still tend to regard this region, as they do virtually anything N of Watford, as mainly industrial and hence mainly dull. By way of confirmation they can point to cities like Birmingham, Derby or Nottingham, whose brash, ugly vitality helped make England 'the workshop of the world' in the 19C, and to areas like the Potteries or the Black Country, whose very names have an uninviting ring. This picture, of course, is no more accurate than one that makes everything S of Watford green and sleekly prosperous. Industrialism has certainly shaped the landscape throughout much of the Midlands, yet countryside has survived too, and often survived close to the cities and the factories. The Midlands owe a lot of their character to this conjunction of rural with urban, pastoral with industrial—the effect so vividly rendered in D.H. Lawrence's novels. And in recent years we have come to realise that industrial culture itself, rather than being an ugly blot to be wished away, can constitute an instructive, even absorbing part of our history. The canal and the railway viaduct, the factory and the warehouse have begun to take their place beside the castle, the church and the country house as significant monuments.

A look at the basic contours of the landscape helps a more precise understanding of this mixture of countryside and industry which now makes up the North Midlands. We can begin by imagining the region in terms of a roughly marked letter U, the broad strokes of the letter being chiefly plain or vale and their inner and outer edges chiefly hill. At the bottom of the U is the limestone belt stretching across southern England from Dorset through Somerset, the Cotswolds and Northamptonshire. It continues up the E fringe of our region to create, in the Leicestershire and Lincolnshire countryside explored in routes from Stamford, the same softly undulating hills and handsome stone-built villages that make Northamptonshire so attractive. Like Northamptonshire, they are also among the least known beauty spots of England. Much better known, as well as more dramatic, is the hilly countryside that marks the W fringe of the region in the Shropshire part of the Welsh Marches. Here limestone is mixed with the ancient Pre-Cambrian rocks of Wales to create famous and sometimes romantically named hills, like Wenlock Edge and the Long Mynd, as well as geological quirks like the extinct volcanic bump of the Wrekin.

If the limestone country around Stamford and the Shropshire hills define the outer edges of the U, its inner edges and central core are the Peak District of Derbyshire and neighbouring counties. The country here is made up of two distinct landscapes, both long popular for the wildness and beauty of their scenery and both now incorporated in the National Park. In the S is the limestone White Peak, with its undulating hills, deep and wooded dales (like Dovedale) and underground caverns. Further N, gritstone (or millstone grit) makes the bleaker country of the Dark Peak.

Marking out the strokes of the U itself between these hills is a much flatter landscape of sandstones and marls, which stretches down through the Cheshire plain and northern Shropshire, crosses Staffordshire, West Midlands, and the northern parts of Warwickshire and Leicestershire, and moves up through Nottinghamshire. Its shape is echoed by the course of the Trent—'the calm and characteristic stream of middle England', as Arnold Bennett called it—as it flows along its broad valley through the Potteries and the brewing town of Burton, swings past Nottingham and turns N through Newark on its way to join the Humber estuary. The red earth ranges from fertile farmland to the thin, sandy soils which support Sherwood Forest in the E and Staffordshire's Cannock Chase in the W.

Most striking of the building materials which characterise this region, and certainly the most surprising to those who would see it as grimly industrial, is the timber from the ancient forests. The forests themselves have largely vanished but have left their permanent trace in the half-timbered buildings throughout the W half of the region, making quite as rich a display as anything the Weald or East Anglia can boast. In a village like Weobley, near Hereford, we can see cottages of ancient cruck construction—with big curved timbers rising from or near ground level to support the walls as well as the roof. Later houses, built on the 'box-frame' principle, show the wealth of decorative ornament and the bold contrast between blackened wood and white infill which have earned them nicknames like 'black-and-white' or 'magpie'. They include country houses like Bramall Hall, near Stockport, and Little Moreton Hall in Cheshire, now made famous by a thousand National Trust tea-towels; town houses like the superb Churche's Mansion in Nantwich; and the rich streetscapes of Ludlow, Shrewsbury and Chester. The Rows at Chester, too, remind the visitor that it was the 'black-and-white' houses of this region, rather than the less dramatic styles of the Weald or East Anglia, which inspired the 19C half-timbered revival. At Wightwick Manor, near Wolverhampton, we find a 19C half-timbered country house whose Pre-Raphaelite interior perfectly matches the promise of its exterior. Sandstone, inevitably, provides the second traditional building material of the region. Bunter Sandstone can be seen at Nottingham, where the tunnels and caves cut into the rock on which the castle stands demonstrate its softness. The lovely rose-coloured Keuper Sandstone gives Lichfield and Chester cathedrals, as well as innumerable parish churches, their distinctive look.

More characteristic than either timber or sandstone is the red brick, fired from the local marl clays, which has left its mark, for good and ill, on most towns of the Midland sandstone belt. Few English building materials are so various in their effect. It can look sedate and mellow in Georgian houses, vivid and exuberant in 19C civic buildings, and pinched and mean in the soot-covered terraced houses which make up so much of the towns and cities of the Red Midlands. Sadly, it is the seemingly endless 19C streets which can dominate the visitor's first and last impressions.

These streets are the most pervasive reminder of the industrial forces which have shaped the history of the Midlands. Yet this 19C result came towards the end of a long process. Early but now almost forgotten industries had included, for example, the Derbyshire lead-mining of which Wirksworth was a centre in the Middle Ages and the Cheshire salt-mining that gave the suffix '-wich' to its chief towns (Middlewich, Northwich, Nantwich). Of early origin, too, is the pottery industry which gave Stoke-on-Trent its familiar name as the Potteries; it still flourishes, celebrating its history and products in several excellent museums. Its crucial period of growth was the 18C, when Josiah Wedgwood came as close as anyone to realising the age's progressive ideal of uniting art and manufacture. Elsewhere, the 18C exploited fast-running water to power the textile mills. The silk mill John and Thomas Lombe built on the river Derwent at Derby in 1717–21 (now the site of the city's industrial museum) is important as England's first true factory, where dependence on a common energy source brought hitherto dispersed workers into an organised community. Yet its city location is less than typical, for the search for water frequently took industry to places that we might now innocently suppose to be unspoiled and rural. Hence we find Richard Arkwright's cotton mill (1771) also on the Derwent but at Cromford near the fringe of the Peaks, and the Quarry Bank Mill (1784) on the aptly named river Bobbin at Styal, near Wilmslow—both of them now among the well-displayed industrial sites of the region. In addition to being a source of power, water also became the chief means of commercial transport. At the end of the 18C and the beginning of the 19C men like James Brindley and Thomas Telford created the canal system which links the Trent with the Thames, the Severn and the Mersey.

The next phase depended on coal, iron and steam. Coal and iron are found at many places throughout the region but had previously been exploited only on a small scale. The two were first brought in vital conjunction at Coalbrookdale, in Shropshire's Severn gorge, when the second Abraham Darby began smelting iron ore with coke rather than with the traditional charcoal in 1709. The Darbys left a permanent monument to their achievement in the famous iron bridge (1779), which now overlooks a complex of museums and displays giving by far the most imaginative introduction to our industrial heritage. In 1775, at the Soho Manufactory in Handsworth, Birmingham, Matthew Boulton and James Watt began those experiments with steam engines that would free industry from its dependence on fast-running water, encouraging it to concentrate in massive, energetic cities like Birmingham or sprawl in dismal conurbations like the Black Country.

These places have survived later changes, though sometimes only with difficulty—becoming cleaner with the advent of electricity, turning away from the production of coal, iron and steel, and depending increasingly on engineering and metal-finishing connected with the motor industry. Modern forms of power, electricity and the internal combustion engine, have in turn created landmarks in the tangled motorway system that includes 'Spaghetti Junction' near Birmingham and in the power stations that line the Trent valley.

61

Birmingham

BIRMINGHAM, with just over 1 million inhabitants, is the second largest city in Britain as well as England and the capital of the industrial West Midlands. A bustling place, it has much to interest the visitor: collections in the Museum and Art Gallery and in the Barber Institute of Fine Arts at the university, a first-rate Museum of Science and Industry and stained glass by Burne-Jones in the 18C St Philip's Cathedral. Good 19C buildings and well-restored canal walks survive 20C redevelopment of the centre, which has a boldness in tune with Birmingham's big-city energy.

TI: 2 City Arcade; Chamberlain Square; Information Desk, Birmingham International Airport; National Exhibition Centre, 9m SE on A45. **Bus Station**: Bull Ring Centre. **Coach Station**: Digbeth. **Railway Stations**: New Street, for London, connecting with Birmingham International, at the National Exhibition Centre and serving the airport and most major cities. Moor Street, local services to Stratford and Leamington. Snowhill Station, connecting with Moor Street. **Airport**: Birmingham International Airport at Elmdon, 7m SE on A45. Passenger services to Aberdeen, Amsterdam, Barcelona, Basle/Mulhouse, Belfast, Berlin, Billund, Brussels, Copenhagen, Cork, Dublin, Dusseldorf, Edinburgh, Eindhoven, Faro, Frankfurt, Glasgow, Guernsey, Hamburg, Hanover, Isle of Man, Jersey, Larnaca, Lyon, Maastricht, Malaga, Milan, Munich, Newcastle, New York, Nice, Norwich, Paphos, Paris, Stuttgart, Tivat and Zurich. **Theatres**: Hippodrome, Hurst St.; Alexandra, John Bright St.; Repertory, Broad St.; Midland Arts Centre, Cannon Hill Park; The Triangle, Aston University. **Music**: City of Birmingham Symphony Orchestra at Symphony Hall. The Royal Ballet, formerly based in London, has become the Birmingham Royal Ballet. **Annual Events**: International Motor Show (October) and many other events at the National Exhibition Centre.

History. Although a market was held and tolls levied before the Conquest, Birmingham is chiefly a modern and industrial city. It was known for its metal workers by 1538, when John Leland found 'a great parte of the towne ... mayntayned by smithes'. Local coal and iron, combined with the presence of 'small masters' skilled in a wide variety of trades, caused its phenomenal growth at the end of the 18C. The population was 35,000 in 1760, 86,000 in 1801, and 233,000 in 1851. Matthew Boulton (1728–1809) formed his partnership with James Watt (1736–1819) to make steam engines at the Soho Manufactory, Handsworth, in 1775. The printer John Baskerville (1706–75), the chemist Joseph Priestley (1733–1804) and William Murdock (1754–1839), the inventor of gas lighting, typified the city's contribution to advances in science and learning. De Tocqueville, a visitor in 1835, found Birmingham 'an immense workshop, a huge forge, a vast shop'. Practically everything metal from pen-nibs to railway carriages and armaments was turned out, with jewellery also an important trade. By this time, too, it was a centre of religious Nonconformity and political radicalism, playing a leading part in Reform agitation in 1832 and Chartism in 1839. Its continued national importance is shown by the names of the radical philanthropist Joseph Sturge (1793–1859); John Bright (1811–89), MP for the city from 1857; and Joseph Chamberlain (1836–1914), Mayor from 1873 and MP for the city from 1876. Chamberlain's 'civic gospel' made Birmingham a byword for enlightened municipal government, a tradition maintained by his son Neville Chamberlain (1869–1940), Mayor in 1915–17 and Prime Minister in 1937–40.

The enlargement of its boundaries in 1911 made the city the second largest in England. In the 20C it has kept its variety of trades, but with cars and accessories industry playing an increasingly important role. The post-war years brought a major campaign of redevelopment which has robbed Birmingham of older architecture and

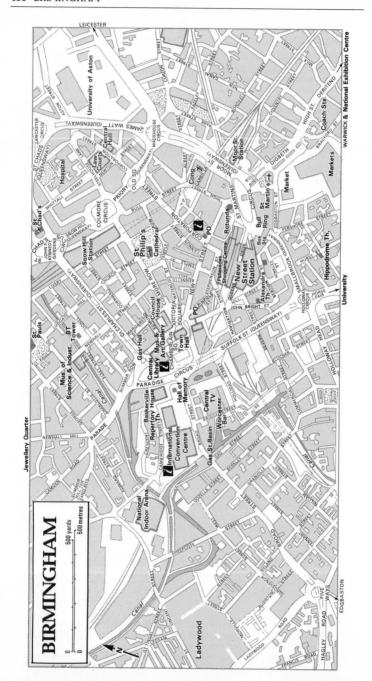

given it distinctively modern landmarks: New Street Station, the Bull Ring Centre, the inner ring road, the International Convention Centre and, amid the motorway system of which the city is now the hub, 'Spaghetti Junction' on M6.

Natives, residents and visitors in addition to those mentioned above. The artists David Cox (1783–1859) and Sir Edward Burne-Jones (1833–98) and the novelist J.M. Shorthouse (1834–1903) were natives. John Henry Newman (1801–90) established the Oratory of St Philip Neri in 1847 and lived there for most of the remainder of his life. Gerard Manley Hopkins (1844–89) was received into the Roman Catholic Church at the Oratory in 1866. Hilaire Belloc (1870–1953) attended the school attached to it. The novelist Henry Green (1905–73) managed his family's engineering works in Birmingham.

The inner ring road, designed by Sir Herbert Manzoni in the 1940s and responsible for devastating much of older Birmingham, tightly encloses the centre in an oval of about ½m by ¾m, with an additional cross link by Colmore Circus. It makes life difficult for pedestrians, who have to cross it by steps and tunnels, and is now being lowered section by section. Paradise Circus and Smallbrook Queensway have been completed so far.

The centre of the city is Victoria Square, just inside the W side of the ring road. The statue of the Queen (1901; Thomas Brock) overlooks a group of 19C civic buildings. The **Town Hall** (1831–35), a timidly correct imitation of a Roman temple, is by Joseph Hansom of hansom-cab fame and E. Welch. On the S side of the square stands the old *Post Office* (1899; Sir H. Tanner), now a TSB branch. The N side is dominated by the elaborate neo-Renaissance *Council House* (1874–79), with its dome. Around the corner in Chamberlain Square is the 1880s façade of the *Museum and Art Gallery* (see below) with the clock tower known as 'Big Brum', linked by a bridge across the street to the Gas Hall (completed in 1919). They face a Gothic monument to Joseph Chamberlain (1880; J.H. Chamberlain, no relation), statues of James Watt and Joseph Priestley, the **Central Library** (1974; John Madin Design Group) and the covered *Paradise Forum*.

The *•Museum and Art Gallery*, one of the best outside London, has rich collections of painting and sculpture, applied art, and archaeology, as well as local and natural history. The Pre-Raphaelite paintings are outstanding.

From the Chamberlain Square entrance, stairs climb past the information desk to the *Round Room*, its walls crowded with canvases in the 19C manner. *Gallery 1*, on the right, contains the museum shop and a taster of the wide variety of the collections. *Galleries 2–7* offer a spectacular vista of Victorian decoration, with cast-iron balconies and staircase and huge gaseliers. They contain applied art: metalwork, ceramics, glass, stained glass, costumes and jewellery. The ceramics collection includes a good representative display of English porcelain and a particularly strong display of pottery and tiles by William de Morgan. The pleasant Edwardian Tea Room at the end of the wing sometimes has music recitals.

From the Round Room a passage leads over the bridge, with its contemporary craft displays, to the Feeney Galleries with the main collection of painting and sculpture. *Galleries 10–11* display Oriental ceramics and applied art. Temporary exhibitions are displayed in the *Gas Hall*, reached by lift or by stairs from Gallery 11, and in *Galleries 12–13*. The English 19C art in *Galleries 14–19* includes the *•Pre-Raphaelite collection: Rossetti (Proserpine; Beata Beatrix), Millais (Blind Girl), Hunt (Valentine Rescuing Sylvia from Proteus; Finding of the Saviour in the Temple), Brown (Last of England; fine landscapes), Alexander Munro (sculpture of Paolo and Francesca), Burne-Jones and their followers, including Arthur Hughes (Long Engagement), Henry Wallis (Stonebreaker) and Charles Rossiter (To Brighton and Back for 3/6d). Other 19C artists represented include Turner (Pass of St Gotthard), Constable, Wilkie, Egg (Travelling Companions), Frith, J.F. Lewis, Leighton, Poynter, Alma-Tadema.

Galleries 20–27 display English and European art of other periods, the room numbers running counter to the chronological order. Medieval and Renaissance work in *Galleries 26–27* includes: Simone Martini (triptych), Memling, the Master of San Lucchese, a 15C Florentine Madonna in polychrome terracotta, a large Pentecost from the studio of Botticelli, a terracotta Madonna from the studio of Verrocchio, Giovanni Bellini, Palma Giovane, Garofalo, Scorel, Boccaccio Boccaccino. 17C art in *Galleries 23–25* includes: Rubens (Head of a Man; oil sketch of James I Uniting England and Scotland), Lely (Cromwell; Susannah and the Elders), David Teniers the Younger, Ochtervelt, William van Velde the Younger, Guercino (Erminia and the Shepherd), Gentileschi (Rest on the Flight to Egypt), Gennari, Crespi, Strozzi, Renieri, Murillo (Vision of St Anthony of Padua), Castiglione, Pellegrini, Reni, Giordano, Dolci, Francisque Millet, Claude (Landscape near Rome; Embarkation of St Paul), and Gaspar Poussin (Classical Landscape). There are also busts by Roubiliac and Nollekens. 18C work continues in *Gallery 22*, with Gainsborough (Miss Isabella Franks), Reynolds (Roffey Family; Mrs Luther), Allan Ramsay (Mrs Martin), Hogarth (Distressed Poet), Joseph Wright, Lawrence, Fuseli, Loutherbourg, Canaletto (two views of Warwick Castle), Francesco Guardi and Boucher. There is sculpture by Rysbrack (bust of Shakespeare), Chantrey and Girardon.

'The Last of England' by Ford Madox Brown, in the Birmingham City Museum and Art Gallery

Galleries 20–21 contain late 19C and 20C art: Sickert, Sisley, Henry Tonks, Mary Cassatt, Degas, Vuillard, Pissarro, Renoir, Fantin-Latour (L'Aurore et la Nuit), Mark Gertler, Jack Butler Yeats, Paul Nash, Stanley Spencer, Vlaminck, Rouault, Braque, Modigliani, Ben Nicholson, Francis Bacon, Ceri Richards, Peter Lanyon and more recent figures. Sculptures include works by Degas, Renoir (bust of Mme Renoir), Gaudier-Brzeska, Rodin, Epstein, Hepworth and Moore (Warrior with Shield).

Galleries 29–30, at street level by the Charles St. entrance, contain local history. The museum's archaeological collection is on the main and upper floors above, with Mexican and Peruvian antiquities on the staircase. *Gallery 32* has finds from Jericho (reconstructed tomb of c 1800 BC), Ur, Nineveh, Nimrud and Cyprus; also Luristan bronzes, a Greek red-figure stamnos (c 460 BC), Roman tombstones and the marble bust of a young girl (2C AD). *Gallery 34*, the balcony above, has Egyptian archaeology: funerary objects, stelae, mummies and the limestone bust of a nobleman (18th Dynasty, 1412–1376 BC). *Gallery 35* is devoted to the archaeology of Birmingham and the West Midlands. A hands-on display introduces cultures from around the world in *Gallery 33*.

The remaining galleries on the upper floor contain tropical birds, butterflies and shells; the Beale collection of birds; zoology; palaeontology; geology; and botany. *Gallery 41* has the Pinto collection, an extraordinary range of wooden objects from matches to a ship's figurehead.

WEST FROM VICTORIA SQUARE TO THE CANAL. Paradise Forum, at the NW corner of Chamberlain Square, leads to a major group of public buildings. On the left is the *Hall of Memory* (1925), devoted to the Birmingham dead of World War I. On the right are the District Council Offices in *Baskerville House* (1939; Cecil Howitt). Beyond lies the brick-paved Centenary Square (1988–91; Tess Jaray and City Architects Design Team), with an imaginative use of street furniture and sculpture. Note particularly Raymond Mason's 'Forward'. On its N side is the *Birmingham Repertory Theatre*. The square culminates in the dramatic *International Convention Centre* (1991; Renton, Howard, Wood, Levine with the Percy Thomas Partnership), which contains the new Symphony Hall, with a mural by Deanna Petherbridge on its external drum walls, best seen from the outside at night.

Broad St., running along the S side of the square, has England's oldest Municipal Savings Bank, founded in 1932, now a TSB branch. An oddcoloured memorial to Boulton, Watt and Murdock (1956; William Bloye) stands outside the *Register Office*. Behind are the *Central TV Studios*.

Gas St., on the left, leads to the *Gas St. Canal Basin*, the very centre of the English canal system. *Worcester Bar* divides the waterways leading N and S. The Worcester and Birmingham Canal goes S via the wooded scenery of Edgbaston and the King's Norton tunnel (see South-Western Suburbs below). The *walk suggested here takes the towpath N under Broad St. and passes an attractive terrace at the back of the International Convention Centre from which barge tours run in summer. At Old Turn Junction the 'main line' continues N via Smethwick to Wolverhampton. Its course, originally designed by Brindley in 1769, was straightened by Thomas Telford in the 1820s. To the right of Old Turn Junction a well-restored stretch of the Birmingham and Fazeley Canal runs between the International Convention Centre and the *National Indoor Arena*. It descends through 13 locks, passing the Museum of Science and Industry and the BT Tower (see the walk N from Victoria Square below) and giving good views of the city, old and new, at many points on the way.

EAST FROM VICTORIA SQUARE. Colmore Row, with 19C banks and insurance offices, is Birmingham's best street. Stone-fronted palazzi from the 1860s survive on the N side between Newhall St. and Church St. On the S side W.R. Lethaby's *Eagle Insurance Building* (1900) is outstanding.

St Philip's Cathedral was built as a parish church by Thomas Archer in 1709–25 and raised to its present status in 1905. The baroque exterior has a tower topped by a dome and cupola. J.A. Chatwin lengthened the chancel in 1883–84. The cool interior, with Corinthian columns at the E end, makes an ideal setting for the *windows by Edward Burne-Jones for Morris and Co. The one at the W end (1897) depicts the Last Judgement; the trio at the E end (1884–90) the Nativity, Ascension and Crucifixion.

Beyond Colmore Circus, Snow Hill Queensway leads past Snowhill Station to St Chad's Circus, which contains a memorial to President Kennedy with a large mosaic by Kenneth Budd (1969). The *Roman Catholic Cathedral* outside the ring road was designed by Pugin and built in 1839–41, the first new RC cathedral in England since the Reformation. It has 15C stalls from Cologne, a 16C pulpit from Louvain and glass (1868) by Hardman in the N transept window.

S of St Philip's Cathedral narrow streets zigzag to the partly pedestrianised New St., the central thoroughfare running from Victoria Square to St Martin's Circus and the Bull Ring. *New Street Station*, off its S side, was transformed with the addition of a tower block and shopping centre in the 1960s.

Corporation St., partly pedestrianised, runs N from this point. It was laid out in the 1870s and 1880s by Joseph Chamberlain's city council as part of a slum improvement scheme. The original buildings have largely been replaced by post-war development but at the N end, beyond Old Square, the *Law Courts* (1887–91; Sir Aston Webb and Ingress Bell) and the *Methodist Central Hall* (1903; E. and J.A. Harper) make a handsome group.

New St. meets High St. below the *Rotunda*, a block of offices (1965; James Roberts). Adjoining is the vast *Bull Ring Centre* (1961–64; Sydney Greenwood and T.J. Hirst), a pioneer inner-city shopping precinct with multi-level shops, offices, car parks, bus station, etc. On a terrace above the open-air market stands Westmacott's statue of Nelson (1809). To the S is *St Martin's*, the city's original parish church, largely rebuilt by J.A. Chatwin in 1873–75 on the 14C plan. It has medieval monuments of the de Birmingham family and a window (1875–80) by Burne-Jones for Morris and Co. in the S transept.

Digbeth and its continuation, Deritend, follow an old but now dreary course SE from St Martin's. The coach station stands on the right-hand side of Digbeth and the half-timbered *Crown Inn* on the left-hand side of Deritend.

Several other points of interest lie scattered about the area E of the ring road. On Stratford Place Bordesley, S of Deritend, *Stratford House* dates from 1601. *St Alban's Church*, on Conybere St., Highgate, further S, is by J.L. Pearson (1881), in one of the first post-war housing redevelopments. N of Deritend, the *Curzon Street Station* (1838; Philip Hardwick) has a fine Ionic portico. In Gosta Green, further N, is the *University of Aston in Birmingham*, formerly the college of advanced technology, chartered in 1966.

NORTH FROM VICTORIA SQUARE. A bridge links the Art Gallery and the Gas Hall. At the corner of Margaret St. is the Gothic *School of Art* (1881–85; J.H. Chamberlain and William Martin). Beyond in Margaret St. is the *Birmingham and Midland Institute*, with a wide range of cultural activities. Edmund St. goes to Newhall St., with the splendid former telephone exchange (1869; Frederick Martin) on the corner. A left turn up Newhall St. leads across the ring road at Great Charles St. Queensway to the *Museum of Science and Industry, in an old factory building by the canal. It graphically illustrates the work of Birmingham engineers and craftsmen with working steam, gas and hot air engines (including the oldest working steam engine in the world, made by Boulton and Watt c 1779), electrical equipment, machine tools and mechanical organs. The transport sections have a steam locomotive and aircraft. 'Light on Science' is an interactive gallery with hands-on experiments.

From here the canal walk described in the route W from Victoria Square (above) can be joined. Near the museum is the *BT Tower* (1966) in Lionel St. *St Paul's*, in the old jewellery quarter to the N, is a church of 1799. *The Discovery Centre* (open) on Vyse St. preserves the old Smith and Pepper factory, closed in 1981.

SOUTH-WESTERN SUBURBS. *Edgbaston*, reached by A456 (Hagley Rd) from the Five Ways junction at the end of Broad St., is a residential suburb with mid 19C houses (notably on Wellington Rd). The **Oratory of St Philip Neri** was founded by Newman in 1847. He lived in the Priest's House and is remembered by a tablet in the Italianate church (1903–09; E. Doran Webb). His grave is at Rednal (see below). The *Botanical Gardens* are S of Hagley Rd. The artist David Cox (1783–1859) is buried at *Harbourne*, 1½m SW. See below for the rest of the way by A456 to Kidderminster.

A38 (Bristol Rd) and A441 (Pershore Rd) both run SW from the inner ring road. To the left of A441 are (1¾m) the *Edgbaston Cricket Ground* and (2¼m) *Cannon Hill Park*, the most pleasant of the city's parks. Its *Nature Centre* has indoor and outdoor enclosures of British wildlife, aquaria, an underwater observation pond, nature trails, etc. The *Midland Arts Centre* is on the N side of the park.

The **University of Birmingham** lies on the right of A38 about 2½m S of the inner ring road. Established in the centre as Mason College in 1875, it moved here on receiving its university charter in 1900. The *Chamberlain Tower* (327ft) is the most striking feature of the original buildings, a rigidly planned red-brick complex by Sir Aston Webb and Ingress Bell (1900–09). Later development, under the supervision of Sir Hugh Casson and Neville Conder, includes University Square, to the N, with their *Staff House* and *University Centre* (both 1962). Further N are the *Sports Centre* (1965–66; Chamberlin, Powell and Bon), the tower of the *Arts and Commerce Building* (1970; Arup Associates) and, at the NE corner, the *Faculty of Education* (1968; Casson and Conder). W of the campus, beyond the railway and the Worcester and Birmingham Canal, rises *Queen Elizabeth Hospital* (1938) with the medical school.

By the East Gate of the university on Edgbaston Park Rd, near A38, is the *Barber Institute of Fine Arts** (open). A statue of George I on horseback by the workshop of John van Nost the Elder (1722), originally on Grattan Bridge in Dublin, stands outside the building by Robert Atkinson (1935–39). Founded under the will of Lady Barber (d. 1933), the institute contains a music room and a small but select art collection. Italian painting is represented by Ugolino da Siena (St Francis), Simone Martini (St John the Evangelist), Giovanni Bellini (St Jerome; portrait of a boy), Matteo di Giovanni (Madonna), Cima, Signorelli, Dossi, Beccafumi, Veronese and Guardi. Dutch and Flemish: Rubens (Landscape near Malines), Frans Hals (Man Holding a Skull, one of his earliest works), Van Dyck (Ecce Homo), Cuyp, Steen, Ruisdael and Van Gogh. French: Poussin (Tancred and Erminia), Claude (pastoral landscape), Watteau (?), Corot, Delacroix, Courbet, Pissarro, Manet (portrait of Carolus-Duran), Monet (Church at Varengeville), Renoir (Young Woman Seated), Gauguin, Toulouse-Lautrec, Bonnard and Magritte. English: Gainsborough (Harvest Wagon; two fine portraits), portraits by Reynolds, Romney and Lawrence, landscapes by Turner and Wilson, and work by Rossetti (Blue Bower), Whistler and Sickert. The collection also includes fine Italian Renaissance bronzes, and sculptures by Giovanni della Robbia (?), Roubiliac (bust of Pope), Louis Barye, Rodin and Degas; silver, ivories, enamels; Greek and Roman antiquities; Oriental, Indian and African works; miniatures, drawings, prints and illuminated MSS; and furniture.

Across Edgbaston Park Rd is **King Edward's School** (open by written appointment). Originally founded in 1552, it moved from New St. in 1936. The Upper Corridor of the demolished New St. building, by Charles Barry and Pugin (1833–37) in the same style as the Houses of Parliament, has been rebuilt as the *Chapel*.

Selly Oak is ¾m S of the university on A38. The ruined 13C *Weoley Castle* (open) lies 1¼m W. **Bournville**, 1m S of Selly Oak, is the site of the Cadbury chocolate works and a 'model village' first laid out for the Cadbury brothers by W.A. Harvey in the 1890s. There is an exhibition centre, *Cadbury World*, next to the factory; the admission fee includes guided tours of two production areas. Two half-timbered 14C houses, *Selly*

Manor and *Minworth Greaves*, have been rebuilt. *King's Norton*, 1½m further S, has a church with 15C spire, an old grammar school (formerly the priest's house) and, to the S, the N portal of the West Hill tunnel (1½m long) of the Worcester and Birmingham Canal. From the Selly Oak junction A38 continues 3½m SW to *Longbridge*, with its motor works. Newman is buried in the little graveyard of the country house of the Oratory Fathers at *Rednal*, 1m S. See Route 54 for rest of way by A38 to Bromsgrove and Worcester.

EASTERN AND SOUTH-EASTERN SUBURBS. In *Yardley*, 3½m E of the inner ring road by A45 and A4040, is the half-timbered *'Blakesley Hall** (open), built between 1573 and 1590. It contains exhibits about half-timbered buildings, rural crafts, etc. At *Tyseley*, 3m SE on A41 (Warwick Rd), the former GWR depot is now a working *Railway Museum* with steam locomotives etc. *Sarehole Mill* (open), the last of Birmingham's 18C corn mills, stands on the river Cole about 3½m SE of the inner ring road via A34. Again fully operational, it has displays of rural life, etc.

NORTH AND NORTH-EASTERN SUBURBS. *'Aston Hall** (open), a Jacobean house, stands in *Aston Park*, 1½m NE of the inner ring road between A38(M) and A34. A red-brick mansion of 1618–35 with gables and chimneystacks, it has a fine staircase, Long Gallery and plaster ceilings. Charles I stayed in the room now named after him in 1642. The Johnson Room contains 18C panelling from the Birmingham home of Johnson's friend Edmund Hector. Other rooms have decoration by James Watt, son of the engineer, who lived here in the early 19C. The house is the original of Washington Irving's 'Bracebridge Hall'. *Handsworth*, beyond A34 about 2m W, can also be reached from the inner ring road by A41. Now a depressed suburb, it was the site of the Soho Manufactory where Matthew Boulton and James Watt demonstrated their steam engine in 1775–1800. Boulton, Watt and Murdock rest in St Mary's Church, the first with a monument by Flaxman, the other two with monuments by Chantrey. *Perry Bar*, 3m N of the inner ring road by A34, has the church of St Matthew (1964; Robert Maguire and Keith Murray).

FROM BIRMINGHAM TO LICHFIELD AND DERBY, 40m. The quick way to Lichfield is by A38, heading NE from the centre via Aston and (3m) the 'Spaghetti Junction' of M6. A slower but more interesting route takes A5127 from the junction through (4m) *Erdington*. About 1½m NW is *St Mary's College*, or *Oscott College*, a Roman Catholic seminary with chapel fittings (1837–42) by Pugin. Lord Acton (1834–1902) was a lay pupil and Frederick Rolfe (Baron Corvo) trained for the priesthood here. 7m: **Sutton Coldfield** (86,500 inhabitants), a pleasant residential town, has a church with a Norman font and the monument of Bishop Veysey (d. 1556), a native and local benefactor. *Moat House*, c 1700, is attributed to Sir William Wilson. *New Hall* (not open), 1½m SE, is a moated mansion partly dating from the 13C. W of the town is *Sutton Park* with the late 19C suburb of *Four Oaks* on its N side. A5127 crosses A5, Watling Street, near the Roman remains at *Wall* (Route 64). 16m: **Lichfield**, see Route 64. A38 follows the Roman Rynkild Street. 20½m: *Fradley*, to the left, is near the junction of the Coventry Canal with the Trent and Mersey Canal. 21m: *Alrewas* has a church with Norman doorways and an Early English chancel. For Elford, beyond the Tame to the SE, see Route 64.

A38 is flanked by the Trent and the canal. 28½m: **Burton-upon-Trent** (47,900 inhabitants; TI) is known for its breweries, which originally flourished because of the high gypsum content of the local water. The *Bass Museum of Brewing*, in a former joinery warehouse of 1866 in Horninglow St., traces the history and technology of the industry. For *Needwood Forest* and *Hoar Cross*, to the W, see Route 64. From Burton to Leicester, see Route 59.

The road crosses the Dove, marking the border with Derbyshire. 32½m: *Egginton Common*. **Repton**, once capital of the Saxon kingdom of South Mercia, lies 2m SE. *St Wystan's Church* has a tall spire, 10C chancel and a 7C (?) crypt. *Repton School*, founded in 1557, has fragments of the Augustinian priory. Pupils have included Christopher Isherwood and Edward Upward. At *Foremark*, 2m E, the church (1662) has early Georgian ironwork by Robert Bakewell of Derby. Foremark Hall (not open) is a Palladian building of 1759–61 by David Hiorns. 40m: *Derby*, see Route 68.

FROM BIRMINGHAM TO LEICESTER, 40m. The quick route is by M6 and M42. A more interesting route takes A47. 10m: *Coleshill*, N of the junction of M6 and M42, has a Decorated and Perpendicular church with a spire rebuilt in the 19C, Norman font and monuments. B4114 leads to (13m) *Shustoke*, with reservoirs to the N, the birthplace of the antiquary Sir William Dugdale (1605–1686), buried in the church. *Maxstoke Castle* (not open), 1m S, is a moated and fortified mansion of 1346. B4114 continues through (14m) *Over Whitacre*. 20m: *Hartshill* and (22m) **Nuneaton**, see Route 64. A47 heads to (27m) *Hinckley* (55,300 inhabitants; TI). At *Bosworth Field* (TI), 4½m N, Henry Tudor became Henry VII by defeating and killing Richard III in 1485. *Stoke Golding*, S of the battlefield, has an early Decorated *church. Dr Johnson worked as an usher in the grammar school at *Market Bosworth*, 2m beyond the battlefield. 40m: *Leicester*, see Route 59.

FROM BIRMINGHAM TO KIDDERMINSTER, 19m by A456. It leaves the city to the SW. At (9m) *Halesowen* the poet William Shenstone (1714–63) established a garden. He is buried in the church. A fragment of the ruined 13C abbey survives (EH, summer season, limited opening). 11m: **Hagley Hall** (open) was built in 1756–60 by Sanderson Miller for George Lyttelton, 1st Lord Lyttelton (1709–73). The severe Palladian exterior contrasts with the plaster decoration by Francesco Vassali inside. The *grounds, laid out by Lyttelton with Shenstone's help and praised by James Thomson in 'The Seasons', have a sham ruin by Miller and a temple by James 'Athenian' Stuart. The church, rebuilt by Miller and altered by G.E. Street, has a monument to Lyttelton's first wife by Roubiliac. The *Clent Hills* (1036ft; NT) rise to the S. **Stourbridge** (54,700 inhabitants; TI), about 2m N, is the centre of a glass-making industry introduced in the 16C by refugees from Hungary and Lorraine. 19m: *Kidderminster*, see Route 66.

From Birmingham to *Warwick*, see Route 52A; to *Coventry*, see Route 52A; to *Stratford-upon-Avon*, see Route 53; to *Worcester*, see Route 54; to *Chester*, see Route 62.

62

The Black Country: Birmingham to Chester

Directions.Total distance 72m. **Birmingham**, see Route 61. A41 to (14m) **Wolverhampton**, (32m) Newport, (52m) Whitchurch and (72m) **Chester**, see Route 63.

The coal and iron industries, practised on a small scale since the Middle Ages, developed on a large scale in the 19C, expanding the towns of the region into one more or less indistinguishable conurbation. Smoke from the furnaces made it as notorious for pollution as the Potteries. In 'The Old Curiosity Shop', where Little Nell's wanderings follow part of the present route, Dickens described it as a modern hell: 'On every side, and far as the eye could see into the heavy distance, tall chimneys, crowding on each other and presenting that endless repetition of the same dull, ugly form, which is the horror of oppressive dreams, poured out their plague of smoke, obscured the light, and made foul the melancholy air. On mounds of ashes by the wayside, sheltered only by a few rough boards, or rotten pent-house roofs, strange engines spun and writhed like tortured creatures; clanking their iron chains, shrieking in their rapid whirl from time to time as though in torment unendurable, and making the ground tremble with their agonies'. Now that motor accessories, engineering and metal-finishing industries have replaced coal, iron and steel production, the Black Country is at least cleaner, though its towns and cities are largely nondescript.

An alternative to the main route to Wolverhampton described below runs further S, on A4123 and A459, via (9m) **Dudley** (187,200 inhabitants; TI). *Dudley Castle* (open), a ruin dating partly from the 14C but mainly from the 16C, has grounds with an open-air zoo. The *Black Country Museum*, on the canal basin near the entrance to the Dudley tunnel, has reconstructed chain-making and glass-cutting workshops, period buildings, etc.

The main route takes A41 NW from the centre of Birmingham, via Handsworth to (4½m) **West Bromwich** (154,900 inhabitants). The *Oak House* (open) has 16C half-timbering. The Old Manor House in Hall Green Rd, about 2m N, is a moated 14–16C building, now a restaurant.

Walsall (178,900 inhabitants), beyond the motorway tangle 5½m N, was the birthplace of Jerome K. Jerome (1859–1927), remembered by a museum on Bradford St. *St Matthew*, rebuilt by Francis Goodwin in 1820–21, keeps a set of 15C misericords. The *Museum and Art Gallery* at the Central Library in Lichfield St. has the Garman-Ryan art collection with works by Epstein.

A41 continues to (8m) *Wednesbury* (34,500 inhabitants), where the museum and art gallery contains local history, 19C paintings, etc. 11½m: *Bilston* (33,100 inhabitants) has a church of 1825–26 by Francis Goodwin. The museum and art gallery contains local exhibits of 18–19C enamels, Staffordshire pottery and industrial history. The poet Sir Henry Newbolt (1862–1938) was a native.

14m: **Wolverhampton** (252,400 inhabitants; TI), the capital of the Black Country and an iron-making centre since the 18C, is an old town, deriving its name from Wulfrun, sister of King Edgar, who endowed a church here in 994. The present *church of *St Peter*, in the centre near Queen Square, is a Perpendicular building which testifies to Wolverhampton's prosperity as a wool town in the Middle Ages.

Apart from remains of earlier work at the crossing, it belongs mainly to the late 15C. The N transept is slightly later, and the W front and E end were rebuilt by Ewan Christian in 1862–55. The nave has double clerestory windows and a Perpendicular stone pulpit and font. The gallery at the W end is Jacobean and the inner S porch is modern. The N transept contains a monument, perhaps by Jasper Latham, to Colonel John Lane (d. 1667), who helped Charles II escape after the Battle of Worcester, and the S transept a bronze statue of Admiral Sir Richard Leveson (d. 1605) by Hubert Le Sueur. Outside stands the Wolverhampton Cross, probably 9C.

The *Museum and Art Gallery*, in an Italianate building (1883; J.A. Chatwin) in Lichfield St., contains temporary exhibitions, Oriental collections and 18–20C paintings, mainly British (Gainsborough, Raeburn, Joseph Wright, Angelica Kaufmann, Fuseli, Cox, Linnell, Danby, Landseer).

The *Bantock House Museum*, SW of the town centre, contains the Balston collection of Staffordshire portrait figures, with other collections. *Willenhall*, about 3m E of Wolverhampton, has a museum of the local lock-making industry. *Moseley Old Hall* (NT), 3m N of Wolverhampton off A449 near M54, is a 17C house clad in 19C brick. Charles II hid here after the Battle of Worcester in 1651. *Penkridge*, 6m further N on the way to Stafford (Route 64), is an old town with a large 13–15C church containing good Littleton monuments. *Wightwick Manor* (NT; pronounced 'Witick'), 3m W of Wolverhampton by A454, is a brick and half-timbered house built by Edward Ould for the paint manufacturer Theodore Mander in 1887 and 1893. The interior has Morris wallpaper and fabrics, glass by Kempe, tiles by William de Morgan and Pre-Raphaelite paintings. *Chillington Hall* (limited opening) lies 8m NW of Wolverhampton on an unclassified road beyond M54. The Tudor house was rebuilt by Francis Smith of Warwick (1724) and Sir John Soane (1786–89), who created a saloon by covering over the courtyard with a characteristic domed roof. The grounds, with 18C garden buildings, were laid out by Capability Brown.

From Wolverhampton to *Shrewsbury*, see Route 65.

Beyond Wolverhampton the route leaves the Black Country, crossing the S tip of Staffordshire on the way into Shropshire. A41 bypasses (21½m) *Albrighton*.

The RAF base at *Cosford*, to the W, has an Aerospace Museum with historic aircraft. Unclassified roads lead NE from Albrighton to (c 2½m) *White Ladies Priory* (EH), a small Augustinian foundation, with the remains of the 12C church. After his defeat at the Battle of Worcester Charles II spent the better part of a week hiding here and at *Boscobel House* (EH, all year except January), a half-timbered 17C hunting lodge about 1m beyond. A descendant of the famous oak tree stands in a field nearby.

At (23½m) *Tong*, just beyond M54, the early 15C *church has many tombs, chiefly of the Vernons and the Stanleys. The 17C antiquarian Sir William Dugdale names Shakespeare as author of the epitaphs on the tomb of Sir Thomas Stanley (d. 1576). Dickens used the church as the resting place of Little Nell in 'The Old Curiosity Shop'. At 26m A41 crosses A5.

Weston Park (open), at *Weston-under-Lizard* 1½m E, is a brick mansion of 1671, with splendid furniture, Aubusson and Gobelins tapestries and paintings which include work by Van Dyck and Jacopo Bassano. Among the garden buildings are a Roman Bridge and Temple of Diana by James Paine (1760); the large park contains various tourist amusements. For Oakengates and Wellington, W along A5, see Route 65.

32m: **Newport** (9000 inhabitants) has a pleasant main street and a *Grammar School* of 1656.

Aqualate Mere, 2m E, is Staffordshire's largest lake. At *Lilleshall*, off A518 3m SW, the church has a Norman font. *Lilleshall Abbey* (EH), to the SE, was founded in c 1148 for canons of the Order of Arrouaisians, which later merged with the Augustinians. The remains include part of the 12–13C church and cloister buildings.

At (43m) *Ternhill* A41 crosses A53.

For the way SW to Shrewsbury, see Route 65. The old town of **Market Drayton** (8900 inhabitants; TI), 3m NE, has half-timbered and Georgian houses and a church with a 14C tower. Lord Clive (Clive of India, 1725–74), who attended the grammar school, was born at *Styche*, 2m NW, and buried at *Moreton Say*, 2m W. At *Blore Heath*, on A53 about 3m E of Market Drayton, the Yorkists under the Earl of Surrey defeated the Lancastrians under Lord Audley in 1459. A53 continues to Newcastle-under-Lyme (Route 67).

52m: **Whitchurch** (7200 inhabitants; TI) has a church rebuilt in 1713, with the tombs of John Talbot, 1st Earl of Shrewsbury (d. 1453), and John Talbot (d. 1550), founder of the grammar school. Sir Edward German (1862–1936) was born here.

Off A49 6m N are the gardens (limited opening) of *Cholmondeley Castle*, a 19C building partly by Robert Smirke. From Whitchurch to Shrewsbury, Ludlow and Hereford, see Route 65.

A41 enters Cheshire on the way to (58½m) *Hampton Heath. Malpas*, 1½m SW, was birthplace of the hymn-writer Bishop Reginald Heber (1783–1826). The Perpendicular church has a beautiful nave roof and good monuments. At (69m) *Rowton Moor*, on the left, the Royalist defeat in 1645 led to the fall of Chester the following year. 69½m: *Christleton*, on the right, has a church (1874–78) by William Butterfield.

72m: **Chester**, see Route 63.

63

Chester

CHESTER (58,400 inhabitants), the county town on the Dee, has long been popular with visitors both for its convenient position on the way to North Wales and for its own sake. With its well-preserved circuit of walls partly following their Roman course, its famous half-timbered 'rows' and its cathedral, the city keeps much of its medieval appearance. The fact that a lot of the picturesque detail is Victorian does not spoil the effect.

TI: Town Hall, Northgate St.; Visitor Centre, Vicar's Lane. **Bus Stations**: Princess St. for local and long-distance services; Delamere St. for coach services. **Railway Station**: off Brook St., NE of the centre and the inner ring road. **Theatres**: Gateway Theatre, Hamilton Place; Little Theatre Club, Gloucester St.

History. The Roman Deva or Castra Devana (the 'camp on the Dee') was founded about AD 48 and became headquarters of the 20th legion. Another name, Castra Legionum, evolved into the Welsh Caerleon and the Saxon Legaceaster, shortened to Ceaster. After the Romans left (c 380) the town was successively in the hands of the Welsh, the Saxons and the Danes until Ethelfleda, Alfred the Great's daughter, rebuilt it in 907. Chester resisted the Normans longer than any other English city, but in 1070 William the Conqueror granted it to his nephew Hugh Lupus, with as much land as he could win from his Welsh neighbours. As Earl of Chester, he was virtually ruler of an independent territory. The earldom reverted to the Crown in 1237 and since 1254 has been one of the titles held by the sovereign's eldest son. Largely because of its port, the town's prosperity grew during the Middle Ages until, as the river began to silt up in the 15C and 16C, trade gradually shifted to Liverpool. The Chester Cycle, one of four cycles of mystery plays to survive in England, was performed from the 14C to the 17C. In the Civil War the town sided with Charles I, but after his defeat in September 1645 at Rowton Moor (about 3m SE) it was starved into surrender the following February. Its prosperity revived in the 19C with the spread of the railways. In this era, too, it became popular with tourists, particularly American visitors arriving at Liverpool.

Natives, residents and visitors. The chronicler Ranulf Higden (d. 1364) was a monk at St Werburgh's, now the cathedral. The artist Randolph Caldecott (1846–86) and Sir Adrian Boult (1889–1983) were natives. Thomas De Quincey (1785–1859) spent part of his wandering boyhood near St John's church. Thomas Hughes (1822–96), author of 'Tom Brown's Schooldays', passed his last years in nearby Dee Hills Park. Swift used the port on his way between England and Ireland; his friend Thomas Parnell died here while making the same journey in 1718. Henry James captures the impressions of 19C American visitors in 'The Ambassadors' (1903) and 'English Hours' (1905).

The city centre is the Cross, at the junction of the Roman roads whose course is now represented by Watergate St., Bridge St., Eastgate St. and Northgate St. The heavily restored *St Peter's Church*, at the corner of Northgate St., stands on the site of part of the Roman praetorium, or camp headquarters. The *Cross* itself is a reconstruction using fragments of the 15C one destroyed in the Civil War. The main feature of the nearby streets is the

*Rows, galleries or arcades forming continuous passages along the first floor of the half-timbered houses and shops. Why this curious arrangement developed, probably in the 13C, is uncertain, but the most likely explanation is that the solid Roman ruins encumbered the site at street level. Some buildings are genuinely old and a few have medieval crypts. More belong to the 19C, though they are not necessarily the worse for that. A particularly spectacular example of 1888 by the chief local exponent, T.M. Lockwood, stands at the corner of Eastgate St. and Bridge St.

WEST FROM THE CROSS. Watergate St., once the main street to the port, has rows on both sides and some of the best buildings in Chester, all on the left. *God's Providence House* is a reconstruction of 1862 incorporating the inscribed beam from the original house of 1652. No. 11 has the city's finest medieval crypt and the 16C *Leche House. Bishop Lloyd's House* is the most richly carved in Chester. *Ye Olde Custom House Inn* (1637) stands at the corner of Weaver St. Opposite, the *Guildhall* (open) occupies the 19C former Trinity Church. Nicholas St., part of the inner ring road, marks the W line of the Roman wall. Beyond is the heavily altered *Stanley Place* (1591), once the residence of the Earls of Derby. For the Watergate, see the city walls below.

SOUTH FROM THE CROSS. Bridge St. has rows on both sides and some particularly attractive houses on the right. 12, a bookshop, has a vaulted crypt. The *Dutch Houses*, near the corner of Commonhall St., date from the 17C but have 13C or 14C fragments. On the same side beyond, Commonhall St. leads to the *Deva Roman Experience*, re-creating Roman and Saxon Chester. In Whitefriars, leading to the right, 1 is an attractive house with a gable of 1658. Opposite Whitefriars the former St Michael's church, mainly 19C, is now the **Chester Heritage Centre**, with displays of architecture and conservation in the city. Lower Bridge St. crosses Grosvenor St. On the corner is the *Falcon*, dating partly from 1626, where Handel stayed in 1741. Opposite is the *Toy Museum*. Further down are the late 16C or early 17C *Tudor House* on the left, and on the right *Ye Olde King's Head*, mainly early 17C, and *Gamul House*, where Charles I stayed in 1645. The *Bear and Billet Inn*, near the Bridgegate at the foot of the street, dates from 1664 and was the town house of the Earls of Shrewsbury until the 19C. For the Bridgegate and the Dee Bridge, see the city walls below.

Castle St., by the King's Head, leads to the former church of St Mary-on-the-Hill, now *St Mary's Centre* (open), with 17C monuments and a timber roof said to have been brought from Basingwerk Abbey. Further on is the entrance to the **Castle**, a handsome group of neo-classical buildings (1793–1820; Thomas Harrison) serving as Assize Court, County Hall, etc. The statue of Field Marshal Viscount Combermere (d. 1865) outside the main entrance is by Marochetti. The *Cheshire Military Museum* is at the NE corner. The only surviving parts of the medieval castle begun c 1070 by Hugh Lupus are a stretch of the inner bailey wall and the early 13C *Agricola's Tower* (EH, all year). The vaulted chapel of St Mary de Castro has spectacular wall paintings.

Grosvenor St. leads back to Bridge St. and the Cross. It passes the **Grosvenor Museum**, on the right, with *Roman inscribed stones and other exhibits of Roman Chester. Upstairs are paintings of local scenes and a silver gallery. The *Georgian House* in nearby Castle St. is also part of the museum.

EAST FROM THE CROSS. Eastgate St., with rows on its right-hand side, is still Chester's main street. Most of its buildings are 19C, though Brown's uses a 13C vaulted crypt as one of its departments. St Werburgh's St., on the left, leads to the cathedral. Eastgate, at the end, is the starting-point for

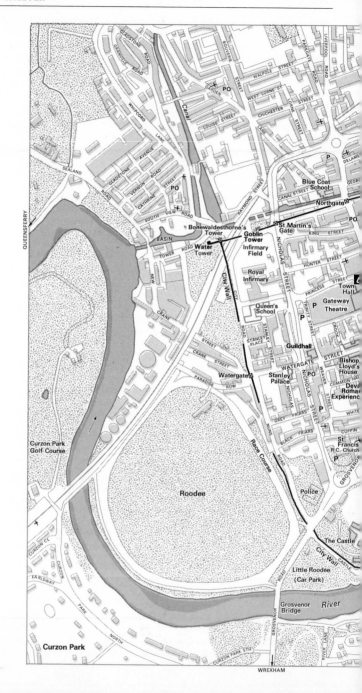

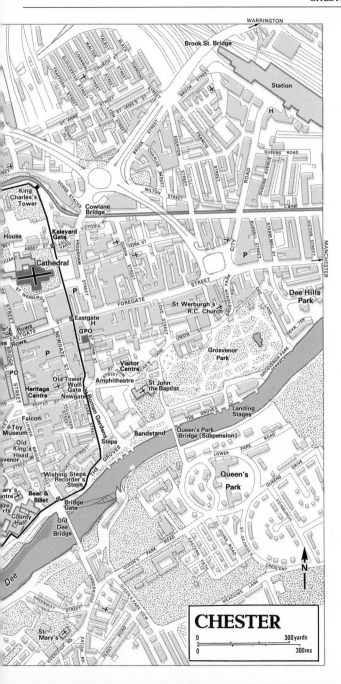

CHESTER

0   300 yards

0   300 ms

a walk around the walls and for points of interest outside the walls. All these are described below.

NORTH FROM THE CROSS. In Northgate St. the rows are mostly on the ground floor. Remains of the Roman praetorium survive in the basement of 23. A window in Hamilton Place, off the same side, allows a view of the Roman strongroom. Beyond, also on the W side of the street, are the Market Square and the Victorian Gothic *Town Hall* (1864–69; W.H. Lynn), with the TI Centre.

There are two interesting old houses on the left-hand side of the street as it continues to the Northgate: the *Pied Bull Inn*, with an 18C frontage and older work behind, and the 15C former *Blue Bell Inn*, now a restaurant. For the Northgate, see the city walls below.

The *Cathedral stands opposite the town hall, its W front almost masked by King's School (1875–77; Sir Arthur Blomfield), now a bank, on the site of the abbot's lodging. It is approached from the N, through the 14–15C *Abbey Gateway* and Abbey Square, or from the S by St Werburgh's St. Both routes emphasise how the W end is hemmed in by streets, just as the E end lies close to the city wall.

The college of secular canons dedicated to St Werburgh (d. c 700) was refounded as a Benedictine abbey in 1092 by Hugh Lupus, Earl of Chester, with St Anselm's help. At the Reformation it became cathedral of the new diocese of Chester. The chief remains of the Norman church are on the N side. Beginning with the Lady Chapel (1250–75), the rest of the building reflects all periods up to the 19C. The choir, largely by Edward I's military engineer Richard of Chester, dates from c 1300, the arcades of the S transept and the S arcade of the nave from the mid 14C, the rest of the nave, the clerestory of the S transept and the top stages of the tower from the end of the 15C. The cathedral was restored in the 19C, notably by Sir Gilbert Scott in 1868–76.

Externally, the red sandstone makes up for the modest site and lack of dramatic features. The two-storied SW porch is Tudor. Worth searching for on the SE corner of the huge S transept are the 19C corbels depicting Gladstone and Disraeli. The apsidal E end of the S choir aisle has a remarkable polygonal roof by Scott. A detached bell tower (1975; George Pace) stands in the SE corner of the precinct. The city wall gives the best view of the E end.

The raised W end of the *Nave* gives a beautiful vista, enhanced by the warm sandstone. The S arcade is Decorated, the N arcade late Perpendicular. A plain frieze takes the place of a triforium, with a late Perpendicular clerestory above. The glass in the W window is by W.T. Carter Shapland (1961). At the W end of the S aisle, in the base of the unfinished SW tower, is the Consistory Court of 1636 with wooden furnishings. The wall of the N aisle, covered by J.R. Clayton's mosaics (1886), is Norman. The Baptistery has a font of Byzantine design brought from Italy in 1885. From both ends of this aisle, doors (the E one Norman of c 1100) lead into the cloisters (see below).

The small *N Transept* was part of the Norman church and is thus the oldest part of the cathedral. The organ loft over the entrance has an organ case by Scott (1876). The windows and roof, with Tudor heraldry, are late Perpendicular. A monument by Sir Arthur Blomfield (1864) to the 17C theologian Bishop John Pearson stands in the centre and a wall tablet commemorates the 19C artist Randolph Caldecott. On the E side a Norman archway with a small row of triforium arches above leads into the Sacristy, where Transitional work replaces a Norman apse. The N side gives access to the vestibule of the chapter house (see below). The huge *S Transept*, with aisles and sidechapels, is 14C Decorated and 15C Perpendicular. It served as the parish church from the early 16C to the late 19C. The great S window (1887) is by Blomfield. There is a charming little monument to Thomas Greene (d. 1602) and his two wives on the NW pier.

The 13–14C *Choir* has a beautiful triforium. The *stalls (c 1390), with their spired canopies, bench ends and misericords, are among the best in England. The bishop's

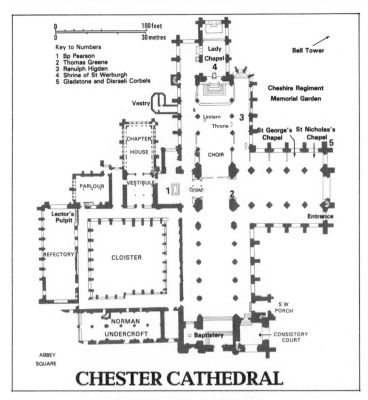

Key to Numbers
1 Bp Pearson
2 Thomas Greene
3 Ranulph Higden
4 Shrine of St Werburgh
5 Gladstone and Disraeli Corbels

0   100 feet
0   30 metres

Lady Chapel
4
Bell Tower

Cheshire Regiment
Memorial Garden

Vestry

Lectern
3
Throne

St George's Chapel   St Nicholas's Chapel
5

CHAPTER HOUSE

CHOIR

PARLOUR   VESTIBULE
1   Organ   2

Lector's Pulpit
Entrance

REFECTORY   CLOISTER

S W PORCH

NORMAN UNDERCROFT   Baptistery   CONSISTORY COURT

ABBEY SQUARE

CHESTER CATHEDRAL

throne is by Scott. Gates of Spanish wrought iron (1558) lead into the choir aisles. Both were lengthened to the E in c 1500, but the *S Choir Aisle* has an apsidal end by Scott. The chronicler Ranulf Higden (d. 1364) is buried in this aisle, and the third window from the W is Pugin's work (1850). The *N Choir Aisle* keeps its Tudor end, now St Werburgh's Chapel, though the line of the original Norman apse is marked in the pavement. Near the entrance are the base of a Norman column and a capital turned over and used as a foundation when the choir was rebuilt. The Early English *Lady Chapel* (c 1275–80), reached from the N choir aisle, has the reconstructed fragments of St Werburgh's shrine and three *bosses.

The *Cloisters* are reached from the N aisle of the nave. They were rebuilt c 1536 and restored by Giles Gilbert Scott in 1911–13, though Norman work survives in the S walk. A graceful vestibule leads from the E walk to the rectangular 13C *Chapter House*. Along the W walk runs a 12C undercroft, part of it now the bookshop. In the N walk the cafeteria occupies the large 13C refectory, with 15C windows and a staircase leading to the *pulpit used for mealtime readings. The hammerbeam roof is modern.

Abbey Square has Georgian houses. St Werburgh's St. has 19C half-timbering and, in Music Hall Passage off its W side, the remains of a chapel originally built c 1280 for the parish of St Oswald, later serving as a wool hall, theatre and concert hall.

THE CITY WALLS. The walk round the *City Walls begins at the *Eastgate*, dating in its present form from 1769 with a clock added to celebrate Victoria's Diamond Jubilee. The Romans defended their fort with turf ramparts and later with stone. In the 12C the system was extended S and

W to protect the castle; more towers were added in the 13C and 14C. An irregular rectangle, built from 15ft to 25ft high in red sandstone, enclosed the old city. Despite alteration and rebuilding, particularly of the towers and gates, a remarkable amount survives, chiefly medieval but with Roman work on the N and E sides. It is worth making the full circuit along the top (about 2m), but in any case visitors should be sure to cover the stretches N from Eastgate to Northgate (600yd) and S from Eastgate to Newgate (250yd) and the Roman remains outside the walls.

From Eastgate steps lead N, along the walls past the modern bell tower and a good view of the E end of the cathedral. At the *Kaleyard Gate*, a postern at the end of Abbey St., it is worth seeing the remains of the Roman wall to the S. The walk rounds the choir school's playing fields. At the NE corner stands *King Charles's Tower* (restored 1658), so-called because he is said to have watched the defeat of his troops at Rowton Moor from here; its other name, *Phoenix Tower*, comes from the crest of the local guilds who once occupied it. It contains a small Civil War exhibition. The N wall, part of which may be Norman with stretches of Roman stone, skirts the Shropshire Union Canal on the site of the former moat. Beyond the canal stands the *Northgate Arena* sports centre. The *Northgate* was rebuilt by Thomas Harrison in 1808. Stretches of Roman wall can be seen from Northgate Bridge, particularly to the W. On the opposite bank is the former *Bluecoat School* (1717).

Morgan's Mount, a square tower, overlooks a flight of canal locks and commands a view of the Welsh hills. The walk crosses St Nicholas St. by *St Martin's Gate* (1966) and reaches the semi-circular *Goblin Tower*, or *Pemberton's Parlour*, rebuilt in 1894. One wing of the *Royal Infirmary*, to the S, stands on Infirmary Field, first a Roman cemetery and later a burial ground for plague victims. The railway cuts across the NW corner of the walls. *Bonewaldesthorne Tower*, at the angle, is linked by a projecting wall to the *Water Tower* (open), built to defend the port in 1322.

The walk descends to street level as it runs S past the Royal Infirmary to the *Watergate*, rebuilt in 1788. On the right lies the *Roodee*, a large open space surrounded by the racecourse where the Chester Races have been run since 1540. Near the SW angle of the walls the Dee is crossed by the *Grosvenor Bridge*, built by Thomas Harrison in 1832.

The irregular S wall runs between the river and the castle to the *Bridgegate* (1782). The medieval *Dee Bridge*, widened in the 19C, has seven arches. The causeway or weir to its E is said to have been constructed by Hugh Lupus to serve the mills, remembered by the song 'The Jolly Miller of Dee', which stood here until the 19C. Salmon fisheries extend downstream. In the suburb of *Handbridge* across the river is the steeple of *St Mary-without-the-Walls* (1885–87).

Soon turning N, the walls pass the *Recorder's Steps* (1700) and the *Wishing Steps* (1785) on the way to the junction of the medieval and Roman walls at the *Newgate*, built by Sir Walter Tapper in 1932 to replace its neighbour, the narrow *Wolf Gate* (1768). The ruined 14C *Thimbleby's Tower*, or *Wolf Tower*, and Eastgate lie beyond.

OUTSIDE THE WALLS. The main points of interest are near Newgate. Foundations of the Roman wall and its SE angle tower (AD 74–96) survive immediately N of the gate. The *Roman Gardens*, to the S, have a reconstructed hypocaust and Roman columns (none in situ). The *Roman Amphitheatre* (EH, all year) dates from c 100 but covers an older wooden site. The largest so far discovered in Britain, it would have seated 9000 people. It is unusual in having a small temple to Nemesis, immediately W of the N entrance.

The unpleasantly commercial *Chester Visitor Centre*, in Vicar's Lane, has TI, restaurant, displays illustrating Chester's history, etc. • **St John's Church**, opposite, preserves the crossing tower and part of the nave of a Norman collegiate church.

Founded c 1075, it was for about its first ten years cathedral of the diocese of Mercia, moved briefly from Lichfield; hence early references to a bishopric of Chester 500 years before St Werburgh's became the present cathedral. The NW tower, already rebuilt in 1523, fell in 1573 and destroyed the W end. In 1881 the detached belfry fell in its turn, crushing the N porch. R.C. Hussey, responsible for most of the Victorian restoration, replaced the belfry with an incongruous structure, but the porch was rebuilt in its Early English form. The stump of the old belfry still stands outside the W end. Beyond the E end are the ruins of the choir and Lady Chapel, with Transitional work. The vaulted 13C 'crypt', perhaps the chapter house, once served as kitchen for a house above, in which the young Thomas De Quincey briefly lived.

The pillars and arches of the nave date from c 1095. The triforium of four arches to each bay and the aisles are Transitional (c 1200), while the clerestory is Early English. A plaque to the right of the entrance commemorates Thomas Hughes (see below). The

The Eastgate clock, Chester

NW corner has Saxon crosses and medieval effigies. The Warburton Chapel, on the S side, has the skeleton monument of Lady Warburton (d. 1693).

Below the S wall of the churchyard is the *Hermitage*, an 18C house on the site of an anchorite's cell where, so a curious tradition maintains, Harold retired after the Battle of Hastings. On the river bank below St John's are The Groves, a shady promenade with landing stages. Pleasure cruises leave from here. To the E extends *Grosvenor Park*, where the 13C Shipgate has been rebuilt. Thomas Hughes spent his last years at 16 Dee Hills Park, immediately E of Grosvenor Park.

OUTSKIRTS. The *Zoo and Gardens* at Upton, 2m N, house animals and floral displays. *Eccleston*, 3m S on an unclassified road following the course of the Roman Watling Street from the Dee Bridge, is the chief village of the Grosvenor estate. The church (1899) is by G.F. Bodley. At *Eaton Hall* (not open), further S, most of the mansion built by Alfred Waterhouse for the 1st Duke of Westminster in 1870–91 has been demolished, though the chapel and stable court survive. The forecourt has a statue of Hugh Lupus by G.F. Watts.

FROM CHESTER TO LIVERPOOL VIA PORT SUNLIGHT, 18m. See Route 73 for an alternative way to Liverpool via Hoylake. Both routes cross the *Wirral*, the peninsula between the Dee and Mersey estuaries. A5116 runs due N to join A41 at 2m. At **Ellesmere Port** (63,100 inhabitants), to the right at 3½m, the Shropshire Union Canal from Chester joins the Manchester Ship Canal. The *Boat Museum* at the docks has warehouses, workshops, hydraulic steam engines and over 50 craft. *Stanlow*, to the E, is site of the Shell oil refinery. A41 continues to (9m) *Eastham*, on the right, where the Manchester Ship Canal joins the Mersey. At the docks tankers discharge their oil for pumping to the Stanlow refinery. 13m: **Port Sunlight** is a model community built in 1888–1914 by W.H. Lever, Lord Leverhulme, around his Sunlight soap factory. The *Lady Lever Art Gallery* has English art (Reynolds, Wilson, Constable, Turner) and particularly work by the Pre-Raphaelites (Ford Madox Brown, Holman Hunt, Millais, Rossetti and Burne-Jones). There is also a superb collection of Wedgwood ware and 18–19C furniture. For *Thornton Hough*, on B5136 3m SW, see the alternative way to Liverpool in Route 73. 16m: *Birkenhead*, and thence through the Mersey Tunnel to (18m) *Liverpool*, see Route 73.

FROM CHESTER TO MANCHESTER VIA NORTHWICH, 40m. A51 leads to (6m) *Tarvin* (Route 64), then A54 past (8m) *Kelsall*. A556 goes left, shortly before (10½m) *Delamere*, in the middle of *Delamere Forest* with quiet meres and pinewoods. *Eddisbury Hill*, on the left, has a well-preserved stronghold attributed to Alfred the Great's daughter Ethelfleda. 17m: **Northwich** (17,100 inhabitants), bypassed to the S, now has chemical factories but was once a centre of the Cheshire salt industry also carried on at Middlewich and Nantwich. There is a *Salt Museum* on London Rd, and the Lion Salt Works (open to visitors) survives at Marston, 1½m NE. *Great Budworth*, beyond Marston 3m N, has a Perpendicular church with 13C stalls and a good 15C font. *Arley Hall* (open), 4m further N, is a 19C neo-Jacobean house with a chapel by Salvin and good gardens.

Beyond Northwich A5033 branches right, crossing M6, to (24m) **Knutsford** (13,700 inhabitants; TI), an attractive town with old houses and a church of 1741. It is the 'Cranford' of the novel by Elizabeth Gaskell (1810–65), who spent part of her childhood here and is buried in the old Unitarian graveyard near the station. *Tatton Park* (NT and Cheshire County Council), 3½m N, is a neo-classical mansion begun in 1780–90 by Samuel Wyatt, brother of James, and finished in 1808–13 by Lewis Wyatt. Much of the furniture was made for the house by Waring of Lancaster. The grounds include a Japanese garden and a deer park. The church of *Rostherne*, on the bank of the lovely mere a little to the N, contains Egerton family monuments. *Tabley House* (open), on A5033 2m W of Knutsford, is a Palladian mansion by John Carr with a good collection of furniture, English paintings and musical instruments. *Peover Hall* (open), off A50 4m S of Knutsford, is an Elizabethan building with fine 17C stables. The nearby church of *Over Peover* contains fine tombs of the Mainwarings. *Lower Peover*, 2m W, has a rare 14C half-timbered *church with a 16C stone tower.

From Knutsford the route follows A556 and, after crossing M56, joins A56 in the pretty valley of the Bollin. 31½m: *Altrincham*, and on to (40m) *Manchester*, see Route 75A.

FROM CHESTER TO WARRINGTON, 20m by A56. 10m: *Frodsham*, on a hill overlooking the Weaver marshes, has a partly Norman church. The road winds back and forth across M56. Runcorn is to the W. 15m: *Daresbury* was the birthplace of Lewis Carroll (Charles Lutwidge Dodgson, 1832–98), commemorated in the church by a window with scenes from 'Alice in Wonderland'. 20m: *Warrington*, see Route 75A.

FROM CHESTER TO WREXHAM. The main road, A483, reaches the Welsh border at (5m) *Pulford*, passes (8m) *Gresford* with its fine church and reaches Wrexham at 12m. A more pleasant route takes B5130 due S from Chester to (9m) *Farndon*, where Edward the Elder died in 924 and the mapmaker John Speed (?1552–1629) was born. *Stretton*, 3m SE, has a working watermill (open). A 14C bridge crosses the Dee to enter Wales at (9½m) *Holt*, with a good church. For (15m) *Wrexham*, and on to *Bala*, *Dolgellau* and *Barmouth*, see 'Blue Guide Wales'.

From Chester to *Bangor*, see 'Blue Guide Wales'; to *Birmingham*, see Route 62; to *Coventry*, see Route 64; to *Hereford* via *Ludlow* and *Shrewsbury*, see Route 65.

64

Coventry to Chester

Directions. Total distance 97m. **Coventry**, see Route 52A. A444 to (8m) **Nuneaton**. A444, A5, A51 to (22m) **Tamworth**. A51 to (29m) **Lichfield**. A51, A513 to (45m) **Stafford**. A34 to (53m) Stone (bypassed). A34, A51 to (77m) **Nantwich**. A51 to (97m) **Chester**, see Route 63.

Coventry, see Route 52A. A444 heads N, crossing M6 at 4m. 5½m: *Griff House* was the childhood home of George Eliot (1819–80), born 2m W at South Farm (see Arbury Hall below). At (7m) *Chilvers Coton*, now a suburb of Nuneaton, the church where she was christened has been rebuilt after wartime bomb damage. 8m: **Nuneaton** (71,500 inhabitants; TI), a dull town, has a centre designed by Sir Frederick Gibberd in 1947. The *Library* contains a George Eliot collection and the *Museum and Art Gallery* memorabilia of the novelist. *St Nicholas*, the handsome church, is Early English and Perpendicular. *St Mary's*, rebuilt in the 19C and 20C, has fragments of the Norman church belonging to the Benedictine nunnery from which the town takes its name.

Arbury Hall (limited opening), 2m SW, has *Gothick alterations made to the Elizabethan house by Sir Roger Newdigate, founder of the Oxford poetry prize, from the 1740s to the 1790s. Sanderson Miller gave advice and Henry Keene was among the architects. There are good family portraits and furniture. The stables are late 17C. George Eliot's father was agent on the estate, and the house appears as 'Cheverel Manor' in 'Scenes of Clerical Life'. There is a country park 2m NW of Nuneaton at *Hartshill*, where the poet Michael Drayton (1563–1631) was born.

From Nuneaton to *Leicester* and to *Birmingham*, see Route 61.

A444 continues N to join A5, following the Roman Watling Street, at 11m. *Fenny Drayton*, ½m N, was the birthplace of George Fox (1624–91), founder of the Society of Friends. *Lindley*, 1m E, where the Motor Industry Research Association has its proving ground, was the birthplace of Robert Burton

(1577–1640) of 'The Anatomy of Melancholy'. A5 heads W. 13m: *Mancetter*, to the left, was the Roman Manduessedum. 14m: *Atherstone* is an old market town with coaching inns. The remains of the Cistercian *Merevale Abbey*, about 1m W, include the 13–14C chapel outside the gate, now the parish church; it contains a Perpendicular screen, early 14C Jesse window and medieval monuments and brasses.

Beyond (18½m) the junction with M42, marking the boundary with Staffordshire, the route follows A51 right. For places further W on A5 as it swings past Wolverhampton on its way to Wellington, see Route 49. 22m: **Tamworth** (64,300 inhabitants; TI) is an old town expanded since the 1960s. Offa, King of Mercia, had a palace and a mint here in the 8C, and the town was fortified by Ethelfleda, Alfred the Great's daughter, in the 10C. The oldest part of the *Castle* (open), near the meeting of the Anker and the Tame, is the Norman shell keep; the great hall and other buildings are largely Jacobean. They contain a local history museum with Saxon coins from Tamworth mint. The light and spacious 14C *Church* has a tower with a double spiral staircase, interesting monuments, and glass by Morris and Co. The delightful *Town Hall* (1701) was paid for by Thomas Guy, founder of Guy's Hospital in London and MP for Tamworth. A statue of Sir Robert Peel (1788–1850), a later MP, stands in front. He is buried at *Drayton Bassett*, beyond A5 1½m S. His house no longer stands but the grounds are the *Drayton Manor Park and Zoo*.

A513 follows a pleasant route along the Tame valley past (4½m) *Elford*, where the church has 1416C monuments. *Alrewas* (pronounced 'Allroz'), 3m further, lies on the way from Birmingham to Burton-upon-Trent and Derby (Route 61).

A51 continues W, passing (26m) *Packington*, with the Museum of the Staffordshire Regiment outside the Whittington Barracks.

29m: **LICHFIELD** (28,700 inhabitants) is Staffordshire's most interesting town. It has a beautiful cathedral and an 18C atmosphere to remind visitors of its connection with Dr Johnson and other literary men of the age.

TI: Donegal House, Bore St. **Bus Station**: Birmingham Rd. **Railway Stations**: City station, off Birmingham Rd, for Birmingham; Trent Valley station, 1m E, for London and Stafford. **Annual Events**: Festival of Traditional Song and Dance (June); Jazz Festival (June/July); Lichfield Festival, with concerts, exhibitions, etc. (July); Sheriff's Ride (September); Johnson Birthday Celebrations and Supper (September).

Natives and residents. Lichfield enjoyed a rich intellectual and literary life, particularly in the 18C. The sites connected with Samuel Johnson (1709–84), are commemorated with proper local pride. Other distinguished Lichfieldians include: the antiquarian Elias Ashmole (1617–92), born in the same street as Johnson; Joseph Addison (1672–1719), who lived here when his father was Dean of Lichfield; and Johnson's friend David Garrick (1717–79), who spent his childhood here. On his frequent return visits Johnson met members of the coterie which included: Erasmus Darwin (1731–1802), scientist and grandfather of Charles Darwin; Anna Seward (1747–1809), poetess and 'Swan of Lichfield'; Richard Lovell Edgeworth (1744–1817), educator and father of the novelist Maria Edgeworth; and Thomas Day (1748–89), author of the children's book 'Sandford and Merton'. The playwright George Farquhar was stationed here as a recruiting officer in 1705. Richard Hurd was Bishop in 1775–81.

The market place has statues of Johnson (1838; R.C. Lucas) and Boswell (1908; Percy Fitzgerald). Edward Wightman, the last person burned for heresy in England, was executed here in 1612. George Fox, founder of the Society of Friends, walked barefoot here in 1651 crying 'Woe to the bloody city of Lichfield'. On the corner of Market St. stands the *Samuel Johnson*

Birthplace Museum, where Johnson's parents lived over the family book-shop, with personal relics and a valuable library. Johnson's baptism is recorded in the register of St Mary's church opposite, since rebuilt and now the *St Mary's Centre* (open), with displays of Lichfield's history. Johnson and Boswell several times stayed at the former Three Crowns Inn, next door to the birthplace. The house beyond was Elias Ashmole's birthplace.

Bore St., at the S end of Breadmarket, has the Gothic *Guildhall* of 1846, the 18C *Donegal House* (the former Guildhall offices, now the TI Centre) and the 16C halftim-bered *Lichfield House* (now the Tudor Café). St John's St. leads S towards the railway station, passing the *Hospital of St John Baptist*, built in 1495, with striking chimney-stacks. The much altered chapel (open) has an E window of 1984 by John Piper. The *Council Offices* opposite stand on the site of the old grammar school attended by Ashmole, Addison, Garrick and Johnson, and incorporate the 17C headmaster's house.

The shortest way from the market place to the cathedral is by Dam St., with Georgian houses and, at the corner of the picturesque Quonians Lane, the site of the dame school Johnson attended. The best way is by Market St. and then Bird St., which has two good 18C inns: the *George*, on the site of the one which Farquhar made the scene of 'The Beaux' Stratagem' (1707), and the *Swan*, where Johnson and the Thrales stayed on their way to Wales in 1774. Beyond the *Arts Centre* (local exhibitions), the walk crosses the bridge flanked by *Minster Pool* and a public garden with Elizabeth Scott's statue of Captain Smith of the 'Titanic'. Past the garden, on the left, is the site of Garrick's childhood home. It is worth continuing a little beyond the entrance to the cathedral close to the house where Erasmus Darwin lived, on the right, and the 16C *Milley's Hospital*, on the left.

The *•Close* has half-timbered houses on Vicars' Close at the NW corner, and the *Deanery* (c 1700) and the former *Bishop's Palace* (1687–88), now the Cathedral School, on the N side. It makes a charming setting for the *•Cathedral*, built of red sandstone from nearby Borrowcop Hill and unique among medieval English churches in having three spires. The central one is a 17C restoration in the style of older W spires, just as the richly decorated *•W front is almost entirely a 19C reproduction of the 13–14C original. They are reminders that the building has been one of the most heavily damaged and restored English cathedrals.

Nothing visible survives of the Saxon church built after St Chad, Bishop of Mercia, moved his bishopric from Repton in the 8C, and only doubtful remnants of the Norman church that succeeded it. The earliest parts are the three W bays of the choir and the sacristy (1195–1208). These, like the transepts and chapter house (1240–50), are Early English, while the nave (1280) is early Decorated, and the Lady Chapel (1320–36) and presbytery (1337) are in the full Decorated style. The cathedral was twice besieged during the Civil War, in 1643 and again in 1646, when the central spire was destroyed and the interior badly damaged. Repairs began during the Restoration. James Wyatt saved the nave walls from collapse in 1795–98, removing much vaulting in the process. 19C restoration was begun by Sidney Smirke and continued after 1857 by Sir Gilbert Scott and his son John Olrid Scott.

Though long in proportion to its width, the interior is graceful and unified, carrying the eye along the unbroken vista of arches to the stained glass of the Lady Chapel. The *Nave*, built in the transitional period between Early English and Decorated, is richly ornamented. The fine carved capitals and stone roof bosses are original, but Wyatt substituted wood-and-plaster groining in most of the roof. The beautiful triforium, with dog-tooth moulding, is unusually large; the clerestory windows are of elaborate and uncommon design. Just inside the entrance, in the NW corner, are wall tablets to Anna Seward and Lady Mary Wortley Montagu (d. 1762), and in the SW corner, now the bookstall, a monument to Joseph Addison's father (d. 1703).

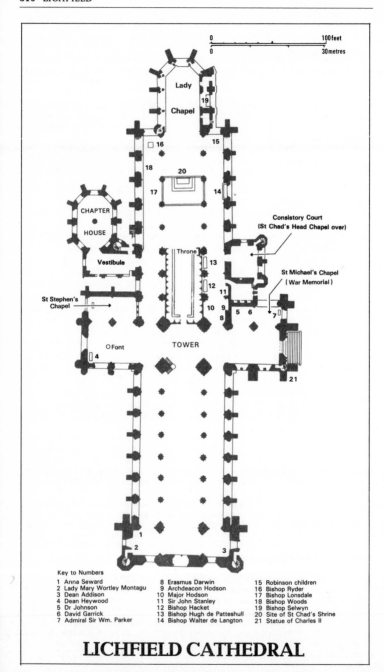

Consistory Court
(St Chad's Head Chapel over)

St Michael's Chapel
(War Memorial)

St Stephen's Chapel

CHAPTER HOUSE
Vestibule

Lady Chapel

Throne

TOWER

Font

Key to Numbers

1 Anna Seward
2 Lady Mary Wortley Montagu
3 Dean Addison
4 Dean Heywood
5 Dr Johnson
6 David Garrick
7 Admiral Sir Wm. Parker

8 Erasmus Darwin
9 Archdeacon Hodson
10 Major Hodson
11 Sir John Stanley
12 Bishop Hacket
13 Bishop Hugh de Patteshull
14 Bishop Walter de Langton

15 Robinson children
16 Bishop Ryder
17 Bishop Lonsdale
18 Bishop Woods
19 Bishop Selwyn
20 Site of St Chad's Shrine
21 Statue of Charles II

0   100feet
0   30metres

LICHFIELD CATHEDRAL

The *Transepts* (c 1220–40) are earlier than the nave, but their stone-vaulted roofs date from the late 15C and are lower than the originals (so the fine rose window in the S gable cannot be seen inside). The Perpendicular windows are 17C and the Early English ones 19C. The N transept has the skeleton monument of Dean Heywood (d. 1492). The S transept has a war memorial chapel, with busts of Johnson and Garrick by Westmacott and, behind the altar, the monument of the last survivor of Nelson's captains, Admiral Sir William Parker (d. 1866). The window above has some Herkenrode glass (see below).

The metal crossing screen (1859–63) was designed by Scott and made by Francis Skidmore of Coventry. The *Choir* is deflected 10° to the N from the line of the nave. The first three bays are Early English and the oldest part of the cathedral. Here the triforium is replaced by high arcaded windowsills with a passage through the piers. The tracery is 17C except for the fine Decorated window on the S side. The *S Choir Aisle* has a small two-storey extension (c 1225): the lower stage, now the consistory court, was the sacristy and the upper, with its charming minstrel gallery, was probably used for displaying St Chad's head to pilgrims. In the same aisle are a medallion to Erasmus Darwin; monuments to Archdeacon Hodson (d. 1855) and Major Hodson (d. 1858) by G.E. Street; the strange effigy of Sir John Stanley (d. 1515); the tomb of Bishop John Hacket (d. 1670), who restored the cathedral after the Civil War; effigies of Bishop Hugh de Patteshull (d. 1245) and Bishop Walter de Langton (d. 1321); and, at the E end, the finest of Sir Francis Chantrey's early works, his *monument to the Robinson children (d. 1812). The window above contains old Flemish glass. At the E end of the *N Choir Aisle* is one of Chantrey's last works, the monument of Bishop Ryder (d. 1836), beneath another window with old Flemish glass. Nearby are the effigy of Bishop Lonsdale (d. 1867) by G.F. Watts and a bust of Bishop Woods (d. 1953) by Epstein.

The Decorated *Lady Chapel* is a polygonal apse with nine tall windows resting on an arcade. The seven easternmost windows contain *glass (c 1530–40) brought from the Cistercian abbey of Herkenrode near Liège. The other two windows have glass of the same period. On the S are three mortuary chapels, one containing the effigy of Bishop Selwyn (d. 1878), after whom Selwyn College, Cambridge, is named.

The *Chapter House* is linked to the N choir aisle by a vestibule with canopied stalls. Completed in 1249, it is an irregular decagon with beautiful arcading and wonderfully undercut capitals, corbels and bosses. It contains the 8C Lichfield Gospels. The Library above has rare Bibles, a manuscript of 'The Canterbury Tales' and a copy of South's sermons (1694) used by Johnson in compiling his dictionary.

A pleasant walk from the Close skirts Stowe Pool on the way to (1m) *Stowe*, where St Chad's church is the burial place of Lucy Porter, Johnson's stepdaughter, and Catherine Chambers, servant to Johnson's parents. The Early English doorway, the Decorated E window and the font of 1455 are worth noting.

At *Wall*, by A5 2m SW, the remains of the Roman settlement of Letocetum include the baths and a museum of finds (EH, all year). *Hanch Hall* (open), 3½m NW of Lichfield off B5104, is 16–19C with a Queen Anne front. The grounds are a bird sanctuary. At *Mavesyn Ridware*, 3m further, the Old Hall has a 14C gatehouse (open by appointment).

From Lichfield to *Birmingham* and to *Burton-upon-Trent* and *Derby*, see Route 61.

Beyond Lichfield the heights of Cannock Chase appear on the left of A51. In the pleasant valley of the Trent, the Trent and Mersey Canal runs beside the river. 36m: *Rugeley* (24,300 inhabitants), with an old church, was home of the poisoner William Palmer, executed in 1856. It has a huge power station.

Cannock Chase, about 30,000 acres stretching between Lichfield and Stafford, was once a royal hunting forest and later a centre for mining coal and iron. It is high moorland with bracken, fern, a few surviving oaks, National Forestry Commission plantations of spruce and pine, and fallow deer.

Abbot's Bromley, beyond *Blithfield Reservoir* 7m N of Rugeley, has half-timbered houses and a church with a neo-classical tower of 1688. The ancient Horn Dance is held annually on the Monday following the first Sunday after 4 September. *Hoar Cross*, 3m E of Abbot's Bromley, has a Gothic Revival *church (1872–76) by G.F. Bodley. *Hoar

Cross Hall (limited opening) is a neo-Jacobean building of 1862–71 with chapel decorations by Bodley. *Needwood Forest*, with oaks and hollies, lies further E.

A51 continues directly from Rugeley to (15m) Stone. It passes (4m) *Great Haywood*, with the picturesque Essex Bridge and the junction of the Trent and Mersey Canal with the Staffordshire and Worcestershire Canal, and (10m) *Sandon*, with an extraordinary monument to Samson Erdeswicke (d. 1603) in the church on the edge of Sandon Park. The route makes a detour S to include Stafford, branching left from A51 at (38m) *Wolseley* along A513 and the N edge of Cannock Chase.

At (41m) *Milford* is the entrance to *Shugborough (NT and Staffordshire County Council).

Originally built for the Ansons at the end of the 17C, the house was several times enlarged, notably in 1745–48 by Thomas Wright of Durham and in 1790–1806 by Samuel Wyatt. Wright added the bow-windowed pavilions and Wyatt the portico, which together dominate the neo-classical entrance front. The interior has rococo plasterwork of the 1740s by Vassali and Wyatt's splendid Red Drawing Room, with French furniture and memorabilia of Admiral Lord Anson (1697–1762).

The service buildings house the *Staffordshire County Council Museum*, with exhibitions of domestic life, etc. The *Park Farm*, to the S, is a museum of agriculture.

Best of all are the *garden buildings added by James 'Athenian' Stuart in 1764–71, among the earliest Greek Revival work. The route through the park passes his Lantern of Demosthenes, Triumphal Arch and Temple of the Winds. His Doric Temple stands in the gardens N of the house, near the Shepherd's Monument, Chinese House, Chinese Bridge and Admiral Anson's monument to his cat. At the NE corner is the Essex Bridge (see Great Haywood above).

From Milford a sideroad leads N to (1½m) *Tixall*, where the 16C gatehouse survives from the house where Mary, Queen of Scots, was briefly held in 1586. *Ingestre*, 1½m further N, has a lovely church of 1676, probably by Wren, close to Ingestre Hall (pronounced 'Ingistry'; not open), with a Jacobean front.

45m: **Stafford** (56,000 inhabitants; TI), the ancient county town of Staffordshire, became a centre of shoe-making in the 18C and of electrical engineering in the 20C. It keeps some old houses.

The Market Square has the handsome former *Shire Hall* (1795; John Harvey). The main street, Greengate St., leads S. Set back from its right-hand side is the large and handsome parish church of *St Mary*, drastically restored by Sir Gilbert Scott in 1841–44, with a central tower, Early English nave and Decorated transepts. It contains a bust of Izaak Walton (1593–1683), a native of Stafford, who was baptised in the remarkable Norman font. Outside the W end are the foundations of St Bertelin's chapel (c 1000) and a replica of the wooden cross found when the site was excavated. Greengate St. continues past the half-timbered *High House* (1555), where Charles I and Prince Rupert lodged in 1642, and the *Swan Hotel*, where George Borrow was ostler in 1825. *St Chad's*, opposite, another church restored by Scott, has a Norman nave and elaborate chancel arch. Further S stands the former *Chetwynd House*, now the post office, where Sheridan used to stay while he was MP for Stafford (1780–1806). Tipping St., just beyond St Chad's, leads to Eastgate St., where the *William Salt Library*, in a beautiful 18C house, has valuable books and manuscripts about the county. Izaak Walton is said to have been born in a house that stood opposite.

The earthworks (open) of the Norman motte-and-bailey castle are 1¼m W, off A518, the Newport road.

FROM STAFFORD TO UTTOXETER, 15m by A518. 4m: *Hopton Heath* was the scene of an indecisive Civil War battle in 1643. At (5m) *Weston* A518 crosses A51. 6½m: The church at *Stowe-by-Chartley*, on the right, has a monument to Sir Walter Devereux (d. 1537) and his two wives, and two memorial tablets by Lutyens. 8m: On the left are the ruined 13C *Chartley Castle* and the 19C successor to the mansion where Mary, Queen of Scots, was held for eight months in 1586, before being taken to Fotheringhay. 15m: *Uttoxeter*, and on to Derby, see Route 68.

From Stafford to *Manchester* via the *Potteries*, see Route 67.

A34 runs due N from Stafford and bypasses (53m) *Stone* (12,000 inhabitants), where the painter Peter De Wint (1784–1849) was born.

At *Shallowford*, near *Norton Bridge* station about 3½m SW, Halfhead Farm was left to Stafford by Izaak Walton for charitable purposes but later sold. The house known as Izaak Walton's Cottage is a museum. *Eccleshall*, about 2m further W, has a fine Early English church and the remains of a castle of the Bishops of Lichfield. Near *Mill Meece*, 3m N of Eccleshall on the way back to A51, is a steam-powered pumping station of c 1905 (limited opening).

Beyond Stone A51 is followed left. The *Dorothy Clive Garden* (open), on the right near (66m) *Willoughbridge*, was begun in 1939. Beyond (68m) *Woore*, in the NE tip of Shropshire, the road enters Cheshire. 77m: **Nantwich** (12,000 inhabitants; TI) was once a centre of the salt industry, like Northwich and Middlewich. The 14C *Church* has *stalls with misericords and a rare stone pulpit. **Churche's Mansion* (1577), a merchant's house with superbly decorated half-timbering in Hospital St., survived the fire which swept the town in 1583. It is now a restaurant. There are many later Elizabethan and Georgian houses in High St. and Welsh Row. The herbalist John Gerard (1545–1612) was a native of Nantwich.

Dorfold Hall (limited opening), off A534 1m W, is a brick Jacobean house with original and 18C interiors. 3m further is *Faddiley* with, to its SW, the little late 17C *Woodhey Chapel* (limited opening).

FROM NANTWICH TO CONGLETON, 17½m by A534. 4m: *Crewe* (47,800 inhabitants) is a railway town, brought into being by the engine works of the old LNWR and the junction of the lines to Birmingham, Manchester, Liverpool and Chester. *Crewe Hall* (not open), to the E, is a 17C mansion rebuilt in the Jacobean style by E.M. Barry after a fire in 1866. 10m: *Sandbach* and (17½m) *Congleton*, see Route 67.

Beyond Nantwich A51 runs beside the Shropshire Union Canal, joined at (80m) *Hurlestone* by its Llangollen branch and at (81½m) *Barbridge* by its Middlewich branch. 83m: *Calveley*. *Bunbury*, 2m W, has a fine collegiate church, Decorated and Perpendicular, with the effigy of its founder, Sir Hugh Calveley (d. 1393). The SE chapel has a Perpendicular screen (1527). Beyond A49 about 2½m further W is *Beeston Castle* (EH, all year), built by the Earl of Chester in 1220 and dismantled in 1646. It stands dramatically on a red sandstone crag, and the *view across the Cheshire plain includes *Peckforton Castle* (not open), built by Anthony Salvin in 1844–50, to the S. A51 crosses A49 near (87m) *Taporley*, to the right, where the main street has handsome houses and the church good 17C monuments. At (91m) *Tarvin* the church has 14C woodwork and a 17C nave roof.

97m: **Chester**, see Route 63.

65

The Welsh Marches: Hereford to Chester via Ludlow and Shrewsbury

Directions. Total distance 94m. **Hereford**, see Route 56. A49 to (13m) Leominster (bypassed), (24m) **Ludlow** (bypassed), (40m) Church Stretton, (53m) **Shrewsbury** and (74m) Whitchurch (Route 62). A41 to (94m) **Chester**, see Route 62 and Route 63. A route through the traditional border country of England and Wales, now the W parts of Hereford and Worcester and of Shropshire.

Hereford, see Route 56. A49 runs N, through the Lugg valley. 1m: *Holmer* church has a detached half-timbered belfry. 6m: *Dinmore Manor* (open), just over 1m W, preserves a 12–14C chapel of the Knights Hospitaller. A49 goes over the wooded *Dinmore Hill* to (9m) *Hope-under-Dinmore. Hampton Court* (not open), ¾m E, is a castellated mansion built with the ransom of prisoners taken at Agincourt in 1415. *Bodenham*, 2m further SE, is charmingly placed on the Lugg.

13m: **Leominster** (9100 inhabitants; seasonal TI), pronounced 'Lemster', is a market town and centre for light industry on the Lugg. It has a number of Georgian and older houses, and a large **Church*, once part of a Benedictine priory, in every style from Norman to Perpendicular. The Norman work includes the nave on the N and the W doorway. The main nave, added in 1239 as the parish church, has a beautiful Perpendicular window. The 14C S aisle has ballflower ornamentation. In the park to the S stands the half-timbered *Grange Court*, the best of the town's old houses. It was built in 1633 by John Abel, the 'King's Carpenter', as the Market House and moved here in the 19C. The *Leominster Folk Museum* in Etnam St., just S of Corn Square, has local collections.

Weobley, 9m SW, has *half-timbered houses, some showing the early method of cruck construction. The 13–14C church with a graceful spire contains a memorial to the regicide Colonel John Birch (d. 1691). *Kinnersley Castle* (open for guided tours), 12m SW on A4112, is an old stone-built border castle rebuilt in the 16C.

FROM LEOMINSTER TO THE WELSH BORDER. A44 leads W to (5m) *Eardisland*, a village on the Arrow with half-timbered houses. *Burton Court* (open), c 1m S, is a modest late 18C house preserving a 14C hall. It contains European and Oriental costumes. 7½m: *Pembridge*, a large village, has a 16C market hall, half-timbered houses and a 14C church with a detached timber *belfry. *Shobdon*, 3m N beyond the airfield, has a Gothick church of 1755. 14m: *Kington* (2000 inhabitants) has some Georgian houses and another good church, Early English and Decorated. Mrs Siddons made her acting début in a barn here in 1772 or 1773. The golf course on *Bradnor Hill* (1284ft; NT), 1½m NW, is the highest in England. *Hergest Croft Gardens* (open), 1m W of Kington, have rhododendrons, azaleas and maple and birch woodland. *Cwmmau Farmhouse*, 4m SW of Kington, is an early 17C building (NT, limited opening and by appointment). For a continuation of the route to New Radnor and Rhayader, and for other routes from Leominster into Wales, see 'Blue Guide Wales'.

FROM LEOMINSTER TO LUDLOW VIA MORTIMER'S CROSS, 18m. A44, in the route to the Welsh border above, is followed to (4m) the junction with A4110, partly following the course of the Roman Watling Street. At (7m) *Mortimer's Cross* the Yorkists led by the future Edward IV defeated the Lancastrians in 1461. At *Aymestrey*, 1m N, the church has a 16C rood screen. From Mortimer's Cross B4362 turns right, passing an 18C watermill (EH, 1 April to 30 September, Thursdays, Sundays and Bank Holidays, 14.00–18.00). 8m: *Lucton* has a school building of 1708. 9m: *Croft Castle* (NT) keeps its 14–15C walls and corner towers, modified in the 16–17C. The interior was largely remodelled in the 18C, with plasterwork by Thomas Pritchard and a Gothick staircase. The little church in the grounds contains the elaborate tomb of Sir Richard Croft (d. 1509) and his wife. A path (1m) leads NW across the park to the large Iron Age hill-fort of *Croft Ambrey*. 11m: B4362 joins B4361. This route heads N. 13½m: *Richards Castle*, on the Shropshire border, has a Norman and 14C church with a detached tower, and (1m NW) a dilapidated motte-and-bailey castle. 18m: *Ludlow*, see below.

The main route passes (16m) *Berrington Hall* (NT) with a fine park, including an artificial lake, laid out by Capability Brown. The house, built by Henry Holland in 1778–81, has marble and plasterwork decoration. It contains 18C paintings of Admiral Rodney's naval battles. *Eye Manor* (not open), 1m W of Berrington Hall, was built in 1680 for Ferdinando Gorges, a West Indian slave-trader. The nearby church, with a 13C porch, contains two 16C alabaster monuments.

A49 enters Shropshire just before (20m) *Woofferton*, in the Teme valley.

FROM WOOFFERTON TO KIDDERMINSTER, 23m by A456. 4½m: *Burford House Gardens* (open), developed since 1954 in the grounds of an 18C house, have unusual plants and a collection and museum of clematis. 5m: **Tenbury Wells** (2500 inhabitants), which enjoyed a brief vogue as a spa in the mid 19C, has half-timbered inns from its days as a coaching stop on the road to Wales. The church contains interesting monuments. 17m: *Callow Hill* has the Visitor Centre for the *Wyre Forest*, 6000 acres stretching N of the road. 19m: **Bewdley** (8700 inhabitants; TI) is a quiet old town on the Severn which lost importance to Stourport (Route 66) in the canal era. It preserves a fine stone bridge (1795–98) by Thomas Telford and 'Georgian buildings on the High St., Load St. and Severnside. Load St. has the Guildhall of 1808 (now a crafts museum) and the George Hotel. The church (1745) is by E. and T. Woodward. The steam service along the *Severn Valley Railway* (Route 53) between Kidderminster and Bridgnorth stops at the station on the E bank of the river. Stanley Baldwin (1867–1947) was born at Bewdley. After it crosses the Severn A546 passes (20½m) the *West Midland Safari Park*. 23m: *Kidderminster*, see Route 66.

24m: **LUDLOW** (7500 inhabitants), on a hill overlooking the Teme and the Corve, is an attractive old place with a castle and half-timbered houses.

TI: Castle St. **Railway Station**: Station Drive, off Corve St. **Annual Event**: Ludlow Festival (music, exhibitions and a performance of Shakespeare in the castle) during last week of June and first week of July.

History. Corve St. and Old St. follow the line of prehistoric and Roman routes. There may have been an ancient settlement, but the present town owed its growth to the castle established c 1086 as a stronghold of the Welsh Marches and made the seat of the Lords President of the Marches in 1475. Built on a grid pattern still apparent today, Ludlow had walls and seven gates by the 14C. The wool trade which made it prosperous in the Middle Ages was replaced, from the mid 18C to the mid 19C, by glove-making and a reputation as a centre for the Shropshire gentry. The railway, which reached the town in 1851, took society further afield and Ludlow declined until the 20C brought light industry and tourism.

The centre is marked by the classical *Butter Cross* of 1743–44 by William Baker. The *Museum* in Church St., to the rear, has local history.

The large, mainly 15C church of **St Laurence**, to the N, testifies to the prosperity of Ludlow's wool trade in the Middle Ages. Note the crossing tower, the early 14C hexagonal porch, the 15C glass in the E window, the reredos, the screens and the monuments to officials and lords of the Welsh Marches in the chancel. The oldest tomb is that of Ambrosia (d. 1574), Sir

Philip Sidney's sister. The misericords include royal emblems, a fox preaching to geese, an alewife cast into Hell and a mermaid. The Lady Chapel has a 14C Jesse Window.

A.E. Housman (1859–1936) is buried in the churchyard beneath the N wall. Opposite the E end stands the picturesque *Reader's House*, a half-timbered Tudor building with a Jacobean porch, incorporating some fragments of a much older stone 'church house'. In the 18C it was the residence of the 'reader', an assistant to the rector.

High St. leads W from the Butter Cross to Castle Square. The *Castle Lodge* has 16C timberwork above 14C stonework.

The ruined *•Castle* (open) stands picturesquely on cliffs overlooking Ludlow's two rivers. Begun c 1086, it was expanded and altered until 1581 and partly dismantled after its capture by Parliament in 1646.

The large *Outer Ward* is entered by a late 12C gateway, above which were the rooms where Samuel Butler, then steward to the Earl of Carbery, wrote much of 'Hudibras' (1661–62). To the left are battlemented Tudor ruins. Ahead is the 13C *Mortimer's Tower*, allegedly the prison of Henry II's opponent Hugh de Mortimer. Beyond the dry inner moat is the smaller *Inner Ward*, entered by a 14C gateway with the arms of Elizabeth I and Sir Henry Sidney, Lord President of the Marches and father of Sir Philip Sidney. To the left of this is the oldest part of the castle, the late 12C Norman *Keep*, with a •view from the top. In the ward stands the exquisite late Norman •*Round Chapel*; the foundations of the chancel and apse on its E side have been exposed. The 13–14C buildings N of the chapel include, from W to E: the suite of rooms where Henry VIII's older brother Prince Arthur died in 1502, the year after his marriage to Catherine of Aragon; the roofless *Great Hall*, where Milton's 'Comus' was performed in 1634; a state apartment of unknown function; the *Armoury*; and the *Pendower Tower*, where the young Prince Edward and his brother were held for nearly ten years until 1483, when they were taken to the Tower of London and murdered.

Dinham runs from the SW corner of Castle Square to the 18C *Dinham House*, now a crafts centre, and the former *St Thomas's Chapel*, with 12C work. Mill St., running S from Castle Square, has Georgian houses.

There are excellent walks down the hill from the Butter Cross. King St. leads E to the Bull Ring, a wide street filled in during late medieval times. The *•Feathers Hotel* (1603) is the most lavish of Ludlow's half-timbered buildings. Corve St., partly Georgian and partly Tudor, with *Foxe's Almshouses* (1593) in stone and many half-timbered houses, leads to the 18C *Corve Bridge*. Old St. drops from the Bull Ring to the *Town Preacher's House* (c 1620) and the 14C *Lane's House*. To the right are fragments of the 13C town wall. •*Broad St.*, starting splendidly at the corner of King St. and running S from the Butter Cross, is one of the best streets in England. It descends through *Broad Gate*, the only survivor (much restored) of the town's seven gates, to the 15C *Ludford Bridge* (•view) on the Teme. The back lanes and alleys are worth exploring.

Ludford House (open by appointment), ½m S on B4361, dates back to the 12C. *Leintwardine*, on A4113 8½m W, is the site of the Roman Bravonium on Watling Street. The church has 15C stalls and the tomb of General Tarleton (1754–1833), who served in the American War of Independence. The return journey can be made via (12½m) *Wigmore*, with the ruined 12–14C castle of the Mortimers, and over the wooded *Bringewood Chase*, SW of Ludlow.

The **Clee Hills**, E and NE of Ludlow, can be explored by taking A4117, the Kidderminster road, and branching left at 1½m on B4364 towards Bridgnorth. *Titterstone Clee Hill* (1749ft; •view) rises to the S of the road, *Brown Clee Hill* (1790ft) to the N. From (10m) *Cleobury North* sideroads swing round Brown Clee Hill via (13m) *Ditton Priors* and (15½m) *Abdon. Heath*, 2m beyond, has a small but complete Norman chapel. B4368 is joined at (21m) *Diddlebury* in *Corve Dale*, the broad valley separating the Clee Hills from the long ridge of **Wenlock Edge** (800–950ft). *Aston Munslow*, ¾m to the right, has the *White House Museum of Buildings and Country Life*, with 13–18C buildings, farm equipment, etc. For the rest of the way to Much Wenlock, see Route 66. B4368 heads left to (27m) *Craven Arms* (see below), passing B4365 for (28½m) Ludlow.

FROM LUDLOW TO KIDDERMINSTER, 23m. A4117 goes along the S side of the Clee Hills via (12m) *Cleobury Mortimer* (2000 inhabitants), where the church has a Transitional Norman tower and good 13C work. Just before (17m) *Callow Hill* the detour from Woofferton described above is joined. 23m: *Kidderminster*, see Route 66.

26m: *Bromfield* has remains of a Benedictine priory, including the 12C gatehouse and the nave of the church, now part of the parish church. The painted ceiling is 17C. 30½m: *Stokesay Castle* (EH, summer season, daily; Wednesday to Sunday in winter, 10.00–16.00) is England's oldest, and probably finest, moated and fortified manor house.

The half-timbered gatehouse (1570) leads into the courtyard opposite the main range of buildings, a hall and solar flanked by two towers. This was largely built between 1285 and 1305, though the lower storeys of the N tower date from c 1240. The roof of the great hall probably includes some of its original timbers, and the solar has a medieval stone fireplace with a 17C Flemish overmantel.

31½m: *Craven Arms* (1400 inhabitants), named after its coaching inn, became important as a junction of the railway to central Wales.

Wenlock Edge (see above) rises to the NE. *Clun*, 8½m W of Craven Arms on B4368, is a remote little town with an old bridge, a ruined 12C castle (EH) and a poorly restored Norman church. A section of Offa's Dyke survives to the SW. *Caer Caradoc*, 3m SE of Clun, is one of many border and Welsh hill-forts bearing Caractacus' name. It may have been the scene of his defeat by the Romans in AD 50 (cf. Caer Caradoc near Church Stretton below). *Bishop's Castle*, 10m NW of Craven Arms, is a small town with old houses but no castle. *Walcot Hall* (limited opening), near *Lydbury North*, 4m SE of Bishop's Castle, is a Georgian house built for Clive of India. The hilly A488 heads NE to (23m) Shrewsbury, following the Welsh border for some of the way. It passes (6m) the little *Mitchell's Fold Stone Circle* (EH) on the left and, on the right in an area once mined for lead and barytes, the quartzite tors of *Stiperstones* (over 1700ft). *Minsterley, at 12m, has a 17C brick church.*

36½m: *Acton Scott*, right of A49, has a farm museum. 40m: **Church Stretton** (3900 inhabitants) stands at 650ft, below the moorland ridge of the *Long Mynd* (1700ft) to the W. The church has Norman work and a powerful 13C roof.

The greater part of the Long Mynd is NT (Information Centre in the Carding Mill valley). There are 15 prehistoric barrows, many either side of the Port Way. This ancient trackway, running the 7m length of the ridge, was used by prehistoric axe traders, became part of the drovers' route from Montgomery to Shrewsbury and still marks the parish boundaries.

The hill-fort at *Caer Caradoc* (1506ft), NE of Church Stretton, is another claimant to be the scene of Caractacus' defeat by the Romans (cf. Caer Caradoc near Clun above). The unclassified road branching right from A49 nearby follows the line of the Roman Watling Street, connecting Leintwardine and Wroxeter, through (4½m) *Frodesley* before veering away from its Roman course to (6m) **Acton Burnell**. The Early English church contains the *brass of Sir Nicholas Burnell (d. 1382), the finest 14C brass in England, and monuments to Sir Richard Lee (d. 1591) and Sir Humphrey Lee (d. 1632), ancestors of the American Confederate general Robert E. Lee. The monument to Sir Humphrey is by Nicholas Stone. *Acton Burnell Castle* (EH) is a ruined manor house built by Edward I's chancellor, Robert Burnell, in 1284. In the timber house which preceded it, he had the previous year entertained the king at the first Parliament to which the Commons were directly summoned. *Langley*, 1½m S, has a Tudor chapel with early 17C fittings (EH, all year). *Pitchford*, 1m N of Acton Burnell, has a church with a remarkable wooden effigy of a knight (c 1250), and a beautiful half-timbered manor house of 1473 (not open). A49 can be rejoined via *Condover*, 3m NW. The church has a late Norman N transept and a 17C nave formed by combining the early nave and N aisle after the fall of the central tower in 1660. Monuments include work by Roubiliac and G.F. Watts. Condover Hall, a stone house of 1598, is a school for handicapped children.

On the way into Shrewsbury A49 passes (44m) *Longnor*, where the timber-framed Moat House (limited opening) dates from the 15C. A49 is less interesting than the detour through Acton Burnell. 48m: *Stapleton*, to the left, has a 13C church originally built with two storeys, later combined. Mary Webb lived at (49m) *Lyth Hill*, to the left. *Bomere Pool*, to the right of (50m) *Bayston Hill*, is the 'Sarn Mere' of her novel 'Precious Bane' (1924). 51½m: *Meole Brace*, a suburb of Shrewsbury at the junction of A49 and A5, was Mary Webb's home in 1902–12. The 19C church where she was married has *glass by Morris and Co. (1870–72).

53m: **SHREWSBURY** (87,300 inhabitants), generally pronounced 'Shrozebury', is the county town of Shropshire. Its lovely position on a hill almost encircled by a loop of the Severn made it strategically important as a stronghold of the Welsh Marches. Shrewsbury's charm for visitors is the wealth of half-timbered houses and old streets, often quaintly named.

TI: The Music Hall, The Square. **Bus Station**: Raven Meadow. **Railway Station**: Castle Foregate. **Theatre**: Music Hall, The Square. **Annual Events**: Shropshire and West Midland Agricultural Show (May); Shrewsbury Regatta (May); International Music Festival (July); Shrewsbury Flower Show (August); British Isles Horse and Tractor Ploughing Championships (first Saturday in October).

History. Shrewsbury's history reflects the violent instability of the Marches in Saxon and Norman times. It may have been settled by local chieftains in the 5C and 6C and even in use as a hill-fort before then. Legend says that as Pengwern it became the seat of the Princes of Powys. Under Offa, King of Mercia, at the end of the 8C the settlement was known as Scrobesbyrig ('fort in the scrub'). The Normans changed this to Sloppesbury, from which 'Shrewsbury' and 'Salop' evolved. At the Conquest Shrewsbury was made part of the Marcher lordship belonging to Roger de Montgomery. It was captured by Llewelyn the Great in 1215 and 1232 and by rebellious barons in 1234. Edward I used it as the seat of his government during his subjugation of North Wales, executing Dafydd, the last royal Welsh prince, here in 1283. Henry Percy (Hotspur), with his father the Earl of Northumberland a leader of the rebellion against Henry IV, was defeated and killed in 1403 at the Battle of Shrewsbury, fought 3m N (see Battlefield church below). In the Tudor era the town traded in wool and flax with the Welsh, and it is from this period of prosperity that most of its half-timbered houses date. During the Civil War Charles I and Prince Rupert briefly made Shrewsbury their headquarters in 1642, and Prince Rupert returned in 1644, but the town fell to Cromwell's troops in 1645.

Natives, residents and visitors. Admiral Benbow (1653–1702), the composer Charles Burney (1726–1814) and Charles Darwin (1809–82) were natives. Sir Philip Sidney (1554–86) and Wilfred Owen (1893–1918) spent much of their youth here. Farquhar wrote 'The Recruiting Officer' (1706), set in Shrewsbury, while staying at the Raven Inn, which stood in Castle St. Lord Clive (Clive of India, 1725–74) was mayor in 1762 and MP from 1761 until his death. The novelist Mary Webb (1881–1927), who lived at Meole Brace and Lyth Hill (see above) and portrayed Shrewsbury as 'Silverton', is buried in the cemetery. See below for famous pupils of Shrewsbury School.

The centre is The Square, with a statue of Clive of India (1860; Marochetti) and the *Old Market Hall*, a stone building of 1596. On the S side is the *Music Hall* (1840), with the theatre and TI Centre. College Hill, further S, has the **Clive House Museum**, in a mainly 18C brick house which was Clive of

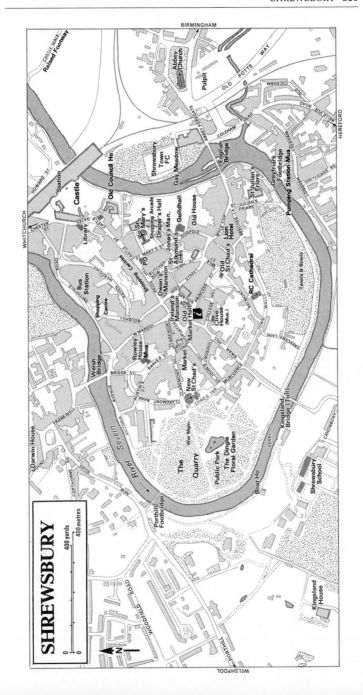

SHREWSBURY

India's Shrewsbury address when he was mayor. It has local history and ceramics (Caughley and Coalport ware).

A walking tour starts by turning left from The Square into High St., which descends between two of Shrewsbury's best half-timbered buildings, *Ireland's Mansion* (c 1580) on the left and *Owen's Mansion* (c 1592) on the right, to Pride Hill. Evans shop, opposite, incorporates part of the medieval *Bennet's Hall*, probably used as a mint by Charles I in 1642. Pride Hill climbs to the *High Cross* (1952; Laurence Gotch), on the site of the earlier cross where Hotspur's dead body was displayed in 1403.

Pride Hill is continued N by Castle St. and Castle Gates. On the right is the *Old Council House* (1625), the meeting place of the Council of the Marches, occupied by Charles I in 1642 and James II in 1687. Just beyond is the entrance to the **Castle**, housing the *Shropshire Regimental Museum*. It has had a chequered history. Completed by Roger de Montgomery in 1083, it was rebuilt by Edward I, partly dismantled after its capture by Parliament in the Civil War, modernised by Telford in 1790 and restored in the 20C. The gateway and part of the main walls survive from the Norman building and the hall, with alterations, from its Edwardian successor. The *Library* on the opposite side of the road occupies the old buildings (1630) of Shrewsbury School. In front is a statue of Darwin. The road goes on to the railway station.

From High Cross, St Mary's St. quickly reaches the redundant church of •**St Mary**, with its tall spire.

The sedile is Norman, the nave is Early English and the N aisle was rebuilt or restored during the Commonwealth. The •glass, from many sources, includes: a 14C Jesse window at the E end, from old St Chad's; 16C glass from St Jacques, Liège, in the Trinity Chapel; and panels made (1500) by the Master of St Severin of Cologne and brought from Altenburg, in the triple lancet on the N side of the chancel and the middle window of the S nave aisle. The Trinity Chapel has a 14C effigy of a knight and 14C alabaster carvings; the N chapel has a tablet to Admiral Benbow.

St Mary's Cottage and *Draper's Hall*, both half-timbered, stand immediately N and S of the church. Church St., opposite, leads to *St Alkmund*, rebuilt, except for its medieval tower, in 1795. Francis Eginton's E window is a copy of Guido Reni's Assumption. On the corner of Church St. and Butcher Row is the 15C *Jones's Mansion*, now a hotel, where Prince Rupert lodged in 1644. Butcher Row has 15C and 16C houses, notably the *Abbot's House* with medieval shopfronts, on the corner of Fish St.

St Mary's St. continues S as Dogpole, with the *Guildhall* (1696) and the *Old House*, occupied by Mary Tudor. At the bottom the street joins Wyle Cop opposite the *Lion Hotel*, a partly Tudor and partly 18C coaching inn. Its guests have included Thomas De Quincey, the future William IV, Dickens and Disraeli; Paganini and Jenny Lind both gave concerts here. Below the Lion is the half-timbered house where the future Henry VII lodged on his way to Bosworth Field. The *English Bridge*, built by John Gwynn in 1769 and widened in 1927, has handsome stonework.

Abbey Foregate, on the opposite bank, is the site of the monastery founded by Roger de Montgomery in 1083. Nothing remains of its domestic buildings except the little 14C *Reader's Pulpit* of the refectory, S of the road. 'The Shrewsbury Quest' is a historical display. The monastery is the setting for 'The Chronicles of Brother Cadford' by the Shropshire author Ellis Peters. Part of the hospitum and the **Abbey Church** survive.

Built of purple-brown stone, it has a Decorated W tower with a Norman base and doorway. The statue above the W window is said to be Edward III. The two W bays of the nave were rebuilt at the same time as the tower; the rest are powerful Norman work. The transepts and chancel, built by J.L. Pearson in 1886–88, considerably shorten the original length of the church. Opposite the N door are fragments from the shrine of St Winifred, showing figures of the saint with St John the Baptist and St

Beuno. The N aisle has a monument to Richard Onslow (d. 1571), Speaker of the House of Commons, and a 13C effigy of a lawyer. The tomb in the S aisle is said to be that of Roger de Montgomery. The war memorial under the tower remembers Wilfred Owen.

The *Coleham Pumping Station* (limited opening) in Longden Coleham, S of Abbey Foregate near the bridge, is a museum of trade and industry, with 19C sewage pumping engines. In Monkmoor Rd, a little beyond the Abbey Church, are the *Shire Hall* and *Whitehall*, a stone mansion of 1582. *Lord Hill's Column*, to the E, was erected in 1816 in honour of Viscount Hill (1772–1842), veteran of the Peninsular War.

The English Bridge leads back into Wyle Cop. Beeches Lane and its continuation as Town Walls branch left. E.W. Pugin's *Roman Catholic Cathedral* of 1856 is on the right; on the left are fragments and the only remaining tower (NT, open by appointment) of the old walls. Murivance continues to *New St Chad's* church, by George Steuart (1792), with a Doric façade and tower, and a circular nave. Below is the **Quarry**, a public park in the loop of the Severn. Its centrepiece, the Dingle, is a flower garden designed by Percy Thrower, parks superintendent in 1946–74.

Shrewsbury School stands on the hill across the river. Founded by Edward VI in 1552, it originally occupied the site of the library, by the castle. Its present buildings are mainly by Sir Arthur Blomfield (1882). Pupils have included Sir Philip Sidney (whose statue is in front of the school), Fulke Greville, Judge Jeffreys, Charles Burney, Charles Darwin and Samuel Butler (of 'Erewhon').

Claremont Bank brings us round to the *Welsh Bridge* (1795). On the opposite bank of the river, Frankwell and The Mount lead to *Darwin House*, Darwin's birthplace in 1809.

Barker St leads back from the Welsh Bridge to The Square. *Rowley's House Museum is a late 16C half-timbered house and its early 17C brick neighbour. Outstanding among the local history, geology, etc. are finds from Viroconium at Wroxeter (see below), which include Samian pottery, an inscribed tablet which stood over the entrance to the forum and a beautifully decorated silver mirror. The modern shopping centre, *New Market Hall*, leads to Shoplatch, from which Market St. goes back into The Square.

Haughmond Abbey (EH, all year) stands 4m NE on a rocky escarpment above the Severn. It was founded for Augustinian canons in 1135 and rebuilt towards the end of the century. Little is left of the 12C church, but remains of the monastic buildings include: the 14–15C abbot's lodging, with a graceful oriel window; the infirmary hall of the same dates; and the 12C chapter house, with a 16C ceiling and windows added when the abbey was converted into a mansion. *Atcham*, on A5 4m SE of Shrewsbury, has a sandstone bridge across the Severn (1771; John Gwynn) and the only church in the country dedicated to St Eata, with 16C glass. *Attingham Park* (NT), N of the village, is by George Steuart (1785) in grounds by Humphry Repton. It contains a picture gallery, largely hung with portraits, by John Nash (1807). **Wroxeter**, 1½m further E, is the site of the Romano-British Viroconium (EH, all year). Founded as a military garrison about AD 60, it developed into a tribal centre of the Cornovii before its decay and abandonment sometime after AD 400. A museum details its history. The chief remains are the 2C public baths and the colonnade of the forum. Wroxeter church has Saxon work using Roman stones and a Norman chancel with 16–18C monuments.

FROM SHREWSBURY TO OSWESTRY, 16m. A5 leads NW, crossing the Severn at (4m) *Montford Bridge*. 8½m: *Nesscliffe* lies at the foot of a wooded hill crowned by an earthwork. *Ruyton-XI-Towns*, 2m N, was formerly a borough made up of the 11 towns of the Manor of Ruyton. *Melverley*, on the Severn 4m SW of Nesscliffe, has a half-timbered church, 15C or early 16C. *Adcote* (open) in *Little Ness*, 2¾m E of Nesscliffe, is a country house of 1876–81 by Norman Shaw, now a school. At (13m) *West Felton* the route branches left from A5, passing the Shropshire Union Canal. 16m: **Oswestry** (13,200 inhabitants; TI) is an old border town and market centre. It is named after St Oswald, King of Northumbria, crucified here in 642 after being defeated by Penda, the pagan King of Mercia. Wilfred Owen (1893–1918) was a native. *Offa's Dyke* lies W of the town. *Old Oswestry* (EH), 1m N, is an Iron Age fort with an elaborate entrance and ramparts. Near *Weston Rhyn*, 4½m N of Oswestry, is *Tyn-y-Rhos Hall*, partly dating from 1711. *Whittington*, 3m NE of Oswestry, has the moat and 13C gatehouse of a castle built by the Peverels. *Ellesmere* (2500 inhabitants), 5m further NE, lies among several of the small meres on the Shropshire plain. From Oswestry to *Welshpool*, and from Whittington to *Chirk* and *Llangollen*, see 'Blue Guide Wales'.

FROM SHREWSBURY TO MARKET DRAYTON, 19m. A49 heads N through (3m) *Battlefield* (see below). A53, branching right, is followed for the rest of the way. 7½m: *Shawbury* has a late Norman church and an airfield. *Moreton Corbet Castle* (EH), 1½m N, has a ruined 13C castle keep and the shell of a house built in 1579. 13½m: *Hodnet* has good half-timbered houses. The church contains a monument by Chantrey to the hymn-writer Bishop Reginald Heber (1783–1826), rector here for 15 years. *Hodnet Hall*, built for the Hebers by Salvin in 1870, has 60-acre •gardens (open) with a 17C tithe barn and dovecote. *Hawkstone Park* (open), to the W, is a fine piece of 18C landscaping, with follies, centred on the ruins of the medieval Red Castle. 19m: *Market Drayton*, see Route 62.

FROM SHREWSBURY TO WOLVERHAMPTON, 30m. A5 passes (4m) *Atcham* and (5½m) *Wroxeter*, described above, where it picks up the Roman Watling Street. 11½m: *Wellington*, at the end of M54, is one of several older towns absorbed by the new industrial town of **Telford** (103,800 inhabitants; TI), whose centre lies beyond the motorway to the SE. Philip Larkin began his career as a librarian here. For the Ironbridge Gorge Museums on Telford's S edge, see Route 66. The **Wrekin** (pronounced 'Reekin'; 1334ft), 2m SW of Wellington, is an isolated extinct volcano with views from its summit. There are Georgian almshouses (1725) at *Preston-upon-the-Weald-Moors*, 4m NE of Wellington. *Rowton*, off A442 6m N of Wellington, was the birthplace of the Puritan divine Richard Baxter (1615–91). From (16m) *Oakengates*, on the E fringe of Telford, A464 leads SE. 19m: *Shifnal* has half-timbered and Georgian houses, which may have inspired the romantic description by Dickens in Chapter 46 of 'The Old Curiosity Shop'. The church of St Andrew, Norman to Perpendicular, has many monuments. A41 is joined at 26m. Route 62 goes to (30m) *Wolverhampton*.

From Shrewsbury to Worcester, see Route 66.

An attractive alternative to the main route N to Whitchurch described below takes A528 to (6m) *Harmer Hill* and follows B5476 through (10m) *Wem*, where William Hazlitt spent much of his youth, and (12m) *Ednaston*, where the church has a Norman door.

The main route follows A49. 56m: The church at *Battlefield*, left of the road, was founded in 1408 to commemorate the Battle of Shrewsbury, fought to the N and W in 1403. It marked the defeat of the rebellion against Henry IV by the Earl of Northumberland and his son Henry Percy (Hotspur). The church contains an early 15C Pietà in oak, probably from the chapel of the nearby moated mansion of *Albright Hussey*. 57½m: *Hadnall* church has a monument to the Peninsular War veteran Viscount Hill (d. 1842), who lived at Hawkstone Hall, further N. 63½m: *Preston Brockhurst* is 1½m E of *Clive Hall* (not open), birthplace of the playwright William Wycherley (?1640–1716). At (74m) *Whitchurch* the route joins Route 62. 94m: **Chester**, see Route 63.

66

Worcester to Shrewsbury

Directions. Total distance 48m. **Worcester**, see Route 54. A449 to (14m) Kidderminster. A442 to (27m) **Bridgnorth**. A458 to (35m) **Much Wenlock** (for **Ironbridge**) and (48m) **Shrewsbury**, see Route 65.

Worcester, see Route 54. A449 runs due N. 3m: *Hawford*, ½m E of the road, has a half-timbered 16C dovecote (NT). 5¾m: *Ombersley* (bypassed) has half-timbered houses. For Witley Court, 5m W, and Droitwich, 3m E, see Route 54. From (9m) *Crossway Green* A4025 bears left for (3m) *Stourport-on-Severn* (19,100 inhabitants), at the meeting of the Severn, the Stour and James Brindley's Staffordshire and Worcestershire Canal (1766–71), which brought it into being. Bewdley (Route 65) is on the Severn 3m upstream. 11½m: *Hartlebury Castle*, to the left, has been the residence of the Bishops of Worcester since the 13C. The state rooms (limited opening) include the 15C great hall and the 18C library built by Bishop Hurd. The N wing houses the *Hereford and Worcester County Museum* (open), devoted to rural crafts, domestic life, etc.

14m: **Kidderminster** (51,300 inhabitants; seasonal TI), known for its carpets, has little of interest except the *Church*, which contains a large early 15C brass and good monuments. Outside stands a statue of the Puritan divine Richard Baxter, minister here from 1641 to 1666. Another statue, beside the town hall, commemorates the postal reformer Sir Rowland Hill (1795–1879), a native of the town. Kidderminster Town Station, next to the BR station on A448 E of the centre, is the S terminus of the *Severn Valley Railway*, which runs a steam service (March to October) along the lovely route through (3½m) Bewdley to (16m) Bridgnorth.

The 16–18C *Harvington Hall* (open), off A448 3m SE, once home of the Catholic Throckmorton family, has priest holes and 17C wall paintings. The pleasant village of *Chaddesley Corbett*, about 1m further, has a Norman font in the church. *Kinver Edge* (NT), 4m N of Kidderminster, is a natural moorland park.

From Kidderminster to *Birmingham*, see Route 61; to *Bewdley* and *Woofferton*, and to *Ludlow*, see Route 65.

A442 runs parallel to the Severn and enters Shropshire. Beyond (23m) *Quatt* is *Dudmaston* (NT), a house of c 1700, perhaps by Francis Smith of Warwick. It contains fine furniture, Dutch flower paintings and modern art. There is a charming garden by the lake.

27m: **Bridgnorth** (11,100 inhabitants; TI) stands picturesquely on the Severn, which divides it into High Town on the W bank and Low Town on the E bank. The two are linked by steps and the steep Castle Hill Railway. High Town was defended by the *Castle* built in 1098–1101, perhaps on the site of a fort used by Alfred's daughter Ethelfleda and the Danes. It was blown up in 1646 after the siege by Parliamentarian troops, which did much damage elsewhere in the town. The only fragment to survive is the perilously leaning tower in the public park at the S end of High Town; there are views over the valley from here. Nearby is the church of *St Mary Magdalene*, designed by Thomas Telford in 1792–97 but with an apse added by Sir Arthur Blomfield in 1876. East Castle St., with the *Governor's*

House of c 1633, leads into the wide and pleasant High St. In the middle stands the *Town Hall* (1650–52), with a half-timbered upper storey on stone arches. Spanning the street beyond is the heavily restored 18C *North Gate*, now a local museum. Church St. leads into the little close surrounding *St Leonard*. Damaged in the Civil War, it has a nave roof of 1662 and contains 17–18C cast-iron monuments but is otherwise largely the result of Victorian rebuilding. *Baxter's House* was home of the Puritan Richard Baxter while he was rector in 1640. The house (1580) where Bishop Thomas Percy was born in 1729 stands near the bridge.

The station off Hollybush Rd, at the S end of High Town, is the N terminus of the *Severn Valley Railway* (see Kidderminster above). The locomotive sheds are open. The grounds of *Stanmore Hall*, on A458 1½m E, have the *Midland Motor Museum*.
From Bridgnorth to *Ludlow* over the Clee Hills, see Route 65.

A458 leads E from Bridgnorth. 30m: *Morville Hall* (NT, open by appointment only) is an Elizabethan house converted in the 18C. *Upton Cresset Hall* (limited opening), 2½m S by a winding sideroad, is a Tudor mansion with delightful chimneys and a detached gatehouse. The roof of the Great Hall can be seen in an upstairs bedroom. 36m: **Much Wenlock** (seasonal TI) is a little town with a good *Church*, Norman to Perpendicular, and a half-timbered *Guildhall* (open) resting on wooden pillars. *Wenlock Priory* (EH, all year) was founded in the 7C as a nunnery with St Milburga as abbess and refounded by the Mercian king Leofric c 1050. It became a priory for Cluniac monks after the Norman Conquest. The substantial remains include a good deal of the Early English church and the 12C chapter house, with Norman blind arcading. The 15C prior's lodging is now a private house.

Ironbridge (TI), on the S boundary of Telford 5m NE of Much Wenlock, was the birthplace of the Industrial Revolution and is now the best-preserved site of industrial archaeology in the country. The rich mineral deposits in the narrow gorge of the Severn were exploited by the first Abraham Darby (1678–1717), who smelted iron ore with coke rather than with the traditional charcoal at nearby Coalbrookdale in 1709. Fifty years later the second Abraham Darby (1711–63) succeeded in making iron suitable for forging as well as casting. In 1779 the third Abraham Darby (1750–89) spanned the river with the world's first *Iron Bridge* (EH). The **Ironbridge Gorge Museum* has restored and re-created the region's industrial past at several different sites. There is an information centre for visitors in the *Museum of the River*, W of the bridge. The *Coalbrookdale Museum of Iron*, ¾m NW of the bridge, explores the history of iron-making on the site of Darby's first blast furnace. E of the bridge are the 18C *Bedlam Furnaces* and the *Jackfield Tile Museum*, in the original Craven Dunnill works. The *Coalport China Museum*, 1½m E, is also devoted to the region's pottery industry, with restored factory buildings, a bottle kiln and displays of Coalport and Caughley ware. *Blists Hill Open Air Museum*, on the Shropshire Canal 1½m NE of the bridge, has re-created a small working community of the late 19C, with rebuilt cottages, shops and industrial buildings.

Buildwas Abbey (EH, all year) stands on the S bank of the Severn 2m W of Ironbridge and 2m N of Much Wenlock. It was founded in 1135 for Savignac monks, who merged with the Cistercians soon afterwards. The 12C ruins include the church, with sturdy piers in the nave, and the elegant chapter house. Thomas Telford's first iron bridge (1795–96), which stood nearby, has been demolished. The novelist Mary Webb (1881–1927) was born at *Leighton*, on the N bank of the Severn 2m further E. *Benthall*

The Iron Bridge

Hall (NT), 4m NE of Much Wenlock off the route to Ironbridge, is a 16C stone house with oak panelling, an oak staircase and decorated plasterwork. The nearby church was built in 1667 and altered in the 19C.

B4378 and B4368 head SW from Much Wenlock, following the S flank of *Wenlock Edge* (Route 65) down Corve Dale to (15m) *Craven Arms*. At 6m the route passes *Shipton Hall* (limited opening), a late 16C house with 18C remodelling inside. It resembles the remote *Wilderhope Manor* (NT, used as a youth hostel but limited opening), 2½m NW.

The main route from Much Wenlock continues on A458, crossing the NE end of Wenlock Edge. 42½m: *Cross Houses*. Near *Cantlop*, 2m SW, is a cast-iron bridge by Thomas Telford over Cound Brook (EH). 48m: **Shrewsbury**, see Route 65.

67

The Potteries: Stafford to Manchester

Directions. Total distance 55m. **Stafford**, see Route 64. A34 to (8m) Stone (Route 64), (18m) Newcastle-under-Lyme (for **Stoke-on-Trent**), (30m) Congleton and (55m) **Manchester** (Route 74).

Stafford and A34 to (8m) *Stone* (bypassed), see Route 64. The route continues N along the industrial valley of the upper Trent. 13m: *Trentham Gardens* (open), site of the mansion designed by Sir Charles Barry in 1833–42 and largely demolished in 1910, has grounds by Capability Brown (1759) and Victorian parterres by W.A. Nesfield. The mausoleum opposite the entrance is by C.H. Tatham (1807). 18m: **Newcastle-under-Lyme** (72,900 inhabitants; TI) is an industrial town with a wide High St. The *Borough Museum* in Brampton Park has local history.

The *University of Keele*, 3m W on A525, was founded as the University College of North Staffordshire in 1949 and granted its university charter in 1962. The buildings grouped around the 19C Keele Hall (by Salvin) include the chapel by George Pace (1964–65). *Whitmore* is a pleasant place 4m SW on A53, the road to Market Drayton (Route 62). The church has a half-timbered bell-tower restored in the 19C. The Mainwaring monuments include the alabaster tomb of Edward Mainwaring (d. 1586) and his wife. *Whitmore Hall* (limited opening) is timber-framed, with a handsome brick front added in 1676. The stable block is late 16C.

The **Potteries**, adjoining Newcastle to the E, are the national centre of the industry from which they take their name. Familiarly known as 'The Five Towns', they consist in fact of six large towns stretching for about 8m along the A50: from S to N, Longton, Fenton, Stoke-upon-Trent, Hanley, Burslem and Tunstall. This ungainly sprawl, amalgamated into **Stoke-on-Trent** in 1910, is now a city of 252,400 people.

Pottery has been made here since the Middle Ages but the industry received its first great impetus when Josiah Wedgwood (1730–95) opened his factory at Etruria in 1769. Other famous names established by the late 18C were Davenport, Minton, Spode and Copeland; Doulton came from London in the 19C. They flourished not so much because of the local marl clay, suitable only for the coarsest ware, but because of the Staffordshire coal needed for firing. China clay was brought from Devon and Cornwall, ball clay from Dorset, flints from Norfolk and felspar from Derbyshire. Brindley's Trent and Mersey Canal was complete by 1777. In the 19C the region became notorious for industrial pollution, its landscape scarred by colliery spoil heaps, marl holes, scraff heaps of broken crockery and above all by smoke from the chimneystacks and distinctive bottle kilns of the 'pot banks'. Arnold Bennett (1867–1931), a native of Hanley, vividly paints this picture in his novels and stories. The Potteries today look very different: electric firing has replaced coal, bottle kilns have all but disappeared, and much of the industrial landscape has been imaginatively reclaimed to make public parks. The chief interest for visitors is the wealth of museums. The Gladstone Pottery Museum at Longton provides an excellent historical introduction, and there are fine collections of pottery, porcelain and ceramics at the City Museum in Hanley as well as at the various factory museums. Many factories also have shops and tours; full details are available from the TI Centre in Stoke.

Stoke (TI) lies 2m E of Newcastle by A52. The church of *St Peter* (1826–29) contains memorials to Josiah Wedgwood, with a portrait medallion by Flaxman, and Josiah Spode II (d. 1827). Some arches of the medieval church survive outside. The *Minton* works in London Rd have a good museum, and there is another at the *Wedgwood Visitor Centre* in *Barlaston*, 4m S. **Fenton**, 1m SE, is the smallest of the towns. The *Coalport* works include a craft centre demonstrating traditional skills. At **Longton**, 1m further SE, the *Gladstone Pottery Museum* occupies a Victorian pot bank with restored bottle kilns, engine house and workshops. Working demonstrations and displays bring the history of the industry to life. At *Weston Coyney*, 2m E of Fenton, old sand quarries have been landscaped as the *Park Hall Country Park*, with good views.

Hanley, beyond *Hanley Park* N of Stoke, is the centre of the region and the largest of its towns. The *City Museum and Art Gallery* in Broad St. has major collections of pottery and porcelain, chiefly from Staffordshire, and of ceramics from many countries, together with exhibits of local history. English 20C painting and English watercolours are strongly represented in the art galleries. Arnold Bennett's childhood home was at 205 Waterloo Rd, N of the centre. At *Etruria*, about 1m SW on the A53 to Newcastle, Josiah Wedgwood opened his factory in 1769 and built his home, Etruria Hall. He chose the name in the mistaken belief that the classical vases which he copied came from Etruria. The *New Victoria Theatre* is beyond.

Burslem, N of Hanley and the *Central Forest Park*, is called the 'Mother of the Potteries'. Josiah Wedgwood was born here and had his first factory on the site of the *Wedgwood Institute* (1869), with handsome terracotta decoration, in Queen St. It housed the school which Arnold Bennett attended. The *Sir Henry Doulton Gallery* in Nile St. displays the firm's ware. *Smallthorne*, about 1½m NE, has the half-timbered *Ford Green Hall*, now a folk museum. A50 continues N from Burslem to (1m) **Tunstall**. The *Chatterley Whitfield Mining Museum*, with underground tours, is off A527 2m NE. The Grange Garden (NT) N of *Biddulph*, 2m beyond, is a rare Victorian survival. The canal-builder James Brindley (1716–72) is buried at *Newchapel*, off A34 2m N of Tunstall.

FROM STOKE TO LIVERPOOL, 49m. A50 goes N from Stoke through Burslem and Tunstall and crosses A34 (see below). At (9m) *Rode Heath* A533 is followed left. For Rode Hall, to the E, see the main route below. 13m: *Sandbach* (14,700 inhabitants; TI) is an old town with two reconstructed Saxon *crosses (EH). 18m: *Middlewich* (8200 inhabitants) was a Cheshire salt town, like (24m) *Northwich*, described in Route 63. 36m: *Runcorn* (64,400 inhabitants; TI), greatly expanded since the 1960s, is a chemical manufacturing town on the Manchester Ship Canal and the Mersey, crossed by a railway bridge (1864–68) and road bridge (1961; Mott, Hay and Anderson). The remains of the 12C *Norton Priory* (open) are off A558 3m E. The site has a Norman doorway and a museum of finds, including mosaic tiles, and monastic life. 37m: *Widnes*, and on to (49m) *Liverpool*, see Route 75A.

From Stoke to *Derby*, see Route 68; to *Ashbourne* via *Alton*, see Route 69B.

Beyond Newcastle A34 crosses the North Staffordshire coalfield and enters Cheshire. 25m: *Scholar Green*.

Mow Cop (1091ft; NT), to the E, is crowned with a sham ruin of the early 1750s. *Rode Hall* (limited opening), ¾m to the W, is a much altered house of c 1700 with work by Lewis Wyatt.

27m: *Little Moreton Hall* (NT) is probably the best and certainly the most striking half-timbered manor house in the Midlands. The range with the Great Hall was built in the late 15C and altered in 1559; the other buildings around the courtyard, including the Long Gallery, were added by 1580. 29m: *Astbury* has a Decorated and Perpendicular church with 17C furnishings. 30m: **Congleton** (23,800 inhabitants; TI), a silk and cotton weaving town in the 19C, has old inns. From Congleton to *Nantwich*, see Route 64. 36½m: *Capesthorne Hall* (open), on the left, is an 18C house by Francis and William Smith of Warwick, rebuilt in the Elizabethan style by Blore in 1837–39 and Salvin in 1861. The chapel of 1720 survives nearby. From the park there is a view of the radio telescopes at *Jodrell Bank* (open), 3m W on A535. The dish of the main telescope is as big as the dome of St Paul's Cathedral. There is a planetarium and science museum. 38½m: *Nether Alderley* has a restored 15C watermill (NT). 40½m: *Alderley Edge* was developed in the 19C. Dean Stanley (1815–81) was born at the rectory. The church has a window (1873) by Morris and Co. The Edge (650ft; partly NT) is a wooded sandstone escarpment with fine views. *Over Alderley*, 2½m E, has the delightful walled garden of Hare Hill (NT). 42m: **Wilmslow** (30,200 inhabitants).

* *Styal* (NT), in the pretty valley of the Bobbin 1½m N, is a wonderfully complete factory community of the early Industrial Revolution centred on the Quarry Bank Mill (1784), now a museum with the water wheels which powered the cotton looms restored to working order. *Lindow Moss*, 1½m W of Wilmslow, has given its name to 'Lindow Man', an ancient body found preserved in a bog here in 1984. *Mobberley*, 4m SW of Wilmslow on the way to Knutsford, has a church with a timber roof of 1450, rood screen of 1500 and memorial window to George Leigh Mallory (1886–1924), who died climbing Everest.

44m: *Handforth*. Handforth Hall (open by written appointment) is an Elizabethan manor house. At (47m) *Cheadle* A34 reaches the suburbs of Manchester. 55m: **Manchester**, see Route 74.

68

Leicester to Derby and Sheffield

Directions. Total distance 63m. A useful connecting route through the centre of the Midlands, dull in itself but giving access to the Peak District (Route 69). M1, following a roughly parallel course, is the fast alternative. **Leicester**, see Route 59. A6 to (11m) Loughborough and (27m) **Derby**. A38, A61 to (51m) Chesterfield. A61 to (63m) **Sheffield**, see Route 75G.

Leicester, see Route 59. Belgrave Rd or St Margaret's Way lead from the inner ring road to A6. 4m: At *Wanlip*, near the Soar and the Grand Union Canal to the right, the brass of Sir Thomas Walsh (d. 1393) in the church is the earliest with an English inscription. At (5m) *Rothley*, on the left, the partly Elizabethan Rothley Court Hotel has the chapel of a preceptory of the Knights Templar. Thomas Babington Macaulay (1800–59) was born here. The parish church has Babington monuments and, outside, a 10C cross. A steam service runs along a reopened section of the Great Central Railway via Woodhouse and Quorn to Loughborough (weekends and Bank Holidays). 6½m: *Mountsorrel* is known for its red granite. 8m: *Quorndon*, or *Quorn* (pronounced 'Corn'), has good 16C tombs in the church.

The kennels of the Quorn hunt are now at *Seagrave*, 4½m E, via (1m) *Barrow-upon-Soar*, where the church has a Perpendicular wooden roof. From Quorn B591 goes W into *Charnwood Forest* (Route 59).

11m: **Loughborough** (47,600 inhabitants; TI), a dull red-brick town, is known for Taylor's bell foundry in Freehold St, with a museum and guided tours for parties. The *War Memorial Tower* (1922–23) in Queen's Park has a carillon of 45 bells. *All Saints* is a spacious Decorated and Perpendicular church restored by Sir Gilbert Scott. *Loughborough University of Technology*, on the Leicester road, was founded as the College of Technology in 1909 and raised to its present status in 1964.

FROM LOUGHBOROUGH TO NOTTINGHAM, 15m by A60. It crosses the Soar and enters Nottinghamshire beyond (3m) *Hoton*. 8m: The attractive village of *Bunny*, rebuilt by the 'wrestling baronet' Sir Thomas Parkyns (1664–1741), has a 14C church with a noble chancel. 10m: *Ruddington* has two museums, one devoted to local history and the other to framework knitting. 15m: *Nottingham*, see Route 70.

A6 descends the Leicestershire bank of the Soar to (16m) *Kegworth*, with a late Decorated church and 19C buildings once used for framework knitting. The church at *Kingston-on-Soar*, on the Nottinghamshire bank to the E, has a 16C chantry displaying the rebus (babe in tun) of the Babington family. From the large junction with M1 N of Kegworth, A453 leads SW to (1½m) *East Midlands Airport*, with passenger services to Aberdeen, Amsterdam, Belfast, Brussels, Dublin, Edinburgh, Glasgow, Guernsey, Jersey, Paris and the Shetland Islands. The Aeropark has aviation exhibits and an information centre. At *Castle Donington*, to the N, is the International Motor Sport Centre with a racing circuit and the Donington collection of racing cars and motor cycles. For A453 to *Ashby-de-la-Zouch* and to *Nottingham*, see Route 70.

17m: *Lockington*, to the left beyond the junction with M1 and A453, has fine woodwork in its church. A6 crosses the Trent, marking the Derbyshire border, and the Trent and Mersey Canal to (21m) *Shardlow*, with a museum of canal history. 23m: *Elvaston Castle Country Park* has beautiful gardens, a working estate museum, etc. The County Show takes place here on Spring Bank Holiday Monday.

27m: **DERBY** (215,700 inhabitants) is the county town of Derbyshire, though no longer the seat of its administration. Given its historic importance and its size, it has surprisingly little to attract visitors. To many it is simply a convenient gateway to the Peak District (Route 69). Apart from the cathedral (originally built as a parish church) and a few 18C buildings (chiefly on Friar Gate), the most interesting aspect of Derby is its varied industrial history, to which the Industrial Museum gives a good introduction.

TI: Assembly Rooms, Market Place. **Bus and Coach Station**: Morledge. City buses also from Market Place. **Railway Station**: Midland Rd, SE of the centre. **Theatre**: Playhouse, Eagle Centre.

History. The Roman station of Derventio was at Little Chester on the opposite bank of the Derwent. In 854 the town was taken by the Danes, who renamed it Deoraby and made it (with Nottingham, Leicester, Lincoln and Stamford) one of the five cities of the Danelagh. Recaptured by the Saxons in 917, it became an important centre in the Middle Ages. In 1745 Prince Charles Edward Stuart penetrated as far south as Derby with his Highland army, but after two days was forced to begin the retreat to Scotland, where the disaster of Culloden awaited him. The silk mill started by John and Thomas Lombe in 1717–21, on the site of the present Industrial Museum, was not just the first to succeed in England but also the first true factory. William Duesbury established the Royal Crown Derby works (now part of the Royal Doulton Tableware Group) in the 1750s. The 19C made Derby a centre of the Midland Railway, with large engineering workshops, and Rolls-Royce Ltd moved here in 1908, two years after its foundation.

Natives and visitors. The painter Joseph Wright ('Wright of Derby'; 1734–97) was born in Iron Gate, Herbert Spencer (1820–1903) in Exeter St. and John Flamsteed (1646–1719), the first Astronomer Royal, at *Denby*, 6½m N. Samuel Johnson married Tetty Porter at St Werburgh's in 1735.

London Rd runs towards the centre past Midland Rd, leading to the railway station on the right, and the *Royal Infirmary* (1891) on the left. Beyond the inner ring road lie the heavily restored 14–15C church of *St Peter* on the left, with a *Heritage Centre* in the Tudor grammar school building, and the Eagle Centre shopping precinct on the right. Cornmarket leads straight ahead into the older shopping area around the Market Place. A devious walk turns left into Victoria St. Between Wardwick and the Strand, beyond, are the *Library* and the **Museum and Art Gallery**.

The *Museum*, largely devoted to local history, has a working model showing the development of the Midland Railway, two natural history galleries and a collection of Blue John. The Prince Charlie Room has oak panelling from Exeter House, where the Young Pretender lodged in 1745. The *Art Gallery* has Derby porcelain and paintings by Joseph Wright.

Nearby *St Werburgh's*, now a shopping arcade, was the scene of Dr Johnson's wedding. It stands at the beginning of Friar Gate, whose 18C houses make it the most handsome street in Derby. *Pickfords House* is a museum of Georgian life

The walk continues N on Bold Lane and turns right into St Mary's Gate, with the handsome *Crown Court*, formerly the *County Hall*, of 1660. At the end rises the lovely Perpendicular *tower of the **Cathedral**. Originally the parish church of All Saints, it was raised to cathedral rank when the diocese was separated from Southwell in 1927.

The tower, built c 1510–30, is all that survives of the medieval church. The rest was demolished to make way for James Gibbs's nave (1723–25); the E end, by Sebastian Comper with windows by Ceri Richards and Patrick Reyntiens, was added in 1965–72. The chief feature inside is the wrought-iron *screen by the local crafstman Robert Bakewell (d. 1752), stretching the full width of the church. The monuments include the effigy tomb of 'Bess of Hardwick' (Elizabeth, Countess of Shrewsbury; d. 1608) in the S choir aisle and, next to it, the figure of Caroline, Countess of Bessborough (d. 1760) by Rysbrack.

Queen St. leads N from the cathedral. Off Full St. to the right is the **Derby Industrial Museum**, in a partly rebuilt version of the silk mill which John and Thomas Lombe opened in 1717–21. The ground floor contains Rolls-Royce aero engines, while the first floor illustrates Derbyshire's wide variety of industries. The first floor also houses the story of railway engineering in Derby from 1839 to the latest research. Queen St. continues to the junction with the inner ring road, spanned by a footbridge leading to Pugin's *Roman Catholic Church* (1838). Between the 18C St Mary's Bridge and the modern bridge carrying the ring road across the Derwent is the 14–15C *Chapel of St Mary on the Bridge*, one of the few surviving bridge chapels in England.

Iron Gate leads down the hill from the cathedral to the Market Place. The *Guildhall* (1842) has been renovated as a concert hall, etc. Behind is the huge barrel-vaulted *Market Hall* (1864), recently restored. On the E side of the square are the *Assembly Rooms* (1970; Casson, Conder and Partners).

The *Royal Crown Derby Works* in Osmaston Rd includes a museum of Derby china from the 1750s; there are tours of the factory. Behind is the *Arboretum*, landscaped by J.C. Loudon in 1840.

Kedleston Hall (NT) stands about 4½m NW of the city. It was built in 1759–65 by Robert Adam, succeeding James Paine and Matthew Brettingham as architect. He modified the original Palladian design to create a masterpiece in his own more sumptuous style. The interior, decorated by Adam with plasterwork by Joseph Rose, has a *Marble Hall with columns of local alabaster and a central rotunda. There are

18C furniture, Italian and Dutch 17C paintings and a museum of Indian art collected by Marquess Curzon of Kedleston (1859–1925) while he was Viceroy of India. The large park has buildings by Adam, including a bridge over the lake and a boathouse. The church has Curzon tombs from the 13C onwards.

Churches near Derby include: *Chaddesdon*, a large suburb 2m NE, rebuilt c 1357 with a screen and a wall lectern, a local characteristic; *Breadsall*, 2½m NE, rebuilt by Caröe in 1915 after arson by suffragettes but keeping its Norman doorway and 14C spire; and *Morley*, 4m NE, with *monuments and 15C glass from Dale Abbey, near Ilkeston (Route 70).

FROM DERBY TO NOTTINGHAM, 16m by A52. At (8m) *Sandiacre*, N of the junction with M1, the church has a 14C chancel. A52 continues through *Beeston* to (16m) *Nottingham* (Route 70).

FROM DERBY TO ASHBY-DE-LA-ZOUCH, 14m. A514 heads S to (5m) *Swarkestone*, where the long 14C bridge over the Trent was the southernmost point reached by the advance guard of Highland rebels in 1745. Beyond (6m) *Stanton-by-Bridge* B587 branches left for the pleasant small town of (7m) *Melbourne*, where the pioneer travel agent Thomas Cook (1808–92) was born. The church has a Norman *interior with mighty arcades. *Melbourne Hall* (limited opening), a 17–18C building with work by Francis Smith of Warwick and his son, was home of two Victorian Prime Ministers, Lords Melbourne and Palmerston. The formal gardens of 1700, overlooking a lake, include a wrought-iron arbour (1706–11) by Robert Bakewell. At *Ticknall*, on A514 2m SW, is the entrance to *Calke Abbey* (NT), a country house largely built in 1701–03 and left virtually unaltered since 1924. Restoration, since the NT opened the property in 1989, has rescued the main state rooms and put some of the house's remarkable contents on view. Visitors are also likely to be intrigued by continuing work on other parts of the house, including the kitchens and servants' quarters. B587 continues to (10m) *Staunton Harold*, where the church (NT) is one of the few built during the Commonwealth. It stands picturesquely beside the 18C Hall (now a Cheshire Home) and above a lake. 11m: The route joins A453, heading SW to (14m) *Ashby-de-la-Zouch* (Route 59).

FROM DERBY TO STOKE-ON-TRENT, 33m. W of Derby A516 branches from A38 and joins A50 at (10m) *Hatton*, on the N bank of the Dove. **Tutbury**, on the Staffordshire bank 1½m S, is known for its alabaster. Mary, Queen of Scots, was a prisoner in the 14–15C castle, now ruined but with 18C additions. The church is the nave of a Benedictine priory founded c 1080, with a Norman *W door of c 1160. 13m: *Sudbury*, left of A50, has a charming village street. *Sudbury Hall* (NT) is a red-brick Restoration house with good plaster decoration and woodcarving inside, including work by Grinling Gibbons. A servants' wing is a Museum of Childhood. The church at *Hanbury*, 3m SE, claims to have the oldest alabaster effigy in England, of Sir John Hanbury (d. 1303).

The route enters Staffordshire before (18m) **Uttoxeter** (9000 inhabitants), where Dr Johnson stood bareheaded in the rain in the market place to expiate his refusal to attend his father's bookstall some 50 years earlier. A bas-relief on the conduit depicts the incident. *Checkley*, on the former course of A50 4m NW, has a church with a Decorated chancel, old glass and three late Saxon crosses. From Uttoxeter to *Ashbourne*, see Route 69B; to *Stafford*, see Route 64.

A50 continues to (27m) *Blythe Bridge*. At *Dilhorne*, 2m N, the Foxfield Railway Society has a museum of steam locomotives, with trips on a former mineral line. A50 enters the Potteries at (29m) *Longton*. 33m: *Stoke*, see Route 67.

From Derby to *Lichfield* and *Birmingham*, see Route 61; to *Manchester* via *Matlock*, *Bakewell*, and *Buxton*, see Route 69A, via *Ashbourne* and *Leek*, see Route 69B.

A38 is joined N of Derby. At Butterley Station near (37m) *Ripley* (18,700 inhabitants) the Midland Railway Centre has steam locomotives and rolling stock from the old LMS railway, with a 3m section of working line. 40m: *Alfreton* (23,100 inhabitants) is a colliery town. A615 leads NW to (8m) *Matlock* (Route 69A). A61 continues N via (44m) *Ogston Reservoir*, on the left, and (46m) *Clay Cross* (9300 inhabitants).

51m: **Chesterfield** (70,500 inhabitants; TI) is famous for the twisted spire of its parish church, caused by the warping of the timbers beneath the lead covering. Inside, the building (c 1350) has good window tracery and 16C tombs. The *Peacock Heritage Centre*, in a half-timbered 16C building on Low Pavement, has local exhibits. George Stephenson (1781–1848), who lived 1m NE at Tapton House, is buried in the 19C *Holy Trinity* on Newbold Rd. The *Stephenson Memorial Hall* houses a civic theatre.

A632 leads E across the colliery-dotted *Scarsdale* to (6m) *Bolsover* (Route 71A); A617 leads SE to (12m) *Mansfield* via *Hardwick Hall* (both Route 71A).

At (53m) *Old Whittington*, to the right of A61, the plans for the overthrow of James II in 1688 were arranged in Revolution House (open), formerly an inn. 57m: The church at *Dronfield* (23,300 inhabitants) has a 14C chancel with the brasses (1399) of two brother priests on the same slab, said to be a unique occurrence.

63m: **Sheffield**, Route 75G.

69

—

The Peak District

Maps: OS Peak District Tourist map (1:63,360 or 1in to 1m) for the National Park and its fringes. Walkers need the OS Outdoor Leisure maps (2½in to 1m) for the Dark Peak and the White Peak.

The *Peak District stands at the S end of the Pennine Chain, bounded roughly by the cities of Derby in the S, Manchester in the NW and Sheffield in the NE. Though it is also often called the Derbyshire Peak, its characteristic scenery extends into Staffordshire in the S and W and, to a lesser extent, into Cheshire in the W, Greater Manchester and West Yorkshire in the N, and South Yorkshire in the NE. About 555 square miles are included in the Peak District National Park, the first National Park to be created under the Parliamentary Act of 1949 and still one of the largest. Its boundaries are marked by the distinctive roadside millstones which greet the many visitors it attracts. On the map the park forms a large oval shape, slightly dented in the SE to exclude the industrialised country around Matlock and Wirksworth and, for similar reasons, more dramatically deformed in the W to omit the wedge of land from Buxton to Whaley Bridge and New Mills. Buxton, though popular as a touring centre, thus lies outside the park. The largest town inside its boundaries—indeed, the only town of any size—is Bakewell.

There is no single hill or range of hills known specifically as the Peak. Rather, the whole region belongs to what geologists call the 'Derbyshire Dome', a conical mass of rock forced up from the bed of the warm, shallow sea that once covered it. The upper stratum was gritstone, also known as millstone grit from its most obvious use for making millstones; beneath lay whitey-grey carboniferous limestone. The way that different parts of this dome have weathered largely accounts for the two distinct types of landscape. Millstone grit survives in the Dark Peak of the W, E and N, creating a wild, treeless scenery of moorland which rises over 2000ft at a few points, notably Kinder Scout. The hills are often guarded towards their summits by low, black lines of crag locally called 'edges' (e.g. Froggatt Edge in the E, and Axe Edge in the W). This country is particularly attractive to determined walkers and climbing enthusiasts. In the centre and S of the region is the White Peak, still hilly but gentler and more accessible, where the millstone grit has been worn away to expose the limestone. The green uplands of this plateau are divided by loose stone walls, built without mortar, into a chequer of fields. In the valleys, the Dove, the Manifold and the Wye have forced their way through the limestone to create the Dales: narrow ravines, often pleasantly wooded and fringed by white cliffs and striking rock formations.

Both the desolate country of the Dark Peak and the gentler landscape of the White Peak have been popular with visitors since the 17C, when Thomas Hobbes and Charles Cotton enumerated their 'wonders' and Cotton fished the trout waters of the Dove with Izaak Walton. By the Romantic era the Peak District was valued, like the Wye Valley and the Lake District, as a miniature equivalent of the Alps. The list of its wonders extended beyond natural features like Mam Tor (the 'shivering mountain' near Castleton), the limestone caverns near Buxton and Castleton, and the spring at Buxton to include the Duke of Devonshire's mansion at Chatsworth. A welcome feature of recent years has been the new awareness of the Peak's industrial heritage: Arkwright's water-powered cotton mill at Cromford, the lead mines around Matlock and Castleton, and the canal and railway systems, including the Monsal Dale railway viaduct. Fittingly, dismantled railway lines now form the High Peak, Tissington and Monsal Trails, which give a pleasant and easy introduction to walking in the region.

The custom of well-dressing, observed or revived in towns and villages throughout the region, probably originated as a pagan thanksgiving for water. The wells are decorated with flower petals pressed into a clay base to form pictures or designs, which are then blessed at a religious service. Ceremonies are held in May at Tissington (Ascension Tide), Etwall, Wirksworth, and Monyash; in June at Ashford (Trinity Sunday), Youlgreave, Hope, Tideswell, Litton, Rowsley and Wyaston; in July at Bakewell, Stoney Middleton, Buxton, Pilsley and Bonsall; in August at Bradwell, Barlow, Eyam and Wormhill; and in September at Whitfield. Exact dates can be obtained from TI Centres and the National Park Office.

There are National Park Information Centres at Bakewell, Castleton and Edale, and seasonal Information Centres at Hartington, Fairholmes, Langsett and Torside. Useful publications listing local events, licensed camping and caravan sites, Youth Hostels, etc. are available from the National Park Office, Aldern House, Baslow Road, Bakewell, Derbyshire DE45 1AE.

A. Derby to Manchester via Matlock, Bakewell and Buxton

Directions. Total distance 68m. **Derby**, see Route 68. A6 to (19m) **Matlock**, (26½m) **Bakewell**, (38m) **Buxton**, (44m) Chapel-en-le-Frith, (48m) Whaley Bridge, (59m) Stockport and (66m) **Manchester**, see Route 74.

Derby, see Route 68. A6 heads N, along the Derwent valley. 4½m: *Duffield* has the foundations of a huge Norman keep razed to the ground in 1266 (NT). Kedleston Hall (Route 68) is about 3½m SW of Duffield. B5023 goes up the Ecclesbourne valley from Duffield to (8m) Wirksworth (see below). 9m: *Belper* developed as an industrial town with the opening of Jedediah Strutt and Richard Arkwright's cotton mill in 1776. The valley becomes more beautiful beyond (11m) *Ambergate*. 13m: *Whatstandwell* lies beneath *Crich Stand* (955ft; *view), about 2m NE. It is reached via *Crich*, with the National Tramway Museum.

Off B5035 1½m NE of Crich, on a steep knoll overlooking the Amber, is the ruined late 15C *Wingfield Manor* (not open) where Mary, Queen of Scots, was imprisoned in 1584–85.

At (15m) *High Peak Junction* are the restored workshops of the Cromford and High Peak Railway (open).

The High Peak Trail follows the disused railway line 17m W and N towards Buxton. It crosses B5036 near the Black Rocks (see below) after 1½m and, about ½m beyond, passes near *Middleton Top*, with a restored 19C winding engine (open) used for hauling wagons up the steep gradient. For the junction with the Tissington Trail near *Parsley Hay*, see Route 69C.

17m: *Cromford* has a rich industrial history. Richard Arkwright established his water-powered cotton mill here in 1771; it is now open, with a small exhibition. Rows of workers' houses survive in North St. There are trips (summer weekends) by horse-drawn narrow boat along a section of the Cromford Canal. To the W runs the wooded *Via Gellia*, built c 1800 by Richard Gell to link his lead mines with Cromford wharf. It gave its name to Viyella, first made at a local mill.

A sideroad leads to the upland village of *Bonsall*, 1½m NW of Cromford, with a market cross and a 14C church spire surrounded by curious 'crowns'. A footpath continues N to Masson Hill (see below).

Wirksworth (5500 inhabitants), beyond the *Black Rocks* on B5036 1½m S of Cromford, was once a lead-mining centre. It is now a market town, though limestone is still quarried nearby. The 19C Moot Hall in Chapel Lane preserves the 16C dish used as the standard measure for lead ore. The 13–14C church has a remarkable Saxon *coffin-lid and, in the S transept, a small carving of a lead miner, apparently 12C. Wirksworth is also connected with George Eliot, who portrayed it as Snowfield in 'Adam Bede'. The *Carsington Reservoir* is to the SW.

A6 continues N to **Matlock** (20,600 inhabitants), the administrative centre of Derbyshire. The general name includes (17m) *Matlock Bath* (TI), in the narrow limestone ravine of the Derwent, and (19m) *Matlock*, at the open end of the ravine beyond. Matlock proper consists of Matlock Bridge by the river and Matlock Bank on the steep hill above. The tepid springs encouraged its development as a spa from the Regency onwards but its great popularity dated from 1853, when John Smedley opened his hydropathic treatment centre at Matlock Bank, in buildings now occupied by the County

Council. Indiscriminate building, tawdry amusements and tourists mar the natural beauty of the setting, particularly at Matlock Bath.

The Pavilion at Matlock Bath houses the *Peak District Mining Museum*, with geology, tools and machinery; nearby is the *Temple Mine* (open). On the W side of the narrow pass between Matlock Bath and Matlock are the wooded *Heights of Abraham* (open), with cable car, Great Rutland Cavern and Nestus Mine, and a view from the Victoria Prospect Tower. Further W is the commanding height of *Masson Hill* (1110ft). Overhanging the opposite side of the river is *High Tor* (673ft; view).

The grounds of the 19C *Riber Castle*, c 2m SE of Matlock via A615 and Tansley, contain a *wildlife park with British and European birds and animals. *Dethick*, about 4m SE off A615 beyond Tansley, has a 13C church with a tower of 1530. *Lea Gardens* (open), S of Dethick, have rhododendrons, etc. in a woodland setting.

Beyond Matlock A6 enters the broad upper valley of the Derwent. 21m: The church of *Darley Dale*, 1m left, has a stone parclose screen, glass by Morris and Co., an early 14C effigy of a knight and two incised 16C slabs of the Rowsley family.

Off the hilly B057, to the NE, is *Hob Hurst's House* (EH), a prehistoric burial mound surrounded by earthworks. About 2¾m SW on B5057 is the pleasant village of *Winster*, with a 17–18C market house (NT Information Centre).

B5056 heads 3¾m N from Winster to rejoin A6 between Rowsley and Bakewell, flanked by gritstone moors rich in Bronze Age remains. The *Nine Ladies Stone Circle* (EH) is on *Stanton Moor* to the E, reached via (1¾m) the sideroad for *Birchover* or (2½m) the sideroad for *Stanton-in-Peak*. At 3m a sideroad branches W for (¾m) *Alport*, where the picturesque limestone valleys of the Bradford and the Lathkill meet. *Monyash*, at the source of the Lathkill 4½m NW, can be reached by road from Bakewell (see below) or A515 (Route 69C). *Youlgreave*, on the Bradford ¾m SW, has a handsome church with a Perpendicular tower, a miniature tomb effigy of 1488, a 12C font and glass by Morris and Co.

The main route enters the National Park by the junction of the Derwent and the Wye at (23½m) **Rowsley**, often pronounced 'Rozly'. The Peacock Hotel dates from 1652.

4m N is ***Chatsworth** (open), the grand classical mansion of the Dukes of Devonshire in its vast park.

The Elizabethan house, begun by Sir William Cavendish and completed by his widow, 'Bess of Hardwick', was replaced by the present building between 1687 and 1707. William Talman designed the S and E sides; the W side with its central pediment and the curved N side, through which visitors enter, probably by Thomas Archer. Wyatville added the N wing (1820–30).

The house contains superb furniture and art. The most striking features of its decoration are the ceiling paintings by Laguerre, Verrio and others, and *wood carving largely by a local artist, Samuel Watson (1663–1715). Both are seen throughout the State Apartments and, to their best advantage, in the *Chapel. Like several other rooms, the State Dining Room has furniture by Kent. The State Drawing Room contains Mortlake tapestries; the State Music Room a door with a trompe l'oeil painting by Jan van der Vaart; and the State Bedroom the bed in which George II died. Beyond the Sketch Galleries, with Mortlake tapestries, Delft ware and modern family portraits (including a fine Sargent), are the Chapel, the curious Oak Room, the Library, Ante-Library and Dome Room. The Great Dining Room has portraits by Van Dyck; work by Franz Hals and Rembrandt hangs in the Sculpture Gallery.

The Orangery leads to the formal Gardens, originally laid out when the present house was built, with a famous cascade and fountains. A maze now covers the site of the conservatory (1836–39) built by the 6th Duke and his head gardener, Joseph Paxton, anticipating his design for the Crystal Palace.

The *Park (11,000 acres) is watered by the Derwent and bounded to the E by moorland. Just N of James Paine's bridge (1762) is a remnant of the Elizabethan house, Queen Mary's Bower, named after the captive Mary, Queen of Scots.

Edensor is a 'model village' of 1839 on the W edge of the park. The church (mainly by Gilbert Scott, 1867) contains a classical monument to the 1st Earl of Devonshire (d. 1625) and a brass inscription to John Beaton (d. 1570), steward to Mary, Queen of Scots. Joseph Paxton is buried in the churchyard. From *Baslow*, a pleasant village on the Derwent beyond the N edge of the park, A621 heads NE to Sheffield (Route 75G).

A6 leaves the Derwent at Rowsley and continues along the lovely winding valley of the Wye. 24½m: It passes the junction with B5056 from Winster (see above). 25m: *Haddon Hall (open), on a wooded slope above the river, is one of the most complete and best preserved medieval manor houses in England.

About the middle of the 12C Haddon passed from its Norman lords, the Avenells, to the Vernons. They were united with another powerful local family in 1558 when Lady Dorothy Vernon married Sir John Manners, though the story of her elopement is probably just a romantic legend. The Manners family, created Dukes of Rutland, moved to Belvoir Castle in Leicestershire about 1700 and left Haddon unoccupied and unaltered for 200 years.

The stone buildings are grouped around two courtyards on different levels. There is a small museum by the gatehouse entrance. The 12–15C Chapel has contemporary wall paintings. The 14C Hall, dividing the courtyards, has a 15C screen and a restored roof. The Parlour has a rare 16C decorated ceiling and panelling. Above is the 17C Long Gallery added by Sir John Manners. From the ante-room nearby run the steps down which Dorothy Vernon is said to have eloped. The terraced *gardens were laid out in the 17C.

26½m: **Bakewell** (3900 inhabitants), an attractive little market town with a five-arched medieval bridge across the Wye, is a popular centre for visitors and walkers in the White Peak. The 17C Market Hall houses the Peak National Park and TI Centre. The *Church*, with a Saxon cross outside, has a Norman W doorway and a S porch with 9–13C gravestones. It contains an elaborate 14C font and, in the S transept, 15–17C monuments of the Vernons and Manners, including those of Dorothy Manners (d. 1584) and her father, Sir George Vernon (d. 1567). The quaint tomb of Sir Godfrey Foljambe (d. 1377) and his wife is in the S aisle. The *Old House Museum*, in Cunningham Place above the church, has a folk collection in a building of 1534 later leased by Richard Arkwright for his workers. 'Bakewell pudding', different from the so-called 'Bakewell tart' found elsewhere, was first made at the Rutland Arms in the 19C. The Bakewell Agricultural Show is held on the first Wednesday and Thursday in August.

FROM BAKEWELL TO HATHERSAGE, 9m. Beyond the Wye, the route heads N on A619, the Baslow road, and branches left on B6001 after ¾m. From (4½m) *Calver*, the road descends into the Derwent valley. Middleton Dale (see below) is to the left, while the millstone grit of *Froggatt Edge* rises on the opposite bank. 6½m: *Grindleford* stands on a lovely reach of the river. For the *Longshaw Estate* (NT), see Route 69D. About 3m SW of Grindleford by B6521, a hilly road with lovely views, is the large upland village of **Eyam** (pronounced 'Eem'). It preserves touching reminders of its devastation in 1665–66, when the plague killed more than 250 of the 350 inhabitants. Led by the rector, William Mompesson, and the ejected minister, Thomas Stanley, the villagers succeeded in isolating their parish and preventing the spread of the disease. A remembrance service is held on the last Sunday of August on the hillside where the villagers worshipped during the plague. There is a Saxon cross, perhaps 9C, in the churchyard. *Eyam Hall* (open) is an appropriately furnished 17C manor house. On A623 ½m S is the rocky gorge of *Middleton Dale*, leading E through the village of

Stoney Middleton back to (2m) Calver. B6001 continues NW from Grindleford to (9m) *Hathersage* (Route 69D).

FROM BAKEWELL TO CHAPEL-EN-LE-FRITH VIA TIDESWELL, 14¼m. B6465 branches right from A6 at (1½m) *Ashford-in-the-Water* (see below), past (3m) *Monsal Head* (see below) to (5½m) *Wardlow*. A623 heads E to Middleton Dale (see above), but this route goes W to (7m) *Tideswell*, where the large 14C *church has a striking W tower, a stone screen behind the altar and the brass of Bishop Pursglove (d. 1579). *Wheston*, 1½m W, has a good 14–15C cross. For Tideswell Dale to the S, see below. 10m: *Peak Forest* has a church of 1657–66 dedicated to King Charles the Martyr. *Tunstead*, 3m S, birthplace of the canal-builder James Brindley (1716–72), has the largest limestone quarry in Europe. 14¼m: *Chapel-en-le-Frith*, see below.

Beyond Bakewell A6 follows the Wye past the pleasant village of (28m) *Ashford-in-the-Water* but leaves the river at (29¾m) *Deep Dale* and does not rejoin it until it has climbed past (30½m) *Taddington Wood* (NT) to (34½m) *Topley Pike*. It thus gives only tantalising glimpses of the *valley to the N.

This is best explored by taking B6465 from Ashford to (1½m) *Monsal Head*, with the viaduct of the disused railway line built in 1863 and denounced by Ruskin for destroying natural beauty so that 'every fool in Buxton can be at Bakewell in half-an-hour'. The Monsal Trail follows the course of the line through (1m) *Monsal Dale* and

The Monsal Dale railway viaduct

(3m) *Miller's Dale* (NT). About 1½m further, beyond B6049, is *Chee Tor*, a crag in a narrow limestone ravine. The trail ends at (7m) the Wyedale car park on A6 near Topley Pike.

38m: **BUXTON** (20,800 inhabitants), outside the National Park, stands on higher ground (c 1000ft) than any town of comparable size in England. Still a popular centre for visitors to the Peak, it has handsome buildings from its days as a spa.

TI: The Crescent. **Buses**: from the Market Place. **Railway Station**: Station Rd, NE of the Crescent. **Theatre**: Opera House, Water St. **Annual Events**: Well dressing in July. Buxton International Festival of Music and the Arts, end of July to beginning of August.

History. The springs, with their warm (28°C), bluish water, attracted the Romans in about AD 79. They named their settlement Aquae Arnemetiae ('The Spa of the Goddess of the Grove'). In the Middle Ages the town became a kind of English Lourdes and the Chapel of St Ann grew rich from pilgrims' offerings. Buxton again developed as a spa under the guidance of the 5th Duke of Devonshire at the end of the 18C.

The centre of the old town, Higher Buxton, on the hill to the S, is the Market Place with the 19C *Town Hall*. Nearby is the *Museum and Art Gallery*, with prehistoric bones from bone caverns, a few local Roman antiquities, Blue John ware (see Castleton, Route 69D) and 17–19C pottery from Stoke. Paintings include work by De Wint, Algernon Newton and Brangwyn. In High St., S of the Market Place, is the unobtrusive church of *St Ann* (1625).

Higher Buxton is linked with Lower Buxton, the spa to the N, by the Slopes, a landscaped hillside with graded paths where patients taking the waters could exercise. Chief among the spa buildings is the *Crescent* (1780–90) designed by John Carr of York to emulate the Palladian architecture of Bath. The *Library* occupies the handsome former Assembly Room. On the edge of the Slopes opposite the Crescent are the drinking fountain known as *St Ann's Well* and the former Pump Room of 1894, now a *Micrarium* (open) displaying natural history through microscopes.

Beyond the NE end of the Crescent is the attractive 19C Colonnade with, further N, the huge domed *Devonshire Royal Hospital*, built as stables by Carr in 1790 and converted in 1859. Station Rd leads E to the *Transport Museum* and the *Peak Rail Steam Centre*, home of the local railway preservation society.

Beyond the SW end of the Crescent is the cloistered Square and the *Opera House*, designed by Frank Matcham and splendidly restored in 1979. The *Pavilion Gardens*, watered by the Wye before it disappears underground, are flanked by a range of 19C spa buildings, including the *Conservatory*, *Octagon* and a swimming pool filled with warm spa water. To the N is Wyatville's church of *St John the Baptist* (1811).

Poole's Cavern (open), in *Buxton Country Park* almost 1m SW, is a natural limestone cave near the source of the Wye. The *Cat and Fiddle Inn*, on A537 about 5m W, stands on high, desolate moorland (1690ft). *Macclesfield Forest* and *Macclesfield* (Route 69B) lie further W. The old road from *Burbage* to the Cat and Fiddle passes the head of the Goyt valley; part of the lower valley is submerged in a reservoir for Stockport.

The bleak millstone grit of **Axe Edge** (1810ft), on A53 2½m SW of Buxton, is the highest point in the neighbourhood. From the surrounding slopes flow the region's major rivers: the Goyt (N), the Wye (N and E), the Dove and the Manifold (SE), and the Dane (SW). *Lud's Church*, a dramatic rock fissure on the Dane 5m further SW, is sometimes identified as the scene of Sir Gawain's encounter with the Green Knight in the medieval poem (but cf. Wetton Mill, Route 69B). The neighbourhood, including the Roaches (Route 69B) and the lower Dane Valley, is the most beautiful near Buxton.

A5002 climbs NW from Buxton directly to (8m) *Whaley Bridge* (see below), passing Combs Moss on the right and the lovely *Goyt Valley* with its reservoirs on the left. It can be explored by walking routes from the car parks at Goyts Lane, The Street, Errwood Hall, Goytsclough Quarry and Derbyshire Bridge. The sideroad linking The Street and Derbyshire Bridge is closed to traffic on Sundays and Bank Holidays between May and September; at all other times the section beyond Errwood is restricted to one-way traffic heading S.

From Buxton to *Ashbourne* via *Dovedale*, see Route 69C.

The main route follows A6 N of Buxton, passing *Combs Moss* (1662ft) on the left, to (44m) *Chapel-en-le-Frith*, an old-fashioned town with market cross and stocks.

FROM CHAPEL-EN-LE-FRITH TO GLOSSOP, 9m by A624. The road heads along the rugged fringes of the National Park through (4½m) *Hayfield*, with Kinder Scout (Route 69D) to the E. 9m: **Glossop** (25,300 inhabitants; TI), with 19C cotton mills, stands on A57, the direct road from Sheffield to Manchester (Route 69D). The Heritage Centre has an exhibition of local history. The *Dinting Railway Centre* (open) is nearby.

From *Chapel-en-le-Frith* to *Sheffield* via *Castleton* and *Hathersage*, see Route 69D.

A6 continues W to (48m) *Whaley Bridge* (5500 inhabitants), with a fine Georgian inn, at the mouth of the Goyt valley (see above). 51m: *New Mills* (9100 inhabitants) is a manufacturing town near the Cheshire border. The church at *Mellor*, 2¾m NW, has a Norman font and a Perpendicular wooden pulpit. B6101 follows the Goyt from New Mills to (4m) *Marple* (23,900 inhabitants), where the aqueduct (1796–1801) of the Peak Forest Canal crosses the valley. 52½m: *Disley* is 2m N of **Lyme Park** (NT).

The originally Elizabethan house was superbly remodelled in 1725 by Giacomo Leoni and altered again by Lewis Wyatt in the early 19C. The rooms are a mixture of 17–19C work, with limewood carving that may be by Grinling Gibbons in the saloon. Beyond the formal gardens is the magnificent *deer park (1320 acres). The Cage, on the ridge to the N, is an Elizabethan hunting tower altered by Leoni. The Lanthorn Tower, in the woods to the E, was removed from the Elizabethan house and rebuilt here in the 18C.

At (57m) *Hazel Grove* A6 is joined by A523 from Leek and Macclesfield (Route 69B). 59m: **Stockport** (136,500 inhabitants; TI) is dominated by the huge railway viaduct (1839–40) across the narrow valley of the Mersey. The high-lying parish church of *St Mary* was rebuilt by Lewis Wyatt in 1813–17 but keeps its Decorated chancel. There is a statue of Richard Cobden (1804–65), Stockport's MP in 1841–47, in St Peter's Square. The church of *St Thomas* on Wellington Rd South is by George Basevi (1822–25). The *War Memorial Art Gallery* has 19–20C British paintings and sculpture, including work by Lowry, and Epstein. The *Museum* in Vernon Park has an award-winning exhibition remembering the area's social and industrial history. A former hat factory houses a *Hatting Museum*, with old machinery, etc.

*Bramall Hall (open), 3m S via A5102, is one of the best black-and-white houses in the country, with rich timber and plaster outside and handsomely preserved rooms inside. In its present form the house dates from 1500 to 1600, though parts of the S wing are earlier, including the chapel with its wall painting.

66m: **Manchester**, see Route 74.

B. Derby to Manchester via Ashbourne and Leek

Directions. Total distance 58m. A route along the S and W fringes of the Peak District and the National Park. **Derby**, see Route 68. A52 to (13m) **Ashbourne**. A52, A523 to (28m) **Leek**. A523 to (41m) Macclesfield and (49m) Hazel Grove. A6 to (51m) Stockport and (58m) **Manchester**, see Route 69A.

Derby, see Route 68. The route takes A52. 4m: *Kirk Langley* is a pleasant village. Kedleston Hall (Route 68) is about 2m NE. 6¼m: *Brailsford* has a Saxon cross in the churchyard, left of the road. 10½m: *Osmaston*, to the left, is a 19C 'model village'.

13m: **Ashbourne** (6000 inhabitants; TI), on the S edge of the limestone country of the Peak, has Georgian houses, particularly on St John's St. and Church St. near the little triangular market place. Opposite the Tudor buildings of the *Grammar School* in Church St. is the house where Johnson often visited his friend Dr John Taylor. The 13C *Church* of St Oswald, the best in the county, has a tall spire, beautiful S arcade with *capitals and double transepts. The monuments include the touching memorial by Thomas Banks to Penelope Boothby (d. 1791) and medieval tombs of the Cockaynes. A traditional game of football is played in the main street on Shrove Tuesday and Ash Wednesday.

FROM ASHBOURNE TO STOKE-ON-TRENT VIA ALTON, 21m. A52 is taken W to (1½m) *Mayfield* (see below), where B5032 branches left. 4¼m: *Ellastone* is identified with 'Hayslope', the chief scene of 'Adam Bede'. George Eliot's father Robert Evans (d. 1849), who spent his childhood in the area, is buried in the churchyard. *Norbury*, on the other bank of the Dove, is the 'Norburne' of the novel. Its church has an impressive 14C chancel with blind arcading and striking tracery, a wealth of 14–15C glass and medieval tombs of the Fitzherberts. The Old Manor (NT, open by appointment) has a 13–15C hall. Beyond Ellastone B5030 forks left to Uttoxeter (Route 68). B5032 continues to (8m) *Alton*, in the wooded Churnet valley. Perched on a sandstone cliff are the scanty ruins of the castle (c 1175) in the grounds of the Convent of the Assumption, built by Pugin in the 1840s. At *Alton Towers* (open), on the opposite side of the glen, the shell of the 19C mansion (also partly by Pugin) and its lovely formal gardens are surrounded by what the management advertises as 'Britain's only world-rated leisure park'. *Croxden Abbey* (EH), 2m S of Alton, was a Cistercian foundation of 1176; the 13C ruins include the W end of the church. 12m: *Cheadle*, a pleasantly situated town, has a Roman Catholic church (1846) by Pugin and a nature reserve on *Hawksmoor* (NT), overlooking the Churnet to the NE. A521 leads to (15m) *Blythe Bridge* (Route 68) and A50 continues to (21m) *Stoke* (Route 67).

From Ashbourne to *Dovedale* and *Buxton*, see Route 69C.

Beyond Ashbourne A52 crosses the Dove into Staffordshire at (14½m) *Mayfield*. 17m: At the fork A523 is followed along the S boundary of the Peak District National Park to (20m) *Waterhouses*.

From the car park at the former railway station walkers (and cyclists) can explore the dramatic scenery to the N, following the Hamps river to its junction with the Manifold at (3½m) *Beeston Tor* (NT), and continuing up the Manifold valley to: (4¾m) *Thor's Cave*, where the river begins the underground course ending at Ilam (Route 69C); (6m) *Wetton Mill*, sometimes identified as the scene of Sir Gawain's meeting with the Green Knight in the medieval poem (cf. Lud's Church, Route 69A); and (8m) *Hulme End* (Route 69C). Some of this country can also be reached by the steep sideroads leading from Waterhouses to (3½m) *Grindon*, (6m) *Wetton* and (8m) *Butterton*.

28m: **Leek** (19,700 inhabitants; TI) is a little industrial town, once known for silk-weaving, among good scenery. The *Brindley Water Mill* (open) was designed by the canal-builder James Brindley in 1752. From the church-yard (with Saxon cross shafts) there is a fine view of the *Roaches*, a range about 5m N, perhaps England's best example of tumbled masses of mill-stone grit.

Cheddleton, 3m S, has a flint mill (open) on the Churnet. There are trips along the canal in narrow boats.

30m: *Rudyard Lake*, from which Kipling took his name, is a long reservoir which has almost the charm of a natural lake. A523 crosses the Dane, marking the Cheshire border, shortly before (35½m) the junction with A54, leading SW to (4½m) *Congleton* (Route 67) and NE to (12m) *Buxton* (Route 69A), with the lower Dane valley and *Lud's Church* (also Route 69A) to the right. 41m: **Macclesfield** (46,800 inhabitants; TI) was once the centre of the English silk industry. *St Michael*, largely rebuilt, contains the Legh and Savage Chapels, with medieval effigies and the 'indulgence brass' of Roger Legh (c 1506).

A537 leads past the wild *Macclesfield Forest* and the lonely *Cat and Fiddle Inn* to (12m) *Buxton* (Route 69A), in a pretty village off A536 4m SW, is a lovely half-timbered manor house of the late 15C, with later additions. The interesting church has 17C monuments of the Fittons, including Mary Fitton (d. c 1620), once thought to be the 'Dark Lady' of Shakespeare's sonnets.

43½m: The pretty village of *Prestbury* lies to the left. The churchyard of St Peter's, the 13–15C mother church of Macclesfield, has a Norman chapel. A half-timbered priest's house stands opposite the church. 45m: *Adlington Hall* (limited opening), to the left, is a 'black and white' house with Georgian brick additions. The late 15C Great Hall has a hammerbeam roof and an organ (c 1670) by 'Father' Smith.

At (49m) *Hazel Grove* A523 joins A6 and Route 69A is followed through (51m) *Stockport* to (58m) **Manchester**.

C.   Ashbourne to Buxton via Dovedale

Directions. Total distance 22m. **Ashbourne**, see Route 69B. A515 to (22m) **Buxton**, see Route 69A. The direct route along A515, passing E of Dovedale, is much less interesting. The Tissington Trail, a footpath along a dismantled railway line closely following the course of A515, runs from Ashbourne to join the High Peak Trail (Route 69A) at (12½m) Parsley Hay.

Ashbourne, see Route 69B. The Buxton road leads due N past the pleasant village of (2½m) *Fenny Bentley*. The church contains the Beresford tomb (c 1550) showing two shrouded adult figures in alabaster with 21 children below. *Bradbourne* church, 2½m NE, has Norman and Saxon carving. 4m: *Tissington*, on the right, is an attractive village with a Norman church tower. 6m: *Alsop-en-le-Dale*, to the right, has a partly Norman church. The Norman church tower at *Parwich*, 2½m E, has a striking tympanum.

A much more attractive way of making this part of the journey takes the sideroad leading NW from Ashbourne across the Bentley Brook to (1½m) *Mapleton*, on the Dove. It then climbs past (3½m) *Thorpe*, with the Peveril of the Peak Hotel, and (4m) the *Izaak Walton Hotel* to (5m) *Ilam*, where the church has a Norman font, the Early English shrine of the local St Bertram, a group by Chantrey and two Saxon cross shafts outside. The 19C *Ilam Hall* (now a Youth Hostel) has beautiful grounds (NT, with information centre and shop) where the Manifold rises from the underground course begun at Thor's Cave (Route 69B).

Thorpe and Ilam stand at the S end of *•Dovedale*, the narrow and wooded limestone ravine through which the Dove forces its way from Milldale, about 3m N. It is the most popular beauty spot in the Derbyshire Dales.

Dovedale was fished by Izaak Walton (1593–1683), author of 'The Compleat Angler', and his friend Charles Cotton (1630–87) of Beresford Hall. Among later generations, it was praised by travellers with tastes as different as Johnson ('he who has seen Dovedale has no need to visit the Highlands') and Byron ('there are things in Derbyshire as noble as in Greece or Switzerland'). The National Trust now owns about 2500 acres of land in the Dove, Manifold and Hamps valleys, with covenants protecting nearly 3000 more.

The entrance lies between the bare summits of *Thorpe Cloud* (E; 942ft) and *Bunster Hill* (W; 1000ft). The footpath up the dale follows the E (or Derbyshire) bank from the stepping stones on the Dove. *Dovedale Castle*, on the W (or Staffordshire) bank, is the first of the fancifully named limestone crags which mark the route, though in summer the trees can make them hard to distinguish. Others include the *Lover's Leap* (E), the *Twelve Apostles* (W) and the jagged *Tissington Spires* (E). Beyond the caves known as *Dove Holes* Dovedale proper ends at (c 3m) *Milldale*.

It is worth following the river about 4m further to *Hartington* (see below), through ravines ending with *Wolfscote Dale* and, most striking of all, the densely wooded *Beresford Dale*. This includes the pool frequented by Izaak Walton and Charles Cotton. Cotton's fishing lodge (1674) stands on private land at the exit from the dale. His pew is among the 17C woodwork in *Alstonefield* church, ¾m NW of Milldale.

Beyond Alsop-en-le-Dale A515 climbs through green countryside intersected by dry-stone walls. After (9½m) *Newhaven*, with a famous coaching inn, the route passes the roads for Youlgreave and Matlock (Route 69A) on the right.

B5054, branching left about ½m beyond, offers an interesting alternative way into Buxton via (2m) *Hartington* (seasonal National Park Information Centre, open weekends and Bank Holiday Mondays from Easter to end of September), on a high plateau near Beresford Dale (see above), and (3m) *Hulme End*, on the Manifold (Route 69B). Shortly beyond, B5053 turns N for (8m) *Longnor*, an excellent centre for the upper Manifold and Dove, and rejoins A515 at 11m.

12m: *Parsley Hay* is near the junction of the Tissington Trail with the High Peak Trail (Route 69A). *Arbor Low* (EH, open at any reasonable time), ¾m E, is a fallen stone circle with a ditch and earth rampart (2500–1700 BC). Nearby is a Bronze Age barrow at Gib Hill. 22m: **Buxton**, see Route 69A.

D.   Sheffield to Manchester via Hathersage and Castleton

Directions. Total distance 46m. **Sheffield**, see Route 75G. A625 to (11m) **Hathersage**, (17m) **Castleton** and, interrupted at Mam Tor, to (24m) Chapel-en-le-Frith. A6 to (28m) Whaley Bridge, (39m) Stockport and (46m) **Manchester**, see Route 69A. A hilly, scenic route along the boundary between the White Peak and the Dark Peak. A57, the direct road from Sheffield to (37m) Manchester, runs via (10m) *Ladybower Reservoir*, (24m) *Glossop* and (30m) *Hyde*. For the section between Ladybower Reservoir and Glossop, see the detour from Bamford below. For an alternative way from Sheffield to Manchester via Penistone, see Route 75G.

Sheffield, see Route 75G. A625 quits the suburbs beyond (3m) *Ecclesall* and enters the Peak District National Park before (8½m) *Fox House Inn*, on the serpentine course of the border between South Yorkshire and Derbyshire.

Carl Wark, an impressive fort on the moor 1m NW, may be late Iron Age or post-Roman. S of A625 stretches the *Longshaw Estate* (NT, Information Centre and shop), 1500 acres of moor and woodland with nature trails. Sheepdog trials take place here in September.

9½m: *Millstone Edge* commands a *view of the upper Derwent valley. 11m: **Hathersage**, beautifully situated, is the 'Morton' of Charlotte Brontë's 'Jane Eyre' and the reputed birthplace of Robin Hood's lieutenant, Little John, said to be buried in the churchyard above the village. The church, mostly 14C, has good 15C brasses of the Eyre family. From Hathersage to *Bakewell*, see Route 69A.

Near (13m) *Bamford*, to the right, A625 leaves the Derwent, which flows down from the moorlands of N Derbyshire.

The huge *Ladybower Reservoir* and *Derwent Reservoir* N of Bamford were constructed in 1937–39, drowning the lower Ashop valley and part of the Derwent valley, including the village of Ashopton. The 'Dambusters' bombing raid on the Ruhr dams was practised on the Derwent Reservoir in 1943. From (9½m) the *Slippery Stones*, a packhorse bridge higher up the Derwent, the Cal-Der-Went Walk continues NE to (16m) *Langsett* (Route 75F) across wild moors whose highest point, near the top of *Margery Hill* (1791ft), commands a *view S and W unrivalled in England for savage desolation. Langsett can also be reached from Bamford by a sideroad (16½m), less wild but very beautiful, leading N from A57 past (7½m) *Strines Reservoir* and (12½m) *Broomhead Hall* to (15m) *Midhopestones*.

FROM BAMFORD TO GLOSSOP, 16m by A6013 and A57, including the tricky Snake Pass. A6013 climbs past *Win Hill* (1523ft; view) on the left. A57 heads left across the reservoir and follows its N shore to the deep and narrow valley of the Ashop, with the savage N escarpment of Kinder Scout (see below) on the left and the moorland of *Hope Forest* (16,555 acres) to the right. From (8½m) *Snake Inn* (1070ft) a well-defined path leads 6½m SW to *Hayfield* (see below and Route 69A), with views from the highest point (1670ft). Beyond the Snake Inn A57 gives a view of the craggy *Fairbrook Naze*, the most striking summit of Kinder Scout. *Lady Clough Forest* (nature trail) fringes the road. 11½m: The flat summit of *Snake Pass* lies between *Featherbed Top* (1785ft) on the left and *Higher Shelf Stones* (2039ft) on the right, with *Bleaklow* (2060ft) beyond. The descent to (16m) *Glossop* (Route 69A) is steep and winding.

Beyond Bamford A625 follows the valley of the Noe, which flows from Edale. In front rise Mam Tor and the other hills round Castleton. 15½m: *Hope* has a 10C churchyard cross.

Near the old lead-mining village of *Bradwell*, in the limestone-quarrying area to the S, is the *Bagshawe Cavern* (open), with stalactites. *Brough*, between Bradwell and the main road, has scanty remains of the Roman Navio. The green and open valley of Edale (nearly 2000 acres NT), NW of Hope, is bounded on the S by Mam Tor and Lose Hill and on the N by the moorland edges of Kinder Scout. *Edale* (National Park Information Centre), 5m from Hope, is surrounded by the wildest scenery in Derbyshire. From here the Pennine Way runs 250m N to the Scottish border.

The broken-edged plateau of **Kinder Scout** (2088ft; NT), NW of the village, is the highest ground in Derbyshire. The Pennine Way crosses it but the route can be difficult and should be tried only in good weather. An easier but still attractive walk W to (7½m) *Hayfield* uses part of the alternative course of the Pennine Way. It follows the valley from Edale to (2m) *Upper Booth* and the end of the lane 1m beyond. A path climbs steeply up *Jacob's Ladder* to (4m) *Edale Cross* (c 1750ft) on the neck between Kinder Scout (right) and *Brown Knoll* (left; 1804ft). The Pennine Way continues N but this walk heads W, down a charming valley to (7½m) *Hayfield*. The walk from Hayfield around the NW side of Kinder Scout to the Snake Inn is described on the detour from Bamford to Glossop above.

17m: **Castleton** (National Park Information Centre) is popular with tourists for the caverns and mines in the neighbourhood. The ceremony of 'Riding the Garland', now connected with the restoration of Charles II but older in origin, is held on the evening of 29 May, Oakapple Day. Perched on the summit of the limestone crag to the S is the small late Norman keep (c 1176) of *Peveril Castle* (EH, all year), originally founded by William of Peveril in 1068. Part of the enceinte wall also survives. At the foot of the precipice is the spectacular mouth of Derbyshire's largest natural cave, the *Peak Cavern* (open), once known as the Devil's Arse, with 400-year-old rope walks. The *Cavendish House Museum* has articles made from Blue John, a local variety of fluorspar with a purple or yellowish colour ('bleu jaune').

A landslide from *Mam Tor* (1700ft; NT), the Shivering Mountain, has blocked A625 W of Castleton. A sideroad climbs through the limestone ravine of *Winnats Pass* ('Wind-gates'; NT) to rejoin A625 at (19m) the bottom of the hill. The *Speedwell Mine* (open), an old lead mine at the entrance to the pass, has a gallery and a natural pothole reached by steps and an underground boat trip. At the top of the pass are the *Blue John Cavern* (open), and the *Treak Cliff Cavern* (open), now the richest source of Blue John.

A625 crosses the flank of *Rushup Edge*. At (24m) *Chapel-en-le-Frith* it joins A6 and Route 69A for (44m) **Manchester**.

70

Stamford to Rutland Water and Nottingham

Directions. Total distance 39m. **Stamford**, see Route 60A. A606 to (11m) **Oakham**, (20m) Melton Mowbray, (39m) **Nottingham**.

Stamford, see Route 60A. A606 heads W, crossing A1 and entering the former county of Rutland, now absorbed into Leicestershire. Just beyond (5m) *Empingham* (seasonal TI) is the NE corner of *Rutland Water*.

It has the largest surface area (3100 acres) of any man-made lake in northern Europe, though Kielder Water in Northumberland has a larger capacity. Begun in 1971 to supply water to the E Midlands, it was formed by damming the valley of the Gwash near Empingham and pumping water from the Nene at Wansford and the Welland at Tinwell. The pleasantly landscaped result, about 5m long and with an irregular perimeter of 24m, also serves as a leisure and recreation centre. There is an Information Centre at Sykes Lane, SW of Empingham, with car parks and picnic sites there and at Whitwell, Barnsdale and Normanton. There are many miles of perimeter footpath for walkers, a nature trail connecting the Whitwell and Barnsdale picnic sites, and a nature reserve at the W end of the Water with a visitors' centre in the public section at Lyndon. Dinghies and sailboards can be launched from the Day Sailing Centre at Whitwell, where a few hire craft are also available; the Rutland Sailing Club is near Edith Weston. Permits for trout fishing are obtained from the Whitwell Fishing Lodge or in advance by post from The Old Hall, Whitwell, Oakham, Leicestershire LE15 8DW; anglers also need an Anglian Water Regional or Divisional Rod Licence.

As well as the main route along the N shore suggested below, it is worth taking the longer way by sideroads round the S shore. At (2m) *Normanton*, with a car park and picnic site, the neo-classical church on a short causeway at the edge of the water makes a striking landmark. Now deconsecrated and housing a water museum, it was built in 1764, extended in 1826 and partly rebuilt in 1911. 3m: *Edith Weston* takes its name from Edward the Confessor's widow Edith. 4m: By the shore N of *Lyndon* is the visitors' centre for the public section of the nature reserve. Beyond (5½m) *Manton* the route joins A6003 heading N to Oakham. 7½m: At *Egleton*, to the right, the church has a *S doorway in the Saxo-Norman style with a carved tympanum thought to be Saxon. 9m: *Oakham*, see below.

The main route from Empingham follows A606 along the N side of the Water past (6½m) *Whitwell*, with car park, picnic site, Day Sailing Centre, Fishing Lodge and nature trail leading 1m W to the car park and picnic site at *Barnsdale*. *Exton*, a pleasant village 1½m N of Whitwell, has a fine park and a church with 16–18C *monuments which include work by Grinling Gibbons and Nollekens. 9½m: A sideroad to the left leads along a spur of land jutting out into the middle of the reservoir to (1½m) the little village of *Upper Hambleton*.

11m: **Oakham** (9100 inhabitants; TI), the former county town of Rutland and a famous fox-hunting centre, is a handsome little place built of local limestone and ironstone. Natives include Sir Jeffrey Hudson, Queen Henrietta Maria's dwarf (1619–82), and Titus Oates (1649–1705), who fabricated the Popish Plot against Charles II.

The chief relic of the *Castle* (open) is the late Norman *great hall. Nailed to its walls are horseshoes presented, in obedience to the local custom, by visiting peers to the lord of the manor. Nearby stand the handsome, mainly 14–15C church of *All Saints*, the original building of *Oakham School* (founded in 1584), refitted as a Shakespeare centre, and the old *Buttercross* and stocks. *Flore's House* in the High St. dates from the late 14C. The *Rutland County Museum* in Catmose St. occupies a former riding school of the Rutland Fencibles, a volunteer cavalry regiment raised in 1794. It contains Iron Age finds from the Rutland Water site, Roman remains from Great Casterton and agricultural equipment.

The Rutland Agricultural Show is held on the first weekend in August at *Burley-on-the-Hill*, a late 17C–early 18C mansion 1½m NE.

There are interesting churches at: *Teigh*, 4m N, with furnishings of 1782; *Market Overton*, 6m NE, with a Saxon tower arch; *Whissendine*, 4m NW, where the lovely late 13–15C building has part of the old rood screen (1516) from St John's College, Cambridge; and *Brooke*, 2½m S, with an Elizabethan interior (c 1579).

A606 leads NW to (20m) **Melton Mowbray** (23,600 inhabitants; TI), another quiet country town which is also a fox-hunting centre. The Early English and Decorated *St Mary's*, one of the county's finest parish churches, has a beautiful effigy of a lady (c 1400) in the S transept. Opposite is a 17C bede house. The *Melton Carnegie Museum* is devoted to the history of the area, including its connection with pork pies and Stilton cheese.

The surrounding Leicestershire Wolds are also explored in the detour from Leicester to Grantham in Route 59.

A606 follows a hilly course into Nottinghamshire. 30m: It crosses A46, the Fosse Way, running from Leicester to Newark-on-Trent. *Willoughy-on-the-Wolds*, off A46 3m SW, has 14–15C tombs of the Willoughby family in its church. The regicide Colonel Hutchinson (see below) is buried at *Owthorpe*, off A46 4m NE.

39m: **NOTTINGHAM** (271,000 inhabitants) is unusual among Midland cities in having a medieval and an industrial past of equal importance. It is more typical in having treated neither very well, leaving their fragments among the inner ring road and modern shopping centres. The site of the castle and the old Lace Market are of most interest. The unusual man-made caves, cut into the sandstone rock on which the city stands, lie mainly beneath private houses but are included in the tours organised by the TI Centre.

TI: 14 Smithy Row; County Hall, Loughborough Rd, West Bridgford. **Bus Stations**: Victoria and Broad Marsh shopping centres. **Railway Station**: Carrington St., ½m S of the centre, beyond Broad Marsh shopping centre. **Theatres**: Nottingham Playhouse, East Circus St.; Theatre Royal, Theatre Square, with Royal Concert Hall adjoining; Arts Theatre, George St.; Lace Market Theatre, Halifax Place. **Annual Events**: Nottingham Festival in June. The Goose Fair is held on the first Thursday, Friday and Saturday of October at the Forest Recreation Ground, N of the Arboretum. Now a fun fair, it originated as a trading fair in the Middle Ages.

History. The Saxon Snotingaham was occupied by the Danes in 868 and became (with Derby, Leicester, Lincoln and Stamford) one of the five Danelagh towns. Edward the Elder recaptured it in 918 and built the first bridge at the strategically important crossing of the Trent. The castle added after the Norman Conquest became the key to the Midlands and a favourite royal residence. Charles I opened the Civil War in 1642 by raising his standard N of its walls on what is now Standard Hill, but the castle was soon seized for Parliament by Colonel John Hutchinson and demolished in 1651.
In the 14–15C Nottingham was known throughout Europe for its alabaster carvings. Its industrial prosperity as a centre of lace- and hosiery-making dated from the invention of the stocking-frame by the Rev. William Lee of nearby Calverton in 1589. Hargreaves came with his spinning jenny in 1768, and Arkwright opened his first mill the following year. The Luddite riots of 1811–16, organised by starving weavers bent on machine-breaking, were at their most violent in Nottingham.

Natives and residents. Natives include Colonel John Hutchinson (1615–64), the artists Thomas and Paul Sandby (1721–98 and 1725–1809), the poets Henry Kirke White (1785–1806) and 'Festus' Bailey (1816–1902), General William Booth (1829–1912), founder of the Salvation Army, and Allan Sillitoe (b. 1928), whose 'Saturday Night and Sunday Morning' is set here. The painter Richard Bonington (1801–28) was born at *Arnold*, 3m NE. Byron lived in the city as a boy (plaque in St James St.). The Chartist leader Feargus O'Connor (1794–1855) was MP in 1847–48. D.H. Lawrence attended the High School and University College in its old building on Shakespeare St. (see below).

The centre is the large, sterile Old Market Square, its E side filled by Cecil Howitt's *Council House* (1928). Cheapside, S of the Council House, has the over-restored *Flying Horse Hotel* with pargeting; the old *Bell Inn*, off the NW corner of the square, is more interesting. Several streets climb from the N side of the square to Upper Parliament St., which has the *Theatre Royal* (1865) with the *Royal Concert Hall* (opened in 1982) immediately behind.

South Sherwood St. leads N between the *Guildhall* (1888) and the buildings of *Nottingham University*, including the original University College (1881) which Lawrence attended, in Shakespeare St. beyond. Shakespeare St. continues NW to the *Arboretum*, a handsome park with aviaries and a statue of Feargus O'Connor. On the S side is the *College of Art and Design*, with a statue of Bonington; on the N side the 19C buildings of the *High School* (founded 1513), where Lawrence was a pupil. The Goose Fair (see above) is held on the Forest Recreation Ground, beyond.

The dreary Lower Parliament St., continuing Upper Parliament St. to the E, goes under a walkway from the huge *Victoria Shopping Centre*. The narrow streets to the S still have medieval names and courses. Broad St. and its extension, Stoney St., lead into the old *Lace Market, with red-brick mid 19C warehouses, the most interesting survival of Nottingham's industrial past. *St Mary*, mainly late 15C, has a massive central tower, wide nave and rich Perpendicular windows; there is a painting by Fra Bartolommeo in the N aisle.

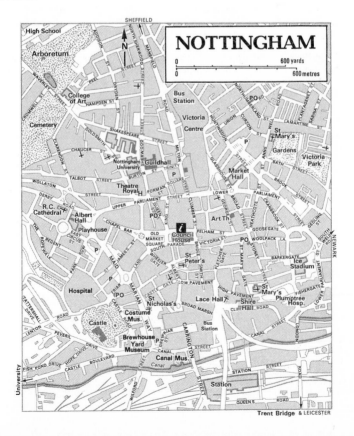

At the corner of Fishergate, a little to the E, is *Plumptre Hospital* (1823; founded 1392) for 13 widows.

High Pavement leads W from St Mary's, past the *Shire Hall* (1770), the *County Record Office* (formerly the Judge's Lodgings) with a façade of c 1833, and the *Lace Hall*, a museum in the former Unitarian chapel. It replaces the building where Bonington was baptised, Coleridge preached and the young Byron worshipped. A plaque opposite marks the site of Henry Kirke White's home. Middle and Low Pavement, with good 19C houses, continue beyond Weekday Cross. The *Broad Marsh Shopping Centre* lies to the S; hemmed in by Marks and Spencer to the N is *St Peter*, partly rebuilt in the 15C.

Castle Gate crosses the ugly Maid Marian Way, part of the inner ring road, with the attractive 17–18C church of *St Nicholas* to the S and the 15C *Salutation Inn* to the N. On the right of the approach to the castle is *Newdigate House*, where Marshal Tallard was held after his capture at Blenheim in 1704. On the left-hand side of Castle Gate a row of 18C houses contains the *Museum of Costume and Textiles*, with period rooms. A half-timbered 16C building moved from Middle Pavement houses the *Lace Centre*.

The grounds of the **Castle** (open) spread up the sides of a steep sandstone rock. Outside the walls are a modern statue of Robin Hood and reliefs depicting episodes from the legends connected with him. The heavily restored late 13C gatehouse is the only major relic of the fortress begun by William Peveril soon after the Conquest. The rest was dismantled in 1651 after Colonel Hutchinson had captured it from the Royalists during the Civil War. The Italianate mansion which the Duke of Newcastle built on the site in 1674–78 suffered a similar fate when it was gutted by fire during the Reform riots of 1831. Restored in 1875–78, it reopened as England's first municipal **Museum and Art Gallery** outside London.

The ground floor displays glass (including the Bles Bowl of c 1685), silver and English ceramics (good Wedgwood), as well as ethnographic and regimental collections. There is an exhibit of local history downstairs. The mezzanine floor has finds excavated at Nemi, near Rome, by Lord Savile in 1885. The picture gallery upstairs has works by Bonington and a range of 18–20C English artists (Richard Wilson, John Crome and other members of the Norwich school, Rossetti, Stanley Spencer). The 'Story of Nottingham' exhibition has interactive displays, videos, archive footage and a multivisual presentation about the history of the castle site.

There are conducted tours of the passages in the rock beneath the castle, including *Mortimer's Hole*, said to have been used by the young Edward III in 1330 when he came to arrest Roger Mortimer, lover of the king's mother Queen Isabella. The *Trip to Jerusalem Inn*, claiming to be the oldest inn in England, adjoins the entrance to another passage at the foot of the rock to the SE. The nearby *Brewhouse Yard Museum*, illustrating Nottingham's domestic and commercial life, occupies a group of restored 17C houses and the caves in the rock behind them.

Canal St. leads E from the bottom of Maid Marian Way to the *Canal Museum*, in a converted 19C warehouse.

The *Park Estate*, W and N of the castle, is a 19C residential area which repays exploration. In the Derby Rd, on its N side, stands the *Roman Catholic Cathedral of St Barnabas*, an impressive building of 1840–42 by Pugin. Close by are the Methodist *Albert Hall* (1909) and the *Nottingham Playhouse* (1959–63; Peter Moro).

Trent Bridge (1869–71), about 1m S of the city centre, crosses the river to the *County Cricket Ground* (left) and the *County Hall* (right) in *West Bridgford*. The Victoria Embankment gardens have pleasant scenery. The grounds of Notts County and Nottingham Forest fooball clubs are on opposite banks of the river. Downstream (E) are the racecourse and park at *Colwick*. Colwick Hall, now a restaurant, was the home of Mrs Musters, Byron's Mary Chaworth (d. 1832). See below for A453, heading SW from the ring road at West Bridgford to Ashby-de-la-Zouch.

A6005, beginning as Castle Boulevard at the S end of Maid Marian Way, heads W from the city via (1m) *Lenton*, where the modern church has a carved Norman *font from Lenton Priory. About 1m further is the **University of Nottingham**, founded as University College in 1881 and incorporated in 1948. It moved to buildings by Morley Horder in this pleasantly landscaped park in 1928. *Beeston*, a former textile village 1m beyond, has striking Boots factory buildings by Sir Owen Williams (1930–32 and 1937–38).

Wollaton Hall (open), 2½m W on A609, was built for Sir Francis Willoughby in 1580–88 by Robert Smythson. Its *exterior combines a symmetrical plan with elaborate ornament in a triumph of Elizabethan bravado. The central tower, containing the hall and rising above the four corner towers, is a conspicuous and unusual feature. The building now houses a *Museum of Natural History*. The large park has an *Industrial Museum* in the 18C stable block and a cast-iron camellia house of 1823.

A609 continues beyond Wollaton Hall to (7m) *Ilkeston* (33,000 inhabitants), a mining and lace-making town in the industrial Erewash valley. The church has an early 14C stone screen and sedilia. There is a local museum in a late 18C house on the High St. At *Dale*, on the moor 3½m SW off A6096, a single arch survives from the Premonstratensian abbey. *Eastwood* (11,700 inhabitants), off A610 and A608 4m N of Ilkeston, is famous for its connections with the early life and work of D.H. Lawrence (1885–1930). His birthplace on Victoria St. is a museum.

FROM NOTTINGHAM TO ASHBY-DE-LA-ZOUCH, 22m by A453, heading SW from the ring road at West Bridgford (see above). 7m: On the right is the Jacobean *Thrumpton Hall* (open to parties of 20 or more). The village of *Gotham*, about 2m E, was famous in traditional jokes for the naivety of its inhabitants. Washington Irving and the Superman comics borrowed the name for New York. 10m: A453 crosses M1 and A6 near *Kegworth*,

The Boots factory buildings at Beeston

the *East Midlands Airport* and *Castle Donington* (all Route 68). 16m: *Breedon-on-the-Hill* has a church with a remarkable sculptured frieze and a cross shaft of the 8C. 22m: *Ashby-de-la-Zouch*, see Route 59.

FROM NOTTINGHAM TO SOUTHWELL, 13½m by A612. 5m: *Stoke Bardolph* lies by the Trent 1m to the right. The main road commands wide views across the valley, which it follows as far as (10m) *Thurgarton*, where the church preserves a W doorway and other remains of a 13C priory. 13½m: *Southwell*, see Route 72.

From Nottingham to *Loughborough* and to *Derby*, see Route 68; through Sherwood Forest to *Doncaster* via *Ollerton* and *Worksop*, see Route 71A; through the Forest via *Mansfield* to *Worksop*, see Route 71B.

71

Sherwood Forest

Sherwood Forest, in the Middle Ages a region of oak woodland, dense bracken and heath held by the Crown under forest law, occupied roughly the whole western part of Nottinghamshire. History has not treated it kindly. Private enclosure, the reclamation of land for farming, the growth of Nottingham and, above all, the development of the Nottinghamshire coalfield have reduced it to a narrow strip lying mainly between A60 and A614, N of Nottingham. Here, among the depressing towns and insensitive plantations of Corsican pine, some lovely woodland has been preserved through its inclusion in the so-called 'Dukeries': the great parks of Welbeck (formerly Duke of Portland), Clumber (formerly Duke of Newcastle), Worksop (formerly Duke of Norfolk) and Thoresby (formerly Duke of Kingston). Worksop and Welbeck are closed but Clumber and Thoresby, and also the park at Rufford, are open. The oak trees here and at Birklands and Bilhaugh nearby are some of the noblest survivors of the ancient British forests.

The outlaw Robin Hood is celebrated in medieval ballads, also making the occasional appearance in folk drama and contemporary chronicles. These place his exploits in Yorkshire and Cumberland as well as Sherwood Forest. He became inseparably linked with Nottinghamshire only in later centuries, when attempts were also made to find a historical basis for the legend. Joseph Ritson, who published the first collection of the Robin Hood ballads in 1795, identified him as Robert Fitz-Ooth, born at Locksley in 1160 and reputed to be the Earl of Huntingdon—doubtful claims which have frequently been challenged and amended. Scott's 'Ivanhoe' (1819) and Thomas Love Peacock's 'Maid Marian' (1822) consolidated the romantic image of the outlaw and his merry men who outwit the Sheriff of Nottingham as they rob the rich to help the poor. Preserved for later generations on film and television, it remains a firm favourite of the local tourist industry.

Of the routes suggested below, the first takes A60 along the W fringe of the region and heads beyond it to Doncaster, while the second goes through the heart of the forest, passing near the Sherwood Forest Visitor Centre at Edwinstowe.

A.   Nottingham to Doncaster via Mansfield and Worksop

Directions. Total distance 42m. **Nottingham**, see Route 70. A60 to (14m) Mansfield, (26m) Worksop and (42m) **Doncaster**, see Route 81.

Nottingham, see Route 70. A60 heads N from the city.

An alternative to the main route below branches left at 1m and follows A611 to (6m) *Hucknall* (28,100 inhabitants), a mining town where Byron is buried in the family vault of the church. *Annesley Hall* (not open), 2m further N, was the early home of the cousin with whom he fell in love, Mary Chaworth. A60 can be rejoined by taking B6011 E from Hucknall through (1m) *Linby*, a pretty place with two village crosses, and branching left on B683 at *Papplewick*, 1m beyond.

A60 continues N past (5m) the turning for A614, followed in Route 71B. 8m: *Papplewick Hall* (open by appointment), on B6011 to the left, is a house by Adam. 10m: Near the *Pilgrim Oak* is the entrance to Byron's ancestral home, ***Newstead Abbey** (open).

The 12C Augustinian priory which Henry II founded was converted into a house by Sir John Byron in 1540 but had largely fallen into decay by the time the poet inherited it in 1798. He made fitful repairs and lived here at intervals between 1808 and 1818, when debts forced him to sell the property.
    A long drive flanked by rhododendrons leads through the park to the lake and the buildings. They owe their present appearance outside to repairs by Byron's successor, Colonel Wildman, though part of the lovely late 13C W front of the priory church is still intact. At the core of the house is the old cloister square with the chapter house which the Byrons made a chapel and the poet used for his menagerie. The main apartments upstairs have mementoes of him.

14m: **Mansfield** (58,900 inhabitants) is a dull town with hosiery mills and collieries, spanned by a large railway viaduct. The 13–15C *Church* has a beautifully proportioned interior.

*Hardwick Hall (NT), off A617 6m NW, is one of the best Elizabethan mansions in the country. It was built in the 1590s, probably by Robert Smythson, for 'Bess of Hardwick', as Elizabeth, Countess of Shrewsbury, was popularly known. Her initials decorate the balustrades above the vast display of windows. Inside, a superb stone staircase rises from the Hall to the High Great Chamber, with a painted plaster frieze, and the Long Gallery, with handsome chimneypieces and a portrait of Mary, Queen of Scots. There is good contemporary furniture and a *collection of tapestries and embroidery. The grounds preserve the original layout of walled courtyards; nearby are the ruins of *Hardwick Old Hall* (EH, 1 April to 31 October, Wednesday, Thursday, Saturday, Sunday and Bank Holidays except Good Friday, 12.30–17.00). The 18C *Stainsby Mill* (NT), in the grounds of the old estate, has been restored to working order. To the N lies the curious little church of *Ault Hucknall*, with early Norman details, where Thomas Hobbes (1588–1679), author of 'Leviathan', is buried. *Sutton Scarsdale Hall*, beyond M1 about 6m NW of Hardwick, is a ruined building of 1724 by Francis Smith of Warwick (EH, exterior only).
    Bolsover (11,100 inhabitants), on A632 about 4m N of Hardwick, stands on the lip of a ridge of magnesian limestone with views W to the distant Peak. ***Bolsover Castle** (EH, all year), originally built by William Peveril in the 11C, was rebuilt and enlarged by Sir Charles Cavendish in 1613–17. He reconstructed the Norman keep on its old foundations in a mixture of Gothic and Renaissance styles, with some heavily decorated marble chimneypieces. The long gallery, now partly ruined, and the riding school were added c 1620–30.

A60 continues N from Mansfield through (15½m) *Mansfield Woodhouse* (26,700 inhabitants) and (18m) *Warsop*, with a good 12–13C church. From (21m) *Cuckney* A616 leads SE to Thoresby and Ollerton (Route 71B) and NW to *Creswell Crags*, a limestone ravine where the caves have yielded rich finds of early Stone Age occupation; there is a display in the Visitor Centre. Beyond Cuckney A60 passes *Welbeck Abbey* (not open), now an army training school.

The 3000-acre park is one of the chief survivals of the ancient Sherwood Forest. The house, on the site of a 12C Premonstratensian abbey, dates mainly from the 17C. The strangest of later additions are the underground rooms and tunnels built by the disfigured 5th Duke of Portland (d. 1879).

A60 passes *Worksop Manor* (not open), where a grand 17C house and its 18C successor once stood, on the way into (26m) **Worksop** (36,900 inhabitants; TI), an industrial town on the edge of the coalfield. The church of *Worksop Priory*, an Augustinian foundation of 1103, has a Norman *nave (c 1150–60), Early English Lady Chapel (c 1240) and S door with elaborate ironwork of c 1260. The transepts and crossing were rebuilt in 1929–35 and the new E end completed in 1965–74. A 14C gatehouse survives S of the church. Mr Straw's House (NT, open by appointment), a semi-detached house in Blyth Grove, preserves the atmosphere of the 1920s and 1930s.

* *Steetley Chapel*, off A619 1½m W, is a little apsidal building with rich mid 12C Norman work. *Thorpe Salvin*, 4m W, has an elaborate *font in the Norman church.

A60 continues N beyond the forest. 29m: *Carlton-in-Lindrick* has a Norman church. At (32m) *Oldcotes*, just before the boundary with South Yorkshire, the road crosses A634.

Blyth, 2m SE, see Route 72. **Roche Abbey** (EH, summer season, daily; winter weekends 10.00–16.00) lies 3m W of Oldcotes. The ruins of the Cistercian monastery founded in 1147 include the transepts of the church. They stand on a beautiful site landscaped in the 18C by Capability Brown as part of the grounds of Sandbeck Park. The church of *Laughton-en-le-Morthen*, 2m SW, has a Perpendicular spire and Saxon N doorway.

34m: *Tickhill* (5000 inhabitants) has a ruined Norman castle, a Perpendicular church of c 1360 containing one of the earliest Renaissance monuments in England (1478), and a domed 18C market hall.

A60 crosses A1, here motorway, and M18 on the way into **Doncaster** (Route 81).

B. Nottingham to Worksop via Ollerton

Directions. Total distance 28m. **Nottingham**, see Route 70. A60, A614 to (19m) Ollerton. A616, B6034 to (28m) **Worksop**, see Route 71A.

Nottingham, see Route 70. The route leaves the city on A60, as in Route 71A, but branches right from it at 5m on A614. 15½m: *Rufford*, on the right, has a country park (open) and the remains of a 12C Cistercian abbey (EH, all year).

Shortly beyond, B6034 branches left to (1½m) *Edwinstowe* with the Sherwood Forest Visitor Centre. The church has a good 13C tower with a later spire and, in the chancel, the fragment of an Early English pillar piscina. Signposted footpaths and trails lead into the surrounding woodland. The main route can be rejoined 1¼m N, through the beautiful forest tract of *Birklands*, where the *Major Oak*, now obviously dying, is reputed to be over 1400 years old.

19m: **Ollerton** (TI), to the right, is an old market centre with *New Ollerton* to its N. A616 heads through the lovely forest of *Bilhaugh*, where B6034 from Edwinstowe joins it on the left. *Thoresby* (not open), on the right beyond, is an extravagant mansion by Anthony Salvin (1865–71) in a handsome park. Lady Mary Wortley Montagu (1689–1762) was born in an earlier house on the site.

Beyond (22m) *Budby*, a 'model village' of 1807, B6034 branches right through a lovely tract of countryside. 23½m: A sideroad on the right leads via *Carburton* and its Norman chapel to **Clumber Park** (NT, Information Centre and shop), 3800 acres of park and woodland with a serpentine lake and an *avenue of lime trees 3m long. The demolition of the house in 1938 spared the *chapel, one of the great achievements of Victorian Gothic, built by Bodley and Garner in 1886–89. The interior is of softly tinted red Runcorn stone, with stained glass by Kempe.

28m: **Worksop**, see Route 71A.

72

Stamford to Doncaster

Directions. Total distance 72m. See beginning of Route 60A for the history of A1. **Stamford**, see Route 60A. A1 to (21m) **Grantham**, (35m) **Newark** (for **Southwell**), (49m) Markham Moor roundabout. A638 to (54m) East Retford and (72m) **Doncaster**, see Route 81.

Stamford, see Route 60A. N of the town A1 enters the former county of Rutland, now part of Leicestershire. The church of (2m) *Great Casterton* is 13C. At (3m) *Tickencote*, on the left, the church has a late Norman *chancel arch and a vaulted choir with boss (c 1160). The exterior arcading (restored 1792), 13C font and 14C wooden effigy of a knight should also be noted. Beyond (8m) *Stretton* the road re-enters Lincolnshire. The oolite of *Clipsham* quarries, 1½m E, makes a famous building stone. Just to the left of (13m) *Colsterworth* is the modest *Woolsthorpe Manor* (NT), where Sir Isaac Newton (1642–1727) was born. 17m: *Great Ponton* has a conspicuous church tower (1509). At *Boothby Pagnell*, 3m E, the late 12C *manor house (open by appointment) is the most complete surviving example of a Norman domestic building in England. A1 bypasses Grantham to the W.

21m: **Grantham** (30,100 inhabitants; TI), the birthplace of Lady Thatcher, is an ancient town that became a railway centre. It keeps some of its old character near the N end of the High St. The *Angel and Royal Hotel*, one of the finest medieval inns in the country, has a late 15C façade. Here King John is said to have held a court in 1213 and Richard III signed the Duke of Buckingham's death warrant in 1483. The 18C *George Hotel*, part of the shopping precinct nearly opposite, was praised in Dickens's 'Nicholas Nickleby'. The nearby market place has a 16C conduit and an old market cross. Grantham's Eleanor Cross (see Lincoln, Route 48) once stood on St Peter's Hill, to the S, where there is now a statue of Sir Isaac Newton. The *Museum* near the statue has local archaeological finds and a Newton collection.

Vine St. branches to the right from the N end of High St., with the medieval *Blue Pig* inn at the junction with Swinegate. The largely 13C parish church of *St Wulfram*, beyond, has a crocketed *spire. Its light and spacious interior has varied window tracery. A library (1598) over the S porch contains chained books. The 14C crypt was probably once St Wulfram's shrine. To the NE of the church is the old schoolroom (1497) of *King's School*, which Newton attended; to the E is the 14–15C *Grantham House* (NT, open by appointment only), with grounds stretching down to the river Witham.

Belvoir Castle (open), pronounced 'Beever', lies beyond *Denton* (Route 59) about 7m SW of Grantham. A coarse exercise in Gothic begun by James Wyatt in the early 19C, it nevertheless makes an impressive silhouette and commands a wide view across the Vale of Belvoir. The *picture gallery contains work by Holbein, Poussin, Gainsborough and Dutch and Flemish masters. There are good family portraits, including work by Reynolds, with tapestry, armour, etc. and a regimental museum of the 17th/21st Lancers.

FROM GRANTHAM TO NOTTINGHAM, 22m by A52 across the Vale of Belvoir. At (7m) *Bottesford* the early Perpendicular church has a tall crocketed spire and a chancel crowded with *monuments to sucessive owners of Belvoir. The church of *Orston*, 2½m NW, has a Restoration font in the Gothic style. 11m: *Aslockton*, to the right, was the birthplace of Archbishop Cranmer (1489–1556). 13m: *Bingham* has an interesting church in a mixture of Early English, Decorated and Perpendicular. From (17m) *Radcliffe-on-Trent* the river winds N to *Shelford*, where the church has memorials of the Stanhopes. W of the town are the National Water Sports Centre and *Holme Pierrepoint Hall* (open), an early Tudor manor house with 17C and 19C work. The nearby church has 17C work in a mixture of classical and Gothic styles, and a memorial to the poet John Oldham (1653–83). 22m: *Nottingham*, see Route 70.

FROM GRANTHAM TO LINCOLN, 25m by A607. 2m: *Belton House* (NT) is a magnificent late 17C building of Ancaster stone. Several rooms keep their contemporary woodwork and plaster ceilings; the Library and Boudoir were altered by James Wyatt in the 1770s. Also of interest are the wall paintings in the Hondecoeter Room, the unusual 18C painted floor in the Tyrconnel Room and the tapestries. The park was landscaped by William Eames in the 18C. The church of *Belton* has good monuments. From (5m) *Honington* A153 heads via (2m) *Ancaster* to (8m) *Sleaford* (Route 48). A607 continues N, skirting the *Cliff* (right), an oolite escarpment crowned by a series of interesting churches. 8m: *Caythorpe* has an unusual Decorated church, partly rebuilt. 10m: *Fulbeck*, where the Hall (limited opening) is mainly 18C. 12m: *Leadenham* has a good late Decorated church. For A17, leading across the escarpment to (9m) *Sleaford*, see Route 48. 16½m: *Navenby* has the finest church on the Cliff. At (22½m) *Bracebridge Heath* A607 joins A15 and follows Route 48 into (25m) *Lincoln*.

From Grantham to *Leicester*, see Route 59; to *Boston* via *Sleaford*, see Route 48.

At (31m) Shire Bridge A1 enters Nottinghamshire. The graceful spire of *Claypole* church rises to the right.

35m: **Newark-on-Trent** (24,600 inhabitants; TI), bypassed to the E by A1, stands at the junction of the old Great North Road and the Foss Way. Natives include the painter Sir William Nicholson (1872–1949) and the actor Sir Donald Wolfit (1902–68). Gladstone first entered Parliament in 1832 as the member for Newark.

The 12–15C *Castle* (not open) guards the river crossing. Now only an impressive shell, it was dismantled in 1646 after three sieges by Parliamentarian armies in the Civil War. King John died here in 1216. The castle grounds contain the *Gilstrap Centre*, incorporating the TI and an exhibition about the castle. In the large *Market Place are the *Town Hall* (open) of 1774–76 by John Carr of York, the restored *Old Town Hall* (1708), two big 18C inns (one now a bank) and the 14C *White Hart Inn*, with carved and painted timberwork. Prince Rupert was living in the half-timbered *Governor's House* in Stodman St. at the time of his quarrel with Charles I. The stately parish church of * *St Mary Magdalene* has a Decorated spire on an Early English tower. The interior is mainly Perpendicular.

The oak rood screen dates from 1505, the choir stalls from c 1525, and the Meyring and Markham chantry chapels, flanking the altar to N and S respectively, from 1500 and 1506. The Markham chantry has a double squint and two painted panels showing a Dance of Death. In the N choir aisle is the large Flemish brass of Alan Fleming (d. 1373).

Wilson St., NW of the church, has Georgian houses. The *Town Museum* in Appleton Gate, to the NE, contains local archaeological finds. It occupies the former Magnus Grammar School, with a Tudor hall (1529), which the composer John Blow (1649–1708) attended. In Devon Park, S of the town, the *Queen's Sconce* is a star-shaped earthwork built as a platform for cannon in the Civil War.

At *Hawton*, 2m S, the church has one of the finest *Easter Sepulchres in England, with sedilia and piscina to match (c 1330). *East Stoke*, on A46 (the Foss Way) 4m SW, is the site of the Roman station Ad Pontem. The Battle of Stoke (1487), at which Henry VII captured the pretender Lambert Simnel, was fought at nearby Stoke Fields. *Holme*, off A1133 about 4m N of Newark, has a church rebuilt in 1485 by John Barton, a Calais woolstapler.

Southwell (pronounced 'Suthall'; 6350 inhabitants) lies about 7m W of Newark via A617 and A612. A dignified little town, it is dominated by the *Minster** which, though raised to cathedral status only in 1884, equals the greatest English cathedrals in beauty.

A church is said to have been founded here c 630 by Paulinus, the first Bishop of York, but the first authentic reference is in a charter of c 956 granting Southwell to Oskytel, Archbishop of York. He established a college of secular canons which, though temporarily suspended under Henry VIII and again under Edward VI, survived until 1840. The new diocese of Southwell was created in 1884 by removing Nottinghamshire from the see of Lincoln and Derbyshire from the see of Lichfield; Derby became a diocese in its own right in 1927.

The minster superbly illustrates three successive styles of architecture. The severe W towers, the low central tower, and the nave and transepts with circular clerestory windows, are all Norman (early 12C), and on the N side is a rare late Norman porch. The choir is beautiful Early English (c 1234–50), while the Decorated chapter house (1295–1300) is the chief glory of the building.

The *Nave*, with its massive Norman piers and big triforium, is brilliantly lit by the Perpendicular W window and the Perpendicular windows inserted in the aisles. The tower arches have cable moulding. The *N Transept* has the fine alabaster tomb of Archbishop Sandys (d. 1588) and, over the door in the W wall, a sculptured tympanum from the Saxon church. The outline of the Norman apse is marked on the floor of the Airmen's Chapel. The *S Transept* has a wooden sculpture of the Virgin and Child (1952) by Alan Coleman.

The Early English *Choir* is separated from the nave by a Decorated stone rood screen (c 1335) with the organ over it. The screen is elaborately carved with miniature human heads (many restored in the 19C), and the stalls behind it have misericords. The capitals of the arch above are carved in what looks a Saxon rather than Norman style. The clerestory and triforium of the choir are ingeniously combined to increase the impression of height. Two heads on corbels on the N side are said to represent Walter de Gray and Henry III, the archbishop and king under whom the choir was built. The E window has two rows of four lancets instead of the more usual three or five; the Flemish glass in the lower lights comes from the old Temple Church in Paris. The brass lectern (c 1500) was recovered from the lake at Newstead Abbey, where the monks had thrown it at the Dissolution. The sedilia on the S side are in the same style as the rood screen, and were likewise restored in the 19C. The S choir aisle has a patchwork window of old glass, perhaps from the chapter house, and a fragment of Roman tessellated pavement, probably from the Saxon church.

A corridor leads N from the choir to the exquisite octagonal **Chapter House* (1295–1300). Oak, maple, hawthorn, vine, ivy and hop, among other types of leaf and blossom, luxuriate over the capitals of the entrance doorway and the canopies of the arcading within. Apart from being the earliest sculpture of its kind in England, this naturalistically carved foliage is also one of the supreme achievements of the mason's art. The building itself is unique among stone-vaulted chapter houses of this type in not being supported by a central pillar.

S of the minster are the remains of the *Palace* (c 1380) belonging to the Archbishops of York, with the 20C Bishop's Manor built inside them.

On the Old Market Place W of the minster stands the *Saracen's Head*, a half-timbered coaching inn where Charles I surrendered to the Scots Commissioners in 1646. Byron lived with his mother in 1803–08 at *Burgage Manor*, a Georgian house on the Green beyond King St. to the N.

From Southwell to *Nottingham*, see Route 70.

The main route rejoins A1 N of Newark. 42m: *Carlton-on-Trent*. Carlton Hall (open by appointment) is a handsome mid-18C house. 47m: *Tuxford*. The medieval field system survives at *Laxton*, 3m SW. The architect Nicholas Hawksmoor (1661–1736) was born at *Ragnall*, 5m NE of Tuxford. From (49m) *Markham Moor* roundabout A1 swings W and then becomes motorway as it bypasses Doncaster. The church at *Blyth*, 10m beyond the roundabout and just short of the motorway, has the early Norman *nave of a Benedictine priory church. A better way from Markham Moor to Doncaster follows A638, the route of the old Great North Road. From (51m) *Gamston* B6387 leads 3m S to the *National Mining Museum* at Lound Hall. 54m: **East Retford** (19,300 inhabitants; TI) is a market town and railway centre. *North Leverton*, 4m E, has a working windmill of 1813. 57m: *Barnby Moor*. Blyth (see above) lies 3m NW. 61m: *Scrooby* claims a connection with William Brewster (1560?–1644), one of the Pilgrim Fathers. At (63m) *Bawtry* A638 enters South Yorkshire. *Austerfield*, 1½m NE on A614, with a Norman church, was the birthplace of William Bradford (1590–1657), the 2nd Governor of Plymouth in New England. Near *Mattersey*, off B6045 4m SE of Bawtry, are the scanty remains of a priory of Gilbertine canons founded c 1185 (EH). 67½m: *Rossington*, left of the road, has a church with a Norman S doorway and chancel arch and a 15C pulpit.

72m: **Doncaster**, see Route 81.

NORTHERN ENGLAND

Northern England, as defined in this section, stretches from the Mersey estuary across to the Humber estuary and up the 'narrowing strand' of England to the Scottish border. Its southern boundary thus runs from Liverpool through Manchester, Sheffield and the industrial towns on the slopes of the Pennines to Hull. In the N, the border runs through wild and often remote countryside between the Solway, near Carlisle, to Berwick-upon-Tweed. The county map, complicated by the boundary changes and new creations of the 1970s, embraces: in the S, Merseyside, Greater Manchester, West Yorkshire, South Yorkshire and the northern half of Humberside; above them, Lancashire, North Yorkshire and County Durham, with Cleveland and Tyne and Wear on the coast; and, bordering Scotland, Cumbria and Northumberland.

Equally intricate, the map of the region's natural contours is dominated by hills and rivers. The Pennine Chain forms a central upland mass, stretching like a backbone from the northern Peak District to the Tyne. The change from millstone grit to mountain limestone along its course typifies the geological variety which makes the other hilly regions of the North, like the Lake District and the North York Moors, distinct and complex units. Their specific composition is described in the separate routes below. Here it is enough to note that chalk, whose smooth and fertile contours so perfectly express the gentle character of most southern landscapes, appears only in the Yorkshire Wolds above Hull. Elsewhere, the northern hills are more rugged than their southern neighbours, often rich in coal or mineral deposits but usually unsuited to arable farming. Their slopes are drained by a network of rivers which help to swell the great estuaries punctuating the coastline—the Mersey in the W and the Humber, the Tees and the Tyne in the E.

Such a landscape lends itself to low-density agriculture or intense indus-trialisation. The hill may be used for sheep pasture or exploited as a mine. The valley may remain a secluded dale or foster a town crammed by the banks of a vital power source and communication artery. The river's mouth may be marked by a compact fishing harbour or a sprawling industrial port. All these various possibilities have been realised, with the result that nowhere else in England is the juxtaposition of the rural and the urban, the pastoral and the industrial, so strikingly apparent. On the one hand, the North preserves remote and beautiful countryside; four of the best and largest tracts—the Lake District, the North York Moors, the Yorkshire Dales and much of Northumberland's hills and forests—are now National Parks. On the other, the region is crowded with towns and cities which burst into energetic, ungainly life during the Industrial Revolution of the 18–19C and are now often withering in the harsher economic climate of the 20C.

The sharpness of the contrast which greets the traveller who heads from the cities and towns near the S end of the Pennines into the Yorkshire Dales, or approaches the Lake District by way of the decayed ports and coalfields on the Cumbrian coast, or enters the North York Moors from the Teesside region, can obscure the length and subtlety of the process which has gone into its making. However emphatically it may have left its stamp, the Industrial Revolution was by no means the only determining event in the region's long and varied history. In Northumberland and Cumbria the ruins of Hadrian's Wall still mark the northern limit of Roman Britain. The medieval castles stretching down Northumberland's coast—at Bamburgh, Dunstanburgh, Alnwick and Warkworth—are monumental evidence of its later history as the disputed outpost of English territory. The medieval 'pele towers' found here and elsewhere in the North provide humbler but equally eloquent reminders of the hazards of border life. These small defensive structures, two or three storeys high and usually with only one room to each storey, survive either by themselves or as the core of buildings expanded into country houses in later, more peaceful times.

In one aspect a stem and remote frontier, Northumberland and its southern neighbour County Durham were also a vital centre where Celtic Christianity first established itself on English soil. From Holy Island (or Lindisfarne), where St Aidan founded his bishopric in 635, it spread to monasteries at Hartlepool, Jarrow and Monkwearmouth. The crosses which still stand at Bewcastle and Gosforth, the church at Escomb and the Saxon crypts at Hexham and Ripon are witness to its wider diffusion. At Whitby the Early English ruins of a later monastery now occupy the clifftop site where the Celtic and Roman churches conferred at the Synod in 664. At Durham the cathedral rebuilt soon after the Conquest marks the final resting place of St Cuthbert, the most revered saint of the early Church, and of Bede, its chronicler.

If Durham, probably the most romantic of all the northern cities, stands as the summative achievement of the Church in its first phase, then York testifies to the power and splendour it achieved later in the Middle Ages. Its minster and parish churches, with their superb stained glass, are famous beyond the need for special praise or introduction. Indeed, their fame has unfairly overshadowed the merits of other Yorkshire churches like Ripon, Selby and, particularly, Beverley. And certainly no part of England is richer in monastic remains or in natural settings which display their ruined glory to such poignant effect. The Cistercian abbeys of Rievaulx and Fountains, in particular, are unrivalled in Europe.

The wealth of Yorkshire's ecclesiastical foundations and market towns was partly derived from wool. The trade became a staple of the region's economy and made cloth centres of towns like Leeds, Wakefield and Bradford long before industrialisation set in. The size and dignity of the late 18C Piece Hall at Halifax shows the importance that such industries could attain even in their cottage phase. Elsewhere in the region, many of the other activities that came to typify the Industrial Revolution can also boast a long pre-industrial history. Lead-mining is one of the oldest: the moors around Pateley Bridge, for example, bear traces of Roman and medieval workings. The hills of the Lake District were being mined for silver, iron, copper and other minerals as well as lead several centuries before tourists began seeking them out for their picturesque beauty; the Keswick pencil industry goes back to the German immigrants who arrived to work the local 'plumbago' mines in the 16C. Sheffield cutlery was known to Chaucer, and by the 17C the folly of carrying coals to Newcastle was becoming proverbial. In the 18C Captain Cook made his first voyage round the world in ships built at Whitby.

The processes which transformed these industries in the 18–19C have already been sketched in the introduction to the North Midlands. In the North, they are summed up by the rise of Manchester. With its wealth and squalour, its brashness and sophistication, it was more completely a child of the Industrial Revolution than any other English city. Fed by the supply of cotton which arrived from America via Liverpool, and stimulated by the advances in spinning and weaving associated with the names of Arkwright,

Crompton, Hargreaves and Kay, it grew into the regional capital of an industry which gave life to the mill towns of Pennine Lancashire. Its canal system spanned the entire history of that era in communications and transport, with the Bridgewater Canal begun by James Brindley in 1759 signifying its modest beginning and the Ship Canal of 1887–94 its ambitious finale. The Liverpool and Manchester Railway—the first line of more than local importance—opened in 1830, some five years after its engineer George Stephenson had pioneered his famous Stockton–Darlington line.

In their own age the cities and towns that grew with the industrial boom of the North simultaneously excited and alarmed contemporaries. Today, they inspire equally mixed reactions, though often of a more melancholy sort. As the introduction to the North Midlands has already noted, England has at last begun to cherish the industrial heritage which previous generations regarded as merely functional or downright ugly. Manchester's Liverpool Road Station is now the centre of an ambitious and expanding museum complex, for example, and Liverpool's Albert Dock has been restored to its former grandeur. By the same token, the architectural achievements of the 19C city are now being cherished, though in many cases the change of taste has come too late to save Victorian centres from a dreadful battering at the hands of post-war planners and developers. Mercifully, the ring roads and shopping centres and gimmicky tower blocks have not swept away the work of John Dobson in Newcastle, or Cuthbert Brodrick in Leeds, or the great town halls of Manchester and Liverpool. Yet admiration for this legacy has come at precisely the time when the cities are also undergoing deep economic and social crisis. The virtual disappearance of the cotton industry and the decline of industries like coal, steel and shipbuilding have bred 20C problems of urban decay in their most urgent form. The northern cities now present a mixture of conservation and dereliction.

73

Liverpool

LIVERPOOL (475,000 inhabitants) has an abundance of 19C banks, office buildings and residential streets, as well as St George's Hall, Liverpool Museum and the Walker Art Gallery, to remind the visitor of its days as a great Victorian city and Atlantic seaport. These monuments testify to an energy, confidence and civic pride which continued long enough into the 20C to produce the Edwardian grandeur of the waterfront and to give the city its two cathedrals, one Anglican and the other Roman Catholic. They now stand alongside new residential, office and shop developments which are gradually replacing the urban decay that followed Liverpool's subsequent decline. The splendid restoration of the Albert Dock has been a catalyst for the regeneration of more than 3m of redundant dockland S of the city.

TI: Clayton Square Shopping Centre and Albert Dock. **Bus and Coach Stations**: The central bus station is on Paradise Street, but most buses stop on Roe St., by St John's Centre. The National Express travel office is in Brownlow Hill, near the Adelphi Hotel.

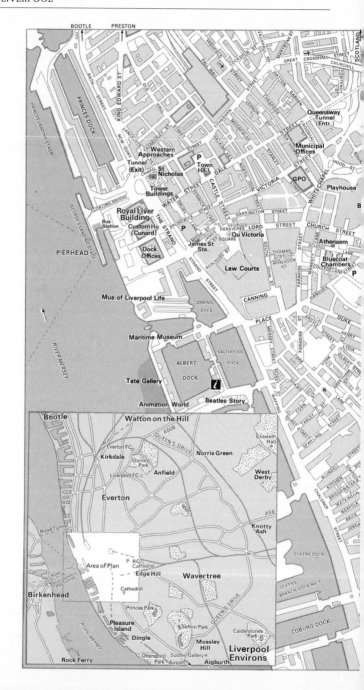

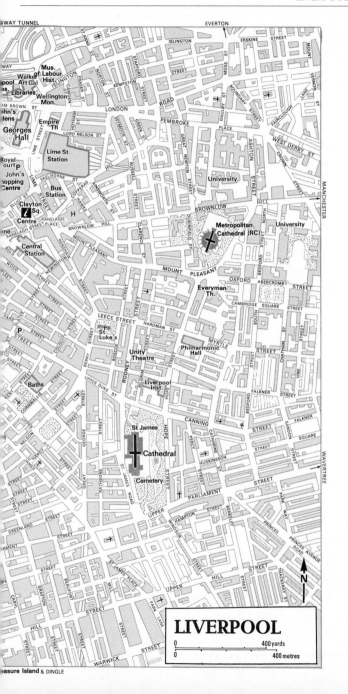

LIVERPOOL

| 0 | | | 400 yards |
| 0 | | | 400 metres |

Railway Stations: Lime Street Station for London and most destinations; Central Station for Merseyrail underground system; Northern Line to Southport, Ormskirk and Hunts Cross; Wirral Line via James Street Station and Birkenhead (Hamilton Square Station) to New Brighton, West Kirby and Chester. **Ferries**: Mersey ferries to Birkenhead (Woodside) and Wallasey (Seacombe) and ferries to Douglas, Isle of Man, from Pier Head. Ferries to Belfast from terminal at Brocklebank Dock, 3m N of Pier Head. **Airport**: At *Speke*, 7m SE of centre via A561. Passenger services to Antwerp, Belfast, Dublin, the Isle of Man, Jersey, London (City), Southampton and Waterford. **Theatres**: Empire, Lime St.; Everyman, Hope St.; Playhouse, Williamson Square; Neptune, Hanover St.; Royal Court, Roe St.; Unity, Hope Place. The Royal Liverpool Philharmonic Orchestra gives regular concerts at Philharmonic Hall, Hope St. **Annual Events**: Liverpool Show (end of May); Lord Mayor's Parade (early June); Mersey River Festival/Festival of Comedy (June); Woolton Show/Beatles Festival (August Bank Holiday).

History. Although King John built a castle and founded a settlement here to serve as a point of departure for Ireland, Liverpool's real growth as a port dates from the 17C to the 19C. The first cargo from the Americas arrived in 1648. Throughout the 18C Liverpool traded with Virginia and the West Indies in sugar, tobacco, cotton and rum, and increased its wealth by the slave trade between Africa and America. The first dock was opened in 1715, and after 1734 further docks spread W into neighbouring Bootle until they stretched in an unbroken line for 7 miles. With the abolition of the slave trade and the introduction of steam Liverpool inherited Bristol's position as England's chief Atlantic seaport, importing cotton from America for the Lancashire mills and exporting the finished goods to the world market. From the 1840s it also became the point of arrival and departure for Transatlantic passenger liners. In the process its population rose from about 6000 in 1700 to about 80,000 in 1800 and about 685,000 in 1900. A city that grew great with the Industrial Revolution and the Empire, Liverpool has suffered inevitable decline in the 20C. The collapse of the cotton trade, the loss of markets provided by the Empire, the rise of Southampton as a passenger port and the development of air transport have all conspired against it. It won itself a fashionable reputation as a centre for popular culture in the 1960s, the era of the Beatles and the 'Liverpool sound', and today has a thriving youth culture fuelled by the growing student population attracted to the city's two universities.

Natives, residents and visitors. Liverpudlians include the painter George Stubbs (1724–1806), the poets Felicia Hemans (1793–1835), Arthur Hugh Clough (1819–61) and Richard Le Gallienne (1866–1947), W.E. Gladstone (1809–98), the architect Alfred Waterhouse (1830–1905), the comedians Tommy Handley (1892–1949) and Ken Dodd (b. 1931), and the Beatles, who first appeared at the Cavern, since demolished, on Mathew St. in January 1961. Sir Francis Bacon (1561–1626), the local solicitor and philanthropist William Roscoe (1753–1831) and William Huskisson (1770–1830) were MPs for the city. Richard Mather (1596–1669), father of Increase and grandfather of Cotton Mather, was minister of the Unitarian church in Park Rd, Toxteth Park. Nathaniel Hawthorne served as US Consul here in 1853–57 and was visited by Herman Melville in 1856. Matthew Arnold died here of a heart attack in 1888. Famous local murders include the Maybrick case of 1889 and the Wallace case of 1931.

THE WATERFRONT AND DOCKS. The finest view of the city is from the Mersey, on one of the ferries or the landing stage at Birkenhead. The waterfront is dominated by the Edwardian office buildings which show Liverpool at the height of its prosperity and by the pinnacled steeple of St Nicholas. The city rises behind them to a skyline crowned with the two cathedrals.

The landing stage for the Mersey and Isle of Man ferries is the surviving fragment of what was once the world's largest floating quay, connected to the river wall by ten hinged bridges and an inclined roadway. Pier Head, the open space behind the terminal, was formed by covering over the old St George's Dock. The *Royal Liver Building* (1910) has two 295ft towers topped by the legendary 'Liver birds' (pronounced 'Lye-ver') which are supposed to have given their name to the city. Next to it are the less ambitious *Cunard Building* (1913–16) and the *Port of Liverpool Building* (1907), with a neo-Renaissance dome. Behind is the ventilating station of the Mersey Tunnel, rebuilt in 1951–52 after wartime damage.

The docks, stretching for several miles either side of Pier Head, are in their present form mostly the work of Jesse Hartley, dock engineer from 1824 to 1860, who built the massive river wall and boundary wall, pierced by gates and lodges of colossal proportions. S of Pier Head the magnificent *Albert Dock, with the adjoining docks, has been restored as a centre for shops, restaurants, offices, museums, etc. Built by Hartley in 1841–45, it has five-storied brick warehouses on huge pillars forming a colonnade round the basin. The *Merseyside Maritime Museum* occupies one warehouse and some of the buildings around *Canning Half-Tide Dock*. Its displays include full-size craft, models, paintings, marine equipment, etc., with special exhibits about the Port of Liverpool, the dock system and emigration from Liverpool in the 19–20C. The *Tate Gallery, Liverpool*, with selections of modern art from the Tate's permanent collection in London, occupies another warehouse. Other attractions include *The Beatles Story* and *Animation World*, with exhibits and displays of cartoon films. Canning Place, across the inner ring road from *Canning Dock* and *Salthouse Dock*, is on the site of Liverpool's first dock, built in 1715 and filled up in 1829.

The Albert Dock, Liverpool

In the memorial garden overlooking the N end of Pier Head stands *St Nicholas*, Liverpool's original parish church, founded in 1360 as a chapel of ease to the mother church at Walton. Only the distinctive steeple (1815; Thomas Harrison) survived an air raid in 1941; the rest is modern Gothic (1952; Edward C. Butler).

FROM THE WATERFRONT TO THE CENTRE (ST GEORGE'S HALL). Water St. leads up from the Cunard Building past some good 19C buildings, notably *Oriel Chambers* (1864; Peter Ellis) on the left. The Georgian **Town Hall** was designed by John Wood the Elder in 1749–54, with a dome (1802) and portico (1811) added by James Wyatt and John Foster. It is open to the public once a year, usually in August. The quadrangle behind, known as Exchange Flags, was the meeting place of cotton brokers before the opening of the Cotton Exchange. A monument to Nelson (1813) stands in the centre. Rumford St. just behind the town hall has the *Western Approaches* (open), the secret wartime headquarters from which the Battle of the Atlantic was directed.

Castle St., opposite the town hall, is lined with Victorian banks and office buildings, notably Norman Shaw's *Westminster Bank* (1901–02), on the right, and C.R. Cockerell's *Bank of England* (1845–48), now a TSB branch, on the left. It leads to Derby Square, on the site of King John's castle, pulled down in 1659, with a statue of Queen Victoria and the *Queen Elizabeth II Law Courts* (1984).

Water St. is continued beyond the Town Hall by Dale St., with a fine range of 19C buildings culminating in the *Municipal Buildings* (1866). The scene beyond is violently disrupted by flyovers and, on the right, the entrance to the **Mersey Tunnel**, or *Queensway Tunnel*, built in 1925–34 to carry road traffic the 2½m journey under the river to Birkenhead. *Kingsway*, a second road tunnel added in 1971, connects Scotland Rd to the N with Wallasey. Facing the Queensway tunnel entry are *St John's Gardens*, with a collection of statues, overlooked on the E by St George's Hall and on the N by the impressive civic buildings of William Brown St.

The **Liverpool Museum**, in a much-altered building of 1857–60 near the lower end of William Brown St., has grown from the natural history collection bequeathed by the Earl of Derby in 1851 to fill five floors of wide-ranging exhibits.

They include: an aquarium; a natural history gallery with plant room; a land transport gallery; sections devoted to the social, industrial and maritime history of Merseyside; and a planetarium with associated displays of time-keeping and space exploration.
   The collections of archaeology and the decorative arts on the first floor include Egyptian, Roman and Greek antiquities, notably the double coffins of Ditamunpaseneb, Attic Red Figure pottery and the Ince Blundell Hall marbles; Anglo-Saxon jewellery, notably the 7C *Kingston Brooch, one of the finest examples of cloisonné work of its period; Chinese cloisonné enamels; classical and medieval ivories; and tribal art from New Guinea and Africa, notably Benin bronzes from Nigeria.

The *City Libraries* next door are housed partly in Cornelius Sherlock's delightful circular *Picton Reading Room* (1875–79). This links the museum building with the *Walker Art Gallery, home of one of the most important art collections outside London.

It includes: Simone Martini (Christ Discovered in the Temple); Ercole de' Roberti (Pietà); Master of Forlì (Christ on the Cross); Pietro Perugino (Birth of the Virgin); Cosimo Rosselli (St Lawrence); Bartolommeo di Giovanni; Spinello Aretino and (?) Vecchietta (St Bernardino Preaching); Francesco Granacci (Life of St John the Baptist); Isenbrandt (Virgin and Child); Lucas Cranach the Elder (Nymph at Fountain); Florentine School (Virgin and Child with St John); Signorelli (Virgin and Child); Master of Aachen (Scenes from the Crucifixion); Master of Frankfurt (Holy Family); Joos van

Cleve (Virgin and Child with Angels); Master of the Virgo inter Virgines (Entombment); Jan Mostaert (Portrait of a Man); French school (Portrait of a Lady with Parakeet); Hans Baldung Grien (Mercenary Love); Rosso Fiorentino (Portrait of a Young Man); Bartolommeo Montagna (Virgin and Child with Saint); Giovanni Mazone (St Mark Enthroned); Giovanni Bellini (Young Man); Girolamo da Santa Croce (Resurrection); (?) Palmezzano (Virgin and Child with Saints); Vicentino (Court of Heaven); Procaccini (Marriage of St Catherine); Studio of Veronese (Finding of Moses); Bonifazio Veronese (Virgin and Child with Saints); Vincenzo Catena (Virgin and Child); Paulus Bor (Magdalen); Solimena (Birth of St John the Baptist); Ciro Ferri (Rest on the Flight into Egypt); Pittoni (Solomon and Queen of Sheba); Carel Fabritius (Portrait); Anton Raffael Mengs (Self-portrait); Govaert Flinck (Portrait of an Oriental); Van Schuppen (Guitar Player); Rembrandt (*Self-portrait; c 1629); Van Dyck (Infanta Isabella; one of several versions); Ruysdael (River Scene); school of Rembrandt (Betrothal); Rubens (*Virgin and Child with St Elizabeth and St John); Nicolas Poussin (*Landscape with Ashes of Phocion); Murillo (La Vierge Coupée); school of Holbein (portrait of Henry VIII); the Pelican Portrait of Elizabeth I (after Nicholas Hilliard); Hogarth (Garrick as Richard III); Stubbs (Molly Longlegs; Horse Frightened by Lion); Richard Wilson (Snowdon; Valley of the Mawddach); Gainsborough (Isabella, Countess of Sefton); Kneller; Lely; Reynolds; Romney; Arthur Devis; Wright of Derby; Turner (Linlithgow Castle; Landscape), Lawrence (Thomas Coke); Benjamin West (Death of Nelson); Constable; Cox; Landseer: Millais (Lorenzo and Isabella); Holman Hunt (Eve of St Agnes; Triumph of the Innocents); John Brett (Stonebreaker); John J. Lee (Sweethearts and Wives); Maclise; Poynter; Watts; W.F. Yeames (And When Did You Last See Your Father?); Luke Fildes; Tissot; Atkinson Grimshaw; Stanhope Forbes; Sir George Clausen; Edward Hornel; Degas (Woman Ironing), Cézanne (The Murder); Monet; Seurat; Matisse; Vuillard; André Derain; Vlaminck; Sickert; Augustus John; Paul Nash; Matthew Smith; Stanley Spencer; Ivon Hitchens; Lowry; Lucien Freud; and David Hockney. Among the sculptures are interesting examples of the 16–18C and works by Epstein, Rodin, Barye, Gaudier-Brzeska, Renoir and Henry Moore (Falling Warrior).

The *Wellington Monument* (1863) stands at the head of Lime St. Beyond is the main façade of *St George's Hall* (open), one of England's best Greek Revival buildings. It was designed by Harvey Lonsdale Elmes in 1839, at the age of 24, and completed after his death in 1847 by Sir Robert Rawlinson and C.R. Cockerell. The Great Hall has a tunnel vault of hollow blocks, a Minton tile floor, a huge organ and statues of local celebrities, including one of William Roscoe by Chantrey. Off the hall is an interesting courtroom and a concert room with a balcony supported by caryatids.

On the plateau in front of the hall are the *Cenotaph* (1930; Lionel Budden) and statues of Victoria and Albert, both on horseback, and Disraeli. The best view of the building is from the terrace of *Lime Street Station* opposite. When it was built in 1867, the cast-iron span of the station's train shed was the largest in the world. The view to the S is closed by the modern shopping precinct of *St John's Centre* with its tall concrete tower.

FROM THE CENTRE (ST GEORGE'S HALL) TO THE ANGLICAN CATHEDRAL. Lime St. continues SE to Ranelagh Place. Brownlow Hill, on the left, climbs past the *Adelphi Hotel* (1912) to the RC cathedral and Liverpool University (see below). Ranelagh St. passes the *Central Station* on its way to the junction with Bold St.

Hanover St. continues straight ahead from the junction. School Lane, to its right, has the attractive building of the former *Bluecoat School* (1716–17), now an arts centre.

The attractive Bold St. begins with Thomas Harrison's *Lyceum Club* (1802), restored as a Post Office and philatelic centre. It ends at the church of *St Luke*, built in 1831 and gutted during World War II. Leece St. climbs to

Rodney St., one of the best of the city's late 18C and early 19C residential streets. The poet Arthur Hugh Clough was born at 9 and Gladstone at 62.

The Anglican **Cathedral** stands high on the ridge of St James's Mount overlooking the city and the Mersey. It was completed after almost 75 years of continuous work in 1978. The architect, Sir Giles Gilbert Scott, was in his early twenties when his design was adopted in 1902 and he worked on the building until his death in 1960—a longer time than Wren spent on St Paul's. Scott's ideas changed greatly as the building progressed, but he held to his original concept of 'a vast hall' quarried out of the local sandstone. The cathedral is the largest church in Britain, and is exceeded in Europe only by St Peter's in Rome and by Milan and Seville cathedrals. Though its Gothic Revival style may seem a hopeless anachronism in the 20C, the building has a strikingly original plan.

It is built N and S, following the line of the rock ridge, but in the description that follows the points of the compass are used in the ecclesiastical sense, with the actual S end referred to as E, etc.

Externally the dominating feature is the huge central tower (1949) resting, unusually, on the outer walls of the building. At its base are the short double transepts and N and S porches. The W front, the last part to be built, was finished more simply than originally planned.

The *Nave* (1948–78) is only three bays long, the two W ones forming a well reached by steps from the side aisles and the E one spanned by the Dulverton Bridge (1961), a huge stone arch supporting a musicians' gallery. They are deliberately subordinate to the huge central space formed by the undertower and the two transept crossings, unobstructed by pillars and capable of seating 4000 people. Particularly striking is the height of the arches of the undertower, with its superb vaulting. The windows (by James Hogan) form two groups of triple lancets surmounted by a rose. The SW transept, the Bapistery, has a marble font by Carter Preston. The S porch contains a brass-rubbing centre. The NW transept is enclosed as a bookstall and the N porch as a cafeteria.

The tall *Choir* (1924), matching the nave in length, has a triforium but no clerestory. The stone reredos, with carved panels by W. Gilbert and L. Weingartner, is unusual in forming an integral part of the E wall. The E window, the largest in England, has stained glass on the theme of 'Te Deum'. The choir aisles, with the two parts of the great organ above their W ends, are connected by an ambulatory. The octagonal *Chapter House* (1924) opens off the NE corner. The *Lady Chapel*, SE of the choir and on a lower level, was the first part to be completed (1910). Its elaborate Decorated Gothic, rising to a stone traceried vault, is markedly different from the rest of the building. The altarpiece is by Scott and Bodley, appointed joint architect during the early stages of the building.

Outside the W end is John Foster's Greek Revival *Oratory* (limited opening), recently rest' ed. Nearby is the entrance to *St James's Cemetery*, romantically laid out in an old .arry below the cathedral. It contains the mausoleum, now neglected, of the politician William Huskisson, killed at the opening of the Liverpool and Manchester Railway in 1830.

FROM THE ANGLICAN CATHEDRAL TO THE RC CATHEDRAL AND THE UNIVERSITY. The direct route goes N from the Anglican cathedral on Hope St., with the *Philharmonic Hall*. A roundabout but more interesting way explores the early 19C streets which extend E and N of the Anglican cathedral towards Abercromby Square (see below). Huskisson St., Percy St., Canning St. and Falkner Square are all worth the detour.

The RC **Metropolitan Cathedral**, on top of Mount Pleasant, was designed by Sir Frederick Gibberd and built in 1962–67. Locally nicknamed the 'Mersey Funnel' or 'Paddy's Wigwam', it consists of a circular skeleton of concrete trusses and flying buttresses, faced with Portland stone and white mosaic, rising to a glass-panelled lantern tower with a crown of slender

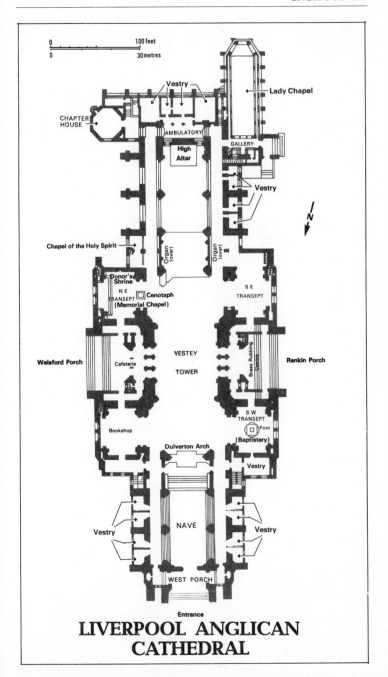

0 100 feet
0 30 metres

Vestry

Lady Chapel

CHAPTER HOUSE

AMBULATORY

GALLERY

High Altar

Vestry

Chapel of the Holy Spirit

Organ (over)

Organ (over)

Donor's Shrine

N E TRANSEPT

Cenotaph

(Memorial Chapel)

S E TRANSEPT

N

Welsford Porch

Cafeteria

VESTEY

TOWER

Brass Rubbing Centre

Rankin Porch

Bookshop

S W TRANSEPT

Font

(Baptistery)

Dulverton Arch

Vestry

Vestry

NAVE

Vestry

WEST PORCH

Entrance

LIVERPOOL ANGLICAN CATHEDRAL

pinnacles. It stands over the vast crypt which is the only completed part of Sir Edwin Lutyens's ambitious design for the cathedral, projected in the 1930s and abandoned after World War II. Gibberd's scheme ingeniously uses the crypt to create an open piazza as well as a podium for his own building.

The entrance is by a porch under the sharply angled belfry, ferociously decorated by William Mitchell. The open pavilion of the interior, lit with stained glass by John Piper and Patrick Reyntiens, has a central sanctuary below a canopy of hanging tubes. The high altar is a slab of white marble from Skopje; the crucifix is by Elizabeth Frink. The spaces between the buttresses form a ring of chapels around the perimeter. Immediately to the right of the entrance is the simple circular Baptistery; diagonally opposite is the Lady Chapel, with glass by Margaret Traherne. The Blessed Sacrament Chapel on the far side from the entrance has windows, tabernacle and altar painting by Ceri Richards.

Lutyens's crypt is entered separately by stairs at the N corners of the piazza. Built of brick in a Renaissance style, it has massive pillars, cavernous vaults and maze-like aisles, with a series of chapels.

The **University** stretches N and E of the RC cathedral on either side of Brownlow Hill. Founded as University College in 1881 and made a constituent college of the Victoria University of Manchester in 1884, it became an independent university in 1903.

Alfred Waterhouse's original *Victoria Building* (1889–92) on Brownlow Hill is surrounded by buildings mostly added since 1950, each by a different architect, showing neither remarkable individuality nor any attempt at cohesion, and prompting the accusation from one unkind critic of 'trying to live down to Waterhouse'. On the opposite corner is the *Students' Union*, the pleasant N end designed by Sir Charles Reilly (1910–13). Of some note are the *Harold Cohen Library* (1936–38; Harold A. Dod) and, next to it, the *Electrical Engineering Building* (1962–65; Yorke, Rosenberg and Mardall); the *Civil Engineering Building* (1958–59; E. Maxwell Fry) in Brownlow St.; the *Chadwick Physics Laboratory* (1957–59; Sir Basil Spence), facing the Green; and Denys Lasdun's striking *Sports Centre* (1963–66) on the corner of Abercromby Square. The E side of the square is filled by the *Senate House* (1966–68; Tom Mellor). Among the early 19C houses opposite is the **University of Liverpool Art Gallery**. Its collection includes English watercolours (Turner, Girtin) and oils, and English porcelain and silver.

See the beginning of this walk for the streets stretching S from Abercromby Square towards the Anglican cathedral.

SUBURBS. As the city plan inset shows, Liverpool's suburbs stretch from *Everton* in the N, known for its toffee and its football team based at Goodison Park, to *Speke* airport in the S. (Speke Hall is described in Route 75A.)

They are well provided with parks and open spaces which, with other points of interest, can be combined into an easy drive of about 15m. From near the Anglican cathedral Princes Rd leads SE to *Prince's Park* (1842), one of the earliest Victorian public parks and Joseph Paxton's first, and the much larger *Sefton Park*, with a lake and superb palm house (1896). By the waterfront, on ground reclaimed by using the spoil from the first Mersey Tunnel, is the attractive *Otterspool Park* and the *Pleasure Island*, laid out for the International Garden Festival in 1984 and now a family leisure park.

Nearby *Aigburth* leads to the Queen's Drive, a handsome boulevard (7m long) encircling the city. In Mossley Hill Rd (right), opposite the parish church, is **Sudley**, a 19C shipowner's mansion with British paintings including work by Gainsborough and Turner. On the E side of Mossley Hill the *Botanic Gardens* at Harthill adjoin *Calderstones Park*. Inside the circuit of Queen's Drive are *Wavertree Playground* and *Newsham Park*, with a lake. To the right of the road at *West Derby*, 5m NE of the centre, is **Croxteth Hall and Country Park** (open). The Jacobean house, with additions of 1702 and 1902, contains period displays, Sefton family portraits, etc. Outside are displays of crafts and carriages, a walled garden, a home farm and 530 acres of parkland with woodland walks. In *Anfield*, to the left, are Liverpool Football Club and *Stanley Park*, enjoying fine views. Beyond Walton Hill Park, on the right, Queen's Drive meets the road leading out to *Aintree*, 5m N, Liverpool's racecourse. The Grand National, the chief event of the steeplechasing season, has been run here in March/April since 1839.

THE WIRRAL: WEST BANK OF THE MERSEY. **Birkenhead** (123,900 inhabitants; TI), on the W bank of the Mersey opposite Liverpool, can be reached by Merseyrail, road tunnel or ferry. A tramway links various sites of interest from the Woodside ferry terminal. The painter Wilson Steer (1860–1942) was a native and the poet Wilfred Owen lived here in 1900–07. Birkenhead developed as a port and shipbuilding town in the 19C. The first iron ship in England was built by Laird & Co. (later Cammell Laird) in 1829 and the famous Confederate privateer 'Alabama' was launched in 1862. The docks, begun in 1844–47, were amalgamated with Liverpool docks in 1855 after a period of intense rivalry. New uses are now being found for the former warehouses and industrial buildings. 'HMS Plymouth' and 'HMS Onyx', veterans of the Falklands War, are open to visitors in East Float.
   The stately Hamilton Square was designed in 1825–44 by J. Gillespie Graham, one of the architects of Edinburgh's New Town. The *Town Hall* was added in 1887. Close to the derelict 19C *St Mary's Church* in Priory St. are the ruins of *Birkenhead Priory* (open), established in 1150, with a chapter house and refectory. The vault of the 19C shipbuilders William and John Laird stands in the churchyard. The *Williamson Art Gallery and Museum* in Slatey Rd has a collection of 18–19C English watercolours and 19C English oil paintings, including work by Wilson Steer; also Liverpool and other porcelain, Della Robbia pottery, and local history displays, including ferry models. *Birkenhead Park* was beautifully laid out by Joseph Paxton in 1843–47 with handsome villas and lodges around the perimeter.
   The borough of **Wallasey** (90,100 inhabitants), beyond the Great Float N of Birkenhead, comprises the towns of New Brighton, Wallasey, Egremont, Seacombe, Liscard and Poulton. *Seacombe*, connected with Liverpool by ferry and the Kingsway tunnel, and *Egremont* are residential suburbs on the Mersey. A riverside promenade leads to *New Brighton* (TI), a resort at the mouth of the Mersey. Sibelius's music was first publicly heard in England at a concert conducted by the composer here in 1899. There is a battery (1827) at Perch Rock, built to guard the approach to Liverpool.

FROM BIRKENHEAD TO CHESTER VIA HOYLAKE, 30m by A553 and A540. For an alternative route to Chester via Port Sunlight, see Route 63. The present route takes A553 inland across the Wirral via (2m) the village of *Bidston*. Bidston Hill is a favourite viewpoint. 8m: **Hoylake** (32,900 inhabitants), at the mouth of the Dee, has the Royal Liverpool golf course. William III embarked from here on his way to the Battle of the Boyne (1690). 9½m: *West Kirby* is a more sheltered resort. The *Hilbre Islands* off the coast are a nature reserve (access by foot at low tide; permit required). Caldy Hill is another good viewpoint. Between West Kirby and Neston the former coastal valley railway line now makes a fine walk through the *Wirral Country Park*. 11½m: *Thurstaston* has the Visitor Centre for the Country Park, as well as a 200-acre common (NT) with heathland and a good hilltop view. The church (1883–86) is by J.L. Pearson. *Arrowe Park*, 2½m NE, was site of the first Boy Scouts' world jamboree in 1929. 15m: *Heswall*. 18½m: *Neston* (18,400 inhabitants), ¾m to the right of A540, was birthplace of Emma Lyon, Lady Hamilton (1763–1815). Nearby *Parkgate*, stranded by saltmarsh, was once the starting-point of the Dublin packet, used by Handel, Swift and John Wesley. At *Ness*, S of Neston, are the splendid *University of Liverpool Botanic Gardens*, with familiar and unusual plants in a parkland setting. *Thornton Hough*, on B5136 2m NE of Neston, is a 'model village' created by Lord Leverhulme of Port Sunlight after he bought the estate in 1891. 30m: *Chester*, see Route 63.

FROM LIVERPOOL TO SOUTHPORT, 20m by A565. The road heads N along the bank of the Mersey, past the docks which stretch to (3m) *Bootle* (62,500 inhabitants). At (4m) *Seaforth*, with a container port, Gladstone spent part of his boyhood at his father's country house. 5m: *Waterloo* is a resort founded in 1815. 6½m: *Great Crosby* has the Merchant Taylor's School. The road continues inland, past (12½m) *Formby* (25,800 inhabitants). The NT owns a 500-acre stretch of wood and dune to the W, where red squirrels can be seen. 20m: **Southport** (89,700 inhabitants; TI) is a resort with a 19C promenade and a pier of 1859, the first in Britain built for pleasure rather than as a landing stage. The handsome Lord St. has Regency villas and late 19C iron verandahs in front of the shops. The Royal Birkdale is the most famous of its golf courses. The old parish church of *Churchtown*, adjoining to the N, contains magnificent woodcarving (c 1704) from the demolished church of St Peter, Liverpool. The botanic gardens have a museum of local history. *Meols Hall* (limited opening) is a 17C house with later additions. *Scarisbrick Hall* (now a school), 4½m SE by the Orsmkirk road, is an astonishing Gothic Revival mansion by A.W.N. and E.W. Pugin (1836–68). *Halsall*, 1½m S of Scarisbrick on A567, stands near the attractive Leeds and Liverpool Canal.

From Liverpool to *Chester* via *Port Sunlight*, see Route 63; to *Stoke-on-Trent*, see Route 67; to *Manchester*, see Route 75A; to *Preston*, *Blackburn*, *Burnley* and *Halifax*, see Route 75B; to *Lancaster* and *Carlisle*, see Route 76.

74

Manchester

MANCHESTER (448,900 inhabitants) is the financial, business and cultural centre of a sprawling conurbation of some 3½ million people which embraces its immediate W neighbour Salford, still anomalously a separate city, and nine other districts (Bolton, Bury, Oldham, Rochdale, Stockport, Tameside, Trafford and Wigan). Despite its ancient origins the city is essentially a child of the Industrial Revolution, when it became regional capital of the Lancashire cotton-manufacturing district. Some great landmarks of its 19C prosperity survive. For the visitor, Manchester's strength lies in the cultural tradition expressed in its concerts, libraries, museums and galleries.

TI: Town Hall Extension, Lloyd St.; International Arrivals Hall, Manchester Airport. **Bus Stations**: Piccadilly and Arndale Centre. Coach station in Chorlton St. The Metrolink system includes a modern tram service connecting various points in the city centre, both railway stations among them, with Bury and Altrincham. **Railway Stations**: Victoria Station (Inter-City), connecting with Salford; Piccadilly Station (Inter-City), connecting with stations at Oxford Rd, Deansgate and Old Trafford, and with a rail link to the airport. **Airport**: 10m S between Altrincham and Wilmslow (connecting spur from junction 5 of M56). Passenger services to Aberdeen, Abu Dhabi, Amsterdam, Bangkok, Barcelona, Belfast, Berlin, Billund, Brussels, Bucharest, Cairo, Cambridge, Cape Town, Cardiff, Chicago, Connaught, Copenhagen, Cork, Dubai, Dublin, Dundee, Dusseldorf, Edinburgh, Eindhoven, Exeter, Fairo, Frankfurt, Geneva, Gibraltar, Glasgow, Guernsey, Hamburg, Hanover, Helsinki, Hong Kong, Inverness, Islamabad, the Isle of Man, Istanbul, Jersey, Johannesburg, Kirkwall, Larnaca, Ljubljana, London (Heathrow and Stansted), Londonderry, Los Angeles, Lyon, Maastricht, Madrid, Malaga, Malta, Melbourne, Milan, Morlaix, Moscow, Munich, Muscat, Newcastle, New York, Nice, Norwich, Oslo, Paphos, Paris, Prague, Pula, Rome, Rotterdam, the Shetland Islands, Singapore, Southampton, Stockholm, Stuttgart, Sydney, Tel Aviv, Tivat, Toronto, Vienna, Warsaw, Waterford, Wick, Zagreb and Zurich. **Theatres**: Opera House, Quay St.; Palace Theatre, Oxford St.; Royal Exchange Theatre, St Ann's Square; Library Theatre, St Peter's Square; Green Room, Whitworth St. West; University Theatre, Devas St., off Oxford Rd; Forum Theatre, Civic Centre, Wythenshawe. Concerts by the Hallé Orchestra in the Concert Hall.

History. Mancunium, or Mamucium, a walled Roman fort on the military road from Chester to York, stood in the Castlefield area at the S end of Deansgate. The later Saxon town, garrisoned against the Danes in 923, lay further N near the cathedral.

Manchester's industrial prosperity had its beginnings in Edward III's settlement of Flemish weavers here in 1375. They worked in wool and linen, though cotton was being imported from the Levant by the 17C. The rise of the Lancashire cotton industry dates from the middle of the 18C, fostered by the moist climate, improvements in machinery and a convenient local coal supply. The first Manchester cotton mill opened in 1781 and Arkwright's mill, established on Miller's Lane in 1783, became the first to use steam power. The transport of raw cotton, coal and finished goods was aided by a system of waterways which began with the Duke of Bridgewater's canal in the mid 18C and, by the early years of the 19C, linked the city with Ashton and Oldham, Bolton and Bury, and Rochdale. The huge Ship Canal (1894), stretching to the Mersey estuary, made Manchester a major inland port. Meanwhile, steam transport had been introduced with the opening of George Stephenson's Liverpool and Manchester Railway in 1830.

To the rest of Victorian England, Manchester became the chief example not only of the prosperity but also of the hardship brought about by the Industrial Revolution, notorious for the unchecked evils of its factory system and the plight of its millhands. At the 'Peterloo Massacre' (1819) the yeomanry killed 11 people in dispersing a mass protest by workers at Peter's Field. The sufferings of later decades were described by Friedrich Engels in 'The Condition of the Working Class in England' (1845) and Elizabeth Gaskell in 'Mary Barton' (1848) and 'North and South' (1855). Opposition to government intervention was a central tenet of the 'Manchester School', led by Richard Cobden (1804–65) and John Bright (1811–89), which played a central role in shaping 19C Liberal politics. Its pressure aided the passage of the 1832 Reform Act which gave the city, until then 'the largest village in Europe', its first parliamentary representation. The Anti-Corn Law League, founded in Manchester, helped bring about repeal of the restrictive corn tariffs in 1846. The modern 'Guardian' newspaper is the descendant of the 'Manchester Guardian', founded in 1821 to advocate the Liberals' belief in parliamentary reform, free trade and non-intervention in foreign affairs.

Natives. Mancunians include Thomas De Quincey (1785–1859), William Harrison Ainsworth (1805–82), Frances Hodgson Burnett (1849–1924), David Lloyd George (1863–1945), James Agate (1877–1947), L.S. Lowry (1887–1976) and Sir Peter Maxwell Davies (b. 1934), who studied at the Royal Manchester College of Music with Sir Harrison Birtwhistle and Alexander Goehr. For famous residents, see the Portico Library, Chetham's Hospital and the university, below.

THE CITY CENTRE. Manchester's most prominent building is Alfred Waterhouse's Gothic *•Town Hall* (1867–76) with its tall central tower. The great hall, included in guided tours, has a double hammerbeam roof and murals by Ford Madox Brown illustrating the city's history. The tower overlooks Albert Square, with the Albert Memorial (1862) and statues of Gladstone and John Bright. To the S are the *Town Hall Extension*, connected to the main building by bridges over Lloyd St., and the rotunda of the **Central Library**, both built in the 1930s. The library is the largest municipal library in the world, housing nine specialised libraries and the *Library Theatre*. The main entrance faces St Peter's Square, with a war Cenotaph by Lutyens (1934).

Mount St. leads S to the former Central Station, now converted into *G-Mex*, the city's exhibition and events centre. Peter St. leads W from Mount St. with an impressive line of buildings on its S side including the former *Theatre Royal* (1845) and the handsome Italianate façade of the **Free Trade Hall**, designed by Edward Walters in 1856 and well restored after wartime bomb damage. The original home of the Hallé Orchestra, it stands on the site of Peter's Field where the Peterloo Massacre took place in 1819 and of the hall where Cobden and Bright delivered their speeches against the Corn Laws. The orchestra's new home is the Concert Hall (to be

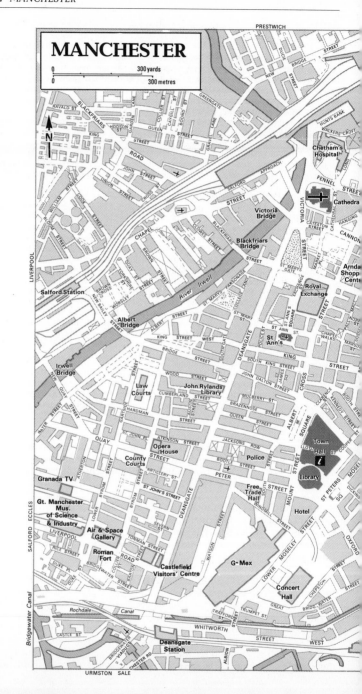

MANCHESTER

0   300 yards
0   300 metres

N

PRESTWICH

Chetham's Hospital

Cathedral

Arndale Shopping Centre

Victoria Bridge

Blackfriars Bridge

Royal Exchange

Salford Station

St Ann's

Albert Bridge

Irwell Bridge

Law Courts

John Rylands Library

Opera House

County Courts

Police

Town Hall

Library

Granada TV

Gt. Manchester Mus. of Science & Industry

Air & Space Gallery

Roman Fort

Castlefield Visitors' Centre

Free Trade Hall

Hotel

G-Mex

Concert Hall

Rochdale Canal

Deansgate Station

Bridgewater Canal

River Irwell

URMSTON SALE

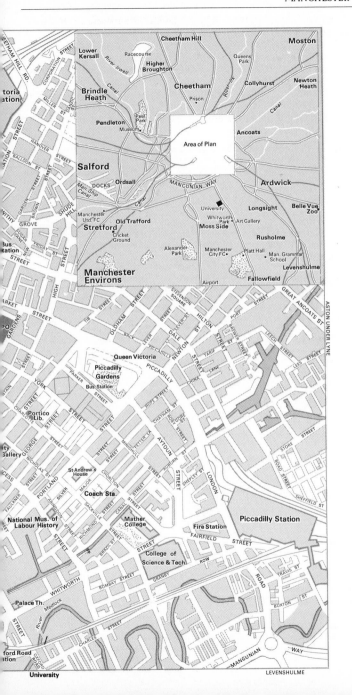

Cheetham Hill
Moston
Lower
Kersall
Racecourse
Higher
Broughton
Queens
Park
Newton
Heath
Brindle
Heath
Cheetham
Collyhurst
Prison
Pendleton
Peel
Park
Museum
Ancoats
Area of Plan
Salford
DOCKS Ordsall
MANCUNIAN WAY
Ardwick
Man Ship
Canal
University
Longsight
Belle Vue
Zoo
Manchester
Utd. FC
Old Trafford
Whitworth
Park
Art Gallery
Stretford
Cricket
Ground
Moss Side
Alexander
Park
Manchester
City FC
Rusholme
Platt Hall
Man. Grammar
School
Manchester
Environs
Levenshulme
Airport
Fallowfield

toria
ation

Victoria
Station

Bus
Station

Queen Victoria
Piccadilly
Gardens
Piccadilly
Bus Station

Portico
Lib.

ty
Gallery

St Andrew's
House

Coach Sta.

National Mus. of
Labour History

Mather
College

Fire Station
FAIRFIELD

Piccadilly Station

College of
Science & Tech.

Palace Th.

ford Road
ation

University

LEVENSHULME

completed 1996; Renton, Howard, Wood, Levin Partnership and Ove Arup), off Lower Moseley St. opposite G-Mex.

Mosley St., running NE from St Peter's Square, soon meets Princess St., running SE from Albert Square alongside the town hall. On the corner stands the *City Art Gallery, in a severely handsome classical building designed by Sir Charles Barry for the Royal Manchester Institution in 1825–29. It houses the city's chief collections of paintings, sculpture, silver, glass and pottery; the remainder are in the branch galleries listed below. The Pre-Raphaelite paintings are outstanding among the British art on display.

The *Entrance Hall* and *Balcony* have been restored to their original neo-classical splendour, with gilded and stencilled decoration on the ceiling and walls. The displays include sculptures by Thorvaldsen and Edward H. Baily and paintings by Etty, Watts, Val Prinsep, Albert Moore, Leighton, Tissot, Poynter and Alma-Tadema. The ground-floor galleries house exhibitions of contemporary decorative and fine arts.

The galleries upstairs are notable for *Pre-Raphaelite and High Victorian paintings, sculpture, furniture and decorative arts. The artists represented include Ford Madox Brown (Work; Stages of Cruelty), Rossetti (Bower Meadow; Astarte Syriaca; Joli Coeur), Holman Hunt (Hireling Shepherd; Shadow of Death; Lady of Shalott; versions of Light of the World and Scapegoat), Millais (Autumn Leaves; Winter Fuel), Burne-Jones, Etty, Leighton, Maclise, Frith, and Watts. Other British artists whose work hangs in these galleries include John Souch (Sir Thomas Ashton), Lely, Stubbs (Cheetah and Stag with Two Indians), Gainsborough (Peasant Girl Gathering Faggots), Bonington, Crome, Cotman, Cox, Constable, De Wint, Etty, Linnell, Samuel Palmer, Turner (Thomson's Aeolian Harp; Now for the Painter) and Sir George Clausen. A Virgin and Child with Goldfinch (c 1380) by a member of the Florentine school and a Crucifixion by a follower of Duccio represent the early Italian schools. Later Italian art includes work by Turchi (Flight into Egypt) and Bernardo Bellotto (View of the Castle of Konigstein). Flemish and Dutch art is represented by the Master of the Magdalen Legend (Virgin and Child), van Ruisdael, Cuyp, van Goyen and Ochtervelt. French art includes work by Claude Lorrain (Adoration of the Golden Calf), Corot, Courbet, Fantin-Latour, Pissarro, Sisley, Gauguin and Rodin.

The **Athenaeum Gallery**, in Barry's Manchester Athenaeum Club building (1839) next door on Princess St., houses a changing programme of temporary exhibitions. The other branches of the City Art Galleries, described in the tours of Outer Manchester, are the Gallery of English Costume at Platt Hall, Rusholme; Wythenshawe Hall, Northenden; and Heaton Hall, Heaton Park. Further down Princess St. is the *National Museum of Labour History*, with exhibits honouring the lives of working men and women.

Mosley St. continues NE from the City Art Gallery. The *Portico Library* (by Thomas Harrison), on the corner of Charlotte St. to the right, opened in 1806 as a social and literary institution. Its first secretary was the Manchester doctor Peter Mark Roget, remembered for his 'Thesaurus' (1852); early readers included De Quincey and Elizabeth Gaskell. Mosley St. ends at Piccadilly, with one of the city's few public gardens and some of its many insensitive modern buildings (1959–65; Covell, Matthews and Partners). The busy Market St. leads left to the Exchange (see below).

NORTH FROM THE CENTRE TO THE CATHEDRAL, AND BACK BY DEANSGATE AND CASTLEFIELD. The busy Cross St. leads N from Albert Square to the Royal Exchange. On the way it is intersected by King St., with some of Manchester's best buildings among the banks and offices to the right. C.R. Cockerell's former *Bank of England* (1845–46), now a TSB branch, and Lutyens's *Midland Bank* (1929) are outstanding. In St Ann St., left of Cross St. beyond the King St. junction, is the lovely church of *St Ann* (1709–12) with a contemporary pulpit and font and Carracci's 'Descent from the Cross'. De Quincey, born in a house that stood at the corner of Cross St. and John Dalton St. nearby, was baptised here. On the right of St Ann's Square, with its statue of Cobden, is the **Royal Exchange** (1914–21), the latest of the city's several cotton exchanges, now a theatre with a spectacular auditorium.

The *Wellington Inn*, a 16C half-timbered house, survives in the otherwise redeveloped Market Place. John Byrom (1692–1763), Jacobite poet, author of 'Christians Awake' and inventor of a system of shorthand, was born here.

Victoria St. continues N to the **Cathedral**, dwarfed by modern tower blocks and looking across the Irwell towards Salford. The old parish church of Manchester was made collegiate in 1421 by a charter of Henry V which also licensed the lord of the manor and rector, Thomas de la Warre, to rebuild. The present church is thus largely Perpendicular, dating mainly from 1422–1520. It was raised to cathedral status in 1847. The square tower was resurfaced and heightened when the building was restored in 1867; further restoration was carried out after damage to the E end in World War II.

The *Nave* is made disproportionately wide by the double aisles, the outer aisles having originally accommodated chantries to Henry V, among others. The tall and graceful tower arch survives from the earlier church. The tower fan vaulting is 19C, and the glass in the W window is by Anthony Holloway (1980). In the NW corner is a 19C statue of Humphrey Chetham (see below). The main beams of the 15C roof are supported by angels with musical instruments, typical of the superb woodwork throughout the church. The beautiful Perpendicular choir screen is also 15C.

The *Choir* has *stalls of c 1485–1506, with a full set of misericords, by the Ripon school of craftsmen who also made the stalls there and at Beverley. Like the splendid 15C panelled roof, they suffered from blast in 1940 but have been well restored. Note the brass of Warden Huntington (d. 1458), the 17C chandeliers and the 18C ironwork.

In the retrochoir a restored screen of c 1440 leads into the *Lady Chapel*, destroyed in 1940 and rebuilt by Sir Hubert Worthington. There is a Madonna by Sir Charles Wheeler on the outside. S of the choir are the *Bishop Fraser Chapel* (1885), the octagonal *Chapter House* (1485) and the *Jesus Chapel*, founded in 1506, with a 16C screen. At the NE corner of the church is the *Chapel of the Manchester Regiment*, built by Bishop Stanley in 1513 and restored after the landmine fell outside its E window in 1940. The modern glass is by Margaret Traherne.

Beyond the cathedral is *Chetham's Hospital**, originally built in 1421 by Thomas de la Warre as a residence for the warden and fellows of his collegiate church. The astrologer John Dee (1527–1608) was warden here. Under the will of Humphrey Chetham (1580–1653) the buildings were converted into a charity school for the maintenance and education of 40 poor boys. The fine collegiate buildings, with 15C refectory and screens passage, are now used by a school for young musicians. The old dormitory wing is occupied by the foundation's *Library* (open).

It claims to be the oldest surviving public library in England, its books having been chained until c 1740. It now comprises some 85,000 volumes (90 incunabula) and many manuscripts, and specialises in the topography of the North-west. The Reading Room contains the 17C portrait of Chetham on which his statue in the cathedral is based, a chained library dated 1655 and a desk used by Marx and Engels.

Chapel St., beginning opposite Chetham's Hospital, is the main street of Salford, explored in Outer Manchester: West, below. N of Chetham's Hospital are *Victoria Station* and the beginning of Cheetham Hill Rd, followed in Outer Manchester: North, below.

Deansgate leads SW. On the right is Basil Champneys's handsome neo-Gothic Deansgate Memorial Building of the *John Rylands University Library of Manchester** (open), endowed and built by Mrs Rylands in memory of her husband and opened in 1900 as the John Rylands Library. In 1972 this merged with the Manchester University Library, on the university campus in Oxford Rd, and the Deansgate Memorial Building is now the rare printed books and manuscripts division of the library.

The watermarking of the red Penrith sandstone in the entrance hall is remarkable. Rare items from the library's collections, changed at intervals throughout the year, are on display. The collection of about 1 million printed books (from a total of over 3 million in the John Rylands University Library of Manchester) includes the Althorp Library of 40,000 volumes collected by the 2nd Earl Spencer (d. 1834) and the Christie Collection of 8000 volumes bequeathed to Manchester University by Professor Richard Copley Christie (d. 1901). The superb collection of early printed books includes the 'St Christopher' block-print (1423), the earliest dated piece of European printing extant; about 4000 incunabula; Bibles in over 400 languages; an outstanding Aldine collection; and many fine bindings. The manuscript collection includes the major portion of the Bibliotheca Lindesiana bought from the 26th Earl of Crawford (d. 1913), some 20,000 items representing around 65 different language groups; the 'St John Fragment' (c AD 120), the earliest New Testament manuscript extant, and the 'Deuteronomy Fragment' (2C BC); and about ¾ million documents and charters.

Hardman St., on the right, leads to the *Law Courts* (1961; Leonard Howitt). Quay St., to its S, has the *Opera House* (1912) and the *County Courts*, built c 1770, Cobden's residence and later the first home of Owens College (see university, below). St John's St., also on the right of Deansgate, has good Georgian houses.

Peter St., to the left, returns to the centre. Before making the return, it is worth continuing S on Deansgate to Castlefield, site of the Roman fort and of Manchester's early canal and railway systems. The neighbourhood has been rescued from decay to become an 'Urban Heritage Park'. On the left of Liverpool Rd is a modern reconstruction of the N gateway of the *Roman Fort*, with displays about Roman Castlefield in the adjoining gardens. On the opposite side of Liverpool Rd the splendid cast-iron market hall (1877) houses the *Air and Space Gallery*, whose exhibits about the history of flight include material on loan from NASA. It is part of the ***Museum of Science and Industry**, which displays its main exhibits in the former Liverpool Road Station, the world's oldest surviving railway station, built in 1830 as the terminus of George Stephenson's Liverpool and Manchester Railway.

Galleries include the Power Hall, a converted goods shed with the world's largest collection of working stationary steam engines as well as vintage cars, steam locomotives, etc.; the Electricity Gallery; the Lower Byrom St. Warehouse, with displays about the textile industry, printing and papermaking; and the restored station platform and First Class Booking Hall, with an exhibition and audio-visual show about the history of the railway. There are also exhibitions about the history of Greater Manchester and 'Underground Manchester'.

Nearby stand the *Granada TV Studios* (open). The tour includes a visit to the set of the soap opera 'Coronation Street'.

S of the museum and the railway lines is the terminus of the **Bridgewater Canal**, begun in 1759 by James Brindley for the 3rd Duke of Bridgewater, the first canal in England to be cut through open country rather than following the course of an existing river. The first section, opened in 1761, runs NW from the city to the duke's coal mine at Worsley (see Outer Manchester: West, below). A later extension runs from Stretford to (26m) Runcorn. Reclamation work has transformed the decayed canal basin, the starting-point for organised boat cruises. There is also a worthwhile walk along the towpath of the Rochdale Canal (1804), leading E to Princess St. See Salford (in Outer Manchester: West, below) for the Manchester Ship Canal.

SOUTH-EAST FROM THE CENTRE TO THE UNIVERSITY. Oxford St., leading SE from St Peter's Square, is continued by Oxford Rd, the main thoroughfare of South Manchester. It passes under the Mancunian Way, part of the ring road.

At 1m is the **University of Manchester**, spreading on both sides of Oxford Rd with a characteristic building by Waterhouse (1873, later enlarged) as the centrepiece of its campus.

Historically the first and today the largest of Britain's civic universities, it developed out of Owens College, founded under the will of John Owens and opened on Quay St. in 1851. The Victoria University was founded in 1880 with Leeds and Liverpool as constitutent colleges. By 1904 these were independent, and Owens College was incorporated as the Victoria University of Manchester. The *John Rylands University Library of Manchester* (on Deansgate; see above) owns editions of Francis Thompson and George Gissing, both students, and of Elizabeth Gaskell, who lived locally. Sir Ernest Rutherford discovered the nuclear structure of the atom at Manchester, and the world's first computer was produced here in 1948. Several departments have exhibitions in their foyers illustrating their work, and the *University Theatre* houses a professional company.

The university's **Manchester Museum**, on the right of the entrance, contains a collection of Egyptian antiquities found by Sir William Flinders Petrie (1853–1942), a rare archery collection, fine Japanese ivories, and a large natural history collection and vivarium.

Elizabeth Gaskell, married to a Unitarian preacher and lecturer at Owens College, lived after 1850 at 84 Plymouth Grove, to the E, leading to the Stockport road. The house is now the University Overseas Centre. Charlotte Brontë several times visited her future biographer here and had earlier begun 'Jane Eyre' (1847) at a house, since demolished, in Boundary St. Emmeline Pankhurst lived at 62 Nelson St., a left turn from Oxford Rd, and launched the suffragette movement at a meeting held here in 1903. The house is now open as *The Pankhurst Centre*.

Nearby in Oxford Rd, on the left, is the *Royal Infirmary*, founded in 1752 and moved here in 1908. Set back from the opposite side of the road is the **Whitworth Art Gallery**, a bequest of Sir Joseph Whitworth (d. 1887) and since 1958 part of the university.

It contains British watercolours (Turner, Girtin, Blake), drawings (Picasso, Van Gogh, Pissarro) prints (Dürer, Mantegna, Rembrandt), sculpture (Epstein, Paolozzi, Frink) and modern art (Lucien Freud, Francis Bacon, Howard Hodgkin). The collection of *textiles, the best in Britain outside the Victoria and Albert Museum in London, ranges from 4C Coptic robes to contemporary knitting. The equally important wallpaper collection has work by Morris, Voysey and Greenaway. A regularly changing exhibition programme continues throughout the year.

OUTER MANCHESTER: SOUTH. Oxford Rd continues S from the university and the Whitworth Art Gallery and becomes Wilmslow Rd. On the right at 1m is **Platt Hall**, a red-brick Palladian building of 1764, now a branch of the City Art Galleries and home of the *Gallery of English Costume*. The collection, ranging from the 17C to the 20C, is the largest and most comprehensive outside the Victoria and Albert Museum in London. *Platt Fields Park* lies to the S. *Hollings College*, opposite, has a gimmicky building by Leonard Howitt (1957–60). Nearby Old Hall Lane leads to the buildings of *Manchester Grammar School*, founded in 1515 by Hugh Oldham, Bishop of Exeter, and moved here from beside Chetham's Hospital in 1931. Pupils have included John Bradford, Humphrey Chetham, De Quincey, Harrison Ainsworth, the playwright Stanley Houghton (1881–1913) and the novelist Louis Golding (1895–1958).

Withington, 1m S, has the interesting church of St Christopher (1935; B.A. Miller). *Didsbury*, about 1½m further, is a well-to-do suburb above the Mersey. The church of St James has a fine monument to Sir Nicholas Mosley (d. 1612), Lord Mayor of London.

Wythenshawe Hall, administered by the City Art Galleries, is by A5103 in *Northenden* about 3m W of Didsbury and 5m S of the city centre. Partly dating from the 16C but several times remodelled, it is furnished as a country house, with displays of 16–17C paintings, furniture, weapons, etc. The *Wythenshawe Estate* is a garden suburb developed by the Manchester Corporation from 1931 onwards and designed by Barry Parker. It has two outstanding modern churches: St Michael's, Orton Rd, by Caichemaille-Day and Lander (1937), and the William Temple Memorial Church, Simonsway, by George Pace (1954–65).

OUTER MANCHESTER: WEST. Chapel St., beginning opposite Chetham's Hospital, is the main street of **Salford** (98,000 inhabitants), Manchester's immediate neighbour on the W bank of the Irwell but still technically an independent city. Among its buildings are the RC *Cathedral of St John* (1844–48) in Chapel St., and the neo-classical *St Philip's Church* (1825; Sir Robert Smirke). The Crescent has some good Georgian houses, one the home of the scientist James Prescott Joule (1818–89) and another now the *Working Class Museum and Library*. The *Art Gallery and Museum* at the entrance to *Peel Park* contains a reconstructed 19C street and the largest collection in the country of paintings by L.S. Lowry, born in Manchester and a resident of Salford for much of his life. The nearby *University of Salford* was opened as a technical college in 1896.

The *Museum of Mining*, on Eccles Old Rd (A576) NW of the centre, has displays and reconstructed scenes from the history of coal-mining. It is housed in a Greek Revival villa of 1825–29 by Sir Charles Barry.

'Coming from the Mill' by L.S. Lowry, from the collection of the City of Salford Art Gallery and Museum

Ordsall Hall (open), S of Salford's centre, is a half-timbered 16C building with appropriate furniture and exhibits of local history. Further S are the docks of the **Manchester Ship Canal**, built in 1887–94, running a 35½m course which connects Manchester with the Mersey at Eastham. Part of the dockland is now being redeveloped after its decline in recent years. On the S bank are the industrial estate of *Trafford Park*, also being redeveloped, and the county cricket ground at *Old Trafford*.

Eccles (37,200 inhabitants) lies 2m W of Salford by A57. *Monks Hall Museum*, in a partly 16C building, has collections of childrens' toys, games and dolls. Industrial exhibits include a Nasmyth steam hammer from the old Britannia Iron Foundry in neighbouring *Patricroft*. At *Barton*, S of A57, a remarkable swing aqueduct carries the Bridgewater Canal over the Ship Canal. The RC church on the opposite bank is a splendid building by E.W. Pugin (1867–68). *Worsley*, near M62 about 2½m NW of Eccles, marks the start of the Bridgewater Canal (see also Castlefield, above). Near the parish church (1846; Gilbert Scott) are the canal basin and the tunnel entrance to the underground system for bringing coal from the duke's mine to the surface. Worsley Old Hall, formerly the home of the Bridgewater family, was almost entirely rebuilt in the 19C and is now a restaurant.

OUTER MANCHESTER: NORTH. From the roundabout beyond Victoria Station, Cheetham Hill Rd (A665) heads N. The old bus garage near (1¼m) the junction with Queen's Rd (A6010) is now the *Museum of Transport*, with a large collection of buses, coaches and memorabilia. **Heaton Hall**, in its park off A576 2½m further N, is a handsome neo-classical house largely built by James Wyatt in 1772. Now administered by the City Art Galleries, it has been restored and furnished in the appropriate style. The Music Room has an organ by Samuel Green (1790) and the Cupola Room superb *painted decoration by Biagio Rebecca.

From Manchester to *Stafford* via the *Potteries*, see Route 67; to *Derby* via the *Peak District*, see Routes 69A and 69B; to *Sheffield* via the *Peak District*, see Route 69D; to *Liverpool*, see Route 75A; to *Bolton*, *Blackburn* and *Settle*, see Route 75C; to *Bury*, *Burnley* and *Skipton*, see Route 75D; to *Rochdale*, *Halifax* and *Bradford*, see Route 75E; to *Huddersfield* and *Leeds*, see Route 75F; to *Sheffield* via *Penistone*, see Route 75G.

75

The Manufacturing Towns of Lancashire and Yorkshire

This densely populated region stretches from Liverpool to Manchester and across the Pennines to Sheffield and Leeds, taking in a host of other cities and towns along the way. Formerly belonging to Lancashire and the West Riding of Yorkshire, it is now divided between Merseyside, Greater Manchester, Lancashire, South Yorkshire and West Yorkshire. Its traditionally industrial character has also changed. Historically, the great activities fostered by the Industrial Revolution were centred here: coal-mining in the southern part of Lancashire and in South Yorkshire, textile production from cotton in Lancashire and wool in West Yorkshire, and steel production in the Don valley. Now the cotton industry has vanished or declined into a much smaller industry dependent on artificial fabrics. Steel and coal have both suffered upheaval and dramatic reduction. The woollen industry alone has proved fairly resilient. The result, where it has not been the economic depression which has left its mark on much of the region, has been diversification, particularly into engineering and chemical works.

Perhaps tourism should be added to the list of new industries. Its traditional image was hardly inviting, but the region has at last begun to establish itself on the tourist map. It certainly has much to offer. The industrialisation of the landscape never completely despoiled its often rugged scenery, and great natural beauty survives in places like Pendle Hill, the Calder valley, Rossendale, the Ryburn valley, the moors near Rochdale and Oldham, and the Colne valley. The towns and cities, however meanly unimaginative most of their ordinary housing might be, expressed their civic pride in grand 19C town halls and public buildings, and in museums and art collections of more than merely local importance. Industrial history, particularly the history of textile production, is remembered in some excellent museums.

A. Liverpool to Manchester

Directions. The direct roads are (34m) M62 and M602, its extension into Salford, and (33m) A580. The routes suggested below pass through the intervening towns.

VIA WARRINGTON, 35m by A57. **Liverpool**, see Route 73. A57 crosses M57 on the way to (8m) *Prescot* (11,000 inhabitants), a centre of the watch trade in the 18–19C, with a Museum of Clock and Watchmaking in the High St. The parish church has a classical exterior (1729) and Jacobean roof. Knowsley Hall, to the N, is not open but its grounds contain the large *Knowsley Safari Park*, entered from the eastbound carriageway of the Prescot bypass. Edward Lear began writing nonsense poetry while employed here to sketch the Earl of Derby's menagerie. At (10m) *Rainhill* A57 crosses the original Liverpool and Manchester Railway. Stephenson's 'Rocket' won the trial of locomotives held here in 1829, the year before the line opened. The RC church of St Bartholomew (1840) is an Ionic temple with a rich interior. 18m: **Warrington** (57,400 inhabitants; TI), on the N bank of the Mersey, is an old town which became a centre for foundries, chemicals and soapworks. The *Town Hall* occupies a mansion built in 1750 by Gibbs, probably also the architect of *Holy Trinity* in 1760. The parish church of *St Elphin*, further E, was rebuilt with a tall spire by Frederick and Horace Francis in 1859–67. The *Museum and Art Gallery* in Bold St. has local history, natural history, antiquities, firearms, and 19C paintings.

Academy St. is named after the Warrington Academy of higher education for the sons of Dissenters, which flourished between 1757 and 1783. Marat and Joseph Priestley were tutors and Thomas Malthus was a pupil. The first premises were in Bridge St., where John Howard lodged while printing his book on prison reform. Both Independent and Primitive Methodism started in Warrington.

From Warrington to *Chester*, see Route 63.

Beyond Warrington A57 crosses M6 and runs close to the Manchester Ship Canal. 31m: *Eccles*, (33m) *Salford* and (35m) **Manchester**, see Route 74.

VIA ST HELENS, 33m by A57, A58 and A572. From Liverpool to (8m) *Prescot* on A57, see above. A58 bears left for (11½m) **St Helens** (98,800 inhabitants), a centre of glass-making since 1773. The *Pilkington Glass Museum*, in the headquarters of the Pilkington glassworks, illustrates the history, manufacture and technology of glass in all forms. The *Museum and Art Gallery* in College St. has bottles and displays of other local industries, as well as local natural history, and a good collection of English watercolours. Sir Thomas Beecham (1879–1971), a member of the family which manufactured Beecham's Pills, was a native of St Helens.

A58 goes on to (5m) *Ashton-in-Makerfield* (29,300 inhabitants), with the racecourse at *Haydock Park* to its S, and continues through (9m) *Hindley* (25,500 inhabitants) to (16m) *Bolton* (Route 75C).

Wigan (79,500 inhabitants; TI) lies 4m N of Ashton by A49. Its reputation as the typical Northern manufacturing town was summed up by the old joke about 'Wigan Pier', made popular by the Wigan-born music-hall comedian George Formby Senior and perpetuated in the title of George Orwell's study of industrial depression in the 1930s, 'The Road to Wigan Pier'. The name is now used for the buildings by the basin of the Leeds and Liverpool Canal, on A49 S of the town centre. They include a Heritage Centre, with exhibits and performances by actors bringing to life the history of the area, and Trencherfield Mill, with the world's largest working mill steam-engine as well as textile and rope-making machinery. *All Saints*, rebuilt in 1845–50, has a partly 13C tower and a S aisle window by Morris and Co. (1868). There are two RC churches in Standishgate, the classical *St John's* (1819) and the Gothic *St Mary's* (1818).

From St Helens A572 goes through (16m) *Newton-le-Willows* (19,700 inhabitants) and then crosses A49 and M6 on the way to (22m) *Leigh* (45,300 inhabitants). 27m: *Worsley* and (33m) **Manchester**, see Route 74.

VIA WIDNES AND ALTRINCHAM, 40m by A561, A562, A50 and A56. **Liverpool**, see Route 73. A561 passes Liverpool airport at (7m) *Speke*. *Speke Hall* (NT and Merseyside Council), also to the right, is one of the finest half-timbered manor houses in the country. Built for the Norris family between about 1492 and 1612, it has four large wings surrounding a cobbled courtyard. Inside, the Great Hall has 16C Flemish panelling and the Great Parlour a carved overmantel and Jacobean plaster ceiling. A561 continues past the motor works of *Halewood*. The churchyard of (10m) *Hale*, on the right, has the grave of John Middleton (1578–1623), the 'Childe of Hale', said to have been 9ft 3in tall. Shortly afterwards A561 joins A562. 13m: **Widnes** (54,400 inhabitants; TI) stands on the N bank of the Mersey opposite Runcorn (Route 67). Its long connection with the alkali and chemical industry is recorded in the *Halton Chemical Industry Museum*, housed in an office building of 1860 on Spike Island.

20m: **Warrington**, see above. A50 crosses the Mersey and at (21m) *Latchford* the Manchester Ship Canal. A56 is then followed left. 25m: *Lymm* (10,400 inhabitants), on the Bridgewater Canal, is a pleasant old place with a 17C market cross and replica wooden stocks. 31m: *Bowdon* (4900 inhabitants), birthplace of the composer John Ireland (1879–1962), has 19C villas and a parish church of 1858 with monuments from its predecessor. *Dunham Massey* (NT), about 1½m W, is a red-brick house of 1732 round an open courtyard, like the Tudor building it replaced. It contains good 18C paintings and furniture and Huguenot silver. The large deer park has ancient trees. Shortly beyond Bowdon A56 turns left, passing (32m) **Altrincham** (39,600 inhabitants; TI), a dormitory town on the fringes of Manchester. Beyond the twin towns of (35m) *Ashton-upon-Mersey* and *Sale* the route crosses the Mersey a second time and then M63. 40m: **Manchester**, see Route 74.

B.   Liverpool to Preston, Blackburn, Burnley and Halifax

Directions. Total distance 71m. **Liverpool**, see Route 73. A59 to (31m) **Preston**. A59, A677 to (41m) **Blackburn**. A679 to (46m) Accrington and (50m) **Burnley** (bypassed; Route 75D). A646 to (64m) Hebden Bridge and (71m) **Halifax**.

Liverpool, see Route 73. As it leaves the city, Scotland Rd (A59) passes (2½m) *Walton* and (5½m) the racecourse at *Aintree*, described in Route 73. The church of *Sefton*, to the left at 7m, has interesting monuments and magnificent 16C screens and stalls. At (12m) *Ormskirk* (27,800 inhabitants) the church, mainly Perpendicular with Norman remains, has a tower and steeple side by side. It contains the burial chapel of the Stanleys, Earls of Derby. 17½m: * *Rufford Old Hall* (NT) is a 16C half-timbered building, with a brick wing added in 1662 and altered in 1821. The Great Hall has a hammerbeam roof and a fantastically carved movable screen, apparently the only one to survive complete. There are also collections of 17C oak furniture and 16C arms, armour and tapestries.

31m: **Preston** (125,800 inhabitants; TI) is the administrative centre of Lancashire. Engineering and other industries have replaced the cotton-weaving on which it once depended. New uses have been found for many of its red-brick mill buildings.

Though it has little to show for its early history, 'Proud Preston' has always been important because of its strategic position on the Ribble astride the lowland route from Scotland. It received its first charter in 1179; the Guild Festival, which dates from that time, is celebrated every 20 years (next in 2012). The town was sacked by Robert Bruce in 1323, captured by the Parliamentary armies in 1643, and occupied by the Old Pretender in 1715 and by the Young Pretender in 1745. Like much of S Lancashire, it remains a stronghold of Roman Catholicism.

Natives include the painter Arthur Devis (1711–87) and the poets Francis Thompson (1859–1907) and Robert Service (1874–1958), the 'Canadian Kipling'. The house where Sir Richard Arkwright (1732–92), another native, developed his water frame in 1768 survives on Stoneygate. Dickens's visit during the cotton workers' strike in 1854, when he stayed at the Bull and Royal Hotel in Church St., gave him useful material for 'Hard Times'.

The town has several modern shopping centres as well as older covered markets. The *Harris Museum and Art Gallery*, in a striking classical building (1882–93; James Hibbert) overlooking the Flag Market, displays local archaeology and social history and 18–20C art, including work by the Devis family. Each August the Flag Market hosts a 'Pot Fair'. Winckley Square, S of Fishergate, is the centre of a pleasant late Georgian quarter. *Avenham Park* and *Miller Park*, further S, slope down to the Ribble. The *County and Regimental Museum*, with regional and military exhibits, occupies the Old Sessions House on Stanley St., E of the centre.

The singer Kathleen Ferrier (1912–52) was born at *Higher Walton*, 3m SE on A675. About 3m further is *Hoghton Tower* (limited opening), pronounced 'Hawton', a 16C fortified house where James I is said to have knighted the loin of beef ('sirloin') in 1617.

B6243 follows the N side of the Ribble valley through (7m) the high-lying *Longridge* and (12m) *Hurst Green*, passing near Stonyhurst College, to (18m) *Clitheroe* (Route 75C). *Chingle Hall* (open), on B5269 3½m W of Longridge near *Goosnargh*, is a small medieval manor house with old beams (said to be Viking), secret rooms and a reputation for ghosts. St John Wall (1620–79), one of the English martyrs canonised in

1970, was born here. There is a country park 5m NW of Longridge at *Beacon Fell* (873ft), with fine views. *Chipping*, a stone-built village 5m NE of Longridge, makes a good centre for walks in the fell country further N. *Ribchester*, by the Ribble 3m SE of Longridge on B6245, has remains of the Roman fort of Bremetennacum with a museum of finds from the site. The 13–15C church and the village centre, with the 18C White Bull inn, are attractive. There are pleasant river walks, with a fine bridge of 1774 1½m upstream. *Stidd*, ½m NE, has a little Norman chapel and early 18C almshouses.

From Preston to *Bolton*, see Route 75C; to *Blackpool* and to *Lancaster*, see Route 76.

The main route leaves Preston by New Hall Lane (A59) and crosses the river and M6. 35m: A59 bears left for Clitheroe (Route 75C). This route follows A677. *Samlesbury Hall* (open), shortly beyond the junction, is a half-timbered 14–16C manor house much altered in the 19C, now a centre for sales and exhibitions of antiques, collectors' items, etc. It was originally built by the Southworth family, best known of whom is St John Southworth (1592–1654), another of the English martyrs canonised in 1970. The hall has a fragment of a carved screen like the one at Rufford.

41m: **Blackburn** (109,000 inhabitants; TI) was once the greatest cotton-weaving centre in the world. It now depends on engineering more than textiles but mill buildings and chimneys survive, notably by the Leeds and Liverpool Canal. The Liberal politician John Morley (1838–1923) was born here.

The *Cathedral* was built as a parish church in 1820–31 and raised to its present status in 1926. John Palmer's Gothic building was enlarged between 1938 and 1967 by new transepts, crossing and E end, with Laurence King succeeding W.A. Forsythe as architect. King designed the corona and needle spire, John Hayward the glass in the lantern and also the huge statue of Christ (1965). The *Museum and Art Gallery* in Museum St. contains medieval illuminated manuscripts and early printed books; Greek, Roman and English coins; local antiquities; and a regimental gallery. The pictures include Japanese prints, 19–20C watercolours and Victorian oil paintings. The adjoining *Lewis Textile Museum* in Exchange St. has working machinery. *Witton Country Park* is 1m W of the town.

B6234, an alternative to the main route below, runs E to Accrington via (2m) *Stanhill* and (2½m) *Oswaldthistle*. James Hargreaves invented the spinning jenny in 1764 at what is now the Post Office in Stanhill. He moved to Nottingham after the mob destroyed his home and machinery.

From Blackburn to *Bolton* and *Manchester* and to *Settle*, see Route 75C.

A679 leads E to (46m) **Accrington** (35,900 inhabitants; TI), another former cotton-weaving town. 'Accrington Bloods', the harsh red bricks popular with late 19C and early 20C builders, are not much in evidence locally. The *Town Hall* (1857) was built in tribute to the politician Sir Robert Peel, descended from a powerful family of local manufacturers. The *Haworth Art Gallery* has the largest collection of Tiffany glass in Europe, with 19–20C English watercolours and oil paintings. Sir Harrison Birtwhistle was born at Accrington in 1934. At 50m the route leaves A679 and bears right on A646, bypassing the centre of **Burnley**, described in Route 75D. The road passes Towneley Hall (also Route 75D), climbs the moors and enters West Yorkshire at (57m) *Cornholme*.

At (60m) *Todmorden* (14,700 inhabitants; TI), a former cotton-spinning town, the imposing neo-Renaissance Town Hall (1870) spanned the York-shire–Lancashire border when it was built. Natives include the cotton manufacturer John Fielden (1784–1849), prime mover of the 1847 Act limiting the working day to ten hours, and Sir John Cockcroft (1897–1967), pioneer of radar and atomic energy.

The walkers' route known as the Calderdale Way links some fine scenery in a 50m circuit of the region, from Todmorden in the W to Brighouse beyond Halifax in the E, with connecting paths to the main centres in the valley. A681 leads W from Todmorden to (4½m) Bacup and Rossendale (Route 75D).

A646 heads along the valley of the Calder, where the Rochdale Canal runs alongside the river. The Pennine Way crosses the road by the prominent Stoodley Pike obelisk. 64m: *Hebden Bridge* (TI) is a typical West Riding mill town, jammed into the narrow valley bottom. The community of weavers from which it sprung was at *Heptonstall* on the shoulder of the moor above; the two are still connected by a steep packhorse way. Hebden Bridge has a working clog mill (open) and a museum of pre-1939 cars, motor cycles and bicycles. Heptonstall has a ruined church, an octagonal Wesleyan chapel of 1764, some handsome houses and an interesting local museum in the old grammar school. Sylvia Plath (1932–63) is buried in the new churchyard. *Hardcastle Crags* are in the NT woods of Hebden Dale, 3m NW. *Haworth* (Route 75H) is 7m N by A6033. The present route, still on A646, follows the Calder to (65m) *Mytholmroyd*, with the pleasant *Cragg Vale* to its S. To the NE are (1m) *Midgley*, one of the villages where the traditional 'Pace Egg Play' is acted at Easter, and (2m) *Luddenden*, with cottages, mills and cobbled streets in a steep little valley. Branwell Brontë, brother of the novelists, drank at the Lord Nelson inn while working as a railway clerk nearby in 1841–42. A646 then climbs out of the Calder valley above *Sowerby Bridge* (Route 75E), passing the distinctive *Wainhouse Tower* of 1877 (limited opening).

71m: **Halifax** (87,500 inhabitants; TI), rising steeply on the slopes of the Hebble valley, has been moulded by the cloth trade. Its best monument is the *Piece Hall* (1779; Thomas Bradley), a vast trading market with 315 rooms opening on to a colonnaded courtyard. An open-air market is held on Fridays and Saturdays. Restored in 1976, the building houses shops, the TI Centre, an *Art Gallery* with changing exhibitions, and the *Pre-Industrial Museum*, tracing the history of the cottage wool industries. The *Calderdale Industrial Museum* in the adjoining 19C mill has early textile and engineering machinery, much of it working, and other relics of the region's past.

The Piece Hall is overlooked from the E by the tall spire surviving from the burnt *Congregational Church* (1857). The low-lying 15C parish church, further E, has oak furnishings and a life-size wooden beggar by the poor box. Market St., to the W of the Hall, has the ornate *Borough Market* (1891–98). Princess St. and Crossley St., to the N, have some handsome 19C buildings culminating in the *Town Hall* (1859–62; Sir Charles Barry and E.M. Barry), with its extraordinary spired tower.

The *National Museum of the Working Horse* is in the old station goods yard off South Parade, S of the church. Gibbet St., W of the town centre, has the base and a replica of the Halifax Gibbet, a precursor of the guillotine, used until 1650 for executing cloth thieves ('From Hell, Hull, and Halifax, good Lord deliver us!'). In Haley Hill (A647), to the N, is *All Souls* (1857–59), which Sir Gilbert Scott considered his best church. Higher up, in Akroyd Park, the *Bankfield Museum* contains English costumes, textiles from the Balkans, Burma, etc., toys, natural history and the museum of the Duke of Wellington's Regiment.

Shibden Hall (open), off A58 1m NE of the centre, is a partly half-timbered 15–17C house standing in an attractive park with a lake in the valley below. It contains a good collection of period furniture and late 16C wall paintings behind the panelling in the dining room. The *Folk Museum of West Yorkshire* in the outbuildings and 17C barn has a brewhouse and dairy, agricultural implements and horse-drawn vehicles, and craft workshops.

Brighouse (35,200 inhabitants; TI on M62), 5m SE of Halifax, has the *Smith Art Gallery*, with temporary exhibitions drawn from a permanent collection of 17C Dutch and Flemish and 19C English paintings.

From Halifax to *Rochdale* and *Manchester* and to *Bradford*, see Route 75E.

The Piece Hall, Halifax, with the spire of the Congregational church behind

C. Manchester to Bolton, Blackburn and Settle

Directions. Total distance 53m. **Manchester**, see Route 74. A6, A666 to (11m) **Bolton**. A666 to (24m) **Blackburn** (Route 75B). A6, A59 to (35m) Clitheroe (bypassed). A59 to (42m) Gisburn. A682, A65 to (53m) **Settle** (Route 86C).

Manchester, see Route 74. The Bolton road begins as A6, leaving the city by Chapel St., Salford. At 3¼m the route bears right on A666 towards the Irwell valley.

11m: **Bolton** (147,100 inhabitants; TI), now with engineering and chemical works, was a textile manufacturing centre specialising first in wool and later in cotton goods. It was the home town of Samuel Crompton (1753–1827), who was born at Firwood Fold and invented the spinning mule at Hall i' th' Wood in 1779, and of the soap magnate Lord Leverhulme (1851–1925).

The imposing classical *Town Hall* was completed in 1873. The nearby *Civic Centre* (1939) contains a *Museum and Art Gallery*; the *Octagon Theatre* is opposite. Churchgate, E of the centre, has Bolton's oldest pub, the Man and Scythe, where the Earl of Derby spent the night before his execution in 1651. Richard Arkwright worked as a barber on Churchgate in the 1760s before returning to his native Preston. N of the centre, the redundant church of *St George* (1769) is a craft centre and the first town hall, known as *Little Bolton Town Hall*, is a museum of local history.

Smithills Hall (open), 1½m NW of the centre, is a picturesque place furnished in the styles of the 16C and 17C. The *Textile Museum*, 2m N of Bolton on Tonge Moor Rd, displays early machinery including Crompton's mule, Hargreaves's spinning jenny and Arkwright's water frame. *'Hall i' th' Wood* (open), off Crompton Way about 2m N of the centre, is a stone and half-timbered manor house dating from the 15C to the 17C, restored and presented to the town by Lord Leverhulme. It contains 17C furnishings and relics of Crompton, who invented the spinning mule here in 1758–82. *Turton Tower* (open), 4m N of Bolton on B6391, is a 15C pele tower with later alterations and additions. It contains a museum of furniture and weapons.

FROM BOLTON TO PRESTON. A675, the direct road (18m), leads across some fine moorland via Belmont, Hoghton and Higher Walton (Route 75B). Another way, 1m longer, begins by taking A673 to (5m) *Horwich* (18,000 inhabitants). To the N are *Rivington Reservoir*, supplying Liverpool, and *Rivington Pike* (1190ft; fine view). The country park on the slopes of the moor includes the splendid *Lever Park*, part of the Rivington Hall estate laid out by Lord Leverhulme for the public in 1904. The village of *Rivington*, beyond the park, has a good 16–17C church and a Unitarian chapel of 1703. A673 crosses M61 and passes through (8m) *Adlington* before joining A6. 11m: **Chorley** (34,700 inhabitants) was the birthplace of Miles Standish (1584–1656), one of the Pilgrim Fathers, and the sugar magnate Sir Henry Tate (1819–99), donor of London's Tate Gallery. *Astley Hall* (open), ¾m NW of the centre, has a 17C façade added to an earlier half-timbered building. It contains extravagant plaster ceilings and interesting collections of furniture and Leeds pottery. *Leyland* (26,700 inhabitants), off A49 4m NW of Chorley, has motor works and a museum of commercial vehicles. The old grammar school building houses a local museum. 19m: *Preston*, see Route 75B.

Beyond (15m) *Egerton* A666 crosses bleak moors diversified by ravines. 19m: *Darwen* (30,000 inhabitants) has petrochemical and plastics works, and the prominent brick chimney of the India Mills (1859–67). 24m: **Blackburn**, see Route 75B.

A666 leaves the industrial district and emerges into the valley of the Ribble, joining A59 at 29m. 31m: *Whalley*, a pleasant village on the Calder, has an interesting church with Anglo-Saxon crosses outside and fine woodwork inside, including 15C stalls with misericords. These come from nearby **Whalley Abbey** (open), founded by Cistercians who moved from Stanlow on the Wirral in the 1280s. Its last abbot, John Paslew, was executed in 1537 for his part in the Pilgrimage of Grace against Henry VIII's religious reforms.

The early 14C outer gateway (EH) lies outside the modern precincts, to the NW. The entrance is from the NE by the late 15C inner gateway. Only the foundations of the large church (1330–80) remain, with a modern high altar marking the place of the medieval one, but more survives of the cloister. The lay brothers' quarters in its W range are used as a Roman Catholic church hall. In the E range is the entrance to the octagonal chapter house. Behind it are some remains of the abbot's lodging, most of which was converted into a private house and is now a diocesan conference centre (not open).

John Mercer (1791–1866), textile chemist and inventor of 'mercerising', was born at *Dean*, 1¾m S. *Great Mitton* (or *Mitton*), 2m NW on B6246, is beautifully situated above the junction of the Hodder and Calder with the Ribble. The church has a 15C rood screen, Jacobean pews and 16–18C Shireburn monuments. Near *Hurst Green*, on B6243 2½m further W, is *Stonyhurst College* (limited opening), a Roman Catholic school founded by the Jesuits at St Omer in 1593 and moved here in 1794. The nucleus of its buildings is the Elizabethan mansion built by Sir Richard Shireburn in 1594–1606. The road continues W via Longridge to *Preston*, see Route 75B.

A59 continues NE, bypassing (35m) **Clitheroe** (13,600 inhabitants; TI), the northernmost of the cotton towns. It is dominated by the limestone outcrop with the shell of its Norman *Castle* (open). The *Castle House Museum* displays local geology, archaeology and history. E of the town rises *Pendle Hill* (1827ft), associated with the 17C 'Lancashire Witches' and George Fox's mission of 1652.

From the pretty village of *Downham*, 3m NE of Clitheroe, a steep sideroad runs across the flank of the hill via (7½m) *Newchurch-in-Pendle* towards (11m) *Nelson* (Route 75D).

A fine moorland route, beginning as B6243, leads W from Clitheroe across the Ribble and then branches N on the unclassified road to Whitewell. 5m: *Browsholme Hall* (limited opening) is a Tudor and Jacobean house with later additions; contents include oak panelling, original furniture and family portraits. 8m: *Whitewell* is in the wooded valley of the Hodder. At (10m) *Dunsop Bridge* the route joins the road leading through the Trough of Bowland from Lancaster (Route 76).

Another good route leads NW from Clitheroe on B6478 via (1½m) *Waddington* and (6½m) *Newton*, with views over Waddington Fell. 8m: *Slaidburn*, a remote village in beautiful country, has a handsome inn, 18C grammar school and a church with Jacobean rood screen and 18C pews and three-decker pulpit. 13m: *Tosside*, on the edge of *Gisburn Forest*, has a bleakly situated little 18C church. B6478 goes on to join the main route described below at (18m) *Long Preston*.

The main route follows A59, passing (38½m) *Sawley Abbey*, or *Salley Abbey*, the scanty remains of a Cistercian house founded in 1148 (EH, all year). At (42m) *Gisburn* the church, adjoining Gisburn Park, has a 13C doorway and 15C chancel screen. The village is the starting-point of the Ribble Way, a walkers' route (42m) following the river SW to its estuary near Preston.

At the charming village of *Bolton-by-Bowland*, 3m W, the church has a Perpendicular font and the tomb of Sir Ralph Pudsey (d. 1481). *Bracewell*, 2m E of Gisburn, has a church with Norman work. For *Barnoldswick*, 1½m further, see Route 75D.

The main route heads N from Gisburn on A682. At (49½m) *Long Preston*, it joins Route 86C and follows A65 to (53m) **Settle**.

D. Manchester to Bury, Burnley and Skipton

Directions. Total distance 41½m. **Manchester**, see Route 74. A56 to (8½m)
Bury, (16½m) Rawtenstall, (23m) **Burnley**, (27½m) Nelson and (29½m)
Colne. A56, A59 to (41½m) **Skipton** (Route 86C).

Manchester, see Route 74. A56 heads N, crossing M62 on the way to (8½m)
Bury (67,500 inhabitants; TI), known for its open-air market and its black
pudding. The market place has a statue of the politician Sir Robert Peel
(1788–1850), born near Bury, whose grandfather introduced calico-printing
into Lancashire. There is a monument at the S end of Market St. to John
Kay (1704–64), inventor of the fly shuttle (1743), who was mobbed by his
fellow townsmen and died a pauper in France. The *Art Gallery and
Museum* has 19C English paintings and watercolours, and local history
displays.

A56 now follows the narrowing valley of the Irwell, 'the most longsuffer-
ing stream in the kingdom'. 12½m: *Ramsbottom* (17,800 inhabitants), on
the left, had the printing works belonging to the Grant brothers, originals
of the Cheerybles in Dickens's 'Nicholas Nickleby'. 15m: To the left of A56
are *Haslingden* (15,900 inhabitants), where the paving stones known as
'Haslingden Flags' used to be quarried, and *Helmshore*, with the Higher
Mill Museum and Museum of the Lancashire Textile Industry. Housed in
old mill buildings, it contains early textile machines, including a water
wheel and fulling stocks, and exhibits of cotton processing and spinning.
A56 bears right, climbing through the moorland *Forest of Rossendale* to
(16½m) **Rawtenstall** (22,200 inhabitants; TI), developed as a mill town by
the Whitehead brothers, with 19C buildings. The Rossendale Museum, in
a former mill owner's house, has local history exhibits.

A681 leads to (4m) **Bacup** (15,200 inhabitants), near the E end of Rossendale, where
the *Natural History Society Museum* has domestic and industrial bygones as well as
natural history. A681 continues to (4½m) *Todmorden* (Route 75B) and A6066 follows
the Whitworth valley S to (6m) *Rochdale* (Route 75E).

A56 heads N. 18m: *Crawshawbooth* has a Friends' Meeting House built in
1716 and enlarged in 1736. 18½m: *Goodshaw* has an 18C Baptist chapel
with furnishings of c 1800 (EH, telephone keykeeper, 091 261 1585, for
details). 23m: **Burnley** (69,900 inhabitants; TI), in a pretty region blackened
by its industries, was the centre of Lancashire cotton weaving by the end
of the 19C. The most interesting survival is the *Weavers' Triangle*, along
the Leeds and Liverpool Canal S of the centre, with weaving sheds,
warehouses, mills, foundries and weavers' cottages. The *Canal Toll House
Heritage Centre* provides an introduction to its history.

Towneley Hall (open), in a large park off A671 1½m SE of the centre, has work of most
periods from the 15–19C. Particularly interesting are the plasterwork (1725–30) by
Vassalli in the hall and the early 16C chapel, moved to its present position in 1712.
The house is now an art gallery and museum with wide-ranging collections which
include pottery, vestments from Whalley Abbey and 18–19C English paintings, notably
Zoffany's portrait of Charles Towneley. The old brewhouse is a museum of local crafts
and industries. *Gawthorpe Hall* (NT), on the outskirts of *Padiham*, 3m NW of Burnley,
is a Jacobean mansion built around a pele tower and remodelled by Sir Charles Barry
in 1849–51. It has a striking long gallery, and contains the Rachel Kay-Shuttleworth
textile collection. The pretty village of *Hurstwood*, 3¼m E of Burnley, is said to have
been Spenser's home while he was writing 'The Shepheardes Calender' (1579).
    From Burnley to *Preston* and to *Halifax*, see Route 75B.

A56 continues to (27½m) **Nelson** (30,400 inhabitants; TI), named after the Admiral. Pendle Hill (Route 75C) rises to the W, with the *Pendle Heritage Centre* at *Barrowford*. The Haworth moors (Route 75H) stretch to the E. 29½m: **Colne** (18,200 inhabitants), once a centre of the wool trade, has a museum about the British in India. A56 branches N to (34m) *Earby*, near the North Yorkshire border, with a museum of lead-mining in the 17C former grammar school (limited opening). At *Barnoldswick*, 3m W, the Bancroft Mill engine of 1922 which drove 1000 looms has been preserved (limited opening). The secluded church of St Mary-le-Ghyll has Jacobean box pews and a three-decker pulpit.

The route changes from A56 to A59 at 37m and continues to (41½m) **Skipton** (Route 86C).

E. From Manchester to Rochdale, Halifax and Bradford

Directions. Total distance 36m. **Manchester**, see Route 74. A664 to (11m) **Rochdale**. A58 to (27½m) **Halifax** (Route 75B). A58, A6036 to (36m) **Bradford**. M62 crosses the Pennines between Rochdale and Oldham, passes over the holding dam of Scammonden Reservoir, SE of Ripponden, and runs between Halifax and Huddersfield, serving Bradford and Leeds by spurs.

Manchester, see Route 74. The route leaves the city by A664. 6m: *Middleton* (51,700 inhabitants), formerly a silk and cotton town, now has plastics and chemical industries. The commanding church, with a curious tower, contains a 16C rood screen, brasses of the Asshetons and a window commemorating Flodden (1513).

11m: **Rochdale** (92,700 inhabitants; TI), both a wool town and a cotton town in its day, has a handsome *Town Hall* (1866–71; W.H. Crossland) modelled after the Flemish cloth halls. The church of *St Chad* has glass by Morris and Co. (1872) in the W window. The *Rochdale Museum*, in the 18C former vicarage, has displays of local history paying particular tribute to two natives, the Liberal politician John Bright (1811–89) and the singer Gracie Fields (1898–1979). The *Art Gallery* on the Esplanade has 19–20C British paintings. The building in Toad Lane where the Society of Equitable Pioneers opened its grocery shop in 1844, thus beginning the Co-operative Movement, has been restored as the *Rochdale Pioneers Museum*. *Littleborough Coach House*, built as a staging post on the local turnpike, is now a Heritage Centre and gallery for arts and crafts. There are attractive moors to the E and NW, with many reservoirs.

From Rochdale to *Bacup* via the Whitworth valley, see Route 75D.

The route takes A58, climbing to the moors beyond (14½m) *Littleborough*. Just before the summit (1269ft), where it crosses the Pennine Way, a *Roman road carries straight on over *Blackstone Edge*. A long stretch of paving keeps the central gutter in which turf was probably placed to give the horses added foothold on the hill. A58 enters West Yorkshire, descending from Rishworth Moor to (22m) *Ripponden* (5100 inhabitants), with an 18C packhorse bridge, in the wooded Ryburn valley. The Ryburn Farm Museum occupies a farmhouse and its adjoining barn. A58 follows the river to (25½m) *Sowerby Bridge* (15,500 inhabitants) with the canal basin of the Calder and Hebble Navigation. A rush-bearing ceremony, dating back to the 17C, is held on the first weekend in September.

27½m: **Halifax**, see Route 75B. Beyond *Shibden Hall* (also Route 75B) the route quits A58 and follows A6036, branching left and climbing steeply via (31½m) *Shelf*, once known for damask and worsted.

36m: **BRADFORD** (280,700 inhabitants) was traditionally a centre of the worsted trade. Though its connection with wool dates back to the 16C, it is essentially a Victorian city and keeps handsome 19C civic buildings, warehouses and mills, together with some good new museums.

TI: Nation Museum of Photography, Film & TV. **Railway Stations**: Interchange Station, Bridge St., for mainline trains. Forster Square Station for Ilkley, Keighley, etc. **Bus Station**: Interchange. **Theatre**: Alhambra, Morley St. **Airport**: Leeds/Bradford Airport at *Yeadon*, 6½m NE. For services, see Leeds (Route 75F).

Natives etc. Frederick Delius (1863–1934), J.B. Priestley (1894–1984), John Braine (1922–86) and David Hockney (b. 1937) were born here. Sir Henry Irving died at Bradford after a performance in 1905.

The Gothic **City Hall** (1869–73), with its striking campanile, is by the local firm of Lockwood and Mawson; the extension to the S is by Norman Shaw (1902–09). The neo-classical *St George's Hall* (1851–53) on the corner of Bridge St., to the E, is also by Lockwood and Mawson. SW of the City Hall, on the opposite side of Princes Way, are the *Alhambra Theatre* (1914), with an Edwardian auditorium, and the excellent **National Museum of Photography, Film and Television** in a building originally designed as a theatre. It has an IMAX screen (the only one in the UK) and exhibits including the Kodak Collection of photographs and television galleries.

Great Horton Rd leads W to the *University of Bradford*, in the buildings of the former technical college, raised to university status in 1966. Grattan Rd, off Westgate to the N, has the inventive *Colour Museum*, in a former wool warehouse, about the science of colour and the history of dyeing and textile-printing.

Market St. heads NE from the Town Hall to the Venetian Gothic **Wool Exchange** (1864–67), by Lockwood and Mawson, on the corner of Bank St. The city's request for advice from Ruskin about the design of the Exchange provoked a magnificent rebuke in his lecture 'On Traffic'. Cheapside is followed to the right from the end of Market St. to Forster Square. Above it stands the **Cathedral**, the 14–15C former parish church, raised to its present status in 1919 and greatly extended by Sir Edward Maufe in 1951–63. It contains a 15C font cover, monuments and some early glass by Morris and Co. (1862) reset in the modern Lady Chapel. The streets to the S make up the merchant quarter known as 'Little Germany', with some fine 19C warehouses.

NW of Forster Square, Cheapside continues as Manor Row, Manningham Lane and Keighley Rd (A650) to Lister Park, about 1m from the centre. The *Cartwright Hall* (open) is an ornate building of 1904 named after Edmund Cartwright (1743–1823), inventor of an early power loom. It contains 19–20C British painting and sculpture, with some earlier English and Continental paintings which include Reynolds's 'Brown Boy'. In Heaton Rd nearby is the grandest of Bradford's mills, the huge *Manningham Mill*, or *Lister's Mill* (1871–73), with an Italianate chimney. Like several other mills in the area, it has a shop open to the public. Church Bank, leading NE from the cathedral, is continued by Otley Rd and Harrogate Rd (A658). Otley Rd passes the interesting 19C *Undercliffe Cemetery*, now being restored. Moorside Rd, off Harrogate Rd 2½m from the city centre, has the *Bradford Industrial Museum* in a former spinning mill, tracing the development of the worsted industry. There are working demonstrations of the steam engines which powered the mill, and the adjoining mill owner's house has been restored. The transport gallery contains locally made cars and motor cycles and the city's last tram.

The old Ludlam St. bus depot in Mill Lane, off Manchester Rd to the S of the city centre, is now the *West Yorkshire Transport Museum* (limited opening), with buses, trams, fire engines, etc. It is the first stage of a project to convert a 5m stretch of railway running through the Spen valley to Heckmondwike into an operating tramway. *Bolling Hall* (open), 1½m SE of the centre on A650 towards Wakefield, is a 15–18C manor house. Now a museum, it contains 17C panelled rooms and oak furniture and, in the Georgian wing by John Carr of York, some pieces by Chippendale.

At *Thornton*, 4m W of the centre by B6145, a house in Market St. was the birthplace of Charlotte, Emily, Anne and Branwell Brontë. *Fulneck*, 4m E of Bradford and 1m S of *Pudsey*, has the oldest Moravian church in England (c 1742–50). Benjamin Latrobe (1764–1820), architect of the Capitol in Washington DC, was born here.

Leeds (Route 75F) is 9m W of Bradford by A647; *Shipley*, in Airedale (Route 75H), is 3m N.

F. Manchester to Huddersfield and Leeds

Directions. Total distance 40m. For M62, the fast alternative, see Route 75E. **Manchester**, see Route 74. A62 to (7m) **Oldham**, (25m) **Huddersfield** and (40m) **Leeds**.

Manchester, see Route 74. A62 heads NE through dreary suburbs. 7m: **Oldham** (95,500 inhabitants; TI) once boasted the largest number of spindles of any cotton town in the world. Several cotton mills are still at work, together with many other textile mills. The *Town Hall* (1841; Joseph Butterworth; enlarged 1879 and 1917) is modelled on the Temple of Ceres near Athens. It stands at the top of Yorkshire St. opposite the *Parish Church* (1823–27; Richard Lane). Cobbett became Oldham's MP in 1832, Sir Winston Churchill in 1900. Sir William Walton (1902–83) was born here.

A669 heads E to join A635, the Barnsley road, which runs to (15m) *Holmfirth* (see below) across the N tip of the Peak District National Park and the bleakly impressive *Saddleworth Moor*, associated with the Moors Murders of the 1960s.

Beyond Oldham A62 climbs over the Pennines. 11½m: It crosses the river Tame. The once important cloth-making centres of *Delph* and *Dobcross*, N and S of the road, have cobbled streets and weavers' stone houses. At (14½m) *Standedge*, the summit of the moor (1271ft), the road crosses the Pennine Way and the West Yorkshire border. Beneath Standedge run railway tunnels and the Huddersfield Narrow Canal tunnel (1811), over 3m long, the highest and the longest canal tunnel in Great Britain. It emerges in the Colne Valley at (17½m) *Marsden*, where the tunnel keepers' cottages have been converted into a Canal and Countryside Centre. The Standedge Trail is a 12m circular walk linking this end of the tunnel with the S end at Diggle. The canal has been restored from Marsden to (20m) *Slaithwaite*, and the towpath can be walked all the way to Huddersfield. A62 follows the river, the canal and the railway to (22m) *Golcar*, on the left, where a group of 19C weavers' cottages have been restored as the Colne Valley Museum (limited opening). The 12m circuit of the Colne Valley Walk starts and finishes here.

25m: **Huddersfield** (123,200 inhabitants; TI), one of Yorkshire's great cloth towns, is strikingly placed among the hills and generously laid out with wide streets. The *Railway Station* (1847–48; J.P. Pritchett) has a neo-classical façade looking out on St George's Square, the centrepiece of Huddersfield's mid-19C development. To the N is the *Brook St. Market* (1887–89) and to the S, on Westgate, the *Byram Arcade* (1880–81), with an elegant entrance. The *Town Hall* (1878–84), further S, contains a concert hall where the Huddersfield Choral Society performs. The Huddersfield Contemporary Music Festival is held in November. The *Library and Art Gallery*, in Princess Alexandra Walk nearby, has a collection of mainly 20C British art.

Off Wakefield Rd (A629), on the E side of the ring road, is the *Apsley Basin* of the Huddersfield Broad Canal, or Sir John Ramsden's Canal (1776), which runs N via a curious vertical lift bridge to join the Calder and Hebble Navigation at Cooper Bridge (see below). The Huddersfield Narrow Canal (see above) heads S. *Ravensknowle Park*, about 1m further E on the Wakefield road, contains the re-erected entrances of the old Cloth Hall (1776) and a hypocaust from Slack (the Roman Cambodunum, 3½m W). The *Tolson Memorial Museum*, also in the park, has displays of natural history, local and social history, transport and textiles. Beyond the park A629 turns S, past the Tudor *Woodsome Hall* (now a golf club). B6116 branches left to (4m) *Kirkburton*, with an early 13C church containing the remains of a Saxon cross. *Skelmanthorpe* church, 2½m further on, has an 11C font. The area is dominated by the fine TV mast by Ove Arup on *Emley Moor*.

NW of the city centre, off Halifax Rd (A629), are the 19C suburbs of (1¼m) *Edgerton* and (2m) *Lindley*, with a striking clock tower (1900–02; Edgar Wood). *Castle Hill*, 2m S of Huddersfield, has an early Iron Age fort and the 19C Jubilee Tower (open). *Almondbury*, E of the hill and 2m SE of the city centre, has a late Perpendicular church.

FROM HUDDERSFIELD TO SHEFFIELD, 26m by A616. From (3½m) *Honley* A6024 climbs to (2½m) *Holmfirth* (21,800 inhabitants; TI), a grim town made famous as the location of TV's 'Last of the Summer Wine', with a postcard museum based on cards produced by the local firm of Bamforths. A6024 continues another 7m over bleak moors to Woodhead (Route 75G), with a fine view near the *Holme Moss* TV mast on the Derbyshire border. A616 crosses the Don at (10½m) *Hazlehead Bridge* and the Manchester–Barnsley road (Route 75G) at (11½m) *Flouch Inn*, skirting the Peak District National Park as far as (12½m) *Langsett* (Route 69D). At (17½m) *Deepcar* it reaches the attractive *Wharncliffe Woods*, also entered from (21m) *Oughtibridge*. 26m: *Sheffield*, see Route 75G.

A62 continues to (28m) *Cooper Bridge*, where the Huddersfield Broad Canal (see above) meets the Calder and Hebble Navigation.

A644 leads left to (2m) *Brighouse* (Route 75B). To the right, it passes through the main centres of the heavy woollen industry, with many mills. 1½m: *Mirfield* (18,700 inhabitants). Charlotte, Emily and Anne Brontë were pupils, and Charlotte a teacher, at Miss Wooller's school in *Roehead* to the N. At (4½m) **Dewsbury** (48,300 inhabitants) the church, rebuilt in the 18C and 19C, has fragments of a Saxon cross and some 13–14C glass. The Dewsbury Museum in Crow Nest Park is largely devoted to the theme of childhood. There is a small canal museum at the basin of the Calder and Hebble Navigation. **Batley** (42,600 inhabitants), 1½m N, originated 'shoddy', a heavy cloth made from reprocessed material. It has a 13–15C church and the Bagshaw Museum, in a Victorian Gothic mansion, dealing with ethnography. *Thornhill*, 2¼m S of Dewsbury, has a church with much 15C glass, 15–20C monuments of the Savile family and fragments of Saxon crosses.

A62 goes on through (31m) *Heckmondwike* (9700 inhabitants), a centre of the blanket industry, and (33m) *Birstall*.

The district is connected with Charlotte Brontë's 'Shirley' (1849). The Elizabethan *Oakwell Hall* (open), ¾m NW, with panelling and oak furniture, is the heroine's home ('Fieldhead'). The 18C Red House (open) at *Gomersal*, ¾m W of Birstall, was the home of Charlotte Brontë's friend Mary Taylor and the model for 'Briarmains' in the novel. *Morley* (44,100 inhabitants), another cloth town, 3m NE of Birstall, was the birthplace of Herbert Asquith (1852–1928).

40m: **LEEDS** (448,500 inhabitants), built across a basin of the Aire, was traditionally a centre of the textile trade. Its industries are concentrated on the flat ground S of the river, while the residential suburbs are on the heights that ring the city to the N. Modern development has left the centre with little sense of history, though some 19C buildings survive, notably the splendid Town Hall.

TI: 19 Wellington St. **Bus Station**: New York St. **Railway Station**: City Station, by City Square. **Airport**: Leeds/Bradford Airport at *Yeadon*, 8m NW. Passenger services to Amsterdam, Belfast, Brussels, Dublin, Edinburgh, Glasgow, Guernsey, the Isle of Man, Jersey, London (Heathrow and Gatwick) and Paris. **Theatres**: West Yorkshire Playhouse, Quarry Hill Mount; Grand Theatre (home of English National Opera North), New Briggate; City Varieties (music hall), The Headrow; Civic Theatre, Cookridge St.; Studio Theatre, Metropolitan University Campus, Woodhouse Lane. **Events**: The Leeds International Concert Season runs from October to June each year. The City of Leeds Open Brass Band Championships are held each May. The Leeds Conductors' Competition is held biennially (next in 1996). The Leeds Musical Festival and the Leeds International Pianoforte Competition are held triennially (next in 1996). The Musical Festival, established in 1858, was conducted by Sir Arthur Sullivan in 1883–98 and heard the first performance of Walton's 'Belshazzar's Feast' in 1931.

History. The monks of Kirkstall Abbey began a trade in wool which was consolidated by Flemish workmen in Edward II's reign. By the 18C Defoe found the Leeds cloth market 'a prodigy of its kind and not to be equalled in the world'. With the advent of steam power the city also became a centre for ready-made clothing, concrete and engineering. Leeds pottery was once famous.

Natives, residents and visitors. Charles I was confined in Red Hall, formerly in Upper Headrow, for a few days while being led captive to London in 1647. The painter Atkinson Grimshaw (1836–93) was born and died at Leeds. The caricaturist Phil May (1864–1903) was born in Wallace St., New Wortley (near the Pudsey road) and Louis le Prince (1842–90), pioneer of the cinema, had his workshop in Woodhouse Lane.

City Square, outside the railway station, is the hub of several busy streets. The statuary in its central triangle includes the Black Prince on horseback (1899; Brock), eight bronze maidens (1899; Drury) and statues of Joseph Priestley, James Watt, John Harrison and Dean Hook. On the E side, overshadowed by tower blocks, is the Gothic *Mill Hill Chapel* (rebuilt in 1847), where Priestley was minister in 1767–78.

Boar Lane leads E to the Georgian church of *Holy Trinity* (1721–27) and, beyond Briggate, the splendid glass-domed *Corn Exchange* (1861–63) by the local architect Cuthbert Brodrick, also responsible for the Town Hall and the Civic Theatre. *Kirkgate Market* (1904), to the N, has a baroque exterior and good iron and glass inside. Kirkgate runs SE under the railway to the parish church of *St Peter*, rebuilt in 1837–41 for Dean W.F. Hook (1798–1875), the High Church vicar and 'Apostle of the West Riding'. It contains a restored Saxon *cross.

The busy Park Row, with some good 19C buildings, leads N from City Square to the broad thoroughfare of The Headrow. In Victoria Square to the left is the classical *Town Hall (1853–58), Cuthbert Brodrick's master-piece and one of the best civic buildings in the North.

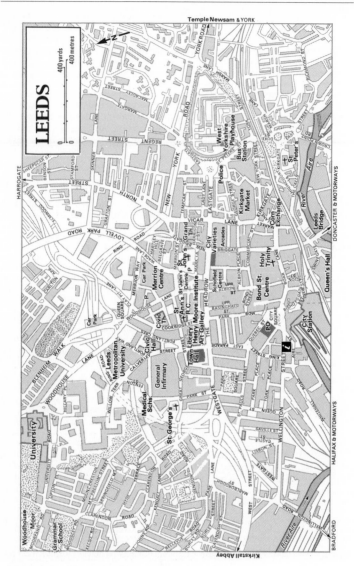

The nearby **City Art Gallery** shows 19C and 20C paintings and sculpture. The Old Masters and decorative arts belonging to the city are housed at Temple Newsam and Lotherton Hall (see below).

The gallery is probably best known for: •English watercolours, prints and drawings; 19C French and British landscapes, including work by Courbet, Sisley, Signac, Derain, Constable, Crome, Corot and Daubigny; Victorian canvases by Leighton, Lady Butler and Atkinson Grimshaw; the Sam Wilson collection, with an Alfred Gilbert fireplace and murals by Sir Frank Brangwyn; and 20C British art, with paintings by Sickert, Nash, Spencer, Piper, Bacon, Hitchens, Wyndham Lewis and Kramer, and sculptures by Moore, Hepworth, Epstein, Arp and Paolozzi. There is a changing exhibition programme, supported by educational activities, films and performance.

The adjoining *Henry Moore Institute* honours the sculptor who studied, with Barbara Hepworth, at the Leeds College of Art under Jacob Kramer. As well as displaying sculptures and drawings, it houses a centre for the study of sculpture and a specialist library. The *City Museum* has collections of geology, natural history, ethnography and archaeology, including Egyptian mummies, Greek and Roman marbles, and local finds, together with a display of coins and medals.

Calverley St. leads N to the twin-towered *Civic Hall* (1933; E. Vincent Harris) and the huge buildings of *Leeds Polytechnic* (by Yorke, Rosenberg and Mardall, begun in 1953). Cookridge St., continuing Park Row N beyond The Headrow, has the Roman Catholic *St Anne's Cathedral* (1904), with a Lady Chapel altar of 1842 by Pugin from the previous cathedral, and the *Civic Theatre* (1865–68; Brodrick), originally built as the Mechanics' Institute.

The Headrow prolongs Westgate eastward across Briggate to Vicar Lane. **St John's** in New Briggate is fine Laudian Gothic, built by the cloth merchant John Harrison in 1632–34. Its woodwork includes the original *screen, pews and pulpit. Beyond Vicar Lane, Eastgate continues to Quarry Hill Mount and the West Yorkshire Playhouse, opened in 1990.

The **University of Leeds** is in Woodhouse Lane, beyond *Leeds Metropolitan University* (the former polytechnic) and the inner ring road NW of the centre. Incorporated in 1904, it grew out of the Leeds School of Medicine (1831) and the Yorkshire College of Science (1874), and was for a time affiliated to the Victoria University (see Manchester, Route 74). The largely undistinguished buildings, begun by Alfred Waterhouse in 1877, include the large *Parkinson Building* (1951; T.A. Lodge). The *Brotherton Library* (open by appointment with the librarian), with its fine circular reading room, was the gift of Lord Brotherton (1856–1930). It contains his personal library (the Brotherton collection, rich in early books and manuscripts, particularly of English literature) amongst some two million volumes in one of the largest academic library systems in the country.

The main residential areas lie to the N of the city, in the neighbourhood of *Headingley*, *Chapel Allerton* and *Roundhay*. **Adel**, about 2¼m N of Headingley, has a little Norman *church with interesting sculptures on the S porch and the chancel arch. The large *Golden Acre Park*, 1m beyond, has gardens, woodland and a lake. See below for the continuation of A660 to Otley. In Roundhay Rd, the approach to the fine *Roundhay Park*, is the remarkable Romanesque church of *St Aidan* (1894) with mosaics by Sir Frank Brangwyn.

A65 follows the river Aire NW from the centre to (1½m) *Leeds Industrial Museum* in the impressive Armley Mills building of 1806. Its displays illustrate the development of the city's major industries, including textiles, clothing, optics and heavy engineering, with reconstructed industrial settings. There is a collection of railway engines, and a 1920s picture palace. *Kirkstall Abbey* (open) lies about 1½m further, in a park by the river. A Cistercian house founded by monks from Fountains in 1152, its ruins are better preserved than those of any other great northern abbey. The chief remains are the church, with its collapsed Perpendicular tower; the late Norman and Early English chapter house, which is almost intact; and the abbot's lodging, a splendid piece of 13C domestic architecture. The restored 12C gatehouse N of the road is the *Abbey House Museum*, with folk collections including toys and games, and reconstructed Victorian streets with shops, cottages and an inn.

FROM LEEDS TO SELBY, 21m by A63. The road crosses the ancient district of *Elmet*, stretching NE towards Tadcaster. 5m: **Temple Newsam** (open) is a Jacobean house altered in the 18C, now containing the *collections of decorative art belonging to the Leeds City Art Galleries. The former house on the site was the birthplace of Lord Darnley in 1545 and the original of 'Templestowe' in Scott's 'Ivanhoe'. The Georgian long gallery and library, and the Chinese drawing room, are outstanding among the interiors. The rich art collections include English pottery, silver and 16–18C furniture; the paintings include work by Paul van Somer, Pellegrini, Reynolds and Morland. Outside are a home farm, seven specialist gardens and a large park laid out by Capability Brown in 1762. See Route 85B for *Lotherton Hall*, by A1 6m NW, also belonging to Leeds City Art Galleries. 10m: A63 meets A1 (Route 85B), which is followed S for 1½m before A63 resumes its eastward course. 13m: *South Milford*, N of A62 on A162, and (14m) *Monk Fryston*, see Route 85B. 21m: *Selby*, see Route 81.

FROM LEEDS TO DONCASTER, 28½m by A639, branching left from A61 S of the city. 7½m: *Methley* church contains 15–17C tombs and effigies of the Waterton and Savile families, and a lectern with an elaborate 16C base. 10m: *Castleford* (36,000 inhabitants), a grimy town at the junction of the Aire and the Calder, was the important Roman station Lagentium. Finds, together with locally made glassware and pottery, are displayed in the small museum in the library. The sculptor Henry Moore (1898–1986) was born here. *Ledston Hall* (only exterior open), 2m N off A656, is mainly 17C. 13½m: **Pontefract** (32,000 inhabitants) is a market town known for its racecourse and for the liquorice lozenges known as 'Pomfret cakes', which take their name from the old pronunciation of its name. Richard II died in the Norman castle in 1400, either murdered by Sir Piers Exton (as in Shakespeare's play) or starved to death. Other prisoners included James I of Scotland and Charles, Duke of Orleans, after his capture at Agincourt. The castle was razed to the ground in 1649 and only a few fragments survive in the recreation ground which now covers its site. *Ackworth School*, 3m S on A628, a Quaker boarding school opened in 1779, occupies the buildings of a foundling hospital of 1758. It is open by appointment during school holidays. Nostell Priory lies 2½m W of Ackworth on the way to Wakefield (Route 75H). At (20m) *Barnsdale Bar* A639 joins A1 (Route 85B), 8½m N of *Doncaster* (Route 81).

FROM LEEDS TO OTLEY, 11m by A660. The route leaves the city via Headingley and Adel and Golden Acre Park (see above). 7m: *Bramhope* has a Puritan chapel of 1649 with contemporary fittings in the grounds of the former Bramhope Hall. 11m: *Otley*, in Wharfedale, see Route 86A.

From Leeds to *Sheffield* and to *Airedale* and *Skipton*, see Route 75H; to *Harrogate*, *Ripon* and *Thirsk*, see Route 80; to *York*, see Route 81.

G.   Manchester to Penistone and Sheffield

Directions. Total distance 41m. **Manchester**, see Route 74. A57 to (9½m) Mottram-in-Longdendale. A628 to (27m) **Penistone**. A629, A61 to (41m) **Sheffield**. The direct way (37m) from Manchester to Sheffield is by A57. For another route via Hathersage and Castleton, see Route 69D.

Manchester, see Route 74. A57 runs E, crossing the Tame beyond (5½m) *Denton* (37,700 inhabitants). 7m: *Hyde* (35,600 inhabitants) is one of a group of cotton and coal towns in the once beautiful Tame valley.

The oldest and most important is *Ashton-under-Lyne* (44,700 inhabitants), 2m N, with *glass of c 1500 in its church. *Dukinfield* (18,100 inhabitants) and *Stalybridge* (26,400 inhabitants) are nearby, with *Mossley* (10,100 inhabitants) further upstream.

9½m: *Mottram-in-Longdendale*, where the painter L.S. Lowry (1887–1976) spent his later years, has a fine Perpendicular church. A57 heads S via

Glossop (Route 69A). The present route takes A628, entering Derbyshire and the Peak District National Park, and following *Longdendale*, watered by the Etherow and almost filled with reservoirs. Beyond (16½m) *Woodhead*, a deserted site where the moorland road to Holmfirth (Route 75F) bears left, is the mouth of the Woodhead Tunnel, which pierces the hard millstone grit of the Pennines and emerges over 3m away in South Yorkshire. The digging of the first tunnel (1840–46), one of the great feats of Victorian railway-building, killed 32 navvies and injured 250 more. This tunnel is disused; a second tunnel (1847–52) has been reopened to carry electricity cables. A new twin-track tunnel has carried the railway since electrification in 1954. A628 crosses the border into South Yorkshire. A long descent past (23m) the *Flouch Inn* (Route 75F) leads to the rocky valley of the Don and (27m) **Penistone** (9000 inhabitants), a bleak little town with steel works and a fine Decorated church.

A628 continues E through pleasant country to the South Yorkshire coalfield. 3m: *Silkstone* has a church with fine woodwork, a monument to Sir Thomas Wentworth (d. 1675) and a memorial to the hydraulic engineer Joseph Bramah (1748–1814). For *Cawthorne* and *Cannon Hall*, to the N, and *Barnsley*, 7m NE of Penistone, see Route 75H.

A629 is followed S from Penistone. 32m: *Wortley*, from which Wharncliffe Woods (Route 75F) can be reached. Beyond Wortley the route joins A61.

41m: **SHEFFIELD** (542,700 inhabitants), the largest city in Yorkshire and the fourth largest in England, has been a centre for producting cutlery since the Middle Ages and high-quality steel since the 18C. Standing at the foot of the Derbyshire hills, where the river Sheaf meets the river Don, it had become 'the foulest town in England in the most charming situation' when Horace Walpole visited it in 1760. It now claims the cleanest air of any manufacturing city in Europe, and has a centre transformed by imaginative planning and architecture. In recent years it has also become an important conference venue.

TI: Peace Gardens; Railway Station. **Bus Station**: Pond St. **Railway Station**: off Sheaf Square, E of the centre. **Theatres**: Crucible Theatre, Norfolk St.; Lyceum Theatre, Tudor Square; Library Theatre, Tudor Place. Orchestral concerts at City Hall, Barker's Pool.

History. Hallam, or Hallamshire, the ancient manor which embraced Sheffield and neighbouring parishes, was already famous for its cutlery in the 14C, when the miller in Chaucer's 'Reeve's Tale' carried a 'Sheffeld thwitel' (knife) in his hose. By the end of the 16C the town had about 60 hallmarks. In 1740 Benjamin Huntsman invented the crucible process of steel production, and in 1742 Thomas Boulsover discovered that silver could be bonded to copper and then rolled into sheets, producing Old Sheffield Plate, later superseded by electroplate. By the 19C the great steel works stretched in an unbroken line down the valley of the Don, NE through the suburbs of Attercliffe, Brightside and Tinsley to Rotherham.

Natives and residents. Mary, Queen of Scots, spent most of her captivity from 1570 to 1584 at Sheffield, partly in the castle and partly in Sheffield Manor. The sculptor Sir Francis Chantrey (1781–1841), born and buried at nearby Norton, had his portrait studio in Paradise Square. The 'Corn Law Rhymer' Ebenezer Elliott (1781–1849), born at Masborough, near Rotherham, established his Sheffield iron foundry in 1821. Joseph Locke (1805–60), the railway engineer, and John Stringfellow (1799–1883), who flew the first heavier-than-air machine, were born at Attercliffe. The composer Sir William Sterndale Bennett (1816–75) was born in Sheffield.

The crocketed spire of the Anglican **Cathedral** in Church St., at the W end of High St., marks the centre of the old town. The diocese was created in 1914, and the core of the building is still the 15C Perpendicular parish church. Already heavily restored in the 19C, it was enlarged in the 1930s and 1940s by Sir Charles Nicholson, who added the chapels and chapter house on the N side, and in the 1960s by Arthur Bailey, responsible for the narthex tower and the W end of the nave. The Wilkinson monument (1805) on the N side of the chancel is Chantrey's first important commission. The Lady Chapel, or Shrewsbury Chapel, contains the tombs of the 4th Earl of Shrewsbury (d. 1538) and the 6th Earl (d. 1590), Bess of Hardwick's husband and keeper of Mary, Queen of Scots. The Chapter House has windows depicting scenes from Sheffield's history.

High St., continuing Church St. to the E, leads to the roundabout of Castle Square, with its piazza-style concourse. The ingeniously planned *Castle Market* (1960–65) by the city architect J.L. Womersley on Waingate, to the N, occupies the site of the castle, of which just a few fragments remain. This was the main fortress where Mary, Queen of Scots, was held captive. The remnants of the Georgian quarter N of the cathedral include the quiet oasis of Paradise Square. John Wesley preached to his largest weekday congregration here in July 1779, and Chantrey had his studio at 24 in 1802.

Facing the cathedral on the S side of Church St. stands the Greek Revival *Cutlers' Hall* of 1832, the third building erected on this site for the Cutler's Company, incorporated in 1624. Open by appointment, it contains the company's collection of silver. The annual feast given by the Master Cutler is held here.

Fargate, which includes the Orchard Square shopping complex, leads S to the **Town Hall** (1890–97; E.W. Mountford), a gabled Renaissance building with a prominent tower topped by a statue of Vulcan, symbol of the city's chief industries. To its S are the *Peace Gardens*, flanked by the *Town Hall Extension* (1977). Facing Barker's Pool, further W, is the **City Hall** (1932), a classical building by E. Vincent Harris with decorations by G. Kruger Gray. Surrey St. heads E from the Town Hall to the *Central Library*, whose top floor houses the *Graves Art Gallery.

Its collections are held in common with the Mappin Art Gallery (see below) and items are subject to removal from one gallery to the other. They include a wide range of European art (Murillo, Procaccini, Ruisdael, Van der Neer); a strong collection of British watercolours (Turner, Girtin); 19C British painting (Turner, Burne-Jones); 20C British painting (Sickert, Nash, Gwen John, David Bomberg); and Chinese ivories. The ivories and, in general, most of the works on paper are kept at the Graves. The Victorian collection is usually displayed at the Mappin. Any visitor wishing to see specific works or groups of works should call the galleries to ensure that they are on show or make an appointment to view. There is also an energetic programme of temporary exhibitions.

Norfolk St. leads N from Surrey St. The *Ruskin Gallery** is housed in an imaginatively converted 19C wine shop. It brings together in a new display the contents of the Guild of St George museum which Ruskin established at Sheffield in 1875 to provide a liberal education for local artisans—a wonderfully eclectic assembly of geological specimens, watercolours, photographs, plaster casts of architectural details, etc. The adjoining Ruskin Craft Gallery has changing exhibitions of contemporary crafts. The *Crucible Theatre*, further N, houses two auditoria. The World Professional Snooker Championships are held here. Nearby is the restored 19C Lyceum Theatre.

The **University of Sheffield** is about 1m W of the city centre in Western Bank. Incorporated in 1905, it had its origin in Firth College, founded in 1879, and the Sheffield School of Medicine, founded in 1828. Modern additions to the original redbrick neo-Tudor buildings (1903–05; E.Mitchel

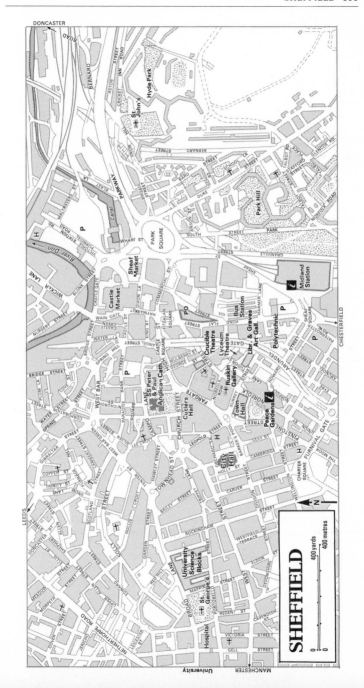

Gibbs) include the dominating *Arts Tower* (1960–65; Gillins, Melvin, Ward and Partners). Just beyond is the beautiful *Weston Park*, with an observatory and a statue of Ebenezer Elliott, the 'Corn Law Rhymer'. The •**City Museum**, in the park, has superb collections of Old Sheffield Plate and Sheffield cutlery, together with local silver and ceramics, archaeology, geology and a wildlife gallery. The adjoining *Mappin Art Gallery* holds its collections in common with the Graves Art Gallery (see above); the 19C paintings are usually displayed here. The university church of *St Mark* in Broomfield Rd was rebuilt in 1958–63 by George Pace, with a W window by John Piper and Patrick Reyntiens.

The *Kelham Island Industrial Museum*, in a former generating station by the river Don NW of the centre, is reached via Corporation St. and Alma St. Exhibits include operational steam and gas engines. Reconstructed workshops are manned by craftsmen demonstrating the skills of the 'little mesters' who once sustained the city's cutlery trade.

A625 leads SW, past (1½m) the handsome *Botanical Gardens* with conservatories of 1837–38 by Joseph Paxton. *Whiteley Wood*, off A625 about 2½m further SW, has the *Shepherd Wheel* (open), a water-powered grinding works on the river Porter. A621 also leads SW from the city to (3½m) *Beauchief*, on the left. The chapel, with its 14C tower and arches, is a relic of a Premonstratensian abbey founded in 1183. The nearby *Abbeydale Industrial Hamlet* (open) preserves an 18–19C water-powered scythe works, with crucible furnace, forges, grinding workshops, office buildings, etc. The road continues to (6m) *Totley*, with the mouth of the Totley Tunnel (3½m), the second longest in England, and to (13½m) *Baslow* in the Peak District (Route 69A). A61, heading S, passes (2m) *Meersbrook Park* with the so-called *Bishops' House* (open), in fact a half-timbered yeoman's house dating originally from the late 15C. At *Norton*, about 2m further S, an obelisk commemorates Sir Francis Chantrey (1781–1841), born and buried here.

Norfolk Rd goes SE from the centre to *Norfolk Park*. To the E are the remains of *Sheffield Manor*, the 16C mansion occasionally occupied by Mary, Queen of Scots, during her captivity. The well-preserved Turret House houses a small museum (usually open by appointment only).

FROM SHEFFIELD TO DONCASTER, 18m by A6109 or A6178 and A630. 6½m: **Rotherham** (82,000 inhabitants; TI) is a murky town on the Don at its meeting with the Rother. The altered 15C bridge has an ancient chantry. The parish church is one of the finest Perpendicular churches in the North, with a crocketed spire, Jacobean pulpit and poppyheads on the chancel stalls. Rockingham china (made at *Swinton*, 3½m N) is displayed at the Art Gallery in Walker Place and at the Clifton Park Museum, in a charming 18C house. The museum also has finds from the Roman fort at *Templeborough* to the SW, now obliterated. The suburb of *Masborough*, to the W, was the birthplace of the 'Corn Law Rhymer' Ebenezer Elliott (1781–1849). About 3½m NW is the grandiose mansion of *Wentworth Woodhouse* (not open), begun by Henry Flitcroft in the 1730s for the 1st Marquis of Rockingham. A630 to (12½m) *Conisbrough* and on to (17½m) *Doncaster*, see Route 81.

From Sheffield to *Derby* and *Leicester*, see Route 68; to *Manchester* via *Hathersage* and *Castleton*, see Route 69D; to *Huddersfield*, see Route 75F; to *Leeds, Airedale* and *Skipton*, see Route 75H.

H. Sheffield to Leeds, Airedale and Skipton

Directions. Total distance 60½m. **Sheffield**, see Route 75G. A61 to (13½m) Barnsley, (23½m) Wakefield and (33m) **Leeds** (Route 75F). A647, A657 to (43½m) Shipley. A650 to (51½m) Keighley (for **Haworth**). A629 to (60½m) **Skipton** (Route 86C).

Sheffield, see Route 75G. A61 heads nearly due N through the now depressed South Yorkshire coalfield. At (12m) *Worsborough* the Mill Museum (open) has a 17C and a 19C mill, both restored to working order. 13½m: **Barnsley** (73,600 inhabitants; TI) is the centre of the coalfield. The *Cooper Gallery* in Church St. contains a good collection of 19–20C English watercolours and work by Eugène Isabey.

At *Cawthorne*, off A635 4½m W, the church has glass by the Pre-Raphaelite Spencer Stanhope in the W window and by Morris and Co. in the N chapel, and two fonts, 11C and Perpendicular. The village adjoins *Cannon Hall* (open), an 18C house mainly by John Carr of York, in landscaped parkland. It is now a country house museum with 17–19C furniture, English, Dutch and Flemish paintings, and good pottery and glass-ware. In the grounds of *Bretton Hall*, 3½m further N, is the *Yorkshire Sculpture Park* (open), with work by Henry Moore and Barbara Hepworth. At *Woolley*, 4½m NW of Barnsley, the church has interesting bench ends. At *Royston* (8,900 inhabitants), 3½m N of Barnsley, the Perpendicular tower of the church has a five-sided oriel. *Monk Bretton Priory* (EH, all year), off A628 2m E of Barnsley, was a Cluniac foundation of c 1154 which later became Benedictine. Remains include the 14C gatehouse and 13–14C buildings around the cloisters, but little of the 12C church.

From Barnsley to *Penistone* and *Manchester*, see Route 75G.

23½m: **Wakefield** (58,500 inhabitants; TI), an ancient city above the river Calder, is the county town of West Yorkshire as it was of the West Riding. A centre of the cloth trade before the Industrial Revolution, it keeps some Georgian houses (in South and West Parade, for example) and has never become as industrialised as its neighbours.

The medieval Wakefield Cycle, one of four cycles of mystery plays to survive in England, includes the famous 'Second Shepherd's Play' by the so-called Wakefield Master. The Battle of Wakefield (1460), at which Richard, Duke of York, was killed by the Lancastrians, was fought near Sandal Castle, 1¾m S. Famous natives include Dr John Radcliffe (1652–1714), the physician and Oxford benefactor; George Gissing (1857–1903), born in Westgate; and Dame Barbara Hepworth (1903–75).

The public buildings on Wood St. include the interesting *Court House* (1810), *County Hall* (1894–98; Gibson and Russell), *Town Hall* (1880; T.E. Collcutt), and the *Museum*, mainly of local history. The *Art Gallery* on Wentworth Terrace to the N has 20C painting and sculpture, including work by Barbara Hepworth and Henry Moore.

Kirkgate leads E to the **Cathedral**, with its tall crocketed spire. Dating mainly from c 1470, it was the parish church until the new diocese was created in 1888. Sir Gilbert Scott rebuilt the spire in the course of heavy restoration in 1858–74, while J.L. and F.L. Pearson added the new E end in 1901–05. Inside, the most striking features are the wooden rood screen of 1635 (with additions by Sir Ninian Comper, 1950), the organ case (1743), the church treasures in the N choir aisle, and the glass by Kempe (1872–1900). Kirkgate continues SE from the cathedral down to the Calder and the medieval bridge with its *Bridge Chapel*, originally built c 1350 (open by appointment). Despite substantial rebuilding by Sir Gilbert Scott in 1847, it is the most important of the handful of medieval bridge chapels surviving in England.

Nostell Priory (NT), off A638 6m SE, was begun in the Palladian style by James Paine in 1733–50 and continued by Robert Adam in 1765–80. The interior, superbly decorated by Paine and Adam, has 'furniture designed for the house by Chippendale, who was for many years the estate carpenter. The dolls' house (1735) is probably his earliest surviving work. The paintings include Holbein's portrait of Sir Thomas More's family. In the park stands *Wragby* church, where Paine was married in 1741, with a wealth of Swiss glass (1514–1751) and a Norman font brought from the vanished church of Auburn on Yorkshire's E coast. Nearly opposite is the site of the Augustinian priory, founded c 1119, which gave its name to the house. At *West Hardwick*, 2½m NE, is the *Top Farm Agricultural Museum*.

Normanton (17,300 inhabitants), on A655 about 4m E of Wakefield, is a grimy town with a large 14–15C church. *Horbury* (9100 inhabitants), on A642 3m SW of Wakefield, was the birthplace of John Carr (1723–1807), who is buried in the church he built at his own expense in 1791–93.

At *Overton*, 6m SW on A642, the Huddersfield road, the redundant Caphouse Colliery has been re-opened as the *Yorkshire Mining Museum*.

Beyond Wakefield A650 heads NW, bypassing Leeds, to Bradford (Route 75E) and Shipley (below). The present route heads due N on A61.

33m: **Leeds**, see Route 75F. The present route leaves the city on A647 and branches right on A657 to follow the largely industrialised lower reaches of **Airedale** to (43½m) *Shipley* (27,900 inhabitants). 44½m: *Saltaire* is named after the river and Sir Titus Salt (1803–76), who moved his mohair and alpaca mills from Bradford in 1853 to create a model industrial settlement with sturdy terraced housing. He is buried in the mausoleum by the Congregational Church. The Victoria Hall contains a museum of 19C reed organs and harmoniums. The 1853 Gallery is an old mill housing works by David Hockney. The route follows A650, which has come directly from Wakefield. 47m: *Bingley* (28,100 inhabitants), a mill town, has a five-rise staircase of locks on the Leeds and Liverpool Canal. 50½m: *East Riddlesden Hall* (NT) is a 17C house in a vigorous local style, with a rose window over the porch and an elaborate fireplace in the hall. The medieval tithe barn has a collection of farm vehicles and implements. A track leads N across *Rombald's Moor* to (5m) *Ilkley* in Wharfedale (Route 86A). 51½m: **Keighley** (pronounced 'Keethley'; 57,500 inhabitants), another mill town, has the *Cliffe Castle Museum and Art Gallery*, with local geology, natural history, social history, pottery, crafts, etc. The *Worth Valley Railway* runs to Haworth and Oxenhope.

Haworth (TI) is 4m SW by A629 and A6033. Imperishably associated with the Brontës, this bleak village on the shoulder of the moors has become a popular tourist centre. The cobbled main street climbs precipitously to the tiny square by the church. The chief attraction is the *Brontë Parsonage* (open), where the Rev. Patrick Brontë brought his family in 1820 and where his children, Charlotte (1816–55), Emily (1818–48), Anne (1820–49) and Branwell (1817–48), spent the majority of their lives. The Georgian building has been restored to its appearance in the Brontës' day, with items of their furniture and many memorabilia, of which the most interesting are the books and manuscripts in the Bonnell Room. The library is open for research by prior arrangement. The *Church*, where Charlotte married the curate Mr Nicholls in 1854, contains the vault of all the family except Anne, who died in Scarborough. Only the tower survives from their time; the rest was rebuilt in 1879–81. The Black Bull Inn was the haunt of the unfortunate Branwell. Walks can be taken across the moors, W to (2m) the *Brontë Waterfall* and (3m) *Top Withens*, perhaps 'Wuthering Heights', or to (2½m) *Ponden Hall*, perhaps the 'Thrushcross Grange' of 'Wuthering Heights', (6½m) the ruined *Wycoller Hall*, perhaps the 'Ferndean Manor' of 'Jane Eyre', and (10m) *Colne*

(Route 75D). Top Withens and Ponden Hall are linked by the Pennine Way. A6033 continues S from Haworth to (7m) *Hebden Bridge* in the Calder valley (Route 75B).

From Keighley A629 follows Airedale to (56m) *Glusburn*. Charlotte Brontë was governess in 1839 at the 18C Stonegappe Hall (not open), the 'Gateshead Hall' of 'Jane Eyre', about 2m W. *Kildwick*, 1m N across the Aire, has a 14C stone bridge and a Perpendicular church. 60½m: **Skipton**, see Route 86C.

76

Liverpool to Lancaster and Carlisle

Directions. Total distance 118m. **Liverpool**, see Route 73. A59 to (31m) **Preston**, see Route 75B. A6 to (52m) **Lancaster**, (74m) Kendal, (99m) Penrith and (118m) **Carlisle**. M6, intertwined with A6, offers a fast alternative.

Liverpool, see Route 73. The route takes A59, following Route 75B to (31m) **Preston**.

FROM PRESTON TO BLACKPOOL, LYTHAM ST ANNES AND FLEETWOOD. *The Fylde*, the plain between the estuaries of the Ribble and the Wyre, separates Preston from the coastal resorts to its W. It is crossed by M55 and A583, both going directly to Blackpool (16½m by either road). A584 branches left from A583 to (12m) Lytham St Annes, then follows the esplanade leading to (20m) Blackpool and (24m) Thornton Cleveleys and continuing as A587 to (29m) Fleetwood.

Lytham St Annes (39,700 inhabitants; TI) is a quiet resort stretching along the shore from Lytham, facing S at the mouth of the Ribble estuary, to the more open St Annes, looking SW. It has several major golf courses and *Lytham Hall* (not open), a Jacobean house altered by John Carr in 1764.

Blackpool (147,900 inhabitants; TI), 'famous for fresh air and fun', is the leading resort in the North-West and one of the most popular resorts in the country, drawing over 16 million visitors a year. Its attractions include: the Illuminations; the Tower (1894) with its ballroom, aquarium and indoor circus; three 19C piers; the 40-acre Pleasure Beach; the 300-acre Stanley Park with boating lake and sporting facilities as well as gardens and conservatories; and several golf courses. It is the only town in England which did not abandon its tram system. Blackpool Airport has passenger services to Belfast, Dublin, the Isle of Man and Jersey.

Thornton Cleveleys (26,100 inhabitants) is a resort on the way from Blackpool to Fleetwood. *Rossall Hall*, 1m N, is a public school where Sir Thomas Beecham was a pupil.

Fleetwood (28,500 inhabitants; TI), looking N across Morecambe Bay from the mouth of the Wyre, is a large fishing port as well as a resort. The history of its industry is told in the museum on Dock St. A ferry crosses the Wyre to *Knott End*, and a seasonal ferry service (primarily for day excursion passengers) goes to Douglas, Isle of Man.

A585, the road from Fleetwood to (22½m) Preston, passes near (6m) *Poulton-le-Fylde* (17,600 inhabitants), a market town with an old cross and stocks and an 18C church.

Beyond Preston A6 runs N through pleasant country. 42m: *Garstang* (TI), a market town on the Wyre and the Lancaster Canal, lies between the plain of the Fylde and the fell country of the Forest of Bowland. 50m: *Bailrigg* makes an attractive site for the *University of Lancaster*, founded in 1964, in mainly low-rise buildings which form a pedestrian precinct (begun by Bridgwater, Sheppard and Epstein).

52m: **Lancaster** (46,300 inhabitants; TI), a historic place, was for centuries the county town of Lancashire until the rise of Preston.

The Duchy of Lancaster, originating in the earldom given by Henry III to his son Edmund in 1265, has been royal since it passed to Henry IV from his father John of Gaunt, Shakespeare's 'time-honoured Lancaster', in 1399. The office of Chancellor of the Duchy of Lancaster is a political appointment normally held by a member of the Cabinet. In the 18C the town became a prosperous port for the West Indies trade and a centre of cabinet-making, known particularly for the work of the Gillow family. The scientist Sir Richard Owen (1804–92), educated at the grammar school, and the poet Laurence Binyon (1869–1945) were natives. George Fox was imprisoned in the castle in 1664.

The *Castle* (open for guided tours), high above the river on the site of the Roman fort, is a much altered building which includes the prison, Shire Hall and Crown Court added by Thomas Harrison and Joseph Gandy in 1788–1823.

The chief medieval remains are the *Gatehouse* (c 1400) and the Norman *Keep*, restored c 1585. One of its turrets is known as 'John of Gaunt's Chair'. The 13C *Hadrian's Tower* contains a miscellaneous collection of prison equipment. The *Shire Hall* and *Crown Court* (not included on the tour when in session) have Gothick interiors and coats of arms.

To the NE of the castle is the *Priory Church of St Mary*. The priory became a cell of the Benedictine abbey at Sées in 1094 and was placed under the jurisdiction of the Bridgettines in 1414. The present building is mainly Perpendicular, but the SW doorway belongs to the 12C church and a doorway in the W wall may be Saxon. The rebuilt tower was designed by Henry Sephton (1754). The interior contains carved oak *stalls (c 1340).

From the W end there is a fine view and a path leading down to St George's Quay, with Georgian warehouses and the Old Custom House (1764; Richard Gillow), now Lancaster's *Maritime Museum*.

Georgian houses, still a feature of the town generally, mark Castle Park and Castle Hill. The *Cottage Museum* on Castle Hill has an interesting period interior. At the top of Church St., the *Judge's Lodging* (c 1630) contains furniture by the local firm of Gillow and a museum of childhood with the Barry Elder doll collection.

The old centre, to the SE, is well documented in the *City Museum* occupying the Old Town Hall (1781–83) in Market Square. It contains models of Lancaster in 1610, 1778 and 1821; a collection of antiquities, with 1–4C Roman pottery and fragments from Cockersand Abbey; and the museum of the King's Own Royal Lancaster Regiment. To its NE, near the bus station, is the redundant church of *St John* (1754) with a tower added by Thomas Harrison in 1784. Harrison also designed *Skerton Bridge* (1783–88), further NE. In Dalton Square, S of the City Museum, stand the *Town Hall* (1906–09; E.W. Mountford) and the *Victoria Memorial* (1907), given by the linoleum tycoon Lord Ashton. To the E, beyond the *Roman Catholic Cathedral* (1859), is another of his gifts, Williamson Park; on the crest of its hill stands John Belcher's splendid *Ashton Memorial* (1906–09), open to the public.

A588 runs SW to (4m) *Conder Green*, beyond which B5290 branches right to (4¾m) *Glasson*, an 18C dock on the Lune estuary, where salmon are taken by 'whammelling' with the drift-net or by the stationary haaf-net. The next right-hand turning off A588, at (5m) *Upper Thurnham*, leads in about 3m to a farm on the coast beside which, in a

The Ashton Memorial, Lancaster

wild and romantic position, is the finely vaulted 13C chapter house of *Cockersand Abbey* (not open), with a few fragmentary remains nearby.

FROM LANCASTER TO MORECAMBE AND HEYSHAM, 5½m by A589, heading NW from the city. 3½m: **Morecambe** (41,200 inhabitants with Heysham; TI), named after its bay, is a resort known for its shrimps, with an 'oceanarium' (performing dolphins), Wild West theme park, etc. For the walk across the bay, see Hest Bank below and Grange-over-Sands, Route 77. 5½m: **Heysham** (pronounced 'Heesham') has a nuclear power station, oil refineries and a ferry service to Douglas, Isle of Man from its harbour. The old village to the N has some interesting houses and a 12–14C church, with a carved 'hog-back' tombstone and a fragment of a Saxon cross in its churchyard. On the promontory above is the ruin of St Patrick's Chapel (9C?); nearby are some early Saxon rock graves with holes for a post or cross.

FROM LANCASTER TO KIRKBY LONSDALE, 16m by A583 along the S bank of the Lune. 1m: A fine aqueduct (1797; John Rennie) carries the Lancaster Canal over the Lune on its way to Kendal. 2¼m: The churchyard at *Halton*, on the N bank, has an early 11C *cross showing episodes from the saga of Sigurd the Volsung. A583 enters the *Crook o' Lune*, the loveliest part of the green valley of Lonsdale, painted by Turner. 8½m: *Hornby* is a centre for anglers. The castle (not open) has a 13C pele tower with additions by Sir Edward Stanley ('Monteagle'; d. 1523), who also built the octagonal tower of the church in thanks for his safe return from the Battle of Flodden. A pleasant alternative way to Kirkby Lonsdale crosses the Loyn Bridge and follows the N bank of the Lune via *Gressingham* and *Whittington*. At (10½m) *Melling* the 15C church has a raised chancel. 12½m: *Tunstall*, see Route 86C. On the left about 1½m beyond the village is the site of a Roman fort, perhaps Galacum. 16m: *Kirkby Lonsdale*, see Route 86C.

From Lancaster a fine moorland road leads SE to (12m) the *'Trough of Bowland* (1000ft), the pass between the Bleasdale Moors on the right and the Forest of Bowland, and then follows the Hodder valley to (15½m) *Dunsop Bridge* (Route 75C).

The main route continues N on A6. 55m: *Slyne* lies ¾m E of *Hest Bank*, the S end of the 'road' across the sands of Morecambe Bay (see Grange-over-Sands in Route 77). 56½m: *Bolton-le-Sands* gives a good view of the bay. At (58½m) *Carnforth* (4800 inhabitants) the old station yards and sheds house the *Steamtown Railway Centre*, which displays a large collection of British and Continental steam locomotives and coaches as a memorial to one of the last homes of steam in Britain, closed in 1968. There are regular train rides in summer along short stretches of standard and 15in gauge track, and occasional excursions on the British Rail line.

Unclassified roads run N and NW to (1½m) *Warton*, below the limestone Warton Crag, with a ruined 14C rectory (EH, all year) and the Washington arms on its church tower; (4½m) *Silverdale*, overlooking Morecambe Bay, where Turner stayed in the 1820s and Elizabeth Gaskell did some of her best work; and (8m) *Arnside*, once a busy port and now a quiet resort on the sandy estuary of the Kent. *Arnside Knott* (NT), 1m S, gives good views of Morecambe Bay and the Lake District fells. *Leighton Hall* (open), in a fine park 1½m N of Warton, has a Gothick façade added by Thomas Harrison in 1800 and contains furniture by the Gillow family, who bought the house in 1822.

A6 enters Cumbria. 65m: *Beetham* has a fine old bridge. 66m: *Milnthorpe* was the birthplace of the regional novelist Constance Holme (1881–1955). At (69m) *Levens Bridge* A590 heads left for the Cumbrian coast (Route 77). For Levens Hall, see below. A6 then joins the course of A591 and passes Sizergh Castle (see below) before A591 branches left for *Windermere* and the Lake District (Route 78A).

74m: **Kendal** (23,400 inhabitants; TI) is an old town known for making shoes and once known for its cloth. 'Kendal Green' was a kind of heavy serge. Narrow 'yards' or alleys lead off the long main street. Catherine Parr (1512–48) was born in the ruined castle on the hill to the E. The painter George Romney worked in Kendal before going to London in 1762 and returned in 1798 to die at a house near the bridge at the S end of the town. He is commemorated by a tablet in the *Parish Church*, where the five aisles enlarge the Perpendicular nave into a rectangular forest of pillars. The Bellingham Chapel has a 13C coffin lid with foliated cross, sword and shield. The *Abbot Hall Art Gallery*, in a handsome building (1759) by John Carr of York overlooking the river, displays portraits by Romney (notably 'The Gower Family'), his pupil Daniel Gardner (1750–1805), a native of Kendal, and other 18C artists, with 18C furniture (Gillow of Lancaster), porcelain, silver and glass. There is also a fine collection of watercolours (Turner, Ruskin), and, shown from time to time, a wide-ranging collection of modern art. The *Museum of Lakeland Life and Industry* in the converted stables has a farming display and reconstructions of craft workshops, period rooms and a Victorian street. The *Kendal Museum*, in a wool warehouse by the railway station at the N end of the town, traces the natural history, archaeology and human history of the region.

Scout Scar (752ft), a limestone ridge on the edge of the National Park 2½m SW, commands a fine view. *'Sizergh Castle* (NT), about 3m S of Kendal, the home of the Strickland family since 1239, consists of a magnificent 14C pele tower, a much altered 15C Great Hall and 16C wings. The Elizabethan panelling and carved chimneypieces are outstanding. Contents include Elizabethan furniture, family portraits and Stuart relics. The grounds have a large rock garden established in the 1920s. **Levens Hall** (open), 2m further S, has a *topiary garden laid out by Guillaume Beaumont in 1692. The house, an Elizabethan mansion added to a medieval pele tower, has splendid plasterwork, panelling and chimneypieces; Cordova leather wall hangings (1692); 17–18C furniture (including pieces by Gillow of Lancaster); a good collection of paintings; and a rare piece of 18C patchwork made from Indian chintz. Mrs Humphry Ward made the house and its surrounding dales the scene of 'Helbeck of Bannisdale' (1898).

From Kendal to *Whitehaven* and *Carlisle* via the Cumbrian coast, see Route 77; to *Windermere, Ambleside, Grasmere* and *Keswick*, see Route 78A; to *Settle, Skipton* and *Ilkley* via Ribblesdale, Craven and Upper Airedale, see Route 86C; to *Hawes, Leyburn* and *Ripon* via Wensleydale, see Route 86D; to *Kirkby Stephen*, see Route 86E.

Beyond Kendal A6, increasingly intertwined with M6, begins the long climb up *Shap Fells*, reaching (83m) the summit at 1304ft. The road is as notorious for winter snows as the railway was in the days of steam for the necessity of 'banking' locomotives and 'doubleheading'. The Shap granite quarries have yielded stone for many famous buildings, including the Albert Memorial in London. To the left there are views of the High Street range and, later, of Blencathra (Saddleback) as A6 descends to (88¾m) *Shap*.

In the Lowther valley 1m SW stands *Keld Chapel* (NT, key available in village), a small 16C monastic building. About ½m downstream are the ruins of *Shap Abbey* (EH), a foundation for Premonstratensian canons moved here c 1199, with a splendid 16C W tower. A fine road leads from Shap to (10m) Pooley Bridge (Route 78B) via (3½m) *Bampton Grange* (Lake District Park local information point), 2m from Haweswater, and the charming village of (7m) *Askham*.

94m: *Hackthorpe*. Beyond *Lowther* to the NW are the ruins of *Lowther Castle* (not open), built in 1806–11 by Sir Robert Smirke for the Earl of Lonsdale, Wordsworth's patron, and demolished in 1957. The church nearby was partly rebuilt in 1686. At (96½m) *Clifton* a 15C pele tower survives from the old hall (EH, all year). 97½m: *Eamont Bridge* has two Neolithic sites, the henge fancifully known as *Arthur's Round Table* and *Mayburgh Earthwork*, with a single stone left in place (both EH). B5320 branches left for *Ullswater* (Route 78B).

99m: **Penrith** (12,200 inhabitants; TI) is a market town built in red sand-stone. Its ruined 14–15C *Castle* (EH, park opening hours) stands in the park opposite the railway station. Outside the dignified church of *St Andrew* (1720–22) are two graves known as the Giant's Grave and the Giant's Thumb, probably c 1000, and the old 16C grammar school briefly attended by William and Dorothy Wordsworth, whose mother came from Penrith. In Great Dockray are the *Gloucester Arms*, perhaps a residence of Richard III and the 16C *Two Lions Inn*, once the town house of the Lowthers. *Hutton Hall* in·Friargate incorporates a 15C pele tower.

Penrith Beacon (937ft), NE of the town, commands a magnificent view. By A66 1½m SE of Penrith stand the ruins of *Brougham Castle*, pronounced 'Broom' (EH, all year; closed Mondays and Tuesdays in winter). The fine late 12C–13C keep and later buildings, restored by Lady Anne Clifford in the 17C, stand near the site of the Roman station of Brocavum. The *Countess Pillar* (EH), by the road about 1m further E, was erected by Lady Anne in 1656 in memory of her parting from her mother, the Countess of Cumberland, in 1616. *Hutton-in-the-Forest* (open), 6m NW of Penrith by A6 and B5305, is a 17–19C house built around a 14C pele tower. It has an early 17C Laudian Gothic gallery wing and a late 17C central façade. The interior, much altered by Anthony Salvin, preserves the splendid late 17C Cupid Staircase. The pleasant grounds are open all year.

From Penrith to *Ullswater* and *Windermere*, see Route 78B; to *Keswick, Derwentwater, Borrowdale, Buttermere* and *Cockermouth*, see Route 78C; to *Scotch Corner*, see Route 86F; to *Alston*, see Route 86G.

A6 continues N past (101½m) the turning for Hutton-in-the-Forest (see above) and (112m) the turning for *Wreay*, 1½m W, where the remarkable church was designed by Sara Losh in 1842 on the plan of a Roman basilica, enriched with carving by the local mason William Hindson.

A more attractive route from Penrith to Carlisle follows A686, the Alston road, to (5m) *Langwathby* by the Eden and then takes the unclassified road to the left. At (6¾m) *Little Salkeld* the old watermill has been restored to working order. Less than 1m beyond are the monolith and stone circle known as *Long Meg and Her Daughters*, with 65 stones, 27 of them still upright. *Little Meg*, ½m NE, is a circle of 11 standing stones. 11m: *Kirkoswald*, a beautifully situated village, has scanty remains of a castle and a church with a detached tower. The College has a fine entrance of 1696. *Lazonby*, just over 1m SW, is reached by a fine bridge of 1763 over the Eden. The attractive village of *Great Salkeld*, 2m further S, has a 14C fortified tower and a Norman doorway. Sideroads continue N from Kirkoswald to (26¼m) *Carlisle* via (12½m) *Staffield*, with the enchanting Nunnery Walks beside the Croglin Water, and (15¾m) *Armathwaite*, on a lovely stretch of the Eden.

118m: **CARLISLE** (71,500 inhabitants), the county town of Cumbria, is an ancient Border fortress with a chequered history remembered in many Border ballads. Though the cathedral, castle and fragments of the city wall survive, the city's atmosphere now owes more to its 19C industrial growth and its modern role as the region's centre of trade and commerce:

TI: Old Town Hall, Green Market. **Bus Station**: Lowther St. **Railway Station**: Citadel Station, S of the Market Square. **Annual Events**: Cumberland Agricultural Show on the third Thursday of July; Carlisle Great Fair in the third week of August.

History. Hadrian's Wall ran through the suburb of Stanwix (Petriana) on the N bank of the Eden. A Roman station was established on the S bank. It later became Luguvalium, which survived into Saxon times, though sacked by the Danes in 875 and constantly beleaguered by the Scots. William Rufus recaptured it from them and began the castle in 1092, though the city was again under Scottish control in 1136–57. During the Civil War it surrendered to the Scottish army under General Leslie after a siege of nine months in 1644–45. Bonnie Prince Charlie entered Carlisle in 1745, proclaiming his father king at the market cross, but the city was retaken by the Duke of Cumberland a few weeks later. Carlisle's industrial development began after the defeat of the rebellion with the establishment of calico-printing works and cotton mills. In the 19C it exchanged its earlier role as port for that of railway centre, with the Newcastle–Carlisle line opening in 1836 and Citadel Station becoming the terminus for seven railway companies.

From Court Square outside *Citadel Station* English St. enters the city, passing between the two huge drumtowers of the *County Buildings* and *Court House*, designed by Thomas Telford and Sir Robert Smirke in 1807–12 but incorporating part of Henry VIII's Citadel. At the end of English St. is the large market square with the *Market Cross* (1682) and 18C *Town Hall*, housing the TI Centre. The half-timbered 15C *Guildhall* is now a museum devoted to the history of the city and its guilds.

Scotch St., with the *Lanes Shopping Centre* on the right, and Rickergate lead to the *Civic Centre* (1956–64; Charles B. Pearson and Partners), with a striking octagonal Council Chamber raised on stilts.

Castle St., where Charlotte Charpentier lodged before her marriage to Sir Walter Scott, leads to the beautiful E end of the ***Cathedral**. Built mainly of red sandstone, it dominates the city. The destruction of most of the nave in the 17C has given it a lop-sided appearance, as well as making it one of the smallest English cathedrals, but it contains many fine details.

The church of the Augustinian priory founded after the Conquest became a cathedral in 1133—the only Augustinian church in England that was also the seat of a bishop. The original Norman building survives in the two W bays, the crossing and the S transept. Replacement of the original presbytery began c 1225 in the Early English style, and continued, after a fire in 1292, in the Decorated style. Bishop Strickland (1400–19) rebuilt the N transept and added the central tower. The original nave was drastically truncated during the Civil War when five bays were demolished and the stone reused. The new *Treasury* (opened 1990), beneath the N aisle of the old nave, houses silver and the 'Christians in Cumbria' exhibition.

The two surviving bays of the *Nave*, serving as a memorial chapel to the Border Regiment, are plain Norman work of 1123. Their arches were distorted by settlement in the 13C. The window over the N door contains fragments of old glass. The small Norman *S Transept* has a Runic inscription on the wall. Bishop Strickland's *N Transept* contains the *Brougham Triptych, a Flemish altarpiece depicting the Passion, probably carved at Antwerp c 1505 and installed here in 1979.

The original E end, only two bays long, was greatly extended in the 13–14C to form the present *Choir* and *Chancel*. The piers of the Early English arcade have superb 14C capitals showing the labours of the months. The special glory of the choir is the Decorated *E Window* (c 1340–45, restored 1983–84). Its tracery lights hold glass of c 1360 showing the Last Judgement; the glass in the main lights is by John Hardman (1861). Below is a monument to the theologian Archdeacon Paley (1743–1805), buried in the N choir aisle. The splendid wooden barrel-vaulted ceiling (c 1360) was restored in the 19C and repainted in 1970. The choir stalls, with misericords, date from c 1420. Their backs were painted c 1484–1507 with the Apostles, and scenes from the lives of St Anthony and St Cuthbert (N) and St Augustine (S). Other woodwork includes the lovely Flamboyant screen of St Catherine's Chapel at the W end of the S choir aisle and Prior Salkeld's *screen (1542) between the presbytery and N aisle. The 16C Flemish *pulpit was brought from Cockayne Hatley in Bedfordshire. In the centre of the choir is the brass to Bishop Bell (d. 1496).

Some remains of the monastic buildings survive in the precinct called The Abbey, to the SW. The *Deanery*, once the prior's lodging, incorporates a 13C pele tower; the first floor has a fine early 16C painted ceiling and the second floor contains the *Education Centre*. The hall known as the Fratry (13C, rebuilt 1482) is now the *Chapter Library*. The *Gateway* was rebuilt in 1527.

Between the cathedral and the castle is the late 17C *Tullie House* (open). It contains displays of Hadrian's Wall, the reivers (cattle thieves), railway history, fine and decorative arts, Cumbrian wildlife and local history. Abbey St., behind, has Georgian and 19C houses.

A pedestrian subway leads under Castle Way to the **Castle** (EH, all year plus Mondays in winter), founded in 1092 but many times altered during centuries of military use. It stands at the NW end of the city, guarding the Anglo-Scottish border. Its walls once connected with the city walls.

The impressive outer gatehouse has a prison on the ground floor. The warden's apartment has on the first floor been furnished in medieval style. The outer bailey contains mainly 19C buildings. Access to the heart of the castle is gained via the inner gatehouse, *Captain's Tower*. The massive Norman *Keep is one of the best of its kind in England. It was begun by Henry I in 1122 and largely completed by David I of Scotland during the Scottish occupation. Changes in later centuries included strengthening in the 16C and the addition of earth ramparts. On the second floor are 14–15C carvings made by prisoners. Later prisoners included Mary, Queen of Scots, in 1568, the reiver, William Armstrong ('Kinmont Willie'), who escaped in 1596, and the defeated Scottish rebels in 1745. The battlements give a fine view.

From Annetwell St., by the entrance to the subway, the city wall can be followed past the back of the Deanery to the *Sallyport Steps*. The 15C tithe barn in Heads Lane, opposite, is the only English tithe barn inside a city wall; it has been restored as the parish hall of *St Cuthbert's Church* (rebuilt 1778). St Cuthbert's Lane leads back into the market square.

Wetheral, on the Eden 5m to the E, has the 15C gatehouse of a Benedictine priory founded in 1106 (EH, all year). On the opposite bank stands *Corby Castle* (not open), a 17–19C house built on to a 13C pele tower. *Burgh-by-Sands* (pronounced 'Bruff'), 5m NW of Carlisle, is on the line of Hadrian's Wall, which continued 7½m further NW to the Solway Firth at *Bowness-on-Solway*. On the marsh about 1¼m N of Burgh-by-Sands a monument marks the spot where Edward I died in 1307 on his way to crush Robert Bruce's rebellion. Beyond *Rockcliffe*, 5m NW of Carlisle between A74 and the estuary, is the late Georgian *Castletown House* (open by appointment).

FROM CARLISLE TO THE SCOTTISH BORDER. A7 heads N through flat country to (8m) *Longtown* (TI), on the Esk about 3m S of the border. About ¾m S is the early 17C parish church of *Arthuret*. Before Longtown A74 branches left from A7 to cross the border at *Gretna*, on the Sark 9m NW of Carlisle. *Gretna Green*, just beyond, was a famous destination for runaway couples seeking immediate marriage under the liberal terms of Scottish law. The country between the Esk and the Sark was the 'Debatable Land', long disputed by England and Scotland. At *Solway Moss*, 3m W of Longtown, the Scots under James V were crushingly defeated in 1542. The present border was agreed in 1552. From Gretna to *Glasgow* or *Edinburgh* and from Longtown to *Edinburgh*, see 'Blue Guide Scotland'.

From Carlisle to *Whitehaven* and *Kendal* via the Cumbrian coast, see Route 77; to *Cockermouth*, see Route 78C; to *Newcastle* via *Tynedale* and *Hexham*, see Route 87A; to *Newcastle* along *Hadrian's Wall*, see Route 87B.

77

The Cumbrian Coast: Kendal to Whitehaven and Carlisle

Directions. Total distance 118m. Closely following the coastal railway for much of the way, this route takes in a mixture of fine views, industry, post-industrial decline and small resorts, with access to the Lake District (Route 78) from several points. **Kendal**, see Route 76. A6 to (5m) Levens Bridge. A590 to (30m) Dalton-in-Furness (for **Barrow-in-Furness**). A595 to (77m) **Whitehaven**. A595, A596 to (85m) Workington. A596 to (91m) Maryport. A596, A595 to (118m) **Carlisle**, see Route 76.

Kendal, and A6 S to (5m) *Levens Bridge*, see Route 76. A590, heading right, enters the S tip of the Lake District National Park on the way to (11½m) *Lindale*.

B5277 leads to Morecambe Bay at (2m) the resort of **Grange-over-Sands** (3600 inhabitants; seasonal TI). From *Kent's Bank*, 2m SW, a 'roadway' leads across the sands of the bay to (9m) Hest Bank (Route 76). The Cartmel monks guided travellers this way, and coaches later used it as a shortcut. It is now a popular walk but, since the bay and the route change with each tide, should not be attempted without the services of the guide at Guides Farm, Cart Lane, Grange.

2m W of Grange, the charming little town of **Cartmel** has a 12C priory *church, now the parish church. The diagonal upper stage was added to its Norman tower in the 15C, when the Perpendicular nave and fine E window were also built. The S choir aisle is Decorated. The choir stalls, with misericords, date from c 1440; the choir screen and stall canopies were installed c 1620. Memorials include the Harrington tomb (1347) and Thomas Woolner's monument to Lord Frederick Cavendish, assassinated in Phoenix Park, Dublin, in 1882. The 14C priory gatehouse (NT) survives in the square. *Holker Hall* (pronounced 'Hooker'; open), near *Cark* 2½m SW of Cartmel, was partly rebuilt by Paley and Austin after a fire in 1871. Its grounds have formal and woodland gardens, a deer park, a motor museum and a rural crafts exhibition.

From Lindale A590 heads inland, climbing to (13½m) *High Newton* on the way to the Leven valley at (16½m) *Newby Bridge*, near the foot of Windermere (Route 78A). The road then follows the Leven, crossing it before (19m) *Haverthwaite* (Lake District National Park local information point). In summer a steam railway runs to Lake Side, connecting with the motor launch service up Windermere to Bowness and Waterhead. 21½m: *Greenodd*.

An attractive route goes up the Crake valley to (10½m) Coniston (Route 78A) via (8m) *Torver*. A5092, leaving the valley at (2m) *Lowick Green*, makes a shortcut with fine views to (8½m) *Broughton* (see below).

A590 leaves the National Park and heads down the Furness peninsula to (25m) the market town of **Ulverston** (12,000 inhabitants; TI). Natives include Sir John Barrow (1764–1848), founder of the Royal Geographical Society, remembered by the monument on *Hoad Hill* to the NE, and Stan Laurel (1890–1965), remembered in the *Laurel and Hardy Museum*. George Fox (1624–91) lived at the Elizabethan *Swarthmoor Hall*, ½m S.

The church at *Pennington*, 2m SW, has a reset Norman tympanum with runic inscription. A5087 takes a pleasant route along the shore of Morecambe Bay to (12m) *Rampside* and (13m) *Roa Island* (see below). It passes (3m) the little resort of *Bardsea*, just S of the early 19C mansion of *Conishead Priory* (now a Manjushri monastery, but open), and (7m) *Aldingham*, where the church stands inside its own sea wall.

30m: **Dalton-in-Furness** (11,000 inhabitants), in the middle of the Furness peninsula, has the 14C *Dalton Tower* (NT). The painter George Romney (1734–1802) was born and buried at Dalton.

A590 continues down to (4m) Barrow at the tip of the peninsula. Hidden away in the 'Vale of Deadly Nightshade', to the left at 1½m, are the lovely sandstone ruins of *Furness Abbey (EH, all year). Founded in 1123 by the future King Stephen, it became second only to Fountains among the great Cistercian abbeys of the North. There is a small exhibition centre at the entrance. Little remains of the church's Norman nave. The transepts, with a fine N doorway, are late Norman and Early English work with 15C windows; the beautiful sedilia and piscina in the choir are Perpendicular, like the W tower. The E wall of the cloister is pierced by rich arches of c 1230, and the elegant chapter house is Early English. The two 13C effigies of knights in armour in the vaulted 14C infirmary chapel are perhaps the oldest in England. To the SE the medieval *Bow Bridge* (EH) crosses the Mill Beck.

Barrow-in-Furness (61,700 inhabitants; TI) was developed from 1846 onwards as an iron and steel town by Sir James Ramsden of the Furness Railway. Its port has shipbuilding and engineering yards, and dock terminals operated by British Nuclear Fuels and British Gas, whose pipeline from the Morecambe Field in the Irish Sea comes ashore here. A bridge leads across to the suburb of *Vickerstown* on the long *Walney Island*, sheltering the harbour, with nature reserves at its N and S ends. To the SE, reached by A5087, are (4m) *Rampside* and (5m) *Roa Island*. A ferry serves *Piel Island*, about ½m offshore, with the ruins of the castle built in 1327 (EH). Lambert Simnel, pretender to Henry VII's crown, landed here in 1487.

A595 runs N from Dalton, making a wide loop round the Duddon Sands. From (41m) *Broughton-in-Furness* A593, a charming road, branches right for Coniston (Route 78A), and from (42m) *Duddon Bridge* sideroads go up both sides of the Duddon valley to Ulpha (Route 78A). From (44½m) *Hallthwaites* A5093 branches 3½m S to *Millom* (7000 inhabitants; seasonal TI), developed as an ironworking town in the 19C but with an interesting church and the remains of a 14C castle. The poet Norman Nicholson (1914–87) lived here.

A595 sweeps round the base of *Black Combe* (1857ft), a distant outlier of the Skiddaw slates which make up the mountains in the N and NW of the Lake District. It then runs parallel to the sandy coast, crossing the Esk just before (59m) *Muncaster Castle* (open), incorporating a 14C pele tower but largely rebuilt by Anthony Salvin in 1862–66.

It contains Elizabethan chimneypieces and 16–17C furnishings. The terrace commands a superb view over the Esk; the grounds have azaleas, rhododendrons and a bird garden.

60m: *Ravenglass* (seasonal TI) is a pleasant place at the junction of the Esk, the Mite and the Irk. Remains of a bath house survive from the Roman fort of Glannaventa (EH). The former station of the Furness Railway is now a railway museum, with a narrow-gauge railway service via Muncaster Mill to (7m) *Dalegarth* in Eskdale (Route 78D). The nature reserve offshore has sand dunes with natterjack toads; visitors should contact the County Land Agent and Valuer, Property Services Department, Cumbria County Council, 15 Portland Square, Carlisle CA1 1QQ.

For *Eskdale*, *Wastwater* and *Scafell*, and *Ennerdale*, reached from A595 between Ravenglass and Whitehaven, see Route 78D.

A595 crosses the Mite, near the restored *Muncaster Mill* (open), and then the Irt on the way to (62½m) *Holmrook*. B5344 leads along the coast to the little resort of (3¼m) *Seascale*. At (65m) *Gosforth* (Lake District National Park local information point) the churchyard has an Anglo-Danish *cross of c 1000, 14½ft high, apparently mixing Norse legend with Christianity in its decoration. The Gosforth Show is held on the third Wednesday in August. To the right of (67½m) *Calder Bridge* is the ruined Cistercian *Calder Abbey* (not open). Near the coast is the *Sellafield* site of British Nuclear Fuels, including Calder Hall, the world's first industrial-size nuclear power station (opened in 1956), the Sellafield nuclear reprocessing plant (called Windscale when it was opened in 1951) and Thorp Hall, a controversial new nuclear reprocessing plant. The exhibition centre by the N Gate is, amazingly, one of the most popular tourist attractions in the region. 71½m: *Egremont* (TI) has a ruined 12–13C castle with a gatehouse on a high mound (open). The Egremont Crab Fair is held on the third Saturday in September; it includes a 'gurning' competition, in which a prize is awarded to the person pulling the ugliest face with his head through a horse collar.

The resort of *St Bees* (Lake District National Park information point), 2½m NW, has a boys' school founded by Archbishop Grindal in 1583 and an interesting collegiate church of c 1120, restored by Butterfield in 1855–58, with a fine but weatherbeaten W doorway. Further NW is *St Bees Head* (462ft), the starting-point of A. Wainwright's 190m Coast-to-Coast Walk, ending at Robin Hood's Bay (Route 84).

A595 reaches the coastal region, now suffering post-industrial decline, where coalmines and ironworks were established in the 17–19C. The last

Cumbrian colliery closed in 1986. 77m: **Whitehaven** (26,700 inhabitants; TI), developed as a coal port in the 17C and laid out in a grid pattern in the 18C, keeps some Georgian and 19C buildings. The Council Offices (open) in Irish St. occupy a Victorian building in the Italianate style. The *Museum* in the former market hall (1880) has exhibits of local geology, archaeology, trade and industry, and a collection of ship models. *St James* (by the engineer Carlisle Spedding, 1752–53) contains galleries, a fine plaster ceiling, an elegant pulpit and an altarpiece by Procaccini. The Sir Nicholas Sekers Theatre at *Rosehill*, 2m NE, presents plays, concerts, etc.

From Whitehaven to *Cockermouth*, see Route 78C. For *Eskdale*, *Wasdale* and *Scafell*, and *Ennerdale*, reached from A595 between Whitehaven and Ravenglass, see Route 78D.

Beyond (81m) *Distington* the route changes from A595 to A596. 85m: **Workington** (27,600 inhabitants; TI), at the mouth of the Derwent, had coalmines reaching under the sea. Mary, Queen of Scots, landed here on her flight to England after the Battle of Langside (1568) and was taken to Carlisle Castle. The church of *St John* (1823; Thomas Hardwick) in Washington St. is a handsome neo-classical building. 91m: **Maryport** (11,600 inhabitants; TI) is a decayed coal and iron port, with a *Maritime Museum*.

FROM MARYPORT TO CARLISLE VIA SILLOTH, 34½m. B5300 continues up the coast via (5m) the resort and fishing village of *Allonby* to (12½m) **Silloth** (seasonal TI) on the Solway Firth. B5302 turns inland to (18m) *Abbeytown*, where the parish church occupies part of the nave of the Cistercian church of Holme Cultram, an abbey founded in 1150 by Henry, son of David I of Scotland. The original work includes the W doorway, massive clustered pillars and newel stair. B5302 joins the main route below near (23½m) *Wigton*.

A596 turns inland for (98½m) *Aspatria*, where the church has a hog's back tombstone and fragments of Anglo-Danish sculpture. 107m: *Wigton* (4800 inhabitants) is an old market town with an 18C church and a market fountain with reliefs by Thomas Woolner (1871). Horse sales are held on the last Wednesday in October. At (112m) *Thursby* the route joins A595 again. 118m: **Carlisle**, see Route 76.

78

The Lake District

Maps: OS Lake District Outdoor Leisure maps (2½in to 1m).

The *Lake District contains some of the best-loved scenery in England. For almost two centuries its combination of fells, lakes and valleys has attracted probably more praise and more visitors than any other region. It is actually quite small: a mere corner of North-West England tucked between the A6/M6 and the Cumbrian coast, measuring about 35m across. Windermere, the largest of the 16 lakes, is just 10½m long; Scafell Pike, though it is the highest mountain in England, reaches only 3210ft. The Lake District's appeal comes from the astonishing variety concentrated in its small compass, and from the wildness and even grandeur achieved by its apparently modest dimensions.

To understand the forces which have shaped the landscape and created its underlying structure we cannot do better than follow Wordsworth's advice in his guidebook to the Lakes. There, in a memorable passage, he recommends that the reader join him in imagination on top of Great Gable or Scafell—or, better still, on a cloud midway between these two mountains and a few feet above their summits. From this vantage point the continually changing vistas which can delight but almost bewilder the visitor to the valley floor fall into a distinct pattern. The lakes and valleys stretch out below like the spokes radiating from the hub of a great wheel. Beginning in the SE and moving clockwise, Wordsworth notes: Langdale and Windermere; Coniston Water, 'a broken spoke sticking in the rim'; the Duddon valley; Eskdale; Wastwater; Ennerdale; Buttermere, Crummock Water and Lorton Vale; and Borrowdale and Derwentwater. These last run due N and, as Wordsworth admits, the NE sector that follows does not conform neatly to his image. But from the top of Helvellyn to the E a fragment of another wheel is represented by: Thirlmere and St John's in the Vale; Ullswater; Haweswater (though it is not actually visible from the top of Helvellyn); and finally, the vale of Grasmere and Rydal Water, bringing us back to Windermere in the S.

As this configuration suggests, the central Lake District was once a great dome, higher than any of the present mountains. Water found its way down the fissures in the slopes, establishing the course that the valleys still follow today. With the coming of the Ice Ages glaciers gouged the watercourses into deeper troughs and, where these were blocked by glacial material, lakes formed. Dry valleys like St John's in the Vale once held lakes which later drained or became silted up. The strip of land which now separates Buttermere and Crummock Water is a clear example of silt deposit that has divided one original lake into two. The tarns on the sides of the fells are meltwater pools filling the scooped-out hollows left at the glacier's head.

These forces were at work not on a homogeneous unit but on several types of rock: their differing reactions gave further variety to the landscape. The oldest rocks are the Skiddaw slates whose softness rounds and blunts the massive outlines of the northern fells overlooking Keswick. In the S another but much younger slate—Silurian slate—makes the peaceful and undramatic scenery of Windermere which forms so many visitors' first impression of the Lakes. The central area is hard volcanic rock—the Borrowdale Volcanic Series—which does not erode smoothly but breaks into peaks and crags or shatters into scree. Its rugged effects can be seen in Borrowdale itself, by the wild shores of Wastwater, and in the great fells which stretch from the Scafell range and Great Gable in the W through Bowfell, the Langdale Pikes, Coniston Old Man (formally The Old Man of Coniston), Helvellyn and the Fairfield range, to the High Street range in the E.

Archaeologists point to significant evidence of early human settlement: Neolithic stone axes in Langdale, the Castlerigg stone circle, and the Roman ways over High Street and the Hardknott Pass, with its fort perched above Eskdale. Etymologists note the strong Scandinavian element still apparent in the local place-names, introduced by the Norse settlers who arrived in the 10C from Ireland, Scotland and the Isle of Man. Yet for centuries the human history of the Lake District was remote from the public life of the nation. Sheep-farming was the mainstay of the rural economy, as it still is today. From the 16C to the 19C the hills were mined with increasing thoroughness for silver, iron, copper, lead and other minerals. The Keswick pencil industry, originally dependent on local sources of graphite, and the shafts and quarries which mark Coniston Old Man are the most obvious reminders of the region's industrial history. So, too, is the loss of the ancient forests consumed as charcoal for smelting.

Far from holding any special appeal, the Lake District could disgust outsiders for whom remote hills and valleys merely signified difficult or dangerous travel, backward customs and bad farmland. Defoe spoke for his age when he dismissed the region as 'the wildest, most barren and frightful in England'. Yet he wrote just before the shift of taste, beginning with the Picturesque Movement in the later years of the 18C and continuing into the 19C with the Romantic Movement, that reversed the judgement of previous generations and made these very qualities attractive. The poet Gray's journal of his visit, published in 1775, shows the first stirrings of the new sensibility. The first guidebook, by Thomas West in 1778, proclaims it as doctrine: 'Such as spend their lives in cities, and their time in crowds, will here meet with contrasts that enlarge the mind, by contemplation of sublime objects and raise it from nature to nature's first source'. The poetry of Wordsworth, most local of the so-called 'Lake Poets', confirmed that the need for nature felt by the new city-dwellers of the Industrial Revolution could best be satisfied by the Lake District. His presence at Grasmere and then Rydal, like that of Ruskin at Coniston in the half century following Wordsworth's death, reinforced the region's intimate bond with literature and landscape art. The list of famous natives, residents and visitors at the end of this introduction shows in summary fashion how a region, geographically marginal, became almost central to the artistic life of the nation from the late 18C until the end of the 19C.

Such popularity brought obvious dangers. Wordsworth himself lived to deplore the new villas which disfigured his view and, memorably but unsuccessfully, to oppose the opening of the Kendal and Windermere railway line in 1847. His protest contained the seed of all the later battles to preserve the region, though their ground would shift from the building of railway lines to the conversion of lakes into reservoirs and the enlargement of local roads into communication arteries. Pioneers in the appreciation of nature gave way to pioneers in its conservation. The National Trust, founded in 1895, grew from the activities of Canon Rawnsley and Ruskin's disciple Octavia Hill, and the generosity of Beatrix Potter, in the Lake District. Since it bought Brandelhow Woods by the shore of Derwentwater in 1902 it has become the largest property-holder in the region, owning more than 120,000 acres with about 12,000 more protected by covenants. It was fitting, too, that the Lake District should have become the largest of the ten National Parks created in England and Wales after World War II.

The four routes below tour the region by the main roads, though the detours which branch from them sometimes tackle narrow or steep sideroads. They take in all the most popular, and often overcrowded, attractions: Windermere, Ambleside, Grasmere and Langdale; Ullswater and Helvellyn; Derwentwater, Borrowdale and Buttermere. They also include less crowded areas like the Skiddaw fells and the western lakes and valleys. Major fells are described briefly and starting-points for popular walking routes are indicated; shorter and easier walks are described in detail when they are the only way of reaching a place that should tempt even the short-winded motorist out of the car. Fellwalkers, rockclimbers, etc. need more detailed advice than the present guide can attempt; hints for obtaining it are given under the appropriate headings below.

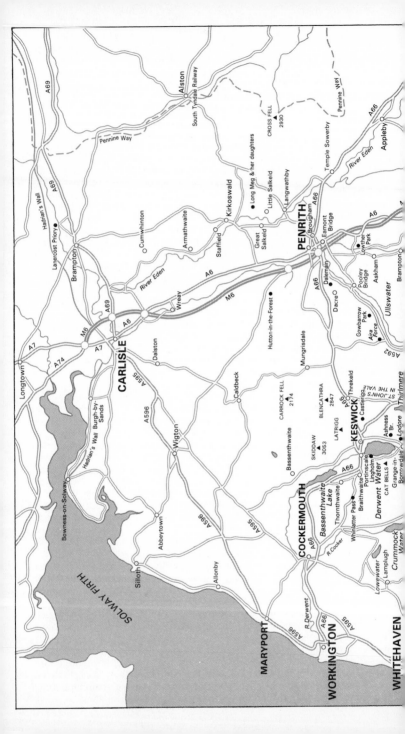

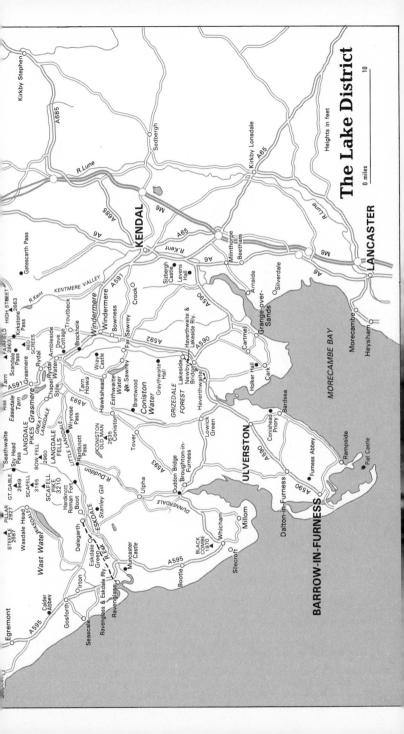

The Lake District

Heights in feet

0 miles   10

Natives and residents. William Wordsworth (1770–1850), born at Cockermouth, brought up partly at Penrith and educated at Hawkshead, lived with his sister Dorothy Wordsworth (1771–1855) at Grasmere in 1799–1813, mainly at Dove Cottage, and then at Rydal Mount until his death; he is buried at Grasmere. Samuel Taylor Coleridge (1772–1834) lived at Greta Hall, Keswick, in 1800–03 and with the Wordsworths at Grasmere in 1808–09. Robert Southey (1774–1843) lived at Greta Hall, Keswick, from 1803 until his death; he is buried at Keswick. The painter J.C. Ibbetson lived at Ambleside and Troutbeck in 1799–1805. The journalist and critic John Wilson ('Christopher North') lived at Windermere in 1807–15. Thomas De Quincey was tenant of Dove Cottage, Grasmere, in 1808–30. The scholar and critic James Spedding (1808–81) lived at Mirehouse, Bassenthwaite. Shelley and Harriet Westbrook lived at Keswick in 1811–12. Felicia Hemans lived near Ambleside in 1829–31. Dr Thomas Arnold lived at Ambleside after his retirement from Rugby until his death in 1842. Harriet Martineau lived at Ambleside from 1845 until her death in 1876. John Ruskin lived at Coniston from 1871 until his death in 1900. Canon Hardwicke Rawnsley was incumbent of Crosthwaite, near Keswick, in 1883–1917. Beatrix Potter lived at Near Sawrey from 1905 until her death in 1943. Sir Hugh Walpole lived near Derwentwater from 1932 until his death in 1941; he is buried at Keswick.

Visitors. Thomas Gray in 1767 and 1769; Arthur Young in 1768; William Gilpin in 1772; Gainsborough in 1783; Ann Radcliffe in 1794; Turner in 1797 and several times later; Constable in 1806; Charles Lamb, Coleridge's guest, in 1802; Keats in 1818; Sir Walter Scott on his birthday in 1825 and other occasions; Edward FitzGerald in 1835, Tennyson in 1835 and 1851 and Carlyle several times, all as guests of James Spedding; Charlotte Brontë, Harriet Martineau's guest, in 1850. Charles Dickens and Wilkie Collins had a dreadful time on Carrock Fell in 1857.

National Park Information Centres. The main Visitor Centre is at Brockhole, near Windermere. There is an Information Centre open all year at Keswick and seasonal Information Centres at Bowness, Coniston, Glenridding, Grasmere, Hawkshead, Pooley Bridge, Seatoller and Waterhead. In addition, there are local information points in post offices or shops at Bampton Grange (Route 76), Elterwater, Ennerdale Bridge, Far Sawrey, Gosforth (Route 77), Haverthwaite, High Lorton, St Bees, Ulpha and Wasdale Head. Written inquiries should be addressed to the National Park Authority, Murley Moss, Oxenholme Rd, Kendal, Cumbria LA9 7RL.

Walking. With 1500 miles of public right of way, the Lake District is ideal walking country. Walkers need the four OS Outdoor Leisure maps (1 to 25,000 or 2½in to 1m). The best guidebooks are A. Wainwright's seven-volume 'Pictorial Guide to the Lakeland Fells' (1955–66) and its various supplementary volumes, which include 'A Coast-to-Coast Walk' (1973), describing a route from St Bees Head to Robin Hood's Bay, and 'Fellwalking with Wainwright' (1984), detailing 18 favourite walks. Two guides by 'John Parker' (the pseudonym of John Wyatt), 'Walk the Lakes: 40 Easy Walks' (1983) and 'Walk the Lakes Again: 38 Easy Walks' (1985), stick to lower ground. The National Park Authority publishes a useful pamphlet, 'Enjoy the Fells in Safety'.

Rockclimbing. The sport was pioneered on Pillar Rock (Ennerdale), Napes Needle (Great Gable), Scafell Crag, Pavey Ark (Langdale Pikes) and Dow Crag (Coniston), and is particularly popular in Langdale and Borrowdale. New routes of extreme technical difficulty are still being opened up. The local Fell and Rock Climbing Club publishes a series of six guidebooks.

Boating. Subject to the necessary permission, boats can be launched on Bassenthwaite Lake, Buttermere, Coniston Water, Crummock Water, Derwentwater, Esthwaite Water (rowing boats only), Grasmere (small boats), Thirlmere, Ullswater and Windermere. Power boats are permitted, subject to speed limits, on Coniston Water, Derwentwater, Ullswater and Windermere. Water ski-ing is allowed on Windermere. The National Park publishes a useful pamphlet, 'Enjoy Water in Safety'.

Sports and Shows. These often preserve Lakeland traditions, with displays of the hardy local breed of Herdwick sheep, Cumberland and Westmorland wrestling, hound trailing and fell running. The largest is Grasmere Sports, held on the Thursday nearest

20 August. Others include: Ambleside Sports on the Thursday before the first Monday in August; Ennerdale Show on the last Wednesday in August; Eskdale Show on the last Saturday in September; Hawkshead Show on the third Tuesday in August; Keswick Show on August Bank Holiday Monday; Patterdale Sheep Dog Trials on August Bank Holiday Saturday; and the Wasdale Head Shepherds' Meet and Show on the second Saturday in October. Also the Egremont Crab Fair, Gosforth Show and Wigton Horse Sales, all in Route 77.

Glossary of local terms. *Band*, raised terrace or ridge between two lower tracts; *beck*, stream; *combe*, hollow; *dodd*, lower spur or foothill, generally rounded; *fell*, hill or mountain; *force* or *foss*, waterfall; *gill* or *ghyll*, narrow mountain stream; *hause*, top of a pass (French 'col'); *holme*, island; *how* or *howe*, low rounded hill; *knott*, rocky knob; *nab* or *neb*, projection; *pike*, peak; *pitch*, steep ascent; *raise*, pile of stones, cairn; *rigg*, ridge; *scar* or *scarth*, crag, steep rock face; *scree*, steep slope of loose rocks; *stickle*, sharp peak; *tarn*, small mountain lake; *thwaite*, clearing; *trod*, sheep path; *wyke*, bay.

Books. Since Thomas West's guide in 1778, travel literature about the Lakes has grown to make a list probably longer than any other English region can boast. Wordsworth's 'Guide to the Lakes' still makes a good travelling companion, particularly in the illustrated edition by Peter Bicknell (1984). In the 20C Norman Nicholson, another poet who lived in the region, wrote several studies, including 'Portrait of the Lakes' (revised as 'The Lakes', 1977). John Wyatt, who also writes as 'John Parker', provides a crisp general introduction in the official Countryside Commission guide to the National Park (1987). A. Wainwright's books, already mentioned above, have a charm and good sense that commend them even to walkers of limited energy. The best-rounded general book is 'The Lake District' (revised edition, 1974) by Roy Millward and Adrian Robinson in 'The Regions of Britain' series.

A.   Kendal to Windermere, Ambleside, Grasmere and Keswick

Directions. Total distance 28m. **Kendal**, see Route 76. A591 to (8m) **Windermere**, (12½m) **Ambleside**, (16m) **Grasmere** and (28m) **Keswick** (Route 78C). A591 is probably the most popular way of entering the Lake District, with many of the most crowded tourist attractions on its course.

Kendal, see Route 76. The main route takes A5284 to join A591 at the edge of the National Park 1½m NW of the town. The road closely follows the course of the Kendal–Windermere railway line, opened in 1847 despite protests from Wordsworth ('Is then no nook of English ground secure/From rash assault?'). From *Staveley*, bypassed at 5m, a sideroad goes N up the charming little valley of the Kent to (4m) *Kentmere*, with a pele tower and restored 16C church, backed by the High Street fells which separate it from Haweswater (Route 78B). Its sister valley of *Longsleddale*, watered by the Sprint, is explored by the sideroad running E from Staveley via (4m) *Garnett Bridge* to (9m) *Sadgill*.

An alternative way of starting the journey takes B5284 via (4m) *Crook* to (7½m) the lakeside road, A592, just S of Bowness and the pier for the Windermere ferry. A third and much more devious route takes the steep sideroad which enjoys marvellous views on its way to (3½m) *Underbarrow* and (6m) *Crosthwaite*, and then strikes SW across the Levens Bridge–Bowness road. Beyond (8m) *Bowland Bridge* the road climbs to an unexpected view before descending to (13m) *Newby Bridge* at the S tip of Windermere. The turning on the left beyond Bowland Bridge leads in 1m to *Cartmel Fell*, above the lovely Winster valley. The church of St Anthony (c 1504) contains good woodwork, a mutilated pre-Reformation Crucifixion, a three-decker pulpit and 15C *glass which may come from Cartmel Priory.

8m: **Windermere** (TI), transformed from a little hamlet by the arrival of the railway, merges with its older neighbour, **Bowness-on-Windermere** (seasonal National Park Information Centre; 8600 inhabitants together), on the E shore of the lake from which they take their name. They are a popular starting-point for tours, though the crowds and resort atmosphere hardly make a promising introduction to the Lakes. The *Windermere Steamboat Museum*, by the lakeside road from Windermere to Bowness, has fine old craft. In Bowness the parish church of *St Martin*, consecrated in 1483, contains late 15C glass from Cartmel Priory in its beautiful E window and a memorial by Flaxman to Bishop Watson of Llandaff (d. 1816) in its S aisle.

Windermere ('Vinandr's lake'), 10½m long but almost as narrow as a river, is the largest lake in England as well as the best known in the Lake District. In summer its surface is often crowded with yachts and power boats. The shores are beautifully wooded and the surrounding hills are much gentler than the dark volcanic crags which overhang the northern and western lakes. *Orrest Head* (784ft), just N of Windermere railway station, and *Queen Adelaide's Hill* (259ft; NT), W of the station, make good viewpoints. Sight-seeing launches cruise the length of the lake from Bowness, Waterhead and Lake Side. They pass the wooded *Belle Isle*, with the circular neo-classical house built by John Plaw in 1774. A car ferry crosses regularly to the W shore from the pier S of Bowness.

FROM BOWNESS TO LAKE SIDE AND THE W SHORE. A592 heads S on a well-wooded route keeping fairly close to the shore. 2m: *Storrs Point* was the scene of a regatta celebrating Sir Walter Scott's birthday in 1825, attended by Wordsworth, John Wilson, George Canning and Southey. Storrs Temple (NT, not open), on the lake, was built in honour of Admirals Duncan, St Vincent, Howe and Nelson in 1804. There is a car park and a good view across the lake near (3¼m) the *Beech Hill Hotel*. 5½m: The road passes beneath *Gummer's How* (1054ft), another splendid viewpoint. 6½m: The sideroad from Bowland Bridge and Kendal (see above) joins A592. By the lake is the *Fell Foot Park* (NT). 7¼m: *Newby Bridge* (also on Route 77) lies just beyond the foot of Windermere. A592 leads right and soon afterwards a sideroad, again to the right, crosses the Leven for (8½m) *Lake Side*, with the pier for the Windermere cruises and the station served by the steam railway from Haverthwaite (Route 77). Sideroads continue up the much quieter W shore of the lake, passing (9½m) the *Stott Park Bobbin Mill* (EH, summer season and 1–31 October), built in 1835 and restored to working order, and (11m) the 19C gardens (open) of *Graythwaite Hall*. At 14m the road joins B5285 just W of the ferry pier. A footpath leads through the wooded *Claife Heights* (NT), N of the road, returning down the shore.

FROM BOWNESS TO HAWKSHEAD AND CONISTON. B5285, on the W shore, can be reached either by the detour just described or by the car ferry from the pier S of Bowness to *Ferry House*, now the laboratory of the Freshwater Biological Association. Skirting Claife Heights, the road climbs to (1m) *Far Sawrey* (National Park local information point). At (1½m) *Near Sawrey* is *Hill Top* (NT), the 17C farm cottage where Beatrix Potter lived intermittently in 1905–13 and wrote some of her best-loved books. One of the most popular attractions in the Lake District, the little house gets very crowded. B5285 continues along the E side of *Esthwaite Water*, one of the smaller lakes (1½m long and about ¼m wide), and passes the pool known as the *Priest Pot*. Cars have to be parked outside **Hawkshead** (seasonal National Park Information Centre), a picturesque little town with half-timbered houses, narrow streets and a network of little squares, often overrun by tourists. The *Beatrix Potter Gallery* (NT), with drawings and illustrations, is in the office where her husband worked as a solicitor. Herdwick sheep can be seen at the agricultural show on the third Tuesday in August. On a hillock stands the 15–16C church, with plain, low-arched arcades, 17–18C murals and interesting monuments. In 1779–87 Wordsworth was a pupil at the old grammar school (open) founded by Archbishop Sandys of York in 1585. The poet apparently lodged, not at the cottage in Hawkshead marked with a plaque, but at the hamlet of *Colthouse*, ½m NE. *Grizedale Forest*, owned by the Forestry Commission, lies S of Hawkshead between Esthwaite Water and Coniston Water. A sideroad runs down to (2¾m) *Grizedale*, with a Visitor Centre and the Theatre in the Forest, and (4m) *Satterthwaite*, where the forest trails include one leading NE to the Windermere ferry.

N of Hawkshead B5285 is joined by the road from Ambleside at (4½m) *Hawkshead Courthouse* (NT), a 15C gatehouse where the manor courts were held, once the property of Furness Abbey. Beyond (5¼m) *Hawkshead Hill*, where a sideroad on the right leads to Tarn Hows (see below), B5285 reaches the highest point of the journey at *High Cross* (647ft) and gives a marvellous view of Coniston Water as it descends.

7½m: The village of **Coniston** (seasonal National Park Information Centre), beautifully situated at the foot of Coniston Old Man and the other Coniston Fells near the head of Coniston Water, is as closely associated with John Ruskin (1819–1900) as Grasmere is with Wordsworth. His home, Brantwood, is described on the drive round the Water, below. He is buried in the NE corner of Coniston churchyard beneath an Anglo-Saxon style cross. The nearby *Ruskin Museum*, opened the year after his death, has paintings, drawings, manuscripts, geological specimens from his collection and personal relics from Brantwood. *Coniston Old Man** (formally *The Old Man of Coniston*, perhaps from the Welsh *Allt Maen*, 'steep or high rock'; 2631ft), usually climbed from the village, is impressive despite the marks of copper mines and slate quarries on its sides. *Dow Crag* (2555ft), beyond the tarn to its W, is a favourite with rockclimbers. **Coniston Water**, just over 5m long and ½–¼m wide, is a smaller and quieter version of Windermere. *Peel Island*, one of three islets, is the 'Wild Cat Island' of Arthur Ransome's 'Swallows and Amazons' (1931). Donald Campbell set a world water speed record of 260.35 mph here in 1959 and died attempting to raise it in 1967. The steam yacht 'Gondola', originally launched in 1859 and renovated by NT, makes passenger cruises to Park-a-Moor and back. There is a superb view down the lake from near *Tarn Hows*, a popular viewpoint in NT land 2½m NE of Coniston village, reached by taking B5285 back towards Hawkshead and branching left through the woods up to the tarn.

A drive round the Water, with views dominated by the Old Man, also begins by taking B5285 but soon branches right, round the head of the lake, to join the unclassified road down the E shore at (1½m) *Tent Lodge*. 2½m: On the left is *Brantwood* (open), which Ruskin bought in 1871 and made his chief home until his death in 1900. There are splendid views from the grounds and from his bedroom in the turret. Though it has lost most of the extraordinary art collection he assembled, the house still contains work by Burne-Jones, Samuel Prout and William Henry Hunt, as well as many paintings and drawings by Ruskin himself, with personal relics, furniture, etc. His boat 'Jumping Jenny' is in the coach house. 3m: There is a fine view from the lakeside picnic site across to the Old Man. Beautiful woodland, most of it NT, flanks the shore almost as far as (6¾m) *High Nibthwaite*, at the foot of the lake. About ½m beyond another unclassified road branches right to cross the Crake and join A5084 from Greenodd (Route 77). The view up the lake, backed by Fairfield and Helvellyn, is superb. At (11¼m) *Torver* the route joins A593 from Broughton-in-Furness (Route 77). 13½m: *Coniston*.

From Windermere to *Ullswater* and *Penrith*, see Route 78B.

From Windermere the main route follows A591 up the shore of the lake, with a fine vista of fells opening ahead and to the left. A592, branching right for Ullswater, and the sideroad for Troutbeck, branching right at (9m) *Troutbeck Bridge*, are described in Route 78B. 10m: *Brockhole*, by the lake shore, is the main National Park Visitor Centre (seasonal), with gardens, exhibitions, lectures and a wide range of activities. 11m: *Dove Nest*, on the slopes of Wansfell to the right, was home of the poet Felicia Hemans in 1829–31. Beyond are the wooded *Jenkin Crag*, with a view over the lake, and *Stagshaw Garden* (both NT). 12m: *Waterhead* (seasonal National Park Information Centre), with the pier for the sightseeing launches which cruise up and down the lake. In Borrans Field W of the car park are the fragmentary remains of the Roman fort of Galava (EH).

12½m: **Ambleside** (2900 inhabitants; seasonal TI and NT Information Centre), in the Vale of Rothay beyond the head of Windermere, is a popular little centre which grew with the influx of tourists in the 19C. The sports festival held on the Thursday before the first Monday in August includes fell running, hound trailing and Cumberland and Westmorland wrestling. The July rushbearing ceremony is depicted in a mural in the church (1850–54; Gilbert Scott), which also contains a Wordsworth memorial chapel. The painter J.C. Ibbetson, who married at Ambleside in 1801, lived here and at Troutbeck in 1799–1805. Harriet Martineau lived at The Knoll, by A591 on the way to Rydal, from 1845 until her death in 1876.

The fells which overlook the little vale include *Wansfell Pike* (1851ft), to the E, with the **Stock Ghyll Force**, a 70ft waterfall, near its foot about ½m from the town. Beyond the Rothay, to the W, rises *Loughrigg Fell* (1099ft). Dr Thomas Arnold of Rugby retired to Fox How, near its foot, in 1834 and his son Matthew Arnold kept up the family connection with the house. To the N, almost encircling the valley of Rydal Beck, is the distinctive horseshoe range which takes its name from the tallest fell, *'Fairfield* (2863ft), on the NW of the arc. Three of its neighbours, *Dove Crag, Hart Crag* and *Great Rigg*, exceed 2500ft. Fellwalkers make the circuit from Ambleside via High Sweden Bridge and *Low Pike* (1657ft) or from Rydal via *Nab Scar* (1450ft).

FROM AMBLESIDE TO CONISTON AND HAWKSHEAD. A593, the direct road to Coniston, heads SW across the Rothay and runs between the foot of Loughrigg Fell and the attractive Brathay river on its way through (1m) the hamlet of *Clappersgate* to (2½m) *Skelwith Bridge*, near the waterfall of *Skelwith Force*. It then crosses the river and climbs to the top of (4m) *Oxenfell Pass* (526ft), with a fine view of the Langdale Pikes. At 5½m the road joins *Yewdale*, beneath the *Yewdale Fells*, and at 7½m it reaches *Coniston*, described on the detour from Bowness, above. An alternative route, taking in Hawkshead, branches S on B5286 at Clappersgate and joins B5285, the Bowness–Coniston road, at (4½m) Hawkshead Courthouse.

A TOUR OF THE LANGDALES FROM AMBLESIDE. It follows a 16m circuit recommended by Wordsworth in his 'Guide' past fells now popular with fellwalkers and rockclimbers. A593, the Coniston road, heads W from Ambleside. Just short of (2½m) *Skelwith Bridge* B5343, the easy road to Great Langdale, branches right. However, this tour follows A593 across the Brathay and branches right at 3½m, just beyond the top of the hill. The little sideroad twists and turns down to (4m) *Colwith Bridge*, where it forks left for the valley of **Little Langdale**, with its waterfall, village and tarn. *Lingmoor Fell* (1530ft; partly NT), to the N, separates it from Great Langdale. At (6m) the fork in the road at the head of the dale, the left branch goes over Wrynose Pass (see below). This tour takes the right branch, which becomes narrow and steep as it crosses the W slope of Lingmoor. A striking view of the Langdale Pikes opens in front. *Blea Tarn* ('dark tarn'), on the left, is the setting of Wordsworth's 'The Excursion' (1814). From the top of the pass the road drops abruptly down to (8½m) the Old Dungeon Ghyll Hotel at the head of the lovely valley of *'Great Langdale*.

To the N the view is dominated by the rugged flanks and crags of the *'Langdale Pikes*, a range of five fells with *Pike o' Stickle* ('the peak with the sharp summit'; 2323ft) at the W end and *Harrison Stickle* (2415ft) near the E end chief among them. *Pavey Ark* (2288ft) at the E end is a favourite with rockclimbers. To the W rises the mass of **Bowfell** (2960ft). *Crinkle Crags* to the SW are more easily reached from the road over Wrynose Pass, described below.

B5343 follows Great Langdale from the Old Dungeon Ghyll Hotel, soon passing near *'Dungeon Ghyll Force*, a waterfall of 65ft framed by the walls of a picturesque gorge, on the slopes to the left. From (11m) *Chapel Stile* a hilly sideroad branches left to (3m) Grasmere past the Youth Hostel at *High Close* (523ft; NT) and down *Red Bank*, with a lovely view of Grasmere lake. B5343 leaves Great Langdale at (11¾m) the village of

Elterwater (National Park local information point), taking its name from the smallest of the lakes, and joins A593 at (13¼m) *Skelwith Bridge*.

FROM AMBLESIDE TO ESKDALE OVER WRYNOSE PASS AND HARDKNOTT PASS. A 14½m route to the western lakes and fells along a steep, narrow and twisting road, sometimes impassable in winter. It follows the Roman way from the fort of Galava at Waterhead to the fort of Glannaventa at Ravenglass. It starts by taking the tour of the Langdales described above as far as (6m) the road fork at the head of Little Langdale. The road to the left climbs up to (7½m) the top of **Wrynose Pass** (1270ft), where the Three Shires Stone marks the old meeting point of Cumberland, Westmorland and Lancashire. To the N is *Pike o' Blisco* (2304ft) and beyond, to the NW, the five **Crinkle Crags**, with their highest summit at 2816ft. The road drops down to (9½m) *Cockley Beck*, in the upper part of the Duddon valley. See below for the left fork of the road following the river to the S. The right fork climbs again to (10¾m) the **Hardknott Pass** (1292ft), between *Hard Knott* (1803ft) to the N and *Harter Fell* (2129ft) to the S. On the right, about ½m beyond the top of the pass, stand the remains of the Roman fort of Mediobogdum (EH), superbly placed on a shelf of rock overlooking Eskdale. The road crosses the Esk at 12½m and at 14½m reaches *Boot* (Route 78D).

At Cockley Beck, between Wrynose Pass and Hardknott Pass, a road heads S down the lovely **•Duddon Valley**, or *Dunnerdale*, quieter than better known valleys like Langdale or Borrowdale. Wordsworth praised it in a popular series of sonnets (1820). From the stony levels near Cockley Beck the river winds through (2m) the wooded cleft at the picturesque *Birk's Bridge* and another fine gorge just before (4m) *Seathwaite*. The churchyard here contains the grave of 'Wonderful Walker', the 18C rector and benevolent despot of the parish. From (7m) *Ulpha* (National Park local information point) a steep sideroad makes a 5m journey over *Birker Fell* (889ft), near *Devoke Water*, to Eskdale (Route 78D). Beyond Ulpha sideroads follow both sides of the valley to (c 11m) *Duddon Bridge* (Route 77).

From Ambleside to *Ullswater* and *Penrith*, see Route 78B.

From Ambleside A591 continues to (14m) *Rydal*, on the right of the road. The church has memorials to Thomas and Matthew Arnold. *Rydal Mount* (open) was Wordsworth's home after leaving Grasmere in 1813 until his death in 1850. He laid out the large, pleasant garden and named the nearby *Dora's Field* (NT), which he bought in 1826, after his daughter. W of the hamlet is *Rydal Water*, a charming little lake less than 1m long and about ¼m across, connecting with Windermere by the Rothay. A591 skirts its N bank, passing *Nab Cottage*, where Thomas De Quincey lived in 1806 and Hartley Coleridge, son of the poet, from 1840 until his death in 1849. Above rises *Nab Scar* (1450ft), which some walkers make the first ascent in their round of the Fairfield horseshoe (see Ambleside, above). Beyond Rydal Water the road turns N to follow the shore of its sister lake, Grasmere, with pleasant views of the vale of Grasmere and its surrounding fells.

16m: The village of **Grasmere** (seasonal National Park and NT Information Centres), left of the main road, is another popular centre for tourists. Its sports festival, held on the Thursday nearest 20 August, is the largest in the Lake District and includes fell running, hound trailing and Cumberland and Westmorland wrestling. The rush-bearing ceremony also takes place in August.

Grasmere, however, is chiefly famous for its connection with William Wordsworth (1770–1850). He is commemorated with a medallion by Thomas Woolner in the church and buried in the churchyard near his sister Dorothy (d. 1855), his wife Mary (d. 1859) and other members of their family. Here also are the grave of Hartley Coleridge (d. 1849) and a memorial to the poet Arthur Hugh Clough, who died in 1861 at Florence. From 1799 to 1808 Wordsworth lived at *Dove Cottage* (open), a little 17C building S and E of the village and main road. A converted barn opposite houses the

Grasmere and Wordsworth Museum. Thomas De Quincey took over the tenancy, holding it for more than 20 years, when the cottage became too cramped to hold the poet, his sister, wife and growing family. The Wordsworths moved first to *Allan Bank*, NW of the church, and then in 1811 to the *Parsonage*, which they left for Rydal Mount in 1813.

  *‌**Grasmere** lake is the roundest in the Lake District, barely 1m long and fully ½m wide, with a little island in the middle. There is a favourite view from the so-called *Wishing Gate*, less than ½m S of Dove Cottage on the old road to Rydal. A pleasant walk round the lake (4m) follows the road on the W shore to *Red Bank*, with a good view, and then takes the lane leading left to *Loughrigg Terrace* (about 300ft; NT), with more good views. The return journey takes the footbridge across the Rothay between Grasmere and Rydal, and follows either A591 or, better, the old road to Dove Cottage.

  Beyond Grasmere A591 climbs, with the Fairfield range on the right, to (19m) the top of *Dunmail Raise* (782ft), the dip between *Seat Sandal* (2415ft) on the right and *Steel Fell* (1811ft) on the left. Tradition maintains that Dunmail, the last king of Cumbria or Strathclyde, was buried here after his defeat by the Saxon King Edmund in 945; in fact, Dunmail died some 30 years later. Below lies **Thirlmere** ('lake in a hollow'), a narrow sheet of water nearly 4m long. It lost much of its character when Manchester Corporation raised its level to make a reservoir in 1894, against the opposition of Canon Rawnsley and others concerned to preserve the Lake District. Both shores are planted with conifers. A sideroad winds around the W bank, with rocky crags and a forest trail. A591 takes the E bank, passing (20m) the church from the drowned village of *Wythburn* and skirting the tree-shrouded base of Helvellyn (Route 78B). It can be climbed from various points along the way, notably Wythburn and (22½m) *Thirlspot*, though the popular routes approach it from the Ullswater side. 23¼m: Beyond *Dalehead* the wooded *Great How* (1092ft) cuts off the view of the foot of Thirlmere, where the sideroad to the W bank crosses the dam.

B5322 branches right for the lovely *‌**St John's in the Vale**, with the *Castle Rock* (about 1000ft) of Sir Walter Scott's 'Bridal of Triermain' on the right and a fine view of Blencathra ahead. At (4m) *Threlkeld* it joins A66 (Route 78C), heading W for Keswick.

A591 crosses St John's Beck. 26¼m: At the top of *Castlerigg* (702ft) a sideroad leads ½m right to the Neolithic or Bronze Age *‌**Castlerigg Stone Circle** (EH), set against a fine panorama of fells. A smaller rectangle of stones stands inside the 100ft circle. 28m: **Keswick**, see Route 78C.

B. Penrith to Ullswater and Windermere

Directions. Total distance 26m. **Penrith**, see Route 76. A592 to (5m) Pooley Bridge, (13m) Glenridding, (14m) Patterdale and (26m) **Windermere** (Route 78A).

Penrith, see Route 76. A66 heads W from the M6 roundabout SW of the town. A592 soon branches left, joining the Eamont as it enters the National Park. 3m: *Dalemain* (open), on the right, has Elizabethan work and the remains of a 12C pele tower behind its 18C façade. Note the 16C panelling, Jacobean plaster ceiling, Chinese drawing room and the gardens. 5m: A592 reaches the head of Ullswater and **Pooley Bridge** (seasonal National Park Information Centre), left of the main road.

An alternative way from Penrith starts by following Route 76 down A6 to (1½m) *Eamont Bridge* and then turns right on B5320, reaching Pooley Bridge in 5¾m. It passes (2½m) *Yanwath*, where the Hall incorporates an old pele tower; (3m) *Tirril*, where the Roman road coming down from the High Street reaches the Eamont valley; and (4m) a turning on the right for *Barton*, where the church has late 13C–early 14C arches strengthening the original Norman arches of its tower.

A detour leads S from Yanwath via (2½m) *Askham* and (6m) *Bampton* (Route 76) to (8m) the foot of **Haweswater** ('Hafr's water'). In 1937 Manchester Corporation made the original, much smaller lake into a reservoir about 3½m long by flooding the valley, church and village of Mardale. The result has very little charm, though there are good views across to the High Street range from the road along the E shore and a fine grouping of fells at the head.

High Street (2718ft) is the tallest of the long line of fells, mainly above 2000ft, which separate Haweswater from Ullswater. The name, also used for the range as a whole, refers to the Roman road between Windermere and Penrith, still running as a clearly defined path for 11m along the ridge.

•Ullswater ('Ulfr's water'; seasonal TI), 7½m long, is second in size to Windermere but quite as popular, its shores often crowded with tourists and its surface with boats. Yet it remains the grandest of the lakes, given a special beauty by the winding course which divides it into three distinct reaches, the scenery growing lovelier towards the head at the S end. A passenger service by motor yacht connnects Pooley Bridge and Glenridding with *Howtown* on the E shore, which can also be reached by the sideroad from Pooley Bridge. A splendid walk (6m) follows the shore from Howtown to Glenridding. This can be varied or made into a circuit of about 9½m from Howtown by following the road inland to (¾m) *Martindale*, with its tiny 17C church, continuing to (3m) the head of *Boardale* and rounding the slopes of *Place Fell* (2154ft) to return along the shore.

A592 follows the W shore, with increasingly fine views across the lake, and skirts **Gowbarrow Park** ('windy hill'; NT), entered from the foot of the Dockray road, A5091, at 10½m.

The park, which covers the whole Ullswater side of *Gowbarrow Fell* (1578ft), is inseparably associated with the daffodils of Wordsworth's 'I wandered lonely as a cloud', whose descendants still bloom here. To the right stands *Lyulph's Tower*, a small 18C shooting lodge. A path climbs from the entrance to the park ½m up to one of the most beautiful waterfalls in the Lake District, *•Aira Force*, 65ft high, in a deep winding ravine. The path continues past another pretty little fall, *High Force*, to (1¼m) *Dockray*, where a fine high-level walk leads S through Glencoyne Park.

Beyond Dockray A5091 climbs past *Matterdale End*, 2½m from the lakeshore, and reaches its highest point at 1124ft, W of *Great Mell Fell* (1760ft), before descending to (5m) *Troutbeck* and A66 (Route 78C).

A592 continues to skirt the lake, passing *Glencoyne Park* (NT) and *Stybarrow Crag* (NT), with the ancient oaks of *Glencoyne Wood* (NT) above it. 13m: **Glenridding** (seasonal National Park Information Centre), at the mouth of its valley, has the pier for the motor launches which cruise the length of the lake. A592 passes a well, on the right, with misty traditions of baptisms by St Patrick, and crosses the mouth of *Grisedale*. 14m: The village of **Patterdale** ('Patrick's Dale') is just beyond the head of Ullswater. Sheep-dog trials take place here on August Bank Holiday Saturday.

•Helvellyn (3118ft), rising W of Glenridding and Patterdale, is the tallest of the range separating Ullswater from Thirlmere. Though Scafell Pike and

Scafell are higher, Helvellyn is the most famous of the Lake District mountains and the one most likely to tempt tourists up from the valley floor. It can be climbed from the Thirlmere side (Route 78A) but the most popular ways to the top start from the road between Glenridding and Patterdale and follow *Striding Edge* or *Swirral Edge*. They both pass *Red Tarn* (2356ft), the highest of the Lake District tarns. Near the summit, with its wide views, stands a memorial to Charles Gough, who fell to his death from Striding Edge in 1805 and whose body was guarded by his dog until its discovery several months later; both Wordsworth and Scott wrote poems about the incident. Another memorial nearby records the landing of the first aeroplane on Helvellyn in 1926.

The fells at the head of Grisedale include *Dollywagon Pike* (2810ft) at the end of the Helvellyn range, *St Sunday Crag* (2756ft) and, to the S, *Cofa Pike*, the N spur of Fairfield.

A592 crosses the Deepdale Beck, Goldrill Beck and Pasture Beck, where it turns right to follow the E side of (16m) *Brothers Water* (NT), popularly supposed to be named after the drowning of two brothers. There is a view back to Place Fell by the head of Ullswater. It then becomes the highest road in the National Park as it mounts rapidly to (19m) the top of **Kirkstone Pass** (1489ft), celebrated in an ode by Wordsworth. Just short of this point, on the right, is the stone whose supposed resemblance to a church gives the pass its name. Just beyond, to the right, a sideroad follows the Stock Ghyll valley to Ambleside (Route 78A). A592 swings to the left and makes its descent above the beautiful Troutbeck valley. At 22m a sideroad on the right leads to Windermere through the village of *Troutbeck*. At its S end is *Townend* (NT), built about 1626, a finely preserved example of a house belonging to a Lake District 'statesman' or yeoman farmer. As well as the range of household equipment typical of such a farm, it contains intricately carved built-in furniture. A592 keeps to the left, crossing the river beyond (23m) the village church, with a stained-glass window by Morris, Ford Madox Brown and Burne-Jones. 26m: **Windermere**, see Route 78A.

C.   Penrith to Keswick, Derwentwater, Borrowdale, Buttermere and Cockermouth

Directions. Total distance 40½m. **Penrith**, see Route 76. A66 to (17½m) **Keswick** (bypassed). B5289 to (30½m) Buttermere. B5289, B5292 to (40½m) **Cockermouth**.

Penrith, see Route 76. A66 leads W, soon entering the National Park. A more interesting start, adding 2m to the journey, follows B5288 via *Greystoke*, a pleasant village with a rebuilt castle. St Andrew's, founded as a collegiate church in the 14C, has misericords and 15C glass in its E window. 9m: For A5091 leading S to Dockray and Ullswater via *Troutbeck* (not to be confused with the Troutbeck near Windermere), see Route 78B. 10½m: The turning on the right leads to *Mungrisdale*, *Mosedale* and *Caldbeck*, on the drive round the Skiddaw Fells described below. From (12m) *Scales* hardy fellwalkers tackle Blencathra (see below); the easier route starts from *Blencathra Centre*, NW of (13¾m) *Threlkeld*. For St John's in the Vale, opening to the S of Threlkeld, and the nearby Castlerigg Stone

Circle, see Route 78A. A66 joins the valley of the Greta, before swinging right to bypass Keswick by a viaduct over the Greta Gorge, part of the road enlargement carried out in the 1970s despite opposition from the National Park Authority and other conservation groups. A5271 heads for the town centre.

17½m: **Keswick** (5600 inhabitants; National Park Information Centre), beneath the Skiddaw Fells and just N of Derwentwater, is a popular tourist centre. The Keswick Show, with cattle, sheep and horse classes, hound trailing and Cumberland and Westmorland wrestling, takes place on August Bank Holiday Monday.

The main streets converge on the narrow market place where the *Moot Hall* (1813) stands on an island in the road. Packhorse Court has an audio-visual display (NT) about Beatrix Potter's work in conserving the Lake District. To the S is the prominent spire of *St John's* church (1813; Anthony Salvin). Sir Hugh Walpole (1884–1941) is buried in the SW corner of the churchyard, which commands a fine view. Station St. leads NE to the delightful *Fitz Park*, bounded by the river. The *Museum* contains: geological specimens; manuscripts and other material relating to Wordsworth, Southey and Sir Hugh Walpole; and Flintoft's scale model of the Lake District (1867).

To the right of Main St., leading NE from the market place, is *Greta Hall* (now part of Keswick School), where Coleridge lived from 1800 to 1803 and Southey from 1803 until his death in 1843. Near Greta Bridge is the *Pencil Museum*, tracing the history of the local industry which began in the 16C. Plumbago, or 'wad', was mined at Seathwaite in Borrowdale. At *Crosthwaite*, near the bypass about ½m further on, the late Perpendicular church stands on the site of the church built by St Kentigern in 553. It contains a brass to Sir John Ratcliffe (d. 1527) and his wife, and a monument to Southey (with an inscription by Wordsworth), who is buried in the churchyard. Canon Hardwicke Rawnsley (1851–1920) was vicar of Crosthwaite in 1883–1917. Shelley lived with Harriet Westbrook in the winter of 1811–12 in a cottage on Chestnut Hill.

N of the town rises the bold mass of the Skiddaw range of fells. Though the name comes from the Old Norse for 'craggy hill', their soft slate gives them gentler, more rounded contours than the jagged Borrowdale Volcanic hills to the S. *Skiddaw itself, the highest (3054ft), overlooks Bassenthwaite Lake at the W end of the range. Fellwalkers usually approach it round the side of its 'cub', *Latrigg* (1203ft), beyond A66 just NE of Keswick. Stiffer routes go from Millbeck or Mirehouse, off A591, by way of *Carl Side* (2400ft). Further E in the Skiddaw range is *Blencathra (2847ft), also called *Saddleback* because of its distinctive shape, best seen from St John's in the Vale (Route 78A) and climbed from Blencathra Centre or Scales, off A66.

*A DRIVE ROUND THE NORTHERN FELLS, 31m. The route takes narrow and sometimes steep sideroads through the fine, remote country at the back of Skiddaw. It returns E along A66 and at 7m turns N on the sideroad running alongside *Souther Fell* (1713ft) to the pleasant hamlets of (9m) *Mungrisdale* and (10m) *Mosedale*. The summit of *Carrock Fell* ('rocky fell'; 2174ft) has a hill-fort, perhaps Brigantian. Dickens and Wilkie Collins described their misfortunes climbing it in 'The Lazy Tour of Two Idle Apprentices' (1857). The route continues along the N fringe of the National Park via (15m) *Hesket Newmarket* to (16½m) **Caldbeck** (also on the detour from Cockermouth to Carlisle, below). The churchyard contains the grave of the fox-hunter John Peel (d. 1854), immortalised in the song. The route follows B5299 to the W, branching left on the Uldale road and left again for (21m) *Longlands*, (22½m) *Over Water* and (22½m) *Orthwaite*. Here the road continues across the valley to join A591 at (25½m) *High Side*. 31m: *Keswick*.

***Derwentwater**, an oval about 3m long and 1m wide, lies between the Skiddaw Fells and the rugged 'Jaws of Borrowdale'. One of the loveliest lakes, it is also, with Windermere, Ullswater and Buttermere, one of the most popular. The shores blend abrupt crags, green fells and wooded slopes, while little islands dot the surface of the lake. The chief ones (all NT) are *Derwent Island*, site of the colony established by the German miners who settled at Keswick in the 16C; *Lord's Island*; the smaller *Rampsholme*; and *St Herbert's Island*, where St Cuthbert's disciple St Herbert (d. 687) is thought to have lived as a hermit. The 'floating island' which periodically surfaces near Lodore is a tangled mass of weeds buoyed up by marsh gas. The NT owns the W half of the lake itself, as well as large stretches of its shore. There are good footpaths on the W shore, served by the motor launches which link the landing at Keswick with jetties at various points around the lake.

*ROUND DERWENTWATER BY ROAD, 10m. B5289 leads S and Lake Rd soon turns left, passing the landing stages at the foot of Derwentwater and *Cockshott Wood* (NT) on the way to ***Friar's Crag** (NT, with Information Centre), a famous viewpoint. It was bought in memory of Canon Rawnsley, a founder of the NT, in 1922. The crag has a memorial to Ruskin, who eloquently recalled his childhood memories of the spot in 'Modern Painters'. *Calf Close Bay* is ½m S. B5289 follows the E shore, passing (¾m) the wooded *Castle Head* (529ft; NT), commanding perhaps the best view of the lake. It passes through the *Great Wood* (NT), with *Walla Crag* (1234ft) rising to the left; beyond it is *Falcon Crag* (1050ft). 2m: The lane on the left leads to Watendlath (see the detour below). In the grounds of *Barrow House*, now a Youth Hostel, to the left, are waterfalls descending over 100ft. 3m: *Lodore Falls*, despite Southey's rhapsodic verses, are disappointing except after heavy rain. B5289 continues S through Borrowdale (see the main route below), but this route follows the unclassified road across the Derwent for (4½m) the popular village of *Grange*. From (5m) *Manesty* footpaths lead up the W shore, giving open views of the lake. On the left, beneath the ridge of *Cat Bells* (1481ft), are the woods of *Manesty Park* and *Brandelhow Park*. They are both NT and Brandelhow, bought in 1902, was the first NT property in the Lake District. The bay between them, where the Brandley lead mine survived into the 19C, gives a good view of the lake. *Brackenburn* was Sir Hugh Walpole's home. Near (6¾m) *Hawes End* a fine view opens across the Newlands valley to the W. Beyond (7½m) *Swinside* Forestry Commission plantations mainly hide the lake from view. *Lingholm Gardens* (open) are down by the shore. 10m: *Keswick*.

The detour to Watendlath branches left from the drive round the lake just before Barrow House. After ½m the Barrow Beck is crossed by *Ashness Bridge*, an old packhorse bridge with a view of Skiddaw. The little road climbs through woods, skirting the Watendlath Beck for much of the way. 3m: *Watendlath* (pronounced with the accent on the second syllable) is a popular hamlet on a small tarn, the setting for much of Sir Hugh Walpole's 'Judith Paris' (1931) in his 'Herries Chronicle'. Walkers may follow the track SW another 1½m to *Rosthwaite* on the Borrowdale road.

FROM KESWICK TO COCKERMOUTH BY A66, 13m. A busy road, best avoided. B5289 heads NW to join A66 at ¾m, just beyond the Derwent. A66 crosses the Newlands Valley and turns N at 2m to avoid *Braithwaite*. The sideroad which now runs parallel to A66 on the left is more pleasant, skirting the foot of the fells of Thornthwaite Forest and passing beneath *Barf* (1536ft), with the rock known as *The Bishop*, usually painted white. 4½m: The sideroad rejoins A66 on the W shore of **Bassenthwaite Lake** ('Bastun's lake'), 4m long and ½m wide, the northernmost of the lakes. There is a good view across the water to Skiddaw but otherwise the traffic on A66, enlarged in the 1970s despite opposition from the National Park Authority and other conservation groups, destroys enjoyment of the shore. 7m: Just before *Dubwath* A66 leaves the lake and branches E. 13m: *Cockermouth*, see the main route below.

FROM KESWICK TO COCKERMOUTH BY A591, 15m. Better than A66. From the A66 roundabout N of Keswick A591 heads for the E shore of Bassenthwaite. Just beyond the roundabout a sideroad branches right for *Ormathwaite*, *Applethwaite* and *Millbeck*, rejoining A591 at (2½m) *Dodd Wood*. Southey maintained that 'the terrace between Applethwaite and Millbeck' offered the best view of Derwentwater. Skiddaw can be tackled from here or from Mirehouse. 4m: *Mirehouse* (open) is a predominantly late 18C–early 19C house between the foot of Skiddaw and the lake. The scholar James Spedding (1808–81) entertained Tennyson, Carlyle and Edward FitzGerald here. The closing scene of Tennyson's 'Idylls of the King' is said to have been inspired, during his visit in 1835, by the lakeside view near the little, partly Norman church of St Bega. There are good walks in the nearby wood and along the shore. At (5½m) *High Side* the drive round the Skiddaw Fells, described above, joins A591. At (7¼m) *Castle Inn* B5291 is followed left, across the Derwent by the Ouse Bridge (good view). 9m: Beyond *Dubwath* B5291 joins A66 for (15m) *Cockermouth*, described at the end of the main route below.

FROM KESWICK TO COCKERMOUTH VIA THE NEWLANDS VALLEY AND BUTTERMERE, 19m. The route takes B5289 and A66 W for (2½m) *Braithwaite*, at the entrance to the little *Coledale*. It then follows the sideroad which heads S along the slopes of the fells flanking the lovely *Newlands* valley. This was the site of the old Goldscope copper mine, which closed in 1864, perhaps a corruption of Gottesgab ('God's gift'), the name used by the German miners who settled here in the 16C. Beyond (5¼m) *Gillbrow* the road climbs to (6¼m) the highlying *Keskadale*, with an ancient oak wood on the right, and then (7¾m) *Newlands Hause* (1096ft), between *Robinson* (2417ft) on the left and *Whiteless Pike* (2159ft) and *Wandope* (2533ft) on the right. There is a good view on the way down to (9m) the village of *Buttermere*, on the main route to (19m) *Cockermouth* described below.

FROM KESWICK TO COCKERMOUTH VIA THE WHINLATTER PASS, 11½m. Like the route through the Newlands valley, it begins by taking B5289 and A66 to (2½m) *Braithwaite*. It then follows B5292 up through *Thornthwaite Forest*, with woodland trails and a Forestry Commission Visitor Centre near (5m) the top of the **Whinlatter Pass** (1043ft), between *Lord's Seat* (1811ft) on the right and *Grisedale Pike* (2593ft) on the left. The descent, with *Whinlatter* (1696ft) on the right, goes via (7¼m) *High Lorton* (National Park local information point) into (8¼m) *Lorton Vale*. Lorton Vale is on the main route to (11½m) *Cockermouth* described below.

From Keswick to *Grasmere*, *Ambleside* and *Windermere*, see Route 78A.

The main route from Keswick follows the drive round Derwentwater as far as (22m) the S end of the lake but, instead of turning right for *Grange*, keeps on B5289 along the bank of the Derwent and into the 'Jaws of Borrowdale'. On the left are *Grange Fell* (1363ft; NT) and the *Bowder Stone* (NT), a marvellously balanced mass of metamorphic rock weighing about 2000 tons, which fell from the neighbouring cliffs. Immediately opposite is the wooded *Castle Crag* (900ft; NT). Further S over Rosthwaite rise *Glaramara* (2560ft) and *Allen Crags* (2572ft) and, to their W, Great End, the N buttress of the Scafell group (Route 78D). The road clings to the river until **•Borrowdale** ('valley of the fortress') suddenly opens out, its level green floor ringed by crags and fells. Ever since early tourists sought it out as the most picturesque valley in the Lake District, it has remained the most popular. 23½m: The village of *Rosthwaite* stands on the pretty *Stonethwaite Beck*, flowing down a little dale with the finely shaped *Eagle Crag* at its head. From Rosthwaite a bridlepath leads NE to (1½m) *Watendlath* (see above). At (25m) *Seatoller* (seasonal National Park Information Centre) B5289 leaves the Derwent, which flows down the dale from *Seathwaite*, about 1¼m S, near the disused plumbago mines which once served the Keswick pencil industry. It climbs to (26½m) the top of the **Honister Pass** (1176ft), with a noble view back into Borrowdale.

•Great Gable (2949ft) rises to the S, though the best view of the mountain is from Wasdale Head (Route 78D). The summit, more or less at the centre of the Lake District, commands a panoramic view. Walkers reach it from the car park at the top of the pass via *Grey Knotts* (2287ft), *Brandreth* (2344ft) and *Green Gable* (2603ft). A more difficult route goes from Seathwaite via the *Sty Head Pass* (1600ft), which the hardy walker can also follow to Wasdale Head or via the Corridor Route to Scafell Pike.

From the top of the pass B5289 drops sharply through wild and bleak country beneath *Honister Crag* (1750ft), scarred by slate quarries, and *Fleetwith Pike* (2126ft) on the left. From (28½m) *Gatesgarth*, at the bottom, a demanding walkers' route leads to the left over the *Scarth Gap Pass* (1410ft), the saddle between *Haystacks* (1750ft) and *High Crag* (2443ft), to Ennerdale (Route 78D). Ahead, the green beauty of Buttermere is suddenly revealed. The road follows the NE shore of the lake to (13½m) the village of *Buttermere*, where it is joined by the route from Keswick via the Newlands valley (see above).

•Buttermere ('dairy pasture lake'; NT), a favourite spot with tourists, and its larger, wilder neighbour **Crummock Water** ('crooked water'; NT) were once united in a single lake about 4½m long. A strip of land formed by alluvial deposits now divides them. On the W the mountains rise abruptly from the water's edge, with High Crag, *High Stile* (2644ft) and *Red Pike* (2479ft) above Buttermere. Paths encircle the lake. At its NW corner, opposite the village, are the thread-like cataracts of *Sour Milk Gill*, flowing down from *Bleaberry Tarn*. In a small ravine SW of Crummock Water is **•Scale Force** (NT), a striking waterfall with a sheer leap of at least 120ft.

Loweswater ('leafy lake'; NT), reached by the sideroad which branches left from B5289 around the N end of Crummock Water, is a charming little lake about 1m long. A path goes through *Holme Wood* (NT) on its SW shore. Beyond Loweswater sideroads continue around the edge of the National Park via (2½m) *Lamplugh* to (7½m) Ennerdale Water (Route 78D).

Beyond (34m) *Brackenthwaite* and the turning for Loweswater the road enters *Lorton Vale*, watered by the Cocker, and beyond (36½m) *Low Lorton* joins B5292, which has come from Keswick over the Whinlatter Pass. 39m: The road crosses A66 and leaves the National Park.

40½m: **Cockermouth** (7100 inhabitants; seasonal TI) is a pleasant little town at the meeting of the Derwent and the Cocker, marked by the ruined 13–15C castle of the Percys. *Wordsworth House* (NT), a handsome 18C building at the W end of the main street, was the birthplace of the poet in 1770 and his sister Dorothy in 1771. Their father, John, is buried in the church.

Fletcher Christian, the 'Bounty' mutineer, was born in 1764 at *Moorland Close*, 1½m SW. *Eaglesfield*, ¾m further on, was birthplace of the scientist John Dalton (1766–1844) and of Robert de Egglesfield, chaplain to Queen Philippa of Hainault and founder of The Queen's College, Oxford. At *Bridekirk*, 2½m N of Cockermouth, the largely 19C church incorporates two Norman doorways and a •font of c 1140, decorated with Norse motifs and signed in runic letters by the artist.

FROM COCKERMOUTH TO CARLISLE, 24½m by A595. The road follows A595 via: (9m) *Mealsgate* (13m) *Red Dial*, on the Roman road near Olenacum, mistakenly known as *Old Carlisle*; and (17½m) *Thursby* where it is joined by A596. 24½m: *Carlisle*, see Route 76.

A pleasant and hilly alternative way from Mealsgate, 5½m longer, follows B5299. 1½m: *Boltongate* church has an unusual tunnel-vaulted 15C nave. The road continues along the side of the fell, entering the N tip of the National Park before (8m) *Caldbeck* (also on the drive round the Skiddaw Fells from Keswick) and striking NE via (17m) *Dalston* to (21m) *Carlisle*.

FROM COCKERMOUTH TO WHITEHAVEN, 13m. The route follows A66 W along the Derwent valley and branches left on A595 for (9m) *Distington* and (13m) *Whitehaven* (Route 77). The western lakes and fells can be reached from various points along A595 between Whitehaven and Ravenglass.

D. Eskdale, Wastwater and Scafell, and Ennerdale

The western lakes and fells are the least crowded but not the least beautiful part of the region. Motorists reach them most easily from various points along A595, the coastal road between Ravenglass and Whitehaven (Route 77). Sideroads also connect Eskdale and Ennerdale with the heart of the Lake District.

Eskdale runs SW to the coast from its source between the Scafell range and the Bowfell range. It has no lake on its floor, but its mountains and waterfalls repay a visit. The Eskdale Show takes place on the last Saturday in September.

The narrow-gauge railway mentioned in Route 77 runs from *Ravenglass* via (1m) *Muncaster Mill* and (4m) *Eskdale Green* to (7m) *Dalegarth*, halfway up the dale. Motorists can take the sideroad up the S bank of the Esk from near *Muncaster Castle* or the sideroad from near *Holmrook*. About 1¼m E of Holmrook a turning on the left leads to *Irton* church, with a fine 9C cross shaft. However, the best routes (both described in Route 78A) come from the E, over Hardknott Pass and Wrynose Pass from Little Langdale and Ambleside, and from the S, over Birker Fell and past Devoke Water from the Duddon valley. Both take steep and twisting roads which are not for timid drivers.

Boot, about ¼m above the railway terminus, is a little village on the Whillan Beck shortly before it joins the Esk on its way down from *Burnmoor Tarn*. The chief attraction nearby is ***Stanley Force**, over the Esk 1¼m S, a 60ft waterfall made particularly charming by its wooded setting. There is a fine view from the open fell above. To see something of Upper Eskdale take the road to the foot of the Hardknott Pass, about 2½m from Boot, and then follow the path along the bank of the Esk, passing the *Esk Falls* after another 2m: Experienced fellwalkers can continue up the Esk, with the Scafell range on their left and Bowfell and *Esk Pike* (2903ft) on their right. The passes from Wasdale, Langdale and Borrowdale meet near the summit of *Esk Hause* (2490ft).

***Wastwater**, the deepest, grimmest and most savage of all the lakes, is approached by the sideroad from *Gosforth* on A595 (Route 77). It reaches the woods by the foot of the lake at 5¼m and continues the 3m length of its N shore. The astonishing range of screes on the opposite side rises almost vertically from the water's edge, culminating in *Illgill Head* (1983ft). The road ends at (9½m) *Wasdale Head* (National Park local information point), in a remote hollow surrounded by mountains. The Shepherds' Meet and Show takes place on the second Saturday in October.

The magnificent views from Wasdale Head are dominated to the SE by the Scafell group, the most impressive in the Lake District. The name, pronounced 'Scorefell', means 'bare fell'. The slopes above 2000ft are NT. ***Scafell Pike** (3210ft) is the highest point in England, and in clear weather the view from its summit includes Snowdon to the S and the Isle of Man and the Mourne Mountains in Ireland to the W. Fellwalkers usually climb it from here or from Seathwaite in Borrowdale (Route 78C) via the Sty Head Pass and the Corridor Route. The summit of *Scafell (3162ft), its neighbour to the S, is reached from Wasdale via Lord's Rake or from Eskdale via Burnmoor Tarn. *Great End* (2984ft) forms the N buttress of the group. *Great Gable* (2949ft), NE of Wasdale Head, can be climbed from Wasdale Head or, more popularly, the Honister Pass or Seathwaite (Route 78C). The best view is from here. *Napes Needle* on its S flank and *Scafell Crag* on the N face of Scafell were among the first challenges tackled by rockclimbers in the Lake District in the 19C.

Ennerdale Water, the westernmost of all the lakes, lies E of A595 between Egremont and Whitehaven (Route 77), though it can also be reached by the detour from Crummock Water via Loweswater and Lamplugh (Route 78C). The Ennerdale Show takes place on the last Wednesday in August.

From *Egremont* A5086 heads NE to (3m) *Cleator Moor*. Sideroads lead to (6m) *Ennerdale Bridge* (National Park local information point), where the churchyard is the scene of Wordsworth's 'The Brothers', and (10m) the car park at *Bowness Knott*.

The lake, about 2½m long, is stern and solemn, encircled by mountains whose lower slopes have Forestry Commission plantations. The North-West Water Authority discreetly uses it as a reservoir. There are forest trails, and a footpath leads round the Water. It is worth walking along the track which goes up the dale from Bowness Knott to (about 4½m) the fine combination of *Steeple* (2687ft) and *Pillar* (2927ft), to the S. The famous *Pillar Rock*, a vertical crag almost 600ft high, was first climbed by John Atkinson, an Ennerdale cooper, in 1826 and is still popular with experienced rockclimbers. The track continues another 1½m to the remote Youth Hostel between the Scarth Gap Pass and the Black Sail Pass.

79

The Isle of Man

The **Isle of Man** (69,800 inhabitants) lies almost in the centre of the Irish Sea, midway between England and Ireland (about 30m from each) but closer to the Scottish than the Welsh coast. The nearest land is 16m N at Burrow Head in Dumfries and Galloway. The island itself is about 33m long and 13m broad. Except for the northern plain, it is largely mountainous, with slate uplands reaching their highest point at Snaefell (2036ft). The wooded river glens and the cliff-bound coast make attractive scenery. The chief coastal towns were developed as resorts in the 19C, when the island added tourism to its traditional occupations of crofting and fishing. Several picturesque railways survive from this period.

The wide range of antiquities extends from megalithic ritual and burial sites of c 3500 BC to 19C mining remains. The *crosses decorated with scenes from Norse mythology and interlaced patterns testify to the Celtic and Viking influences which shaped Manx culture. The island has more runic inscriptions (usually displayed in the parish churches) than Norway. However, the Scandinavian flavour persisted chiefly in personal and place names, the Manx language being akin to Irish and Scottish Gaelic. It now has about 60 fluent speakers.

History. Ellan Vannin or Mannin (perhaps 'middle isle') was first settled c 6000 BC by hunter-gatherers using microlithic flint implements. At the time of their conversion to Christianity the Manx apparently spoke a Brythonic Gaelic, and were then increasingly subject to Norse influence. Godred Crovan, a Norseman and perhaps the 'King Orry' of Manx legend, won a decisive victory in 1079 and united the island with the Hebrides. It was handed over to Scotland in 1265 but Edward I soon brought it under English control. The first viceroys, the Montacutes, Earls of Salisbury, called themselves 'Kings of Man'. In 1406 Henry IV bestowed the island on the Stanleys, Earls of Derby; the 4th changed his title to 'Lord of Man' in 1505, on the ground that he would rather be a great lord than a petty king. The 7th Earl's wife held the island on his behalf for the king during the Civil War, but after the Earl's execution in 1651 it was surrendered by the receiver-general, William Christian, the Illiam Dhône ('brown-haired William') of Manx history. In 1765 the Duke of Atholl, descendant and successor of the Earls of Derby, sold his sovereignty to the Crown. The Three Legs device was probably adopted by the 13C, though the earliest example to survive is on the 14C Maughold cross. The Manx motto 'Quocunque jeceris stabit' ('Wherever you throw it, it stands') appeared on the earliest known Manx coinage (1668).

Administration. The Isle of Man is constitutionally separate from the UK. Its legislative and executive authority is the Court of Tynwald, the world's oldest parliament with continuous traditions. The name comes from the Old Norse 'tingvöllr', meaning 'assembly' and 'field'. It consists of the House of Keys (24 elected members) and the Legislative Council (the Attorney General, the Bishop of Sodor and Man, and nine members elected by the House of Keys). British Acts of Parliament do not apply to the Isle of Man unless expressly so enacted, but the laws of Tynwald require Crown approval and must be proclaimed on Tynwald Hill. **Practical Details**. The Manx government issues its own notes and coins, though English, Scottish and Northern Irish money is also accepted. The island has its own postal authority; UK stamps are not valid. Customs duties and VAT are in line with Westminster. **Annual Events**. The open-air assembly of Tynwald is held at Tynwald Hill, near St John's, on 5 July (old Midsummer Day). The Isle of Man TT (Tourist Trophy), an international motorcycling competition, takes place in late May/early June. Dating from 1907, the races cover a mountain course of 37¾m beginning and ending at Douglas. The Southern 100 road races take place in July, and the Manx Grand Prix (the Manx Amateur Motorcycle Road Races) in late August/early September. The Manx International Rally in September is one of the top ten car rallies in Europe. The Isle of Man International Cycling Week is held in June. **Ferries**. By Isle of Man Steam Packet Co. Ltd to Douglas from Heysham, the chief point of departure, throughout the year; from Liverpool, Fleetwood, Belfast and Dublin from May to September. **Air Services**. Passenger flights to the Isle of Man (Ronaldsway) Airport, 1½m NE of Castletown, from Belfast, Birmingham, Blackpool, Cork, Dublin, Glasgow, Jersey, Leeds/Bradford, Liverpool, London (Heathrow), Luton, Manchester and Newcastle.

DOUGLAS (22,200 inhabitants), on the E coast, is the island's capital and chief resort. Backed by hills, it stands just below the confluence of the Awin Dhoo and Awin Glass (the 'dark' and 'light' rivers). In its wide bay rises Conister (or St Mary's) Rock with its *Tower of Refuge* (1832) for shipwrecked sailors.

TI: Sefton Information Bureau, Harris Promenade.

The chief attraction is the seafront, a 2m promenade stretching from Victoria Pier to the *Derby Castle* terminus of the Manx Electric Railway (see Douglas to Ramsey, below) and the *Summerland* indoor leisure, sports and entertainment complex. The promenade passes many of the town's main hotels and entertainment centres, including the restored *Gaiety Theatre* (1900; Frank Matcham). The journey can be made by the Douglas Horse Tramway, opened in 1876.

The oldest part of town, W of Victoria Pier, has some handsome Victorian terraces and the chief public buildings, including the *Town Hall* (1899) and the *Legislative Buildings* (1894; guided tours), with the chambers of the Legislative Council, the House of Keys and the Tynwald Court. *St George's* church stands a little SW.

The **Manx Museum** in Kingswood Grove, above the junction of the Loch and Harris Promenades, is the island's national museum. Its contents, wholly Manx, cover a wide range: natural history, archaeology, social history, fine arts and applied arts. Further N in Upper Douglas is *Noble's Park*, with the grandstands overlooking the start and finish of the Isle of Man TT.

On *Douglas Head* (view), reached by the swing bridge at the end of Parade St., are a lighthouse, the Manx Radio station and a *Camera Obscura* (open). The lifeboat station at the foot stands near the site of the house owned by Sir William Hillary (1771–1847), founder of the Royal National Lifeboat Institution. The *Marine Drive* along the cliffs to (3½m) *Port Soderick*, with its pretty glen, has been closed to vehicles because of rock falls but is still open to walkers.

The N suburb of *Onchan* (pronounced 'Oncan'; 8500 inhabitants), beyond the official residence of the Lieutenant Governor at *Government House*, has a 19C church with a pretty spire. Captain William Bligh of the 'Bounty' was married in its predecessor in 1771. *Kirk Braddan*, 1½m NW of Douglas, has runic crosses in the old church, 18C with an earlier tower. The churchyard contains interesting monuments and the grave of the painter John Martin (1789–1854). *Braaid*, about 4m W of Douglas, has *St Patrick's Chair*, an early Christian monument, and the so-called *Stone Circles*, in fact an exceptionally large Norse boat-shaped house with subsidiary buildings and a large, presumably earlier, round house.

FROM DOUGLAS TO PORT ERIN, 14½m by road. Between May and September the journey can also be made by the Steam Railway, originally opened in 1874. A5 leads to (5m) *Santon*. On the coast 1m S is the pretty bay of *Port Grenaugh*, with a Viking promontory fort on the clifftop. 5¾m: The *Fairy Bridge* gets its name from the local superstition that travellers should greet the fairies as they pass over it. At (8m) *Ballasalla* the modest ruins of *Rushen Abbey*, an offshoot of Furness Abbey founded by Olaf I in 1135, stand by the Silverburn river. Upstream are the medieval monks' bridge and the pretty *Silverdale Glen*.

A5 continues W to (6m) Port Erin via (3½m) *Colby*, about ½m S of the pretty *Colby Glen*.

A8 branches S from Ballasalla, skirting the *Isle of Man (Ronaldsway) Airport*. On its edge is *King William's College*, the island's chief independent school, founded in 1668. Pupils have included the Manx poet T.E. Brown (1830–97) and Dean Farrar (1831–1903), author of 'Eric: or Little by Little'.

10m: **Castletown** (3200 inhabitants; TI), the capital of the island until 1869, is a compact old town with attractive shopping streets and a tidal harbour. *Castle Rushen* (open seasonally), dating perhaps from the time of Magnus (1252–65) or somewhat earlier, was developed by successive kings and lords of Man. Bridge St. has the interesting *Nautical Museum* (open seasonally), with an 18C armed yacht in her original boat cellar.

Scarlett, to the S, has a Visitors' Centre and geological nature trail, with a footpath leading round the point to the Iron Age/Norse promontory fort at *Poyllvaaish*. On the E side of Castletown is *Hango Hill*, where William Christian was executed in 1663 for his surrender of the island. Further on is *Derbyhaven*, a small village at the neck of *Langness*, the promontory which forms the E side of Castletown Bay. It has a golf course and great wildlife interest.

A7 heads W from Castletown to (11½m) *Balladoole*, where the fortified hilltop at Chapel Hill is a major archaeological site, with Bronze Age burials and a 9C Viking ship burial overlying early Christian graves. The site also includes a 12C 'keeill', or chapel. At (13¾m) *Gansey*, A7 continues directly to Port Erin (see below). The present route branches ¾m left to **Port St Mary** (1800 inhabitants; TI), a fishing village and centre for golf, watersports and yachting on the W side of *Bay ny Carrickey*, with a harbour and breakwater 400yds long.

A lovely *coast walk (3m) heads down the SW tip of the island, with its perpendicular cliffs and caves, via *Perwick Bay*; the remarkable series of fissures known as the *Chasms*; *Black Head* and *Spanish Head* (Manx NT), where the cliffs rise to 400ft; the *Burroo Ned* promontory fort; and *Calf Sound*, with earthworks. A31, the direct road to the Sound, passes through (1½m) *Cregneash*, with the *Cregneash Village Folk Museum* (open seasonally) in the characteristic old houses of a crofting and fishing community, centred on the cottage of Harry Kelly (d. 1934). Offshore is the *Calf of Man* (616 acres; Manx NT), reached by boat from Port St Mary or Port Erin, a bird sanctuary and observatory, also with grey seals. About ¾m to its SW is the automatic lighthouse on the *Chicken Rock*.

15m: **Port Erin** (3000 inhabitants; TI), one of Man's oldest and most attractive towns, stands among fine scenery on a square bay protected by a ruined breakwater. It has excellent bathing and golfing. The Steam Railway terminus contains a *Railway Museum* and there is an interpretation centre (open seasonally) at the *Marine Biological Station*. Milner's Tower, crowning *Bradda Head* on the N side of the bay, gives a fine view. A footpath continues along the coast c 2m N to *Fleshwick Bay*.

FROM PORT ERIN TO PEEL, 14m. An interesting route by A36 and A27. A36 passes close to (4m) *The Stacks*, with a good cliff view. 6½m: *South Barrule* (1585ft) has a huge late Bronze Age hill-fort and a fine view over the S half of the island. A36 continues round the hill, with mining remains to the N and more traces of silver and lead mines at (4m) *Foxdale*. A27 branches left for (9m) *Dalby*, a quiet village about ½m inland of *The Niarbyl*, commanding the best coastal view on the island. 11m: *Glen Maye* is a delightful wooded spot with pretty waterfalls. A walk leads up the coast to Peel via *Contrary Head* and the folly on *Corrin's Hill*. 14m: *Peel*, see below.

FROM DOUGLAS TO PEEL, 11½m by A1. Beyond (5m) *Crosby*, on the slopes of *Greeba Mountain* (1383ft) to the right, are *Greeba Castle*, where the writer Sir Hall Caine died in 1931, and the ruins of *St Trinian's Church*. 8½m: *St John's*, where the Tynwald Mills produce and sell the traditional Manx tweed.

On the right are the *Tynwald National Park* and **Tynwald Hill**, a tiered artificial mound where, in accordance with ancient Scandinavian custom, new laws are proclaimed in Manx and English at the open-air assembly held on 5 July.

From St John's to *Ramsey*, see below.

11½m: **Peel** (3800 inhabitants; TI), the most attractive town on the island, has grown up around the fishing village at the mouth of the Neb. It is the main centre for curing Manx kippers. 'Odin's Raven', which made the crossing from Trondheim to Peel in 1979, is on display at the *Viking Longship Museum*.

On *St Patrick's Isle*, connected by a causeway to the W arm of the harbour, *Peel Castle (open) stands inside a stout 16C wall.

To the right, beyond the *Keep* and the *Guard Room*, are the roofless 13–14C ruins of *St German's Cathedral*, founded by Bishop Simon (1230–48). Other remains include the *Old Palace* of the bishops, with a banqueting hall; *Fenella's Tower*; the *Round Tower*, resembling those in Ireland; and the roofless 9C *St Patrick's Chapel*. Finds from recent excavation include the rich contents of a woman's grave of the Viking period, now in the Manx Museum at Douglas.

From Peel to *Port Erin*, see above.

FROM PEEL TO RAMSEY, 19½m. Beyond (3m) *St John's*, on the way into Peel from Douglas (see above), A4 branches N up the valley of the Neb. 5m: A4 passes the mouth of the wooded *Glen Helen* with the *Rhenass Falls*. The road descends to the coast at (9½m) *Kirk Michael*, where the conspicuous parish church has fine Norse cross slabs. A3 heads N, passing (11m) *Bishopscourt*, formerly the residence of the Bishop of Sodor and Man. 12¼m: *Ballaugh*, pronounced 'Balláff', lies about 1½m S of its old 17C church, with an 11C cross and a curious font. A3 continues inland, passing (13¾m) the *Curraghs Wildlife Park* (open), with rare species of otters, deer and many water birds. From (14½m) *Sulby* A14 runs up the narrow *Sulby Glen*, the 'Manx Switzerland', to the *Tholt-y-Will Inn* in beautiful grounds with waterfalls. 15½m: *Sulby Bridge* is a favourite fishing centre. 17m: *Lezayre* is near the site of the battle which gave Godred Crovan ascendancy over the island in 1079. 19½m: *Ramsey*, see below.

FROM DOUGLAS TO LAXEY AND RAMSEY BY THE *MANX ELECTRIC RAILWAY. Opened in successive stages between 1893 and 1899, this 3ft gauge electric railway runs in summer from the Derby Castle Station at the N end of Douglas promenade. It passes through scenery offering a superb combination of coastal views, mountains and glens. Beyond *Banks Howe* (393ft) it reaches the beautiful (2½m) *Groudle Glen*. From May to September the reconstructed miniature *Groudle Glen Railway* (1896) connects *Lhen Coan* with the coast at 'Sea Lion Cove'. 4¾m: *Garwick Glen* and the megalithic *Cloven Stones*, to the E. 7m: **Laxey** (1400 inhabitants), now a resort, was once a centre of lead, zinc and silver mining. The mine buildings survive, including the *Laxey Wheel* (1854), built to pump water from the underground workings. The St George's woollen mill, producing Manx tweed, can be visited.

In summer the *Snaefell Mountain Railway*, opened in 1895, climbs from Laxey to (5m) the top of **Snaefell** (2036ft), the island's highest mountain. The line crosses the mountain road from Douglas to Ramsey at (3½m) the Motorcycle Museum (see below). The summit, with a café and gift shop, commands a *view which takes in the whole of the island and, in good weather, the Lake District peaks in England, the Mull of Galloway in Scotland, the Mourne Mountains in Ireland and the Snowdon group in Wales.

The Ramsey line returns to the coast along the N side of the valley, passing on the left the so-called *King Orry's Grave*, a Neolithic chambered cairn of c 3500 BC. It then gives a *view of *Bulgham Bay*, 400ft below. There are waterfalls at (10½m) *Dhoon Glen*, (12m) *Glen Mona* and (13m) the unspoilt *Ballaglass Glen*. About ½m S of Ballaglass Glen is *Cashtal yn Ard*, a chambered cairn contemporary with King Orry's Grave. *North Barrule* (1860ft) appears on the left, *Maughold Head*, pronounced 'Mack'ld', (373ft) on the right. 18m: *Ramsey*, see below.

FROM DOUGLAS TO RAMSEY BY THE MOUNTAIN ROAD, A18. It branches left from the Laxey road at (1½m) *Governor's Bridge* and makes the laborious climb past (4½m) *Keppel Gate*, with magnificent views, to (8m) the foot of Snaefell at the junction with the Snaefell Mountain Railway (see above). The *Motorcycle Museum*, near the highest point on the TT course, has a large collection of old bikes and memorabilia. From here A15 descends to the left, through *Sulby Glen*, and joins A3 at (15m) *Sulby* (see Peel to Ramsey, above). A18 descends to the right, crossing the E slopes of Snaefell and the W slopes of North Barrule. Ramsey is 20m from Douglas by the former route, and 15m by the latter.

Ramsey (6500 inhabitants; TI), on a magnificent bay, is a popular resort. It has a sandy beach, a long pier and *Mooragh Park*, with a boating lake etc. *The Grove Rural Life Museum* (open seasonally), near the N edge of the town, is an early 19C house with Victorian furnishings and, in the outbuildings, agricultural equipment appropriate to larger Manx farms, including a horse-powered threshing machine.

The background of mountains makes the surroundings of Ramsey attractive. Walks can be taken to the *Albert Tower*, with a view, about ¾m S; and SW via *Glen Auldyn* or over *North Barrule* and along the ridge to (c 4m) *Snaefell*.

A15 runs SE along the coast via *Ballure Glen* and *Port Lewaigue* to (3½m) *Maughold* (pronounced 'Mack'ld'), where a coastal footpath (Manx NT) leads past St Maughold's Well. The churchyard contains three separate early chapels, or 'keeills', as well as the site of a fourth, the parish church; also early cross slabs and a 14C standing cross with the earliest version of the Isle of Man's Three Legs emblem. The path continues to the lighthouse at *Maughold Head*, with good sea birds. A10 heads N from Ramsey to (4½m) *Bride*, with a *cross carved with the image of Thor. A16 branches right to (7½m) the *Point of Ayre*, the N tip of the island, with a lighthouse. A visitors' centre near *Ballaghennie* explains the wildlife value of this unique area of heathland. Nesting birds include terns. A9 heads NW from Ramsey to (4m) *Andreas*, where the collection of Celtic and Viking crosses in the church includes *Sandulf's Cross, with beasts and inscriptions. There are more Viking crosses at *Jurby*, 8m NW of Ramsey, mainly by A13. The former World War II aerodrome nearby has secondhand shops, etc.

80

Leeds to Harrogate, Ripon and Thirsk

Directions. Total distance 37½m. **Leeds**, see Route 75F. A61 to (8m) Harewood (Route 86A), (15m) **Harrogate**, (26m) **Ripon** (for Fountains Abbey and Studley Royal) and (37½) Thirsk.

Leeds, see Route 75F. A61 runs N through *Chapel Allerton* and climbs to (5m) *Alwoodley*, passing near the *Moortown* golf course. It then descends to cross Wharfedale at (8m) *Harewood*, described in Route 86A, and enters North Yorkshire.

15m: **HARROGATE** (66,500 inhabitants), with hotels, public gardens and good shops, was once the leading spa town in the North and has now become an important conference venue. It makes a convenient base from which to tour the surrounding countryside.

TI: Royal Baths Assembly Rooms, Crescent Rd. **Bus Station and Railway Station**: Next to each other in Station Parade, E of the war memorial. **Theatre**: Harrogate Theatre, Oxford St. Concerts in International Centre; morning coffee concerts in Royal Baths Assembly Rooms. **Annual Events**: The Great Yorkshire Agricultural Show in July at Harrogate Showground, SE of the town; International Festival of Music and Arts in July/August.

History. Harrogate has nearly 90 springs in all, 30 of them in Bogs Field (Valley Gardens), where sulphur and iron wells occur close together and yet are quite distinct. They seem to have been used locally in earlier times, but the town's development as a spa began with the rediscovery of the Tewit Well by William Slingsby in 1571 and St John's Well by Dr Michael Stanhope in 1631. Smollett's 'Humphry Clinker' testifies to its vogue in the 18C. Harrogate reached the height of its popularity in the Victorian and Edwardian era, and its reputation began to fade after World War I. Agatha Christie spent most of her much-publicised disappearance in 1926 at the Hydropathic Hotel.

The 200-acre common known as *The Stray* lies immediately S of the town centre and is connected to it by West Park. The *Royal Baths Assembly Rooms* (1897, with later additions), facing Crescent Gardens, house Turkish Baths and the TI. In Kings Rd to the N is the *Royal Hall* (1903) with its modern adjunct, the *International Centre*. To the W is the *Royal Pump Room* (1842), now a museum of local history with costumes, pottery and Victoriana. Water from the old sulphur well in the basement can be tasted. Further W are the *Valley Gardens*, with formal floral displays and a path leading to (1m) *Harlow Car Gardens*, the ornamental gardens and woodlands of the Northern Horticultural Society. *Birk Crag* is to the N.

Almscliff Crag (750ft), a good viewpoint, lies off A658 about 4m SW. *Spofforth*, off A661 about 5m SE of Harrogate, has a ruined 14C castle of the Percy family (EH, all year). A661 continues via (6m) *Stockeld Park* to (8m) *Wetherby* (Route 85B).

W of Harrogate A59 runs over the moors via (9m) *Blubberhouses*, in the Washburn valley, to (16½m) *Bolton Abbey* (Route 86A). At about 3m the road passes the turning for *Hampsthwaite*, 1m N, the home of Thackeray's ancestors.

From Harrogate to *York*, see Route 81.

A61 crosses the Nidd just before (19m) *Ripley*, on Route 86B through Nidderdale from Knaresborough to Grassington.

26m: **RIPON** (14,300 inhabitants; seasonal TI) is a pleasant little cathedral city which claims to have been granted its first charter by King Alfred in 886. St Wilfrid's Feast is celebrated, with a procession through the streets, on the Sunday before the first Monday in August.

The spacious Market Place has a 90ft obelisk erected as a monument to himself by William Aislabie of Studley Royal in 1781. The *Town Hall* (1801; James Wyatt) bears the city's motto, referring to the 'wakeman', or watchman, who lived in the timber-framed but much altered *Wakeman's House*, now selling local crafts. The ancient custom of sounding the nightly curfew on a horn is still observed at 21.00, and a handbell still announces the opening of the market at 11.00 each Thursday.

Kirkgate leads to the **Cathedral**, small and not particularly impressive at first sight, but of great interest for its variety of building styles (Saxon to Perpendicular) and for its beautiful choir stalls.

A monastery was founded c 660 at Ripon, which Bede calls Inhrypum. St Wilfrid (634–709) built a church about ten years later, and for a short time (681–86) Ripon was a bishop's see. It became a cathedral again in 1836, when the diocese was separated from York. The crypt of Wilfrid's Saxon church survives, though the Danes destroyed the rest of the building in the 9C. The second Saxon church was destroyed by the Normans in 1069. They soon built a third church, part of which survives in the apsidal chapel at the E end of the chapter house and the undercroft below it. The present church, the fourth on the site, was begun by Archbishop Roger of York (1154–81) as a church for secular canons. His plan, unique in England, included an aisleless nave, an aisled choir, transepts with E aisles only, and a central tower. Archbishop Walter de Grey (1215–55) probably built the present W front, with its twin towers and rows of lancet windows. It is the only Early English example of a twin-towered façade of its kind in England, for at Wells the towers stand clear of the aisles. Some have found its severe restraint flat and lifeless but, like the whole outside of the church, it must have had more impact before the loss of the leaded spires to all three towers in the 1660s. The E end of the choir is a Decorated reconstruction of the last quarter of the 13C. The SE corner of the central tower collapsed c 1450, and the S and E sides were rebuilt in the Perpendicular style, leaving the Transitional work of the N and W sides unaltered. Finally, the nave was enlarged by the addition of aisles at the end of the 16C.

The *Nave* and aisles are now unusually wide, the Perpendicular alterations contrasting with the much older work from Archbishop Roger's time at the E and W ends. The base of a pillar from the 10C cathedral survives in the N aisle. The pulpit is a fine work of 1913. The *Transepts* keep Archbishop Roger's design in fair completeness but the rebuilt Perpendicular S and E tower arches give the crossing an unfinished look. The Gothic pulpit in the N transept was originally above the rich stone screen (c 1480, with later statues). The organ case above the screen is by Sir Gilbert Scott (1860).

The *Choir*, with its unusual glazed triforium (or double clerestory), is a remarkable mixture of three building periods: Transitional, Decorated and Perpendicular. The Geometric tracery of the great E window, and the naturalistic foliage of the capitals in the two E bays, are Decorated at its finest. The roof has some superb gilded bosses (c 1300). The stalls, with their *misericords, were carved c 1489–94 by the local school which also made the stalls at Manchester and Beverley. Scott restored them in the 19C. The ornate reredos is by Sir Ninian Comper (1922). The choir aisles end in chapels; that of St Wilfrid, on the N, is believed to have contained the saint's shrine.

On the S side of the choir is the apsidal Norman *Chapter House*. The undercroft below was restored in 1948–60 as a chapel and choir vestry. The Decorated Lady Chapel, or Lady Loft, in a very unusual position above the Chapter House, now houses the *Chapter Library* (open by request).

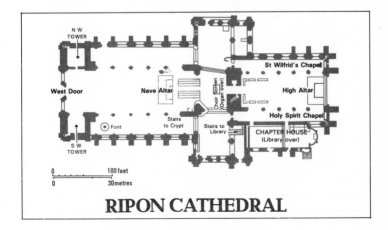

RIPON CATHEDRAL

The *Crypt, one of the half-dozen Saxon crypts in the country, was built by St Wilfrid, like the one at Hexham. Now containing church treasures, it has a central chamber for displaying relics and wall niches for holding lights. The narrow hole on the N side is known as 'St Wilfrid's Needle'; the ability to crawl through it was once taken as a proof of chastity.

The pleasant buildings in Minster Rd on the N side of the cathedral include remains of the medieval Canon Fee Court, with the 19C *Courthouse* behind, and the *Old Deanery*, a much altered 16C building now a hotel. Bedern Bank leads from the W end of the cathedral down to the river Skell. High St Agnesgate, on the left, has the ruined 15C chapel of *St Anne's Hospital*. Low St Agnesgate and St Marygate, where the old jail (1816) is now a *Prison and Police Museum*, lead N from the end of the street to the chapel of the *Hospital of St Mary Magdalen*, founded for lepers by Archbishop Thurstan (d. 1140), near the Ure bridge.

The landscaped gardens of ***Studley Royal** and the lovely ruins of ***Fountains Abbey** lie off B6265 to the W of Ripon, with sideroads leading to entrances at 1½m and 3m respectively. First linked as one great estate in the 18C, they are now reunited in a single NT property of 680 acres.

Close by the W entrance to the abbey stands *Fountains Hall* (open), a handsome Jacobean mansion built mainly of monastic stone. The ruins beyond, among the largest and best preserved in England, are beautifully sited in the wooded valley of the little river Skell. The abbey was founded in 1132 by a breakaway group of Benedictines from St Mary's, York, but taken over by the Cistercians in 1135. It had become the wealthiest Cistercian foundation in England by the middle of the next century. The buildings, on a scale which everywhere reflects the abbey's importance, belong to four main periods. To the first (1135–47) belong the nave and transepts of the church; to the second (1147–79), the gradual reconstruction of the domestic buildings; to the third (1220–47), the rebuilding of the church's E end; and to the fourth (1498–1526), the addition of the church's tall Perpendicular tower.

Substantial remains of the *Church* survive, notably the austere Cistercian nave, 11 bays long and complete to ceiling height. Note the pointed arcade above the solid Norman piers. The delicate *Chapel of the Nine Altars at the extreme E end is close in date to the similar chapel at Durham Cathedral. The Perpendicular tower stands in an unusual position, at the end of the N transept. In the vestry off the S transept is the tomb of a knight (c 1300) of the Percy or Mowbray family.

The most remarkable of the buildings around the cloister is the *undercroft of the *Lay Brothers' Dormitory* on the W side, supported on a central row of 19 pillars, Now open from end to end, it was originally divided into the *Lay Brothers' Refectory*, storerooms, etc. The size of the refectory, the dormitory above, its extension across the river, and the *Lay Brothers' Infirmary*, spanning the river further W, are all reminders of how large a lay community was attached to Cistercian monasteries. On the E side of the cloister is the *Chapter House*, with three fine entrance arches and abbots' tombstones. Next to it are the parlour and undercroft of the *Monks' Dormitory*. On the S side are, from the E: the *Warming Room* with its huge fireplace, the only heated room in a Cistercian monastery; the fine *Monks' Refectory*, with tall lancet windows and a laver outside the door; and the small *Kitchen*. Above the Warming Room is the *Muniment Room*, reached by the monks' day stairs. E of the cloister buildings, and built partly across the Skell, are the foundations of the huge *Monks' Infirmary*.

A lovely walk along the valley E of the ruins leads to the landscaped gardens of Studley Royal, developed by John Aislabie, MP for Ripon and Chancellor of the Exchequer, after his involvement in the South Sea Bubble forced his retirement from public life in 1720. His designs, on the grand scale and in the formal Dutch manner, exploited the picturesque prospect of the ruins and in 1767 his son William Aislabie, who continued the work, added Fountains to the estate.

The Skell is canalised to supply a series of striking water gardens: the *Crescent Pond*, the *Moon Pond*, cascades and a lake. The *'surprise view' of the abbey is the best of several contrived vistas. The garden buildings artfully dotted about the landscape include the *Temple of Piety*, the *Octagonal Tower* and the *Banqueting House*—the last, like the stables, probably by Colen Campbell, pioneer of English Palladianism. Beyond the water gardens are the deer park and the sumptuous *St Mary's Church* (EH, summer season, daily 13.00–17.00) built by William Burges in 1871–78. It looks along the avenue of limes to the towers of Ripon Cathedral. Aislabie's house does not survive.

Beyond Fountains B6265 continues SW to (9m) *Pateley Bridge* (Route 86B).

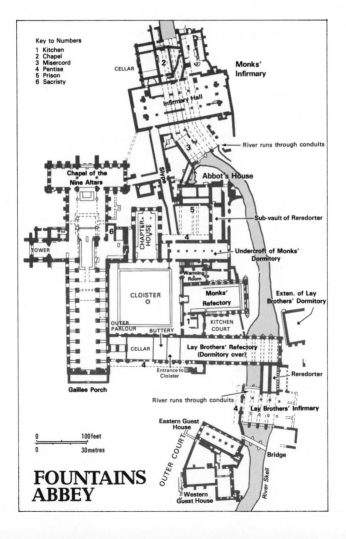

Key to Numbers
1 Kitchen
2 Chapel
3 Misercord
4 Pentise
5 Prison
6 Sacristy

Monks' Infirmary

CELLAR

Infirmary Hall

River runs through conduits

Chapel of the Nine Altars

Abbot's House

Sub-vault of Reredorter

TOWER

CHAPTER-HOUSE

Undercroft of Monks' Dormitory

Warming Room

CLOISTER

Monks' Refectory

Exten. of Lay Brothers' Dormitory

OUTER PARLOUR BUTTERY

KITCHEN COURT

CELLAR

Lay Brothers' Refectory (Dormitory over)

Entrance to Cloister

Reredorter

Galilee Porch

River runs through conduits

Lay Brothers' Infirmary

Eastern Guest House

0   100 feet
0   30 metres

Bridge

FOUNTAINS ABBEY

OUTER COURT

River Skell

Western Guest House

There are several good country houses near Ripon. *Markenfield Hall* (limited opening), off A61 3½m SW, is an early 14–16C manor house with a moat. *Newby Hall* (open), off B6265 4m SE, is a Queen Anne house remodelled by Robert Adam in 1767–80. His *interior contains plasterwork by Joseph Rose, one of only five sets of Gobelins tapestries made for an English house, and a sculpture gallery housing the collection of the dilettante William Weddell. There are pleasant gardens and grounds, with *Skelton* church (1871–72; William Burges) the counterpart to his church at Studley Royal. *Norton Conyers* (open), off A61 3½m N, is medieval in origin but largely 17–18C in appearance, with a fine park and walled garden. The family legend that a mad-woman had been confined in the attic during the 18C may have suggested the fate of the first Mrs Rochester to Charlotte Brontë, who visited the house in 1839.

From Ripon to *Wensleydale*, via *Leyburn*, *Hawes* and *Kendal*, see Route 86D.

The main route continues on A61 from Ripon, crossing the Ure, then (30m) A1 (Route 85B), and finally the Swale at (32½m) the pleasant little village of *Skipton-on-Swale*. 37½m: **Thirsk**, see Route 85A.

81

Doncaster to York

Directions. Total distance 34m. **Doncaster** is at the end of Route 72, up the A1 from **Stamford**. A19 to (20m) **Selby** and (34m) **York**.

Doncaster (288,600 inhabitants; TI), by the river Don on the site of the Roman Danum, has been known for horse-racing since the 17C and railway engineering since the Great Northern Railway established its workshops in the 19C. The racecourse still flourishes, though the Plant Works (as they were known locally) no longer play a major part in the town's industry.

The parish church of *St George* (1853–58), replacing a medieval church destroyed by fire, is one of Sir Gilbert Scott's grandest works. The *Mansion House* (1745–48; James Paine) is one of only three official Lord Mayor's residences in the country; the other two are in York and London. The *Museum and Art Gallery* on Chequer Rd has local history, geology and natural history; glassware and ceramics, including Yorkshire pottery; Dutch paintings; horse-racing exhibits; and a gallery of the King's Own Yorkshire Light Infantry Regiment.

The racecourse, on the Town Moor to the E, has a modern grandstand and exhibition centre. Its oldest classic race, the St Leger, was established in 1776 and is run during the second week of September. The William Hill Lincoln Handicap in March begins the flat-racing season in Britain.

Cusworth Hall Museum, off A638 about 2½m NW, occupies a mid-18C house by George Platt and James Paine set in its own parkland. Its collections illustrate the everyday life of local people over the last 200 years. The chapel and billiard room have plasterwork by Joseph Rose. The interesting church at *Sprotbrough*, 3m W of Doncaster, has good woodwork and a curious stone seat in the chancel, apparently 14C and perhaps a sanctuary chair.

Conisbrough stands in the valley of the Don 5m SW of Doncaster by A630. The Norman castle built c 1180 by Hamelin, half-brother of Henry II, has perhaps the best circular *keep in England (EH, all year). The parish church has fine capitals and a carved 12C tomb chest. A630 continues to (11m) Rotherham and A6109 or A6178 to (17½m) *Sheffield*, both in Route 75G.

FROM DONCASTER TO HULL. The fast way, avoiding Goole, is by M18 and M62. The slower way (46m) takes A630 NE from Doncaster to join A18. 7½m: *Hatfield*, with a good 12–15C church, is in *Hatfield Chase*, part of the district known as the 'Levels', mostly under water until drained by Cornelius Vermuyden in 1626. A18 joins A614 on the way to (10½m) *Thorne*, a small town with a church of c 1300, on the W edge of a peat moor. The large church at *Fishlake*, 2m W, has a late Norman S *doorway of c 1170. A614 skirts the Don, canalised lower down by Vermuyden as the Aire and Calder Navigation, and touches the Aire at (17½m) *Rawcliffe*. 20½m: **Goole** (18,400 inhabitants), created by the opening of the docks in 1826, stands at the meeting of the Don and the Ouse not far from the point where the Ouse joins the Trent to form the Humber. The Aire and Calder Navigation Company built the conspicuous church in 1843–48. From Goole to Lincoln, see Route 48. 22m: *Boothferry Bridge* crosses the Ouse. 23m: *Howden* and on to (47m) *Hull*, see the detour from Selby below.

From Doncaster to *Nottingham* via *Mansfield* and *Worksop*, see Route 71A; to *Stamford*, see Route 72; to *Leeds*, see Route 75F; to *Sheffield*, see Route 75G; to *Durham*, *Newcastle* and *Berwick*, see Route 85B.

Beyond the Don A19 bears right and continues N across a system of rivers and canals to (18½m) *Brayton*, where the 14–15C church has a fine tower, chancel arch and S doorway with carving of c 1150.

20m: **Selby** (10,700 inhabitants; TI), a market and manufacturing town by the tidal Ouse, is a dull place except for the *Abbey Church*, one of the most perfect monastic churches in England.

The Benedictine abbey was founded in 1069. The first stage of church building, c 1100–c 1230, embraced the transition from Norman to Early English. The choir was rebuilt on a grander scale and the nave windows enlarged, in the Decorated style, in c 1280–1340.

The W front has a superb Norman doorway with Early English blind arcading above. The window is a Perpendicular insertion and the two towers were raised a storey by J. Olrid Scott in 1935. The nave belongs to several periods. Norman work (c 1100–1123) appears in the four E bays on the N side and two on the S side, and the four tower arches. At the W end the architecture becomes Transitional, with pure Early English in the S triforium and both clerestories. The *S Transept* was rebuilt by Scott in 1912 on the site of the transept ruined by the fall of the central tower in 1690. The *N Transept* has a Perpendicular window with 20C glass.

The *Choir* is Decorated throughout, though of more than one period, with the remains of rich sculpture and a charming triforium balustrade. The sedilia were almost certainly designed c 1380 by Henry Yevele, architect of the nave at Canterbury. The *E window (c 1340) is a Jesse window with a fine Doom in its beautiful Flamboyant tracery. The arms of the Washington family appear in a window of the S choir clerestory. The War Memorial Chapel S of the choir contains a 15C alabaster *Deposition by the Nottingham school. The N porch has a Norman doorway as good as the one on the W front; its upper storey is decorated with Early English blind arcading.

Drax, off A1041 6½m SE, is dominated by its power station. The partly Norman church has carved figures and 16C bench ends. A1041 continues to *Snaith*, 7½m further, with a 13–15C church with Dawnay tombs.

FROM SELBY TO HULL, 34m by A63. The road branches E from A19. At (5m) *Hemingbrough* the 12–15C church has a tall *spire, good woodwork and a set of bench ends. *Wressle*, to the left beyond (7m) the Derwent bridge, has the ruins of a 14C castle belonging to the Percys, Earls of Northumberland. 10m: **Howden** *church, one of the most important in the region, was rebuilt after it was made collegiate in 1267. It is thus Decorated, but of different dates. The *W front (1306–11) is a beautiful composition, and the crossing tower (completed in the 15C) is one of the finest in Yorkshire. The nave and crossing are used as the parish church. The Saltmarsh Chapel contains family tombs from the 14C to the 20C. Though ruined, the 14C choir and early Perpendicular chapter house keep many beautiful details. The chronicler Roger of Hovedon (d. 1201?) was rector of Howden, and his statue stands in front of the market hall. The novelist Nevil Shute (1899–1960) worked with Barnes Wallis on the design of the R100, Britain's last successful airship, here in 1923. Beyond Howden A63 continues as B1230, running alongside M62 past (11½m) the turning for *Eastrington*, with an interesting church. At (19m) the end of M62, the route joins A63 again and bears S near the foot of the Wolds. 24m: *Brough*, to the right, is the site of the Roman station of Petuaria. The fort guarded the ferry by which Ermine Street crossed the Humber. 34m: *Hull*, see Route 82A.

From Selby to *Leeds*, see Route 75F.

B1223 and B1222, heading N from Selby, offer an alternative to the main route to York described below. 4½m: *Cawood* has the 15C gatehouse to the palace of the Archbishops of York, where Wolsey was arrested in 1530. 7½m: *Stillingfleet* church has a Norman 'S doorway, with ironwork on the door showing Viking influence, and the 14C effigy of a knight. 14½m: *York*, see below.

The main route crosses the Ouse by the Selby toll bridge and continues N on A19 through flat countryside.

34m: **YORK** (98,700 inhabitants) is one of the most attractive old cities in England, despite dull patches of 19C and 20C development close to the centre and despite the tourists who have made its historic quarters increasingly self-conscious. The city walls enclose streets which follow their narrow and irregular medieval course, with overhanging rows of old buildings and parish churches whose glass echoes the chief glory of the city's great Minster. The local purple-grey brick is used to particularly handsome effect in the 18C houses which evoke York's prosperity in a later age.

TI: De Grey Rooms, Exhibition Square; Railway Station. **Bus Station**: Rougier St. **Railway Station**: Station Rd, S of the river. **Theatre**: Theatre Royal, St Leonard's Place.

History. The Brigantian settlement was garrisoned by Vespasian's nephew Quintus Petillius Cerialis in AD 71 and, as Eboracum, became headquarters of the 6th Legion and capital of the province of Lower (i.e. Northern) Britain. Stone city walls replaced earth ramparts in the early 2C. Hadrian was the first emperor to visit York, in AD 121, while Septimius Severus and Constantius Chlorus both died in the city (211 and 306). On the latter's death Constantine the Great was proclaimed Emperor of Western Rome here, the only time an emperor was proclaimed in Britain. Eoforwic, the Saxon town which emerged after the Romans' withdrawal in AD 407, played a leading role in the spread of Christianity throughout Northern England. Paulinus baptised King Edwin of Northumbria here in 627 and York became one of the chief centres of European learning while Alcuin (734–802) was 'Magister Scholarum'. Danish invaders captured the city in 867, naming it Jorvik and making it an important port and trading centre. The suffix '-gate' in street names is a legacy of their presence (cf. the modern Danish '-gade').

William the Conqueror established two castles; city gates and walls were built in the 12–14C. As capital of Northern England, York was favoured by the Plantagenets: Henry I granted its first charter, Henry II and Edward II held parliaments here and in 1328 Edward III married Philippa of Hainault in the Minster. The Duke of York became the title of the sovereign's second son. The Minster and several monastic foundations made York a religious centre, while its prosperity as a port and a staple town of the wool trade fostered powerful guilds. These were responsible for the York Mystery Cycle, 48 plays dating from about 1340 and making up one of the four surviving cycles in England. They are still performed in York about every three or four years.

During the Civil War the city surrendered to the Parliamentary forces under General Fairfax after the Royalist defeat at Marston Moor in 1644. The 18C made York a fashionable social centre, where the gentry of the North maintained town houses. George Hudson, the fraudulent 'Railway King', was Lord Mayor in the 1830s and 1840s, and his influence made York headquarters of the North-Eastern Railway. In the 19C, too, the chocolate-making firms of Rowntree's (taken over by Nestlés) and Terry's (taken over by Kraft) expanded to occupy their present importance in the city's industrial life.

Natives, residents and visitors. Natives include the conspirator Guy Fawkes (1570–1606); the sculptor John Flaxman (1755–1826); the painters William Etty (1787–1849) and Albert Moore (1841–93); the architect and inventor of the hansom cab J.A. Hansom (1803–82); and the poet W.H. Auden (1907–73). Margaret Clitherow, canonised as St Margaret of York in 1970, was pressed to death in 1586 after being accused of sheltering Jesuit priests. Laurence Sterne lodged here in the 1740s and a Stonegate printer first issued 'Tristram Shandy' (1760–67). The highwayman Dick Turpin was tried and hanged at York in 1739, and the murderer Eugene Aram in 1759. Turpin's famous ride to York was in fact made by Swift Nick (William Nevinson) in the 17C and added to the Turpin legend by William Harrison Ainsworth in his novel 'Rookwood' (1834).

THE MINSTER AND ITS ENVIRONS. ***York Minster**, in the N corner of the old city, is the largest English medieval cathedral and ranks second only to Canterbury in ecclesiastical importance. The Archbishop of York holds the title Primate of England (Canterbury is Primate of All England), and his sway extends over 14 dioceses in the North Midlands and the North. Though called a minster (from the Latin *monasterium*), the cathedral was never monastic and so lacks a cloister or domestic buildings. Its architecture covers three periods: Early English (transepts), Decorated (nave and chapter house), and early and late Perpendicular (choir and towers). As at Canterbury, the atmosphere suffers from the large number of visitors.

The present Minster is the latest of several to stand on the site. The first was the wooden chapel put up for the baptism of King Edwin of Northumbria and his court by Paulinus on Easter Day 627. Its stone successor was destroyed in the troubles following the Norman Conquest. Thomas of Bayeux, the first Norman archbishop, began rebuilding c 1080, though his choir was soon rebuilt again by Archbishop Roger of Pont-l'Evêque (1154–81). The present building gradually replaced this Norman church. Archbishop Walter de Grey (1215–55) rebuilt the S transept (c 1220–40) and began the new N transept (1240–60). A new nave was started in 1291 and completed c 1345. The Norman choir was replaced by the present one in 1360–1405. The W towers were complete by 1474 and the central tower by c 1480, bringing to an end the labour of nearly 250 years.

After structural investigation in the 1960s showed that the central tower was in danger of collapse, the foundations of its four supporting columns were encased in reinforced concrete. The Minster has also suffered several damaging fires: in the choir (1829), nave (1840) and the roof of the S transept (1984).

The best view of the exterior is from the city walls (see below). Its finest parts are the *W façade, particularly the great window and finely sculptured portal; the N transept, especially the façade and 'Five Sisters' window; the octagonal chapter house; and above all the *central tower.

The glory of the Minster inside is its **glass, mainly by a well-defined local school of artists and craftsmen. The *Nave* is unusually tall and broad, with the piers widely spaced and the triforium virtually suppressed to create the largest possible area of glass. The design presupposes a stone vault which was never built, and the present wooden roof (part of Sydney Smirke's restoration after the 1840 fire) continues the earlier deception by being painted to look like stone. There is superb tracery in the large clerestory windows and particularly in the *W window (1338). Unlike the nave, the aisles are stone-vaulted. Their W windows have fine glass. Besides the 14C glass elsewhere in the aisles, the remains of 12–13C glass in the clerestories are worth studying. All round the nave and choir, below the triforium, are painted stone shields of Edward II and the barons who met in parliament at York in 1309–10.

The tall Perpendicular lantern at the crossing and the spacious transepts, with aisles on their W as well as their E sides, create an impression of size which is hardly lessened by the obtrusive triforium and correspondingly mean clerestory. The *S Transept*, with a rose window of c 1500 and the tomb of Archbishop de Grey, has been restored after the fire of 1984. The *N Transept* is dominated by the tall lancet lights of the *'Five Sisters', with 13C grisaille glass. The wooden vaulting dates from 1934–51 but incorporates bosses and ribs from the 15C ceiling. The astronomical clock (1955; Sir

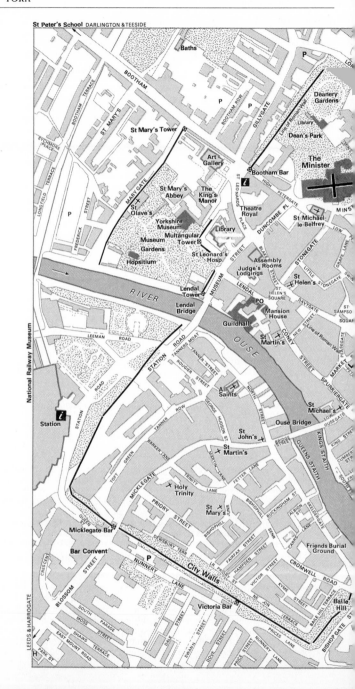

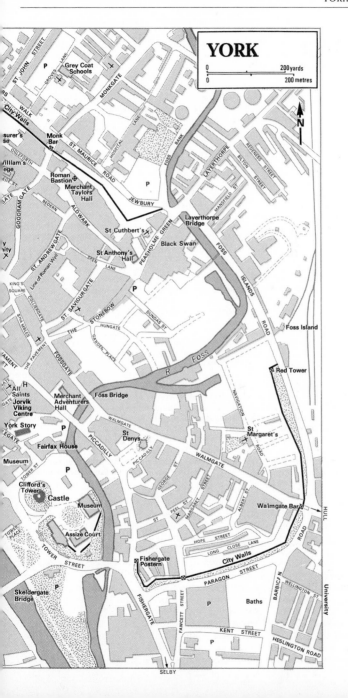

YORK

| 0 | | 200 yards |
| 0 | | 200 metres |

N

St. John Street
Groves Lane
Grey Coat Schools
Monkgate
P
City Walls
Walk
Monk Bar
St. Maurice Road
Ogleforth
/illiam's ege
EGE ST.
Hospital Lane
Foss Bank
Layerthorpe
Bedford Street
Redness Street
Roman Bastion
Merchant Taylors Hall
Jewbury
P
Mansfield Street
Layerthorpe Bridge
St Cuthbert's
Peasholme Green
Black Swan
Foss
Foss Islands Road
Foss Island
St Anthony's Hall
Spen Lane
Line of Roman Wall
KING'S SQUARE
St. Andrewgate
St. Saviourgate
Stonebow
Dundas St.
Hungate
Garden Place
R. Foss
Red Tower
Navigation
Fossgate
The Pavement
All Saints
Jorvik Viking Centre
York Story
Foss Bridge
Merchant Adventurers Hall
Walmgate
St Denys
Piccadilly
St Margaret's
Fairfax House
Piccadilly
Museum
George St.
Margaret Street
Albert St.
Tower St.
P
Clifford's Tower
Castle
Museum
Peel St.
Hope Street
Long Close Lane
Walmgate Bar
HULL
Assize Court
Tower Place
Tower Street
Fishergate Postern
City Walls
Paragon Street
Barbican
Wellington St.
University
Skeldergate Bridge
Fishergate
Fawcett Street
P
Baths
Kent Street
Heslington Road
P
SELBY

Albert Richardson) is a memorial to the airmen based in North-East England who died in World War II.

From the E aisle of the N transept a *vestibule leads to the *Chapter House* (fee). Built in 1260–1300, both are among the finest Decorated work in England, second only to their counterparts at Southwell Minster. They preserve contemporary glass of rare quality set in lovely tracery, and over 250 carved stone heads and almost 300 foliage capitals and pendants. The octagonal chapter house is unsupported by any central column, though (unlike Southwell) the vaulting is of wood rather than stone.

In the SW corner of the S transept is the entrance to the *Undercroft Museum* (fee) in the space excavated during the repairs of 1966–72. The reinforced concrete encasing the foundations of the central piers contrasts powerfully with the exposed foundation walls of the present Minister, its Norman predecessor and the Roman headquarters building. Pre-Conquest sculpture and capitals from Archbishop Thomas's cathedral, unearthed during the repairs, are on display. The adjoining treasury in part of the original Norman crypt contains, among its magnificent church plate and domestic silver, the 11C Horn of Ulph and the mazer bowl traditionally connected with Archbishop Scrope (see below).

The *Choir* is separated from the nave by a stone rood screen, traditionally dated c 1475–1500, with life-size statues of English kings (all original except Henry VI). The vaulted entrance has a central boss of the Assumption of the Virgin (c 1150), Byzantine in manner. The glass in the great *E window, by John Thornton of Coventry (1405), forms the largest expanse of medieval glazing in England and probably the world. The soaring windows of the E transeptal bays contain 15C glass showing the lives of St Cuthbert and St William of York, whose shrine is believed to have stood behind the high altar. All the woodwork in the choir was destroyed in the fire of 1829 and the stalls, by Sir Robert Smirke, are an approximate reproduction of the originals. The traceried altar screen (1831) is a free copy of its 15C predecessor.

The N choir aisle has the monument of Archbishop Savage (d. 1507), with a restored chantry, and the damaged but finely wrought effigy tomb of William of Hatfield (d. 1336), Edward III's son. The *Lady Chapel* has the tomb of Archbishop Bowet (d. 1423); opposite is the plain, restored monument of Archbishop Scrope, beheaded in 1405 (see Shakespeare's 'Henry IV, Part 2'). The S choir aisle has monuments of Archbishops Dolben (d. 1686) and Lamplugh (d. 1691) by Grinling Gibbons and of William Burgh (d. 1808) by Westmacott. Steps lead down from this aisle to the Zouche Chapel (1352).

The late Norman *E Crypt* is entered from the choir aisles. Its structure shows the extent of Archbishop Roger's choir and the pillars, probably dating from the time of Archbishop Thomas (c 1080), have capitals with Romanesque carving. The font marks the site of Paulinus's original wooden chapel. Beneath a trapdoor is the base of a pillar of the Roman praetorium.

Dean's Park, N of the Minster, has a fragment of the cloister belonging to the Norman Archbishop's Palace. Its 13C chapel, built by Archbishop de Grey, has been used since the 19C as the *Minster Library* (open), now connected with the University of York. The exhibition of its main treasures includes the baptismal entry for Guy Fawkes from St Michael-le-Belfrey (see below).

Immediately E of the Minster is *St William's College* (open when not in use). Originally a prebendal house, it was enlarged c 1461 for the chantry priests attached to the Minster and much altered after the Dissolution. Restored in the 20C as the meeting place of the Northern Convocation, it is now used for meetings of all kinds. It keeps a fine timbered roof and carved figures. To the left in Minster Yard stands the *Treasurer's House* (NT), a 17C building on a site used since Roman times, with good 17–18C furniture.

Opposite the S transept of the Minster a Roman column from the headquarters of the 6th Legion has been re-erected. The late Perpendicular church of *St Michael-le-Belfrey* has some magnificent 14C and 16C *glass; Guy Fawkes, probably born at what is now Young's Hotel in Petergate, was baptised here in 1570. Nearby Stonegate, reached by the alley between the column and the church, is one of York's prettiest streets. A passage leads from it to the remnant of a Norman house, now an open courtyard. Low

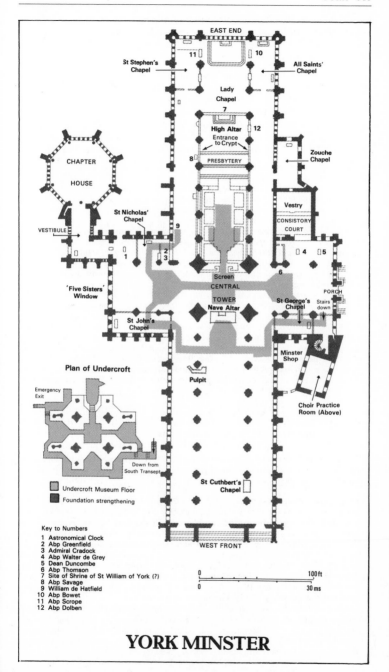

EAST END

11   10

St Stephen's
Chapel

All Saints'
Chapel

Lady
Chapel

7

High Altar   12
Entrance
to Crypt

CHAPTER

HOUSE

8

PRESBYTERY

Zouche
Chapel

St Nicholas'
Chapel

VESTIBULE

Vestry

CONSISTORY
COURT

9

1   2
3

4   5

'Five Sisters'
Window

Screen
CENTRAL

6

PORCH
Stairs
down

TOWER

Nave Altar

St George's
Chapel

St John's
Chapel

Minster
Shop

Plan of Undercroft

Pulpit

Choir Practice
Room (Above)

Emergency
Exit

Undercroft Museum Floor

Foundation strengthening

Down from
South Transept

St Cuthbert's
Chapel

Key to Numbers

1 Astronomical Clock
2 Abp Greenfield
3 Admiral Cradock
4 Abp Walter de Grey
5 Dean Duncombe
6 Abp Thomson
7 Site of Shrine of St William of York (?)
8 Abp Savage
9 William de Hatfield
10 Abp Bowet
11 Abp Scrope
12 Abp Dolben

WEST FRONT

0   100 ft

0   30 ms

YORK MINSTER

Petergate leads from the beginning of Stonegate to Goodramgate and the 13–14C *Holy Trinity*, York's quaintest church, with box pews and a fine E window of 1470–80. The mid 14C houses of Lady Row further along Goodramgate are the oldest in York.

THE CITY WALLS. Goodramgate continues NE to Monk Bar and the *City Walls, among the finest medieval city fortification to survive in Europe. Much restored in their present form, they date mainly from the reign of Edward III (1327–77), though the gates (or bars) incorporate Norman work and the N section of the walls follows the line of the smaller Roman system built in the 2C. The full circuit of about 2½m is worth making, and the stretch between Monk Bar and Bootham Bar is particularly attractive.

Monk Bar (open), probably taking its name from a nearby monastic house, is the tallest of the four main gates and, like the others, has a Norman core. It was encased in the 14C, when the portcullises were added. The walk heading left along the wall round its N angle gives lovely views of the Minster, more than compensating for the dull prospect outside. *Bootham Bar*, the only gate on the site of a Roman one, was rebuilt in the 18C and 19C but keeps its Norman archway.

Museum Gardens, with its fragment of the Roman wall, is described later in the tour of the city. The present walk leaves the wall and follows St Leonard's Place and Museum St. to Lendal Bridge, with the *Lendal Tower*, largely rebuilt in the 19C. The wall continues at the *North St. Postern* on the opposite bank of the river. There is a good view back to the Minster from the stretch leading to *Toft Tower* at the W corner. *Micklegate Bar* (open), shortly beyond, is the chief of the four original gates. Richard of York's head was displayed here in 1460–61 and those of Jacobite rebels in 1746. Beyond the 19C *Victoria Bar* and the S angle, the wall skirts the mound of *Baile Hill*, where one of William the Conqueror's two castles stood. Beyond the river, spanned by the iron *Skeldergate Bridge*, are the *Castle* (see below) and the Foss, or canal. The wall resumes at *Fishergate Postern* (c 1505), in a dreary neighbourhood. The walk passes *Fishergate Bar* and *Walmgate Bar*, the only one which still has its barbican or outwork. The stretch between the brick 16C *Red Tower* and *Layerthorpe Bridge* was never walled, as a marsh here protected the city. The final stretch of wall between the bridge and Monk Bar passes, both on the left, the *Merchant Taylors' Hall* and the foundation of the Roman E bastion (see below).

THE CITY ART GALLERY AND MUSEUM GARDENS. The starting-point for this tour is Bootham Bar, reached on the walk along the city walls or by taking High Petergate from the W end of the Minster, past the house where the Cavalier and traveller Sir Thomas Herbert (1606–82) died.

The **City Art Gallery** dominates Exhibition Square. Its wide-ranging collection illustrates most developments in Western European painting from the 14C to the present.

Continental painting is displayed in the *Main Gallery* on the ground floor. Among the Italian pictures are a group of good early Florentine and Sienese panels, including part of a predella with two scenes from the life of St Clement by Fungai, and works by Bacchiacca (Agony in the Garden), Parmigianino (Portrait), Domenichino (Monsignor Agucchi) and Bellotto (View in Lucca). Among the Northern European pictures are some good early panels, including Bernhard Strigel's Sleeping Soldier, and works by Baburen (Roman Charity), van Streek (Vanitas), van Goyen (Peasants and Horsemen) and Snyders (Game Stall). Spanish painting is represented by Valdés Leal (Jesuit Conversion) and Meléndez (Still Life); French painting by J.F. Millet (Nobleman of Capernaum), Watteau (Le Defilé) and Gravelot (Le Lecteur).

British painting is displayed in the *South Gallery* on the ground floor. The interesting collection of early portraits includes works by George Gower (?), Van Dyck, Edward Bower and Lely. The 18C section includes work by Francis Cotes, de Loutherbourg, William Marlow, Philip Mercier, Reynolds and Andrea Soldi. A room is devoted to nude studies, historical subjects and other works by William Etty, born in York.

The *Burton Gallery* on the first floor has a wide range of 19–20C art: apocalyptic landscapes by John Martin and his followers; genre pictures by Frith and others; canvases by G.F. Watts and Albert Moore; late 19C French paintings, including Barbizon school landscapes and work by Ribot, Bonvin, Boudin and Fantin-Latour; and paintings by most important British artists of the period 1900–50, notably Sickert, Gilman, Gore, Gwen John and Nash.

The *Pottery Gallery* on the first floor contains the finest holding of Staite Murray's work, and important examples by Bernard Leach, Shoji Hamada and other potters of the period 1920–60. There is a continuous programme of temporary exhibitions, mostly shown in the *Exhibition Gallery* on the first floor.

Next door is the lovely **King's Manor**, originally the abbot's lodging of St Mary's Abbey (see below) and assigned after the Dissolution to the Lord President of the Council of the North. Founded c 1270 but dating mostly from an enlargement of 1485–90, it was visited by Henry VIII, James I, Charles I and occupied by Strafford while he was Lord President in 1628–40. The building is now used by the University of York; its courtyards and public rooms are open.

Across St Leonard's Place are the De Grey Rooms, with the TI Centre, and the *Theatre Royal*, opened on this site as the New Theatre in 1740. The building, several times altered since the 18C, incorporates the 12C vaulted crypt of St Peter's Hospital, founded by Athelstan and rebuilt by William Rufus.

At the end of St Leonard's Place a right turn into Museum St. leads to Museum Gardens. Stretching down to the river, these pleasantly laid-out grounds of the Yorkshire Museum contain an interesting medley of ruins and old buildings. On the right of the entrance are the remains of *St Leonard's Hospital*, founded by Archbishop Thomas (d. 1116) to replace Athelstan's 10C hospital. The ruined passage, undercroft and chapel date from the 13C. At the corner of the city wall beyond is the *Multangular Tower*, medieval in its upper stages and 4C Roman below. The inside, with a collection of Roman coffins unearthed in various parts of the city, can be seen from the grounds of the *Public Library*.

The **Yorkshire Museum** is housed in William Wilkins's building for the Yorkshire Philosophical Society (1830). It contains an outstanding *collection of archaeology together with displays of natural history and geology.

The Roman Life gallery has the central fragment of Trajan's gateway (AD 107–08), mosaics, tombstones, altars, the preserved hair of a Roman lady and a reconstructed Roman kitchen. The Anglo-Saxon and Viking Life gallery has an impressive array of Viking artefacts, including the 8C silver gilt Ormside Bowl and the Gilling Sword. The collection also boasts the Middleham Jewel, the finest piece of medieval gold jewellery found this century. In addition there is a large display of Yorkshire pottery, natural history exhibitions and a geology gallery, 'Time Club'.

The museum's basement is built around the fireplace and part of the chapter house of the Benedictine **St Mary's Abbey**, founded c 1080 by Stephen of Lastingham and enlarged by William Rufus. The ruins of the *Abbey Church* begun by Abbot Simon of Warwick in 1259 consist chiefly of the N wall and part of the W front. The foundations of the E end of the original Norman church, with seven apses, have been partly excavated. The N door of the nave looks into the churchyard of *St Olave's*, with Etty's tomb. The church has 15C glass. The *Abbey Gatehouse* (not open) adjoins it and the precinct wall runs from the river around the N corner of the gardens, originally meeting the city walls at Bootham Bar. The abbey's 16C *Hospitium*, or guesthouse, by the river is administered by the Yorkshire

Museum and is open for special exhibitions as advertised. A fragment of the water-gate stands nearby.

SOUTH FROM MUSEUM GARDENS TO THE CASTLE AND BACK. Lendal and Blake St both lead S from Museum St. to St Helen's Square. The former *Judge's Lodging*, now a hotel, in Lendal is a fine building of 1718–25. The *Assembly Rooms* (open except when in use for functions) in Blake St. were built in 1732–36 by the 3rd Earl of Burlington, the patron of Palladianism in England. Inside is an Egyptian Hall with double rows of columns, as derived by Palladio from Vitruvius. The murals of Roman York in the Rotunda endow Constantine the Great with Burlington's features. St Helen's Square, the centre of modern York and site of the main gate to the Roman city, is overlooked by the church of *St Helen's*, which has some 15C glass. The *Mansion House* (open by prior arrangement), facing the church, was built in 1725–26 as the official home of the Lord Mayor; the only other Mansion Houses in England are at Doncaster and London. The 15C *Guildhall* (open), by the river behind the Mansion House, has been rebuilt on the old lines since World War II bomb damage.

Coney St. heads S from the square, passing *St Martin-le-Grand*, a late Perpendicular church partly rebuilt by George Pace after wartime bomb damage. In Spurriergate, beyond, the 12–15C church of *St Michael* was truncated by road widening but still has medieval glass. Nessgate continues Spurriergate.

Castlegate, heading further S, has a heritage centre, the *York Story*, in the redundant 13–15C church of St Mary. Beyond is *Fairfax House (open), built by John Carr for Viscount Fairfax of Emley in 1755–62 and restored by the York Civic Trust. It has superb plaster ceilings and wrought ironwork, and now houses the Noel Terry collection of 18C furniture, paintings, porcelain and clocks. Carr also built *Castlegate House* (1763) opposite.

The **Castle**, one of the two established at York by William the Conqueror, is now largely replaced by John Carr's Crown Court (1773–77) and the museum. The chief remaining medieval fragment is the 13C *Clifford's Tower* (EH, all year plus Mondays in winter), with its remarkable quatrefoil ground plan, on the mound thrown up by the Conqueror. The wooden Norman keep was destroyed during the anti-Jewish riots of 1190, in which 150 Jews who had fled here for sanctuary were killed. The *Castle Museum (open) is in the former Female Prison (1780; John Carr) and the old Debtors' Prison (1705). Its rich social history collections were begun by the far-sighted Dr J.L. Kirk of Pickering (d. 1940).

The outstanding feature is Kirkgate, a reconstructed 19C street with cobbles, shops and a hansom cab. There are also 17–20C interiors, an 18C automaton clock, Victorian royal commemorative ware and 19–20C kitchen, domestic and consumer items. The Debtors' Prison has military, costume and toy displays as well as a reconstructed Edwardian street. Dick Turpin's condemned cell, craftsmen's workshops and a water mill, working in summer, complete the displays. Part of the castle's outer wall, protecting the city between the Ouse and the Foss, survives behind the museum and the Crown Court.

The walk now heads back from the castle along Castlegate and turns right into Coppergate. In the shopping centre, to the right, the popular **Jorvik Viking Centre** occupies the site of the Danish Viking neighbourhood excavated by the York Archaeological Trust. It contains interesting displays of the objects unearthed and the archaeological techniques employed, but the gimmicky presentation—with journeys by electrically operated train through a reconstructed Viking street—cheapens its subject. *All Saints*, where Castlegate meets The Pavement, is a partly rebuilt 15C church with an elegant octagonal lantern on its square tower and a curious brass knocker on the N door. In The Pavement itself stands the half-timbered Jacobean house where Sir Thomas Herbert was born in 1606.

The *Merchant Adventurers' Hall* in Fossgate, leading S from the E end of The Pavement, was built by York's most powerful guild, which controlled the northern cloth-export trade in the 15–17C. The Great Hall (1357–68) has splendid timberwork. Underneath is the Hospital, once occupied by the guild's pensioners, with massive wooden piers and a 15C chapel, altered in the 17C. There is a pleasant garden. Beyond the bridge Fossgate is continued by Walmgate, with two interesting churches: *St Denys*, with a Norman S doorway moved from its original place and 14C glass, and *St*

Plaster decoration from the great staircase at Fairfax House, York

Margaret (not open), rebuilt in the 19C but with a *porch of c 1160 brought from the demolished church of St Nicholas.

The Stonebow, leading E and N from The Pavement, is continued by Peasholme Green with the half-timbered 17C *Black Swan Inn*. Opposite is the partly 15C *St Anthony's Hall*, built by the ancient Guild of St Anthony and now headquarters of the Borthwick Institute of Historical Research, part of the University of York. The main hall, with a good timber roof and bosses, is open. The nearby church of *St Cuthbert* (not open) incorporates Roman stones. Aldwark leads back to the Minster via another guild hall, the *Merchant Taylors' Hall* (open when not in use), with a 14C roof behind the 17–18C exterior.

There are two ways, both interesting, of making the walk N from The Pavement. The Shambles, York's narrowest and quaintest street, leads to the pleasant little King's Square at the bottom of Low Petergate. Parliament St., the only wide street in the centre of York, leads via Davygate to St Helen's Square. It passes through St Sampson's Square, where the *Roman Bath Inn* takes its name from the Roman remains in the basement.

WEST OF THE RIVER. There are some interesting churches across the Ouse, best reached by following High and Low Ousegate W from The Pavement. *St John the Evangelist*, beyond the bridge, is now an arts centre. The late 12–15C *All Saints*, North St., has angel corbels and *glass in the N aisle depicting the Fifteen Last Days, in illustration of the 14C poem 'The Pricke of Conscience', and the Corporal Acts of Mercy, besides other glass of great beauty. Micklegate, continuing W, has Georgian houses and two more churches: *St Martin-cum-Gregory*, with good glass, and *Holy Trinity*, the much-altered fragment of a great priory church, with a memorial to Dr John Burton (d. 1771), the original of Dr Slop in Sterne's 'Tristram Shandy'. Performances of the medieval mystery plays began their circuit of the city outside the gateway. *St Mary*, in Bishophill Junior to the S, has a tower with Saxon work. The stones of its demolished sister church, St Mary in Bishophill Senior, were used by George Pace to build a new church (1965) in the NW suburb of *Acomb*. Beyond Micklegate Bar (see the city walls, above) the Georgian architecture continues in Blossom St., where the *Bar Convent* (1760; Thomas Atkinson) has a museum of 13–19C church embroidery, plate and illuminated manuscripts.

The *National Railway Museum* is W of the railway station in Leeman Rd. A branch of the Science Museum in South Kensington, it displays the record-breaking 'Mallard', royal carriages used by Queen Victoria, Edward VII and the Queen Mother, and replicas of Stephenson's 'Rocket' and a section of the Channel Tunnel. The Balcony Galleries have paintings depicting life on the railways and a reconstruction of the manager's office from the Wolverton carriage and wagon works.

SOUTH-EASTERN OUTSKIRTS. The **University of York**, opened in 1963, is 1½m SE of Walmgate Bar at *Heslington*. Attractively laid out around an artificial lake, the campus incorporates the 19C Heslington Hall (now administrative offices) among new buildings mostly in the modular system, CLASP. The university also uses several buildings in the city centre, notably King's Manor and St Anthony's Hall (see above).

SOUTH-WESTERN OUTSKIRTS. The racecourse, at the *Knavesmire*, about 2m SW of the city by A1036 (the Leeds road), is one of the finest in the country, with a history dating from 1731. Flat-race meetings are held between May and October, and the racing museum in the grandstand is open on race days. The city gallows, where Dick Turpin and Eugene Aram were executed, stood at the Knavesmire until 1801.

FROM YORK TO HARROGATE, 19½m by A59. The road follows a Roman course to (8m) the Skip bridge over the Nidd. To the S lies *Marston Moor*, where Cromwell won his decisive victory over the Royalists in 1644. To the left, just beyond the river, is *Kirk Hammerton*, where a Saxon church forms the S aisle of the 19C church. *Nun Monkton*, 3m NE at the meeting of the Nidd and the Ouse, has a beautiful little conventual church (Transitional and Early English) with glass by Morris and Co. (1873) in a pleasant village setting. 13m: A59 crosses A1 (Route 85B). 16m: *Knaresborough*, see Route 86B. 19½m: *Harrogate*, see Route 80.

FROM YORK TO LEEDS, 23m. A1065 leads past the racecourse (see above) to join A64, followed for the rest of the way. 10m: *Tadcaster* (5900 inhabitants) is a brewing town on the Wharfe. The church has an E window with glass (1875–80) by Morris and Co. *Towton*, 2½m S, is near the battlefield where the Lancastrians were defeated in 1461. *Bolton Percy*, 3½m SE of Tadcaster, has a good church of 1424 with fine original glass in the E window and an Elizabethan sundial in the churchyard. The manor house of *Nun Appleton* (not open), on the Wharfe 1½m further SE, has been rebuilt since it was the home of General Fairfax (1612–71) and the subject of Andrew Marvell's 'Upon Appleton House'. Fairfax's tomb is preserved in the 19C church at *Bilbrough*, 4m NE of Tadcaster. At (13m) *Bramham Moor* A64 crosses A1 (Route 85B). At 15m a sideroad leads left to *Barwick-in-Elmet* (1½m), with some remarkable Norman mounds. 23m: *Leeds*, see Route 75F.

From York to *Hull*, see Route 82A; to *Bridlington*, see Route 82B; to *Scarborough*, see Route 83; to *Whitby*, see Route 84; to *Durham, Newcastle* and *Berwick*, see Route 85A.

82

The Yorkshire Wolds

The **Yorkshire Wolds** are the northernmost chalkland in Britain, the last outpost of the belt sweeping up from Salisbury Plain through East Anglia and Lincolnshire. Here it forms a crescent extending from the Humber estuary a few miles W of Hull to the cliffs between Flamborough Head and Filey. The Wolds are at their steepest on the western and northern escarpments which rise out of the York plain and the Vale of Pickering, but their highest point, Garrowby Hill, is only 807ft and their characteristic landscape is gentle and undulating. Many of the villages in these dry uplands feel surprisingly remote when the sky is not being invaded by RAF practice flights. In the S and E the Wolds trail off into the plain of Holderness and the boulderclay coastline between Spurn Head and Bridlington.

A. York to Hull

Directions. Total distance 38m. **York**, see Route 81. A1079 to (19¼m) Market Weighton. A1079, A1035 to (29¼m) **Beverley**. A1174, A1079 to (38m) **Hull**.

York, see Route 81. A1079 heads E from Walmgate Bar, passing the junction with A64 and A166 (the Bridlington road, Route 82B) at (3¼m) *Grimston*. Beyond (6¾m) *Kexby* it crosses the Derwent, marking the boundary between North Yorkshire and Humberside. At (11¼m) *Barmby Moor* B1246 branches left for (2m) *Pocklington*, a small town where William Wilberforce (see Hull, below) went to school. The fine 13–14C church, with a Perpendicular tower, contains a 14C cross head. *Stewart's Gardens and Museum* (limited opening), in the grounds of *Burnby Hall*, are named after their creator Major P.M. Stewart (d. 1962): the gardens include lakes with an abundance of water lilies and the museum houses sporting trophies and an ethnographical collection. A sideroad runs 5½m N from Pocklington via Bishop Wilton to A166 (Route 82B).

19¼m: **Market Weighton** (3800 inhabitants; pronounced 'Weeton') is at the foot of the Wolds.

About 1½m NE is *Goodmanham*, the 'Godmundingaham' of Bede, where the partly Norman church probably stands on the site of the pagan temple destroyed after the Great Council of 626. Note the chancel arch and 16C font. *Nunburnholme* church, 4¾m N of Market Weighton, has an interesting 10C cross. *Kiplingcotes*, 3¾m E of the village, is the starting-point of the Kiplingcotes Derby, the oldest and longest horserace in England, run yearly since 1519 on the third Thursday in March. The present 4m course has been used since 1667. A peculiarity of the race is that the winner usually receives less prize money than the runner-up. *North Newbald*, 4m SE of Market Weighton, has perhaps the finest Norman *church in the region.

Beyond (26¾m) *Bishop Burton* A1079 swings S to bypass Beverley. A1035 continues into the town.

29¼m: **BEVERLEY** (16,400 inhabitants; TI), once the county town of the East Riding of Yorkshire and now the administrative centre of Humberside, is an old-fashioned market town with a racecourse, attractive houses and two splendid churches. The martyr Bishop John Fisher (1459–1535) was born and Mary Wollstonecraft (1759–97) spent much of her childhood here.

Within the restored red-brick *North Bar* (1409), only survivor of the five town gates, stands *St Mary's Church*. Its Decorated chancel dates from c 1300, while the nave and tower were rebuilt in the Perpendicular style after the original tower collapsed in 1520.

The W front (c 1380–1411) spans the transition from Decorated to Perpendicular. The S porch has an outer Early English arch (perhaps not in situ), surmounted by a Decorated canopy, and an inner Norman arch. The nave was carefully restored by Sir Gilbert Scott; its roof was renewed in 1937. The hoodmould stops in the N aisle arcade record the contributors to rebuilding in the 1520s: note particularly the delightful group of minstrels. The panelled ceiling of the chancel was painted with the figures of English kings in 1445; George VI was added when it was restored in 1939. The rood screen and misericords (c 1445) deserve attention. The NE chapel (1330–49) has elaborate vaulting and flowing window tracery. The rich sculpture throughout is well preserved, and includes a rabbit said to have inspired Lewis Carroll's White Rabbit.

The Saturday Market, the town's main square, has a charming *Market Cross* of 1711–14. The main street leads S to the Minster past the Georgian *Guildhall* (limited opening). Its courtroom has a fine stucco ceiling. Above the *Library* in Champney Rd, to the right, is the *Art Gallery*, with work by the local artist Frederick Elwell (1870–1958).

Beverley Minster equals some English cathedrals in size and outstrips many in splendour. As well as its superb early 16C choir stalls, it boasts a great achievement in stone-carving from each of the main Gothic eras: the Early English choir and transepts, the Decorated Percy tomb and the Perpendicular W front.

In 721 John of Beverley, Bishop of Hexham and later of York, was buried at the monastery he had founded here on the site of a chapel of St John the Evangelist. He was canonised in 1037 and kings, from Athelstan to Henry V, conferred benefits on the church in gratitude for victories won after pilgrimages to his shrine. The first

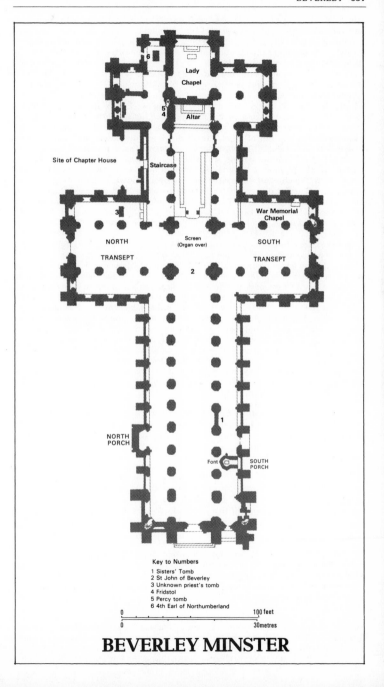

Site of Chapter House

Staircase

Lady
Chapel

Altar

6

5
4

3

NORTH TRANSEPT

SOUTH TRANSEPT

War Memorial
Chapel

Screen
(Organ over)

2

NORTH
PORCH

1

Font

SOUTH
PORCH

Key to Numbers

1 Sisters' Tomb
2 St John of Beverley
3 Unknown priest's tomb
4 Fridstol
5 Percy tomb
6 4th Earl of Northumberland

0   100 feet
0   30 metres

BEVERLEY MINSTER

minster was destroyed by the Danes in 866, and its successor disfigured by fire in 1188 and the fall of the central tower in 1213. Rebuilding began soon afterwards and continued for two centuries—spanning the Early English, Decorated and Perpendicular styles but keeping a remarkable unity of design. The Perpendicular *W front with its slender twin towers, probably the finest of its kind in England, marked the completion of work in c 1420. Hawksmoor's restoration saved the church from ruin in the 18C; further work was carried out by Sir Gilbert Scott in 1866–68 and more restoration began in 1977.

In the *Nave* the W bay is Perpendicular and the two E bays are Early English; the rest is fine Decorated work of c 1300–50. Here, as throughout the church, the stone-carving deserves careful attention: note, for example, the musicians on the hoodmould stops in the N aisle. The W doors are decorated with figures of the Evangelists added during Hawksmoor's restoration. The S aisle has a massive late Norman font of Frosterley marble, with an elaborate cover of 1726, and the Decorated 'Sisters' Tomb'. St John of Beverley is buried at the E end of the nave. The central tower above the crossing still houses the medieval treadwheel crane used for lifting stones. The Snetzler organ (1769) was restored when Scott designed the screen in 1880. The Early English *Great Transepts* have both E and W aisles, like the transepts at York. In the S arm is an early 17C painting of Athelstan, and in the E aisle of the N arm a remarkable 14C tomb with the effigy of a priest, possibly Gilbert de Grimsby (d. 1306).

Like the Great Transepts, the *Choir* and its E transepts are Early English work at its purest and loveliest. The N choir aisle has a rare double staircase, which led to the Chapter House (since destroyed). The *Stalls* (c 1520–24) were carved by the school whose work also survives at Ripon and Manchester; the array of 68 misericords is the largest, and one of the best, in England. The canopies were much renovated in the 18C. The front of the Decorated altar screen was renewed in 1826 and adorned with statues and mosaics in 1897. On the N side of the altar stands the 'Fridstol', or sanctuary chair, said to date from Athelstan's time (924–39). Also on the N side of the altar is the *Percy Tomb, lacking a chest or effigy on its slab but thought to be the tomb of Lady Idoine Percy (d. 1365). Its canopy, carved with figures, foliage and heraldic emblems, is one of the masterpieces of medieval art. The lovely *Retrochoir* has an E window inserted in 1416 which contains 13–15C glass, some collected from other windows. The back of the reredos has vaulting and blind arcading (c 1340), with Flamboyant tracery. The small 15C *Northumberland Chapel*, to the N, holds the mutilated tomb of the 4th Earl of Northumberland (d. 1489).

In Friars Lane beyond the E end of the Minster stand the restored buildings of the Dominican friary founded in c 1240, now partly used as a Youth Hostel but also open to other visitors. Flemingate, leading SE from the Minster, has the *Museum of Army Transport*, with over 100 vehicles on a 5-acre site.

S of Beverley A1174 rejoins A1079.

38m: HULL (252,000 inhabitants), officially *Kingston upon Hull*, stands where the river Hull flows into the Humber. For centuries it has been the leading port on the estuary. The old town, centred on the splendid parish church near the meeting of the rivers, has much more character than the modern centre and, despite the loss of Queen's Dock and now of Prince's Dock, the surviving dockland and wharves are being rescued from neglect.

TI: City Hall, Carr Lane; Central Library, Albion St.; King George Dock, Hedon Rd; North Bank Viewing Area of Humber Bridge, Ferriby Rd, Hessle. **Bus and Coach Station**: Ferensway. **Railway Station**: Paragon Station, Ferensway. **Theatres**: New Theatre, Kingston Square; Spring St. Theatre. Concerts in the City Hall and Middleton Hall (University). **Ferries**: From King George Dock to Rotterdam (Europoort) and Zeebrugge.

History. Originally called Wyke, the town was refounded and laid out as a seaport in 1293–99 by Edward I—hence the 'King's Town' in its official name. Defended by walls and ditches, it outstripped its rivals on the Humber and became England's chief seaport by the 14C. Its refusal to admit Charles I in 1642 was the first open act of rebellion in the Civil War, and it resisted Royalist sieges in 1643 and 1644. In the late 18C and early 19C the medieval ditches were replaced by the chain of Town Docks, whose course across the angle between the two rivers marks the extent of Hull before its expansion.

Natives and residents. Natives include the anti-slavery crusader William Wilberforce (1759–1833), the pioneer aviator Amy Johnson (1903–41) and the poet Stevie Smith (1902–71). Andrew Marvell (1621–78), born at nearby Winestead, was educated at the old grammar school and served as MP for Hull from 1658 until his death. Philip Larkin (1922–85) worked as librarian at the university.

THE CITY CENTRE: QUEEN VICTORIA SQUARE AND QUEEN'S GARDENS. From the handsome *Paragon Station* (1848) the broad Paragon St. leads E to Queen Victoria Square, the centre of Victorian and modern Hull, with the *City Hall* (1903–09; J.H. Hirst). On the S side is the **Ferens Art Gallery**. A lively programme of special exhibitions occupies the recent extension.

The permanent collection includes Humberside marine paintings, 20C British art (Moore, Hepworth, Hockney and a group of portraits) and popular works by the Beverley artist Frederick Elwell (1870–1958). Earlier English painting is represented by Hoppner, Constable and Bonington. One gallery permanently displays Netherlan-

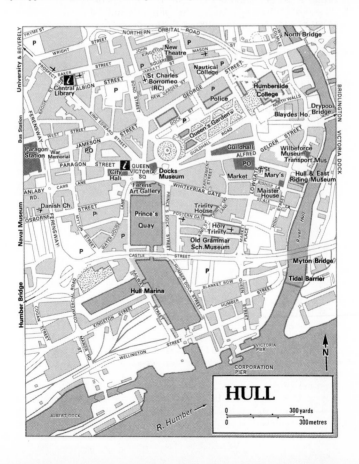

dish Old Masters: portraits by Frans Hals and van der Helst; works by Volmarijn (Supper at Emmaus) and Barent Fabritius (Dismissal of Hagar); still-life paintings by C.N. Gysbrechts and P.J. Elinga; and interiors by de Blieck and Egon van der Neer. Other foreign schools are represented by an early Canaletto and works by José Ribera, Guardi and Maffei.

On the E side is the *Town Docks Museum, housed in a prominent, triangular building with three domes, the former offices of the Hull Dock Company (1871; C.G. Wray). Displays show the history of whaling, trawling and Hull's mercantile past, with collections of scrimshaw, maritime paintings and ship models. The splendid, many-columned courtroom of the former Dock Company houses temporary exhibitions. Its view takes in Queen's Gardens, to the E, and Prince's Quay, to the S, now a shopping centre.

Queen's Gardens is a spacious square created in the 1930s on the site of Queen's Dock and slowly being surrounded by modern development. On the N side are *Portcullis House* and the *Police Headquarters*. At the E end is the *Wilberforce Monument* (1834), backed by the *Humberside College of Further Education* and the *University of Humberside Fine Arts Campus*. The *Nautical College* is in George St., behind a multi-storey car park, and the skyline to the N is dominated by the tower of *Kingston House*.

The RC church of *St Charles Borromeo*, on Jarratt St. just S of Kingston Square, has baroque late 19C decoration.

FROM QUEEN VICTORIA SQUARE TO HOLY TRINITY AND THE OLD TOWN. Whitefriargate leads SE. Parliament St., on the left, preserves some 18C façades. Trinity House Lane heads right. *Trinity House* was founded for distressed sailors in the 14C, rebuilt in 1753 and used for training seamen since 1787. Just beyond is *Holy Trinity, one of the largest and longest parish churches in England.

The transepts and chancel, begun c 1300, are important for their early use of brick. The nave was added c 1400 and the fine central tower c 1500. The interior has interestingly varied window tracery, with glass by Walter Crane (1897 and c 1907) in the S aisle. The font and some of the bench ends in the choir are c 1370. A tomb in the S choir aisle is thought to belong to Sir William de la Pole (d. 1366), first mayor of Hull and ancestor of the Earls and Dukes of Suffolk. The retrochoir has a communion table of 1770.

In King St. at the W end of the church an open-air market is held on Tuesdays, Fridays and Saturdays. SW of the church is Hull's oldest secular building, the *Old Grammar School Museum* (1583), where Andrew Marvell and William Wilberforce were pupils. The E end of Holy Trinity looks out on Market Place, with a gilt statue of William III (1734; Peter Scheemakers).

THE OLD TOWN: SOUTH FROM MARKET PLACE. From the statue Queen St. leads S to *Victoria* or *Corporation Pier*, where the Hull flows into the Humber. Nearby is a statue of William de la Pole. The *Minerva Pier* makes a good look-out point for the Humber, the riverside docks and the distant Humber Bridge. To the E, the Hull is spanned by the *Tidal Surge Barrier* (1980) just below the *Myton Bridge*. A riverside walk, parallel to High St. (see below), continues up past the wharves to *Drypool Bridge*. To the W, the Humber Dock (1803–09; John Rennie) and Railway Dock (1846; Jesse Hartley of Liverpool) have been reclaimed as the *Hull Marina*. The old *Spurn Lightship* (1927) is moored here. A promenade with marine artefacts and modern sculpture is on the E side; the lock-keeper's cottage survives at the S end and a seven-storey warehouse by the junction of the two docks, to the W.

THE OLD TOWN: NORTH FROM MARKET PLACE. Lowgate continues Market Place to the N, past the *Market Hall* (1902–04) and the *Hepworths Arcade* (1894) on the left. Beyond, on the right, the pavement cuts through the tower of the Perpendicular church of *St Mary* (enlarged by Sir Gilbert Scott in 1861). The narrow Bishop Lane leads to High St., once the city's main street, between Lowgate and the river. *Maister House* (NT), a merchant's house of 1744, has a Palladian entrance hall and *staircase, decorated by Joseph Page with ironwork by Robert Bakewell of Derby; the rest of the building is not open.

In the former Corn Exchange, opposite, is the **Hull and East Riding Museum**, with horse-drawn vehicles, early motor cars and motor bicycles. The *prehistoric, Roman and Saxon antiquities include an Iron Age log boat discovered near Holme-on-Spalding Moor, late Bronze Age/early Iron Age images from Roos Carr and a Viking sword from Skerne. The Roman collection is shown with a display of Romano-British mosaics from both sides of the Humber, notably the mosaic from Horkstow and pavements from Rudston and Brantingham.

Further on are the *Nelson Mandela Gardens*, a walled enclosure around a pool containing a statue of Minerva. A new *Transport Museum* is being built behind the garden; the first phase (opened in 1988) houses Hull's only surviving tram, the Kitson steam tram (c 1882), and the Ryde Pier tram (1871). N of the garden is ***Wilberforce House** (open), a 17C merchant's house where Charles I was entertained in 1639. It was Georgianised shortly before William Wilberforce was born here in 1759. Its displays deal with the history of slavery and the campaign for its abolition. The museum extends into the neighbouring Georgian houses, restored after wartime damage; the complex includes period rooms with Hull silver, costumes, arms and artefacts. A yard at the rear, with a chemist's shop (c 1900) removed from Leeds, leads to a garden giving on to the riverside wharves.

Further N in High St. a section of the old wood-block paving has been renewed. The warehouses, now converted into flats, include the city's earliest industrial building, *Pease Warehouse* (1759). The return to the modern centre can be made via Alfred Gelder St., to the left, past the site of the new Crown Courts and the *Guildhall* (1907–16; Sir Edwin Cooper).

In High St. N of Alfred Gelder St. stands the Georgian *Blaydes House* (open by appointment). Remains of the medieval walls have been excavated in North Walls, opposite. The citadel (1541), one of Henry VIII's last defensive works, has been excavated on the E bank of the Hull close to the site of the old *Victoria Dock*, filled in during the 1970s. High St. is continued N by Dock Office Row and, beyond North Bridge, Wincolmlee. Charterhouse Lane, on the left, has the *Charterhouse Chapel* (open) in the 18C almshouses.

WESTERN OUTSKIRTS. In Cottingham Rd, 2¼m NW of the centre, is the **University of Hull**, founded as University College in 1925 and raised to university status in 1954. *Middleton Hall* contains the University Art Collection, largely of British art from 1890 to 1940. Further W, the old village of *Cottingham* has a fine Decorated and Perpendicular church with the over-restored brass of Nicholas de Luda (d. 1384), the rector who built the chancel.

A63, the Selby road, leads W from Hull to (4½m) *Hessle* and (7½m) *North Ferriby*, the starting-point of the Wolds Way, a long-distance footpath leading to (79m) Filey (Route 82B). From Hessle the **Humber Bridge** (toll; TI at North Bank Viewing Area), opened in 1981, crosses to *Barton-upon-Humber* (Route 48).

HOLDERNESS. This flat region stretches S and E of Hull between the Humber and the North Sea, with resorts at *Withernsea* (6000 inhabitants), 20½m E, and *Hornsea* (7200 inhabitants; seasonal TI), 18½m NE. *Hornsea Mere* has a bird sanctuary.

A1033, the main road to Withernsea, runs via (6m) *Hedon* (4500 inhabitants), a port before Hull was dreamt of, and (16m) *Patrington*, each with an excellent church. Hedon *church, known as the 'King of Holderness', has a Decorated nave, Early English choir and transepts, and a Perpendicular tower. The tracery in the windows of the three E bays of the nave is exceptionally fine. Patrington *church, the 'Queen of Holderness', with a tall central spire, is Decorated work. The W window, the vaulted Lady Chapel in the S transept, the Easter Sepulchre and the capitals should all be noted. Andrew Marvell (1621–78) was born at the rectory in *Winestead*, 1½m NW of Patrington. From Patrington B1445 goes on to (6m) *Easington*, where the North Sea gas pipeline comes ashore. The coast ends in *Spurn Head*, 13m from Patrington or Withernsea, a causeway of sand and pebbles overgrown with sharp-pointed rushes. The last 4m of the road run through a nature reserve, with a bird migration observatory. No trace has survived of the port of *Ravenspur*, where the future Henry IV landed 'upon the naked shore' in 1399 and Edward IV arrived on his return from exile in 1471, nor of its Danish predecessor *Ravenscar*, the 'Hrafnseyrr' of Icelandic saga, from which Olaf, son of Harald Hardarda, set sail after his father's defeat at Stamford Bridge in 1066. The medieval cross of *Kilnsea*, another eroded village, still stands at Hedon.

B1238 branches E from A165, the main Hull–Bridlington road, to (8m) *Sproatley* and (12m) *Aldbrough*, where B1242 continues up the coast to Hornsea. *Burton Constable Hall* (open), 1½m N of Sproatley, is an Elizabethan house altered in the 18C, with work by Thomas Lightoler, Thomas Atkinson and James Wyatt inside. Beyond Hornsea the coast road continues to (14m) Bridlington (Route 82B) via (5½m) *Skipsea*, with a large motte-and-bailey castle (EH).

From Hull to *Lincoln* and *Peterborough* via the *Humber Bridge*, see Route 48; to *Selby* and to *Doncaster*, see Route 81.

B. York to Bridlington

Directions. Total distance 40m. **York**, see Route 81. A1079 to (3¼m) Grimston. A166 to (28m) Great Driffield and (40m) **Bridlington**.

York, see Route 81. A1079 heads E from Walmgate Bar. At (3¼m) *Grimston* A166 branches left. The *Yorkshire Museum of Farming*, occupying an 8-acre site at *Murton*, on the left, has livestock, exhibitions, crafts and special events. 8m: *Stamford Bridge*, over the Derwent and the Humberside border, was the scene of King Harold's victory over Harald Hardrada of Norway shortly before his defeat at Hastings in 1066. A166 reaches the Wolds. The sideroads leading N to Malton (Route 83) and S to Pocklington (Route 82A) run through out-of-the-way country and quiet villages. There is interesting Norman work in the local churches, for example at *Bishop Wilton*, a charming village in a combe 1m S of (12½m) *Garrowby Hill*, and at (19m) *Fridaythorpe*, on top of the Wolds.

B1251 branches NE from Fridaythorpe to (5½m) *Sledmere*. Sledmere House (open) was begun in 1751 and completed by the agricultural reformer Sir Christopher Sykes in the 1780s. The plaster decoration by Joseph Rose was restored after a fire in 1911, when the Turkish room was also added. There is a good collection of 18C furniture and paintings. In the park laid out by Capability Brown stands the parish church (1898; Temple Moore) and in the village, a memorial to the Yorkshire Waggoners, the regiment raised by Sir Mark Sykes in 1912, and an imitation Eleanor Cross (1900; Temple Moore) converted into a war memorial.

Several interesting routes lead over the Wolds from Sledmere. The first goes NW on B1253, continued by B1248, to (11½m) Malton (Route 83). At 4m it passes *Duggleby*, about 3m NE of the deserted medieval village and church of *Wharram Percy* (EH). At (7m) *North Grimston* the church has one of the crudely carved Norman *fonts for which the district is noted. The second follows B1253 E to (16½m) Bridlington (see below). At 2½m it passes the turning on the right for *Cowlam*, with another Norman font. At 5m it crosses B1249, about 1½m N of *Langtoft*, with the Norman font from the disused church at nearby Cottam. At 10½m it passes *Rudston*, with an early Norman church tower and, in the churchyard, a huge menhir 25ft high. The third route from Sledmere goes SE on B1252 to rejoin A166 at (5m) Garton-on-the-Wolds (see below), passing (2½m) a good viewpoint at the striking memorial to Sir Tatton Sykes (d. 1863) on *Garton Hill*.

The church at (25m) *Garton-on-the-Wolds* was rebuilt by J.L. Pearson (1856–57) and G.E. Street (1871–80), with frescoes by Clayton and Bell. It is perhaps the most impressive result of the campaign by Sir Tatton Sykes and his son, also Sir Tatton. 28m: **Great Driffield** (9100 inhabitants), often just called Driffield, is a pleasant agricultural town with a fine 15C church tower.

Kirkburn, 3½m SW, has a Norman *church with rich carvings, a Norman font and an unusual tower staircase (c 1200). *Bainton*, about 2m further SW, has a church of 1335 with the elaborate tomb of Sir Edmund de Mauley (d. 1314).

At (33¼m) *Burton Agnes* the church contains the extraordinary monument of Sir Henry Griffith (d. 1654). He built *Burton Agnes Hall* (open), a red-brick mansion designed by Robert Smythson, in 1598–1610.

The entrance is by a splendid turreted gatehouse. The house itself contains a Great Hall with carved stone screen, a fine oak staircase, a Long Gallery and, throughout the house, good ceilings, panelling and chimneypieces. The collection of paintings is particularly strong in Impressionist and Post-Impressionist work. Nearby stands the original Norman manor house, altered in the 17C and 18C (EH, all year).

40m: **Bridlington** (29,300 inhabitants; TI) is a resort on the wide sweep of Bridlington Bay. William Kent (1685–1748) was born here. The *Church in the old town to the N uses the Early English to Perpendicular nave of the old priory church, founded for Augustinian canons in 1113. Note the W façade, the N porch and elegant arcades. The neighbouring *Bayle Gate* dates from c 1388.

FROM BRIDLINGTON TO THE FLAMBOROUGH PENINSULA. B1255 runs NE past the turning for (2m) *Sewerby Hall* (open), on the cliffs to the S, a Georgian mansion in a fine park. 3½m: The *Danes' Dyke*, in fact a pre-Roman earthwork, runs across the peninsula. 4m: *Flamborough* church, partly Norman and Early English, has a 16C *rood loft. B1259 continues to the headland at the sheer chalk cliffs of (6m) **Flamborough Head**, a sanctuary for sea birds during the breeding season. The best scenery (rock stacks, caves, etc.) is on the N side, reached by B1255 from Flamborough village. It was off Flamborough Head that the American privateer Paul Jones captured the British ship 'Seramis' after a bloody fight in 1779; his own ship, the 'Bonhomme Richard', sank the next day. From here B1229 runs along the cliffs via (3m) *Bempton* and (6m) *Speeton* to join the Bridlington–Scarborough detour described below.

FROM BRIDLINGTON TO FILEY AND SCARBOROUGH, 17m by A165. The road leaves Humberside for North Yorkshire and is joined by the road from Flamborough Head just before (6½m) *Reighton*, where the church has a fine Norman font. 10½m: **Filey** (5700 inhabitants; seasonal TI), to the E, is a resort on Filey Bay at the NE tip of the Wolds. Two long-distance footpaths meet here: the Wolds Way (79m), heading S to North Ferriby and Hessle Haven on the Humber (Route 82A), and the Cleveland Way (93m), heading up the coast and round the North York Moors National Park to Helmsley (Route 84). The beach stretches below the cliffs to the low rocky spit of *Filey Brigg*. The church of St Oswald mixes Early English with traces of Norman work. At

Hunmanby, a large and attractive village 3m SW, the partly Norman church has 19C furnishings. There are good sea views on the way to (17m) *Scarborough* (Route 83).

From Bridlington to *Hull*, see Route 82A.

83

York to Scarborough

Directions. Total distance 41m. **York**, see Route 81. A64 to (17½m) Malton (bypassed), (41m) **Scarborough**.

York, see Route 81. A64 heads NE across the York plain. 10½m: *Barton Hill* lies 1m SE of *Foston*, where Sydney Smith was rector in 1809–29.

The unclassified road going N from Barton Hill is continued by the five-mile avenue of *Castle Howard (open), the vast baroque mansion which Sir John Vanbrugh, helped by Nicholas Hawksmoor, built for Charles Howard, 3rd Earl of Carlisle.

Vanbrugh produced his first designs in 1699 and finished the main body of the house by 1712, though he was still at work on the grounds and garden buildings when he died in 1726. The fact that he came to the project apparently without architectural experience has provoked speculation about the extent of Hawksmoor's contribution. The N and S fronts and the striking central dome show the same blend of monumentality and exuberance as Blenheim Palace, the other great fruit of Vanbrugh and Hawksmoor's collaboration. The W wing was completed in a more restrained Palladian style by Sir Thomas Robinson of Rokeby Park (Route 86G) in 1753–59.

Inside, the magnificent Great Hall has an elaborate chimneypiece and a painting by Giovanni Pellegrini in the dome. The room was restored after the fire which badly damaged the S front in 1940, though the Music Room and the Tapestry Room also keep some of their original decoration. The impressive collection of pictures and furniture is shown to its best advantage in the Orleans Room, with paintings by Rubens and Domenico Feti, and the Long Gallery, added in 1800, with portraits by Holbein (Henry VIII; the 3rd Duke of Norfolk), Van Dyck, Lely and Kneller. The Chapel, altered in 1870–75, has a bas-relief by Sansovino and stained glass by Morris and Burne-Jones.

The stable block (1781–84; John Carr) to the W of the house contains the largest private collection of historic costume in Britain, with original specimens mainly from the early 18C to the present day; also costumes from the Diaghilev Russian ballet.

With its magnificent avenue, obelisks, gatehouses and lakes, the park creates a formal 18C landscape on the grandest scale. The garden buildings include, both SE of the house, Vanbrugh's Temple of the Four Winds and Hawksmoor's *Mausoleum.

Sheriff Hutton, 4m W of Foston, has the ruins of its 14C castle. The church contains 14–15C effigies, one of them probably of Richard III's son Edward (1471–84), and the brass of two babies (1491).

11½m: *Whitwell-on-the-Hill* is to the left. To the right, in an attractive setting on the opposite bank of the Derwent, are the scanty but beautiful ruins of *Kirkham Priory*, an Augustinian foundation of 1122 (EH, all year). They include the sculptured gatehouse and the *lavatorium in the cloister, both late 13C, and the Romanesque refectory doorway. To the left of A64 further on is another turning for (3m) Castle Howard, via *Welburn*.

17½m: **Malton** (4100 inhabitants; seasonal TI), bypassed by A64, is a market town on the Derwent, with two partly 12C churches. It stands on the site of the Roman Derventio, and the *Museum* in the 18C former Town

Hall has a good Roman collection. Across the river is *Norton* (5900 inhabitants). At *Old Malton*, 1m NE, the late Norman and Early English parish church with a beautiful W front and aisleless nave is a relic of the Gilbertine priory founded c 1150.

Castle Howard, 6m SW, is reached by the sideroad which passes (3m) *Easthorpe Hall* (not open), the home of Dickens's friend Charles Smithson (d. 1844), who entertained the novelist while he was writing 'Martin Chuzzlewit'.

A169 heads N to (7m) Pickering (Route 84), past (4½m) the turning for *Flamingo Land*, a zoo and amusement park at *Kirby Misperton*, 1½m W.

FROM MALTON TO HELMSLEY, 15m by B1257. 4½m: *Barton-le-Street* has a rebuilt church with Norman carving. 6m: *Slingsby* has the ruins of an early 17C country house. 8m: *Hovingham*, a pleasant village, has a church with a Saxon tower, cross and sculptured stone panel which may have been part of an altar or tomb. *Hovingham Hall* (open to parties only, by appointment) is a Palladian house designed c 1750 by its owner, Sir Thomas Worsley. *Nunnington Hall* (NT), by the Rye 2½m N, is a 16C and late 17C manor house with a fine staircase, panelling and chimneypieces. It contains a collection of miniature rooms furnished in the style of different periods. From (12m) *Oswaldkirk* Route 84 leads to (15m) *Helmsley*.

From Malton to *Sledmere* and *Great Driffield*, see Route 82B.

A64 skirts the northern escarpment of the Wolds, with the flat Vale of Pickering on the left. Beyond (22½m) the attractive spire of *Rillington* church the road passes, on the left, the park of *Scampston Hall* (1803; Thomas Leverton). 27½m: *East Heslerton* church was built in 1877 by G.E. Street for Sir Tatton Sykes of Sledmere (Route 82B). The spire has statues of the Four Latin Fathers designed for Bristol Cathedral but rejected as unProtestant. There is a fine view from the Wolds escarpment above (33½m) *Staxton*. Shortly beyond, A1039 branches right for Filey (Route 82B). A64 goes N via (36½m) *Seamer*.

41m: **SCARBOROUGH** (53,600 inhabitants), the most popular resort in the North-East, is splendidly situated on two bays separated by a rocky headland crowned with the ruined castle. The seafront is laid out with pleasant irregularity, and the cliffs of both bays are covered with gardens.

TI: St Nicholas Cliff. **Coach Stations**: Westwood and William St. **Railway Station**: Junction of Valley Bridge Rd and Westborough. **Theatres**: The Spa (see below); Royal Opera House, St Thomas St.; Futurist Theatre, South Bay; Library Theatre, Vernon Rd; and Theatre in the Round, Valley Bridge Parade, known for its premieres of plays by Alan Ayckbourn.

History. The headland has been the site of an Iron Age settlement, a Roman beacon, Saxon and Norman chapels, and the castle, built in a seemingly impregnable position 300ft above the sea. The fishing village developed as a spa town after the discovery of mineral springs in 1620 and as a seaside resort in the second half of the 18C—probably the first place in England where sea-bathing became fashionable. Smollett's 'Humphry Clinker' (1771) and Sheridan's 'A Trip to Scarborough' (1777) testify to its early popularity.

Natives, etc. The painter Lord Leighton (1830–96) and Dame Edith Sitwell (1887–1964) were born here and the painter Atkinson Grimshaw lived here after 1876. Anne Brontë (1820–49) died at a house on the site of the Grand Hotel and is buried in the detached churchyard of St Mary.

The main street, known as Westborough, Newborough and Eastborough, descends NE from the *Railway Station* to the old fishing harbour on **South Bay**. Nearby are the house (c 1350) where Richard III is said to have stayed and the 17C *Three Mariners Inn* (open).

To the N the broad Marine Drive sweeps round the base of the headland and continues as Royal Albert Drive to (1½m) the quieter **North Bay**, with *Northstead Manor Gardens*. Above are *Alexandra Gardens* and *Peasholm Park*, with a boating lake and glen.

The only way that a Member of Parliament may resign his seat is by accepting the stewardship of the Manor of Northstead, or that of the Chiltern Hundreds in Buckinghamshire, both offices of profit under the Crown and incompatible with parliamentary duties.

Immediately above the harbour the steep streets of the old town climb to Castle Rd. Here stands the parish church of *St Mary* (c 1180), with four vaulted 14C chapels opening off the S aisle. Its choir and N transept were destroyed during the siege of the castle in 1645. Anne Brontë is buried in the detached part of the churchyard, E of the church. Of the ruined **Castle** (EH, all year), the chief remains are the keep (1158–64) and the 13C barbican by which it is approached across the moat. On the cliff are foundations of the 4C Roman signal station.

Piers Gaveston was besieged and captured here by the Earl of Pembroke in 1312. Parliamentarian sieges during the Civil War starved the castle into surrender in 1645 and 1648. It was slighted after its final capture, and further damaged when a German battleship bombarded it in 1914. George Fox, the Quaker, was imprisoned here in 1665–66.

SW of the headland and the harbour the sweep of South Bay begins with *St Nicholas Cliff* and its gardens, and continues with the steep ravine of the *Valley Gardens*. St Nicholas St., on top of the cliff, has the *Town Hall* in a converted mansion (1852; H.J. Wyatt). Further inland, the early 19C Crescent has the *Art Gallery*, with local scenes and work by Lord Leighton and Atkinson Grimshaw, and the *Natural History Museum* in Woodend, once the Sitwell family's villa. The *Rotunda Museum* in the Valley is an early purpose-built museum (1829), with displays of local archaeology and social history. Overlooking the sea stands the monumental *Grand Hotel* (1863–67; Cuthbert Brodrick of Leeds).

The Valley is spanned by *Valley Bridge* and, nearer the sea, *Spa Bridge*, leading to the *Spa* and its gardens at the foot of the South Cliff. It includes a concert hall, theatre, restaurant and ballroom. The pretty *South Cliff Gardens* (views) stretch along the cliff face. The church of *St Martin-on-the-Hill* (1863; G.F. Bodley) has a splendid Morris and Co. interior, with stained glass, pulpit, altar and reredos by Morris, Burne-Jones, Rossetti and Ford Madox Brown and a huge organ case by Bodley himself.

Off the Filey Rd, further S, is *Oliver's Mount* (500ft) with a prominent war memorial and wide views.

The Cleveland Way passes through Scarborough on its way up the coast from Filey (Route 82B). To the S, *Cornelian Bay* (2½m), *Cayton Bay* (3½m) and *Gristhorpe Cliff* (5m) lie on its course; to the N, *Cloughton Wyke* (4½m) and *Hayburn Wyke* (6m; see also Route 84).

From Scarborough to *Filey* and *Bridlington*, see Route 82B; to *Pickering* and to *Whitby*, see Route 84.

84

The North York Moors: York to Whitby

Directions. Total distance 57½m. **York**, see Route 81. B1363 to (20m) Oswaldkirk. B1257, A170 to (23½m) Helmsley. A170 to (36½m) Pickering. A169, A171 to (57½m) **Whitby**. Walkers need the two OS Outdoor Leisure maps (2½in to 1m).

The **North York Moors** stretch from the sharply defined western escarpment of the Hambleton Hills and Cleveland Hills across to the coast between Scarborough and Staithes, N of Whitby. The central hills, covered with heather, rise to about 1400ft and create an open landscape with wide views. The drainage runs off in deep parallel valleys—long to the S, where all the streams eventually join the Derwent, and short to the N, where they flow into the Esk. In the dales the scenery is green and sometimes wooded. Here, too, the sandstone and limestone which predominate among the moorland rocks can be seen in the houses which line the characteristically wide village streets and in the ruined abbeys which are among the region's great attractions. Both the dales and the moors make excellent walking country. As well as many shorter excursions, there are several long-distance routes: the Cleveland Way (108m), starting at Helmsley, the Lyke Wake Walk (40m) from Osmotherley to Ravenscar, and the eastern part of A. Wainwright's Coast-to-Coast Walk, from Osmotherley to Robin Hood's Bay.

Since 1952 the region has been a National Park, with a Visitors' Centre at Danby and information centres at Sutton Bank and Helmsley. Further information can be obtained by post from the National Park Authority, The Old Vicarage, Bondgate, Helmsley, York YO6 5BP.

York, see Route 81. B1363 heads due N to (8m) *Sutton-on-the-Forest*, whose name recalls the old royal Forest of Galtres. Sutton Park (limited opening) is an early Georgian house with good plasterwork, furniture, pictures and porcelain. Laurence Sterne was vicar from 1738 and lived here until 1759. In 1741 he also acquired the living of (10½m) *Stillington*. The road climbs to (15½m) the summit of the *Howardian Hills* and then drops down to (18m) *Gilling*, or *Gilling East*. The castle (hall and Great Chamber open) stands on medieval foundations but is chiefly interesting for its Tudor and Georgian alterations. The *Great Chamber (c 1575–85) has a decorated plaster ceiling, painted frieze, wood panelling and chimneypiece, and painted glass. At (20m) *Oswaldkirk*, on the edge of the National Park, B1363 joins the detour from Malton in Route 83.

An unclassified road leads W beneath the limestone escarpment of the Hambleton Hills to (2m) *Ampleforth*, where there is a Benedictine priory, founded in 1802, with a public school. 5m: **Byland Abbey** (EH, all year), one of Yorkshire's great Cistercian foundations, established itself here in 1177. The chief remains are the striking W front, with the fragment of a rose window above the row of lancets, and the S transept of the church, which has 12–13C *tiles. The museum displays carved stones and tiles. 6½m: *Coxwold* is a delightful village, popular with visitors. Sterne was perpetual curate here from 1760 until his death in 1768, writing part of 'Tristram Shandy' and 'A Sentimental Journey' at the house he renamed Shandy Hall (open). The building dates from c 1450.

Sterne's pulpit still stands in the Perpendicular church, with its unusual octagonal tower. His body was reburied near the S wall in 1969. *Newburgh Priory* (limited opening), just SE, is a 16–18C house on the site of a 12C Augustinian foundation. It preserves a tomb said to contain the headless body of Oliver Cromwell. *Kilburn*, 2¼m NW of Coxwold beneath Roulston Scar and the 19C White Horse, housed the village workshop of Robert Thompson (d. 1955) whose woodcarving, signed with a mouse, adorns many Yorkshire churches.

B1257 and A170 lead N from Oswaldkirk to (23½m) **Helmsley** (1400 inhabitants; seasonal TI and National Park office), a pleasant little town at the foot of the Hambleton Hills and a popular centre for visitors to the moors. To the W of the large market place are the ruins of the 12C *Castle* (EH, all year), with large earthworks and a range altered in the 16C. The house and gardens of the 18–19C *Duncombe Park*, under 1m SW, are open.

*Rievaulx Abbey (EH, all year plus Mondays in winter) stands in a beautiful setting in *Ryedale*, off B1257 2½m NW of Helmsley. Its name, pronounced 'Reevo', preserves the Anglo-Norman form of the valley's name. Founded in 1131, the earliest of Yorkshire's Cistercian houses, it grew to become one of the greatest. Its ruins are as substantial and well preserved as those of Fountains and Kirkstall, and perhaps more beautiful.

The slope of the valley forced the monks to build their church on a N–S, rather than W–E, axis (though in the description which follows the ecclesiastical rather than the actual compass points are used). Of the Norman nave (c 1140), which had a galilee porch at the W end and side chapels in the aisles, little remains except the base of the outer walls and the stumps of the pillars. The transepts combine Norman with Early English work, while the *choir (c 1230) is Early English at its best.

Of the domestic buildings to the S, the most interesting are grouped around the main cloister, where a fragment of the original arcade has been reconstructed. The late 12C Chapter House in the E range is apsidal, an unusual feature in a Cistercian foundation; the shrine of the first abbot, William (d. 1148), is by the entrance. Between the warming house and kitchen in the S range stands the massive Early English Refectory, with remains of a lavatorium on either side of the door and of a pulpitum inside.

Rievaulx Terrace (NT), entered separately from B1257, was laid out as part of Duncombe Park in the 1750s to command a *view of the dale and abbey ruins. There are two classical temples, one Doric and one Ionic.

Beyond Rievaulx B1257 skirts Ryedale on the E and continues up *Bilsdale*, at the head of which *Urra* earthwork runs along the crest of the hill for c 3m. The road crosses the Cleveland Hills en route to (20m) Stokesley, on the detour from Whitby to Teesside described below. At 1½m a sideroad on the left leads across the valley to (4½m) *Hawnby*, at the E foot of the Hambleton Hills.

A charming lane climbs W from Rievaulx to join A170, the main Helmsley–Thirsk road, a little short of (4m) the top of *Sutton Bank* (TI), where a wide and sudden view extends across the York plain to the Pennines. The descent to Thirsk (Route 85A) is notoriously steep and perilous.

The Cleveland Way, a long-distance footpath (108m), takes a circuitous route from Helmsley along the W and N escarpment of the moors to Saltburn-by-the-Sea and then down the coast through Whitby and Scarborough to Filey (Route 82). Its first stage passes Rievaulx on the way to Sutton Bank; here it turns N to join the old drove road across the Hambleton Hills via *Hesketh Dike* and many earthworks and standing stones to (c 10m) *Osmotherley*, near Mount Grace Priory (Route 85A). Osmotherley is also the starting-point of the Lyke Wake Walk to Ravenscar and the North York Moors section of A. Wainwright's Coast-to-Coast Walk to Robin Hood's Bay.

From Helmsley to *Malton*, see Route 83.

At Helmsley the main route turns E on A170, skirting the S fringe of the moors and the National Park. Beyond (26¾m) *Nawton* a sideroad branches ½m N to the prettily wooded *Kirkdale*, where St Gregory's Minster has a *sundial commemorating the rebuilding of the church in the reign of

Edward the Confessor (c 1050). In the quarry face by the ford stood the Kirkdale Cave, discovered in 1821, which yielded a rich haul of lion, hyena, rhinoceros and mammoth bones of the pre-glacial period. 29½m: *Kirkbymoorside* has a handsome High St. off the main road.

A sideroad runs N to (3m) *Gillamoor*, with a surprise view of the moors just beyond the church, and continues up the W side of *Farndale*, noted for its daffodils. Beyond (7m) *Low Mill* the route is one-way and can be crowded in spring. There is also a pleasant riverside walk (3m) from the car park at Low Mill to Church Houses. Motorists can return down the E side of the valley to *Hutton-le-Hole*, a charming village popular with visitors. The Ryedale Folk Museum has exhibits illustrating daily life in the region, and a splendid open-air section with reconstructed buildings (medieval cruck house, 16C manor, 18C cottage, etc.).

Lastingham, 2m E of Hutton-le-Hole, is a pretty village beneath Spaunton Moor. Its church, begun c 1078, has an early Norman *crypt with pre-Conquest stone-carving. Beneath it is buried St Cedd, founder in 654 of the original Saxon monastery destroyed by the Danes. *Appleton-le-Moors*, 2m S of Lastingham, keeps its medieval plan. *Cropton*, 2m SE of Lastingham, has a ruined castle with a view of Rosedale.

A fine *road heads N from Hutton-le-Hole along *Blakey Ridge* to (13m) Castleton (see below), keeping above 1000ft for much of the way. At (8m) the crossroads, with wide views, stands Ralph Cross, one of the traditional crosses which mark boundaries and routes on the moors. Another, the curious Fat Betty, stands on the Rosedale Abbey road just to the right.

Rosedale Abbey, 4m NE of Hutton-le-Hole by the direct road, is another popular village. Its churchyard has a fragment of the Cistercian nunnery founded here in the mid 12C. The crests of the surrounding hills were worked for ironstone in the 19C and early 20C, and the course of the railway line which linked the mines makes an interesting walk. Impressive mine ruins can be seen on the path leading from Hill Cottages, 1½m up the dale from Rosedale Abbey.

Rievaulx Abbey from the south east

35m: *Middleton* church has three 10C wheel-head crosses. 36½m:
Pickering (5900 inhabitants) is a plain little town with a *Castle* (EH, all year)
where Richard II was held for a time after his abdication. It has a 13C shell
keep and 14C curtain wall. The Norman and Decorated *Church* has a
Norman font, but its chief interest is the series of wall paintings (c 1450) in
the nave, drastically restored in the 19C. The *Beck Isle Museum*, in a
Regency house, has exhibits of local history and folk life.

Between April and October the privately owned *North Yorkshire Moors Railway*
operates a regular steam and diesel service up the narrow, wooded *Newtondale* to
(18m) Grosmont in Eskdale (see the detour from Whitby to Middlesbrough, below). It
stops at Levisham, Newtondale Halt and Goathland, and connects at Grosmont with
the BR service between Whitby and Middlesbrough. The moors railway was built as
a horse-drawn tramway by George Stephenson in 1836 and converted to steam by
George Hudson, the Railway King, in 1845.

FROM PICKERING TO SCARBOROUGH. A170, the direct road, takes 17m. 6m: *Ebberston
Hall* (open), on the left, is a little villa by Colen Campbell (1718). At (9¼m) *Brompton
Wordsworth* married Mary Hutchinson in 1802. 10½m: *Wykeham* (pronounced
'Wickam') has a church built by Butterfield in 1853. 17m: *Scarborough*, see Route 83.
   A more interesting alternative route branches N from A170 at (2½m) the charming
village of *Thornton Dale* and takes the forest drive (toll) via (5¾m) *Low Dalby* (Forestry
Commission Visitor Centre), (11m) *Bickley* and (13m) *Langdale End* to (15m) *Hackness*.
By the late 18C Hackness Hall (not open) stands the Norman and Early English parish
church, with a Perpendicular font cover, Jacobean pulpit, and monument by Chantrey
to Mrs Johnstone (d. 1819). A Saxon cross bears inscriptions in Latin and what is
apparently a variant of Ogham. There are several ways of completing the journey from
Hackness to Scarborough. The shortest (21m in all) goes E to (16m) *Suffield* and then
descends, with a superb view, to join A171 at (18m) *Scalby*. A second route (23½m)
follows the Derwent and the lovely wooded *Forge Valley* to rejoin A170 at 19m,
between *West Ayton* and *East Ayton*. A third route (22m) branches E from the Forge
Valley to A171 via Lady Edith's Drive.
   From Pickering to *Malton*, see Route 83.

A169 heads N from Pickering and climbs to the open moor. 42m: A steep
sideroad leads left to the moorland villages of (½m) *Lockton* and (1½m)
Levisham, with unusual views of the deep dales below them. Levisham
church, with a Saxon chancel arch, stands by the Beck. 45½m: *Saltergate
Inn* stands on the old pack route by which Whitby salt was taken to
Pickering market for distribution throughout Yorkshire, and near the head
of the *Hole of Horcum*, where the moor has been eroded by the springs that
rise on its slopes. On the descent to (47½m) *Eller Beck Bridge* the ominous
white radar domes of the Ballistic Missile Early Warning Station (1963)
dominate *Fylingdales Moor* to the right.

Beyond the bridge a road branches left across the moor to (2½m) *Goathland*, a good
centre for walking. The village maintains a tradition of folk dancing by the Plough
Stotts (sword dancers). The 70ft drop of *Mallyan Spout* is 1m SW. On *Wheeldale Moor*,
3m SW, over 1m of *Roman road has been exposed (EH).

A long, steep descent leads to (53m) *Sleights*, where the road leaves the
National Park. In a wooded setting on the Little Beck 3½m SE is the 40ft
waterfall of *Falling Foss*. For the network of sideroads leading W through
Eskdale, see the detour from Whitby to Middlesbrough below. A169 crosses
the Esk and, at 55m, A171 heads E.

   57½m: **WHITBY** (13,800 inhabitants; TI), a fishing port and once a centre
for whaling and ship-building, is probably the most handsome town on the
NE coast. Red-tiled houses rise up the steep banks of the Esk above the

busy harbour. The East Cliff is crowned by the superb combination of parish church, graveyard and abbey ruins, the West Cliff by the holiday resort developed in the 19C.

The two William Scoresbys, father (1760–1829) and son (1789–1857), were both natives. Captain Cook (1728–79) served his apprenticeship with a local shipping firm and made his first voyage round the world in Whitby-built ships. Elizabeth Gaskell made Whitby the 'Monkshaven' of 'Sylvia's Lovers' (1863), while in Bram Stoker's novel (1897) Count Dracula makes his landfall in England during a storm in the harbour and takes refuge in St Mary's churchyard. The novelist Storm Jameson (1891–1986) was born at Whitby.

The road from York passes Pannett Park, where the *Museum* contains a good collection of local geology, archaeology and natural history, a section devoted to Captain Cook and other Whitby sailors, and a display of Whitby jet ornaments. The neighbouring *Art Gallery* has local paintings. Baxter-gate leads to the swing bridge (1908) over the Esk. On the opposite bank is Grape Lane, to the right, with the *Captain Cook Memorial Museum* in the late 17C house where he served as an apprentice. The picturesque Church St. is the main thoroughfare of the old fishermen's quarter. From its N end a flight of 199 steps climbs to *St Mary's Church* on top of the East Cliff, its interior a charming muddle of 17–18C galleries and box pews and a three-decker pulpit. The Cholmley Pew (c 1700) almost obscures the Norman chancel arch. The churchyard contains weatherbeaten 18C tomb-stones and a 19C cross commemorating the poet Caedmon (d. c 680), a monk at the abbey.

*Whitby Abbey** (EH, all year plus Mondays in winter) lies beyond the churchyard, romantically placed on the cliffs 200ft above the sea.

The house for monks and nuns founded in 657 by St Hilda of Hartlepool became important enough to serve as host to the Synod of Whitby (664), at which repre-sentatives of the Roman and Celtic churches met to discuss differences in custom and practice. The abbey was destroyed by the Danes in 867 but refounded for the Benedictines in 1078.

Nothing visible survives of the Saxon abbey, which lay slightly to the N of later buildings; the outline of the apsidal Norman church is marked within the walls of the present ruin. This is largely Early English, begun c 1220, though the change to Decorated (in the 14C) can be seen towards the W end. The central tower and much of the S side have vanished, and the W end was further damaged by a German battlecruiser in 1914. However, the N side of the nave, the N transept and the E end, with its rows of lancets, testify to the magnificence and delicacy of the building. A row of arches from the nave has been re-erected by the boundary wall to the N. The domestic buildings, which stood to the S, have gone but part of their site is occupied by the late 17C mansion of the Cholmleys, now derelict.

The West Cliff, its top marked by whalebones and a statue of Captain Cook, is the holiday quarter of Whitby, with a promenade and the so-called *Spa* (concert hall, theatre, etc.). East Terrace (c 1850; John Dobson of Newcastle) is part of the early development of the resort undertaken by George Hudson, the Railway King.

FROM WHITBY TO SCARBOROUGH, 19½m by the hilly A171. From (2½m) *Hawkser* B1447 leads left to the coast at (2m) **Robin Hood's Bay**, a picturesque fishing village on a steep slope, overrun with tourists in summer. A. Wainwright's Coast-to-Coast Walk via Osmotherley from St Bees Head ends here. A171 crosses *Fylingdales Moor*, with its radar domes conspicuous on the right (see above). From (14m) *Cloughton*, on the edge of the National Park, a sideroad leads N via (1½m) *Hayburn Wyke*, a wooded dell laid out with a labyrinth of walks, and over *Staintondale Moor* to (5½m) *Ravenscar*, a resort at the N end of a range of fine cliffs. The Lyke Wake Walk from Osmotherley ends here. 19½m: *Scarborough*, see Route 83.

FROM WHITBY TO MIDDLESBROUGH VIA ESKDALE. A171, the main road, goes via Guisborough and misses Eskdale, which lies to the S. This route turns S from it on A169 to (4½m) *Sleights* and then heads W on hilly and meandering sideroads. 7m: *Grosmont* is the terminus of the North Yorkshire Moors Railway from Pickering (see above), connecting with the BR line from Whitby to Middlesborough. Near (9m) *Egton Bridge* is the ornate Roman Catholic church of St Hedda (1866). It was the parish of Father Postgate, executed for his faith in 1679 at the age of 83. 11½m: *Glaisdale* stands at the mouth of a beautiful side valley. The Beggar's Bridge (1619) crosses the Esk nearby. The present route crosses the Esk at (13m) *Lealholm* to reach (17m) *Danby*, with the North York Moors National Park Centre. To the NE rises *Danby Beacon* (981ft); to the SE lies the ruined 14C *Danby Castle* (not open but visible from the road), near the medieval Duck Bridge over the Esk. 19m: *Castleton*, a good centre for moorland walks, stands at the N end of the road along Blakey Ridge from Hutton-le-Hole (see above). The church (1924–26) has woodcarving by Thompson of Kilburn. 21½m: *Commondale* is another good starting-point for walks. The route leaves the Cleveland Hills at (24m) *Kildale* and the National Park on the way to (26m) *Easby*. The church at *Ingleby Greenhow*, 2m S of Easby, is Georgian with Norman fragments. 29m: *Stokesley* is a little market town with a fine wide street. A173, the Guisborough road, leads 3m NE to *Great Ayton*, near the conical *Roseberry Topping* (1051ft). Captain Cook attended the village school here and the schoolhouse, rebuilt in 1785, now contains a museum. The site of his cottage, removed to Melbourne in 1934, is marked by an obelisk of Australian granite. A 60ft obelisk erected in his honour in 1827 stands on Easby Moor. B1257 heads S from Stokesley to Rievaulx and Helmsley (see above). A172 heads N from Stokesley and enters Cleveland on the way into (38m) *Middlesbrough* (Route 85B).

FROM WHITBY TO MIDDLESBROUGH VIA THE COAST, 32m by A174. 3m: *Sandsend* is a little resort. 4m: *Lythe* has a superb view S over Whitby and the bay, and a church with many Saxon fragments. *Mulgrave Castle* lies in a wooded valley 1m S. From (9m) *Hinderwell* ('Hilda's Well') sideroads lead to the magnificent *Runswick Bay*, 1m SE, and to *Port Mulgrave*, 1m NE, with the decayed remains of the harbour where iron ore from the nearby mine was loaded. 10½m: **Staithes**, a pretty village set partly at the bottom of a deep ravine, became a favourite haunt of painters, including Dame Laura Knight, in the early 20C. Captain Cook was apprenticed to a draper here before he moved to Whitby. *Boulby Cliff* (666ft), to the W, is the highest cliff on the E coast of England. A174 leaves the National Park on the way to (14½m) *Loftus* (8500 inhabitants), a beautifully situated but grimy town. 19m: *Saltburn-by-the-Sea* and on to (32m) *Middlesbrough*, see Route 85B.

85

York and Doncaster to Durham, Newcastle and Berwick

A. From York

Directions. Total distance 143½m. **York**, see Route 81. A19 to (23m) Thirsk. A168 to (32m) Northallerton. A167 to (48m) **Darlington**, (66½m) Durham, (81m) Newcastle and (143½m) Berwick, see Route 85B.

York, see Route 81. A19 heads N. 3½m: *Skelton* has a beautiful little Early English church of c 1247. From (5¼m) *Shipton* a sideroad leads 2½m W to *Beningbrough Hall* (NT), built for the Bourchier family in 1716. It contains: a fine staircase, woodwork and plaster; a well-preserved Victorian laundry; and portraits on loan from the National Portrait Gallery. 12½m: *Easingwold* (seasonal TI) has a pleasant market place away from the main road.

At *Alne*, 4m SW, the 12C •doorway of the church is carved with animals from the bestiary. *Raskelf*, 2m NW, has the only wooden church tower in the county. For *Stillington* and *Sutton-on-the-Forest*, E of Easingwold, see Route 84.

23m: **Thirsk** (6800 inhabitants; seasonal TI) is a traditional Yorkshire market town with a good Perpendicular church, a racecourse and a local museum in the birthplace of Thomas Lord (1755–1822), founder of Lord's Cricket Ground. The country vet stories of 'James Herriot' are set in Thirsk and its surrounding region. Several 'Herriot trails' follow the locations.

Kirby Wiske has *Sion Hill Hall* (open), an early 20C house in the Lutyens style, with interesting collections. Thirsk lies W of the *North York Moors*, reached by following A160 up the perilous Sutton Bank, at the edge of the Hambleton Hills, to *Helmsley* (Route 84). From Thirsk to *Ripon*, *Harrogate* and *Leeds*, see Route 80.

FROM THIRSK TO MIDDLESBROUGH OR STOCKTON-ON-TEES. A19 runs N, skirting the foot of the *Hambleton Hills* and the *Cleveland Hills* and the edge of the North York Moors National Park (Route 84). Shortly before (11m) the Cleveland Tontine Inn a turning on the right leads to •**Mount Grace Priory** (NT and EH, all year), founded in 1398, the most perfect Carthusian monastery in England. Its ground plan—two large courts with the church between them—reflects the fact that Carthusians led a solitary rather than communal life, each monk having a small house and garden. Part of the domestic buildings were converted into a private house in the 17C. At 17m, as it enters Cleveland and approaches the depressed industrial region along the Tees estuary, the road forks. A19 bears right for (25m) *Middlesbrough* (Route 85B). A67 bears left to (20m) *Yarm*, an old town on a loop of the Tees, dominated by the brick arches of its railway viaduct (1849). It keeps a broad High St. and many inns from the days when it was an important stage on the coaching route. The first meeting of the promoters of the Stockton and Darlington Railway, opened in 1825, was held at the George and Dragon. A67 crosses the river and A135 branches right, passing the Preston Hall Museum on the way into (24m) *Stockton-on-Tees* (Route 85B).

N of Thirsk the main route bears left on A168. 32m: **Northallerton** (9600 inhabitants) is the county town of North Yorkshire. A large market is held in its broad High St. on Wednesdays and Saturdays. The fine church, mostly 12–13C, has a striking Perpendicular tower.

A684 heads SW, crossing the A1 near *Leeming Bar* (Route 85B) and joining Wensley-dale at *Leyburn* (Route 86D).

A167 continues N, passing (34½m) the site where King Stephen defeated the Scots at the Battle of the Standard in 1138. At (44½m) *Croft-on-Tees* the road crosses the winding river and enters County Durham. The Old Rectory was Lewis Carroll's boyhood home.

Byron spent his honeymoon at *Halnaby Hall*, now demolished, 3m SW. *Sockburn*, with a ruined church containing Anglian fragments, is attractively placed on the Tees 5m SE. Wordsworth and Coleridge stayed here in 1799.

48m: **Darlington**, and on to (66½m) *Durham*, (81m) *Newcastle* and (143½m) *Berwick*, see Route 85B.

B. From Doncaster

Directions. Total distance 175m. **Doncaster**, see Route 81. A1 to (15½m) Ferrybridge, (32m) Wetherby, (44m) Boroughbridge, (71m) Scotch Corner. A1, A1(M), A66(M), A66 to (79½m) **Darlington**. A167 to (98m) **Durham** and (104m) Chester-le-Street. A6127 to (112½m) **Newcastle**. A6125 to (119½m) Seaton Bur, (127m) Morpeth, (145m) Alnwick and (175m) **Berwick**.

This route continues the journey up the A1 begun in Route 60A (London to Stamford) and Route 72 (Stamford to Doncaster). A1 bypasses the villages and towns, including Doncaster, that lined the former *Great North Road*, and crosses many of the transverse roads by flyovers or underpasses. Beyond Scotch Corner a short section of the old alignment is designated motorway but, beginning with the Darlington bypass, the motorway follows a new alignment: bypassing Durham to the E, briefly coming close to its old course near Chester-le-Street, and then veering E again to avoid Newcastle and cross the Tyne by the tunnel below Jarrow. It returns to its old alignment at Seaton Burn. The present route follows the course of the Great North Road, successively relabelled A167, A6127 and A6125, where most points of interest lie.

Doncaster, see Route 81. Beyond the river Don A638 heads NW. *Adwick-le-Street*, right of the road at 3½m, has a 12–16C church with the tomb of James Washington (c 1580).

A638 continues to Wakefield (Route 75H) but the present route joins A1 at (5½m) the end of the Doncaster bypass. At (8½m) *Barnsdale Bar* A1 leaves the Roman line, which runs W as A639 and A656 through Pontefract and Castleford (Route 75F). *Robin Hood's Well* (rebuilt by Vanbrugh), 1m S, marks the centre of the former forest of Barnsdale, which legend makes a favourite haunt of the outlaw. 10¾m: *Wentbridge* is bypassed to the E by a fine viaduct (1962). 12½m: *Darrington* church has a remarkable Lady Chapel with a small gallery above its entrance and 15C glass. At (15½m) **Ferrybridge** A1 crosses the Aire by a modern bridge, leaving John Carr's bridge of 1797 for foot traffic. The ugly industrial landscape is dominated by the eight huge cooling towers of (16m) *Brotherton*. Particularly unpleas-ant are the stagnant scummy pools used for chemical settlement.

A162 branches right for Tadcaster and York (Route 81) through the ancient district of *Elmet*. 3m: It crosses the Selby road, A63, just W of *Monk Fryston*, where Richard Monckton Milnes, Baron Houghton (1809–95), entertained Swinburne, Sir Richard Burton and Charles Kingsley and employed the American Henry Adams as his secretary at the Hall, now a hotel. 4m: *South Milford*. To the W is the 14C gatehouse of *Steeton Hall* (EH, all year). At (5½m) *Sherburn-in-Elmet* the partly Norman church contains a 15C *cross head, cut in half in the 19C.

The little *church at *Birkin*, 3½m E of Brotherton, is an unspoilt late Norman building (c 1140) with a carved doorway and capitals and a vaulted apse.

19m: *Ledsham*, to the W, has a church with Saxon and Norman work, and *Kippax*, 3m further W, a Norman church. 24m: *Aberford*, ¼m W, stands on the line of the Roman road shortly before it veers towards York. Parlington Park has an arch built by Sir Thomas Gascoigne in 1783 to celebrate 'liberty in North America triumphant'.

Lotherton Hall, 1m E of A1, is a museum of the decorative arts administered by the City of Leeds. It contains the Gascoigne family's collection of silver, porcelain, racing cups, jewellery, furniture and paintings (Pompei Batoni's portrait of Sir Thomas Gascoigne); 18–20C costume; English 19C porcelain and furniture; 19–20C arts and crafts, including pottery by Bernard Leach and his school; early Chinese ceramics and other Oriental works.

At (26½m) *Bramham Moor* A1 crosses A64, the Leeds–York road (Route 81). 28½m: *Bramham*. To the SW is *Bramham Park* (open), a Queen Anne house restored early in the 20C, with good pictures and furniture. The early 18C garden is a rare survival of the formal French style. 32m: **Wetherby** (10,200 inhabitants; TI), bypassed to the E, is a dull town on the Wharfe. Its racecourse lies off B1224, the York road, E of A1.

A661, the Harrogate road, passes (2m) *Stockeld Park* (limited opening), a fine little Palladian house of 1758–63 by James Paine. 3m: *Spofforth* and on to (8m) *Harrogate*, see Route 81.

From Wetherby to *Ilkley*, *Grassington* and *Hawes* through Wharfedale, see Route 86A; to *Knaresborough* and *Grassington* through Nidderdale, see Route 86B.

At (35½m) *Walshford*, A1 crosses the Nidd, and at 39½m the York–Harrogate road, A59 (Route 81). 44m: **Boroughbridge** (seasonal TI) was once the major crossing point of the Ure, where the Roman Dere Street rejoined its N line after branching E to York. Edward II defeated the Duke of Lancaster here in 1322, and in 1569 the Rising of the North, the Catholic rebellion against Elizabeth I, came to an abortive end at the Crown, then the Tancreds' manor house. The *Devil's Arrows*, three Bronze Age monoliths, stand about ¼m SW of the village.

Aldborough, ¼m E, occupies the site of Isurium Brigantium, a Brigantian settlement developed by the Romans as a camp for the 9th Legion in the 1C and as a major town in the 2C. Part of the Roman wall and two mosaic pavements survive, with an exhibition of finds (EH, summer season). The 14–15C church has a large 14C brass. For *Newby Hall*, 2½m NW of Boroughbridge, see Route 80.

50½m: A1 crosses the road from Leeds, Harrogate and Ripon to Thirsk. 60m: *Leeming Bar*, on the right. Northallerton (Route 85A) is 6m NE by A684.

A684 heads W to Wensleydale. 7¾m: *Bedale* (seasonal TI) has a good church, mainly 13–14C, with a defensive tower and 14C Fitzalan tombs. The 18C Bedale Hall contains a local museum. *Thorp Perrow Arboretum* (open), off B6268 about 2½m S, contains rare trees and shrubs. *Snape*, ½m further, has the remains of a 15–16C stronghold of the Nevilles and the Cecils. 11¼m: *Patrick Brompton* church has a beautiful 14C chancel. 15m: *Constable Burton Hall* is a handsome Palladian house of 1762–68 by John Carr, set in large informal gardens (open more often than the house). 12½m: *Leyburn* in Wensleydale, see Route 86D.

66m: *Catterick*, on the right, has a good 15C church. 67m: *Catterick Bridge*, also on the right, has a racecourse and a 15C bridge over the Swale.

On the moor 3m W is *Catterick Garrison*, the 'Aldershot of the North'. The road to it passes some traces of the Roman camp of Cataractonium and (2½m) *Hipswell*, probably the birthplace of John Wyclif (c 1330–84).

70m: *Moulton Hall* (open by appointment), E of the road, is a 17C house with a fine staircase. 71m: **Scotch Corner** (seasonal TI) is a major junction. Route 86E takes A6108 SW to *Richmond* and then follows Swaledale to *Kirkby Stephen* and *Brough*. Route 86F takes A66 over the Pennines to *Penrith*. Dere Street continues as B6275 through Piercebridge (Route 86G). The present route stays on A1, which soon becomes motorway and bears right. 75½m: A66(M) branches right for Darlington, crossing the Tees into County Durham.

79½m: **Darlington** (99,700 inhabitants; TI) is a market town which grew into an industrial centre after the opening of Edward Pease and George Stephenson's Stockton to Darlington Railway, the world's first passenger line, in 1825. The *Darlington Railway Centre and Museum* in the North Road Station (1842) displays Stephenson's No. 1 'Locomotion', which drew the first train at a rate of 10–13mph, the 'Derwent' engine (1845), and other early relics. The former *Town Hall* and *Market* are by Alfred Waterhouse (1861–64). •*St Cuthbert*, originally collegiate, is a fine Early English building (1180–1250) with a 14C spire. It contains a curious stone rood screen added to strengthen the central tower, stalls and misericords of the time of Bishop Langley (1406–37) and a 17C Gothic font cover. Church Lane to the N is a relic of old Darlington.

From Darlington to *Barnard Castle* and through Teesdale to *Alston*, see Route 86G. *Bishop Auckland*, 11m NW, is the starting-point for Route 86H through Weardale to *Alston*.

Teesside Airport, 6m E of Darlington on A67, has passenger flights to Aberdeen, Amsterdam, Belfast, Humberside, Jersey, London (Heathrow and Gatwick), Newcastle, Norwich and Wick.

FROM DARLINGTON TO STOCKTON-ON-TEES, MIDDLESBROUGH AND SALTBURN. The suburb of *Haughton-le-Skerne*, 1½m NE of the town centre, has an attractive green and a Norman church with 17C woodwork. A66 heads E and enters (6m) the county of Cleveland, a creation of the 1974 boundary changes, dominated by the heavily industrial and now badly depressed towns along the Tees estuary. They developed, thanks to the Stockton and Darlington Railway, as ports handling coal from the Durham coalfield and then, with the discovery of iron in the Cleveland Hills, as steel and ship-building centres. The 20C added oil refineries, petrochemical works and, near the N tip of the estuary, the Hartlepool nuclear power station. The last shipyard closed in 1987.

11m: **Stockton-on-Tees** (86,800 inhabitants; TI) keeps some of its Georgian character in the broad High St. with the parish church (1710–12) and Town Hall (1735). The *Green Dragon Museum*, off Finkle St. by the Georgian theatre, has local history displays. The cabinet-maker Thomas Sheraton (1751–1806) was born in Stockton; John Walker invented the friction match here in 1827; and Harold Macmillan, Earl of Stockton (1894–1986), took his title from the borough he represented in Parliament for most of the years between the wars. The *Preston Hall Museum*, off A135 2¼m SW, has Victorian interiors and a re-created Victorian street with working craftsmen; also pewter, arms and armour, and toys. A135 continues to Yarm (Route 85A). *Norton*, on the Hartlepool road 2m NE of Stockton, keeps much of its character as a prosperous village, with 18–19C houses around the green and pond; the church, Stockton's parish church until the 18C, has a Saxon crossing and the 14C effigy of a knight. *Billingham*, further on, is a modern industrial town with ICI petrochemical works. The church, enlarged in 1939, has a 10C Saxon tower.

12m: *Thornaby* lies across the Tees from Stockton. 15m: **Middlesbrough** (pronounced as in 'Edinburgh'; 149,800 inhabitants; TI) developed in the 19C as a port and an iron and steel town. The *Dorman Museum*, with natural history, local history and Linthorpe pottery, and the *Middlesbrough Art Gallery*, with changing exhibitions from its collection of 20C British art, are in Linthorpe Rd. The *Cleveland Gallery* in Victoria Rd mounts changing exhibitions from collections which include decorative art, maps, geology and contemporary art. The *Newport Bridge* (1934), the first vertical lift bridge in England, crosses the river to Billingham. The *Transporter Bridge* (toll), opened in 1911, crosses to *Port Clarence* for Hartlepool. *Ormesby Hall* (NT), off A171 about 3m SE, is a mid 18C house with good plaster ceilings and a stable block attributed to John Carr. *Marton*, 1½m to its W, has the *Captain Cook Birthplace Museum* in Stewart Park near the site of the cottage where the explorer was born in 1728. *Newham Grange Leisure Farm*, off A174 another 1m W, is a working farm with rare breeds of farm animals.

A1085 continues past the Wilton ICI petrochemical works and the Redcar British Steel works to the coast, with A174 following a parallel course to the S. 24m: **Redcar** (36,700 inhabitants) is a 19C resort with a racecourse in the centre and, on the seafront, a lifeboat museum with the oldest surviving lifeboat in the world, put into service in 1802. *Kirkleatham*, 2½m S in the shadow of ICI's Wilton works, has a fascinating array of 18C buildings. The *Old Hall Museum*, a free school endowed by Sir William Turner (d. 1692) and built in 1710, has displays about the region's social and industrial history. The Turner Hospital, founded by Sir William in 1676 and remodelled in the 1740s, contains a fine chapel by James Gibbs (open on request). The church of St Cuthbert has Gibbs's mausoleum of Marwood William Turner (d. 1739) with good 18C monuments, including work by Scheemakers.

A1085 skirts the dunes to (25½m) *Marske-by-the-Sea* and then turns inland to join A174 on the way to (28½m) **Saltburn-by-the-Sea** (20,000 inhabitants; TI), developed as a resort in the 19C. *Hunt Cliff* (549ft) rises to the E. *Skinningrove*, 3½m down the coast, has the *Tom Leonard Museum* on the site of an old ironstone mine. To Whitby, see Route 84.

The return to Middlesbrough can be made on A174 to (1½m) *Brotton* and A173 to (4m) *Skelton* (16,200 inhabitants together), where the 18C Gothick castle was a favourite haunt of Sterne and the 'Demoniac Club'. There is a truncated Norman church near *Upleatham*, 2m NW, and a working watermill at *Tocketts Mill*, on A171 1½m W of Skelton. A171 continues to (8m) *Guisborough* (19,900 inhabitants; TI), a pleasant town at the foot of the Cleveland Hills. *Guisborough Priory* (EH, all year) was founded for Augustinian canons c 1119. The scanty ruins include the Decorated E end of the early 14C church. For A171 to Whitby, see Route 84. A171 heads N to (18m) Middlesbrough via Ormesby Hall.

From Stockton A19 and A689 lead to **Hartlepool** (pronounced 'Hartleepool'; 94,400 inhabitants; seasonal TI), which developed during the 19C into England's third largest port and a major shipbuilding centre. The novelist Sir Compton Mackenzie (1883–1972) was born here. The *Gray Art Gallery and Museum* in Clarence Rd has archaeology, local history, natural history, Chinese porcelain and 19–20C paintings, with reconstructed buildings in the grounds. The original and much more interesting settlement, NE of the docks, dates from the foundation of a Saxon convent c 640. St Hilda was its abbess c 649–57. A headstone from her time is preserved in the Early English church of *•St Hilda*, which has a heavily buttressed tower. Towards the sea a gateway and section of the 13C town walls survive. The *Hartlepool Maritime Museum* traces the port's history.

From Stockton to *Durham*, and to *Sunderland* and *Newcastle*, see below.

Beyond Darlington A167 follows the course of the old Great North Road. 84½m: *Aycliffe*, on the Skerne just after the junction with A1(M), has a 13C church and two carved Saxon crosses (one with St Peter, head downwards). *Newton Aycliffe* (24,700 inhabitants), beyond, is a new town developed since 1947. 91m: *Ferryhill* is on the edge of the coalfield centred on *Spennymoor*. There is a good view as A167 crosses the Wear near (94m) *Croxdale*. Durham can be approached either by branching right on A1050 to enter the city by New Elvet, or by continuing on A167 to (97m) *Neville's Cross*, where the Nevilles and the Percys defeated David II of Scotland in 1346. A right turn leads into Durham by Crossgate, past the partly Norman church of *St Margaret*.

98m: **DURHAM** (26,400 inhabitants), in romantic contrast to the often depressed and depressing industrial region that surrounds it, is the most beautiful city between York and Edinburgh. It stands on a bold peninsula of rock almost encircled by the Wear, its great cathedral and castle towering above the steep and richly wooded banks.

TI: Market Place. **Bus Station**: North Rd. **Railway Station**: Above the city to the NW. **Annual Events**: Miners' Gala in July; Folk Festival and City Carnival in August.

History. Durham grew up, somewhat like St Albans, round the nucleus of a cathedral built on virgin soil in 995 (see below). Its name first appears as Dunholm ('hill-island') about 1000, developing its final form through Norman influence. The prince-bishop held his own courts of law and ruled with the powers of a petty sovereign, in return for defending the northern marches of the kingdom, so that the city had, almost from the first, a double aspect: 'half church of God, half castle 'gainst the Scot'.

The railway station, high above the city on the NW, gives a *view across the river to the cathedral and the castle. North Rd, below the railway viaduct (1857), descends to a famous *view from the Wear at *Framwelgate Bridge*, rebuilt by Bishop Skirlaw c 1400 and widened in 1856. Silver St. climbs to the triangular Market Place, with the church of *St Nicholas* (1857), the *Town Hall* (1851) and a spirited equestrian statue of the 3rd Marquess of Londonderry (d. 1854).

The direct route then follows Saddler St. and Owengate up to the Palace Green, where the cathedral and castle confront each other. The 17C buildings by Bishop Cosin on the other sides include, on the W, the former grammar school (now the *University Music School*) where the poet Christopher Smart, Shelley's friend Thomas Jefferson Hogg, and R.S. Surtees, the creator of Jorrocks, were pupils.

A longer route branches left from Saddler St. and crosses the Wear by the 13C *Elvet Bridge*, widened in 1804–05 but keeping a few old bridge-houses. On the farther side is the 18C 'suburb' of Elvet. Old Elvet, with the *Royal County Hotel*, the 19C *Old Shire Hall* (now the university's administrative offices) and several fine houses, leads to the *Courthouse* (1809–11), near an unexpected view of the cathedral. New Elvet, to the right, leads past *Elvet Riverside* (1962–66; Architects' Co-Partnership), housing the university's arts and modern language faculties, and *Dunelm House* (1961–65; Architects' Co-Partnership), with the Students' Union and the Staff Club. *Kingsgate Footbridge* (1962–63; Ove Arup), crosses the river. Hallgarth St. leads left to the *Prison*; some medieval tithe barns near it have been converted into a social club. The main route continues by Church St. to *St Oswald*, a late 12C–15C church partly rebuilt in 1834, with a Morris and Co. W window by Ford Madox Brown (1864–65). The path across the churchyard gives a *view of the cathedral and continues beside the river along the delightful 'Banks' to *Prebends' Bridge* (1772–78), with another *view. South Bailey climbs steeply to the cathedral, passing *St Mary-the-Less* (rebuilt 1847), which has a fine 13C Majesty.

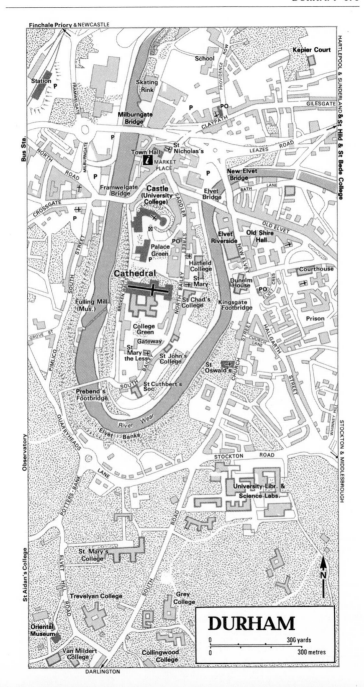

Finchale Priory & NEWCASTLE

HARTLEPOOL & SUNDERLAND & St Hild & St Bede College

Station
P

Bus Sta.

Skating
Rink

School

Providence Row

Kepier Court

GILESGATE

Milburngate
Bridge

P

PO

Claypath

LEAZES ROAD

MILBURNGATE

NORTH ROAD

Town Hall
i
MARKET
PLACE

St
Nicholas's

New Elvet
Bridge

BATH LANE

Framwelgate
Bridge

P

Castle
(University
College)

SADDLER STREET

Elvet
Bridge

CROSSGATE

P

OLD ELVET

Elvet
Riverside

Old Shire
Hall

PO

Palace
Green

NEW ELVET

Courthouse

SOUTH STREET

Cathedral

Hatfield
College

St Mary

Dunelm
House

PO

HALLGARTH STREET

Prison

Fulling Mill
(Mus.)

NORTH BAILEY

St Chad's
College

Kingsgate
Footbridge

CHURCH LANE

GROVE ST

PIMLICO

College
Green

Gateway

SOUTH BAILEY

St
Mary
the Less

St John's
College

St
Oswald's

CHURCH STREET

NEW ELVET

WHINNEY HILL

STOCKTON & MIDDLESBROUGH

Prebend's
Footbridge

St Cuthbert's
Soc.

QUARRYHEADS LANE

Elvet Banks

River Wear

STOCKTON ROAD

Observatory

POTTERS BANK

ELVET HILL

LANE

University Libr. &
Science Labs.

SOUTH ROAD

St Aidan's College

St Mary's
College

N

Trevelyan College

Grey
College

Oriental
Museum

Van Mildert
College

Collingwood
College

DARLINGTON

DURHAM

0 _____ 300 yards
0 _____ 300 metres

On the outer bank the path continues N up to Framwelgate Bridge, with a branch leading left up to a *view of the W end of the cathedral from Silver St. On the inner bank a path also continues N to Framwelgate Bridge past the *Old Fulling Mill* (open), housing a museum of local archaeology. Another follows the loop of the river round to Elvet Bridge.

The * *Cathedral** is beyond doubt the greatest piece of Norman work in the British Isles and commands the best site of any English cathedral, unrivalled even at Lincoln.

The monks of Lindisfarne fled when the Danes raided their island in 875, taking with them the body of their bishop, St Cuthbert (d. 687). They settled at Chester-le-Street in 883 and found a final refuge at Durham in 995. Little or nothing remains of the Saxon cathedral built by Bishop Aldhun and consecrated in 998. Bishop William of St Carileph (or St Calais) began the present great Norman church in 1093 with the choir, transepts and crossing; Bishop Ranulph Flambard (1099–1128) finished the nave. The rib vaulting of the choir may be the first in Western architecture; its main vault (c 1104) was rebuilt in the early 13C, but original work (before 1096) survives in the choir aisles. The pointed transverse arches of the nave, probably the earliest (c 1130) in a high vault anywhere in Europe, mark another approach towards Gothic, though again without compromising the massively Romanesque character of the building. The Galilee at the W end was added as a Lady Chapel by Bishop Pudsey (or Le Puiset; 1153–95), while the two W towers were probably built between 1150 and 1226. The original three apses at the E end were replaced between 1242 and 1279 by the Chapel of the Nine Altars, paralleled only at Fountains Abbey. The great central tower (c 1260) was partly rebuilt c 1464–88.

Though the building has kept most of its Norman glory undiminished, later hands did not always treat it well. 18C restorers pared down the walls (N side, E end, W towers) by several inches, removing much detail in the process. In the 1790s the most barbarous of James Wyatt's suggested changes—adding a spire, knocking down the Galilee—were successfully opposed by the London Society of Antiquaries. Anthony Salvin misguidedly cleared out Bishop Cosin's 17C woodwork in the 1840s but most of it has been put back again. Sir Gilbert Scott's restoration (1870–77) added the present choir screen.

The figure of a cow, outside at the NE end, perpetuates the legend that a woman looking for her dun cow guided Bishop Aldhun in choosing the site for his church. The entrance is by the NW porch, spoilt when its upper storey was removed in the 18C. The mid 12C sanctuary knocker (replica here, *original in the Treasury) is a reminder that the cathedral was a place of sanctuary in the Middle Ages.

Inside, the uninterrupted view from the W end makes a powerful impression. No other great English church keeps its original Norman bulk so comparatively un-touched, and nowhere else is the Norman work so strongly individualised—an effect due largely to the great circular columns (7ft in diameter, 22ft in circumference) with their incised ornament and to the abundance of zigzag moulding. The *Nave* alter-nates single circular columns with clustered ones. Quadripartite rib vaulting spans each bay, and the pointed transverse arches spring from the clustered piers. The W window was inserted c 1346. The towering tabernacle of the Renaissance font is part of the magnificent woodwork with which Bishop John Cosin (1660–72) endowed his cathedral. The Frosterley marble in the pavement to its E marks the point beyond which women could not enter. The S aisle has the case of the organ built by Father Smith (1683) to stand on the choir screen, the Miners' Memorial (1948) and two battered effigies surviving from the former Neville chantry.

The graceful, many-pillared *Galilee*, entered from the W end of the nave, is Transitional work, begun by Bishop Pudsey in 1175 and altered by Bishop Langley (d. 1437), who built his altar tomb in front of the W door. It contains the tomb of the Venerable Bede, who died at Jarrow in 735 and whose remains were brought to Durham in 1020. The 12C wall paintings in the bay of the E wall may be of St Cuthbert and St Oswald.

The open lantern above the crossing is unusually tall and dignified. The original Norman ends of the *Great Transepts* were altered in the 14C (N) and 15C (S) by inserting the present windows, but the vaulting of both transepts is original (c 1105).

The S transept has Sir Francis Chantrey's statue of Bishop Barrington (d. 1826) and Prior Castell's Clock (c 1500, several times restored).

The *Choir* is separated from the crossing by a light, open screen of coloured marbles by Sir Gilbert Scott, replacing Bishop Cosin's mid 17C screen which Salvin removed. Cosin's fine stalls, however, survive. On the S is the Bishop's Throne, the 'highest in Christendom'; its lower part serves as the monument of Bishop Hatfield (1345–81), who erected it. The magnificent stone *Altar Screen* (c 1375), with its lofty open pinnacles, was the gift of John, Lord Neville.

Though wholly different in style, the *Chapel of the Nine Altars* (1242–78) harmonises admirably with the choir. Its slender polished shafts are of Frosterley marble. The tracery of the E rose window is neo-Gothic tampering by Wyatt (1795). The rich Bede Altar in the central chapel was designed by Stephen Dykes Bower (1935). The fine 13C stone cross, to the S, came from the vanished abbey of Neasham,

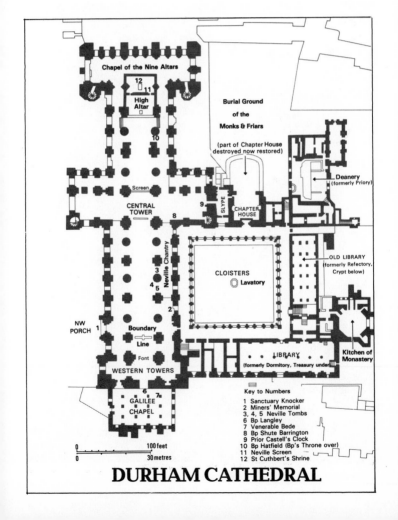

Key to Numbers

1 Sanctuary Knocker
2 Miners' Memorial
3, 4, 5 Neville Tombs
6 Bp Langley
7 Venerable Bede
8 Bp Shute Barrington
9 Prior Castell's Clock
10 Bp Hatfield (Bp's Throne over)
11 Neville Screen
12 St Cuthbert's Shrine

0 _____ 100 feet
0 _____ 30 metres

DURHAM CATHEDRAL

near Darlington. St Cuthbert's shrine behind the High Altar was destroyed at the Reformation and the saint now rests beneath a simple marble slab with candlesticks and tester by Sir Ninian Comper (1949). The plan of the original Norman apse is outlined on the floor.

Durham was established as a secular church, but Bishop St Carileph made it monastic in 1083 by bringing Benedictines from Jarrow and Monkwearmouth. The monastic buildings are grouped round the *Cloister* (c 1388–1418), S of the nave. Both doorways from the church are worth remark, especially the Monks' Door (W) with splendid ironwork of c 1130. The W range consists of the *Monks' Dormitory* (open), built by Bishop Skirlaw (1388–1404), still with its original timber roof. It contains a fine display of 7–11C sculptured stones, mainly crosses, from Durham and the surrounding region (Hexham, Hartlepool, Jarrow, Monkwearmouth, Escomb, etc.). The *Treasury* (open) in the 13C undercroft displays fragments of *St Cuthbert's carved wooden coffin, made before 698, in which his body was carried on its wanderings, and the relics found inside

The nave of Durham Cathedral

it: an exquisite mid 7C pectoral cross, 7C portable altar, 10C vestments, and 11C(?) comb. Also on view are the original *sanctuary knocker and the cathedral's collection of illuminated manuscripts, seals, documents, plate and vestments. The refectory on the S side was rebuilt c 1684 as the *Chapter Library* (open to scholars only). The *Chapter House* (not open) in the E range was completed under Bishop Geoffrey Rufus (1133–41), partly destroyed in 1796 and restored in 1895.

Across College Green from the cloisters is the *Gatehouse* (c 1500), leading to the attractive houses and college buildings of North and South Bailey. In North Bailey *St Mary-le-Bow* (1685), with a screen of 1707, is now a Heritage Centre.

The *Castle stands opposite the cathedral on Palace Green, guarding the exact neck of the peninsula. Begun in 1072, it served as the palace of the prince-bishops until the 1830s, when it became the University College of the newly founded university (see below). It has kept the motte-and-bailey plan of a Norman fortress through all its mutations. Guided tours are given throughout the year, but during longer hours in the Easter and summer vacations.

The outer arch of the main *Gateway* is Norman but its upper floors, like the outer walls of the castle, were rebuilt by James Wyatt. The *Keep* (not open), on the mound to the right of the courtyard, was rebuilt in the 1830s. On the left of the courtyard, Bishop Cosin's Ionic porch leads into the screens passage. The *Kitchen*, with its huge fireplaces, was adapted from the 12C building by Bishop Fox in 1499. The *Great Hall*, now the college's dining hall, keeps its original 14C roof among alterations by virtually every succeeding age. The splendid *Black Staircase* added by Bishop Cosin in the 1660s leads up to *Tunstal's Gallery* (1530–39). The *doorway from Bishop Pudsey's 12C hall is richly decorated Norman work. It now leads into the state rooms (not open). *Tunstal's Chapel* (c 1542) at the end of the gallery contains fine woodwork. On the next floor is the *Norman Gallery*, with open wall-arcades and decorated arches belonging to the upper floor of Pudsey's hall. A spiral staircase leads down to the earliest part of the castle, the *Norman Chapel* (c 1080), with interesting capitals.

The **University of Durham**, England's third oldest university, was founded in 1832 by Bishop Van Mildert, the last episcopal count palatine, who gave up the castle and part of his princely revenue for the purpose. Its organisation modifies the Oxbridge system, with residential colleges responsible for the students' social and domestic life and faculties responsible for their teaching.

Like *University College*, in the castle and neighbouring buildings, the other early foundations were in the heart of the city: *Hatfield College* (1846) in 17–20C buildings in North Bailey and *St Cuthbert's Society* (1888) in a 19C building in South Bailey. Later growth has extended beyond the peninsula. S of the river are: *St Mary's College* (1899; main buildings by E. Vincent Harris, 1952); *St Aidan's College* (1947; buildings by Sir Basil Spence, 1964); *Grey College* (1959; buildings by T. Worthington, 1960–61); *Van Mildert College* (1965; buildings by Middleton, Fletcher and Partners, 1966); *Trevelyan College* (1966; buildings by Stillman and Eastwick-Field, 1967); and *Collingwood College* (1972; buildings by Richard Sheppard, Robson and Partners, 1973). The *College of St Hild and St Bede*, off Leazes Rd N of the river, was formed by a merger of two independent colleges of education and fully integrated into the university in 1979. It has a fine chapel (1939; Mottistone and Paget). *St Chad's College* (1904) in North Bailey and *St John's College* (1909) in South Bailey are Church of England colleges which also admit students to the full range of university courses. All the colleges are co-residential except St Mary's and Trevelyan, which admit women only. King's College, Newcastle, was part of Durham University from 1937 until 1963, when it became the University of Newcastle in its own right.

Views of the cathedral and castle from Grey College and St Aidan's are worth seeking out. The *Oriental Museum*, on Elvet Hill below St Aidan's, has collections of art and archaeology. The *Botanic Garden*, off Hollingside Lane near Collingwood College, has 18 acres of worldwide trees, shrubs, cacti, etc., with a tropical collection and a Visitors'

Centre. The church of *St Giles*, off Gilesgate near St Hild and St Bede, contains early and late 12C work and an unusual 16C effigy. Off Gilesgate further on a 14C gatehouse survives from *Kepier Hospital*, founded by Bishop Flambard in 1122.

Near the *County Hall*, 1m NW of the centre by Framwelgate on the way to A167, is the *Durham Light Infantry Museum and Arts Centre*, with a lively programme of exhibitions. *Finchale Priory* (EH), pronounced 'Finkle', is charmingly situated on the bank of the Wear about 4m N of the city, reached by lane and footpath or by the sideroad branching E from A167. It was founded c 1195 by Bendictines from Durham on the site of the cell where St Godric had spent his last years and died in 1170. The ruins include the 13C church, with the tomb reputedly belonging to the saint, and the 14C cloister buildings, notably the refectory and its undercroft.

Sherburn Hospital, 2½m E of the city, has the gatehouse of the hospital founded by Bishop Pudsey in 1181. *Ushaw College* (not open), beyond Neville's Cross 4m W, was founded in 1808 in direct succession to the dispossessed seminary for Roman Catholic priests at Douai. *Brancepeth* lies on A690 3½m SW of Neville's Cross. Its castle (not open), mostly rebuilt in the 19C, was the seat of the Neville family until 1569. In the grounds stands the 12–14C church of *St Brandon*, with remarkable Neville monuments and *woodwork by the future Bishop Cosin, rector here in 1626–44.

Bishop Auckland, 11m SW of Durham by A167 and A688, is the starting-point for Route 86H through Weardale to *Alston*.

FROM DURHAM TO STOCKTON-ON-TEES, 19m by A177. The route crosses the Wear near (1½m) *Shincliffe*, with a pleasant main street. 5½m: *Coxhoe*, where Elizabeth Barrett Browning (1806–61) was born at the Hall, since demolished. 10½m: *Sedgefield*, with the 18C grounds of Hardwick Hall Country Park and the racecourse to the right of the road. The church has a Perpendicular tower and a good 17C screen and stalls in Bishop Cosin's manner. 19m: *Stockton*, see above.

FROM DURHAM TO SUNDERLAND, 13m by A690. 1m: A sideroad leads from the roundabout to (2½m) *Pittington*, right of A690, where the church has an interesting N arcade of c 1175. 2m: The road crosses A1(M). 7m: *Houghton-le-Spring* (31,000 inhabitants), in Tyne and Wear, has 16–18C houses and a 13C church with the tomb of Bernard Gilpin (d. 1583), the 'Apostle of the North'. A690 continues straight to (13m) *Sunderland* (see below).

A longer route, adding 7m, takes A182 N from Houghton to (13m) **Washington** (50,900 inhabitants), developed as a colliery New Town and now home of the Nissan motor works. The *Old Hall* (NT) in Washington Village is an early 17C building with fragments of the medieval house of the Washington family. The *Washington 'F' Pit Museum*, in the winding house of the former colliery, has an 1888 steam engine. The *Waterfowl Park* designed by Sir Peter Scott, on the Wear to the E, has a view across the river to the *Penshaw Monument* (NT), a Greek temple built in 1844 to commemorate 'Radical Jack', the 1st Earl of Durham. A1231 heads along the N bank of the Wear, passing near the airport and Hylton Castle on the way into (20m) *Sunderland* (see below).

FROM DURHAM TO NEWCASTLE BY THE DERWENT VALLEY, 27m. A pleasant alternative to the main route below. A691 heads NW from the city. 7½m: *Lanchester* has a Norman and Early English church with Roman columns in the N arcade and a Roman altar (AD 244) in the porch, and, ½m SW, remains of the Roman Longovicium. 11½m: A691 meets A692, which leads 2m W to *Consett* (33,400 inhabitants), a steel town until the works closed in 1980. The main route continues straight ahead on B6309, following the line of the Roman Dere Street. 14m: *Ebchester* stands on the site of Vindomara fort above the Derwent, and has Roman stones in its church tower. R.S. Surtees (1803–64), the creator of Jorrocks, is buried here. A694 goes E along the Derwent valley to (15m) *Hamsterley*. Surtees spent much of his life at the 18C *Hamsterley Hall* (not open), in the woods about 2½m SE. A694 passes the 18C *Derwentcote Steel Furnace* (EH, summer season). The road crosses the river for (19m) *Rowlands Gill*, on the Country Park walk which follows the route of the former Derwent Valley Railway between Consett and the Visitors' Centre at Swalwell, near A69. Just beyond Rowlands Gill it offers views of the ruined home of the Bowes family and the tall Liberty monument (1757) in the Gibside estate (not open). Off B6314 S of Rowlands Gill is the beautiful *Gibside Chapel* (NT), designed as the Bowes family mausoleum by James Paine in

1760 and converted in 1809, with a three-decker pulpit. 22½m: A694 joins A69 and the Tyne near *Swalwell*. 27m: *Newcastle*, see below.

The main route leaves Durham by Framwelgate, past the Durham Light Infantry Museum (see above) and the County Hall, and joins A167 at (99m) *Framwellgate Moor*. 104m: *Chester-le-Street* (20,500 inhabitants) is on the site of the Roman fort of Concangium. The Lindisfarne monks came here with St Cuthbert's body in 883, moving on to Durham in 995. The church is notable for its spire, Lumley monuments (mostly Elizabethan imitations of medieval work) and anchorite's cell, now housing local history exhibits.

*Beamish, The North of England Open-Air Museum (TI), 3m W on A693, re-creates life in the North of England early this century on a 200-acre site. Buildings from other parts of the region have been re-erected and furnished as they once were to form a town, colliery village, home farm and railway station. The *Causey Arch* (1725–26), about 1½m NW of the museum, was built for the horsedrawn wooden waggonway that linked Tanfield colliery with the Tyne at Gateshead and so is arguably the world's oldest surviving railway bridge. The course of the metal railway that replaced it runs N to (½m) the junction with the Bowes Railway (see below), near the *Tyneside Locomotive Museum*, with locally built engines. In summer steam locomotives haul passenger trains along the stretch between Marley Hill and Sunniside.

About 1m E of Chester-le-Street is *Lumley Castle* (now a hotel), a fine 14C castle of the local type, altered by Vanbrugh.

The old road continues N as A6127, with A1(M) running alongside. It enters the county of Tyne and Wear, created in 1974 from the once great North-East coalfield and the Tyneside and Wearside ship-building region, now badly depressed, which used to belong to County Durham and Northumberland. Shortly beyond (107½m) *Birtley* the road crosses relics of the old Bowes Railway, a rope-hauled colliery line whose first section was designed by George Stephenson in 1826. The *Bowes Railway Heritage Museum* at *Springwell*, 2m NE of Birtley, has locomotives, rolling stock, displays of rope-haulage and steam rides along a short stretch of track. 112m: **Gateshead** (81,400 inhabitants; TI) has lost its former industrial base as a port for the Tyne coalfield and a centre of heavy engineering, particularly railway workshops. The *Metro Centre* (1986–88), said to be the largest drive-in shopping centre in Europe, is the latest attempt to help revive the region's economy. The *Shipley Art Gallery* has changing displays from a permanent collection which includes the Dutch school and 19C British painting. From Gateshead to Jarrow and South Shields, and to Sunderland and Stockton, see below. The road enters Newcastle by the Tyne Bridge.

112½m: **NEWCASTLE UPON TYNE** (192,500 inhabitants), never hyphenated and usually abbreviated to *Newcastle*, is the unofficial capital of the North-East. It keeps a lively big-city atmosphere despite its recent economic problems. The quayside and river, where coal-exporting for centuries gave Newcastle its identity, now combine picturesque decay with signs of redevelopment—a familiar picture throughout Britain's dockland and waterways. The city centre that rises up the steep N bank of the Tyne has its share of insensitive modern replanning, but also a continually surprising skyline and, above all, the superb streets built by the speculator Richard Grainger (1798–1861) with John Dobson (1787–1865) and other local architects.

TI: Central Library, Princess Square; Main Concourse, Central Square; Newcastle Airport. **Railway Station**: Central Station, Neville St. **Bus and Coach Stations**: Eldon Square Bus Concourse, Haymarket, Marlborough Crescent, Worswick St., Gallowgate. **Metro**: Monument Station is the main interchange for the rapid transit system. There

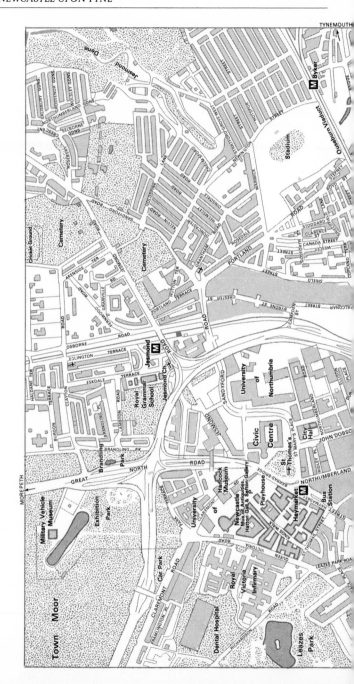

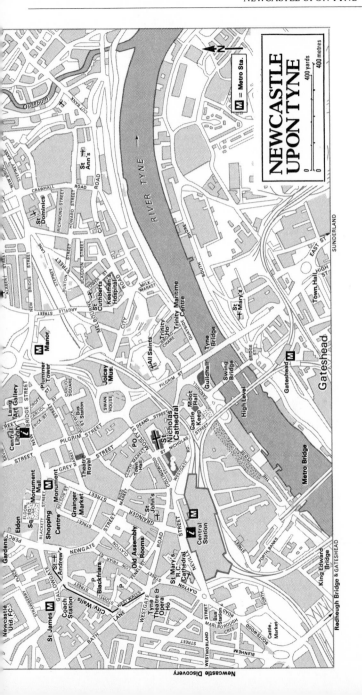

NEWCASTLE
UPON TYNE

M = Metro Sta.

400 yards
400 metres

RIVER TYNE

Ouseburn

St Ann's

St Dominics

CRAWHALL ROAD

RICHMOND STREET

HOWARD STREET

CITY ROAD

NEW BRIDGE STREET

ALBERT STREET

STEPNEY BANK

NEW BRIDGE STREET

BUXTON STREET

ARGYLE STREET

MELBOURNE STREET

CITY ROAD

St Cuthberts
Keelman's Hospital

MILK MARKET

Trinity Maritime Centre

Trinity Ho
QUAYSIDE

St Mary's

SUNDERLAND

EAST ST

HIGH ST

Town Hall

Gateshead

Manor

Plummer Tower

Joicey Mus.

All Saints

PILGRIM ST

Tyne Bridge

BRIDGE ST

Guildhall
Swing Bridge

Gateshead

M

High Level

Laing Art Gallery

Central Library

NEW BRIDGE STREET

CARLIOL SQUARE

SWAN HOUSE

PILGRIM STREET

POLY

DEAN STREET

St Nicholas Cathedral

Castle Moot Hall
Keep

THE SIDE

BRIDGE ST

Metro Bridge

THE CLOSE

NEW BRIDGE STREET

SAVILLE

GREY STREET

Theatre Royal

MARKET STREET

COLLINGWOOD STREET

Town Hall

SANDHILL

QUAYSIDE

Eldon Gardens

Monument Mall

Monument

GREY STREET

GRAINGER STREET

MARKET ST

St John's

WESTGATE

ST NICHOLAS

Shopping Centre

ELDON SQ.

Eldon Sq.

Grainger Market

BLACKETT STREET

NEWGATE STREET

CLAYTON STREET

GRAINGER STREET

M

Central Station

FORTH BANKS

St Mary's R.C. Cathedral

Old Assembly Rooms

Blackfriars

LOW FRIAR ST

NEVILLE STREET

NEWGATE STREET

St Andrew's

P

P

Newcastle Utd. F.C.

St James

Coach Station

City Walls

GALLOWGATE

STOWELL STREET

WESTMORLAND ROAD

BATH LANE

WEST WALLS

Tyne Theatre & Opera Ho

WESTGATE ROAD

MARLBOROUGH CRES.

Bus Station

SCOTSWOOD ROAD

FORTH

Cattle Market

BLENHEIM

WESTMORLAND STREET

PERCY STREET

STRAWBERRY PLACE

King Edward Bridge

Redheugh Bridge & GATESHEAD

Newcastle Discovery

are BR interchanges at Central Station and at Heworth on S Tyneside. **Ferries**: Local ferries across the Tyne between South Shields and North Shields. Passenger ferries from Tyne Commission Quay, about 7m downstream near Percy Main, North Shields, to Esbjerg, Gothenburg, Bergen, Stavanger, Hamburg. **Airport**: At Woolsington, 6m NW. Flights to Aberdeen, Amsterdam, Belfast, Bergen, Birmingham, Bristol, Brussels, Dublin, Dussledorf, Frankfurt, Guernsey, the Isle of Man, Jersey, London (Heathrow, Gatwick and Stansted), Manchester, Oslo, Paris, Plymouth, Stavanger, Teesside and Wick. **Theatres**: Theatre Royal, Grey St.; Newcastle Playhouse, Barras Bridge; New Tyne Theatre and Opera House, Westgate Rd; People's Theatre, Stephenson Rd. Annual visit by Royal Shakespeare Company to Theatre Royal and other theatres each spring. The City Hall, Northumberland Rd, is home of the Northern Sinfonia of England and the main venue for concerts. **Annual Events**: Jazz Festival in May; The Hoppings, a travelling fair, on Town Moor (N of the centre) in last full week of June; Film Festival in October.

History. Newcastle was the Roman station of Pons Aelius on Hadrian's Wall. It took its present name from the castle Robert Curthose, William the Conqueror's eldest son, built in 1080. The city suffered more than once at the hands of the Scots, and held out against them on Charles I's behalf for ten weeks in 1644. Two years later the Scots sold Charles to the English Parliament here. At first a centre of the wool trade, Newcastle flourished on coal-mining and coal-exporting from the Middle Ages onwards: the sarcasm 'to carry coals to Newcastle' was familiar by the 17C. The 19C added ship-building, steel production and engineering. The 'Rocket' was built at George Stephenson's Newcastle works.

Natives and residents. The composer Charles Avison (1709–70), the poet Mark Akenside (1721–70), Admiral Collingwood (1750–1810), the politician Lord Eldon (1751–1838), the arms manufacturer Lord Armstrong (1810–1900), Dickens's friend and biographer John Forster (1812–76) and Hugh Stowell Scott (1862–1903), who wrote historical novels as Henry Seton Merriman, were all born here. The engraver Thomas Bewick (1753–1828), born near Eltingham (Route 87A), worked in Newcastle and died at his home in Gateshead.

FROM THE CATHEDRAL SOUTH TO THE TYNE AND BACK. The **Cathedral** stands in Mosley St., midway between the Tyne Bridge and Central Station. Formerly one of the largest parish churches in England, it was raised to cathedral status in 1882. The W tower with its *spire delicately supported in mid-air by flying buttresses is the chief landmark of central Newcastle. The earliest and best example of a 'crown spire' in Britain (c 1448 but since rebuilt), it set the pattern for similar spires, notably at St Giles's, Edinburgh.

The interior is mainly 14–15C. Unusually, the columns of the nave (1330–60) lack capitals. Beneath the striking lierne vault of the tower stands the font; its superbly carved *canopy (c 1500) has a miniature vault and boss inside. Nearby is a bust of Admiral Collingwood, Nelson's second-in-command at Trafalgar, who was baptised and married here. St Margaret's Chapel, interrupting a series of low arched recesses in the S aisle, has a roundel of 15C glass. The lectern dates from c 1500, and the upper part of the organ case survives from the original Renatus Harris organ of 1676. The S transept has an elaborate 17C monument of the Maddison family. The *Flemish brass commemorating Roger Thornton (d. 1429) and his wife, one of the best and largest in the country, now hangs on the wall of the S choir aisle—too high to be properly appreciated. The crypt has 14C rib vaulting and a small internal 'wheel' window. The cathedral's treasures include the so-called Hexham Bible of c 1220. Charles Avison was organist from 1736. Bewick's workshop was at the SE corner of the churchyard.

St Nicholas St. leads S to the remains of the *Castle (open), on a site cruelly cut in two by the railway.

The *Black Gate*—named after a person, not its colour—is a barbican of 1247 with a 17C upper part. The handsome though not very big *Keep*, on the other side of the railway, was built by Henry II in 1172–77 on the site of Robert Curthose's 'new castle'

(1080). An outside staircase over the forebuilding mounts to the restored entrance (1848) at second-floor level. This arrangement is paralleled only at Dover and may be the work of the same mason. The *Hall* occupies most of the interior of the keep. Stairs lead up to the 19C battlements (with a view of the city and river) and down to the beautiful but much restored *Chapel* (c 1168–78) in the forebuilding, and the so-called *Garrison Room*, with its central pillar. Chambers and passages in the walls can also be explored.

The crown spire of Newcastle Cathedral

The walk crosses Castle Garth and, passing the *Moot Hall* (1810) on the left, goes through the S postern gate to descend the steep Castle Stairs to the river by the *Swing Bridge* (1876), on the site of the Roman and medieval bridges. Downstream is the *Tyne Bridge* (1925–28; Mott, Hay and Anderson). Upstream are the superb *High Level Bridge* (1845–49; Robert Stephenson), with the road suspended beneath the railway, and the new *Queen Elizabeth II Bridge* carrying the Metro.

The tall 16–17C houses in Sandhill, to the left, include *Bessie Surtees House* (EH, all year plus Mondays in winter). The *Guildhall*, opposite, was built by Robert Trollope in 1658, classicised in the 18C and given its rounded E end by Dobson in 1823. Quayside, where an open-air market is held on Sunday mornings, leads under the Tyne Bridge. There is a fine view up the river bank to *All Saints' Church* (1786–96; David Stephenson) with its striking steeple and elliptical nave. Shortly beyond stands the *Custom House* (1766, altered by Sydney Smirke in 1838). Broad Chare has the *Trinity Maritime Centre* (open) and *Trinity House* (not open), a foundation of 1492, with 16–19C buildings.

Milk Market leads into City Rd and an area several times battered by change. Opposite are the Dutch-style buildings of the *Keelmen's Hospital* (1701). Further E is *St Ann's Church* (1764–68; William Newton). City Rd heads up towards the Swan House roundabout, passing a corner tower of the medieval town walls on the left. Hemmed in by later development stands the Holy Jesus Hospital, an arcaded and Dutch-gabled almshouse of 1681–83, restored as the *John George Joicey Museum*. Devoted to the social history of Newcastle, it contains audio-visual displays, 17–19C period rooms, swords and sporting guns made in the North-East, and regimental collections. Pedestrian passages lead to Mosley St. below the monstrous and barren *Swan House* (1970; Robert Matthew, Johnson-Marshall and Partners in association with George Kenyon), entombing a fibre-glass replica of Dobson's *Royal Arcade* (1831).

FROM THE CATHEDRAL NORTH TO THE CIVIC CENTRE AND THE UNIVERSITY, AND BACK. *Grey St., climbing N from Mosley St. in a gentle curve of classical façades, is one of England's finest streets (1835–38; John Dobson, John Wardle, George Walker, Benjamin Green). On the right stands the *Theatre Royal* with its splendid portico (1837; Benjamin Green). On the left is the entrance to the well-preserved Edwardian *Central Arcade* (1905). At the top of the street stands the *Grey Monument*, also by Green, commemorating the 2nd Earl Grey (1764–1845), the Liberal Prime Minister responsible for the Reform Bill of 1832. His statue is by Edward H. Baily. *Monument Station* is the main interchange for the Metro, the city's rapid transit system.

Grainger St. and the Eldon Square Shopping Precinct, to the left, are visited later in this walk. It now takes New Bridge St. to the right, passing Northumberland St. on the way to the modern John Dobson St. This leads N between the *Central Library* (1968; Sir Basil Spence), with the main TI Centre, and the **Laing Art Gallery** in a neo-baroque building of 1904.

It contains wide-ranging collections of British art from the 18C to the present, including paintings by Gainsborough, Reynolds, Landseer, Burne-Jones (Laus Veneris), Holman Hunt (Isabella and the Pot of Basil), Stanley Spencer and John Hoyland, and a good display of work by John Martin. The award-winning 'Art on Tyneside', telling the story of the region's art over 400 years, displays an extensive collection of paintings, watercolours, ceramics, silver and glass, including 18C enamelled glass by William Beilby. The Laing also has a childrens' gallery and a programme of temporary exhibitions.

In Croft St., opposite, is the *Plummer Tower*, a relic of the medieval wall altered in 1742.

Northumberland St., a busy shopping street, continues Pilgrim St. N to Barras Bridge, where Dobson's Gothic Revival church of *St Thomas* (1825–30) forms the focal point between the Civic Centre and the university.

The **Civic Centre** (1960–68; George Kenyon) has a quasi-monastic plan in the shape of a cross, with a central tower, and an arcaded cloister or quadrangle enclosed by the administrative wings.

A *Ceremonial Way*, lined with tall flambeaux and dominated by a huge bronze symbolising the Tyne, leads to the elliptical *Council Chamber*. At the N end of the quadrangle stands the plain and massive *Banqueting Hall*, with deep-set slit windows. The *Tower* has a copper lantern, decorated with sea horses and crowned by the three castles of the city's arms.

The **University of Newcastle** grew out of the College of Medicine (1834) and the College of Physical Science (1871), later Armstrong College. In 1937 they united to form King's College, part of Durham University until granted university status in its own right in 1963. Among the new buildings are the *Physics Building* (1961; Sir Basil Spence), the *University Library* (1982; Faulkner-Brown), and the *Medical School* (1984; Robert Matthew, Johnson-Marshall). The campus has several good museums.

The *Museum of Antiquities* contains a splendid collection, particularly of finds from Hadrian's Wall.

It includes: the late Bronze Age Whittingham sword; Iron Age finds from Ryton; the Celtic Aesica brooch (AD 75–80) from Hadrian's Wall, and other similar brooches; a gladiator and the *Bear cameo (3C), both from South Shields, and a set of bronze Roman military cooking vessels (2C) found near Ponteland; Roman altars, inscriptions and relief sculpture; an Anglo-Saxon hanging bowl (the most northerly in England); the Falstone Latin/Runic inscription (8–9C); and part of a 10C cross from Alnmouth. Note also: the scale models of Hadrian's Wall; original and reconstructed Roman body armour; a reconstruction of the Carrawburgh Mithraeum; and a facsimile of the Corbridge Lanx (original in British Museum).

The *Hatton Gallery* has 16–18C European paintings, a large relief by Kurt Schwitters and African sculptures. The *Greek Museum*, open on application to the Department of Classics, houses a small but important collection of Mediterranean antiquities. The *Mining Museum* in the Department of Mining Engineering has a good collection of miners' lamps. The *Hancock Museum*, in Barras Bridge to the N, has large collections of geology and natural history, with a Thomas Bewick Room.

Further N is the large *Town Moor*. Before the little *Brandling Park*, on the E side of the Great North Road (subway), stands the *Royal Grammar School*. Overlooking the pleasant *Leazes Park*, SW of the university, is the dignified Leazes Terrace (1829–30; Thomas Oliver). The St James's Park ground of Newcastle United Football Club adjoins it.

From Barras Bridge the busy Haymarket (with a Metro station and bus station), Percy St. and Newgate St. lead SW, passing the huge *Eldon Square Shopping Precinct* (1976; Chapman, Taylor and Partners) on the left. *St Andrew's Church*, on the right, has a good chancel arch and a carved 15C font cover like the one in the cathedral.

The remains of the medieval *Town Walls* (1265–1307) begin in the churchyard and continue, with towers, along West Walls and Bath Lane to Westgate Rd. *Blackfriars*, between Friars St. and Monk St., incorporates the restored buildings of a Dominican friary founded before 1239 and later used by craft guilds. Nearby Fenkle St. has the *Old Assembly Rooms* (1776; William Newton).

Newgate St. curves SE to the junction with Grainger St., which has a handsome stretch of buildings (partly by John Wardle, 1835–39) leading up to the Grey Monument. The *Grainger Market* (1835; Dobson) on its left-hand side is a good covered market. Westgate Rd and Neville St., on the walk W from the cathedral (below), can be reached by taking Grainger St. to the right from Newgate St. The walk can also be finished by following Bigg Market and Cloth Market to Mosley St. and the cathedral.

WEST FROM THE CATHEDRAL. Mosley St. is continued W by Collingwood St., with *Lloyd's Bank* (1891) and the *Literary and Philosophical Society* (1822–25). George Stephenson demonstrated his miners' safety lamp at the earlier location of the society in Groat Market in 1815, and Sir Joseph Swan demonstrated his electric light bulb here in 1879. J.G. Lough's statue (1862) of George Stephenson stands at the fork of Neville St. and Westgate Rd. **Central Station** (1848–50) is a fine building by Dobson, with elegantly curved train sheds behind its classical entrance.

The 14–15C church of *St John the Baptist*, at the junction of Westgate Rd and Grainger St., has a Jacobean pulpit and beautiful font cover. Bewick was married here. The Old Assembly Rooms, Blackfriars and the medieval walls, all described above, can be reached from Westgate Rd.

Neville St. leads to the junction with Clayton St. and Pugin's *Roman Catholic Cathedral*, built as a church in 1844 but elevated to cathedral status in 1850. The spire was added by J.A. Hansom. Westmorland Rd continues to Blandford Square and the **Newcastle Discovery**. Its permanent displays deal with: the history of motive power, with working models; the history of the Tyne, with a model of the river in 1929; and Tyneside's industrial pioneers, including George and Robert Stephenson, Sir Joseph Swan and Lord Armstrong.

SOUTH TYNESIDE: FROM NEWCASTLE/GATESHEAD TO JARROW AND SOUTH SHIELDS, 10½m by A184, A185. From Gateshead the road skirts the S bank of the industrial Tyne. 7m: **Jarrow** (27,200 inhabitants; TI), whose name recalls unemployment and the Hunger March of 1936, has ship-repair yards and oil installations. The *Tyne Tunnel* (1967; toll) takes the A1 under the river to Willington Quay and North Shields. Part of the basilica founded here by Benedict Biscop in 682 survives as the chancel of *St Paul's Church*, with its 11C tower, to the E of the town. The dedication stone of 685 can be seen above the chancel arch inside; the N aisle has interesting displays of pre-Conquest sculptured stones. The Venerable Bede ('the monk of Jarrow') lived in the adjoining monastery from 682 until his death in 735, writing his 'Historia Ecclesiastica' here. The chair in the chancel is traditionally said to be his, though dendrochronology has shown it to be only about 800 years old. The *Bede Monastery Museum*, in a late 18C mine-owner's house, displays Saxon and medieval finds, as well as temporary exhibitions. The property is EH (ruins open at any reasonable time; museum open 1 April to 31 October, Tuesday to Saturday and Bank Holidays 10.00–17.50, and Sundays 14.30–17.30, and from 1 November to 31 March, Tuesday to Saturday 11.00–16.30, and Sundays 14.30–17.00). The popular novelist Catherine Cookson was born at Jarrow in 1906, and much of the South Tyneside region advertises itself to tourists as 'Catherine Cookson country'.

10½m: **South Shields** (87,200 inhabitants; TI), at the head of the estuary, developed as a coal port and resort in the 19C. The local ferry crosses the Tyne to North Shields. Near the seafront the Roman fort of Arbeia has been excavated and its gateway rebuilt. The *Roman Museum* displays building, military, household and personal items from the site. The *Central Museum and Art Gallery* has local history exhibits, including a section about the invention of the lifeboat at South Shields. The author and naturalist

Ernest Seton Thompson (1860–1946) was born here, but went to Canada at the age of five.

FROM NEWCASTLE/GATESHEAD TO SUNDERLAND AND STOCKTON, 11½m. A184, relabelled A1 for part of the way, leads SW from Gateshead. At (7m) *East Boldon* the route turns S on A1018. 10½m: *Monkwearmouth* is an unattractive suburb of Sunderland. *St Peter's Church* preserves the tower, W wall and porch from the Saxon church of the monastery founded by Benedict Biscop in 674. Bede entered the monastery in 680 at the age of seven, moving to Jarrow in 682. Monkwearmouth Station (1848), with a lovely neo-classical façade, is now a museum of land transport. The booking office and other parts of the building have been restored to their original condition. *Roker*, an Edwardian seaside suburb 1m NE, has a church by E.S. Prior (1906–07) with Arts and Crafts furnishings which include an altar tapestry by Burne-Jones and tablets by Eric Gill. *Whitburn*, on the coast 1½m further N, has a statue of Lewis Carroll, said to have written 'The Walrus and the Carpenter' while walking on the beach here. The Souter Lighthouse (NT) was opened in 1871. The Wear is crossed by a bridge (1929; Mott, Hay and Anderson) replacing one of 1793–96, then the boldest iron bridge of its time.

11½m: **Sunderland** (196,200 inhabitants; TI), at the mouth of the river, developed as a coal port and a centre of ship-building and engineering in the 19C. Sir Joseph Swan (1828–1917), who in 1878 narrowly anticipated Edison in inventing the electric light bulb, was born here. George Hudson, the fraudulent 'Railway King', became its MP in 1845, and Sir Henry Irving made his first stage appearance here in 1856. The *Town Hall* and *Civic Centre* (1968–70) were designed by Sir Basil Spence, Bonnington and Collins. The *Museum and Art Gallery* in Mowbray Park has exhibits of local and maritime history, Sunderland glass and pottery, English silver and 18–20C British painting. *St Michael's Church* (enlarged by W.D. Caröe, 1932–35) in High St. West and the parish church of *Holy Trinity* (1719) near the docks are worth seeking out. The *Grindon Museum*, off A183 3m SW, has reconstructed 19–20C interiors. *Hylton Castle* (EH, all year), off A1290 3m NW, is a 15C gatehouse-keep with the arms of the Washington family on its front. From Sunderland to Washington and Durham, see above.

A1018 continues S. At (14½m) *Ryhope* the Pumping Station Museum has the original beam engines of 1868. *Seaham* (21,100 inhabitants), 2½m S, is a coal port with a badly polluted coastline. In 1815 Byron was married at Seaham Hall, to its N. A1018 turns inland and joins A19 at (16½m) *Seaton*. At (20½m) *Easington*, with a 13C church, the Hartlepool road bears left. It passes the mining town of *Peterlee* (22,800 inhabitants; TI), founded in 1948 and named after the miners' leader Peter Lee (1864–1935). A19 heads right to (29½m) the roundabout near *Wingate*. The castle (limited opening) at *Castle Eden*, about 1m left, is an 18–19C building. A19 continues to (36m) *Billingham* and (39m) *Stockton*, both described in the detour from Darlington, above.

NORTH TYNESIDE: FROM NEWCASTLE TO TYNEMOUTH AND WHITLEY BAY. The quickest route (9½m) takes A1058, leaving Newcastle via (1½m) *Jesmond Dene*, a lovely park in the Ouseburn valley. The route below (11m) takes A193, linking up the industrial towns on the N bank of the Tyne. 3½m: *Wallsend* (44,700 inhabitants) is so called because Hadrian's Wall reached the Tyne here. The site of the fort of Segedunum lies near the Heritage Centre and Swan Hunter's ship-building yard. A193 crosses the N approach to the Tyne tunnel and passes the road for Tyne Commission Quay, with the passenger ferry terminal (seasonal TI). 7½m: *North Shields* (seasonal TI), with a ferry service across the Tyne to South Shields. *The Fishing Experience*, on Fish Quay, re-creates the area's connection with the North Sea. At (8½m) **Tynemouth** (60,000 inhabitants with North Shields) the head of the estuary was guarded by the *Castle and Priory* (EH, all year). There was a monastery here by the 7C, refounded c 1090 as a Benedictine priory. The ruins consist chiefly of the Early English presbytery and 15C Percy Chapel, enclosed by the castle wall and 14C gatehouse. A193 continues up the coast past (9½m) the former fishing village of *Cullercoats* to (11m) the resort of **Whitley Bay** (37,100 inhabitants; TI). On its way further N to (7m) *Blyth* (see below) the coast road passes (3¼m) *Seaton Sluice*. To its W stands *Seaton Delaval Hall* (limited opening), built by Vanbrugh in 1718–29 and, though gutted by fire in 1822, still ranking as one of his masterpieces. The little church is Norman.

FROM NEWCASTLE TO THE SCOTTISH BORDER AT CARTER BAR, 45m by A696 and A68. A lovely route through remote countryside. It passes Newcastle Airport on the way to (7½m) *Ponteland* (10,700 inhabitants) in Northumberland. 13½m: *Belsay Hall and Castle* (EH, all year), to the left, consist of a 14C pele tower attached to a ruined 17C mansion, and a Greek Revival house of 1810–17 built by the owner, Sir Charles Monck, with the help of the antiquary Sir William Gell and John Dobson. 17m: *Shaftoe Crags* are on the right. *Capheaton Hall* (not open), 1m left, is a beautiful house of 1668 by Robert Trollope of Newcastle. Swinburne spent part of his childhood here with his grandfather. 19m: *Kirkharle*, to the left, was the birthplace of Capability Brown (1716–83). He started work as a day labourer and later landscaped the grounds at *Wallington* (NT), 2m N, a late 17C house with good 18C plasterwork inside. The central hall, added for Lady Pauline Trevelyan by John Dobson in 1855, has painted decoration by William Bell Scott, Ruskin and others. There are good paintings, furniture, needlework and dolls' houses, and a superb collection of fine porcelain. 21m: *Kirkwhelpington*, on the edge of the wild Northumbrian moors. 30m: **Otterburn** was the scene of the Scottish victory over the English in 1388, remembered in the English ballad of 'Chevy Chase' and the Scottish ballad of 'The Battle of Otterbourne'. Douglas, the Scottish leader, was killed and Hotspur, the English leader, captured. There is a National Park village information point at the Border Reiver café and shop. At (31½m) *Elishaw* A696 joins A68, the Roman Dere Street from Corbridge (Route 87A), and enters the Northumberland National Park (see note to Route 87). The road follows the wild valley of *Redesdale* past (34½m) *Rochester*, with the Roman station of Bremenium ½m right, and (42m) *Catcleugh Reservoir*, created in 1896–1906. One of the original workers' huts has been preserved and restored (open by prior arrangement with the National Park headquarters). Between Rochester and the reservoir A68 is joined by the drive (11m; toll) through the Border Forest Park from Kielder (Route 87A). 45m: **Carter Bar** (1371ft), at the SW end of the Cheviot Hills, marks the border. The last border skirmish, the Raid of Reidswire, took place here in 1575. From Carter Bar to Edinburgh via Jedburgh and Melrose, see 'Blue Guide Scotland'.

From Newcastle to *Carlisle* via *Tynedale* and *Hexham*, see Route 87A; via *Hadrian's Wall*, see Route 87B.

A6125 heads N from Newcastle. At *Killingworth*, E of (117m) *Gosforth Park* racecourse, George Stephenson built his first locomotive in 1814. At (119½m) *Seaton Burn*, on the Northumbrian border, the road joins A1. 127m: **Morpeth** (14,500 inhabitants; TI) is a pleasant little town on the Wansbeck. The 14C church of *St Mary* contains a restored Jesse window, and an adapted 15C gatehouse survives from the *Castle*. The 13C *Chantry* near the river has been converted to house a local history museum and the TI Centre. Vanbrugh's *Town Hall* (1714) in the Market Place was altered in 1869–70. The 15C *Belfry* in Oldgate rings a curfew at 20.00 every evening.

Mitford, 2m upstream where the Font flows into the Wansbeck, and *Bothal*, 3m downstream, both have ruined castles and interesting churches.

Roads run SE from Morpeth to (5m) *Bedlington*, with an attractive High St., and (9m) the colliery and ship-building port of *Blyth* (36,500 inhabitants); and E to (9m) the small seaside resort of *Newbiggin-by-the-Sea* (12,100 inhabitants). N of Newbiggin are the towns of (2½m) *Lynemouth* and (3½m) *Ellington*, with the world's largest undersea mine. The winding B roads leading SW from Morpeth to (26m) *Corbridge* (Route 87A) pass (6m) *Whalton* and (16m) *Stamfordham*, two good villages with long greens. Whalton church has 13C work. *Belsay*, where the route crosses A696 between Whalton and Stamfordham, lies on the detour from Newcastle to Carter Bar, above.

FROM MORPETH TO COLDSTREAM, 45m. After briefly joining A1, the route branches left on A697 about 2½m N of Morpeth. At (9m) *Weldon* the road crosses the Coquet, explored in the detour from Felton below, and beyond (10½m) *Longframlington* it climbs over the moors of *Rothbury Forest*. 15m: A697 is crossed by B6341, heading SW to Rothbury and NE to Alnwick via Edlingham, all described later in this route. 19m: *Bridge of Aln Inn*. The church at *Whittingham* (pronounced 'Whittinjam'), 1½m W, has traces of Saxon work. *Callaly Castle* (not open), 2m SW of Whittingham, is a 17–19C mansion built round a pele tower. Beyond (22m) *Powburn* the valley of the Breamish leads W into the Northumberland National Park (see note to Route 87), with a seasonal Information Centre at (2½m) *Ingram*. Further on lies the prehistoric settlement of *Greaves Ash*, scattered over about 20 acres, and, 4m from Ingram, the fall of *Linhope Spout* in the heart of the desolate Cheviot Hills. 31m: **Wooler** (seasonal TI) is a small, grey market town on the edge of the Northumberland National Park and the Cheviots. *Humbleton Hill*, where Hotspur defeated Earl Douglas in 1402, rises 1½m W. *The Cheviot* (2674ft), about 6m SW, is the highest hill in the group, with a wild and desolate view. *Chillingham Castle* (open), 6m SE of Wooler, keeps the square corner towers of the 14C fortress, with 15–19C additions including an Elizabethan Long Gallery. The grounds include formal gardens, landscaping by Sir Jeffrey Wyatville (1753) and lovely woodland. The small church contains the elaborate table-tomb of Sir Ralph Grey (d. 1443). *Chillingham Park* (open) has a unique herd of wild white cattle. From (33¼m) *Akeld* B6351 heads W along the valley of the Glen past *Yeavering Bell* (1182ft; •view), on the left, above the site of Edwin of Northumbria's 7C palace. Beyond (2¾m) *Kirknewton* it crosses the College Burn. From (5m) *Kilham* a sideroad goes on up the Bowmont Water to (11m) *Kirk Yetholm* in Scotland, at the end of the Pennine Way. Beyond Akeld A697 follows the valley of the Till past (38m) *Ford*, with its partly 14C castle (not open), on the opposite bank. The village was improved in the 19C by Ruskin's pupil Louisa, Marchioness of Waterford, whose paintings are displayed in the former village school. *Etal* (pronounced 'Eetle'), a pleasant little place 1½m NW of Ford, has the remains of a 14C castle (EH, summer season, daily; grounds open in winter). 39¼m: *Crookham*. About 1½m W is the battlefield of *Flodden*, where the English defeated the Scots in 1513. A monument to 'the brave of both nations' stands near *Branxton* church on the spot where James IV of Scotland is supposed to have fallen. 43m: *Cornhill* and (45m) *Coldstream*, see below.

Beyond Morpeth A1 crosses the Coquet near (137m) *Felton*.

For *Warkworth*, on the river about 7½m E, see below. B6345, A697 and B6344 follow the river W. 6½m: *Brinkburn Priory* (EH, summer season), founded c 1130 for Augustinian canons, stands on a lovely site by the river. Its handsome late 12C church spans the transition from Norman to Early English. The nearby Georgian house incorporates part of the cloister buildings. 11½m: **Rothbury** (1700 inhabitants; seasonal TI) is an attractive town. The church font stands on part of a 9C cross. •*Cragside* (NT), splendidly sited on a hillside 1m NE, was largely designed by Norman Shaw in 1869–85 for the Newcastle arms manufacturer Lord Armstrong. The fine interiors contain work in the Pre-Raphaelite taste, including pottery and tiles by William De Morgan and paintings by Evelyn De Morgan, as well as Victorian technology (central heating, electric light, hydraulic lift, etc.). The wooded grounds run to 900 acres. The heather-clad *Simonside Hills* (1447ft) rise SW of Rothbury.

B6341 continues through the beautiful moorland scenery of •*Coquetdale*. 4m: The sideroad to the right enters the Northumberland National Park beyond (6½m) *Sharperton*. Near *Holystone*, about 1m S, is a well (NT) in which Paulinus is said to have baptised 3000 Northumbrians in 627. In the beautiful parkland of Holystone Grange stands *Woodhouses Bastle*, a fortified 16C farmhouse. Beyond (9m) *Harbottle*, with the remains of a late 12C castle, and (10½m) *Alwinton*, the sideroad reaches the boundary of the vast Redesdale Firing Range (closed during firing practice) and continues to (19½m) *Blindburn*, 3m from the Roman camp of *Chew Green* on Dere Street, near the Scottish border. After the turning for Sharperton B6341 crosses the Coquet and goes through (12m) *Elsdon*, with a pele tower near the church and the earthworks of a Norman castle, on the way to (15m) *Otterburn* (on the Newcastle–Carter Bar detour, above).

145m: **Alnwick** (pronounced 'Annick'; 7200 inhabitants; seasonal TI) is an unspoilt old town above the Aln. The 15C *Hotspur Gate*, with *Pottergate* near the church, is the only relic of the medieval walls. *St Michael* contains good capitals, 14–15C effigies and a Flemish chest in the vestry.

Alnwick Castle (open), overlooking the river, makes a marvellously romantic spectacle. This is largely the result of 19C rebuilding, though the medieval plan and some good details survive.

The original 12C shell-keep and curtain wall were strengthened and enlarged when the Percys, later Earls and then Dukes of Northumberland, bought the castle in 1309. Robert Adam rescued it from disrepair in the mid 18C but his work was expunged a century later, when Anthony Salvin gave the exterior its present baronial appearance and Italian workmen created the ornate interior.

The entrance is near the *Barbican* and *Gatehouse* (c 1440). The early 14C *Abbot's Tower* in the Outer Bailey contains a regimental museum. The 14–15C *Middle Gateway* leads into the Middle Bailey, where the *Constable's Tower*, *Hotspur's Seat* and *Postern Tower* are early 14C. The Postern Tower houses prehistoric and Roman archaeology, with Celtic and Viking material. The mid 14C *Octagonal Towers*, with a Norman arch beyond, lead to the *Keep*. The 19C state rooms, in the style of a Renaissance palace, contain a fine art collection (Andrea del Sarto, Tintoretto, Titian, Claude Lorrain, Van Dyck, Canaletto, Turner). The grounds are by Capability Brown.

Only a 14C gatehouse remains of *Alnwick Abbey*, beyond the Aln, founded in 1147 for Premonstratensian canons. *Hulne Priory*, on a hill above the river 3m NW, is reached on foot through the beautiful grounds of Hulne Park either from Alnwick or from B6346 (admission pass from the Estate Office, Alnwick Castle). It is privately occupied but can be seen with the tenant's permission. Founded c 1240, Hulne is the earliest example of a Carmelite friary in England, and the ruins are the most perfect of their kind.

B6341, the Rothbury road to the SW, passes near (6m) *Edlingham*, where the castle ruins by the railway viaduct include a handsome 15C tower (EH).

A1068 leads E to (4½m) **Alnmouth**, a resort on the estuary of the Aln. B1339, heading N, passes the turnings for (4½m) the beautiful gardens (open) of *Howick Hall* and (5½m) the fishing village of *Craster* (seasonal TI), known for its kippers, with a tiny harbour and a medieval tower. Near Dunstanburgh Castle B1339 joins B1340, on the alternative route from Alnwick to Belford, below. Beyond Alnmouth A1068 continues another 3m down the coast to *Warkworth*, a lovely village on a loop of the Coquet, with a medieval bridge and a partly Norman church. The spectacularly sited *Warkworth Castle* (EH, all year) was founded in the 12C and became a stronghold of the Percys in 1332. The ruins include the walls, gatehouse and vestiges of the great hall (all before 1215), the Lion Tower (c 1400) with the lion emblem of the Percys, and the marvellous 15C keep. About ½m upstream is the remarkable 14C *Hermitage* cut into the cliff (EH, opening details from castle). 2m beyond Warkworth the road reaches *Amble-by-the-Sea* (5400 inhabitants; seasonal TI), a port at the mouth of the Coquet. About 1m offshore is *Coquet Island*, the site of a cell of Tynemouth Priory, with a lighthouse.

A1 from Alnwick to (160m) *Belford* (seasonal TI) is not interesting and the alternative route nearer the coast, described below, is recommended. *Preston Tower* (open), right of A1 at 153m, is a late 14C pele tower with tunnel-vaulted rooms.

The alternative way from Alnwick to Belford, 8m longer than the main route, takes B1340 to (7¼m) *Christon Bank*. About 2m E is *Embleton*, with a vicar's pele tower (14C). On the rocky headland 2m beyond, and 1m from the end of the road, are the striking ruins of **Dunstanburgh Castle** (EH, all year). One of the largest border castles, it was begun in 1314 and strengthened by John of Gaunt, then Lieutenant of the Scottish Marches, in 1380–84. The Wars of the Roses hastened its ruin. The Lilburn Tower and parts of the curtain walls survive but the boldest feature, dominating the beautiful coastline, is the twin-towered *gatehouse-keep*. For Craster, to the S, see above. B1340 joins the coast at (13m) *Beadnell* and continues to (14½m) the resort of *Seahouses* (seasonal TI).

In summer there are boat trips from the harbour to the *Farne Islands (NT), an archipelago of about 28 small islands forming the E tip of the dolerite scarp known as the Great Whin Sill. They are a breeding place for the grey seal and about 20 species of seabirds. The *Inner Farne*, c 2m from the coast, is the nearest and largest. St Aidan often withdrew here from Lindisfarne for prayer and contemplation, and St Cuthbert lived from 676 to 684 in a hermitage whose site is marked by a 14C chapel, returning to die here in 687. The *Longstone Lighthouse*, on one of the remotest islands, was the scene of the rescue by Grace Darling (1815–42) and her father of the survivors of the 'Forfarshire' in 1838.

17½m: **Bamburgh** was the Saxon capital of Bernicia and, for a time, of the united kingdom of Northumbria. The *Castle (open), romantically placed on a dolerite crag by the shore, served for generations as a royal fortress. The magnificent keep is Norman and much of the curtain wall dates from before 1250, but the Newcastle arms tycoon Lord Armstrong rebuilt most of the remainder in the late 19C. There is a fine view of the coast from the ramparts. The *Church* on the opposite side of the village has a lovely 13C choir. St Aidan died here in 651, though he was buried on Holy Island. The tomb of Grace Darling stands in the churchyard and her lifeboat is preserved in the museum named after her.

B1342 heads inland past the S tip of *Budle Bay* to join A1 just before (23m) *Belford*.

A1 continues past *Beal*, to the right at 166½m on the direct route. *Holy Island, or Lindisfarne, can be reached from here by a causeway (about 3m) uncovered at low tide. The tables posted at each end should be consulted.

King Oswald of Northumbria gave the island to St Aidan (d. 651), a missionary from Iona, who became the first Bishop of Lindisfarne in 635. Under him and his successors, who included St Cuthbert (d. 687), Holy Island became one of the earliest and most shining centres of Christianity in England. A glorious relic survives in the famous Lindisfarne Gospels (c 698), now in the British Museum. When the Danes descended in 875, the monks fled with the body of St Cuthbert, finding a final refuge at Durham in 995.

Nothing remains of this first monastery. The existing *ruins (EH, all year) belong to the Benedictine priory founded as a cell to Durham in 1083. Despite erosion by nine centuries of sea weather, the red sandstone church remains a superb example of Norman work, remarkable for its fortified character and very like the mother church at Durham. Note the incised decoration of the nave pillars and the diagonal rib vault between the crossing piers. The domestic buildings to the S are 13–14C. Nearby are a small museum displaying carved stones and other remains from the priory, and the Early English parish church with its massively buttressed bell-tower.

The fine view from the ruins takes in Bamburgh Castle on the mainland to the S and, on a dolerite rock E of the priory, *Lindisfarne Castle* (NT), a small 16C fort ingeniously converted into a private house by Sir Edwin Lutyens in 1903. It contains 17C oak furniture, and the grounds include a walled garden by Gertrude Jekyll.

At (174m) *Tweedmouth* A1 crosses the Tweed by the high concrete New Bridge (1925–28), supplementing the 15-arched Old Bridge (1611–34). To the left is Robert Stephenson's Royal Border Bridge, built for the railway in 1850.

175m: **Berwick-upon-Tweed** (pronounced 'Berrick'; 12,200 inhabitants; TI) is an old border town at the mouth of the Tweed.

Alternately English and Scottish for centuries, Berwick had changed hands at least 13 times when it was finally surrendered to England in 1482. It was then made a bastion against the Scots and organised as a kind of extra-territorial community with a government of its own. Its autonomy was recognised until the 19C.

The town centre is enclosed by *Ramparts* (EH) begun in 1555, among the earliest northern European examples of the new military engineering pioneered in Italy. The N front was complete in 1569; the rest is a later extension, not finished until 1747. They enclose a much smaller area than Edward I's wall, of which only traces survive. The *Castle* where Edward judged in favour of John Balliol's claim to the Scottish crown in 1291 was largely demolished to make way for the railway station in the 19C, but a few fragments still stand nearby (EH). The fine *Ravensdowne Barracks* (EH, all year), built in 1717–21, are perhaps by Vanbrugh. They contain the local museum and art gallery, an exhibition about the history of the British infantry soldier from 1660 to 1880, and the regimental museum of the King's Own Scottish Borderers. *Holy Trinity* (1648–52) is one of the few churches built during the Commonwealth; the outside is marred by 19C turrets, but the inside has good woodwork and a reredos by Lutyens. The church-like *Town Hall* (1754–60) preserves its original jail cells on the upper floor. In the grounds of the early 18C Governor's House, overlooking the pleasant Palace Green, is the *Lindisfarne Wine and Spirit Museum*.

At *Halidon Hill* (537ft), 2m NW, a Scottish army attempting to raise the English siege of Berwick was defeated with great slaughter in 1333.

FROM BERWICK TO KELSO, 23m by A698 and B6350. The road follows the S bank of the Tweed, marking the Scottish border. 6½m: **Norham** lies in a bend of the river 1¾m NW. Its ruined *Castle* (EH, all year) was the border stronghold of the prince-bishops of Durham. Bishop Pudsey built the fine Norman keep (c 1160). In the church (with a Norman chancel) Edward I opened the assembly to decide the rival claims of Bruce and Balliol to the Scottish throne in 1290. 9¾m: The deep ravine of the Till is crossed by the 15C *Twizel Bridge*, over which the English vanguard passed safely before the Battle of Flodden (1513). The 'castle' above is a ruined folly (1770). At (13m) *Cornhill-on-Tweed* A698 is joined by A697, which crosses the river into Scotland at *Coldstream*. B6350 continues along the S bank via (15½m) *Wark-on-Tweed*, with the scanty remains of its once formidable castle, and enters Scotland shortly beyond (17½m) *Carham*. 23m: *Kelso*, see 'Blue Guide Scotland'.

From Berwick to *Edinburgh* via *Dunbar* and *Haddington*, see 'Blue Guide Scotland'. A1 crosses the border 3m N of Berwick at *Lamberton Bar*, where the tollkeeper performed the same offices for runaway couples as the Gretna Green blacksmith.

86

The Dales

Maps: Walkers need OS Outdoor Leisure maps (1:25,000 or 2½in to 1m) for the Yorkshire Dales (three sheets) and Teesdale (one sheet).

The Pennine Chain, the loosely linked series of hills forming the so-called 'backbone of England', stretches N from the Peak District to the river Tyne in Northumberland. It is never very broad, avoided by the A1 on the E and the A6, intertwined with M6, on the W. Nor is it particularly high, its hills rarely exceeding 2000ft; the tallest rise in the W, where Cross Fell (between Appleby and Alston) achieves 2930ft. Its geological structure shows the same mixture of gritstone, or millstone grit, and limestone as the Peak District, described in the introduction to Route 69. Millstone grit predominates in the S, sometimes weathered into fantastic shapes which enliven the moorland. The limestone region begins near Skipton and the Aire Gap, where the Craven Faults create dramatic effects at Malham Cove and the local 'scars'. Further N, in Teesdale, is the S edge of the Whin Sill (or Great Whin Sill), the intrusive scarp of hard igneous rock over which the waterfall at High Force hurls itself.

This upland landscape of fell, moor and rock is varied by the dales, the winding valleys of the rivers which make their way down the Pennine slopes. Most flow eastwards, though the Ribble perversely heads S before issuing into the sea on the W coast near Preston. The southern reaches of the dales have proved a natural breeding-ground for industry since the 18C; they are toured on the way through the Yorkshire and Lancashire manufacturing towns in Route 75. The present routes follows the largely agricultural dales further N: Wharfedale (Route A), Nidderdale (Route B), the upper stages of Airedale and Ribblesdale (Route C), Wensleydale (Route D) and their many tributary dales. Here the countryside remains wild or wooded or just pleasantly green. Bolton Abbey in Wharfedale is the best-known example of the picturesque combination of water, wood and ruin which the dales can offer, just as Grassington, higher up the same valley, typifies their charming stone-built towns and villages. Lead-mining has left its trace further N, in Swaledale (Route E) and Teesdale (Route G), but only Weardale (Route H) bears the scars of industry.

These routes repeatedly interconnect and, in their possible combinations with each other, offer drivers a choice of many different ways over the Pennines, linking points on or near the A1 (Route 85B) with points on or near the A6 (Route 76). But the character of the landscape, with its often steep and narrow roads, hardly suits long-distance travellers or car-bound sightseers: they are better advised to cross the Pennines by the high-lying A66 (Route F) between Scotch Corner and Penrith, or to follow A69 (Route 87A) along the Tyne valley from Newcastle to Carlisle. The dales attract climbers, pot-holers and, above all, walkers. In addition to the various short walking detours suggested in the routes that follow, several long-distance footpaths are worth noting. The Dales Way (81m) connects Ilkley with Bowness-on-Windermere in the Lake District, following Wharfedale, Dentdale and the valleys of the Lune and the Kent. The central section of A. Wainwright's Coast-to-Coast Walk, 190m from St Bees Head to Robin Hood's Bay, follows Swaledale. The central section of the Pennine Way, which starts at Edale in the Peak District and ends at Kirk Yetholm over the Scottish border, goes via Malham (Upper Airedale), Horton-in-Ribblesdale, Hawes (Wensleydale), Keld (Swaledale), Middleton-in-Teesdale and Alston.

Most of the Yorkshire Dales toured in Routes A–E are part of the National Park established in 1954 and covering 650 square miles. There are National Park Information Centres at Aysgarth Falls, Clapham, Grassington, Hawes, Malham and Sedbergh, with smaller local information points in village shops, post offices, cafés, etc., at Askrigg, Bolton Abbey, Buckden, Burnsall, Dent, Garsdale, Gunnerside, Hebden, Horsehouse, Horton-in-Ribbesdale, Kettlewell, Kilnsey, Langcliffe, Litton, Muker, Reeth, Stump Cross Caverns and Thoralby. Further details are available from Colvend, Hebden Rd, Grassington, Skipton, North Yorkshire BD23 5LB.

A. Wharfedale: Wetherby to Ilkley, Grassington and Hawes

Directions. Total distance 58m. **Wetherby**, see Route 85B. A58 to (1½m) Collingham. A659 to (14m) Otley. A660, A65 to (20m) **Ilkley**. A65 to (23m) Addingham. B6160 to (26m) Bolton Abbey, (36½m) **Grassington** and (46½m) Buckden. Unclassified roads to (58m) **Hawes** (Route 86D).

Wetherby, see Route 85B. A58 heads SW to join A659 near (1½m) *Collingham*, which can also be reached directly from A1. The church has the remains of 9C Saxon crosses.

Bardsey, off A58 2¼m SW, was the birthplace of William Congreve (1670–1729) and has a late Norman church with a Saxon tower.

A659 heads W along the broad and not very interesting valley of **Lower Wharfedale**, where the river divides West Yorkshire from North Yorkshire. 6m: *Harewood*, in the sharp bend where the Leeds road joins A659, is a model village by John Carr (1760) outside *Harewood House (open).

The mansion was built in 1759–72, with Robert Adam modifying Carr's original, severely Palladian design. Sir Charles Barry remodelled the S façade and added a third storey in 1843. Inside, only the Entrance Hall is decorated by Carr; the rest of the house keeps some of Adam's best interiors, reaching a superb climax in the Gallery. The plasterwork is by Joseph Rose and the painted wall panels are by Angelica Kauffmann, Antonio Zucchi and Biagio Rebecca. Much of the *furniture was made for Harewood by Chippendale (see Otley, below). The paintings include work by Turner, Thomas Girtin, Bellini, Catena, Pollaiuolo, El Greco, Titian, Veronese and Tintoretto, and family portraits by Gainsborough, Reynolds, Hoppner, Romney and Lawrence. There are also superb collections of Sèvres porcelain and Chinese porcelain.

Outside, the formal terrace and parterre by Barry and Nesfield, to the S, contrasts with the landscaped park by Capability Brown which extends to the N. It contains a *Bird Garden* with exotic species, the ruins of *Harewood Castle*, and the Perpendicular *Church*. Among the fine monuments here is the tomb of Chief Justice Gascoigne (d. 1419), said to have committed the future Henry V for contempt of court (see Shakespeare's 'Henry IV, Part 2').

From Harewood to *Leeds* and to *Harrogate*, *Ripon* and *Thirsk*, see Route 80.

14m: **Otley** (13,800 inhabitants; TI) is an industrial market town on the Wharfe. The cabinetmaker Thomas Chippendale (1711–79) was born here. The restored Perpendicular church contains 17–19C monuments of the Fairfax and Fawkes families, and fragments of 9–11C Saxon crosses. The churchyard has a monument with a scale model of the Bramhope Tunnel, in memory of the railway navvies killed during its construction in 1845–49. The *Chevin* (841ft), rising to the S, gives a good view of the Wharfe valley and the hills to the NW.

The view from the Chevin takes in *Farnley Hall* (not open), about 1½m NE of Otley, an Elizabethan house with a wing added by John Carr in 1786–90. Turner frequently visited his friend Walter Fawkes (a descendant of Guy Fawkes) here, and used a view of the Chevin during a thunderstorm in his painting of 'Hannibal Crossing the Alps'. To the E of Farnley Park is *Leathley*, with its early Norman church tower and 18C Hall and almshouses. Beyond Farnley B6451 follows the Washburn valley, partly filled by reservoirs, to (7m) *Blubberhouses* on the Harrogate–Bolton Abbey road (Route 80).

Guiseley, 2½m S of Otley, has a gabled rectory (1601) and a partly Norman church, where the parents of the Brontë sisters were married in 1812. Ancestors of the American poet Longfellow are buried in the churchyard.

From Otley to *Leeds*, see Route 75F.

A660 heads W from Otley to join A65 outside (16½m) *Burley-in-Wharfedale*. On the other side of the Wharfe beyond the village lies *Denton Park* (not open), rebuilt by John Carr in 1778, where General Fairfax was born in 1612.

20m: **Ilkley** (24,100 inhabitants; TI) spreads from the S bank of the Wharfe towards the high moorland made famous by the Yorkshire song. The late Perpendicular parish church of *All Saints* has three Anglian crosses in the churchyard. The *Manor House Museum* behind it is a 15–17C building on the site of the W gate of the Roman fort of Olicana. Part of the Roman wall has been exposed nearby. The collection includes archaeological finds as well as 17–18C farmhouse furniture.

The neighbourhood is also rich in Bronze Age remains. The *Panorama Stone*, a rock carved with the distinctive 'cup and ring' motif, is in the public gardens opposite the 19C *St Margaret's Church* in the S part of the town. The most famous of the Bronze Age stone circles on the breezy moors further S is the *Twelve Apostles*, beyond the *White Wells* about 1½m from Ilkley. The *Swastika Stone*, on *Addingham High Moor* about 2m SW of Ilkley, may be from the Iron Age. The *Cow and Calf*, above Ben Rhydding about 1m SE of Ilkley, are blocks of millstone grit weathered into fantastic shapes.

The track from Ilkley to (5m) East Riddlesden Hall and (6m) Keighley (Route 75H) crosses the highest part of *Rombald's Moor* (1321ft), 2m S. A pleasant little road follows the N bank of the Wharfe from Ilkley via *Nesfield* and *Beamsley* to (5½m) Bolton Abbey (see below).

From Ilkley to *Skipton*, *Settle* and *Kendal*, see Route 86C.

At (23m) *Addingham*, with the shaft of a late Anglian cross in its church, A65 goes on to Skipton (Route 86C). The present route bears right on B6160 for the Yorkshire Dales National Park and *Upper Wharfedale*, one of the loveliest valleys in England. At (25m) *Bolton Bridge* the route crosses the Skipton–Harrogate road (A59).

At *Beamsley*, off A59 ¾m E, the hospital founded by the Countess of Cumberland in 1593 provided accommodation in almshouses opening off a little circular chapel. The *Beamsley Beacon* (1314ft), a good viewpoint, rises across the valley of the Kex Beck.

26m: *Bolton Abbey* (National Park local information point) is the misleading name for the village which includes *Bolton Priory* (open). The ruin stands on a promontory of level parkland in a loop of the Wharfe, with craggy hills on the opposite bank—a setting which inspired a famous watercolour by Turner and which Ruskin thought the most beautiful of any English ruin.

The priory of Augustinian canons was founded at Embsay, outside Skipton, by Cecily de Romille in 1120 and moved here by her daughter, Lady Alice, in the 1150s—to commemorate the drowning of her son in the Strid (see below), claims a sentimental legend. The nave of the *Church* has been used as the parish church since c 1170 and so was spared at the Dissolution. It is entered by the magnificent Perpendicular W front, added by Prior Moon in 1520 and intended as the base of a tower which was never completed. This masks the 13C front. The Early English nave and its single aisle end at the blocked-up crossing arch. Outside, the transepts, choir and E window (minus its tracery) survive nearly to roof level, but the monastic buildings to the S have almost entirely disappeared. The 19C *Bolton Hall*, W of the ruins, incorporates the medieval gatehouse.

The lovely wooded banks of the Wharfe stretching N of the priory are well worth exploring. A footbridge and stepping stones cross from the ruins to the E bank, with its fine views, where paths and tracks can be followed up to (3m) Barden Bridge (see below). At 1¼m a charming detour on the right follows the Posforth Beck, with its waterfalls, to (¾m) the *Valley of Desolation*. The nature trail along the W bank is reached from the right fork in the road at the Cavendish Fountain, about 200yd beyond the entrance to the priory ruins. It passes (2m) the narrow cleft of the Wharfe known as the Strid ('Stride').

B6160 also continues along Wharfedale to (29m) *Barden Bridge*. High up on the left is *Barden Tower* ('Boarden Tower'), which Henry, Lord Clifford, the 'Shepherd Lord', rebuilt in Henry VII's reign and used for alchemical studies. It was restored in 1658–59 by Lady Anne Clifford, who added the little parish church attached to the cottage on the S. From the bridge an unclassified road follows the E bank to Burnsall, passing *Simon's Seat* (1529ft; view). B6160 takes the W bank to (33m) **Burnsall** (National Park local information point), on a lovely reach of the Wharfe. It has an old Grammar School (1602) and a church with a Norman font and Jacobean pulpit. 35½m: *Linton*, to the left, is a pretty village with a packhorse bridge and an old clapper bridge across the stream, and Fountain's Hospital (1721) in the style of Vanbrugh. The partly 12C church stands beside the Wharfe ¾m NE.

B6160 crosses the river to (36½m) **Grassington** (1300 inhabitants; 650ft; National Park Information Centre), a charming little town apt to get crowded during the tourist season. In the tiny square on the hill two former lead-miners' cottages house the *Upper Wharfedale Folk Museum*.

From the E end of the bridge a path leads ½m upstream to *Ghaistrill's Strid*. B6265 crosses the Wharfe to *Threshfield* and leads via Linton and (3¾m) *Cracoe* to (9½m) Skipton (Route 86C).

From Grassington via *Stump Cross Caverns* to *Pateley Bridge* in Nidderdale, see Route 86B.

39½m: *Conistone*, on the E bank of the Wharfe, has a heavily restored church with pews by Robert Thompson of Kilburn. A fine limestone gorge lies to the E. Recrossing the Wharfe B5160 reaches (40m) *Kilnsey*, at the base of the overhanging *Kilnsey Crag* (see Route 86C), a notorious challenge for rockclimbers.

FROM KILNSEY TO MALHAM TARN OR STAINFORTH. There are several ways leading W, by small and sometimes perilous roads, to Malham Tarn and Stainforth in Ribblesdale (both in Route 86C). Walkers can reach the Tarn by Mastiles Lane, the old drovers' road running across *Kilnsey Moor* (about 5½m). Drivers should take the unclassified road which branches left from B6160 beyond Kilnsey and follows the Skirfare to (4m) *Arncliffe*, attractively laid out around its village green. From here a steep moorland road swings left to (9m) Malham Tarn. The name of *Fountains Fell*, to the right of the road, recalls that it marked the W boundary of the land in Wharfedale belonging to Fountains Abbey. Another road continues from Arncliffe up the E bank of the Skirfare through the lovely *Littondale* to (6m) *Litton* (National Park local information point) and (8½m) *Halton Gill*, where a steep moorland road heads left, passing between Fountains Fell and *Pen-y-Ghent* on the way to (16m) Stainforth.

B6160 crosses the Skirfare. 42½m: **Kettlewell** (700ft; National Park local information point), a large village on the E bank of the Wharfe, is a good centre for anglers and walkers.

Great Whernside (2308ft; view) rises to the E. A steep and rough road skirts its N flank and that of *Little Whernside* (1984ft) on the way to Coverdale, with a National Park local information point at (8m) *Horsehouse*, and (13m) Coverham (Route 86D).

B6160 continues up the E bank to (44½m) *Starbotton* and (46½m) **Buckden** (780ft; National Park local information point).

FROM BUCKDEN TO AYSGARTH, 8m by B6160. Beyond Buckden the road bears right and climbs rapidly along the Cray Beck, with waterfalls and a good view back, to

(1½m) *Cray* (1050ft). About 1½m further on, a track, unsuitable for cars, bears left via the *Stake Pass* (1832ft) for Semer Water and (10½m) Bainbridge (both in Route 86D). B6160 climbs to about 1390ft before descending into *Bishopdale*. 5m: *Newbiggin* lies on the opposite side of the dale from *Thoralby*, with a National Park local information point and a traditional forge in working order. 6½m: *West Burton* is an attractive village with a large green, a 19C cross and an old packhorse bridge below Walden Beck waterfall. 8m: *Aysgarth*, see Route 86D.

The final stage of the way to Hawes is by unclassified roads which grow progressively rough and steep. From Buckden the road crosses the Wharfe and continues up the dale, here called *Langstrothdale*. 47¾m: *Hubberholme* has a small 12C church with a rood loft of 1558 bearing the Percy arms. The stalls are by Robert Thompson of Kilburn. At (50m) *Deepdale* the route crosses the river. At (51m) *Beckermonds* (970ft) two streams unite to form the Wharfe. The route turns sharply to the right, climbs to (53¾m) the summit of *Fleet Moss* (1934ft) and then drops down to (58m) **Hawes** in Wensleydale (Route 86D).

B. Nidderdale: Wetherby to Knaresborough and Grassington

Directions. Total distance 32m. **Wetherby**, see Route 85B. B6164 to (7m) **Knaresborough**. B6165, B6265 to (22m) Pateley Bridge. B6265 to (32m) **Grassington** (Route 86A).

Wetherby, see Route 85B. B6164 goes NW, crossing into North Yorkshire and joining the valley of the Nidd at (4½m) *Little Ribston*.

7m: **Knaresborough** (13,400 inhabitants; seasonal TI), where a railway viaduct crosses the steep ravine of the Nidd, is an old-fashioned town with 18C houses. High above the river in Castle Gardens (*view) are the remains of John of Gaunt's *Castle*, where Richard II was imprisoned in 1399. Its best preserved part is the 14C keep, which (uniquely) also served as gatehouse between the inner and outer wards. The *Old Court Museum* has local history displays. The church of *St John*, Early English to Perpendicular, contains 17C monuments of the Slingsby family and glass by Morris and Co.

To the N of High Bridge is the public park of *Conyngham Hall*, with a zoo. High Bridge leads across to delightful walks on the opposite bank of the river. In the *Dropping Well Estate* (open) to the S are *Mother Shipton's Cave*, where the prophetess is said to have been born in 1488, and the *Dropping Well*, famous for its petrifying properties. On the other bank, below Low Bridge, is the curious *Chapel of Our Lady of the Crag* (open), a shrine cut into the rock c 1408, with a roughly carved figure of a knight at its entrance. Above is a late 18C house, also partly cut into the limestone.

About 1m downstream, near Grimbold Bridge, is *St Robert's Cave*, or *Eugene Aram's Cave*, where Aram hid the corpse of his victim Daniel Clark in 1745. Aram's body was returned to Knaresborough and hung in chains after his execution at York in 1759. At *Farnham*, 2m N of the town, the church has a Norman apse.

From Knaresborough to *York*, see Route 81.

B6165 crosses the Harrogate–Ripon road (Route 80) on the way into (11½m) *Ripley*, a 'model' estate village built by Sir William Amcotts Ingilby in

1820–30. The churchyard has the remains of a cross, perhaps 13C, with niches for kneeling at the base. *Ripley Castle* (open) has a 15C gatehouse, 16C tower, late 18C additions and a serpentine lake. Cromwell spent the night here after the Battle of Marston Moor. B6165 rejoins the course of the river before (18½m) *Summer Bridge*. On the moors 2m N are *Brimham Rocks* (NT), grotesquely shaped crags of millstone grit scattered over 60 acres.

B6165 joins B6265 shortly before (22m) **Pateley Bridge** (1900 inhabitants; seasonal TI), a pleasant little town set among beautiful scenery. The ruined church of *St Cuthbert*, high above the town, has wide views. The *Nidderdale Museum*, in the Council Offices opposite the 19C church of St Mary, has exhibits of local life. The Nidderdale Agricultural Show takes place here on the Monday nearest 20 September.

Nidderdale proper lies to the N, reached by steep and narrow sideroads. Part of the dale is filled by *Gouthwaite Reservoir* between (1½m) *Wath* and (4½m) *Ramsgill*. The murderer Eugene Aram (1704–59) was born at Ramsgill and kept school at Gouthwaite Hall, now submerged. 6½m: *Lofthouse*, with the *How Stean* gorge and caves (open) to the W. 7½m: *Middlesmoor* has a good view of the dale. Rough tracks (no cars) continue to the head of the dale, 6m further on, at *Angram Reservoir* beneath *Little Whernside* (1984ft) and *Great Whernside* (2308ft), also seen on the way from Kettlewell through Coverdale in Route 86A.

About 1½m S of Pateley Bridge, beyond *Bewerley*, is the 19C Yorke's Folly.

From Pateley Bridge to *Fountains Abbey*, *Studley Royal* and *Ripon*, see Route 80.

B5265 crosses the Nidd and goes W over the steep *Greenhow Hill* to the Yorkshire Dales National Park and Wharfedale. The hill has been mined for lead since the time of the Brigantes, and traces of Roman and medieval workings survive on either side of the road. 26½m: *Stump Cross Caverns* (open; National Park local information point), discovered by lead-miners in the 19C, have fine stalactites and stalagmites. 30¼m: *Hebden*, with another National Park local information point. 32m: **Grassington**, see Route 86A.

C. Upper Airedale, Craven and Ribblesdale: Ilkley to Skipton, Settle and Kendal

Directions. Total distance 54m. **Ilkley**, see Route 86A. A65 to (9½m) **Skipton**, (25m) **Settle**, (41m) Kirkby Lonsdale and (54m) **Kendal** (Route 76).

Ilkley, see Route 86A. A65 is followed W, skirting the S edge of the Yorkshire Dales National Park, explored on several of the detours described below. Beyond (3m) *Addingham*, where Route 86A turns right to follow Wharfedale, the present route stays on A65 and leaves West Yorkshire for North Yorkshire. The road crosses the watershed into the upper reaches of **Airedale**, whose lower, largely industrialised course is followed on the journey N from Leeds via Keighley to Skipton in Route 75H.

9½m: **Skipton** (13,200 inhabitants; TI) is a fine old market town with a broad main street leading up to *Skipton Castle* (open).

The Norman castle built by Robert de Romille in 1090 was rebuilt by Robert de Clifford in the early 14C. A Tudor range (not open) was added in 1536. Beginning in the 1650s, Lady Anne Clifford restored the whole building after it had been besieged and then slighted by Parliamentarian troops during the Civil War. Her additions include the lettered balustrade above the entrance displaying the Clifford motto 'Désormais' ('Henceforth'). With their six round towers, the main buildings survive in remarkably good condition, roofed and floored throughout. In the centre is the pleasantly irregular *•Conduit Court*, created by Henry, Lord Clifford, the 'Shepherd Lord', in Henry VII's reign and restored by Lady Anne, who planted the yew tree. The archway leading into the court belonged to the Norman castle.

The *Church* contains Clifford tombs, with heraldic decoration, and a fine screen of 1533. The *Craven Museum* in the Town Hall illustrates local geology, archaeology and social history. The old railway station at *Embsay*, 1½m NE, is headquarters of the *Yorkshire Dales Railway*, with steam locomotives and goods vehicles. Visitors can make a 4m round trip to Holywell Halt, on a preserved stretch of the Skipton–Ilkley line.

Skipton is the capital of the Mountain Limestone region of **Craven**, stretching from the sources of the Wharfe and the Ribble to the borders of Lancashire. The upland scenery to the N is some of Yorkshire's finest, particularly wild and dramatic at the crags, scars and broken limestone 'pavements' of the Craven Faults, which run from Wharfedale (see Kilnsey, Route 86A) past Malham and Settle to Kirkby Lonsdale.

FROM SKIPTON TO MALHAM, 11m. A65 is followed NW. From (4½m) *Gargrave* (see below) and (6m) *Cold Coniston* unclassified roads turn right for (9¾m) *Kirkby Malham*, with an interesting Perpendicular church. The Parliamentarian general John Lambert

The conduit court at Skipton Castle

(1619–83) was born here. A narrow road, with a *view, leads over the moor (1272ft) past (3¼m) the beautiful waterfall of *Scaleber Force* to (5m) Settle. 11m: **Malham** (National Park Information Centre), set among wild hill scenery near the source of the Aire, is an attractive village, popular with tourists.

Two of the most dramatic features of the Mid Craven Fault lie beyond. *Gordale Scar*, about 1¼m NE by road and footpath, is a deep ravine (about 300ft) formed by the collapse of a cave system. Energetic walkers can climb the rocks by the side of the waterfall to reach the upper valley. Across the road to the S of the Scar is the waterfall of *Janet's Foss* (NT). *Malham Cove*, ¾m N of the village by road and footpath, is a limestone amphitheatre, 300ft high, with markings on the pavements of its upper level showing where a waterfall once flowed over its lip. A stream—not the Aire, as is sometimes supposed—issues fully grown from its base. The little country road passing near the cove continues almost to the secluded upland lake of *Malham Tarn* (NT), another 2½m N, where Charles Kingsley set the opening scenes of 'The Water Babies' (1863). Tarn House, on the N shore, is used by the Field Studies Council. The Tarn nurses the Aire, for the stream which drains it to the S and disappears underground a little way beyond at Water Sinks reappears at Aire Head, just S of Malham. From the crossroads W of the Tarn steep and narrow routes lead W to (5m) Settle and N to (5m) Arncliffe in Littondale (Route 86A). Walkers can take Mastiles Lane, the old drover's road, E from the Tarn across Kilnsey Moor to (c 5½m) Kilnsey in Wharfedale (Route 86A).

From Skipton to *Burnley*, *Bury* and *Manchester*, see Route 75D; to *Leeds* and *Sheffield*, see Route 75H; to *Grassington* in Wharfedale, see Route 86A.

A65 continues NW from Skipton to (14m) *Gargrave*, where the road, the railway and the Leeds and Liverpool Canal meet in the Aire Gap. The detour to Malham described above branches right from here or *Cold Coniston*, 1½m further. A65 crosses into **Ribblesdale**. At (21m) *Long Preston* it is joined by the roads from Clitheroe and Slaidburn, both described in Route 75C.

25m: **Settle** (2300 inhabitants; TI) is a pleasant little town which makes an excellent centre for exploring the surrounding country. The *Shambles* in the market square is partly 17C, and the distinctive local style of 17–18C building, with its curious doorway arches and playfully shaped columns, is splendidly illustrated by the *Folly* (1694), now an antique shop. The *Museum of North Craven Life* is in Chapel St. Natives of Settle include George Birkbeck (1776–1841), founder of the Mechanics' Institutes and the London university College which bears his name, and Benjamin Waugh (1839–1908), founder of the National Society for the Prevention of Cruelty to Children.

Giggleswick, about ¾m W on the opposite bank of the Ribble, has a public school founded in 1512. Its domed chapel (1897–1902) is the masterpiece of Sir T.G. Jackson.

The Mid Craven Fault marks the landscape from Settle E to Malham. The best and most accessible of the caves in *Langcliffe Scar*, about 2m above the town, is the *Victoria Cave* which, with the nearby *Jubilee Cave*, has yielded traces of occupation from mesolithic to Roman times.

FROM SETTLE UP RIBBLESDALE TO HAWES, 21½m by B6479 and B6255. This *route crosses the wildest corner of Yorkshire. Its first stage follows the Ribble to its source and runs alongside the Settle–Carlisle line (1875), the most arduous stretch of railway building in England. ¾m: *Langcliffe* (National Park local information point). 2½m: *Stainforth*, where the Ribble flows through a narrow gorge, has a waterfall and single-arched 17C bridge (NT) on the old drovers' road from York to Lancaster. *Catrigg Force* is about 1m E above the village. A sideroad branches NE to (7½m) Halton Gill and (12m) Arncliffe in Littondale (Route 86A). 6m: *Horton-in-Ribblesdale* (TI), in a region scarred by quarrying, is a popular centre for walkers, cavers and potholers in the 'Three Peaks': Pen-y-Ghent (2273ft) to the E, *Ingleborough* (2373ft; see below) to the W, and Yorkshire's highest point, *Whernside* (2419ft; see also Route 86D), beyond.

Horton church is mainly Norman. B6479 crosses the Ribble as it leaves the village. At (11½m) *Ribblehead* the railway crosses the barren moor by a breathtaking *viaduct (24 arches; ¼m) before disappearing into the Blea Moor Tunnel (1½m long). For B6255 heading left to Ingleton, see below. The present journey takes B6265 to the right. It passes (15m) the turning on the left for Dentdale and Sedbergh (Route 86D), and descends *Widdale* to (21½m) *Hawes* (Route 86D).

From Settle to *Blackburn*, *Bolton* and *Manchester*, see Route 75C; to *Malham*, see above.

Beyond Settle A65 climbs past *Giggleswick Scar*, on the South Craven Fault, with the *Ebbing and Flowing Well*. 31m: **Clapham** (National Park Information Centre), an attractive village at the S foot of Ingleborough, is a popular starting-point for excursions into the hills.

Ingleborough Cave (open), 1½m N through the pleasant *Clapdale Woods*, has chambers and passages 800yd long, filled with glittering stalactites and stalagmites. Another mile further up the hillside is the mouth of *Gaping Gill*, a cavern 350ft deep, into which a waterfall flings itself. From here it is an easy climb of 1½m to the top of **Ingleborough** (2373ft), the most striking though not the highest of the Yorkshire hills, with a panoramic *view. The level summit has the remains of an Iron Age fort, with part of the walls still standing, and the foundations of circular huts of the 1C. The descent can be made N to (2m) Chapel-le-Dale or SW to (3m) Ingleton.

35m: **Ingleton** (seasonal TI), another attractive village and popular centre for visitors, stands where two streams unite in a ravine spanned by a railway viaduct (1859, now disused). A lovely walk of about 4m follows the wooded banks of the streams, with their waterfalls.

B6255 heads NE to (6m) Ribblehead (see above) around the flank of Ingleborough and past limestone scars and caves which include (1½m) *White Scar Cave* (open) and *Weathercote Cave*, a rocky chasm with a waterfall, at (4m) *Chapel-le-Dale*.

A65 crosses the NE corner of Lancashire. At (39½m) *Cowan Bridge* Charlotte and Emily Brontë entered the Clergy Daughters' School in 1824 but were withdrawn the following year after their elder sisters, Maria and Elizabeth, died of typhus contracted here. Part of the building survives N of the bridge over the Leck and is marked by a plaque. It appears in 'Jane Eyre' as 'Lowood' and its headmaster, the Rev. William Carus Wilson, as 'Mr Brocklehurst'. An 'exposed and hilly road' leads SW to (2¼m) *Tunstall*, 'Brocklebridge' in the novel, with the church attended by the pupils of the school. From Tunstall to *Lancaster*, see Route 76. A65 enters Cumbria and crosses the Lune just below the 15C *Devil's Bridge*. 41m: **Kirkby Lonsdale** (1500 inhabitants; TI) is an old town in a beautiful spot by the river, painted by Turner and praised by Ruskin as 'one of the loveliest scenes in England'. *Ruskin's View* is near the churchyard. The church has Norman work.

A683, a beautiful road, goes up Lonsdale via (1m) *Casterton* to (11m) *Sedbergh* (Route 86D). From Kirkby Lonsdale to *Lancaster*, see Route 76.

47m: A65 crosses M6. 54m: **Kendal**, see Route 76.

D. Wensleydale: Ripon to Leyburn, Hawes and Kendal

Directions. Total distance 61m. **Ripon**, see Route 80. A6108 to (14m) Jervaulx Abbey and (19½m) **Leyburn**. A684 to (26¼m) Aysgarth, (35m) **Hawes** and (50m) Sedbergh. A684 to (61m) **Kendal**, see Route 76.

Ripon, see Route 80. A6108 heads up the valley of the Ure, which beyond Kilgram Bridge becomes *Wensleydale. Broad and green in its lower stages, with tributary rivers creating side valleys to the N and S, it runs among wilder fells near its head beyond Hawes.

The road crosses the Ure at (5½m) *West Tanfield*, a pleasant village with the Perpendicular gatehouse of the Marmions' castle (EH, all year). The church contains Marmion effigies, including those of Sir John (d. 1387) and his wife under an iron hearse. There is also woodcarving by Robert Thompson of Kilburn. The road meets the river again at (9m) *Masham*, with a large market place once used for sheep fairs and a 12–16C church with Danby tombs. 14m: **Jervaulx Abbey** (open) was founded by Cistercians who moved here from Aysgarth in 1156. The name, pronounced 'Jervo', is Norman French for 'Yoredale', or 'Ure valley'.

The picturesquely overgrown ruins look confusing from the entrance, but the foundations of the large church can be traced at the N of the site. The monastic buildings are arranged around the cloister to its S in the usual Cistercian pattern, with the chapter house and monks' dormitory (two-storied wall) on the E side. *Kilgram Bridge*, about 1½m E of the abbey, marks the point where the Ure valley becomes Wensleydale.

From the pretty village of (15½m) *East Witton* a sideroad leads W to (2m) the 17C *Braithwaite Hall* (NT, open by appointment). 17½m: *Middleham* has racing stables and the imposing ruins of *Middleham Castle* (EH, all year), once the stronghold of Warwick the Kingmaker and a favourite residence of Richard III, whose son Edward died here in 1484. The space between the large Norman keep (c 1170) and the 13C curtain wall is extraordinarily narrow. To the SW is the site of an earlier castle on higher ground.

A6108 crosses the Ure again on the way to (19½m) **Leyburn** (675ft; TI), an old market town high up on the N bank and a centre for excursions in E Wensleydale. It is the venue for the Wensleydale Agricultural Show in August and two fairs, in May and October.

A footpath which begins just N of the Bolton Arms leads ¼m W to the *Leyburn Shawl* (800ft), a green terrace running along the N side of the valley and giving an exceptionally fine view of Wensleydale. About halfway along the walk is the *Queen's Gap*, where Mary, Queen of Scots, is said to have stopped during her attempted escape from Bolton Castle.

FROM LEYBURN TO RICHMOND. The direct way to (9m) *Richmond* (Route 86E) takes A6108 to (3½m) Halfpenny House and branches right across *Hipswell Moor*, past (4½m) *Hartleap Well*, the scene of Wordsworth's poem, and the firing ranges in the military training area W of *Catterick Garrison* (Route 85B). A better way, about 1m longer, stays on A6108 to reach Richmond via an attractive stretch of Swaledale.
From Leyburn to A1 at *Leeming Bar*, see Route 85B.

20½m: *Wensley*, once a market town but now only a village, gave its name to the dale. It has a 15C bridge and a 13C church containing a Flemish *brass of a priest, Sir Simon de Wenslaw (d. 1394), choir stalls with carved poppyheads (1527), and fragments of 14C wall painting. The Bolton pew incorporates an old parclose (1506–33) from the Scrope chantry at Easby Abbey; near the door is a unique wooden reliquary (of St Agatha?), also from Easby. On the opposite side of the village green from the church are the entrance gates of *Bolton Hall* (not open), 1m W.

Roads follow both sides of the dale to Aysgarth, in the Yorkshire Dales National Park beyond Wensley. A684, on the S, goes through (22½m) *West Witton* and under *Penhill* (1792ft; view).

The route along the N side of the dale, about 3m longer, is more interesting. It passes below *Scarth Nick* (*view) and descends to (3¼m) *Redmire*. About 1m NW is ***Bolton Castle** (open), the late 14C fortified manor house of the Scropes. Mary, Queen of Scots, was held here in 1568–69. The battlements give a lovely view of Wensleydale. A left turn at (6½m) *Carperby* crosses the river to Aysgarth.

26¼m: **Aysgarth** (National Park Information Centre at the Falls) stands on a hill above charming scenery where the Ure, crossed by a 16C bridge, flows over a series of flat limestone edges, forming the *Upper Falls* above the bridge and the **Middle and Lower Falls* ½m below. The nearby church has a superb rood screen and two carved pew ends, apparently from Jervaulx Abbey. The old mill displays horse-drawn carriages, etc.

The *Walden Valley* and the pleasant *Bishopdale* open to the S. Buckden (Route 86A) in Wharfedale can be reached by a good road through Bishopdale or a rough track from Bainbridge.

31½m: *Bainbridge*, at the foot of the flat-topped *Addlebrough* (1564ft), is a pleasant village with a large green. A horn is blown here every evening at 21.00 from Holy Rood (28 September) to Shrove Tuesday to guide benighted travellers. Brough Hill, to the E, is site of the Roman fort of Virosidum.

The river Bain leads 2½m SW to Yorkshire's only natural lake, **Semer Water**, beautifully situated at the foot of *Raydale*. The local legend of a submerged village may derive from the Iron Age settlement which stood here. A track leads from Semer Water over the Stake Pass to Bishopdale (see above). N of Bainbridge a bridge crosses the Ure for (1½m) **Askrigg** (National Park local information point), once a centre of hand-knitting and clockmaking, with a late Perpendicular church, a market cross and 17–18C houses. The TV series 'All Creatures Great and Small' was filmed here. For the fell road to Muker, see Route 86E.

35m: **Hawes** (1300 inhabitants; 800ft; seasonal TI), a popular centre for visitors, is a grey little town with a big livestock market and the Duerley Beck cascading through its E end. The *Upper Dales Folk Museum* is housed in the former railway station. About 1½m N is *Hardrow Force, a 90ft waterfall painted by Turner.

From Hawes to *Wharfedale*, see Route 86A; to *Settle* and *Ingleton*, see Route 86C; to the *Buttertubs* and *Muker*, see Route 86E.

Beyond (36m) *Appersett* A684 passes the pretty waterfall of *Cotter Force*, on the right. At (40½m) the *Moorcock Inn* (1063ft) A684 leaves the Ure, which rises to the N.

B6259, the Kirkby Stephen road, heads this way. It passes (2¼m) *Lunds Fell* (2186ft), with the source of the Ure, and (2¾m) the striking ravine of *Hell Gill*, where the river Eden begins as Hell Gill Beck. The road then descends *Mallerstang*, the green valley of the Eden, between *Wild Boar Fell* (left; 2324ft) and *Mallerstang Edge* (2328ft). Between the road and the river lies *Pendragon Castle* (open), a 12C pele tower restored in the 17C by Lady Anne Clifford, which legend says was built by Uther Pendragon, father of King Arthur. 10m: *Kirkby Stephen*, see Route 86E.

A684 enters Cumbria and descends *Garsdale*, with *Baugh Fell* (2216ft) to the N. A more interesting way to Sedbergh follows the moorland road on the left through the parallel *Dentdale*, the valley of the Dee, and *Dent* (National Park local information point), a pleasant village with narrow cobbled streets, once famous for its cottage knitting industry. The Cambridge geologist Adam Sedgwick (1785–1873) was born here. The fells on the left culminate in *Whernside* (2419ft; *view), Yorkshire's highest point and the northernmost of the 'Three Peaks' (Route 86C). 50m: **Sedbergh** is a popular place, in a beautiful mountain site. Its public school was founded in 1525 by Roger Lupton, Provost of Eton. *Briggflatts*, 1¼m SW, has an early Friends' meeting house (1675).

From Sedbergh to *Kirkby Lonsdale*, see Route 86C.

A684 crosses the Lune, marking the W boundary of the Yorkshire Dales National Park, and then (56m) M6. 61m: **Kendal**, see Route 76.

E.   Swaledale: Scotch Corner to Richmond, Kirkby Stephen and Brough

Directions. Total distance 40½m. **Scotch Corner**, see Route 85B. A6108 to (4m) **Richmond**. A6108, B6270 to (14½m) Reeth. B6270 to (23m) Muker and (36m) **Kirkby Stephen**. A685 to (40½m) **Brough** (Route 86F).

Scotch Corner, see Route 85B. A6108 leads SW to (4m) **Richmond** (7700 inhabitants; TI), a splendid old town on the Swale with much to remind the visitor of both its medieval and its 18C prosperity. It has given its name to many other places, including Richmond-upon-Thames. Lewis Carroll attended school here before going on to Rugby.

The *Castle (EH, all year) stands on a precipice sheer above the river.

Originally built c 1071 by Alan Rufus, the 1st Norman Earl of Richmond, it keeps many features from this period: curtain wall, gatehouse, chapel and Scolland's Hall, a rare survival of a Norman great hall ('very probably the oldest in England', says Pevsner). The magnificent keep over the gatehouse was added in 1171–74; the top commands a good view.

The large, cobbled market place has a cross of 1771 and several 18C buildings around its sides. The former church of Holy Trinity is now the *Green Howards Museum*, devoted to the North Yorkshire Regiment. The *Georgian Theatre* to the N is one of the oldest theatres in the country, built in 1788 and reopened in 1963 after 100 years of disuse. It is open in summer when a play is not being staged, and contains a theatre museum. The Perpendicular *Tower in Friary Gardens, off Victoria Rd, is the only relic of the Greyfriars' monastery founded in 1258. The *Richmondshire Museum*, in Ryder's Wynd to the E, has local history exhibits which include carved Saxon stones, craftsmen's tools, etc. The heavily restored church of *St Mary*, which stood outside the town walls, has Perpendicular choir stalls with misericords brought from Easby Abbey. Frenchgate and Pottergate both have good Georgian houses. Hill House was the home of Frances l'Anson, the 'Lass of Richmond Hill' in the 18C song.

*Easby Abbey** (EH, all year), in a beautiful setting by the Swale 1m SE, can be reached by B6271 or a pleasant riverside walk. It was founded for Premonstratensian canons in 1155 and dedicated to St Agatha of Sicily. The picturesque ruins have an unusual and irregular ground plan. Very little remains of the church, but the 13C refectory on the S side of the cloister still stands almost to its full height. On its W side are the monks' dormitory and guests' solar. The 14C gatehouse, to the SE, is substantially intact.

Hudswell, 2m SW of Richmond, can be reached by a pleasant walk through NT woods along the S bank of the Swale. The old road climbing the N bank to (5m) Marske (see below) gives good views and passes between (2½m) broadcasting aerials and *Whitcliffe Scar*, with Robert Willance's monument (1606) giving thanks for his escape when his horse went over the escarpment.

From Richmond to *Leyburn*, see Route 86D.

A6108 follows the winding course of *Swaledale**, the deepest, wildest and one of the loveliest of the Yorkshire Dales. Norse influence lingers in many of the place names, and there are traces of lead-mining. 5½m: The road crosses the river and enters the National Park. 8½m: The picturesque Dunnerholme Bridge leads across the Swale to *Marske*, 1m NW, with an 18C Hall (not open) and a 15C bridge across the Marske Beck. At 9m A6108 heads left to Leyburn (Route 86D). The present route follows B6270, passing the scanty ruins of two nunneries: (11m) the Cistercian *Ellerton Priory* and, on the opposite bank 1m beyond, the Benedictine *Marrick Priory*, now part of a Youth Centre. 13½m: *Grinton* has the mother church of Upper Swaledale, with Norman to Perpendicular work. The route crosses the river again. 14½m: **Reeth** has an attractive green and the *Swaledale Folk Museum*.

A hilly road goes up the side valley of *Arkengarthdale*, with disused lead mines, and crosses the moors via (11m) *Tan Hill Inn* (1732ft), the highest pub in England, to (20m) *Brough* (see below). Another road branches right from Arkengarthdale at 4m and leads via the forested ridge of the *Stang* (1677ft), with good walks, to (15m) *Barnard Castle* (Route 86G).

Though still dotted with villages, Swaledale grows wilder beyond Reeth and the road becomes hilly. 17½m: *Feetham*. At (20m) *Gunnerside* (National Park local information point) B6270 crosses the river. *Ivelet*, 1m W, has pretty falls. 23m: **Muker** (National Park local information point) is a quaint village in a beautiful situation. The Swaledale Agricultural Show takes place here in September.

There are two steep sideroads to Wensleydale (Route 86D) from this part of Swaledale. One starts about ¾m E of Muker and leads over the fells (1633ft) to (5m) *Askrigg*. The other, more interesting and with *views, starts 1m beyond Muker, passes the four deep limestone holes known as the *Buttertubs* and makes its way over the *Buttertubs Pass* (1726ft) to (6½m) *Hawes*.

At Muker B6270 leaves the Swale and follows the Muker Beck to (24½m) *Thwaite* and (26½m) *Keld*, where it rejoins the Swale. Walkers can follow the track along the W bank past *Kisdon Force*, in a romantic site ½m below Keld. The head of Swaledale beyond Keld is much less impressive, but B6270 commands a fine view of the Eden valley from (32½m) the top of the pass, marking the end of the National Park and the border with Cumbria.

36m: **Kirkby Stephen** (1500 inhabitants; seasonal TI) is a pleasant town on the Eden. The church, with a Perpendicular tower, contains 15–16C tombs of the Musgraves and Whartons and an Anglo-Danish cross shaft showing Satan in bonds.

A685 leads to (23½m) *Kendal* (Route 76) via (4½m) *Ravenstonedale* (pronounced 'Rassendale') and (11½m) *Tebay*. From Kirkby Stephen to the *Moorcock Inn* and Wensleydale, see Route 86D.

A685 leads to (40½m) **Brough**, where A66 and Route 86F continue to Penrith.

F. Scotch Corner to Penrith

Directions. Total distance 49m. **Scotch Corner**, see Route 85B. A66 to (9m) Greta Bridge (for Barnard Castle, Route 86G), (15m) Bowes, (28m) Brough, (36m) Appleby and (49m) **Penrith** (Route 76). Not a Dales route as such, but a useful cross-Pennine route connecting with the Dales to the N (Teesdale from Greta Bridge) and S (Swaledale from Brough) and offering a fine contrast of scenery between Pennine moorland and the Eden valley.

Scotch Corner, see Route 85B. A66 follows the line of the Roman road connecting the garrisons at York and Catterick with those at Penrith and Carlisle. For *Stanwick Fortifications*, N of the road at 2m, see Route 86G. 7½m: After running along the county boundary, A66 leaves North Yorkshire for County Durham. 9m: *Greta Bridge*, *Rokeby Park* and, 3½m NW, *Barnard Castle*, see Route 86G. 15m: **Bowes** has the ruined Norman keep of its castle inside the earthworks of the Roman fort of Laventrae (EH). The school which suggested 'Dotheboys Hall' in 'Nicholas Nickleby' occupied the low stone building at the W end of the village.

A66 follows the upper valley of the Greta, spanned at 17½m by the natural limestone formation called *God's Bridge*. The desolate waste of *Stainmore Forest* reaches its summit (1436ft) at (21m) the Roman camp of Rey Cross, where the route enters Cumbria. A *view opens across the valley of the Eden to the distant fells of the Lake District, and the road descends rapidly. 28m: **Brough** (670 inhabitants) has a ruined castle, built c 1170 inside the Roman fort of Verterae and restored by Lady Anne Clifford in the 17C (EH, all year; closed on Monday and Tursday in winter).

From Brough to *Kirkby Stephen* and Swaledale, see Route 86E; through Lunedale to *Mickleton* in Teesdale, see Route 86G.

36m: **Appleby** (2400 inhabitants; TI), properly *Appleby-in-Westmorland* and formerly the county town of Westmorland, is a charming place with a steep High St. The castle (open), overlooking the Eden, was restored by Lady Anne Clifford in the 17C but still has a fine Norman keep. The church has monuments to Lady Anne (d. 1676) and her mother, the Countess of Cumberland. The organ was brought from Carlisle Cathedral in 1684. For *High Cup Nick*, see Route 86G.

A66 follows the valley of the Eden, with the Lake District fells in the distance on the left and the Pennine Chain on the right. *Cross Fell* (2930ft), the highest point of the Pennines, rises NE of (42m) *Temple Sowerby*. The gardens of *Acorn Bank* (NT), 1m N of Temple Sowerby, include orchards and a herb garden. The 16–18C manor house is open by arrangement. Beside (47½m) *Brougham Castle* (Route 76) the road crosses the Eamont. 49m: **Penrith**, see Route 76.

G. Teesdale: Darlington to Barnard Castle and Alston

Directions. Total distance 48½m. **Darlington**, see Route 85B. A67 to (16m) **Barnard Castle**. B6277 to (26½m) Middleton-in-Teesdale and (48½m) **Alston**.

Darlington, see Route 85B. A67 runs W up the valley of the Tees. 5m: *Piercebridge* lies within the Roman fort on Dere Street, now B6275, extending N from Scotch Corner to Bishop Auckland. The remains of a drainage system (NW of the green) and some mounds of the walls survive, together with some fragments of the abutment and piers carrying the 2C timber bridge across the Tees (EH). 8m: *Gainford* has a 13C church beautifully situated above the Tees. 10m: *Winston*, with a fine bridge of 1764, is 2¼m S of Staindrop (see below).

Stanwick Fortifications (EH) lie 4m SE of Winston and 3½m SW of Piercebridge. The Brigantes built the earthwork, enclosing 850 acres, in the 1C AD and used it as a rallying point against the Romans.

16m: **Barnard Castle** (6000 inhabitants; TI) is an attractive market town in a lovely site on the N bank of the stony Tees. Below the *Market Cross* (1747) stands the 16C *Blagraves House*. Dickens stayed at the *King's Head Hotel* in 1838 on a trip investigating northern private schools. A watchmaker's shop nearly opposite sugggested 'Master Humphrey's Clock'.

The ruined *Castle* (EH, all year) from which the town takes its name is strikingly placed above the Tees near the old *County Bridge*.

The castle was founded c 1125–40 by Bernard Balliol and confiscated in 1296 after the revolt by John Balliol, King of Scotland, against Edward I. Its best features are the 12–14C Mortham Tower, the 13C hall range partly improved by Richard III (bearing his emblem of the boar) and the 13C Round Tower.

The ***Bowes Museum**, off Newgate E of the centre, looks unexpectedly like a French château. It was built by the colliery owner John Bowes of Streatlam and his wife Josephine, Countess of Montalbo, in 1869–76 as a museum for their art collection. Durham County Council now administers it.

The collection is particularly strong in Spanish painting (El Greco, Goya), porcelain (Chantilly) and French 18C furniture and works of art. The mechanical silver swan makes a prominent exhibit. Later additions include paintings by Canaletto and displays of dolls, toys, costumes, English decorative art and local archaeological finds.

FROM BARNARD CASTLE TO BISHOP AUCKLAND, 14½m by A688, partly following the line of the Roman road. 6m: *Staindrop* has an 11–14C *church with monuments of the Neville and Vane families. Close by is the entrance to *Raby Castle* (open), a 14C castle modified by later generations but keeping its romantically medieval silhouette. It passed to the Vanes from the Nevilles after the leading role played by Charles Neville, Earl of Westmorland, in the Rising of the North against Elizabeth I in 1569. Particularly impressive are: the Neville gateway; the Barons' Hall, lengthened by William Burn in the 1840s; the medieval kitchen; Burn's octagonal drawing room; and the Gothick entrance hall, part of John Carr's alterations in 1768–88. There are good pictures, particularly portraits, and French 19C furniture. Outside are walled gardens, carriages (in the stables) and a deer park. 14½m: *Bishop Auckland*, see Route 86H.

From Barnard Castle to *Reeth*, see Route 86E.

* **Teesdale** stretches from the meeting of the Greta and the Tees, 3m below Barnard Castle, to Cauldron Snout, 20m above it. Before continuing N on the main route it is well worth making the detour S described below.

FROM BARNARD CASTLE TO GRETA BRIDGE, a 10½m round. Crossing the river to the suburb of *Startforth*, the route follows the S bank of the Tees to (1¾m) the picturesque ruins of **Egglestone Abbey** (EH), a daughter house of Easby Abbey founded for Premonstratensian canons in 1195–98. A good deal of the Early English church still stands. 2m: The *Abbey Bridge* (1773) commands a lovely view in both directions. About 1m further on a lane leads left to the superbly romantic *meeting of the Greta and the Tees, painted by Cotman and Turner, and *Mortham Tower*, a 14C pele tower with later additions. A66 (Route 86F) skirts *Rokeby Park* (limited opening), a Palladian house which the amateur architect Sir Thomas Robinson built for himself in 1735. It contains good furniture, paintings and needlework pictures, and once housed the 'Rokeby Venus' by Velasquez, now in the National Gallery. Sir Walter Scott's visits in 1809 and 1812 inspired his poem 'Rokeby'. 3¾m: *Greta Bridge*. A pleasant walk follows the river SW via (2½m) the wooded *Brignall Banks* to (7m) *Bowes* (Route 86F). The return to Barnard Castle can be made via *Whorlton*, 2½m NE of Greta Bridge and 1m W of *Wycliffe*, where the church has 13–15C glass. John Wyclif's family may have taken its name from the village, though the reformer himself was probably born at Hipswell (Route 85B), near Richmond.

The main route goes N up Teesdale, following B6277 along the SW bank and passing *Deepdale* on the left. 20m: *Cotherstone*, a Quaker village at the foot of *Baldersdale*, had a school of the 'Dotheboys Hall' type where Richard Cobden was a pupil in 1814–19. 22m: *Romaldkirk* is an attractive village with the 12–15C mother church of this side of Teesdale. 24m: Beyond *Mickleton* B6277 crosses the foot of *Lunedale*.

B6276 follows the dale towards (14m) *Brough* (Route 86F). On the right beyond (7m) *Grains o' th' Beck* the Lune flows from its source on the slopes of *Mickle Fell* (2591ft; view), the highest hill in County Durham.

B6277 crosses the Tees to (26¼m) the former lead-mining town of **Middleton-in-Teesdale** (1200 inhabitants; 750ft; TI) and follows the narrowing valley into the wilder landscape of upper Teesdale. 29½m: *Bowlees* has a Visitor Centre and picnic area. Behind the village the Causeway Sike tumbles over several waterfalls, notably at *Gibson's Cave*, about ¾m N. *Low Force* is S of the village on the Tees. Wynch Bridge, just below the falls, crosses to the S bank, where a stretch of the Pennine Way can be followed 1½m upriver to * **High Force**, not the highest but perhaps the most majestic waterfall in England, where the Tees hurls itself over a 70ft cliff into a wooded valley. The dolerite rocks are the exposed S edge of the igneous scarp known as the Whin Sill (or Great Whin Sill), which stretches up into Northumberland to form the landscape of Hadrian's Wall and the Farne Islands. A shorter but less interesting approach to High Force, via the N bank, is from B6277 at (31m) the *High Force Hotel*. At (33½m) *Langdon Beck* a track leads across the Tees to (2¾m) *Cow Green Reservoir*. A nature trail follows the shore to (1½m) the dam at its S end and, just beyond, *Cauldron Snout*, also part of the Whin Sill, where the Tees cascades down a wild dolerite ravine. Mickle Fell (see above) rises to the S.

In good weather walkers can follow the Pennine Way over the fells W of Cauldron Snout to (5m) *High Cup Nick*, a savage ravine between the dolerite cliffs of the Whin Sill. The Pennine Way then descends to (9m) the pleasant village of *Dufton*, from which footpaths continue S to (12½m) *Appleby* (Route 86F).

Just beyond Langdon Beck a steep unclassified road heads N over the fells to (5m) *St John's Chapel* in Weardale (Route 86H).

B6277 becomes one of the highest roads in England after it leaves Teesdale, climbing over (40m) *Yad Moss* (1962ft) on the Cumbrian border. The infant waters of the South Tyne flow down the other side of the fell through (44m) *Garrigill*, on the left. 48½m: **Alston** (1900 inhabitants; TI), at about 950ft, is the highest market town in England. The highest point of the Pennines, *Cross Fell* (2930ft), lies on the Pennine Way to the S.

The *South Tynedale Railway*, a narrow-gauge tourist line on the trackbed of the old BR line to Haltwhistle, runs excursions from Alston station along the valley to (1½m) Gilderdale Halt. An extension is planned.

A686 heads SW to (20m) *Penrith* (Route 76) via (5¾m) *Hartside Cross* (1903ft; *view). A686 heads NE to (15½m) *Langley Castle* and (17m) *Haydon Bridge* (both Route 87A), past (11m) the head of *West Allen Dale* and *East Allen Dale* (Route 86H). A689 follows the wooded South Tyne Valley N to (19m) *Brampton* (Route 87A). It passes (2m) *Whitley Castle*, on the left, with the remains of a Roman fort on Maiden Way, here joined by the Pennine Way. For A689 SE from Alston to Weardale and *Bishop Auckland*, see below.

H.   Weardale: Bishop Auckland to Alston

Directions. Total distance 38m. Bishop Auckland is roughly equidistant between Darlington and Durham (Route 85B) and Barnard Castle (Route 86G). A689 and unclassified road to (5½m) Witton-le-Wear. A68, A689 to (18m) Stanhope. A689 to (38m) **Alston** (Route 86G).

The colliery town of **Bishop Auckland** (32,600 inhabitants) has been the chief country residence of the Bishops of Durham since the 12C. Their palace, *Auckland Castle* (limited opening of state rooms and chapel), is mainly 17–18C but its beautiful *chapel was built from the ruins of the late 12C banqueting hall by Bishop Cosin (d. 1672), who is buried here. The Bishop's Park (open) has an 18C gatehouse and a deer shelter (EH).

About 1¼m SE is the large and handsome 13C mother church of *St Andrew Auckland*, with a reconstructed 9C Northumbrian cross. *Escomb*, on the S bank of the Wear about 3m W of Bishop Auckland, has a small and simple 7C *church, one of the earliest in England. It was built partly with stones from the Roman fort of Vinovia (open) at *Binchester*, 1m N of Bishop Auckland. The site includes an excavated bath system. *Shildon*, 3m S of Bishop Auckland, has the *Timothy Hackworth Museum* in the restored home and workshop of the engineer to the Stockton and Darlington Railway.

From Bishop Auckland to *Barnard Castle*, see Route 86G.

The route follows the N bank of the Wear as closely as possible, taking A689 to (3¾m) *High Grange* and then branching left on the unclassified road to (5½m) the attractive village of *Witton-le-Wear*. Its striking but altered castle of 1410 stands S of the river; the grounds are a public park with a camping and caravan site.

Hamsterley Forest, beginning about 4m W, has 1100 acres of Forestry Commission land open to the public, with a Visitor Centre, forest drive and forest walks.

The route takes A68 N and at 8½m rejoins A689. At (12½m) *Wolsingham* (2800 inhabitants) it meets the river again where the valley narrows to form **Weardale**. Its natural beauty has been scarred by a long industrial history of stone quarrying, mining for lead and iron ore, and steel and cement works. 15m: *Frosterley* is known for its 'marble', really a black, fossil-rich limestone, used in the North (in the Chapel of the Nine Altars at Durham Cathedral, for example) as Purbeck 'marble' is in the South. 18m: **Stanhope** (TI), among limestone quarries, is the centre of upper Weardale and a good headquarters for walks over the moors. The church, mainly 13C, contains a Roman altarstone found on nearby Bollihope Common. Bishop Joseph Butler, author of the 'Analogy', was rector in 1725–40. The landscape grows wilder and industry less intrusive as the route follows the dale through (20½m) *Eastgate* and (23¼m) *Westgate*, marking the boundaries of the hunting park which belonged to the Bishops of Durham. A689 crosses to the S bank of the river shortly before (25m) *St John's Chapel*, a charming little place. A steep fell road leads S to (5m) *Langdon Beck* in Teesdale (Route 86G). At (26¼m) *Irehopesburn* the minister's house attached to the 18C Methodist chapel is now the *Weardale Museum*, with reconstructed period interiors and a collection of minerals. A689 crosses back to the N bank at (27m) *Wearhead*, where Burnhope Burn and Killhope Burn unite to form the Wear. 28m: *Cowshill*.

B6295, heading N, follows the wooded *East Allen Dale*. 3¼m: *Allenheads* is a delightfully secluded village, and (10½m) *Allendale Town* a good centre for walks in the dale and nearby *West Allen Dale*. 14½m: A686 heads NE via *Langley Castle* to (16½m) *Haydon Bridge* (Route 87A). The lovely NT woodland where the Allen meets the South Tyne is most easily reached from A69 (Route 87A).

30½m: *Killhope Wheel* (open) is a well-preserved 19C lead-mining site, with a large water-wheel. Surrounded by bleak hills, A689 becomes the highest main road in England as it climbs over (32m) *Killhope Cross* (2056ft; fine views) on the Cumbrian border. The river Nent flows down the side of the fell from (33¼m) the former lead-mining village of *Nenthead* to join the South Tyne. 38m: **Alston**, see Route 86G.

87

Newcastle to Carlisle

The **Northumberland National Park** covers much of the county from Hadrian's Wall in the S to the central Cheviot Hills in the N, and from the Simonside Hills in the E to Kielder Water and the Forestry Commission's Border Forest Park in the W. Its wild and remote border country, almost roadless in its northern reaches, includes the upper valleys of the Rede, the Coquet and the North Tyne. The Pennine Way enters the Park at Greenhead and follows the line of the Roman Wall before heading N via Bellingham to end at Kirk Yetholm.

Route 87B follows the S fringe of the Park along Hadrian's Wall, while Route 87A includes a detour up the valley of the North Tyne from Hexham via Bellingham. The detours from Newcastle to Carter Bar, from Morpeth to Coldstream and from Felton along Coquetdale, all in Route 85B, also cross the Park.

There are seasonal National Park Information Centres at Once Brewed, Rothbury and Ingram; a jointly operated centre at Housesteads (with NT, open April to October and weekends in March and November); and a village information point at the Border Reiver café and shop in Otterburn. Further information can be obtained by writing to the Northumberland National Park, Eastburn, South Park, Hexham, Northumberland NE46 1BS.

A. Via Tynedale and Hexham

Directions. Total distance 58½m. **Newcastle**, see Route 85B. A695 to (17½m) Corbridge and (21m) **Hexham**. A69 to (48½m) Brampton and (58½m) **Carlisle**, see Route 77.

Newcastle, see Route 85B. A695 runs along the N bank of the Tyne to (3m) *Scotswood*, where its crosses the river. 7½m: *Crawcrook*. At *Wylam*, 1½m NW, the former school-house is now a railway museum; the cottage (NT) where George Stephenson was born in 1781 lies about ½m E of the village, by the river and near the course of the 18C waggonway. 10m: *Prudhoe* (11,800 inhabitants; TI) has a ruined 12C castle on a cliff (EH, all year). *Ovingham* (pronounced 'Ovinjam'), across the Tyne ¾m NW, has an Early English church with a Saxon tower. At its foot lies the engraver Thomas Bewick (1753–1828). His birthplace at Cherryburn House near the hamlet of *Eltringham*, about 1m W of Prudhoe, is a museum (NT). The valley becomes more attractive. Opposite (13m) *Stocksfield* is *Bywell*, a beautifully situated village with a 15C gatehouse, an 18C Hall by James Paine and two fine 11–13C churches, one with a Saxon tower.

17½m: **Corbridge** (3100 inhabitants; seasonal TI) is a pleasant old town on the N bank of the Tyne, spanned by a bridge of 1674. The church, rebuilt in the 13C, has an 8C Saxon 'porch tower' and windows and a Norman S doorway. The TI Centre occupies a 13C vicar's pele tower. Like the tower arch in the church, it is built of stones from *Corstopitum* (EH, all year), ½m NW, a Roman garrison town and supply depot that grew from a late 1C fort guarding the main crossing of the Tyne.

The remains include two granaries; a fountain and aqueduct; two military compounds whose walls were later combined with a defended gateway; the remains of earlier temples; a headquarters building with a strongroom like the one at Chesters and, over it, an unfinished storehouse with rusticated masonry, one of the largest Roman buildings to survive in Britain. The first-class collection in the museum includes the *Corbridge Lion, a 3C sculptured fountainhead.

At *Newton*, off A69 3½m E, the *Hunday National Tractor and Farm Museum* has probably the largest collection of vintage tractors in Europe, as well as engines, a narrow-gauge railway, crafts and animals. *Aydon Castle* (EH, summer season), off A68 or B6321 1m NE of Corbridge, is a 13–14C fortified manor house.

A68, roughly on the line of the Roman Dere Street, runs N from Corbridge through lonely country, crossing the Wall at (2¾m) *Stagshawbank* (Route 87B). At (16½m) *West Woodburn*, on the edge of the National Park, the road crosses Redesdale near the Roman fort of Habitancum. 22½m: *Elishaw* is on the way from Newcastle to Carter Bar (Route 85B).

From Corbridge to *Morpeth*, see Route 85B.

18½m: The ruined *Dilston Castle*, on the Devil's Water to the left, was the original seat of the Earls of Derwentwater, the last of whom was executed for his part in the Jacobite rising of 1715.

21m: **Hexham** (9600 inhabitants; TI) is an ancient and attractive town. Next to the Market Place with its 18C *Shambles* stands the ***Priory Church**, larger than some cathedrals and one of the great achievements of the Early English style.

The first church was built by St Wilfrid in 674. The foundations of its apse and some fragments of its nave survive, together with the *crypt, among the best Saxon crypts in England; inscribed Roman stones from Corstopitum can be seen in its walls. The cathedral of a bishopric from 681 until 821, this Saxon church was sacked by the Danes in 876. It was succeeded by an Augustinian priory, founded in 1114, whose canons built the beautiful choir and long transepts (c 1175–1225). The S transept still has the canons' night stair from the dormitory. The nave, destroyed by the Scots in 1290, was rebuilt by Temple Moore in 1907–09.

The church contains rich furnishings of several periods. The rood screen with its painted panels commemorates Prior Smithson (d. 1524). In the choir are 15C misericords and also the stone Saxon *Bishop's Chair, which later served as a sanctuary chair (cf. Beverley Minster). On the N side of the chancel is the 15C Leschman Chantry and on the S side the Ogle Chantry with a triptych altarpiece; a 15C screen in the sanctuary has painted panels showing bishops and a Dance of Death. In the S transept are the sculptured tombstone of the Roman standard-bearer Flavinus and the Saxon *Acca Cross (c 740).

Some partly restored priory buildings survive to the S, while Cowgarth, off Market St. to the NW, has the ruins of the late 12C gateway.

E of the Market Place stands the 15C *Moot Hall*. Beyond are the *Manor Office* (open), built as a prison in 1330 and now containing displays of border history, and the former *Grammar School* (1684). Fore St. and Market St. are also rewarding.

Hexham makes a good base from which to explore Hadrian's Wall. In the school summer holidays a special bus service (890) runs from Hexham to Haltwhistle via the Military Road (B6318), stopping at or near the major Roman sites along the way. Timetables are available from National Park information centres and headquarters.

B6306 runs SE from Hexham, crossing the Devil's Water above the gorge of Swallowship Hill and the Dilston woods, and passes near the site of the Battle of Hexham (1464), at which the Yorkists defeated the Lancastrians. It then climbs across the moors to (10m) **Blanchland**, a charming village in the secluded Derwent valley. The parish church preserves the choir and N transept of the church belonging to the Premonstratensian abbey founded in 1165. The late 15C abbey gateway leads into the unusual square, centrepiece of the 'model village' laid out on the site of the monastic buildings by Lord Crewe in the 1750s.

FROM HEXHAM TO BELLINGHAM, KIELDER WATER AND THE SCOTTISH BORDER. A69 runs W along the N bank of the Tyne and A6079 heads N past (4m) *Wall* and the Roman wall. B6318 branches left across the North Tyne to (5m) *Chollerford* (Route 87B). A sideroad leads to (5½m) *Humshaugh*, pronounced 'Humshalf', and follows the beautiful wooded valley past (6½m) the partly 13C *Haughton Castle*. B6320 continues N, passing the 18C *Nunwick House* and, on the opposite bank, *Chipchase Castle* with its 14C tower and 17–18C additions, on the way to (11½m) *Wark*. The road climbs to a view of the wild *Redesdale* before crossing the North Tyne for (17m) *Bellingham* (pronounced 'Bellinjam'; TI) on the Pennine Way and the edge of the National Park. The church has a curious 17C stone-vaulted nave. B6320 continues N to Otterburn on the Newcastle–Carter Bar road (Route 85B). The present journey takes unclassified roads up the lonely valley of the North Tyne towards its source on the desolate slopes of *Peel Fell* (1975ft). 21m: The sideroad branching right for *Greenhaugh* continues to (3m) *Black Middens Bastle House* (EH), a fortified 16C farmhouse near the junction of the Tarset and Black Burns. 26m: The road reaches **Kielder Water** and the *Border Forest Park* (Kielder Forest), with a Visitors' Centre run by the Northumbrian Water Authority at *Tower Knowe*. The forest, developed by the Forestry Commission over the last 60 years, is the largest man-made forest in Europe. Kielder Water, completed in 1982, has the largest capacity (44 billion gallons) of any man-made lake in northern Europe, though Rutland Water has a larger surface area. As well as supplying water for the North-east and generating a small amount of electricity for the National Grid, it also serves as a recreational centre, with ferry cruises, boating, water sports, fishing, etc. The road leading across the dam near Tower Knowe gives access to forest trails along the N shore of the Water. 34m: *Kielder Castle*, an 18C former hunting lodge at the N tip of the reservoir, houses an information and exhibition centre run by the Forestry Commission. A forest drive (11m; toll) leads NE to join the Newcastle–Carter Bar road (Route 85B). An unclassified road leads to (36m) *Deadwater*, just before the Scottish border, and joins B6357, the Carlisle–Jedburgh road, at (40m) *Saughtree*.

The main route follows A69 past (23½m) *Warden*, at the meeting of the North and South Tyne rivers ¾m to the right. The 11C church tower has a Roman arch. 28½m: *Haydon Bridge*, on the opposite bank, was the birthplace of the painter John Martin (1789–1854).

A686 heads SW to (17m) *Alston* (Route 86G). It passes (1½m) the mid 14C *Langley Castle* (not open) and (2m) the junction with B6295, which follows *East Allen Dale* (Route 86H).

31½m: From the car park S of the road and river, walks lead into the lovely NT woodland on the banks of the Allen near its meeting with the South Tyne. 32½m: *Bardon Mill* is 3½m S of Housesteads (Route 87B). 37m: *Haltwhistle* (TI) is a pleasant little town with an Early English church.

Unthank Hall (not open), 2m SE, was the birthplace of the martyr Bishop Ridley (1500–55). *Featherstone Castle* (not open) is splendidly situated by the bank of the stony South Tyne, 3¼m SW.

A69 leaves the South Tyne and, beyond (40½m) *Greenhead* (Route 87B), follows the line of the old military road into Cumbria. 47m: **Naworth Castle** (limited opening), on the right, was built around a central courtyard in 1335 and tactfully restored by Anthony Salvin after a fire in 1844. It contains a large Great Hall hung with French tapestries, a Long Gallery and a library with a gesso relief by Burne-Jones.

Beyond Naworth the sideroad continues N past the medieval bridge spanning the Irthing to (2m) *Lanercost Priory (EH, summer season) in remote countryside near the Roman Wall. It was founded c 1166 for Augustinian canons. The S and E cloister buildings and the choir and transepts of the church are ruined, but the Early English nave has survived as the parish church. Its N aisle has glass by Morris and Co. The W front is particularly fine, with elegant arcading and tall lancets. The W range of the cloister is known as Dacre Hall, after Sir Thomas Dacre, who converted it in the 16C. For *Banks*, 1m NE of the priory, see Route 87B. From Banks the moorland road continues about 7m N to *Bewcastle*, where the remote church and ruined castle are built on the site of a Roman fort. The church has a late 7C *cross, 14½ft high, decorated with figures, beasts, birds and vine scrolls and bearing a runic inscription.

49¼m: **Brampton** (seasonal TI) is an old-fashioned market town, with a country park at *Talkin Tarn*, 2m SE. A689 follows the wooded South Tyne valley E and S to (19m) *Alston* (Route 86G). A69 completes the journey to (58½m) **Carlisle** (Route 77).

B.   Along Hadrian's Wall

Directions. Total distance 60½m. **Newcastle**, see Route 85B. A69 to (4¼m) West Denton. B6528 to (7½m) Heddon-on-the-Wall. B6318 to (23m) **Chesters** (31m) **Housesteads**, (33½m) Twice Brewed (for **Chesterholm/Vindolanda**) and (42m) Gilsland. B6318 and unclassified road to (43½m) Birdoswald. Unclassified roads to (50½m) Brampton (Route 87A). A69 to (60½m) **Carlisle**, see Route 87A.

Maps. OS Hadrian's Wall map (1:31,680 or 2in to 1m).

*Hadrian's Wall, the most impressive monument to the Roman Empire in Britain, stretches 73 miles from Wallsend on the Tyne estuary, E of Newcastle, to Bowness-on-Solway, W of Carlisle. Building started in AD 122 following the Emperor Hadrian's visit, and the Wall was still being modified when he died in 138. The purpose was to control the movement of people in and out of the province, to enforce regulations governing entry to the Empire and to prevent petty raiding. The Wall was made of local stone, mortared on the outside and filled on the inside with rubble originally held together by clay, replaced by a core of mortar in the late 2C. It probably rose to a height of about 15ft. As building work progressed, its thickness was reduced from 9½ft (10 Roman ft) to 6–8ft; for some stretches this narrow wall stands on broad foundations. The section W of the river Irthing at Willowford was originally made of turf but replaced in stone; near Birdoswald the turf and stone walls follow different courses. The Wall was patrolled from mile-castles built a Roman mile (1875 yds) apart, with two smaller observation turrets or towers regularly spaced between each pair. In the course of building it was decided to replace the forts that already stood to the S with forts astride the Wall itself, placed at roughly 7m intervals and together capable of holding about 10,000 men, who could defend the province against a major invasion. N of the Wall runs a ditch about 27ft wide, missing only where natural features like the Whin Sill made it unnecessary or the rock proved too hard to dig out. At varying distances to its S run the so-called Vallum, in fact a flat-bottomed ditch 20ft wide between mounds 80ft apart, and a military way linking the forts along the Wall, added in the late 2C. The Vallum was apparently designed to control access to the military zone. A little further S lay the earlier road which the Saxons called the Stanegate. A chain of coastal watch-towers and mile fortlets extended the line of the Wall SW along the Solway Firth, certainly to Maryport and perhaps as far as St Bees Head.

Shortly after Hadrian's death the Romans again moved N, establishing a new frontier on the Antonine Wall between the Forth and the Clyde. This was abandoned about 165 and Hadrian's Wall recommissioned. Though some bases were still held to its N into the 4C, it remained the frontier of the Empire until the end of Roman Britain in 409. Modifications were carried out after the barbarians had crossed it in the 180s, and by Constantius Chlorus in 297 after the defeat of Carausius and Allectus' bid for power. Theodosius carried out a final restoration after the barbarian conspiracy of 367.

The most interesting and popular sites are the forts and civil settlements at Corbridge (Corstopitum), Chesters (Cilurnum), Housesteads (Vercovicium) and Chesterholm (Vindolanda). Though the Wall itself nowhere stands to full height, many long sections survive. The finest stretches march across the countryside of the Whin Sill between Sewingshields and

Birdoswald, where the Vallum is visible for much of the way. The sites of two important forts lie E of Newcastle: Segedunum at Wallsend and Arbeia, with a reconstructed gateway, beyond the Tyne at South Shields (both in Route 85B). There is little to see W of Carlisle.

The best way to explore the Wall is on foot, with the help of the special OS map. (The long-distance footpath proposed by the Countryside Commission has been opposed by those worried about damage to the fragile earthwork of the Vallum mounds.) During the school summer holidays a special bus service runs between Hexham and Haltwhistle via the Military Road, stopping at or near the major sites along the way. The brief itinerary below is designed for motorists and takes in all the major points of interest; unless otherwise noted, it can be assumed that they are administered by EH and are open at any reasonable time. The Roman collections in the Museum of Antiquities at the University of Newcastle and the Tullie House Museum at Carlisle make an excellent start and finish to the trip.

Useful books include 'Hadrian's Wall' (3rd edition 1987) by David J. Breeze and Brian Dobson.

Newcastle, see Route 85B. A69 is followed W from the city. 2m: *Benwell*, site of the fort of Condercum, has a small apsidal temple to the god Antenociticus and a causeway across the Vallum, the only one now visible. 3½m: *Denton Burn* has a turret (7b), with fragments of the Wall to the W. At (4¼m) *West Denton* the route changes to B6528 and passes another stretch of the Wall on the way to (7½m) *Heddon-on-the-Wall*, which has a church with Norman work. B6318 now follows the course of the Wall. This is the Military Road which General Wade built by quarrying the Wall in 1751 after its predecessor had proved inadequate to bear his artillery during the 1745 rebellion. 9m: *Rudchester*, site of Vindovala fort, on the left. Further on, S of the reservoirs, is the pele tower of Welton. 16½m: *Halton Chesters*, site of Onnum fort. To the S is the border stronghold of *Halton Castle*. There are magnificent views at (17¼m) *Stagshawbank*, or *Portgate*, where the Military Road and the Wall are crossed by A68, following the line of the Roman Dere Street. *Corbridge*, 2¾m S, and a detour 19¾m N to *Elishaw*, are described in Route 87A. 21m: *Planetrees* is near *Heaven Fields*, where St Oswald recovered the throne of Northumbria by defeating the heathen King Cadwallon of Gwynedd in AD 633. Beyond Planetrees the road passes a section of the Wall which includes a point where the broad wall is reduced in width and then, near *Brunton House*, a well-preserved turret (26b) with another stretch of the Wall.

B6318 crosses the North Tyne at (22¼m) *Chollerford*. The *abutment of the Roman bridge and, when the river is low, the bases of some piers can be seen about ½m S of the present bridge. The church of *Chollerton*, 1½m NE, has Roman columns in the S arcade and a Roman altar made into a font. For *Hexham*, 5m S, and the detour N from Chollerford to *Bellingham*, the National Park and the Scottish border, see Route 87A. In (23m) the park of **Chesters** are the excavated remains of *Cilurnum, claimed as the best surviving example of a Roman cavalry fort in the whole Empire (EH, all year plus Mondays in winter). The headquarters building has a well, beside which is a carved phallic stone. The strongroom keeps its vaulted roof. Also exposed are the commanding officer's house, parts of three barrack blocks, and several gates and towers. Near the river is a well-preserved *bath-house. The *museum has sculptures, inscriptions and everyday objects from the Wall. B6318 enters the Northumberland National Park and passes (25m) *Black Carts* turret (29a), with a stretch of wall, ditch and the Vallum. 26m: *Carrawburgh*, site of the fort of Brocilitia, with a 3C temple to Mithras outside its walls.

At (28¼m) *Sewingshields*, with a turret (33b), the Military Road crosses the Vallum and leaves the Wall, which now becomes fairly continuous, mounting the crest of the dolerite Whin Sill and commanding wide views. The ditch ends at Sewingshields farm, and along this section turrets and a mile-castle (35) are visible. The Vallum diverges considerably to the S of the Wall. At (31m) **Housesteads**, with a seasonal Information Centre jointly run by NT and the National Park Authority, are the considerable remains of the infantry fort of *Vercovicium (NT and EH, all year plus Mondays in winter). They include the headquarters building, commanding officer's house, granaries, barrack blocks, hospital, flush-water latrine and four impressive gates. The museum contains finds and displays about the history of the fort. To the S stood a large *vicus*, or civil settlement; six buildings are now on display. A good walk leads W along the Wall towards the Steel Rigg car park, passing the well-preserved mile-castles 37 and 39 (NT). To the N are the small Northumbrian lakes, in desolate moorland crossed by the Pennine Way. 33½m: *Twice Brewed*, with the Once Brewed Youth Hostel and a seasonal National Park Information Centre. At *Peel Gap* an extra tower has been excavated between turrets 39a and 39b. The Wall reaches its highest point (1230ft) on *Winshield Crags* to the W. At **Chesterholm**, 1½m SE of B6318, are the well-preserved remains of the 3C fort of Vindolanda (EH, all year; access controlled by the Vindolanda Trust), with the headquarters building, a bath house and a Roman milestone still in situ on the Stanegate. The *vicus* outside its walls, excavated by the Vindolanda Trust, is particularly interesting, with an inn, houses, workshops, etc.; also a replica of a section of the Wall at its full height and a *museum. 36m: *Cawfields* mile-castle (42) is about ½m to the N, near the car park with the seasonal National Park information van. To its W is *Great Chesters*, the site of Aesica fort. *Haltwhistle* (Route 87A) is about 1½m S of B6318. The Wall crosses the broken dolerite cliffs known as the *Nine Nicks of Thirlwall*; a good stretch survives at *Walltown*, with an unusual turret (45a) from a signal system pre-dating the Wall. 39½m: *Carvoran*, the site of the fort now identified as Magnis, with the *Roman Army Museum*.

B6318 leaves the Northumberland National Park just before (40m) *Greenhead*. From here A69 heads directly to (58m) Carlisle, as described in Route 87A. However, Wall enthusiasts should continue on B6318, which follows a winding course to the right. 42m: *Gilsland*, near the Cumbrian border in the Irthing valley, was a small but fashionable spa in the days when Sir Walter Scott first met his future wife here. He described the neighbourhood in 'Guy Mannering' (1815). By the railway bridge to the S is the *Poltross Burn* mile-castle (48), one of the best preserved; a section of narrow wall on broad foundations continues about 1m W, through the former vicarage garden and past turrets 48a and 48b, to the abutment of the *Willowford* bridge which carried it across the Irthing (EH; access controlled by Willowford Farm). *Upper Denton* church, about 1¼m SW of Gilsland, has an ill-fitting chancel arch of Roman stones. 1m beyond Gilsland an unclassified road turns left from B6318 for (43½m) *Birdoswald*, with one of the largest and most interesting forts on the Wall, traditionally identified as Camboglanna but more probably Banna (partly EH, summer season, and 31 October, 10.00–5.30). From *Harrow's Scar* mile-castle (49), by the Irthing about ¼m E of the fort, the turf wall and the stone wall which replaced it follow different courses for about 2m. The road passes a stone-wall turret (49b), turf-wall turrets at *Piper Sike* (51a) and *Leahill* (51b), a signal tower at *Pike Hill* and another turf-wall turret at *Banks East* (52a) on the way to (46½m) *Banks*. A fragment of wall stands 9ft high about ¼m W of the village. The detour N from Banks to *Bewcastle* is described in Route 87A.

From Banks the main course of Route 87A can be joined by taking the road SW via *Lanercost* and the turning for *Naworth Castle* to (50½m) **Brampton**, from which A69 continues to (60½m) **Carlisle**.

INDEX

This index uses the following abbreviations for counties, etc, in those cases where it is necessary to distinguish between two or more places of the same name or very similar names:

People are limited to major English figures and major foreigners connected with England by visits, prolonged periods of work or expatriation. Minor English figures and foreign artists, otherwise unconnected with England, whose work is represented in galleries and museums are not included. Saints, kings, queens and people who take their name from a place (Geoffrey of Monmouth) appear under their first names. People best known by their pen- or stage-names (George Eliot, Cary Grant) are indexed in this form.

ATLAS SECTION

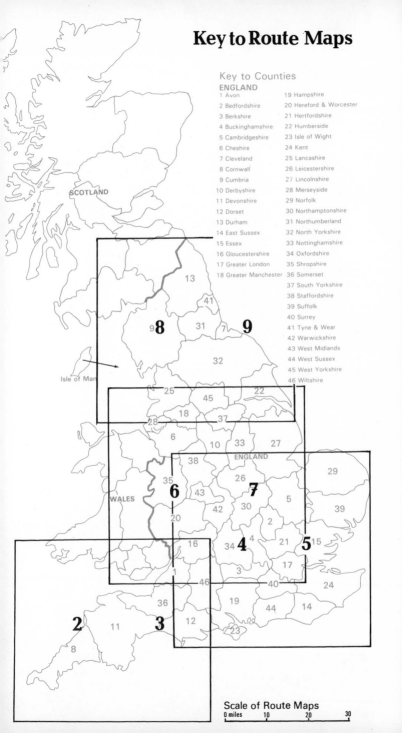

Key to Route Maps

Key to Counties

ENGLAND

1 Avon	19 Hampshire
2 Bedfordshire	20 Hereford & Worcester
3 Berkshire	21 Hertfordshire
4 Buckinghamshire	22 Humberside
5 Cambridgeshire	23 Isle of Wight
6 Cheshire	24 Kent
7 Cleveland	25 Lancashire
8 Cornwall	26 Leicestershire
9 Cumbria	27 Lincolnshire
10 Derbyshire	28 Merseyside
11 Devonshire	29 Norfolk
12 Dorset	30 Northamptonshire
13 Durham	31 Northumberland
14 East Sussex	32 North Yorkshire
15 Essex	33 Nottinghamshire
16 Gloucestershire	34 Oxfordshire
17 Greater London	35 Shropshire
18 Greater Manchester	36 Somerset
	37 South Yorkshire
	38 Staffordshire
	39 Suffolk
	40 Surrey
	41 Tyne & Wear
	42 Warwickshire
	43 West Midlands
	44 West Sussex
	45 West Yorkshire
	46 Wiltshire

SCOTLAND

Isle of Man

ENGLAND

WALES

Scale of Route Maps

0 miles   10   20   30

2

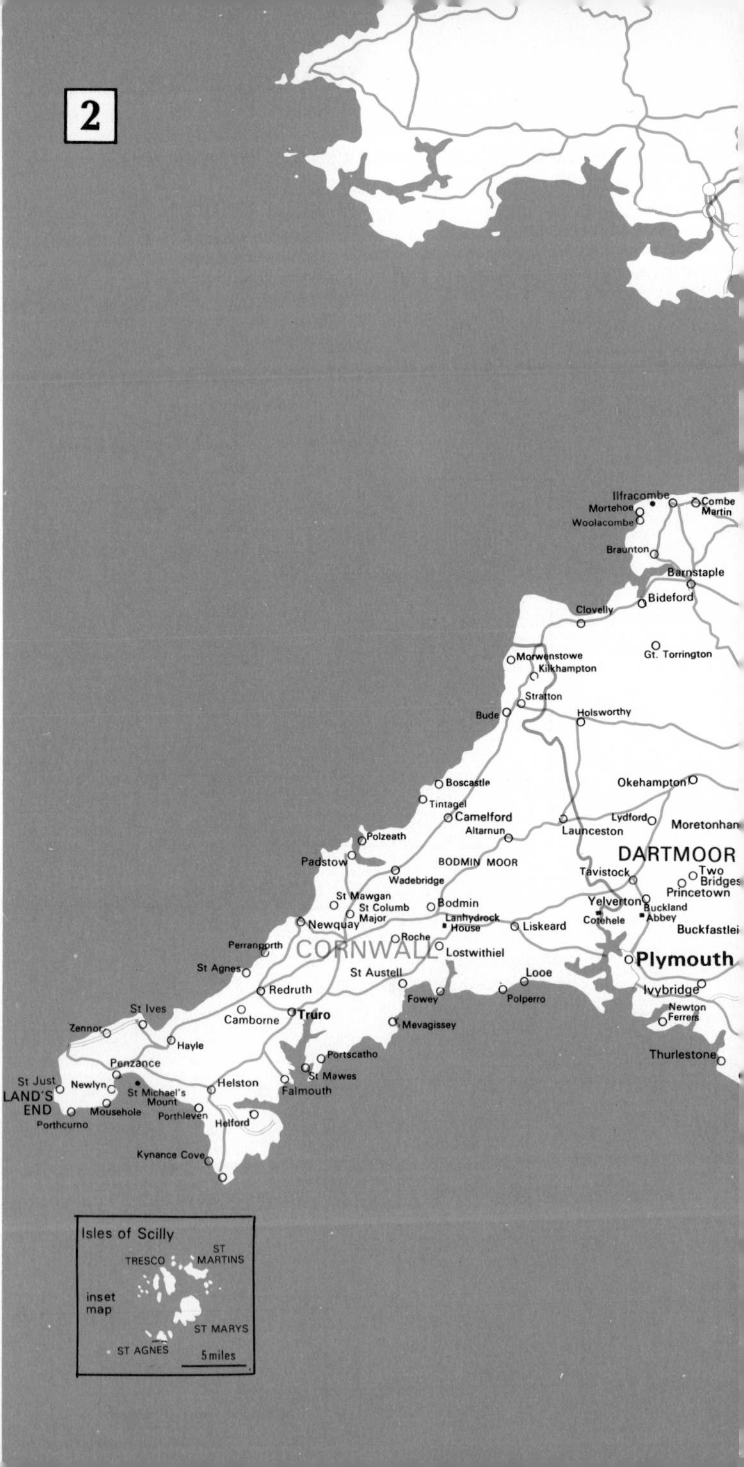

Ilfracombe
Mortehoe
Woolacombe
Combe Martin

Braunton
Barnstaple
Bideford

Clovelly
Gt. Torrington

Morwenstowe
Kilkhampton
Stratton
Bude
Holsworthy

Boscastle
Tintagel
Camelford
Altarnun
Okehampton

Lydford
Launceston
Moretonham

Polzeath
BODMIN MOOR
DARTMOOR
Tavistock
Two Bridges
Princetown

Padstow
Wadebridge
Yelverton
Buckland Abbey
Corehele
Buckfastlei

St Mawgan
St Columb Major
Bodmin
Lanhydrock House
Roche
Liskeard

Newquay
Plymouth

Perranporth
CORNWALL
Lostwithiel

St Agnes
St Austell
Looe
Ivybridge

Redruth
Fowey
Polperro
Newton Ferrers

St Ives
Camborne
Truro
Mevagissey
Thurlestone

Zennor
Hayle

Penzance
Portscatho

St Just
Newlyn
St Michael's Mount
Helston
St Mawes

LAND'S END
Mousehole
Porthleven
Falmouth

Porthcurno
Helford

Kynance Cove

Isles of Scilly
ST MARTINS
TRESCO
inset map
ST MARYS
ST AGNES
5 miles

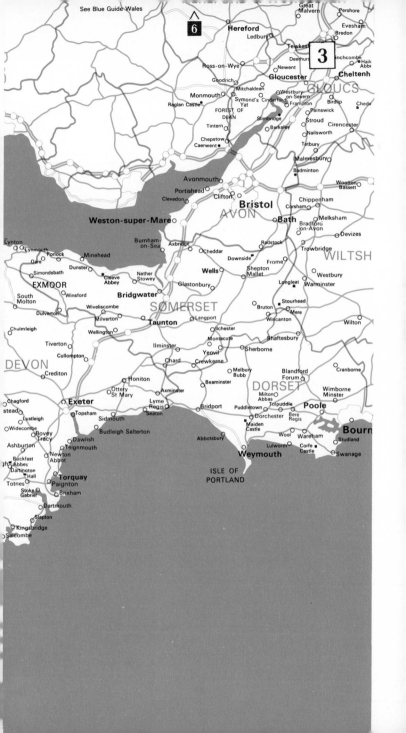

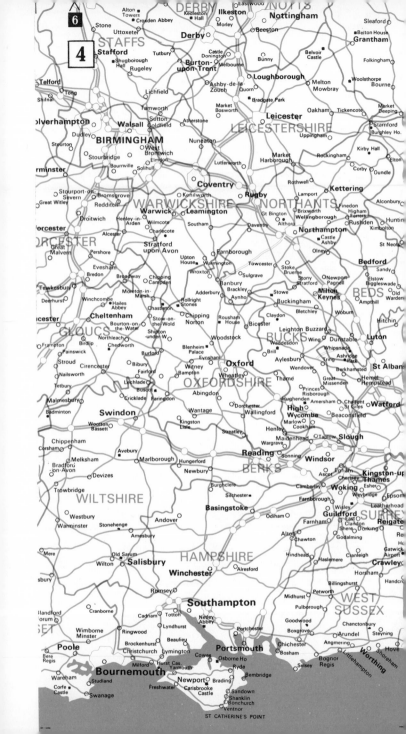